THE WORLD OF MAN

THE WORLD OF MAN

JOHN J. HONIGMANN

Professor of Anthropology,
University of North Carolina,
and
Research Professor of Anthropology,
Institute for Research in Social Science

HARPER & ROW, PUBLISHERS

NEW YORK, EVANSTON, AND LONDON

Library of Congress catalog card number: 58–13969

B-R

11/13/68

. . . It is evident that the war has, in more ways than one, paved the way for an economic and, as a corollary, a semi-political internationalism. All those spheres of activity that relate to the satisfaction of immediate ends, which, from the vantage point that we have gained, are nothing but means, will tend to become international functions. However the internationalizing processes will shape themselves in detail, they will at bottom be but the reflection of that growing impatience of the human spirit with the preoccupation with direct ends. . . . Such transnational problems as the distribution of economic goods, the transportation of commodities, the control of highways, the coinage, and numerous others, must eventually pass into the hands of international organizations for the simple reason that men will not eternally give their loyalty to the uselessly national administration of functions that are of inherently international scope. As this international scope gets to be thoroughly realized, our present infatuations with national prestige in the economic sphere will show themselves for the spiritual imbecilities that they are.

Edward Sapir (1924:427)

CONTENTS

vii

PART SIX: GROWTH OF WESTERN CULTURE

PART SEVEN: MAN AND CULTURE

"WORLD OF MAN" refers to those aspects of our planet created by man living in society. Government, science, rearing of children, housing, gardening, hunting, and dress all belong to the world created by that distinctive animal—man. Collectively they are referred to as culture. To study the world of man and the organism responsible for its creation is the business of anthropology.

More and more is heard about anthropology from daily newspapers and college catalogs, and in the corridors of international organizations, hospitals, and psychiatric clinics. Perceptive readers who have never taken a college course in the subject will recognize names like Margaret Mead, Ralph Linton, and Clyde Kluckhohn. Anthropology is impressing more and more people with the vitality of its approach to man and his world. The present book is designed for any reader who wants to understand culture.

Experience gained in teaching a considerable portion of this book to college students suggests that from it one may obtain a better idea of the systematic nature of social life: the way in which any culture is organized, how innovation in social behavior is facilitated and limited, why contradictions occur in community living, and how groups maintain their integrity and morale.

Anthropology is not purely science. It contains strong humanistic currents which, it is hoped, will be perpetuated. Many understandings of culture originate with nonanthropologists; the bibliographic citations in this volume refer the reader to many perceptive observers, including novelists and poets, who have enriched our understanding of the world of man. Cultural anthropology is the central field of anthropology. Hence the book proceeds first to that topic. Biological evolution and one of its end products —man—are surveyed largely from the standpoint of a cultural anthropologist who is interested in the relationship between culture and man's biological nature. Considerable effort has been spent in dealing with technical concepts extant in anthropology. If concepts are the tools by which to manipulate the phenomena which one studies, then it is important to have relatively precise meanings for terms like "myth," "technique," "religion," "art" and others. The value of words increases when they are defined clearly, rigorously, and, above all, with a view to making them useful for moving from one culture to another. The manner in which certain phenomena have been conceptualized should not unduly concern the reader. If for anthropological purposes it is useful to classify Christmas with the Fourth of July or Memorial Day, it is not denied that for other purposes these days can be thought of differently. It is the business of science, in trying to discover a predictable order in the universe, to reclassify familiar facts.

The professional anthropologist will discover that certain subjects have been treated more systematically than others. The former, of course, reflect subjects possessing special appeal for the writer. Frankly, this book is written more in order to share with the layman what has appeared to be an enlightening view of culture than it is designed for fellow anthropologists. Few persons today can control the whole field of anthropology. No doubt occasional facts are wrong and some interpretations no longer warranted. To have these pointed out will be welcome.

Now a few notes on using this book, whether in college classes or outside. Meaningful assimilation of anthropological knowledge demands some geographical awareness of where places on the earth's surface are located. As yet there exists no comprehensive ethnographic atlas (see, however, R. F. Spencer, 1956). A good geographical atlas is quite indispensable for the reader whose knowledge of the subject is rusty. Consulting maps frequently will enhance the meaning of what is read and aid in remembering facts about diverse peoples and world areas. Teachers using the book in college classes undoubtedly will find points to amend, discard, or amplify. For example, someone may want to deëmphasize methodology. He can move from Chapters 1 and 2 to Chapter 9. The book should not be difficult to outline for study. The references scattered in the text may be useful for students assigned to write short papers or reports on special topics. The short lists of available films are intended primarily for the college teacher. Unfortunately, not all these films can readily be secured on loan in this country. The poverty of anthropological films dealing with points of theory is appalling. How much longer will it endure?

Possibly some readers may wish to consult primary sources to find out more about peoples and areas mentioned in the following pages. Major bibliographical tools available for this purpose include: Murdock, *Ethnographic Bibliography of North America* (1953), which is an exhaustive guide to literature about North America's aboriginal people. For the location of American Indian tribes, their initial contacts with the Europeans, and the various names by which they have been known, see Driver, *et. al.*, *Indian Tribes of North America* (1953), and Swanton, *The Indian Tribes of North America* (1952). South America is covered in the 7-volume *Handbook of the South American Indians* published by the United States Bureau of American Ethnology and edited by Julian H. Steward (1946–50). Murdock's *Outline of South American Cultures* (1951a) furnishes a briefer guide and short bibliography. The areas and subareas of Africa are succinctly summarized with attendant bibliographies in numerous volumes making up the *Ethnographic Survey of Africa*, edited by Daryll Forde. For tribal locations in that continent see C. Bruce Hunter, *Tribal Map of*

Negro Africa (1956). Peter H. Buck provides *An Introduction to Polynesian Anthropology* (1945) with selected bibliography. C. R. H. Taylor, *A Pacific Bibliography* (1951), includes Melanesia and Micronesia as well as Polynesia. Southeast Asia (including Assam, Burma, Cambodia, and Vietnam) are covered in Embree and Dotson's two-volume *Bibliography of the Peoples and Cultures of Mainland Southeast Asia* (1950). Kennedy's *Bibliography of Indonesian Peoples and Cultures* (1945) guides the reader through the island world lying off the southeast coast of Asia.

Generally, except in French and Spanish and bibliographical citations, diacritical marks have been omitted from foreign words. The German *umlaut* has been transcribed by inserting *e* after rounded vowels.

Much collaboration is involved in writing a book. For critical reading of parts of the manuscript much gratitude is expressed to Louis Binford, Joffre Coe, John Gillin, John Gulick, Carroll Riley, and Irving Rouse. The Bibliography indicates many of the teachers, most of whom I have never seen, to whom I owe much of my knowledge of anthropology. Conrad Arensberg, Robert F. Bales, Frederick Johnson, Felix Keesing, Daniel O. Price, the Forest Products Laboratory of Canada's Department of Resources and Development, and the Swedish Royal Ministry of Foreign Affairs among others answered inquiries pertaining to special matters. Marijane Allen gave permission to use her sonnet, "Neanderthal," and Joseph H. Greenberg to reprint a portion of his unpublished "Violence Texts." To my graduate students I am especially grateful for stimulating discussion of many points incorporated in the following pages. As Director of the Institute for Research in Social Science, University of North Carolina, Gordon W. Blackwell (now Chancellor of The Woman's College of the University) expedited my work. More, perhaps, than he is aware did membership in, and opportunities offered by, the Institute contribute to my education as a social scientist. The Wenner-Gren Foundation for Anthropological Research sponsored several field trips to Great Whale River, Quebec, and Attawapiskat, Ontario. I have drawn on the material collected during those expeditions. The following organizations generously offered their films for preview: Australian News and Information Bureau, British Information Services, California Texas Oil Company, National Film Board of Canada, New Zealand Embassy, Quebec Tourist Bureau, and United States Indian Service. The following publishers have given permission to reprint or quote from material they have published: Cambridge University Press; F. S. Crofts and Co., E. P. Dutton and Co., Oxford University Press, Random House, Charles C. Thomas, and Harcourt, Brace and Co.

The reference staff of the Wilson Library, University of North Carolina were ever graciously helpful. Assistance in completing the manuscript was provided by the Institute for Research in Social Science. This will acknowledge my appreciation of the cooperation provided by Katharine Jocher,

Assistant Director; Frances Schnibben, and her secretarial staff. Critical reading, checking, and typing were also undertaken by Irma Honigmann despite pressure to prepare for an extended visit to Pakistan.

JOHN J. HONIGMANN

Chapel Hill
January, 1959

THE WORLD OF MAN

Part One

NATURE AND SCOPE

OF ANTHROPOLOGY

The discoveries of science . . . have changed the way men think of things. . . . We have learned from the natural history of the earth and from the story of evolution to have a sense of history, of time and change. We learn to talk of ourselves, and of the nature of the world and its reality as not wholly fixed in a silent quiet moment, but as unfolding with novelty and alteration, decay and new growth. We have understood something of the inner harmony and beauty of strange primitive cultures, and through this see the qualities of our own life in an altered perspective, and recognize its accidents as well as inherent necessities. . . .

J. ROBERT OPPENHEIMER (1953)

Western Civilization has paid dearly with the blood and tears of millions because of the facile belief that civilization is not a process of trial and error. . . . Time and again those who thought themselves the "good," the "chosen," the "élite," or, as divinely appointed emperors or tyrants, made the . . . mistake of regarding civilization as dependent only on them, or on their abstract concepts of perfection. . . .

S. H. FRANKEL (1953:162)

1.

What Is Anthropology?

THE phrase "man and his works" succinctly sums up the scope of anthropology and indicates the very wide boundaries of the discipline. "Man"; the anthropologist attends to the physical structure and biological functioning of the human being. "Man's works"; anthropology covers the whole range of human life. In theory as well as in practice, the subjects, man and man's works, cover a large and heterogeneous ground. "Anthropology is bounded only by the limits of what anthropologists do and use" (Tax, 1955:519).

DIVISIONS OF ANTHROPOLOGY

In practice few anthropologists attempt to exploit the full scope of man and his works. Some specialize in the biological aspects of human beings. They make up the division of physical anthropology. Others study the regularities of human behavior from one part of the world to another. They pursue cultural anthropology.

Physical Anthropology

Physical anthropologists are concerned with the similarities and differences linking man and the other animals. How did man acquire biological features like upright posture, flexible hand, specialized foot, and large brain? How are these and other aspects of the human organism reflected in culture? What is the significance of those variations in mankind called racial?

Not only the fact that physical anthropology studies the human organism, and so deals with tissue and bones rather than with an ephemeral phenomenon like behavior, but also its relatively precise methods of measurement assert the close ties of this division with the biological and natural sciences. Cultural anthropology, with its interest in human ways of life, has its firmest links with the humanities and social sciences.

Cultural Anthropology

Cultural anthropology has been called the central field of anthropology (Tax, *et al.*, 1953:361–362). As a discipline it studies the whole range of

3

human behavior—subsistence, manufacturing, marriage, family life, government, values, religion, and medicine. For such a total way of life the
anthropologist uses the term "culture." In speaking of the culture of a
people—for example, the Central Eskimo—he means the whole system of
interrelated behaviors practiced by those people together with the sleds,
cooking utensils, clothing, and other artifacts which they employ.

Cultural anthropology, then, is devoted to the study of whole cultures.
In addition simply to describing total ways of life the anthropologist is
concerned with the dynamics of culture, that is, with how culture persists
in time, changes, and grows. Finally, many anthropologists probe deeply
into selected parts of culture, divisions like kinship organization or sexual
behavior, subjects which other academic disciplines tend to neglect or
pursue only in the context of Euroamerican culture. The variety of such
interests is indicated by the following topics, each of which refers to one
or more actual pieces of research:

> Political Organization in Negro Africa
> Ceremonies of the American Indians
> Eskimo Law
> Economics of a Rural Guatemalan Population
> Basket-making Among American Indians
> Traps and Trapping Methods
> Personality of Chinese and Americans
> House Forms in the Southwest Pacific
> The Origin and Distribution of the Plow
> The Ruins of Yucatán
> Proverbs of an African People
> American Indian War Veterans and Their Values
> Religion and Myths in New Guinea
> Agriculture in Madagascar
> The Dance Among Various African Peoples
> Fishing in Northwestern North America
> Tribal Organization in the Mountains of Northern Iraq
> Changing Forms of the Family in India

To pursue topics as diversified as these, anthropology has attracted
people with varied interests. Newcomers to the profession have constantly
reached out after fresh topics. The field "always has been as broad in
conception as it is possible to be; in wandering correspondingly widely for
its data and tools, it absorbs in the tradition of the discipline those new
men with special ideas who accept the breadth of anthropology" (Tax,
1955:319).

Cultural anthropology may be regarded as a federation of some half-
dozen subsidiary fields, namely: (1) archeology, (2) ethnology, (3) eth-

nography, (4) sociological anthropology, (5) linguistics, and (6) culture and personality.

1. Prehistoric Archeology. Prehistory, or, as it is also called, prehistoric archeology, seeks to uncover the remains of former ways of life which have left no written records. Evidence of no longer extant cultures often helps in tracing historical relationships between regions of the globe and also illustrates concretely how culture has changed and grown. The techniques are examined in Chapter 4. According to a survey conducted by the U.S. Department of Labor, about one-third of the country's anthropologists are specialists in archeology.

2. Ethnology. Anthropology is best known for the study of "living" cultures, that is, ways of life which remain available for direct observation. Like the archeologist, the ethnologist, too, inquires into how parts of culture, like a dance, house type, or forms of family, change. His ultimate goal is to understand how total cultures are constituted and how they work. The word "anthropologist" will be used freely in the following pages where "ethnologist" would be more accurate. In England students of living cultures tend to be called "social anthropologists" (Radcliffe-Brown, 1946a, 1952a). About one-fourth of American anthropologists classify themselves as specialists in ethnology or social anthropology.

3. Ethnography. Field work, or ethnography, means the process of actually acquiring data about a living culture. The techniques of ethnography, which involve active participation in an exotic way of life, will be described in Chapter 5.

4. Sociological Anthropology. This area of specialization in ethnology is marked by a tendency to focus on the forms of relationships between people to the almost total exclusion of other parts of culture (R. Firth, 1951; Beattie, 1955). In sociological anthropology little attention is paid to man as a toolmaker, hunter, or farmer. Man is studied as a group-living animal. Perhaps the strongest development of this point of view has been in Great Britain and some other British Commonwealth countries. Spokesmen for sociological anthropology claim that it is easier to describe social relationships in different parts of the world than to compare more abstract customs, like religion (Evans-Pritchard, 1951b:40). Actually, a great deal of abstraction also enters into the analysis of kinship behavior, political organization, and other sorts of groupings studied by workers in this subfield.

5. Linguistics. Another specialism within ethnology is devoted to exploring that very restricted division of culture, language. The linguist studies language as a system of sounds agreed upon to possess significance. He looks for the units of language, the rules which speakers of any language follow in combining sounds, how those rules change, the spatial relationships between languages, and the degree to which thought may depend on language. Linguistics is not concerned directly with teaching people to use their own language more effectively or correctly nor with helping them to acquire command of foreign languages.

6. Culture and Personality. An ethnologist tends to study a way of life as it is manifested by people acting in concert. The student of culture and personality pursues much the same data as an ethnologist but studies culture as it is manifested in the personalities of individuals. To say that the United States is a productive country is to make a very terse statement about culture. Describing Americans as animated by needs for achievement, conformity, and control of the material environment is a statement about personality. An abstract type of individual—"the American"—is frequently imagined for purposes of personality description. Among millions of citizens not one will be identical with the type. Culture and personality research goes further. It seeks the relationship between some aspect of culture and certain features of personality. For example, does a high rate of production somehow depend on a driving need for achievement? About 5 percent of a sample of American anthropologists list themselves as specialists in this subfield.

Archeologist, ethnologist, ethnographer, linguist, and physical anthropologist—all may be united in the same person. More and more, however, anthropologists have begun to specialize in one or a few of these interests. Some physical anthropologists, for example, concentrate so intensively on human biology that they have quite lost touch with what cultural anthropologists are doing. The same, of course, holds for many cultural anthropologists. The future, probably, will encourage further specialization. There are sound reasons for expecting this trend. Few men can find the time and energy to learn the techniques which each of the subfields requires for effective mastery. Then there is the problem of finding time to read the voluminous literature being accumulated in anthropology as a whole. On the other hand, self-conscious and deliberate efforts to counteract the trend of specialization are also apparent. No graduate school is willing to turn out a professional anthropologist who does not possess general familiarity with all the diverse fields. "It is obvious that, with the growing diversity of interests and the growing perfection of techniques, we cannot all do everything. We cannot certainly be, at the same time, linguists who are rated as such by the specialists in that field, ethnographers, physical anthropologists, and prehistorians. We can and I think we must, however, take an interest in all these branches . . ." (Lowie in Tax, *et al.*, 1953:68).

WHY STUDY ANTHROPOLOGY?

A complex play of motives impels most behavior. A college student may be motivated to climb the social ladder at the same time that he seeks a college degree; he may choose courses that arouse his curiosity as well as those that appear not too difficult because he wants to maintain a certain average grade. What are some goals that motivate people who are attracted to anthropology?

Solution of Practical Problems

In college, people not exceptionally choose subjects like anthropology or sociology because of a strong drive for social amelioration. They "desire to change the world for the better and 'solve' social problems" (R. N. Wilson, 1954:28). Soon, however, the student discovers how enormously difficult it is to direct social change. He wrestles with the question, what is social improvement? At this point he may abandon the subject, often expressing intense dissatisfaction with the futility or pedantry of scholarship. As one young man put it to the author: "While the world is destroying itself, professors disagree on how to define technical terms!" Other students accept the accumulation of knowledge about human behavior as a worthwhile goal in itself. Reform may continue to be an ultimate aim but often it recedes more and more into the background as the desire to learn comes to dominate. People so motivated argue that the "paramount reason for studying anything . . . is a matter of intellectual passion" (Homans, 1950:2) or "for most scientists . . . the justification of their work is to be found in the pure joy of its creativeness; the spirit which moves them is closely akin to the imaginative vision which inspires the artist" (Conant, 1952:58).

The individual with a desire to use knowledge for the solution of practical problems may find applied anthropology a congenial field in which to work. Unfortunately, he had better understand at the outset, rarely does the professional man have both the opportunity to design solutions and the power to put those solutions into practice. All through human history the successful social engineer has generally also been an administrator of social affairs. It is likely, therefore, as Plato also thought, that the most effective application of any knowledge can be made by someone who occupies a position of authority. One disadvantage with such merging of positions lies in the fact that the administrator is too busy making day-to-day decisions to examine a problem thoroughly from the standpoint of existing knowledge. Hence, the applied anthropologist makes his appearance. He is usually a social engineer who works for a responsible administrator, helping the latter achieve certain ends by advising on the difficulties to be encountered and reporting on the grass-roots progress of administrative decisions. The applied anthropologist seldom decides what goal an administrator should adopt. When working in a colonial administration, for example, he accepts the ends of the government and helps to execute them. Sometimes, in association with other technical experts in forestry, agriculture, health, and animal husbandry, he may help the government to design certain policies, but even then the overall goal—a contented population or increased output—is set by the administration. The technical experts are expected merely to implement that policy. If the anthropologist does not believe the particular end to be in the best interests of the subject population he has little recourse but to resign and work as a private citizen against the program in question.

Dynamics of Social Life

An observer of the world of man may want to know why human beings behave as they do. His interest is scientifically oriented rather than primarily concerned with the applicability of knowledge or motivated by humanistic curiosity.

Although no discipline by itself, nor even all disciplines together, can fully account for human behavior, there is a fair chance that the reader will finish this book a little wiser about certain elementary principles of culture. He will learn, for example, that the complexity of a government depends on the number of people living together. He will discover that change in a way of life is not haphazard but that its course can to some degree be anticipated. Ritual will become less a matter of traditional forms and more a living process which knits together human aggregates. The reader will see that any culture is related to how the human animal is constructed.

A great deal of scholarly effort in any field goes toward sharpening tools and methods of inquiry. Hence, the reader who wants to understand culture will be expected to spend some time learning the concepts that an anthropologist uses as tools of inquiry and the methods which help him in uncovering relevant knowledge about human behavior.

Appreciation and Curiosity

Some people are attracted to anthropology simply because they want to broaden their acquaintance with man's nature: to know how he has evolved, what he has done in the past or in various parts of the world, and what he is now up to. Questions about the origin of culture, how Samoans live, how man arrived in the New World, or what the life of a Muslim woman is like may imply no more than a lively curiosity about human behavior. Such curiosity ought to require no defense. Unfortunately, in the predominantly scientific climate of our time, humanistic endeavor has been relegated to a subordinate position. How unjustified this is will be clear to the reader who believes that the humanities broaden the base of human action. They widen the perspectives with which we live, lending tolerance and sophistication to our judgments. An anthropologist through a world-wide survey of cultures reveals that divorce is "easier and more prevalent in other societies than our own" (Murdock, 1950:200–201). What humanistic significance may reside in this fact? Let the anthropologist himself reply:

"The cross-cultural evidence makes it abundantly clear that the modern American family is unstable in only a relative and not an absolute sense. From an absolute, that is, comparative, point of view, our family institution still leans quite definitely toward the stable end of the ethnographic spectrum. Current trends could continue without reversal for a considerable period before the fear of social disorganization would acquire genuine justification."

2.

Culture

WORDS point to events or things in the realm of experience, or else they designate relationships between such events. In the language of semantics, words have referents. What referents has the term "culture"?

The label "culture" has been employed in anthropology with over one hundred different meanings (Kroeber and Kluckhohn, 1952). Clearly, everybody does not use the word to refer to precisely the same thing. Little will be gained at this point by listing a hundred definitions of culture. But it must be clear how the word will be used in these pages.

REFERENTS OF CULTURE

The term "culture" enjoys both technical and nontechnical meanings. In its nontechnical sense, with which this book will not be concerned, the word (it may be written "culture$_n$") refers to certain features of living, including a taste for literature; participation in music, painting, or drama; and the support of those activities in a community. The concept culture$_n$ possesses a strong normative flavor because it designates not only what exists but what is desirable. In this sense culture is "something which man as a rational being ought to achieve in life, a good which should be pursued for its own sake" (Das, 1953:71). Presumably all people do not equally share culture$_n$, that is, everybody is not equally cultured. In its more technical or anthropological usage, on the contrary, culture is as universal as human life itself. It would be ridiculous to deny anyone the right to employ the notion of culture$_n$. More and more, however, that usage is falling into abeyance and the anthropological, or technical, concept is taking its place. In this latter sense culture refers basically to behavior and artifacts.

Culture Patterns

When an ethnographer describes a living culture, what specifically is he talking about? The bulk of his report deals with recurrent forms of behavior, together with descriptions of the types of objects, which he found to be extant in a particular group of people. In a word, the field worker deals with culture patterns.[1] The word "pattern" designates a sequence of behavior

[1] Only one of several anthropological usages of the word "pattern" is represented here. For a review of the diverse meanings assigned that term see Rioux, 1956.

which is repeated from one individual to another. "The people of Pakistan believe that Mohammed was the prophet of one, almighty God" is an example of a culture pattern. "Americans brush their teeth upon arising" illustrates another pattern. One might say that a pattern represents behavior that is shared between two or more individuals. Of course, each individual executes the pattern in his own fashion, with minor idiosyncratic peculiarities. Such minor variations, however, do not prevent the ethnographer from being able to abstract the basic form of the behavior and to express it as a regularity. The word also designates the common form and attributes shared by the objects which a community makes and uses. "American homes generally contain several rooms which are specialized according to use" is an example of a culture pattern that applies to a man-made object.

Although anthropologists report patterns, the word "culture" is not clearly defined by saying that it refers to patterns. The events to which a field worker attends when he is constructing patterns are the basic referents of "culture." Three kinds of phenomena make up culture.

1. **Activities.** Culture includes socially standardized actions. These may be undertaken with the limbs, torso, head, speech organs, or any other body part that is susceptible to group influence. Thus in northwestern Pakistan, the spoken greeting, "Remain happy," the technique of guiding an ox-drawn plow, swimming across the Indus River supported on an inflated animal skin, and carrying a pistol or rifle "for fashion" all constitute acts which an individual acquires as a member of a group. Hence, they are socially standardized. They help make up the culture of the Pathan people in northwestern Pakistan.

2. **Ideas.** Socially standardized thoughts and feelings represent the second order of phenomena in culture. Although theoretically distinct from activity, thoughts and feelings actually are closely involved with most acts. In a Pathan village the excitement accompanying a holiday, the ideal of defending one's personal honor, one's fear of being attacked in the maize fields by armed robbers, and the belief that nobody should give his daughter in marriage to a man belonging to another occupationally named group all illustrate socially standardized thoughts or feelings which contribute to the make-up of Pathan culture.

Two classes of referents of the term "culture" have so far been designated: overt actions and covert thoughts and feelings. Together these may be referred to as "behavior." The word "custom" designates a recurrent form of socially standardized behavior—a shared act, thought, or feeling. It is the custom of Pathans to be proud of their honor and it is also customary for Pathans to plow with oxen.

3. **Artifacts.** Socially standardized artifacts represent the third and last order of cultural referents. An "artifact" is any man-made characteristic of the environment, like the Pathan's turban, plow, or even his cattle, as long as the latter are regarded as *domesticated* animals (Braidwood, *1946*).

Social Standardization

Practically everything man does, even his breathing, is acquired while he is a member of society and is conditioned by social factors (Sapir, 1927: 116–117). Culture refers to the activities, thoughts and feelings, and artifacts which man acquires as a member of society (Tylor, 1891:I, 1). By definition any activity, idea, or artifact is socially standardized if it has been influenced by membership in some human aggregate.

Practically Everything Man Does Is Conditioned by Social Factors (courtesy, New Zealand Embassy).

"Culture" often is defined as referring to learned behavior. It is more precise to substitute the words "socially standardized" for "learned." If each generation acquires an idea of a proper house, then that house when it is built will be socially standardized. Further, the house, in turn, will influence whatever behavior occurs in its context. Learning is too narrow and ambiguous a term to apply to all the ways in which social factors directly or indirectly influence behavior and artifacts.

A word of warning is in order. The word "standardized" does not mean only extremely tight proscriptions on activities such as extinguish practically all originality and suppress individual variation. Standardization is a quite normal phenomenon and a universal feature of social life. From the moment of birth the individual modifies his behavior to meet the expectations and other conditions of his group. Later if he travels, further modifications are assumed in response to the social conditions of a foreign community. The process of being socially influenced lasts until death and is continuous from one generation to the next.

Do other animals than man have culture? A later chapter examines the animal basis of culture (Chap. 44). Meantime let the reader note that this book is concerned specifically with human culture. There is little question but that some behavior of all animals (how much is not clear) is modified by social interaction and hence constitutes culture by definition. It is perfectly clear, too, that man alone passes on a major portion of his customs to succeeding generations.

Culture as a System

Culture points to socially standardized actions, thoughts, feelings, and artifacts. An anthropologist generally deals with these several classes of elements as they reveal regularities or patterns. In addition the culture concept contains yet one more important implication, namely, that the socially standardized units of behavior constitute at least a partial system (i.e., configuration). That is to say, the various activities, thoughts, feelings, and artifacts characteristic of a group of people are in some degree interrelated. As a result, change in one area of culture will be associated with changes in other areas. Now, this is not to say that everything is related to everything else directly (F. E. Williams, 1940:400–412; 1951:15, 33). By no stretch of the imagination can the methods of cost accounting practiced in a large American corporation be related directly to the religion of a snake-handling cult in the Piedmont district of the Carolinas. Perhaps a radical change in the former complex would in time be followed by changes in the latter, but the relationship is indirect at best. The two are linked through many intervening activities rather than being in a state of direct mutual dependence. Thus elimination of cost accounting might be followed by a serious loss in business efficiency which would be reflected in mill-town unemployment and eventually increase participation in the snake-handling cult.

Most areas of culture possess some degree of autonomy in relation to other areas. This means that they can withstand certain amounts of change in other parts of the system before they themselves undergo modification. The relative degree of autonomy of any part of culture varies. Grammar, meaning the rules for forming words and larger utterances, is highly stable in any culture and has often remained relatively unchanged despite thoroughgoing and revolutionary changes in other areas of a way of life. On the other hand, the words of a language (vocabulary) change readily with other changes in culture.

The systematic nature of culture may be illustrated by showing how the prestige system, tools, and human skills are related to the food-getting system in different cultures. In northwestern Pakistan prestige for Pathans comes from landowning as well as movable wealth which, in turn, is acquired from farming. The important tools are those used in making a living off the land: scythe, plow, and the oxen which supplement human energy. Men learn to use these tools in order to cultivate the land. From such cultivation, in turn, their own and their families' prestige derives. In a band of Arctic Eskimo hunters prestige is tied to other activities, namely, hunting and fishing. Little wealth exists in the form of portable goods; the wealthy man remains an unknown figure. Important tools include the harpoon, kayak, sled, and, today at any rate, the gun. A man must learn the techniques for using these implements effectively and in that way he can acquire renown as a successful hunter.

Silkworm cultivation in China is bound up with a number of other items of Chinese culture including means of forecasting the crop of silkworms (astrologers make a living through performing this service), worship of a spirit that controls the silkworms, and celebrations that come at certain points on the sericulture cycle (Liu, 1952:155–163). The culture of a silkworm-raising village would be quite different if sericulture were excised from its way of life.

The systematic nature of culture may be studied (1) with historical data or (2) by observing the relationships between parts of culture at a single moment in time.

1. Use of Historical Data. From a historical viewpoint a cultural system is indicated when, following a change in one part of the way of life, other nonautonomous areas also alter. For example, when Winnebago Indian children began to grow up in houses floored with lumber and started to wear diapers or "training pants," the earlier, lax attitudes toward toilet training became sharper (Oestreich, 1948:91). Indian parents began to train the children in the fashion of middle-class white Americans. Apparently, the time required to launder diapers and to clean the wooden floors had something to do with the shift in toilet training. Toilet training thus is seen to be dependent on the kind of houses in which one lives, the clothes worn, and the standards of cleanliness adopted. Another historical test of the systematic nature of culture is furnished by the Cayuá Indians in southern Brazil (J. B. Watson, 1952). When they first met the white man they gave up stone for metal tools, and subsistence agriculture for commercial farming. Quickly a host of other, related changes entered their way of life. For example, in association with the new type of farming the woman became economically less important so that her occupational role altered. With women's labor less important, the custom of a man's marrying several wives disappeared, although other factors were no doubt also at work urging monogamy on the people. The new system of agricultural production put more stress on individual efficiency; hence former patterns of group cooperation disappeared from the way of life.

It is not necessary to go far afield to study the systematic nature of culture from the standpoint of change through time. In Europe and America the rise of large business corporations, for example, helped to weaken the force of Judaic and Christian moral principles. Apparently such principles were not suited to the new ways of doing business. According to some observers, God simply had to quit business (Childs and Cater, 1954:86). Morality, therefore, seems to bear a close relationship to the way in which people interact with one another in the course of making a living.

2. Use of Contemporary Data. If culture is indeed a system, then relationships between certain parts of a culture should also exist at any single moment in time. An illustration has already been given in comparing the skills and tools of Pathan farmers and Eskimo hunters. One also can point to the simple, easily constructed houses associated with nomadic hunting peoples and the generally more substantial houses of settled farmers. A relationship between house type and mode of subsistence is indicated. Or notice how a people's vocabulary reflects their occupations and interests. An Air Force bomber squadron, for example, will use many words (like "ops room," "prop," "mission," "briefing," and "GCA") the meanings of which are scarcely comprehensible to other English speakers. (Of course, military service for millions of men has helped to disseminate many of the specialized terms of military argot into the population.)

Culture as an Abstraction

Much dismay has been provoked by calling culture an abstraction. The "abstraction conception of culture," it is held, will hinder "a return to the scientific tradition of a direct and immediate concern with objective things and events: Culture is the name of a class of things and events in the external world . . ." (Leslie A. White, 1954b:467). But surely an electron is also an abstraction rather than an objective thing! Yet physicists find no difficulty carrying on atomic research simply because of the "abstraction conception" of the electron.

What is meant by claiming that culture is an abstraction? Nobody observes a culture directly. Anthropologists "observe" words, actions, and things. By systematically putting these observations together they reach the idea of some kind of system called "Pathan culture," "American culture," or simply "culture." In other words, culture conceived of as a whole includes more than the discrete elements which a field worker observes. He combines and organizes these in his mind and on paper. Thereby he constructs an abstraction which is at least one step removed from the raw data of experience. To say that culture is an abstraction is to say that (like an electron) it is not tangible, occupies no space (except figuratively), and exerts no mechanical force. The raw data of culture—for example, a specific chair or a punch in the nose—are tangible enough.

Only figuratively and for convenience can culture be said to have power to make people do, or not do, things. "Islamic culture prohibits the Muslim from eating pork" is only a figurative way of speaking. All that one can ever observe is one Muslim instructing or warning another to avoid pork. Such behavior may be customary. Yet it is not the custom one observes but rather each discrete instance. From a number of such instances the ethnologist constructs the pattern and out of many patterns he derives his idea of a culture.

HUMAN AGGREGATES STUDIED FOR CULTURE

The anthropologist studies culture from the vantage point of some human aggregate, living or vanished. The terms "community" and "society" designate two main types of such aggregates, although another type of aggregate which has been investigated will also be discussed. It is necessary to fix clearly in mind the distinction between culture as a way of life and the people who manifest it. To say that "societies differ" is inaccurate when one means to say that ways of life are different. A phrase like "he went to live in another culture" really means that somebody went to join another aggregate of people. A community and society are essentially aggregates of individuals; culture, however, refers to what people do, say, or feel.

Community

A community is an aggregate of people to some degree localized in time and space and manifesting a relatively intense common life (G. Wilson and M. Wilson, 1945:30). The term points, first, toward people and, second, toward a characteristic of their mutual relationships, namely, intensity. Any such aggregate may be studied for its culture. "Community" may be used to designate a single village or tribe, or a number of villages bound together by a feeling of common membership in a larger community. New York City may be regarded as a community for the purpose of ethnography, although it is broken up into a nearly countless number of distinct groups whose customs often vary. But a community is not necessarily synonymous with a local group—that is, with a village, town, or city. In North Burma one anthropologist dealt successfully with an interacting series of 9 villages, 6 dialects, and 500 people (Leach, 1954:66–281). For many analysts the tribe, traditional unit of ethnography, continues to represent the most useful focus of cultural analysis. But the Victorian era in England might also be regarded as an area of relatively close common life. So could any modern nation. It is possible to apply the term to so specialized an area of work and life as a factory (Jaques, 1951), psychiatric ward or mental hospital (Caudill, Redlich, Gilmore, and Brody, 1952; Stanton and Schwartz, 1954), sanatorium (Wilmer, 1953), or United States Air Force bomb squadron (Honigmann, 1954d).

Archeologically, the existence of communities may be inferred from the skeletal and artifactual remains of the people who occupied a definite spatial locale at some point in time. "During the Bronze Age . . . Europe was divided up among a multiplicity of distinct communities or peoples. These may be distinguished from one another by burial sites, architecture, art and the types of tools, weapons, vessels, and ornaments they used. The distinctive metal, bone, stone and pottery types (artifacts), regularly found associated in graves and settlements over a given geographical area, together with the peculiarities of the domestic and funerary structures in which they occur, constitute what is called a culture" (Childe, 1930:41–42).

A few indicators of close common life, or of social intensity, may be suggested as signs by which to gauge existence of a community. (1) Common life is revealed by the interdependence of individuals—whether manifested through customs of trade, specialized occupations, political rule and subjugation, intermarriage of clans, or rivalry between constituent subgroups. (2) People living in community may distinguish themselves in some way: by name, garment, or emblem. Such symbolization expresses their distinctiveness or unity. Finally, (3) a community may be recognized through the common interests and goals which motivate members. Building automobiles, maintaining national sovereignty, even just a desire to remain together are all goals around which the interaction of people is focused. Note that social intensity does not imply frictionless relationships. Communities never lack opposition.

Communities persist in time even though membership does not remain stable. Members die and, in time, may be forgotten; individuals migrate in and out, and the community increases or decreases in size. Racial composition may change as a result of immigration, even though interbreeding between racial populations may never occur.

Anthropologists are often content to study only one ethnic group in a community. To study only the Navaho Indians is not to study the whole community of which the Navaho are a part. The area of Navaho common life may include not only those Indians but also other Indians like the Hopi, white traders, and missionaries who serve those people.

Society

In recent years anthropologists have become increasingly aware that they know a great deal about relatively small communities but very little about the larger social systems, like nations or regions, in which the former are incorporated (Leach, 1954:290–291). "There is no people and no state which is not part of another society, more or less unlimited, which embraces all the people and all the States with which the first comes in contact either directly or indirectly . . ." (Durkheim, 1915:426). In other words, a community exists in a society. It is part of a larger social area, one also anchored spatially and temporally, and characterized by a relatively unintense common life. A society may be defined as referring to all the people of whom the community is aware. In such a definition it is assumed that the society will always be specified from the vantage point of a particular community. From that community it derives its name (G. Wilson and M. Wilson, *1945*:31, 39–41).

Obviously the societies of different communities vary in range or scale. Two hundred years ago those Kaska Indians living in the upper Liard, Frances, and lower Dease River valleys of British Columbia were aware of a relatively narrow society (Fig. 2:1). Mountains hemmed them in and shut them off from the Indians to the north, east, and west. Some vague ideas of inhabitants beyond these frontiers existed among the Kaska but these ideas were largely stereotypes or fantasies, perhaps akin to our image of Martians. The people across the mountains were scarcely human. Relationships with them were thin. Not even intense warfare linked the Kaska with neighboring Indians. A few men traveled to the Pacific coast and they must be taken into account when setting the precontact boundaries of Kaska society. In the eighteenth century Indians from the Pacific coast started coming to the Kaska seeking furs which would be sold to Europeans. In the nineteenth century European and Canadian fur buyers opened trading posts in closer proximity to the Kaska and in the late nineteenth century American and Canadian gold seekers poured into the country (Honigmann, *1949a*:39–50). A Roman Catholic missionary came to live with the Indians in 1924. In 1942 the Alaska Highway was built to bisect Kaska territory and a large military airport opened in the area. The Kaska had by now come to meet people from relatively distant places. They had discovered how their lives were affected by a far-reaching network of social relationships. They learned about Canada, the United States, and Europe. From the missionary they became aware of events that happened in the Middle East nearly 2000 years ago. Kaska society has expanded during the last 200, and especially during the last 20, years. Yet the Indians are scarcely as wide in their range of social relations as a typical university community in the United States. On the other hand, the presence of a dozen or so white men living quite closely with the Indians

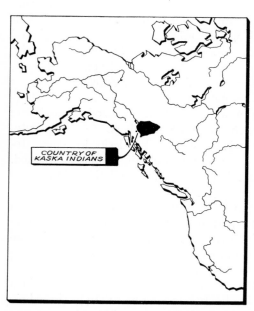

FIG. 2:1.   Map Showing Location of Kaska Indians.

should not be overlooked in setting the social scale of the community. Include them in the community and Kaska society is considerably larger in scale than it was 200 years previously.

A society includes a number of constituent communities. It is quite possible to find one of these communities more dominant than the others. A society may be dominated intellectually by the idea systems originating in one community, financially by the money loaned from another, and politically by the power emanating from a third. Or all such influences may stem from a single, powerful community. Culture is continuous in society. Despite the isolation of the Kaska Indians in aboriginal times, their culture was not very different from that of other Indians to the east and north, although it did diverge rather sharply from the culture of people who lived on the Pacific coast, across the Continental Divide.

Status Category

One can approach a culture from the standpoint of people who occupy a particular status (i.e., position) in a community or society. The aggregate—whether women, men, Polish immigrants, scientists, Indians, or Negroes—is called a status category. A category is an aggregate of people who possess one or more attributes in common but who do not form a group (see p. 356). Do they also share other patterns of culture? Several writers have described patterns of women's life in Australia (Kaberry, 1939), the American Deep South (Hagood, 1939), India (Cormack, 1953), and Pakistan (Honigmann, 1957b). Sociologists and anthropologists have written about American white-collar culture (Mills, 1951) and about that of the British middle class (Maude and Maude, 1950). To be part of the middle or white-collar class is also to occupy a social status.

Part Two

METHODOLOGY

Many persons study so imperfectly the spirit and character of the different nations that inhabit the earth, and the influence of climate on their manners, customs, predilections, and usages, that they are astonished to find how widely such nations differ from each other. Trammelled by the prejudices of their own surroundings, such persons think nothing well regulated that is not included in the polity and government of their own country. They would like to see all nations of the earth placed on precisely the same footing as themselves. Everything which differs from their own customs they consider either uncivilized or ridiculous. Now, although man's nature is pretty much the same all the world over, it is subject to so many differentiations caused by soil, climate, food, religion, education and other circumstances peculiar to different countries, that the system of civilization adopted by one people would plunge another into a state of barbarism and cause its complete downfall.

J. A. DuBois (1924:27–28)

3.

Approaches to Culture

CULTURAL anthropology has no single method for studying culture but combines a miscellany of approaches (Redfield, 1946). Some anthropologists work to discover the historical antecedents of a given culture, to trace the origins of its parts. Others are content with life as it is lived at a particular time and place. A third emphasis is on discovering regularities, or laws, which hold from one culture to another. The three approaches may, of course, be combined in a single person. Many anthropologists agree that it would be regrettable for one approach to become entrenched so firmly that all others were rejected. Each produces its own unique kind of knowledge.

HOW ANTHROPOLOGY HAS CHANGED

Anthropology became established in the Victorian era. The new discipline emerged as part of the intellectual ferment accompanying the era of exploration, Industrial Revolution, birth of geology, and Darwin's doctrine of animal evolution (Forde, 1950; Daniel, 1950). From its start anthropology characteristically sought to confront people with striking, unfamiliar phenomena or teach them to look at familiar phenomena in a fresh way. Nineteenth-century students of man confronted startled Victorians with man's great antiquity and the slow growth of human culture. Both bits of knowledge upset people who had been reared on Biblical chronology and had accepted the story of Eden's perfection terminated by Adam's fall.

When the nineteenth-century ethnologists began to work with culture what they did with their data was influenced strongly by Darwin's still recent theory of animal evolution. They interpreted culture to show its evolution. At every stage of its progression from simple to complex, culture had left survivals. These way-markers could be found in existing ways of life "full of meaning for those who can decipher their signs." By consulting them carefully "the European may find among the Greenlanders or Maoris many a trait for reconstructing the picture of our primitive ancestors" (Tylor, 1891:I, 21). The fossils of biological evolutionists, however, constituted surer evidence than the supposed way-markers of culture. That some communities personified trees and water or endowed natural phenomena with souls scarcely constituted evidence that religion had originated in such conceptions of the world. Nineteenth-century evolutionary anthropologists treated exotic cultures as though the latter were fossils. That is, they arranged contemporary ways of life in a supposed order of age and evolutionary development. Australian aborigines' culture was put at the early end of the presumptive sequence, there to be consulted by anybody who wanted to know how man had lived at his most primitive stage. A culture that included cities, the plow, domesticated animals, and writing approached European civilization so closely that it obviously belonged near the apex of the progressive record of culture history.

Fossils come in rock strata whose relative age can be determined by geologists. Cultures do not fossilize. They constantly change. Therefore any attempt to rank "living," or relatively contemporary, cultures as more or less ancient or as representing the survival of some primitive stage of human existence is fallacious. It is quite true that the general form of certain elements in a way of life may persist over long periods. The alphabet, which serves much of mankind, has persisted for some 2000 years in its fundamental pattern. On the other hand, no existing alphabet, living religion, form of marriage, contemporary form of the plow, bow, or house can be taken as accurately mirroring the original form of that element. To know the past requires clear-cut evidence either in the form of historical documents or in the form of the remains excavated by archeology.

Although early anthropologists, seeking to interpret ethnological data evolutionarily, got off on the wrong foot, they successfully introduced a new discipline. From them stems the tradition of collecting the facts of culture, of regarding human behavior as empirically as other disciplines regard other branches of nature. Certain nineteenth-century scholars, like Edward B. Tylor, also combined in their work attention to man as a physical organism while at the same time focusing on his culture. The unity of anthropology as a discipline concerned with both these aspects of humanity also derives from this period (Tax, 1955).

Evolutionism gave place to a surer kind of culture history. During the Victorian period archeology began to emerge as a substitute for presumptive reconstructions of culture growth. From the stratified evidence of successive human occupations prehistoric archeologists have succeeded in reconstructing the history of nonliterate peoples in Asia, Africa, Europe, and America. Ethnologists, too, devised new means for determining the past of people who possessed no written records. Great interest was devoted to examining the distribution of cultural elements on the earth's surface with the intention of determining their origin and course of migration (see pp. 94–97). Using such methods, anthropologists wrote the first installments of the long story of human migrations and contacts between people.

All of the new anthropologists were not historically minded. Another brand of scholarship concentrated not on trying to reconstruct history in the absence of written records but on studying the form and organization of living cultures. The facts examined by nineteenth-century evolutionists had come largely from the reports of travelers and other nonprofessional observers. Now anthropologists themselves began to go into the field to collect their own ethnographies. Some of these accounts of culture were sheerly descriptive with little attempt at interpretation. Others increasingly sought to show the interrelationships between such parts of culture as chieftainship, religion, land tenure, and the cycle of the individual's life from birth to death (Lowie, 1937).

Diachronic and Synchronic Emphases

Modern cultural anthropology still shows both of the tendencies which waxed with the decline of evolutionary theory: interest in the history of the forms of human behavior and strong devotion to studying total cultures as they exist at a given moment in time. Sometimes both approaches appear in a single work but often one point of view predominates. This is the case, for example, in George A. Pettitt's *The Quileute of La Push: 1775–1945* (1950), in which a historical interest in culture change appears on practically every page. Bowers' *Mandan Social and Ceremonial Organization* (1950), on the other hand, is relatively timeless and ahistorical even though he writes about a vanished period of Mandan Indian life. Bowers describes a rather small sector of Mandan culture as it might have been observed by a visitor to those Missouri Valley villages in the years immediately following white contact, late in the eighteenth century. Working with 14 informants, men who recalled the past from accounts which their fathers or grandfathers had related, Bowers reconstructs the culture of a bygone era. He is not concerned with present-day Mandan Indian culture. Bronislaw Malinowski followed much the same approach to the culture of the Trobriand Islanders (living off the coast of New Guinea) and has described it ahistorically in several books, including *The Sexual Life of Savages* (1932). One difference between the two men is that Bowers reconstructed a former way of life which he did not directly experience, whereas Malinowski reported on things which he had directly experienced during his stay with his Melanesian hosts. Both are synchronic in their method, whereas Pettitt is diachronic. The synchronic approach (*syn* expresses concurrence; *chronus* means "time") captures a picture of culture as it exists at one moment in time; a diachronic study (*dia*, "through") follows culture through time.

Anthropology is quite unique among disciplines like sociology, psychology, and history in studying social behavior from both diachronic and synchronic positions. Most ethnologists feel at ease whether talking about human culture 8000 or 600,000 years ago or about the way of life of some existing community. Occasionally a dissenting voice has compared historical research unfavorably with the study of living cultures. Ethnologists, it is claimed, must work only with first-hand data that have been perceived directly. They must reject indirect evidence of how people lived in the past (Malinowski, 1945:114; Gluckman, 1949:3). Attempts to reconstruct history by examining the spatial distribution of particular cultural elements have been attacked with the argument that all elements in a group's way of life are related. Hence, "no element or aspect can be scientifically understood in isolation" from its cultural context (Piddington, 1950:28–29). On this principle is urged abandoning efforts to trace the travels and modifications of cultural elements like weapons, the alphabet, agriculture, or ceremonies. The argument is difficult to rebut because one is not clear about the meaning of "scientific." The term sounds suspiciously as if it embodies a hidden value judgment. If so, then the word "good" might freely be substituted for "scientific," leaving the argument resting on one man's opinion of what is desirable. Other anthropologists do not agree with the rejection of the diachronic emphasis. ". . . For social anthropologists to . . . slip into the habit of ignoring the time dimension altogether, is surely exceedingly unwise. Indeed I should call it scientifically indefensible. To restrict anthropological field work to peoples whose real history does appear at present more or less unknown is a convenient, and sometimes popular, way of running away from the time dimension. But were it to become a universal habit, anthropology would become quickly ruined" (Hawkes, 1954:163).

Value is seen in both the synchronic and diachronic approaches of anthropology. Each supplements the other. Defenders of a historical approach, however, often are insistent in arguing that a knowledge of how past events succeeded one another is essential for understanding the present. Useful, yes; but essential, no. One may come to understand an existing culture (or, in fact, any event) without knowing its antecedents. But to do so means being able to identify carefully all the relevant factors in the current situation. For example, one can understand relations between the northern and southern states of the United States without reconstructing the Civil War but not without being aware synchronically of any still extant attitudes which appeared through the Civil War. In the same way a psychiatrist may treat a patient without knowing the latter's childhood as long as he knows the relevant traits of behavior which originated in childhood. Obviously, knowledge of the history of a community or person may provide a short cut for identifying such relevant features in the contemporary system being studied.

HUMANISM AND SCIENCE

It is easier to distinguish the diachronic and synchronic interests of anthropologists than to explain the humanistic and scientific strains which cut across that dichotomy. An unfortunate connotation of desirability has become part of the word "science." Hence practically everybody who observes human behavior prefers to call his labor "scientific." Nevertheless, many historians are adamant in insisting that their work lies in the domain of the humanities. Classicists, philologists, and many students of comparative religion are also content to be identified with this long-established division of knowledge (Benedict, 1948; Redfield, 1953b; R. F. Spencer, 1954).

The Humanistic Tradition

Humanists often are witty, insightful, and plausible. For example, after suggesting that man's loss of hair increased man's sexual pleasure and so early men began to breed unconsciously for hairlessness, David Cort (1954:171) suggests "that civilization was created primarily to provide an improved alcove for sexual dalliance, and that this is the true function of architecture. If this sounds flippant, it is necessary only to remember that it is nakedness that requires architecture and clothing. Furthermore, it is probable that cave life weakened man's hairy covering, so that natural architecture may be charged with having created nakedness."

The idea sounds plausible and even logical; but is it true?

The essence of the humanistic approach to man and culture rests in its concern with (1) uniqueness, (2) valuation, and (3) a logical rather than an experimental approach to truth.

1. Uniqueness. Interest in the unique event characterizes the historian. In anthropology this is reflected in the concern with cultural diversity for its own sake. The unique and diverse stirred men like Herodotus as well as that trio of pilgrims, Fa Hien, Hiuen Tsang, and I Tsing, who visited India from China during the fifth to the eighth centuries (Gokhale, 1952:102–105; Coon, 1948:452–463). The same values appeared, too, in a small group of Sarsi and Blackfoot Indian men who, after traveling south from Alberta all summer in 1850 crossed a great river and came upon a region of low "hills" (Fig. 3:1). On top of one of

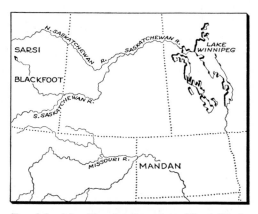

Fig. 3:1. Map Showing Location of Sarsi, Blackfoot, and Mandan Indians.

these "hills" a man suddenly appeared. Quickly the figure disappeared into the earth again, like a gopher. Then other men emerged, one of whom invited the strangely clad visitors to climb down into what turned out to be a semisubterranean dwelling. The guests received meat of the prairie deer to eat. They had come to the territory of the Mandan Indians in the Missouri

Valley. The Sarsi and Blackfoot men became terribly embarrassed when they discovered in the houses women who were naked except for an apron-like loincloth. "Ashamed" at the firm bosoms of the young girls and the sagging breasts of the old women, the tourists hid their eyes. How familiar, to hear that the visitors believed they were among people who lived like animals! They agreed among themselves to stay for only one night, lest they be killed.

Travel and new experiences broaden one's outlook and encourage tolerance. But the example of the Sarsi and Blackfoot Indians indicates that new experience is not immediately liberating. College students who in anthropological films see Eskimo tear raw seal meat with their teeth or observe an Eskimo mother wash her baby with spittle also often react with involuntary shock or disgust.

2. Valuation. Another keynote of the humanities is a tendency to react with appreciation or, less often, with some feeling of disparagement to the phenomena being studied. So, for example, civilizations like Egypt and Greece may be compared with avowedly evaluative overtones such as would strenuously be avoided by the scientist. Intuition and emotion are conceived to be valid, humanistic bases of knowledge capable of promoting agreement among observers whose tastes are carefully trained. When treating parts of culture—sculpture, poetry, painting, or even political systems—and even entire ways of life that have stood the test of time, the humanist's attitude is often one of admiration and pleasure. ". . . Humanism is that belief . . . that nothing which has ever interested living men and women can wholly lose its vitality—no language they have spoken, nor oracle beside which they have hushed their voices, no dream which has once been entertained by actual human minds, nothing about which they have ever been passionate, or expended time and zeal" (Pater, 1925:49). However, within the humanities disciplines differ somewhat in the frankness with which subjective impressions are set forth. History is probably the most objective and nonevaluative of the humanities.

3. Logical Thinking. Like science, the humanities seek relationships between phenomena being studied. Great pains may be taken to set down the facts fully and objectively. Witness how the historian carefully tests documents (his principal source of data) against each other, trying to discern bias in the writers. The data of the humanist, it must be kept in mind, usually represent unique events—for example, the particular occurrences that preceded the outbreak of hostilities in the American Civil War. Using extreme care, advancing the soundest reasons which he can muster, and guided by rigorous use of logic, the historian links such particular occurrences and shows how they combined to produce the Civil War. In anthropology the same rational procedure is followed when the ethnologist demonstrates how the annual Sun Dance dramatized an American

Plains Indian community's most "important social value"—individual prestige. The ceremony provided a stage on which the strong interest attaching to a man's personal rank could be expressed (Shimkin, 1953:431–432). Or the ethnologist may describe the "effects" of the coming of the white man to a formerly isolated group of Brazilian Indians (J. B. Watson, 1952). The unique nature of the event being studied, a particular war or specific Indian community, means that the historian and ethnologist must be content with reason alone to prove that certain antecedent events produced particular subsequent conditions. He does not ask if *similar* events are predictably associated with similar consequences. The student of the Sun Dance is working with only one community. Therefore he cannot generalize and then test the conclusion that ceremonies in *any* community provide opportunities for dramatizing important social values. Similarly, the investigator studying white influence in Brazilian forest culture offers a clear and cogent statement of what happened to a specific group of Indians in Brazil. But he does not test those conclusions by going to other communities where Europeans also have intervened. Hence his demonstration of validity rests only on reason. The aim of science is to generalize laws that apply to all societies. Relationships obtained in a particular context furnish hunches, hypotheses, that sometimes can be tested by larger masses of data to see whether they will recur more often than can be ascribed to chance alone. Logical proof is insufficient for science.

The Method of Science

The distinguishing feature of science, then, lies in the search for recurrent relationships between objectively perceived facts. An extensive discussion of scientific method in cultural anthropology will be given in Chapter 6. Now the method will be examined only briefly to note how the scientist obtains generalizations from the descriptions of unique cultures or communities.

In the grassy Sudan of West Africa live the Hausa-speaking people (M. G. Smith, 1952). Population in parts of Hausa country is quite dense—35 persons to the square mile in some places. The Hausa put great stress on cereal cultivation and practice crop rotation as well as manuring. Plows have not yet taken hold; the men cultivate only with hoes. A group of neighbors or kin coöperates for large field tasks but little help is hired by the individual farmer. In addition to farming, men practice hereditary part-time specialisms like trading, potmaking, ropemaking, matmaking, and others. Markets exist to distribute these products in exchange for money or food.

In contrast to the Hausa are the Attawapiskat Cree Indians living in the forest of northeastern Canada (Fig. 3:2; Honigmann, 1956a). Until recently they subsisted almost entirely on fish taken from rivers and lakes and on what moose, caribou, or smaller game could be speared, snared, or taken with bow and arrow. Specialization by occupation such as the Hausa practice never existed among the Cree Indians; every man and woman had to master many tasks in order to remain alive. Markets were also lacking

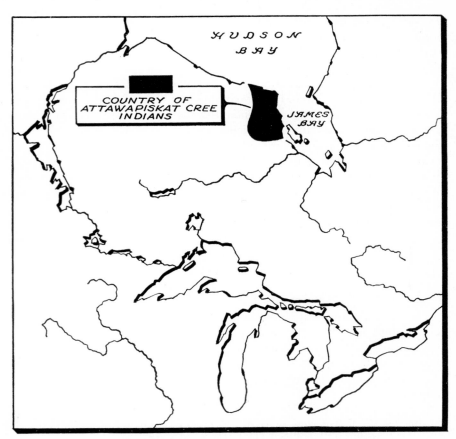

FIG. 3:2. Map Showing Location of Attawapiskat Cree Indians.

before Europeans came to open stores. Population density remained very low—less than one person per square mile.

Another community, the Pilagá, lives in the tropical forest of South America (Henry, 1951). Devoting most of their time to hunting, the Pilagá also cultivate a little food using a digging stick as the sole farm implement. Population density is very slight; specialization and markets remain unknown.

In extreme contrast stands a village in West Pakistan, where men guide the plow behind a pair of strong oxen and raise wheat, millet, sugar cane, and cotton. Nearly every village contains a small store or market as well as a variety of hereditary specialists—like carpenter, blacksmith, priest, and potter. Much food is exported from the village and manufactured products are imported. Populations are quite dense; in what was formerly Punjab Province the average is 300 persons on each square mile.

For each of these communities information has been given about four variables: the subsistence techniques, extent of occupational specialization of labor, amount of trade (or presence of markets), and density of population. Table 1 illustrates a rough quasi-statistical experiment which is

TABLE 1.   Relationship Between Variables in Four Communities

Communities	Subsistence Techniques	Population Density	Occupational Specialization	Trade or Markets
Hausa	Cereal agriculture	High	Yes	Yes
Attawapiskat Cree Indians	Hunting, fishing, and gathering	Low	No	No
Pilagá	Hunting and incipient agriculture	Low	No	No
Pakistan	Cereal agriculture	High	Yes	Yes

designed to show whether any predictable relationships exist between these variables. The number of cases treated is far too small to yield any significant results, but the purpose is to illustrate a method rather than to perform an actual experiment. Roughly the same kind of subsistence technology—agriculture—found among the Hausa recurs among the West Pakistan peasants. In both places it is associated with relatively high density of population, occupational specialization of labor, and trade. In the other two communities an emphasis on hunting or food gathering is related to low population density, lack of occupational specialization, and no trade or markets. In this manner the scientific anthropologist looks for predictable, universal relationships (or laws) between sociocultural phenomena. The reader should understand clearly why in order to obtain evidence of generalized relationships it is necessary to deal with more than one instance of a phenomenon. In the humanities repetition is impossible precisely because attention is devoted to unique, nonrecurrent events.

Anthropologists who are strongly humanistic in their sympathies, as well as those who for other reasons regard cultures as incomparable (see p. 89), reject the search for laws. Sometimes these dissenters claim that certain kinds of truth cannot be verified by the scientific method but can be grasped only in some other way.

ANTHROPOLOGY IN CONTRAST

A basis has already been provided for understanding how anthropology differs from the other humanistic and scientific disciplines that deal with social behavior—political science, psychology, and sociology. The terms "social science" and "behavioral science" have become common for referring to those disciplines collectively. One should not overlook the fact that each of these fields contains both humanistic and scientific elements. In other words, the social sciences are scientific only to the extent to which they rely on scientific method.

Anthropology and the Social Sciences

Three major distinctions separate anthropology from the other disciplines concerned with social life.

1. **Concern with Total Culture.** Anthropology is devoted to studying whole cultures, regarding them as systems of interrelated parts. Other disciplines characteristically limit themselves to a small sector of culture, like political organization or social groups. Here, perhaps, is the most significant distinction between anthropology and its nearest academic neighbors. On the other hand, there are times when the ethnologist also chooses to focus on less than a total culture and concentrates on law, political relations, religion, or some other limited area. He may not even attempt to relate that area to other sectors of the way of life.

2. **Diachronic Emphasis.** The most historical (i.e., diachronic) of all the disciplines which study human behavior is anthropology. Yet not one of the other fields is wholly ahistorical. Psychology, for example, is historical when it takes into account how children learn to behave as adults. But this, indeed, is very short-range history. Sociology, psychology, and political science rarely find it necessary to secure data from the far end of the long corridor of time which anthropology exploits, a corridor that stretches back to man's first appearance on earth.

3. **Nonsocial Bases of Behavior.** More than the other behavioral sciences (except, perhaps, psychology) anthropology seeks to discover the relations of human behavior to biological features of the human organism, as well as to factors of geography and demography. Psychology pays much heed to the biological basis of behavior but is rather less concerned with the physical environment. It is quite sound to say that anthropology stands closer to the natural sciences (zoölogy, biology, and geology) than do the other disciplines with which anthropology is usually classified. The recent years may have been accompanied by some weakening of the natural-science ties of cultural anthropology as sociological interests increasingly influenced the work of younger men (Kroeber, 1955a).

Anthropology and Sociology

The difference between anthropology and its closest academic neighbor, sociology, deserves more comment. Genealogically speaking, the two are sister disciplines, having diverged from a common parental stem.

What distinction is made between anthropology and sociology varies from one country to another (de Bie, 1954:16–28). In the nineteenth century, men like Darwin, Spencer, Durkheim, and Sumner were not clearly distinguished as sociologists or anthropologists (Murdock, 1954: 15–17). They sought to apply to man and society the naturalistic methods of other disciplines. The break came about 1900 when sociology abandoned the comparative approach, preferring to concentrate on the social phenomena of western society which anthropology tended to ignore. Organizationally speaking, anthropology, despite its growth, has not yet fully emerged as an independent discipline (Lévi-Strauss, 1954b:97). Professional sociologists, in the United States at least, probably teach anthropology more often than anthropologists teach sociology. Although frequent interaction between members of the two disciplines has tended to draw them close together, differences between the approaches remain apparent. The holistic interest in total culture; the comparative approach that, intellectually speaking, takes the anthropologist out of the country more often than the sociologist; the anthropologist's firmer interest in history, as well as differences in method—these traits mark a border line between the two fields.

4.

Archeology

AN ARCHEOLOGIST secures data in a fashion quite different from that of the ethnologist. The latter, it will be pointed out (see Chap. 5), attaches himself as an observer to communities of living people in order to record ongoing ways of life. The archeologist depends on the material remains of bygone cultures which he removes from the earth.

TWO KINDS OF ARCHEOLOGY

Archeology may be prehistoric or classical. Prehistory covers the period for which there are no written records, for writing itself was unknown. The classical archeoloigst has the advantage of working with written records —clay tablets, carved monuments, or papyri—which he supplements with other data, like buildings, tools, ceramics, and sculpture. In Europe, the Middle East, and South Asia, as written records increase in number and fullness with the approach to more recent times, the work of the archeologist overlaps the span of the documentary historian. Archeology always remains distinctive, however. Where historians enjoy access to quite complete records describing the fortunes of kings and nations, archeology concentrates on the art and other objects that remain from everyday life.

The type of evidence unearthed by the prehistorian differs from that often sought by the classical scholar. From sites formerly occupied by Indians who hunted, fished, or precariously raised maize, an American archeologist recovers large quantities of broken pottery, stone projectile points, flakes of stone apparently discarded in making those points, and charcoal, the evidence of hearths where meat was cooked and water boiled. He does not often excavate imposing public buildings with tile floors, monumental statues, or extensive cemeteries full of elaborate objects deposited with the dead. But these are the very kinds of discoveries that have made classical archeology a glamorous profession and in pursuit of which museums send out expeditions.

Whereas a prehistorian collects any kind of data that will help to reconstruct past ways of life or movements of people, a classicist often values the objects he uncovers for their own sake. The artifacts possess intrinsic value. Spectacular artifacts of this type come not only from the city sites of Italy, Greece, Egypt, and Southwest Asia but also from parts of the New World, like Central America and the Andean Highlands of South America. Hints of buried art objects, especially when coupled with the rumor of precious metals, stirred up the avarice of commercial grave robbers long before archeology became a serious profession.

The difference between prehistoric and classical archeology is one of degree rather than of kind (cf. C. F. Hawkes, 1954:157–160). Between these ends of the continuum is parahistoric archeology, which concerns people who themselves left no writing although they maintained relations in a society that included literate communities. Thus, Europe in about 4000 B.C. had relations with the Middle East at a time when written records were maintained in the latter region. Artifacts transmitted from the Middle East reached preliterate Europe. Understanding the use and significance of those objects sometimes is facilitated by knowledge of Middle Eastern writings. Sometimes, too, the culture of a period without writing comes to be described in the literature of a succeeding, literate period.

Mindful of the strategic value of former habitation sites for gaining knowledge about the past, the archeologist encourages their protection by governments. All excavation involves some destruction of primary records, but the loss is especially great when that destruction is undertaken by inexperienced persons or excavators who will not make available their findings.

EXCAVATION[1]

Archeology basically consists of excavating a site of human occupancy in order to reconstruct the culture or history of the site. Especially when history is an object in research, careful attention is paid to the layer of soil with which any excavated artifact is associated. Some of these layers may have been laid down by man, like the mound of broken shells along a seacoast. Others are attributable to natural processes, like the blanket of sand covering a formerly busy Middle East village. The excavator identifies the layers that are uncovered and notes the position of each discovered object.

Digging and Recording the Finds

There is no single technique for recovering the remains of former ways of life. The research problem and the type of site dictate how excavation is carried out. Although "there is no right way of digging . . . there are many wrong ways. Amongst the latter our successors will no doubt include

[1] Much of this section is adapted from Kenyon, 1952, and A. J. H. Goodwin, 1953: Chaps. 6, 7, 10. See also Brade-Birks, 1955.

ways which we regard today as relatively right . . ." (Wheeler, 1954: Chap. 1).

The first task is to find a place where men lived and worked. One of the simplest to locate is the open-air site, at which artifacts are distributed over the surface of the soil. Two kinds of open-air sites are recognized: deposits made by man and left undisturbed, and artifacts which had been laid down elsewhere and were redistributed by natural agents. For example, they may have been washed down to a lake shore from higher land. The open-air site may be the remains of a camp, village, quarry that provided stone for tools, or workshop where implements were fabricated. Deduction based on acute observation is the only way in which the original use of a site can be determined. Of course, the problem is not inevitably difficult. A locale containing traces of house posts, hearths, burials, finished stone tools in abundant assortment, and large accumulations of refuse quite probably is a village, while a place containing mainly broken and roughly worked stone implements together with scraps of stone, but without evidence of quarrying, is probably a workshop. The kitchen-midden site is a rubbish heap left behind by a prehistoric settlement. Excavation of any of these sites, provided people occupied them long enough, may reveal a rich record of successive phases of culture. Much knowledge about the past has been derived from cemetery sites. Graves in which burials are accompanied by a profusion of implements, pottery, weapons, and tools reveal practically the whole visible part of a bygone culture. Another important site is the cave or rock shelter which provided human shelter. Several layers of cultural remains in such a place testify to its long occupancy.

In any site the oldest data normally will be at the bottom, subsequent levels representing later periods of occupancy. During nonoccupancy falling earth and wind-blown debris may have settled on the locale, giving rise to so-called sterile layers of soil that separate one period of settlement from another. Excavating a stratified site is like peeling off and studying the contents of successive pages of a book.

Before excavation begins the archeologist makes a simple ground survey, mapping features of the locality. The survey lays out a grid over the site. Later this serves as a guide for classifying excavated materials. A grid is simply a site plan marked off in squares of a yard or a meter each. Each column and row of squares is given a letter or a number. This grid will be applicable to each successive layer peeled off the site.

Once mapping is finished and a grid has been laid out, excavation of the artifactual evidence can begin. Assuming that the site is stratified and that the archeologist aims to recover a historical record of culture change, he may begin by digging a narrow exploratory trench toward and across the inhabited area. This permits inspection of the stratified layers. Following the test trench comes the real excavation. No step in the sequence that starts with mapping is normally taken in a hurry. The prehistorian is fully aware that a site can be excavated only once and that errors may have serious consequences. Digging can extend over several seasons and often involves more than a single worker. Hired laborers may help to sift each spadeful of dirt and to sort out artifacts from useless debris. Of course photographs are taken at various stages of work and careful record is kept of where specific artifacts have been recovered. The letters and numbers of the grid squares facilitate such identification (Fig. 4:1). Each square may be subdivided further into numbered feet for finer identification.

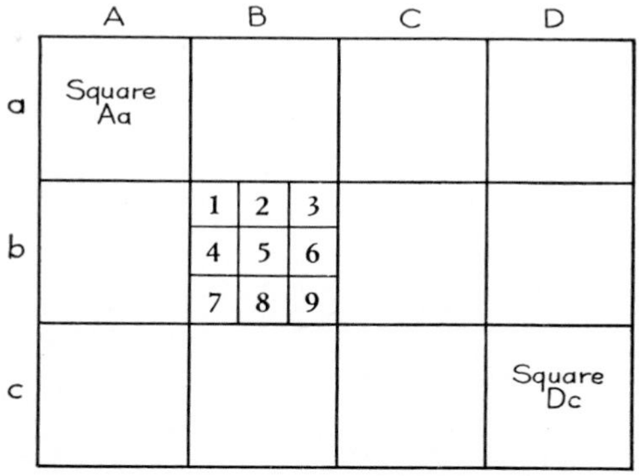

The grid, however, classifies only the horizontal surface of a site. In addition, vertical levels must be identified for chronological classification. Often the natural strata in which the objects are found suffice for vertical classification. But the earth

FIG. 4:1.   Sketch of a Grid Laid Out over a Site.

of a site may also be peeled away in layers of equivalent depth, each of which is identified by letter or number. By such horizontal and vertical allocation, the provenience of each artifact can be specified before it is packed for shipment to the laboratory.

Archeologists are interested not only in what can be measured and taken away from a site. Qualitative impressions of the locality as a whole, its environment, and the position of artifacts also are recorded and may be useful for cultural interpretation after the site has been destroyed.

In certain European and South African cave sites, wall paintings have been found. These are described for color, form, content, grouping, and other characteristics. Superposition of one painting over another serves, like stratigraphy, to reveal changes through time. The paintings are photographed and traced on cellophane, using exactly mixed shades of color. Later they will be retraced on glass. Similar techniques are applied to petroglyphs—engraved or pecked pictures and designs found on rock surfaces. When the outlines of the markings are deep enough to be felt by touch, a plaster cast may be obtained or the outline can be traced by rubbings.

CLASSIFICATION[2]

Prehistoric archeologists normally do not deal with specific artifacts. No more than a hardware dealer sells particular nuts or bolts are archeologists

[2] Much of this section has been derived from Childe, 1956.

much interested in specific pots, pins, or stone blades. The individual objects which have been excavated are instances of general types that begin to form in the archeologist's mind as soon as he sorts his data. For example, out of a collection of several hundred projectile points there might be the following three types: leaf-shaped point, stemmed point, and notched point. These are illustrated in Figure 4:2.

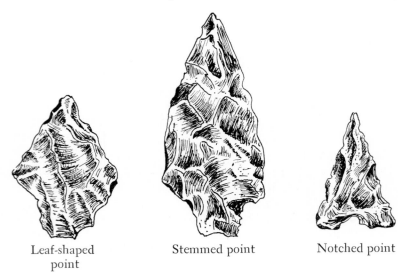

Leaf-shaped   Stemmed point   Notched point
point

Fig. 4:2. Types of Projectile Points.

Types (analogous to the patterns of the ethnologist described on pp. 64–68) normally indicate that the people who made the artifacts did so in a socially standardized fashion. They manufactured points or knives, shaped pots, plowed fields, and interred corpses according to certain norms and within a limited range of variation. Compared to the prehistorian, the classical archeologist is less interested in constructing types. For reasons already pointed out (p. 27), he often treats particular artifacts as significant in their own right.

The prehistoric archeologist classifies data in several ways. He may group artifacts by the material of which they are made; by form (flakes, cores, microlithic implements);[3] by technique (stone artifacts made by chipping versus those that took shape through grinding the material); by decoration (white-on-black painted pottery distinguished from black-on-red or plain ware); and by use: vessels, weapons, vehicles, ornaments, and ceremonial

[3] Here belong the types of large stone (megalithic) monuments common in western Europe but also found in Asia: namely, menhirs (erect stone slabs), dolmens (tabletop-like slabs set on uprights), and cromlechs (large stones set in a circle). These terms are compounded from Breton words. (See pp. 759–760.)

objects, for example. It is true that the use to which an object has been put cannot be discovered as directly as the material of which it consists. Sometimes use can only be inferred from the context in which the object was found; hence the importance of keeping careful records during the excavation process. A small clay animal figurine found in graves is probably a mortuary offering rather than a toy. Charred animal bones found near a hearth probably represent food. In certain cases knowledge of former use may be derived from observing similar objects in "living" cultures. Deduction from the known present to the unknown past is not always satisfactory. A large wooden wheel made in three sections probably served the same purpose of transportation in ancient Mesopotamia that it still does today in parts of Pakistan, but who can feel equally sure that stones with narrow grooves cut into a flat face, such as were found in Scotland, served to sharpen bone pins simply because similar stones were so used among the American Indians? Apparently they weren't pin sharpeners at all but served for casting sparks while making fire by the strike-a-light method (Childe, 1956:49).

Grouping by Phases and Industries

When several sites in a region have been excavated, artifacts of the same age and types often are observed regularly to recur together; for example, certain kinds of daggers recur with certain kinds of graves, houses, clay vessels, and bead necklaces. Such a recurrent assemblage is a phase (Phillips and Willey, 1953:620)—a systematically interrelated way of life that recurs from site to site, from one locality to another, in a certain delimited region.[4] The region over which a number of artifacts recur may be merely a valley, or it may cover an island group or portion of a continent. Phases succeed each other in time. Along the central east coast of Florida, for example, 7 periods (i.e., phases) have been distinguished archeologically, one succeeding the other. The second of these, called the "Orange period," is known from shell heaps; orange-colored pottery, some of it decorated by being incised; as well as a variety of stone vessels, implements, and ornaments. These objects recur at some 20 different locality sites (Rouse, 1951:240–243). A single item or a few nondiagnostic items whose distribution is far-flung (like barley together with saddle-shaped grinding stones) cannot signify a cultural phase. The assemblage of artifacts must be more inclusive and contain artifacts falling into a variety of use-type categories.

Particular types of stone tools, which practically alone survive from the early Stone Age of Europe, sometimes have been held to indicate distinct

---

[4] More usually such recurrent assemblages have been called "cultures," but culture is reflected at even a single site so another word is needed to designate areal or temporal units of culture.

Abbevillian (formerly called Chellean). Known in Europe from very early Ice Age (Pleistocene) times, or about 500,000 years ago. The name derives from Abbeville, on the Somme River of northern France. The industry designates mainly a particular type of stone tool, called a hand ax, which was held in the clenched fist. These implements were more or less chipped on both surfaces; the cutting edge tends to be irregular. Forms vary somewhat, although a type is easy to recognize. A few flake implements characterize the industry also. Hand axes of the same industry occur across Europe and have also been found in Egypt, East Africa, Southwest Asia, and India-Pakistan. There is also a South African version which differs somewhat in detail.

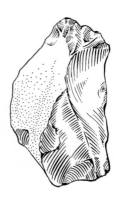

Clactonian. Very early Pleistocene times in Europe but later than Abbevillian. The name derives from Clacton-on-Sea, in southern England. The industry refers to a rough, small, flake tool struck from a core of stone, as well as a roughly made chopping tool—a nodule of flint worked on one end into a cutting edge (illustrated). Sometimes only one side of the upper edge was sharpened by chipping. Length ranges from 2 to 4 inches. This tool is mainly limited to western Europe although an Egyptian version is recognized.

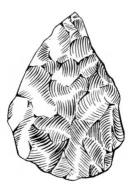

Acheulian. Very long-enduring in Europe, from early Pleistocene times to late Pleistocene times. The name comes from St. Acheul in the Somme Valley. The industry consists of a hand ax of roughly oval-like shape which reveals much more control over stoneworking than does the Abbevillian industry. The cutting edge tends to be more regular. Flake tools, especially one resembling a scraper, also characterize the industry. The industry extends into North and East Africa; there is also a South African version and it may be recognized in Southwest Asia and India-Pakistan.

FIG. 4:3. Three Early Old Stone Age Lithic Industries. (Sources: Movius, 1956; Oakley, 1952.)

phases of culture even though other artifacts, devoted to different purposes, have not been discovered in association with them (see pp. 736–740). The term "industry" better designates assemblages consisting only of one or more types of tools. Three well-known early Old Stone Age (or Paleolithic) industries are summarized in Figure 4:3. In comparison one may consider the much later Magdalenian phase of culture found recurrently in western Europe. This consists of bone javelin points; bone harpoons; bone needles; a spear-throwing device; a variety of stone tools, including blades and engraving instruments; cave wall engraving; both monochrome and polychrome cave painting; stone, bone, antler, and ivory carving; and engraved decoration on certain bone implements. In this richness of artifacts one perceives the difference between a more or less widely distributed way of making stone tools—an industry—and the recurrent assemblage of artifacts that constitutes an archeological phase.

Phases and industries must not be confused with another type of temporal classification in which broad cultural periods, like the Old, Middle, and New Stone ages, or the Bronze and Iron ages, are designated. Each of these categories includes a number of phases and industries covering long moments of time. Industries and phases making up the Old Stone (Paleolithic) Age feature stone artifacts manufactured through chipping the raw material; the phases making up the New Stone (Neolithic) Age include artifacts made by grinding stone and also pottery, plant domestication, and animal husbandry. It does not follow that these temporal periods occurred in every part of the globe. Europe and much of Asia reveal successive cultures that can be classified into Paleolithic, Neolithic, Bronze, and Iron categories. But no Mesolithic (Middle Stone) or Bronze Age appeared in native North America, and the use of iron, coming with the arrival of Europeans to the New World, meant the thorough dislocation of native cultures.

Once a number of phases or industries are ordered into larger categories, the latter become useful for dating cultural innovations in relative fashion. That is, one can say that the wheel first came into use in the Middle East during the Bronze Age or that the invention of weaving dates from the Neolithic period. This scarcely is different from saying that certain thinkers or their works flourished during the Renaissance or that particular ideas made headway during the Victorian era.

DATING

Generally speaking, the prehistorian assumes that remains found higher in the earth's surface are younger than those found below them. Yet instances are recognized where this assumption cannot be applied. Erosion, for example, may have washed out artifacts at a site and laid them down somewhere else *above* other deposits of much more recent vintage. For other reasons, too, successive phases of a community's way of life may not show up in the same site. Following war, for example, people may have moved from a devastated town to resettle elsewhere. The latter site will obviously be later than the first, although dating it relative to the former presents special problems.

The following example illustrates some of the problems and techniques of dating. Near Delhi, in northern India, is a site called Hastinapura which reveals four clearly marked levels of occupancy (Lal, *1952*). One way of dating would be to rely on purely relative methods and simply list the succession of cultural phases from one level to the next, more recent, one. However, archeologists prefer, whenever possible, to follow more absolute methods of dating; that is, they try to reckon the age of a culture or industry in terms of solar years. The top, or fourth, level of Hastinapura offers little trouble in this respect. Its age can be dated from coins containing the images of kings who are known, through written history, to have reigned from 1266 to 1287 A.D. The third level from the bottom (the second to be excavated) also contains coins. These picture kings known to have ruled from the second century before the Christian era to the second century after Christ. The next level contains artifacts of iron. In itself this offers no clue for absolute dating. However, the second level from the bottom also contains weights of chert and a highly polished form of black pottery such as has also been excavated at Kausambi, some 200 miles farther south. Written texts indicate that Gautama, the Buddha, visited Kausambi. This bit of information allows the conclusion that the latter town must have existed at about 500 B.C., the period when the Buddha lived. Thus, the lower levels of Hastinapura are perhaps as old as Kausambi, or at least date from the sixth century before the Christian era. But what about the lowermost level? Evidence indicates that occupancy on this level came to an end after a heavy flood of the nearby River Ganges. Reoccupation did not come much later than the sixth century B.C. (for reasons argued above). This fixes the flood at a date *before* 500 B.C. Excavation revealed a layer of earth containing no artifacts between occupancy-layers I and II. Can it be estimated that it would take a hundred years to lay down such a layer of earth? If we accept this guess, then Hastinapura I was abandoned not later than the seventh century B.C. The occupational layer itself is about 8 or 10 feet deep. In the present state of knowledge it is very difficult to say how long it takes a community to lay down this much evidence of occupation. Perhaps two or three centuries is a fair guess. That leads to the conclusion that the original settlement lasted from about 1000 to 700 B.C., at which approximate time the Ganges flooded and destroyed the town.

Types of Dating

As already suggested, dating methods fall into two classes: relative and calendrical (or absolute). Relative dating merely places a phase of culture or an artifact relative to other, earlier or later, phenomena occurring at the same site or in the same region. A well-stratified site, like the mound of the Biblical city Jericho, contains its own sequence of events each of which can be dated relatively by the level in which it occurs. Calendrical dating seeks to specify the year or century when a culture or artifact existed. In recent decades several technical procedures have been developed for discovering approximate calendrical dates in the absence of written records. The most exciting of these, radiocarbon dating, is based on the discovery that the death of organic material (like wood or bone) is followed by disintegration of radioactive carbon (C-14) atoms. Since this disintegration proceeds at a steady rate, age can be determined by measuring the degree of radioactivity remaining. This and other common techniques for absolute dating are described briefly in Table 2.

TABLE 2. Some Common Techniques for Dating the Past

Technique	Description
Geological dating	In this technique, especially useful for very ancient sites, the prehistorian secures a geological identification of the stratum (or period) of earth history associated with an artifact or site. The geologist then attempts to date the period relative to some other earlier or later one, or in absolute terms. The four glacial advances are valuable aids to dating the early industries and cultures of Europe (see pp. 733–735). In Africa rainy (pluvial) and dry periods correlated with glacial advances or retreats serve the same end.
Paleontological dating	This approach will be illustrated solely as applied in pollen analysis. Following the close of the glacial period, climates changed. With each new climate, different species of plants flourished. The climatic periods have been reconstructed from the succession of microscopic fossilized pollen grains recovered in ponds and bogs. Paleontological dating also is used in conjunction with geological methods. Old Stone Age industries associated with warm-weather animal fossils indicate a warm, interglacial climate, such as marked the epochs between European glacial advances (see chart, p. 852).
Dendrochronology	Where rainfall is irregular, trees produce distinctive annual rings: thick in a well-watered year, thin when there is drought. A master chart of rings, counting back from a known date, forms the basis of dendrochronology. Tree-ring dating works only when a site contains remains of timbers. The rings are first diagramed and then compared to the master chart. The outermost ring of a specimen, when compared to a matching ring of known

TABLE 2 (*Continued*)

Technique	Description
	date on the chart, indicates the year when the tree was cut. For want of ancient trees, dendrochronology has not been helpful in European archeology and has been little applied outside of North America.
Radioactive dating	The most common type of radioactive dating requires testing an organic substance found at a site for the amount of radioactive carbon (C-14) which it contains. All living plants absorb a constant stream of radioactive carbon atoms, the source of which lies in the action of cosmic rays on nitrogen taking place in the high atmosphere. Animals eating plants build radioactive carbon into their tissues. With death the C-14 atom begins to disintegrate at a steady rate, half in every 5760 years or so.
	Since the amount of radioactive carbon which an organism possessed when alive is known, and since the disintegration of the atoms proceeds at a steady rate, which is also known, it becomes possible at any given time to compute the organism's age since death from the amount of radioactivity which remains. A beam fashioned from a tree felled 5600 years ago will show about half as much radioactivity as a beam from a tree felled last year. The technique is not useful for periods beyond about 30,000 years and the dates established by it are not precise ones.[a]
Chemical dating	A common means of chemical dating is to measure the amount of fluorine in prehistoric bone or tooth. The technique is directly helpful to the paleontologist working with fossilized skeletal material and only indirectly useful for prehistory. Although fluorine content increases with time, the technique is primarily useful in distinguishing the *relative* age of different bones in the same site, preferably a site located in an environment where fluorine is not very abundant. In one study, animal bones *known* to date from a lower glacial period contained 2 percent of fluorine; a human cranial bone of unknown age also carried that amount. Its early date was thereby authenticated. On the other hand, bones of Piltdown Man, a fossil for which an early age had been claimed, contained only about 0.1 percent of fluorine or none at all. Hence, Piltdown Man could not belong to the early Ice Age.

[a] Recent research suggests that the carbon-14 atom has not been produced at a constant rate. An increase in the intensity of cosmic rays during the last 2000 years, due to weakening of the earth's magnetic field, if true, may mean that at least 240 years will have to be added to the asserted age of objects dated as 2000 years old by this technique and 1000 years or more may have to be added to objects previously considered to be 5000 or 6000 years old (*New York Times,* Dec. 26, 1956).

SOURCES: Heizer, *1953;* Johnson, *1951;* Zeuner, *1952;* Titiev, *1954*:170–174; *New York Times,* Jan. 11, 1960.

INTERPRETATION

As used here, interpretation refers to going beyond the datum of a physical artifact itself in order to infer something about its use or about the kind of nonmaterial culture to which it once belonged. Interpretation has already been introduced in talking about the classification of artifacts by use (see pp. 38–39). Reconstruction of the culture in which tools or other implements were used can come only by rational deduction plus disciplined imagination (Childe, 1951:Chaps. 1–5; 1956).

Owing to the incompleteness of the record with which he works the prehistoric archeologist possesses few clues for reconstructing the larger cultural whole of which his data formed part. He is like a student trying to reconstruct American life from a Sears, Roebuck catalog that lacks every page which shows an artifact that would disappear after 200 years' burial in wet forest ground (Fejos in Tax, *et al.*, 1953:194). Reconstructions made from such an impoverished record never can be certain. The interpreter must know from a comprehensive knowledge about different ways of life what kinds of cultural configurations go with hunting, elaborate burials, plows, or palaces. Many archeologists make little effort to reach beyond the bare facts of objects to reconstruct the nonmaterial characteristics of a bygone way of life. A few are determined to wrest from the concrete data as complete a picture of the vanished culture as possible and are not deterred by the fallibilities sure to reside in such attempts.

The process of interpretation is illustrated by what happened when Charles Johnson, an amateur English archeologist, found in the mud of the Thames River a jug dating from the time of Charles II (i.e., 1660–85).

Jugs of this kind are quite common, but it is unusual to find an unbroken one in the river. And when Mr. Johnson saw that it still had a clay stopper in it, he was even more pleased with his find. He then realized that there was something inside the jug, and when he removed the stopper, out fell a handful of rusty nails. But something else still remained inside, and would not pass through the narrow neck of the jug. When this was eventually extracted, with the aid of surgical forceps, it was found to be a piece of felt, cut in the shape of a heart, and in it were stuck several brass pins. It was obviously either a charm prepared by a would-be witch, or more probably a charm against witchcraft. It is likely that some unfortunate person, who believed that he was bewitched, was trying to cast the spell back against the witch who sent it. In the seventeenth century, or perhaps even later, "witch bottles," containing pins, nails, and water, were used for this purpose in various parts of the country.[5]

Note how the interpretation of the jug in the light of seventeenth-century culture was aided both by previous discoveries of such jugs containing nails, pins, imitation hearts, and human hair and by knowledge of how sorcerers manipulate symbols in order to effect death or illness in diverse parts of the world (see pp. 627–628).

[5] *The Listener* (1954), 51:414.

Interpreting Belt Cave

To put together a few things discussed in this chapter the record of
Belt Cave, an important site on the shores of the Caspian Sea in Iran, may
be examined. The complete report on Belt Cave is, of course, far more
technical and detailed than is reported here.[6]

A sketch of the successive levels of the site appears in Figure 4:4. The
stratigraphic levels are numbered along the right-hand margin of the

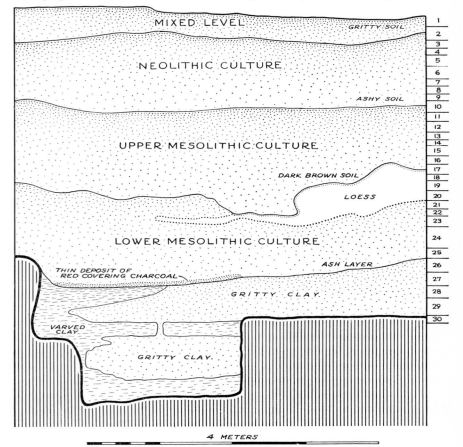

FIG. 4:4.   Cross Section of an Excavation in Belt Cave, Iran (After Coon, 1951b:30).

diagram. Table 3 offers a quantitative picture of 27 artifact-bearing levels.
The table reveals what the excavator found when he penetrated the site
and moved backward in time by peeling off one layer of soil after the

---

[6] For another reference to this site see pp. 697–698. The following account is based on
Coon, 1951b. See also Coon, 1957.

TABLE 3. Quantitative Analysis of Excavated Levels from Belt Cave, Iran

Level			Flint Implements	Flint Sickle Blades	Number of Bones						Pottery Sherds
					Gazelle	Ox	Sheep	Goat	Pig	Seal	
1	Neolithic Period	(Ceramic)	18	3		1	1	3	2		155
2			16	3	2	4	2	5	1		61
3			14			1	1	2	1		50
4			13			1	1	4	2		12
5			9	2		1	3	5	1	2	6
6			9		1		2	10			9
7			10	1	1		3	7			6
8		(Lower)	5	1			1	4			
9					1		1	5		1	
10			8			6	10	5			1
11	Mesolithic Period	(Upper)	25		67	20	4	4			
12			43		106	37	8	3			1
13			45		236	22	5	1			
14			33		123	31	3	1		3	
15			40		169	5	4	3		2	
16			11		28	18	1				
17			25		16	1		1			
18		(Lower)	13		14	2			1	5	
19			18		9	1				1	
20			26		3						
21			13		6	1				2	
22			6		2	2				2	
23			14		1	1					
24			51		3	1				11	
25			36							7	
26			19							1	
27			22		2	1					
RÉSUMÉ											
Ceramic Neolithic 1–7			89	9	4	13	13	36	7	2	299
Lower Neolithic 8–10			13	1	1	6	12	14	—	1	1
Upper Mesolithic 11–17			227	—	745	134	25	13	—	5	1
Lower Mesolithic 18–27			220	—	40	9	—	—	1	29	—

SOURCE: Coon, *1951b:*36 ff.

other. Note how sickle blades; the bones of sheep, goats, and pigs; and pottery sherds all decrease with time, indicating that they were late innovations. Bones of the gazelle and seal, however, increase in frequency as one travels further into the past. Apparently man increasingly came to neglect these resources in his environment, perhaps in favor of the domesticated sheep and goat. Blades suitable for mounting on a sickle hint that agriculture began to be practiced around the time when level 8 was laid down but they also may have been used to harvest wild grain. Still more refined analysis of particular artifacts is possible and reveals, for example, a change in the types of flint implements. Blades disappear around level 18, their place being taken by rather small, geometrically shaped bits of flint such as are characteristic of the Middle Stone Age in Europe, Asia, and Africa. Ground stone implements (heralding the Neolithic) join those made of chipped stone in level 4. Another mode of analysis is shown in Table 4, where the bones of sheep and goats are separated to reveal the

TABLE 4.   Analysis of Maturity of Animal Specimens, Belt Cave, Iran

Levels	Sheep		Goat	
	Immature	Mature	Immature	Mature
1–7	20	16	9	4
8–10	8	3	1	7
11–17	3	4	—	6
18–27	—	—	—	—

SOURCE: Coon, *1951b*:47.

number of immature and mature specimens. The frequency with which immature animals came to be killed seems to increase with time, suggesting that the people were sparing adult sheep and goats for wool or milk. But how was such foresight possible if at the same time the consumption of seal, gazelles, and oxen fell off? Assuming that the population at the site remained constant, the explanation may well lie in the sickle blades. That is, if the sickle blades are interpreted as pointing to agriculture, then an explanation for the other facts comes to hand. The people could spare adult goats and sheep and devote less time to hunting because farming had brought them new resources which allowed indulgence in luxuries like milk and wool. The example is instructive in showing how logical reasoning is applied to archeological facts in order to reconstruct nonartifactual aspects of a bygone way of life. Such reasoning, of course, is never better than its assumptions. The reader will note in Figure 4:4 how the relatively natural strata of the earth in Belt Cave are grouped into larger culture periods—like the Mesolithic and Neolithic.

AVAILABLE FILMS

The University of Arizona, Visual Aids Bureau, distributes *Point of Pines* (21 min., color). The picture deals with the University's archeological field school located on the San Carlos Indian Reservation and illustrates some procedures in prehistoric archeology. *Carbon Fourteen* explains radiocarbon dating techniques and the use of the C-14 atom in biology (12 min., b. and w. or color). It is produced by Encyclopædia Britannica Films.

5.

Ethnography

AS A process, ethnography refers to the empirical description of culture through the medium of living informants. Furthermore, it designates the manuscript or published record resulting from that activity. The stock of already published ethnographic monographs, representing accounts of several hundred world cultures (some no longer existing in the original, recorded form) is a precious resource of anthropology (Chapple, 1952).

Ethnologists entertain a confirmed bias in favor of field work with a living community, regarding this as a preferred means of gaining information about culture. Many universities are reluctant to grant a graduate degree in anthropology to someone who lacks actual archeological or ethnological field experience. Ethnologists tend to deplore learning about culture from books, letters, or newspaper files. They also discourage placing too great reliance on printed interview schedules and psychological tests in field work when those techniques are used in place of observing ongoing behavior. Some anthropologists also feel strongly the need to undertake more descriptive studies before European and American cultures make further inroads on exotic lifeways. As much as 50 years ago ethnologists were told that "now is the time to record. An infinitude has been lost . . . and a very great deal is now rapidly disappearing" (Haddon in Iyer, 1909:27). Then apathy was blamed for the neglect of field work. Today high publishing costs are partly responsible for the failure of much detailed ethnography to be printed.

THE IDEAL OF NATURAL HISTORY

When he adopts a meticulously careful, highly detailed, and relatively objective attitude toward his data—a community's socially standardized behavior and artifacts—the anthropologist is acting in the role of a natural historian. The natural historian is not using full-fledged scientific method. Only confusion is encouraged when the word "science" is bestowed on any careful, systematic, scholarly activity whether or not it pursues generality.

In zoölogy, botany, and anthropology the object of natural history is to observe and describe all the relevant facts of the phenomenon under study

49

as dispassionately and faithfully as possible and to distinguish carefully the observed from that which is not observed directly. Where some link in a sequence of behavior cannot be observed directly, the natural historian will indicate the process of reasoning or deduction through which he derives and supplies it. The primary goal of natural history is utter objectivity in reporting. That is, the report of one's observations should be written in such a way that the facts can readily be corroborated or disproved by another, future observer working with similar empirical data. In a word, the report should be reliable.[1]

Difficulties with the Natural-History Method

Actually, and although not all anthropologists are ready to admit it, complete reliability is not attainable in ethnography. The natural-history method is difficult to realize in full when one works with man rather than with other animals or plants. Snails and mice don't share the zoölogist's human nature and the latter cannot enter into interpersonal relations with them. Such interpersonal ties, the essence of ethnography, bring out distinctive behaviors in the people being studied by the anthropologist which cannot be predicted to occur should another observer form a different kind of relationship with those same people. Also, as one ethnologist writes: ". . . What I see men do, and understand . . . is seen often with a valuing of it. I like or dislike as I go" (Redfield, 1953a:165). If these sentiments emerge in the finished ethnography, then to the extent that they are present the report will not possess complete objectivity. Nor is it easy to test the reliability of an ethnography when the writer through empathy acquires insights into the socially standardized sentiments of his people, sentiments which they themselves scarcely can verbalize (see pp. 122–123). The observer may hardly know by what method such insights are derived and certainly he does not in detail report the steps by which he acquired his knowledge. Then how can the observation process be duplicated?

Despite these limitations on attaining the goal, ideally reliability is quite highly valued by anthropologists. Therefore attempts are made to control subjectivity and to report facts in such a way that they can be verified readily. Most anthropologists hold a conception of truth according to

[1] Objectivity in anthropology also has a second meaning which frequently will be used in Chapters 34 to 37. In this second sense the word means to describe some portion of culture from the standpoint of the anthropologist rather than with the meaning held by the community under study. Thus a community subjectively may believe that sucking an illness from a patient's body is effective in promoting cure. Objectively the sucking may be understood as a form of suggestion. The cure works (if and when it does) not by virtue of the sucking itself but through its psychological influence on the patient's organism. Some measure of subjectivity appears in all ethnographies and is highly desirable, since the community's perception of behavior constitutes a cultural datum. However, if all accounts of culture were written only subjectively, comparison between different ways of life would become very difficult (Goodenough, 1956).

which the only way an ethnographic fact can be proved true (more precisely, reliable) is to have another observer, possessing relatively the same training and experience and following the same method of observation, make similar observations in the same community. With such a conception of truth is it any wonder that anthropology avoids a full commitment to the highly intuitive position of the humanities? The originality and force with which a poet sees, say, suburban life need no further test of truth to prove their validity.[2] But an anthropological description rarely is appreciated the way a poem is. The truth it possesses is ascertained through some assessment of reliability.

Because most professional anthropologists value objectivity, ethnographies tend to be formidably cold and aloof, despite the intimacy of the social life with which they deal. More emotional and insightful descriptions of culture frequently carry the names of authors who, although alert and sensitive, have not been trained in anthropology and do not belong to its fraternity.[3] On them the natural-history method sits most lightly. In the manner of the humanities these writers often reveal much of the character of human life, although their insights may also be accompanied by opinions that annoy, especially when they run against one's own.

The first two of the following accounts describe a Hindu temple (not the same one). Neither is by an anthropologist but one author is a devout Hindu and the other a foreigner. The former looks, as it were, from within the culture while the latter is manifestly an outsider who makes little effort to control his subjective opinions. Following these is a third description written by an anthropologist of a temple ritual among the Coorgs, a South Indian tribe.

THE HINDU

Suddenly, we turned a corner and beheld the tall temple of ochre-colored stone leap like a golden red column into the deepening emerald dusk of the sky, while at its foot surged and pulsated the throng of worshipers clad in saffron and green and gold. They too were entering the

THE FOREIGNER

The drums are beating violently as he approaches, and wild music of strange sorts is issuing from the equally strange building before him. He is admitted (after he has taken off his shoes), and beholds a sight as extraordinary as is the noise that accompanies it. On the walls of the

---

[2] These lines from MacNeice's "Birmingham," for example:

"Splayed outwards through the suburbs houses, houses for rest
Seducingly rigged by the builder, half-timbered houses with lips pressed
So tightly and eyes staring at the traffic through bleary haws
And only a six-inch grip of the racing earth in their concrete claws;
In these houses men as in a dream pursue the Platonic Forms
With wireless and cairn terriers and gadgets . . ." (MacNeice, 1940:22–23).

[3] For examples the reader should see the excerpts from Doughty, Lawrence, Grinnell, Melville, and Freuchen in *Primitive Heritage* by Mead and Calas (1953).

temple for the even-song. Fearing that we would find no seats if we lingered, my brother and I entered the shrine, though I was longing to stay without and feast my eyes on the phantasy of color that was fast sinking into the black silence of night.

Within, the odor of *dhoop* (incense) and *dhoona* (frankincense) greeted our breath, and far away beyond us over the heads of the worshipers, gleamed the half-lit inner shrine where the two large sapphire eyes of the God glowed above his robes of crimson brocade. . . . What a sense of art the priests had, I thought, to dress in crimson a God whose eyes were glowing blue stars. At this moment, a silver bell rang from afar; it sounded like large drops of water falling on a tranquil lotus pool. It stilled the worshipers into an inert mass . . . [Mukerji, 1924:19–20].

room are hideous images, carved in stone and daubed in red paint, one representing a monkey, one a creature with a fat human belly and an elephant's head, each with an offering of yellow marigolds before it; while in the most prominent place is a stone pillar, rounded off on top, wet with the pouring of much Ganges water, bedaubed with spots of paint, and surrounded with green leaves, uncooked rice, a few coins and more yellow marigolds. . . . The noise becomes louder, and [an] old priest seizes a lighted lamp and brandishes it about in front of the muchbedaubed pillar, while the audience follow his motions with obvious excitement; and at the close of the hocus-pocus he distributes to them some of the rice which has been collected at the foot of the sacred object. The performance has been utterly unintelligible to our visitor, but the most astonishing thing about it all is the attitude and aspect of the worshippers . . . [J. B. Pratt, quoted in Bouquet, 1951:153].

THE ANTHROPOLOGIST

On the ninth afternoon the villagers go in state to the Bhadrakāli temple, accompanied by the three "horses."[4] The latter run round the inner shrine thrice. After this is over, Coorg men dance the "torch dance" (bolakāt)—actually they hold in their hands swords (*kadatalés*) or *chauris* (yak-tail whisks). Four Coorg drummers stand in the centre of the circle formed by the dancers, beating their small drums. As they beat the drums they sing the Bhadrakāli song. The outer circle of dancers do not, however, sing this song, but a different one which consists mostly of the names of deities interspersed with short interjections such as *"ho!" "ha!"* and *"he!"*: people dancing the torch dance always sing such a song.

After the dance is over, the Brahmin priests treat the Coorg devotees to coffee, and a dish made of parched rice mixed with jaggery and grated coconut. Coorgs

---

[4] Bhadrakāli is a female village deity; the "horses" are hollow figures made of bamboo. In the middle of the back of such a figure is an opening large enough for a man's head and shoulders to pass through. One man sits on the shoulders of another and the head and shoulders of the top man pass through the opening of the bamboo figure. The whole image is garlanded with flowers. The ritual being described lasts 10 days and is performed annually or every few years to propitiate the deity.

sit on the steps all round the shrine and the Brahmins serve them, taking care, however, not to touch them. Only the priests may enter the kitchen or the inner shrine [Srinivas, 1952:191].

CONCEPTS

Ethnography consists in fact collecting. By a "fact" is meant any verifiable characteristic of experience. That is, a fact is an event which can be observed directly or indirectly by the aid of some sense organ, perhaps in conjunction with an instrument which extends that organ's range of sensitivity.

Nature does not impress itself on man; rather, man meets nature with a frame of relevance comprising a number of systematically related concepts. An important task of concepts is to help formulate observed facts in the observer's mind and to help him set them down in writing. In other words, ethnographers come to know the facts of culture by conceptualizing (categorizing or labeling) them. Quite literally concepts help one to see. Without concepts to distinguish between, say, a tree and a person, one would experience only forms, shades, and colors. There would be no persons, trees, or the other familiar objects of experience. An anthropologist and a nonprofessional person perceive different elements in the same phenomenon because the former possesses specialized concepts with which to refine experience. In the same way the Eskimo has concepts that help him to designate many more kinds of snow than the average urban American can. Similarly, members of different disciplines attend to different aspects of the same experience by applying different concepts in the act of observation. Obviously, concepts are powerful tools for acquiring knowledge about the world.

Kinds of Concepts

Anthropologists utilize a broad range of concepts extending from concepts by inspection to concepts by postulation. A concept by inspection designates events that may be apprehended directly, like verbal statements, physical actions, or objects in the environment. To say that the Kaska Indians live in log cabins is a concept by inspection. Such concepts may be verified by pointing directly to the phenomena which they designate, in this case human existence in log cabins. A Cree Indian's *verbal statement:* "We believe in a cannibalistic giant with heart of ice called Wiitiko" may be verified directly by receiving the same verbal statement again. Asking questions or using sense organs enables ethnographers to check the reliability of one another's concepts by inspection.

A concept by postulation points to unseen events which can only be inferred from some more immediately observed phenomenon. Thus anxiety in a community is inferred when the members verbally express worry about the future, bolt their doors at night, and believe that surrounding space is crowded with invisible hostile beings. Inferred events analogous to anxiety are used widely in the physical sciences—for example, in atomic physics. A concept by postulation is a fact whose reliability can be established only after its observable manifestations have been stated clearly and unequivocally—that is, after the concept is defined. If anxiety is defined as a state of terror accompanied by thoughts of threat and insecurity, then, as the definition implies, one verifies the existence of anxiety by ascertaining in any convenient way whether people actually feel threatened and uncertain about their capacity to manage experience.

Ideal types are another special kind of concept. Examples include large- and small-scale communities, as these terms will be defined (see pp. 149–151), hunting and collecting communities (see pp. 305–308), and even the way humanism and science have been defined. An ideal type is based on many instances of the phenomenon in question—for example, communities that live by hunting and collecting. The type is defined not by what such communities most frequently reveal (i.e., not by their modal characteristics) but by any characteristics which any of the communities reveal provided that those attributes set them apart from communities pursuing life in different fashion. In actuality no particular hunting and collecting community may manifest all the characteristics given in the ideal type. Sometimes ideal types lie at opposite poles of a continuum. Large- and small-scale communities are of this nature. It is not expected that any particular community will correspond perfectly to either of these two extremes; rather it will fall toward one or other end of the continuum (Redfield, 1955:Chap. 9).

Disciplines may be divided into those using relatively unspecialized concepts, i.e., their language is close to that of everyday speech, and those possessing highly specialized concepts which are difficult for the uninitiated to understand. The criticism sometimes is made that anthropology uses difficult jargon in referring to commonplace things.[5] Compared to that of biology and physics, the language of anthropology is unspecialized. As a result it is also relatively unprecise and forced to use vague and ambiguous concepts like "nation," "tribe," "religion," and "art." Precise, clear observation of the kind that lends itself well to reliability testing is difficult with everyday English. Take a proposition like "All meat is cooked." What exactly do these words mean if they appear in an ethnography without further clarification? The term "to cook" does not specify whether the food is prepared in boiling water or in hot grease, baked in coals or in a hot oven, or grilled by an electric cooker. Does the concept "meat" in-

[5] See Chinoy, 1954; Blue, 1955; and Wooton, 1950:13.

clude insects and fish or only mammals? Some common-sense terms of English may designate very different phenomena in different cultures. Crime, for example, is known only from the laws enforced at a particular time and place. To compare "crime" in the Soviet Union and the United States is meaningful only if by that concept is meant the different acts which are defined as criminal in each country. They will not invariably be the same acts.

Sometimes common terms like "religion" are redefined in anthropology (as the physicist redefines "space" and "time") in order to render them sharper and more suitable for application from one culture to another. Much more reinterpretation of such concepts will probably appear even though familiar concepts used unfamiliarly also arouse prejudice in some quarters. This is particularly true when the redefined concept already enjoys some technical meaning.[6] Such intolerance is strange among persons who profess to be dedicated to the improved pursuit of new knowledge. It is unlikely that any single or highly standardized usage of concepts can be legislated. The most to be expected is that concepts will be defined clearly so that a subsequent observer who wishes to check on what his predecessor has done will know what referents are designated by the other worker's language.[7] In the last analysis all definitions are arbitrary and cannot be treated as superior or inferior to one another. From this it follows that a concept—the meaning attached to a term—cannot be true or false. Only the events to which the concept refers are subject to verification, as has been explained. Is there any test of more or less *adequate* concepts? Just that in reporting on a specific piece of work an observer should employ concepts consistently and in such a way as to give a coherent picture of the events being studied. His stock of concepts should be sufficiently large to include all of the relevant information, but unnecessary terms which lead to redundancy are to be avoided.

STANDARDS IN ETHNOGRAPHY

What makes a man or woman a skillful ethnographer? Training and experience, though essential, probably are not sufficient. Training in fieldwork methods is too recent an innovation, and too slightly developed in graduate schools, to account for many products of skillful ethnography. Many capable professional field workers have never taken such courses.

[6] For an instance of a dispute over this point see Bernard Karsh's review of a book in the *American Journal of Sociology* (1955), 61:269–271, and the author's reply in the same journal (1956), 62:62–63.

[7] Of course, terms not only possess referents but also have uses. Some words stand neither for concepts by intuition nor for concepts by postulation. Simple examples are the words "but," "and," "or." One must know how a word is used to perceive whether or not it possesses a referent.

Perhaps the most important element in an observer is sensitivity. There have been anthropologists who used their whole organisms—eyes, ears, and viscera—as recording instruments and then sought to conceptualize their experience on paper. Such observers have not escaped the charge of being too subjective.[8] To heighten sensitivity a field worker deliberately may adopt a "feeling of strangeness" toward the phenomena being studied (Muehlmann, 1938:4). Also required is willingness to put up with conditions that often involve discomfort and even risk to life, health, and emotional security. It is not accurate to say that the anthropologist sacrifices his comfort for field work. He often enjoys the opportunity to live unconventionally.

Most anthropologists probably would agree that the satisfactory ethnography is restrained in its handling of subjective values and reveals a quality of detachment. Yet "it is surprising how many anthropologists hold high this motto of detachment when they refuse to condemn native customs, yet forget all about its existence when they praise them" (F. E. Williams, 1940:414) (see also p. 115 *infra*).

The satisfactory ethnography is also comprehensive, but there is no agreement about what comprehensiveness entails. One man values "massiveness of factual contribution" (Lowie, 1956), but this ideal often is ignored in favor of selective reporting. Whether his details are massive or not, the anthropologist who writes on a culture is expected to know quite fully the way of life on which he is reporting. Like the novelist describing character, the ethnographer may offer his reader not so much a full explanation of a culture as the feeling that it is all explicable (Forster, 1927:Chap. 3).

The successful ethnography is more than a listing of behavior and artifacts arranged in some formal series of categories. The anthropologist faces the problem not only of collecting directly observable and inferred facts of culture but also of reporting those facts in a coherent and systematic manner. Furthermore, in addition to the descriptive passages the ethnography very probably will point out relationships between the observed phenomena or discuss their historical significance. Such interpretations, of course, are not observed by the most skillful field worker but represent his examination of data in the light of a general knowledge about culture. How data are handled in scientific and historical anthropology will be examined later (Chaps. 6 and 7).

TECHNIQUES OF ETHNOGRAPHY

The following account of the procedures followed by the ethnological field worker should help the reader visualize the process through which

---

[8] That the field worker's total experience, including his internal processes, is part of his data is the thesis of *die verstehende Soziologie,* a position relatively neglected in American social science (M. Weber, 1922).

cultural facts are collected, classified, and reported. It is not contemplated that this brief review will be sufficient to teach those techniques.

What the Field Worker Looks For

Any investigator selects out of the mass of phenomena in the universe certain ones that he perceives to be significant for study. What he selects and how he describes the phenomena depend not only on such matter-of-fact considerations as available time and energy but also on the concepts which constitute his frame of relevance (see pp. 91–92). *The Outline of Cultural Materials* (Murdock, *et al.*, 1950) constitutes a nearly exhaustive frame of relevance to guide field-work observation. No ethnographer in a single lifetime could collect full information about the more than 70 categories of cultural and noncultural facts to which it calls attention. Indeed, not all of the categories in the *Outline* are applicable in every kind of community. The Central Arctic Eskimo do no "marketing" and lack "political behavior" worth describing, and there is little to say about their social stratification. However, comprehensive ethnography requires that attention be paid to a majority of the following key topics:

Geography
Human biology (racial affinities, musculature, stature, etc.)
Personality
Demography
History and culture change
Language
Subsistence techniques (hunting, agriculture, etc.)
Food processing and consumption
Clothing and adornment
Buildings and construction
Settlement plan
Tools, appliances, machines
Property system
Exchange and marketing (including gift giving)
Travel and transportation
Recreation
Social stratification
Marriage
Family and other kin relationships
Community organization
Government
Law and offenses
War
Sickness and its treatment
Religion
Ideas about nature and man
Sex

Reproduction
Infancy and childhood (including socialization of the child)
Old age

Observation

Observing culture entails not merely acts of looking and questioning but keeping a careful record of what is learned through those processes. The new field worker faces the difficult task of acquiring an ability to write quickly while at the same time overcoming fear of writing in the presence of others. Sometimes, of course, he may realize that a particular situation is quite incompatible with note-taking. The field worker must be ready to record similar data a second, third, or fourth time—as many times as necessary—until he can predict correctly the circumstances under which an object or behavior will appear. There is little inherent pleasure in recording or in transcribing the day's rough notes. Small wonder that one is tempted to reduce recording to a minimum and to rely on memory for the rest. Actually, even with the most assiduous note-taking, much information will be absorbed in other ways, to be played back later via memory. Field workers who do not work in this way but who know only what is in notes tend to brand as "intuitive" and "unsystematic" workers who rely on recalling the full context of sensory impressions (Mead, 1953c:12). Yet, obviously, such recall may involve a relatively large amount of subjectivity.

The ethnographer self-consciously relies upon his own senses—especially sight—to experience life in the community chosen for investigation. Using sensory cues he maps the settlement; takes a census of the houses; describes activities, vehicles, clothing, and other artifacts; and notes what people say and do in specified situations. The most difficult task in observation is recording certain fleeting moments of behavior—how an arm is held, a smile flashes, or a woman reacts who has dropped and broken a pot. Repeated exposure to such behavior will stamp into the observer's system empathically some of the nuances that always fail to get into field notes.

Although concentrating on details, a field worker does not neglect holistic impressions of a scene, village, or dance. A daily journal is useful for recording some of the more holistic as well as the relatively unprecise, personal, and impressionistic reactions to life in the community. Here the field worker may write as he pleases, without fear that others will go over these personal lines as they might have a right to inspect the primary data in field notes. Many months later, when the anthropologist writes up his report, he finds very useful the chronological journal record with its global descriptions of people, food, weather, and the exhilaration he himself experienced during a festival.

A field worker who lives close to his subjects soon discovers that his judgments increasingly tend to reflect the community's judgments and values. More and more his role comes to be shaped by the behavior of the community's members toward him and by the expectations they have for his actions. Every anthropologist in this way becomes partially assimilated to the exotic culture he studies. Nonanthropological visitors to a foreign community often try self-consciously to protect themselves from such assimilation, perhaps by restricting their interaction with natives. Not so an anthropologist. He typically will refuse to establish himself in a tourist's bungalow where the natives are brought for questioning. The ethnographer values increasing participation in native life because it promotes him toward his final goal. "Empathic understanding of the problems faced by the people under study cannot be obtained fully through hearing about experiences from others or even from direct observation" (Katz, 1953:72). Hence the field worker tries to blend observation with participation, even if the participation is limited to relatively incidental activities, like driving a plow or holding a busy housewife's baby. Nor is the participant-observer merely trying to erase awareness of his presence from the situation being studied. However desirable it may be to encourage people's "natural" behavior, an observer tries always to be aware of how his role influences the field-work situation. Even physics has discovered that observation which does not account for the observer is invalid.

What is significant for observation obviously differs from one community to the next. As the observer becomes familiar with a way of life his appreciation of phenomena worth recording increases. "Indicator phenomena" begin to appear—events that are eloquent in revealing more than at first glance might seem to be the case. Take, for example, the number and age of cars parked in front of four churches on one Sunday morning in Lost Lake (Table 5). The figures support the conclusion that the Presby-

TABLE 5. Number of Cars of Various Ages Parked in Front of Four Churches on One Sunday

Year	Presbyterian	Christian	Full Gospel	Latter-Day Saints
1949	5	2	1	0
1947–48	7	2	7	1
1940–41	5	4	3	2
1938–40	1	0	4	1
1936–38	0	0	4	2
Pre 1936	0	0	2	2
Pick-up Truck	0	1	2	3

SOURCE: A. R. Beals and T. McCorkle, 1950:48.

terian (Community) Church "is the church of the elite" while the Full Gospel Church corresponds to the church of transients and the poor. The "Christian Church is an attempt to compromise between the lower class

Table 6. A Short Modified International Phonetic Alphabet for Consonants

	Labial	Labiodental	Interdental	Alveolar	Alveolar Palatal	Velar	Uvular	Glottal
Stops voiced	b			d		g	ɢ	
unvoiced	p			t		k	q	ʔ
Spirants voiced	β	v	ð	z	ž	ɣ		h
unvoiced	φ	f	θ	s	š	x		ʜ
Nasals voiced	m			n	ɲ	ŋ		
unvoiced	ᴍ			ɴ	ᶮ	ᴺ		
Laterals voiced				l				
unvoiced				ł				
Flaps voiced				r			ʀ	
unvoiced				ʀ			r	
Affricatives voiced				ds	dž, dł			
unvoiced				ts	tš, tł			
Semivowels voiced					y	w		
unvoiced					ʏ	w		

SOURCE: Adapted from Pittman, *1948*:14, 53–54. There are many modifications that can be indicated by suitable diacritics including nasalization, fronting, backing (for example, t may not be alveolar but, as in Urdu, palatal; this is indicated by a dot under the sign), lengthening, trilling, aspirating, glottalizing, and others.

church and the dignity of the upper class church" (A. R. Beals and T. McCorkle, 1950:48). Other information bearing out the conclusion that the churches cater to different social classes independently supports the automobile data. If much reliance were to be placed on the diagnostic value of cars as indicators of church membership, a suitable statistical test might be employed to discover if the differences shown in Table 5 are significantly greater or less than what could be expected to occur by chance alone.

"Observing" Language

Observation extends to the language of a community. The field worker learns to use this language and, if that is his interest, describes its sounds and processes (Lounsbury, 1953).

To describe the sounds of a language accurately requires a special system of notation, one capable of recording practically any sound that might be produced. An alphabet of this type is illustrated in Tables 6 and 7. Many

TABLE 7. Some Basic Vowels

	Front	Central	Back
High			
close	i (be)		u (Ger., *gut*)
open	ɪ (lid)		ʊ (wood)
Mid			
close	e (late)	ə (sofa*a*)	o (go)
open	ɛ (met)	ʌ (mud)	Ω (Ger., *Kopf*)
Low			
close	æ (fat)		ɔ (law)
open	a (Brit., laugh)	ɑ (cot)	ɒ (Brit., top)

a Last vowel sound.

SOURCE: Pittman, *1948*:35. Abbreviations used in illustrations are: Ger., German; Brit., British English. Other illustrations are standard English. Modifications of these basic forms include lengthening, rounding (German *Buecher* contains a rounded high front vowel), nasalization, and more or less tenseness.

of the signs are taken from the International Phonetic Alphabet (IPA), a system designed for the precise notation of speech sounds.[9] Note how the phonetic alphabet contains signs for vowel differences significant in English (like the vowels in "hot" and "go") which ordinarily are written with the same sign. Transcribing sounds of language accurately depends on a knowledge of how those sounds are produced. Table 6 indicates that speech fundamentally consists of releasing air from the lungs and then disturbing

[9] For the "complete" IPA and comprehensive accounts of how speech sounds are produced see Pittman, 1948; Bloch and Trager, 1942; and Laird, 1953:125–126. The IPA may be extended further by use of diacritical marks to permit the notation of many distinctions in the way sounds are produced.

it (stopping, spirantizing, nasalizing, or blocking it in some other way) at
certain points in the oral cavity (with the lips, lips and teeth, between the
teeth, on the gum ridge behind the teeth, or farther back in the mouth).
The glottal stop is made deep in the throat, as in the break between the
first and second syllables of "coördinate" and in Brooklynese "bottle."

Interviewing

Interviewing in ethnography differs somewhat from the interviewing
used by Gallup pollsters or sociologists. Rarely does a printed form lie between interviewer and subject. Often life goes on while ethnographer and
informant chat back and forth, the former trying to find out why the
people are doing something; how they formerly did something; what will
happen when winter comes, when the fishermen return, or what would
have occurred in a quarrel if the police patrol had not just arrived. Interviews tell the anthropologist about phenomena which he cannot readily
observe, such as the courtship of lovers and how administrators reach
policy decisions, and throw light on activities not performed during the
term of the anthropologist's visit. Talking to informants brings out the
values, beliefs, and rationalizations of a culture.[10]

A special problem is encountered when interviewers, armed with printed
schedules, seek to obtain precisely comparable information from two or
more communities that differ considerably in culture. They may discover
that some questions prepared for one culture lose their meaning when
transposed to another setting (Stoetzel, 1955:22–24). For example, Attawapiskat Cree Indians are not accustomed to thinking in generalities.
Hence they couldn't answer satisfactorily when the author asked them
questions like "What do people like you eat nearly every day?" This question had worked well in nutrition surveys carried out in the United States.

Testing

A psychological test is actually a kind of interview schedule designed
for obtaining relatively specialized data of the same type from a series of
subjects in the same or different communities. The use of tests in field
work started in the area of culture and personality. Anthropologists sought
techniques that would reduce the degree of subjectivity involved in describing covert states of personality.[11] For such procedures they turned to
psychology, a field that faced the same problem of controlling subjectivity
in personality description. The technique sought had to be one that would
enable personality to be studied as a total system, rather than one that
measured only intelligence or some other segment of the individual's

---

[10] See Katz, 1953:69–74; Paul, 1953a; Rivers, 1900 and 1910; and J. A. Barnes, 1947.
[11] Discussion follows Henry and Spiro, 1953. See also Hallowell, 1945; and Honigmann,
1954b:122–126, 160–162.

reaction system. The technique, also, could not be limited to the community in which it had been invented. Intelligence tests, for example, measure intellectual processes in terms of the problems of western (and often urban or middle-class) culture. They are useless when applied to individuals reared to solve extremely different types of problems. A technique possessing all these qualities was found in the projective tests of psychology. These instruments elicit from a subject responses that are assumed to give a valid picture of his feelings about himself and the world around him. The subject figuratively projects himself into the relatively amorphous stimuli of the test. What he projects is then interpreted in terms of his personality system. Among the most widely used projective tests are Rorschach's Inkblot Test and the Thematic Apperception Test. Administration is relatively simple but scoring and interpreting the responses present considerably greater difficulty and require careful training. Neither technique has been completely validated. That is to say, only limited confidence may be put in the meaning assigned to a particular type of response, especially when subjects are from exotic communities.

Since tests are severely limited in the kind of data which they produce, they obviously cannot substitute for other elements of the field-work process. However, they supplement traditional ethnography in providing many valuable clues to the thoughts and feelings of informants.

Documentary and Other Records

Ethnology, like other disciplines which study human behavior, uses two kinds of data: those which the anthropologist himself collects when he is doing field work in a particular community and those reported by other disciplines, the press, or government services and others of the people's store of written records. A popular study of Middletown, in addition to observation and interviewing, utilized census records; city and county records; court files; school records; minutes of organizations; newspaper files; city, state, and county histories; diaries; and other printed material (Lynd and Lynd, 1929). One difficulty with documentary evidence lies in its very volume. A large amount of time often is required to make an adequate analysis and to extract useful material from the great deal that is merely trivial.

Caution must be exercised in using documentary sources. One cannot assume, for example, that newspapers report all crimes, because criminals of all social classes may not be brought to court with equal frequency. Speeches in the daily paper reporting a prosperous and efficient municipal administration may conceal quite another state of affairs. So, too, the student must learn to detect and, perhaps, reject accounts of travelers who never saw what they describe but who parrot actual visitors to the community (Tax, et al., 1953:81). In studying certain documents—like scriptures or constitutions—the ethnographer must be clear concerning whether they are to be used for the meaning they had when originally written or for their present-day significance. One or both approaches are possible but the fact that such documents acquire different meanings to successive generations makes it important to know which point of view is adopted (Waley, 1949:12–13).

Documents as well as other products of human behavior may be studied for the attitudes, ideals, and aspirations they reveal. To this kind of study the term "thematic analysis" has been applied. Motion pictures, plays, radio dramas, and, of course, popular literature (oral and written) are examples of behavioral products that contain themes (see pp. 127–128). Analysis of themes from such sources has aided anthropologists who were prevented by war and other difficulties from first-hand study of certain cultures (Mead and Métraux, 1953). Again, care is needed when studying material like drama, literature, and films not to confuse the community's image of itself with the community's manifest behavior (see pp. 123–124). Perhaps Germans only like to think of themselves as ruthless and unconventional idealists (McGranahan and Wayne, 1948). In actuality they may remain quite conventional.[12]

PATTERN CONSTRUCTION

Ethnographers do not attempt to deal only with the immense number of individual events which they observe and note. Rather, uniformities of behavior are constructed from the discrete incidents which were observed. The presentation of these uniformities, or patterns, constitutes the bulk of a published ethnography. Remarkably little has been written about the process by which the observer of behavior and artifacts moves from the observation of relatively discrete events to patterns of behavior and artifact. Yet this process constitutes the essence of ethnography (Mead, 1953c; Gorer, 1953). A pattern refers to a class of activity, thought or feeling, or artifact (F. A. Logan, et al., 1955:34). But it does more than to class behavior under categories like "hand-shakes," "anxiety about witches," or "beehive-shaped houses." In the case of behavior, at least, the pattern also specifies the dimensions of the response (the speed, vigor, seriousness, or some other property of the behavior). Thus: "People shake hands loosely and with a weak grip." The frequency with which the behavior or artifact occurs may also be included (perhaps merely in words like "rare" or "often"), and the probability that it will occur under certain conditions may be stated.

[12] More on working with documentary and other behavioral records will be found in Albrecht, 1954; Honigmann, 1954b:128–134; and with greatest detail Mead and Métraux, 1953.

It is important to understand, first, that patterns are not part of the immediately given, objective world; they are not "straight" sense impressions but rather are the product of the ethnographer's organizing his empirical data. Second, in testing ethnographic statements for their reliability, it is patterns and not the discrete, recorded events that are verified. Hence much depends on the sharpness with which patterns are delineated.

How Patterns Are Derived

An ideal paradigm of data handling in ethnography includes the following steps: (1) observation and interviewing to acquire information about particular acts, thoughts, and feelings—observations are recorded; (2) transferring the contents of the notebook to slips—ideally one discrete event, or statement by an informant, to one slip; (3) generalization (or "construction") of patterns from the evidence in the slips.

In preparation for the third step the slips are sorted. Similar events are seen to recur. For example, older siblings, parents, and other adults repeatedly were reported or seen to scold children who displayed aggression. Sorting the slips helps a pattern to emerge from the data, namely: "Parents, older siblings, or unrelated adults [in this particular community] reprimand fighting and order it to cease."

Although nobody has yet succeeded in determining precisely what operations an ethnographer goes through in constructing patterns, simple models of the process are easy to devise. For instance, let the reader examine half a dozen whiskey or automobile advertisements and generalize the printed message which is regularly stated in such announcements. No doubt different field workers proceed with pattern construction in somewhat diverse fashions.[13] There are times when one instance of an event becomes the basis of the pattern, perhaps because the event did not occur more often. *One* informant's condemnation of the Commissioner of Native Affairs is accepted as a type attitude; *one* wedding becomes the pattern of all weddings. More often the pattern is an ideal type based on a great number

---

[13] Much of the paragraph which follows is based on Gorer, 1953:60–62. It is only fair to indicate that still more varied conceptions of pattern exist. To some students of culture the midpoint or average of a series of incidents is a pattern. Thus, if some men in an office go to lunch from 11 to 12 and the rest from 12 to 1, then lunch at 12 noon may be cited as the pattern. Sometimes the mode is made equivalent with the pattern: If 2 men go to lunch at 11, 5 at noon, and 8 at 1, then lunch at 1 becomes the pattern because this is the most frequent type of behavior. Another anthropologist, taking the latter set of facts, would generalize that men go to lunch from 11 to 1, making pattern synonymous with the range.

Wermlund (1951) points out how the word "pattern" is used in diverse senses. Sometimes it designates that people have patterns for behavior, and sometimes the same word designates the possibility of discovering patterns of, or in, behavior. The latter is the sense in which the word is used here. Such usage does not, of course, deny that people act according to norms, standards, or ideals.

of observed instances. Thus, the statement that "men are the hunters, ivory carvers, and butchers of large game. Their recreation is found in dancing and playing the fiddle at dances" refers to an ideal type of man since most men in the community presumably never combine hunting, ivory carving, dancing, and playing the fiddle at dances. An ideal type pattern, therefore, possesses more characteristics than any concrete case on which it is based. Still a third type of pattern is one which possesses fewer characteristics than any specific event observed during the field-work process. For example, it is not unusual to enter a landlord's men's house in what was formerly Sind Province, Pakistan, and to see the occupants smoking, eating, reclining, arguing on occasion, giving orders to laborers, or playing with children who have come from the women's apartments. These diverse activities may be condensed, the pattern saying that "wealthy men take their leisure in the *otak*, where they also receive guests, conduct business, and take meals." A few illustrative behaviors become keynotes of a presumably greater variety of qualitatively similar acts.

Can You Describe the Pattern of These Water Pots? They are found in nearly every home of Pakistan and India and serve to keep drinking water cool (courtesy, Government of India).

Some patterns represent statements about the *range* of permitted variation for some behavior. Exceeding the limits of that range calls attention to behavior and may bring reproof. The field worker thus gets help in constructing such patterns by noting when scolding, gossip, or some other kind of attention is drawn to behavior. These devices indicate that the limits of permitted variation have been exceeded. The pattern, then, will describe only what occurs within the range. However, one must recall that disapproved behavior, which automatically carries censure when it is discovered, may also fall into patterns. For example, illicit brewing is a pattern in modern-day Kaska Indian life. White-collar crime in the United States also constitutes a pattern of crime.

Sometimes, especially when the community is culturally heterogeneous, the anthropologist finds it convenient to identify the pattern with the ideal culture of the community—the norms which specify what all people should do or what all would like to do if circumstances permitted (see pp. 123–124). The ideal may be carried out directly by some persons in actual behavior, it merely may be espoused, or it may be expressed inversely, as when certain individuals react against the norm. The ideal may only be approximated:

. . . If you enter the simplest, the most deviant American house, the unsealed sharecropper's cabin with the pine knots blazing on the hearth, the cold-water flat without furniture except rugs brought from the Near East . . . you are likely to find, if not a modern crib, at least a mail-order catalogue or a calendar with a picture of a modern crib. Where the material objects and the new ways that go with them have not penetrated, because the way of life of that family is too firmly rooted in some old traditions, or because the way in which the family earns its bread leaves no money to approximate an American standard of living, you find that the image of the new ways, of the modern ways, of the standard American ways, has come. It has come in the mail-order catalogue, over the radio, in the moving pictures, even if they are seen but twice a year [Mead, 1949b:246].

Obviously an attempt to assess the reliability of a pattern derived from ideals is likely to fail if carried out by inspecting only what people actually do. Yet the author of the pattern may insist on its reliability! The subsequent investigator must know the source of the generalizations before he can hope to replicate the process of the original field worker (J. W. Bennett, 1946).

The generalizations that the anthropologist offers in print are those which he believes to be warranted by the number of cases observed or because they were reported "ready-made" by a number of trustworthy observers. There appears to be no way of specifying the absolute number of cases that should be observed before risking a pattern generalization. In part, volume of evidence depends on the kind of data. In one or two days of field work a pattern of recreation—like ball playing at evening-time—may be established firmly. Then comes a search for exceptions to the pattern. Who doesn't participate in the ball game and under what conditions (e.g., seasons or weather) does the game not occur? Where ready-made patterns are secured from informants or documents, such sources will usually be tested against each other before the pattern is accepted as corresponding to actual behavior. In cases in which only one event of its kind is reported by informants or observed, the incident may be reported as a discrete case rather than as a pattern. While patterns are the essence of the anthropologist's report, emphasis on them does not imply total neglect of idiopathic data. Also useful for comparative work are zero-patterns, that is, statements which read "There is no . . ." It is quite important to note the absence of regularities which the anthropologist had expected to find in a culture. An ethnographer usually also gives at least a little space to generalizing about geographical events, size and distribution of population, and descriptions of the people themselves. But the bulk of his writing is devoted to regularities of artifacts and of overt and covert behavior.

By patterns of artifacts we refer to the recurrent characteristics of man-made things. Thus a traditional winter house among the Cree Indians of James Bay was conical and covered with brush and turfs. The Cree Indians of the Great Plains, however, lived in a conical house covered with buffalo skins and provided with an "ear" to help create a draft for the fire.

Figure 5:1 illustrates how artifact types may be presented graphically. The example is taken from archeology but is applicable to ethnography.

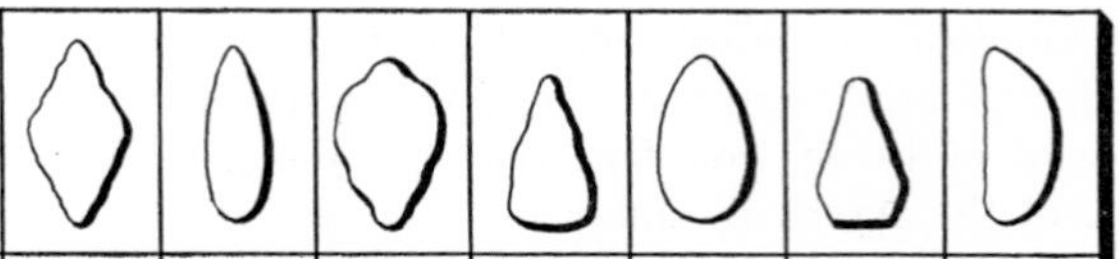

SITE 1 N = 337	4	21	2	5	52	1	15
SITE 2 N = 67	3	22	5	6	57	3	5
SITE 3 N = 24	4	13	0	17	37	0	29

FIG. 5:1. Seven Types of Stone Blades (in percentages) (from Thomas E. Lee, 1954:109).

Over 400 blades were discovered in three sites. These were classified into 7 patterns or types. The 7 types are sketched and the proportion of specimens corresponding to each is given for each of the 3 sites. The patterns could also be designated verbally, although not without danger of ambiguity, as large diamond-shaped blades, narrow leaf-shaped blades, and so on. The figure at the head of the seventh column is a semilunar blade.

Phonemic Analysis

Phonemic analysis designates the process of discovering the significant sound classes of a language from the discrete sounds transcribed while listening to speakers of that language (Pittman, 1948:57). The basic technique is indicated by the following oversimplified steps (Pike, 1947:67–71). In the field the linguist records, as carefully as possible, using a phonetic alphabet, utterances in the language which he was studying. He then prepares a phonetic chart of all the kinds of sound units which he has recorded. For example, in a hypothetical language we have the following words with their English equivalents:

mafsa	whale
tasa	walrus
mama	house
katasa	garden

The phonetic chart will look like this:

	LABIALDENTAL	ALVEOLAR	VELAR
Stops		t	k
Spirants	f v	s	
Nasals	m		
Vowels		a	

Next comes a listing of all pairs of sounds which are suspicious because they are phonetically similar and might freely be interchangeable (i.e., might prove to be members of a single sound class or phoneme). Two such are:

f   and   v

Now those sound units are listed which do not occur in suspicious pairs and which, therefore, may tentatively be regarded as separate phonemes:

/t k s m a/

Intensive work is required with the suspicious pairs (in this case only f and v) in order to determine whether they constitute different phonemes or whether they are nonsignificant variants of a single basic sound class. Basically such analysis involves discovering whether the similar units, f and v, ever occur in identical sound environments. Analysis of more data turns up the following words:

fama   man
vama   seed

From this it would be concluded that /f/ and /v/ are indeed separate phonemes for they cannot be used interchangeably in the same environments.

To distinguish phonemes from the actual sounds of a language they are enclosed in diagonals.

WHY SO MUCH TIME WITH EXOTIC CULTURES?

So closely is the anthropologist associated with the study of exotic ways of life that his discipline is sometimes defined as pertaining only to the study of "primitive cultures." The word "primitive" enjoys a variety of meanings, but in this case it refers to isolated ways of life that anthropologists have traditionally investigated. In the last few decades, however, the ethnologist came to define his task as including the study of culture everywhere. Anthropology, therefore, cannot be differentiated from the other disciplines which study human behavior by subject matter as much as by the approach adopted to social behavior. Yet the anthropologist, while not neglecting his own culture, obviously is engrossed with exotic ways of life. At least five reasons may be suggested to explain his interest in ways of life different from his own.

To Acquire Universal Knowledge

If one of the goals of anthropology is to pursue knowledge about culture wherever culture may be found, then the ethnologist cannot remain concerned only with the forms of behavior current, say, in Europe and America. Whereas in zoölogy, for example, it may be possible to learn the structure of all dogs from the anatomy of one member of the species precisely because all dogs are so homogeneous as to constitute a species, knowledge about culture requires sampling a relatively large number of different ways of life. Hardly any two cultures are similar!

To Combat Ethnocentrism

To study exotic cultures extensively is to discover how broad is the range of cultural diversity and how often people disregard what western communities regard as normal or essential. Cultural diversity emancipates the observer from the blindness inflicted by habituation to only one way of life. He discovers that not all languages categorize nouns into masculine, feminine, and neuter genders, as his does; not all people expect premarital chastity, and the small, western type of family is not the only basis on which to erect lasting relationships between men and women. Anthropologists can say with assurance that Euroamerican culture is but one of a series of possible ways for insuring survival and other satisfactions.

To Promote Objectivity

Dealing with foreign ways of life is expected to nourish a spirit of objectivity toward all cultures but particularly one's own. Even brief exposure to anthropology often enhances one's ability to look at familiar things —eating habits, marriage customs, sexual mores—from new perspectives and with greater sophistication. Why is it easier to learn to be objective about culture by studying it among exotic peoples?

In the first place, everyone is likely to be too much involved emotionally with certain aspects of his own way of life to maintain objectivity toward them. It is hard, for example, to think of western man's devastating wars as possibly related to the maintenance of certain values and *esprit de corps*. But a little familiarity with other cultures indicates how war may reinforce other behaviors. In a typical Indian community of the western Great Plains of North America, war provided the proving ground for masculine virtues. The bold warrior became the cynosure, eligible for political office as well as for espousing a chaste and proper girl. Life pivoted around the war parties which kept alive values like bravery, tribal patriotism, and even female chastity.

In what is now the United States, warfare, like predation in wild life, functioned toward the ecological harmony, and more complexly than predation in wild life, it functioned toward the shaping of virile, structured, unafraid, truly noble personality, which counted one's separate life and fate as of no great moment.
Yet while Indian warfare was limited, not unlimited or excessive, the Indian and his society "lived dangerously." The extreme of effort, of discipline and resourcefulness, hardest of realism, might at any time be demanded of every member of the little society. The Indian made it his business to have fullness of life within material meagreness, and within a deep insecurity which his wisdom did not even want to see terminated [J. Collier, 1947:102].

Given these values of living fully, dangerously, and resourcefully, with no competing ideology of pacifism, warfare could constitute a vital part of the configuration of Plains Indian life. One need neither condone nor condemn Plains Indian warfare in order to see its integration with other elements of behavior. This analysis helps to explain the collapse of Indian morale after United States administration put an end to tribal warfare. Things are not too different in modern America. "It is a mistake to believe that the American people hate war to the extent that they derive no satisfaction from it. Verbally and superficially they disapprove of war, but this is only partly revealed in their deeper feelings. In simple terms, most of them had more fun in the Second World War, just as they did in the First, than they have had in any other period of their lives" (Warner and associates, 1949:287).

From Simple to Complex

The anthropologist's concern with exotic cultures further stems from a conviction that learning wisely proceeds from the simple to the complex. The anthropologist wants to understand both simple and elaborate ways of life. Preparation for the latter is sought by working with communities which contain few people, a limited number of alternative forms of behavior, simpler forms of organization, and hardly any conflicting values or beliefs. Such communities probably are easier to understand at the present stage of knowledge than those at the opposite end of the continuum.

Preference

In all honesty it must be admitted that an additional reason exists for the anthropologist's preoccupation with the exotic. Many ethnologists joined the profession because of an emotional leaning toward ways of life that are remote and different. Even in studying his own culture the anthropologist often looks for elements that are nearly completely hidden from untrained members of his community.

"The anthropologist is the astronomer of the social sciences; his task is to discover a meaning for configurations which, owing to their size and remoteness, are very different from those within the observer's immediate purview. . . . He can also be called upon to take part, alongside specialists of other disciplines, in the study of phenomena which exist within his own society but which are also characterized by 'distanciation,' either because they concern only one section of the group and not the whole of it, or because, even though they are of an overall nature, they are deeply rooted in the unconscious" (Lévi-Strauss, 1954b:123).

Nowhere is it implied that exotic communities, no matter how small and isolated they may be, are investigated because they represent survivals of human society as it existed at the "dawn of civilization." All cultures have an equally long history and none can be taken as closer than any other to man's earliest ways of life (Lévi-Strauss, 1952:Chaps. 4–6).

6.

Data Handling in Scientific Anthropology[1]

DRAWING mainly on ethnological examples, this chapter outlines briefly the procedures of science as they may be applied to anthropological data. The greatest emphasis is given to describing how scientific propositions are tested and how testable hypotheses may be derived from reliable ethnographic facts.

Science means a search for recurrent, or predictable, relationships between objectively perceived facts (see pp. 29–31). In anthropology it makes little difference whether those facts stem from one's own or another investigator's archeological or ethnographic field work. The facts, usually patterns, must be reliable if the attempt to extend their truth value is to be undertaken seriously. In scientific analysis one moves beyond knowledge of the individual fact to the general truth which emerges when particular facts are found to be related predictably to one another. Scientists assume that such truths cannot be deduced through reason or logic alone. Science insists on *testing* the predictive, or truth, value of hypotheses which posit a connection between two or more facts.

WORKING WITH HYPOTHESES

No matter how many insightful ethnographic monographs are published, they cannot by themselves yield scientific explanations of how culture operates. Similarly, the most painstakingly excavated and dated archeological site cannot by itself provide verified knowledge about how culture changes. Attainment of such generalized knowledge requires crossing from natural history to science.

There are many definitions of science, each emphasizing somewhat different aspects of that activity. A synonym for scientific method might be "generalizing method," designating the scientist's goal of generalized knowledge about some segment of natural phenomena—in this case, culture. However, that definition conveys nothing about the steps taken to

[1] The beginner may find this chapter a bit difficult. If so, let him read only through p. 76 now and return to the chapter after he has read more (or all) of the book.

attain generalized knowledge. Intuition also yields generalized knowledge and scientists sometimes use intuition. But then they go further. They test their hunches empirically. Testing means to verify or confirm, disprove or throw out. Hence science is defined as the search for predictable (that is, verifiable) relationships between facts. Note that this definition ignores the acts of collecting and verifying patterns of a particular culture, a task belonging at the natural-history stage of inquiry. Science begins when particular facts are handled in order to make them yield more generalized truths.

A case study of science in action may make the process clearer.

Animal Names for Human Groups[2]

Some of the tribes who live in the interior of New South Wales, Australia, divide themselves into two parts, or halves, named after the eagle-hawk and the crow. There is a rule that a man should take a wife only from the division other than his own. Children in turn will be identified with the division of the mother. Technically such divisions are called exogamous matrilineal moieties (see pp. 398–399). A kind of mild opposition exists between the moieties and is expressed, for example, in joking. Members of opposite divisions are expected to taunt one another and each side provides opponents for competitive games. In this description are several relatively independent facts to deal with. Two may be singled out. One is the fact that the divisions are named after birds, the eaglehawk and crow, the other that a degree of socially regulated opposition links the halves. Now a close parallel to the South Australian state of affairs occurs among the Haida Indians of the Queen Charlotte Islands, which lie off the northwest coast of North America. Here the community is divided into two moieties named after the eagle and the raven. In other parts of Oceania similar divisions appear. They only sometimes are called after birds, also being identified, as in other parts of Australia, with two species of other animals. Opposition between the divisions is common wherever moieties exist. Evidence is lacking that adventurous sailors carried the pattern between aboriginal Australia, New Ireland, northwestern America, and wherever else it may be found. Hence, it is reasonable to propose that the invention of the pattern occurred independently in Australia, Melanesia, and northwestern America.

So far no scientific problem confronts the reader. Lack of sufficient knowledge about the prehistoric past killed off a potential historical problem. This leaves only the distribution of a "complex" (see pp. 126–127) in several parts of the world. A. R. Radcliffe-Brown, facing this distribution,

---

[2] This section is based on Radcliffe-Brown, 1952a.

asked a scientific question: How did these social divisions come to be identified by species of birds or other animals? Clearly he could not, as a quick reading of the question suggests he may have wanted to, turn to history for an answer. Even if knowledge of the past had been adequate, answering in terms of the historical origin of moieties and their animal identification would only push the scientific question back in time. The scientist would still be faced with the problem: What factors help to explain the identification of these social divisions with birds or other animals? Radcliffe-Brown demanded to know the principle by which such pairs as eaglehawk and crow, eagle and raven, coyote and wildcat are chosen to represent the dual divisions.

Let the reader imagine that while the ethnographer is still in the field in New South Wales he sits down with an informant and asks the latter for some traditional stories. The informant obliges and suddenly the anthropologist hears something that makes him pay sharper attention:

Eaglehawk was the mother's brother of Crow. . . . Eaglehawk told his nephew to go and hunt wallaby [kangaroo]. Crow, having killed the wallaby, ate it himself. . . . On his return to camp his uncle asked him what he had brought, and Crow, being a liar, said he had succeeded in getting nothing. Eaglehawk then said, "But what is in your belly, since your hunger belt is no longer tight?" Crow replied that to stay the pangs of hunger he had filled his belly with the gum from the acacia. Then uncle replied that he did not believe him and would tickle him until he vomited. . . . The Crow vomited the wallaby that he had eaten. Thereupon Eaglehawk seized him and rolled him in the fire; his eyes became red with the fire, he was blackened by the charcoal, and he called out in pain "Wa! Wa! Wa!" Eaglehawk pronounced . . . "You will never be a hunter, but you will forever be a thief," and that is how things now are.

Note that the story plot employs the same two animals after which the moieties are named.

Anthropology from its start has followed some form of the comparative method.[3] Such methods entail relating communities, cultures, or parts of cultures to each other.

It rests on the sound principle that the way to explain a particular fact is to relate it to others, to proceed from the particular to the general and from the general to the still more general until, in the end, we see the particular phenomenon not as unique or isolated but as an instance of a universal human tendency. But the comparative method must be used with great care and caution and the items compared must be genuinely and not just superficially

---

[3] The comparative method is not limited to scientific analysis of data. It also serves for historical analysis. See Chapter 7.

similar; and to ensure this the function as well as the form of a custom or an institution must be taken into account [Macbeath, 1954:218].

Back home while working over his field notes, the field worker continues to read accounts dealing with native life in other parts of Australia. In an account of another community that also possesses dual divisions he reads:

Wombat [an opossum-like creature] and Kangaroo lived together as friends. One day Wombat began to make a "house" for himself. (The wombat lives in a burrow in the ground.) Kangaroo jeered at him and thus annoyed him. Then one day it rained. . . . Wombat went into his "house" out of the rain. Kangaroo asked Wombat to make room for him, but the latter explained that there was only room for one. Thus Wombat and Kangaroo quarreled and fought. Kangaroo hit Wombat on the head with a big stone, flattening his skull. Wombat threw a spear at Kangaroo which fixed itself at the base of the backbone. The wombat has a flattened skull to this day and the kangaroo has a tail; the former lives in a burrow while the kangaroo lives in the open; they are no longer friends.

Again opposition between two anthropomorphized animals who represent the dual divisions! It is time to become imaginative—a quite essential component of science! In both these communities the exogamous moieties linked through opposition are named after animals which the folk tales describe as having once been enemies or which remain at loggerheads with each other. The scientist is ready to advance a hypothesis, one not only applying to his Australian data but of more general scope. *Dual divisions engaged in mild opposition,* he predicts, *are named after animals believed to be (or to have been) opposed to one another.*

Now comes the task of verifying or testing the hypothesis that moieties are named after animals manifesting opposition to each other. Further comparative research reveals that accounts very much like the Australian stories about eaglehawk and crow or wombat and kangaroo are repeated in other world regions where opposed, exogamous moieties exist. The tales are similar in that they tell of animal species anthropomorphically entering relationships of friendship and antagonism. Then comes a startling discovery. Dual divisions are also named after heaven and earth, or simply after the directions up and down. The hypothesis is not denied by these additional facts, but it must be modified in the direction of still greater generality in order to accommodate the new facts. It is concluded, therefore, that moieties tend to be named after natural phenomena which the members of a community regard as somehow opposite or contrary to each other. Future discoveries may overturn this proposition, but for the present the principle of "contrariety" (as defined in the preceding sentence) explains in a nonhistorical manner how social divisions happen to be identified with natural species. Nothing is said about which phenomenon occurs first, the dual division named after opposites or the conception of contrary phenomena. Logically, the latter ideas would seem to have been earlier, but such a hunch is practically impossible to substantiate.[4]

Qualitative and Quantitative Research

Quantification and statistical method are widely employed in scientific work. In order to treat facts statistically it usually is necessary that they have been collected in quantitative form. Only to a slight extent do anthropologists obtain quantitative data. Rarely do they count or measure the events they observe. Hence, in comparing facts recorded in one community with those acquired in another, it is usually possible only to count up the number of communities in which they are present or absent, or roughly to gauge their importance numerically to the community's members.

Quantitative procedures are not indispensable in scientific method. Nonquantitative studies summarizing a relatively large number of observations can also indicate relationships. For example, a famous study of college and street-corner groups identifies the college boy as more frequently interested in social advancement, parliamentary procedure, saving money, and a willingness to give up friendship with those who do not advance as he does. The street-corner boy, on the other hand, more often is associated with different values. He is interested in his neighborhood, favors informal ways of doing things, likes to spend money, and is unwilling to disrupt group ties (W. F. Whyte, 1943). The researcher may go further and explain the relationships found in each case with another hypothesis. The data suggest the hypothesis that saving is useful to the college youth because it provides an avenue to social advancement. Saving does not offer this reward to a street-corner boy, for whom upward mobility holds little promise. Street-corner boys see little to save for (C. Kluckhohn, 1949a:211). This conclusion, like the explanation for moieties' being named after contrary natural phenomena, involves no quantitative data and requires no

[4] There are, of course, other explanations of totemism (see pp. 366–367). For Malinowski (1948:44–46), totemism rests on a keen interest in animal nature that leads man to invest animals with particular sentiments. Radcliffe-Brown's hypothesis is not in contradiction to Malinowski's but is somewhat more specific and testable. Psychoanalysis has another explanation for the identification of groups with rivalrous animal pairs. The rivalry is seen as a disguised form of rivalry between father and son, the latter having incestuous wishes for exclusive possession of the mother. But the women of the mother's moiety are barred to the son (at least in communities where moiety membership follows the mother). This exogamous rule provides the sons of the community with a defense against the anxiety which their incestuous wishes arouse. They will never come into open rivalry with the father over possession of his woman because sexual relations with women of the same moiety are strictly forbidden (Róheim, 1925:Chap. 1). It is difficult to see how such an explanation for the identification of moieties with opposed pairs of animals can ever be proved true or false by application of comparative testing. To psychoanalysts, however, it is logically highly satisfactory.

statistical procedure. For that reason its predictive value is difficult to gauge precisely. The reader will also note that generalization in this instance is on a lower level than in the case of the moieties. The latter explanation, based on data from a few particular cultures, is world-wide. The former, based on data from a few individuals in an American city, presumably is limited to the United States.

Comparative qualitative analysis can be elaborated to a point at which conclusions drawn from one instance can be tested tentatively against a control case. In a study of this type witchcraft (see pp. 641–642) is compared in four African communities (Nadel, 1952). Two of the tribes, Nupe and Gwari, are neighbors in an identical environment of West Africa. They also possess the same system of social organization and similar indigenous religions. Both believe in witches who "eat" the "life-souls" of victims. Among the Gwari, witches may be either male or female. In Nupe, however, the witches are believed to be always women, although they may be assisted by men. The men, however, are never blamed for their role. Since the two communities are alike in so many factors it may be that the differences in witchcraft can be accounted for by reference to other points of difference between them. Clearly not *any* other difference will be sought but one which can meaningfully be related to the divergence in witchcraft beliefs. The relations of men to women suggest themselves as fruitful in this respect. Marriage is relatively tension-free in Gwari, which now serves as a kind of control group, but is full of stress and hostility in Nupe. Here opportunities for women to engage in trade lead wives to assume responsibilities ideally expected of men alone. The situation frustrates men, who also resent their trading wives' reluctance to bear children. While the women no doubt live by values of their own, the values of the two sexes are in conflict. We are now ready to state the hypothesis in specific terms: Among the Nupe frustration by women who do not conform to male expectations of female behavior is related dynamically to a tendency to make women solely responsible for witchcraft. The frustration which men experience in marital life, it is reasoned, finds expression in witchcraft accusations. Such reasoning to explain the facts is congenial with what has become known as the frustration-aggression theory of psychology plus the theory of stimulus generalization. In still more general terms, phrased to make the proposition amenable to cross-cultural testing, the hypothesis may be stated as follows: Witchcraft accusations are leveled against people whose behavior generates frustration. A simplified statement of these steps is given in the accompanying diagram.

Does the sequence of accusing of witchcraft persons who do not conform to social expectations and so arouse frustration recur? This question is essential since it tests the predictability of the relationship. If these facts do recur together, then some support also is given to the theory underlying

DIAGRAM ILLUSTRATING THE FORMULATION OF A
HYPOTHESIS WHILE USING A CONTROL GROUP

Experimental Group	Control Group
Nupe	Gwari

Both these groups are matched as far as environment, social organization, and religion are concerned.

Step 1. *Fact to be explained (the dependent variable):*

Witches are predominantly female.

Witches are not predominantly female.

Step 2. *Facts serving as an explanation (the independent variables):*

Men are frustrated by wives' behavior.

Husband-wife relationship relatively tension-free.

Step 3. *Statement of the hypothesis:*

The identification of women as witches among the Nupe is related to the man's frustration by the woman's behavior. (*Note that the explanatory condition [independent variable] is lacking in the control group and so is the condition to be accounted for [the dependent variable].*)

Step 4. *Generalization of the hypothesis:*

Persons whose behavior arouses frustration will be accused of witchcraft.

the relationship, although that theory cannot itself be proved true or false in this simple manner.

In East Africa live the Korongo and the Mesakin, two neighboring communities inhabiting the same environment and possessing similar ways of life. The Korongo lack any semblance of witchcraft beliefs while the Mesakin "are literally obsessed by fears of witchcraft . . . and witchcraft accusations are frequent." Here is a favorable situation in which to test the hypothesis that witchcraft accusations tend to be directed against persons who do not fulfill social expectations and thereby arouse frustration. Among the Mesakin witchcraft accusations are usually structured between relatives, not necessarily women; among these relatives the accusation frequently occurs between mother's brother and sister's son. Especially is the former believed to be prone to use witchcraft against his nephew. Is a mother's brother or sister's son a source of frustration among the

Mesakin but not among the Korongo? Note how the latter community constitutes a control group. It turns out that the relationship of mother's brother to sister's son among the Mesakin is connected to the socially standardized conception of aging. The Korongo and the Mesakin diverge in how they regard the process of growing old. In both communities men are not fond of old age but the Korongo on the whole accept graciously the decline in physical vigor associated with growing old. Not so the Mesakin, among whom aging is frustrating and the frustration is exacerbated by certain ceremonial duties assigned old men. Now, in both Korongo and Mesakin cultures the pattern is for the nephew to inherit from his mother's brother. Demand that the inheritance be paid represents a sign that the owner of the property is perceived to be growing old. This demand and its attendant meaning are relatively acceptable to the Korongo man but are resented by the Mesakin. There the frustrated mother's brother tries to hold on to his wealth as long as possible. In turn he arouses frustration in the sister's son. The men accuse each other of witchcraft. The hypothesis has moved another step toward confirmation.[5] The theory to explain the relationship between frustration and witchcraft appears to be a useful one.

These examples of finding hypotheses to explain the naming of dual divisions, saving, and witchcraft are all weak not because they are qualitative in nature but because they rely on *post hoc* reasoning. Except in the case of the Mesakin, certain relationships between phenomena were presumed to be meaningful and a theory "after the facts" was then invented to explain those adhesions. Such a procedure is not very convincing. Explanations are easy to find after an event has occurred. History, for example, is continually finding fresh data to explain certain events of the past. Ideally in scientific procedure a theory suggests why two or more facts should be associated more often than could be accounted for by chance alone.[6] Then the scientist proceeds to collect data to see if the predictable relationship (i.e., hypothesis) indeed holds true. If it does, then the hypothesis is verified and the theory is proved useful.

An example of such research which also illustrates quantitative methods is found in the study undertaken to see if sorcery (see pp. 627–628) and social control are associated predictably (B. B. Whiting, 1950).

A sample of exotic communities studied from published reports revealed two main types of social control: coördinate and superordinate. In communities manifesting coördinate social control no individual or group of individuals possesses authority to settle disputes or punish offenses. Rather,

[5] Other evidence supporting the hypothesis will be found in C. Kluckhohn, 1944; Marwick, 1952 and 1956; and M. Wilson, 1951b. The intracultural source of Gwari witchcraft remains to be explained; perhaps the same theory could be applied.
[6] The meaning and use of theory is further examined below, pp. 89–92.

social control relies upon retaliation administered by the injured party or his kin. Superordinate social control means that certain persons (like chiefs) hold responsibility for deciding disputes and punishing wrongs. Among the Paiute of southeastern Oregon sorcery and coördinate control are found together. Sorcery actually constituted a device for retaliating against a wrongdoer among these people. Seemingly it took the place of persons with clearly designated authority to keep order. Can the hypothesis that coördinate control will generally be found in association with considerable use of sorcery be verified? If so, it will also throw light on the theory that sorcery is useful as a form of retaliation in communities lacking specialized agents of law and order. To test the hypothesis 50 communities were divided into those in which members avenged wrongs without first securing permission from an individual or group (i.e., showing coördinate control) and those in which a troublesome matter or dispute was referred for settlement to a chief or court (i.e., settled with superordinate control). Each of these two categories was then subdivided into communities in which sorcery was given as a cause of illness (sorcery, it could be assumed, was "important" in these) and those in which sorcery was not so cited. Here the practice of sorcery was assumed to be unimportant. The results are grouped in Table 8. Next, a tetrachoric correlation between the four variables was made to ascertain the degree of relationship. The coefficient

TABLE 8.   Relationship of Coördinate and Superordinate Control to Sorcery

	Coördinate Control			Superordinate Control	
Sorcery important	Apache	Hill Maria	Murngin	Ashanti	
	Arunta	Gonds	Orokaiva	Fiji	
	Azande	Ifugao	Paiute	Lamba	
	Barama Caribs	Jivaro	Tiv	Sanpoil	
	Buka	Kamilaroi	Trobriands	Venda	
	Chagga	Kiwai	Witoto		
	Chuckchee	Kutchin	Yurok		
	Copper Eskimo	Kwakiutl	Zuni		
	Delaware	Kwoma			
	Dieri	Lesu			
	Dobu	Mala	N = 30		N = 5
		Maori	% = 60		% = 10
Sorcery unimportant	Kazak			Bali	Tanala
	Lango			Cayapa	Tikopia
	Masai			Cheyenne	Tonga
				Crow	
				Japan	
				Lepcha	
				Ontong Java	
			N = 3	Riff	N = 12
			% = 6	Samoa	% = 24

SOURCE: B. Whiting, *1950*:87.

of correlation turned out to be .85, a high index. This suggests that a very predictable relationship exists between the importance of sorcery and co-ordinate social control as well as between the unimportance of sorcery and superordinate social control. Further statistical treatment indicates that there is less than one chance in a hundred that the correlation obtained with the sample of 50 communities can be due to chance. Other samples would, in over 99 cases out of a hundred, reveal the same relationship.

The reader will note an obvious advantage of quantitative and statistical research over qualitative methods. Judging from the example just given, the former procedures are better suited to reveal the precise degree to which facts go together. Qualitative inspection of Table 8 reveals merely a positive association between types of sorcery and social control. The use of correlation and of a test of significance brings out the magnitude of the correlation as well as the probability that such an association is not simply accidental or due to chance.[7] Instead of being due to chance, the relationship is probably "lawful." That is, there is something about the two variables, social control and sorcery, which makes them vary in a certain way. One is in a sense dependent on the other. The theory says that the secret of their interdependence lies in the way sorcery can serve to maintain order in a setting of coördinate social control. Presumably under a condition of superordinate control sorcery is unnecessary for this function and may even be undesirable. This reasoning helps to explain the correlation which it suggested in the first place. The correlation, however, merely states that the variables are predictably related. It says nothing about the reason for the interdependence which was discovered. Yet, had the correlation come out negatively or with an insignificant measure of probability, the theory would no doubt have been discarded as unproductive or not useful.

MORE ABOUT RELATIONSHIPS

Not all the hypotheses suggested by anthropological theory are immediately testable. The variables believed to be predictably related may have been reported by too few anthropologists to provide sufficient cases for statistical analysis. Or for some other reason the relationship is merely stated but cannot be verified. What is important is that the hypotheses should be verifiable cross-culturally. Hence the definition of science is given as the search for *verifiable* relationships between phenomena.

In speaking of a relationship between the importance of sorcery and coördinate control there is no implication that one of these phenomena

---

[7] We shall not attempt to go further into statistical theory or procedures. The interested student may consult Ackoff, 1953; L. Cohen, 1954; David, 1953; or Hagood and Price, 1952.

causes or produces the other. There is no better ground for interpreting the correlation as indicating causality than there is for saying that totemic groups produce a people's conception of contrary animal pairs. These relationships merely state that one factor is predictably related to another factor. The evidence is that the two variables, *a* and *b*, regularly concur, that is, with a frequency significantly greater than could be ascribed to chance alone. Actually three types of relationships between phenomena may be distinguished, only two of which need serious consideration.[8]

Causal Relationships

Relationships in which it is held that one variable, say *a*, is sufficient by and of itself to cause the appearance of another variable, *b*, may be called "causal relationships," although the word "cause" has acquired many other meanings and few people are sure what they mean by that word. Causal thinking is by no means uncommon in everyday experience. It is nevertheless very dubious, at least for the realm of social and cultural phenomena, that one factor is ever sufficient by itself to produce any effect. Saying this does not deny the assumption that social and cultural events are determined or that the determinants may be known. Investigation suggests, however, that multiple rather than single conditions always determine human behavior. One factor, whether it is frustration, war, delinquency, or contact with another way of life, is never sufficient to instigate any behavior. Many other conditions, including at least an intact biological organism, are also required to operate in order that behavior may occur in response to a particular stimulus.

Causal relationships imply that one variable is sufficient to produce another and therefore that the connection between them is somehow necessary or inevitable. A more tenable assumption holds that the relationships tested by science are always more or less probable but never absolute, necessary, or unfailing. In science to speak of a necessary or inevitable connection between two variables usually means that two things are related by definition or that one is arguing in a circle (Bridgman, 1938:65–66). Thus, totemic groups *always* have natural phenomena associated with them. The phenomena consist of plants, animals, or, sometimes, celestial elements like the sun and moon. But such a relationship between totemic groups and natural phenomena *must* be true (and therefore always is true), simply because totemic groups are defined as groups which are named or otherwise symbolized by natural phenomena! The relationship of these variables, therefore, cannot be tested. In a different category is the proposition which says that the natural phenomena associated with moiety divisions are con-

---

[8] Much of the following discussion is based on Ackoff, 1953:65–68.

ceived of by the community as somehow contrary or opposed. There is no reason to expect that this second relationship will always be true. Certainly it is not given in the definition of a moiety.

A relationship which asserts a necessary bond between one variable and another is easy to disprove. Thus in the early part of the present century the restlessness of adolescent youth, its conflict and distress, were sometimes ascribed to the period itself. "Adolescence was characterized as a period in which idealism flowered and rebellion against authority waxed strong, a period during which difficulties and conflicts were absolutely inevitable" (Mead, 1928a:2). The anthropologist had little trouble in showing that conflict and distress did not inevitably occur with adolescence. A relationship between adolescence and restlessness was apparent in America, a country of conflicting standards of conduct, but could be seen much less clearly in the older parts of Europe and didn't appear at all among the girls living in American Samoa. "The adolescent girl in Samoa differed from her sister who had not reached puberty in one chief respect, that in the older girl certain bodily changes were present which were absent in the younger girl. There were no other great differences to set off the group passing through adolescence from the group which would become adolescent in two years or the group which had become adolescent two years before" (ibid., p. 196).

Producer-Product Relationships

Another kind of relationship states that the presence of a given variable, a, will under certain conditions (specifiable as $x, y, z \ldots n$) give rise to b, while the absence of a (the other conditions remaining constant) is predictably associated with the absence of b. In other words, a produces b. Discovering producer-product relationships entails some form of controlled experiment in which factors $x, y, z \ldots n$ can be held constant while only a is varied in order to test its crucial relationship to b. The relationship may be symbolized as follows:

$$a(x, y, z \ldots n) \rightarrow b.$$

Devising experiments in ethnology to test producer-product relationships promises to be difficult. For example, supposing the relationship between importance of sorcery and form of social control is revised so that the rise of superordinate forms of control (that is, forms of government) is made responsible for the suppression of the importance of sorcery. It is, of course, assumed that superordinate social control is not operating independently in producing a decline in the importance of sorcery but occurs only in a context of other relevant factors. Testing this producer-product hypothesis might be done through the following procedure:

STEP 1: Secure an adequate sample of communities with superordinate control and count the incidence of communities in that sample in which sorcery is important.

STEP 2: Secure a control group of communities which as far as certain relevant factors are concerned (size, mode of food production, religious notions) is quite closely matched with the experimental group. *Superordinate control is absent in the control group.* Now count the incidence of communities in the control group in which sorcery is important. For the hypothesis to be true, the incidence of communities having sorcery important should be significantly greater than in the former, or experimental, group.

Even a reader only moderately sophisticated in anthropology will recognize the difficulty of finding a control group of communities lacking superordinate social control but for even a few relevant factors closely matched with the experimental group. When superordinate control is present, many other conditions are also likely to be present which would very probably be absent with coördinate social control. It is nearly impossible to manipulate only one variable in ethnological analysis, holding others constant. Culture is a system; there is rarely an alteration in one part without an alteration also in other sectors of the configuration (see pp. 13–15).

Another procedure often adopted to test producer-product relationships might be applied to the present problem:

STEP 1: Discover communities without superordinate control or records of such communities. It is to be expected that sorcery will also be important in most of these.

STEP 2: Observe what happens in these communities when superordinate control is added. One thing that is predicted should happen if the hypothesis is sound: sorcery should decline in importance.

The trouble with the second procedure is not the difficulty of finding communities to study which have been or are changing in the direction of superordinate control. Many reports of changes are published and available and may provide at least a partial sample for analysis. The more serious difficulty is that when superordinate control appears in these communities the rest of the culture usually does not remain constant but also changes. Hence, even if sorcery is found to be reduced in importance following the introduction of superordinate control, how can it be maintained that this change is produced by a change in the form of social control? A major condition of the controlled experiment is absent—constancy in other relevant factors. Despite this difficulty, historical changes which recur from one culture to another are often explained in producer-product terms as being derived from other changes.[9] Simply as a means of suggesting pro-

[9] Historians are not referred to here. Because they usually work only with a single community at a time they will ascribe even nonrecurrent changes (a particular war, inflation, emigration, or change in style of painting) to certain antecedent phenomena, and

ducer-product hypotheses for some kind of more crucial testing such a procedure is defensible. Quite definitely it proves nothing about determinism.

In ordinary language a producer-product hypothesis linking variables a and b is often loosely referred to as a's "giving rise to," "developing," "causing," "producing," "stimulating," or "maintaining" b. Sometimes b is called a "consequence" of a or a is spoken of as governing the persistence of b. Such language must be understood as implying that other factors are also operative in the particular relationship being studied.

Many hypotheses stated to be producer-product relationships have never been verified as actually being in that category. Hence, they constitute hypotheses of unknown predictive value. Whether they can ever be tested depends on whether the anthropologist's skill in handling comparative data will increase. To say that producer-product relationships are hard to verify cross-culturally is no reason to avoid offering such hypotheses.

Functional Relationships

Distinct from producer-product relationships are statements of correlation which imply only that two or more variables covary: a covaries with b.

The reader will recall that correlation provided the subject of an earlier section in this chapter. Coördinate control and sorcery, for example, were shown to be strongly correlated (the index of correlation, .85, being quite high). Correlations are far easier to verify in anthropology than are producer-product relationships. On the other hand, it is also apparent that a knowledge of tested producer-product relationships allows a greater degree of control over a situation than does knowledge of correlations. However, knowledge of correlations also allows control, although it is of a more limited kind. If one knows that coördinate control and importance of sorcery go together, then the appearance of one variable allows the prediction that the other will also probably be present. Such knowledge is a kind of control.

Under certain limited conditions a significant correlation can quite unambiguously indicate a producer-product relationship. This occurs when the producing factor is already known from more elemental, experimental work in another science. Thus, size of a crop correlates with number of sunny days. That the latter probably constitutes the productive agent in the relationship is known from verified research in plant physiology (A. M. Rose, 1954:287). Logic may also strongly suggest the producing agent to

---

they assume the antecedent produced the subsequent. But historians are a special case. They do not pretend to be working in the field of science, where truth lies in predictability. They defend the truth of their statements by logic alone (see pp. 28–29). It is true that some cultural anthropologists emulate the method, including the assumptions, of history, but in this chapter the application of scientific method to ethnology is being discussed.

reside in some sequences of events. For example, to test whether crowding on land produces emigration from a community, we compare communities to see if crowding and emigration are regularly correlated. There follows strong presumption that crowding produces emigration; at any rate, it cannot logically be the other way around! However, all such short cuts to producer-product relationships substitute the method of reasoning about phenomena for the scientific method of relating those phenomena empirically.

Correlations in social science are often designated as functional relationships. The correlated variables are functions of one another, one varying or appearing with the other. Symbolically such a relationship may be written as follows:

$$a = f\,(b)$$
$$b = f\,(a)$$

The first equation is to be read as stating that a is a function of b, where a and b stand for hypothetically related phenomena. The second equation states that b is a function of a. Obviously both statements mean the same thing—a and b covary. In the first example, however, the investigator for some reason focuses his attention on factor a, while in the latter b has become the dependent variable.

It may be unnecessary to warn the discerning reader that the literature by no means always rigidly distinguishes producer-product from functional hypotheses. Often one variable is spoken of as "governing," "determining," or "helping to maintain" another when, according to the evidence, at best a functional relationship is indicated. A theory may trace the presence of one factor, say, the declining importance of sorcery, to the action of another, for instance, superordinate social control. The former may be described as a "consequence" of the latter. The proof, however—namely, a comparative correlation analysis such as that shown in Table 8—will indicate clearly that in the course of being tested the producer-product relationship was converted into a far more manageable functional relationship. The reader has no alternative but to become sophisticated about the operations available for demonstrating relationships in science and to pick out the one which has been, or can be, used in a specific situation regardless of the words chosen to describe the relationship.

Independent and Dependent Variables

In dealing with producer-product relationships as well as with correlations it sometimes is useful to distinguish the independent from the dependent variable. Perhaps the subject under discussion is social organization. One wants to know something about conditions producing or governing different forms of social organization. For example, under what conditions do large kingdoms and empires come into being? Paraphrasing this

question one may ask: On what is complex tribal, or intertribal, social organization dependent? Here social organization becomes the dependent
variable. Those conditions which theory suggests are explanatory of complex social organization are the independent variables. Diagrammatically:

$$Complex\ social\ organization = \text{f}\ (?)$$

or, in a producer-product hypothesis:

$$?(x, y, z) \longrightarrow Complex\ social\ organization$$

Or one may ask what depends on complex social organization. What else
varies when empires grow and bureaucracy increases steadily? Here complex social organization becomes the independent variable, and the other
conditions predicted by hypotheses are the dependent variables. To symbolize this:

$$? = \text{f}\ (Complex\ social\ organization)$$

or, in a producer-product hypothesis:

$$Complex\ social\ organization\ (x, y, z) \rightarrow ?$$

The independent variable, then, is the variable which is manipulated,
varied, or removed in order to learn what it controls. Although there are
other ways of stating such relationships, for the sake of consistency the
independent variable, in parentheses, will always be written on the right side
of functional equations.

The Problem of Determinism

The admission that predictable relationships link events in social life
stimulates the question whether people possess free will or human behavior
is determined. For if it were not determined, how could statistically significant relationships be discovered? But if behavior is determined, then do
people not possess choice?

It is quite true that correlations or producer-product relationships involving human behavior imply some kind of limits for the range of variation. With superordinate control present in the community people are apparently not as likely (or are unable) to attach importance to sorcery as
when coördinate control is present. Does this mean that people do not
have the free will to choose one or the other course of action?

Proper attention cannot be devoted to this venerable and recurrent
philosophical problem in a book purporting only to introduce cultural anthropology (cf. Tylor, 1891:I, 2–5). Generally speaking, the fact that anthropologists do succeed in discovering predictable relationships in culture
does not mean that individuals living in a particular community are unable
to exercise decision-making powers over their own behavior. People in a

community with superordinate control are as free to attach importance to sorcery as are people living under coördinate control. All the correlation says is that people under superordinate control do not choose to attach the same significance to sorcery as people living under the other set of conditions do. Scientific laws do not deny that man has the power of choice. As a matter of fact, that very power limits social science. The laws of social science are far less certain than the laws of inanimate nature.

Culture is basically a product of man (Bidney, 1953:14, 120–124). Although man can and does alter this culture, choice always is confined by the limits of one's awareness of resources, both cultural and noncultural. Bedouin living in the Arabian Desert are not likely to choose to shower-bathe daily, nor will Americans select sorcery as a vehicle for retaliation. The overwhelming proportion of man's choices are made within the limits of the culture of the community in which the individual lives and within the limits imposed by his organism and the geographical environment.

DISSENTERS

Not all anthropologists admit to the possibility of finding predictable relationships in culture. Sometimes it is maintained that "cultural phenomena are of such complexity that it seems . . . doubtful whether valid cultural laws can be found." Therefore "the material of anthropology is such that it needs must be a historical science," meaning a humanistic study that seeks to understand individual phenomena (i.e., particular cultures) rather than to pursue general laws (Boas, 1932:257–258). Part of this denial that there can be a science of culture stems from the belief that any cultural phenomenon is relatively unique and comprehensible only in its particular context. If one cannot assume that sorcery is in some respect the same from one community to another, then sorcery cannot be compared from one community to another. Those who dissent from trying to build a science of culture see no possibility of abstracting general elements from a series of truly unique events.[10] "Every event, every being is in the final sense unique. Nothing quite the same ever recurs; no two beings are ever entirely alike. It is only because they can be thought of abstractly that their differences can be lost from sight and their points of likeness held in mind" (de Grange, 1953:81).

GENERALITY AND THEORY

How does the cultural scientist proceed to generalize a universal hypothesis from the facts found in a particular community? Consider the proposition that the aboriginal Kaska Indians, a community which obtained its

[10] Marxists also deny that there can be a science of social life (Schaff and Ehrlich, 1950: 330).

food by plant collecting, hunting, and inland fishing, exhibited practically no domestic or foreign trade and no specialization of occupation (see p. 18). Let *FG* ("food gathering") summarize a mode subsistence based on collecting, hunting, and fishing in the equation

$$\overline{S}\,\overline{T} = f\,(FG_1)$$

Here, $\overline{S}$ and $\overline{T}$ stand for the absence of occupational specialization and trade respectively, the line over the symbols indicating absence. Thus the hypothesis reads that the absence of occupational specialization or trade (the dependent variables) is a function of food gathering (as contrasted with food production through such techniques as farming and animal husbandry) in *one* particular community. The subscript numeral following the symbols *FG* indicates that the facts apply to only one case. Sampling additional communities in other parts of the world (like the Australian Bushmen, Cree Indians of northeastern Canada, Eskimo, and the Ona of Tierra del Fuego) reveals that they also live by collecting, hunting, and fishing and possess unelaborated patterns of specialization and trade. In other words:

$$\overline{S}\,\overline{T} = f\,(FG_1)$$
$$\overline{S}\,\overline{T} = f\,(FG_2)$$
$$\overline{S}\,\overline{T} = f\,(FG_3)$$

More cases will, of course, be sought. The hypothesis may now be generalized to read:

$$\overline{S}\,\overline{T} = f\,(FG)$$

Here *FG* indicates food-gathering communities in general. The generalized hypothesis says that the absence of specialization and trade is dependent functionally on a subsistence technology that rests solely on collecting, hunting, and inland fishing.

To read anything further into such an equation is to increase the number of propositions that call for verification. Thus, it may be reasoned that food-gathering communities possess populations that are too sparse or widely scattered to support occupational specialization and trade. At the present stage of social science, it is not likely that such a statement can be tested as a producer-product hypothesis but it can be expressed as a correlation—absence of occupational specialization and trade is associated with sparsely distributed populations. Such a relationship may also be tested. The result would throw light on the original hypothesis and help to explain why people who secure their subsistence in this way lack occupational specialization or trade.

The reader may have noted in the hypothesis dealing with population density a shift from exclusive concern with cultural facts to consideration of a variable which is by no means covered in the definition of culture. The sparsity of a population is neither a socially standardized artifact, activity, nor thought, although it may well be dependent on such facts. Any discipline by definition specializes in dealing with certain more or less restricted types of phenomena. Cultural anthropology specializes in the study of culture. A science ordinarily will pursue generalizations as long as they involve such phenomena but will not move out of its area to deal with the phenomena studied by another discipline. Cultural anthropologists, as a rule, do not seek to discover relationships that involve chemical, physical, or even demographic phenomena. But sometimes it is felt to be worth while to leave the core area of a discipline in order to relate facts from that area (in this case cultural facts) to phenomena which, strictly speaking, are the business of other disciplines. The hypothesis associating occupational specialization and trade to population density is an example of such a move.

The Business of Theory

"The success of any scientific endeavor depends on three elements: a clear identification of the objects to be investigated, an imaginative theory as to how they hang together, and clear insight into the specific problems of evidence and proof most adequate to the subject at hand" (Lazarsfeld, cited in Hyman, 1955). Here the second element, to which some attention has already been given, will be examined from the standpoint of how it is represented in scientific anthropology.

Theory helps to guide scientific research by offering some very broad, more or less systematically arranged, formulations and concepts which are so general they cannot hope to be tested in their existing form. An example of such a general formulation, or postulate, would be: "Culture is a function of the human organism." The assumption that culture constitutes a system of mutually related parts illustrates another type of general proposition which, although it cannot be proved or disproved by any simple set of operations, can have its worth-whileness demonstrated by the degree to which it guides productive research. Also a theory contains a certain number of strategic unit concepts that enable the scientist to group, or deal with, the diverse phenomena of nature. In anthropology the concepts useful for this purpose are cross-culturally applicable, enabling the researcher to recognize what are, in effect, similar phenomena even though they may have different appearances or occur under different circumstances. The concepts of a science constantly are added to and undergo inspection, redefinition, and rejection in order to accumulate a conceptual arsenal more and more adequate for discovering verifiable relationships between facts. Common-sense terms are not as adequate for this purpose as is the much maligned jargon of scientific disciplines. Often, despite the outsider's confusion, words in everyday use (in physics, "space"; in anthropology, "group," "magic," or "ritual") are redefined in order to make them sharper for identifying phenomena to be investigated.

Chemistry and physics are sciences in which research is guided nearly exclusively by a relatively few, highly general propositions together with conclusions (hypotheses) deduced from those broad principles. Observation and experiment occur as an outgrowth of deductive reasoning, the specific hypotheses for testing being deduced from the general propositions. Anthropology scarcely fits in this category. Hypotheses here are often formulated for testing because the postulates of another discipline (psychology or psychoanalysis, for example) suggest them to be true. Sometimes the justification for, or meaningfulness of, a particular hypothesis rests on little more than a hunch; the investigator may not even be aware of how his hunch is derived from the basic assumption that culture constitutes a system. Absence of a well-formulated, systematic theory also leads anthropologists to explain each relationship afresh, often without reference to other verified relationships already discovered by other research workers. Sometimes historical explanations are substituted for scientific explanations. For example, it has been noticed that pottery and maize agriculture tend to be correlated; that is, they recur from one culture to another. Nothing in anthropological theory offers a ready basis for explaining this association. In such circumstances ethnologists fall back on a historical explanation: "The most likely explanation . . . is that the maize and pottery complexes were evolved in the same center and at about the same time. Their coincidence is then in the nature of an historical event" (Wissler, 1923:65). Such an explanation, which says little more than that both elements appeared, and continue, together, could scarcely satisfy a scientist unless it also were maintained that things which evolve in the same center at about the same time tend to persist in association (which obviously is not true).

7.

Historical Analysis of Data

WHERE science tries to predict events in highly general terms history seeks precise knowledge of particular events that occurred in the past. Fully extended, "history" covers not only human behavior but also the record of former animal life as pieced together by paleontologists, earth history as studied in geology, and reconstructions by philologists of languages no longer spoken.

Human history, in the strict sense in which the word will be used in this chapter, depends for its knowledge about the past primarily on written documents which constitute, as it were, eyewitness accounts of past events. Some day photographs, motion-picture films, and recorded speeches will provide auxiliary sources from which historians may understand contemporary times. But many communities lack written literature and hence maintain no documents from which history can be written. Writing, after all, dates back only some 5000 years, while culture has existed for almost 600,-000 years. As already indicated in Chapter 4, the prehistoric past is known primarily from material artifacts recovered from the earth. In the case of past unwritten languages, not even artifacts provide primary data for historical reconstruction. To reconstruct an extinct language is possible only when known descendants of that language exist, in speech or writing, and can be consulted by the philologist, who works from the known to the unknown.

In many cases the reconstruction of the past as accomplished in the absence of written records is possible only because the geologist, culture historian, or philologist is also a scientist. He applies a theory which explains his phenomenon—the earth's crust, culture, or language. Acting upon verified knowledge he interprets data from subsequent points in time to see if they fulfill scientific predictions. Often enough the theory is derived from common sense. The culture historian assumes, for example, that what is more elaborate must be later than that which is simpler. Reconstructions of the past which go beyond direct, documentary evidence must lack certainty.

In most of what follows attention will be focused on how events in prehistory are discovered when they are not indicated by directly documentary or archeological materials. By now the archeologist has secured his data. A particular site has been excavated and the way of life followed by the people interpreted as far as possible. Now larger questions come to be asked of the data bearing on the historical problem under investigation.

THE EVIDENCE OF DISTRIBUTIONS

One means for reconstructing what happened in prehistory consists in mapping the spatial and temporal relationships of a culture trait. The object may be to infer where specific traits originated and the routes they traversed to achieve their subsequent distributions. Sometimes a negative proposition is tested by such means—namely, establishing the impossibility of contact between two areas and hence confirming the independent invention of the traits in question. The map summarizes and relates available information (Fig. 7:1).

The Spread of Culture

Simple examples of how spatial-temporal distributions help to reconstruct past movements of cultural elements are shown in Figure 7:1 and Table

Fig. 7:1. Spread of Papermaking. The map pinpoints strategic dates and connects particular areas to show how papermaking spread from China to Europe and Japan. Much data must be examined before such a summary map can be drawn (after N. E. Lee, 1955:66).

9. The latter sums up data showing that the wheel (or wheeled vehicle), potter's wheel, and plow were each in use earlier in Mesopotamia than in other regions lying east and west of that country (the dates given are very approximate).[1] The conclusion that these traits each originated in Meso-

TABLE 9. Distribution of Three Major Early Inventions

	Wheel	Potter's Wheel	Plow
Mesopotamia	3500 B.C.	3500 B.C.	3500 B.C.
India	2500	—	1300
Crete	2000	1800	—
Greece	1600	1600	1300
China	1400	1400	—
Scandinavia	1400	—	—
Britain	800	50	800
Scotland	—	400 A.D.	—
America	1500 A.D.	—	1500 A.D.

SOURCE: Childe, 1944, modified by the author.

potamia agrees with the premise that the region where a widely distributed trait is earliest often is also the point where it originated.

Three criteria govern the historical interpretation of distributional data: the criteria of quality, quantity, and continuity (Schmidt, 1939; Sieber and Mueller, 1950). Do these criteria support the conclusion that the wheel, potter's wheel, and plow originated in the Middle East?

1. **Quality.** The criterion of quality insists that two traits found in different areas are likely to be connected historically (i.e., genetically) if they resemble each other in both form and purpose. Similarities between them must be discounted if they arise simply out of the nature of the object or the material from which it is made. Huge pyramids occur in Egypt and Mexico but serve as tombs in the former area and as temple platforms in the latter. Purpose and form are dissimilar. Baked pottery vessels are relatively impervious to water everywhere in the world because this is the chemical nature of baked clay; that characteristic cannot be used as proof of historical connection. The potter's wheel and plow in Table 9 appear to satisfy the demands of the criterion of quality. Wheeled vehicles do, too, but it is instructive to point out that in ancient Mexico wheels were used only on toys. Prior to the sixteenth century there is no coincidence of form and purpose with respect to the wheel in the Old and the New World. Few anthropologists believe that the wheels used on toys in precontact Mexico originated in the Old World.

2. **Quantity.** The criterion of quantity refers to the number of criteria of quality that link two areas. The conical dwelling (tipi), is found in both

---

[1] Some idea of the isolation of Africa is indicated by the fact that the plow did not reach the sub-Saharan peoples until after 1850 A.D.

By the Criterion of Quality Both These Mosques (*Top*, Lahore, West Pakistan, *Bottom*, Ivory Coast, West Africa) Are Historically Related to Each Other (courtesy, Pakistan Embassy and French Cultural Services).

North America and northern Asia. Relationship between these or any other areas would be much more probable if more elements were shared by both. In fact, other culture traits do link these regions of the circumpolar world. The hunting bow, tailored skin garments, semi-underground dwelling, tambourine drum, the shaman (see pp. 636–637), and ritual directed to slain bears are half a dozen items found in northern Asia and North America (Bogoras, 1929; Montandon, 1937:188–247). Historical connection between the two areas is suggested strongly. (Note, however, that the direction and chronology of movement are not indicated in a dateless spatial distribution of traits.) The case for any single item in Table 9 is strengthened by the simultaneous distribution of the other two traits in most of the areas covered. These areas do seem to have been in contact with one another. A longer trait list would make the case even stronger.

3. Continuity. The criterion of continuity emphasizes the possibility of contact or migration between one place and another. The Central Pacific Polynesians *could* have had contact with the west coast of the Americas because they possessed seagoing vessels and were accustomed to long sea voyages. Whether they actually came so far east is, of course, not proved simply by establishing the possibility of contact. The demands of the other two criteria must be met also. The places where the wheel, potter's wheel, and plow have been discovered all were accessible from Mesopotamia or intervening regions.

The criterion of continuity also implies that the area between a presumed point of origin and subsequent locations of a trait should whenever possible show traces of the trait's passage. The three traits in Table 9 show a constant distribution in the area over which they are presumed to have traveled.

Reconstructing Polynesian Culture History

Sometimes only an undated synchronic distribution of elements exists from which to reconstruct historical change. Various assumptions, based on common sense or representing more or less tested principles of culture, may help in such cases. The culture history of Polynesia has been reconstructed by working from the assumption that greater elaboration in culture proceeds from lesser elaboration (see Table 15, p. 143). On the basis of such reasoning Goldman (1955) divided 19 Polynesian island communities into three culture types—traditional, open, and stratified. The age of none can be dated directly; they all existed synchronously in Polynesia at the time when the area was opened to white contact. But each successive phase is more elaborate than the previous one. Following the assumption it is deduced that the traditional type of culture is oldest, the open next, and the stratified most recent. Islands of the traditional type suggest what the way of life must have been like during the earliest stage of Polynesian culture. They reveal concern for the relative rank of individuals but no crystallized class structure. In communities with an open-type culture, rank can be achieved through war. They are transitional between the traditional and stratified stages of Polynesian life. The communities marked by a stratified-type culture consolidated conquests by imposing an aristocracy over commoners.

These three culture types may now be compared to show how the conception of property, deities, and even the afterlife possibly changed as communities became first open and then stratified. Such comparison suggests that wealth became progressively more unevenly distributed, deities more vengeful as well as more diversified, and the next world conceived of in more unpleasant terms. Religion was taken over to become an arm of the government, kinship bonds weakened, women gained political rights, and sexual orgies grew prominent during the stratified phase, all as functions of aristocratic ascendancy over commoners. Warfare, of course, became more serious and the priesthood tended toward more complex organization. Concern with omens increased.

While ingenious, such an undocumented reconstruction of history is not without problems and uncertainties. One danger to be faced in all reconstructions of history from purely synchronic data is the possibility that in any given area, say, Polynesia, the original phase of culture actually was more elaborate than later phases. In other words, if one assumes that cultural decline rather than elaboration took place, then a correct temporal ordering of the communities would be from most to least elaborate. Before arranging the synchronic data chronologically the investigator must assure himself that cultural decline did not take place (see p. 282). The brief occupancy of the Polynesian islands prior to European contact, according to archeological evidence, makes unlikely such a course of events for that particular region.

A more serious problem of undocumented history is the difficulty of proving that any of the existing cultures in fact resemble the prehistoric stage which they are supposed to represent. Culture always is changing, although not revolutionarily to be sure. One may assume that the so-called open and transitional communities in Polynesia, no less than their stratified contemporaries, have undergone rather constant change. How safe is it, then, to assume that the contemporary open-type culture is reasonably like the original stage of Polynesian culture out of which the transition took place?

Comparative analysis using scientific method has not yet proved that changes in the conception of deities or the afterlife, the weakening of kinship bonds, and sexual orgies are associated predictably with a stratified social organization dominated by a conquering aristocracy. To assert such associations in the cultural reconstruction of Polynesia is to assert hypotheses which still await cross-cultural testing. True, it makes little difference for the accuracy of the reconstruction of Polynesian history should such relationships hold only for that region and not be recurrent. But if that is the case then the conjunction of these items with aristocratic control cannot be used as proof that they too are late innovations. For such an assertion to be sustained, independent evidence is required proving that aristocratic control in different cultures is regularly associated with vindictive deities, weakened kinship bonds, and the other elements.

The Age-Area Hypothesis

No wholly satisfactory method exists for dating cultural elements solely on the basis of their synchronic spatial distribution. The problem has aroused much interest, however, and there are several common-sense assumptions for dealing with it. For example, it may be assumed (1) that the older of two or more related elements will be found surviving farthest from its point of origin and (2) that of two or more related forms of a culture trait the more elaborated and specialized will occupy the more restricted distributional range. In other words, the geographical spread, elaboration, and specialization of culture are assumed to require time. Together these assumptions are referred to as the age-area hypothesis.

Caution must be used in employing such very general reasoning in historical analysis (Kroeber, *1931*). Unrelated items of culture, like the telephone and radio, cannot be dated relative to one another by distributional evidence alone. The radio (at least the receiving set), for technical reasons, probably is more widely distributed than the telephone. It also is a more elaborate piece of equipment. But documentary evidence indicates that it is not the older of the two traits. It is likewise impossible to infer the relative age of birds and snails from their distribution, but zoölogists frequently can date the appearance of different kinds of birds or various species of snails from distributional evidence. One cannot say that Islam is older than Judaism simply because Islam has spread into more world areas and converted more people. The two elements are too diverse. The method, however, works when applied to elements of orthodox Islam like prayer five times daily compared to the specialized doctrines of the Ahmadiya sect. The latter remains concentrated largely in western India and West Pakistan, near the village of Qadian where the sect began. The traits of orthodox Islam have a far wider distribution. A simple example of the age-area hypothesis is provided by the telephone. In remote parts of the world tourists may still come across old-fashioned hand sets. The most specialized type of telephone equipment, however, will be found in the research laboratories of the Western Electric Company.

The Spread of Language

The value of language in reconstructing culture history derives from two characteristics: the high degree of persistence manifested by language and its orderly course of change. By comparing the areas where related languages are spoken it often is possible to infer human migration or other forms of culture contact.[2] Only a few Athapaskan Indian languages are spoken in the southwestern United States but many in northwestern North America. A continuous trickle of Athapaskan languages links Alaska and western Canada with the southwestern United States. The facts satisfy the three criteria of relationship (pp. 95–97) and support the inference that the ancestors of the present-day Navaho and Apache, Athapaskan-speaking

---

[2] We ignore for the moment the task of establishing historical connections between languages—i.e., that they derive from a single parent. For a discussion of this subject see pp. 102–104.

Indians living in Arizona and New Mexico, originated in the northwest corner of the continent. Other evidence quite confirms this conclusion.

Another method demonstrates how language distribution may offer clues to migration and culture history (Voegelin, 1945). The basic assumption (similar to Goldman's on p. 97) holds that time is related directly to language differentiation. The older a language family, the more differentiated languages it will contain. Such an assumption is supported by knowledge of what has happened to language in Europe. With time, languages that separated from parent tongues, like French and Spanish, tended to diverge widely in vocabulary and pronunciation.

North American Indian languages fall into six very general types, each type consisting of a number of related families. In numerous cases proof that certain families belong together as members of a type is still lacking. Each family in turn contains a number of related languages. The relevant facts are given in Table 10. A glance at the six types makes it quickly apparent that some are more diversified than others (i.e., contain more com-

TABLE 10. North American Language Types and Their Components

Types	Number of Related Families	Number of Separate Languages
I. Eskimo-Aleut	2	4
II. Algonkian-Wakashan	8	50
III. Na-Déné (Athapaskan, Tlingit, and Haida)	4	33
IV. Uto-Aztecan-Tanoan	4	19
V. Penutian	16	29
VI. Hokan-Siouan	25	60 ($\pm$ 30)

SOURCE: Voegelin, 1945:232.

ponent families or languages). In order of diversity, the order is: VI, V, II, III, IV, I. Hokan-Siouan heads the list and comprises at least 60 distinct languages, whereas Eskimo-Aleut comes at the foot. Applying the assumption one concludes that Hokan-Siouan was the earliest language to begin differentiating in North America. It must have reached here relatively long before the Na-Déné and Eskimo-Aleut types. To switch to a distributional approach, which types are most discontinuous in their spread? Here the underlying assumption holds that more discontinuous types are older than those found less discontinuously distributed. The former, it is reasoned, over a longer period of time have been subject to the intrusion of other linguistic types. Arranged in succession from most to least discontinuous the order is: VI, II, V, IV, III, I.

The correlation between this and the arrangement by diversity is high. It is probably safe to conclude that Hokan-Siouan speakers, linguistic ancestors of the present Indians who speak Dakota, Crow, Pomo, Yuman, Iroquoian, and Pawnee, were among the earliest arrivals on the North American continent. They were closely followed by the Algonkian-Wakashan speakers (ancestors of the modern speakers of Fox, Cree, Blackfoot, Cheyenne, Kwakiutl, and other languages) or by Penutian speakers (relatives of the people who still talk Chinook or Tsimshian). Then came either the original Na-Déné speakers (from whom stem modern Navaho, Apache, Kaska, Tlingit, Haida, Chipewyan, and many other languages) or the Uto-Aztecan-Tanoan speakers (from whom Hopi, Tiwa, Kiowa, and Comanche are traced). Finally the Eskimo-Aleut speech type entered the New World. This still retains a very limited distribution across the Arctic littoral.

HISTORICAL LINGUISTICS

One of the aims of historical analysis, as has been stated, is to discover how various parts of culture came into association and whence they originated. In historical linguistics the aim is to learn how different speech families became separated from each other.

A fundamental achievement of nineteenth-century language research, one paralleling in significance the discovery of biological evolution, was the realization that certain similarities between language were not fortuitous but indicated specific historical connections.[3] The basic assumption making it possible to establish linguistic relationships holds that any relationship between the meaning of a word and its sound is arbitrary. There is no natural way of expressing any idea. By virtue of this assumption it is deduced that whenever resemblances between meaning and form in two or more languages occur significantly more often than can be accounted for by chance alone the languages must be related historically. That is, the resemblances are to be accounted for as due either to common origin (the relationship is genetic) or to borrowing. There is a slight tendency for certain combinations of sounds to be connected with certain meanings more frequently than could be expected by chance alone (notably in the words "father" and "mother"), but the number of such correspondences is light and the significance of the fact not clear. Words in different languages corresponding in both form and meaning and deriving from a common heritage source are called "cognates." Noncognatic resemblances are irrelevant for establishing such relationship.

To establish historical relationship between languages it is necessary to determine the extent and nature of resemblances between meaning and form by examining a suitable sample of vocabulary. Given many cognatic resemblances, the problem still remains: Is the relationship between the

[3] This section is based on Greenberg, 1953:267–269, 274.

languages due to borrowing or is it genetic? To answer this question three kinds of language elements may be distinguished: (1) fundamental vocabulary, containing terms for body parts, pronouns, and similar concepts, (2) cultural vocabulary, containing words for artifacts, the nature of which might be expected to change readily or to vary with environment, and (3) parts of speech used to inflect or modify words. Empirical observation indicates that borrowing far more frequently involves cultural words than fundamental vocabulary or inflectional particles. Hence resemblances in fundamental vocabulary and inflectional particles not accompanied by resemblances in cultural vocabulary indicate a strong likelihood of genetic relationship.

Discovering Language Relationships

The following examples grossly simplify the comparative methods used to verify genetic relationships between languages. Proof of the common origin of languages, it has been stated, depends on more correspondences between form and meaning (criterion of quality) than could arise through chance alone (criterion of quantity). It is relatively common to encounter a few chance resemblances between distant languages. English "moose" and Cree *muus* appear to be cognates, but careful search produces only few additional correspondences in form and meaning between these languages. The pattern of inflecting words is very different, as may be illustrated by English plural, "moose"; Cree, *muusak*. Hence it is concluded that resemblances between Cree and English are due to borrowing rather than to a common origin.

How different the results when German and English are compared. The number of correspondences is very great. To take only obvious ones: drink/*Trink*; dance/*Tanz*; man/*Mann*; cold/*kalt*; green/*gruen*; cow/*Ku*, and so on. Furthermore, the resemblances extend into fundamental vocabulary and inflectional particles: hand/*Hand*; blood/*Blut*; will go/*wird gehen*; has remained/*ist geblieben*, and many others. Independent evidence not connected with comparative linguistics confirms the relationship of English and German. Evidence also exists for the relationship of English to Russian, although here the cognates are not apparent so immediately: thou/*ty*; thousand/*tysiaca*; sour/*syroi*; mouse/*mysi*; now/*nyne*. However, the correspondences between English and Russian are regular; English ou or ow regularly corresponds to Russian y, and English th to Russian t. This leads to the indubitable conclusion that the two languages are connected genetically (S. E. Mann, 1946; see also Table 11).

Much more work remains to be done in tracing relationships between many world languages. Satisfactory methods for the job have been invented but "the greatest single obstacle to the rapid growth of the field . . . is . . . the lack of trained people in sufficient number to provide descriptive

TABLE 11. Main Representatives of the Indo-European Language Family

Derivatives of Proto-Indo-European	
Eastern (Satem) Branch	Western (Centum) Branch
Main subbranches are:	Main subbranches are:
1. *Indic*, from which Sanskrit and modern Indian languages, Pashto, and Iranian are derived.	1. *Hellenic*, which eventually gave rise to modern Greek.
2. *Balto-Slavic*, from which Lithuanian, Lettic, Polish, Czech, and the Russian dialects stem.	2. *Italic*, whence Latin derived; from Latin, in turn, stem such Romance languages as French, Spanish, and Italian.
3. *Albanian* (or Albanese).	3. *Celtic*, which gave rise to Gaulish, Welsh, Gaelic, the latter revived in contemporary Ireland.
4. *Armenian.*	4. *Germanic* (or *Teutonic*), from which derive (a) *North Germanic*, and, in turn, the modern Scandinavian languages Norwegian, Swedish, and Danish, and (b) *West Germanic*, the parent of English, Dutch, Flemish, and modern German.

SOURCE: Bloomfield, *1933:*312; Hencken, *1955:*4–5.

data for a vast number of languages, some of them near extinction" (Greenberg, *1953:*285). Students of languages have tended to specialize in European and related languages, leaving few workers for large unworked areas like South America or Oceania.

An important object in comparative linguistics is to reconstruct parts of a no longer spoken parent language from which living languages derive. The Algonkian language family is based on many easily recognized correspondences between sister languages. Take, for example, the word for "big" or "much" (Bloomfield, *1946:*89):

Fox	*kehtši*
Cree	*kistši*
Menomini	*keeqtš*
Ojibwa	*kitštši*

Many other cognates are found between these four languages. The numerous resemblances linking them extend into fundamental vocabulary and inflectional particles. Clearly the languages are related genetically and on that basis they have been classified together. There remains the task of reconstructing the forms of words like "big" or "much" in the remote parent language—Proto-Algonkian. It will be noted that each of the above words begins with k and each, except Menomini, possesses a final i. Therefore, it is reasonable to assume that these sounds existed in the parent language as well. The sound tš also occurs in all four languages preceded by an h, s, q, or tš. The corresponding cluster in Proto-Algonkian may be represented by qtš. Similarly the vowel sound that originally occupied the place of internal e, i, and ee may be represented by e. This leads to *Keptši as the Proto-Algonkian form of the word. An asterisk is used to symbolize such reconstructions. The pronunciation of this word, of course, remains unknown because Proto-Algonkian no longer is spoken and has left no records. The symbols by which the acoustical elements of the word are represented "are merely labels for correspondences" (Bloomfield, 1933: 310). This does not mean that the linguist guesses at the form of words when he reconstructs parent languages. He draws on scientific knowledge concerning the kind of change likely to occur in a particular language as well as in language generally. This tested knowledge is applied in the particular case under analysis. Students of European languages have an advantage in tracing cognates to parent forms. Written documents often afford direct information about earlier forms.

Lexicostatistic Dating[4]

Language cannot change too quickly, or intelligibility would be destroyed. A fundamental vocabulary, as has been discovered, not only changes slowly but does so at a relatively constant rate. The situation is akin to radioactive carbon atoms in living substances which disintegrate at a relatively steady rate after an organism dies (see Table 2, p. 43). Just as elapsed time since death can be ascertained for organic matter by computing the amount of radioactivity still present, so "morphemic decay," measured by the percentage of retained elements in a test vocabulary of about 200 fundamental words, can be used to count elapsed time since the separation of one language from another.

When a speech community splits into two or more parts the percentage of common fundamental vocabulary retained by both constitutes an index of time since divergence. Comparison of modern German and English using a basic list of about 200 terms reveals 124 cognates or 58.5 percent retention. Tests of a number of cases in which the actual elapsed time since divergence is known independently indicate that from 76 to 85 percent of a fundamental vocabulary tends to survive in every 1000 years. If 81 percent is tentatively taken as the proportion of vocabulary surviving over a millennium, 58.5 percent retention indicates that the two languages separated 1236 ± 246 years ago, roughly between 470 and 960 A.D. Independent evidence indicates that German speakers migrated to England in 449 A.D., and it is reasonable to assume that the languages began to diverge shortly after that date. Eskimo and Aleut are shown to have separated about 2900 ± 400 years ago. Analysis of radioactive carbon in organic material from the earliest settlements known in the Aleutian islands indicates an elapsed

---

[4] Based on Swadesh, 1951, 1952, 1955; Lees, 1953. The technique often is called "glottochronology." See also Kroeber, 1955b.

time of 3018 ± 230 years—practically coinciding with the lexicostatistic date.

Although lexicostatistic dating remains in an experimental stage, it has a number of impressive interpretations to its credit. Along with comparative linguistics it promises to illuminate many problems of prehistory. On the other hand, some puzzling inconsistencies indicate that the technique must be used cautiously. Lucumí, the speech of the Santeria religion in Cuba, is genetically related to Yoruba, a language still spoken in West Africa. Indisputable cognates amount to only 48.5 percent. Yet the languages have been separated for only about 300 years (Olmsted, 1953:163).

From Linguistic to Nonlinguistic History

The vocabulary of a language reflects the culture and environment of its speakers. Applying this rule to certain words that survive from the past, or that were part of a now extinct language, gives insight into a vanished culture and the environment in which it was spoken (Hoijer, 1946b:226).

Vocabulary analysis indicates that the Sumerians who lived in Mesopotamia about 3200 B.C. (prior to the arrival of Semitic-speaking Babylonians) originally came from a northern region in which grew firs and pines (Hooke, 1953:16). Their language retained words for those trees. Similarly, cognates for snow are found in many Indo-European languages (German, Greek, Sanskrit, and others). This feature suggests that a word for snow also occurred in Proto-Indo-European, the parent language. Although analysis shows that snow probably was familiar to the speakers of that language we still are not sure whence they came. The possibility that India south of the Himalayas was the original home of Proto-Indo-European speakers is, however, ruled out. Cognates for cattle, milk, and wheeled vehicles similarly are widespread in the Indo-European languages. They attest to cattle domestication and use of the wagon by the original speakers. Other words in Indo-European languages suggest that the ancient Indo-Europeans tracked bears in the snow, feared wolves, recognized only three seasons (spring, summer, and winter), sat under conifers, but knew nothing about living in tropics (Laird, 1953:24).

Athapaskan Indian languages (spoken in the southwestern United States, western Canada, and Alaska) share similar words for "dog" but differ from one another in designations for the horse. This tends to confirm something already known from other evidence, namely, that speakers of Proto-Athapaskan knew the dog but not the horse.

Vocabulary may reflect contacts between cultures. It is easy to recognize in the Japanese words *besuboru, karenda,* and *koto* the English words "baseball," "calendar," and "coat" (Norbeck, 1954:202–203). It is reasonable to infer that these cultural terms, like the artifacts to which they refer, were borrowed from an English-speaking country. Other evidence proves quite conclusively that the donor was the United States. Similarly English "rouge" corresponds closely to French *rouge*. The particular sound cluster found in *rouge* does not exist in many English words but is common in French, suggesting that the word was borrowed from French along with the substance it designates. The Brazilian terms *boxeador* for prize fighter, *tenista* for tennis player, and *polista* for polo player are similarly interpreted (*New York Times*, Mar. 17, 1955).

OTHER SOURCES ABOUT THE PAST

For reasons already given, anthropologists often have little opportunity to use direct documentary sources about the past. Classical archeologists concerned with the ancient Middle East, Greece, or Rome, on the other hand, rely much on surviving records of stone, clay, or other materials. Ethnologists working with cultures in the Orient and the Middle East also may take advantage of written records. Often, though, such records possess limited value for a student of culture. They mainly are full of political events and dynastic genealogies. Other data must be eked out, often by reading between the lines. Much the same thing is true of daily newspapers, which, surprising as it may seem, yield limited information about regularities of behavior (Honigmann, 1956c).

Classical archeologists often find their records fragmented, scattered, or partly indecipherable—severe conditions under which to reconstruct a complicated epic or business document. The task amounts to putting together a jigsaw puzzle of the first magnitude. "It is as if all the books of the Latin writers had been torn first into pages and then most of the pages into small fragments, and the whole accumulation of torn pieces of paper thoroughly mixed up and only a handful of them given to someone who has to reconstruct them into a whole" (Chiera, 1938:115–116). Fortunately scribes who wrote in the Middle East 5000 years ago made not one but many copies of important clay tablets. The chances, therefore, are good that important texts will have survived. But if they have survived the different copies probably have been carried off to different Oriental institutes and museums around the world. Hence, a scholar may be able to finish reading an Assyrian text only by traveling from a Chicago museum to another museum in Philadelphia or London which possesses other parts of another copy of the same document.

Where only textual fragments are available and the specific referents of words (especially the names of plants, animals, or people) cannot be defined, great caution must be exercised in using documentary sources. Imagine how an archeologist from India might someday reconstruct one aspect of twentieth-century American culture from newspaper sources (Greenberg, n.d.):

. . . Who then were the masked creatures who at various ceremonial stations such as the right field, the left field, the inner field, the outer field, and the "mound," doubtless a raised sacrificial altar, sacrificed winged animals? They must surely have personified sacred beings. The names themselves are strange and for the most part uninterpretable as is so often the case with names of divinities of other cultures. A notable feature is the frequency of the suffix -sky in these names. Among the surviving texts we find Jablon-sky, Herman-sky, Pe-sky and Repul-sky. A hypothesis presents itself. Our Funk and Wagnall under "sky" gives "heaven" as a synonym. Now, in such phrases as "Heaven forbid" the word "heaven" obviously means god, or divinity. Hence sky in ritual language might easily have this same meaning. In the case of Repul-sky the interpretation "divine being who repels or drives back," . . . the enemy, suggests itself. Herman-sky means "the god Herman." Another divine name, "Slaughter," doubtless refers to a war-god. Most of these names, unfortunately, still remain obscure.

Oral Literature

Many people without written records pass on to succeeding generations oral accounts of past events. Anthropologists have become wary about accepting native legends as reliable evidence of what actually occurred. The danger of distortion in such accounts is real unless evidence indicates that extraordinary care has been taken to prevent any alteration. The presence of supernaturals or superhuman heroes in oral tales suggests how large a nonhistorical and, perhaps, wish-fulfilling component these sources may contain. Nearly every field worker collects oral literature from the people whom he studies but he does not regard such data as trustworthy sources of objective history.

A case in point is the tale told by Sarsi Indians (now on a reservation outside of Calgary, Alberta, but formerly living farther north around Edmonton) about how they separated from the Beaver Indians, who still live to the north in Alberta. The Athapaskan language of the Sarsi Indians is related closely to that of the Beaver. Linguistically the two communities undoubtedly are related. Westward-penetrating explorers discovered them several hundred miles apart, separated by a wedge of Cree (Algonkian-speaking) Indians who had arrived in the country about 1750. But by 1600 the Sarsi probably had already quit the northern forest and moved onto the plains, there absorbing the culture of their Blackfoot Indian neighbors. Here is the Sarsi account of the separation from the Beaver as told to the author by Pat Grasshopper in 1942:

"A long time ago the Beaver Indians and the Sarsi were all camping together on the shores of this lake. One day the whole camp moved. Some people were already crossing the lake on the ice and were half-way across. A woman and child were going behind to cut out this horn for him. The mother refused but the child insisted, claiming he wanted the horn badly. The woman started to chop out the horn. She struck it twice. On the second blow the horn began to move and the ice broke. Some people were caught in the breaking ice and were drowned. Those who had not yet started to cross remained on the opposite bank."

"That is how the people split," Pat explained, adding that the Sarsi moved south while the Beaver continued toward the north. It is unlikely that this is accurate history. Tales containing incidents of travelers' separating to form tribes or running into trouble once they find a horn in a frozen lake surface are not uncommon in American Indian literature (cf. Lowie, 1953). The Sarsi version happens to correspond to a migration which is demonstrable from other evidence, especially the closeness of their language to that of the Beaver.

8.

Application and Values

APPLYING knowledge means to make practical use of it. Engineers apply knowledge about the physical world when they design a bridge, dam, or tunnel. An inventor who comes up with a new insecticide has made practical use of chemistry and of his knowledge about the parasite's life cycle. To make worth-while inventions may require a great deal of preliminary research when available knowledge is not sufficient for solving a practical problem. At that point any hard and fast distinction between "pure" and "applied" knowledge breaks down. Just as practical undertakings often add to the fund of knowledge, so pure research in many cases opens up vistas of potential applicability.

APPLIED ANTHROPOLOGY

Cultural anthropology may be "applied" in two senses. A person makes practical use of his knowledge about the world of man when from this background he perceives his own way of life, or the world in which he moves, in a new light and with new insight. If this book gives the reader a better understanding of his own culture, it has promoted application of anthropology. In a more specific sense, applied anthropology signifies using knowledge about culture deliberately to direct (or alter) the processes of some culture. Directing is what an administrator does. The applied anthropologist, then, is somebody who provides an administrator with certain relevant facts on which to base decisions which redirect a way of life. Usually an anthropologist acting as consultant draws upon an intimate knowledge of some community in order to supply the administrators with workable recommendations. Each such recommendation constitutes a hypothesis that predicts what will happen if certain changes are made in a system of customs. Obviously, acting upon such recommendations and at the same time observing what follows may greatly enrich understanding of social life. Here, again, one sees a close relationship between applied and pure science.

ANTHROPOLOGY FOR THE ADMINISTRATOR

In 1952 certain administrators of the Department of State pondered the question of extending American overseas informational activities in order to reach millions of peasants in rural South Asia. Motion pictures, already being shown in cities, seemed to be a promising vehicle for reaching that audience. Since the Department already employed specialists to write, produce, and exhibit information films, it was logical that it should turn to another specialist to discover whether rural audiences would be able to understand the information films that were already available. The specialist also would offer recommendations for the more effective production and exhibition of such motion pictures. An anthropologist was selected to make an investigation in Pakistan (Honigmann, 1953b). He assumed that communication through motion pictures would be influenced by the cultural milieu of the audience. Therefore he spent considerable time in ethnographically studying three Pakistan villages. Special attention went to those cultural factors that in theory would influence the communication process. Into each of the three villages also went a team sent by a United States overseas agency to exhibit specimen films. Interviews, guided by a schedule of open-ended questions, sought to learn how a random sample of subjects in each village had experienced the pictures or why certain people had not attended the performance. The final report to the State Department contained two kinds of statements: First, it sought to make the planning and production staff in Washington aware of village life in South Asia and of what happens when a field crew moves into, and exhibits films in, such a setting. The anthropologist suspected that few policy makers possessed much of this kind of knowledge. Second, the report made recommendations which predicted how the aims of the administrators could be achieved better if they adopted certain specified procedures or changed others in the production and exhibition of motion pictures intended for rural audiences in Pakistan. For example:

Those pictures will best be comprehended, the content of which is familiar in the experience of the people or compatible with their milieu. Films concerned with irrigation, health, child care, agricultural methods fit in this category.

Closely related to successful communication is the capacity of a picture to tell its story through action rather than to rely heavily on spoken narration.

Certain techniques, when they play a crucial part in developing a story, should be avoided because they are not understood. These include use of culture-bound symbols and use of historical allusions. References to the San Francisco Charter or the Berlin Airlift are in the latter category.

Note that the applied anthropologist accepted the aims of the administrative group, namely, in some degree to change Pakistani citizens' ideas and attitudes. He provided data and recommendations that he believed would be useful for achieving those aims.

Strange as it may sound, it often is difficult to get administrators to be explicit about aims which they take for granted. As a result initial field work must be devoted to exploring the culture of the very people who hire the anthropologist! This field work seeks to discover what the administrators are doing and what results they want to accomplish (Gouldner, 1956a:173–179). An understanding of the administration's culture cannot be neglected because applying anthropological knowledge often involves bringing together the divergent values or aims of administrators and dependent people. Management interacting with labor, colonial officials with natives, American foreign policy makers with rural Pakistani villagers —in each of these cases some kind of collaboration is to be effected between both members of the pair. The applied anthropologist's job, as often as not, is to explain contradictory aims or orientations and point out opposition in values as well as to recommend steps by which the aims of the two parties may be reconciled.

Diretlo Murder in Basutoland

In another case involving the application of anthropology, the British High Commissioner for Basutoland and other South African native protectorates in 1949 appointed an anthropologist (G. I. Jones) to report on the nature and significance of a large number of murders which had recently occurred in Basutoland. He was directed to discover "the proximate and underlying causes of the apparently increased incidence of the crime" and to recommend steps by which the administration could remedy the situation (Great Britain, 1951).

The report of the investigator begins with a sketch of the history of the Basuto nation and then examines the nature of the murders. It is pointed out that the killings were intended to secure portions of the victims' bodies which could be used to prepare *lenaka* (loosely translatable as "medicine") that would be effective in safeguarding the user from threat and anxiety. In pre-British times protective *lenakas* had relied on animal flesh, plants, and, for special power, the flesh of enemies (*ditlo*) killed in battle. After tribal wars had ceased even a fellow tribesman who possessed specific attributes might be killed for such use of his flesh (which is called *diretlo*). An increased search for more powerful *lenakas* probably also occurred following the arrival of the British, and the greater part of the report is devoted to discovering factors related to their use.

The anthropologist seriously examined some popular beliefs about the cause of *diretlo* murders (murders undertaken for the purpose of securing human flesh to be used in compounding *lenakas*). He exonerated the Christian religion, Johannesburg underworld, and police from responsibility for the murders, pointing out, however, that such suspicions, while wrong, were not illogical and could be generated in the culture of modern Basutoland. Most of the killings seemed to be traceable to subordinate chiefs of the Basuto. Their position had been rendered highly insecure by the higher chiefs' practice of placing subordinate authorities of their own choosing in territories at the expense of the local leaders. In attempting, some time previously, to control the "placing" system, the British authorities had introduced a number of administrative changes which inadvertently further threatened the rank and responsibility of these lesser chiefs. The uncertainty and anxiety felt by the latter were expressed in the use of protective *lenakas*, the purpose of which often was to insure political stability for oneself. Faith in the *lenakas* rested on strongly traditional, but logical, foundations in the belief system of the Basuto. The report concludes that until the Basuto realize that *lenakas* "are incapable of performing the functions attributed to them there will always be a certain number of people who will value them more highly than they do human life, and who will be prepared in certain circumstances to go to any lengths to obtain . . . *diretlo*." At the same time the insecure tenure of the minor chiefs must be kept in mind in trying to control the *diretlo* killings. Closer ties between the British and native administrations and decentralization of political powers are two steps recommended to allay the anxiety of the lesser chiefs.

Other Applications

Recently anthropologists have begun to apply their discipline through participation with physicians in medical schools, clinics, hospital wards, and public health departments. The aims behind such collaboration have been threefold: first, to help the physician see the role of cultural factors in the onset and treatment of disease; second, to facilitate the introduction of health programs by noting points where such measures conflict with established values; and third, to study the culture of hospital communities as it is related to the process of getting well (Caudill, 1953; Mead, 1953a: Chap. 4). Industry is another area in which anthropologists are asked to apply their skills to practical problems involving relationships between people who have relatively different lifeways (Chapple, 1953; Jaques, 1951; F. L. W. Richardson, 1955).

In company with psychiatrists, anthropologists have begun to explore the cultural sources of mental illness (Marvin Opler, 1956). In that area, however, the cultural investigator finds himself in a quandary. Is mental health indicated when a patient can adjust to the demands of his community, whatever those demands may be? Or may a culture itself be "so 'sick' that, in order to adjust to it, one has to be very sick indeed" (Devereux, 1956a)? If one adopts the latter viewpoint, namely, that cultures may be unhealthy, then there must be an ideal, or optimal, culture. But how is such a culture to be known? As a moralist the anthropologist may prescribe for society (pp. 116–117), but such a role is different from what is expected of the applied anthropologist who provides tested knowledge for the solution of practical problems. Objectively speaking, the discipline knows nothing about what kind of culture is optimally suited to man.

Responsibility

At the present stage of anthropological science any application of knowledge about culture is very much an art, one compounded of common sense, extraordinary intuition, and prayerful thought. Certainly this is true when the anthropologist is asked to advise on current political events. All the information on which a sound interpretation might be based will rarely be available until long after the crisis is finished. Then, perhaps, the relevant documents will emerge from secrecy and find their way into print, and historians will discover other facts on which judgments should have been based. Were the Chinese Communists in 1947 separable from the Communists in Moscow? Is a given premier to be trusted when he states his aims? Will disunity in a nation intensify the will of the people to stand up under adversity or will it demoralize them? These are some of the kinds of questions that have to be answered before policy can be determined. But on what facts or theory (other than common sense) shall the answers be based? Even working in a government bureau the "cultural expert" has no chance of getting all the relevant knowledge. Yet he is expected to bear responsibility for the advice he gives. So intensely may this responsibility be insisted upon, especially in time of tension and fear, that an error may become grounds for branding the expert as disloyal. Perhaps it is too early to apply knowledge of human behavior in practical situations with any pretense of expertness. The ideal solution would be, first, to develop social science in order to obtain better knowledge. Until that goal is realized, if it can be, caution is important.

VALUE JUDGMENTS

In helping to solve practical problems which involve human behavior the anthropologist is trying to achieve a goal, either that of an administrator or, more commonly, his own version of the administrator's goal which he urges his client to adopt. The applied anthropologist, then, is dealing with some conception of the *good* toward which he bends his knowledge and skills. This is very different from the image of a research worker as somebody pursuing knowledge of what *is* without regard for what *ought* to be.

How Values Enter

The following propositions specify the place that values occupy in anthropology. Not all students of culture are equally tolerant in allowing valuation to enter their work. Many, it is suspected, are actually unaware of the extent to which values do enter into what they do.

1. *The anthropologist cannot help valuing as he works.* No human being, regardless of how objective he wishes to be, can wholly dispose of valuing (Redfield, 1953a:156–157). The desire to be objective or detached is, of course, a value. The researcher may like or dislike the circumstances of his work, the people he is studying, or the method being applied. The archeologist, depending on whether he is classical or prehistoric in his orientation, prefers to work with one kind of data rather than another. If he is a classical archeologist he stops digging in a site after "treasures" peter out. The ethnographer values clear-cut results or relative completeness in his data. He prefers to work in one community rather than in another. The anthropologist quite frankly rejects ethnocentrism. That is, he rejects those judgments which interpret exotic behavior as unreasonable, inadequate, or inferior (Paul, 1953b). Instead he values respect for cultural differences. These examples all illustrate how anthropologists become value-involved in their work. Such involvement also occurs in other disciplines, even in the physical or natural sciences. The worker in the most exact science makes decisions that rest on valuing. The process of valuing is fundamental to every activity in which man engages.

Anthropologists, however, often recognize a danger inherent in value judgments. Will a committal to respect cultural differences lead to glossing over a form of ritual mutilation which, if reported in detail, might confirm the ethnocentric bias held by a nonprofessional reader? Will the ethnographer read rationality into behavior that actually may be quite nonrational, because of his own preference for rational behavior? Will a dislike or affection for a people, climate, or culture influence his reporting? In lieu of a team of observers, the anthropologist can only hope that constant awareness of possible bias will guard against serious subjectivity in eventual disagreement with others who may check his work.

2. *The ethics of the anthropologist are values.* How much information to publish without identifying actual informants and subjecting them to unpleasant notoriety, and what methods to use in obtaining data are ethical questions facing anthropologists as well as other students of human behavior. To help answer them codes of ethics have been drawn up. Such codes correspond to a series of value judgments about what is right for a professional investigator. The most rigorous laboratory scientist does not object to ethical codes in general. Researchers may, however, object to particular paragraphs in such instruments—for example, the promise to follow only investigations that benefit society. In the first place,

benefit can be visualized only in terms of an existing idea of the good. This idea may change as social conditions alter. Furthermore, it is not always possible to tell how the discovery resulting from investigation will ultimately be applied. What is "society"? Are a nation's enemies part of the country's society? Should they be destroyed if destruction helps the nation but clearly does not help them?

3. *Anthropologists evaluate culture.* Ethnographic descriptions based on field work are rarely as detached or nonevaluative as sometimes is claimed. In descending order of frequency the ethnographer avoids giving his opinion about the morality, truth, or beauty of what a community does or believes. Periodically, however, a practice, like a technique of healing, which the ethnographer believes to be unreliable is branded as erroneous. More frequent are references in anthropological monographs to "attractive" designs on costumes or "pleasing" forms of singing and dancing. Such judgments are influenced by the standards of the observer's own culture.

Certainly anthropologists rarely brand as evil, indecent, or immoral behaviors they observe. Comparatively few anthropologists ever appraise the laws or customs of people according to whether they are unjust, nor do they speak of the economic system as wasteful or inefficient. Field workers are especially careful to avoid judging an exotic religion as false, nor would they condemn socially accepted premarital sexual intercourse as immoral. In other words, their objectivity is likely to take the form of avoiding *unfavorable* value judgments. Students of culture often are sympathetic toward the people they study. A botanist or chemist is less likely to become fond of his sources of data. But the observer who lives with his subjects, observes them finding satisfaction in their way of life, and through isolation depends on them closely for the satisfaction of his emotional and other needs is less able to remain detached.

4. *Cultural relativity may be phrased as a value judgment.* Anthropologists have propagated the notion of cultural relativity to generations of college students and to the general public. The meaning of cultural relativity is by no means clear. In one sense the term states that every community possesses a way of life in which it believes and to which it is emotionally committed. Such a definition says nothing about whether cultural relativity is desirable or undesirable.

As soon as lessons are drawn from this descriptive statement of cultural relativity—for example, when a particular cultural difference is made the basis of urging tolerance for that difference—then the line into normative judgments is crossed. Sometimes cultural relativity is expressed in the opinion that cultures are in some way equal to each other: are equally valid or equally good (Herskovits, 1953:4–8). Such opinions represent value judgments. They imply more than that every community possesses its own standards of truth, morality, or efficiency.

What is meant by saying that cultural relativity, "in recognizing the values set up by every society to guide its own life, lays stress on the dignity inherent in every body of custom . . ." (Herskovits, 1948:76)? Does this mean that a system of culture in which one category of people is degraded or persecuted deserves respect even by people who feel such degradation to be intolerable? Is the author saying that in this chaotic world everything and nothing is significant (E. Williams, 1947:85–86)? Few members of one community are able to grant precisely the same significance to another way of life that they attach to their own. No philosophy or religion has yet been devised that will enable such an extreme degree of tolerance, although such a philosophy would be very appropriate at the present stage of human history.

5. *Some anthropologists are moralists.* It sometimes is said that members of the academic professions exert little leadership in public affairs. They have not, it is held, despite guarantees of academic freedom, spoken out sufficiently to help shape public opinion in areas where they might claim special competence. The foregoing discussion of cultural relativity suggests that some anthropologists have not been reluctant to urge new standards of conduct. In writings and public addresses many anthropologists tirelessly seek to teach the importance of cultural understanding, tolerance for cultural differences, and respect for race. Many more anthropologists exercise such moral leadership while teaching college classes. The anthropologist has come to occupy a prominent place on panels, at conference tables, and in discussion groups, often along with the psychiatrist and psychologist. These three specialists speak a remarkably similar language.

What do anthropologists say when they play the role of publicist? They advise people to respect foreign ways of life and warn that intolerance of other cultures may lead to hostility. They urge grammarians and purists to stop interfering with the natural changes occurring in all languages (R. A. Hall, 1950; Carpenter, 1957). They predict that some changes introduced into another way of life may have profound traumatic consequences for people who follow those customs (Mead, 1953a:286–303). Certain such statements are testable. For example, the prediction that too rapid culture change may destroy psychological stability is a potentially verifiable proposition. But when anthropologists become moralists they do not make such statements as hypotheses that remain to be proved or disproved. The implication is given that people who attempt to change human behavior—whether by trying to raise national exports or in well-baby clinics, schools, or abroad—must be careful lest their too rash efforts damage personal integrity. In other words, a strongly normative element colors such statements.

Or consider this statement, in which the growth of responsibility in marriage and family living is being discussed: ". . . If such responsible new patterns are to develop, then it is crucial that in theory, and in practice, the fact that divorce may come to any marriage—except where the religion of both parties forbids it—must be faced. The stigma of failure and sin must be removed" from divorce (Mead, 1949b:365). Here the intention is not simply to state the hypothesis that responsible adulthood is functionally related to freedom of an individual to terminate his marriage. Such a hypothesis is buried in the anthropologist's message. The message as a whole is hortatory. It *urges* action. It may be argued that the statement intends only to say that the stigma of sin surrounding divorce must be removed *if* a stronger sense of family responsibility is to be encouraged. But the whole context suggests that this is more than an objectively stated hypothesis. A distinguished anthropologist is drawing upon her experience and best reasoning to urge more moral patterns of behavior.

It is not implied that such evaluative activity on the part of an anthropologist is improper. In an age of great indecision and uncertainty, when many people have lost confidence in religion, professional persons who exert popular leadership may be rendering a valuable service. Their power and prestige are likely to be greater than a clergyman's, to whose role moral leadership traditionally has belonged.

Part Three

NATURE

OF CULTURE

Man is no longer satisfied merely to acquire knowledge; while accumulating more of this, he contemplates himself as the "knower" and his research is daily brought a little more to bear on the two inseparable factors constituted by a humanity that transforms the world and a humanity that, while it acts, is transforming itself.

LÉVI-STRAUSS (1954b:108)

9.

Dimensions of Culture

CULTURE has been defined as referring to socially standardized behaviors and artifacts organized in a system (pp. 10–16). Usually the attention of the ethnologist is devoted to the patterns, or regularities, of behavior and artifacts, that is, to those which are shared by some specific aggregate of people.

FACIES OF CULTURE

A culture might be conceived of as analogous to a crystal. It possesses several facies as well as an overall unity or organization. A recognition of these facies can help in understanding social behavior. Ten facies of culture will be examined in this section.

Overt and Covert

Overt culture refers to actions and artifacts which may be perceived directly. Examples include the houses, clothes, vehicles, books, and speech forms employed in a community; postures executed in various situations; sports, songs, curing practices, and the externally manifested signs of deference or respect. On the contrary, covert culture—sentiments, beliefs, fears, values—is not amenable to direct observation though it may be known through what people say or do. So one learns about a Pakistani's ambivalent tendency to absorb western values from the way he speaks about the West or invidiously compares western culture to the Muslim way of life. The reader will appreciate how easily one may err in proceeding from overt phenomena to the covert level of culture. People do not always express quite what they feel or believe. Hence caution must be used in studying covert culture.

Superorganic and Organic

Every culture normally outlives the particular generation of people who carry it and so persists from one generation to another. In this sense culture constitutes the "social heritage" of each new generation and is superorganic. But without doubt any system of socially standardized behavior and artifacts remains rooted ultimately in the biological organism. For without people to act, think, feel, or to make and use things, there would be no culture. At least no new artifacts would be added to those which previous generations have discarded and which are in the process of becoming part of the earth. In this sense culture is organic even while it is superorganic.

The meaning of "superorganic" applied to culture should not be misunderstood. Culture is superorganic to the extent that it outlasts particular generations of individuals. This does not imply that its origin is other than natural (Durkheim, 1915:347). Culture is man-made and dependent on human choice and energy for its continuity. Any way of life, theoretically speaking, can be altered through a man-made decision. But this does not mean that it is easy to change a culture. Arbitrary interference with customs is often fraught with peril, as the trial and execution of Socrates, various inquisitions, persecutions of heretics, Congressional committee hearings, and threats of committal to a mental hospital fully attest.

Also the application of "organic" to culture should not be exaggerated. To point out the organic basis of culture is not to claim that everything people do or make can be explained by reference only to biological needs or physiological structure (L. A. White, 1950). One cannot explain hunting and agriculture solely in terms of the human being's animal need for food; circumcision cannot be explained fully by man's possession of a foreskin, and the idea of God cannot be accounted for simply in terms of an allegedly universal feeling of human helplessness. Culture is organic in the sense that it ultimately derives from man's nature. Once created, however, it becomes more profitable to explain culture at least partly in cultural, rather than exclusively biological, terms. Cultural explanations of human behavior are a major aim of this book.[1]

Explicit and Implicit

Explicit culture includes those elements of behavior that can be verbalized, described, or criticized readily by the persons who hold or practice them. For example, many qualified Americans can describe how a grand jury is selected, how a radio is put together, and how the table should be set for a formal dinner. But there are other, covert and overt forms of socially standardized behavior about which Americans cannot give coherent accounts. These are behaviors that they perform with little or no self-consciousness (Sapir, 1927:122). For example, it is not likely that many Americans can express how they greet persons of lower or higher rank than themselves. Americans tend not to think explicitly in terms of rank and hence remain quite unaware of how they relate to people possessing

[1] However, see Chapter 44, where an attempt is made to show relationships between culture and the structure and functioning of the human organism.

relatively more or less prestige. In other parts of the world it would be possible for a man to tell in detail what grammatical forms and gestures he employs when speaking to somebody whose rank is higher or lower than his own. Grammatical rules present another example of largely implicit culture. Few people in any community can state them in detail, although this is the business of grammarians. Yet speakers, with few exceptions, conform to socially standardized usages in putting words together. They possess the rules implicitly. Similarly speakers of unwritten American Indian languages experience no difficulty in dictating word by word to anthropological field workers. This ability suggests that they possess an implicit criterion for distinguishing words, even in the absence of writing (C. E. Osgood and T. A. Sebeok, 1954:60). Another example of the implicit was revealed when survey interviewers asked Japanese for a definition of *giri*, a word which refers to the obligation assumed by a person who has received a favor from a friend and thus becomes the latter's "debtor" (Stoetzel, 1955:193–194; Benedict, 1946:116). One-third of the sample of persons interviewed could not state the word's meaning. Apparently they were not ignorant of its definition but could not find the words to express themselves.

Ideal and Manifest

Ideal culture refers to how people say they should behave, the way they would like to live, or how they believe they do live. Attawapiskat Cree Indians from the west coast of James Bay identify generosity as the mark of a good person; they also claim 10 dogs are needed to make a good sled team, and seriously affirm that everyone in the Indian community lacks enough to eat. These are three ideal sentiments that anthropologists will take not as matters of fact but as important socially standardized opinions. On the manifest (real) level of culture the Attawapiskat Cree are not especially generous, dog teams with less than 10 animals pull heavily loaded sleds, and not all Indians are hungry chronically. In other words, here as in other communities a discrepancy exists between the ideal and the manifest.

Ideal sentiments are especially important in ritual where behavior is often in terms of the way one is supposed to behave in that particular situation (say at a wedding or funeral) rather than expressive of the way one actually feels (see pp. 509–510). Similarly, not every ruler who invests a minor ruler in office is actually an overlord with real power to appoint. The whole investiture may be an empty pageant and yet clung to with the feeling that it is appropriate. Among the Melanau people of Sarawak there are five ranked *bangsa* between whom marriage is not supposed to take place. A child takes his father's rank or *bangsa*. If this ideal formulation were actually observed, the *bangsa* would become fixed groups or castes. But no Melanau deceives himself into believing that this formal system of organization really exists (H. S. Morris, 1953:54–60). In the rural Welsh parish of Llanfihangel the ideal is for the youngest son to remain at home to succeed his parents and to postpone his marriage until they die (Rees, 1950:68). While this is actually the most frequent single pattern of succession followed, it is outweighed by alternative patterns, as Table 12 indicates. Some communities may have more such discrepancies than others.

TABLE 12.   Succession in Welsh Families, Llanfihangel Parish

Parents Succeeded By	Number of Cases
Daughter (there being no sons)	3
Daughter (although there were sons)	3
Only son	7
Youngest son	15
Eldest son	7
Intermediate son	2
Two bachelor sons (jointly)	2

SOURCE: Rees, 1950:68.

By some people each such discrepancy has to be accounted for carefully; elsewhere it can be passed over lightly (Mead, 1947c:174–176).

Sometimes people seek to make the manifest conform to the ideal. Such behavior has been reported for the United States Air Force. In some units of the Air Force, reporting to higher echelons of command is in terms of what the latter ideally expect a squadron to carry out in training rather than of what the fliers have actually accomplished. Also, in Russia ". . . falsification takes many forms, even within a single factory. One informant described his wife's experience. She worked in a silk artel which listed itself as a whole as overfulfilling the plan by 110 per cent, when actually the plan had been only 65 per cent fulfilled. Within this artel, his wife's unit had actually overfulfilled by 250 per cent, but this was only credited as 121 per cent, since over 120 per cent warranted a premium" (Mead, 1951:45).

People also have ideals (in the technical sense of the term) that they know to be immoral and that are rarely brought into practice. In this category of ideal culture belong the sexual daydreams of people, which may be socially standardized through pornography and in more subtle ways as well. Only rarely do such fantasies find opportunity to be dramatized in erotic behavior (Mead, 1949b:203–206). Deep ambivalence may characterize some ideal patterns in a community. Many people in Asiatic nations like western clothing better than native clothing and can even afford western dress. Yet this ideal is not realized in practice, partly because wearing western dress may be criticized but also because, despite being preferred, it is considered to be less attractive (Norbeck, 1954:76).

A few ethnographers prefer to deal nearly exclusively with ideal rather than manifest culture. That is, they inquire about rules and values without being much concerned to find out what people actually do (Creedy, 1939:360; R. L. Beals and H. Hoijer, 1953:219).

Facilitating and Restraining

Through culture (more specifically, for example, through machines or forms of social coördination) man transcends the limited resources of his own biological nature and increases his control over nature. He may also extend the range of satisfactions at his disposal. Culture facilitates life by enlarging human potentialities or increasing their chances for satisfaction. On the other hand, every culture includes rules and limitations that restrict certain forms of human behavior. In other words, culture is at least partly a system of proscriptions (Bidney, 1953:11). Rules against aggression exist in all communities. Similarly with regard to the expression of man's sexual impulse. In all communities certain persons are forbidden to him as sexual partners, and many other restrictions may also be imposed on how he satisfies the sex drive.

STRUCTURE OF CULTURE

This section introduces concepts useful for dealing with culture analytically, that is, for separating a cultural system into constituent units and aspects.

Trait

A trait (or element) is a significant unit of socially standardized behavior or an artifact singled out for some purpose. How small a unit one isolates depends largely on the purpose for which analysis is carried out (Herskovits, 1948:170). For one purpose it might be sufficient to state that subsistence traits in Attawapiskat Cree culture include hunting, fishing, and berry picking, but if two cultures with the same three techniques were to be compared, the various implements and techniques of hunting, fishing, and berrying would be listed in detail. Similarly the presence of a wedding ceremony may be selected as a trait of a culture. But for comparative purposes it may be useful to break down this trait according to where and when the ceremony is held, who brings gifts, and when the presents are brought. Table 13 includes a small section of a trait list comparing 6 tribes of the Oregon, Washington, and British Columbia plateau region. Notice that comparable information for all the tribes could not be obtained. The total trait list from which this brief section was taken contains over 7633 items and covers 17 tribes.

Defining a trait as the "unit of observation" does not distinguish this concept sharply from a pattern (Wissler, 1923:50). Some measure of overlap between the concepts cannot be avoided. The difference between them lies not in different parts of culture to which they refer but in different operations performed by the anthropologist. Pattern designates the regular-

TABLE 13.   Traits of the Marriage Ceremony in the Plateau Culture Area

Trait and Number	Cl[a]	Um	Sh	Th	Ku	Co
5355. At home of bride	−	+	+	−		−
5356. At home of groom	+	−	−	+		+
5357. At home of wealthiest parents				−		
5358. At home of chief (R?)				−		
5359. During daytime				+		+
5359a. During evening				+		
5360. Relatives and friends present	+	+	+	+	+	+
5361. Of bride only		−	+	−		
5362. Gifts brought	+	+	−			(+)
5363. Promised gifts brought		+	−	(+)		(+)
5364. Brought on preceding or following day		−				+
5365. Groom and bride present	+	+	+	+	+	+

ᵃ Abbreviations stand for Lower Chinook, Umatilla, Shuswap, Thompson, Kutenai, and Coeur d'Alêne respectively. A plus indicates presence of the trait and a minus sign absence or denial of its presence. Parentheses indicate that the informant qualified his testimony by a term such as "sometimes" or "a few."
SOURCE: Ray, 1942:209.

ities derived by a field worker when he observes several people acting or examines a series of homologous artifacts. A trait denotes the parts that an analyst isolates from an already formulated system of patterns. Pattern construction is the process of formulating a way of life. Element analysis enumerates the constituent items of that configuration. It is quite true, however, that in actual use the two words are often used interchangeably to refer to units constituting a culture (Gillin and Murphy, 1950–51).

Complex

Combinations of traits sometimes can be perceived. The elements are organized in larger complexes. A culture complex consists of a series of traits that "organically" hang together. Therefore they tend to persist as a unit or to be transmitted as such from one group to another. The plow complex provides a good example. This unit, comprising draught animal, harness, instrument, and male operator, has reached nearly every corner of the world following its first appearance in Mesopotamia some 3500 years before the Christian era. Other complexes include the automobile, alphabet, and monotheism. What distinguishes these trait aggregates "is a specific interrelation of their component parts, a nexus that holds them together strongly, and tends to preserve the basic plan; that is, in distinction to the great 'loose' mass of material in every culture that is not bound together by any strong ties but adheres and again dissociates relatively freely. . . .

"As we mentally roam over the world or down the centuries, what is impressive about these systematic patterns is the point-for-point correspondence of their parts, plus the fact that all variants . . . can be traced back to a single original form" (Kroeber, 1948:313).

The alphabet, for example, was invented once by a Semitic-speaking people in Southwest Asia. The principle of the alphabet is having one letter stand for each minimal speech (i.e., sound) unit. No matter how specialized or decorative the letters of the alphabet may become, the system remains basically the same. Monotheism, as found in Judaism, Christianity, and Islam, constitutes another complex. Included are such traits as a single deity characterized by unlimited power, living apart from man, concerned with morality, and proclaimed by prophets.

Theme

A theme is a special kind of trait or pattern (depending on the use to which the concept is put). Speaking operationally, a theme is an objective generalization based on an available corpus of data (for example, motion pictures, books, or spoken utterances) that expresses how the members of a community conceive of the world or of themselves. From a slightly different standpoint, a theme is a postulate that finds expression through activity or embodiment in artifacts (Morris E. Opler, 1945:198–200).[2] Government officials in Pakistan are fond of publicly reiterating in one way or another that "people do not exert themselves enough." This is one theme in Pakistan culture (Honigmann and Carrera, 1957). The Lipan Apache Indians believe that culturally they are distinct from all other communities and morally superior (Morris E. Opler, 1946). This theme is expressed in various ways. For example, the Lipan attribute the Catholic Church to a postulated being, Earth Slayer, who is said to have instructed the first padre. Another Lipan theme maintains that "industry, generosity, and bravery are cardinal moral-social virtues." Such a theme is echoed in the midwife's prayers for the new baby, in parents' tutorage, in the praise bestowed on a generous warrior, and in myths concerning Earth Slayer's bravery.

One theme in French culture (R. Métraux and M. Mead, 1954:Chap. 2) says that children must be "formed" by parents; development is a lifelong process. This notion was expressed by a French girl who compared the handling of an American child with her own education, saying that the

---

[2] There is another usage of the word in anthropology referring to the way in which some event of general human significance (for example, the conflict between father and son or the relationship of mother and son) is phrased in a particular culture or in a work of fiction (cf. Wolfenstein, 1953).

former receives no "moral basis for action from her parents. While [my] parents were always telling me what to do, at the same time they tried to develop my own judgment and good sense. This education is much better than giving complete liberty to children . . ." (*ibid.*, p. 31).

Focus

A focus of culture consists of an area of behavior about which the members of a community show much concern. Their preoccupation with the focus is manifested in the way the subject figures in speech or thought as well as in the amount of time actually spent upon the activity (Herskovits, 1948:544).

Among the Comanche Indians of eastern Texas war and the desire of warriors to excel constituted two related focal areas of culture. Men of fighting age commanded the greatest prestige, but within the ranks of warriors further increments in social standing came through exemplary fighting behavior. ". . . The wars of the Comanche were mainly offensive ones, and there can be no question that they were waged primarily to enable warriors to gain prestige." A man wore his war record proudly in some distinctive piece of dress or equipment—like a feathered war bonnet (Linton, 1936:444-450). Widespread in East Africa is the cattle focus. For the South African Swazi cattle have a multitude of uses. They provide food and clothing, serve as currency and as sacrificial offerings to departed ancestors, and form a gift with which to ratify marriage. Epigrams and riddles are built around cattle and there exists a rich vocabulary to describe the various types. Even men are referred to in terms of cattle, and cattle are praised by the same terms used for people. The king is referred to as the "bull" of the nation. Children play at herding, using clay models. Cattle are extolled in folk tales, and many practices are known for improving the health and fertility of the herds (Kuper, 1947:150-151). Farther north the Nandi of Kenya regard cattle as the main support of life, and the animals furnish the major topic of interest. A large vocabulary exists for referring to cattle and their products; people's personal names are derived from animals. The herds are the only form of wealth that counts; by means of cattle a man secures a bride, shows his respect for relatives, and can indemnify another person for an injury (Huntingford, 1950:39-42). "The absorption of the Nandi in their cattle has not so far been lessened by agriculture, contact with Europeans, or any other outside influence. . . . All the Nandi whom I came across in the Army, no matter where they had been or what they had done, had their minds as firmly fixed upon cattle as if they had never left home."

Cultures may readily be compared in terms of contrasting foci. For example, the Middle East lacks such foci of western culture as the factory system, mass education, public safety systems, and sanitation-hygiene

(Patai, 1953:32 ff.). It is interesting to note that the spread of western culture into the Middle East and other parts of Asia largely consists of traits making up these foci.

Individual members of a community perceive a focus as a powerful stimulus to behavior. In the language of psychology, the focus includes those activities which possess strong drive value. For the Nandi cattle "provide the only stimulus to action." The strong stimulus value exerted by the focus makes it highly receptive to change. The focus invites "the greatest variation in custom, manifest in the greatest complexity of form" (Herskovits, 1948:544). New and additional techniques for handling books can be expected in a library, an organization whose focus is books. New concepts for treating culture are constantly appearing among anthropologists. A focus not only attracts variation but repels modifications anywhere in the cultural system that people perceive as threatening the major interest. Factories resist whatever limits productivity; Pakistan fears western customs that threaten Islamic values; and in an army basic training squadron, illness and incapacity, behaviors which threaten the focal goals of inculcating masculine toughness and ruggedness, are rejected (D. M. Schneider, 1947:330).

Ethos

Culture may be described in terms of what people have, do, think, and feel. It may also be presented in terms of the emotional quality revealed in behaviors and artifacts. In addition to describing the emotional aspects of culture, an observer may probe further to discover the needs, aspirations, themes, or motives that prompt people to react toward experience with certain emotions. Ethos, therefore, is defined operationally as the designation of culture in terms that carry emotional meaning.

A memorable study contrasts the Indians of the western plains and those living in southwestern villages (i.e., Pueblos) in terms of a Dionysian and Apollonian ethos respectively (Benedict, 1934:Chap. 4). How are these terms defined? "The desire of the Dionysian, in personal experience or in ritual, is to press through it toward a certain psychological state, to achieve excess. . . . He values the illuminations of frenzy. . . . The Apollonian distrusts all this, and has often little idea of the nature of such experiences. . . . He keeps to the middle of the road, stays within the known map, does not meddle with disruptive psychological states" (ibid., p. 79).

"Dionysian" designates the quality of reaching beyond the commonplace to extraordinary states. "Apollonian" denotes an emphasis on restraint, safety, or moderation. The contrast of the Plains and Pueblo (chiefly Zuñi) Indians in terms of these qualities is summarized in Table 14. There one sees how different areas of culture—war, religion, political organization, death, and the handling of menstruation—share a common

TABLE 14.   Dionysian and Apollonian Ethos Contrasted

Plains Indians	Pueblo Indians
The following customs have a Dionysian quality:	*The following customs have an Apollonian quality:*
1. Fasting is endorsed as a means of bringing on a vision.	Fasting is a means to ceremonial cleanliness.
2. Self-torture is an important experience that brings a vision, good fortune, or protection.	Self-torture is absent, although in excitement a man may sometimes hurt himself.
3. The dance is used to induce ecstatic states or temporary oblivion.	Dancing is monotonous and intended to promote the growth of crops.
4. Great value is placed on the self-reliant man who has won honor and prestige by show of initiative. He assumes authority.	The ideal man is mild-mannered and affable. He never tries to lead but rather avoids office.
5. Death promotes uninhibited grief and self-torture; mourning is prolonged.	Death promotes sorrow but people try to make as little of the event as possible.
6. The war-slayer is honored and envied.	The war-slayer is someone in danger. He also puts the community in danger until he is purified.
7. Men sometimes vow suicide.	Tales of suicide can scarcely be believed.
8. Menstruation is associated with danger. The menstruant is isolated to reduce danger of contamination.	Menstruation makes no difference in a woman's life.

SOURCE: Benedict, *1934:*Chap. 4.

emotional quality. The same tendency is revealed so that the total configuration comes to be colored by a consistent atmosphere. Something of the same tendency has been noted in English culture. British people who are willing to delay cleanliness training until a baby is at least 12 months old "are also markedly permissive about pre-marital experience; those who advocate training from birth or during the first two months of life are more rigid in this attitude toward sexual experience before marriage" (Gorer, 1955:124).

An ethos may alter in time. In 1954 American life showed marked emphasis on conformism. This came after a serious depression and major war. The stress on conformity expressed a "growing passion for economic security" and was probably not unrelated to the recent "mass organization of labor, and the passing of the unorganized man."[3] The United States once placed far more value on nonconformism.

Tradition

The term "tradition" has been used mainly in archeology to designate a persistent trait or artifact (P. Phillips and G. R. Willey, 1953:626–627). A tradition refers to any segment of culture which, in a particular community or world area, has maintained itself for a relatively long time. Such usage is fairly close to the common-sense meaning of the word, as when

[3] Dorothy Thompson's syndicated column in the *Durham* (N.C.) *Morning Herald*, Mar. 31, 1954. Cf. Commager, 1949.

rice throwing is called a traditional part of a wedding ceremony. A tradition is the diachronic complement to a focus. Tradition may undergo change in time but a characteristic unity manages to be preserved despite change. For example, painted pottery constitutes a tradition in the southwestern United States. Within the painted pottery tradition several trends are apparent. "The gradual chronological shift from large, bold, broadly-lined designs to finer-lined, more complex layouts is such a trend" (Willey, cited in Wheat, 1954:589).

INTEGRATION OF CULTURE

It is by no means easy to explain how a culture becomes integrated so that the parts fit together like the works of a clock or come to be pervaded by a similar logic or a common emotional quality. Partly the failure of anthropology to work out a comprehensive theory of integration is related to the diverse meanings of the word "integration" (Sorokin, 1947:337–341). A theory that explains integration as the product of people's trying, for the sake of efficiency, to avoid incompatible activities or values (Mead, 1953a:10) is insufficient. For example, an American enters social relationships in his home, a factory, club, and on the national political level. In each he expresses some of the same general attitudes—admiring success and perseverant activity. Similarly, the child who learns these attitudes in the family comes to express them in later life in adult relationships. Thus, there is integration between modes of child rearing and adult forms of behavior. However, it is not likely that this theory of integration can explain all forms of integration found in culture. It cannot

The Large Assortment of Toys Possessed by American Children Links Playtime with Many Elements of Adult Culture: Tables, Chairs, Telephones, Literature, and American Indian Lore.

explain why food gatherers tend to have few possessions and tend to share both food and wives (see p. 307).

This section will not try to explain integration in general. Discussion will concentrate on how an observer goes about describing the integration which he perceives in a particular way of life. Operationally speaking, integration is a process carried on by an observer. This point of view is consistent with our definition of culture as an abstraction derived from observed data (pp. 15–16).

Any ethnography is by itself an essay in integration, an attempt to grasp the traits of a culture, each in terms of its place in the total configuration. An ethnography also discusses traits in terms of the meaning they acquire from the total context in which they occur. More specifically integration refers to a deliberate attempt to link together as many parts as possible of a cultural whole. In this section four bases of integration will be examined: (1) ethological, (2) logical, (3) contextual, and (4) life-cycle linkage. Other bases of linkage will be referred to more briefly. It should be understood that the essence of any attempt at integration is selection. No observer can hope to find absolutely everything in a culture related to everything else except in the most general and impressionistic terms. Galvanized water pails in the culture of a Midwest farming community are difficult to see in a meaningful relationship to television quiz programs.

Ethological Linkage

Ethos was defined as referring to the emotional quality expressed in series of behaviors. For example, among the Kaska Indians of northern British Columbia the husband-wife relationship, the approach of lovers to one another, and the parent-child relationship all reveal a quality of emotional aloofness or isolation (Honigmann, 1949a:287–290). This quality is a conspicuous note in Kaska ethos and one which links additional areas of Kaska culture. Folk tales are narrated with little emotional expression, social dancing is restrained, disturbing situations are shut out by the person, and the appreciation of children is expressed in terms of material advantage rather than emotional need. Ruth Benedict's (1934) method of contrasting Pueblo and Plains Indian culture by showing how the Apollonian ethos links a large series of traits in the former culture while a Dionysian ethos does so among the Plains tribes is another example of integration attained through ethological linkage. In Dobu, an island off New Guinea, it is also "possible to show a unity of feeling throughout. Jealousy of possession is the keynote to the culture. In social organization this jealousy is found in a conflict between the kin and the marital groupings. In gardening this jealousy obtains between gardeners. All illness and disease and death are attributed to jealousy, and provoke recrimination. It is also possible to show that poverty and a great pressure of population upon land accords well with the prevalent tone of jealousy of possession" (Fortune, 1932b:135; Benedict, 1934:Chap. 5).

Logical Linkage

Logical linkage consists in finding common premises or assumptions about the order or structure of nature expressed in different areas of culture. The premise that the world is both knowable and malleable links a variety of elements in American culture; especially does it run through the basic and engineering sciences. It also appears in contemporary philosophy, which is less normative than philosophy was several generations ago and more concerned with the nature of truth and knowing.

In aboriginal Kaska Indian culture the assumption that danger to men inheres in feminine physiological functions was revealed in the isolation of the menstruant (especially at menarche or initial menstruation) and also of the woman at childbirth. Before going on a search for big game the hunter abstained from coitus lest he become contaminated and undesirable to the animals he sought. The integration of these behaviors around the premise of contamination by feminine functions is logical. However, should the central premise not be accepted, then similar behavior would be highly irrational (see pp. 678–680). The irrationality which western observers have sometimes attributed to exotic communities actually may have stemmed from the observers' ignorance of the premises under which the members operated. This is equally true in the modern world. The censorship of books, rewriting of history, and, at one time, strait-jacketing of certain lines of scientific research in the Soviet Union strike Americans as a betrayal of truth. However, Americans lack a premise similar to one found in Soviet culture, namely, that nothing can be true which conflicts with the Communist party line and that this line accurately forecasts the future (Mead, 1951). Granting this premise, it is logical to tailor day-to-day discoveries in order to make them conform to the line.

Navaho Indians who are attracted to American technology also become dissatisfied with the native dwelling and want to build a white-style cabin, acquire farm machinery, and carry a watch so that they will be on time for appointments. They are acting on relatively atypical premises compared to their contemporaries on the reservation. The traditional Navaho view of the world holds that man is subjugated to nature (rather than in potential control over nature) and that the present (not the future) is the significant time dimension. Navaho Indians who come under white influence, however, reorient their lives in accordance with new premises, which are also held by the Indians' white neighbors (Vogt, 1951). From this example it is clear that the premises integrating behavior may change, perhaps under alien cultural influence. A community may contain two or more categories of people, each governed by different values and assumptions. What is logical to one group may appear quite irrational to the other. Integration, therefore, has to be sought in several divisions of a community rather than in terms of overall consensus.

Contextual Linkage

Traits may be linked by showing how they occur together in a single context. The frying pan, rolling pin, and teakettle are related because they constitute kitchen equipment. A well-known book, *The Sexual Life of Savages*, demonstrates how marriage, mortuary customs, pregnancy, childbirth, the organization of the family, fantasies, and folk tales may be related meaningfully around the context of sexual relations (Malinowski, 1932). The author successfully

. . . showed that the behavior patterns in any community formed an interlocking, interdependent unity; that the "culture" of any people is not to be seen as a set of parts, each separately investigable, but rather that we should see the whole mass of behavior and artifacts and geographical circumstances as an interlocking functional system, such that, if we started from, say, the food-getting behavior—the system of agriculture, hunting, fishing, and the rest—and examined that system carefully, we should find that the functioning—the effective, continual working of the agricultural system—interlocks at every step with the religion of the people, with their language, with their magic, with the geographic circumstances of their life, etc., and similarly, that their religion interlocks with all other phases of their behavior; their economics likewise; and their kinship likewise. . . . Malinowski, in fact, laid a basis for an organismic approach to cultural phenomena. . . . Malinowski demonstrated that everything in a cultural system was, if not a cause, at any rate a necessary condition for everything else [Bateson, 1944:717].

While it is true that culture traits may be understood more richly when presented in context than when they are simply described and listed, for certain purposes form rather than contextual meaning may be the object of cultural analysis.

Life-Cycle Linkage

A special form of contextual linkage is accomplished by showing how behavior and artifacts are integrated by virtue of their impingement on the individual between birth and death. For example, *Coming of Age in Samoa* (Mead, 1928a) reveals the linkage of large segments of Samoan culture around the career of the growing girl. "Matters of political organization which neither interest nor influence young girls are not included," says that author (*ibid.*, p. 17). A life history or autobiography of a single individual showing the successive socially standardized experiences which he encounters also brings together many sectors of culture—for example, childbirth, family relations, kinship behavior, subsistence activities, sex play, initiation ceremony, and marriage.

Other Approaches

There are other avenues to presenting culture in an integrated fashion. Event analysis is a device for presenting large portions of modern national culture which would be difficult to describe in traditional ethnographic fashion (Kimball, 1955:1140). The method requires the selection of some situation, like the attempt of a community to organize for better health, a riot, or some other violent explosion of feeling, and systematic exploration of its relationship to other areas of socially standardized behavior. The Moscow purge trials of 1937–1938 have been shown in their relationship to Soviet ideology and other facets of Russian culture (Leites and Bernaut, 1954:Chaps. 1–15).

Status linkage shows how culture is integrated around some single social status—like that of the woman (Hamamsy, 1957; V. R. Jones and L. B. Jones, 1941).

Juxtaposed photography may be used to bring out integrated aspects of life (Mead, 1956b). This has been done to show parallels between the stimulation and frustration of the child in Bali which lead to temper tantrums, and the drama played by figures masked as a witch and a dragon. The stylized trance seizures undergone by the accompanying dancers appear to be equivalent, in a certain sense, to the infant's temper tantrums (Bateson and Mead, 1942; Belo, 1949:35–39). ". . . The teased baby of the witchlike human mother watches the witch on the stage, and the teasing mother, even as she teases her baby, also sees the witch, attacked, apparently destroying, but in the end doing no harm" (Mead, 1955:45).

10.

Classifying Cultures and Communities

A CULTURE has been defined as a system of socially standardized actions, thoughts and feelings, and artifacts characteristic of a community (pp. 10–11). A community, in turn, refers to an area of relatively intense social relations located within the boundaries of a society possessing a

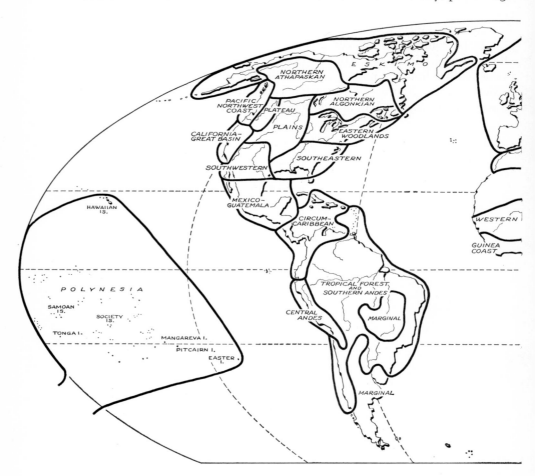

FIG. 10:1. World's Main Culture Areas (after Bacon, 1946; Herskovits, 1924; Naroll, 1950; Wissler, 1938; Kennedy, 1943; Krieger, 1943; Weckler, 1943; Steward, 1949b, with Additions). See Table 15.

certain breadth and depth (pp. 16–17). Cultural systems may be classified in terms of their continuity in space or time. Communities may also be classified on the basis of certain selected characteristics of their culture.

CULTURE AREAS

One of the most common bases of ordering data in cultural anthropology consists in the geographical mapping of culture by culture areas. Such an area represents a portion of the earth's surface in which a series of communities share a significantly large number of cultural traits (Klimek, 1935:16). For example, in northern North America the Eskimo culture area is set off from the northern Athapaskan area. The two certainly share

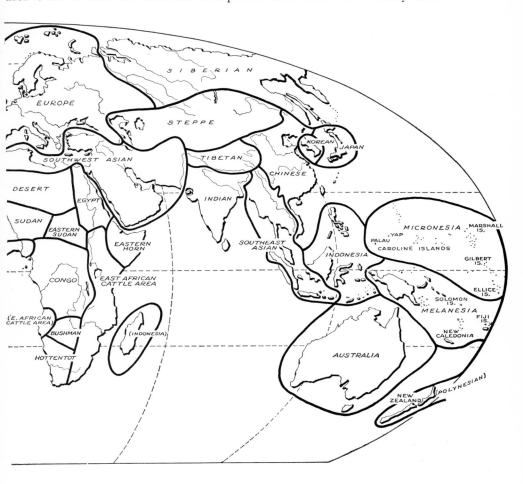

some features in common, but they can also be distinguished if a moderately large assemblage of elements is taken into account. Eskimo culture possesses traits like hunting on sea ice, dependence on sea mammals, the use of the snow house, sled, saucer-shaped oil lamp, bow and arrow, skin garments, and a distinctive language. Northern Athapaskan culture also contains some of these same elements (bow and arrow, skin garments, for example) but is oriented to forest hunting and inland fishing; houses are bark, brush, or skin covered; the toboggan rather than the sled serves for transportation, and the language spoken is again distinctive.

A limited number of only the more distinctive features of the world's main culture areas are included in Table 15 (see also Fig. 10:1). Continuing research promises to lead to revision of areal boundaries in both Asia and Africa. Other schemes for the organization of the cultures of South America are already available (Murdock, 1951b). Despite its lack of detail, Table 15 offers an idea of how culture, although relatively continuous in time and space, falls into rather sharply demarcated geographical tracts. A culture area constitutes the end result of historical influences and is functionally related to its environmental setting (Kroeber, 1931; 1948:261–265).

The culture areas extant in the contemporary world did not always possess their present distributions. Nor has the same population alone continued to reproduce itself within the borders of a culture area. Culture area maps, like those in Figures 10:1 and 10:2, are static. They hold time constant and do not deal with the fact that culture is always changing. Certainly the Plains Indians of the United States (Fig. 10:1, area 6) no longer use a horse and travois. At one time they lacked horses. Table 15 describes that area as it was shortly before European contact, when the Indians had acquired the horse after Spanish penetration in the south. More ancient cultures of the Great Plains are known to archeologists.

Phase, Variety, and Climax

A continental map of culture areas reveals that culture tends to alter from one point in space to another. The relatively small variations of culture occurring from one place to another within a culture area constitute phases (P. Phillips and G. R. Willey, 1953:620).

A phase is a systematic assemblage of cultural traits found within a given culture area. The contemporary United States and southern Canada compromise a distinct culture area, within which one may distinguish a southern and a northern phase of American culture (in addition to others). Both phases share a great many items but they differ in dialect, architecture, relations between whites and Negroes, and attitudes toward the Civil War. Within the Eskimo culture area there exists an Alaskan (or western) phase of culture and a northern, littoral, phase. The former far more closely resembles the Pacific Northwest Coast (Fig. 10:1, area 4) than it

TABLE 15.   Some Characteristics of the World's Main Culture Areas

Area	Distinctive Cultural Elements

A. ABORIGINAL NORTH AMERICA

1. Eskimo
Winter camps on sea ice; seal primary food resource; two boats—kayak for hunting and umiak for family travel; saucer-shaped lamp; snow house; semilunar woman's knife; family the unit of social and political life; Eskimo-Aleut language stock.

2. Northern Athapaskan
Hunting and fishing for food; woven spruce-root vessels; snowshoe; toboggan; large and small bark canoes; house covered with brush, skin, or bark; band organization; some tribes have matrilineal descent groups (see pp. 396–398); Athapaskan language; fear of the Nakani.

3. Northern Algonkian
Hunting and fishing for food; snowshoe; toboggan; large and small bark canoes; band organization; shaking-tent for predicting future events; cradleboard; Algonkian language; fear of the Wiitiko.

4. Pacific Northwest Coast
Great dependence on sea food, especially salmon, with some land hunting; large rectangular gabled houses of upright cedar planks; wood carving; large seagoing dugouts; armor; social organization of nobles, commoners, slaves; unilinear descent groups; village the maximal political unit; potlatch; secret associations; elaborate ceremonial life.

5. Plateau
Extensive use of salmon, deer, and berries; salmon pulverized with roots for storage; semisubterranean winter house; summer house of mats or rushes; basketry; bark fiber clothing; armor; village maximal political unit.

6. Plains
Dependence on bison for food, skins, and bone for tools; conical dwelling covered with skin (tipi); travois drawn by dog and later horse; flat skin bag (parfleche) for storage; circular shield; large-band organization; emphasis on warfare, especially after introduction of the horse; military associations; great linguistic diversity.

7. Eastern Woodlands
Hoe cultivation of maize, squash, and beans; hunting also important; rectangular bark house in summer; dome-shaped house of bark or mats for winter (wigwam); secret associations; fortifications; skin clothing; relatively elaborate ceremonial life.

8. California–Great Basin
Acorns chief vegetable food supplemented by wild seeds and some hunting; simple dwelling of brush and grass; basketry; reed raft for ferrying; feet generally bare; elaborate girl's puberty ritual; gifts burned in mourning rituals; band organization.

9. Southwestern
(Pueblo used as the type-culture.) Maize main domesticated plant; hoe; turkey raised; upright loom; painted pottery; elaborate ceremonial life including head-washing, masked dancers, and underground ceremonial structure (kiva); cotton cultivated for textiles; apartment house dwellings; village is basic political unit. (The Navaho, Apache, Pima, and Papago vary from this type.)

TABLE 15. (Continued)

Area	Distinctive Cultural Elements
10. Southeastern	Intensive cultivation of maize, cane, pumpkins, melons, tobacco by hoe; domestication of turkey; persimmon bread; rectangular house; fortified towns; blowgun; sun worship; elaborate ceremonial life; confederation of tribes as maximal political unit.
11. Mexico-Guatemala	Dependence on hoe agriculture; maize, potatoes, gourds, tobacco, and cotton cultivated; cotton textiles; bees domesticated; water drum; two social divisions—Indians and Ladinos, the latter identifying with a Spanish-type culture (see pp. 456–457); extensive ceremonies connected with the saints and other Catholic concepts. In precontact times work in gold, silver, and copper; writing; calendar; extensive empires raised by Maya and Aztecs; large towns; elaborate ceremonial life; human sacrifice.

B. ABORIGINAL SOUTH AMERICA

12. Circum-Caribbean	Hoe agriculture sufficiently intensive to support large permanent villages; hammock; loom weaving of cotton; work in gold, silver, copper; class organization with nobility based on military distinction; ceremonials involve temples and idols; ancestor worship; conquest led to small, unstable empires; human sacrifice.
13. Central Andes	Developed agriculture; foot plow; loom for weaving cotton and wool; domestication of llama and alpaca; work in gold, silver, copper, bronze, platinum; elaborate painted pottery; occupational specialization of labor; large public buildings; hereditary class system; war for conquest led to Inca empire; elaborate ceremonial life.
14. Tropical Forest and Southern Andes	Kinship primary basis of social organization; hoe agriculture; hammock; blowgun; loom weaving of cotton; use of rubber; dugout canoe; metal received by trade; village basic political unit; passage rites main form of ritual (see pp. 512–514). In the southern Andes villages were fortified and metals worked.
15. Marginal	Dependence on hunting and fishing with unintensive hoe agriculture; kinship primary basis of social organization; small temporary shelters; no use of salt; warfare primarily for defense; passage rites main form of ritual; adornment of body more important than clothing except in the south; band organization.

C. AFRICA

16. Desert	Camel and horse pastoralism; caravan transportation; sharply stratified classes with the pastoralists acting as overlords over peasants; oasis cereal cultivation; raising of dates; Islam. The region is generally a blend of African and Middle Eastern elements derived from the north; Hamito-Semitic languages are spoken.
17. Egypt	Irrigation farming along the Nile and desert pastoralism; cereals main crop; plow; intensive division of labor based on skill; Islam the prevailing religion; the Arabic language belongs to the Hamito-Semitic family.

TABLE 15. (*Continued*)

Area	Distinctive Cultural Elements
18. Western Sudan	Subsistence based largely on cereal agriculture with hoe and cattle domestication; a number of empires maintained relatively stable existences here in pre-European times; round houses with thatched roofs enclosed in compounds; markets; large towns or cities; secret associations; Islam widely accepted.
19. Eastern Sudan	Cereal hoe agriculture and domestication of cattle, horses, and camels; camel milk important in desert regions; round houses with thatched roofs; pastoral people live in tents; Islam widely accepted though pagan enclaves remain.
20. Guinea Coast	Root crops and maize are important for food; hoe cultivation; large towns and cities; markets; iron and brass work in the hands of specialists; relatively large empires; elaborate ancestor rituals involving human sacrifice; many deities associated with their own temples and priesthoods; languages belong to Niger-Congo family.
21. Congo	Root crops and maize cultivated with hoe; chickens raised; Pygmy tribes are primarily hunters; cannibalism; houses often rectangular with gabled roof but also round houses; markets; men weave on upright looms; iron working; ancestor rituals with human sacrifice; bridewealth of hoes or cowrie shells; village tends to be maximal political unit; Bantu language belongs to Niger-Congo family.
22. East African Cattle Area (also 22a)	Hoe agriculture; domestication of cattle, sheep, goats; milk often drunk soured; men tend cattle; prestige correlated with size of cattle herd; bridewealth paid in cattle; round houses with grass roof; iron work; large-scale political organization under kings found in some regions; polygyny common; ancestor ritual; Bantu language belongs to Niger-Congo family. Coastal towns show influence of the Middle East.
23. Eastern Horn	Desert pastoralism and, in highland Ethiopia, cereal agriculture with use of plow; women tend cattle, men work with camels; markets; iron work; animal bridewealth; languages are primarily of the Hamito-Semitic family.
24. Bushman	The Bushmen are hunters who work only in wood and stone; dog only domesticated animal; simple shelters; realistic animal painting; bullroarer used in ceremonies; band organization; language belongs to Click family.
25. Hottentot	The Hottentots are cattle pastoralists living in dome-shaped mat houses; ox transportation; villages in a territory are governed by a hereditary chief; language belongs to the Click family.
D. EURASIA	
26. Southwest Asian	(Excluding the desert pastoralists.) Area is marked by cereal cultivation; use of the plow; irrigation; wheat and barley main crops; ox, ass, horse, and camel used for transportation or draft

TABLE 15. (*Continued*)

Area	Distinctive Cultural Elements
	purposes; goat and sheep raised for food; mud houses; untailored garments; Islam main religion; languages primarily belong to the Hamito-Semitic family, except in Iran, Afghanistan, and Pakistan, where Indo-European languages are spoken.
27. Steppe	Horse domesticated for transportation, milk, hides, and prestige; also sheep, goats, camel; dome-shaped tent; large-band organization; Islam.
28. Siberian	Coast: Subsistence closely tied to fishing and sea mammal hunting; semisubterranean house; dog sled. Interior: Hunting and fishing important; snowshoe; conical skin dwelling (tipi); tailored skin clothing; reindeer domestication practiced by some people; reindeer-drawn sleds.
29. Japan	The original Ainu culture was pushed to the northern periphery by mainland migrants bringing influences from China and Korea. Subsistence based on wet rice cultivation with plow; Euroamerican contact has introduced intensive industrial manufacturing and other changes.
30. Korean	An indigenous stratum of culture, including elements like the seclusion of women, men's topknot, slight emphasis on religion, alphabet, female exorcists who cure spirit possession and are themselves possessed, and bull packing, is blended with many Chinese influences.
31. Chinese	Millet and wheat cultivated by a plow are staple crops in the north; wet rice in the south; houses of mud or sun-dried brick; domestication of cattle, sheep, horses, pig, fowl; balance pole for carrying; weaving of textiles; ancestor ritual in addition to Buddhism, Taoism, and Confucianism; traditional bureaucratic administration with a divinely sanctioned sovereign at the head.
32. Tibetan	Sedentary plow farming; pastoral nomadism; Buddhism; many cultural influences from India and China blend here.
33. Indian	Plow used to cultivate wheat, barley, and legumes; irrigation; mud houses except in the east, where bamboo takes over; caste organization sanctioned by Hindu doctrine; empires, but village council retained autonomy in local affairs until British conquest; southern languages are Dravidian, those in the north mainly Indo-European.
34. Southeast Asian	Wet and dry rice form staple crops; water buffalo is draft animal; bamboo houses, especially in south; Hindu Indian influences are apparent as well as Chinese; religions include Hinduism, Buddhism, and Islam; languages primarily belong to Sino-Tibetan family.
E. OCEANIA	
35. Indonesia	Dry rice the main crop; chickens, pigs, water buffalo, cattle, horses, sheep, goats domesticated; people live in small villages that sometimes shift when the land under cultivation becomes

TABLE 15. (*Continued*)

Area	Distinctive Cultural Elements
	exhausted; bamboo houses with thatched roofs; cotton clothing; tattooing; blowgun; bow; matting and basketry; weaving; outside of areas influenced from mainland Asia, the village was the maximal political unit in aboriginal times; Islam has been adopted by 90 percent of the population; languages belong to Malayo-Polynesian family. While the languages in Madagascar belong to this family, the culture of that island is partially transitional to that of Africa.
36. Australia	Subsistence in aboriginal times depended exclusively on hunting and food collecting; simple shelters; band organization; ceremonies to increase the game supply and commemorate heroes of the Dream Time; male initiation ceremonies important; genital mutilations; men naked.
37. Melanesia	Subsistence dependent on taro, yams, and the sago palm; pigs raised; fishing and hunting contribute to diet; cannibalism; elaborate men's houses with steep gabled roofs; pile dwellings in some places; grass-fiber skirts; kinship groups the primary units of organization; villages politically independent; trade journeys for the exchange of ceremonial goods; languages belong to Malayo-Polynesian family.
38. Micronesia	Coconut, pandanus, breadfruit, and taro the main crops; fishing important for food; pigs and chickens domesticated; great skill in navigation with outrigger canoes; rectangular houses of wood and thatch; cotton cloth woven only in west; tattooing; grass skirts; matting; sling and spear; administrative units under kings tended to grow through conquest; languages belong to Malayo-Polynesian family.
39. Polynesia	Aboriginally and today reliance on fishing; pigs and chickens domesticated; taro, breadfruit, coconuts, bananas, yams, sugar cane cultivated; paper mulberry tree cultivated for bark to provide clothing; use of kava (see pp. 520, 525); grass skirt; matting; tattooing; great consciousness of rank; conquest led to large political units; premarital sexuality; languages belong to the Malayo-Polynesian family.
40. Europe	Dominance of industrialism; subsistence based on fishing, cattle and pig domestication, and (except in far north) plow agriculture; considerable food imported in exchange for manufactures; large political units; colonialism; languages primarily Indo-European; Christianity. The same culture is found today in North America, having replaced aboriginal lifeways.

does the Arctic littoral phase of Eskimo culture. There is also an inland phase of Eskimo culture located on the Barren Grounds west of Hudson Bay.

Local varieties constitute the components of phases. Yankee City, for example, is the fictitious name of a large town in New England whose culture represents a local variety of the northern phase of modern American culture (Warner and Lunt, 1941). Plantation County contains a variety of the southern phase (Rubin, 1951). Great Whale River, a trading post in the southeast corner of Hudson Bay, is the site of a variety of Arctic littoral Eskimo culture (Honigmann, 1952).

The northern Athapaskan culture area (area 2) has been subdivided into two relatively distinct parts, the Pacific and Arctic drainage subareas (Fig. 10:2). The names refer to the oceans where the waterways of the country find outlets to the sea. Athapaskan culture becomes generally

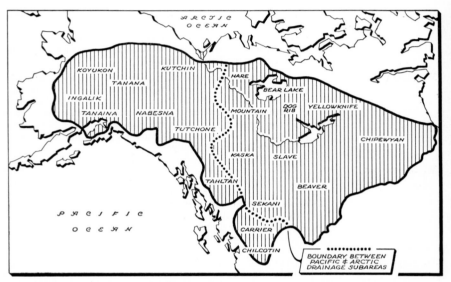

FIG. 10:2. Northern Athapaskan Subareas and Phases (from Cornelius Osgood, 1936).

more elaborate moving from east to west (Honigmann, 1954c:143; Cornelius Osgood, 1936:21). Within each of these subareas, as shown in Figure 10:2, a number of phases (commonly called "cultures" and "tribes") are recognized. A more detailed map showing local groups would give the local varieties into which most of those phases can be divided.

Despite its phases and localized varieties, culture within any culture area remains relatively uniform. Within the boundaries of the areal unit it often is possible to distinguish one point with a particularly high degree of cultural elaboration or intensity. The point of maximum cultural intensity marks the climax of the area. Although primarily a cultural concept, an areal climax is recognized through its correlation with a relatively dense population. In the southern United States a late prehistoric climax occurred in the Mississippi Valley of northern Louisiana and Mississippi shortly before white contact with the Indians. A new, improved variety of maize and greater dependence on agriculture allowed a spurt in population growth at the same time that the people's widespread contacts introduced a wide variety of new ideas. Cultural florescence followed (P. Phillips, J. A. Ford, and B. Griffin, 1951:453–454). Cultural elaboration, richness, or florescence implies increase in the number of elements making up a way of life and, of course, their systematic organization. A relative poverty of cultural materials (such as characterizes the Arctic littoral phase of Eskimo culture) cannot be systematized highly. There simply aren't enough elements. The climax of an area is both a center, from which traits radiate to other points within the area, and a point marked by the greatest absorption of alien cultural traits. For "as a culture becomes richer it also tends to become more highly organized, and in proportion as its organization grows, so does its capacity to assimilate and place new material, whether this be produced within or imported from without" (Kroeber, 1939:222; also 1936a). Climax points tend to persist in the same part of an area (barring a major cultural upheaval) for long periods of time.

CLASSIFYING COMMUNITIES

Instead of plotting the distribution of cultural elements on a map and demarcating relatively uniform culture areas, the anthropologist often selects one trait, or a number of related cultural elements, as a basis for classifying the communities he studies. Theoretically there are as many ways of classifying people as there are cultural elements or meaningful characteristics of culture. People with tattooing, wheeled vehicles, pottery, or premarital sex relations might, for some reason, be classified apart from people lacking those traits. An organized priesthood, domesticated animals, or the richness of a total cultural assemblage might also be diagnostic. In actual practice, however, the most used categories have been based on things like the presence or absence of literacy, rate of change (or homogeneousness), degree of isolation, and scale. These and one or two other kinds of classification will be discussed in the balance of this chapter.

Literate and Nonliterate

Communities possessing writing or having members who can read are literate. Many of the small-scale, exotic communities that anthropologists study lack both these traits in their cultures. A community in which only a small proportion of people is literate (like modern Pakistan or India) would still be classified as literate. The total cultural configuration of those countries is influenced heavily by the literate element in the population.

Anthropologists increasingly are devoting attention to literate communities, particularly as more and more of the world's people acquire skills of reading and writing. Often these skills are introduced by missions and colonial administrations. Even the Eskimo have been taught to read and write their language and are provided with religious and other literature (Canada, Department of Mines and Resources, 1949). Literate communities may be subdivided into those in which "the dominant com-

Indonesian Muslims Read the Quran in a Mosque. In some communities the dominant literature consists of sacred books or commentaries upon them (courtesy, Indonesian Embassy).

ponents are *sacred* books of presumably divine origin" and those in which "secular literature, without claim to sacred origin, predominates" (Znaniecki, 1952:11). The Eskimo, like the Cree Indians of Attawapiskat, still belong primarily in the first category. Their literature has been prepared mostly by missionaries and consists of readings and devotions used in church or in the home.

N and N̄ Type

When anthropologists ceased being concerned exclusively with tribes or villages and began to study factories and other specialized organizations, they discovered that certain features associated with the former units were lacking in the latter. The cultures of villages, bands, and tribes, for example, contain procedures for dealing with birth and other aspects of reproduction. These are absent in, say, the culture of an Air Force squadron or a trailer colony of elderly, retired persons in Florida. It is useful to speak of an N type of community, in which membership is perpetuated, at least in part, through mating and reproduction, and an N̄ type (i.e., non-N type) of community, in which membership primarily is perpetuated through some form of recruitment.[1] The distinction between these types is not absolute. For refined analysis intermediate types might be warranted.

Homogeneous and Heterogeneous

Culture in a homogeneous community offers its members choice among relatively few alternatives of behavior. Practically all men are farmers or hunters, and women rear their own children and share similar domestic roles. Change is slow and migration unknown. The ordinary experiences of an individual prepare him for almost any future eventuality (Mead, 1947b). He does not leave his community to confront exotic customs, and the slow rate of culture change does not present him with experiences unfamiliar to his parents. In precontact times every Kaska Indian in northern British Columbia trapped or hunted for food while his wife made clothes, set fish nets, and cooked. Techniques and implements for these tasks scarcely altered from one generation to another. In modern Pakistan life is more heterogeneous. The son of a farmer may never adopt his father's occupation. He may join the army, learn a profession, or migrate to seek work in an urban factory.

In a heterogeneous community change from one generation to another tends to be rapid. Hence less opportunity exists to prepare the child fully for its future roles. The range of choice open to an individual is wide. It becomes difficult to choose from the variety of competing religions, philosophies, and attractive occupations that confront him (see pp. 258, 355). The distinction between homogeneous and heterogeneous is, of course, a matter of degree—as, in fact, is true of all the other ideal types of communities discussed in this chapter.

Folk and Urban

The folk-urban continuum overlaps not only with the homogeneous-heterogeneous dichotomy just defined but also with the notion of scale discussed below (pp. 149–155). Such overlap indicates that the three bases of classification have much in common. In fact, they may be merely different words designating pretty much the same referents.[2]

The theoretical end points of the folk and urban continuum may conveniently be summed up in two parallel columns.[3]

[1] The symbol N stands for "natural," a word used analogously to its meaning in law.
[2] Cf. Chinoy, 1954:31–33. These concepts also overlap with the distinction between *Gemeinschaft* and *Gesellschaft* (Toennies, 1940; Loomis and Beegle, 1950) and between "sacred" and "secular" communities (H. E. Barnes and H. Becker, 1938:Chap. 1).
[3] Based on Redfield, 1947, 1953a, and 1955; Odum, 1953. Recently an intermediate peasant-type community has been proposed. See Kroeber, 1948:284; Firth, 1951:Chap. 3; Redfield, 1956b.

FOLK COMMUNITY	URBAN COMMUNITY
1. It is small enough in size so that people in interaction know one another personally.	The population tends to be large and social relations are highly impersonal.
2. People neither travel in nor communicate with the wider society.	Travel and communication in and with the larger society are frequent.
3. There is considerable similarity in what people do and think.	There is much variety in what people do and think.
4. Social interaction depends mainly on a feeling of belonging together (e.g., rests on a sense of kinship or tribal oneness). Group relations are based on "mechanical solidarity."	Social relations are guided by values of expediency or by the advantages to be found in associating together. Their basis, then, is "organic solidarity."
5. Production is for use; hence, there is little trade.	Production is largely for trade.
6. Behavior is traditional, automatic, and unquestioned.	Readiness exists to reflect on behavior and to consider one's actions objectively and critically.
7. Traditional behavior is valued as an end in itself.	Behavior is evaluated in terms of efficiency, whether it makes for "progress" or provides satisfactions for the greatest number of people.

Symbiotic Communities

Two or more communities are symbiotic to one another when they are related in such a way that the culture of one is dependent very closely upon that of the other. A relatively drastic modification in one way of life would demand a reorganization in the second. Social symbiosis is illustrated in those parts of the Middle East where nomadic Bedouin tribes raise camels and sheep and trade the animal products with sedentary Arab farmers. The latter, in turn, produce a surplus of grain and fruit for exchange. The Pygmies together with their taller Negro hosts in the Ituri forest of the Congo provide another example of symbiosis. The Pygmies supply their neighbors with meat and elephant ivory in exchange for metal tools and bananas. Many communities in modern large-scale society exist in some degree of mutual symbiosis.

The Loosely and Tightly Structured Community[4]

Behavior in a community may reveal a general lack of regularity, discipline, regimentation, respect for administrative efficiency, neatness, and

[4] Based on Ryan and Straus, 1954; the concept of structure here bears little relationship to the way in which that concept is used in connection with social organization (see pp. 341–342, infra). See also Embree, 1950.

walking in step. The community, then, is said to be loosely structured. In Thailand, Ceylon, and other parts of Southeast Asia, where loose structuring is found, a great number of alternative channels of behavior exist in which people can express conformity to norms. Behavior going beyond the acknowledged sphere of the normative is condoned readily or at least tolerated. Lying, for example, will be accepted as well as bribery. Formal organization of groups (see pp. 358–359) is little encouraged in such a cultural climate.

Americans and most Europeans are more familiar with a culture in which much more conformity in individual behavior is socially standardized. The behavior specified for particular situations is closely limited, and any transgression of the norms must be rationalized carefully if it is to escape social pressure. Respect for administration and for formal rules governing organizational life are developed highly in a tightly structured social system.

CLASSIFICATION BY SCALE[5]

The reader will recall the definition of a community as part of a larger social area, the society, which includes all the people of whom members are aware (pp. 17–19). The societies of different communities vary in range or scale. A large-scale community, then, is first of all one that participates in a relatively large society.

Criteria of Scale

Scale refers, first, to the number of people in conscious relations in a society. If a community increases in population, it has increased in scale since the community is part of the society and the latter thereby grows in size. If a community expands its former limits of interaction so that members enter relationships with more people, again it is increasing the size of its society. Second, scale is indicated by the intensity of interpersonal relations in the society.

How can the intensity of societal relations be discovered? Intensity in this sense means the degree to which the community coöperates, communicates, or identifies emotionally with those people, whatever the number, of whom it happens to be aware. A community that believes all other people in the world to be barbarians, with whom there can be nothing to exchange or communicate because they possess nothing of value, has very unintense relations with its society. It is, therefore, relatively small in scale. Diachronically, intensity is measured by the degree to which there

[5] Much in this section follows G. Wilson and M. Wilson, 1945:Chaps. 2, 4.

is awareness of, identification with, and inheritance of wealth or knowledge from, the past. "History is a link uniting each of us as an individual with a whole greater than ourselves" (A. Robertson, 1952:1).

The intensity of a community's societal interaction may be judged by reference to five criteria.

1. Economic Coöperation with Contemporaries in the Form of Joint Production, Trade, Gift Exchange, and Loans or Inheritance from the Past. The area of close economic coöperation of a small-scale community is small; the capital inherited from past generations is also limited. This criterion is illustrated by Europe in the early Middle Ages when "there was comparatively little trade between distant places; industrial production had fallen drastically; and agricultural output was primarily for local consumption. To make matters worse, the Mohammedan conquest of a large part of the Mediterranean at the beginning of the eighth century and the antagonism of Christian Europe to this rival religion brought trade between the Mediterranean and Western Europe almost to a standstill" (Clough, 1951:166). However, some parts of Europe, like Venice, continued to maintain far-flung trade relations and prospered.

2. Communication of Fact Through Speech or Writing with Contemporaries or from the Past. The area of communication is, of course, quite small when the community is illiterate. A small-scale, illiterate community possesses only meager oral traditions of past events. By comparison, twentieth-century scholars know more about the history of Mesopotamia 3000 years before the birth of Christ than did the ancient scribes working in the Mesopotamian city of Ur in 2000 B.C. (Childe, 1949:11).

3. Communication and Expression of Feeling or Emotion. Emotion may be expressed beyond the boundaries of a community through visiting dancers, exchange of representational art, or the circulation of literary productions. In a small-scale society "communication of feeling barely extends beyond personal contacts, for there is no literary art, and each small group being largely self-sufficient, the manufactured articles which circulate are few" (G. Wilson and M. Wilson, 1945:26–27). In comparison to later times, the many distinct, local modes of decorating pottery in prehistoric Greece around 3000 B.C. suggest little circulation of such objects between the small fortified villages. The numerous localized physical types confirm the impression of a high degree of local isolation. Historically, the communication and expression of emotion are limited by the absence of written records and of lasting media.

4. Identification with Contemporaries or Continuity with the Past. A small-scale community is suspicious or afraid of distant contemporaries and does not trace its continuity to a society stretching far back in time. A large-scale community, on the other hand, values much broader identification. But even in large-scale modern nations religious inclusiveness often is limited by race or nationalism, though a universal society is valued by some people. In a small-scale community continuity with the past "is limited by the absence of traditions going back more than ten or twelve generations" (*ibid.*, p. 27; cf. Cunnison, 1957). Unity and continuity may be asserted ritually through the use of a single name, common form of dress, single flag, or common ceremonies.

5. Social Pressure Exerted by People on One Another. In a small-scale society power is exercised only within a comparatively small community—

Chuckchee Hunters of Northeastern Siberia Study *Pravda*. What are the implications for scale? Note conical dwelling in the background (courtesy, Sovfoto).

perhaps an autonomous village. "The area in which any ruler can exert pressure by force of arms, and in which law is effective, is limited. . . . In civilized societies the range of social pressure is much greater. The military power of large groups extends over the world, and law is effective over wide areas" (G. Wilson and M. Wilson, 1945:29).

As already suggested, people are by no means always ready to increase the intensity of their relations with outsiders. A village that resents the government-appointed schoolmaster, a state legislature that tries to restrict teaching about the United Nations in its public schools, a patriotic association that presses for laws against display of the U.N. flag in classrooms, restrictions on foreign travel, book burning, and immigration quotas all illustrate means by which people have sought to limit their degree of participation in society.

Correlates of Scale

Communities often seek to expand or limit scale with a view to gaining or avoiding certain consequences. This suggests that scale is associated predictably with certain correlates. What can be predicted to occur as a society expands in size and the relations of its members become more intense? Six major correlates associated with increasing scale have been suggested.

1. **A Large Degree of Occupational Specialization.** In a large-scale community hardly anybody can supply all of his needs unaided. The rest of the society, from which many resources are imported, also shows great specialization. Some men spend their working hours making shoes, baking bread, growing wheat, practicing medicine, or teaching school. The product of, or service rendered by, each of these specialists is exchanged for the surplus produced by the others. Money provides a convenient medium to facilitate the great amount of trade that flourishes in association with a large degree of division of labor based on skill.

2. **Realization and Appreciation of Cultural Variety.** The large-scale community not only is in a position to include in its culture a large variety of alternative religions, philosophies, dance styles, games, dramatic styles, or musical types but approves and expects such variety. "In England, for example, a considerable degree of variety is valued. Polemics against the evil of a 'dead uniformity' are frequent, and the proverb that it 'takes all sorts to make a world' is not only an expression of resignation to unavoidable differences. It is widely held that absolute truth cannot be fully stated in human speech; that creeds, while they may point to the nature of reality, cannot contain it; and that all of them, therefore, are in some degree relative" (*ibid.*, p. 85).

3. **Technical Development.** A large-scale community possesses the means to protect itself against floods and variations in rainfall; it can avoid drought by means of irrigation and maintains soil fertility through fertilization. It has prodigious power resources with which to supplement the energies of men. The capital goods required to maintain this degree of control over the physical environment represent a considerable investment of wealth. In short, a large-scale community is a wealthy community and, generally speaking, one that enjoys a high standard of living.

4. **Nonmagicality.** Magic refers to the belief that certain artifacts or actions possess unfailing significance or that they are absolutely indispensable (see pp. 684–688). Ideally speaking, in a small-scale community there is only one way to do a task. Alternatives, if discovered, are rejected in favor

of traditional modes of behavior without prior investigation of whether they possess advantages lacked by traditional procedures. Actually, of course, no people are so exclusively magical or unchanging in their culture (see pp. 188–189). People in a large-scale community, familiar as they are with variety, take little for granted and constantly search for more efficient ways of doing things. When there is choice, behaviors are weighed in terms of their relative advantages. Through the origination of new elements at home and the borrowing of traits from abroad, variety in the culture constantly is maintained. One result is a relativistic attitude toward truth (Wissler, 1923:Chap. 16). When the pagans in the remote Hindu Kush Mountains of Afghanistan and Pakistan came under the influence of the outside world their attitude toward traditional customs changed. ". . . The young portion of the community [is] inclined to be somewhat sceptical . . . sacred ceremonies are frequently burlesqued or scoffed at . . ." (G. S. Robertson, 1896:379). The tolerance of a large-scale community for religious variation is well expressed in the general policy of the Roman Empire. Rome readily acknowledged the religions of her subject people, although she forbade some ritual practices on the ground of morality. On the other hand, it was expected that the subjects would be equally tolerant and show homage to Rome and the emperor. This the Christians and Jews refused to do. However much their integrity may be admired, their refusal to affirm unity ritually with Rome reveals a relative narrowness in the intensity of their social relationships with Rome (de Burgh, 1947:Chap. 9).

   5. Impersonality. Most social relations in a large-scale society occur between people who are relative strangers to one another. The psychological test becomes the basis of hiring and promotion; people are assigned numbers and addresses, and the possessions of a family constitute indices to its relative social standing. These things take the place of the personal knowledge of one another which people in a small-scale community possess. With increased scale the conception of the universe ceases to be cast in terms of personalized, anthropomorphic movers but is phrased impersonally (see pp. 594–595).

   6. Autonomy Increased in the Narrow Circle of Relations and Decreased in the Wider. A large-scale community allows the individual to retain considerable local freedom in regard to such things as selecting his clothes, choosing a job, practicing religion, selecting a wife, or striking out independently to make a living. At any rate, the power of parents and local authorities is limited as police, law courts, and other agencies of the superordinate government take over (A. R. Beals, 1955:92). Behavior and satisfactions in the large-scale community are governed by many outside and even distant factors, including availability of raw materials, ability of foreign markets to absorb imports, and stability in international relations, to name only a few. Decisions made in the Soviet Union have repercussions in London, Washington, and Delhi; the tastes of Latin Americans influence the production of motion pictures in Hollywood.

Increase of scale . . . though necessarily involving greater centralization, produces not less but more freedom in personal relations; not less but more local autonomy; not greater inequality but greater mobility. The freedom of a primitive man is limited at every point by the pressure of neighbours and kinsmen, living and dead, from whom he cannot escape. He has little privacy. His position in society is largely fixed by sex, age, and blood. The freedom of the civilized man from neighbours and kinsmen, and from the immediate past, is much greater than that of a primitive; not only does he live relatively aloof in his house, but he can escape the living by moving. . . . On the other hand, he is dependent upon distant groups—upon banks and cartels, upon his heritage from ancient Greece and Rome, Palestine and China—in a way in which a primitive man is not dependent [G. Wilson and M. Wilson, 1945:115].

A dependable relationship links scale on the one hand and these six correlates on the other. Each correlate of scale is functionally dependent on the others (Hobhouse, 1924:31–32). For example, increased scale implies a surrender of autonomy to distant groups through which the community derives new ideas. These ideas in turn help to undermine magicality as they promote variety. In Southeast Asia growing control over environment through the use of trucks, motorcars, and aircraft encourages further travel. Formerly "for most of the people, over the hill and beyond the next village was out of the world" (Landon, 1949:172). Not by accident was the ferment of change which affected Europe at the turn of the seventeenth and the beginning of the eighteenth centuries associated with a passion for travel. Global exploration and contact with new ways of life undermined assumptions on which traditional philosophy had reposed. As a seventeenth-century observer put it, "a new conception of things will inevitably be called for" (Hazard, 1953:5–6, 8, 11, 17).

We repeat that no inevitable compulsion demands that a community expand its scale. Nor can scale increase indefinitely, at least not beyond the point where maximum use is being made of the society's members. People often seek to restrict social relations in order to avoid fatigue, too intense cultural variety, impersonality, or contact with disagreeable alien behaviors. Modern governments fear the consequences of having their power weakened by enhancing the authority of an international administration. Generally, however, a community will welcome the technical development encouraged by participation in a wide society. People often are ambivalent about the degree of intensity with which they participate in society, valuing some fruits of participation but rejecting others.

It must be kept in mind that groups in a society, or even individuals in the same community, may not be equally wide in scale. Hence, sectors within a community will be affected differently by the correlates of scale. Conflict often breaks out between categories and groups of people who are unevenly matched for scale.

CIVILIZATION

Civilization always implies a considerable range of scale. As used here, the concept refers to a relatively high degree of elaboration and technical development characterizing a community. For a community to constitute a civilization, the culture must also include that complex of cultural elements which first appeared in culture history between 8000 and 6000 years ago. At that time, on a basis of agriculture, stock raising, and metallurgy, intensive occupational specialization began to grow up in the river valleys of Southwest Asia (see Chap. 40). Writing appeared, as well as relatively dense urban aggregations that accommodated administrators, traders, and other specialists. The cities had a decidedly high standard of living. These are the specific characteristics of civilization: food production (plant and animal domestication), metallurgy, a high degree of occupational specialization, writing, and cities. Such characteristics have emerged in several parts of the prehistoric world: Mesopotamia, Egypt, China, Greece, Rome, India, Highland Peru and Bolivia, the valley of Mexico, and Guatemala (Steward, 1949a). They were never fully realized in America north of the Rio Grande prior to European colonization.

11.

The Cultural Field

A FRUITFUL theory of culture can be founded profitably on a few general propositions or postulates. Each of these, in turn, possesses implicit consequences which can be deduced from it. The explicit deductions become useful for guiding observation, formulating more specific hypotheses (of a sort that can be proved true or false far more readily than can the postulate itself), and explaining phenomena. The postulates of a theoretical system constitute the points from which research takes off. They predict, in a general sort of way, the nature of that portion of the universe which is being studied. Deduction of more specific hypotheses from the postulates actually means refining those broad propositions. If hypotheses deduced from a given set of postulates regularly fail to hold up, then, perhaps, the theory ought to be discarded and a new one created.

SOME GENERAL POSTULATES

The following six propositions, each fairly inclusive, cover much that will be said in this book:

1. Human behavior and artifacts are socially standardized. (Socially standardized behavior and artifacts will be referred to collectively as culture.)

2. The constituent elements of culture are functionally related to the conditions of the geographical environment of a given society.

3. The constituent parts of culture are functionally related to the size, composition, and other demographic characteristics of population in a given society. (Society has been defined on pp. 17–19.)

4. The constituent parts of culture are functionally related to the structure and functioning of the human organism in a given society.

5. The conditions of the geographical environment, structure and functioning of human organisms, and the size and composition of population in a given society together constitute a system. This means that they too are functionally interrelated. Collectively these three classes of variables will be referred to as the cultural field.[1]

[1] Some very fundamental assumptions are implicit at this point, namely, that the conditions of environment, structure and functioning of the human organism, and the size

6. The various elements of culture are functionally related to one another. We have already referred to the systematic nature of culture (pp. 13–15).

Postulates 2, 3, and 4 state that culture is dynamically related to three noncultural factors: the geographical environment (also referred to as "geographical milieu," "habitat," or "the environment"), the demographic properties of the society, and the biological nature of the human organism.[2] Understanding any culture depends partly on examining its relationship to the conditions simultaneously extant in the cultural field. It is assumed that a change in a field factor—say, in size of population—will be accompanied by a concomitant cultural change. Conversely, any cultural change will be accompanied by a modification of the field. Causality, of course, is not suggested simply by such statements (see pp. 83–87).

ENVIRONMENT

The geographical milieu includes variables like climate, soil, and topography. Wild plant or animal life also constitutes part of the environment. No absolutely rigid boundary can be drawn between culture (at least its artifacts) and its environment. Hence, on occasion doubt may arise concerning whether a specific phenomenon—say, plowed ridges—should be regarded as geographical factors or artifacts. Either point of view is possible. Selection will depend on the perspective from which the particular variable is to be studied.

Considerable debate has centered on the question of whether the geographical environment limits, directs, or influences culture. For a while the reaction against the position that environment could indeed produce cultural phenomena was so strong that anthropologists came dangerously close to throwing out any consideration of even possible relationships between culture and habitat. As the reader is by now aware, it is fruitless to talk of the production of anything by environment unless data are available to test such a producer-product relationship experimentally (see pp. 84–86). Hypotheses linking a specific environmental feature—say, amount of annual rainfall—to a discrete element in culture—yellow raincoats, for example—are not likely to prove cross-culturally verifiable. Logically, of

---

and composition of population may be handled individually as relatively self-contained phenomena despite their interrelationship. Also, socially standardized behavior and artifacts may for certain purposes be handled apart from the field in which they exist, and each trait in isolation from the others. For the average reader these assumptions may not seem important but for a philosopher they are significant (cf. Bidney, 1953:39–53).

[2] Gillin (1948b:208) includes a foreign culture, whenever present, as an element of what he calls the "cultural situation." In that way, however, he fails to limit the concept to noncultural variables only. The relationship of a foreign culture to the one being studied can better be treated under the concept of acculturation (see Chapter 17 below).

Farming on Mountainside Terraces Is Found in Several Parts of the World. The terraces and nearby ruins of Machu Picchu shown here belonged to the Inca Empire (courtesy, Grace Line).

course, one may assert a "fit" between such variables. To say that the northern forest environment is responsible for the Attawapiskat Cree Indians' custom of fur trapping is nonsense. In the first place, the custom did not always possess the importance which it currently enjoys. Furthermore, all communities in the northern forest do not make a living by trapping.

Two principles should be kept in mind. First, several relatively different modes of relating to the same milieu may be manifested by the same community at different times of its existence. Three hundred years ago the Cree Indians secured their entire subsistence from the habitat. They drew from the land materials for clothing, tools, and shelter. Today the same community reveals a quite different way of life. People have altered their previous relationship to the habitat. The bulk of subsistence is now secured from distant environments which the Indians do not visit directly. At home they trap large quantities of animal furs which are exported in exchange for flour, tea, canvas, clothing, guns, and traps. Second, different groups in the same environment may relate to the habitat in quite different fashion. Near Attawapiskat is a radar outpost whose staff perceives values in the climate, flora, and fauna of the sub-Arctic environment quite different from those of the Cree Indians. It is apparent that the geographical milieu cannot be held predictably responsible for behavior.

The relationship between culture and environment is complicated by the fact that the response of a community is a function of the range of other environments which its members directly or indirectly exploit. Canadian troops in the treeless Arctic tundra live in plywood barracks built with lumber obtained from a radically different milieu. The Eskimo, without such resources, use caribou skins, stone, and turf for shelter. The scale of a community, therefore, is significant for understanding how people deal with the problems posed by a particular habitat. Large-scale communities have access to a large variety of geographical resources drawn from different corners of the world. Small-scale communities are highly specialized in the way they relate to a given habitat.

Much can be learned about human behavior in specific communities by observing how the two factors, environment and culture, are functionally associated. By this is meant only that change in one area will be accompanied by change in the other. By making environment the independent variable one can observe how its alteration is reflected in a way of life. Or the process can begin with culture, in which case the geographical milieu becomes the dependent variable (pp. 161–162). From a number of such relationships studied in specific communities it may be possible to arrive at more generalized hypotheses, still of a functional or correlational nature. We shall attempt to formulate these when possible.

Environment, the Independent Variable

History chronicles many instances in which change in culture is geared to changes in the geographical setting. For example, in 1425 A.D. the herring off the coast of Europe suddenly shifted their run and began to spawn in the North Sea instead of the Baltic. Hanseatic German fishermen found their lives profoundly dislocated while the Dutch became prosperous, their culture growing in overall richness (Kroeber, 1948:388). Here is another instance: during the last few decades, oat and stock farming have

been moving northward accompanying the rising temperature of the oceans
and the lands of Europe and Greenland (A. Lee, 1954:779). A quite different phenomenon occurred in Iron Age times when the postglacial warm
spell ended, to be followed by very cold winters (see p. 781).

Without evidence of an actual change in the geographical environment
and a concomitant modification in culture, one can logically perceive
culture-environment relationships. Common sense indicates that irrigation
is related to a desert environment. Logically speaking, the technique would
be unnecessary if the area received sufficient moisture by rainfall. Pakistan's
concern with restoring the nitrogen and organic carbon content of the
soil is a response conditioned by a chemically impoverished environment.
Man's socially standardized response to cold and heat occurs in practically
all environments, but certain aspects of the form it takes may be understood as a function of the particular habitat. The Eskimo expeditiously
constructs a shelter of snow blocks in a territory which, in winter at least,
reveals few other resources. In northern Scotland and the Orkney Islands,
where wood for building is also scarce, its place has long been taken by
stone. In Southwest Asia the thick-walled, earthen dwellings built by peasants, containing small windows that can be closed by wooden shutters, represent an adjustment to a treeless environment and are well suited to
keeping out the intense summer heat. In Washington, D.C., the papers
often give tips for coping with the summer heat.

Moving now to a level of greater generality: it is usually true that
clothing is light or nonexistent where climate remains moist and hot all
year round. Heavy and windproof clothing tends to be found where winters
are sharp and chill. The correlation is, of course, not perfect. Some tropical
people, rather than allow the air full play on hot skin, employ Mother
Hubbard dresses to hide the nakedness of which missionaries have taught
them to be ashamed. Another general relationship between environment
and culture has been suggested by economists. They point out that a
greater proportion of wealth, time, and effort will be expended for clothing
and shelter in a relatively rigorous geographical milieu. ". . . A Swede or
a Canadian requires heavy and expensive clothing and a well-built and well-
heated house, while an Indian or an Egyptian can obtain the same level
of well-being with light clothing and makeshift shelter" (Woytinsky and
Woytinsky, 1953:379).

A change in environment is likely to boost cultural innovation. (Generally, however, a drastic change of this sort comes about only through
migration from one habitat to another.) The previous way of life, to the
extent that it involved dealing with certain, no longer present natural
resources, becomes unfeasible. New raw materials are utilized and, perhaps,
new artifact forms or techniques come into being. These, in turn, can condition still further changes in the cultural system (Dixon, 1928:42–46).

Environment, the Dependent Variable

Lasting modifications of a people's habitat may be related to socially standardized activities (W. L. Thomas, 1956). Guns in the hands of Indians and frontiersmen on the western plains of the United States practically destroyed the bison on which the Indian had depended for food, raiment, and shelter. In this instance the sequence leads from a cultural fact to an environmental modification and then back to cultural innovation. For following the devastation of the herds, Indians turned to other sources for clothing and shelter. Beef cattle and other foods supplanted bison flesh. The Blackfoot Indians in Canada tried to feed themselves by stealing cattle belonging to white settlers. When this behavior was punished they contemplated migrating to places where bison still survived. Finally they settled down to imitate their white Canadian neighbors, raising maize, wheat, potatoes, and beef (Hanks and Hanks, 1950:14–28).

The case of the Plains Indians is not unusual. One of the nearly inevitable processes coinciding with man's occupation of a habitat is the progressive exhaustion of certain natural resources. In many parts of the world devastating erosion followed intensive plowing and overgrazing. The extension of farming and the concomitant removal of forest cover from vast areas have also stimulated erosion. Clearing the land bares its surface to the action of wind and water, which carries the topsoil away. Increase in population, bringing with it pressure on the land to produce more food or fodder, can in time wear out the fertility of a region (Batten, 1954:I, Chap. 12). Counteracting these tendencies are efforts incorporated in culture to maintain the stability of environment. Through manuring or by the addition of chemical compounds to the soil man renews the fertility of cultivated soil; reforestation and contour plowing protect the land from erosion. Not all communities try, or are able, to maintain environmental stability to the same degree, nor can all resources be renewed (see pp. 277–278). Some scientists predict that industrial air pollution and atomic bomb explosions will contaminate the atmosphere and reduce precipitation. They point out that a relationship exists between the cleanliness of the air and the likelihood of rain. The dirtier the atmosphere the more difficult it seems for rain droplets to form in clouds and become big enough to fall (*New York Times*, Apr. 25, 1957).

Man also modifies his habitat more deliberately. The American Indian's custom of burning the vegetation cover to further successful hunting converted millions of acres of woodlands to grass. Periodic grass fires thereafter helped to preserve the prairies by preventing the forest from returning. Some disagreement exists over whether burning actually increases game supply (Stewart, 1954:244).

Evidence of conservation has already been cited, indicating that man's modifications of the geographical milieu are by no means always exploitive. The New Zealand government has planted over 550 square miles in pine forest, transforming a former wasteland; Ontario and other Canadian provinces have stocked depleted woodlands with fish, beaver, and other fur-bearing animals important for the northern Indian's livelihood; harbors have been constructed since 2000 B.C. in the Middle East and elsewhere (Klimm, 1956). Through domestication new races or species of animals are brought into being. Inadvertently man constantly renews life-giving elements in nature through organic wastes and, eventually, by depositing his own body in the earth.

DEMOGRAPHIC CHARACTERISTICS

A society, like its constituent communities, is made up of people who may be enumerated by age or sex, or as totaling a certain number. These figures may be expressed as ratios. Or a population may be compared to the area of land which it occupies. Fifty persons on 100 square miles of territory yield a density of 0.5 person per square mile. Density is calculated by the formula: P/A (population divided by area). People have a specific life expectancy. An average woman's fertility may be calculated in terms of the number of live children to which she gives birth. Such indices express demographic characteristics by means of which populations can be compared. On the whole, little work has been done to relate such variables to elements of culture. Research along these lines may turn out to be a productive trend in future anthropology.

Size as Independent and Dependent Variable

Sheer size has been perhaps the best studied of all demographic variables in terms of its association with culture. The number of persons in interaction is, as already pointed out (pp. 152–154), closely related to the kind and amount of social interaction that can occur. The smaller the size of a specific group, the less opportunity for occupational specialization or trade to build up between individuals (G. Wilson and M. Wilson, 1945:83; Chapple and Coon, 1942:86–92, 266–272). The relationship holds even for the family: a large family reveals more specialized occupational roles than a small family. Since occupational differentiation in turn promotes interdependence (i.e., social solidarity), a large group will tend to be knit together more tightly than a small one (Bossard and Sanger, 1952:7–8; Durkheim, 1933).

In the same way that a change in environment stimulates innovation by offering new resources or presenting new problems, so any change in population size and density encourages culture change (Dixon, 1928:43–45). The urbanization of a community implies not merely the growth of an urban-dwelling population but also the appearance of many new, specialized patterns of culture that go with urban living. A falling population is also a dynamic factor in culture (Wagley, *1940*). Invention and cultural borrowing tend to increase as population grows, but the rate of cultural innovation declines when the total number of people declines (E. Rose, *1947–48*). Careful study shows how art, philosophy, and other areas of culture depend, functionally speaking, on the number of persons in interaction (Kroeber, *1944*). In 1767 the town of Hilltown, New England, consisted of 150 people; in 1850 it reached a peak of 1825 persons; in 1945 population fell to about a thousand. "We must note, for what significance it may have, that the decades in which towns like this were most prosperous and populous were also the ones in which New England literature and philosophy reached their full flower in Emerson, Thoreau, and Hawthorne" (Homans, *1950*: 340–342). Size, of course, cannot produce an elaborate culture; organization of people is also important. A million people divided into a hundred geographically scattered and isolated communities will possess a different culture from that of a million people asserting their unity and organized under a central authority (Kroeber, *1948*:272–273).

Sheer number is related directly to organization. English parishes in rural South Devon which contain large villages are also associated with a "lively and effective form of local government" (G. D. Mitchell, *1952*:98). A large local population engages in relatively intensified communication with the wider society, and local government mediates a considerable part of this communication. This is similar to saying that where many people live together government finds more work to do and so becomes strong and active. Where population density is extremely low, as in the Eskimo and northern Athapaskan culture areas, true government is practically absent (see pp. 480–481).

Clearly, a two-way rather than unilateral relationship exists between population size and culture. The growth of culture may be favored by a relatively large population, but the size of a human aggregate also depends on adequate means for providing food, clothing, and shelter. Not only must culture provide a sufficient amount of food; quality is also important. Dense populations have grown up where protein foods existed in dependable supply. In the Old World dairying and animal husbandry represented such sources after about 8000 B.C. while in the prehistoric New World beans fulfilled the same function (Linton, *1940b*).

Population Movement

An increase or decrease in population at a given time normally is a function of cultural arrangements. The depopulation of Hilltown and other New England small towns after 1850 accompanied the development of rail transportation westward in the United States, growing industrialization of New England cities, the coming of automobile transportation ending the days when a small town would also be a retail center, and new standards of living which could not be realized in the Hilltowns (Homans, 1950: 342–358).

A relationship has been demonstrated between population growth and changing traits of character structure. In communities where births and deaths are both high and where population remains stationary or increases at a very low rate, people are closely attached to tradition. Little room exists for personal choice. As population begins to expand rapidly (perhaps following innovations in sanitation and medicine) an inner-directed character structure appears. Tradition continues to limit choice, but each individual possesses, as it were, an inbuilt gyroscope by whose aid he makes choices in unfamiliar situations. These choices are made in terms of values that were instilled early in life. Currently the western world seems to be settling down, after a period of rapid demographic expansion, to a period of incipient population decline. The dominant character type is now other-directed. Behavior is chosen to conform to what others expect. Figuratively speaking, a radar set has been substituted for the internal gyroscope. By its aid the individual becomes highly sensitive to the expectations of others. In a given social situation he suits his behavior to those cues (Riesman, 1950:7–24). An era of more intense conformity and adjustment to the values of one's peers has begun (Viereck, 1956; W. H. Whyte, 1956).

Upward or downward movement of population depends on at least three interacting demographic factors: birth rate (i.e., the number of children born in a given interval compared to the total population), death rate, and migration (Dice, 1955:Chap. 5). Population will increase if births exceed deaths and if immigration exceeds emigration. All three of these factors are highly sensitive to cultural arrangements. For example, birth rate is tied in with age of marriage. In India and Pakistan a girl begins her reproductive career early. This gives her a relatively longer time in which to bear children, and the subcontinent's birth rate is proportionally high (K. Davis and J. Blake, 1956). Raising the age of marriage, as is urged by some South Asians, would reduce the birth rate and, other things being equal, slow down the rate of population growth. Some communities manage to control conception mechanically or chemically. Successful use of such controls also limits birth rate but their employment depends on several cultural factors, including values and the readiness of husband and wife to talk about such things as family planning (Stycos, 1955). Deliberate contraception is not practiced with equal frequency by different categories in a community. Americans who have been to college produce fewer children than Americans who have not, presumably because the former make more use of contraceptive devices.

Historians have tended to conceive of a community with a rising population as satisfied. Conversely, a declining population indicates that cultural conditions do not provide many rewards. ". . . A rapidly growing city is usually a prosperous and happy place, while a city of declining population is normally not very prosperous or optimistic" (J. C. Russell, 1948:377). A problem lies in testing such hypotheses cross-culturally. What are unequivocal signs of prosperity, happiness, and optimism? Is early marriage in South Asia evidence of fundamental satisfaction with life? It probably is true that population growth accompanies an increasing production of wealth. But not everyone is ready to accept material prosperity as indicative of general satisfaction or happiness. Nor do people whose standard of living is rising necessarily feel prosperous. Often their wants grow proportionately and they may become quite pessimistic about satisfying them.

Age and Sex Ratios

Every culture, at least in an N-type community, includes certain behavior patterns and artifacts specialized for different age levels. The whole area of child care is a function of the fact that children are being born into, and live in, the community. A shift in the proportion of the population in one age category to another may be accompanied by compensatory shifts in culture. As the proportion of old people in North America increases, new culture patterns put in an appearance. Gerontology, a specialized discipline concerned with studying aging and the aged, is an example. Trailer colonies in Florida or California for the retired, growing concern over what is the best age of retirement, and social security programs are functions of the country's growing number of old folks. Similarly, many Americans in 1957 were made conscious of an expanding juvenile population. As the number of school-age children increased, provision had to be made for additional teachers, schoolrooms, and play space.

Experience indicates that any drastic alteration in the proportion of men to women in a population will be associated with cultural rearrangements. The customs of America's western frontier were suited to an extreme disproportion of men to women. Homosexuality in prisons and harems illustrates the same point. Military organizations are likely to include predominantly members of one sex. The culture that appears, for example, in an Air Force squadron of men is likely to be preoccupied with the topic of the opposite sex (Honigmann, 1954d).

Life Expectancy

Long life is likely to appear more frequently in certain family lines than in others; hence longevity probably possesses a genetic basis. However, families with a tendency to longevity are equally distributed in a society (Goldstein, 1954:85–86). Hence, variation in life expectancy between communities, or between categories of people within a community, probably reflects cultural differences (Table 16). During the forties the average North American citizen could expect to live 65 years, the average Japanese or Mexican only 35 (United Nations, Statistical Office, 1951:526–539). That more people in the United States achieved middle and old age in 1950 compared to 1900 is related to more effective means of infant care that have

TABLE 16.   Variations in Life Expectancy, Selected Countries and
Population

Country or Category	Number of Persons out of 100,000 Born Alive Who Would Survive to Age 70	
	Male	Female
Canada	55,020	66,576
United States	49,950	64,873
Ceylon	48,684	48,022
Japan	46,446	56,525
El Salvador	35,313	38,653
Brazil	26,654	42,634
Union of South Africa (Asian population)	25,901	24,728
Belgian Congo (African population)	13,716	17,865

SOURCE: United Nations, Statistical Office, 1954:626–629.

reduced infant mortality, application of enhanced knowledge about health and disease, and growing self-consciousness regarding diet.

The Negro in the United States cannot be proved biologically less fit than his white contemporary. His numbers have grown threefold since 1870. Yet the Negro's life span in 1950 amounted to only 59 years, some 7 years below the country's average life expectancy. Such a differential can be explained readily by cultural differences between the Negro and his white contemporaries; the Negro's reduced opportunities to share health and other facilities available to fellow citizens is undoubtedly of prime importance (see also W. P. D. Logan, 1954).

BIOLOGICAL ORGANISM

The human organism constitutes the last of the three noncultural variables related to culture. Compared to habitat and demographic characteristics, the biological organism is very constant from one part of the world to another. Excluding the minor hereditary traits distinctive of race (on the basis of which cultural forms of discrimination may be built up), man constitutes a single species, *Homo sapiens*. Culture in all its diverse forms is functionally dependent upon the structure and functioning of that common organism. This is a topic to be examined in some detail in Chapter 44. Here we look at the organism only as it may be dependent upon culture.

Organism, the Dependent Variable

Many communities shape or mutilate the human body in certain socially standardized ways. These include deliberate fattening (Hiroa, 1934:89), circumcision and other genital operations, removal of the teeth, and head shaping (see pp. 573–574). How the body shall be used in walking, sitting, swimming, and other activities also is socially standardized, though these things have been studied relatively little (Mauss, 1950:365–368). Metabolic rates vary with culture. For example, they are low among Chinese. Americans who adopt a Chinese style of life show a lower rate of metabolism than Americans at home.

Human illness, which represents a special condition of the biological organism, is not infrequently dependent upon culture. The spread of western culture seems to be associated with an increasing incidence of caries, pyorrhea, gum infections, and abnormal formation of the teeth. Apparently these conditions are related to the relatively slight use made of the masticatory apparatus under western ways of life (Armattoe, 1949). Indigenous ways of life also do their part in encouraging disease. In parts of Africa diets which are nutritionally deficient in protein underlie kwashiorkor, a disease with heavy mortality (Brock and Autret, 1952). Coronary thrombosis, "a modern epidemic," is not fully understood. Indications suggest, however, that clotting of the blood in the main coronary artery, which provides nutrients and oxygen to the heart muscle, is related to culture. Rural Guatemalans, Bantu-speaking Africans, Okinawans, and Jamaicans have relatively little coronary thrombosis. In Europe and the United States the incidence is comparatively high for both Negroes and whites. The difference correlates with variation in diet. In both latter places about 35 percent of total bodily energy is derived from fat. Poverty-stricken populations in Africa, Latin America, and elsewhere secure only 15 percent or less of total bodily energy from that source. Occupation appears to be another variable in coronary thrombosis. In Europe the incidence of fatal coronary thrombosis is greater among professional and business men than among agricultural workers. In other words, active people are less likely to die of coronary thrombosis than are sedentary workers (J. N. Morris, 1955). Cancer in the United States is also tied to certain occupations. The rate of cancer among men exposed to soot (furnace men, boiler firemen, and stokers) is three times that found among white-collar workers (Hueper, 1948:8). There is no question but that the radiation produced by man, including x-rays and the radiation released in nuclear explosions, is potentially dangerous (Auerbach, 1956). Precautions are normally taken to protect populations from direct exposure to such radiation. In 1957 the question was still being debated whether experimental tests with atomic and hydrogen bombs endangered the ordinary citizen. According to some physicists the radioactive fall-out produced in these explosions would damage body cells in susceptible individuals. The United States Atomic Energy Commission, on the other hand, denied that the radiation released in such tests constituted a serious danger.[3]

A more complex relationship between culture and biology is illustrated with respect to a man's ability to impregnate a woman. Even fertile men do not constantly produce fertile semen. A period of 1 to 3 days may be necessary after intercourse to produce sperm necessary for fertilization. A man who copulates daily is unlikely to be in condition to fertilize an egg cell (see pp. 872–873). For biological reasons men normally are not motivated to copulate daily. Cultural arrangements often operate to insure further that they will not do so. Hunting or trading trips take the man away from home, and ceremonies impose temporary continence. These are cultural means that allow male fertility to be restored following sexual intercourse (Coon, 1950:247).

[3] See editorial "Loaded Dice" in *Science* (1957), 125:963.

Part Four

PROCESSES
OF CULTURE

Every time, every culture, every code and tradition has its own character, its own leniencies, its own rigours, its beauties and ugliness; accepts certain sufferings as a matter of course, puts up patiently with certain evils. Human life is reduced to real suffering, to hell, only when two ages, two cultures and religions overlap.

HERMANN HESSE (1929:36)

. . . It must not be forgotten that when a higher civilization impinges upon a lower both sides are affected. A double diffusion takes place. The barbarian learns many of the vices, and also, we may hope, many of the virtues of the civilized man, who in his turn is enriched in proportion as he serves the barbarian and debased in so far as he descends to his level.

E. W. SMITH (1927:54)

12.

General Functions of Culture

THE processes of culture include not only those by which a way of life changes or resists change but also those that promote human survival and adjustment. It is quite true that "culture . . . must be understood as a means to an end, that is, instrumentally . . ." (Malinowski, 1944:67). However, we must also consider whether such a position is not too one-sided. Perhaps no instrumental functions can be found for some elements in culture, while for others the functions may be stressful rather than stress-reducing.

THE ENDS OF CULTURE

The instrumental ends (i.e., general functions) of culture have been conceptualized variously. Sometimes the components of culture are referred to needs which they satisfy. A distinction is then drawn between (1) primary drives, like hunger and sex, which stem from the biological make-up of the human organism; (2) derived needs, or the learned requisites through which the biological drives may be satisfied—needs for tools, vehicles, food procurement, and cleanliness; and (3) integrative needs for adequate forms of social organization through which people are assisted in satisfying both their primary and their secondary needs (Piddington, 1950:15–16). Or a different set of needs may be proposed: for freedom to act without undue fear and uncertainty, for self-expression and recognition, and for change from monotony. Each culture provides somewhat different means for meeting these claims (E. J. Krige and J. D. Krige, 1943:282).

Functional Prerequisites

Longer lists of so-called "functional prerequisites" have been offered that look at culture from the standpoint of community survival. Six fundamental prerequisites of social life are:

1. Maintenance of the biological functioning of the community's members (including provision for health and care of the young).
2. Production and distribution of goods and services (including clothing, food, and shelter, as well as adequate rewards for the specialists who provide these things).

3. Reproduction of new members.
4. Socializing new members into responsible adults.
5. Maintenance of internal and external order.
6. Maintenance of meaning and motivation (that is, providing the community's members with a desire to live together and with certain central social values) [J. W. Bennett and M. M. Tumin, 1948:Chap. 4].

It should be kept in mind, however, that culture is endowed with the ability to induce tension as well as to reduce it. Also, culture may serve noninstrumental (or expressive) functions—for example, in play—as well as the instrumental ends of food, shelter, rest, and social organization.

Three General Functions

The rest of this chapter will deal with three general processes of culture: adaptation, adjustment, and stress. Many more specific cultural functions will be encountered in succeeding chapters, but the three listed here are broad enough to include all others. This analysis of the general functions of culture will remain objective. It makes no difference whether the members of the community see some bit of their behavior as adaptive or stressful, the way the analyst does. A man's purpose in hunting, worshiping, or engaging in any other socially standardized behavior may or may not coincide with the functions that an observer perceives in the behavior. Also we do not intend to imply that adaptation and adjustment are good while stress is bad.

ADAPTATION

Adaptation is the process of furthering survival. Many customs promote survival. Some protect the individual from mortal danger. Examples include the use of heavy gloves and other safeguards when working with high-voltage electricity, and automobile safety belts. In the sampan (boat) colony living on the Pearl River in the heart of Canton, China, "Children old enough to walk but not old enough to have much sense wear buoys of light, brightly painted wood, attached to shoulder harnesses, over their pajama suits. The idea is not only to keep the child from sinking if he falls overboard, but to catch the eye of his mother or a neighbor when he goes, so that he may be spotted at once and hauled out" (Rand, 1949:56). Other elements of culture, like the radar network strung across Arctic and sub-Arctic North America or the weapons installed on a merchant ship during time of war, protect group survival. Individual and group survival need hardly be identical. The adaptation of a group may be secured through the sacrifice of individual lives. Among some hunting people, like the Eskimo, for example, very old and sick people who could not keep up with the band in its search for food were formerly abandoned. The infirm were sacrificed to give the more hardy people a greater chance to live (see pp. 583–584). Cultures vary in the importance they attach to group, as compared to individual, survival. Authoritarian countries explicitly hold the individual to be subordinate to the national group. In time of war practically all modern nations enforce the idea of individual sacrifice in order that national integrity may be protected. On a level exceeding anything known among small-scale communities, they then demand the lives of thousands of healthy young men. People who are shocked at the Eskimo's willingness to abandon an oldster nevertheless accept this aspect of war. They rarely question the value of national integrity.

No culture is (and, probably, ever can be) perfectly adaptive. If it were, nobody living under that way of life would ever die. On the other hand, all cultures available for examination in some measure help people to survive. Theoretically, a culture may stand at any point along a continuum from relatively precarious to relatively efficient adaptation. That is to say, cultures may be classified in terms of their capacity to promote survival. Further discussion of this concept occurs on pp. 274–276.

Meeting Adaptive Threats

Adaptation protects people from at least four types of lethal problems. These are shown in Table 17 together with examples of specific threats and

TABLE 17.   Four Types of Lethal Problems Related to Adaptation

Type of Problem	Specific Threats	Illustrative Cultural Solutions
Threats arising mainly from the nature of the human organism	Vulnerability to accidents	Safety programs
	Hunger	Subsistence techniques and food preparation
	Infant helplessness	Child care
	Illness	Sanitation, medication, and surgery
Threats arising mainly out of the geographical environment	Low and high temperatures	Fire, air-conditioning, clothing, shelter
	Drought or desert	Irrigation
	Exhaustion of soils	Fertilization
Threats arising mainly out of demographic factors	Low density	Family self-sufficiency
	Great density	Rules to reduce danger of interference between people
	Great proportion of aged in population	Means to care for, or abandon, the aged
	Rapid rate of increase	Research for new ways of food production or of birth control; infanticide
Threats arising mainly out of culture itself	Destruction of natural resources	Planned reforestation or conservation
	Dangerous machines, radiation, high voltage	Guards and rules of procedure

Examples of Adaptation and Adjustment in a Marine
Environment. *Above:* A British frogman goes overboard to
locate an underwater obstacle. *Right:* The grocery boat
provides a means whereby boat-dwelling families on the
Rhine River are able to secure supplies (courtesy, British
Information Services and the United Nations).

illustrative, socially standardized solutions. A few remarks about the table
may be helpful.

1. Problems do not arise simply out of the nature of the organism or from
the environment or from demographic factors but from a combination of
several variables. If people were not constituted biologically as they are,
then a fall down cellar stairs, low temperatures, hunger, or high voltage
would not be dangerous. It is merely for convenience that the threats have
been categorized.

2. The middle column of Table 17 could list a nearly indeterminate number of threats instead of only a few examples. Specific threats to survival
also vary considerably from one geographical area and culture to another.
Fur trappers in the Northwest Territories of Canada are threatened by low
temperatures in winter; farmers along the northwestern frontier of Pakistan

are threatened by the intense summer sun. Cultural solutions obviously also vary.

3. To come now to the third column: adaptation is not dependent on single activities, as the table seems to indicate. Subsistence techniques involve more than hunting or planting. Tools must be provided; the requisite knowledge mastered; the food transported, milled, or processed; and persons at each step of the sequence motivated to do their part if survival is to be assured for anyone.

ADJUSTMENT

Adaptation refers to coping successfully with lethal threats. Adjustment means reducing the nonlethal tensions which disturb an individual or deliberately increasing the level of such tension for the satisfaction it brings.

Adaptation and adjustment are related. Adaptation implies a certain measure of adjustment. On the other hand, the persistent failure of an organism to secure relief from anxiety, win social acceptance, or enjoy a measure of self-esteem can interfere with survival. Certain adjustive satisfactions may kill an organism. The great overlap between lethal and nonlethal problems has led some observers to abandon any distinction between them. Doing so, however, means failure to recognize that the adjustive component in human behavior is distinctively human and distinguishes man from other animals (Spiro, 1954:24–25).

Most of the specific nonlethal tensions reduced by culture are acquired through learning. People acquire appetites for particular foods. Americans find satisfaction in accumulating wealth, but in other communities the periodic giving away of wealth is adjustive. Competition is avoided by Hopi Indians, but in many parts of the United States successful competition is rewarding. Such wants or aspirations, socially standardized in a particular community, constitute the nonlethal tensions for which appropriate cultural solutions will usually be available. The learned needs, therefore, being themselves socially standardized, constitute part of culture.

To study adjustment requires asking, first, what goals a particular community inculcates and then what satisfactions particular culture traits afford. Rituals, beliefs, trimming the front lawn, books, pictures, the search for knowledge, singing, playing musical instruments, fixing output in a factory in response to the work group's norms, and wearing modest or revealing attire are all adjustive. For some of these elements the motivating tensions cannot be specified clearly. Presumably these are acts whose reward lies in their very performance; they are more expressive than instrumental.

Rooted in human biology is at least one nonlethal tension, the sex drive. It is nonlethal because failure directly to satisfy the drive does not, like unsatisfied hunger, threaten the organism's life. In fact, some organizations provide rewards and punishments the object of which is to help members forgo direct sexual satisfaction. The Sarsi Indians of Alberta promised a girl honor if she remained a virgin. Relatives supervised her behavior carefully to prevent deviation from this ideal (Honigmann, 1956d). However, the question is not how sexual satisfaction may be renounced but what avenues of adjustment to the drive are culturally provided. Heterosexual coitus is the most common means of achieving sexual satisfaction. Communities vary in the degree to which they restrict this outlet to marriage or allow it to occur before marriage as well. A few communities are tolerant enough also to permit homosexuality or masturbation as channels of sexual satisfaction, especially when opportunities for coitus are lacking (see pp. 578–579). No community allows untrammeled freedom for securing sexual gratification.

Another universal problem lies in maintaining an adequate feeling of self-esteem (i.e., sense of social acceptance). Self-esteem in some communities comes from being bold, dominant, and assertive. In other groups people are most highly regarded when they don't strive too ambitiously, or compete, boast, or seek power.

All cultures include means for providing adjustment by reducing anxiety. The sources of this tension vary. An Eskimo hunter is anxious about finding sufficient food, a Pakistan farmer worries about having enough water for his crop, the college student is concerned about grades, and the hospitalized patient about his health. Resources for reducing anxiety also differ. Security may be found in carrying amulets or lucky pieces, in dancing or parading for rain, in prayer, or in psychotherapy. In large-scale communities specialists —priests, psychiatrists, family counselors, or industrial relations experts— may be available to facilitate reduction of anxiety or to repair social relationships that promote frequent distress (F. Watson, 1956). It is not unusual for different groups in a community to pursue incompatible adjustive satisfactions.

Measuring the relative ability of different cultures to provide adjustment is more difficult than devising such ratings for adaptation. Wide fluctuation in the kinds and numbers of nonlethal tensions, the great variety of adjustive satisfactions, and the difficulty of recognizing whether or not they really work are some of the obstacles facing such a task.

STRESS INDUCTION

Some customs are carried out for the sake of the tension they create in the organism. To suggest this somewhat paradoxical form of adjustment, familiar to the reader of mystery stories, is different from saying that culture induces stress. Only undesirable stress is denoted by the latter proposition. Stress induction is the very opposite of adaptation and adjustment, though it does not deny the simultaneous operation of those processes. An objective view of any culture recognizes that it not only permits people to reduce lethal and nonlethal tensions but also provides sometimes quite unbearable distress from which the individual cannot readily escape. Even fulfilling such ordinary day-to-day goals as preparing lessons, digging ditches, tending an assembly belt, teaching classes of students who have other motives than learning, rearing children, and providing for a family, despite whatever satisfaction they give, also involves quite a bit of stress. There is no reason to suspect that conditions are otherwise in small-scale, exotic communities. Anthropologists, however, have often neglected the stressful functions of culture and unwittingly contributed to the myth of natural man popularized by Rousseau.[1]

[1] In 1762 Rousseau wrote: "Compare without partiality the state of the citizen with that of the savage, and trace out, if you can, how many inlets the former has opened to pain and death, besides those of his vices, his wants and his misfortunes. If you reflect on the mental afflictions that prey on us, the violent passions that waste

Sources of Stress

Four conditions of culture are common instigators of stress.

1. Inadequacy of Cultural Arrangements to Promote Adaptation and Adjustment. As already pointed out, no culture is perfectly adaptive or provides unmitigated satisfaction for all members of a community. Illness, accidents, smog, and war still exist despite the contributions of medical research and accident prevention, not to speak of powerful defensive weapons and diplomacy. Few communities are able to manage social relations well enough to avoid disturbing conflicts or costly breakdowns in collaboration. Many times a community simply does not know how to avoid certain sources of stress. The culture, then, is inadequate by virtue of human limitations or ignorance. Sometimes stress is the price paid for the sake of other rewards. The wrap-around windshield on recent models of American automobiles distorts vision, creates glare, and tires the driver—but it sells cars.

2. Unrealizable Goals. Where everybody seriously is expected to achieve outstanding success, high marks, perfect peaceableness without a trace of hostility, or unflinching bravery, some people are certain not to achieve the goal. They therefore feel distressed. When the community, in addition to demanding high achievements from everyone, makes it impossible for an unlimited number to reach the goal (perhaps because of the rule that only 10 percent of the class may receive A's while another 10 percent must receive D's or fail), then stress is further assured. One category of people may be favored above others for achieving success in some field. Middle-class American children are better prepared than lower-class children to succeed in school. The ostensibly democratic "social system does not provide all competitors with equal opportunities" (Hollingshead, 1949:452). It is not unlikely that a considerable measure of unrest, or stress, in the modern world derives from the assumption that there can be an indefinite increase in material abundance and in the standard of living. This is a comparative

---

and exhaust us, the excessive labour with which the poor are burdened, the still more dangerous indolence to which the wealthy give themselves up, so that the poor perish of want, and the rich of surfeit; if you reflect but a moment on the heterogeneous mixtures and pernicious seasonings of food; the corrupt state in which they are frequently eaten; on the adulteration of medicines, the wiles of those who sell them, the mistakes of those who administer them, and the poisonous vessels in which they are prepared; on the epidemics bred by foul air in consequence of great numbers of men being crowded together, or those which are caused by our delicate way of living, by our passing from our houses into the open air and back again, by the putting on or throwing off our clothes with too little care, and by all the precautions which sensuality has converted into necessary habits, and the neglect of which sometimes costs us our life, or health; if you take into account the conflagrations and earthquakes, which, devouring or overwhelming whole cities, destroy the inhabitants by thousands; in a word, if you add together all the dangers with which these causes are always threatening us, you will see how dearly nature makes us pay for the contempt with which we have treated her lessons" (Jean Jacques Rousseau, 1913:241–242).

newcomer among human ideas, one less than 200 years old (Vickers, 1956: 1113).

3. Postulated Terrors. Man has a fecund brain which permits him to create postulated sources of anxiety that are none the less vivid for their invisibility. The variety of such terrors is diverse, including gods of small-pox, deities associated with destruction, devils who rob souls and commit them to damnation, and ghosts eager to hasten the living toward an uncertain future. Neighbors are credited with witchcraft or other forms of malignancy or suspected, without sound evidence, of sedition and treachery. Beliefs about enemies in the community's midst tend to be especially abundant when the group is beset by other kinds of difficulties or problems. It is characteristic of such invented terrors that relatively little attention or interest is paid to their empirical verification.

4. Opposition in Ideas and Social Expectations. Man's fertile brain also allows him to invent ideas and values which come into opposition with traditional beliefs still endorsed by contemporaries. The introduction of heresies or radical new philosophies, while it contributes to the growth of knowledge, also complicates the job of living together harmoniously (see pp. 467–470).

Functions of Stress

The possibly adaptive uses of the socially standardized feeling of stress are not to be overlooked. Punishment and the threat of punishment are used universally in social life to maintain order and derivative satisfactions, including life itself. Children are socialized into the community's culture partly through the satisfaction furnished by learning but also by threat and punishment. Every known culture seems to make some use of undesirable stress in order to maintain the dependability of social relations and to sustain faith in values that bind men in solidarity (see pp. 496–499). All stress induction, however, cannot be explained in these terms.

GRATIFYING FOR WHOM?

Most western readers endorse a philosophy of maximizing adaptation and adjustment and reducing stress to a minimum. This value should not be projected ethnocentrically on other people. It is not even always acted upon in the western world. During time of war, adjustment in many areas of life is deliberately sacrificed for the sake of group adaptation. Of course, strenuous propaganda and even legislation are required to induce people to make the sacrifices. Other communities reveal no such consistent effort to maximize adjustive gratifications. For one thing, a small-scale community hardly can afford to support specialists who work to devise softer beds, more comfortable chairs, fresh sources of amusement, and new taste sensations.

Until recently many of the world's communities hardly realized that culture could be changed through deliberately looking for new adaptive or adjustive elements.

Customs may, for a time at least, provide adaptive and adjustive rewards for only a part of the community while constituting sources of stress for some other, even larger, section of the population. For example, in parts of former British India the complex of owning large holdings of land and exercising power over many tenant farmers was highly gratifying—to landlords. Land helped a landowner to secure other forms of wealth. The customs associated with being a landlord were not adjustive for the poorer peasant but rather were stressful. The latter dared not resist the landholding squire, even when the landlord sought more land at the peasant's expense. " 'If he attempted to do so, his cattle would be driven, his women folk carried off, himself prosecuted before an honorary magistrate on a charge of cattle theft, and in a short time he would be glad to hand over his land and secure protection on any terms' " (Darling, 1947:99). Segregation of Negroes in parts of the United States was similarly adjustive for one set of people but stressful for another. Bitter conflict may ensue when, through legislation, civil disturbance, or revolution, attempts are made by the injured parties to get rid of obnoxious culture patterns.

13.

Cultural Persistence and Change

EVERY culture is always changing even while, in whole or part, it persists as a recognizable entity over long periods of time. Sometimes change is slow, many elements remaining relatively unaltered from one period to another. More often change merely appears slow (or even nonexistent) to an alien observer whose own way of life has undergone rapid change. But even in the rapidly changing ways of life of Europe and America certain traits, despite modification, have remained recognizable for millennia.

Neither persistence nor change is a completely random process. Both are orderly events with whose dynamics students of social behavior are becoming increasingly better acquainted. It is the object of this and the next four chapters to outline the anthropologist's understanding of cultural persistence and change.

PERSISTENCE

The term "persistence" applied to a cultural process can be misleading if by it the reader understands that some elements of culture remain free from change. Culture in all its traits and aspects involves constant change. Persistence implies a kind of change that allows certain elements to be recognized sometimes for very long periods of time.

Cultural persistence is mainly of two kinds: general and sectional. In a culture which is characterized by very slow and gradual change in nearly all its areas and in which the members of the community seem intent on limiting or resisting change in a wide area of life, general persistence is operative. The Old Order Amish of Pennsylvania reveal relatively general persistence in their way of life (Kollmorgen, 1942). Convinced that God's people do not conform to the world, Amish men and women wear a traditional garb and coiffure that they refuse to alter. Hooks and eyes substitute for buttons and men's coats have no lapels. Water on farms is provided through wind power. Automobiles, bicycles, telephones, radios, and musical instruments have no place in the community. Customs of mutual aid allow the Amish to care for their poor. Capital is invested within the community at low rates of interest. Pacifism is another Amish value that has persisted over a long time. Children are deliberately reared to perpetuate traditional forms of behavior and to avoid radical change. The people regard consolidated schools as a danger. Education through high school or college is perceived as a threat to the old order that these Amish cherish. To maintain general persistence "the lives of the Old Order Amish are thoroughly regimented by a multiplicity of church regulations and discipline. Some of these regulations are giving rise to increasing irritation and dissatisfaction" (*ibid.*, p. 12). Indications are plain, however, that the conservative Amish have not resisted all change. They have accepted new

Bear Ceremonialism, Still Practiced by the Japanese Ainu, Is an Old Trait in Circumpolar Culture (*Life* photo by Alfred Eisenstaedt [c] 1946 Time Inc.).

crops, like tobacco and tomatoes, and dairying has increased. Tractors have already been adopted, and the ban on automobiles and telephones is one of the regulations promoting dissension. On the whole, however, conservatism is certainly a keynote of this way of life. The people are having trouble maintaining their unique existence. One reason is that a rural way of life remains essential if the Amish are to survive as a culturally distinct group. But land is limited. Holdings cannot be expanded as new farmland becomes increasingly difficult to find. Under such circumstances "resistance to urban opportunities may further weaken. Once factory and urban jobs are accepted the peculiar and rural ways of life are seriously threatened" (*ibid.*, p. 104).

A high degree of general persistence is also manifested by the Fulniô tribe of Indians who live in the scrub forest of northeastern Brazil. Emphasis is put on speaking the native language in preference to Portuguese. Strangers are kept out of the territory, and if an Indian of another tribe marries into the Fulniô community he is put under restrictions. These people regard themselves as intrinsically superior to all neighboring tribes, an ethnocentric belief that helps to conserve the culture. Like the Amish, they are highly self-conscious about preserving aboriginal customs. Certain matters are secret and dare not be revealed to Neo-Brazilians for fear of death. A three-month ceremonial cycle attended by every adult helps to perpetuate many aspects of tradition. The Fulniô have consistently refused to recognize the authority of the Brazilian government. They have even changed their territory in order to avoid official harassment (Hohenthal and McCorkle, 1955).

Sectional persistence means the perpetuation of select features of culture. These are the "hard" parts of the way of life that resist drastic change (Bartlett, 1946). Sectional persistence is illustrated by the reluctance of manual workers to enter nonmanual occupations after the Russian Revolution (Feldmesser, 1953), the continued use of dogs for transportation among American Plains Indians even after acquisition of the horse (Roe, 1955:20–22, 62), and maintenance of the village ground plan, with separate quarters for different castes, in some industrial cities of India (G. Murphy, 1953:38). In 1941 only three bears were killed by the Ojibwa Indians of the Lac Court Oreilles Reservation in Wisconsin, but the hunters still directed rituals of respect to the animals. Bear ceremonialism is an old trait in those cultures of Asia and North America that girdle the polar region (Casagrande, 1952; Hallowell, 1926). The reluctance of people in the United States to modify the Constitution and their attempts to preserve a large measure of state and national sovereignty also exemplify sectional persistence. Language is one of the most conservative areas of any culture and so are legal norms.

Certain elements in Euroamerican culture have had extraordinary longevity. These include phonetic writing, heavy drinking in boisterous male company, gladiator sports and tournaments (football games are in the tradition of Roman gladiator contests), sea raiding (the Greek and Viking pirates are reflected in modern military submarines), and epic poetry (Wissler, 1923:232–237). Note how persistence resides in the way a basic form of an element or complex is preserved. At the same time there have been extensive accretions and alterations of detail. The phonetic alphabet has remained basically the same since its invention a thousand years or so before the Christian era. But the basic form has been adapted to many different languages. Type designers have drastically altered the shapes of the signs. So, too, with the masked Kachina dancers in Pueblo ceremonialism; the underlying pattern has persisted along with great variation in detail (F. Anderson, 1955).

An examination of similarities in three complexes of culture—canoe building, house building, and tattooing—between five Polynesian communities shows that fundamentally the same techniques have been conserved for, probably, hundreds of years. However, a wide range of variation exists in the forms of the objects, in decoration, and in tattoo designs. The rank of

Certain Aspects of Euroamerican Culture, Like Heavy Drinking in Boisterous Male Company, Have Had Extraordinary Longevity (courtesy, British Information Services).

the craftsmen carrying out a particular technique and of the priests who collaborate in the activities also varies from one community to another (Mead, 1928b).

Partial (i.e., token) persistence represents a special type of sectional conservatism. It refers to the vestigial continuity of some element in culture. Perhaps the custom is carried out with reduced frequency or only under restricted circumstances. An immigrant in the United States may revert to traditional dishes only at Christmas and Easter. Token persistence is also illustrated in the band that surrounds a man's hat. This has been regarded as a vestigial turban (Bell, 1949:42–43). In the same way decorative living-room mantels conservatively recall more utilitarian fireplaces, while the arrow pointing to an exit derives from the projectile point (Borges, 1955). South Yorkshire miners used to refuse to go to work if a woman crossed the pit yard while they waited to descend into the mine. Today this belief survives in the feeling that it is unlucky to meet a woman while on the way to the pit (Dennis, Henriques, and Slaughter, 1956:219–220). Folklorists are much interested in customs that represent the attenuated persistence of what were once more important elements of culture. Customs like dancing around the Maypole, coloring eggs at Easter, or the use of mistletoe (formerly the all-healing plant) persist with only attenuated meaning or restricted use. Hence they are sometimes referred to as "survivals," connoting that they possess relatively thin significance (Frazer, 1922:Chap. 65; Marett, 1920:109–112).

General and sectional persistence are different in degree, not in kind. Whether a particular culture is seen as more or less persistent depends partly on the position of an outside observer and the degree of change to which he is accustomed. Members of a community may not agree with an anthropologist whose culture is undergoing rapid change and who perceives extreme conservatism in the culture he is studying (Lévi-Strauss, 1952:26).

Tarriance

Tarriance denotes the persistence of cultural elements in association with geographical isolation (i.e., geographical marginality). The marginal cultures of extreme southerly South American Indians (Yahgan, Ona, Tehuelche, and others) have been regarded as retaining numerous old elements and complexes. These include tattooing by drawing a needle and thread under the skin; fire making with stones; the complex of scratching-stick, drinking-tube, hoof rattle, and ashes used in the girl's puberty observance; making water boil with the aid of preheated stones; cooking in an earth oven; and, perhaps, occasional marriage of a woman to two or more men simultaneously (polyandry). The assumption is not that the entire way of life of these marginal peoples persisted. The Indians certainly must have accommodated themselves to new environmental conditions when they reached their present habitats. The principal evidence that these particular elements have been retained for a long time lies in the recurrence of the same traits in other refuge areas of North and South America and Asia. For example, they recur in the Arctic, which has been called "a marginal area culturally as well as geographically, a refuge area where ancient culture patterns have persisted long after they have been discontinued elsewhere" (Collins, 1954:106). The number and specificity of the resemblances are quite impressive.

Three criteria are useful for ascertaining tarriance (Cooper, 1941:63–65).

1. When a cultural element (e.g., use of alcoholic beverages) is widespread among nonmarginal people but consistently absent from contemporary marginal cultures, then probably it was not archaic.

2. When a cultural element (e.g., abandonment, or killing, of the aged and sick) is consistently found among present-day marginals, it probably also was present in archaic cultures.

3. When an element (e.g., occasional polyandry) is irregularly found among present-day marginals but cannot clearly be established as an innovation recently derived from some other, nearby culture, it probably also was present irregularly in archaic times.

Other Conditions Favoring Persistence

Apart from tarriance, the persistence of culture is basically a function of people's reluctance to change or their lack of exposure to conditions that invite major change. Persistence also occurs when existing arrangements serve adaptation and adjustment better than would available substitutes. British miners remain in mining, and therefore contribute to the persistence of that trait, because unskilled jobs are limited and the pay is high enough for the standard of living which miners expect (Dennis, Henriques, and Slaughter, 1956). Many Haitian peasants did not perceive in Catholicism a full, satisfactory substitute for *vodun* ceremonies. Left to themselves they would have preferred to follow both ritual systems rather than to drop the latter in order to be admitted officially to the former (A. Métraux, 1953).

Seven somewhat more specific, but overlapping, factors that underlie persistence will be mentioned.

1. *Cost in time or energy is involved in learning new behaviors.* People do not possess unlimited time. Energy available for shifting from one form of behavior to another is also limited. Motivation must be high for people to learn complicated new habits, or else substantial, tangible rewards need to be assured. The latter was the case whenever the steel ax was introduced to stone-tool-using people. We guess, however, that sitting on a chair instead of on the ground rarely promises such tangible rewards. Persistence, therefore, is favored whenever people refuse to spend their limited energy and time on learning new routines. The lack of available energy encourages persistence not only on the level of individual behavior but on the community level as well. A community controlling little wind, water, or steam power will have little time to spare for new learning. People remain too busy making a living.

2. *A threat is perceived in relinquishing an element of culture.* After the advent of the horse the American Plains Indians continued to pack goods on dogs or dog-drawn travois for transportation. Apparently they did

so in order to preserve horses for more valuable work in hunting (Roe, 1955:20–22, 62). In modern times the buildings trades prefer to build traditional houses requiring 2500 and more hours to construct. A serious threat is perceived in mass-produced, prefabricated housing which could dispense with many construction specialists. Yet far cheaper prefabricated houses have been designed, one of which could be constructed in 405 factory hours and set up in another 1090 hours (*Illustrated London News*, Nov. 12, 1949, p. 740).

Persistence and Change in Attawapiskat, Ontario, Are Shown in the Conical Dwelling Persisting with Modifications from Aboriginal Times While Indians Are Learning to Build Multiroom Modern Houses.

Political parties and leaders remain firmly opposed to simplifying the fragmented court system in the United States. The purpose of such simplification would be to reduce the number of officials. But the effect, where those officials are appointed, would be to limit the amount of patronage that could be bestowed (Mayers, 1955:69). The Mamluk dynasty of Egypt, which ruled until the sixteenth century, when the Ottoman Turks took over, was slow to adopt firearms. One reason lay in the pride which the military elite took in the handling of traditional weapons like the lance and sword (*London Times Literary Supplement*, Sept. 7, 1956, p. 528). The introduction of automatic machinery has aroused apprehension in some workers and leaders of organized labor. Generally, the more insecure a worker feels in his job the more he is inclined to insist on traditional modes of procedure. Changes, in other words, threaten to bring risk and insecurity (Blau, 1955:197).

The existing railroad system in America represents an investment of about $100 billion in standardized equipment. A 150-mile-an-hour mono-railway that could cross an abyss on a steel cable offers advantages in speed and efficiency unmatched in existing railroads, but "would greatly disrupt the going system" (Barber, 1952:214). Much invested capital would become useless. Hence, while marked changes have appeared in railroad equipment, the basic forms of rail transport remain basically unaltered.

Even in small-scale, exotic communities a threat to vested interests may favor persistence. One of the factors permitting rapid change in Manus, an island off the coast of New Guinea, between 1928 and 1953 was the Second World War, which isolated young men away from the village (Mead, 1956a:221–230). Under ordinary circumstances the youths gradually would have become active participants in the native economic system. Their vested interest in the system would have made it hardly amenable to radical change. But the war prevented their induction into adult roles. Instead the young men were exposed to a new way of life in which they learned much. It is not surprising that when they returned to the villages and sought to introduce changes in the traditional culture they had to overcome opposition from the still entrenched older men.

3. *Fear of linked changes may favor persistence.* Change ramifies, one novelty bringing other innovations in its wake (see Chapter 16). People may not mind a particular change as much as the linked changes which they believe will follow. The Old Order Amish do not object to all that is taught in higher education. They fear mainly the new attitudes which children will learn in high school and beyond, attitudes that might seriously disrupt their peculiar way of life. A devout Muslim in Pakistan does not object to the profession of nursing but he hardly is willing that his daughter should leave off the veil, appear in public, and minister to unrelated males. Hence the slow growth of the nursing profession in that country. The fact that the linked change may be improbable does not make a person's fear less real.

4. *An idea of necessity may be attached to a traditional element.* Persistence is favored whenever, in the face of available substitutes, one form of behavior or artifact alone is regarded as proper. Such an attitude, being itself socially standardized, is not encountered with equal frequency in all communities. Some people are more magical than others (see pp. 684–688). Many Muslims in Pakistan are repelled by the thought of having their wives and daughters mingle freely and publicly with fellow citizens of both sexes. Seclusion of women (i.e., purdah) is regarded as most strongly necessary. Hindus visiting Europe in the nineteenth century sometimes

insisted on preserving as meticulously as possible many traditional arrangements. Often their insistence on seclusion of women or special procedures in cooking involved them and their hosts in great expense and inconvenience. Magical attachment to existing procedures is by no means unknown in modern America. For instance, a strong sense of necessity is felt toward representative government, state sovereignty, and belief in God.

5. *Strong emotional attachment to some part of tradition may be felt.* Attachment to an element of culture may not be so strong that it is regarded as absolutely necessary. The custom may be retained mainly out of sentimental regard. Immigrants nostalgically retain knickknacks, dishes, and traditional garments or dances from the old country.

6. *An element may be involved strongly with other elements in culture.* The value which Americans place on material rewards is not self-consciously perpetuated. Maximizing material satisfaction, however, is implicit in education and in much of the advertising that the citizen daily encounters. To value success measured in material terms is a lesson the American child learns from an early age. The learning is reinforced consistently in later life. Patriotic rituals keep alive certain positive images of Washington, Lincoln, and other historic figures. Hindus believe that the Absolute can be known only through meditation. This definition of the Absolute contributes to perpetuating in Indian culture both the value of and practice of contemplation or meditation. In the same way education, newspapers, and diplomacy in modern nations assume that war constitutes a practical means of solving certain problems of international relations. By this attitude war is perpetuated as an element in culture. Although robbery is not exactly condoned in Tibet, a number of elements in culture tend to perpetuate it. For example, theft from a member of the out-group is not regarded as a great wrong. Furthermore, there are relatively few ways of acquiring wealth with which to reëstablish oneself in the pastoral economy after having given away one's wealth in ritual or to a monastery. Giving for these purposes is so highly meritorious that it readily offsets whatever degree of disapproval is felt for stealing from a stranger. In addition, to bestow wealth for the sake of religion is itself an act of atonement in which the guilt of theft can be erased. Hence, there are many factors in Tibetan culture that make for the persistence of robbery (Li An-Che, 1949:28).

7. *Early learning favors retention.* Behavior learned in infancy or early childhood, it has been suggested, tends to be most resistant to change (Bruner, 1956:194). An examination of the culture of the modern Mandan-Hidatsa Indians reveals that elements showing greatest persistence (like kinship behavior or conceptions of roles and values) were learned early. The primary agents of socialization were members of the child's own

kinship group. Ceremonial activities, on the other hand, which no longer exist, were learned quite late in life.

It should be clear that for cultural elements to persist they need not lack stress-inducing properties. The separation of the executive and legislative aspects of government in the United States continues despite the fact that administration practically ceases on important issues when the President and Congress possess different polit (Osburn, 1950:149–150).

SCOPE OF CHANGE

A way of life may alter in several ways. There may be addition of new elements or the discarding of traits from culture. Existing elements may be modified or their performance and use may vary quantitatively, that is, in frequency. With respect to change in social relations two kinds of innovation have been distinguished: change in the form of organization (i.e., structural change) and change in the content of existing relationships that in no way alters the organizational framework. The second is illustrated when a Mandan-Hidatsa Indian man shows respect to his mother-in-law by offering her not the traditional enemy scalp and ammunition war bonnet purchased from a mail-order house. The same relationship, however, remains as part of the social structure. Structural change among these people occurred when they shifted from densely and locally groups (villages) to localities marked by widely dispersed households (Bruner, 1955:846). The concept of social structure is taken up again on p. 341.

Persistence in culture basically is related to its open and its people's failure to perceive innovation as rewarding. Closure, on the other hand, is rooted in largeness of scale. It implies that people are rewarded for doing things in different ways or for adopting new styles of behavior and new artifacts. Those times when a community is a window on the world are most widely open reveal the most intense change. Among such periods were the Elizabethan Age in England; the European Renaissance; the Mauryan Empire of India, which coexisted with Alexander's invasion (326 B.C.); and nineteenth-century China, when that country came up against the expanding nations of the West.

Degree of Change

Culture change may manifest itself with various degrees of thoroughness. At one extreme stands revolution, "a change suddenly precipitated with more or less violence, affecting a considerable total portion of a culture" (Kroeber, 1948:408). At the other extreme is a change in the style of something. (A civil war which is mainly a scramble between rivals for political power is not a revolution in the cultural sense.)

Revolutions may be violent or peaceful. The violent kind, in which the leaders use force to impose far-flung innovations in technology, social organization, and ideas, often ends by being considerably less extreme than its original blueprint. Elements adopted in the heat of the revolt later are abandoned. This happened to the new calendar after the French Revolution, although the simultaneously innovated metric system has survived to the present. The Russians discontinued free divorce and abortion soon after the Bolshevik Revolution. Cultural continuity lasting through revolutions may be understood by recalling three things: (1) Revolutions are made by men reared in a specific cultural tradition. Their very program and ambitions are limited by their previous experience. (2) If a violent revolution succeeds, the leaders try as soon as possible to reëstablish government which curtails further radical innovation. All governments are alike in pursuing relative stability and for that reason "stand at the opposite pole of thought and action to revolution: once the revolution has obtained its goal and enthroned itself in the seats of authority . . . a halt has to be called to further revolutionary change" (Carr, 1955:697). If government secures stability, another feature making for continuity appears. (3) The administration resumes its foreign relations, diplomatic and commercial. Such intercourse depends closely on the geographical location and resources of the country. These conditions of the cultural field are highly constant and remain unaffected by revolution. It is in foreign relations "that continuity with the policy of previous governments is most rapid and conspicuously asserted."

Nonviolent revolutions include the food-producing revolution ushered in some 10,000 years ago with the discovery of agriculture and animal husbandry, the seventeenth-century switch to use of coal and steam for manufacturing, and the less dramatic economic revolution in twentieth-century Great Britain.

The food-producing revolution that took place in Southwest Asia changed mobile hunters into sedentary farmers who invented kingship, priestcraft, metallurgy, and empires and then entered a period of urbanization (see pp. 697–700 et seq.).

The Industrial Revolution with its mass production of goods meant additional material possessions for more people, and more wealth which could be spared for scientific and other research. From research new ideas emerged to transform additional vast sectors of life. Internationally the revolution helped to weaken the idea of national sovereignty and inaugurated a still not fully accepted era of international political organization.

The British economic revolution, like the others, had spread from its original home. In some countries the welfare state is hailed; in others it is condemned as "creeping socialism." In Great Britain the revolution brought about a profound redistribution of wealth: three-quarters of the nation's households in 1954 earned from 2 to 5 times what they had earned 15 years previously and paid the least proportion of taxes. One-quarter of the households, however, had been forced to spend less and to pay a larger share of taxes. While the invention of agriculture or steam-powered machinery had mightily affected the content of culture, the British Socialists provoked mainly quantitative variation in the way certain people participated in certain areas of culture. For the three-quarters of the population whose economic position improved, more travel, smoking, radio listening, television viewing, entertainment, use of cosmetics, and household equipment have become available. They are able to make greater use of educational and health services than previously. The richer quarter, by being forced to reduce spending for travel and luxuries, also altered its way of life, abandoning large homes, big corps of servants, and other patterns of conspicuous consumption. The fact that the British revolution came into existence through legislature while the other two appeared less deliberately has no particular significance (Hutton, 1954).

Let us consider less thorough changes. A style is a briefly enduring modification in a single cultural trait. By this definition style becomes recognizable only after it changes. Modification may involve alteration in the size of the parts belonging to the trait, in the material out of which the trait is constituted, or in the number of parts. It may involve a change in the rate at which certain words are used from one period of time to another. Variations in the length of women's dresses, or the height of the waistline, are examples of style changes. Styles in what people wear occur in a community with ranked social classes (see pp. 448–450) and function not only to distinguish one class from another but also to demarcate one period of time from another (Simmel, 1957).

Style also characterizes academic disciplines, especially those in which research is communicated primarily verbally rather than mathematically or through formulas. Preferences arise for certain words and phrases. These for a time give the impression of carrying greater precision, but eventually their freshness becomes exhausted. Then they are abandoned in favor of other terms. "Function," "model," and "structure" are words currently enjoying a considerable vogue in sociology and anthropology. "Dynamic" and "integrated" were more fashionable recently than they are today.

Exactly how long an innovation must endure to be called a style is difficult to specify. Some styles are cyclical. Beards appear, become unfashionable, and then reappear; dresses lengthen, shorten, and lengthen again. Another characteristic of style lies in the fact that usually it is of small practical significance. Wearing last year's dress may seriously affect a woman's prestige, and dressmakers survive through the grace of fashion, but such changes do not involve drastic, concomitant modifications in other areas of culture.

Distinct from style is the long-term trend. The trend toward tailored clothing has been apparent for the past several hundred years. For a long time the world has been turning to maize and wheat at the expense of millet. The trend from food gathering (hunting and fishing) to food production (agriculture and pastoralism) started about 10,000 years ago and still has not reached some of the world's people. Another trend has been the substitution of inanimate, mechanical energy for human and other forms of animal energy (Sorre, 1948:385; 1951:274). Trends may be localized rather than worldwide. In England there has been a long-term trend away from drinking in pubs and bars to home drinking (Mass Observation, 1943:74–77, 215–219).

Cultural Drift

Despite the persistence of culture, manifested, for example, when the child learns to wash, eat, speak, spell, and relate himself to his parents and teachers in traditional ways, many small variations always creep into the way in which each generation executes its social heritage. Sometimes these minor variations in culture are dependent on other changes in a way of life. Parent-child relations altered with the introduction of television into the home. But all such small changes are not products of synchronization (see pp. 233–246).

The process whereby minor variations arise, accumulate, and spread in society is called, very aptly, cultural drift (Herskovits, 1948:Chap. 48). The modifications appear simply as alternative ways of pronouncing a word, signing a letter, wearing a hat, designing a book, or expressing pleasure and disgust. Sometimes the changes will be adopted widely in a community, becoming universal culture patterns. A large number of such small changes universally adopted in time add up to a highly significant transformation of culture. Often, though, minor variations remain restricted to a portion of the community. They occur only in a particular family, neighborhood, or parts of a tribal area. In time they disappear without leaving a trace. Drift in culture can be broken down into a number of component processes like origination, diffusion, and reinterpretation. These will be examined in the following chapters.

14.

Origination

THE process by which new elements of culture are discovered or invented, as distinguished from their circulation within or between communities, will be called origination. In anthropological usage the transmission of elements through borrowing or learning is diffusion. Origination and diffusion together make up the two main processes of innovation, a word used in the most general sense to designate any process whatsoever whereby a new, socially standardized behavior or artifact comes into being in, circulates in, or is distributed between cultures.

A word about the nature of novelty. Newness cannot be defined absolutely. It resides in the degree to which a culture trait is different from any previous trait. A narrowly defined conception of novelty only succeeds in making innovation a very rare process, and man turns out to be very uncreative (Barnett, 1953:7–19). When mechanical pencils first appeared they were only relatively different from standard pencils; the thin-lead mechanical pencil represented a further degree of novelty. The pencil that writes with liquid graphite is another new trait. Compare such minor novelties with the startling distinction between food production and food gathering. In accordance with previous definitions it is assumed that novelties constitute part of culture when they are influenced by social conditions (pp. 12–14).

DISCOVERY AND INVENTION

It is sometimes useful to recognize discovery and invention as two distinct steps in origination.[1] A discovery represents an addition to knowledge, whereas an invention utilizes the new knowledge in some novel form. (It should be noted that these terms, like "innovation," "origination," and others to be introduced, may signify both processes and end products of processes. At present attention is focused primarily on process.)

A conjectural but helpful example of how a discovery led to invention involves the origination of pottery. Perhaps once a man found that footprints in clay hardened as the earth dried under the heat of the sun.

[1] The following distinction follows Linton, 1936:Chap. 18.

Perhaps spatters of mud dried hard on his bare skin, or he may have noticed how fire had hardened the clay of the hearth site. The knowledge that heat converts plastic, wet clay into a substance that is hard and relatively unaffected by water probably was discovered several times in culture history (Childe, 1944:31). Application of the knowledge to the manufacture of pottery vessels did not follow in a single step. Ceramics involved many cumulative inventions, such as means of preparing clay, building up vessels, drying them, and, finally, firing the pottery in a kiln that would drive out any moisture still in the clay. Another invention (cited as a warning that this process is not limited to technical processes or artifacts) followed the discovery that dreams are not haphazard but are related dynamically to the dreamer's problems (Freud, 1913:Chap. 2). In 1895, when Sigmund Freud was treating Irma psychoanalytically, he dreamed of meeting her at a party. There he reproached her for not getting well but then learned that she was suffering from an infection. In the dream her illness was attributed to a careless injection by Freud's colleague, Otto. Puzzled that the dream should have come precisely at a time when he felt depressed about his inability to cure Irma of certain somatic difficulties, Freud proceeded to analyze what he had dreamed. The meaning of the dream flashed on him. It fulfilled several wishes of the dreamer. For instance, it freed him of responsibility for Irma's condition by referring her illness to an infection brought on by the carelessness of Otto, a man whose reproaches Freud had come to fear. Similar successful dream interpretations supported Freud's conclusion that dreams fulfill wishes. Later he applied this discovery in treatment. Analysis of a patient's dreams to learn the dreamer's often unconscious desires, which, in turn, are related to his illness, remains a part of the psychoanalytic method.

Discoveries do not always represent sudden flashes of insight. Some, like Einstein's theory of relativity, on which the harnessing of atomic energy is based, involved long thought, extensive mathematical calculation, and experimentation. Even after a long period of growth discoveries may contain contradictory features (as did the pre-Newtonian theory of gravitation). Only intensive reanalysis and reorganization of the facts will enable a subsequent investigator, like Isaac Newton, to clear up puzzling features and inconsistencies. Even when discoveries occur as flashes of insight, careful reasoning and testing may be required to carry the discovery over into some useful application. Complex inventions, like deriving energy from the nucleus of the atom, represent not one but hundreds of discoveries, although one new bit of knowledge (in this case the identity of energy and matter) may have been of major significance. Not infrequently originations embody rediscovered knowledge. Even the invention may have been made before, independently. Reserpine, a drug recently discovered to be useful for treating mental illness, was in use long ago. Healers in southern Asia (where among other names it is known as Asrol) had long ago discovered its soothing properties. More will be said about parallel invention later (pp. 206–208).

Abundant experience shows that invention need not keep pace with discovery. Around the middle of the nineteenth century Gregor Mendel discovered that inheritance was due to genes (see pp. 823, 864). This knowledge was not applied to plant and animal breeding until the early twentieth century. DDT had been discovered in 1874 but was not utilized as an insecticide until 1939 (Kluckhohn, 1949a:57). Modern architects possess skill sufficient to adapt the design of buildings to their intended use. Their knowledge often cannot be applied because the owners demand Colonial and other traditional designs for schools and commercial buildings.

Some Difficulties

The distinction between discovery and invention seems to be neat and sharp. Intensive use, however, brings out certain difficulties in distinguishing one process from the other. In some sciences, like astronomy, little practical use may exist for knowledge. Yet are not discoveries applied when they replace previous theories? When a discovery upsets an earlier theory and lands in the textbooks, is it an invention or still only a discovery? Making the difference between a discovery and an invention rest on an increasing degree of purposefulness manifestly offers no solution. Not in an era when discovery is purposefully pursued in university and government laboratories (Dixon, 1928:34).

Another difficulty arises in deciding what is the knowledge that constitutes a discovery. Disciplines which study nature not only make and apply discoveries but also devise definitions, create concepts, and reorganize existing knowledge. Are new definitions, fresh concepts, and a new way of ordering familiar facts discoveries? A new definition hardly contributes to knowledge the way discovery of a hitherto unknown fossil or chemical element does. What about a hypothesis which connects two or more known facts? Hypotheses stimulate the search for new knowledge. But a hypothesis can also be proved false. Can it, therefore, be considered a discovery? For some purposes the distinction between discovery and invention may be fruitful. Often it will be satisfactory to use the more general term "origination" for any process by which an element of culture comes into being.

CLASSIFYING ORIGINATIONS

Originations occur in all areas of life and in all societies. As already suggested, the process may be spontaneous or deliberately fostered. The originations themselves may be more or less fundamental. They may make little difference in, or may revolutionize the rest of, a cultural system. These points will be developed further in this section. Throughout the discussion the reader is urged to bear in mind that originations sometimes run counter to the normative expectations of a community. Of course, widespread acceptance of an initially disapproved trait also may take place.

Universality

In popular usage discovery and invention are often restricted to scientific research or to the realm of technology. It is less common to talk of originations in social organization, language, ritual, disposal of the dead, or the realm of ideas. We emphasize that origination occurs not only in all cultures but in all contexts of life. Restricting origination to gadgets and technical processes distorts the distribution of human creativity and makes some groups of people more ingenious than others. Only propaganda is served by such a restrictive approach (Barnett, 1953:19). Unemployment insurance, lend-lease, zoning, coöperatives, collective bargaining, and workmen's compensation schemes were all inventions. It has been suggested that social inventions of this type are especially frequent in a democracy. A democratic system of government makes it readily possible for people to insist that solutions be found for problems like unemployment or industrial accidents. Effective pressure can be put on administrators to cope with these and other widespread difficulties. Hence origination is encouraged (Dahl and Lindblom, 1953:7). The heightened pace of social originations in the modern world stems, too, from the great increase in social interdependence stimulated by the Industrial Revolution. In order to maintain a constant rate of production and distribution of goods in a closely knit economy, and to reduce conflicts that threaten those interlocking relationships, social originations like collective bargaining, workmen's compensation, and others have occurred. Their general function is adjustive, namely, to maintain a relatively high level of satisfaction that will motivate people to continue working together.

The circumstances stimulating particular social inventions in small-scale, exotic communities are often unknown. One case for which information is available concerns a bank introduced among a people who had only recently become familiar with money (Mead, 1956a:299–301). Borrowing of money became a problem for the people of New Peri, a village on the coast of Manus, which is an island off New Guinea. Apparently the Manus, unfamiliar with handling money, found it difficult to refuse one another's requests for loans. Granting such requests, however, might leave a person short of ready cash. So the villagers created an informal bank by depositing funds with the most trusted man. The banker received no remuneration for his task. He also came to find his role highly inconvenient.

Sometimes people drew money out of the bank and returned it twice in one day. Some people demanded to see their money periodically. The banker complained that he could never go anywhere because he had to remain at home guarding people's money and showing it on request.

From India comes a revealing example showing one way in which deities originate. The anthropologist inquired in dozens of houses seeking to learn the identity of the goddess Naurtha. Those people willing to risk an identification gave contradictory answers but tended to identify the goddess with other, more widely popular, female deities. No one asked could give the explanation that seemed to be obvious from a linguistic analysis of the word. Naurtha in the local dialect is *nava ratra*, meaning "nine nights," the Sanskrit name of a festival that these people celebrated. Apparently what happened was that over a long time the original meaning of *nava ratra* had been forgotten. The word came to be redefined and a local goddess was born (Marriott, 1955:201).

Deliberate and Spontaneous Origination

Western countries have made research a highly specialized part of life. Certain industries maintain research laboratories, as does the federal government, which also offers research contracts to universities. University faculties also pursue independent studies in the sciences and humanities. A distinctive American development has been the rise of private organizations like the Ford, Rockefeller, and Commonwealth foundations, which finance research without expecting to profit from knowledge that might be forthcoming. The foundations often suggest topics for research. In 1955 the Fund for the Advancement of Education (Ford Foundation) offered financial encouragement to educationalists willing to look for new and more efficient means of teaching college students. Foundations may be set up to support only certain kinds of research. The Carnegie Endowment for International Peace has the abolition of war as its general goal while the Wenner-Gren Foundation is devoted to anthropological studies. Fear has recently been expressed that some foundations, by the direction which they give to research, possess power to shape American culture great enough to challenge the power of the government (Reece, 1954).

Such purposeful organization for discovery and invention remains unthinkable for many communities (Linton, 1936:307–312). Formal research in western culture is designed to reward the originators through salaries, grants-in-aid, royalties, higher profits, or increased power. In small-scale communities where occupational specialization is absent and production is for use, not for trade, these advantages are meaningless. Even prestige may not be bestowed on the man who originates something. Under such circumstances the rate of origination is low. The situation alters if the community discovers some inadequately met need or encounters radical opposition of ideas (see pp. 470–471). Rare as such a case may be under normal conditions, it frequently occurs when the society comes to include alien people to whom new adjustments are required, when migration carries a community into a new environment, or if population increases. Invention will be encouraged under such conditions unless, of course, ready-made, acceptable solutions to the newly created problems can be borrowed from another culture. Note what happened to the Maori after they left their tropical Pacific island homeland and migrated to New Zealand (Birket-Smith, 1946:48; Weckler, 1943:37). They had been accustomed to make bark-cloth clothing by beating the fibers of the paper mulberry tree. This plant did not grow in the new environment. The Maori tried to work with the bark of other trees, but research showed that these would not serve the same purpose. Finally, they discovered that New Zealand flax, while it could not be fabricated into cloth by beating, possessed fibers suitable for weaving. In that way the bark-cloth garments found elsewhere in Polynesia were replaced by woven clothing in New Zealand.

Basic and Secondary Originations

Sometimes a discovery or its application opens up new and vast potentialities for change and becomes the foundation for a large number of other innovations which "improve," or secondarily elaborate, the origination. This is a basic origination. Agriculture, pottery making, metallurgy, the steam engine, the internal-combustion engine, open-hearth steel furnace, dynamo, wireless, and atomic energy were basic originations in culture history. New crops, new devices making engines more efficient, automatic controls, and devices which insured smoother operation were secondary originations. Basic originations are relatively rare, often revolutionary, and sometimes troublesome for they render much previously accumulated capital obsolescent and require workers to learn new skills. It has even been suggested that in America this troublesomeness is responsible for turning the attention of researchers toward new devices which will merely provide more beauty or a larger measure of convenience rather than constitute radical innovations. Basic originations offer man greatly enhanced control over nature. They are developmental (see pp. 273–274).

Secondary origination introduces modifications in an existing process, form of organization, or artifact. It may also constitute a reorganization and clarification of some earlier, basic ideological discovery. Hand and dial telephones are examples of secondary originations which modified the basic process of telephony. Most of the patents granted annually by the United States Patent Office protect secondary elaborations. Basic originations are even more uncommon in the social area of culture and in the realm of ideas. New story plots are rare while new twists to hackneyed plots are common. Original philosophies appear very occasionally, and science rarely hits upon fundamentally original conceptions.

Integration of Originations

Originations in culture, whether fundamental or secondary, may be integrated closely or scarcely at all with other elements in a way of life. Chlorophyll chewing gum, quiz programs, and filter-tip cigarettes add pleasure to living. Their appearance failed to revolutionize culture and their disappearance would likewise not be accompanied by far-reaching repercussions (Lévi-Strauss, 1952:44). The automobile or steam power on the other hand could not be removed without a fundamental reorganization of the way of life.

CULTURAL BACKGROUND OF ORIGINATION[2]

Origination is related to a number of specific cultural factors, conditions that favor or limit the frequency of discovery and invention. The manipulation of these factors, it may be predicted, will be followed by dependent changes in the rate or intensity with which originations appear.

Size of Cultural Inventory

The greater the number of cultural traits on which originators may draw, the greater the frequency of discovery and invention. A community that is richly provided with means of fastening things, releasing physical energy, measuring, counting, noting, that possesses well-stocked laboratories and stockrooms, well-endowed foundations, extensive libraries and collections of documents, has advantages for origination denied to people less well provided with such resources. The size of the accumulated inventory of artifacts, techniques, organizations, and ideas obviously varies from one community to another. Therefore, the limits within which originators operate also vary. The possession of writing directly facilitates the accumulation of ideas and hence significantly influences the rate at which knowledge is reassorted, recombined, or leads to new knowledge.

Funneling of Ideas

The ease with which ideas about a given topic reach an interested individual influences the frequency of origination. Such funneling does not occur automatically. In order that potentially combinable discoveries and inventions may reach persons likely to utilize them, certain opportunities for ideological dissemination must be provided. The freedom of individuals to travel, absence of restrictions on contacts between people of different

[2] Based on Barnett, 1953:Chaps. 2–3.

rank or from different nations, and publicity for newly created knowledge all "multiply the chances that new thoughts will occur" (Barnett, 1953:42).

Socially Fostered Collaboration

The degree of collaborative effort socially fostered in working with ideas is closely related to opportunities provided for the funneling of ideas just discussed.[3] Professional meetings of learned societies at which papers are read, conferences, and study groups encourage collaborative working with ideas. The standardization of measurements and terminologies facilitates collaboration by making ideas more readily comprehensible when they are exchanged between culturally different communities. Conversely, preventing scholars from attending the national or international meetings of professional groups or failing to provide for an exchange of books and journals interferes with collaboration and hinders origination.

The rapid exchange of technical information in the modern world often leads to parallel originations. Widely separated research workers draw upon the same fund of knowledge in reaching a solution to a problem. A kind of informal, international coöperation is created which makes parallel solutions to the same problem not unusual.

Conjunction of Differences

The existence of conflicting values, ideas, or customs favors origination. Conflict produces stress that encourages innovations to reconcile the opposition (G. Wilson and M. Wilson, 1945:133). The very existence of different modes of thinking and doing, even when these are not incompatible, promotes origination through encouraging fusion or syncretism (see pp. 241–242). The blending of an indigenous and an alien belief constitutes a genuinely creative process, one that has often enriched cultural inventories. As already suggested, the extent of variety in culture, whether compatible or incompatible, will increase with scale (see p. 152). It follows that scale correlates with rate of origination.

Expectation of Change

Communities vary in the degree to which they expect or welcome change. A favorable attitude to change encourages looking for originations. Communities like the Amish and certain Pueblo Indian tribes do not anticipate change and reject many novelties. The Navaho Indians, neighbors of the

---

[3] This book will often find it useful to distinguish collaboration from coöperation. People coöperate when they work together for a single, shared goal, one in which they will all participate. A group collaborates for the goal of one of its members. Or there may be several goals (profits, wages, and creative satisfaction are goals operative in a factory) distributed among different members.

Pueblo people, "expect new developments in their culture; and their history, in so far as it is known, reveals that they have been receivers and adapters of alien customs throughout the period of their occupation of their present habitat" (Barnett, 1953:56; cf. pp. 267, 540 *infra*). In Samoa there exists almost complete freedom for the individual to originate novelty. Imitation is warmly disliked, for an individual is expected to be unique in many things that he does. It is understandable that Samoa should reveal considerable improvisation in songs, dance steps, house building, design making, and even religion. Yet most changes are slight and nondescript. For a small origination is as welcome as a large one, and a good deal easier to achieve. "The whole flexibility of Samoan culture, which at first blush looks so favourable to the display of individuality, so pliant to the moulding hand, is also a powerful conservative force" (Mead, 1928c:495).

In modern American culture the expectation of change, which creates the atmosphere favorable to origination, in turn depends on faith in progress and on the belief that, generally speaking, change is more likely to be beneficial than injurious.

Freedom of Inquiry

Absolute political power implies the existence of rigid limits to which origination must conform. Only those novelties will be rewarded which further the ends of the administrators, like fictions glorifying the regime or military inventions. Absolutism also allows an administration to limit some of the conditions previously cited which encourage origination. Even in the absence of political absolutism, and despite an ideal open-mindedness for new ideas, the pursuit of certain originations may be discouraged socially. Certainly no modern country allows all lines of inquiry to be pursued with equal encouragement. Even professional colleagues may devaluate certain originations—for example, when they are very radical. It is sometimes difficult for professional men to decide whether a new theory merely is eccentric or marks a significant addition to knowledge.

Competition

Competition between rivals for rewards encourages origination. The competition may be between business associations for customers. Originations are then favored that cut costs of production, enhance the attractiveness or quality of the product, or confer some other advantage on the competing parties. International competition for power favors the origination of new types of weapons and new kinds of propaganda that "sell" a favorable image of the country. Competition that turns into war favors military innovation. During the First World War the United States granted three times as many patents for weapons and war implements as during the prewar period; patents for nonmilitary inventions shrank (Rossman, 1931). Entertainment artists are engaged in a competitive struggle to hold and gain large audiences. Doing so successfully requires nearly constant improvisation, originality (of a sort), and fresh twists. The advertising profession puts a similar premium on men who can come forward with copy that is flavored with the spirit of newness.

Deprivation

To be cut off from some desirable object, and even the threat of being so deprived, stimulates a search for substitutes. Originations are sought that will allow behavior to continue as usual. Common sources of deprivation include war, disaster, and limited natural resources. In winter Kaska Indians, who have gone into the forest to trap furs, are deprived of access to stores from which they might replace lost or broken tools and implements. Their isolation often promotes ingenious inventions. One young man discovered that nobody in the little settlement where he lived possessed a drill bit with which he could complete wooden snowshoe frames. He manufactured his own bit out of the handle of an old file. Another man departed from camp on a hunting trip but forgot his knife. After succeeding in killing a moose, he retrieved the shell of the cartridge and, using the back of his ax, beat the metal into a crude

Lack of Timber for House Building in the Treeless Arctic Environment Probably Contributed to the Origination of the Eskimo Snow House (courtesy, National Film Board).

blade. This allowed him to butcher the game. The isolation of far northern Canada is related to a widespread readiness on the part of missionaries, traders, and natives to improvise when equipment fails or is lacking. As more and more specialized equipment comes to be used in the Arctic and sub-Arctic, for whose care specialized training and parts are required, independent resourcefulness probably will decline.

The factors of deprivation, isolation, and competition may be generalized by saying that crises of any kind stimulate origination. On the other hand, evidence indicates that in time of stress origination tends to be confined narrowly to those points of life where pressure is felt. It declines in areas of behavior unconnected with the emergency.

Origination as a Variable

Origination begets origination. The basic factor here is that an innovation often renders other, previous behaviors or artifacts awkward or impossible. Pressure is therefore introduced to reduce the incompatibility between an origination and other aspects of culture through further modification. New possibilities of behavior are realized, and neglected areas in culture come to be exploited. A kind of chain effect is created (see also pp. 243–246).

The early use of heavy Pullman cars on American railroads led to strengthened roadbeds on many lines. The radio has been accompanied by widely ramifying changes in American culture. It promoted the glorification of the American athlete and magnified the role of football coaches. In Palau new buildings, like Quonset huts with solid floors, created a problem for men accustomed to chew betel and spit. In the traditional native house numerous cracks in the floor had accommodated spitters. Some Palauan genius solved the problem by introducing empty tin cans, secured from the anthropologist's garbage dump, as spittoons.

Other Factors

Among additional important factors favorable to origination first place must go to the extent of occupational specialization in a society. "Invention is helped by all specialization of labor . . . whether between (a) regions, (b) firms or (c) workmen, since these all enable a more intensive, full use of the capital required to devise, build, and operate an invention" (Gilfillan, 1935:9; cf. Boas, 1932:160).

A country attracting talented immigrants may be encouraging a rich crop of originations. The United States is a case in point. Inventions at least partially contributed by immigrants include long-distance telephony, electricity, the typewriter, sugar beet, ironclad ship, screw propeller, electric elevator, underwater tunnel, automatic rifle, steamboat, and automobile (Handlin, 1955:172). Immigrants have also contributed ideas to American anthropology, physics, and other disciplines.

When an ethnic group finds itself rejected, devaluated, humiliated, and frustrated, as did the American Indians, a situation favorable to a certain kind of origination appears. Revitalization movements, a function of which is to restore a favorable self-image, are likely to arise. Examples of such movements include the Great-Shaker Message of the Iroquois Indians, the Shaker Cult of the Northwest Coast, and the Peyote Movement among the Plains Indians. All originally preached a new way of life that promised to restore the shattered sense of personal dignity. They contained a reformulation of the people's view of their situation. In such movements "the battleground of human failure and success shifts from a struggle against external forces to a struggle against the self" (Voget, 1957:371; cf. Wallace, 1956b). Here one glimpses how new religions can come into being.

INCENTIVES TO ORIGINATE[4]

In the previous section attention was devoted primarily to cultural factors associated with origination. The focus will now be somewhat more psychological. What motivates an individual or a group to pursue research leading to discoveries and inventions?

Major Incentives

Nine major incentives to origination have been suggested.

1. Conscious Goal Orientation. The originator may be motivated by a conscious desire for credit, social approval, or a tangible, material reward.

2. Unconscious Peripheral Motives. A motivation of this kind can be expressed in playful doodling, fingering, poking, and other random manipulations which, in some instances, lead to valuable discoveries. The inception of the backward-folding airplane wing was a product of absent-minded fiddling with a paper clip by an inventor who, it is important to add, also happened to be preoccupied with the problem of devising a space-saving, collapsible wing.

3. Unconscious, Central Motives. Self-realization through creative work, an unconscious search for power through achieving renown, and relief from an overpowering sense of guilt illustrate central, subliminal wants underlying origination. The intensity with which somebody works to devise new arguments denying the existence of God, or which will prove a professional colleague's theory to be wrong, may spring from unconscious motives. New doctrines coined by a prophet or philosopher perhaps express deep-seated ego-needs of the author.

4. Conflict of Motives. The originator may be driven to reconcile two or more conflicting wants which are simultaneously operative in his make-up (see pp. 470–471). In 1954 many white Southerners in the United States began to look for some way in which they could reconcile racial segregation in schools with the desire to comply with the Supreme Court decision holding segregation to be unconstitutional. Among solutions that have been forthcoming was one calling for private schools to be partly subsidized by the state.

5. Compensation for Blocked Goals. The Kaska Indian who substituted a makeshift blade for the knife he had forgotten illustrates origination arising from the desire to reach a blocked goal by roundabout means. Crutches, braces, hearing aids, spectacles, wigs, telescopes, microscopes,

[4] Based on Barnett, 1953:Chaps. 4–6.

and false teeth were once originations that allowed the human body to perform activities which it could not otherwise have carried out.

6. Creativity. An origination, ideological, artistic, or technical, may be devised primarily for its own sake, without thought of additional reward or practical utility. New paintings and poems sometimes represent products springing from this incentive.

7. Relief from Existing Nonphysical Discomfort. Examples of nonphysical discomfort include boredom and distracting sounds. A new form of play or a device to reduce the distraction constitutes the adjustive response.

8. Desire for Quantitative Variation. A person who engages in study or research may be motivated by the desire to raise business profits, lower costs, reduce personnel, increase personnel ("empire building" this sometimes is called), or increase the volume of fresh air.

9. Vicarious Want Satisfaction. The originator may be motivated by any of the foregoing needs, but without feeling them for himself as much as for another person. The professional research worker does not directly experience his employer's need for power or lower costs, nor may he mind the distracting noise on the sound track of a film. Nevertheless his job calls for coping with those problems. The motives of the employer vicariously become his own.

PARALLELISM

Similar cultural elements are sometimes found in cultural areas too remote to make an explanation of single origin plausible. For example, closely similar blowguns occur in South America and Melanesia. Sometimes such parallelisms are products of successive changes converging toward a similar, final form. Originations in two or more cultures independently moving in a parallel direction result in what is called convergence.

Convergence is based on the limited possibilities governing change in a given situation. Limitations may arise from the material out of which the object is made, from the purpose for which it is intended, or from the nature of the human organism that will use the element in question. Blowgun bores of nearly the same diameter and similar sized darts for that weapon in South America and Melanesia reflect the channeling of secondary innovation according to the peculiar demands of the complex (i.e., the purpose for which it was intended) (Riley, 1952:319). Bores greater than a certain size would result in loss of efficiency. In one way or another such a point of diminishing effectiveness must have been noted in both the Southwest Pacific and South America. Hence the weapons remained within fairly small limits (Linton, 1936:319).

The universal correspondence between the forms of paddles, harpoons, and springpole snares is explicable by the same principle (Goldenweiser, 1937:120–126). Here is an analysis of why oars possess parallel forms all over the world (*ibid.*, 124–125).

It may be observed here . . . that the operative conditions, or the uses to which an article is to be put, often provide limiting conditions which in a sense predetermine the technical solution, thus leading to comparable results whenever such a solution is reached. Take, for example, an oar. Abstractly speaking an oar can be long or short, light or heavy, circular in cross-section or flat, wide or narrow, of even width throughout its length or otherwise; also it can be made of more than one material. Now, in accordance with local conditions or chance, most of these shapes and materials may have been used for oars at one time or another and a variety are still being used in a pinch, including even the human arms when a rower or paddler permits his tool to slip into the water and, perhaps, be carried off by the current, leaving him stranded in his boat. But if you want a *good* oar—and this is what at length you do want—the end result is limited by the conditions of use. The oar must not be so short as not to reach the water, or only barely so, nor must it be too long, for that would make it too heavy or clumsy as a lever; it must not be so heavy as to impede its operation, nor so light as to cut off the resistance it should offer in a measured rhythmic movement. It must not, finally, be either brittle or pliable, for this would unfit it for use against a dense resisting medium. The manner again in which an oar is used, which is the only manner in which it can be effectively used in a sitting position, precludes uniformity of shape throughout its length. The blade, in order to offer proper resistance to the water and thus induce propulsion, must be either flat or preferably somewhat curved longitudinally and laterally, like a shallow spoon open at the end, with the concavity facing in the direction opposite to the movement of the boat. Anyone who has tried to row a boat with a stick will know what is meant here. The butt end of the oar, on the other hand, must be adjusted to manipulation: preferably it should not be flat or angular but more or less circular in cross-section. Also it must not be too bulky for a firm grip nor too slight, or it would tend to slip during rowing. The middle section of the oar is the connecting link between the blade and the butt; its length is determined by the proper length of the oar; it must be strong enough to withstand the stresses, and so on. It is desirable, finally, that the oar be made of a material that could float, so that the oar could be readily recovered from the water.

The principle of limited possibilities cannot explain all parallelisms for which evidence of common origin is also lacking. It cannot very well account for pottery vessels with conoidal bottoms found in Neolithic Europe and among eastern North American Indians. Parallelism occurs when two different communities independently hit upon similar cultural elements. Circumcision occurs in several parts of the world. Tie-dyeing represents a parallel trait serving similar functions in South Asia and Peru. The process consists in pinching or bunching small pieces of cloth and tying the pieces tightly with a waxed cord or a line that has no affinity for color. Then the cloth is dipped in dye and dried with the result that the original color of the fabric forms the background for irregular patches of color (Dixon, 1928:127). Social groups opposed through a feeling of rivalry, and symbolized by animals which also connote rivalry, illustrate another case of parallelism (see pp. 74–77). Aztec and Egyptian pyramids constitute parallels in form alone, for the use of each was different. The Egyptian structure provided burial chambers, while in Mexico the pyramid formed a temple mound.

Among the striking parallelisms from our own time is the independent origination of calculus by Newton and Leibnitz and the discovery of the periodic nature of the chemical elements by Dimitri I. Mendelyeev, a Russian, and Lothar Meyer, a German. Parallel origination is likely to occur when the attention of closely collaborating specialists in a literate society is focused on a specific common problem. The preliminary steps to the goal are equally known to all parties. Successive steps in reaching the solution will also be limited by the common point of departure, a common system of thought, and similar materials (see pp. 200–201).

Substantial resemblance is required before cultural elements can be accepted as *true* parallels. Ideally both form and use should be similar. This requirement is not met by the Egyptian and Aztec pyramids. Mummification in ancient Egypt included removing the viscera of a corpse, drawing out the brain through the back of the head, soaking the body in brine, rubbing it with oil, adding aromatic substances, and, after certain other steps, drying by heat. In Peru so-called mummification consisted simply of desiccating the body in dry air without any artificial preparation (Dixon, 1928:213–217). The two processes do not really parallel each other. The classification of dissimilar elements under a single concept, say "hour-glass drums," even though all members of the class are not closely similar, should not be confused with parallelism (Lowie, 1912:32–38).

AVAILABLE FILMS

Educational movies dealing with discovery and invention are often elementary. *The Story of Dr. Jenner* by Teaching Film Custodians (10 min., b. and w.) describes the discovery of smallpox vaccination. *Steam Engine* (Young America Films, Inc., 10 min., b. and w.) tells the story of how that device developed. The significance of coöperation and collaboration in origination is brought out in the March of Time documentary *Atomic Power* (19 min., b. and w.).

15.

Diffusion

ONLY a small part of the content of any culture can be accounted for in terms of originations made by members of the particular community.

Progress, degradation, survival, revival, modification, are all modes of the connexion that binds together the complex network of civilization. It needs but a glance into the trivial details of our own daily life to set us thinking how far we are really its originators, and how far but the transmitters and modifiers of the results of long past ages. Looking round the rooms we live in, we may try here how far he who only knows his own time can be capable of rightly comprehending even that. Here is the "honeysuckle" of Assyria, there the fleur-de-lis of Anjou, a cornice with a Greek border runs around the ceiling, the style of Louis XIV and its parent the Renaissance share the looking-glass between them. Transformed, shifted, or mutilated, such elements of art still carry their history plainly stamped upon them . . . [Tylor, 1891:I, 17].

The process by which elements are transmitted from one culture to another is diffusion.

Diffusion certainly represents an important source of culture change. Yet man is not quite as uninventive as the extreme proponents of cultural borrowing have suggested. Members of the German-Austrian Culture-Circle School (*Kulturkreislehre*) have maintained that a vast number of similarities between cultures can be traced to several original culture circles which, like ripples in a pond, spread around the world. In some cases they fused with one another.[1] The fact that contacts between communities possessing similar traits could not always be established by concrete evidence did not deter members of the Culture-Circle School. They nevertheless affirmed a common source for the traits. Or else they postulated that such noncontiguous people as the Ona in southernmost South America, Pygmies of

[1] Three early primitive culture and three later primary culture circles were postulated. "The crossings of the different primary cultures with one another and with earlier cultures produced the secondary cultures" (Sieber and Mueller, 1950:332). For example, the conquest of the primary village-dwelling farmers by pastoralists, who constituted another primary culture circle, gave rise to cultures marked by great economic activity. "The control of large herds was a capitalistic undertaking. Conceptions of wealth were introduced by the stockholders. This connection with livestock is even preserved in our language today. . . . 'Capitalism' indicates its original relationship to heads of cattle; 'pecuniary' . . . derives from the Latin word 'pecus' which means stock" (*ibid.*, p. 341).

Congo Africa, and Veddah of Ceylon had migrated from some original homeland to these distant places. The migrants carried with them traits like hunting, monotheism, and monogamy, all elements of the so-called primitive culture circle. Another group of extreme diffusionists, the Heliolithic (Pan-Egyptian) School, a now defunct English group, sought to derive from ancient Egypt a number of superficially similar cultural elements, like mummification, pyramids, high value set on gold, and others. It made no difference where the elements were found, whether in Africa, America, or Asia, their original home was the ancient civilization on the Nile. The excesses of diffusionist thought can be avoided without forgetting that borrowing constitutes a very important source of culture change.

DIFFUSION DEFINED AND ILLUSTRATED

Generally speaking, diffusion is the process by which culture traits circulate. When this circulation occurs inside a community, as when people accept an invention made by one of their fellows, it may be called internal (or "primary") diffusion (Dixon, 1928:Chap. 3). Obviously internal circulation at least partly corresponds to what psychologists call learning. Cultural elements circulating from one community to another illustrate external (or "secondary") diffusion. Usually the term "diffusion" is used to designate this second type of cultural transmission. It is likely, though, that many of the same factors govern both the internal and external varieties (Barnett, 1953:292). Once the boundaries of the community are passed, diffusion proceeds from communities who themselves borrowed the new trait to still others (this is illustrated in Table 46). Agriculture, starting in Southwest Asia, passed from one people to another, region to region, until it was blocked by an as yet insurmountable barrier—the Atlantic. In this transmission successive receivers no doubt modified the elements of plant cultivation. The potato followed a similar gradual progress, passing from western to northern and eastern Europe after its diffusion by Spaniards from South America. Reaching Spain around 1560, it was cultivated in England by 1586; Ireland, 1590; Germany, 1651; Scotland, 1683; Sweden, 1725; and Russia, 1744 (Tjomsland, 1950:1262–1263). Internal diffusion, exemplifying the same ripple effect, is illustrated in Table 18. The diffusion of workmen's compensation laws in the United States, shown in the table, also serves as a reminder that artifacts and technical processes are not the only culture traits susceptible to diffusion. New systems of social relations, legal norms, values, and other ideas have all been borrowed successfully.[2]

[2] Secondary originations in workmen's compensation legislation have been conspicuously slight. In many states the early experimental legislation still remains in force. "The laws . . . generally have not grown with a more enlightened social point of view" (Kossoris, 1953:366).

When diffusion just begins, the ripples scarcely may be noticed. A day or so after the Supreme Court rejected an appeal against a federal court order ending bus segregation by race, a reporter in a North Carolina city noticed little change in bus seating. Negroes who entered a bus automatically seated themselves in the rear, as formerly. The new seating pattern has not yet diffused. Only during rush hours did a new pattern begin to emerge. At one point a Negro woman took a front seat opposite a white woman. The Negro "looked ill at ease" and watched the rear of the vehicle until she saw a vacant seat. Quickly she got up to occupy it (*Durham Morning Herald*, Apr. 26, 1956).

TABLE 18.   Diffusion of Workmen's Compensation
Laws, U.S.A.

Year	Number of Units[a] with Laws Enacted	Year	Number of Units[a] with Laws Enacted
1908	1	1918	42
1909	2	1919	46
1910	3	1920	47
1911	13	1927	49
1912	17	1928	50
1913	24	1929	51
1914	26	1935	53
1915	35	1939	54
1916	36	1948	55
1917	41		

[a] The word "unit" includes territories as well as states and the District of Columbia, in which a law covering federal employees existed in 1908.
SOURCE: U.S. Department of Labor, *1940*:219; *Monthly Labor Review*, *1948*:639.

Caste organization is currently in process of diffusing to marginal tribes in India as these are losing their isolation and adopting Hinduism. How this sometimes works is shown in the following case. About 1909 the Mech, a low-ranking Assamese tribe, during visits to Calcutta became impressed by the teachings of a Hindu *guru*, Sivanarayana. Tribesmen returned home and taught the Hindu doctrines which they had learned. The people, whose tribal name meant "Barbarians," were eager to advance their rank. They accepted Hindu doctrine, changed their name, set themselves up as a Hindu caste, and cut themselves off from people whom they perceived to rank below them. That is, they refused to eat or intermarry with certain tribal neighbors and in this way advertised their own relatively superior rank. It is ironical that Sivanarayana heartily disapproved of caste (Farquhar, *1929*:134).

Diffusion does not always occur gradually. In conjunction with an invasion by a culturally very different community, transmission may be swift and voluminous. Such extensive diffusion followed the Roman invasion of Britain in 55 B.C. (Winbolt, 1945) and the arrival of the British in India (Griffiths, 1952). During the past few decades swift and voluminous diffusion has marked the western Piedmont and mountain regions of North Carolina. The instruments which promoted this diffusion were the same ones simultaneously breaking down immigrant enclaves in the rest of the United States—radio, television, and motion pictures.

Not only do rate and volume of cultural transmission vary from one time or place to another. Qualitative differences may also be recognized. Where the relationship between two communities primarily involves trade, cultural exchange will be confined largely to artifacts. The Indians and Eskimo of northern Canada, who trade furs at stores operated by the Hudson's Bay Company, secured metal tools, guns, ammunition, foodstuffs, and other products from this source. Naturally they do not learn the techniques for making the objects from the trader. The transmission of new artifacts is sometimes distinguished from another, "true," kind of diffusion in which knowledge of manufacturing process is transmitted (Dixon, 1928:118).

Culture traits easily cross the boundaries of adjacent communities without actual resettlement of people. Spanish explorers migrated to America and from them the domesticated horse entered the southwestern United States. Thereupon the horse complex passed from tribe to tribe until it reached the northernmost Plains Indians in what is now Canada (Ewers, 1955b).

Diffusion is not inevitable. Little occurred in the early relations between Indonesians and Australian natives of Arnhem Land (R. M. Berndt and C. Berndt, 1954:38, 44–45). At various other times in history communities have shut the door on cultural borrowing (see pp. 181, 266). When cultural transmission does occur, the borrowed element by no means always continues to possess the meaning or use in the new configuration that it held in the old. This subject will be examined later (see pp. 237–241). Finally, it is well to keep in mind that although the initial reaction to an innovation is favorable, subsequent experience may uncover problems connected with the new custom. If these are serious, the novelty may swiftly be abandoned.

Types of Diffusion

Some classification of diffusion has already been attempted in making a distinction between internal and external cultural exchange, gradual and rapid diffusion, and the circulation of artifacts versus the diffusion of techniques for making them. Four other types are worthy of comment.

1. **Nonstrategic and Strategic Diffusion.** New elements can be borrowed which require no drastic changes in the culture as a preliminary step. The

use of perfume, new patterns of clothing, and smoking tobacco are relevant examples. Some traits cannot be diffused unless extensive preparatory modifications first take place in the host's way of life. Automobile transportation requires the provision of roads, filling stations, and trained mechanics. For a country to industrialize demands a considerable shift in food production, banking, government, transportation, and training of industrial workers.

2. **Stimulus (or Idea) Diffusion.** Because of the degree to which it involves the inventive ingenuity of the host community, stimulus diffusion overlaps with origination. In stimulus diffusion it is not the artifact, technique, or some other action pattern that circulates. Instead, for one reason or another, only the idea of the trait diffuses. The receiving community then devises its own means for producing the same result (Kroeber, 1940; 1948:369). Idea diffusion is a matter of degree since all diffusion usually is followed by some modification in the form or use of a newly acquired element (Barnett, 1953:330–331). A classic example of stimulus diffusion comes from the early nineteenth century when a Cherokee Indian, Sequoia, perceived the principle underlying writing. This man had followed a portion of the Cherokee nation to Indian Territory, or Oklahoma. There he saw the white man graphically representing spoken sounds (see pp. 550–551). Sequoia himself was illiterate and hence, by definition, barred from understanding the full nature of the technique which he witnessed. But he understood the idea of writing and became literate in 1821 by virtue of single-handedly inventing the Cherokee Syllabary. This he brought east

SIGN	PHONETIC VALUE
T	i
У	gi
Ꭿ	hi
Ꮲ	li
Ꮋ	mi
Ꮒ	ni
Ꮽ	gwi
Ꮀ	o
A	go
Ꮏ	ho
Ꮆ	lo
Ꮐ	mo
Z	no

Fig. 15:1. Portion of Cherokee Syllabary (from Diringer, 1948:175).

and introduced to the Cherokee Indians who had remained in Georgia. A syllabary is not an alphabet, in which, ideally, one sound is represented by one sign. Rather, signs stand for syllables more than for discrete sound units. Type for the Cherokee Syllabary of 85 signs (a portion is shown in Fig. 15:1) was provided through the agency of New England missionaries. They also provided the Indians with a printing press. The Cherokee were not slow in using the press to fight Georgia's westward expansion into what was still Indian country. The Georgia militia punished such sedition by destruction of the press and type fonts.[3]

[3] Cherokee resistance to Georgia reached the Supreme Court, which, under Chief Justice Marshall, decided in favor of the Indian nation in 1830. The Federal Executive used interposition on that occasion. President Andrew Jackson, despite his oath of office, reported to the Court: "John Marshall has rendered his decision; now let him enforce it" (J. Collier, 1947:207).

Yet the syllabary remains in limited use by Cherokee speakers up to the present time.

The alphabet which the reader is now using originated in the extreme southwestern corner of Asia over a thousand years before the Christian era and reached many parts of the world through stimulus diffusion. Another instance of idea diffusion appears in the deliberate attempts made in Europe after 1500 A.D. to emulate Chinese porcelain. The final achievement of porcelain on that continent was not completed until 1709, by which time kaolin, a clay of the proper type, had been found and its use mastered (Kroeber, 1948:369).

The difference between stimulus and pure diffusion may not always be easy to recognize. When disciplines like political science and sociology began to look for hypotheses to test empirically and in other ways emulated physical science methods, did the idea of those methods diffuse? Or was there an actual diffusion of scientific method, that is, a set of techniques that could be learned and applied to any subject matter? Some historians of science believe that certain operations performed in physical science were applied more or less analogically to social facts. In other words, stimulus diffusion occurred. Anyone who holds that scientific method is one and indivisible, no matter to what subject it happens to be applied, might argue differently.

3. Nondeliberate and Planned Diffusion.   Diffusion need not be the unconscious, unplanned process that it often has been. An agent may deliberately set out to introduce certain traits in a culture. Missionaries, teachers, advertising agencies, and technical development officers do this. Or a community deliberately may examine the merits and disadvantages of some new item. This is certainly what industrial concerns do before they invest in new material, machines, or processes. In British India the less conservative princely states, like Baroda, carefully watched legislative innovations which the British-controlled government introduced in areas under its administration. Those perceived to be worth while were adopted. The same rational note dominated the Manus in the Admiralty Islands off New Guinea who decided to become Catholic rather than Protestant. They reached this decision after careful thought. Catholic missionaries offered to teach them writing in the *lingua franca* of pidgin English instead of, as Protestants proposed, in their own, purely local, language. The skill thus acquired promised to facilitate access to the wider world. The Catholic missions also did not demand heavy contributions, being largely self-supporting. The Manus were influenced further by the fact that Catholics practiced confession to a single person (the priest) rather than to the entire village. This proved attractive to a people who themselves had practiced public confession but did not particularly enjoy it. Despite their careful deliberation, the people did not remain Catholic long but soon established their own church (Mead, 1956a:92). Planned diffusion does not always work out according to plan. Social engineering as yet contains little knowledge comparable to mechanical engineering. In India attempts were made to revive village panchayats (i.e., councils) and make them instruments of democratic self-government. Consensus, representing village-wide norms, was to determine policy in the local government bodies. The panchayats came to be used in a somewhat different fashion. They served as means whereby socially important families could stabilize their positions. Rival families employed them to exert their claims and under-privileged groups to exercise a bid for power and influence (Dube, 1956: 27).

4. Active and Passive Diffusion. Some diffusion can occur only with the active participation of the borrowers. The horse, which came to the Plains Indians from the Spaniards, served as a riding mount, and Europeans smoked the tobacco deriving from the American Indian. Nowadays, however, diffusion often invites spectatorship. Recorded jazz is heard by African and European audiences, and American and British films are watched abroad. This is not to deny that such imported traits influence exotic music or other areas of culture. Of course they do. But what diffuses is less an element of behavior than the behavior of specialists to which audiences respond by more or less passive listening or looking.

Agents of Diffusion

An agent signifies any personal or impersonal medium (see pp. 345–346) through which cultural content is circulated. A missionary who teaches his doctrines to a native congregation, an agricultural agent explaining new seeds or methods of cultivation, and a salesman extolling a new machine to the purchasing agent of a factory illustrate actual or potential diffusion occurring through interpersonal interaction. The shift from wine to beer among Italians of New Haven occurred when these people began to shift their drinking from the home to public places. In restaurants run by non-Italians they found it easier to secure beer than the more traditional drink (P. H. Williams and R. Straus, 1950:622). In the same way food introduced to an American family is controlled by whatever "gatekeeper" happens to do the shopping (Lewin, 1951:174–187). The agents in these situations are persons. Rarely does diffusion occur without either inter-personal or mediated interaction. True, the Eskimo in the eastern Arctic secured metal from the remains of wrecked ships, and ancient tombs provide objects for modern museums, but this is a relatively rare kind of diffusion.

The selection of elements for transmission will tend to be related to the status of the personal agent. In the Southwest Pacific native peoples in 1944 saw much of American troops. Melanesian culture still contains items that diffused via the military channel: a rusted, tracked vehicle serves as a ladder to a pile dwelling; the blackboard of an Air Force briefing room and airplane fuselage provide wall material, and other parts of aircraft make pig troughs (*New York Times*, Jan. 5, 1955). More elements of culture will diffuse if both sexes constitute the sources of transmission. From the wives and children of Hudson's Bay Company traders some Eskimo

Foreign-Aid Programs and Companies with Overseas Branches Promote Considerable Diffusion (courtesy, Caltex).

have learned English nursery rhymes and accompanying games. What will diffuse is also clearly dependent on the agent's motivations. Traders do not offer the same "goods" as public-health workers. Since prehistoric times, however, merchants have been responsible for diffusing more than their stock in trade.

In studying agents of diffusion it is well to remember that not all merchants or missionaries are alike. Some differences are individual in nature. Others arise from the policies of the organization to which the agent belongs or depend on the style of life he follows. Upper-middle-class representatives of the British Universities Mission in Central Africa seek to disseminate somewhat different norms pertaining to dancing and drinking than do the lower-middle-class English Baptist missionaries (Brown, *1944*).

CONDITIONS FAVORING DIFFUSION

Two very general factors may be cited at the outset as favorable to cultural transmission. First, diffusion from the wider society is encouraged in a nonmarginal geographical location. Second, the psychological reward value attached to a given element motivates its acceptance.

The more a geographical situation provides opportunities for contact with other ways of life, the greater the chances that new elements will enter the culture. The importance of location is shown by the fact that cultures manifesting the smallest degree of control over nature, and possessing the smallest content, are also generally the most marginal. It follows that the scale of a community relates closely to the frequency of cultural borrowing (Leiris, 1951:30–35). Of course, geographical position does not promote diffusion automatically. Indeed, none of the variables upon which diffusion depends operates wholly independently of another. To take a concrete situation, in Ceylon the Karava, a fishing caste, have embraced Christianity more than any other caste (Ryan, 1953:105). One factor in their Christianization undoubtedly has been a coastal position. However, it is also likely that Christianity found a favorable reception among the Karava because as takers of life they could only have been inconsistent Buddhists. Christianity showed greater compatibility with Karava culture than did Buddhism. It did not require the fishermen to rationalize their occupation. The relatively low rank of the caste may also have favored conversion. It had less to lose and more to gain from a switch in religion than would a caste of high prestige.

Health Programs May Encourage Construction of Pit Latrines and Outhouses, but Reports from Several Parts of the World Indicate That Such Structures Once Built Are Not Always Used.

Real or perceived reward value as a factor promoting cultural borrowing needs little comment. The hypothesis that reward favors diffusion derives from the psychology of learning. Experiments indicate that learning a new habit depends on the reduction of some drive or state of tension (for example, hunger) in the organism. The term "reward" (also called "reinforcement") designates drive reduction. To generalize from learning experiments: Acceptance of new elements into a cultural system depends, among other things, upon the reinforcement which the new elements afford or which they promise. In other words, new cultural elements will be accepted and retained when they maximize adaptation or adjustment and reduce stress. No concrete experimental evidence exists to sustain this logical extension of learning theory. Furthermore, the theory has been tested mainly by animal experiments rather than with human beings. In anthropology a great deal of carefully oriented research remains to be done if the reinforcement concept is to be tested. Attention will have to be focused upon individuals and their motivations for accepting new elements of behavior and artifacts (Putney and Putney, 1954:Chap. 5). Perhaps it is not the specific novelty that promotes reward but the total situation which is created when the borrowed trait is added to culture. The whole cultural system seems to work more smoothly.

The following more specific factors which favor diffusion do not purport to be exhaustive. Overlap between several factors will be perceived. It should be recalled that in any given situation limiting conditions may be exerting simultaneous counterpressure and will slow down or block diffusion. (Limiting factors are examined on pp. 225–232.)

Felt Inadequacy

For people to perceive that a novelty possesses adaptive and adjustive advantages not met by elements in the existing culture is favorable to diffusion. In practically all cases where stone-tool-using people were confronted by corresponding metal implements they readily saw advantages in and added the latter. Similarly the bow has practically always given way to the gun. Today members of the elite in India, Pakistan, and South America have begun to question the indigenous systems of medicine. Their awareness of the accomplishments of western medicine is promoting dissatisfaction with native curing, which they perceive to be less reliable. These people are financially well enough off to adopt the new modes of curing (Erasmus, 1952). In Pakistan native practitioners themselves are turning to western remedies, like penicillin, whose efficacy they recognize. As some local Ecuadorians put it, "you cannot deny what you see with your own eyes" (ibid., p. 417). The advantages of new therapeutic traits can be observed quite readily, especially when dramatic recoveries follow. Preventive medicine, on the other hand, in which the advantages are less apparent, does not diffuse as readily as curative practice.

After their arrival in India the British did not borrow indiscriminately from the native culture. Among elements that did diffuse was the underground chamber (taikhana) that served as a retreat against summer heat and the marble baths of Moghul dwellings (Spear, 1951:151–152). Another felt inadequacy is illustrated by the anarchy that broke out on Truk, an island group in Micronesia, following withdrawal of the Spanish colonial administration. People saw no way by which to control the intermittent, destructive wars which were being fought with newly acquired guns. Obviously the Trukese were ready for a workable solution that promised stability. In 1899 Spain sold her Pacific possessions, including Truk, to Germany. One of the first orders that the new administration issued called on the Trukese to turn in their guns and to cease warfare. ". . . This was apparently all that was required of the people who had created for themselves an intolerable condition which they did not know how to stop" (Gladwin and Sarason, 1953:41). The Trukese accepted foreign suzerainty readily and brought their disputes before district chiefs as ordered.

Prestige Symbolized by the Innovation

How several factors may operate simultaneously in promoting diffusion is illustrated by the readiness with which the elite in certain underdeveloped countries have adopted western medicine. In Ecuador, as was pointed out, the elite perceive western medicine to be more effective than native curing. But they also patronize western-trained physicians out of the realization that in doing so they are acting as the "better people" because only people of inferior rank use herbal remedies or go to native curers (Erasmus, 1952:420). Closely related to this is the feeling in some communities that certain alien traits will facilitate upward social mobility.

The horse complex in southern Brazil readily diffused to German immigrants in that country after 1824. The immigrants came mostly from lower-ranking strata of rural Germany. Many had known serfdom or had been landless laborers; later, however, artisans began to arrive in larger numbers. The large Brazilian landowners and cattle breeders tried to ascribe to the newcomers a very low social rank. The immigrants fought for higher prestige. They secured it partly by borrowing certain elements from the native setting. The gaucho culture (a cattle-breeding, cowboy way of life) carried relatively high prestige in Brazil. From this system the Germans made their choice. The horse complex, of course, was focal in the gaucho assemblage. In Germany owning and riding saddle horses had been privileges of noblemen. These traits, therefore, in Germany also symbolized high prestige. Thus the complex seemed highly desirable in the eyes of the rank-conscious immigrants and motivated them to borrow it (Willems, 1944).

Prestige Enjoyed by an Innovator

Modern advertising makes familiar the device of promoting sales by associating the product—cigarettes, whiskey, or automobiles—with somebody of high rank. The figure may be a real person or merely symbolic of great prestige, like the "man of distinction" or the well-groomed people shown in advertisements of expensive cars. People with prestige apparently help to sell goods in western markets. In the same way sponsorship of an innovation by respected persons in exotic communities facilitates diffusion. In parts of Africa light skin constituted proof of favor with God. On the prestige thus gained by Europeans rested much of their power to further innovation (E. W. Smith, 1927:73).

In 1897, when controversy over cholera inoculation raged in Bombay, the Aga Khan, venerated leader of the Ismaili Muslims, had himself publicly inoculated. He put his leadership to a crucial test and discovered that it survived (Sultan Muhammed Shah, 1954). A concealed danger lurks in this. A leader with prestige may lose some power by advocating innovations that followers find distasteful. In Sind, a former province of West Pakistan, a powerful, deeply respected, wealthy landlord found it difficult to arouse enthusiasm among his tenant cultivators when it came to planting trees. Nor did he push them to comply with his wishes for he recognized that doing so would lower the respect he commanded. Many leaders have discovered their prestige to be insufficient to advocate successfully unpopular measures. Others, like Kemal Ataturk in Turkey, succeeded in achieving at least surface compliance, not so much through prestige as with coercion (Barnett, 1953:319–320). Force, however, also is limited. It cannot be abused without endangering its effectiveness.

Cultural Compatibility

We include here the compatibility of an origination with conscious and unconscious values, existing techniques, and current forms of social organization.

Business gives the most careful attention to insuring certain kinds of compatibility in borrowing. Even folk products must be geared to alien tastes if they are to be marketable abroad. In India a technical-assistance expert recommended that handicrafts intended for western markets should be made with fast dyes, according to standardized measurements, and that silk brocades should contain less gold. Certain design changes were advised as well (Willis, 1955). Western nations face a similar difficulty when they try to introduce elements in exotic communities. European white and black spotted pigs excited little interest when they were introduced among hill tribes in Southeast Asia. Pigs there possess great value as sacrificial objects, but sacrificial pigs must be black (International Institute of Differing Civilizations, 1953:348). Congruity as a factor accelerating diffusion operates in music. African and western styles of music, which share many common characteristics (including the diatonic scale and harmony), have mutually influenced each other through the exchange of elements (Merriam, 1955:34). The same cannot be said for Chinese music, which is extremely different from music familiar to western ears.

Acceptance of the potato by the Salish Indians of coastal Washington and British Columbia may have been hastened by the fact that these people possessed a culture into which potato cultivation could enter without requiring serious readjustment. Roots already provided a source of food and were stored. Furthermore, the people lived in sedentary local groups, a condition favorable for planting and tending gardens. The new vegetable also proved to be useful for trading with whites, on whose goods the Indians were becoming increasingly dependent (Suttles, 1951:281).

Among the Siuai of Bougainville, Solomon Islands, the Australian administration has encouraged road improvement. The administration is most successful in its efforts to diffuse good roads as an element of native culture in those neighborhoods where a tradition of teamwork has long existed. In other words, this technical innovation is favored by compatible forms of social organization (D. L. Oliver, 1955:312). Imported forms of social organization also diffuse better when they are compatible with existing culture elements. Communism, for example, possessed features congruent with traditional Chinese values. These included strong loyalty to a doctrine (traditionally Confucianism but now also Communism); a monastic, ethnocentric belief in exclusively possessing a proper style of life—all else was barbarism; readiness to subordinate the individual to larger social units; and no high importance set on personal freedom (Fitzgerald, 1952:31–32). The school is an alien organization in many world areas. Of two clans among the Ibo people in southern Nigeria, the one in which literacy fitted into an already existing trend of emigrating for jobs showed the keener desire to adopt schools. The clan with the more favorable geographical environment, but whose members tended to stay at home, showed little interest in schooling (Chadwick, 1949:9).

Internal ideological diffusion and compatibility are illustrated in the spread of conditioning psychology (i.e., Watson's behaviorism) in the 1920's. Why did this theory of learning, which held children to be extremely malleable creatures whose personality development it was relatively easy to control, become so popular in America? Partly because Americans were accustomed to thinking in terms of manipulating the external world, shaping it rather than growing into it (Mead and Macgregor, 1951:10). Behaviorism could be integrated into that system of thought. In Russia a similar psychology associated with I. P. Pavlov suited the Marxist assumption that most behavior arose out of the way people organized for production. Russia represented a revolutionary kind of social structure. A new type of person should also make his appearance, according to Marxist theory. Pavlov's psychology theoretically allowed for revolutionary changes in behavior and was, therefore, quite timely (Wortis, 1950:Chaps. 2–3).

Relief from Social Pressure

The housewife who gives in, buying a gadget partly to get rid of an insistent salesman, and the native who escapes missionary criticism by accepting clothing both exhibit conforming behavior in response to social pressure (cf. Chap. 30). The western South Australian natives felt no embarrassment in their nakedness. Missionaries, however, convinced them that they ought to be ashamed. Now a "superficial feeling of modesty has replaced the natural and conscious acceptance of nudity" (R. M. Berndt and C. Berndt, 1942–44:320). Yemenite Jews in an Israeli immigrant camp hid the shoes which they had been issued. They preferred to walk barefoot. Not until the authorities threatened expulsion did the Yemenites "slowly get used to wearing shoes" (Patai, 1953:208). Pressure may invoke financial penalties. Where a colonial administration levies a hut tax, plural wives housed in separate domiciles within a compound turn out to be an uncomfortable expense. Monogamy is encouraged by such measures.

At first glance social pressure, especially in the form of law (see pp. 489–499), may seem a very effective means of promoting diffusion. A shortcoming lies in the antagonism that social pressure may arouse, particularly when it is not accepted as just or moral. Social pressure is likely to work most effectively in a small population where personal supervision is exercised over individuals. Such supervision is impossible when the ratio of administrators to subjects is very wide. Schemes like the Village-AID (V-AID) Programs of India and Pakistan, in which many village workers in the program are each given responsibility for relatively few people, exhibit one means of insuring close supervision.

Nature of the Origination

It would seem that some elements of culture diffuse more readily than others. In particular those traits are most likely to diffuse which (1) are readily perceived to be useful in terms of existing needs, (2) for some other reason attract special interest, and (3) are introduced with special emphasis (Putney and Putney, 1954:323–325).

On the whole, specific utilitarian artifacts have diffused more readily than elaborate systems of ideas. Techniques likewise find easier acceptance. But by no means does it follow that ideas never cross cultural boundaries. European immigrants to the New World, for example, did not hesitate to accept American legal norms or the high value placed on success (Sorokin, 1947:579–580). Where a technique constitutes a joint system of action plus idea the action patterns may be transmitted without their supporting understandings and values. Antisepsis is carried out in many parts of the world where western medical knowledge has reached. The underlying germ theory, however, has not been taken over as a firmly integrated part of the total complex. Hence in Pakistan the author saw vaccinators use the same needle for several persons while wiping the arm with a piece of gauze that had become quite soiled. In religion, objects and gestures diffuse without appreciation of their symbolic meanings (Social Science Research Council, 1954:991).

Language is another area in which unequal readiness for borrowing shows up. Usually it is easier to learn vocabulary items than grammatical systems.

Characterological Factors and Social Climate

The socially standardized character structure of a people may favor or limit change. It is, however, necessary to say that this is a subject about which practically nothing is known. Curiosity certainly is an element in personality significant in borrowing. The Australian aborigines, who are taught not to be curious, consider the ways and possessions of the white man to be "his secret, his own possessions, and . . . not to be taken by storm or imitated." Imitation among these people is further inhibited by a strong current of traditionalism. They want to follow behaviors that have continuity with the mythological past (Elkin, 1951:164). In contrast, American Athapaskan Indians (like the Navaho and Kaska) show great "cultural receptivity" (Birket-Smith, 1930:27; Morice, 1928:77). The Japanese represent another people marked by a strong readiness for borrowing.

The Manus, living in the Admiralty Islands off New Guinea, possessed a distinctive attitude which disposed them to change. In conjunction with other facilitating conditions operative between 1928 and 1953, this orientation helped the Manus to reshape their culture thoroughly (Mead, 1956a). What was this characterological factor? They believed that change could be for the better and that their way of life could be reshaped deliberately to make it work more satisfactorily (ibid., pp. 92–97). This is an extraordinary attitude to uncover in a near Stone Age people—one, however, that rings familiarly on an American ear. The characterological readiness to change in Manus adults was related to their discontinuous childhood experiences (ibid., pp. 158–159). After a period of nearly untrammeled freedom, the growing child was subjected to a very different climate, one marked by puritan values and "tyrannical" obligations. Young people did not accept the transition easily. They felt miserable even as they worked to meet the demands of the adult world. Their dissatisfaction prepared them to remake their culture when the opportunity arose during World War II.

Characterological factors favorable to diffusion may also be observed as they color the "climate" of business organizations. As already pointed out, fear discourages change (pp. 186–188). In a civil-service bureaucracy people with secure job tenure and limited, clearly demarcated responsibilities are quite ready to admit new ideas and practices, especially if the innovations promise to overcome existing irritants (Blau, 1955:198–200). In a United States bomb squadron studied by the author even major innovations in procedure tended to be received in a way suggesting that the men expected their customary behaviors to be only temporary (Honigmann,

1954d:Chap. 7). Readiness for change pervaded the squadron and there was little inclination to regard any existing procedure as inviolable. Implicitly, at least, squadron members acknowledged that almost any other procedural form might work just as well or better. Of course, the centralized administration in the Air Force, through which change can be ordered at will, must also be taken into account to understand the squadron's attitude toward change. Not all new traits were equally acceptable. Procedural innovations that threatened to undermine a supervisor's power or break up groups and end privileges encountered considerable hostility.

Other Factors

Size of the community may favor diffusion whether it is small or large. When the number of people in association is small, supervision can be personal, and this helps to spread new cultural elements. But a small community is usually more homogeneous than a large one. Variability is limited. This might limit the spread of innovation unless it were to be accepted by everyone. Where population or its density is great, contacts between people and between communities are likely to be frequent, providing numerous opportunities for cultural exchange (Dixon, 1928:116).

Social organization vitally affects cultural transmission. Four examples will be cited. (1) Groups in a community whose specialized object is partial reform or revolutionary change of culture may exert a potent force for borrowing. Such a group may search out originations that further its aims and then intensively seek to promote their acceptance (A. Rose, 1956:331, 347–360). (2) As already suggested, diffusion benefits from vigorous leadership which will inspire willingness to try a novelty or can control active resistance to it. The coöperative farm organized experimentally at Casa Grande, Arizona, under federal auspices in 1936 failed to survive partly because it lacked dedicated leadership (Banfield, 1951:Chap. 15). (3) Rules requiring exogamous marriage for members of a group favor the circulation of cultural traits. Exogamy means that the individuals must seek spouses from some other group (another family, clan, or village). Each such group in a community, it may be assumed, possesses a few peculiarities of behavior and artifacts. Exogamy, therefore, involves establishing a new relationship with a social unit that follows a somewhat different way of life. Each of the parents in the newly founded family will draw on a somewhat different cultural heritage. "Culture is borrowed," under such circumstances, "through the very mechanism by which it is transmitted" from parent to child (Murdock, 1955a:365). The rapid diffusion of the potato, which women grew, among the Salish Indians may have been aided by the custom of securing wives from other villages (Suttles, 1951:282). (4) Finally, group support is an important matter in accomplishing diffusion. Hence, the initial technique of changing any aspect of culture might well be to promote a positive attitude toward the innovation in the group as a whole. Such an attitude cannot be forced. A leader can help the group see advantages which he expects will follow from the novelty—say, less tooth decay after fluoride is added to drinking water—but the decision to act is a group process (Putney and Putney, 1954:Chaps. 10–11; Lewin, 1952).

Like origination (see pp. 204, 243), diffusion works in the manner of a chain reaction: successful borrowing accelerates more borrowing. Therefore the degree of adoption that has already occurred in a particular community constitutes an index of cultural transmission likely to ensue in the future (Mead, 1956a:287).

FACTORS LIMITING DIFFUSION

The world contains many cultures. Many different ways of life are in daily contact yet cultural differences do not disappear. Cultures do not mix indiscriminately and the reader readily can detect in his own life clear resistance to borrowing. Newly discovered foods, a treatment for illness, and even scientific ideas may be bitterly attacked and fought. In the nineteenth century when J. Vogt offered his theory of matter as a disturbance of the ether, his colleagues thought him demented. In the early twentieth century fundamentally the same view, holding matter to be a special state of energy, became a firm part of physics (Kahn, 1954:36–38). It is said that the world of Vogt's time was not ready for his radical discovery. Can one be more specific about why cultural transmission is slowed down or blocked? This section discusses some factors which limit cultural diffusion.

Actual or promised reinforcement constitutes a basic psychological variable favorable to diffusion. The perception of pain or punishment similarly motivates resistance to borrowing. So general a proposition offers little scope for predicting precisely what traits will be rejected and under what circumstances. It must be made more specific.

Failure to Perceive Advantages

Failure to perceive an advantage in a novelty will constitute grounds for rejecting the element. A campaign during World War II to reduce gasoline consumption so that there would be enough fuel for all motorists eventually failed. American citizens did not believe the message of the campaign or read in it the intended significance. Motorists could get gas when they wanted it, couldn't they? What more would the campaign give them (Mintz, 1953)? Programs of inoculation against illness, as well as other forms of preventive medicine, fail when people see no tangible or immediate gain following from compliance. George Bernard Shaw's phonetic alphabet, containing 40 signs borrowed from the Greek and Phoenician alphabets, created scarcely a ripple of interest. Phonetic systems of writing don't promise any advantage to the ordinary layman, and the linguist already uses a satisfactory International Phonetic Alphabet.

An innovation not only may be neutral, promising no advantage, but may be feared as a direct threat. Industrial organizations are familiar with workers' resistance to new procedures that will abrogate some previously held, desirable advantages.

An example of an innovation whose advantages were not recognized comes from a Canadian town where a mental-health education program was instituted. One of the aims was to allay anxiety about mental illness. Instead the program stirred up anxiety and created intense hostility toward the educators. Little or nothing diffused. What had happened? The people of Prairie Town possessed their own way of thinking about what to them was an anxiety-laden topic, mental illness. Partly they refused to think about it at all; they pushed it out of mind. The mental-health program, however, deliberately focused attention on the subject. Also, most people in the community believed that the mental hospital took adequate care of the mentally sick. They did not like to be told about the inadequate supply of psychiatrists, which made therapy practically nonexistent in the hospital. Learning these things carried no rewards. Rather the education was threatening. Prairie Town reacted with understandable hostility (Cumming and Cumming, 1955).

In a United States Air Force bomb wing through channels of command an innovation was introduced that withdrew from the ground crew attached to each giant bombing plane much responsibility for inspecting and maintaining the individual aircraft. Under the old system a crew chief and his assistant mechanics remained in charge of a single plane. Under the new system an aircraft would be checked by a large group of men called a dock crew. They moved from plane to plane and did not remain attached specifically to any one. The aim, of course, was more efficient maintenance and inspection. Both the flight personnel and the ground crews (who were left with minor inspections) predicted the new "dock system" was bound to fail in its purpose. Each dock crew would tend many aircraft, they pointed out. Emotional identification between men and machines could not occur under the new system as it had under the old. Loss of identification with the plane would undermine the sense of personal responsibility and lead to less careful workmanship. Men's lives were going to be endangered. Regardless of the merits of these charges and pessimistic fears, it is clear that a threat rather than an advantage was perceived in the new maintenance system. Something that had been instituted to increase efficiency struck enlisted men and officers as carrying a potential danger. Of course the order to start the new system was obeyed. But the quality of compliance was unenthusiastic (Honigmann, 1954d:103–104).

Ideological Incompatibility

Abundant evidence indicates that resistance is probable when an innovation is perceived to be incompatible with existing ideas, whether consciously or unconsciously. Thus, techniques of contraception do not diffuse to Catholics who believe the practice to be a grave sin, equivalent to murder. Deliberate control of conception is likewise not welcomed by people who place value on numbers of offspring. Social dancing in the western mode is rejected by the Chinese, who conceive of any kind of intimate contact between unrelated men and women as offensively sexual in nature. These examples of conflict between a novelty and existing value-laden ideas are obvious. So (at least when one thinks of it) is the rejection of the principle of majority rule by the Indians of Isleta Pueblo in New Mexico (French, 1948:37). These people prefer to reach decisions by unanimous assent. Unfortunately unanimity, relatively easy to arrive at in a homogeneous, slowly changing community, becomes practically impossible when, as in Isleta, conflicting viewpoints exist in a group. Hence decisions on important matters cannot be reached. A similar difficulty exists among the Doukhobors, a minority religious sect in western Canada (Hawthorn, 1955:33). Yet in both communities the practice of majority rule remains in disfavor and does not diffuse, while unanimous consent continues to be valued.

Consider the plight of the children from dingier parts of English cities who came to school from bookless homes. Their background contained nothing that prepared them for the middle-class juvenile fiction found in the school libraries. The children were alienated from books peopled by heroes with whom they could not identify and replete with themes they did not understand (*London Times Literary Supplement*, Nov. 13, 1956, p. ix).

Lack of Available Resources

Diffusion often requires a supply of "risk capital" that includes money, costly apparatus, and highly trained personnel (Useem and Useem, 1955: 106). The leaders of underdeveloped countries, like Pakistan or Iraq, are aware that public-health measures can prolong life and reduce illness. Such countries, however, spend little money on acquiring public-health experts and know-how from abroad. They prefer in many cases to spend limited funds to build up production. Then, when they are able to produce greater wealth, money will be available to send students abroad for public-health training.

A vicious circle is struck when available resources scarcely permit importing capital goods and experts with whose aid domestic production can be expanded. Namhalli, a village in South India, is in this plight. The people

TABLE 19.   Training Awards and Experts Provided Under Various
Assistance Plans (1951—June, 1955)

Country	Training Awards	Experts
Australia	916	115
Canada	311	59
Ceylon	11	1
India	340	14
Japan	11	3
New Zealand	226	44
Pakistan	8	—
United Kingdom	853	157
United States	3,025	949
United Nations (and specialized agencies)	1,458	2,373
Total	7,159	3,715

SOURCE: *The Task Ahead, 1956:39.*

could increase agricultural wealth by adding fertilizer to the soil and employing electric irrigation pumps. Lack of capital keeps them from adopting those innovations (A. Beals, 1955:98). A partial answer to this dilemma has been found in international technical aid programs. In these
schemes highly productive countries freely give or lend a portion of their
wealth for the purpose of developing the resources of other nations. Sometimes workers from underdeveloped areas are trained abroad or else experts
are loaned to a country seeking to develop its resources (Table 19). The

TABLE 20.   Rise in Production Under Colombo Plan in South and
Southeast Asia

Commodity	Output (thousand metric tons) 1953	1954	Percentage Increase
Tea	494	528	7
Natural rubber	1,505	1,561	4
Coal	39,036	40,032	2
Petroleum crude	15,552	16,080	3
Steel	1,542	1,730	12
Tin in concentrates	103	109	5
Cement	5,435	6,337	17
Sugar	3,047	3,200	5
Cotton yarn	737	797	8
Jute manufactures	934	997	6
Electricity[a]	9,336	10,560	13
Cotton[b]	5,122	5,352	5

[a] Million kilowatt-hours.
[b] Million yards.
SOURCE: *The Task Ahead, 1956:16.*

Colombo Plan, sponsored by nations belonging to the British Commonwealth, has led to gains in agricultural and other production as well as to a higher output of power in the nations of southern Asia (Table 20; cf. *Progress in Asia, 1953*).

Lack of Suitable Skills and Facilities

Even when resources are available to pay for innovations or techniques, without requisite skills the novelty will remain useless. There may be resistance to discarding old skills and substituting new ones (see pp. 188–189). A Yorkshire coal mine introduced a conveyor belt replacing cable-drawn tubs for hauling coal to the surface. The new technique promoted a flood of grievances but one especially is pertinent: the conveyor meant that the miners had to cease thinking about coal in terms of tons or hundredweights and appraise production by cubic feet of coal removed. The miners found the new ability difficult to come by. " 'There is no one below ground who can work out all this cubic measure,' " said a union leader (Dennis, Henriques, and Slaughter, 1956:107).

Of a somewhat different order is the failure of the Japanese to accept rhymed tonal poetry from China. The rejection is explicable by differences between the Chinese and Japanese languages. Chinese is a tone language, in which the tone of an utterance contributes to meaning. In rhymed tonal poetry the tones are rhymed. Japanese is not tonal. Hence rhymed tonal poetry was thoroughly incompatible, and nearly impossible, for a Japanese speaker (Kroeber, 1948:416).

Techniques require facilities. Complicated cooking routines are impossible where houses lack stoves with ovens, several burners, or temperature controls. Northern Canada's Indians and Eskimo have accepted the baby-feeding bottle with its rubber nipple. Sterilizing these or precisely measuring the ingredients of a formula is quite impractical because the people lack facilities to perform these operations.

Incompatibility with Social Organization

Cultural transmission is slowed down by other than ideological or technical incompatibility. The new element may prove to be incompatible with existing forms of social relations in a community.

An innovation promising to upset the existing system of prestige or power will probably be resisted as strongly by people who perceive the threat to their rank as it will win support from individuals hoping to gain prestige and influence. In Europe and America rank and power are tied closely to wealth. Changes in the system whereby wealth is distributed, owned, and taxed are among the most strenuously resisted innovations of modern times (Ogburn, 1950:167). A person in public office scarcely is permitted publicly to discuss radical transformations in this sector of culture. Such resistance is not, of course, evenly distributed through the American population. On the other hand, if already powerful groups oppose, and relatively powerless people support, a change, then the opposition is likely to be favored from the start. In underdeveloped countries economic development sometimes poses a threat if it advances the rank of traders and craftsmen, making these positions equal or superior to that of a landholding farmer (Linton, 1952:85). If an item is a prestige symbol its transmission to persons holding lower rank may be resisted. In the Nilgiri hills of South India live the Badaga, an agricultural people, and the Kota, lower-ranking artisans. The former wear the turban. Some Badaga once ambushed and beat up Kota who sought to adopt that headgear (Mandelbaum, 1941:19–20).

The Japanese did not accept from Chinese culture the civil-service system with its merit examinations (Kroeber, 1948:416). Japan was organized on the principle of hereditary descent for rank and office. A merit system could have little place in such an organization. Not until the hereditary aristocracy lost power in Japan did that country adopt the civil service. Many South Asian countries set great value on kinship loyalties. Relatives are trusted far above strangers. Basic loyalty is reserved for the family, village, or region. Despite western constitutions and other political forms, identification with the nation remains weak. It is not surprising that primary identification with kinsmen, villagers, or tribesmen should limit the degree to which a rationalistic, western-type civil service can operate in those countries (Northrop, 1953:114–121). The basic distrust of strangers also is related to the slow rate of capital accumulation. People are reluctant to invest in corporations composed of strangers. Although Pakistanis are not accustomed to investing money in corporate enterprises, when they do they often place more reliance on foreign-owned or foreign-managed concerns than on domestic enterprises (United States Department of Commerce, 1954:42). A similar instance of incompatibility is provided by the early attempts of Spaniards in Peru to introduce individual landholding among the Aymara Indians. The concept of private ownership of land was largely unintelligible to a people organized around land held in common. When finally accepted, the new pattern led to fractionation of landholdings, breakdown of coöperation between relatives, and dissolution of the extended family (Tschopik, 1951:161). A new social organization emerged, one congruent with private ownership of land.

Social Pressure

The use of social pressure to limit diffusion needs little discussion. It is illustrated when punishment and ostracism are threatened by the priestly administrators of highly conservative Pueblos in the southwestern United States (Waters, 1942). Zuñi Indian veterans returning from World War

II brought with them new elements of behavior that rarely became incorporated in the cultural web. Gossip, rumor, and ridicule restricted their innovative tendencies. One veteran wanted to establish a branch of the American Legion in the pueblo. Rumors that he would appropriate the dues for private ends helped to cut short the plans. Those young men unwilling to conform to traditional customs leave the village and become lost as agents of change (Adair and Vogt, 1949:551).

Blocked Communication

When people cannot understand each other diffusion will be affected. Under this condition artifacts are more likely to be transmitted than underlying ideas. Language alone may not be the barrier. Also lacking can be channels of communication between groups and categories of people along which innovations could be transmitted.

In many underdeveloped countries which are largely illiterate, programs of planned culture change are stymied because of difficulty in reaching people through the printed word. Use of radio receivers centrally located in villages and educational films shown by mobile projectors are recently innovated solutions to that difficulty.

Geographical Marginality

Diffusion, as already pointed out, depends on the geographical location of a community. Conversely, geographical marginality limits cultural exchange. Marginality, referring to a community's spatial isolation from some center of innovation or cultural elaboration, is governed by the techniques of transportation and communication available elsewhere in the world. Fifty years ago the Arctic regions were far more marginal than in 1958, when aircraft, supply ships, and winter tractor trains supplied far-northern trading posts, weather stations, radar installations, and military airfields. Radio has put the most isolated fur trader in daily touch with his regional headquarters. Always speaking relatively, marginal areas still exist in the modern world—including the upper Amazon Valley, the northeastern frontier of India, interior Dutch New Guinea, and much of northern Canada. Diffusion to these regions is slow, sometimes practically nonexistent.

Environmental Incompatibility

Marginality often works hand in hand with geographical incompatibility to restrict diffusion. Not till 4000 years after its invention in Southwest Asia did agriculture penetrate into the northern zone of Europe (see pp. 698, 754). Marginality did not operate alone. Climate remained too cold and moist for the available cereal crops and this factor still operates to exclude the Mediterranean olive, fig, and date from those regions. Use of northern lands for farming had to wait for the development of hardy and early maturing plants.

Other Factors

The circumstances in which an innovation enters channels of transmission can influence its subsequent diffusion. When cold storage first began in the United States (about 1890), unfit products were sometimes stored under poor refrigeration conditions. The consumer blamed refrigeration for the poor quality. A prejudice against cold storage appeared that lasted for many years and limited acceptance of the complex (O. E. Anderson, 1953: Chap. 9).

Perhaps the nature of certain cultural elements limits their diffusion. Ideas which cannot be understood without a large number of underlying premises that establish their logicality fall in this category. For this reason action patterns often diffuse more readily than the ideological elements of a complex.

Sometimes no plausible reason can be suggested for failure of a trait to spread. Why did the Pawnee Indian custom of sacrificing bison flesh by burning not diffuse to neighbors of the Pawnee who also hunted that animal (Wissler, 1923:140)?

AVAILABLE FILMS

Forgotten Village (67 min., b. and w.) by Brandon Films describes resistance to sanitation and vaccination in a Mexican village. The same theme, this time concerning a maternity home, is carried out in *Daybreak in Udi* (45 min., b. and w.). The latter picture, produced by British Information Services, was filmed among the Nigerian Ibo (*Overseas Education*, 1948, Vol. 19, No. 2).

16.

Synchronization of Change

ORIGINATION and diffusion constitute the primary processes through which novel elements enter culture. Once an innovation appears, through one or both of these sources, it will activate other, secondary processes: displacement, reduction-segregation, reinterpretation, and syncretism. In other terms, innovations set up a series of synchronized ramifications in a way of life.

DISPLACEMENT

Displacement occurs when a trait disappears from culture. The log cabin, perhaps a contribution of German settlers in the New World, is rapidly disappearing from the American scene. Horse-drawn vehicles, the icebox, hand-driven lawn mower, and commercial sailing ship have been displaced largely from western ways of life.

Complete and Partial Displacement

Like persistence, displacement may be complete or partial. Complete displacement occurs rarely. Even the knight's armor has not been dropped entirely from western culture. It survives—with a very different use, of course—in museum cases. It is fairly safe to cite buffalo hunting as a completely displaced trait, one that has vanished from the overt culture of the American Plains Indians. Even here, however, the trait persists in memory.

Partial displacement is manifested, first, in the reduction of the frequency with which some behavior occurs and, second, in the loss of particular meanings or usages formerly connected with a trait. Partial abandonment of breast feeding in twentieth-century America and Europe illustrates the first type (Jelliffe, 1955:15–16). So does the displacement of polygyny among the Saulteaux (Ojibwa) Indians of Canada (Table 21). The second variety of partial displacement is demonstrated in the example of medieval armor and the retention of the bow and arrow as toys among many American Indian tribes.

TABLE 21. Displacement of Polygyny in
Three Bands of Saulteaux Indians

Years	Proportion of Polygynous Men[a]
1875	17.6
1876	15.2
1877	12.1
1878	11.3
1879	10.1
1880	9.8
1881	8.4

[a] Polygyny means marriage to 2 or more women simultaneously.
SOURCE: Hallowell, *1938*:240.

Factors in Displacement

All displacement involves change in culture but it is not always correlated with innovation. A change in the geographical environment may be followed by abandonment of those elements of culture which hinged on a specific environmental variable. The Maori had little choice but to discontinue bark-cloth making after they arrived in New Zealand where the requisite tree did not grow. Displacement may also follow boredom or disinterest in a trait ("cultural fatigue" [Kroeber, *1948*:403–405]). The Melanesian Banks Islanders are supposed to have given up canoes after they lost interest in ocean travel.

Considered as a synchronized adjustment to changes deriving from one of the primary processes (i.e., origination or diffusion), displacement occurs when (1) a new trait substitutes for an old one or (2) cultural conditions alter in a way that makes an element incompatible with the new way of life. In addition, (3) displacement may grow out of social pressure.

1. Substitution. Much displacement arises from the appearance in culture of what is perceived to be a more satisfactory substitute for a given trait. The Silex coffee maker came on the market and partly displaced the percolator, the steel ax drove out the stone ax in practically all parts of the world, guns have substituted for bows and lances, and in America commercial baby foods to some extent have usurped the place of mother's milk.

2. Incompatibility. Italians in America have begun to abandon the manufacture and use of wine. Americans of Italian descent identify with Americans in general. Wine drinking is not an American custom. Also operative is a lack of space in which to manufacture and store the traditional Mediterranean beverage (P. H. Williams and R. Straus, *1950*:622–624). In Truk, a Micronesian island group, young men used to carry love sticks, slender rods about two feet long, useful for awakening a sleeping girl to call her to a lovers' tryst (Gladwin and Sarason, *1953*:106–107). The objects became useless after the frame house replaced the thatch dwelling. Today the sticks persist only as curios. Among the White Knife Shoshoni of Nevada the appearance of permanent houses and a keener appreciation of the value of accumulating wealth ended the custom of destroying a dead man's house and goods. Now houses are taken down and reassembled following death (Harris, 1940:95). In parts of India a combination of many innovations has encouraged displacement of the extended family. In Namhalli, a Mysore village, losing the help of married sons, their wives, and children meant less labor for cultivation with the result that the acreage devoted to orchard and garden crops decreased, representing a partial displacement of those activities (A. R. Beals, 1955:93).

With the diminished importance of hunting in Siberia, hunting rites have disappeared. Where displacement did not occur immediately, the rituals have been deprived of some of the conviction with which they were held formerly (Lot-Falck, 1953:11). The displacement of beliefs which are not amenable to testing (and hence cannot be proved to be true or false empirically) comes about when new premises for reasoning are adopted in a community. The new assumptions, based on recently discovered knowledge, may contradict a traditional belief or challenge its underlying premises. The conception of God or the ancestors as responsible for every drop of rain that falls is not very compatible with meteorological knowledge.

3. Social Pressure. When pressure is directed against some portion of a way of life it may, by depriving the element of reward value, extinguish it. This frequently occurs in culture contact. Missionaries in Melanesia refused to admit natives to church unless the latter wore more than loincloths (Durrad, 1922:10). Legal force together with moral suasion, in this and other parts of the world, ended both cannibalism and human sacrifice. In Natal, South Africa, scolding and propaganda have been used to wage war against plural marriage, girls' initiation ceremonies, ancestor propitiation rites, and other customs (Jaspan, 1953:116). In the western United States the federal government resolved to end the traditional religious ceremonies of the Plains and other Indian tribes. Laws were enacted in 1884 which made hitherto sacred rituals criminal offenses. Army troops intimidated worshipers and relief rations were withheld from people who insisted on worshiping together illegally. Before the repressive legislation was suspended, the Sun Dance and other native ceremonies had practically disappeared (J. Collier, 1947:230–232).

REDUCTION-SEGREGATION[1]

The rate of displacement rarely equals the pace of origination plus borrowing. Only if such a balance were maintained could the content of cul-

[1] This section is based on Kroeber, 1948:370–374.

ture remain at a constant level. Instead of constancy, however, culture manifests a cumulative tendency. The volume of world culture has increased enormously since Stone Age times. Of course, not all cultures expand their content at equal rates nor does accumulation proceed at a steady rate from one period to another. Areas within a particular culture rarely expand equally. Cultural accumulation confronts people with the problem of managing an enlarged volume of activities, types of groups, ideas, and artifacts. Reduction-segregation constitutes a process for dealing with the expanded content. It consists in reducing the sheer number of traits which any particular individual is obliged to handle.

One way in which this goal may be achieved is by segregating the increased volume of elements among different specialists. Ancient beliefs and knowledge about stars were allocated between two specialisms: astronomy and astrology. Those ideas which pertained to the location and appearance of various stars and planets went into the former category. Other ideas, which connected various heavenly bodies with human fate, went into the other. What seems to have happened is that during, or shortly after, the Persian Empire some scholars in Babylonia decided to slough off omens and portents from other types of star lore. They chose to deal with the heavens mainly in terms of what could be observed directly. Astronomy was born as a separate science. Astrology was left to occupy itself with less directly verifiable ideas.

Reduction-segregation is also accomplished by systematizing knowledge into a lesser number of concepts or by combining several overlapping concepts. "Knowledge advances . . . by artificial simplification . . ." (Flexner, 1930:114). Sometimes such recombination involves the synthesis of formerly distinct concepts. The results may be quite strange and, therefore, encounter trouble in winning acceptance. An example comes from contemporary anthropology. Here culture is defined as including socially standardized ideas. Personality also is defined as embracing socially standardized covert behavior traits (i.e., ideas). Obviously the two terms overlap. Yet anthropologists are reluctant to adopt a system of thought in which the two concepts would be merged. They continue to speak of culture "acting on" personality as though each concept referred to an independent referent (Honigmann, 1954b:28–29).

The reader will perceive reduction-segregation to be a more complex process than displacement. It contains the principle of displacement and also reveals a tendency toward genuine origination. Reduction-segregation sometimes occurs in a highly systematic and planned fashion, as when management experts are invited by an industrial concern to study, and make recommendations to simplify, a complicated system of organization, one that evolved piecemeal over several decades.

REINTERPRETATION

Reinterpretation designates the process through which a culture element is modified in form, meaning, or use in order to make it applicable under relatively new conditions. Reinterpretation also takes the form of restructuring new experiences to make them compatible with some existing feature in culture.[2] Reinterpretation introduces an element of considerable indeterminacy into cultural transmission. The precise form, use, or meaning which will be assigned to a borrowed element cannot be predicted easily. It can be said with assurance that, despite the volume of diffusion that has occurred in culture history, "no culture is a simple copy of any other" (Malinowski, 1927:42).

Any simple reassignment of value or meaning is not reinterpretation. A distinction must be drawn between it and metataxis, in which a cultural element spontaneously undergoes a change in evaluation or "standing," and also metalepsis, the spontaneous assignment of new meaning to a trait (Marett, 1920:109–112). Both these processes are illustrated by the case of masks, formerly "of sacred import" and later used to decorate actors. They also operate when a charm against the evil eye becomes converted into an ornament. After the Ghost Dance had failed to promote return of the ancestors and extinction of the whites, the Ute Indians of Colorado burlesqued the once sacred ceremony. Disillusioned and disappointed, the Indians parodied the old dance in a new one. They even burlesqued the act of falling into a trance, one of the elements in the ceremony (Marvin K. Opler, 1940:190). Like certain other distinctions, that between reinterpretation, metataxis, and metalepsis cannot always be made with assurance.

Reinterpretation and Diffusion

An important function of reinterpretation is to facilitate cultural borrowing by overcoming incompatibility between a new element and other factors in a cultural system. It is easy to see how this happens. John de Brébeuf, a French missionary in the New World, sought to tell the story of the Nativity to his Huron Indian congregation. He wanted to put the story in the light of their special experience. Here is a translation of words he wrote for a Christmas carol:

> Within a lodge of broken bark
> The tender Babe was found,
> A ragged robe of rabbit skin

[2] In psychological theory a process similar to reinterpretation is called "cognitive restructuring." This means that a person perceives and interprets matters differently under different circumstances (Allport, 1954:29).

Enwrapped His beauty round.
The chiefs from far before Him knelt
With gifts of fox and beaver pelt.

A more complex illustration of the process is seen in how the school was modified (reinterpreted) to make it congruent with Tuareg life. These Saharian pastoralists herd camels and travel with their tents. The French educational authorities made the school equally mobile, moving it as the families and children shifted pasture grounds (Blanguernon, 1954; see also Gast, 1954). The case illustrates a recasting of the traditional form of the western school, overcoming those elements of the trait incompatible with mobile life. Information is not available to indicate whether the new, mobile school is as efficient as the traditional kind. The question is not an idle one. Considerations of cost or effectiveness may render impractical the most ingenious reinterpretations.

The question of practicality is unlikely to arise when only the meanings of borrowed elements are reinterpreted, leaving their form and operation unaltered. Jewish culture contains many traits derived from communities in which the Jews at one time or another found themselves. They reinterpreted the traits for meaning. "By depth and ingenious reinterpretation they sought always to convert the popular customs . . . of their neighbors into instruments for . . . fulfilling, in daily practice and usage, their fundamental commitment to serve as the witnesses of God among men" (Gaster, 1955:xi). For example, the breaking of the bride's wineglass by the groom (a light bulb may be substituted in modern America) is distributed widely in the world. Usually it signifies destroying the powers of evil. Jews, however, have given it another meaning. It reminds them, first, of Nebuchadnezzar's destruction of the Temple (in 586 B.C.) and, second, of the fact that even joyous occasions must be tempered by sober recollection of that sad event (ibid., pp. 119–121). In the same manner the individualistic Navaho Indians, after arriving in the southwestern United States from an original northern homeland, borrowed and reinterpreted Pueblo rituals. They converted the group-centered ceremonies of the coöperative village Indians into individually oriented practices benefiting not the whole community (as among the Pueblo) but mainly those persons for whom the rites were performed.

What original meanings will be assigned to a borrowed novelty may be related to the conditions under which the innovation was introduced. Very special attitudes were reserved by the natives of Gela, an island in the Solomon group, for books and writing. ". . . The power of books is enhanced from the obvious fact that the administrators continually refer to them during court cases to obtain guidance on points of law. Thus it was more than mere spite that caused the Melanesians of Gela to burn the law books in the Judicial Commissioner's house after the European evacuation of Pulagi" during the Second World War (Belshaw, 1954:73).

As a wealth of illustrations suggests, reinterpretation often alters the meaning of borrowed traits rather than their form. Also use is altered more readily than form. Roman Catholic Christmas ceremonies in the Mackenzie River Valley trading posts remain the same whether performed in December, when the Indian population is dispersed on trap lines, or in summer, when the people have returned to the post. Only the actual celebration is shifted to another season. Several reasons may be suggested for more tenacious persistence of original form. First, in the case of artifacts, form is transmitted more easily from one culture to another than are complicated instructions for use or complex meanings. Second, it is easier to alter meaning or use and still have a trait that remains suited to a given end than to change the form. Finally, alteration of form is difficult—if not impossible—when the community does not manufacture the artifact which is borrowed.

Although reinterpretation usually is nondeliberate, it may be otherwise. A number of Muslims in late nineteenth-century India deliberately set out to make the Muslim way of life more compatible with European culture (W. C. Smith, 1946:31–32). The religion of Islam, they maintained, principally demands worship of a single God and honor to the memory of his prophet, Mohammed. All else—like the avoidance of interest, keeping women in seclusion, and prayer in Arabic—was superfluous. Their reinterpretation of Islam, known as the Aligarh Movement, came quite near to European values. Although it did not succeed entirely, the movement helped to narrow the gap between certain Indian Muslims and the British ruling class. In the same deliberate vein a professor of religion claims that a truly African branch of Christianity is needed. But it can come only through "African ways of worship, and African formulations of Christian doctrine and theology . . ." (Welch, 1953). He offers a small suggestion for securing more compatible forms of worship. An Anglican hymn invoking praise from all created things appeals to " 'O ye frost. . . . Bless ye the Lord. . . . O ye snow, bless ye the Lord.' " This he has altered to " 'O ye waving palm trees, Bless ye the Lord.' " The carol quoted earlier is also a deliberate reinterpretation.

Other Aspects of Reinterpretation

Situational reinterpretation is shown by the Lovedu of the Transvaal, South Africa, who have seen their reserve grow overcrowded and land become scarce. Yet "the people act as if the old abundance of land still prevails." New conditions are reinterpreted in the light of traditional optimistic values. "They attribute ordinary shortages, not to scarcity of land, but to the indolence of the modern generation, thus rephrasing their difficulties in a manner which is congruous with" the value they place on coöperation (E. J. Krige and J. D. Krige, 1943:286). By their perception of the existing situation the Lovedu also reduce the danger of competition for the scarce room remaining on their reserve.

Probably in every community each generation reinterprets some of the cultural heritage received from the past. Conditions change and the content of culture is redesigned quite unconsciously to make it compatible, continually adaptive, or maximally adjustive in the new situation. This happened with the Sun Dance among the Ute Indians. These people in northeastern Utah adopted the Sun Dance only relatively lately, perhaps about 1890, when their culture already had undergone drastic change under Euroamerican influence. In reinterpreting the dance they made it a symbol of defiance of the whites—a meaning which it did not possess among neighboring tribes. The conception made the ceremony quite compatible with the sentiments extant among the Ute in 1890. By 1932 the Sun Dance had become a commercialized tourist attraction and the defiant features had disappeared. But by 1937 a new spirit for collective action came over the tribe and the Sun Dance once again was reinterpreted nativistically. It has become a "binding factor for all the northern Ute who have remained culturally Indian. Those who became oriented toward White values do not partake. It is the symbol of the native culture which has practically disappeared . . ." (J. A. Jones, 1955:256).

Reinterpretation operates when events accounted for one way by priests or in scriptures are parochialized in daily life. Sacred ceremonies in India acquire meanings in village culture that they do not possess in strictly orthodox belief (Marriott, 1955:199–201). The legal norms of a culture are constantly reinterpreted in a heterogeneous community to make them congruent with changed conditions or new knowledge (see pp. 492–493).

Not all reinterpretation succeeds. Factors of cost and lack of efficiency have already been cited as handicaps. Resistance may greet the reinterpretation. Many Indian Muslims saw no positive worth in the Aligarh Movement and resented its unorthodoxy. In France more recently the worker priests had to discontinue their activities for somewhat the same reason. The rationale for the latter lay in the changes which the urban community had undergone since the onset of industrialization. City people had lost their feeling of parish membership, yet priests continued to be assigned to parish units. Most of the clergyman's parishioners remained strangers to him, even when they attended Mass on Sundays. Some industrial workers, of course, had ceased to carry out the obligations of Catholics. A new missionary movement grew up. Priests would live and work among the people, sharing their houses, dressing like workers, and even entering factories and labor unions. The Roman Catholic authorities, however, feared that such activities placed the priests in moral jeopardy. After operating for a few years the movement was ordered to cease.[3]

SYNCRETISM

"It is not merely that one nation borrows a god from another with its proper figure and attributes and rites. . . . The intercourse of races can produce quainter results than this" (Tylor, 1891:254). With those words an early anthropologist called attention to the process by which a trait belonging to one cultural configuration becomes fused with an analogous element in another culture. This process is called syncretism.

Haitian culture retains some West African deities—presumably derived from Africa at the time of the slave trade—and also it includes the Catholic Trinity and saints. In some cases identification has occurred between concepts deriving from each of these cultural traditions. The god Legba, of African origin, has undergone fusion with Catholic Saint Anthony (Herskovits, 1948:553). The analogy between these two concepts, Legba and Anthony, lies in the fact that each traditionally has been associated with poverty. Legba conventionally is conceived as clad in tatters while Saint Anthony represents a patron of the poor. In Africa, however, Christian missionaries syncretized Legba with the Christian devil (Herskovits, 1941a: 253). They probably acted on the conception of Legba as a trickster, with emphasis on his fondness for playing pranks on men and his reputation for balking the other gods in carrying out their duties. In the missionaries' ideology the devil, symbol of evil, also nearly counterpoises God, the symbol of good. Legba, Saint Anthony, and the devil, of course, possess other characteristics than those which entered into the syncretization process. The additional features, however, are less relevant for understanding the identifications which took place.

In another type of fusion the ceremonies of two religious traditions merge. Romans celebrated the Lupercalia near the middle of February. For this festival men selected women to be their partners. On February 15 a dog and a goat were sacrificed; the thongs made from these animals remained efficacious for curing female sterility. In 270 A.D., on February 14, occurred the martyrdom of Valentine. Henceforth Christians observed the anniversary of that event on February 14. The holiday gradually came to be fused with the meanings of the Lupercalia and Saint Valentine became a symbol of sexual love. Christmas and Easter are each celebrated at periods when pre-Christian Europe carried out midwinter and spring ceremonies. In Rome the midwinter festival included games, dancing, the exchange of

[3] This account is based on Emmanuel, 1954. See also Dubalen, 1955, and *The Worker-Priests: A Collective Documentation*, 1956.

gifts, and other forms of merrymaking. Those elements have entered into the celebration of Christmas and are reflected in the traditional seasonal greeting: "Merry Christmas!" In some parts of the Soviet Union antireligious agitation took the form of arranging mass festivals of socialist culture at Christmastime (Yaroslavsky, 1956:275). In Zulu Zionist churches of

Syncretism Has Occurred to Promote a Complex Mixture of Maya and Catholic Ritual in Modern Guatemala (*Life* photo by Dmitri Kessel [c] 1947 Time Inc.).

South Africa the Hebraic-Christian tradition of prophecy fused with traditional forms of diagnosis (i.e., divination). Accompanied by hymns and a chorus of "Amens," the prophet or prophetess uncovers the source of an illness, discerns an evildoer, and reveals hidden sin. Such diagnosis is said to be sponsored by "the Lord" (Sundkler, 1948:253–259). Gnosticism, appearing in Alexandria, Egypt, about the second century after Christ, represented a deliberate attempt to fuse Christian, Platonic, Buddhist, and Hindu ideas. Had it succeeded, the Christian faith today might include belief in reincarnation. Islam, the faith of Muslims, is, like other world religions, a product of fusion. Drawing on the resources of Christianity, and Arabian paganism, it relegates Jesus to the rank of a Hebrew prophet. The *Quran*, its sacred scripture, includes Old and New Testament incidents, like the accounts of Moses and Noah and the promise of a Last Judgment. The book reports the words which the Prophet Mohammed heard from God (Pickthall, 1930:Surah XXV). Treating Islam or any other ideology as syncretic is not to devaluate it. The special value which such beliefs possess for their adherents must be kept in mind even while analyzing their syncretic nature.

RAMIFICATION OF CHANGE

It is time to put together some of the primary and secondary processes of change to see the complex interrelations which may link an innovation with changes in the rest of the cultural configuration and cultural field. Because culture and its field constitute systems that are mutually dependent, each with interrelated parts, changes in one area of either system are likely to ramify into other areas. Intensive plowing of the American plains promoted erosion of the topsoil, an environmental change, which in turn led to considerable thought and many socially standardized measures devoted to soil conservation. Some amount of migration from the afflicted area took place as well as a nation-wide redistribution of occupations as people who fled from the dust bowl assumed new positions in the American community.

When a South Asian rice cultivator learns to use a chemical insecticide to get rid of environmental pests he may also give up prayer as a symbolic means of preventing plant infection. European rule in colonial territories often has been accompanied by a weakening of not only the power of traditional leaders but people's faith in supernatural powers. In retrospect it is easy to understand how these things happened. The European administrator was powerful. He committed acts forbidden in the traditional code, yet the expected automatic retribution, which people had been taught to fear, did not follow. The natives themselves lost their fear of the forbidden acts, and and this, in turn, weakened faith in the postulated beings supposed to sanction conformity (Speiser, 1922:37–41). Ramification may be less complex but equally unpredictable. Photography after its origination changed painting. The need no longer existed for paintings which faithfully would represent or imitate nature. Impressionistic techniques appeared and also an art which frankly sought to distort familiar things.

Ramification of change is inevitable. One sector of culture, however, need not always keep pace with others. This will become clearer after the discussion of unequal culture change (pp. 247–251). Before turning to that subject we will look at some other illustrations of ramifying culture change.

Ramification of Change in the Mato Grosso[4]

Among the Cayuá Indians, living in the southern Mato Grosso of Brazil, agriculture became more important in the way of life following 1850. At

[4] This account of Cayuá culture change is from J. B. Watson, 1952:98–123.

that time contacts with Brazilians of European extraction brought about a cessation of intertribal fighting as well as relief from preoccupation with defensive measures. The point here is not simply that one change produced the other. The network of interrelationships is more complex. Let the reader at this point cease to think solely of Cayuá culture and bear in mind the way of life in the Mato Grosso, regardless of ethnic group. Clearly that way of life, together with numerous elements of the cultural field, changed following the immigration of fresh people who possessed new values and assumed the role of peacemakers. From Neo-Brazilian culture diffused the machete, hoe, and ax, which, in the hands of Indian men, very much facilitated agriculture. More time and effort devoted to agriculture meant reduced intensity of hunting and gathering activities, a restriction further reinforced by the fact that the Brazilians tended to confine the Cayuá to reservation lands. The Cayuá no longer planted crops only for their own use; in part the expanded landholdings were intended to allow participation in trade. Through the newly opened market more items of European origin reached the Indians. Acceptance of these products meant a decline in certain native types of manufacturing and the consequent reallocation of specialists to other crafts, especially those whose products could be sold to the Brazilians. Out of these shifts in work appeared an increasing tendency among men to value individual effort rather than coöperative endeavor. The new tools allowed a farmer to work alone while yet remaining reasonably efficient. The profit motive, combined with the newly created need for money in order to secure imported manufactured goods, weighed still further in favor of individual male work and against the previous pattern of coöperation. For one reason, trade goods, like pots, tools, and items of clothing, could not be distributed as easily as jointly produced garden crops.

The individualism fostered by the new tools and through trade relations with Brazilians encouraged still further change. They affected the form of the family. With the breakdown in group farming, husband and wife began to constitute an independent economic unit, one cut off from both parental families. A man no longer served out a work term in his bride's family, an insisted-upon condition of marriage in former times when women had performed much of the agricultural work. The shift in family form involved derivative changes in obligations to kinsmen. These need not be followed through here.

Other Instances of Ramified Change

Urbanization is another variable regularly accompanied by a large series of interrelated changes and one that is spreading rapidly in the modern world.

The fact of high density in small space gives rise to traffic and sanitary difficulties, to housing problems, to crime conditions, to organized special interests.

All of these have to be dealt with in one way or another, and the innovations made sometimes give rise to new patterns of political and social control which can be diffused to the rural population. Furthermore, the competition for space and for special advantage within the urban milieu gives an advantage to individual innovation, to regionalistic calculation, and to individualism—all of which tends to stimulate a faster pace of cultural change than is likely to be seen in a peasant setting [K. Davis and H. H. Golden, 1954:24].

A single, comprehensive ideological system may embody principles affecting a large area of behavior. Conversion to such a system demands in advance or leads to thoroughgoing culture change. The introduction of Protestantism in Brazil through proselytism has been accompanied by many innovations (Willems, 1955).

Senegal Farmers Have Entered a Money Economy by Producing a Cash Crop of Cotton (courtesy, French Cultural Services).

Although literacy is by no means undesirable in the estimation of the Catholic Church, the latter body does not impel people to secure literacy as strongly as does the Protestant movement. The ability to read and write, in turn, has become a medium for the secularization of Protestants. Through the insistence of the church, members refrain from alcoholic beverages, tobacco, and forms of gambling, including the national lottery. The new religion thereby influences economic behavior, something it also does through prohibiting aids to devotion like statues of the saints, candles, rosaries, and banners. In a country where much business depends on debt and bills are not paid regularly Protestants live up to a moral obligation to discharge their debts. They are recognized as dependable and honest. Their strict rules of chastity and marital fidelity, while quite in line with Brazilian values prescribed for females, contrast sharply with the type of sex behavior traditionally expected from men.

When new culture elements are possible only in return for raw materials, capital goods, or money, accumulating these adjuncts illustrates a type of ramification. The point is illustrated on the Melanesian island of Malekula. The diffusion from one tribe to another of certain ceremonies, by means of which a man could promote himself in rank, demanded a simultaneous increase in the production of pigs. The rituals required the use of pigs (Layard, 1928:144). Innovations like the shorter work week and the two-week vacation in America have been accompanied by an increased output of sporting goods, the wherewithal by which many people enjoy their new leisure.

Like reinterpretation, all the cultural and field ramifications of a change are difficult to predict. Hence even the most carefully planned diffusion may be followed by unexpected phenomena (Mead, 1956a:448). What student of culture would have predicted that the introduction of western culture to Africa would be accompanied by not a decrease but an increase in the African's preoccupation with witch beliefs (cf. pp. 641–642)? This is exactly what has happened. The explanation lies in the interpersonal rivalries and tensions encouraged by culture change. Witchcraft accusations had constituted a traditional means of damaging a rival's reputation as well as a channel for draining off tension. The same ready vehicle remained available for coping with new stresses accompanying European contact (Marwick, 1956).

UNEVEN CHANGE

All ramifications of an innovation do not spread evenly through a cultural system, encouraging complementary displacements or insuring compatibility through the reinterpretation of traditional traits. Nor does change flow evenly through a community, bringing the sentiments of different social groups and categories into harmonious alignment. If both these things regularly happened much of the stress accompanying culture change could be avoided. It might then not be true that "human life is reduced to real suffering, to hell . . . when two ages, two cultures and religions overlap" (Hesse, 1929:36).

Innovations are often deliberately resisted by some sections of a community. They may be accepted only incompletely, the necessary accommodations in other areas of life not being forthcoming. Sometimes members in a community adopt contradictory innovations so that mutually incompatible expectations confront people. Among the Southwest Pacific Manus, when economically dependent young men ceased to be available to work for a rich patron outside of the family, the role of adolescent sons was reinterpreted to include the obligation of food getting. A man now needed the labor of his sons to replace the services of youths whose marriage he formerly financed. At the same time, however, the villagers of New Peri, in Manus, opened a school. The school's demands on adolescent boys conflicted with their roles in fishing and other economic activities. The Manus may be accused of planning their culture change poorly, but it is very rare for any community, outside of western factories or similar specialized organizations, to guide change rationally and to inquire beforehand whether an innovation will mesh with other elements in culture.

Change becomes uneven in a community not because one section of culture, or one set of people, remains completely unchanging or static. Remember that change is constant, affecting everyone and everything in a community. When one section of people or an area of culture lags behind another it is because the *rate* of change between them is not proportionate, or the directions of innovation may be divergent.

Readers will note that a distinction has been drawn between uneven

Unequal Culture Change Is Suggested by This Scene in an Eskimo Tent at Lake Harbor, Baffin Island (courtesy, National Film Board).

change taking place in a system of behavior and artifacts—that is, in culture—and uneven change between the groups, categories, or individuals constituting a community. The former constitutes uneven *culture* change; the latter, uneven *social* change. The same situation often may be perceived as representing both uneven culture and uneven social change.

Uneven Culture Change

A simple form of uneven culture change occurs when overt behavior alters without a corresponding, complementary change in values. Thus, the frequency with which unmarried youth engages in sex relations appears to have increased in America during the last few generations (Kinsey, Pomeroy, Martin, and Gebhard, 1953:298). But community attitudes opposing premarital sexuality have not changed proportionately. A more complex example of uneven culture is reported from New Peri in Manus (Mead, 1956a:297–302). During the past 25 years these Melanesians made the transition from a production-for-use type of economy to one dependent upon money and trade. When this happened many of their requirements came to be imported from Europe and America. But the people have not learned to guard an extra supply of purchased goods from neighbors who run short. In the old days a man might keep his house full of property needed for some future exchange or ceremony. He could then with good conscience refuse to lend or give away anything on the ground that his wealth was pledged for a particular purpose. People understood the wealthy man when he argued that supernatural punishment would strike him if his obligations were not discharged properly. Today the old exchanges of wealth, the ceremonies for which much food and other valuables were formerly required, as well as their supporting beliefs have disappeared from Manus culture. Yet the transition to a European-type economy remains incomplete.

Take for instance the question of mantles for pressure lamps. These mantles are delicate little bits of silken net; they cost two shillings each, and once on a lamp they are likely to break at a sudden jar from the impact of any insect or a sudden shift in temperature. Any man who depends upon fishing with a pressure lamp is well-advised to have at least one spare mantle. But if he has a spare mantle, and is known to have a spare mantle, then he is subject to pressure to sell it to anyone he knows whose mantle breaks. Here it is not so much a question of other people's begging for one's property as the simple question of availability of necessary and scarce goods. So people tend not to take the trip to Lorengau or Ndropwa to buy spare objects until after they need them. With uncertain weather and many days when canoe voyages are almost impossible, this means long periods without necessary objects, particularly food.

Apparently the people of New Peri need a retail store where food for the next meal could be bought or a broken mantle replaced without having to make a long sea journey. For various reasons (mainly having to do with the amount of capital and licenses required) no store has yet appeared.

Another instance of uneven culture change comes from Ceylon, where a revolution in ideals occurred under British influence. Legally and economically the Ceylonese accept the principle of equality. People live where they please and economic discrimination is forbidden. Yet castes ranked as superior and inferior to one another survive, although the growing impersonality of social life makes the full observance of caste restrictions unenforceable. In an urban area, especially, one may not even know the caste to which one's neighbor in a bus or tenement belongs. In the past inferior castes probably accepted discrimination as natural and without complaint. Today such acceptance has quite disappeared and caste constitutes an anachronism when seen alongside the egalitarian values of modern Ceylon (Ryan, 1953:338–340). A roughly parallel situation exists in the modern United States, where the Fourteenth and Fifteenth Amendments to the Constitution were deemed necessary in order that all men might secure legal rights. These amendments by 1958 had not ended formal and informal

The Revival of *Eisteddfods* Represents a Conscious Attempt to Preserve a Portion of the Welsh Cultural Heritage (see p. 262) (courtesy, British Information Services).

customs of discrimination directed against the Negro in both northern and southern states.

In Central Africa, among the Nyakyusa, monogamy has replaced plural marriage among Christian natives. Yet the old value on generous hospitality remains in force and governs both Christians and non-Christians. Also the pattern of hoe agriculture, with women working in the fields, persists. A modern Nyakyusa family head, who is a Christian and therefore possesses only one wife to tend the growing crops, cannot produce as much food as previously. Therefore he cannot readily furnish the entertainment on which his social standing still depends. On the other hand, if he takes more than a single wife he loses the respect of his fellow Christians. No modification of the value system consistent with the acceptance of Christianity has appeared, nor any change in agricultural technology which might help a household to produce the same amount of food as previously while utilizing only a single woman's work (G. Wilson and M. Wilson, 1945:126).

Modern life in Europe and America furnishes many examples of culturally uneven change. As American government assumed more and more specialized tasks (which now range from regulating developments in atomic energy to rehabilitating narcotics addicts), citizens also became increasingly educated for their role as informed participants in democratic government. Yet, despite universal literacy and a large proportion of adults educated through high school and college, voting behavior remains personal or is done on a party basis. The typical voter chooses the man he likes, generally someone who possesses personal appeal. American elections (except when constitutional amendments come before the public) are scarcely based on intensive study of issues or of the policies which a man promises to implement when he secures office. The privately owned radio and television networks in the United States devote little time to reviews of policy, the owners presumably recognizing that such programs would not be popular. It is fair to conclude that the American voter does not inform himself in order better to direct the complex government which is partly his responsibility (editorial, *New York Times*, Nov. 10, 1956). It may be that the ever increasing scope and elaborateness of government demand more knowledge than even the college-educated voter possesses and mean the end of popular democracy. Most Americans, however, hardly are willing to accept that conclusion.[5]

Another instance of uneven culture change appears in every modern nation's role in international affairs. New forms of transportation, economic interdependence of countries, and powerful, deadly weapons have combined to reduce each nation's effective sovereignty. An independent country today is less free than ever before to do what its citizens and leaders desire at home or abroad. Yet the claim to sovereignty persists. International forms of organization, like the United Nations and its specialized subgroups, avoid any suggestion of interfering with a member country's claim to sovereign status. Despite international interdependence, modern nations have not changed their antiquated modes of dealing with one another. In an atomic age when mistakes can be more costly than ever before, the efficiency of the diplomatic and consular services has not become better suited to deal with international problems (Ogburn, 1950:246–247).

Uneven culture change can promote personality conflict. The same individual wants certain advantages conferred by an innovation but is reluctant to accept its other implications. Americans value rapid forms of

---

[5] Various other solutions have been proposed, so far unsuccessfully. A suggestion is that people vote for representatives who hold different points of view, rather than for men representing political parties. This might focus more attention on the issues (Van den Bergh, 1956).

communication and transportation but resent the notion that mankind's closeness demands new ways of relating to foreign neighbors, including more limitations on national sovereignty. In the same way the individual Nyakyusa is in a quandary when he faces the competing attractions of Christianity, with its obligation of monogamy, and social acceptance based on generosity, which is more readily realized through pagan forms of marriage. Uneven culture change, therefore, often means intrapersonal stress for individuals caught in it.

Serious conflict between incompatible elements in culture may be avoided, of course, by some kind of scheduling. The discrepant behaviors are restricted to separate situations. In the United States equality for all people long remained a constitutional ideal rather than an insisted-upon norm in daily living. People may not even be able to adopt the necessary perspective enabling them to see the conflicting tendencies in their way of life. But though the opposition is kept from impinging too directly on consciousness, its presence in a culture will be felt periodically, especially by thoughtful persons able to adopt a viewpoint of distanciation (Lévi-Strauss, 1954b:123).

Uneven Social Change

Uneven social change implies that categories, groups, or individuals modify their behavior or artifacts independently of one another. Some persons alter certain elements of culture faster than, or in different directions from, others. Whereas uneven culture change often promotes intrapersonal tension, uneven social change is likely to produce misunderstanding and conflict between the members of a community.

A familiar type of unequal social change involves a widening gap between two generations, the members of each valuing relatively different kinds of experience. In many parts of Africa the attendance of children at European schools has driven a wedge between them and their parents. During the period of heavy European immigration the same situation was common in the United States, where, of course, it continues to be found. Change may also proceed unequally in diverse regions of the community, or may affect different social classes unevenly. In an industrial establishment management may favor the impressive advantages of a new process while workers perceive it as a threat. Many of the frictions apparent in the 40-year-old Hawaiian homestead community of Anahole are related to remnants of ancient culture patterns persisting among a few families while having been displaced in other people. The Hawaiian woman who criticized her neighbor's children, saying they ran around without proper supervision, showed how far she had come from the traditional, permissive mode of child rearing. The commercial fisherman who did not invite his neighbors to assist him and share in the catch was resented for his apparent selfishness, even though he lived by new values that were congruent with a money economy. The unevenness of change in Anahole contributed to the isolation of families from one another and so to the decline of enterprises jointly carried out (Fried, 1955:56–57).

Uneven social change may be studied fruitfully in a society as well as in a community. From the societal point of view, communities may originate or borrow traits at different rates or may alter their cultures in divergent directions. Misunderstanding and conflict between tribes, nations, and cities, as well as between urban and rural populations, are often illuminated when studied in relation to uneven change.

Sources of Uneven Change

Basically uneven culture change depends on the unequal willingness or ability of people to alter, through origination or borrowing, some aspects of life in comparison to others. Correspondingly, uneven social change arises from differential readiness of people to adopt new lines of conduct. Both types of unevenness are likely to appear in communities undergoing rapid change. The rapidity of innovation means that certain innovations are accepted eagerly without time for the necessary modifications to be introduced in other areas of the way of life. The need for such secondary modifications may not be perceived.

A few testable propositions that render uneven change more predictable follow.

1. Uneven change often follows when modifications appear in the technological area of culture without being accompanied by compatible changes in social organization and ideology (Ogburn, 1950:73). This principle constitutes more a description of "culture lag" than an explanation. However, it does indicate where at least one source of unevenness lies. The special readiness of technology to change may be due to the fact that technological change is more cumulative than change in other areas of culture. A novelty in social organization or ideology relatively rarely builds on previous elements of behavior but rather will encourage their displacement through substitution. In the case of techniques and their accompanying artifacts, however, secondary innovations frequently are added to a basic invention. Whether the cumulative nature of technical change is responsible for any significant proportion of uneven change deserves more study. May it not, in addition, also be true that many people welcome technological change for the tangible and immediately perceived rewards which it brings, while the reward value of new values, idea systems, and forms of social relations remains less apparent?

2. It has been suggested that man, largely by virtue of his early social experience, possesses a strong desire for satisfactory interpersonal ties with other people (Scott and Lynton, 1952:29–30). Under rapid technical change, undertaken in pursuit of lower costs, increased output, shorter hours

of work, and higher earnings, such social satisfactions tend to be ignored. Highly mechanized, rational, efficient, but impersonal ways of mass production are adopted without much concession to men's desire for close human relationships. Workers find themselves among strangers and derive little sense of accomplishment from their work. They possess little control over what they produce. Signs of human unhappiness under such conditions include absenteeism, illness, and passivity. The presence of these symptoms in the factory or community obstructs the execution of the most efficient and rational techniques. If this analysis is true, "Can modern industry with its repetitive processes, rapid changes, specialization and large size, provide community satisfactions?"

3. The unevenness of change to some extent rests on man's tendency, in times of stress, to retain elements in his way of life which possess strong emotional or symbolic value. The retention of kinship terms, privileges, or attachments to certain groups may persist in times of rapid culture change because these things bestow security and prestige or emphasize the distinctiveness of certain individuals (R. Firth, 1952; Allen, 1955:10).

4. Primarily with reference to uneven social change, an obviously important factor in unevenness is differential experience. If individuals, groups, or categories for whatever reason (social rank, financial resources, or migration) are exposed to different situations in which varying degrees and rates of change are experienced, then uneven social change will occur. Any social barrier that restricts interaction between people in a society, thereby reducing common experiences, increases unevenness (see Chapter 27).

It would be repetitious to repeat them here, but the factors contributing to the persistence of any element in culture as well as factors which limit diffusion (see pp. 185–190 and 225–232) also condition uneven change, provided that some elements in the way of life are simultaneously undergoing modification.

How Uneven Change Affects Further Change

The stress occasioned by uneven change constitutes an incentive to innovate behavior and artifacts that promise to reduce the unevenness (G. Wilson and M. Wilson, 1945:133–134). These solutions often go only half the way so that they do not really cope with the fundamental problem.

Uneven change tends to favor piecemeal rather than rapid and relatively total change and to slow down new learning (Mead, 1956a:445–450). The old traits surviving in culture exert pressure to reinstate or maintain others "and so continually act as a drag on the establishment of new habits." The Melanesian people of Manus, on the other hand, show wholesale, rapid, and relatively easy change. "The people . . . all changed as a unit—parents, grandparents, and children—so that the old mesh of human relations could be rewoven into a new pattern from which no thread was missing" (ibid., p. 452). Change in European immigrants to America revealed much the same speed and thoroughness. Potential drags on change and anchors to the past had been left in a foreign country.

There was no old house style to remind one that the old social relationships no longer held. Instead, a different kind of house, lived in by those who practised the different kind of relationship, was ready to support the change. Children who came home from school to insist that a good American breakfast contained orange juice and cereal stormed up American steps and banged American doors; children, become far more active and free in the American environment, jumped on American sofas. . . . Unfamiliar foods were cooked on a new kind of stove, and served in a new kind of dish, whose pattern and design evoked no nostalgia for the old. Each detail of the new life supported each other detail [*ibid.*, p. 446].

Scale and Uneven Change

It may be assumed that cultural change always involves some change in scale (see pp. 149–151). Directly or indirectly the change has been made possible by, or gives rise to, some modification of the number of people in relation or of the intensity of social relations (G. Wilson and M. Wilson, 1945:132). Uneven social change also implies unevenness in scale. Some people in the community or society are larger in scale than others. This means that the correlates of scale (see pp. 152–154) will also be distributed unevenly in the population. From the standpoint of scale theory, the resolution of uneven social change without social fragmentation requires either that one side catch up with the other or that the latter give up some portion of its wider scale. Because reduction in scale involves change in the correlates of scale, and because many correlates tend to be valued, it is often a particularly difficult and costly matter for people deliberately to choose to reduce scale. Social fragmentation, of course, also brings with it a costly reduction in scale. To avoid that price (reflected, for example, in a nation's weakened political or economic power) attempts at social fragmentation are likely to be resisted most strenuously, even to the point of civil war.

AVAILABLE FILMS

Many films deal with the changes that have followed the acceptance of foreign culture traits by small-scale, exotic communities, but very few illustrate much theory. A notable exception is *Father and Son* (20 min., b. and w.), released by British Information Services. The father's conversion of a compass, given to him as a gift by his son, into a charm dramatically highlights reinterpretation. The setting is coastal Kenya. Syncretism in the celebration of Christmas and in other ceremonies carried out by Brazilian Bahians is shown in *Fêtes à Bahia* (15 min., b. and w., 35 mm. only, in French), produced by H. Beauvais. See also the films listed in the following chapter.

17.

Acculturation

HEAVY diffusion and related culture change in the modern world are transforming radically many small-scale communities. Currently South America, Africa, and the Southwest Pacific islands are experiencing the full force of contact with European and North American cultures. Much the same situation confronted the North American Indian starting 350 years ago when European immigrants arrived in the New World. In the eighteenth century a different kind of culture contact ensued for the Sarsi Indians as they moved south from the forested region of northern Canada and entered the western plains. Here they came into contact with the culturally highly divergent Blackfoot Indians. In contemporary Israel, people of many cultural backgrounds live and work together closely. Anthropologists have become much interested in observing such plural communities, in which two or more distinct ways of life coexist and in which many of the previously mentioned cultural processes operate. The term "acculturation" designates in general what happens during culture contact of this kind.

ACCULTURATION—SITUATION AND PROCESS

Acculturation refers mainly to a situation marked by relatively continuous interaction between two or more cultures. From the standpoint of process, however, acculturation designates all the processes that ensue when two or more cultures come into lasting direct or mediated contact. A number of those constituent processes have already been introduced and will require only brief identification in this chapter.

In actuality one sees not cultures but people in contact. It is more precise to refer to communities being in, and adjusting to, one another. As already suggested in connection with diffusion, the status of the active participants in a situation of culture contact influences what transpires in acculturation. University-trained colonial administrators are likely to instigate somewhat different processes in a native community from those set in motion by labor recruiters or an invading army.

Acculturation must not be confused with diffusion. The latter does not depend on direct contact. In diffusion, community X may transmit its artifacts to community Y through a series of intermediary communities. In that case X and Y are spatially remote from each other. Direct culture contact occurs when colonial administrators, missionaries, shopkeepers, immigrants, migrant laborers, or refugees—people characterized by a relatively distinct way of life—settle down near people with another way of life. European immigrants to the New World and Sarsi migrants to the plains exemplify the process. Contact may also be mediated by the printed word, radio, motion pictures, or other mass media (Herskovits, *1941b*). Many rural enclaves in the United States have become aware of urban or national behavior patterns following the advent of the radio. Acculturation does not exist until culture contact is relatively continuous. The brief annual call of a mission ship to an isolated island scarcely creates an acculturation situation. A resident foreign trader on the same island is a much better example of continuous contact. A conquering army that remains in occupation is in the same category.[1]

Occasionally the adjective "acculturated" is used to designate an individual or community that has for a long time been in an acculturation situation and assimilated many elements from another way of life. Such a usage will be avoided in this chapter mainly because acculturation is not always marked by intensive diffusion or assimilation. We prefer to use "assimilated" to refer to the state of having absorbed many elements from an exotic way of life.

Aspects of Acculturation

Acculturation situations vary with respect to certain features.

1. Power. Culture contact may be marked by equal or unequal social dominance of the communities involved. (Cultural dominance is something else again and will be discussed on p. 259.) China's position vis-à-vis the Soviet Union in 1956 was marked by relatively equal dominance compared to Germany's postwar relationship with the United States or the relationship of the Cayuá Indians with the Brazilians (see pp. 243–244). In a situation of unequal dominance one of the parties controls by force or some other kind of power a disproportionate number of the responses made by the subordinate community. In equal dominance the relationship is between peers.

2. Mutual Respect. Culture contact may be marked by varying degrees of mutual appreciation. At one extreme is a situation in which each party respects the way of life of the other. If one is larger in scale and possesses

---

[1] The Social Science Research Council Summer Seminar on Acculturation (*1954*:974) would add that any cultural system involved in acculturation must "not require another system for continued functioning." This is confusing. Certainly a nation which administers a colonial empire is not autonomous. The intention of the Seminar is, perhaps, to exclude relations between classes and castes from acculturation. This might as well be done frankly, in so many words.

greater social power and more knowledge, these resources are used not autocratically but to help the other party develop in whatever direction the latter chooses. Such a relationship exists as the ideal in colonial policy. In practice, however, the policy scarcely may be apparent. At the opposite extreme one community is interested primarily in exploiting the other. The situation is marked by fear, rivalry, or ethnocentrism. Neither values the other's language. Change is regarded either as something to be avoided at all costs or as necessary in order to eradicate an unwholesome way of life.

3. Hostility. Acculturation that is hostile features not only violence but also discrimination and rejection. In the western United States during the Second World War American-born Japanese experienced considerable prejudice from local Americans. After they migrated to Chicago they entered a situation of low discrimination that seemingly fostered a high rate of cultural borrowing (Caudill, 1952:8). In northwestern Manchuria contacts between Russian Cossacks and Tungus reindeer herders began with the military defeat of the Tungus in 1603 and 1615. Recollection of this event · practically disappeared with time, and relations between the two groups remained amicable for 200 years. An anthropologist heard no expression of fear, contempt, or hatred expressed by either side. Contacts are confined mainly to trade; the Russians (who possess the greater prestige), numbering about 150, merchandise goods to the 160 herders. Neither party is able to command the other's language (Lindgren, 1938). The hypothesis that the amicability characteristic of this situation depends on the individualistic character of Tungus and Cossack social life plus the complementary nature of their basic beliefs is confirmed by a comparative study of a community where Guatemalan Indians live with Ladinos (Redfield, 1939; Tumin, 1952:Chap. 17; cf. pp. 456–457 *infra*).

4. Regulation. Controlled acculturation means that the culture contact situation is regulated deliberately. The purpose of such regulation is to govern the rate of change and maintain a fairly high degree of general persistence or stability. The rules may be formulated by the subordinate community or by any other party involved. The joint agreement between the United States and Canada to build radar stations and airstrips in far northern Canada contains a provision that "all contact with Eskimo, other than those whose employment on any aspect of the project is approved, is to be avoided except in cases of emergency" (Agreement, 1956:28). Greenland similarly regulates the contact of American military visitors with Eskimo.

The Hutterites, a religious sect akin to the Amish, seek to control acculturation. Any basic change in the culture demands first a change in the formal rules. Such a modification can be introduced only by an elite leadership and requires a majority vote of baptized males for adoption.

The leadership is not likely to introduce new rules until a point is reached where failure to do so would promote much rule breaking (Eaton, 1952). This suggests that controlled acculturation requires a powerful administration of a type also found in industrial and other organizations. Controlled acculturation does not mean blocking all novelties. Change related to acculturation is very much evident in a Hutterite community. The move to make all local Hutterite churches subordinate to a central organization is exactly such an innovation, one designed to slow down innovation on the local level!

5. Primary-Secondary Contacts. Cultural contact exists on a continuum from primary to fully secondary (Mead, 1949a). In primary culture contact individuals reared in a homogeneous community, through migration or otherwise are faced with the problem of adjusting to the way of life found in another homogeneous group (see p. 147). Intermediate secondary culture contact means that a party from a homogeneous setting is placed in heterogeneous conditions. Examples include rural Sicilian immigrants in New York or the first American Indians to be placed on a government-managed reservation. The response may be to cling to the past, reinterpret the new experiences in familiar terms, or violently reject the past in favor of rapid acceptance of the new. Full secondary culture contact involves interaction between two or more parties, all reared in heterogeneous circumstances. People in such a situation tend to be highly mobile, accustomed to cultural differences (though not necessarily tolerant of them), and ready to reduce values to some quantitative basis of measurement (like measuring the worth of a particular way of life by the number of deaths from t.b., or kilowatt-hours of electricity associated with it). They possess a tentative attitude toward life and regard experience as atomized into thousands of unrelated bits (Honigmann, 1954b:352–354).

Immigrant Acculturation

The cultural response of immigrants depends on the situation, cultural and noncultural, into which they enter (Handlin, 1955). In Great Britain, European immigrants entered a community with a highly traditional and relatively homogeneous culture. Despite regional differences, they, like their hosts, exhibited a strong tendency to conform to national patterns. In the United States newcomers encountered a different situation. Here diversity of origin was something taken for granted, no deeply rooted traditions existed, and the immigrant experienced less pressure to conform than in England. Despite his rapid and thorough cultural change in America, the immigrant felt encouraged to join organizations whose members possessed the same ethnic background he had. Immigrants maintained a foreign-language press. The organized immigrant life which developed in America under these conditions remained until recently, when

the rise of mass media, combined with the influence of compulsory education, led to the rapid assimilation of the immigrants' children. In Brazil
and Argentina the migrants joined rural communities living on extensive
frontiers. Here, as well as in provincial towns, it was easy for them to remain isolated. The members of the host community remained unaggres-
sive culturally. The immigrants at first developed a way of life little influenced by the hosts' culture. However, in the second quarter of the
twentieth century, following road building and industrialization, growing
national consciousness and the progressive unity of the countries reduced
the isolation of immigrant enclaves and stimulated assimilation.

GENERAL CULTURAL PROCESSES IN ACCULTURATION

The first group of processes likely to be found in conjunction with acculturation are those which have been discussed already: diffusion, origination, displacement, reinterpretation, and others. It is not hard to see why
continuous contact between different ways of life should encourage these
mechanisms of culture change. A few brief remarks about the operation of
three of these in acculturation may not be unduly repetitious.

Diffusion

One is likely to think of diffusion as the major event in culture contact.
Often voluminous diffusion indeed does occur. But two cautions will prevent exaggeration of its importance. First, borrowing is not manifested
equally by all communities which are party to the contact situation. The
flow of elements may be one-sided, proceeding from the dominant culture. Euroamerican culture has frequently exhibited cultural dominance
when carried to exotic communities by traders, administrators, and missionaries. On the other hand, an individual American frontiersman living
with native people may adapt and adjust by rapidly assimilating the exotic
way of life. In that case cultural dominance lies with the natives. Second,
diffusion is not automatic. It can be resisted and does not inevitably
continue but may slow down as a protest against loss of cultural identity.
The borrowers may become satiated. Unless further incentives for diffusion are inculcated, or new resources become available to pay for additional goods and services, diffusion will halt (Belshaw, 1954:122). Conversely, the inclination of people to assimilate all that can be obtained
from another culture is an extremely powerful factor in diffusion.

Origination

Acculturation favors origination. The culture contact situation confronts
each interacting party with new problems that it would not otherwise have
encountered. It may be impossible to borrow ready-made solutions from

another culture and so origination is encouraged. To take a simple example, an impinging culture may offer new goods that the formerly isolated community desires. The latter must learn ways to acquire the goods and then must work out appropriate patterns for using them. At the same time compensatory modifications occur in other areas of life. In Africa, natives who obtain public employment or become house servants do not wear European clothing but are assigned uniforms which represent an origination made by Europeans in the culture contact situation. "The clash and interplay of the two cultures produce new things" (Malinowski, 1945:22, 25). The Mende of Sierra Leone observed that firing the house thatch was one of the common ways by which the British imposed their power. So they learned to take down the thatched roofing when an attack was expected and further deprived the British of jungle cover by clearing the bush for several hundred yards in front of a stockade. These tactics count as genuine originations in Mende culture (Little, 1951:50–51). Many originations in acculturation are bound up with the process of stimulus diffusion, reinterpretation, or syncretism.

Displacement

Displacement is encouraged by several factors in acculturation situations. The death from introduced disease or the loss through migration of craftsmen who did not transmit their skills to many members of the next generation tends to extinguish those techniques. So does the absence of youths at school or elsewhere at a time of life when ordinarily they would be learning adult skills. The displacement of roles, like those of curer, diagnostician, and others, follows the introduction of more effective systems of therapy as well as new bases of knowledge and belief. It is not uncommon for young men and women able to master the language and customs of a colonial power to become guides for their elders in the new situation. The prestige acquired by the youths in this role makes them independent; they become strong enough to resist learning traditional customs.

ACCULTURATION AND THE CULTURAL FIELD

Acculturation often promotes culture change whose repercussions are very evident in the cultural field. Three common field-related processes encouraged by culture contact are environmental alteration, demographic change, and organismic change.

Environmental Alteration

In many parts of the world contact with western civilization has been accompanied by the introduction of new powerful weapons, new techniques of plant cultivation, like plowing, and intensified use of land for money crops. The new artifacts and practices help alter the geographical environment. Powerful weapons, for example, lead to the extermination of game, erosion is encouraged by certain kinds of plowing, and the fertility of land becomes seriously depleted under intensive cultivation (Batten, 1954:I, Chaps. 7–13). In Australia the immigrant Europeans introduced sheep and cattle herding that interfered with the aborigines' traditional means of using land by hunting and collecting. Apart from game being driven off, land formerly exploited by the natives was removed from their control. The aborigine's response was to seek work from the white man (Elkin, 1951:166).

Demographic Change

Fluctuation in population, birth rate, death rate, and other demographic indices may follow from altered diets, introduced diseases, and additional facilities for medical treatment. Also labor recruitment policies that separate men and women interfere with reproduction. These are not uncommon conditions appearing with acculturation. Often the indigenous population curve, following the onset of culture contact, begins to decline. In Tasmania, where the aborigines were sometimes hunted for sport, the decline continued until the community had completely disappeared (Murdock, 1934:16–18). More often, however (as Table 22 indicates), a point of stability is achieved. The people acquire resistance to the new diseases, medical care becomes effective against novel viruses or bacteria, and, perhaps, some kind of protective policy designed for the welfare of the indigenous community is instituted. These things came about in the New World. Although early estimates mostly are guesses, and by no means is it easy to identify who is an Indian (racial purity, clearly, is not indicated by such an appellation), the Indian population of the Americas in 1940 probably exceeded that of the time when Columbus landed (Table 22).

TABLE 22. Variation in the Indian Population of the Americas

Year	Population	Increase or Decrease
1492	13,385,000	
1570	10,827,150	−2,557,850
1650	10,035,000	− 792,150
1825	8,634,301	−1,400,699
1940	16,211,670	+7,577,369

source: International Labour Office, 1953:31.

Changes in the Organism

Modifications in physical structure follow from changes of diet under acculturation. Quite spectacular are the relatively lasting changes in body build that have accompanied acculturation of European immigrants in the New World. Out of 13 studies comparing stature of immigrants with nonimmigrants, in 10 the former were significantly taller, in no case were they significantly shorter, and in 3 cases no significant differences could be ascertained. Out of 13 comparisons of the stature of immigrants with American-born descendants, in 9 the American-born were significantly larger in stature, in 2 they were significantly shorter, and in 2 no significant difference showed up (Kaplan, 1954). These changes, it should be emphasized, involved no genetic change. That is, they are not evolutionary but only reflect the influence of different cultural conditions (especially diet) on the *expression* of already given genetic potentialities.

SPECIALIZED PROCESSES IN ACCULTURATION

In this section two processes will be discussed that are relatively specialized as far as occurrence in culture contact situations is concerned. These are nativism and culture conflict. Ways in which acculturation situations terminate also will be discussed.

Nativism

Narrowly, nativism is defined as a more or less deliberate attempt by a community to revive or perpetuate selected aspects of its culture (Linton, 1943:230). That definition, however, fails to include movements such as have recently occurred in Melanesia, Turkey, and elsewhere which emphasized destruction of elements from the past in favor of more rapidly assimilating another way of life (Berndt, 1952–53:150). It also does not cover resistance to a foreign political power and the ensuing struggle for independence. Nationalistic movements of this kind have even shown up among the Greenland Eskimo (Frederiksen, 1952). If all these related manifestations are to be grouped under one heading, nativism must be defined more broadly as referring to any social movement arising under culture contact in which members of a community assert cultural or social identity, affirm dominance, or effect psychological readjustment. Such movements take different typical forms from one culture area to another (Wallace, 1956b:276).

An example of a nativistic phenomenon is the revival of Gaelic as a literary language in Ireland at a time when the people in other ways, too, sought to assert their independence from England (O'Faolain, 1947:Chap. 11). Attempts made by speakers of a language to get rid of foreign words reveal a somewhat parallel tendency. So does the revival of *Eisteddfods* in Wales (see p. 249). The Welsh reinstituted these contests of Welsh speech, poetry, and music as a conscious attempt to preserve a portion of their traditional heritage (Kroeber, 1948:437). The nativistic movement may consist of little more than some men's custom of pridefully wearing their hair long in order to underscore their native heritage and avoid being identified with another category of people. The Swadeshi (or Khadi) Movement, a small episode starting in 1905 in the larger struggle for Indian independence, illustrates nativism on a more political level (Desai, 1954:292; Griffiths, 1952:291–292). The movement, which demanded heavy sacrifices on the part of its supporters, aimed at boycotting European (specifically British) products in favor of indigenous manufactured goods. Students did much to enforce that aim. In one case some ripped a shirt of foreign cloth from a schoolfellow's back and in another students refused to take an examination on foreign-manufactured paper supplied by the college authorities. Gandhi symbolized the goal of the movement by encouraging professional people to spin thread and weave homespun cloth or *khadi* (Gandhi, 1940:Chap. 39). In somewhat the same category is the decision of Japan in 1638 to cut herself off from intercourse with other nations (Sansom, 1951:177–178). Underlying this move was an attempt by the rulers to preserve their powerful positions. Japanese shoguns feared that European ideology would inspire domestic uprisings. Whether intended to do so or not, their exclusionist policy favored the persistence of native culture elements.

Sometimes nativism is spearheaded by prophets or messiahs, who marshal energies and symbolize their followers' aspirations. The nativistic attempt may carry a strong religious flavor, like the Ghost Dance of the American Indians or religious revivals among the Delaware Indians.

The essential doctrine of the Ghost Dance held that the world was old and worn out. The time for renewal had come. Wovoka (also named John Wilson) arose as the prophet of the movement. He himself was the son of a Paiute prophet, Tavibo. Born about 1856, Wovoka grew up under the patronage of a white rancher, from whom he learned some elements of Christianity. At about the age of 18 he received a great revelation. Falling asleep in the daytime he was carried to another world where he saw God and all the people who had died long ago. They were engaged in their old-time games and occupations, living happily and remaining young eternally. God told Wovoka to tell the living Indians that they must be good, love one another, live peacefully, and remain at peace with the whites. If they did these things they would be united with their friends in the next world. Such a message came opportunely to a community that was undergoing difficult new learning in a world drastically changed under white influence. The Ghost Dance religion consisted of a cultural and social hearkening back, and expression of nostalgia for the old way of life. Wovoka also received dances to teach his people. Through them the dancers could hasten the coming of the millennium, when they would be united with the departed. So the Ghost Dance was born (Mooney, 1896). Here is a Paiute Ghost Dance song pleading poverty:[2]

> My father, I am poor.
> My father, I am poor.
> Our father is about to take pity on me.
> Our father is about to take pity on me.
> Our father is about to make me fly around.
> Our father is about to make me fly around.

The movement assumed quite different forms as it diffused from the Paiute eastward across the mountains and into the Plains culture area. The underlying doctrine became a belief that all the Indians, living and dead, were soon to be reunited on a regenerated earth and would live in aboriginal happiness—free from death, disease, and misery. The white race would have no place in the new scheme of things and might even cease to exist. Some shamans as part of the movement preached active resistance to further white encroachment. Among the Sioux Indians, where frustration ran high, the movement took a most hostile turn. Here all adherents of the movement wore a special ghost shirt, usually at dances but also underneath the regular garments. They believed the shirt to be impenetrable to bullets but learned differently at the battle of Wounded Knee.

Among the Delaware Indians, after their lands had been lost to the whites and other elements of native culture disrupted through warfare, "panic stricken" attempts were made to identify with the whites in religion along with equally desperate attempts to revive traditional rituals. After 1760 more and more emphasis came to be put on the revival of modified forms of the old-time religion and the exclusion of Christianity. Prophets appeared to preach these doctrines. They also advocated a morality founded on sexual chastity and abstinence from alcohol. One function of their teachings was to restore an integrated view of experience and repair the self-esteem of the Delaware Indians that had been shattered under culture contact (Wallace, 1956b).

Among the most recent forms of nativism to gain world-wide attention has been the Cargo Movement in Melanesia (also called Vailala Madness).[3] The most striking element in the movement is the belief that a "cargo" of European goods will soon arrive by ship or plane as a gift of the

---

[2] "This song refers to the present impoverished condition of the Indians, and to their hope that he is now about to take pity on them and remove them from this dying world to the new earth above; the feathers worn on their heads in the dance being expected to act as wings . . . to enable them to fly to the upper regions" (Mooney, 1896:999).

[3] The following discussion is based mainly on Berndt, 1952–53 and 1954. See also Worsley, 1955.

ancestors or some other spirits. These will be goods like those that the European trader regularly receives when his cargo is delivered and on which the native people have become highly dependent. The people are unable to secure all such goods that they would like to own. In the rituals of the Cargo Movement, which sometimes consist of ancestor ceremonies revived from the past, attempts are made to influence the ancestors to send the cargo promptly. Involuntary, intermittent trembling characterizes participants; this is explained as possession by ancestral spirits. Less frequent elements in the complex include, in the Central Highlands of New Guinea, the construction of a large building (called the "store") in which symbolic European goods are kept. These will be converted into real goods by the action of the ancestors. Or "wireless houses" may be built, complete with aerial poles, to receive messages from ancestors. Sometimes drills are held with dummy rifles to prepare the people for the forcible overthrow of the Europeans. In some places pigs, ceremonial goods of the traditional culture, and other possessions have been destroyed while awaiting the imminent arrival of the vessels with the cargo. Storehouses may be built to receive the goods. Naturally, when the cargo does not come a serious situation develops. Hostility may be directed against Europeans, they being blamed for having diverted the ships.

The Cargo Movement seems to express a desire to alter radically the existing way of life by securing as rapidly as possible the full measure of European goods. The Cargo Movement, then, is not regressive. It does not, like the Ghost Dance, hanker after a bygone culture. It has broken out in an area of the world where culture change under acculturation has been particularly spectacular, rapid, and thorough. The old way of life in Melanesia has been dislocated thoroughly, leaving the men (who formerly did the fighting, performed war ceremonies, went on trading expeditions, and built defensive stockades) with considerable unspent time and energy. Transition to a new way of living has not been rapid enough for Melanesians who cannot secure jobs or provide themselves with other means through which to assimilate more fully to the new way of life. "It is possible that the conscious desire for material goods led to a wish to establish rapport with the spirits, as the only way of achieving this end" (Berndt, 1952–53:156). In other words, the people use partly traditional culture patterns symbolically to reach desired ends in the new situation (Berndt, 1954:271). But this is not all. Political tendencies in the Cargo Movement also are apparent. These include a desire for liberation from alien control, including freedom from missionary pressure. In any area where it has occurred, the Cargo Movement facilitated the emergence of new leaders who spanned several clusters of kinsmen or villages and thus ushered in wider-scale social organization than has been customary in Melanesia. These leaders in some cases have become active in implementing other culture change. Their roles have not failed to arouse the suspicion of Australian and other administrators. There are sufficient grounds for considering the Cargo Movement the forerunner of a less symbolic and more politically active type of Melanesian nationalism.

Nativism that seeks to stop the course of change may be divided into perpetuative and revivalistic types (Linton, 1943). In the former, a community in an acculturation situation decides to resist *further* change in culture and to perpetuate remaining elements in the social heritage. In revivalistic nativism, however, elements of the past, usually those (like dances or rituals) which do not require extensive preparatory modifications in culture, are revived. They give distinctiveness to the community. Symbolically they help the people to assert themselves culturally and serve as symbols of social unity. In either of these two subtypes resentment of foreign political domination may or may not appear. Of course, not all general or sectional persistence is self-conscious enough to be classed as nativism.

It will be apparent that all nativistic movements cannot be ascribed to any single independent variable like economic deprivation or nostalgia for the past. Similarly the dependent functions will vary somewhat between different movements. The following are some dependent functions of nativistic movements (all need not apply to any single movement).

1. The movement may increase self-confidence as it boosts morale and in-group coöperation (Lesser, 1933:109; Voget, 1956).

2. In situations where people are powerless to attain goals by direct coping techniques, nativistic movements allow the pursuit of goals through safe indirect means. The people engaged in the movement adopt symbolic techniques and act as though these are sufficient to attain the desired ends. These techniques also provide dissatisfied people with an outlet for their energies. They support the conviction that *something* is being done toward achieving a desired state of affairs or ending intolerable conditions.

3. By providing a focus for group activity the movement, whether regressive or progressive, canalizes and organizes social energies. It helps leaders to emerge and identify themselves. In short, the nativistic movement, despite its primarily symbolic character, prepares the way for greater social dominance which, perhaps, will be attempted through less symbolic means (Worsley, 1955).

4. A nativistic movement which tries to regulate diffusion may be a means of reducing the effects of uneven change. The progressive elements in the community are slowed down and kept in leash. The speeding up of diffusion advocated in such a movement may effect the same end.

Culture Conflict

Acculturation brings with it conflict between disparate values, identifications, and loyalties. It poses difficult problems of relearning, involving discrimination of one community by another, and introduces wants that cannot always be supplied.

In eastern Nigeria youngsters who are barely literate learn to despise the traditional occupation of farming and hope to land clerical jobs. Both they and their parents suffer disappointment when such jobs turn out to be unavailable. At the same time limited funds and shortage of staff restrict opportunities for secondary education, the avenue to clerical employment, and so encourage more frustration (M. Mann, 1953).

In the Aleutian village of Nikolski off the coast of mainland Alaska the school has been a great source of stress (Berreman, 1955:54–55). Schooling includes suppression and ridicule of Aleut activities and values, and the extolling of those of the Euroamerican teacher. Urgent wants are inculcated in pupils that the village is unable to help realize. Leaving the village for jobs in Alaska or the United States solves the problem for some youngsters. However, the cost of emigration and fear of ridicule keep many people at home.

Akutan, an Aleutian village one hundred and twenty miles east of Nikolski, provides another example in which an unprecedented situation, similar to that in Nikolski today, has not had disintegrative results. There the traditional culture has been largely replaced, but the village is apparently thriving. This is partly because Akutan is closer than Nikolski to the mainland and, therefore, to the source of supply and of cash income which provide means to satisfy the new wants. The unprecedented situation has brought adjustive mechanisms with it. Other factors which have helped promote community integration in Akutan include these: the village is unincorporated and therefore is not subject to many unpredictable outside administrative controls; it has only the traditional chieftainship and no potentially conflicting council; it has legal rights to its own land and water; it has had an enlightened schoolteacher who helped procure these rights. Traditional local controls have been maintained to a considerable extent. Projection to the new way of life has been possible within the village, and as a result the community has prospered [*ibid.*, p. 58].

Prosperity by itself is no guarantee against culture conflict. Shiprock, New Mexico, is the most prosperous area of the Navaho Indian Reservation (D. Leighton and C. Kluckhohn, 1947:122–126). Income derives from irrigation agriculture, livestock raising, and wages. White influence has been strong in Shiprock and so has the pressure of missionaries and administrators. "No group on the Reservation has been exposed to so many years of high-pressure administration. It seems likely that this is partly responsible for the fact that Shiprock is the center of anti-white feeling and resistance to government programs for the Navajos." Suspicion of witchcraft is also common. Yet there are more people in this area than elsewhere in Navaho country who act like white people.

Dilemmas in culture contact are felt not only by the socially subordinate community. New Zealand, which administers a portion of the Samoan

islands for the United Nations, has become involved in a perplexing conflict of values. The Samoans have become nationalistic and seek self-government within the framework of their own customs. New Zealand is not
unwilling to grant independence but wants such cherished western values
as universal suffrage and wide democratic participation in decision making
to diffuse into a Samoan constitution. The islanders remain cool to these
proposals. Among them, decisions are arrived at formally by assemblies
of titled men called *matais*. There is no place for mass democracy. New
Zealanders also believe that no innovation which has not the full support
of a dependent people can hope to win acceptance.[4] Ideally they believe
in the right of the Samoans to follow traditional customs. Manifestly they
are quite unable to accept the perpetuation of certain of those customs
(M. Boyd, 1956).

Recent work by students of culture and personality provides insight into
how individuals actually experience culture conflict. On the reservation of
the Menomini Indians of Wisconsin several personality configurations can
be discerned: the (1) native oriented, (2) peyote, (3) transitional, (4)
lower-ranking assimilated, and (5) elite assimilated (Spindler, 1955:170–
202). One end of this continuum represents people who seek to retain as
much of traditional culture as possible. At the other extreme are Menomini
who have adjusted successfully to a new system of living. The three middle
categories contain those caught in culture conflict. They reveal reactions to a stressful situation. Each of the 5 categories reveals a distinct personality configuration, as shown in Table 23. The peyotists come close to

TABLE 23.   Five Menomini Personality Configurations Revealing Culture Conflict and
                    Successful Adjustment

Category	Main Cultural Features	Personality Configuration[a]
1. Native oriented	Subsistence by wage work, hunting, fishing. Also dances put on for white tourists. Kinship ties are consciously maintained and provide a basis for social cohesion. Traditional ceremonies are retained. All persons speak Menomini and old men know little English.	A passive orientation toward life but not compounded of hopelessness. The personal- ity is unsuited to competitive struggle or to social relation- ships that require inter- personal aggression. Emo- tional expression is withheld.
2. Peyote	Subsistence mainly through wage work in mills or lumber camps. Membership in peyo- te ritual group provides a	The old culture exerts a strong hold on the individual, yet he doubts the efficacy of the old ways and feels impelled

[4] In American Samoa only titled men, that is, the traditional leaders, are returned to
an elected legislative which possesses limited powers. Yet theoretically anyone is eligible
to hold office.

TABLE 23 (Continued)

Category	Main Cultural Features	Personality Configuration[a]
	basis for social cohesion. The ceremony is not traditional but fosters emotional release through expressive behavior and visions.	to adjust to the new way of life. A quality of hopeless, passive soul-searching expresses the individual's anxious reaction to culture conflict.
3. Transitional	Subsistence mainly by working in jobs connected with lumbering. These people have no ties with the old culture and have not adopted a full measure of the new. They have few identifications with stable groups in the Menomini community.	In some persons nostalgia for the old way of life is revealed but there is also identification with Euroamerican culture. Compared to the native-oriented, the personality is less passive and more aggressive. This reflects the individual's greater participation in competitive social relations. Anxiety is present but is not dealt with through hopeless soul-searching. Aggression sometimes takes the form of explosive hostility.
4. Lower-ranking assimilated	Subsistence partly in skilled occupations connected with lumbering, often in low-supervisory statuses. Belong to Catholic Church but reveal little group cohesion.	The individual is not passively oriented. Signs of deep disturbance exist. He is not strongly rooted in the past, identifying readily with Euroamerican symbols.
5. Elite assimilated	Subsistence through supervisory jobs connected with lumbering; other managerial tasks. Belong to Catholic Church, the men to the high-ranking Holy Name Society. Constitute a strongly cohesive group with many contacts off the reserve.	Emotional expression is readily forthcoming. The individual does not show signs of disturbance like the transitional or peyote categories. Hostility is controlled effectively. The personality is marked by controlled activity rather than passivity. People are familiar with Euroamerican culture, to which they have effectively adjusted.

[a] Personality insights were obtained through use of the Rorschach Inkblot Test (see pp. 62–63).
SOURCE: Spindler, 1955:59–103, 170–199.

finding adjustment in a nativistic movement which reduces anxiety. The transitionals are caught in a dilemma of choice between the old and the new, a dilemma they are unable to resolve successfully. The low-ranking assimilated category have chosen the new way of life but are unable to realize all of its constituent goals. They are assimilated but possess relatively low prestige on the reservation and feel deprived despite (or, perhaps, because of) their strong drive toward achievement.

Terminal Processes

Acculturation may be resolved by four processes: (1) the socially subordinate community may be exterminated; (2) each of the communities in contact may go its own way despite some continuing diffusion; (3) interdependence between the communities may grow up; (4) social and cultural assimilation may blend all distinctions existing between them.

1. Social Extermination. Extermination came to some socially subordinate communities, especially those which sought to resist a more powerful invader by force. The ravages of disease or internal wars fought with newly acquired firearms destroyed others (Speiser, 1922:36). Today 25 Trumaí Indians remain in the northern Mato Grosso of Brazil (Murphy and Quain, 1955:Chap. 6). Respiratory infections transmitted by the white man primarily were responsible for depopulation, which, however, also made the Trumaí progressively more vulnerable to attacks from neighbors seeking women. The decline following from illness also reduced the yield from fishing and so led to deteriorated nutrition that helped further to lower resistance to disease. All factors leading to the practical extinction of the Trumaí did not originate outside of the community. The traditional custom of spacing births far apart and the people's ineffectual social organization constituted contributory cultural factors.

2. Stabilized Pluralism. Many Pueblo Indians in the southwestern United States illustrate the tendency to retain cultural individuality despite culture contact. These people regulated cultural borrowing and also stabilized the direction in which they allowed change to originate. Preserving a large part of their traditional heritage they continue to go their own way, isolating themselves from interaction with the socially dominant community—the United States—as much as possible. Of course, acculturation continues in the sense that awareness of the larger American nation has not been eliminated. Stabilized pluralism may well represent only a temporary process, one that will be replaced by another.

3. Symbiosis. Often acculturation brings two or more communities into a state of complex interdependence or symbiosis. Each culture becomes specialized in a different direction but finds itself dependent on the roles or services provided in the other. The Indians of northern Canada manifest such specialization. During the winter they trap furs, which are exchanged for practically all resources that the people need to live. Food, clothing, tools, weapons, housing material, outboard engines, and fuel oils are imported from the outside and paid for through furs. Complementary specialized elements have also appeared in Eurocanadian culture. These include procedures for administrating the Indians, trading organizations that deal in furs, and special products destined for the northern trade. However, the consequences of any disruption of the symbiotic relationship would be far greater for the Indians than for the national community. In other words, the northern Indians are the more specialized of the two parties in contact. Arms of the Eurocanadian community reach into the North, where missions and trading posts are highly specialized innovations whose distinctive culture would disappear if by some chance the Indian popula-

Commercialized Forms of American Indian Ritual Designed to Appeal to White Tourists Are End Products of American Indian Acculturation. This photo was taken at the annual Inter-Tribal Indian Ceremonials at Gallup, New Mexico (courtesy, Santa Fe Railway).

tion were wiped out. In Australia the specialized response of the aborigines to the new community has been still more one-sided. It takes the form of pauperism—a parasitic life which was encouraged unintentionally by the way the Australians dealt with the natives (Elkin, 1951). The commercialized forms of American Indian ritual, designed to appeal to white tourists who visit Indian reservations, illustrate another symbiotic development (Gamble, 1952).

4. Assimilation. Biological and sociocultural assimilation should be distinguished. In cultural anthropology assimilation means at least relatively intense social interaction and cultural fusion so that a single way of life emerges from a situation of cultural pluralism. Of course, as members of different cultural backgrounds begin to interact freely, without discrimination, biological assimilation probably also will occur. On the other hand, fairly heavy cultural assimilation may take place with relatively little social acceptance or biological mixture. This has been the case with West Indian Negroes in Great Britain. Cultural assimilation is limited by the extent to which any party in the culture contact situation rejects another. In some cases assimilation may be achieved locally under favorable circumstances— for example, when the total interacting population is small—but remains highly incomplete on the larger national level (Willems, 1955).

Assimilation is favored by five conditions (Deutsch, 1953:91–93, 130–136).

a. There is already considerable similarity and compatibility between linguistic and other cultural elements belonging to the interacting parties.

b. At least one party is ready to learn from another.

c. Contacts, direct and mediated, are frequent between parties.

d. Assimilation is rewarded (e.g., by employment, promotion, higher income, security, and prestige).

e. Symbols and rituals exist that express unity in place of emphasizing social distinctions. The readiness of European immigrants in India to think of themselves as "British" slows down assimilation. So do other nationalistic symbols. Nativistic movements that one-sidedly emphasize cultural identity also do so.

AVAILABLE FILMS

Two films dealing with specific cases in culture contact are *Daybreak in Udi* (45 min., b. and w.) and *They Planted a Stone* (27 min., b. and w.), both distributed by British Information Services. The first picture describes a district commissioner in Nigeria who encourages a village to build a nursing station that encounters resistance from a few conservative men. The second film deals with an irrigation project in the Egyptian Sudan and what it means for a desert village. The same organization releases *Partners* (17 min., b. and w.), showing how "the needs of East Africa are gradually being met by a partnership with the white man." The New Zealand Embassy describes *Western Samoa* (17 min., b. and w.) as a "picture of Samoan life which makes use of beneficiary European services and still preserves its own customs and traditions." *Citizen Varek* (12 min., b. and w.) tells the story of the disillusions and discouragements of a European immigrant in Canada. It is distributed by the National Film Board of Canada. Tunisian nomads in the towns of North Africa and a program for nomad resettlement are the themes of *Fixation des nomades en Tunisie* (35 min., b. and w., in French), produced by T. Grejebine. *River People*, produced by the United States Indian Service (25 min., color) excellently shows culture conflict among the Pima Indians.

18.

Development, Elaboration, and Decline

THE processes designated in the title of this chapter refer to certain directional tendencies manifested in culture. These processes may follow from originations locally made or may be instigated through borrowing. Often they are associated with acculturation.

DEVELOPMENT

Let the reader not think of development as good or bad, desirable or undesirable. Development refers to those conditions in culture that enhance a community's control over the material environment. The word also designates the *process* of enhancing such control. All communities possess some degree of development however much it may vary from one people to another. Through the ages development in culture has taken such forms as controlling heat and cold (through means ranging from a simple open fire to air conditioning), spanning distance (by use of a bow, gun, wireless, or rocket), controlling energy (through the sail, horse, steamboat, and, most recently, nuclear fission), curing or arresting illness, and increasing the length of life. These are areas of culture in which technical development is apparent.

It is not at all clear that in gaining ever increasing mastery over the material world man has also increased his ability to control social relationships. Enhancement of social control through the ages, or at least its eventual possibility, is sometimes affirmed (Childe, 1953:Chap. 1; Clough, 1951:253–256) at the same time that it is denied by equally competent students of culture. In support of the thesis that social development has indeed taken place, proponents point to the ability of man to coördinate an ever increasing number of people and harness their energies, the growth of predictable forms of industrial management and other forms of administration, the increasing scope of empires, and the more effective use of words in propaganda and education. It is held that even if social control remains rudimentary, man can study his history and so learn to introduce greater order in social relations. Opponents of this position point to man's manifest inability to control wars, strikes, and other breakdowns in coöperation. Furthermore, their argument goes, with reference to the material world, man is outside the system which he seeks to control. This offers him an advantage. But man cannot learn to control the course of history (or culture) because he is himself a dependent variable in the cultural situations he seeks to master. His behavior is dependent on the very processes he might like to control. In view of the unsettled nature of this question, it is well to remain cautious in extending the concept of development from technical to social matters.

Measurement

If two or more people wish to measure development they must agree on certain indices or standards. Initially it will be assumed that the reader accepts the indicators furnished by the author. The problems related to the selection of agreeable standards will be discussed immediately thereafter.

If we keep in mind that development refers to the degree of control which a community possesses over the material world, indices of development may be conceived which are direct or indirect measures of such control. Directly showing control is an indicator like the amount of energy employed for work in a community. It is clear from Table 24 that by this indicator

TABLE 24.   Two Indicators of Development in Selected Countries

Country	Consumption of Energy from All Fuel and Water Sources Expressed in the Equivalent of Pounds of Coal Consumed Annually per Person (1949)	Deaths Annually per 1000 People (around 1950)
United States	16,100	9.6
Canada	15,600	9.0
France	4,970	12.6
Chile	2,160	15.7
Venezuela	1,830	11.0
Spain	1,580	10.8
India	770	16.0
Egypt	700	20.3
Afghanistan	550	—
Ethiopia	550	—

SOURCE: Woytinsky and Woytinsky, 1953:942, 230.

the United States in 1949 possessed nearly 30 times more control over the material environment than did Afghanistan and Ethiopia. While quantification is useful, it is not essential in measuring development. One can refer to the fact that prior to the white man's penetration of the Arctic the Eskimo were dependent mainly on the energy created by fire, their own bodies, and dogs. The people of ancient Egypt around 3500 B.C. utilized wind, cattle (for drawing the plow and cart), fire, and their own bodies as energy sources. It is reasonable to deduce, therefore, that Egypt possessed a more developed culture than did the aboriginal Eskimo. Such a comparison is very crude. For one thing it neglects the efficiency with which animal or human power is applied through tools or vehicles.

Indirectly development is measured through the consequences that can logically be assumed to follow from enhanced control over the material world. For example, if the causes of death or illness are regarded as residing in the material world (including the nature of the human body), then annual rates of infant or adult mortality, life expectancy figures, and rates for specific illnesses represent indirect indicators of control over the material environment. Table 24 in fact shows death rates to be correlated inversely with energy consumption. From the viewpoint of process, development lies in reducing mortality indices and increasing life expectancy. Such demographic movements actually are occurring in many parts of the world simultaneously with increasing energy consumption.

Maternal and Infant Welfare Clinics in the Northern District of Papua, New Guinea, Have Led to Improvement of Health in Mothers and Children and a Decrease in Infant Mortality (courtesy, Australian News and Information Bureau).

Following are some direct and indirect indicators that might be considered for measuring development:

DIRECT INDICATORS	INDIRECT INDICATORS
Energy consumption	Death rate
Caloric consumption	Life expectancy
Miles of track, road, telephone or telegraph wire	Standard of living
	Deficiency diseases (rate)
Efficiency of tools and machines	Units of output in agriculture or manufacturing
	Incidence of famines

On a more qualitative level, the presence in culture of food production (for example, agriculture) rather than food gathering (i.e., hunting, fishing, or collecting) may be regarded as a very general indicator of greater development.

The reliability of any given technique, if it can be appraised, serves a similar purpose. Reliability exists when the repetition of an act is followed by similar desired events in a satisfactory number of cases. It is likely that treating malaria by western drugs is more reliable than treating it by the methods of Ayurvedic medicine, a traditional system of curing practiced in much of India. It is likely, too, that western medicine is ordinarily more reliable than techniques of curing which depend mainly on prayer, singing, or the manipulation of other symbols. Hence, western medicine may be taken as more developed than these other forms (see pp. 648–649).

Problems in Measurement

Certain problems in measuring development are inherent in the definition which has been adopted. Three specific problems will be examined.

1. **Relativity of Control.** The word "control" in the definition of development suggests overcoming certain limitations in human potentialities —for example, in man's ability to lift weights. But extension of control over the material world cannot continue indefinitely to free man from all his limitations. Furthermore, the Eskimo continues to be bound by the limitations of his block and tackle, the western man by his crane—its power, length of life, and associated dangers. Control is always relative, never complete, and not to be confused with perfection.

2. **Ethnocentrism.** The direct and indirect indices of development which are deduced from the definition do not recognize that some communities may value other goals than harnessing energy or controlling nature. The criteria of measurement make no allowance for such contrary values. Hence, two or more communities may be compared in terms of output per unit worker. Yet one may be attracted to leisure or a standard of living sufficient to get by while the other wants as much production as possible in order to engage in trade. Of necessity the former will be ranked as relatively undeveloped. The anthropologist can compare only small parts of culture—in this case actual output. The value placed on leisure is not being dealt with. In comparing communities for level of development it is assumed that the standard is applicable equally to all, regardless of whether they share the underlying values. Different values placed on technical development actually constitute one reason why communities differ in the level of development attained (see below).

3. **Environment.** A problem arises when an index is applied in contrasting environments. Supposing rice production is selected as an indirect measure of development. The per acre yield of a village in the tropical monsoon area of Southeast Asia might be heavier than that realized by farmers in a desert oasis. Actually the latter may have surmounted more environmental limitations than the former. Is it meaningful to categorize the Southeast Asian farmers as more developed when in some degree their

higher production is favored by their habitat? The same difficulty is reflected in asking simply how well people can overcome a climatic problem like cold. The Eskimo do it very effectively. But in other parts of the world cold is not a problem at all! Canada uses a considerable portion of its fuel to produce warm clothing and to heat the interiors of houses. Egypt does not face these problems. Yet no account is taken in Table 24 of the difference between the situations of Egypt and Canada. The two countries are compared only in terms of the amount of energy consumed annually per capita. Can two such areas be compared in terms of energy consumption? Yes, they can, if one recognizes that environment is, after all, the variable in relation to which development takes place.

Factors Related to Development

In order to have ever increasing development, sufficiently high value must be set on goals like greater prosperity, health, leisure, and energy (W. A. Lewis, 1955:37–51). Basically, two divergent attitudes to these goals may be adopted. In the Soviet Union, North America, and parts of Asia the people or their leaders seek the swiftest possible building up of wealth and health, the quickest possible reduction of burdensome human labor (*London Times Literary Supplement*, Feb. 24, 1956, p. 1). Other countries have chosen different values. They reject too great efforts in behalf of material prosperity, or do not wish to pay the costs of development. An economist, V. Rao, from one of the most rapidly developing countries of Asia states his belief that a ceiling should be placed on increasing standards of living in order to provide more opportunity for what he calls creative work (*Durham Morning Herald*, May 14, 1956).

1. Clearly development rests on certain kinds of wants. People's wants motivate them to produce goods more efficiently. Then they consume more, meaning that the standard of living rises. But if development still continues it is because people's wants

The Incidence of Livestock Mortality and Disease Constitutes a Measure of Agricultural Development. A community development worker in West Pakistan is vaccinating a villager's hens.

continue to rise—paradoxically dissatisfaction remains high. Of course, the increase of wants may also slow down (as may be occurring in contemporary England and France). This brings a slowing down in development.

2. Equally important, development cannot occur without the requisite knowledge to apply toward the control of the material world. Such knowledge, as the reader is aware, originates in a community less often than it is secured through diffusion. Opportunities for diffusion, however, are not equal for all people, nor are all communities equally receptive toward all kinds of new knowledge. These factors, therefore, also govern development. A relatively developed community tends to be larger in scale than one that is less developed. Largeness of scale promotes contacts on which cultural transmission depends and itself is made possible by a high degree of control over nature.

3. Social organization is essential for the enhanced control of environment. Machines, environmental resources, and sheer numbers of people without organization are of little significance. Naturally, not just any kind of social organization will suffice. After a certain point development may require the individual to free himself from obligations to relatives who in undeveloped countries cut into savings by consuming the wealth he produces above his own needs (J. C. Mitchell, 1956:647). Social relationships in highly developed countries are more rationalized and less traditional than in undeveloped countries. Their bonds are organic rather than sheerly mechanical (see p. 148).

In many of the so-called underdeveloped countries of the modern world only a vast change in beliefs and practices will make possible substantial increases in development (Frankel, 1953:69–70). Africans have to breed and utilize their cattle for dairy products, Indians need to surrender narrow caste allegiance in favor of working with strangers of whatever caste, and more people will have to postpone immediate gratification in favor of self-denying attitudes that encourage saving. There must be created a willingness and financial ability to spend long years in school as well as greater readiness to take risks, whether with capital or through migration to cities and frontiers in search of work and a higher standard of living. Is development worth these costs?

Development and Stress

It is unnecessary to emphasize that development enhances adaptation and adjustment. Enough has also been said to suggest that development cannot be confused with any simple notion of happiness. It is very intimately bound up with its own characteristic stresses. That development and personal happiness are not highly correlated is suggested dramatically by a medical report presented to the American Public Health Association

(*New York Times*, Oct. 13, 1954). Based on two American occupational categories, female telephone operators and telephone craftsmen, the report suggests that one-third of the adults in the most developed country of the world are unhappy, ineffective, and upset. These conditions impose a severe burden on the rest of the community.

ELABORATION

Elaboration refers to increasing variety in, and the systematic organization of, what people make, use, do, feel, and believe. It is only as new artifacts and behavioral traits are added to a way of life that the culture becomes more elaborate or "productive" (Bogoras, 1929:581, 597). The concept is used objectively, without any implication of desirability. Elaboration is not inevitable but may deliberately be restricted in a community which fears variety or certain of its consequences. Even though no single individual can participate in the full content of a highly elaborated culture, such a culture offers potentially more opportunities for diverse experience and congenial activities than a way of life containing few alternatives or specialisms. Variety, however, often brings with it the problem of regulating disharmonious or incompatible differences. In this respect, elaboration can become a source of stress.

By definition the accumulation and systematic organization of elements in a culture—outside the area of language—marks elaboration.[1] Instead of a general tool for digging and cutting, specialized tools for these purposes appear. Instead of one costume for all statuses and for wear on all occasions, people occupying different social positions wear different forms of dress and change their apparel for special circumstances. Types of musical instruments increase; so do dances and songs. Buildings become specialized for use and contain more parts. Foods multiply. Philosophies increase and compete with one another in claiming truth. New systematic assemblages of dress, food, or other items appear. Certain foods go together for particular meals and certain ideas are incorporated in a single ideological system.

What is here called elaboration has also been referred to by terms like "intensity" and "complexity." "What we call intensity of culture . . . means both special content and special system. A more intensive as compared with a less intensive culture normally contains not only more ma-

---

[1] We would reject linguistic elaboration for the following reason: In comparison to English the languages of many small-scale communities include more words for relatives and are more intricate by virtue of possessing many prefixes for categorizing nouns and verbs. Experience indicates that such linguistic features do not, like other kinds of elaboration, correlate with other cultural phenomena. In other words, this kind of linguistic elaboration is not helpful in formulating a scientific understanding of culture.

terial—more elements or traits—but also more material peculiar to itself, as well as more precisely and articulately established interrelations between the materials" (Kroeber, 1939:222).

Factors Related to Elaboration

1. Cultural elaboration depends in part upon the cumulative process in culture. Culture is cumulative when certain basic elements persist and have secondary parts added. The basic form of the wheeled vehicle has persisted for thousands of years, successively changing into the carriage and automobile. Not all parts of culture, however, are equally cumulative. Science and technology are very much so but forms of marriage are more often substituted for, rather than added to, one another (H. C. Moore, 1954).

2. Sheer numbers of people influence cultural elaboration because people generate ideas or borrow new traits. Generally speaking, a large-sized community will have a more elaborate culture than a small one. In small groups variety is discouraged by size alone. A hypothesis that could be verified experimentally, perhaps in a small group laboratory, holds that a small number of people with variegated customs would become less variegated after they began to interact as a group.[2]

3. Elaboration can occur only if there is something to elaborate. As variety increases, more potentialities become available for further elaboration (see pp. 152–153). Once organizations with distinctive rituals appeared among the American Plains Indians, the way was open to elaborate those rituals and the forms of organization.

GROWTH

Development and elaboration share certain features in common. Both depend directly on the number of people who are associated; they are aided by diffusion and are self-perpetuating (development encouraging more development and elaboration further elaboration). Each process seems to be correlated with the other; development is functionally related to elaboration. It will therefore often be convenient to use a single term when the concerted action or result of both of these processes is indicated. Growth designates not only the processes of development and elaboration but also the levels which these processes have achieved at any given time. No analogy is intended with biological growth. Culture growth cannot be compared meaningfully to an individual's career from fetus through maturity to death.

The conditions favoring growth are, of course, those that favor development and elaboration. Increase in scale is the most general of these (see

[2] This hypothesis is consistent with experiments in perception. A similar reduction of genetic variability occurs in small, breeding populations (see pp. 867–868).

pp. 149–152). One of the outstanding characteristics of growth is its uneven distribution in the world. The level of growth varies from one period
to another in the same community and also between communities. Experience suggests that high growth levels are of relatively short duration.
So-called "classical" or "florescent" eras come to an end rather quickly,
the growth curve slowing down or actually reversing itself.

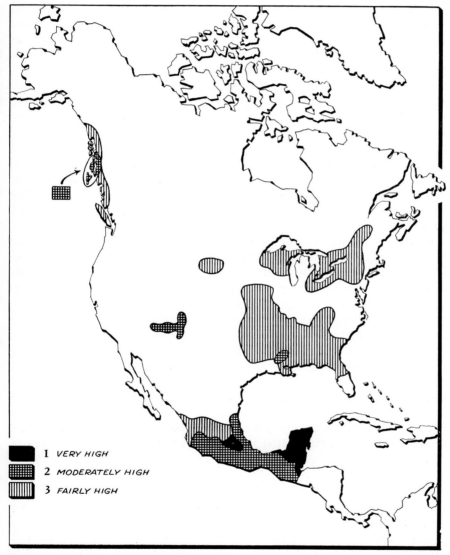

FIG. 18:1.   Areas with High Growth Levels in Native North America (after Kroeber,
1939:222).

Growth levels can be mapped. Figure 18:1 indicates areas of the North American continent which in precontact times were marked by relatively intense development and elaboration.

CULTURAL DECLINE

Do cultures decline as well as develop and become more elaborate? For human culture as a whole, growth has been increasing since the dawn of the Old Stone Age, about 600,000 years ago. But while culture history as a whole reveals a constant though by no means evenly distributed record of development and elaboration, particular cultures have shown reversal or decline. Probably no large area of the world has ever become completely cultureless, but the content of particular ways of life has shrunk (Kroeber, 1944:818) and development has been turned back at least temporarily. Epidemics, alteration of the geographical environment (perhaps through increasing cold or worsening drought), and military invasion are some circumstances that have brought about decline (Birket-Smith, 1946:57–58). The process of decline, as defined here, must not be confused with simple loss of political power or with subjective conditions like deterioration of the arts or "immorality and degeneration." Decline should also be distinguished from a mere arrest or slowing down of culture growth.

A simplification of culture may have occurred in the extreme southwest corner of Asia after Islam appeared there (Kroeber, 1945:11–13). The new ideology incorporated much that was of Greek and Christian origin but also rejected much. Among the Cuna on the Isthmus of Panama decline occurred after the Spanish conquest (Steward, 1955:60–61). Military conquest eliminated the upper class and confiscated its wealth. Human sacrifice and the state religion were forcibly displaced but Spanish rule and Catholicism were not substituted effectively. The Cuna resumed life on a smaller, local-group basis; production for the upper class was abandoned and came to be primarily for use. Certain techniques permanently disappeared. The Acolhua domain in the valley of Mexico underwent similar "cultural devolution" (Wolf and Palerm, 1955:277). Of course, decline need not be permanent. It is possible for a people to begin a new course of development and elaboration following the smashing of a former way of life.

AVAILABLE FILMS

Several films already mentioned earlier illustrate development programs. *Father and Son* (British Information Services, 14 min., b. and w.) very effectively demonstrates certain obstacles that may face technical development. *Desert People*, a film dealing with the Papago Indians of the American Southwest, shows the United States Indian Service at work among a people whose way of life has strong currents of persistence. It is produced by the U.S. Indian Service (25 min., color). *Productivity: Key to Plenty* relates America's high rate of production and high standard of living to the machine (20 min., b. and w., Encyclopædia Britannica Films).

Part Five

DIVISIONS

OF CULTURE

By the conjunction of forces, our power is augmented; by the partition of employments, our ability increases; and by mutual succour, we are
less exposed to fortune and accidents. It is by this additional force, ability,
and security, that society becomes advantageous.

DAVID HUME (*1911*:II, 191–192)
(originally published 1740)

Man has opened the secrets of nature. . . . If he uses them wisely, he
can reach new heights of civilization; if he uses them foolishly they may
destroy him.

H. S TRUMAN (*New York Times*, Jan. 5, 1950)

19.

Divisions of Culture

MANY ways of dividing the content of a particular culture are possible. The ethnographer can make a simple but nearly exhaustive list of discrete traits (see pp. 125–126). Or the culture may be presented in terms of its own distinctive ethos (see pp. 129–130). The divisions of culture adopted in this book are intended not for an ethnography but to help the reader who wants to understand better how any way of life is ordered. They are analytical, not descriptive concepts.

IDEALS OF CULTURAL CLASSIFICATION

Ideally any categories for ordering culture content which are intended for analysis should be universally applicable and possess theoretical utility.

Universality

Categories which are too narrowly derived from the anthropologist's own culture may not be applicable cross-culturally. Take, for example, the categories "technology," "art," and "religion." An answer to the question whether all people have a technology, an art, or a religion depends in large measure on the definition of those terms. With a customary definition the concepts may not distinguish relevant phenomena in an exotic culture. Not many years ago some students of language unsuccessfully sought to impose the categories of Latin grammar on all languages. Cultural anthropologists still work with some relatively culture-bound concepts. Unless these become redefined and more universal they will be difficult to use for other cultures. To define religion as including beliefs or ceremonies involving a deity leaves little provision for handling ceremonies that are political or bound up with kinship and that serve functions analogous to the former. Redefinition, however, also presents difficulties. The word "religion" has a certain common-sense currency in everyday speech. To expand it beyond those ordinary limits may be disconcerting. By no means do all anthropologists encourage growth of a technical argot that will cut off the discipline from uninitiated, nonacademic folk.

Theoretical Utility

Theory is a prerequisite for science and includes concepts by means of which relevant areas of experience may be categorized and then related to one another in the form of hypotheses. From the point of view of theory it is desirable that the categories used in classifying cultural content should be strategically planned for scientific analysis (C. Kluckhohn, 1953:507). This means deliberately choosing or defining categories in a way that best promises to contribute to knowledge of dependable relationships in culture or between culture and the cultural field (E. T. Hall and G. L. Trager, 1953a and 1953b).

It would be naïve to claim that the divisions of culture suggested below perfectly meet these ideals. More careful thought must be given before a set of maximally heuristic concepts for ordering cultural content will be found.

MAJOR DIVISIONS OF CULTURE

In the chapters which follow, three major categories of culture will be isolated: technology, social organization, and ideology. The full definition of these major divisions must be reserved for subsequent chapters. Briefly, however, technology refers to the activities and associated artifacts with which man manipulates the material world (including his own and other bodies); social organization, to the activities and apparatus used when man interacts with other men; and ideology, to the beliefs, knowledge, and values by which man lives (including the material embodiment of these in artifacts). Any given social situation includes all three divisions. A Kaska Indian hunts with his brother-in-law in a social relationship that is motivated by a variety of covert considerations and values. Hence, these three divisions are far too broad to be useful in classifying particular cultural events. They do, however, designate the threefold nature of cultural content. The categories certainly overlap. Some acts, like tattooing another person or performing dentistry on a patient, are partly technical and partly social. They represent techniques to the degree that the subject of the action is regarded as a body rather than a person. All acts imply the existence of a purpose or underlying value that is ideological in nature. Because of this overlap we say that technology, social organization, and ideology are only relatively distinct divisions of culture.

A number of other concepts will be used in the following pages to distinguish pertinent features of technology, social organization, and ideology. For example, reference will be made to forms of residence in marriage. The correlation of these with particular ways of procuring subsistence will be explained. Types of groups will be spoken about and equilibrium will be examined as a property of group life. Under ideology types of world views are fo be distinguished.

Apart from the major divisions of culture are concepts like communication, ritual, and the life cycle. These categories of culture content possess universal applicability but are not as embracive as technology, social organization, or ideology. Nor do they fit into, or amplify, any one of those areas. They more than overlap divisions. They cut across all three of the major divisions. Communication, for example, involves some kind of technical manipulation, perhaps of a telegraph key or of the speech organs (Chap. 32). A social relationship is also usually implied in the act of communication, and a set of agreements must exist concerning what sounds and combinations of sounds are significant or will have meaning. Communication, thefore, is equally a technique, an element in social relations, and intimately bound up with ideology. Ritual refers to the expression in action, often with the aid of technical manipulations, of sentiments that people feel, or are supposed to feel, on certain occasions (Chap. 31). Social interaction is often a vital part of ritual expression. People get together in a party to celebrate or in a congregation to express dependence on a deity. All cultures can be analyzed in terms of the life cycle: the typical course of events experienced by the normal individual between birth and death (Chap. 33). The life cycle is a vantage point from which to see a culture as it impinges on the maturing individual. Obviously the life cycle includes relevant techniques, like birth, play, or those pertaining to occupations; relationships to other people; and beliefs or values.

20.

Technology

TECHNOLOGY is a popular word but its everyday meaning must be distinguished from the more specific use to which it will be put here. In popular usage the word designates machines or manufacturing with the aid of power-driven devices. "Technological civilization," a term used in admiration or dismay, means a community in which many people are engaged in operating powerful machines. Sometimes the word is used more broadly to include any tools, not only machines. "The technology of the So-and-So" then means the tools of a people, how they make and/or employ them. Technology in this book refers, in still broader fashion, to any socially standardized technique, including its associated artifacts or tools. Technology, in other words, designates the techniques of a community.

WHAT IS A TECHNIQUE?

A technique is any socially standardized action by which man manipulates the world, including his own or another's body. ". . . 'Technique' is used by the violinist as well as by the skilled soldier; it is revealed by the surgeon's use of his tool, as well as by the priest handling such paraphernalia of worship as the chalice or the prayer wheel" (Gerth and Mills, 1953:30). Strictly speaking, therefore, techniques are not limited to the production of food and goods but are found in all areas of culture. Except in certain kinds of ritual, art, and recreation, techniques are means to ends rather than ends in themselves.

Technology covers any act by which man handles, gathers from, or modifies his geographical environment as well as the practices by which he modifies his own or another human body—for example, by tattooing, painting, or embalming it or by surgery. Walking is a socially standardized technique (Mauss, 1950:365–370) as much as pottery making or weaving. Exactly where one technique leaves off and another begins, like the question of what constitutes a unit trait (see pp. 125–126), depends on the particular problem under discussion. For some purposes stone toolmaking may be called the technique; for another purpose, however, the technique may be chipping or grinding. A possible classification of techniques in culture is given in Table 25.

It is not possible to draw a firm boundary between technology on the one hand and the other two major divisions of culture, social organization

TABLE 25.   A Classification of Some Techniques[a]

Food Gathering	Maintenance Techniques
Hunting	Cleaning
Collecting	Warehousing, etc.
Fishing, etc.	

Food Gathering
Hunting
Collecting
Fishing, etc.

Food Producing
Incipient agriculture
Intensive manual agriculture
Plow agriculture
Irrigation agriculture
Animal husbandry, etc.

Domestication of Nonedible Plants
Floriculture, etc.

Domestication of Nonedible Animals
Fur farming, etc.

Collecting, Mining, or Quarrying of Nonedible Resources

Manufacturing

On basis of power source:
Handicraft manufacturing
Industrial manufacturing

On basis of type of material:
Leather working
Ceramic manufacturing
Metallurgy, etc.

On basis of product:
Food processing
Clothing manufacturing
Printing
Refrigeration, etc.

Travel and Transportation
Burden carrying
Walking
Animal transport
Ship transport, etc.

Maintenance Techniques
Cleaning
Warehousing, etc.

Manipulation of Weapons
Dueling
Artillery
Bone pointing, etc.

Analytical Techniques
Weighing
Measuring, etc.

Techniques Involving Manipulation of One's Own Body
Spitting
Locomotion
Burden carrying
Sexual techniques
Sports
Verbalization, etc.
Posturing

Techniques Involving Manipulation of Another's Body
Surgery
Embalming
Petting, etc.

Ritual Techniques
Slaughter
Posturing, etc.

Games and Sports
Athletic sports
Table games, etc.

Communication Techniques
Verbalization (speech)
Telegraphy
Radio, etc.

Expressive Techniques
Carving
Painting
Adorning, etc.

---

[a] Overlap between these categories is readily acknowledged. There are different ways to classify the same acts. Whatever classification is adopted will presumably be related to the classifier's interests. All possibilities of classification are not exhausted in this table.

and ideology, on the other. People execute few techniques without some idea or value underlying the activity, giving it meaning, or standardizing the outcome. Many techniques are beyond the capacity of a single individual. Or they are carried out individually on the behalf of other persons. The best that can be done is to emphasize that a technique refers to an action taken on directly perceivable objects: the hunter kills game, the farmer plows land, the scribe writes on paper, and the dentist extracts or fills a tooth. In studying techniques the analyst is not primarily concerned with the idea that has been written down or with the dentist's attitude toward the patient as a person (Flexner, 1930:16).

Studying Technology

Technology is not synonymous with economy. Technology refers to techniques—actions on, and manipulations of, the material world. An economy, however, is a system of social relations concerned with the production and distribution of wealth.

There is more than one way of studying technology in culture. The constituent techniques of a community might be described. Or they can be analyzed into a few basic elements (see pp. 330–332). Thus it has been suggested that man acts on the material world in combinations of four basic ways: by means of heat, fire, air, and the application of pressure (Leroi-Gourhan, 1943:43–88). Another way of studying technology is to isolate techniques with a view to discovering their correlates (i.e., functions) in other areas of culture. This primarily will be the method adopted here (cf. Hobhouse, Wheeler, and Ginsberg, 1915; Hobhouse, 1956; Krause, 1924).

THEORY OF TECHNOLOGY

If culture is a system, then it follows that technology is related to other areas making up a way of life. Taking technology as the independent variable, one notes that techniques often constitute a pivot around which people organize into groups. Americans form many groups when they make automobiles, mill flour, or print books. Far smaller groups of Eskimo are organized for shorter periods of time to hunt walrus or catch fish. Cities grow up around factories, villages around the cultivation of adjacent land. Even interaction between family members is related to the techniques which they perform. A change in techniques means a change in family interaction. Weapons enable one nation to maintain power over another; an empire is created. Nobody believes that cultivation of the potato with the aid of chemical fertilizers was sufficient to produce World Wars I and II. Yet "the rise to a great power of Germany in the 19th Century was, in part, based upon agricultural intensification, which increased, manyfold, the amount of food produced, especially from the light, sandy lands of the North German Plain. Here, aided by copious, nitrogenous and phosphatic fertilizers (partly produced from the mines at Stassfurt), the potato flourished, and enabled farmers not only to rear more animals—notably pigs—but permitted the German nation to become much more numerous" (Lebon, 1952:123).

Ideology may also be dependent on given techniques. The Kamar pattern of agriculture is conducive to a present-time orientation.

In his economic pursuits the Kamar is concerned primarily and almost wholly with the present. The motive of making provision for future needs . . . plays a very minor part in his economic life. . . . If he has enough to satisfy the need of today, he would seldom worry about tomorrow. When his *bahi* [field][1] crops are harvested, for a time he gives up his other economic pursuits such as food gathering from the forest, basket-making, etc., sits at home and eats the fruit of his labour. . . . When he takes to settled plough cultivation and domestication of animals, he does not remain contented with a hand to mouth living . . . but begins making provisions for the future [Dube, 1951:28].

This is reminiscent of what has been said about cotton cultivation: "The seasonal and cyclical nature of the money income [in cotton cultivation] not only serves to give the cotton grower a shifting standard of living, but also serves to prevent him from acquiring habits of thrift" (Vance, 1929:305).

To take technology as the dependent variable, it can be maintained that the very practice of a technique depends upon certain patterns of organization. Railroad refrigeration, for example, grew up in America after the rise of seaboard cities (O. E. Anderson, 1953:14–36). The corporation is a group of people, a form of organization, that finances power-driven machinery for modern manufacturing. "Even steam and electricity are far less important than the limited liability corporation, and they would be reduced to comparative impotence without it" (Butler, 1912:82). Of course, public or state financing of industry is another form of organization on which industrial manufacturing may be founded.

General Functions of Technology

Culture in general serves adaptation and adjustment and these functions are very much shared by technology. Technology is a means for directly coping with the environment and sustaining life. It has even been proposed to "regard cultures as systems formed in one fashion or another to organize and utilize a particular technology" (Beardsley, 1953). Activities like food

[1] The word refers to a field that is cleared by fire, is used for a few seasons, and then, its fertility exhausted, is abandoned for another field. Such agriculture is referred to as shifting cultivation, or slash-and-burn cultivation (see p. 312).

production, clothing manufacture, surgery, and eating represent techniques that directly serve survival; techniques of communication, transportation, and sanitation may be related more indirectly to adaptation. Techniques contribute to adjustment when they help to reduce nonlethal tensions in the individual. For example, dancing, painting, hunting, and practically any other activity often help in satisfying a learned desire for prestige. They also provide channels of recreation or help to reduce anxiety. Sexual techniques are primarily adjustive from the standpoint of the individual. In a later chapter a further refinement in the theory of man's coping activities will be introduced (pp. 623–625). There a distinction is drawn between techniques that serve for coping directly with problems, and another form of coping, used, perhaps, when adequate techniques are unavailable. This latter is called indirect coping.

Technology also contributes to stress. In any community a technique may prove inadequate for a given end. Indians in the northern forest of Canada burn wood in stoves to heat tents and log cabins. Their houses and resources for heating are not adequate to maintain comfort in outdoor temperatures of 30, 40, or more degrees below zero. Modern techniques of warfare inflict extensive suffering, often on nonbelligerents. Some techniques encourage disease. Chemicals used in industry poison an unknown number of workers annually (Sawyer, 1951:153). Certain techniques favor accidents more than others. In 1948 only about 2 percent of the American population was engaged in mining and quarrying but the accidental death and injury rates of these were the largest for any work force in the country. In much of South America a large proportion of labor on large plantations is invested in the cultivation of rubber, sugar cane, and coffee. Relatively little time is spent in the cultivation of subsistence plants, and income does not allow purchase of a proper diet. Malnutrition is rampant in those areas and follows from the way the people allocate time to their techniques.

The Marxist Position

We recognize a dynamic relationship between three sets of cultural variables: technology, social organization, and ideology. Any of these areas of culture may be taken in turn as the independent variable to note how it conditions the others. In this and the following chapter technology is regarded in that light. None of the three is more important than the others. Culture involves the dynamic interplay of them all.

Marxist theory, on the contrary, would make the technological factor primary.[2] Not only is culture divided into constituent parts that are functionally related but the relative importance of the parts is weighted. Failure

[2] The rest of this section is based on B. J. Stern, 1949.

to evaluate the relative importance of facts is one of the criticisms which Marxists direct against anthropological theorists who do not adhere to the principles of "historical materialism." Among all variables in culture the economic ones are regarded as truly decisive.

The meaning of this statement must be examined carefully. "Economic" here refers to certain, but not all, technological routines as well as to those social relationships which revolve around wealth. "The economic factor has reference to modes of production by which people acquire their means of subsistence, and the contention of historical materialism is that other forms of social relations and cultural patterns are basically dependent upon such economic activities" (B. J. Stern, 1949:348). The organization of society, for example, depends on what is produced and how it is produced, as well as on how the product is exchanged. What Marxists designate as the economic sector of culture, therefore, is something more than what this chapter calls technology. The technological factor is but part of the concept of economy. In making the economic factor the decisive variable in culture, Marxists do not assume that this is the only determining variable. All the areas of culture are dynamically interrelated; yet the economic element "asserts" itself in culture more than the others.

The major difficulties with such a position lie first in its confusion of correlation with determinism and second in its subjectivism. The historical materialists have no trouble demonstrating that the mode of production is related to other areas in culture. "Comparative studies of culture substantiate the fact that the forms of social relationships, the religion and political institutions and practices, the arts and the techniques clearly tend to be correlated with the type of economic life . . ." (*ibid.*, p. 348). This is true. But it does not follow that economic factors are primarily responsible for determining the rest of culture. Nor that they are decisive for "the nature and rate of development of cultures." The ritual system may lend morale for carrying out production, and art may help to promote relaxation or fortify meaning and motivation. Machines and economic organization are useless if workers are not motivated to collaborate and to operate the instruments of production.

ENERGY AND TECHNOLOGY

Energy is a useful concept with which to explain the functions of technology.[3] Energy, whether in its thermal, electrical, or mechanical guise, provides the power to act or work. It may also be transformed from one guise into another. One of the most important features of energy is that

[3] Much of the following section is based on Egerton, 1951, and Cottrell, 1955. See also L. A. White, 1949:Chap. 13, and 1954a.

it can be measured in units, various types of which have been employed. Most familiar of such units are the horsepower and the kilowatt-hour.

Sources of Energy

Man requires energy to maintain life or to behave. Inasmuch as culture refers ultimately to overt or covert behavior, a very intimate relationship exists between culture and the energy available to, and employed by, a given community.

Everywhere man secures a portion of the energy on which culture rests from food which he eats. Ultimately the source of the energy in food, like the energy in coal and oil, derives from the sun. The sun radiates a tremendous stream of energy, of which only about one two-thousand-millionth ever reaches the earth. Even some of this energy is again reflected back into space. Of the absorbed energy only a small percentage ever reaches man and that chiefly becomes available to him through photosynthesis, the process by which plants absorb sunlight and convert it into materials needed for growth. It has been calculated that an acre of land (say, sown with wheat) receives 15,000 kilowatt-hours of solar energy daily; about 5 of those hours enter into the photosynthesis every day. The nonhuman animals inhabiting land and sea subsist on the energy in plants or, like man, in part on the energy of other animals. Carnivorous animals ultimately derive energy from the plants eaten by their smaller prey.

Solar energy reflected back from the earth produces changes in temperature, evaporation, wind, and rain. Approximately half the energy from the sun entering the earth's atmosphere becomes involved in those processes. Less than $\frac{1}{20}$ of the earth's water power is harnessed for use.

Man neglects some energy sources but he has learned to make generous use of energy laid down ages ago, the plant materials that have been converted into peat, natural gas, coal, and more limited supplies of oil. These resources represent stocks of stored sunlight concentrated with the aid of vast geological processes. Replacement of such stocks still goes on but only at a very small fraction of the rate of their withdrawal from the earth. Resources in the form of stored sunlight confer great advantages on communities which use them, but they are distributed very unequally throughout the world. Their distribution bears virtually no relationship to the need for them. Also the scale by which they are transferred from "have" to "have-not" nations is slighter than might be supposed (McCabe, 1951; Ailleret, 1950).

Other sources of energy available to man are not derived from solar radiation. Included here are the tides and the heat of volcanoes derived from the intensely high temperatures in the core of the earth. Neither of these energy sources is used to any considerable extent (though in Italy,

The Gasoline Engine on Canoes and in Aircraft Means a New Source of Energy in Arctic and Sub-Arctic Canada (Top Photo, courtesy, National Film Board).

California, and Iceland a little steam and hot water are derived from volcanic heat). Finally, there is nuclear energy, released when matter ceases to be matter. This source of power man has just learned to tap. The potentialities of atomic power are enormous. A pound of uranium$_{235}$, for example, can produce 3,000,000 kilowatt-hours of energy.

Utilization of Energy

Man cannot convert potential energy into usable form without expending energy in the process. The basic problem becomes one of putting out as little energy as possible for the maximum return. The human body is one instrument which performs the function of converting solar energy into a usable form. Other converters are erected or manufactured and constitute part of culture. They include the harnessed animal, sail, wind-mill, water wheel, steam engine, hydroelectric generator, and atomic reactor. More and more efficient forms of converters have appeared in an attempt to restrict the energy inevitably lost during the conversion process (Eichelberg, 1950). The consumption of energy in the world has increased steadily in the course of culture history as man discovered new ways of drawing on power external to himself. Energy converters are among the most important artifacts in the technological sector of a culture. Possession of them distinguishes man from other animals who depend only on plant and animal food for life and who harness power from no other sources.

Since energy is produced and put to work through techniques, the technologies in different communities vary in terms of the amounts of energy they produce and utilize. Energy, it will be seen, is an important variable with which to explain how techniques in different cultures condition other factors in the way of life.

21.

Subsistence Techniques

ONE of the most advantageous and best-explored perspectives for under-standing culture is subsistence technology. How people secure their food has been called the "core of culture," although this does not mean that subsistence techniques constitute a cultural focus in all communities (Steward, 1955:37) or that these are the most decisive factors in culture. Their biological importance, of course, is self-evident. Changes in the mode of procuring subsistence are often easy to detect in archeological remains. From these changes much has been learned about the transforma-tion of human culture, from Stone Age hunting to modern large-scale farming and animal raising.

The important fact that mankind commenced at the bottom of the scale and worked up, is revealed in an expressive manner by their successive arts of sub-sistence. Upon their skill in this direction, the whole question of human supremacy on the earth depended. Mankind are the only beings who may be said to have gained an absolute control over the production of food; which at the outset they did not possess above other animals. Without enlarging the basis of subsistence, mankind could not have propagated themselves into other areas not possessing the same kinds of food, and ultimately over the whole surface of the earth; and lastly, without obtaining an absolute control over both its variety and amount, they could not have multiplied into populous nations. It is accordingly probable that the great epochs of human progress have been iden-tified, more or less directly, with the enlargement of the sources of subsistence [L. H. Morgan, 1877:19].

Subsistence techniques fall into two broad categories: food gathering and food production. There are perhaps about a million people in the world still securing at least a portion of their food simply by hunting, fishing, and gathering wild fruits, roots, or other edible materials. Often all three of these techniques are combined in a culture. Such food gatherers include the Eskimo, Pygmies, the Australian aborigines, Bushmen, and certain aboriginal people of India. These populations illustrate the subsistence pattern of early man. They follow a way of life that has endured for 600,000 years and long preceded the innovations of agriculture and animal hus-bandry (see Chapter 41). Food producers who domesticate plants and animals constitute the vast majority of the extant populations of Asia, Oceania, Europe, and the Americas. Food production originated only about 8000 B.C. (see pp. 697–698).

Each category may be further subdivided, giving rise to the seven subsistence systems shown in Table 26. Rarely does a culture secure food

TABLE 26.   World's Major Subsistence Systems

Based on Food Gathering	Based on Food Producing
Hunting, with collecting (usually in conjunction with some fishing) Intensive fishing with hunting and collecting	Incipient agriculture Intensive manual agriculture Plow agriculture Irrigation agriculture Large-scale pastoralism

entirely within the bounds of only a single one of these systems. People who farm with a plow usually also raise a few barnyard animals; they may even fish or hunt for auxiliary food. The people of Oceania who do intensive fishing in Pacific lagoons and on the open sea also carry on fairly intensive farming, although they lack the plow. The seven systems represent ideal types constructed for theoretical purposes. Actually such types will often be found mixed.

DYNAMICS OF SUBSISTENCE

The relationship of subsistence techniques to other elements of culture depends on the operation of four main interrelated variables, namely: surplus, energy, dependability, and social organization (including the sexual division of labor).

Surplus

The operation of a subsistence technique in culture varies according to the economic surplus of food it yields. Some forms of agriculture produce a large surplus in one community but less in another. Soil or moisture conditions may be different or the technique may be pursued with differing intensities by the two peoples. Generally speaking, however, agriculture produces a larger surplus than hunting; the latter allows a family to spare practically no food from immediate consumption.

Surplus refers to that portion of a yield which an individual worker or his family is willing to relinquish in exchange for other wealth, in tribute, or for charity. The surplus normally finds its way to members of the society who do not pursue the technique. In rural Pakistan and India grain is given to reward the blacksmith, barber, oil presser, and carpenter for their services. It may leave the village in trade, as tax, or as foreign aid. In a modern national community a large part of the agricultural surplus is converted into money. A share of that money, representing crops, finds its way to the administrators (i.e., the government), who, in turn, carry out duties in behalf of the nation as a whole.

Energy

Subsistence techniques require energy but, if they are efficient and practical, provide more energy than they consume. The relationship of any technique to other areas of culture is understandable in terms of the energy it yields. This energy may be in the form of steam or electric power, fish, other animals, or plant food. Perhaps the energy will be harnessed, stored, and traded, before being consumed. Agriculture, generally speaking, provides more energy than hunting and collecting. Hence, agricultural communities are more populous, are larger in scale, and possess greater wealth and power. Of course, the energy yield of farming also depends on geographical conditions in a given area—for example, rainfall—and on the intensity with which it is carried out. Intensity, in turn, is governed in part by motivation. Energy and surplus are not different things but represent two ways of conceptualizing the same phenomena.

Dependability

A dependable technique is reliable. It achieves its goal in a satisfactory number of cases. Agriculture becomes more dependable when, through irrigation, cloud seeding, fertilization, seed selection, and weather prediction it can be counted on to produce a given yield. Agriculture, generally speaking, is more dependable than hunting and collecting. Hunters often seek vainly for food and cannot foretell the results of their activity reliably. Dependability, along with relatively large surpluses and high energy yields, allows a community to take risks. People feel free to experiment with new forms of production. They devise new techniques, extend irrigation, carry on research, and bring new land under cultivation, paying for these things out of future yields. Hence development and cultural elaboration are associated with dependable subsistence techniques. Care should be taken not to confuse low reliability with complete unreliability. Hunting, for example, is not a wholly uncertain venture. People who carry out relatively undependable techniques are not constantly in a state of high uncertainty or stress. They adjust to relative undependability, the full measure of which may not become conspicuous until a more reliable, alternative technique becomes available.

Organization

Some techniques are carried out individually. They require little collaboration, coöperation, or systematic social interaction. Others, like irrigation based on dams, require considerable organization of personnel in order to maintain the technical apparatus and provide the requisite services. The relationship of technique to other elements of culture varies with the degree of social organization involved. If the subsistence techniques of a community directly involve organized human effort, such effort is facilitated and guaranteed by overall organization.

A technique may also foster social organization indirectly through the amount of surplus energy it yields. Highly productive subsistence techniques will encourage a dense population, which in turn requires more organization than a small, scattered aggregate of people. Subsistence techniques that produce large surpluses or that, like camel and horse herding, provide small surpluses but an abundant supply of energy in the form of riding mounts give rise to considerable organized social interaction that serves to distribute the farmers' surplus or helps the herders to augment their food supply through pillage.

The allocation of subsistence roles by sex is an aspect of social organization. Whether these techniques are allocated mainly to men or women depends on several factors, including the conception of the fitness of each sex and the nearly constant responsibility of women to care for young offspring. In some degree, however, nearly all subsistence techniques are specialized between the sexes in all communities (see pp. 353–354). The allocation of such roles in turn conditions the relative social importance of each sex. When men regularly participate in a prestigeful technique, like hunting, their normally greater social importance is enhanced. When women make a proportionately large contribution to the available food supply, their importance is raised. The relative importance attaching to roles of men and women will influence the pattern of marital residence (Murdock, 1949:36–38). The groom joins his bride's family after marriage when the social importance of women is great. When subsistence techniques enhance the normal importance of men, or depend on a man's knowledge of the country in which he grew up, residence will be with the husband's people. Other forms of marital residence will be explained when they arise (see also pp. 382–385). Where women contribute a large proportion of the available food supply, marriage generally involves the transfer of wealth from the groom's to the bride's family.[1] It is reasonable to interpret this "payment" as compensation for the loss of the bride's services (Murdock, 1949:19–21). In fact, many people themselves acknowledge this purpose. The subsistence contribution of women further influences the practice of polygyny, i.e., the custom of being married to two or more women simultaneously. Polygyny tends to be found in communities where women play a relatively large part in providing food.

---

[1] This paragraph is based on an unpublished paper by Heath, 1955.

Other Intervening Variables

Another variable that links subsistence techniques with other areas of culture is the elaborateness of the technique. By this is meant the number of relatively distinct processes entering the operation being performed. Irrigation agriculture is more elaborate than rainfall agriculture. But is agriculture in general more complex than hunting? More study is needed before elaboration can be measured so precisely.

The focal value attached to a particular technique is also important as a variable governing the relationship of subsistence activities to the rest of culture. The size of the capital investment required by a technique obviously conditions the build-up of certain forms of social organization around the technique and in other areas of social life; banks, stock exchanges, and regulatory bodies of the government illustrate such forms.

HUNTING AND COLLECTING

Communities that depend on hunting and collecting are highly diversified (Lowie, 1952). Some subsist primarily through collecting fruits or other vegetable products and devote little time to procuring animal food —for example, the Semang (Forde, 1949:11–19) and northern Maidu (Coon, 1948:263–292). Other people rely heavily on fish caught with nets or seek larger game on land or in the sea. The Kaska Indians (Honigmann, 1954c), Blackfoot Indians (Forde, 1949:24–31, 45–68), and seal-hunting Eskimo might be put in this category. The diversity of hunting-collecting systems is related in part to the fact that they are found in practically every type of environment, from the polar region to the tropics.

Means of Food Gathering[2]

The food-gathering techniques to be discussed in this and the next section involve a large number of devices and operations. Hunting equipment tends to be quite specialized for particular game and environments. A summary of the chief such means, excluding simply use of the hands to pluck fruit or gather shellfish, follows.

1. The knife, basic cutting tool of mankind (see pp. 329–330), also serves as a weapon for dispatching game and for cutting vegetable products free from branches. An equally general weapon is the club, used for small prey.

2. Much hunting is carried out with weapons that are thrust or thrown, but without use of additional mechanical devices. The lance is in this category. Its chief disadvantage is that the hunter must approach closely the

[2] This section is based largely on Leroi-Gourhan, 1945:13–95.

animal he wants to kill. Many animals become dangerous when cornered. The harpoon, except when installed on a gun, also belongs in this class. It commonly is found in northern North America, among both Indians and Eskimo, as well as on the North Pacific coast of America and Asia. Cordage is the principal element in a thrown weapon like the bola. This consists of a series of connected cords each weighted at one end. When a bola is flung the cords wrap around the legs and so trip a running bird or other animal. The boomerang, used for hunting in Africa and Australia, is another thrown weapon.

3. Weapons propelled with human energy augmented by mechanical devices include the arrow, propelled by a bow, and the spear, thrown with the aid of a spear-thrower (i.e., atlatl). The vanes of an arrow keep the missile on a straight course. Bows are of various types, including the simple self-bow of nearly universal occurrence and the composite bow made up of several pieces of wood or bone mortised together. A concentrated stream of air is the mechanical energy used to propel darts from a blowgun, a device generally limited to the tropical forests of Africa, South America, and Southeast Asia.

Much Hunting Is Carried on by Weapons That Are Thrust or Thrown. Hunters of the Kimberly region, Australia, use spears thrown with the aid of a *womera*, an implement on which the haft is laid (courtesy, Australian News and Information Bureau).

4. Today hand-propelled weapons, except for fishing spears, harpoons, and bird darts, have been largely displaced by the gun, a device which relies on chemical propulsion. Since all people who use guns to secure subsistence do not make the weapon or its ammunition, they must engage in trade in order to secure these goods. Products of the chase or simply labor is offered in exchange for such capital equipment.

5. Toxic substances, usually of a vegetable nature, serve as poisons in hunting and fishing. They are applied on the points of weapons, like the spear, arrow, and dart, or added to a body of water to kill or stun fish, which then float. Both uses of poison are common in tropical Africa, South America, and Southeast Asia but also occur in Europe (Karrer, 1955).

6. Lures, familiar to the American sportsman who angles for game fish, may consist only in imitating the call of an animal—for example, the mating call of a moose. The sound lures the animal to where the hunter has

concealed himself, bringing it within range of his weapon. Bait represents a common lure. In some places hunters masquerade in skin or antlers in order to creep close to their prey. Employment of lures and disguises is based on knowledge of animal curiosity, combativeness, sociability, or hunger. The use of torches in certain kinds of hunting and fishing can be included under this heading, for they, too, are designed to promote a particular response in the game being sought.

7. Traps constitute very efficient aids in hunting. The difference between a weapon and a trap is that the latter operates without the presence of the hunter. Therefore he can set a relatively large number of traps and leave them to work in his absence. Apart from metal traps using springs, three common devices of this type are the snare, deadfall, and pitfall. The snare consists of a noose planted and secured in such a way that it will tighten and hold an animal entering it. The deadfall utilizes a weight of logs or stones to pin down the prey, while in a pitfall the animal tumbles into and is held in a specially dug, camouflaged pit. Another variety of trap consists of a large fence or pen built to accommodate a herd of grazing animals. These are driven into the surround and then dispatched by concealed hunters. Caribou were formerly hunted in this manner by the Indians of the Canadian North.

Correlated Factors

Despite differences between various hunting-collecting people, certain general statements can be made about the ideal-typical community that relies considerably on this form of subsistence system. The following generalizations do not apply to seed or plant collectors who do little hunting, or to hunters, like the Blackfoot Indians, who use horses in the chase. The operation of hunting and collecting in culture and the cultural field is governed by the fact that these techniques provide an uncertain basis for adaptation. Little food is produced beyond the needs of the hunter and his family. A hunter rarely supports more than four nonhunters (Hallowell, 1949; Honigmann, 1952:510). The sources of energy in such a community are limited to the plants or animals found. The supply of these generally is limited and their exploitation undependable. Very little organization enters into the performance of hunting and collecting. Individuals work alone or with a partner, the latter often serving more for company than to furnish aid. Husband and wife coöperate in many activities and children are also useful. Rarely do tasks arise which require the concerted, geared interaction of a number of workers. Building a surround to trap a herd of grazing animals is one such task.

Small surplus, relatively slim sources of energy, undependability, and little organization help to explain the small populations found among hunting-collecting people. Densities (i.e., the ratio found through dividing population by size of area) are everywhere small; the ratio works out at less than one person per square mile (cf. Kroeber, 1939:134–142). Life expectancies in the population are short. Such people are often hungry but, unlike some agricultural peoples, their hunger is less one for specific nutrients than for food itself (Lebon, 1952:87). Periodic famines are probably instrumental in keeping down the population to a point that the environment can support; hence, densities vary considerably from one geographical zone to another. Diet as well as other habits depends closely on seasonal changes.

Culturally speaking, hunters and collectors are limited to an effective social organization embracing only the mobile band totaling about 50 persons.[3] Frequent movement by such a local group means portable housing, or at least shelter that requires little expenditure of energy, since it frequently will have to be renewed. Accumulation of possessions is also slight. These people do not build large shrines or monuments. Most of their time and energy are bound up with techniques directly or indirectly related to adaptation. Although built around a core of related families, membership in the local band is unstable. Frequent shifts occur from one unit to another. Marriages cement ties between bands, especially within an area where the same language is spoken. But clear-cut tribal organization remains absent. If government be defined as the ability of an individual or group to direct the behavior of unrelated persons, then these communities lack government. Sometimes, however, hangers-on, who are nonkin, may join a band and follow a leader. Leaders among hunting-collecting folk tend to give advice rather than issue orders (see pp. 480–481).

Of course, hunters do not fail to apply pressure on one another in order to induce conformity. Law, however, is not enforced by specialized agencies, like police or courts. Individuals, with the consent of public opinion, tend to punish offenses committed against them or their kin. In other words, private retaliation constitutes an approved form of punishment.

Monogamy prevails among the food gatherers who live on a hunting-collecting level of existence. Plural marriage, however, is not forbidden. A man simply cannot afford a large family of several wives and their children. Following marriage a woman may join her husband's family (thereby insuring that he stay in the country where he has learned to hunt). The pattern of shifting from one band to another also leads to a married couple's living first with the parents of one spouse and then with the parents of the other. "A family may pitch its tent or erect a hut near the father's relatives at one campsite and near the mother's at the next, or if they belong to different bands it may reside with either or shift from one to the other (Murdock, 1949:204). This gives rise to bilocal marital residence,

[3] The rest of this section draws mainly from Grosse, 1896; Jacobs and Stern, 1947; and Murdock, 1949.

a form not yet discussed (see pp. 378, 383). Marriage involves little or no "consideration." No wealth is given by the groom to the bride's people, no dowry from the bride's family to the groom. A young hunter may, however, work for his father-in-law for a period of time before claiming his bride. Sometimes he takes a wife whose brother marries the first man's sister in a kind of exchange.

Cultures not producing a surplus evidence little or no occupational specialization—no men who make canoes or boats and exchange those objects for a hunter's meat or fish. What manufacturing exists is exclusively handicraft. There are no machines driven by wind or water power. Hence manufacturing surpluses also tend to be small or, since no market exists for them, nonexistent. There is practically no trade in such a community or between it and the larger society. A man may swap an ax for a bow, or a number of men may offer soapstone to a neighboring tribe lacking this resource in exchange, say, for cordage. But such trade is very occasional. Sometimes a symbiotic relationship develops between adjacent groups, as in the case of the Pygmies who supply agricultural Negroes with meat, skins, and ivory in return for vegetable food, iron tools, and cloth. As the proportion of time increases which a hunting people spends in collecting nonedible materials—for example, to the point found among modern northern Canadian Indian fur trappers—we cease to deal with people who live by hunting and collecting. Such communities are commercial specialists symbiotically linked with the wider society, whence they secure food and other resources.

Hunters are widely known for sharing. Food and even wives and children are shared, the latter through adoption. The sharing of gustatory and sexual satisfiers probably functions to preserve the social cohesion of the small local group. The utility of children for tasks like getting wood or water, and the difficulty faced by a man in feeding a large family are facts related to the frequency of adoption in association with this subsistence system.

Anthropologists find little distinction between rich and poor in hunting-collecting communities, although differences in individual ability manifestly are recognized by the people. The scale of the band stays small. Even warfare, in the form of raids carried out by a few individuals, tends to be unimportant for relating the local group to a large society. Genealogical memory is short and dead ancestors are soon forgotten. Hence scale also remains small in its historical aspect. Slight heed is given to inheritance. Very little exists to be transmitted to survivors, the land never being owned individually.

Hunting enhances the importance that people normally attach to males. The distinction between the sexes in hunting-collecting communities is enhanced further by avoidance rites that isolate women at certain periods of life, like menstruation and birth, from contact with the hunters, food, or hunting implements (see pp. 576–577). Other ritual is concerned primarily with the passage of an individual from one status to another. In other words, interaction beyond the narrow kin group rarely builds up around festivals or ceremonies. Every man is a potential or actual ritual specialist and there are no full-time priests.

INTENSIVE FISHING

People who intensively exploit large lakes and ocean fishing grounds often secure part of their subsistence from agriculture. The Central and Southwest Pacific, as well as Southeast Asia, are populated by many such communities. Communities that fish intensively while also practicing hunting or collecting but no agriculture—in other words, true food gatherers—are much more rare, being limited largely to the southern coast of South America and the North Pacific coast of North America. In the latter area they extend from northern California to western Alaska. Tribes include the Tlingit, Nootka, Haida, Bella Coola, Kwakiutl, and Alaskan Eskimo (Forde, 1949:69–95; Benedict, 1934:Chap. 6; Drucker, 1951; Murdock, 1934:Chap. 9). It is with these people that the present section mainly will be concerned.

Means of Fishing

A number of operations in fishing, like the use of lures and harpoons, have already been discussed under hunting. Actually the two techniques overlap considerably. Not only are hunting and fishing both aspects of food gathering but among the most valuable sea animals, from the standpoint of human diet, are mammals like the seal and whale. These are hunted, rather than fished.

Hooks and cordage make up major devices used in fishing. Hooks may be carved from a single piece of bone or wood or cast from metal; they may be compound structures in which several pieces of material are joined. Barbed hooks have a very wide distribution and, of course, hold the prey more securely than the unbarbed variety. Fishing people also use arrows, and multipointed spears. For seal, whale, and other large sea mammals harpoons and retarders are important. The latter consist of inflated skin floats that slow down and weaken the animal after it has once been lanced or harpooned but not killed. Their use occurs along the North Pacific coast and in the Arctic. Employment of trained animals, especially sea birds, to aid in taking fish is generally restricted to eastern Asia (Hornell, 1950:Chap. 3).

Traps are often used in fishing as well as in hunting. Fish traps may entail blocking a stream so as to leave only a narrow opening where the trap is located. Nets are more common in fishing than in hunting. They may be fixed along the banks of streams, thrown from boats, or thrown by fishermen standing in shallow water. The latter two types of net fishing are common among people who fish intensively and export some of their catch in commerce. The widespread distribution of nets in the world undoubtedly is related to their great efficiency for securing relatively large numbers of fish which are aggregated in schools.

Correlated Factors

Over half of the world's fish are found close to shore, their supply in any given area depending on the nutritive value and temperature of the water. The regular appearance of fish year after year and the abundance of shellfish on readily accessible ocean shores make the exploitation of these resources a fairly dependable basis of subsistence (Hewes, 1948). When large seasonal supplies of fish or other marine products are taken, the catch may be stored to tide a population over less productive months. Fish are easily stored when dried or smoked. Especially when other techniques, like farming, are followed for additional subsistence, intensive exploitation of the sea readily produces a surplus beyond what a given worker or his family can consume. This becomes available for trade. Fish and other sea food are rich in energy. They provide much energy compared to that expended in obtaining them. Nutritionally speaking, sea food furnishes many substances needed for efficient human adaptation. In general, intensive fishing bears relatively little resemblance to marginal subsistence techniques like hunting. The yield from fishing is far more dependable than that from hunting. (This is also true of inland fishing; hence many hunters and collectors depend for a large proportion of their food on the animal resources of streams, rivers, and lakes.) Ocean fishing also requires more elaborate technical equipment than hunting. The provision and use of such equipment involve an individual in social relationships. Large boats, for example, are often built by specialists and owned jointly by a number of partners.

The following description of the culture associated with intensive fishing is based primarily on the Pacific Northwest coast culture area (Table 15, area 4). The date line for this account is, of course, the period before white contact.

Densities in northwestern America along the Pacific shore tended to be high (cf. Kroeber, 1939:135). This reflects the fact that much edible energy could be secured fairly close to the shoreline villages. Periods of hunger were rare and came only when a run of fish was late and the stock of preserved food had all been consumed.

The local group was the sedentary village facing the sea and containing from 1500 to 2000 people.[4] While villages were abandoned temporarily in order to allow the dwellers to exploit distant resources, like a salmon creek, houses were substantially built. Each village retained a large degree of political autonomy. Rarely did effective social organization encompass several such local groups. Thus, here at least there is no association of intensive fishing with the growth of complex political organization such as appears in conjunction with intensive agriculture. Even within the village, effective organization mainly was limited to groups of extended kinsmen who responded to hereditary leaders. There were no persons or agencies who applied law; the offended individual or his kin settled disputes that arose. Men frequently took more than one wife and these women played a useful role in collecting minor food from the beach. Often a man brought his wife to live in his own or his mother's brother's house, where he himself resided. Marital residence tends to follow the more important sex. Along the North Pacific coast, where men did the fishing, why did not a husband always bring his wife to his father's home? Apparently certain Indians came to this area with matrilocal residence, the custom having been for men to join their wives' families after marriage (Murdock, 1955b). Under pressure of factors that enhanced male importance, a compromise with patrilocal residence was reached by those tribes with matrilocal residence. A man took his spouse into the home of his mother's brother, a male equivalent to the father but on the mother's side of the family. The new custom scarcely upset the prevailing value which was felt for those kin on the distaff side (Murdock, 1949:211).

Occupational specialization on the Pacific Northwest coast remained moderate. Some men specialized part of the time, spending the rest of their days in fishing and hunting in order to accumulate a small surplus of food for exchange. Woodworkers, canoe makers, and basketmakers offered their products in trade. They found in the large village and adjacent territory a sufficient number of clients to keep them occupied. A form of shell currency facilitated the exchange of goods. All manufacturing was carried out by handicraft, without the aid of power tools or machines. A little regional specialization also appeared, certain villages exchanging shells for pounded dry salmon, furs, or slaves.

The social equality typical of a hunting band gave way on the Pacific coast to a rank system that included nobles, commoners, and slaves. Each of these strata constituted a social circle into which one could not move without the proper prerequisites—wealth, birth, or rights to certain rituals. Nor did every man have equal access to productive resources. Rules of inheritance were defined carefully. Considerable wealth existed, to be passed on by one generation to another. War became important as a means

---

[4] The following material is adapted from Jacobs and Stern, 1947.

of getting domesticable human beings who could be put to work. War, like trade, was fairly frequent and involved many men. Hence the scale of the village exceeded that of a hunting band.

With the rather populous local groups and an abundance of food, it is not surprising to discover long and elaborate ceremonies in the Pacific Northwest. One function of these was to intensify the solidarity of the village even as they served to mark the passage of an individual from one status to another. Clubs or associations grew up, the members of which also joined together in ceremonies. Such associations probably helped to control fissiparous tendencies in village life arising from loyalty to different kinship groups.

When a community specializes in fishing in a society where large agricultural surpluses are produced, the fishermen normally exchange a large part of their product with farmers (Brelsford, 1946; R. Firth, 1946).

THE TRANSITION TO AGRICULTURE

Farming does not automatically mean larger surpluses, more control over the food supply, and a greater supply of energy than food gathering. Much depends on the intensity with which plant cultivation is pursued. If crop tending receives relatively little attention alongside of hunting, collecting, or fishing, then none of the functions associated with large-scale farming will appear. As far as surplus, energy, and control over food supply are concerned, people engaged in such farming are about equal to those in communities devoting all their time to hunting and collecting. Agriculture carried on as a part-time activity in conjunction with hunting and collecting is indicated in Table 26 by the term "incipient agriculture." The Siriono of eastern Bolivia follow this subsistence pattern. Farming "is subsidiary . . . to both hunting and collecting; one of the reasons for this may be that the game supply of an area becomes scarce before the rewards of agriculture can be reaped, thus entailing a migration of the band to other areas to search for game" (Holmberg, 1950:28). Many of the Kamar of the Central Provinces in India also still practice agriculture only incipiently (Dube, 1951:36). Densities of population as well as cultural correlates naturally vary with the intensity of cultivation. At the present time the Kamar spend about six months of the year in farming. They live in villages and their culture resembles that of more intensive manual agriculturalists, to be discussed in the next section. On the other hand, the Siriono, who cultivate more casually, live in mobile bands. Their way of life closely parallels that of hunters.

Incipient agriculture doubtlessly often represents a transition to a new way of life. Until the new skills can be learned and fairly sufficient harvests assured, the people continue with a subsistence technique that provides auxiliary food, is familiar to them, and yields products they enjoy. Administrative pressure from the larger society, dwindling game resources, and new values the realization of which requires money turn the people increasingly to cultivation, gradually dissolving the old way of life.

Among the Siriono four factors underlie the persistence of hunting and collecting as bases of subsistence: (1) Clearing land for farms is very difficult with existing tools in the tropical forest. (2) The short supply of game limits continued residence in any area. People are forced to move before they can reap what they have sown. No reward is consistently forthcoming from the energy put into cultivation. (3) The Siriono regard gardening as a man's work. Men, therefore, face conflict between scheduling time for planting and also providing meat through hunting. Often incipient agriculturalists allocate gardening to women while men continue to hunt and fish, but the Siriono did not apply that solution. (4) The tropical forest is relatively bountiful with game. Hence, starvation never occurs and there is no very strong motivation to farm.

Operations in Agriculture[5]

The domestication of plants, together with animal husbandry, began about 10,000 years ago, presumably in the Middle East. Since that time new species of plants have been brought under domestication in many other parts of the world. Yet the number of such plants is relatively small. Out of about 350,000 plant species, not 600 are domesticated (Sorre, 1951: 123).

One of the rapidly disappearing forms of agriculture is that requiring frequent shifting of gardens and destruction of forested tracts by cutting and burning (Conklin, 1954). The plants subsequently sown benefit from the ash and the practically virgin soil. After the fertility of a particular ground again has been exhausted through several harvests, a new territory is cleared in the same way. The previously used fields are allowed to return to forest. This practice, variously called slash-and-burn, swiddin, or shifting cultivation, requires an abundance of available land. It tends to be associated with relatively low population density. Formerly it was common among the tropical farmers of Africa, Asia, and South America. Colonial governments have tended to forbid shifting cultivation with the aim of protecting forests. With continuous use of the same soil, restoration of fertility becomes a problem for the farmer unless, as on a flood plain, the land is renewed regularly by deposits of fresh alluvial mud. Restoration of nutrients to land may be accomplished by periodically giving rest to the fields (which is also the function of slash-and-burn cultivation), planting crops whose roots fix nitrogen in the soil, and adding organic or chemical

---

[5] Much of this section is based on Leroi-Gourhan, 1945:122–146.

materials. Long periods of fallowing are not practicable where population density is high. The use of organic fertilizers in addition to brief periods of rest constitutes solutions widespread among the contemporary agriculturalists of Europe and Asia. Animal manure makes a good fertilizer and one that is available to farmers who keep barnyard animals. Plant refuse plays the same role and is used widely in the Middle East.

The four principal operations in agriculture are: (1) preparation of the soil, (2) sowing, (3) caring for the crops, and (4) harvesting.

1. A simple digging stick is the most elementary instrument used for preparing soil. It resembles an implement used by food gatherers in search of roots. In Melanesia and Polynesia the digging stick was the main planting tool and it is still the principal such device used by marginal farmers of India and the tropical forest of South America. In the Inca Empire of Peru the digging stick was developed through the addition of

The Plow Helps to Increase the Area That a Family Can Cultivate (courtesy, Pakistan Embassy).

a foot bar that gave additional leverage and converted the tool into a spadelike implement. The spade itself originally belonged to Europe and the Far East (if the analogous snow shovel of the circumpolar Indians of North America is excluded). The hoe is distributed more widely and possesses a longer history. The length of hoe handles varies. In parts of Africa a short-handled hoe requiring the worker to bend nearly double is preferred to the longer variety introduced by Europeans. Stone, bone, wood, and metal provide materials for blades. By using the hoe, West African cultivators are able to support relatively dense populations. The digging stick, spade, and hoe utilize only human energy. The plow, being animal-drawn, greatly increases the area which a family can cultivate. For over 4000 years this instrument remained limited to Europe, North Africa, and Asia. Only recently has it diffused to farmers in Africa below the Sahara and in the New World. Levelers, also drawn by animal power, follow the plow and smooth the soil for planting. Hitching the plow and other instruments of cultivation to an oil-burning tractor is a secondary origination that has further extended man's power to utilize the land. Farm machinery, however, at present is expensive and can be used efficiently only on large fields. Its increasing employment may well spell the end of peasant farming in Europe and Asia. Small-scale farming already has tended to disappear in the United States and the Soviet Union.

2. Sowing requires little specialized apparatus apart from a container to hold the seeds. The seeds may be dropped into holes made with a digging stick or into ground prepared by hoe and plow. Broadcast sowing of grain occurs when large tracts of land are cultivated with plows. The addition of a seed drill to that implement leads to sowing in a straight line. In South Asia and the Far East other crops are sown between rows of grain, thus making fuller use of scarce land. Some plants, like the taro grown as a staple in the Southwest Pacific and the banana in Africa, are not grown from seeds but from shoots or cuttings of the plant itself.

3. Once plants have appeared above the ground surface their care begins. This includes weeding and, when irrigation is practiced, bringing water to the standing crop. Whereas the more severe tasks of preparing the soil and sowing are allocated to men, cultivation of the growing plants is frequently a female specialism. Exceptions occur; for example, in parts of India and, more generally, in Europe laborers often are employed on large farms in preference to the cultivators' women, who remain at home. Even here, however, women often assist in harvesting. Protection of grain fields from human and animal marauders may be included under cultivation. In eastern Asia people often move into the fields and live there until the crop is reaped. Protection against frost and strong sunlight is less practical and farm crops remain highly vulnerable to destructive weather. The period during which plants are nearly mature or above ground is ever a precarious one. In few places is insurance available to safeguard the cultivators from serious loss and famine.

4. For the farmer whose crop successfully survives the growth period, and most crops do, the harvest brings great satisfaction. Much harvesting requires mainly use of the hands for plucking or digging. For grain, a cutting tool of some kind—the sickle, for example—is employed. Except where mechanical equipment has been introduced, harvesting involves considerable labor, especially since, like planting, it often must be done

quickly before a change in weather destroys the crop. Once harvested, grains and certain legumes, like lentils, require threshing before being stored. This operation may be carried out by animals, a pair of oxen, for instance, being walked over the spread-out grain, which is then winnowed in the wind.

INTENSIVE MANUAL AGRICULTURE

People who spend considerable time cultivating plants through their own energy, perhaps in addition to domesticating a few animals, like pigs, cattle, and chickens, are intensive manual farmers (Curwen and Hatt, 1953:Chaps. 11–14). In this category are people who sow seeds of wheat, millet, rice, maize, and other grains as well as those who plant root crops, like taro, cassava, bananas, or yams in land that is worked without plows. Manual farmers exploit a wide variety of soils in many different climates. They are found in Africa south of the Sahara, prevail in Oceania and South America, and formerly lived in North America (Forde, 1949:131– 286). These differences will be ignored for an ideal picture that generalizes from many cases but applies perfectly to none. The following generalizations are not intended to cover the special conditions created by irrigation.

Correlated Factors[6]

In most environments manual farmers can produce a surplus beyond what they can, or wish to, consume. In other words they produce a supply of energy that can be exchanged or used to retire other individuals from food production. The surpluses are not, however, as great as those turned out with the aid of a plow; hence the expansion of population remains limited. With the surplus energy manual agricultural communities devote themselves to tasks other than providing subsistence. Men specialize as ritual leaders, in administration, manufacturing, or trade. The population is large enough to support such specialists and to provide them with work to do. The reader will recall, however, that deep-sea fishing on the Pacific Northwest coast also provided conditions favorable to a moderate degree of specialization.

Farming is more dependable than hunting. A sower can predict his probable harvest better than a hunter can predict the success he will meet on the trail. The implements of the manual farmer are simple, consisting essentially of the ax to clear ground, digging stick or hoe, and harvest knife. Complex social organization builds up around garden work when men from several families collaborate in clearing one another's land. The

[6] What follows is derived largely from Chapple and Coon, 1942; Grosse, 1896; Jacobs and Stern, 1947.

large population capable of being supported by farming in turn encourages social organization, particularly when cultivators are nucleated in villages. Density of population is greater among intensive manual agriculturalists than among hunters and collectors (cf. Kroeber, 1939:135–141).

The minimal unit of effective social organization under manual agriculture is a village of about 20 families. These units sometimes do not combine but remain well-nigh autonomous. In parts of East and West Africa, however, many villages are organized under a single administrator (a king). Through war or voluntarily, several such administrative units may combine into a yet larger aggregate, giving rise to a maximum unit of social organization called an empire. Empires found in association with manual agriculture are small compared to those which appear in conjunction with use of the plow. Local groups in West Africa include both small villages and larger aggregates, towns or cities, where specialist manufacturing is carried on and where the administrators have headquarters. Similar tendencies toward urbanization are apparent in the prehistoric Middle East, Mississippi Valley, and highland South America.

Frequent and well-organized warfare, whose further significance will be discussed in a moment, helps extend and protect the power of the king or emperor. Law under these conditions comes to be allocated at least partially to specialist agencies. Police are lacking but courts function to redress grievances and restore equilibrium. In the presence of kings, warfare, or focal interest in breeding cattle for wealth (three conditions that enhance the normal importance of men), marriage in manual agricultural communities is often followed by the wife's residence in her husband's household. Otherwise, especially if women possess a large share of responsibility for the crops, men join the wife's parents after marriage. Polygyny is frequent, again particularly when women constitute the agricultural labor force.

Specialization under intensive manual agriculture may be quite diversified, some men engaging in ceramics, hunting, woodworking, curing, divining, trade, and administration. Their food comes from the surplus produced by the cultivators. Manufacturing is primarily with handicraft methods, although mechanical devices like the potter's wheel and bellows help to speed up production. Trade is proportionate to the amount of specialization. With increase in the volume of trade, media of exchange facilitate the interchange of dissimilar goods. Social organization builds up around trade, including its financing. For example, periodic markets occur at designated places where specialists bring their wares. War becomes very important as a means of protecting trade routes, maintaining power in the society, or protecting sources of wealth. In lieu of war, diplomacy is employed to secure advantages in international affairs. With the maximal intensity of manual agriculture people are divided into ranked segments between which marriage may seldom or never occur. Farmers give explicit attention to how land, the principal resource, shall be used or inherited. But private ownership of land is not customary. Instead each family enjoys the right to the use of cultivatable ground or pasture according to its needs. Ritual continues to be associated with the passage of the individual from one status to another, but other ceremonies, too, are performed that involve more than a man and his kin. Often they honor a symbol of the maximal political unit, perhaps the king or his ancestors, and therefore serve to reinforce the solidarity of that unit. A few specialized ritual leaders are supported by the surplus derived from the fields.

PLOW AGRICULTURE

Cultivation with the animal-drawn plow has long been characteristic of North Africa, Europe, and Asia, including Indonesia but not Melanesia, Polynesia, and Micronesia (Fig. 21:1). Currently it still is being introduced to manual farmers in marginal areas.

Correlated Factors[7]

Plow-using farmers are often called peasants, a term that designates their commercial involvement in urban life (Redfield, 1956b). This involvement is attributable directly to the dynamics of the plow. Whether drawn by horse or ox (the ox needs fewer calories than the horse and walks more slowly; anyhow, a fast animal is not needed in plowing), the plow can provide relatively large surpluses of food. Its use frees considerable manpower from cultivation and for service in manufacturing or other specialisms. Hunting becomes relegated to a sport as the animal energy drawing the plow helps bring large land areas under cultivation and institutes dependable production.

The productivity of plow agriculture may be judged from the following figures. A family of 5 Burmese can cultivate from 2 to 3 acres of dry riceland by manual techniques while a group of the same size easily can plow 16 acres of wet riceland (Leach, 1949:26–28). In a Mexican village cultivation of 2.5 acres of land by hoe culture occupies from 143 to 180 man-days. The same land takes 35 to 78 days to cultivate by the ox-drawn plow (O. Lewis, 1949). Because a farmer can cultivate more land with a plow than manually, wherever the extra product can be exchanged for other desirable goods land becomes scarce and subject to sale and purchase. More land makes possible a larger output but of course no time is available for the farmer to provide other requirements of living. Here we see how surplus production encourages specialization. The plow enables many

[7] The following material is largely derived from Edward Hughes, 1952, and Jacobs and Stern, 1947.

Fig. 21:1. Old World Distribution of the Plow. Limits are prior to recent diffusion (from Thurnwald, 1950:Tafel 8).

potential workers to retire from food production, and the tractor still more. An efficient Iowa farmer can produce corn to feed enough livestock to supply over 300 townsfolk with meat and livestock products. For every 15 persons engaged in agriculture in America 100 work in other pursuits. In Ghana, West Africa, the ratio is 50:100. Hoe farmers could not turn out surplus food to feed so many nonproducers.

The maximum appearance of the cultural correlates of plow agriculture are found only when markets exist which can absorb the agricultural products. In Europe from the seventh to the tenth centuries there was little trade. The plow-using manors constituted practically independent communities, each with its own corps of specialists. When markets opened up, the farmer became merely another full-time specialist, one engaged in growing food and, perhaps, other commodities for exchange.

The plow does not itself make agriculture more dependable than the hoe, but the increasing attention given to fertilization, crop rotation, fencing, and seed selection has had this influence. Plow cultivation, however, directly encourages intensified social organization. The implement is usually made and repaired by specialists. The surplus produced by the farmer involves him in trade relations with other specialists. Government sees to it that the network of interdependence thus created is kept in relative equilibrium. Also the plowman is assisted by hired labor to carry out short-term tasks like weeding and harvesting. The farm laborer is paid with a part of the cultivator's surplus and uses it to supply his other needs.

Communities that have long used plows reveal some of the greatest densities so far encountered, sometimes 1000 persons per square mile. Of course, these densities also reflect soil and climate conditions as well as the influence of industrial manufacturing where it is present. Purely rural densities are misleading, for the urban population increases prodigiously under plow agriculture.

The cultural concomitants of plow agriculture are largely an intensification of those found under intensive manual farming. Mechanization accentuates these still further. With the plow comes a further expansion of the maximal unit of effective social organization. Very large empires appear, like those of Babylonia, Greece, Rome, Britain, and France. Government becomes a far more complex process than before. Matters of law are quite effectively removed from private hands and placed in the hands of specialists. Specialization in the community becomes intense and even local groups or regions specialize in particular commodities. Particularly are specialists numerous in cities. Trade is enormous, and the social organization that grows up around commerce is complex. Inns or hotels operate to serve mobile traders. Within already specialized crafts further specialization occurs as one man performs only a single process in the course of manufacturing. The assembly line appears.

The custom of a man's simultaneously marrying two or more women does not necessarily disappear under plow agriculture, but its function alters. No longer do the number of women in a household govern the number of cultivated acres. Area can increase without adding to mouths that have to be fed whether or not there is work to do (Schapera, 1943: 134). In rural areas the bride usually goes to live with the husband's family and compensation is paid to her family. But in urban areas this pattern is replaced by independent residence of the married couple and no compensation is offered for a bride.

Plow-using communities may be divided into those in which manufacturing is carried on by hand, perhaps with added animal energy, and those which make goods with the aid of inanimate energy—for example, steam power. More will be said about the dynamics of these systems in the next chapter. Social strata based on differential wealth and influence continue under plow agriculture, despite the appearance of idealistic doctrines that stress political and social equality or equality in the sight of God. Perhaps more than under any other system, sharp differences in the mode of adaptation appear between these ranked strata. The poor are malnourished, ill housed, and poorly clothed despite signs of affluence in the society. "Class war," or organized expression of dissatisfaction with the distribution of wealth, prestige, and power, shows up. Such expression has been followed by a closing of the economic gap between the extremes of poverty and wealth, for example in England and the United States. Wars between empires or nations become more expensive, world-wide in scope, and are waged by highly specialized armies supported by the plow's surplus. The plow-using community with its tremendous energy resources can readily subordinate food gatherers and manual farmers, and many elements of the community's culture diffuse to the latter. Scale is large. Widespread literacy further contributes to people's range of social awareness. Land, primary source of wealth, tends to become individually owned and, of course, subject to sale and inheritance (Batten, 1954:Chap. 5). (However, a recent trend to collective and coöperative ownership should also be noted.) Individual ownership not unexpectedly leads to the concentration of land in relatively few hands. The landless people supply their labor to the landlords.

Rituals function to integrate the large, diversified social units. In the nation itself ceremonies affirm that common loyalties shall prevail over the segmental tendencies promoted by class, occupational, regional, or other allegiances. The ceremonies often express the social importance of men and warriors as well as of the occupants of powerful positions. Full-time ritual specialists are prevalent. A part of the agricultural surplus is also employed to retire from production ideological specialists, men whose business it is to cultivate and execute new ideas: poets, writers, historians, painters, and scientists. The application of scientific discoveries to practical problems rapidly enhances development in the plow-using community.

IRRIGATION AGRICULTURE

Irrigation denotes the artificial application of water to plants. As an auxiliary technique it may be practiced with either manual or plow farming. Irrigation practices themselves vary and several types have been distinguished. In broadest terms a distinction may be drawn between relatively small-scale hydroagriculture and large-scale hydraulic agriculture; the latter comes about when waterworks grow in size and are kept in operation by mass labor (Wittfogel, 1957:Chap. 1). Hydroagriculture includes farming with the aid of flood water. The water is taken from a river only during the season of high water and directed onto the land where crops have been planted. This is, perhaps, the simplest of all types of irrigation for it need involve little or no construction or social organization. It is also the least amenable to control and direction. Sometimes terraces are built connected by small ditches, the object being to conserve flood water running off a steep slope. Simple canal irrigation leads water over land from a well or river. A Persian wheel, lever, or oil-powered pump may lift the water. Sometimes the well runs dry or the river level falls. Then the crops cannot be watered. Hence this form of irrigation also is quite undependable. The Persian water wheel, by means of which the power of oxen or camels is

Some 5½ Million Square Miles of Desert Were Converted to Farmland by Canals Leading Off from Sukkur Barrage, Which Spans the Indus River (courtesy, Pakistan Embassy).

used to lift water from a well, has been employed since the pre-Christian era. It may still be seen in West Pakistan and North India. This device is notoriously wasteful for it loses much power through friction and spills back a large amount of water.

The line to hydraulic agriculture is crossed when a dam or barrage is stretched across a river, the held-back water being released as needed to feed the canals. Modern dams of this type are complicated works the building of which is very expensive. They tend to be found in areas where output is relatively large, although they may be built out of surpluses produced by richer members of a society for people whose productivity is less. Two-thirds of the cultivated area of West Pakistan is irrigated, in many cases through large-scale waterworks. In India plans have been drawn to double the amount of irrigated land. They call for an outlay of over $2 billion and their realization will take 20 years. India is not a rich country. Even $5 per inhabitant spread over 20 years will not be an easy sum to pay in order to provide barrages and canals (Government of India Information Services, Aug. 8, 1953). But the gains expected from this capital investment are proportionately great.

Irrigation, generally speaking, is a mark of intensive farming, although, as we have just seen, different intensities of irrigation can be distinguished.

Irrigation that is efficient and dependable makes possible great population density. The concomitants of agricultural intensity mentioned previously will then also appear. Specialization and trade grow, government holds sway over large aggregates, social inequalities become conspicuous, and warfare is important. Widespread disorganization and cultural decline are likely to follow should the large-scale irrigation works be destroyed and the people be left too disorganized to rebuild them. This happened in the Middle East after the Mongol invasions of 1258 A.D. Today, still, the desolation of formerly fruitful regions remains unrelieved (Gruber, 1948:71).

Large-scale irrigation demands complex social organization. The canals or ditches must be dug and periodically cleaned out, and the dam must be repaired and protected. The supply of water has to be regulated, and disputes which arise must be kept in check. A small population cannot install complex hydraulic works, and people with little organization cannot maintain them efficiently. Therefore large-scale irrigation directly encourages complex social organization—a strong administrative center that can maintain the waterworks on which the community is dependent for survival. The social interdependence promoted by intensive irrigation has been called "similar to a modern factory production line where each successive operation is dependent on the one preceding it" (F. L. W. Richardson, 1949:482). An attempt to protect the operation of the waterworks may involve a community in aggressive acts against a neighbor who is perceived to threaten the supply of water. Victory in such an encounter may mean conquest and a spurt in the size of the political unit. Other devices than war and conquest, of course, have been used to guarantee water rights. The agricultural Pokot of northwestern Kenya have created a federation of autonomous villages for control of the irrigation system. The pastoral Pokot, although they are like the farmers in many respects, do not need irrigation and remain far more individualistic in their social organization (Peristiany, 1954). Among the Doukhobors, a religious sect in southern British Columbia, elaborate irrigation works have failed and now stand in disrepair. One reason has been the lack of authority and cooperation in maintaining and repairing hydraulic systems. The Doukhobors idealistically reject authority and resist the power of the government (Hawthorn, 1955:233). In western New Mexico the Mormons farm with irrigation. They also place far more value on coöperative community action than do the neighboring Texans, who practice dry farming (Vogt and O'Dea, 1953). Investigation reveals, however, that the Mormons adapted a preëxisting coöperative system to irrigation. The system did not grow out of the latter technique. Furthermore, when the individualistic Texans moved to irrigated farms they retained their value on individual action. They even invented an irrigation meter to measure the flow of water, making unnecessary highly organized, coöperative arrangements.

LARGE-SCALE PASTORALISM

Any large-scale pastoral community, whether a cattle ranch manned by cowboys in Wyoming, a band of Bedouin in Saudi Arabia, European Lapp reindeer herders, or a Kazak tribe of sheepherders in Central Asia, is likely to be linked closely to nonpastoral groups, like commercial towns or agricultural villages (Coon, 1948:142–170, 380–407; Coon, 1951a; Forde, 1949: 287–370; Murdock, 1934:135–162). In other words, such people do not, like hunters, subsist on animal and other local resources alone. Unlike farmers they do not use as food only what they themselves produce. They use the products of their herds in trade for other food and for manufactured goods.

Comparative studies of pastoral people are scarce (cf. Patai, 1951, and Sorre, 1948:633–660). An ideal-type picture of the way of life followed by large-scale pastoralists therefore is not easy to draw. Instead, as with the system of intensive fishing, one or two areas of the world will be selected to illustrate some of the dynamics of pastoral technology. This section will be concerned mainly with the herders of the horse and camel who live in Central and Southwest Asia. In addition these people normally also raise herds of sheep and goats. Perhaps 5,000,000 of the world's remaining pastoral nomads live in Central Asia, many in the Soviet Union. Attempts are being made to persuade them to settle in villages and on farms. Another 2,000,000 live in Southwest Asia and North Africa—the Middle East. The four animals mentioned above constitute only a small proportion of the 43 animal species domesticated by man (out of a total of about 2,000,000 species, according to Sorre, 1951:123).

Many more than these 7,000,000 large-scale pastoralists domesticate only a few animals along with farming. (Hunters and collectors, as a rule, raise only dogs and have done so since Stone Age times.) Where farming and herding are joint bases of subsistence the custom of transhumance is sometimes found. That is, the livestock not needed for work or food are driven out to pasture seasonally by village herdsmen while the rest of the local group remains to till the soil. Often these pastures are located on the slopes of mountains, land that is unfit for plant cultivation. In historic times transhumance has been found in Scandinavia; along the mountain massifs of the Pyrenees; in the Jura, Vosges, and Tyrolean Alps; Balkans; Caucasus; Iranian highlands; and northern Pakistan and India (Krader, 1955: 302).

Correlated Factors

In the form of meat and dairy products, pastoralism yields only a limited surplus of food energy. Even this amount is more costly to produce than

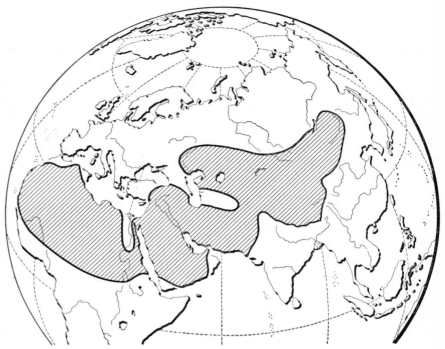

Fig. 21:2.   Distribution of Large-Scale Pastoralism (from Lebon, 1952:End Paper).

an equivalent supply of plant food. Herders who domesticate camels, horses, or reindeer, however, are provided with a source of energy that can be put to work. The animals are driven or ridden. Pastoralism is a fairly dependable technique for what it produces. Illness and drought, of course, are constant threats that may decimate a man's herds. Organization builds up around the operations of pastoralism to the extent that herds are put under a common guardian, or several owners coöperate for a task like castration or slaughter. Generally it would seem that pastoralism does not directly involve much interpersonal interaction. But the fact that herders are unable or unwilling to subsist solely on meat and dairy products, and are too nomadic to farm, forces them to trade with, or plunder, other groups in the society. Hence, large-scale pastoralists are quite wide in social scale. Recognition of how land and stock have been transmitted from remote ancestors, after whom the tribe may be named, contributes to their range of social awareness in time.

Dense populations are not associated with large-scale pastoralism. These people often occupy relatively dry steppes or deserts where densely aggregated farmers cannot live. Furthermore, pastoralism requires large grazing territories. In Mongolia only four persons exist to a square mile of territory.

The local group is a band consisting of one or more extended families who live for at least part of the year in portable dwellings. The band possesses its own administrative system but for some purposes recognizes the overriding authority of a larger unit into which it is mechanically incorporated—the tribe (cf. Lambton, 1953:Chap. 15). On the level of the tribe still wider units of effective organization may build up. One tribe conquers another or establishes power over an oasis or commercial town, from which tribute is then collected. Tribes also confederate diplomatically. Relatively large systems of political power therefore tend to appear with large-scale pastoralism. The government is often autocratic, especially toward subordinate groups outside of the tribe. But within the tribe all the adult male members participate in decision making. Special agencies for the administration of law are rare. Therefore a large measure of feuding keeps the pastoral society in a state of perilous equilibrium. From the standpoint of adjacent agricultural people, the pastoral areas are "lawless" and "unsettled." Strenuous efforts may be made to bring them under law but the vast territory occupied by herders makes the task of "settlement" a difficult one for police or troops. The pastoral country remains a "land of insolence" (Coon, 1951a:Chap. 16). Reasons for the desire to bring the herders under control will be apparent in a moment.

Herders are usually monogamous. Women contribute little to subsistence. Since the activities associated with herding enhance the normal importance of men it is common for a bride to reside in the household of her husband. Marriage occurs only after the man has furnished a handsome consideration, usually in the form of animal wealth, to her parents.

When seen in the framework of the larger society pastoralists are specialists. They draw supplementary rations, weapons, riding gear, containers, and clothing from the society. To pay for the goods they need, herders put on the market a modest surplus of cheese, live animals, hair, wool, skins, and meat. The herders themselves reveal little further internal specialization. Many horse- and camel-raising tribes, however, have further ways of gaining wealth. They use their mounts to act as transport agents or offer armed protection to caravans that fear being pillaged by other pastoral tribes. Some tribes make a career of pillaging. Many collect tribute from prosperous farmers and market towns. Carrying on these activities demands organization. The tribal chief who collects tribute or provides an armed guard must be able to control his own team.

Central Asiatic nomads are stratified into three social levels: aristocrats, commoners, and a servile slave class. The southwestern Arabs, or Bedouin, possess no explicit class structure in the tribe except as far as captured slaves are concerned. Tribes, however, are ranked and marriage rarely occurs across tribal lines. Taking their society as a whole, one can say that all pastoralists recognize gradations in rank, the artisans or farmers in towns and villages being regarded as far inferior to the herders themselves.

Obviously these folk place great value on animals, which are the focus of the culture. The animals frequently are valued for their number, that is, as ends in themselves. Little interest is taken in breeding, say, sheep for richer wool or goats for larger yields of milk. A man takes pride in the size of his herd, a pride that is quite distinct from the security of knowing that the herds constitute a source of milk or skins. ". . . Wherever livestock is herded in large units, whether the animals be cattle, horses, camels, or reindeer, the attitude of the owners to the value of the animals cannot be expressed merely in terms of utilization or exchange" (Steiner, 1954:118). It is not unreasonable, therefore, that pastoralists should be reluctant to kill their animals for food. They will do so only under special circumstances, perhaps on the occasion of a ceremony. The animals are individually owned and their inheritance carefully regulated.

Many of the world's large-scale pastoral people today profess the faith of Islam, for whose ceremonial expression no ritual specialists are required. Most Islamic rituals may be performed individually and require no costly appurtenances. They are therefore congruent with mobile life, a limited surplus, and sparse density of population.

AVAILABLE FILMS

A number of excellent films show some elements of the culture of hunters. The Australian News and Information Bureau releases *Tjurunga* and *Walkabout* (18 and 17 min. respectively, color) showing incidents in the life of the central Australian aborigines. There is some duplication between the two, and the first picture may be found preferable. (Other pictures about the Australian hunters are described in *Oceania* [1954], 25:123). For the central and eastern Arctic Eskimo and Canadian Indians, the National Film Board of Canada has produced nearly a dozen documentaries. *Eskimo Summer* (17 min., color or b. and w.) illustrates fish spearing and the hunting of whales, seals, and a polar bear. *The Caribou Hunters* covers the Cree Indians of northern Manitoba and their search for large game (18 min., color and b. and w.). *Indian Hunters* (9 min., b. and w.) deals with the people of northeastern Canada, and *Land of the Long Day* (38 min., color or b. and w.) splendidly encompasses the round of an Eskimo year. *Hunters of the North Pole* (10 min., b. and w.) concerns the most northerly Thule Eskimo and features a dramatic encounter with a polar bear. The Museum of Modern Art Film Library distributes the 6-reel *Nanook of the North* of which a 55-minute black-and-white version is available from many university film libraries (including New York University and the University of North Carolina). The Museum also releases *Grass*, dealing with the nomadic Baktyari of Iran (7 reels, b. and w.).

22.

Manufacturing

MANUFACTURING, the process of acting on raw materials in order to fabricate useful products, occurs universally and in association with every kind of subsistence system. However, its intensity and the way it is related to other elements in culture vary. This chapter examines how two systems of manufacturing—handicraft and industrial production of goods—are each related to characteristic cultural features.

THEORY OF MANUFACTURING TECHNOLOGY

Four overlapping factors—surplus, energy, capital, and organization—help to explain how manufacturing influences other areas of culture.

Surplus

Of primary importance is the economic surplus turned out by the manufacturer or craftsman. When a man produces more goods than he personally cares to utilize, that surplus can be used to secure other specialties made or grown by other workers in the community. A share of the goods produced can be reserved for administrative and similar specialists who themselves produce no wealth. The surplus also can be channeled beyond the community, being used to secure goods and raw materials not available locally. For exchange and surplus to flourish requires a sufficient number of buyers. The search for profitable markets, through exploration, war, or diplomacy, accompanies any increase in the manufacturing surplus.

Energy

Basic to any manufacturing and, of course, to the production of a surplus is energy or power. The simplest energy universally available is that provided by the human body. Other sources of power are domesticated animals, wind, water, coal, oil, and the nucleus of the atom. As more energy is produced in a community, people's power to produce goods is augmented. More wealth can be manufactured, goods can be moved more swiftly and efficiently, and the work force can be reduced or the working day shortened. The community then not only turns out great wealth but has time to

devote to activities that are not directly productive. The division of manufacturing into two broad classes, handicraft and industrial, is based primarily
on the source and amount of energy consumed in production.

Capital

All manufacturing requires capital, whether in the form of tools, machines, raw materials, or labor. The amount of required capital varies with
different occupations and with different types of manufacturing. Remember
how the intensive exploitation of marine resources involves equipment that
a man cannot readily fabricate or operate himself. Social organization builds
up around supplying the fishermen with capital or around operating the
equipment. This is equally true in certain kinds of manufacturing. The
greater the capital investment, the more numerous the social groups that
spring up to supply, guarantee, and operate it. Offering capital itself becomes a specialized service. The persons who invest it in large amounts reap
rich rewards. New systems for raising capital, like state ownership or co-
operatives, are experimented with. Opinion comes to be divided concerning the rights of investors and the best way of capitalizing production.

Organization

Social organization may be fostered directly or indirectly by manufacturing. In general, the more social interaction directly involved in producing
goods, the more complex will be the social organization of the total community or society. The modern factory produces goods through the collaboration of men working in the power plant and in the receiving, assembly, finishing, and shipping rooms. Coördinating these subsystems is the job
of the administration, which has its own specialized subdivisions. But the
factory does not produce its own materials and machines, nor does it sell
the finished product to the ultimate consumer. Production indirectly depends on producers of cotton, wool, steel, or other raw materials, as well as
on shippers and other transportation establishments. Also it depends on
jobbers and buyers who dispose of the factory's output. A break at any point
in these social links blocks the manufacturing process. The government,
therefore, does many things to assure stable social conditions. Through its
own specialized organizations it regulates freight charges, wages, compensation for injured workmen, labor's rights to collective bargaining, and
even the prices at which goods may be sold to the factory or by the factory
and its outlets. But when manufacturing is carried on by an individual
craftsman and his son, and the product is directly sold in the town or its
close-in environs, the social organization directly and indirectly involved in
manufacturing is much less.

BASIC TOOLS AND OPERATIONS

Basic Tools and Their Correlates[1]

The primary instruments used in manufacturing are cutting tools. These, of course, are themselves manufactured, but once made they enter into a wide variety of constructions and operations, ranging from cooking to building a railroad car. With cutting tools the hunter makes his weapons, toboggan, and boat. The agriculturalist's digging stick, hoe, and plow and the irrigator's spade are made with similar implements. Cutting tools, in the form of machine tools, underlie the machines and armaments of western civilization. Many people will recall the high priority attached to work in the machine-tool industries during the Second World War.

Cutting tools fall into three main classes: those constructed by chipping flint or some other easily fractured stone, those made by finishing a close-grained stone through pecking and grinding, and metal tools. Each of these classes will be described briefly and their cultural significance indicated.

1. Chipped Stone Tools. An easily fractured stone, like flint or obsidian, is simple to work into the shape of a blade or ax. The substance, perhaps after being dislodged from a core, is chipped or flaked into a socially standardized form. The process takes only a short time, 5 minutes sufficing to make a knife blade (Martin, Quimby, and Collier, 1947:31). But the advantages associated with easy working turn out to be the principal limitation of the tool. A flint implement cannot stand heavy pressure; an ax of this material readily loses its cutting edge.

Communities that use cutting tools of flint or a similar substance, but practically none made of closer-grained stone or metal, generally secure subsistence only through hunting and collecting. The rest of the cultural system found in association with these implements can be predicted by the reader familiar with what was said in the preceding chapter (pp. 305–308). Such communities remain small in scale, possess few specialists, engage in little trade, and reveal very simple forms of political administration.

2. Polished Stone Tools. Fine-grained stone is worked into a cutting tool by first pecking it roughly into a desired shape and then adding a sharp edge and polish by grinding the implement against an abrasive surface, like another stone. If an axhead is being made, the artifact will be hafted in a handle. To make an implement out of a very hard pebble occupies from 1 to 3 hours of a skilled workman's time. But the finished tool will stand up under much rougher use than flint. It can be used to fell trees and hollow out logs as well as for other constructions. With this instrument a pine log

[1] This section is based on Chapple and Coon, 1942:96–104.

5 inches in diameter can be cut through in 2 to 8 minutes. People whose tool kits include polished-stone implements often also possess chipped-stone artifacts. Such communities follow a wide range of subsistence systems. Hunters, herders, and manual agriculturalists fall into the category. In comparison with an easily fractured rock, the close-grained stone gives them greater control over the resources used for manufacturing. Often the culture includes well-developed forms of transport, like the sled, toboggan, or ship.

3. **Metal Tools.** Metal is less fragile than stone. A metal cutting tool can be sharpened or hammered back into shape if it becomes dull or bends. Metal can be cast into a variety of specialized forms suitable for manufacturing particular objects. But the ores are not distributed as widely as is stone suitable for chipping or grinding. Therefore, the working of some metals—for instance, bronze, a mixture of tin and copper—involves a community in trade and helps institute relatively large-scale relationships. Iron ore, however, is more abundant and cheaper. Hence it has become the most common metal employed in making primary tools. To make metal cutting tools demands more elaborate methods of fabrication than does work in stone. Therefore, use of metal encourages more specialization. The metallurgist probably was among the first occupational specialists.

Metal quickly replaces stone when it is introduced to people who are using the latter. However, all people who use and prefer metal do not manufacture it. Communities that smelt ores and cast metals secure their food by intensive manual or plow agriculture. They possess complex forms of social organization and developed forms of land and sea transport, and they often domesticate animals which are a source of power. A far greater diversity of people, including modern hunters and pastoralists, make use of metal implements that are secured in trade. The desire for the more durable cutting tools makes these people willing to part with a portion of their surplus and links them in trade relations with other communities in a far-flung society.

Some Basic Operations[2]

Four somewhat overlapping operations constitute the bases of manufacturing: the application to a substance of pressure, fire, water and other liquids, and air.

1. **Pressure.** Much manufacturing involves the application of violent force in order to split, hammer, cut, polish, or grind material. Several kinds of pressure may be distinguished. In the first, pressure is applied steadily to the material, as in cutting with a knife or a saw, until the desired form is achieved. In the second, pressure is applied intermittently, as when the carpenter hammers a nail or adzes a board. Third, pressure may be applied

[2] The following section summarizes briefly pp. 43–88 of Leroi-Gourhan, *1943*.

steadily through the action of a separate driver, like a mallet which repeatedly strikes the head of chisel. Apparently this final type found its way into the human repertory of technical operations relatively late. Circular pressure, illustrated in a mill wheel or a bow drill, constitutes a special type of steady pressure.

2. Fire. The use of fire or heat is the second basic operation constituting manufacturing. It enjoys a long history. Apart from use of the modern chemical match, two ways of making fire (both using pressure) are widely employed: first, creating friction with two stones, catching the resultant sparks in tinder, and, second, producing friction with two pieces of wood, and again using the resultant heat to ignite tinder. Fire may be used directly in manufacturing, an object being put into the heat, or indirectly, as when a liquid, solid, or air is interposed between the object and the source of the heat.

3. Liquids. The third basic manufacturing process involves the use of water or other liquids. Here discussion will be confined to water. It is interesting that ice and steam play a negligible role in manufacturing, at least outside of those world areas in which modern industry operates. When water is employed, it generally serves for washing, wetting, dissolving, refrigerating, and heating. Materials as diverse as iron, clay, and wood may be processed by wetting them, that is, by soaking them in water. Dissolving occurs when a pigment is added to water to form a paint or dye. Water, usually at its normal temperature, serves to cool; for example, a metallurgist dips an implement into the liquid and thereby tempers the artifact.

4. Air. Air serves a variety of functions. It provides a drying agent and acts as a solvent—for example, when solids are burned to produce smoke. Indians give tanned hides their golden color and render them somewhat impervious to water by smoking the material. Air helps to cool and it is also applied in a strong draft to intensify the heat of a fire. Many means are known for bringing air (oxygen) in conjunction with fire. Prior to modern widespread diffusion, the chimney was limited to Europe and Asia. Blowing up or fanning a blaze is widely practiced. Pipes, into which the worker blows, and bellows have been associated with the manufacturing of metals for many thousands of years. When air is used for drying it is obviously the heat of the sun that promotes desiccation rather than the air itself.

Materials

The materials used in manufacturing can be divided into five categories: raw, separated, extracted, compounded, and constructed substances (Harrison, 1954). (1) Raw materials are procured in a state of readiness for shaping into artifacts. They may be stone, wood, clay, native gold, or natural copper. (2) Separated materials are those that have been removed from a plant or animal. Such materials include plant fibers, skin, bone, bark, and sinew. Usually they undergo preliminary processing before being ready for use. Common preparatory processes include shredding, beating, tanning, and drying. (3) Extracted material is obtained with the aid of chemical processes, usually with the application of intense heat. Metals are extracted from ores in this way. (4) Compounded materials are obtained through compounding or alloying simpler substances; thus bronze is a combination of tin and copper. (5) Constructed materials are elaborate artifacts, the constituent parts of which have already undergone extensive work, used in the preparation of further artifacts. Thus woven textiles are employed in making apparel, cordage is employed in a variety of artifacts, and the separate parts of an engine are combined on the assembly line in making an automobile. Culture history shows that man has tended to move from animal to plant and finally to synthetic materials for the substances he uses in manufacturing. There has been a gradual and as yet incomplete shift from the organic to the inorganic.

HANDICRAFT MANUFACTURING

Handicraft designates the processing of raw materials with the aid of human power alone or with hand- and foot-operated machines.[3] Energy and capital employed in this system of production are slight, and little social organization is fostered directly or indirectly. Output, therefore, remains limited compared to the real and potential yield under industrial manufacturing. However, handicraft manufacturing frequently does yield a surplus beyond the wants of the individual worker, particularly in association with dependable subsistence techniques that themselves produce large surpluses: intensive fishing, intensive manual farming, and plow agriculture. For this reason it is useful to distinguish, from the standpoint of the amount of surplus distributed, two types of handicraft: housework and commercial handicraft (Buecher, 1901:151–157, 182). Housework produces for domestic or family consumption with little or nothing left over for trade. Commercial handicraft, on the other hand, turns out a surplus for trade. Communities with commercial handicraft, and even those using industrial processes of manufacturing, always retain a certain amount of housework. In what follows the reader should bear in mind that housework, commercial handicraft, and industrial manufacturing differ one from another in degree rather than in kind. No culture contains a pure industrial or handicraft system of production.

In distinction to industrial manufacturing, handicraft is found in the com-

---

[3] We ignore as a separate system the harnessing of animal, wind, and water energy in manufacturing. To add such a system would merely introduce another step in the continuum from handicraft to industrial production but nothing very new would be learned.

pany of subsistence systems ranging from food gathering to plow cultivation. Among hunters and collectors and incipient agriculturalists dominated

by hunting, handicraft is limited to housework. Commercial handicraft, as already stated, appears in societies that produce dependable surpluses of crops or animals for trade. Relative to industrial manufacturing, however, trade in manufactured goods remains slight and division of labor limited. Specialization increases at all points along the continuum from housework to industrial production. The limited amount of trade under handicraft means that self-sufficiency is high, although it declines if metalworking is included in the craft repertory (see pp. 330, 709). This form of production is carried out by members of a family or larger kin group. As the intensity of production increases under commercial handicraft conditions, relations with nonkin build up around the fabrication of goods and the work may shift from the home to a nondomestic building located nearby.

Commercial Handicraft Turns Out a Surplus for Marketing. Navaho Indian women weave blankets to exchange for coffee, flour, and other goods at nearby trading posts (courtesy, Santa Fe Railway).

INDUSTRIAL MANUFACTURING

When raw materials are processed with tools or machines powered by inanimate sources of energy that largely replace the human body, we speak of industrial manufacturing. Under this system of fabrication there occurs an enormous stepping up of productivity. Each worker easily produces a vast surplus of shoes, radios, or pencils beyond his family's capacity to consume in a lifetime. The output of the machines, which are powered by steam or electricity, remains governed by factors like the number of consumers in the society, the capacity of those consumers to buy, and the possibility of increasing the scale of the society by making a greater effort to reach more consumers. In order that potential consumers will have sufficient buying power they may be aided by the government, money being secured primarily from taxes paid by people engaged in manufacturing. The consumers are aided to produce a surplus of grain, cotton, furs, coal, wood, or other raw materials. Such goods will be exchanged for the manufactured products. When a large enough market cannot be found the manufacturer must reduce his output. Startling increases in amount of capital and degree of interpersonal organization required for production occur under industrial manufacturing.

Correlated Demographic Factors

Striking demographic phenomena are associated with the shift from handicraft to industrial manufacturing. Population increases rapidly, largely on account of the declining death rate and partly because of increased life expectancy. But the increase in population gradually slows down and, if there is no immigration, the population in the industrial community tends to become stationary or threatens to decline, principally because the birth rate falls. These trends are illustrated in Tables 27 and 28.

TABLE 27.   Population Movement and Energy Consumption
in Sweden—1871–1935

Year	Annual Rate per 1,000 Population			Consumption of Coal and Coke (000 tons)
	Births	Deaths	Increase	
1871–1800	30	18	9	759
1881–1890	29	16	4	1,344
1891–1900	27	16	7	2,409
1901–1910	25	14	7	4,076
1911–1920	22	14	6	4,170
1921–1930	17	12	3	5,167
1931–1935	14	11	3	3,570[a]

[a] The use of hydroelectric power and liquid fuel expanded rapidly in this period at the expense of coal, much of which had to be imported (Montgomery, *1939*:137).

SOURCES: Montgomery, *1939*:136, 189. Coal-coke consumption figures for the three decades from 1911 are based on information supplied by the Swedish Royal Ministry for Foreign Affairs.

How can these changes be explained? The matter is complex. The declining death rate and increased life expectancy no doubt are mainly products of increasing attention to health. Such attention is readily possible in a rich community, i.e., one that produces large surpluses of food and other goods. Scientific research, supported by a portion of the surplus, delves into the agents of morbidity, and man learns to control their growth and action.

The matter of the falling birth rate is primarily a product of some kind of control exercised over conception. Such control is readily secured through mechanical contraception with the use of the condom, diaphragm, and chemical adjuncts. But why do people seek to limit offspring? Three main motivational factors appear to underlie contraception in a community with industrial manufacturing: (1) Children have little significance in individual life goals. For example, fathers do not desire sons to perform ancestral rites and no prestige is attached to a woman's demonstrated

TABLE 28. Population Growth and Coal Production in Great
Britain After the Industrial Revolution—1800–1947

Year	Population in Millions	Percent of Increase	Coal Produced (tons per capita)
1800	10.5	—	1.0
1850	20.8	98	2.1
1900	37.0	76	6.2
1920	42.0	13	5.5[a]
1940	46.9	12	5.1
1947	48.0	2	4.2

[a] Petroleum and hydroelectric power became increasingly important from this time on. However, fuel consumption measured in coal ton equivalents may have declined from 1941 to 1950. In 1950 the United Kingdom's 47 million people *consumed* the equivalent of 230.5 million tons of coal or 5.0 tons per head of population (Egerton, *1951*:38).

SOURCE: Egerton, *1951*:26.

fecundity. (2) The importance of family coöperation for adaptation and adjustment diminishes. For many tasks the individual is dependent on nonkinsmen. The plow or tractor on the farm reduces the need for young adults to supply cheap labor. (3) High value is placed on material comforts, and people fear lest the realization of that value be curtailed for themselves and their offspring. They seek to maximize advantages for a few children (Meadows, *1950*:1–63). In addition to these motivational factors, it must be realized that many tasks performed in the industrial community require a high level of skill. This is imparted through long, gradual training in schools. Another function of such training is to prepare the child in a general fashion for participation in a variety of specialized occupations. The individual for a long period of his life remains uncertain about his career and unable to work. Now, in association with the long preparatory period accompanying growth in an industrial community, marriage comes to be delayed. This shortens the period of child rearing and limits the children that can be borne during a woman's reproductive career (Lorimer, *1954*:Chap. 6).

Correlated Cultural Factors

Industrial manufacturing ushers in substantial displacement of handicraft manufacturing in the society. Handicraft techniques are displaced largely because they cannot compete with the industrial products; demand increases for the latter at the expense of the craftsman's artifacts, and new artifacts appear that cannot readily be produced by handicraft (Buecher, *1901*:192–204). Even the handicraftsmen may prefer the industrial product. For example, the Balahi, a specialist weaving tribe of the Central Provinces of India, prefer mill cloth for many purposes because it is softer (Fuchs, *1950*: 332). A certain amount of homework remains under industrial manufacturing. How much further the displacement of cooking, home dressmaking, and the preserving of food will go in the American family is hard to predict.

Agriculture in an industrial culture reveals progressive intensification and development. This takes several forms. For example, farming becomes mechanized through adoption of the gasoline engine, artificial fertilizers become available in large quantities, and pumps distribute water more efficiently to the fields. All of which means that agricultural production goes up while man-hours go down. In 1880 about 20 man-hours were required to harvest an acre of wheat in the United States. The mechanical reaper had already been invented. Secondary originations applied to that machine cut the time to 12.7 man-hours between 1909 and 1916 and to 10.7 between 1917 and 1921. By 1936 the figure had fallen to 6.1 man-hours (Giedion, 1948:162). Despite increases in cultivated acreage, manpower easily can be spared from the fields once agriculture is mechanized. Population migrates from rural to urban centers or to more industrialized communities in the society. Some of the labor is absorbed in industrial production. The rest fills the rapidly increasing number of places available in commerce and transportation. How labor is redistributed may be seen in Table 29.

TABLE 29.   Relationship of Production to Distribution of Workers in Sweden

| Year | Wheat Production (000 quintals)[a] | Steel Production (000 tons) | Proportion of Workers in | | |
			Agriculture and Subsidiary Occupations	Manufacturing and Mining	Commerce and Transport
1870	910	—	72	15	5
1880	900	—	68	17	7
1890	1,100	320	62	22	9
1900	1,300	460	55	28	10
1910	1,900	560	49	32	13
1920	2,400	620	44	35	15
1930	4,600	607	39	36	18

[a] A quintal equals 100 kilograms or about 220 pounds.
SOURCE: Montgomery, 1939:141, 154, 170. Figures in the last 3 columns do not add up to 100 because the tally of workers in "other" occupations is omitted.

Handicraft tends to be family-anchored; industrial manufacturing is carried on in a new form of social organization—the shop or factory. A factory is a group of people that assembles regularly in a special building for the purpose of fabricating goods with tools and machines. Rarely do the members of the factory constitute a kin group. With the aid of power-driven resources the workers produce a great surplus of goods whose sale enables them to secure the necessities for living. The factory, however, includes not only people directly engaged in manufacturing but also administrators who manage the enterprise, and "staff-line" persons who keep the plant's records and act as salesmen to promote new markets for the goods produced. These people, too, are rewarded with a share of the workers' output.

Related to the factory is another new grouping that appears in conjunction with industrial manufacturing—the corporation. The corporation is a group of people organized around the capitalization of production. They finance shares of the very considerable capital that is required to organize a factory. They start the productive process rolling and are rewarded for their role (which sometimes involves a considerable element of risk) by a further share of the industrial output. Usually the owners of the corporation, the capitalists, do not themselves run the factory which they have financed. They hire administrators to take charge. There is a growing tendency for this management to refer to itself, rather idealistically, as "stewards" tending an enterprise for the sake of the stockholders, employees, and consumers (Maurer, 1955). Actually, the factory is not run solely for the sake of any party to the enterprise—not for the stockholders, employees, management, or the consumer. The ultimate goal of the factory, as deduced from management's behavior, is the survival of the factory group itself. Capital to finance industrial production may be supplied not by private individuals or banks but by a national community as a whole. The government then organizes capitalization. This form of state ownership is familiar from the Soviet Union but many other nations provide some capital for production.[4]

Industrial production encourages the rapid expansion of that dense aggregation of factories, commercial centers, transport depots, and homes of workers and managers called the city. Cities also accompany commercial handicraft. But industrial cities are larger. They serve industry by conveniently providing the labor and other facilities which the factory needs. Banks and corporation offices are located in the metropolis, often occupying well-defined zones away from the factory district. The population, too, lives in residential areas informally zoned by social rank (G. Taylor, 1951; Warner and Lunt, 1941:Chap. 5).

In the industrial city large families are of slight importance. Work is carried on outside of the home, which becomes a place specialized for eating, sleeping, child rearing, and fellowship. In this setting marriage involves neither having a bride move in with the groom's parents nor having a man join his wife's folks. Rather, each married pair occupies an independent residence. Residence is neolocal, not patrilocal or matrilocal.

Occupational specialization in a factory and in the industrial community as a whole is finely broken down. No longer are many such broad specialists found as shoemakers, metallurgists, and clothing makers. Within each of these jobs there is an extensive subdivision of operations. One man spends

[4] Moneylending or banking is found in association with commercial handicraft as well as industrial manufacturing. In communities with the former manufacturing system people often borrow to invest in ceremonies or other nonproductive ends. Among such people the moneylender is an odious figure. This attitude alters with industrial manufacturing. People borrow in order to invest the funds to create fresh wealth. The banking profession then comes to be held in high esteem (Cottrell, 1955:77).

his time at some very specific task connected with making shoes. He passes along the partially assembled artifact to another worker, who performs another specified task that contributes a little more toward completion. The assembly line, as this system of superspecialization is called, is not totally unknown in commercial handicraft, but its extent is far greater under industrialization (Giedion, 1948:77–78, 87–89).

With the factory, corporation, and assembly line, other patterns of organization appear in the culture. These are groups concerned with trade, with increasing and regulating production, or with protecting the interests of the various parties engaged in manufacturing. Relationships build up around raising the efficiency of the factory, as when management consultants are called in. The community contains trade associations, unions of workers, associations of factory owners, and other interest groups. The same point can be expressed by saying that an increase occurs in the number of positions (statuses) which have to do with the production and exchange of goods (Theodorson, 1953). Sometimes these organizations use their power to interfere with production, as when unions of workers call strikes against owners. The complexity of relations just described is paced by the growing complexity of government. The duties of government also increase as it regulates the intricately specialized community. The extension of governmental power often encounters strenuous resistance from both the workers and management, for as this type of control increases, the factory, family, and other groups lose power effectively to regulate their own behavior (Theodorson, 1953:478–483; G. Wilson and M. Wilson, 1945:108–113).

The industrial manufacturing community places great reliance on study and experimentation. It is rationalistic rather than traditional (see pp. 148, 153). Emphasis is put on finding the right man for the job, the most efficient mode of production, and the most economic number of workers. The epitome of rationalism is found in the new field of operations research, a method for providing quantitative data which can be used by a responsible administrator to make decisions. Operations research tells management the cost, chances of success or failure, and probable rewards to be expected in following a series of alternative courses of production. On this information management bases its policy. Traditional allegiance to kin, tribe, or caste has little priority when efficiency is the goal, as it is in industrial production. In India "for the growth of industry, it was necessary to have plenty of labour supply. The rigid rule of caste forcing its every member to follow the hereditary occupation came in the way of the plentiful labour supply for industry" (Desai, 1954:221). Rationalism is a well-nigh essential element for the rapid change that constantly affects industry. To a considerable extent, however, industrial change is held back by high capital investment. Changes which would render that capital obsolescent tend to be resisted, no matter how worth while they otherwise might be.

Character structure acquires a distinctive cast under industrial manufacturing. Children are reared to be affable, sensitive to other people in the environment, and able to get along with others (Riesman, 1950:17–24). "False personalization," this may be called. Actually the industrial society is a highly impersonal place in which one spends considerable time with strangers. The selection of people who can work and live together harmoniously therefore comes to be of great importance. The ideal person is one who can get along with a variety of strangers and who does not upset the applecart by becoming temperamental, adopting radical ideas, or fighting for causes. Self-discipline is expected of such people. Readers know how this self-discipline acts when they hasten not to be late to work and to finish a job on time. These are the people who make trains run on schedule. The style of life common in modern industrial America is not easy to acquire in a community just beginning to industrialize. People find it difficult to work methodically, by the clock, and conscientiously under impersonal conditions. Perhaps people are not born for the machine (Gerschenkron, 1952:7).

Research into the order of nature constitutes a highly valued activity in the industrial community. The knowledge produced by the research worker can often be utilized in the manufacturing process. The great wealth of the industrial community also supports research into matters of health. Means are made available to implement this knowledge, too, in the form of clinics and public-health programs. Therefore, the death rate in the industrial community falls and life expectancy increases. The question gets asked: How can "modern industry with its repetitive processes, rapid changes, specialization and large size . . . provide community satisfaction?" Meaning: How can more personal rather than highly impersonal groupings be promoted (Scott and Lynton, 1952:34)? Some sociologists believe that close personal associations contribute to high output in a factory and are also valued by the individuals concerned. This approach shades into applied research conducted objectively to ascertain the conditions affecting production or the stability of the industrial plant (D. C. Miller and W. H. Form, 1951). Philanthropy, too, becomes a well-endowed field in the rich industrial community. However, it may be curtailed as taxes mount and the government assumes increasing responsibility for welfare.

The industrial community includes ideological specialists who produce a thoughtful literature in defense of, or in protest against, industrial manufacturing (Todd, 1933:2–4, 7). Sometimes they produce poetic conceptions of the system, like this one: "In these spacious halls the malignant power of steam summons around him his myriads of growing menials, and assigns to each the regulated task, substituting for painful muscular effort on their part, the energies of his own gigantic arm, and demanding in return only attention and dexterity to correct such little aberrations as casually occur in his workmanship" (Ure, *1835*:18). Sometimes, however, an angry attack is forthcoming. It may urge remodeling of the system. Tawney (*1920*), for example, argues that modern industry, by virtue of a philosophy of individualism, is conceived of by its owners and workers only as an opportunity to maximize individual advantages. Any thought of producing for the benefit of the society as a whole is a by-product of this selfish point of view. Industry, he urges, should be carried on for the public and not to maximize advantage for property owners. Capital should be employed as cheaply as possible, for its purpose is to assist production and not to earn profits.

AVAILABLE FILMS

The National Film Board of Canada has produced a short picture, *Making Primitive Stone Tools* (11 min., b. and w.), and another, *Eskimo Arts and Crafts,* dealing with representative manufactures of one house-work-practicing people, the Eskimo (22 min., color or b. and w.). The Province of Quebec, Tourist Information Bureau, releases two fine short pictures dealing with the processing of *Moose Skin* and the making of a *Birch Bark Canoe* (10 min. each, color). *Machine Maker* describes the significance of modern machine tools (Encyclopædia Britannica Films, 10 min., b. and w.). Two films dealing with North African handicrafts are available from the Office des Arts Tunisiens. They are *Ktifa des hamama* (20 min., b. and w., silent, French titles) and *Les poteries, moulées des Ouled Abd-el-Krim* (8 min., color, silent, French titles). The former deals with carpetmaking and the latter with pottery. *The City,* distributed by the Museum of Modern Art Film Library (30 min., b. and w.), is a vivid picture showing some aspects of urban life.

23.

Social Organization

WHY do people relate with other people? They do so for the value or satisfaction inherent in, or expected from, such behavior (G. Wilson and M. Wilson, 1945:46–47). Fundamentally social organization rests on the fact that everybody is different from everybody else. The differences, provided they complement one another, give rise to social interaction. No two businessmen could find anything useful to exchange if they used resources in utterly different, or in precisely identical, ways. No pair of theologians could find anything worth discussing if their assumptions were utterly different or completely alike. Social relations (i.e., social organization) arise out of the complementary diversities which exist between people in every society. By virtue of these, rewards come to reside in interacting with others.

SOCIAL ORGANIZATION AND SOCIAL STRUCTURE

Often what purports to be a study of social organization is limited to the bare forms within which social interaction occurs: there is description of the form of the family, larger groups, or of responsibilities inherent in specific pairs of relationships like king-subject, father-son, father's sister-brother's son. The description includes the mutual and largely ideal expectations which govern such groups and relationships. This is an interest in social morphology, or social structure, rather than in social organization. It is an attempt to lay bare the skeleton of relationships within which actual interaction occurs. The distinction between social organization and structure is a subtle one. The following quotation sums up the concept of social structure by claiming that it "stresses not so much the actual relations between persons or groups as the expected relations, or even the ideal relations. According to these views, what really gives a society its form, and allows its members to carry on their activities, is their expectations, or even their idealized beliefs, of what will be done, or ought to be done, by other members. There is no doubt that for any society to work effectively, and to have what may be called a coherent structure, its members must have some idea of what to expect" (R. Firth, 1951:30).

Social organization is a broader concept, designating, as it does, every-thing that transpires in a web of established relationships (i.e., in the social structure). A change in socially oriented behavior need not imply a serious alteration of the social skeleton. The behavior between a father and son may alter but the relationship does not disappear and traditional expectations may persist, even when they are not realized in manifest be-havior. If too great changes occur in a given relationship, a structural change may be indicated. That is, an alteration is perceivable in the texture of the web of social relationships. This may happen when a relative—say, the father's sister—ceases to be recognized as warranting special be-havior or as possessing special rights with reference to her brother's son. It also comes about when a group ceases to attract membership and dis-appears, as the large family is vanishing in many parts of the world.

Social structure represents canalized energy (Hobhouse, 1924:84). The skeleton coördinates the abilities of people so that they can act as a team. So long as the manorial communities, which dotted western Europe in the Middle Ages, remained independent their potential total energy was dis-sipated. After the eleventh century consolidation began, largely in defense against lords ambitious to extend their power. Three hundred years later consolidation had produced national states. "Incalculable" energy had come under control. What the states did with this energy is a familiar story to the reader of modern history. "Most . . . had no sooner per-fected their internal structure than they launched a program of expansion" (Whittlesey, 1949:83). Shaw (1945:159–160) expressed the matter more cynically when he said: "Let six hundred and seventy fools loose in the streets; and three policemen can scatter them. But huddle them together in a chamber in Westminster; and let them go through certain ceremonies and call themselves certain names until at last they get the courage to kill; and your six hundred and seventy fools become a government." In some respects coördination of people is analogous to the control of physical energy (Thurnwald, 1951:22).

To show how individuals actually carry out structurally prescribed relationships is to study social organization. One cannot, however, study social organization without at the same time, at least implicitly, paying regard to the content or functions of those relationships.

GENERAL FUNCTIONS OF SOCIAL ORGANIZATION

If complete ignorance of the functions of social organization is pre-tended, then this section can begin by claiming that nothing less than life itself depends on this area of culture. The adaptive function of social organization is easily revealed by the mother-child relationship. The human infant, helpless at birth and for a long time thereafter, could not survive without the mother's coöperation. Her own survival, while she cares for the baby, would be threatened if there were not a male to help her (see pp. 811–812). The well-nigh universal distribution of the family logically is related to its survival value. This group also endows the child with the basic values and attitudes that are foundations of consensus and mutual harmony in social life. Cemented by the possession of common values first acquired in the family, people remain in coöperation. Thereby they protect their survival chances. Whatever the source of lethal threats, if they can be met, then organization helps to overcome them.

Social organization also aids people to reduce nonlethal tensions and to win adjustive satisfactions. Play groups, ritual gatherings, or simply interactions with congenial people contribute such satisfactions. Sexual tension normally is reduced through social relations. The enjoyment of property and a measure of freedom are contingent upon having the help of others, if necessary, to protect those satisfactions. The role of certain people as comforters in time of crisis illustrates another adjustive function of social organization. Funeral ceremonies nearly universally provide for some kind of organization through which the bereaved are aided in controlling their grief and helped to carry on more or less as before.

Of course, social organization at times is a source of stress. Organized enemies within or outside a community hamper and threaten survival. Even dependence on others may be threatening, especially when new circumstances demand that the relationship be terminated. Marriage destroys some individuals' dependence upon parents. Thus, in making an individual less capable of surviving or adjusting independently, dependent relationships carry the seeds of stress. Stress resides in the application of social power, even though the power may be designed for adaptive and adjustive ends. These are some ways in which social organization induces stress, often simultaneously with promoting adaptation and adjustment.

An important function of social organization lies in its relationship to personality. In his relations with others the child and adult modifies his behavior; he acquires a certain conception of himself and of the external world. Human nature, as it is studied by psychologists, psychiatrists, and other students of social behavior, in large part is the product of group membership, or a function of social organization (Ogburn and Nimkoff, 1946:Chaps. 5–8; Honigmann, 1954b:Chaps. 8–9).

SOCIAL ORGANIZATION AND TECHNOLOGY

Some observers come close to seeing technology as the master of human relations (see pp. 294–295). Especially is subsistence technology given paramount significance in this theory. It is certainly true that by increasing his control over the food supply man increases in number, spreads, and acquires more elaborate patterns of group living and more embracive forms of social organization. Unless one can set up carefully controlled producer-product experiments (see pp. 84–86), the question of which comes first, technology or social organizational forms, remains meaningless. In dealing with a system of mutually interdependent parts, like culture, practically any part of the system can be treated as the independent or the dependent variable. No part need be ascribed absolute priority. We propose to follow this approach with respect to the relationship between social organization and technology.

Organization, the Independent Variable

Tools, machines, and technical procedures originate and depend for their use on people in groups. How else could a dam be built? How else could people in each generation of the Old Stone Age have made the time-tested hand axes and blades which they utilized for survival? The point is easy to illustrate for the highly specialized modern world. Without appropriate forms of organization the most powerful, fully automatic, highly developed appliance remains but a promise of potential energy. Somebody instructs the operator in its use. Other people provide the fuel and keep it in repair. A market is organized to absorb the products turned out by the machine. The more elaborate or powerful the instrument, the more complex the organization required to keep it at work.

Social organization can facilitate or limit technological change. Such limitation occurs on a small scale when patent holders do not market new appliances for fear of destroying capital investments. It also occurs when nations renounce the use of certain military weapons and techniques or when a conservative peasant village rejects the use of manure. This is akin to saying that the actual technology in a community is always socially regulated. No man can use the full horsepower of his automobile within city limits—nor, indeed, on the open road. There are speed limits that must be obeyed. Among the Attawapiskat Cree Indians nobody was supposed to build fish weirs at a point upriver from where a fish weir was already located—unless an intervening stream fed into the river. The same rule has been noted for the Tonga in Northern Rhodesia (Allan, Gluckman, Peters, and Trapnell, 1948:118). These legal norms are designed to protect survival and adjustment from the selfish use of technological processes. They illustrate the way techniques are regulated by social organization.

Organization, the Dependent Variable

It has been more popular to consider social organization as it might be dependent on techniques, tools, or machines than vice versa. This may be a reflection of how intellectual problems are related to the modern world's cultural focus on technology. Chapters 21 and 22 pointed out how different subsistence and manufacturing systems condition quite different forms of social organization. Those points need not be repeated.

Changes in technology manifestly bring with them changes in human relationships. In Yankee City the tools for shoe manufacturing changed from a few basic, hand-used ones to machines placed in an assembly line (Warner, 1947). Output increased from a single pair of shoes daily per worker to thousands. Formerly shoes were made in and for the family. Today the job has come to be divided between many persons organized in a factory where materials and tools are supplied by the owner-manager. The products are marketed throughout the country and even abroad. Workers are organized in labor unions which include similar workers located in distant cities. In much the same way has the development of new military weapons, including bomber aircraft, given rise to more embracive forms of organization for defense. Small nations have sought security by becoming satellites of great powers or combining into new units of strength.

SOME ASPECTS OF SOCIAL ORGANIZATION

In examining the following facets of social organization, the aim is to understand better how people are organized. We seek also to learn the principles which govern the way organized relationships function in society.

Social Interaction[1]

Human relations, or social organization, is constituted out of acts in which one person responds to an initiation by another. A greeting may be taken as a simple form of interaction. An American says "Hi" or "Good morning" while waving an arm or touching his hat. In the former province of Sind, Pakistan, a person of subordinate status need say nothing when he greets a person of higher rank. He simply stands for a moment with hands pressed together and raised before his face. This, too, is interaction.

1. *Social interaction may be direct, mediated, or indirect.* The foregoing examples of greeting illustrate direct social interaction in which one individual initiates action to other persons who are face to face with him. Lecturing to a class which responds by listening and note-taking is another example of direct social interaction and so is the following act in the marriage of the people of Dobu: ". . . His mother-in-law gives him [the groom] a digging stick with the command, 'now work'" (Benedict, 1934: 134).

Social interaction is mediated when a product that is instigated by another person's action serves to promote a response in the absence of that

---

[1] Much of this section is based on Slotkin, 1950:Chap. 2. See also Goffman, 1956.

person himself. Such products include clear-cut printed signs, written letters, a radio broadcast, flowers or candy sent to a girl on Valentine's Day, and a Christmas gift. Notice that it is not even necessary for the initiator to manufacture the stimulus by which he evokes a response. Probably in all groups social interaction is sometimes mediated by property (Herman, 1956).

The culture history of the world is marked by an increasing reliance on mediated social interaction, especially following the origination of writing, that has accompanied coördination of larger and larger aggregates of people. Relatively recent originations allow mediated social interaction to occur simultaneously with millions of people. The importance of the radio for coördinating the behavior of millions of citizens became apparent in both the dictatorships and the western powers during World War II. Motion pictures are another medium through which large numbers of people can be reached (Fig. 23:1).

Indirect social interaction occurs when an individual initiates to others through one or more intermediate persons. The manager of a factory interacts with workers through several intermediaries. A chain of command is created in large groups, the function of which will become clear as the reader continues. Indirect interaction is also revealed when a creditable person obtains a warrant for the arrest of another person and police are instructed to take the latter into custody. The reader will perceive that indirect social interaction is not likely to occur where communities are small or people are sparsely distributed. In other words, like mediated social interaction, it is not found in all societies to the same degree. Although indirect interaction may operate in a small group, its special importance lies in the fact that it is well-nigh indispensable for the coördination of large numbers of people.

2. *Interaction ranges from primary to secondary.* Primary social interaction is close, intimate, and personal. The actors in the social situation share a rich fund of common experiences. The understanding they possess of each other derives from long and close association. Family interaction has this quality and so, generally speaking, do relations in a Pueblo Indian village or a northern Canadian Indian band. These people have grown up together. Even with opportunity for more impersonal relations, people in small-scale societies often prefer primary interaction. The Chinese, for example, "has little active interest in wider entanglements except where the latter enhances his position among his family members, relatives and fellow villagers . . . or . . . become necessary to protect himself or these same groups." In contrast the American is less committed to a primary social core. He "participates in a wide variety of relationships none of which is his final anchor . . ." (Hsu, 1953:217). The Spanish-Americans of New Mexico reveal similar preferences (Mead, 1953a:177).

Secondary social interaction tends to be distant and impersonal. The

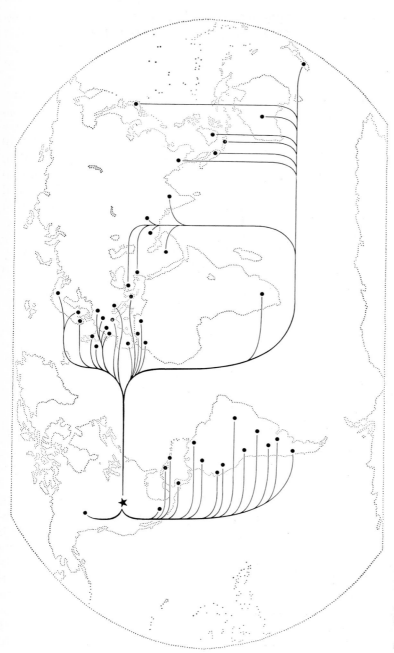

Fig. 23:1. Mediated Social Interaction. United States newsreels are distributed around the world. They bring international public figures, sports heroes, and common folk into interaction with millions of other people, providing recreation and information (from Baechlin and Muller-Strauss, 1952).

interacting parties share relatively few common experiences, though they are likely to make the most of those present—like the fact that both once vacationed at the same summer resort or prefer the same flavor of ice cream. However, much in the background of each person remains unknown and not to be revealed. The hotel clerk's or airplane hostess' interaction with the traveler is highly secondary despite its deliberately cultivated cordiality. As indicated, not all people participate in secondary interaction to the same degree. Clearly, the degree of secondary interaction in a society is a function of population size or density (see pp. 305–306). Secondary social interaction must not be confused with emotional detachment, indirection, or reserve. The Kaska Indians, numbering 200 or so, engage in primary interaction with one another but suppress strong emotion. This gives social relations an impression of being distant but the distance is different from that existing between an airplane hostess and the passenger whom she never before saw but now greets so warmly. In many Asian countries people do not express unfavorable criticism directly for fear of offending. Even refusal is expressed indirectly. Such behavior occurs in both primary and secondary social relationships.

3. *Social interaction may be harmonious, in conflict or opposition, or neutral.* Harmonious social relations occur when people passively or actively aid one another to reach mutual or different goals. They coöperate or collaborate in the interests of all or of one. For example, a number of farmers may combine their labor and work successively on each member's fields; thereby every individual in the team gets the benefit of all the others' energy. Such coöperative work groups are familiar in Africa, where they are associated with primary social interaction (Nadel, 1942:248–251; E. J. Krige and J. D. Krige, 1943:26, 52–54). The reader no doubt is more familiar with collaboration furnished by workers in a factory or business organization in exchange for a share of the value of the ultimate product. Maintaining harmony in social relations, or balancing harmony favorably with conflict, is a universal problem.

No less than harmony, disharmony is a recurrent feature of social life. In games, the conflict element is deliberately fostered in interaction. It becomes an end in itself; without it there could be no game (Simmel, 1955: 35). Whenever people hinder or oppose each other, they are in conflict. Two men compete for a single office; two nobles are rivals to see who can distribute the largest amount of wealth and so acquire the greatest prestige; a thief demands another man's wealth; veterans returning to an Indian pueblo after foreign war service contradict their elders over the propriety of certain customs—these are examples of disharmony. But they are not all of a kind, and a later chapter will elaborate further distinctions in this sphere (pp. 465–470).

Social interaction is neutral when the actors are neither mutually helpful nor in conflict.

Social Isolation

Social isolation implies a reduction in social interaction. In practically all communities there are people who at certain times or under prescribed conditions are to some degree isolated. Among the Kaska Indians a man tends to reduce his initiations to a married daughter and she to her father; they become "shy" with each other. Among the same people a man avoids talking to, or eating with, his wife's mother, or even meeting her face to face. In the United States Air Force, as in practically all military organizations, fraternization between enlisted men and officers is explicitly disapproved. Arrangements on an air base studied by the author include separate clubs, dormitories, and even latrines for these two classes (Honigmann, 1954d).

The purposes behind social isolation vary. A man who avoids direct interaction with his mother-in-law among the Kaska Indians thereby shows his respect of her. An army officer or executive on the other hand seeks to retain effective power over his subordinates and avoid undue familiarity with them by isolation. Sometimes a person is avoided because he is presumed to be dangerous; the menstruating woman among the Kaska Indians used to be isolated lest she interfere with a man's hunting ability. People who threaten harmonious social interaction may be deported from the community or incarcerated within it, thereby becoming isolated. To take a more general point of view: (1) Social isolation helps people to carry out responsibilities by reducing distraction or conflicting claims. (2) It is also a means of guarding against undesirable behaviors. Avoidance of a mother-in-law reduces the possibility of incest or bickering between that woman and the daughter's husband. (3) Social isolation that involves groups or categories of people encourages stereotypes (i.e., generalizations based on few or no reliable facts). Airmen who do not know their officers will conceive of them as selfish or conceited; upper-class people in Yankee City, Massachusetts, claim that lower-class people live like animals. (4) Finally, social isolation slows down internal diffusion and encourages unequal social change. Further opportunity to study social isolation will be provided in Chapter 27 and on p. 522.

Status and Role

Interaction may be considered as taking place not only between individuals but between categories of individuals. Each member of the same category occupies the same definite position in the social structure. Mr. Monroe's interacting with Mr. Brown is an instance of individual interaction. The interaction of Monroe, manager of the plant, with Brown, supervisor of the plant's maintenance staff, is an instance of interaction between two social positions.

Any social position recognizable with reference to other positions in a society is a status.[2] A status may be defined by the patterns of behavior generally manifested by occupants of such a position. Certain attitudes and actions, for example, distinguish the American father, mother, and Air Force officer. A status carries with it certain rights and duties. We behave toward another person according to the rights warranted by his status in a given situation and by the duties attached to our own status in that situation. This means that every individual occupies several statuses but all of them are never operative in the same situation. When a person executes behavior appropriate to his status in any given situation he is performing the role associated with that position. No two individuals play the same role—say, the role of father—in quite the same manner. Sometimes, in the opinion of other members of the community, a person may not play his role at all adequately. He may then be removed from his position. Or perhaps he is punished by losing some prestige for failing to live up to the role expectations. Status and prestige, it is important to emphasize, are not synonymous, despite their confusion in popular speech (see below).

Culture change may be followed by the creation of new statuses and displacement of others. A new technique will generally introduce a new position. Population increase which favors specialization involves the creation of new statuses—the positions of specialists. Even more common than such structural changes, however, are changes in content of existing statuses. Housewives in America play a very different role in 1957 from the one they played in 1857. The content of the status has changed synchronously with changes in other sectors of social life. Individual variation in role playing between occupants of the same status may promote change in the definition of the status. In time the consistent deviation from behavior ideally expected from the occupant of a position may be accepted as quite appropriate to the status.

As noted already, an individual does not occupy only a single status. The same man in a Pakistan village may be a farmer, father, husband, Muslim, citizen of West Pakistan province, national citizen, debtor to his bank, and plaintiff in a lawsuit directed against the local landlord, whom he accuses of having stolen a portion of his land. Some of these statuses are active simultaneously in a single situation while the others are latent. When two or more statuses are operative simultaneously, the Pakistan farmer may discover that the roles demanded by each interfere with one another. He experiences conflict. For instance, attending court could inter-

---

[2] The definition follows Linton, 1936:Chap. 8.

fere with plowing. Some kind of scheduling is called for to reduce such conflict. Alternatively, certain roles may be neglected, but the cost may be high for the individual, the community, and his society as a whole. When farmers are expected both to play their agricultural roles and to be prepared to defend the country from external attack, the provision of food for the community may suffer, the export of raw materials may be slowed down, and people in other communities may be thrown out of work. The behaviors performed in each status occupied by an individual are usually linked or integrated. That is, a father's role is colored by virtue of the father's also being a Muslim and a Pakistan citizen. Therefore any role tends to reflect all the roles acted out by an individual in a specific community.

Caution is required in delineating statuses that a community does not recognize explicitly. Because administration is important to us, we may expect every group to reveal a clear-cut community leader. Leadership is by no means universal. That is to say, every culture does not contain clear-cut, explicit recognition of the position of leader. A status found in one culture may be broken up into several positions in another culture. Where one community recognizes only one kind of cousin other people distinguish between different kinds of cousins and prescribe quite different behaviors to and for each. When a man marries more than one wife he may for purposes of inheritance distinguish between sons born of the same or different women (between uterine and nonuterine sons). Some statuses are recognized more readily by an alien observer than others. A woman among the Coorgs of South India, it is easy to see, occupies the statuses of woman and, perhaps, also of wife or daughter. She may also occupy the status of one who is impure because she is menstruating. The stranger will not be aware of any such position in the culture whereas somebody familiar with Coorg life, observing that she is omitting certain customary behaviors of women, will be quite aware of her current status (Srinivas, 1952:102).

Certain statuses are assigned (i.e., ascribed) to an individual automatically, quite without reference to his inclinations. The status of man or woman, child or adult, is in this category. So are hereditary statuses symbolized by titles which pass, for example, to an eldest son. Positions based on kinship also fall in this category. A man cannot choose the status of son, cousin, or nephew. If a family with one son through birth acquires another, the first child automatically is ascribed the status of brother or sibling. He has little choice in the matter. Sometimes a community makes limited provision whereby a person can rid himself of an ascribed status which he does not want to occupy. The American Indians allowed a man who felt attracted to woman's status to become a sort of woman (see pp. 574–575). In 1955 the son of a British viscount, who was married to an American woman, tried to escape inheriting the title of "Lord" when his father died. The man pleaded for 90 minutes before a committee of the House of Lords.

He claimed that his wife had little desire to acquire the complementary status of "Lady." The House of Lords, however, turned down the request (*New York Times,* Feb. 19, 1955).

Statuses are achieved when the individual lands in them by competition or by virtue of his performance. All achieved statuses are not voluntarily sought nor are they all desirable. An inept sergeant, it will be appreciated, usually has no desire to be demoted to the rank of private because of poor performances.

Prestige

Status, as the word is used here, corresponds to a position. A status system is the web of social positions knitting together a community or society. Observation of a status system in operation reveals that not all the positions are esteemed equally. Prestige refers to the social worth which is placed on different social statuses or their occupants. Relative prestige is an important aspect of social organization. It may be conceived of as adding a second dimension to the web of social structure. Height is given to certain statuses corresponding to the esteem in which they are held.

High prestige often attaches to positions that constitute a focus of the culture, like the warrior among the American Plains Indians or the hunter among the Kaska Indians. But every community also assigns social worth on the basis of age and sex. With few exceptions adults enjoy higher prestige than subadults or children, undoubtedly partly because many responsible tasks, as well as the training of children, rest on adult shoulders. There is also a universal tendency for greater prestige to be allocated to males than to females. The greater esteem normally accorded to males may be enhanced further in some communities by the kind of responsibilities and tasks assigned to that sex—for example, fighting or stock raising. Women can also enhance their prestige by performing socially valued tasks. The greater prestige attached to men probably follows from the biological differences between the sexes. Men are not regularly disadvantaged for work by pregnancy or child rearing. Furthermore a male normally can subdue any female (see below). In a very few communities where men are much more highly esteemed than women—for example, in parts of Japan —boys ideally possess more social worth than girls and even outrank adult women. Positions involving a large share of power in social relationships nearly always carry higher rank than statuses associated with slight power.

There are many other bases for social worth. These include the race to which an individual is supposed to belong, his length of membership in the group, language spoken, and the amount of wealth he possesses. Some people show very little concern with calculations of relative prestige. The Indians of northern Canada and also the eastern Eskimo are in this category. Other communities are obsessed with the matter of relative rank.

People are constantly anxious lest they do, wear, or say something that will lower their esteem in the eyes of others. They cling tenaciously to symbols of high rank. In the Middle East, for example, to work with the hands is held to be demeaning. Western anthropologists arouse consternation when they pitch in to change a tire on a car. No local citizen of equivalent high rank could perform this task without risking loss of prestige, perhaps only in his own eyes.

Specialization

What people do in social organization may be allocated to them on the basis of age, sex, or distinct occupation.

1. **Age.** Specialization by age is universal. Children and adults in all communities perform different roles. The aged, too, possess peculiar obligations by virtue of their ascribed status. The universality of age specialization doubtlessly is related to the different capacities and abilities of people at various points in their lives. Children cannot hunt or do many other tasks as effectively as adults. Old people gradually lose their strength and often their health. Hence such relatively simple tasks as hauling water or fetching small sticks of firewood are often relegated to children while old people occupy themselves with sewing and other sedentary work.

2. **Sex.** Specialization by sex also appears in all cultures. In every community woman's role behavior differs from man's, despite the fact that the excluded sex might be fully capable of performing a particular task. Sex specialization is related partly to the physiological differences between men and women. Pregnancy and nursing hinder women at times in their lives. A woman who must nurse a child can't go off for several days hunting game. The child is an encumbrance; its cries would frighten the game. Sex-allocated tasks are also related to such things as the male's larger bones, muscles, lungs, heart, and the greater frequency of red blood corpuscles in each cubic centimeter of a man's blood. Together these variables allow "surges of activity" (LaBarre, 1954:108). Physiological differences or even variations of strength are far from explaining all sex specialization. Dogmatically, certain incapacities frequently are ascribed to women. The Cree Indians of Attawapiskat say that women are too shy to be effective as public leaders. Women may or may not agree with such beliefs. Arbitrary convention may be responsible for the allocation of some role behaviors; Americans feel it is improper for a woman to ask a man to dance. Sex specialization is not enforced with the same rigor in different communities. But wherever it occurs in a substantial measure it functions to emphasize the distinction between men and women. Such a distinction tends deliberately to be blurred in America and Europe, where sex specialization is also not rigorously enforced. That the distinction between the sexes cannot be completely suppressed is strongly indicated by the experiment of

the *kibbutzim* (collective farms) in Israel. Differences in physical ability and occurrences like pregnancy keep women from attaining the ideal of equality with men. In one *kibbutz*, out of 113 physically able women only 14 work permanently in farming. The remaining 88 percent are in service jobs, like laundry and cleaning, performing roles in which they are unhappy (Spiro, 1956:225).

A comparative study of sex specialization involving a total of 283 communities reveals that gathering of fruit and vegetable foods and plant cultivation are subsistence techniques frequently allocated to women; fishing, dairying, and, of course, hunting more frequently remain in the domain of men (Heath, 1955). If woman's contribution to subsistence is ordered on a scale ranging from no contribution (zero) to 100 percent, then in no community does a woman contribute as much as 90 percent of subsistence. Her contribution is often so slight as to be inconspicuous. These points are brought out in Table 30. The figures help explain why

TABLE 30. Subsistence Contribution of
Women in 289 Communities

Percent of Subsist- ence Contributed by Women	Communities	
	Number	Percent
0– 20	113	39
30– 50	136	47
60– 80	40	14
90–100	—	—

SOURCE: Heath, *1955*.

in practically all communities women are held in lower esteem, or possess less social worth, than men. Feminine rank, it may be suggested, is correlated with the relatively attenuated contribution which women make to subsistence.

3. Occupation. Specialization by skill or occupation (so-called "true" specialization) is not universal. It appears in conjunction with a relatively dense population and food production. Occupational specialization means that different people in a community specialize in particular skills and services. People engaged in such specialisms produce a surplus of something, or a service, that is exchanged for the products or services of others. Even a university exemplifies this principle. The professor lectures in return for the services and products given to him by the students' parents. But in the community with a money economy the products are sold. A share of the money earned is paid for tuition or, in a state university, in taxes. A portion of that money reaches the instructional staff. Such specialization and exchange, as already pointed out (Chapter 21), are not possible without a relatively dense population together with provisions for transporting surplus goods.

For convenience three degrees of occupational specialization can be distinguished (Chapple and Coon, 1942:253–254): (1) practically none, in which case the family provides nearly everything needed for adaptation

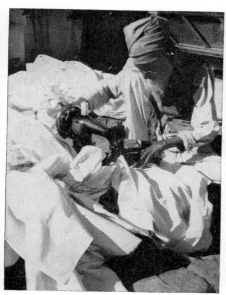

Two Kinds of Specialization in West Pakistan: an Outdoor Tailor with Portable Sewing Machine and Two Afghan Girls Begging.

and adjustment, (2) part-time, in which only part of an individual's time is spent producing a surplus or rendering a service for exchange, and (3) full-time, the individual spending practically all his working time producing a surplus or service which is exchanged for other goods and services. The third condition is, of course, characteristic of modern Europe and America. Even regions of modern national communities specialize: North Carolina produces tobacco and tobacco products as well as textiles; Corona, a town some 40 miles east of Los Angeles, California, produces more lemons than any other region in the world. Some persons specialize in illegal acts; illustrations are American gangsters and so-called criminal castes of India.

What are the functions of specialization in social organization? To the extent that the services of two or more people supplement each other, they become interdependent. Specialization promotes social solidarity (Durkheim, 1933:56–63). Sex specialization accomplishes in family life what occupational specialization does in society. Even more basically, specialization diversifies people. Social organization is founded upon human diversity, for if everybody were precisely like everybody else—fantastic as it sounds—what would be the point of anybody's interacting with anybody else? What value would reside in social organization?

GROUPS

Social interaction occurs in and between groups (i.e., organizations). Two people of the same status interacting casually for a moment form a group. Other groups in society are comprised not of two but of thousands or millions of people who are divided into hundreds of thousands of coördinated statuses. Society is structured into relatively enduring groups that form the stable skeleton maintaining orderly and dependable interaction. For the individual who conforms to, or shares, the values of his group, the latter becomes a reference point, in terms of which he orders his other behavior. Culture—socially standardized behavior and artifacts— arises under this condition.

What is a group? Any two or more people who actually, or are potentially likely to, interact constitute a group (Ackoff, 1953:377–380). They may not be interacting at a given moment, but their relationship is such that interaction can be predicted for them with some assurance. The interaction may, of course, be direct, mediated, or indirect. Among many Plains Indians the tribe constituted an actual group only during a relatively brief period in the summer when bison could be killed in large enough number to feed many people gathered in a restricted territory. During the rest of the year the tribe existed latently; the members were split up into smaller extended families and bands which traveled over a wide region in search of subsistence. Sometimes the potentiality of interaction is very slight indeed. All the men who belong to the Washerman *khel* in Tordher, a village near the northwest border of Pakistan, never meet as a whole, but any two Washermen are more likely to come into relationship than any two men taken at random. They may give their children in marriage, for example.

In any community an individual normally belongs to several enduring groups. However, as will be seen, the number of enduring groups by no means is equal in all communities. The fact that in a large community each person belongs to many groups contributes to the solidarity (i.e., cohesiveness) of the whole. Multigroup membership makes for interdependence of people, it balances groups so that no one group is able to overcome all others, and it inhibits factional strife. Two factions are less likely to quarrel openly when in other situations the opposed persons interact in the same groups (Gluckman, 1955a:Chap. 1).

A mere category (i.e., plurel) of people must be distinguished from a group. Just as status and prestige are frequently confused in popular speech, so little care is taken ordinarily to specify whether an aggregate of people constitutes a group or a category. If the latter, then the aggregate is identified only by the fact that members possess one or more characteristics in common. They are not related through actual or potential interaction (Dodd, 1947:53–63). A category is a class of people founded solely on things like sex, age, marital status, occupation, income, literacy, schooling, intelligence, language, health status, and any other trait. However, some categories are potential groups. If members of a category are treated as though they were organized, then they might well become a group.

How Groups Differ

It is useful to consider groups in terms of certain attributes. The degree to which groups sharing these attributes occur in a community is a function of other cultural characteristics or conditions of the cultural field.

1. *Groups differ in the quality of their interaction.* A primary group features primary social interaction; a secondary group reveals a large amount of secondary interaction (see pp. 346–348). The family ordinarily is a primary group in every community and so are all the people who call themselves Kaska Indians. When a group gets much above 200 people, however, all the members no longer have intimate knowledge of one another and secondary interaction increases. Secondary groups multiply in a community as population increases. They also increase with use of the plow in cultivation, under industrial manufacturing, and with large-scale societal relations that promote contact with strangers. Barring brief, chance meetings with strangers, an isolated hunting band will reveal no secondary groups. Contrast this situation with human relations in factory cities like Pittsburgh, Pennsylvania, or Manchester, England!

2. *Groups differ in duration.* Transitory and enduring (i.e., long-standing) groups occur in all communities. Kaska Indians who met at a summer evening dance exemplify a relatively transitory group. Once the dance breaks up the members will probably not again reassemble *as a group* although they remain members of the Kaska tribe, an enduring group of larger size. If a group is defined in terms of actual and potential interaction, then a briefly enduring assembly of people is scarcely a group. Groups are matters of degree.

An enduring group remains in actual or latent interaction over a long period of time and despite change in membership. Perhaps it meets intermittently, like a tribe of Plains Indians. Or it may be kept in constant interaction through mediated and indirect interaction, in the fashion of a modern nation or army. Whereas transitory groups rarely are differentiated by sign or symbol, enduring groups usually are identified through a name, sign, or emblem. "Crew Thirteen of the Twenty-second Bomb Squadron, Seventh Bomber Wing, Strategic Air Command" is a rather lengthy label covering four interlocking groups, the last of which fits into a still larger group, the United States Air Force. Among the Indians of the North Pacific coast, kin groups identify themselves in a more complicated fashion with animal figurines carved on so-called totem poles (see pp. 366–367). The animal, perhaps an eagle, bear, or raven, represents the form that had been adopted by a specific supernatural being who is believed to have helped the original ancestors of the group (Drucker, 1955:109, 179–181). Any enduring group loses even its latent existence if interaction between members does not occur with some frequency or if members are not kept aware of membership. Signs or symbols of identity constitute one device for maintaining awareness of the group's existence. Periodic get-togethers serve the same function. Ceremonies that bring together relatives from far-flung places illustrate a type of get-together.

Increase in the types of longstanding groups in a community is an aspect of cultural elaboration and occurs as a function of population growth, largeness of scale, intensive food production, and industrial manufacturing.

3. *Groups differ in formality.* In an informal group what people do is relatively spontaneous or flexible. Individuality counts a great deal as far as behavior in such a body is concerned. The bands constituting a Plains Indian tribe, like the Gros Ventre of Montana, were quite informally organized. Their names changed and the clustering of bands into larger units was highly spontaneous and unpredictable. Although there were no prescribed procedures for election, an effective band leader usually emerged. Consultation between this leader and other men preceded any important decision but such meetings themselves were informal, not governed by rules (Flannery, 1953:Chap. 2). The visiting of neighbors in an American town is a socially standardized phenomenon, of course, but much of what transpires in the visiting group depends on *who* comes calling and on the spirit that develops spontaneously between the actors in the situation. How different is such a group from a factory or the House of Representatives, where rules of organization minutely prescribe procedures to be followed! Qualifications for membership are explicitly specified. Individuality still counts in such groups, but it is not counted on. Ideally in a formal group variation in behavior between persons occupying the same status should be slight. People are supposed to be interchangeable, at least in positions that carry slight decision-making power. Groups approaching this type are frequently found in association with plow agriculture and industrial manufacturing.

Despite formal rules governing procedure, informal patterns of organization often develop in formal groups. They are carried out by unplanned and unanticipated groupings of people that are called cliques. Informal organization of this type is a very important element in the modern factory and other business organizations. It must be counted on by anyone seeking to understand how such organizations operate (D. C. Miller and W. H. Form, 1951:Chaps. 5–9).

4. *Groups differ in degree of departmentalization.* Sometimes a group is subdivided into segments that perform specialized tasks which are related to the overall purpose of the group. Such a group may be described as departmentalized (cf. Coon, 1948:604–614). Some Plains Indian war parties were made up of three divisions: fighting men, scouts who moved ahead of the main force, and young attendants, who guarded pack horses while the fighters closed in on the enemy. The modern factory shows much more departmentalization, each arm of the enterprise being geared formally into the working of the total organization. At the opposite extreme are undivided or nondepartmentalized groups. The fighting men making up the Plains war party were not further segmented; the family consisting of parents and children is also an undivided group.

Departmentalized groups include indirect social interaction; each segment has a head who transmits orders that originate from a central coordinator. If the overall group is large and dispersed in space, mediated interaction links the segments into overall organization. Departmentalization will occur only when a group is sufficiently large. As a community grows in size departmentalization within its component groups increases. It has been a marked concomitant of the Industrial Revolution. As such groups appear they present new administrative problems, particularly problems of coördination, since failure of a single segment to collaborate in expected fashion with other segments can render the whole group inoperative.

5. *Groups vary in hierarchic administration.* In single-command groups members interact with not more than one administrator, or level of leadership, at any given time. If the group is informal, like a small family, then even that leader may not be designated clearly. At the other extreme are extended-command, or hierarchic, groups, in which members interact indirectly as well as directly with more than one executive level (Jaques, 1951:274). In a "street corner gang," for example, Doc was the acknowledged leader, but Mike and Danny served as his lieutenants, and the rest of the gang were followers (W. F. Whyte, 1943:162). When administration is through several levels of leadership the information which a member receives must pass through a chain of command. Naturally, all links in the chain do not possess equal skill or power to make decisions. Hierarchic organization may be centralized, with a few policy makers holding nearly all of the power, or decentralized, in which case the subordinate figures in the command chain possess considerable influence in decision making. Modern society shows an apparent paradox. More and more peo-

ple are being brought into intense interaction but the number of really powerful decision makers apparently is becoming smaller (Deutsch, 1954:10).

6. *Groups differ in the significance attached to genealogical and affinal relationships.* A kin group consists of members most of whom are related to one another by genealogical or affinal relationship. Children in a family, for example, can trace genealogical connection to parents, who are related through marriage, as well as to genealogical and affinal kin of the parents. But members of a sib merely affirm genealogical descent from a common ancestor; they are unable to trace specific relationship to each other (see pp. 397–398). In Tordher village of West Pakistan, all men who belong to the *khel* of Washermen claim to be related. Experiment indicated, however, that they could not trace their several known lines of descent back to a single actual ancestor. They merely affirmed their mutual kinship. Kin groups fade off into nonkin groups. Between the two extremes, perhaps, are fraternities and sororities, the members of which occasionally refer to one another by kinship terms ("brother" and "sister") but do not seriously claim genealogical relationship. At the other end of the continuum is a group, like the factory or nation, which manifestly is not linked by real or affirmed kinship.

The types of nonkin groups increase in communities with plow agriculture and industrial manufacturing. Commercial handicraft also sees many such organizations. Not only the frequency with which an individual interacts with nonkin but, perhaps, also the number of kinsmen whom an individual can even identify distinguishes a large- from a small-scale community. Theoretically every person possesses about 180 primary, secondary, and tertiary relatives (see pp. 407–408), not all of whom will have been acquired by a specific person. For example, he may have no siblings although, theoretically, he can be related to at least two—a brother and a sister. It is reasonable to assume that the average young adult possesses over 50 and probably nearer 100 fairly close, living kinsmen. Yet a sample of 200 Vassar College students coming mostly from the northeastern United States could identify only 30 to 33, of whom about 6 or 7 were deceased (Codere, 1955). This sparse knowledge of kin probably means that there are very few relatives on whom an individual in the urban Northeast depends, from whom he learns, or to whom he extends help. It is seriously to be doubted whether a similar condition obtains in many of the small-scale, exotic communities that have been studied by anthropologists.

7. *Groups may be corporate.* A corporate group possesses marks like the following: it is enduring (outlasting a single generation), carefully selective and stable in membership, confers specific rights and duties on members not possessed by outsiders, and is identified clearly. The members work together for specific goals, the group owns wealth independently of in-

dividual members, and in its name members can be disciplined and rewarded. Clear-cut leaders are characteristic of corporate groups. Perhaps most enduring groups have some degree of corporateness, but the quality of corporate organization certainly varies between, say, an Eskimo family and the United States Steel Corporation. Corporate groups are often conceived of as though they were individuals; the legal norms of Europe and America treat corporations in this way. On the Micronesian atoll of Truk there are also groups that operate as individuals in relation to property (Goodenough, 1951:30–33). Ideally such corporate groups consist of brothers or sisters; if other people constitute the group they pattern their organization after the relations of siblings. The corporate group of siblings jointly produces and inherits wealth. Property is administered by the eldest brother and no member can put wealth to use without that man's permission. The senior man represents the group to others. To violate the unity of the sibling group is a very serious moral breach to the Trukese.

Complexity in Social Organization

By the combination of certain aspects of social interaction and the attributes by which groups may be differentiated, we can arrive at a useful basis for distinguishing a special aspect of cultural elaboration—organizational complexity. Social organization in a community may be either simple or complex.

1. **Simple Social Organization.** In ideal terms, simple social organization includes few people and is marked by such features as the following: interaction is primary; all enduring groups are primary groups; there are few ascribed statuses but many achieved positions; there are few nonkin groups; no formality, departmentalization, or hierarchy marks the existing groups. Specialization in a system of truly simple social organization is limited to age and sex. A system of simple social organization "tends to be very exclusive and parochial. Its special respect for the individual as a human person, and its treatment of persons as human beings with human needs and wants, tends to be limited to its own members. The individual outside it is a stranger. He is to be regarded with suspicion and even with hostility" (Little, 1953:89).

2. **Complex Social Organization.** Somewhat more complex social organization is revealed in a group of American civilians interned by the Japanese on the Philippine Islands during the Second World War (Vaughan, 1949). The 148 prisoners were divided into family kin groups and organized themselves under a single elected director. He represented the group to the Japanese. A specialized executive group came into being when the director chose 8 men to serve as his advisers. Later a cooking staff with a manager increased further the degree of departmentalization and added an element of hierarchy. A food buyer further added to the

degrees of specialization. Still later the whole group split into informal factions and a variety of committees was appointed to help coördinate the segments. The prisoners' camp can be evaluated as more complex than, say, a Kaska Indian band because it included many people who were not kin; interaction was more secondary (although no doubt it became more primary with time), and attributes of formality, departmentalization, and hierarchy became more apparent as specialization increased. Departmentalization, of course, meant an increase in the number of enduring nonkin groups within the overall organization. It is quite likely that even today the Kaska Indians would not know how to create an organizational structure like that of the American prisoners in the Philippines.

As an ideal type, complex organization may be defined as including a large number of ascribed statuses and a large number of enduring secondary groups. These groups are highly formalized, heavily departmentalized, and hierarchic in administration. Much time is spent in nonkin groups. While age and sex specialization continue, there is a large amount of occupational specialization.

A grossly oversimplified sketch of only the maintenance structure in a U.S. Air Force bombardment wing is given in Figure 23:2. It shows an elaborate system of extended command and an extreme degree of departmentalization. Power devolves from the wing commander and his group, the headquarters squadron, to a number of other squadrons, each of which is further departmentalized into what are here called units. Each unit has a hierarchy of command. The reader must imagine the formal rules of procedure, represented by a shelf of volumes that specify the duties of each status and unit. Several thousand men, who essentially are strangers to one another, through secondary interaction maintain the wing organization as a going concern. Many of them are working to keep intricate flying machines—bombing planes—in ready condition. "Out of the complexity of the airplane grows the complexity of air base organization. . . . The four engines alone require the work of many men with varying skills, while the electrical system requires still different specialists, and so on . . ." (Bates, 1953:2).

The basic variables on which complex social organization depends should by now be clear. Complexity increases with food production, industrial manufacturing, and scale. It follows permanent conquest, in which one system of organization is imposed over that of another. Complex organization in turn implies extreme rationality applied to human relations so that they may be planned and coördinated effectively to reach stated goals. Complex social organization enables the energies of many people to be utilized for such ends as cultural development, elaboration, war, and further increase in scale. It tends to be dynamic, encouraging rapid change. It

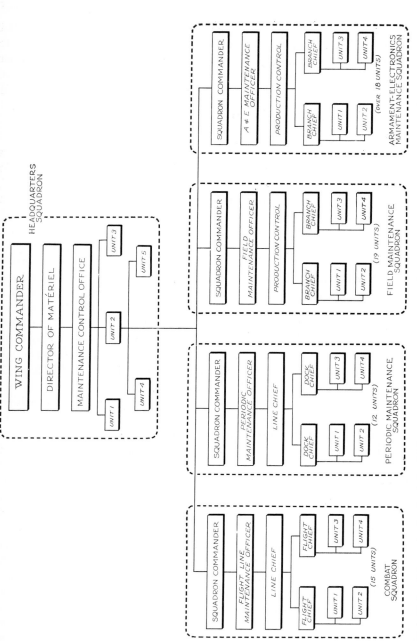

FIG. 23:2. Schematic sketch of the Maintenance Structure of a U.S. Air Force Bombardment Wing (from Bates, 1953:Fig. 2).

also is unstable, producing frequent problems and crises. One segment refuses to work with another or the subadministrators fail to coördinate their activities. The instability, in turn, is associated with a large number of socially standardized devices—systems of record keeping, administration, personnel selection and training, and rituals—the purpose or function of which is to maintain the total system in relatively stable equilibrium.

The Charter

Enduring groups over time adopt a charter, that is, a set of basic values and beliefs by which the relations of members may be ordered and in terms of which the group relates itself to other groups (Malinowski, 1944:48, 52–53). A national constitution is the explicit, written charter of a nation. In addition to such written principles there may exist an unwritten, implicit charter. In Pakistan the explicit charter recognizes in its preamble the existence of "fundamental rights including rights such as equality of status" (Pakistan, 1956:1). The day-to-day relations of citizens belonging to the Islamic Republic of Pakistan, however, do not reveal equal treatment of persons in all walks of life. There are even class A and B jail accommodations in that country. Such inequality of status is justified by the traditional, implicit charter. The class system of the United States similarly reveals that American citizens implicitly do not regard all people to be equal, despite contradictory ideas in charters like the Constitution and Declaration of Independence (Warner and associates, 1949:Chap. 2; Hollingshead, 1949:Chap. 4).

The charter of a group may include scriptures, myths, and beliefs which, regardless of whether they rest on sound empirical evidence or not, govern the social relations of members. Thus in a factory, a former plant manager may be idealized despite the fact that quite contrary feelings existed toward him while he was around. The myth functions to compensate workers for the unhappiness they are experiencing under the current plant manager (Gouldner, 1954:79, 83; see also Dubin, 1951:336–345). Among the most vital ideas in a charter are those which validate the right of certain men to administer other men and which justify the often severe power exercised by a leader (see pp. 477–479). The charter need not be unchanging. On the other hand, reinterpreting charters to make them compatible with altered conditions often presents a truly formidable problem.

Whether it is ideal or manifest, the charter furnishes a basis of consensus on at least a few issues. Such consensus is helpful if a group is to endure. The charter also binds together numerous specialists in an organization, restraining them from unduly emphasizing their narrow professional interests. Finally, a charter helps the group to defend itself in the face of external criticism (Selznick, 1949:50–51).

SOLIDARITY

Social solidarity (i.e., cohesiveness) refers to the satisfaction that motivates people to remain associated in a group. Operationally speaking, solidarity exists when people are reluctant to see their interaction end. The very fact that a group endures, actually or latently, means that it possesses some degree of solidarity. The existing solidarity may be growing stronger or weaker (Nadel, 1951:165–168).

Conditions of Solidarity

Two types of social solidarity have been distinguished: mechanical and organic (Durkheim, 1933). Mechanical solidarity is founded on the sentiment of belonging. Like ascribed status it is associated strongly with groups based on genealogical descent or heredity membership. It is mechanical solidarity which knits together the family and tribe.

Organic solidarity rests on the voluntary choice to join a group and on rewards found in social interaction. People remain together not because they belong together but for the advantages which accrue from their relationship. A stronger element of rationality dominates this form of solidarity. Organic solidarity binds a man to his job and ties the factory to other business organizations in the community. Through specialization of labor, organic solidarity links a wife to her husband and a child to its parents. Organic solidarity increases as the number of groups to which an average individual belongs increases and also as groups in complex social organization grow more interdependent. The factors underlying complexity, therefore, also condition organic solidarity. A potent factor in organic solidarity is some form of reciprocal exchange. For example, in many parts of Africa south of the Sahara women from one kin group are given as brides to another in return for cattle. The exchanges firmly bind the kin groups to one another. In other places reciprocal exchanges of gifts, feasts, and visits are the forces that hold people in association and help to maintain organic solidarity.

Both mechanical and organic solidarity are strengthened through doing things together in face-to-face groups. Mediated or indirect interaction does not seem to possess the same cementing power as direct interaction for creating enduring organizations.

Solidarity also rests on differentiation of the group from nonmembers, usually through a sign (like a flag, circumcision, or other emblem) or a name. The many ways by which groups mark themselves as distinct from one another is revealed by clans among the Heiban, a Nuba tribe in the Egyptian Sudan (Nadel, 1947:92–99). Not only do Heiban clans have names but each further is identified by particular ritual practices. Thus, one faces west in certain rites, employs 7 as its ritual number, obtains its "ritual fat" from goats, and shaves the hair of mother and child 3 days after birth. The other clans follow other observances or employ some of these in different combinations. Among the Nuba, as elsewhere in the world, groups also differentiate themselves through prohibitions on eating with other groups. Of course strength-giving emblems, things which signify in-group membership, may be conceived of very unfavorably by nonmembers. They may help to instigate hostility and aggression toward the group whose solidarity they underlie.

A measure of consensus, particularly about basic values, strengthens solidarity, while radical opposition makes social interaction close to intolerable (see pp. 467–470). Consensus scarcely means that everybody thinks alike in all respects or that change is not valued. Nor does all opposition weaken solidarity. Controlled competition in an organization may be relied upon to maintain a high degree of solidarity. Opposition to an out-group, such as occurs in war, is well known to strengthen social bonds within each of the contending systems.

The significance of rituals in maintaining group solidarity will become clearer when that subject is discussed systematically (see Chap. 31). In some ceremonies the loyalty of members to one another is dramatized and periodically renewed. At the same time the ceremonies insure transmission of such sentiments to new members. In China extended family loyalties are cemented through ceremonies directed toward the group's dead ancestors. In Australia local groups (bands) engage in rituals at those places in a group's territory where some Dawn Being is supposed to have entered the earth. Purposively the ceremony is intended to increase the supply of game in the territory. Functionally speaking, the rituals express the unity and individuality of the group and promote its solidarity (Radcliffe-Brown, 1952b:Chap. 8).

Totemism

Much has been written about totemism, a subject to be considered here mainly in relation to social solidarity. A totem (the word comes from Ojibwa, an Algonkian language) is a particular species of bird, other animal, plant, or a natural phenomenon (for instance, the rainbow), with which a group identifies or to which it believes itself somehow to be linked. Perhaps descent is traced from an original totemic ancestor. Totemism refers to the behavior through which a group expresses its relationship to a totem. For instance, the name of the species or phenomenon may be borne by the group, in which case one speaks of an eponymous totem. The Kaska Indians have two divisions, called moieties, one named Wolf and the other Crow. There is no belief that the people in these divisions descended from the eponymous animals. Among the

Orokaiva of New Guinea, clans as well as individuals are frequently linked to plants although again there is no thought of descent from a plant. Yet the plant is referred to as an ancestor (F. E. Williams, 1930:Chap. 8). In the recent world wars the Rainbow Division and Flying Tigers illustrate totemism marked with somewhat different attitudes but serving the same function it does among the Kaska, namely, promoting group identification. Note that in one of these illustrations the species is imaginary—flying tigers are not real—but that does not interfere with the function of the concept. Totemism frequently is revealed in the respect shown toward the totem. The group may avoid eating the animal or may eat only sparingly of it.

Totems are signs by which groups symbolize their unity and identity, setting themselves apart from other groups. In Australia each sex has a totem, as well as each moiety, clan, individual,[3] and local group (i.e., band). A child inherits the local-group totem of his father, provided he was conceived in the territory of his father's band. If he was conceived while his mother was on a visit to the territory of another band, then it is that totem he acquires. In that group he holds "totemic membership" regardless of where he dwells (Elkin, 1954:138–139). Australians classify not only people but even nature in totemic categories. For instance, the kangaroo is a symbol of a group as well as of grass, water, and the Pleiades. All belong in the same category (ibid., p. 197). Totemism probably is associated more frequently with kin groups than with groups of nonkin. In Euroamerican culture relatively abstract and nonnaturalistic signs, like trademarks, have replaced the naturalistic totems of small-scale, exotic communities.

SOCIAL CIRCULATION

A group continues to exist despite the fact that individual membership constantly turns over through loss and recruitment. The process through which individuals join or retire from groups, or shift from one group to another, is called social circulation (G. Wilson and M. Wilson, 1945:58–61, 98–99).

Three basic factors, operating separately or together, condition social circulation. (1) Biological changes, like birth, death, and aging, obviously influence the patterns of membership in groups. (2) Social circulation is conditioned by the satisfaction and rewards that men hope to secure by associating together. In the expectation of higher salary or more desirable working conditions employees change from one business organization to another. The promises attached to marriage condition movement from one family into another, newly founded one. An energetic missionary among a

[3] The relationship of an individual to an animal is better called nagualism than totemism.

non-Christian people may induce converts to join his congregation in the hope of winning salvation or forgiveness of sin. (3) The desire to escape persecution or social pressure may motivate movement away from a group. Among the Indians of Zuñi Pueblo, "An important aspect of the postwar period . . . has been a drift of the younger men from the pueblo—twenty-three of their number were living on the outside in the summer of 1947. . . . Those who leave the village and live on the outside are the ones who are the least willing to conform with the sentiments of the group and who are made to feel uncomfortable by the gossip occasioned by their deviant behavior. To get along in Zuñi society at least outward conformance is necessary. The result is that many of the most 'progressive' members of the pueblo leave . . ." (Adair and Vogt, 1949:551).

Actually this example illustrates better a type of social circulation, called social fragmentation, in which a sizable portion of the group splits off the parent body. Fragmentation occurs when population has outgrown local resources; it is also promoted by internal opposition, as in the Zuñi instance. Both parent and daughter groups may remain separate or both may fuse with other existing organizations. Social circulation undertaken to escape from the necessity of conforming often involves painful sacrifice. The individual may lose prestige and even wealth as he shifts. He is forced to acquire new customs in the group where he hopes his heterodoxy will be accepted. Within groups internal circulation operates when occupants of existing statuses are transferred to new positions where they assume new roles.

In some degree social circulation, including fragmentation, exists in every society. In a small-scale society the importance set on primary and kin ties restricts movement between groups. Even marriage may be restricted to certain cousins or to a narrow territory. Group membership is regulated by age and sex, so that movement between groups is limited to people who meet the requirements. In a large-scale society the great number of nonkin groups which compete for membership by advertising inducements invites heavy social circulation. Consequently, in groups so constituted there are likely to be more secondary interaction, organic social solidarity, and impersonality. The power of group members or administrators to compel conformity tends to weaken as the individual's freedom to quit a group increases. Autonomy exists when a person is free to change his allegiance or job.

AVAILABLE FILM

Totems, produced by the National Film Board of Canada (11 min. b. and w. or color) illustrates some totem poles found in British Columbia Showing the picture needs careful preparation if it is to be useful for anthropological purposes.

24.

Residential Kin Groups and Marriage[1]

AMONG the most enduring groups for promoting adaptation and adjust-ment in the communities frequently studied by anthropologists are those based on kinship ties. Such groups fall into two main types: (1) The members may form a residential unit, living in a common house or cluster of houses set off in a walled compound. The various forms of the family found throughout the world illustrate residential kin groups. (2) The mem-bers may not be localized but are united through real or affirmed genealogi-cal descent. This type is illustrated by consanguineal kin groups: the lineage, sib, and moiety. A compromise kin group, the clan, may be ignored for the present (see p. 405). Genealogical descent binds the members in the family as well as in the lineage or sib. But in the family the unifying bonds include marriage as well as consanguinity. The tie between husband and wife is affinal, whereas between parent and child it is consanguineal. In contrast the members of consanguineal kin groups are united only through directly traceable or affirmed consanguinity (see pp. 393–394).

Residential kin groups, consisting of various forms of the family, are the main subject matter of the present chapter. The family in general is a group characterized by common residence, economic coöperation, re-production, and the rearing of children. Normally it is formed or main-tained through some form of marriage (see pp. 385–391). Three basic family types will be distinguished (see the accompanying diagram).

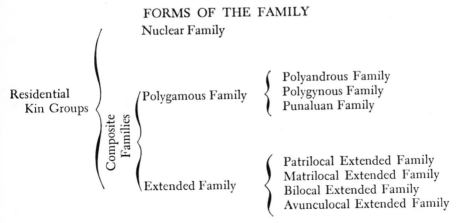

FORMS OF THE FAMILY

Nuclear Family

Residential Kin Groups — Composite Families — Polygamous Family { Polyandrous Family / Polygynous Family / Punaluan Family

Extended Family { Patrilocal Extended Family / Matrilocal Extended Family / Bilocal Extended Family / Avunculocal Extended Family

[1] Much of the first part of this chapter follows Murdock, 1949:Chaps. 1–2.

nuclear, polygamous, and extended forms. Since the last two include two or more nuclear families aggregated together, they may be called composite forms of the family. Out of a world-wide sample of 192 communities for which sufficient information was available, 47 normally possess only nuclear families living independently. That is, no composite family types appeared. In 53 communities only polygamous families with plural spouses occur, and 92 include some form of extended family (Murdock, 1949:2). Clearly the European and American pattern of nuclear families living alone, a pattern doubtlessly spreading into industrialized areas of South America, Asia, and Africa, is relatively uncommon.

NUCLEAR FAMILY

The nuclear family consists of a married man and woman together with their offspring (Fig. 24:1). A couple who have not produced offspring may be called an incomplete nuclear family. The nuclear family, either existing as an independent social group or aggregated into larger, composite, residential kin groups, is practically universal. Attempts to displace it, however, are not unknown. The most recent such attempt has occurred in the *kibbutz*, an agricultural collective found in Israel (Spiro, 1954). The main features of the *kibbutz* are communal living, collective ownership of all property, and collective rearing of children. Marriage is primarily entered for the comradeship and intimacy that it promises. The husband and wife do not depend on each other for support nor do the couple fully rear any children they produce. For this purpose the *kibbutz* includes a nursery with a trained staff. Here the mother goes to feed the child while it still nurses. Both parents visit the infant upon their return from work each day. After six months the child may be taken to the parents' one-room apartment for brief visits but it continues to sleep in the children's house. Teachers gradually replace nurses as child rearers. However, parents do play a role in the emotional development of the child. They are its most important objects of identification and provide it with a certain security and love that it receives from no one else. The *kibbutz* leaves the physical care and education of children, duties normally undertaken by the family, to persons other than the parents. It also separates offspring from parents. They alone share the common residence. Also in the

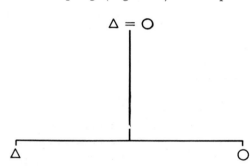

FIG. 24:1.   Diagram of Nuclear Family with Offspring.

kibbutz the married couple does not, like the family in general, practice economic coöperation. To the degree that these usual characteristics of family life are lacking, the married couple in the *kibbutz* differs from the family as it usually is organized. The attenuated functions of the *kibbutz* family also make it highly vulnerable to dissolution. Apart from companionship, love, and physical charm few bonds hold the couple together—indicating the importance of multiple role specialization for social solidarity (Spiro, 1956:233–234).

Functions of the Nuclear Family

The universality of the nuclear family is related to the functions it serves. These usually include (1) provision of sexual satisfaction for the spouses, (2) technological coöperation based on age and sex specialization, (3) the care and education of the young, and (4) provision of mutual companionship and other emotional satisfactions. These ends not only serve individual survival and adjustment but, the first and third particularly, maintain the continuity of the community itself. None of these functions by itself explains the universality of the family. Sexual intercourse springs from a powerful drive. The satisfaction it provides helps to cement the bond between husband and wife; but many of the sample of the world's communities allow sexual relations to occur before marriage or outside of the family as well. The majority of communities do not object strongly to having one or both spouses find sexual satisfaction outside of the family, provided that the partner is a particular relative. Hence, sexual satisfaction by itself cannot be the motivation for founding, or remaining in, a family. We have seen that a couple marries in an Israeli *kibbutz* despite the fact that men and women do not depend on one another for support. In the Trobriand Islands of Melanesia a family receives its main support from the wife's brother, the husband having similar responsibility to provide subsistence for his sister and her family (Malinowski, 1932). Important as the sex specialization of subsistence and other technical roles may be, it is not sufficient to explain the family. In the *kibbutz* the third function of the family—rearing children—has also been taken over by nonfamily members without destroying the family itself. Europe and America have seen the family shorn of many former tasks, while compulsory-school laws deprive it of the right to rear fully its own children. Formerly a husband produced food and relied on a wife who kept the home. But even sexual division of labor now has become less sharp. Often both spouses go to work daily. Mass media of communication in the home or outside reduce somewhat the need for companionship. Yet the family has not disappeared. It continues to provide sexual gratification and is an area in which parents and children mutually provide each other with emotional satisfactions. Emotional satisfaction is at least as important as the other functions of the family. It may be one which becomes more important in an impersonal, large-scale society where the other functions are provided by extrafamilial groups.

Incest Rules

Practically universally the nuclear family imposes incest rules. The importance of these lies in their function of making the nuclear family discontinuous in time and thereby instigating the formation of new nuclear families every generation. If brother-sister marriages were usual, the nuclear family would be permanent. Siblings would not have to look outside their residential group for spouses. The individual would not belong to both a family of orientation, in which he was born, and a family of procreation, established through marriage. Incest rules, therefore, help to give rise to rules of residence, some of which produce extended families (see pp. 382–384). In no community is it customary or permissible for father and daughter, mother and son, brother and sister to have sexual intercourse or marry. Occasionally, as in ancient Egypt, in aboriginal Hawaii, and among the preconquest Inca of highland South America, aristocrats practiced brother-sister marriage (Westermarck, 1921:II, Chaps. 19–20). The custom expressed a prestige so high that no suitable mate equal in rank could be found outside of the family. Azande nobles are permitted to marry their daughters, and elsewhere in Africa ritual intercourse sometimes is allowed between father and daughter. But these are exceptional customs and must not be allowed to obscure the fact that practically universally the nuclear family is governed by incest rules (cf. Cooper, 1932; L. A. White, 1948).

In response to the question why incest rules occur universally various answers have been given. (1) Formerly the weight of explanation was put on a biological aversion governing mating between close relatives. The weakness of this argument lies in the fact that no community expects incest rules to operate automatically. Punishments are threatened for incest; hence repugnance for incest cannot be innate. Also damaging to this theory is the fact that incest does occur. In rare cases, as indicated, it is even expected between members of the nuclear family. To postulate a biological mechanism, or instinct, which deters people from incest is simply incompatible with the facts known to anthropology. (2) The theory that people universally avoid incest because of the danger that weak offspring may be produced by parents who are close relatives is likewise undemonstrable. In the first place, if healthy genes are involved in sexual relations between close relatives they will produce healthy offspring. The plant and animal breeder knows this when he deliberately breeds healthy strains from the same parentage to obtain offspring possessing certain desirable qualities. Many communities known to anthropology have for generations not only allowed but encouraged the marriage of children of brothers and sisters (see pp. 386–388). The evidence indicates no frequent or obvious damage in the offspring of such matings. (3) The universality of incest rules can best be understood functionally. By making the nuclear family and other exogamous kin groups discontinuous, incest rules in each generation encourage alliances between such groups. These alliances widen the circle of the in-group and provide an additional number of people who can be relied on for adaptation and other satisfactions. Incest rules also avoid the danger that the nuclear family or other exogamous kin group will be destroyed through aggression generated from sexual jealousy and frustration.

THE POLYGAMOUS FAMILY

Polygamy refers to any form of plural marriage, whether of a woman to two or more men simultaneously (polyandry) or of a man to more than one wife at the same time (polygyny). Group marriage is a third, and very rare, form of polygamy in which several men are married to several women. Polygamous families are composite because they affiliate two or more nuclear

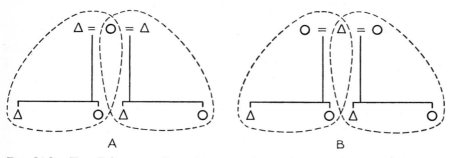

Fig. 24:2. Two Polygamous Composite Families. Dashed lines surround constituent nuclear family segments. A, polyandrous composite family; B, polygynous composite family.

families through a common spouse. This is shown in Figure 24:2. Notice how in the polyandrous family a woman is the common wife and mother of two nuclear families, whereas in the polygynous group the man acts as the link between two groups.

Polyandry and the Polyandrous Composite Family

The polyandrous family is relatively rare, although its distribution is fairly worldwide and not limited to particular culture areas. It constitutes a normal type among the people of Marquesa, a Polynesian island, and among the Toda of South India. Tibet is also prominently associated with polyandry, but monogamy actually is far more common there (Hermanns,

1953). In Tibet the union of a woman to two or more men, who are also brothers, is especially frequent among the poorer peasants. They use polyandry to maintain land and herds undivided. If the brothers married independently the pressure to divide the land between them would presumably be greater than it is when they establish a common polyandrous household. The oldest brother usually constitutes the principal husband and becomes the social father of all the children. The other brothers, regardless of possible biological parenthood, are referred to as "little fathers." Among the Toda, female infanticide leads to a shortage of women for the available male population. This is overcome by having a group of brothers, or unrelated men, marry a woman in common (Rivers, 1906:477–480). Betrothal is often celebrated in behalf of a specific man but there is a ritual enabling each husband successively to establish his social fatherhood regardless of who the biological genitor may have been.

Polyandry must be distinguished from wife lending and sexual hospitality, whether these customs obtain between brothers or unrelated men. In parts of Liberia, for example, a man married to a large number of women secures an extraordinary advantage on the labor market "by lending ('giving,' is is called) his 'superfluous' wives to other men." He is able to attach these men to himself in a form of "servitude" (Schwab, 1947:186). The polyandrous family is an enduring composite group which, like any family, practices economic coöperation, shares a common residence, allows sexual rights to all the men, and, of course, rears children. These characteristics are not associated with wife lending. Mostly polyandry is fraternal, the co-husbands being brothers. In Marquesa, however, a number of unrelated men become spouses of a woman of high prestige. The first husband outranks all subsequent men, who, in a sense, are merely workers in the senior husband's household. In return for their labor they are allowed sexual satisfaction. The function of polyandry here is similar to wife lending in Liberia. It is claimed that Marquesan women could always show a child its genitor (Linton in Kardiner, 1939:155–156).

Generally speaking, polyandrous families seem to be related to a shortage of women and to sex specialization in which the woman makes only an insignificant contribution to subsistence (Heath, 1955). Actually, studies of communities with polyandrous marriage are few. Therefore available material on which to base generalizations is limited.

Polygyny and the Polygynous Composite Family

Socially recognized residential cohabitation, economic coöperation, and sexual association between a man and two or more women simultaneously constitutes polygyny (Fig. 24:2). This definition is intended to remove any doubt concerning whether American "serial monogamy" and the keeping of a permanent mistress are to be regarded as forms of polygyny. The polygynous composite family may exist ideally as well as manifestly. That is, the group may be an ideal which remains unattainable to the majority of men. Ignoring manifest incidence of the trait, out of a sample of 250 communities, 193 can be characterized as polygynous. In 2 out of 250 polyandry is the ideal and 43 prefer monogamy (Murdock, 1949:28). In communities where polygyny or polyandry is the ideal, monogamous unions may be more common by far, perhaps because men do not produce sufficient food for more than one woman and her offspring. Also the number of women is normally far too small to allow every man to possess more than one wife. Generally in a community with polygyny the number of marriageable women is increased by reducing the age of marriage, but even this is not sufficient to provide women for all men. Table 31 furnishes

TABLE 31.   Percent of Polygyny in Selected Communities

Community or Region	1 Wife	2 Wives	3 Wives	4 Wives	5 Wives	6 or More Wives	Source
Portuguese Guinea[a]	59.0	28.2	8.5	2.6	0.8	0.7	Carreira, 1953
Lamba[b]	95.2	4.0	0.8	—	—	—	J. C. Mitchell and J. A. Barnes, 1950:46
Tallensi[c]	60.4	27.0	5.4	6.3	0.9	—	Fortes, 1949:65
Ashanti[d]	50.5	32.2	12.2	2.7	1.0	1.0	Fortes, 1954:286
Hehe	62.1	27.6	6.9	2.0	0.8	0.4	Brown and Hutt, 1935:107
Kufana[e]	59.9	31.8	6.9	1.3	—	—	M. G. Smith, 1953:315
Caribou Eskimo	81.4	18.6	—	—	—	—	Birket-Smith, 1946:274
Keraki Papuans	55.1	37.2	5.1	2.6	—	—	F. E. Williams, 1936:149

[a] Rural areas; in urban districts nearly 67 percent of families are monogamous, and 24 percent consist of a man with two wives.
[b] Survey based on 16 villages.
[c] Based on 61 families.
[d] Information available for 660 men of Agogo township; no data on 27 additional married men.
[e] Represents one village of 229 married men.

some idea of the actual extent of polygyny in a few communities. Polygyny may involve only women who are sisters, in which case it is called sororal polygyny. Nonsororal polygyny involves unrelated women. Sororal polygyny integrates well with matrilocal residence, where a number of sisters remain at home to marry a single husband. Mitigated are such universal problems of the polygynous family as rivalry, sexual jealousy, and disputes over the allocation of feminine tasks. Most polygynous communities try to prevent rivalry and sexual jealousy by providing separate dwellings for each co-wife, superior rank for one of the women (usually the first wife married), who is then given supervisory authority over the others, and strict rotation of sexual relations. A man is expected to spend time regularly with each of the co-wives. The Muslim scripture quotes God as warning the prospective polygynist: "If ye fear that ye will not deal fairly by the orphans, marry of the women, who seem good to you, two or three or four; if ye fear that ye cannot do justice (to so many) then one only . . . (Pickthall, 1930:*Surah* 3). The problems anticipated by such rules and injunctions are less serious in the case of sororal polygyny because the sisters who are co-wives already have learned to get along. They introduce into the family of procreation an established bond of solidarity. Therefore, it is not surprising that sororal polygyny should be widespread. In 18 out of the 21 communities where the polygynous family is exclusively sororal, the women do not even occupy separate houses, while in 28 out of 55 with non-sororal polygyny separate accommodations are the rule (Murdock, 1949:31).

Functions of Polygyny

An unprejudiced understanding of polygyny may be difficult to acquire by people who idealize monogamy to the point of making all polygamy illegal. In many cultures the value placed on polygyny is related to its dependent functions. These are mainly economic, sexual, reproductive, and prestigeful in nature. (1) Additional women in a household mean more hands to produce wealth. This is easily seen in Africa, where women often cultivate the growing crops. More women produce more food, some of which can be traded or used to enhance a man's reputation for hospitality. The frequent occurrence of polygyny in communities where women make a large contribution to subsistence is consistent with this generalization (Heath, 1955). (2) Plural wives facilitate sexual adjustment. In most communities sexual relations are ruled out during menstruation and the later stages of pregnancy. For a man polygyny avoids the sexual deprivation bound up with such periods under monogamy. (3) Where offspring are valued, as they are by many people, polygyny enables a man to produce many children during his lifetime. On the other hand, polygyny does not particularly favor high female fertility. When a man disperses his sexual acts among several women the chances are high that he may not for a long time copulate with any one of his wives at the proper point in the ovulation cycle for conception to take place. However, empirical data on this point are ambiguous (Lorimer, 1954:98–99). (4) The wealth or number of children which a man produces in a polygynous family, and even the number of wives he possesses, may contribute to his prestige in the community. This is an important motivation in polygyny.

There are even satisfactions for women in polygyny. A second wife reduces the work load of the first woman. In communities where the sexes are segregated and where men usually do not associate with spouses in leisure-time activities, polygyny creates a group of women who may enjoy one another's companionship at home (Ingrams, 1952:82–83). For some upper-class women in Pakistan and India this adjustive function of polygyny remains as important today as in 1832 when an observer noted:

To ladies accustomed from infancy to confinement this is by no means irksome; they have their employments and their amusements, and though these are not exactly to our taste, nor suited to our mode of education, they are not the less relished by those for whom they were invented. . . . Be that as it may, the Mussulmaun ladies, with whom I have been long intimate, appear to me always happy, contented, and satisfied with the seclusion to which they were born; they desire no other, and I have ceased to regret they cannot be made partakers of that freedom of intercourse with the world we deem so essential to our happiness. . . . Female society is unlimited, and that they enjoy without restraint [Ali, Mrs. Meer, 1917:168].

Punaluan Composite Family

Early anthropologists, working with limited data collected by untrained observers, made much of group marriage and the resultant punaluan family. They thought that these traits represented survivals of the original form of human marriage and the earliest type of social group.[2] More careful investigation reveals no communities in which the punaluan family, based on the common marriage of several men to several women, is normal. It occurs sporadically, for example, among the Kaingáng of Brazil. Here 8 percent of all recorded unions were of the group type compared to a 14 percent incidence of polyandry. The hunting and gathering Kaingáng live in bands whose membership is constantly shifting. There are few enduring relationships (Henry, 1941:Chap. 4). Sex is a basis of social cohesion, and women become the nucleus of a group of males which may disintegrate as the women die. If only one woman unites a number of men, the band is equivalent to a polyandrous family. Sometimes, however, another woman is added to such a menage. "Through the years the family would expand and contract. . . ." The co-husbands constitute one of the strongest groups in this community. Something like the punaluan family has been reported for the northeast Asiatic Chukchee, where 4 or 5 couples sometimes shared spouses but did not reside together.

THE EXTENDED FAMILY

The extended family comes into existence when offspring remain at home after their marriage. Generally, only offspring of one sex remain with the

[2] The term "punaluan" is from L. H. Morgan, 1877:Pt. 3. It is by no means entirely clear that among the anthropoid apes—man's closest animal kin—indiscrimate breeding occurs between several males and females (see Table 58). Rather, the tendency among apes and monkeys is toward polygyny, with the dominant male securing the largest number of females (Ford and Beach, 1951:110). Tendencies to monogamy have been noted among certain subprimate mammals, like the dog and fox.

family of orientation. A rule of marital residence, specifying who shall move, is an important factor determining the type of extended family which will be founded. The custom may be for daughters to remain with the family of orientation, creating matrilocal extended families, or sons may stay at home, creating patrilocal extended families.[3] When either son or daughter may remain at home, bilocal extended families are created. These and one other extended family form, created through avunculocal residence, are described in Table 32.

TABLE 32.   Extended Family Types in Relation to Rule of Marital Residence

Rule of Marital Residence and Incidence[a]	Associated Form of Extended Family and Incidence[a]
Patrilocal Residence Bride regularly leaves her parental home to live with or near the groom's parents; 146 cases.	*Patrilocal Extended Family* The binding link is the father-son relationship, the son remaining at home and the daughter moving out after marriage; 52 cases.
Matrilocal Residence Groom regularly leaves his parental home to live with or near bride's parents; 38[b] cases.	*Matrilocal Extended Family* The binding link is the mother-daughter relationship, the daughter remaining at home and the son moving out after marriage; 23 cases.
Bilocal Residence The couple may live with or near the parents of either spouse, depending on circumstances or inclination; 19 cases.	*Bilocal Extended Family* The binding link may be between father and son or mother and daughter depending on which spouse remains at home; 10 cases.
Avunculocal Residence The couple regularly lives with or near the home of the groom's mother's brother (maternal uncle); 8 cases.	*Avunculocal Extended Family* The binding link is between nephew and maternal uncle; the former will probably inherit wealth or other privileges from his mother's brother; 7 cases.
Neolocal Residence The couple regularly establish their domicile independently of the homes of either set of parents; 17 cases.	None

[a] The total sample is 250 but relevant information is not available for all communities.
[b] In 22 communities matrilocal residence lasts only during the first year of marriage, or until the birth of a child, and is then followed by permanent patrilocal residence. Such a practice is called matri-patrilocal residence.
SOURCE: Murdock, *1949*:16–17, 34–35.

An extended family may include polygamous families or monogamous nuclear families or both. Taking the world as a whole, out of a sample of 250 communities, 92 communities possess extended families (Murdock, *1949*:35). An extended family always includes two or

[3] A few British anthropologists prefer the terms virilocal and uxorilocal for patrilocal and matrilocal residence respectively (Adam, *1948*:12).

more generations. Whereas in polygamous families a spouse is the link between two or more nuclear families, in the extended family a son or daughter links the nuclear segments of the larger group (Fig. 24:3). The extended family may endure indefinitely while the nuclear and polygamous families are transitory.

Table 32 indicates that a rule of residence does not guarantee extended families. The residence expected may be merely temporary. Tuscarora

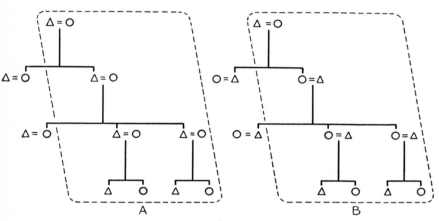

Fɪɢ. 24:3. Extended Composite Families. A, patrilocal extended family; B, matrilocal extended family. Note that unmarried children of both sexes remain in the family of orientation until marriage, when those of one sex move. The sex of the individual who moves is specified in the rule of residence.

Indians of New York State admit to no preferred rule of residence, yet 53 percent of a sample of 78 marriages in the last generation remained matrilocal during the first year or two of marriage, 28 percent were patrilocal during this period, and 19 percent remained neolocal from the outset. Unilocal residence among these people generally gives way to neolocal residence after one or two years (Wallace, 1952:18).

Patrilocal Extended Family

The patrilocal extended family, most common of all extended residential kin groups, may be described as it occurs among the Nupe of northern Nigeria (Nadel, 1942:241–248). The group occupies a compound and includes, normally, one or more brothers, their wives, unmarried daughters, and unmarried or married sons, the latter with their wives. These persons coöperate in work, the men laboring under the direction of the senior male, either a father or father's elder brother. The leader, who enjoys more leisure than his subordinates, supervises and plans the order of activities. The men organized under him build up the ridges in the field for planting, weed the crops, and secure raw materials for manufacture. If the family head cannot himself work, then leadership devolves on the next senior male. The wealth created in this coöperative fashion is turned over to the family head, who holds sole rights over its disposal. Rules, however, limit his actions. New tools must be purchased when needed and the male labor force, together with their dependents, housed, fed, and clothed. Some money must be reserved for taxes, and a sum is set aside to use in securing brides for the unmarried sons. Any individual in the extended family may, on his own time, use land or tools to earn an independent income. Should he ever leave the extended family he will be provided with tools, land, and, for the first year, food by the head of the household.

All over the world the extended family appears to be undergoing displacement in favor of smaller residential kin units. The same forces are at work among the Nupe; in the decade preceding 1941 many patrilocal extended families disappeared as coöperative work groups. Their land was divided among the individual male members to be worked independently. What forces have been at work? While a certain efficiency attaches to relatively large work units, the efficiency, among the Nupe at least, never entirely compensated for certain inconveniences. As new values appeared in a community, values emphasizing individual responsibility, together with a growing market ready to absorb more of what certain craftsmen and farmers could produce, members preferred to use their own discretion in planning and to receive the total product which their output bought. They also preferred to choose their own profession rather than remain on the farm or in the father's craft. The inability of the extended family head to supply bridewealth for marriageable sons or to meet taxes also has influenced the growth of independent enterprise. Competition from European-produced goods has reduced the market for some products which were manufactured coöperatively in the family. As income fell so did the satisfactions that the group was able to provide. A tradition of individual production had been present among the Nupe, a man working for himself in his spare time. This may have contributed to the speedy dissolution of the extended family system.

In China too the extended family has begun to disappear. The factors underlying its displacement include the fact that "intellectuals who have the responsibility of upholding the traditional model of the family are no longer interested in traditional ways of life" (S.-C. Lee, 1953:279). Functions have been taken away from the extended family, especially in cities, through the rise of schools. In the rural areas the family could not retain its land and produce enough goods to supply members with the satisfactions they demanded. Sons and daughters of all but the wealthiest landowners left to secure jobs elsewhere. It is doubtful that extended families ever constituted more than a dimly realized ideal among peasants. Therefore the real breakdown has occurred in the large-scale, wealthy strata of the community where new values made their strongest impact.

Matrilocal Extended Family

A matrilocal extended family does not refer to a residential kin group in which power lies in the hands of females. In a matrilocal family the in-marrying men stand as relative strangers among women whose solidarity is largely determined by common descent. But many decisions are made, and economic assistance is furnished, by sons and brothers who have moved out of the household. Similarly the husbands of the women continue to bear responsibilities for their sisters. Among the Navaho Indians men often leave sheep and other property at their maternal household and contribute to the ceremonies carried out there (C. Kluckhohn and D. Leighton, 1946:57). Strain over such divided loyalties is not unusual. The in-marrying husband may resent criticism from the wife's father. A brother-in-law may feel that the husband shirks responsibilities. A father may object to the way in which his children are disciplined by their mother's brother.

The Avunculate and Avunculocal Extended Family

The relationship of a person to his mother's brother is called the avunculate. Much has been written about the conflict expressed by the occupant of the latter status, who must divide his loyalties between his own and his sister's children. The conflict may not be less severe for the youth who, for example, helps his father develop a plantation. The two jointly market the produce. But when the man dies the son will see the land inherited by his father's sister's son. Among the Ivory Coast Agni, the nephew fears lest his mother's brother do the forbidden thing and favor his own son in exactly the way the nephew wants his own father to favor him (Koebben, 1954). The stressful aspects of the avunculate have probably been intensified on the Ivory Coast with the rise of a market economy and greater dependence on money. It is also exaggerated there by the rule of patrilocal residence.

Avunculocal residence mitigates somewhat the conflicts inherent in the avunculate. Instead of working with his father to develop resources that will be transmitted to the older man's nephew, under avunculocal residence a youth at an early age begins to coöperate with his mother's brother. This means permanent leave-taking of his own home. In the new residence he marries and rears his own children until the sons are ready to leave for the home of their mother's brother. Meanwhile he receives his sister's son. If in any generation a man lacks a sister to produce a son, the avunculocal family may cease, just as matrilocal or patrilocal families may cease without female or male births.

The avunculocal extended family is illustrated on Losap atoll in the Caroline Islands of Micronesia (Fischer, 1955). Here a census showed 53 couples were living in avunculocal residence, 22 matrilocal, 16 patrilocal, 2 neolocal, and 1 unknown. Close coöperation is maintained between a brother and sister after each marries. Both live in proximity to one another, making it easy for a brother to supply food for the woman and her children. Brother and sister do not, however, form a residence group.[4] As a boy becomes able to work, his mother's brother exercises increasing power over him. Sometime between puberty and marriage he may move to his uncle's house and there brings his bride.

On What Do Residence Rules Depend?[5]

The form of the extended family is highly sensitive to other elements in the cultural configuration. Primarily the influence of these is exerted through rules of residence. Changes in technology, trade, relationship to property, government, and religion can all "alter the structural relationships of related individuals to one another," leading to modifications in residence, to extended family form, and to factors dependent on the extended family (Murdock, 1949:202).

1. **Patrilocal Residence.** A shift to patrilocal residence in a community is favored by any change in culture or the cultural field which enhances the normal importance of men. Such a change may come in technology, giving the men a subsistence contribution larger than women's.[6] The introduction of cattle or the plow exerts pressure in the same direction. Among collectors, migration to an area containing abundant game, so that game usurps the place formerly held by plant collection as the chief subsistence technique, will exert a similar influence. The assumption is that collecting usually is women's work. Polygyny favors patrilocal residence; hence the introduction of Islam, which gives scriptural sanction to plural marriage, could press toward patrilocal residence. Large amounts of any form of movable wealth, such as can be accumulated in quantity by men, warfare, slavery, and complex forms of government all operate in favor of men and therfore are associated with patrilocal residence, and, in turn, with patrilocal extended families.

2. **Matrilocal Residence.** When women make a large subsistence contribution—for example, in agriculture—residence is often matrilocal. It is also found where women own certain types of wealth or other rights that enhance their importance. Other variables congenial to matrilocal residence

---

[4] Siblings form a residence group among the Nayar, a high-ranking caste in Kerala, southern India. Wives remain in their brothers' households to be visited there by husbands, whose primary responsibility in turn is to their sisters.

[5] This section follows Murdock, 1949:Chap. 8, as well as pp. 16–22.

[6] Statistical examination, however, fails to bring out a definite correlation between patrilocal residence and a low subsistence contribution by women (Heath, 1955).

include little warfare and a relatively simple political system without kings or powerful chiefs.

3. Matri-Patrilocal Residence. This form of residence is conditioned by the same factors that favor patrilocal residence when, in addition, elements exist in the culture which continue to press toward matrilocality. For example, the custom of bride-service may obtain. That is, the husband is expected to spend a period of time after, or shortly before, marriage working for his wife's family. Should this custom be present together with matrilocal residence at a time when conditions are created which enhance the normal importance of men, a compromise between the matrilocal and patrilocal forms may be devised—namely, matri-patrilocal residence. Matri-patrilocal residence is also favored in cases where bridewealth—goods given to a bride's parents in recognition of marriage—is paid in installments. Matrilocal residence may then endure until the full wealth has been turned over.

4. Bilocal Residence. Encouraging bilocal residence is the migratory life of food gatherers living in unstable bands. The instability and migratoriness mean that sometimes a nuclear family pitches camp near the husband's parents and sometimes near the wife's. The family may even shift from one band to another if the spouses' parents belong to different units. The approximate equalization of men and women in things like ownership of wealth or rights to inheritance also favors residence with either of the spouses' families. Residence will normally be with the spouse possessing the greater wealth. Bilocal residence is compatible with customs like primogeniture or ultimogeniture that favor certain children regardless of sex. If wealth is inherited by the first-born child, whether male or female, or if higher rank is ascribed to the first-born child than to subsequent children, then each sex has a chance of falling into the favorable status and so remaining at home upon marriage. In brief, the rule of bilocal residence allows various circumstances to be taken into account in deciding where the newly married couple shall live. This is seen in a modern Netherlands village where "if there are several grown sons, the family will be glad if a daughter can live with her husband's people, because there is neither need nor room for a son-in-law. On the other hand, a son-in-law may be welcomed as a helper where there are only one or two daughters, and may even be looked upon as the future head of the farm" (Keur and Keur, 1955:107).

5. Avunculocal Residence. Residence with a mother's brother generally represents replacement of a pattern of matrilocality. The conditions pressing for such a change include the identical factors favoring patrilocal residence, except that these occur in association with a previously matrilocal rule and, perhaps, with the avunculate. Avunculocal residence constitutes a kind of a compromise between matrilocal and patrilocal forms.

"Every advantage which males can achieve under patrilocal residence—polygyny, slaves, wealth, political power, military prestige—they can acquire equally well under avunculocal residence" (Murdock, 1949:208). The two systems, then, are functionally equivalent although different in form.

Dependent Functions of Residence

Residence that endures creates extended families which help to give rise to certain consanguineal, nonresidential kin groups that remain to be examined (see Chapter 25). Primarily they do so by assembling in one locality a specific aggregation of genealogically related persons. These people may be males and their children, or women and children, or with avunculocal residence, men related through women. From such alignments lineages, sibs, and clans come into being as well as rules which specify whether membership in these groups will be inherited through the father or mother. To summarize at this point, the following correlations obtain between extended families and systems of descent:

Patrilineal descent = f (Patrilocal extended family)
Matrilineal descent = f (Matrilocal or avunculocal extended family)
Bilateral descent = f (Bilocal extended family)

Bilateral descent also occurs in connection with neolocal residence.

Patrilocal residence, whereby the bride leaves her home to join another residential kin group, is generally accompanied by some form of consideration. This takes the form of wealth ("bridewealth") offered to the woman's parents. Cattle provide a common type of bridewealth, although in many places money has come to play an increasing part in such exchanges. In lieu of consideration a sister or other female relative is sometimes offered in exchange for the bride, or the husband may spend some period working for the bride's family. Rarely, if ever, does the payment of bridewealth signify that people secure a bride as they would a chattel. The symbolic meaning of bridewealth will be discussed below (p. 390).

Extended families are coöperative groups serving the general functions of adaptation and adjustment. Naturally, tensions also are generated in such aggregates. Extended families, however, are not only means to ends. In many parts of the world they possess enormous value and become ends in themselves. An elder is pleased to see his sons and brother's sons living around him with their wives and children. He may strive by sound administrative practice to keep the group intact throughout his lifetime. The theme of preserving the extended family is a popular one in Indian films and novels.[7] As with polygyny, not everybody may find a large extended family equally possible. Only people who possess sufficient wealth—for example, in the form of land—may realize the ideal and the prestige it

[7] See, for example, Abbas, 1955, and Chitale, 1950.

brings. Where such an ideal is strong, dissolution of an extended family may promote strong shame (S.-C. Lee, 1953).

Fraternal Joint Family

The term "joint family" is often used when an extended family is indicated. The label is applied more specifically to a relatively rare, composite family consisting of two or more brothers with their wives and offspring. This group, which dissolves with the death of the males, is one form of residential kin group formerly found among the Manus of New Guinea. It grew up where an elder brother, rather than a father or uncle, assumed economic responsibility for a younger brother's marriage. Ideally a father would have undertaken this role, but owing to the short life span of a Manus man, a father rarely lived to see his sons married. The husband of the junior family not only provided for his wife but also worked to repay the elder brother, who, by providing thousands of dog's teeth and other valuables, had helped him to secure a bride. The junior wife and her elder brother stood in the same relationship as a daughter-in-law and father-in-law (Mead, 1930:Chap. 12; 1934:264–270, 275–277, 292–295).

MARRIAGE AND THE FAMILY

Marriage and the family indeed form closely related topics but they are not precisely identical. Marriage designates the socially recognized, and sometimes legally enforced, relationship between a couple who establish a nuclear family. The couple, in rare instances, may be comprised of two women, one assuming the masculine status (E. J. Krige and J. D. Krige, 1943:Chap. 9), a spirit of a deceased person and another spirit (Evans-Pritchard, 1951a:109–111), or even a human being and an object. Similarly the nuclear family so established may be merely a convenient assumption, as in the case of spirit marriage. Atypical forms of marriage will be ignored in this section.

Marriage will be studied as it involves the selection of a spouse, with consideration of sanctions, and in terms of its duration.

Selection of Spouses

In most of the world, even in communities which allow young people to engage in premarital sex relations, marriage is regarded as something more than the selection by an individual of a congenial partner. The western reader is familiar with personal mate selection. More commonly marriage is regarded as not primarily the business of two individuals, but a matter involving their families and even other kin. When potential mates are allowed to choose one another, a strong power of veto remains with parents or other kin. The alliance to be cemented through marriage is so vital that the arrangements cannot be left to young people alone. In Southwest Asia, including Pakistan and parts of Hindu India, women are secluded from an early age. Therefore they cannot be proposed to by boys. All arrangements for marriage are made by parents, perhaps with the assistance of marriage brokers. The young people, however, are expected to give their consent. The couple may first see one another through photographs and not have opportunity to meet until the wedding ceremony has been completed. Even in those countries, however, a distinction is made between a man's primary and secondary marriage. For subsequent unions greater initiative in selecting a spouse is exercised by the husband.

With personal mate selection, the individual nowhere has unlimited freedom of choice. In the first place, residential proximity influences the selection of a spouse. A boy and girl must be able to meet before they can marry. Once they meet, cultural variables become important. The couple must have an opportunity to understand each other. This requires that they share a certain number of values and other behaviors. Even in the United States, marriages tend not to be between distant social classes as often as they occur between people of relatively the same rank and culture (see pp. 450–451). Incest rules, which extend out from the nuclear family to include other kin, are another limitation on mate selection.

Marriage often is preferred with certain relatives, especially cousins. But all cousins are not preferred equally. Sometimes certain cousins are rigorously forbidden to marry while others represent ideal partners. Obviously, people who make distinctions of this sort do not classify cousins in the way that English speakers normally do. They recognize a distinction between parallel and cross-cousins. All cousins are the children of siblings. Parallel cousins are offspring of brothers or sisters respectively; cross-cousins, children of siblings of opposite sex (diagramed in Figure 24:4). There the father's brother's and mother's sister's children are labeled as parallel cousins

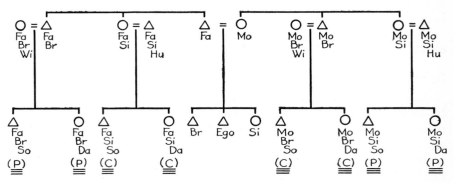

FIG. 24:4.   Diagram Showing Ego's Parallel and Cross Cousins. The abbreviations are: Fa, father; Mo, mother; Br, brother; Si, sister; Wi, wife; Hu, husband; So, son; Da, daughter; P, parallel cousin; and C, cross-cousin.

(P) of Ego (speaker). The father's sister's and mother's brother's children are Ego's cross-cousins (C).

Cross-cousin marriage is symmetrical when either paternal or maternal cross-cousins are eligible or preferred marriage partners. Unilateral (i.e., asymmetrical) cross-cousin marriage, in which a man is expected to marry either his mother's brother's or his father's sister's daughter, is rare. Often it exists merely as an ideal, because marriageable cross-cousins are not in all instances available (cf. Schapera, 1950). Preferred marriage with a mother's brother's daughter is more common than with a father's sister's daughter. Generally, the former type of unilateral cross-cousin marriage occurs when the social organization includes nonresidential patrilineal kin groups (see pp. 394–398). The converse form, marriage with the father's sister's daughter, is correlated with matrilineal descent groups. The explanation for these correlations is interesting. With patrilineal kin groups, warmth and intimacy develop between Ego (male) and his mother's brother, and his daughter becomes a spouse. The father's brother possesses authority and power. He must be treated with respect. In matrilineal kin groups the mother's brother occupies a position of leadership and authority. Warmth and intimacy now link Ego and his father's sister, whose daughter comes to be a preferred marriage partner (Homans and Schneider, 1955). Often where the father's sister's daughter is preferred for a man to marry, his paternal aunt is called mother-in-law from the start. That is, in the kinship system of the particular community, both statuses are terminologically equivalent (Murdock, 1949:173–174). Cross-cousin marriage is found in all continents except Europe (Lowie, 1948:107).

A general explanation for preferred cross-cousin marriage lies, first, in the fact that people who possess simple social organization and are closely attached to kin do not like to see offspring marry strangers. Strangers are not trusted by small-scale people (Titiev, 1956:856). Second, such preferred marriage, when it occurs in every generation, links two kin groups in an enduring relationship. A man marries his mother's brother's daughter. She moves to her husband's residential kin group but her brother is left behind to marry. The woman's child has a claim on his mother's brother's daughter, and this, ideally speaking, will be paid when that child is old enough to marry. In the meantime the relationship between both intermarrying kin groups is kept alive by periodic exchanges of gifts or through visits (De Jong, 1952; Lévi-Strauss, 1949).

Parallel cousins rarely wed. A conspicuous exception to this generalization is seen among the Arabs and other Muslim peoples of Southwest Asia. Here paternal parallel cousins are preferred mates. Partly such marriage is related to the scarcity of women which, in turn, may follow from polygyny. With women rare, a man will ordinarily be forced to offer considerable wealth to secure a desirable bride, i.e., one who is a virgin and comes from a family of unblemished reputation. The solidarity linking brothers in the extended family makes these relatives ready to exchange daughters for only a small consideration.

Is marriage to a first cousin biologically detrimental? Meaning, does it lead to unfavorable inheritance? The answer a biologist would give is: not necessarily and only very rarely. Such unions are likely to produce defective offspring if both cousins carry a recessive gene for some fatal or severe inheritable disease. Theoretically, two first cousins are more likely to carry such genes than unrelated persons. But such genes are not common. The danger inherent in cousin marriage, therefore, is trivial.

Secondary marriages often are governed by the sororate and levirate. In many communities if a man loses his wife through death he possesses a claim on her family. That group must replace the girl with an unmarried sister. This custom is known as the sororate. The levirate involves inheritance of a widow by her deceased husband's brother. The functions of these forms of marriage should not be overlooked. The bond of solidarity linking sisters will probably condition the second woman's affection toward her dead sister's children. She will treat them more warmly than a stranger might. The levirate assures security for the widow and children of a deceased man.

Prohibited forms of marriage normally include unions between parents and children or between siblings. In general it can be said that no prohibition on marriage to a person outside the nuclear family is universal (Murdock, 1949:285). A son's wife or daughter's husband, however, is very widely prohibited as a secondary spouse. Prohibitions of marriage to kin tend to apply with diminished intensity as relatives are further removed from the nuclear family. The intensity with which incest rules are applied beyond the nuclear family is related to the terms by which relatives are designated. Thus, persons addressed as "mother" or "sister," regardless of actual relationship, rarely will be available to a man as potential mates.

Sanctions of Marriage

Marriage may be initiated with no stronger or more obvious sanction than its recognition by a community. That is, people in general are made aware of the fact that a marriage has taken place and a new family established. It may be sufficient for both parties publicly to take up residence together. Such simple marriage formerly was found among Indians of northern Canada, like the Kaska and Attawapiskat Cree. Among the former, however, a period of bride-service further sanctioned the couple's relationship. Ceremonies, usually involving a feast to which relatives are invited, constitute a common means of securing public recognition of a marriage.

The transfer of property as a sanction of marriage has been mentioned.

Marriage May Be Initiated with Some Kind of Ritual. In West Pakistan the groom and his younger brother sit veiled and garlanded at a feast being given in the bride's house. Throughout the ceremony the groom is accompanied by his best friend. A modern Attawapiskat Cree wedding shows the bride outside of church wearing ceremonial dress.

Several types of transfer can be distinguished. Bridewealth is property transmitted to a bride's relatives in recognition of her marriage. The rationalizations offered for bridewealth vary. Sometimes it is offered explicitly to compensate the girl's family for the loss of a worker; sometimes it signifies a legal right to her offspring; or it may be simply a sign of respect for the girl and her parents who reared her. The acceptance of bridewealth is not regarded in the same light as payment for a chattel. What sometimes is called "bride purchase" only under the rarest and most aberrant circumstances is construed to be the sale of a woman. In some communities with bridewealth, commercial transactions based on payment are unknown. It cannot be expected that such people would think of a girl as being worth so many cattle or horses or so much salt.

Dowry is wealth in money or goods settled on a bride by the bride's kin group. Among Muslims a man may also settle wealth on the girl he marries. Or he may promise her wealth to be paid at a future date. This custom is neither bridewealth nor dowry but may be called dower (Parsons, 1906:66) or designated by the Arabic term *meher*. In rare cases a woman may relinquish her right to *meher*, perhaps in consideration for the right to divorce her husband should she at a future date desire to do so.

One function of all transfers of wealth accompanying marriage is to stabilize the union. The investment is not jeopardized readily. The relatives who have given or received wealth will seek means to prevent dissolution of the marriage. Stability is recognized explicitly as a function of *meher* even though the bride may give up her right to this settlement in exchange for the privilege of divorce.

Other sanctions of marriage include service, the groom spending a term working for his bride's family; exchange, the husband giving a sister to the wife's kin in exchange for its loss of a woman; and divine sanction, in which the attention of deities is directed to the union. Bride-service and sister exchange would seem to be alternatives for bridewealth. A significant correlation exists between bridewealth, bride-service or exchange, and a woman's appreciable contribution to subsistence (Heath, 1955). It is as though her family were being recompensed for the loss of her productive services. Dowry tends to occur where women make a very small contribution to subsistence.

Marriage by capture has received unwarranted attention. It occurs among warlike people, like the Indians of the American Great Plains, but it is not a normal basis for securing a wife in any community. In aboriginal Sarsi Indian culture it served as an expression of license. Generally, no doubt, a captured girl was one with whom a man had already been intimate (Honigmann, 1956d:28–29). Symbolic, or ritual, capture is more common than real abduction. The bride or her relatives simply pretend to resist the groom when he comes to claim his bride. An attenuated form of this drama occurs when a husband today carries his wife across the threshold of their new home. No evidence suggests that ritual abduction is a survival of actual marriage by capture which existed at some earlier period in culture history. If anything, it is probably a survival of more elaborate forms of symbolic abduction. The function of this ritual is to allow the bride and others to express the ambivalence which they are supposed to feel (or, perhaps, actually do feel) on the occasion of marriage. The custom also emphasizes the change in status taking place.

Elopement cannot be considered a sanction of marriage since it occurs when permission to marry is denied.

Duration of Marriage

Most communities are interested in the stability of marriage but not all try to maintain it in the same degree. The marriage relationship, therefore, is dissolved more readily among some people than others. Divorce is sometimes a simple matter. Among the Kaska Indians (if a church marriage has not taken place) it is accomplished merely through the physical separation of the couple, children being apportioned to one or the other parent. Where relatives and, perhaps, the total community adopt a stronger interest in the responsibilities incurred through marriage, divorce ceases to be so easy. Mere separation no longer dissolves all the responsibility of a husband and wife or that which devolved upon certain of their relatives with the marriage (D. M. Schneider, 1953a). Some of these responsibilities still may be enforced legally; failure to observe them will be punished by community-approved physical or economic sanctions.

If divorce is defined as any disruption of the husband-wife relationship, then it can be said that practically all communities make some provision for terminating marriage through divorce (Murdock, 1950). Apparently some men and women the world over cannot avoid being disappointed in a marriage choice they or their elders have made. The Inca of highland South America are among the few people opposed to any dissolution of the marital tie. Out of a sample of 40 communities, in 30 it is impossible to detect any substantial difference between the right of a man or a woman to terminate a marriage. Only 6 cultures give men rights superior to women in this respect; 2 of these are Muslim in religion. In Islam, although divorce is reprehensible, a man can end his marriage by thrice pronouncing the words "I divorce thee." He may do so only during a period when his wife is not menstruating and he need offer no reason. Nor must he secure permission from the community. The wife does not even have to be present when he announces his decision. A Muslim husband may delegate this power of divorce to his wife. Unless he does so, she does not, unless civil legislation to the contrary exists, possess rights equal to his (Fyzee, 1949). In only 4 communities are women able to initiate divorce more readily than their spouses. The divorce rate in 24 communities out of the sample of 40 appears to exceed that of contemporary United States; only in 6 exotic communities is marriage noticeably more stable.

AVAILABLE FILMS

Motion pictures illustrating family organization (but not structure) include: A *Balinese Family* (New York University Film Library, 17 min., b. and w.), *Children of China* (Encyclopædia Britannica Films, 11 min., b. and w.), *Eskimo Children* (Encyclopædia Britannica Films, 11 min., b. and w.), *Life on a French Farm* (Coronet, 10 min., b. and w.), and *Lima Family*, a view of an upper-class group produced by the Office of Inter-American Affairs (20 min., b. and w.). Covering the annual cycle are *Alexis Tremblay, Habitant,* showing life in French Quebec (National Film Board, 38 min., b. and w. or color), and *From Father to Son,* dealing with the same region and produced by the same Canadian organization (26 min., b. and w.).

Lobola (26 min., b. and w.) describes the problems of marriage in changing South Africa. The title refers to the cattle bridewealth which a man offers to his bride's kin and which validates marriage. The picture is distributed by Contemporary Films.

25.

Consanguineal Kin Groups and Kinship[1]

COMMUNITIES vary in the degree to which they emphasize the genealogical ties of an individual to the relatives of one or both parents. Some people, like the contemporary Cree Indians of northeastern Canada, the Central Arctic Eskimo, or English-speaking Americans, emphasize primarily the relationship of husband and wife, parents and children. Stress is put on the nuclear family. Larger groupings of consanguineal kin are recognized only weakly or may be absent from the culture. Other communities put stress not only on some form of residential kin group but on a wider circle of relatives who do not reside together. A child learns to identify with, and is taught loyalty to, his father's or mother's kin, or, simultaneously, to both lines of descent. Those relatives, in turn, recognize specific rights and responsibilities toward the child. Common undertakings, symbols and emblems of solidarity, coöperative rituals, and leadership help to fashion such consanguineal kin groups.

BASES OF CONSANGUINEAL KIN GROUPS

The residential kin groups described in the previous chapter are characterized by common residence and mixed consanguineal and affinal ties. A consanguineal tie is one based on descent. The links between a man and his mother, father, father's brother, or mother's brother are consanguineal. The groups to which attention now is directed consist of people related consanguineally. Generally speaking, common residence is not associated with consanguineal kin groups. At times certain members of consanguineal kin groups are localized in a circumscribed territory but they do not share a common dwelling or compound. Another difference between a residential and a consanguineal kin group lies in the fact that the former, i.e., the family in its most general sense, never includes both brothers and sisters after marriage. Either of these siblings normally moves out at maturity. However, the descent tie between siblings allows them to enjoy common membership in the consanguineal group. Exactly the op-

[1] Much of this chapter follows Murdock, *1949*:Chaps. 3, 6–8.

posite situation obtains with regard to husband and wife. They belong to a single residential kin group but, because of the rule of exogamy governing many groups of that type, rarely to the same consanguineal descent group.[2]

The general functions of the two types of kin groups are similar. Both provide for adaptation and adjustment. The common descent group often provides labor and wealth for some undertaking that its members cannot essay unaided. Even in some modern nations such groups continue to be active, nepotically securing jobs and other advantages for members. These organizations have been called "the individual's second line of defense" (Murdock, 1949:43). Where kin groups are important, the individual without known kin may feel quite helpless.

Rules of Descent

An individual's kin ties ramify endlessly. Nobody can trace his own out fully. In no community does an individual expect assistance from all relatives. Selection is made between kinsmen. The form of a consanguineal kin group depends in part on how this selection is accomplished.

Extended families, it will be recalled, arise from bilocal or unilocal residence. Consanguineal kin groups, while not unaffected by marital residence, are related more directly to rules of descent. By definition descent rules allocate a newborn individual to some specific portion of relatives, whether on his father's or mother's side, or both. There are three basic ways in which such social affiliation is made. These constitute the three primary rules of descent.

1. Patrilineal Descent.   Patrilineal descent disregards genealogical ties with the mother's relatives and unilinearly affiliates the child with the consanguineal kin of the father—the father's brothers, father's sisters, and, of course, their father. This rule, sometimes called agnatic descent, is observed in 105 out of a sample of 250 world communities; 97 of the 105 also practice patrilocal or matri-patrilocal residence and only 8 bilocal or neolocal. None are in the matrilocal or avunculocal categories (Murdock, 1949: 59). In association with patrilineal descent considerable authority and power for disciplining children normally rest in the hands of the father or father's elder brother. In contrast, the mother's brother has little authority over a sister's child. He is a kind of male mother, the link between maternal uncle and sister's child being marked by considerable intimacy (Homans and Schneider, 1955:22).

2. Matrilineal Descent.   The second descent rule works in reverse fashion. In matrilineal descent (sometimes called uterine descent), the father's relatives are discarded and the individual is allocated socially to his mother's consanguineal kin. They include his mother, mother's sisters, and mother's

[2] Consanguineal kin group endogamy does sometimes occur. The preferred marriage of parallel cousins among the Arabs is an expression of lineage endogamy.

brothers. Out of 52 communities with matrilineal descent in the sample, 33 have matrilocal or avunculocal residence, 15 patrilocal or matri-patrilocal, and 4 neolocal or bilocal. Often, but not inevitably, in association with matrilineal descent authority and power over children are vested in the mother's brother. When this is the case, he is the head of the extended family, even though he lives elsewhere, and the relationship between him and his sister's children is marked by constraint. Sometimes authority over children may reside in the father, even though descent is matrilineal. Then the child's relationship with his mother's brother may be relaxed and comradely (Homans and Schneider, 1955:47).

3. Bilateral Descent. The pattern of descent may omit any unilinear placement. In bilateral descent some of the father's consanguineal relatives and some of the mother's are disregarded. The child is affiliated with a rather small number of kin from both mother's and father's sides. These are usually the nearest genealogical kinsmen, represented in America by those relatives whom the bride must invite to her wedding or who come for Christmas dinner. In Euroamerican culture bilateral descent is common. It also is found in 75 out of a sample of 250 communities. Of this number 13 have matrilocal or avunculocal residence, 39 patrilocal or matripatrilocal, and 23 neolocal or bilocal.

This completes the primary rules of descent. However, some people combine matrilineal and patrilineal tracing of descent. This gives rise to a fourth, composite, descent rule.

4. Double Descent. In double descent the community affiliates children with patrilineal kinsmen for one purpose and mother's kin for another. For example, in Manus a child patrilineally inherits membership in his father's clan. In the process he acquires a clan name, clan avoidances, and the father's rank. Patrilineal clan membership also makes him invulnerable to the curse of his father's sister. Some degree of affiliation with the mother's side also occurs. It is indicated in the avoidances which the child inherits from the mother's consanguineal kin, the special relationship acquired toward the maternal uncle, and a weak sense of membership in the mother's clan which confers on him certain rights (Mead, 1934:230). Some cultures provide that girls will be allocated to matrilineal kinsmen and boys to the father's consanguineal kin. Only 18 out of the sample of 250 communities practice double descent. None of these have matrilocal or avunculocal residence; 17 are patrilocal or matri-patrilocal, and 1, probably, bilocal.

The correlations enumerated above between unilinear descent rules and certain rules of residence deserve to be noted carefully. "Matrilineal descent is normally linked with matrilocal residence, patrilineal with patrilocal" (Linton, 1936:169). The explanation for such correlations is as follows: Where spouses of a particular sex continue to live with their consanguineal relatives, the manifestly equal biological relationship of a child to both of his parents tends to be minimized or overlooked. He is allocated to the parent and parent's kin dominant at the place where he is reared. When such clear-cut aggregations of maternal or paternal kin do not occur (they don't, remember, in a community with bilocal or neolocal residence), the emergence of a rule of bilateral descent is favored. This rule agrees with the biological fact that a child is the product of both parents.

TYPES OF CONSANGUINEAL KIN GROUPS

Basically rules of descent are unilinear or bilateral. Unilinear descent rules help to produce unilinear kin groups like the lineage, sib, moiety, and phratry. Bilateral descent underlies only one consanguineal group, the kindred. Each of these groups will be described briefly and illustrated.

Lineage

The lineage represents a consanguineal kin group that includes only those persons who can trace their common relationship through a specific series of genealogical links to a known ancestor. They trace their descent according to whatever primary rule of descent operates in the community. A patrilineage includes the relatives who trace descent patrilineally, whereas members of the matrilineage are affiliated through matrilineal descent. Usually the smallest corporate segment of a lineage consists of unilinearly related persons of the same sex forming the core of an extended family. However, the lineage also includes married siblings of opposite sex who reside elsewhere.

Among the Kurds of Southwest Asia, the maximal lineage, or *tira*, goes back 9 or 12 generations. It is divided into a number of smaller lineage segments. The maximal lineage owns agricultural land and grazing territory. Formerly it mobilized in total when external attack threatened any segment (Barth, 1954).

Truk, a Micronesian atoll, offers a good illustration of how matrilineages are organized and operate (Murdock and Goodenough, 1947; Goodenough, 1951:66–73, 137–145). The lineage includes those people who can trace descent matrilineally from a remembered ancestor together with a few adopted members. Genealogies which contain the names of known ancestors in the lineage descent line form an important kind of knowledge which is best developed in old people but is taught to the young. A lineage averages 30 or 40 members. These people form a corporate group which owns its own territory in the form of named tracts. A lineage also corporately owns an earth oven and a common men's house where unmarried boys above the age of puberty formerly slept. Formerly a sequestration hut into which women retired during menstruation and childbirth also constituted lineage property. A lineage used to live together in a hamlet (at one time even in a common house partitioned off into apartments). Since the Japanese occupation of Truk, houses of the same lineage have tended to form a cluster within a village. The hamlet formerly contained, and the village ward today consists of, a corps of women and girls together with their unmarried sons. The head of the lineage, however, is the most senior male. He administers the corporate property, calls meetings of the lineage membership, can veto a proposed marriage of a lineage member, and has other rights and duties. The office normally is inherited by a younger brother and then an elder sister's eldest son. Fellow members of the lineage regard one another as siblings. Males of the matri-lineage are organized into one loose group and their sisters and mothers into another. In the latter subgroup the oldest woman directs joint activities. In each subgroup thus constituted, individuals are ranked by relative age or, better, by birth order. Responsibility and power follow this ranking so that the youngest adult is at the beck and call of all other members of the group. Lineages are also ranked. The political system of Truk rests on lineage rank in the following manner: Truk is divided into small districts. In such a district land might be owned by several lineages, some possessing more than others, depending on age. The highest-ranking group, which is usually also the largest landholding body, provides the district chief, who is himself a lineage head. He collects tribute from other lineages, sets the dates of ceremonies, and formerly acted as war leader. The district is endogamous, the men being linked bilaterally through kinship. Such bilateral ties, however, are insignificant compared to the strength of the lineage ties.

Lineages may be weak or strong. A strong lineage is a corporate group with recognized administrators, the members of which carry out many activities in common. Among the most important of such activities, at least from the standpoint of strengthening the solidarity of the corporate body, are ancestor ceremonies.

Sib

In the sib is found a group of consanguineal kinsmen who affirm a bond of kinship which is traced in either the paternal or the maternal line. But all these people cannot trace actual genealogical connection with one another. It is as though all persons calling themselves Smith affirmed their common descent. Some could demonstrate genealogical links to one another but most could not. In a patrisib membership is traced through males (i.e., is inherited from the father), while a matrisib includes only people related through females.[3] In place of the known ancestor of a lineage, the sib often postulates an ancestor, perhaps a species of animal or plant. Living representatives of the species may be treated with special

[3] In ethnographic literature a patrisib is often referred to as a gens, and a matrisib as a clan. See the discussion of clans on p. 405.

respect, being avoided as food and figuring prominently in rituals. Totemism, as this complex of customs is called, helps to give identity to a sib
(see pp. 366–367). Normally sibs include several lineages but such segments
may not be structured as clear-cut groups.

Matrilineal sibs were numerous among the Indians of the Creek Confederation in the southeastern United States (Swanton, 1946:654–664).
Totemic, the groups bore names like these: Alligator, Arrow, Bear, Beaver,
Bird, Bison, Cane, Corn, Deer, and about 30 more, including Red Paint,
Spanish Moss, and Wind. All the Creek sibs were divided into two divisions, called Whites and People of Different Speech (the latter symbolized
by the color red).

On the Micronesian island of Yap an exogamous matrisib is organized
by a belief in a common place of origin and through a sacred place where
rituals may be executed (D. M. Schneider, 1953b:217). Such sibs are scattered over the island. They operate by regulating marriage through the
rule of exogamy, providing sanctuary to members in time of war and hospitality in time of peace, and, finally, constituting a widespread group of
last resort, one in which wealth can be borrowed or various kinds of
favors secured. An individual's sib membership is treated as a secret matter,
a subject discussed only between mother and child and not to be brought
up with a stranger. The function of secrecy probably is to enhance the
importance of sib membership in general. It bolsters the significance of
belonging to such a group.

Phratry and Moiety

When two or more sibs affirm a unilinear bond of kinship, they constitute
a consanguineal unilinear kin group called a phratry. However, if only two
phratries exist, every person belonging to one or the other, they are called
moieties. Should the community possess only two sibs, each also is referred
to as a moiety. Patrilineal descent in a moiety gives rise to patrimoieties
while matrimoieties are the result of matrilineal descent.

The bonds uniting the phratry or moiety are usually weaker than the
solidarity existing in a sib. The former groups also are not as frequently
exogamous. Among the Kaska Indians of northern British Columbia two
matrimoieties, Wolf and Crow, are founded on the belief that the members
in each are somehow related in much the same way that brothers and sisters are related (Honigmann, 1949a:133). By virtue of such affirmed common descent, the moieties are exogamous. Occasionally the members of
one group extend a feast (i.e., potlatch) to the other division. People without moiety affiliation marrying into the Kaska tribe eventually are informally classified with one side or the other—for example, at a potlatch when
it is decided whether they will be hosts or guests. True moieties are distinguished from the pseudomoieties that appear when a village is divided

in half without thought of kinship or genealogical descent. Such dual divisions, as these groups may be called, are less likely than true moieties to be exogamous. "Political moieties" are also in this category (Murdock, 1956).

Sections[4]

In communities with double descent both patrilineal and matrilineal descent groups can exist simultaneously, although relatively more emphasis may be put on one type than the other. In Manus, for example, strongest

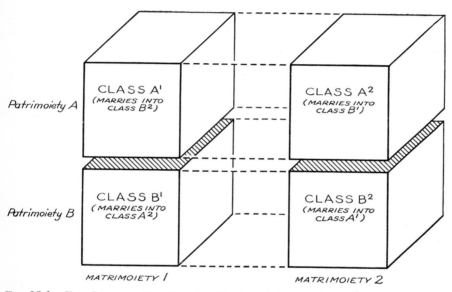

FIG. 25:1. Four-Section System Showing Marriage Role for Each Section. Patrimoieties are placed in horizontal columns A and B; matrimoieties in vertical columns 1 and 2. Each cell represents a section or a marriage class. Cross-cousins are in the section into which Ego is obliged to marry.

identification is with the patrilineal descent group, membership in the mother's clan being relatively submerged. Communities which affiliate the newborn individual with two unilinear kin groups simultaneously offer no special problems. This system can be understood in terms of what has already been said.

When, however, a person is affiliated with an exogamous moiety derived through one parent, say, the father, and simultaneously with an exogamous moiety in which descent is traced through the opposite parent, then some-

[4] The following discussion is based largely on Layard, 1942:Chap. 5. The reader who finds the organization of sections difficult to follow, perhaps because of the abstract nature of the discussion or the foreignness of the component customs, is assured that sections have relatively little significance as far as the working of culture in general is concerned.

thing novel is added. The community is divided into equal halves patrilineally and again matrilineally (Fig. 25:1). Patrimoieties A and B coexist
with matrimoieties 1 and 2, so that each individual in the community is at
once a member of one patrimoiety and another matrimoiety. The possibilities are limited to membership in class A-1, A-2, B-1, or B-2. Because
these four classes are exogamous they may be called marriage classes or, as is
customary, sections. A section, then, is a marriage class arising from the
simultaneous operation of two or more sets of unilinear descent groups, the
individual holding a status in each set. Regulation of marriage is the major
function of these descent groups. In the system diagramed in Figure 25:1,
which represents a situation found in parts of Melanesia and among Australian aborigines, the community contains only four sections. The individual
may marry only into one of the four unilinear kin groups:

A man in section A-1 marries a woman of B-2; following descent rules, children fall into class A-2.
A man of A-2 marries a woman of B-1; their children are A-1.

Conversely:

A man of B-1 marries a woman of A-2; their children are B-2.
A man of B-2 marries a woman of A-1; their children are B-1.

The 4-section system here described, and, in fact, any section system, is
highly congenial with marriage by
sister exchange. Figure 25:2 shows
the working of the section system
and reciprocal exchange of sisters
over three generations. A man receives a bride from the opposite
patrimoiety and appropriate marriage class and in turn bestows his
sister on his bride's brother. This
occurs in every generation.

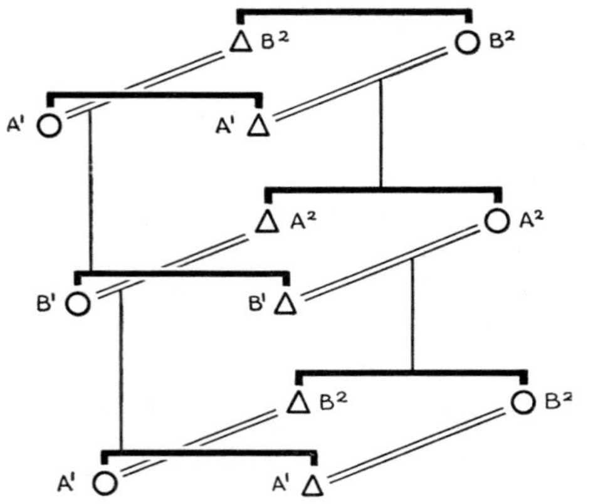

Somewhat more complicated is
the 6-section system which is
made up of 3 exogamous descent
groups; for example, 3 patrisibs
coexist with exogamous moieties
following an opposite rule of de-
scent. This arrangement, sketched in Figure 25:3, represents another common system of kinship organization found in Melanesia and native Australia. The diagram again reveals the section, or marriage class, from which a
spouse must be secured. If children belong to the moiety of the mother and
the unilinear descent group of the father, to what section will a child belong if the father is A-1 and marries a woman who is C-2?

FIG. 25:2. Section System Operating with
Sister Exchange.

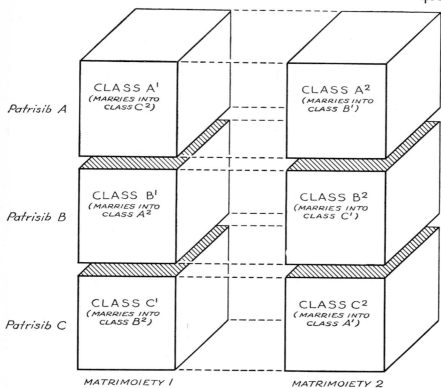

Patrisib A

CLASS A¹
(*MARRIES INTO CLASS C²*)

CLASS A²
(*MARRIES INTO CLASS B¹*)

Patrisib B

CLASS B¹
(*MARRIES INTO CLASS A²*)

CLASS B²
(*MARRIES INTO CLASS C¹*)

Patrisib C

CLASS C¹
(*MARRIES INTO CLASS B²*)

CLASS C²
(*MARRIES INTO CLASS A¹*)

MATRIMOIETY 1   *MATRIMOIETY 2*

Fig. 25:3. Six-Section System Showing Marriage Rule for Each Section. Patrisibs are placed in horizontal columns A, B, and C; matrimoieties in vertical columns 1 and 2.

Progressively more complicated section systems arise when 4 exogamous, unilinear descent groups exist with 2 exogamous moieties, giving rise to an 8-section system. In Figure 25:4 the moieties are matrilineal while the sibs follow patrilineal descent.

Even 12-section systems occur in Melanesia and also existed in China between 1000 and 300 B.C. (Layard, 1942:151). As shown in Figure 25:5, the system includes 2 exogamous matrimoieties, each of which is divided into 3 matrilineal descent groups (X, Y, and Z). Each of the resultant 6 sections is then divided between patrimoiety A and B. An individual belongs to one of the resultant 12 marriage classes and marries into a prescribed section. The prevailing descent rules allocate the offspring of the marriage to a specific section. Knowing the rules of marriage and of descent operating in each section, a reader can work out the social allocation of children resulting from particular unions. This might seem like a complicated system to live by but it is thoroughly familiar to people who learn it from childhood and to whom it possesses more than academic significance.

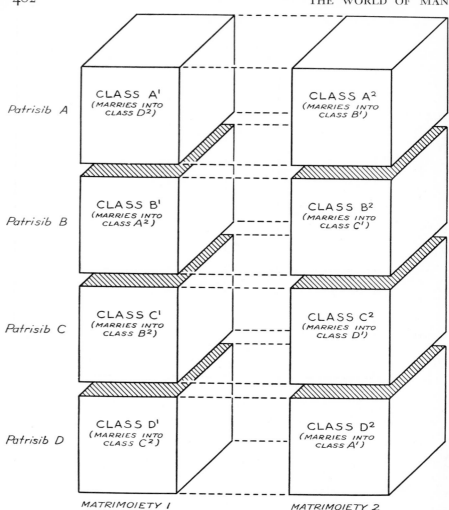

Fig. 25:4. Eight-Section System Showing Marriage Rule for Each Section. Patrisibs are shown in horizontal columns A, B, C, and D; matrimoieties in vertical columns 1 and 2.

Kindred

Not all communities with consanguineal kin groups follow a rule of unilinear descent. In modern America, for example, bilateral descent affiliates a newborn child with both the mother's and father's sides of the family. When some of these relatives interact as a group, for example, exchanging invitations to family reunions and weddings or visiting each other, a kindred is operating.

Study of 200 young, upper-middle-class Vassar College students from the

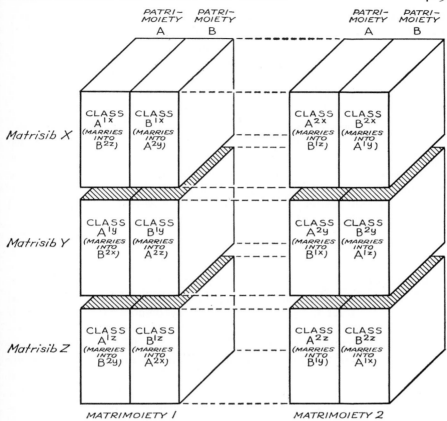

FIG. 25:5. Twelve-Section System Showing Marriage Rule for Each Section. Note matrisibs X, Y, and Z in horizontal columns while patrimoieties A and B and matrimoieties 1 and 2 are placed in vertical columns.

northeastern United States reveals that the kindred in this part of the country includes not more than 25 persons—at least that is the number of living relatives whom they could readily identify (Codere, 1955). Kindreds rarely are reported in the ethnographic literature, largely because their theoretical significance as a bilateral kin group has not been appreciated until recently. Anthropological thinking has been dominated by unilinear kin groups.

Kindreds especially are frequent with bilocal residence and occur when husband and wife reside neolocally after marriage. One kindred always overlaps another. For example, a nuclear family may customarily invite the mother's sister and her husband to Christmas dinner. But very probably the mother's sister's husband also is somebody's brother. In that status he is in another kindred and receives similar invitations. Kindreds do not form distinct groups in a community like lineages or sibs. Nor are they continuous in time. They cannot very well be corporate, owning property or possessing a well-defined system of administration. The kindred usually lacks a name. The individual who belongs to two sets of relatives, maternal and paternal, often becomes involved in conflicting obligations to each set. When relatives from both branches of the family quarrel, a person is pressed to align himself with one side or the other. Such antagonisms weaken a kindred. In a community with unilinear kin groups the individual knows with greater certainty where he stands. In case of a dispute between two "members of his own kin group, he is expected to remain neutral. . . . If neither is a member, the affair is none of his business. If one is a member but the other is not, he is expected to support his sibmate regardless of the rights in the matter. In short, most conflict situations are simply and automatically resolved" (Murdock, 1949:61).

Deme

The kindred is roughly comparable in size to a small segment of a lineage. The deme, another bilateral group in which descent often is affirmed or suspected, rather than being genealogically demonstrable, corresponds more closely to a sib. Demes have practically never been described in anthropological literature. The concept emerges as a useful one from comparative analysis of many cultures. By definition a deme refers to a spatially localized aggregate (for example, a village, band, small tribe, or inhabited valley) the members of which are by preference endogamous and lack any rule of unilinear descent (i.e., the deme is bilateral). By virtue of endogamy combined with isolation from similar groups, it is likely that everyone in the deme is related to everybody else. Beyond the family the individual's strongest sense of identification is with the deme itself.

The deme exists among the contemporary Aymara Indians who live around Lake Titicaca in Peru and Bolivia (Tschopik, 1946:531–541). These people are divided into local groups, called *ayllus*, which usually bear descriptive place names and possess myths by which the inhabitants are assigned to a common place of origin. Strangers are not welcomed in an *ayllu*. The group owns grazing land in common and recognizes an annually rotated headman. Each *ayllu* includes a number of related, extended families founded through patrilocal residence. The *ayllu* generally is endogamous and, therefore, corresponds to a deme.

When members of a deme, following widening of scale and increased participation in society, remain intact but cease to marry endogamously, the deme becomes exogamous. A rule of residence is adopted, giving rise to patridemes or matridemes out of which clans may arise.

THE CLAN: A COMPROMISE KIN GROUP

The previous chapter described kin groups based on residence combined with genealogical and affinal relationships. The clan is based on both common residence and genealogical descent. Therefore it is called a compromise kin group.

The clan by definition must meet three major specifications: (1) It is characterized by a unilinear rule of descent which forms the binding force of membership. But this does not distinguish clans from lineages, sibs, or moieties. Something more is necessary. (2) The clan is characterized by residential unity, the rule of residence agreeing with the rule of descent. But, the reader may object, how can a unilinear descent group have residential unity? Do not some siblings move away after marriage? The existence of a rule of residence indicates that some members certainly do leave upon marriage. Then why does not the clan become nonlocalized, like the lineage and sib? The reason lies in another factor. (3) Siblings who leave the clan upon marriage lose their identification with the group. In this way clans differ from kin groups like sibs and moieties. The out-marrying siblings come to be recognized as integral members of the clan into which they marry. A clan, therefore, includes in-marrying spouses but not out-marrying siblings. In this sense clans exist in 87 out of a sample of 250 communities but are absent in 131. Information is insufficient for the remaining 32 communities (Murdock, 1949:71). Patriclans far outnumber any other type, being present in 72 out of 87 communities. There are 11 cases of matriclans and 4 of avunculans.

Clans may arise quite simply through operation of a unilocal rule of residence. This rule assembles in one locality a number of unilinearly related adults of one sex plus spouses and children. When an explicit rule of descent is added, and the localized aggregate—including spouses—begins to act as a group—for example, executing common rituals or recognizing a single leader—then a clan is formed. Extended families founded through unilocal (but not bilocal) residence and exogamous demes already possess the requisite patterns of organization. They need only the appropriate descent rule in order to become matriclans or patriclans. When the rule of descent later is extended to include even out-marrying siblings, the clan becomes a lineage or sib.

SOME PRINCIPLES OF KINSHIP

Individuals related through ties of kinship are organized in kin groups. All people related by ties of kinship, however, do not form a group automatically. The purpose of this section is to examine kinship independently of kin groups.

In every vocabulary there exists, as a means of designating people who are consanguineally or affinally related, a set of kin terms. A kin term consists of one or more words by which relatives address or refer to one another.

Classification of Kin Terms

There are three ways of classifying kin terms.

1. By Mode of Use. According to mode of use we may distinguish terms of address, used in speaking to another person ("Hey Mom!" in the United States), and terms of reference, employed in referring to another person ("My father said . . ."). Relatives, of course, are sometimes also referred to by personal name ("Mary") as well as by somebody else's personal name joined to a term of reference ("John's aunt"). Teknonymy is the technical word for the custom of referring to a parent by the name of his or her child ("The father of John . . ."). In India spouses show respect for one another by never referring to one another by kin terms. They never use personal names either but practice teknonymy.

2. By Linguistic Form. According to linguistic form there are three types of kin terms: elementary terms (like English "father"), which cannot be analyzed into component elements possessing kinship meaning; derivative terms (English "grandmother"), which are compounded out of an elementary term plus some other linguistic element ("grand") which does not primarily possess kinship meaning, and descriptive terms (English "mother's brother's daughter"). Anthropologists studying kinship employ many descriptive terms because the ordinary elementary and derivative terms of English (for example, "cousin") are very unclear. In any language, however, speakers can resort to descriptive terms when ordinary terms of reference are ambiguous. The Kaska Indians customarily refer to parallel cousins by elementary terms also used for brother and sister. When the writer wanted to discover whether the relative in question was biologically a sibling, informants adopted the custom of specifying descriptively their relationship to that person. In any kinship system, derivative and descriptive terms apply with increasing frequency as relatives come to be further and further removed from Ego. This is illustrated in Table 33. The reader will note that not all the kinship statuses listed there are significant in modern Europe and America. A woman does not, for example, recognize a husband's wife (HuWi). However, where polygyny is practiced this status occurs quite normally.

It is worth repeating that despite a person's potentially great number of relatives few of these are ever known. Table 33 indicates 151 potential tertiary relatives, not all of whom occur in every individual's genealogy. Yet 200 Vassar College students, knowing only 30 to 33 living and dead kinsmen, could identify practically no one who fell in this category (Codere, 1955:77).

3. By Range of Application. Denotative terms apply only to relatives in a single kinship category, the category being specific for age, sex, and genealogical connection. In English the kin term "father" is ordinarily not applied to any relative outside the status of biological genitor, who must

TABLE 33. Classification of Relatives in Terms of Distance from Ego and Showing Increasing Frequency of Derivative and Descriptive Terms as Distance Increases

Class of Relatives	Members of the Class[a]
Primary relatives. These belong to the same nuclear family as a particular person (Ego).	Fa, Mo, Br, Si, Hu, Wi, So, Da.
Secondary relatives. These are the primary relatives of Ego's primary relatives.	FaFa and MoFa (grandfather), FaMo and MoMo (grandmother), FaBr and MoBr (uncle), FaSi and MoSi (aunt), FaWi (stepmother), MoHu (stepfather), FaSo and MoSo (half-brother), FaDa and MoDa (half-sister).
	BrWi (sister-in-law), BrSo (nephew), BrDa (niece), SiHu (brother-in-law), SiSo (nephew), SiDa (niece).
	WiFa and HuFa (father-in-law), WiMo and HuMo (mother-in-law), WiBr and HuBr (brother-in-law), WiSi and HuSi (sister-in-law), WiHu and HuWi (co-spouse), WiSo and HuSo (stepson), WiDa and HuDa (stepdaughter).
	SoWi (daughter-in-law), DaHu (son-in-law), SoSo and DaSo (grandson), SoDa and DaDa (granddaughter).
Tertiary relatives. The primary relatives of secondary relatives.	The 151 possibilities include 8 great-grand-parents, 8 first cousins, and the spouses of uncles, aunts, nephews, nieces, and grand-children.

[a] Abbreviations listed alphabetically are: Br, brother; Da, daughter; Fa, father; Hu, husband; Mo, mother; Si, sister; So, son; and Wi, wife.

SOURCE: Murdock, *1949*:94–95.

be older than Ego. When the social father is not the biological one, the designation "stepfather" may be used as a term of reference. Classificatory terms, however, apply to persons who occupy two or more kinship categories. For example, the English term "grandfather" is classificatory because it applies equally to mother's father and father's father (note how, by descriptive terms, one can make clear the specific individual who is being designated). The English term "cousin" also is classificatory, covering 8 distinct kinship positions. It is primarily through the generous use of classificatory terms that all communities reduce the individual's potentially large number of relatives to some easily manageable number of statuses—usually 25 or so.

The reader will understand how misleading it is to describe the kin-term systems of exotic communities as either descriptive or classificatory, although the terms often are used in that way. Every known kin-term system employs some classificatory terms.

How Kin Terms Arise

Denotative or descriptive kin terms are based on the recognition of one or more fundamental distinctions between relatives. Failure to heed these distinctions for reasons like those to be discussed below (p. 412) results in classificatory terminology. Nine criteria of distinction may operate in assigning an individual to a kinship category. These are:

1. **Generation.** The biological fact of reproduction automatically aligns an individual in a generation different from the one occupied by his parents or parents' siblings. In Ego's own generation are his brothers, sisters, and cousins. In the first ascending generation, his parents, their siblings, and

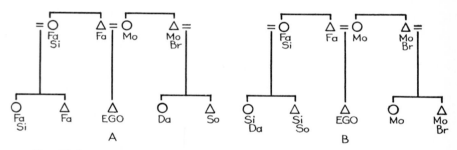

FIG. 25:6. Crow and Omaha Kin-Term Systems. A, Crow type; B, Omaha type.

their cousins. The first descending generation includes Ego's sons, daughters, nephews, and nieces. The second ascending generation contains grandparents and the second descending generation includes the grandchildren. Most kin-term systems pay some heed to generation differences between relatives. A notable exception is found in two rather widespread kinship complexes, the first the Crow Kinship System and the other the Omaha Kinship System. In the Crow system (A in Fig. 25:6), maternal cross-cousins are dropped one generation while paternal cross-cousins are promoted to the first ascending generation from Ego. In the Omaha system (B in Fig. 25:6), the reverse occurs. The maternal cross-cousins are elevated one generation and the paternal cross-cousins dropped one generation.[5]

[5] For an explanation of such overriding of generations see Hoebel, 1949:254–255, or Titiev, 1954:370–375.

2. Sex. The biological difference between male and female relatives very frequently gets taken into account in kin-term systems. The English terms "mother" and "father" distinguish on the basis of sex two people occupying parental status. The English term "cousin," however, fails to take sex differences into account.

3. Affinity. The universality of incest rules means that consanguineal relatives rarely are also relatives by marriage. Hence a distinction between two kinds of relatives—those connected to Ego consanguineally and those who become his kin through marriage (i.e., affinal kin)—quite frequently is recognized in kin-term systems. English recognizes affinity when the term "father-in-law" or "brother-in-law" is applied to certain persons related to Ego through a spouse. But English sometimes ignores this criterion, as when the terms "aunt" and "uncle" are applied to parents' siblings and to the spouses of those relatives.

4. Collaterality. Among an individual's consanguineal relatives some will be biologically closer than others of the same generation and sex. Parents, for example, are closer to Ego, biologically speaking, than parents' siblings or cousins. The parents are lineal, the latter collateral, kin. An individual's children are closer to him than his brother's and sister's children. Surprisingly, a majority of cultures to some degree do not take the trouble to distinguish collateral from lineal kin. English rather faithfully recognizes the distinction. Any grouping of lineal and collateral kin under a single term is called merging. Kin most frequently merged, and the kin with whom they are merged, include:

Parents merged with their siblings of the same sex. In many kin-term systems Mo is terminologically equated with MoSi and FaSi.
Siblings merged with parallel cousins of the same sex. The effect is to give greater prominence to cross-cousins, who emerge with distinct terms while parallel cousins are classed as siblings.
A wife merged with her sister. This is congenial with sororal polygyny and the sororate.
Children merged with sibling's children. So is terminologically identified with BrSo and SiSo; Da with BrDa and SiDa. Note that this is congruent with the merging of parents and parents' siblings.

5. Bifurcation. Among the secondary and more remote kin of Ego (see Table 33) are relatives related to him through either a male or a female connecting relative. The biological fact of such bifurcation is taken into account by most communities in assigning labels to certain relatives. This may come as a surprise to speakers of English, for in that language the sex of a connecting relative is ignored in assigning kin terms. The label "grandfather" is applied to both the mother's father and the father's father, quite ignoring the intervening kinsman. Similarly the terms "uncle," "aunt," "cousin," "nephew," and "niece" fail to make a distinction that is not often neglected.

6. Polarity. A social relationship involves at least two persons. It is not different with kinship relations. A kin term links Ego to at least one other person. If a community fully recognizes this fact, there will be a separate term for each of the two statuses. For instance, a child will apply a different term to the parent from the term the parent applies to him. "Father" and "son," in English, recognize the polarity of the parent-child relationship, as do the terms "uncle" and "nephew" or "niece." Occasionally polarity is ignored, especially when the relatives are two generations removed. Ego is two generations removed from his grandparents and in many communities one reciprocal term applies to both of these relatives. The grandfather addresses the grandson by the very term which the latter uses for his father's or mother's father.

7. Relative Age. Relatives of the same generation rarely are identical in age. A brother is normally younger or older than his sibling. A parent's sibling is nearly always older or younger than the parent. In English differences of age within a generation are ignored in the kin-term system. Most communities pay more regard to relative age. Especially do they distinguish older and younger siblings of the same sex.

8. Speaker's Sex. In the case of some kin terms, cultures may include alternative terms, one to be used by a male speaker and the other by a female speaker. English never does this, but among the Haida a son and daughter employ different denotative terms when designating the father.

9. Decedence or Other Condition of Life. Bifurcation, it has been pointed out, distinguishes between relatives on the basis of the sex of the connecting relative. When the crucial point becomes not sex but whether the connecting relative is alive or dead, or some condition of his life, then a relatively rare basis of distinction comes into being. The criterion of decedence sometimes occurs where the levirate is practiced. The death of an elder brother alters the surviving widow's status (she may now wed the deceased husband's brother); hence, he applies a new term to her. Decedence frequently operates in the kin-term system found on the Micronesian island of Yap (D. M. Schneider, 1953b:221). Here as long as Ego's father is alive he alone is referred to by the term "father" and he alone plays the role of father. When Ego's own father dies, then the father's brother replaces the father socially and is also referred to by that term. If a father's brother is lacking, Ego's elder brother assumes the role and status of father and the customary kin term for elder brother is dropped.

Significance of Kin Terms

Kin terms designate statuses in a social structure. A status, it will be recalled, is bound up with rights and duties which show up in role playing (see pp. 349–352). It follows that different behavior is expected of people who occupy different kinship positions and is also due to occupants of different kinship statuses. Generally speaking, "Persons to whom ego behaves in the same manner he will call by the same term; . . . persons to whom ego behaves in a different manner he will call by different terms" (Tax, quoted in Murdock, 1949:107).

This broad generalization must be modified. Differences in behavior between kinsmen covered by the same kin term follow when the degree of intimacy between them also differs. On Yap a father's sister is referred to as a "mother." But she is treated with special respect, different from the respect accorded to the emotionally closer, biological mother. The latter woman alone is addressed by the term "mother," the father's sister being called by a distinct kinship term (D. M. Schneider, 1953b:223). Among the Kaska Indians, where the mother's sister is also classified with the mother, everybody can distinguish his biological mother and behaves toward her in a special manner that is derived from the intimacy bound up with her since infancy. A Kaska Indian also calls his parallel cousins "brother" or "sister." But he clearly is aware of a distinction between biological and classificatory siblings and behaves to parallel cousins with somewhat attenuated warmth, especially if the classificatory sibling is the child of a father's brother. Children of a mother's sisters are likely to be known far more intimately owing to common residence.

Terminological distinctions may exist in the absence of manifest role differences—for example, in a community which has abandoned asymmetrical cross-cousin marriage. The two cross-cousins no longer represent different possibilities as marriage partners. To this extent their roles have become similar. Yet the custom of distinguishing between them by special terms may be retained.

It has been suggested that kin terms used as terms of address impose on a relationship a kind of sanction, or expectation, which helps to maintain behavior close to the ideal, structural definition of the relationship (D. M. Schneider, 1953b:228; D. M. Schneider and G. C. Homans, 1955). That is to say, when an individual calls another individual "father" or "brother" he is not only symbolizing a status verbally but declaring the existence of a specific relationship governed by certain norms. Where personal names are employed, structure is played down and the sanctioning element is absent. It is significant that Americans tend not to employ kin terms as forms of address between husband and wife, uncle *to* nephew, father *to* son, and between siblings. These relationships are also loosely defined. Even in the relationship of son *to* father, a tendency to equality may be noted in the use of informal words like "dad" or "pop" in place of "father." When, as on the island of Yap, kinship terms are not customarily used as terms of address, the actors have wide latitude in how they manage kinship relationships. Considerations of a personal nature play a large part in the interpersonal behavior of Yap kinsmen. However, there as elsewhere kinship positions are recognized by terms of reference, and an awareness of certain expectations, rights, and duties continues to be attached to those statuses.

KINSHIP IN RELATION TO OTHER ASPECTS OF CULTURE

Classificatory kin terms arise when one or more of the nine criteria of differentiation is overlooked (pp. 408–410). How do criteria come to be overlooked? Cross-cultural research demonstrates that overriding of generations, overlooking of collaterality, and neglect of other criteria do not occur randomly but are subject to lawful explanation. Only a very summary account of these explanations will be presented.[6]

Generally speaking, two or more kin positions tend to be classified together, in disregard of criteria which distinguish them, when regular or perceptible similarities characterize the occupants' relationship to one another and to some other particular relative. In other words, certain similarities exist between the kinsmen. These similarities are then emphasized by the application of a single term to both. Conversely, regular and significant differences between two relatives will be associated with different kin terms.

How do kinship statuses become equated to one another? Similarities arise from customs of marriage, rules of marital residence, rules of descent, and the presence or absence of kin groups in a community. Sororal polygyny, a form of marriage, tends to equate a wife to her sister; both relatives, then, tend to be called by a single term. The relationship of a child to his mother's sisters is influenced by matrilocal residence, which creates matrilocal extended families. The child grows up in a family that regularly includes the mother and her sisters. The latter women care for him, and his mother helps to care for her sisters' children. A similarity between the two statuses—mother and mother's sister—is emphasized. The mother's sister tends to be called "mother," and the maternal parallel cousins are categorized with siblings. The common classification of the women tends to equate their children with one another.

It follows that changes in forms of marriage, rules of residence, and types of consanguineal kin groups will be followed by changes in the kin-term system. Such correlated changes have been observed. They provide another illustration of the systematic nature of culture. How forms of marriage (for example, polygyny) and rules of residence in turn are dependent on the role of women and on subsistence techniques must also be kept in mind to understand how kinship systems are functionally related to other elements in culture.

[6] The most concise and detailed summary will be found in Murdock, 1949:Chap. 7.

26.

Local, Maximal, Instrumental Groups, and Associations

IDEALLY speaking, the groups referred to in the present chapter are nonkin in type. However, with simple social organization, nonkin organizations are not conspicuous. To the person reared in Europe or America a village is typically a nonkin group. Comparative research frequently reveals villages whose members are actually related to one another or, like the Israeli *kibbutz*, behave as though they were (Spiro, 1956:90). Emphasis in the present chapter is put on the morphology of nonkin groups. Processes occurring in these and other organizations are reserved for separate discussion (Chaps. 29–31).

No more than lineages, sibs, or other consanguineal kin groups do the groups referred to in the following pages occur everywhere. Sedentary local groups, like the village, as a rule appear with agriculture; maximal territorial organizations, like the nation or empire, depend on considerable technical development, which, in turn, rests on a large population adequately provided for by a dependable subsistence system. The following types of organizations will be surveyed: (1) local groups, (2) maximal territorial groups, (3) instrumental groups, and (4) associations.

LOCAL GROUPS

A local group ideally consists of several unrelated families occupying, or identified with, a circumscribed territory. Here their houses are built and fields laid out. Or over it they hunt and collect resources. A local group may be constituted primarily of relatives. But even if a village or band consists essentially of a localized segment of a lineage together with in-marrying spouses, its essential characteristic is not kinship.

Bands

Local groups may be mobile (i.e., nomadic) or sedentary. The mobile local group, found among people who depend on fishing and collecting for subsistence and also among pastoralists, is called a band. Out of 241 communities studied in a world-wide survey of social organization, for which relevant information is available, 39 are organized in bands (Murdock, 1949:80; cf. Steward, 1955:Chaps. 7–8). Bands are generally small, averaging about 50 persons among hunting and fishing folk. This number usually exploits a large territory. Bands among food gatherers also are unstable. That is, members regularly fall out to join or form another band. The remnant that is left either reorganizes or merges with yet another unit. Such shifting is less common among pastoralists.

The nature of the band among hunters and collectors may be illustrated by the aboriginal Cree Indians who lived west of James Bay in northern Ontario (Honigmann, 1956a; cf. MacNeish, 1956). Sometimes a joint family of two sisters and their husbands or a patrilocal extended family lived

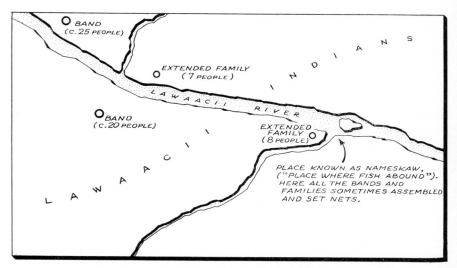

Fig. 26:1. Schematic Sketch of Bands Belonging to One River Drainage in Northern Ontario.

alone, but often from 1 to 9 such units joined together to form a band. If the band was moving in search of game it seems to have been limited to from 2 to 5 families. In winter or summer Indians sometimes gathered around a rich fishing site to set nets; then the temporarily sedentary unit swelled to 8 or more families. Resources were available at such a place to support the larger aggregate while in the bush people spread out more thinly to take advantage of the available game. Most of the members of the band were related either genealogically or through marriage. They also recognized one or more leaders whose advice carried more weight than the words of other men but who never sought to compel obedience. The band kept to a more or less vaguely defined territory, usually a river drainage, which it shared with other, similar units who spoke the same dialect and, no doubt, included kin (Fig. 26:1). That group which occasionally collected around a rich fishing site constituted practically all the inhabitants of the larger territory. The Cree Indians had no specific words to designate any of these groupings. We will find it convenient to distinguish between the scarcely corporate, unstable, small, local groups, which might be called microcosmic bands, and the larger composite unit occupying a river valley, the macrocosmic band. Since the latter corresponds to a maximal social unit it may also be called a tribe (see pp. 419–422). A macrocosmic group usually was named by neighbors after the river basin or other geographical feature of the tract they occupied. In Figure 26:1 the designation "Lawaacii Indians" actually means "People living along the Lawaacii River." The smaller, less stable, microcosmic bands were not named. Following contact with traders, missionaries, and governmental officials the people living in the northwest corner of James Bay came to assemble around the church and store located near one of the former summer fishing sites. Officially the macrocosmic bands of the several river valleys came to be designated collectively as Attawapiskat Indians after the name of the town and the river on which it was located. Sentiments associated with the smaller river-drainage units have persisted. The location of families which makes up the neighborhood pattern in Attawapiskat roughly corresponds to the macrocosmic bands. In winter these bands are resuscitated partially as people leave town to trap on territories with which they have been associated from childhood.

Another kind of band occurs among the pastoral Kurds of Southwest Asia (Barth, 1953:Chap. 2). Here the tribe is divided into camps (bands), called *khels*. The core of each band consists of a lineage, or segment of a larger lineage. In addition to kinsmen, the *khel* also includes unrelated workers. Leading the band is an older man with outstanding prestige.

Band organization is disappearing rapidly from the modern world as formerly nomadic people adopt sedentary residence and new occupations. Bands, however, continue among desert Bedouin of the Middle East, gypsies in many parts of the world, and the nomadic trading castes of India (Bose, 1956).

Homestead, Village, and City

At the outset it must be recognized that a village is not the smallest local group even among sedentary people. Among the Land Dayaks of Sarawak the longhouse occupies this position (Geddes, 1954). The longhouse contains 100 or more people who form a kindred. Two or three such houses form a village. Among the Nandi and many other East African people, as well as in parts of Bengal, the homestead, a kin group, lives in relative isolation (Huntingford, 1950:15). A group of Nandi homesteads forms a *koret*, or parish, a unit administered by a council of old men. Beyond the parish is the district comprising a number of parishes and also possessing a council. Districts in turn are grouped into counties, divisions with scarcely any corporate organization. Rural farm neighborhoods in the United States represent another unit on the subvillage level.

It is common to distinguish several types of sedentary local groups, usually on the basis of size. Population aggregates below 2500 are often referred to as villages unless the number of people goes below 250, when the unit is called a hamlet. Any aggregation of over 2500 people in the United States counts as a city, especially if it is incorporated. The word "town" has less

Sedentary Local Groups, Like Taos and Other Southwestern Pueblos, Are Found When Subsistence Activities Permit People to Remain Aggregated in One Place (courtesy, Santa Fe Railway).

precise meaning but usually is applied to a sedentary local group intermediate in size between a village and a large city. Out of 241 communities for which information is available, 189 contain villages or towns (Murdock, 1949:80–81). Another 39 communities have families living in scattered, semi-isolated homesteads more or less grouped around an administrative or market center.

Sedentary local groups, it has been pointed out, tend to be found when the subsistence or manufacturing system permits or requires people to remain aggregated in a relatively tight cluster for an extended period of time. Of course, people may occupy several villages during different parts of the year. The Nootka Indians of Vancouver Island possessed sheltered winter villages from which they exploited the sea and forest and in which they spent the months of torrential rain and storms. With summer they moved to other villages located on salmon streams and on the lowest reaches of inlets as well as along outer beaches (Drucker, 1951). Transhumant farmers live most of the year in valley villages, but a part of the population quits these in summer to pasture sheep or cattle on high mountain slopes.

Under conditions of simple social organization the sedentary local group is small and essentially a collectivity of kin. The size of Lamba villages in Northern Rhodesia is shown in Table 34. The average number of people

TABLE 34.   Size of Lamba Villages

Population of Village	Number of Villages	Number of Huts in Village	Number of Villages
Below 20	2	5–9	6
20–29	2	10–14	1
30–39	3	15–19	3
40–49	2	20–24	5
50–59	5	25–29	1
60–69	1		
Over 70	1		

SOURCE: J. C. Mitchell and J. A. Barnes, 1950:21, 29.

in a village is about 40; the largest local group contains 27 huts, the smallest 7. Each Lamba village possesses a headman whose office is inherited matrilineally by a brother or sister's son. The daughters and sisters of the headman, or his sister's daughters, together with their husbands and children, account for a large proportion of the village inhabitants—about 60 percent of the total membership. Twelve percent of the villagers belong to the same clan as the headman but not to his lineage. Twenty percent belong to lineages living in the village and related to the lineage or clan of the headman through marriage. Only 8 percent are not related to members in one of these ways (J. C. Mitchell and J. A. Barnes, 1950:35–36).

Apart from size, one of the points of difference between a city and a village lies in the relatively narrow influence of the latter compared to the surpassing influence of a large metropolis. People in a village identify with their local unit in day-to-day activities; but for buying, selling, administration, or pleasure they often look to the city. Historically, villages appeared before cities, urbanization largely being dependent on agricultural practices capable of supporting many specialists. The specialists, people engaged in administration, ritual, commerce, and manufacturing, live by exchanging their products and services for rurally produced food. Or else they levy taxes on the farmers. Cities possess other distinctive attributes. With their greater size goes more cultural heterogeneity. The urban individual as he matures faces many choices involving job, place of residence, and spouse. Of

course, strong emphasis on hereditary transmission of roles, and other barriers to mobility, may restrict such choices. Cities are more impersonal than
rural units. T. S. Eliot (1934:21) wrote:

> And no man knows or cares who is his neighbour
> Unless his neighbour makes too much disturbance. . . .

Compared to the villager's, a large proportion of the urban dweller's income
goes to maintain the outward signs of status (Veblen, 1912:Chap. 4). Perhaps this is related to urban impersonality. For in a village a person is
known through long acquaintance and family history, but in cities how one
impresses others, and the symbols employed in doing so, contribute mightily to one's identity.

Cities depend heavily on immigration from the countryside, not only
for subsistence but for population maintenance and growth. Rural people,
in turn, are attracted to urban centers by advantages which they desire.
Consequently the metropolis encourages culture change and all the processes of change may be studied in an urban context.

MAXIMAL TERRITORIAL GROUPS

Maximal territorial groups are difficult to define. Primarily the term designates tribes and nations. Such units are territorially localized, although
the localization of all parts need not be contiguous. Alaska is part of the
United States despite its separation from the other states. So are the Hawaiian Islands and Puerto Rico. Pakistan is divided into two wings separated by
the 1000-mile breadth of the Indian Union. Maximal groups are the large,
formal or informal, social divisions with which thousands or even millions
of individuals identify and through which a person's status is very much
affected. An Englishman's life and duties are different by virtue of the fact
that he belongs to the Commonwealth of Nations from what they would be
if this collectivity did not exist. It is not denied, of course, that the Englishman is profoundly more influenced by membership in the British nation
than by Commonwealth membership. Culture history is a record of constantly enlarging maximal groups. As technological development increased,
the size of nations and empires also expanded, in terms of both population
and land area (Hart, 1948; Sorre, 1948:167–208). Obviously an organization
of several million members is different from one with 50 or 300 persons. An
individual can have direct contact with every other member of a band or
small village. But he may be unaware of the existence of millions of people
who help form his nation. Much of the interaction of people in these large
groups is mediated and indirect. Millions of people listen when an American
President gives a radio talk. Yet they never directly meet the President.
Despite the great degree of impersonality, persons usually are keenly aware

of belonging to the specific nation and of their rights and duties as citizens.

The size of maximal territorial groups varies greatly and serves as a useful indicator of scale. The aboriginal population of the several tribes in northern British Columbia and southern Yukon Territory who today call themselves Kaska Indians may have been less than 200. Australian aboriginal tribes average about 1000 persons. In West Africa 4 million Ibo tribesmen are bound together by a common language, culture, and sense of group membership, though they lack any central political system. Modern national communities are similarly variable. The principality of Monaco consists of 21,000 people, Syria of 3,500,000, and the Union of Soviet Socialist Republics of 193,000,000.

Individuals may hold membership in several maximal territorial groups simultaneously, the units fitting into one another like a series of smaller and smaller boxes. Americans who belong to the city of "Middletown," a local group in the state of Indiana, also belong to the United States, a nation. A Pathan identifies with the unorganized category of people who speak Pashto,[1] belongs to the Province of West Pakistan, is a citizen of the Pakistan nation, and is a member of the British Commonwealth. Different degrees and kinds of loyalty may be felt to these different units, some of which may be subdivided into administrative units.

Tribe and Nation

As is often the case with relatively nontechnical concepts, the distinction between a tribe and a nation is hardly a sharp one. Tribes vary considerably. In the northern forests of Canada, from British Columbia to Labrador, each major river-drainage area contained one or more unorganized aggregates of people named from some geographical feature of their territory. Within the aggregates smaller bands were constantly forming and breaking up (see pp. 413–415). Often the larger, or macrocosmic, band spoke a dialect different from that of its neighbor, reflecting rather severe isolation. Such large divisions bounded by geographical landmarks may be called tribes. Following European contact, visits to the trading store and treatment by government officials as a single unit helped to merge these macrocosmic units. The separate dialect groups became better acquainted with one another; the members started to intermarry; they perceived that all spoke an essentially common language and, perhaps, through knowledge of other people whose language differed radically from their own, learned to regard themselves as a distinct unity. Out of this widening scale emerged a new group in which the earlier dialect divisions, while not forgotten, tended to disappear. People came to identify themselves as Attawapiskat

---

[1] He may also recall his membership in a specific Pathan tribe. But the quickening pace of detribalization means that many Pathans are being weaned away from tribal identification.

Cree, or Kaska Indians. Today these new tribes rarely possess any formal social structure; there are no chiefs. If the Canadian government insists upon a chief, his authority is limited.

The Indians who lived on the great plains of North America possessed a different kind of tribe. Here, too, there were bands moving over tracts of territory. Each band possessed a headman. The bands identified with a larger unit, the tribe, which frequently possessed one or more chiefs or a council. The Omaha Indians, for example, recognized an unlimited number of Lesser Chiefs whose power was confined mainly to the sib of which they were distinguished members (Fletcher and LaFlesche, 1911). From the Lesser Chiefs, seven Superior Chiefs were recruited, ideally representing men of unruffled temper. They formed a council presided over by the two highest-ranking members. Two heavily ornamental pipes symbolized the authority of the council and also symbolized Wakonda, the name designating the order in the universe. Hence, the council of Superior Chiefs was linked up with one of the very important beliefs of the people, just as the idea of divine monarchy in Europe related kings with God. The council acted mainly to preserve peace within the tribe and operated through a police force. The duties of the Superior Chiefs also included making peace with other tribes and entertaining distinguished foreign visitors. The Omaha tribe was far more corporate and formally organized than the river-drainage unit among the northern forest Indians of Canada.

Still another kind of tribe appears among the nomadic Kurds of Iraq (Barth, 1953:Chap. 2). The term "Kurd," like "Ibo," refers to a noncorporate collectivity within which more effective tribal units are organized. Each tribe among the Kurds consists of a group of kinsmen. It is a maximal patrilineage whose component sublineages constitute the component bands into which the larger division is divided. Each tribe owns grazing land in common and possesses a headman who is at the same time headman of the highest-ranking sublineage. This lineage segment exercises power over the others as long as the hereditary office of tribal headman remains in its control. Similar patterns of tribal organization occur among the Bedouin of Southwest Asia and gave strength to the conquest of Jenghis Khan and his Mongols. All the Kurds, all Bedouin, or all Mongols, however, do not constitute one maximal territorial group. They and similar people, like the Ibo, Pathans of Pakistan, Cree Indians of North America, and Berbers of North Africa, are better called ethnic groups. An ethnic group possesses little prospect of ever acting in concerted fashion. Hence it is, properly speaking, a social category (see pp. 356–357).

As the foregoing examples indicate, not all tribes are politically organized under a headman, king, or council. Formal governmental machinery cannot be taken as an essential criterion of a maximal territorial group (see p. 480–481).

Only relatively distinct from the tribe is the nation. Theoretically a citizen can quit or be expelled by his nation. Ideally speaking, this is not true of the tribe, in which solidarity is mechanical rather than organic. There exist clear-cut, formal procedures for gaining national citizenship. Although adoption into a tribe occurs, such transfers of allegiance are not normally expected in the tribal pattern of organization. Nations as groups are governed more by formal rules than are tribes. Other characteristics of the nation may be cited without further comparison to tribes. Nations often refer to themselves objectively in the third person: "Her Majesty's Government cannot agree with the view that . . ." is an example. Sovereignty is affirmed by the nation and is taken to mean that a government "may assume to regulate by legislation any persons or property within its borders, to adjudicate through its courts any controversy it may see fit, and to execute, within its own boundaries, any resultant judgements or decrees resulting from these courts" (Mayers, 1955:37–38).

The distinction between tribes and nations should not be exaggerated. A single term for both units would serve quite well for many purposes. Both types of groups invite a strong identification of the individual and through both the person is enabled to strive vicariously for greatness and other ends (Creedy, 1939:154–168). Tribe and nation are closely fused among the Sotho peoples of South Africa.

A Sotho tribe is a composite group containing not only those persons who acknowledge a common descent from the ancestor of the tribe and a common tribal totem . . . but a number of other members drawn from other tribes as well, but who become full members of this tribe through their allegiance to its chief. Thus the Ngwato tribe of Bechuanaland Protectorate contains a nucleus of 20,742 true Ngwato and 80,739 persons of . . . other tribes. The bond that unites these people is their allegiance to the chief of the Ngwato and their feeling of a common political unity and autonomy. The Basuto nation is merely an enlarged group of this type held together through their allegiance to the Paramount Chief, the head of the nation. But the Basuto nation is six times the size of the Ngwato, and whereas the Bechuana Sotho stress membership of a tribe and allegiance to a tribal chief, the Basuto emphasize allegiance to the Basuto Nation and to the Paramount Chief and Head of this nation. . . . The policy of the Paramount Chief . . . has been to break down any form of tribal allegiance . . . [Great Britain, 1951:5–6].

By our definition the Ngwato and the Basuto are both nations, much as Pakistan is a nation although it is populated by many ethnic groups (Punjabis, Sindhis, Pathans, Baluchis, and others). Some of these ethnic groups are themselves divided into tribes which possess corporate organization. As in Basutoland, the emphasis of the Pakistan government is to counteract tribal loyalties by arousing national patriotism.

Where formally organized nations in the modern world exist in proximity

to tribal units, there is a steady tendency of the former to reduce the autonomy of the latter. More and more areas of tribal life are controlled by the
national administration. Quite deliberate attempts are made to replace the
sense of tribal identification with national loyalty. The process has been
carried very far among American Indians and, perhaps, in the Soviet Union.
It is still nascent on the northern rims of Iraq, Iran, Afghanistan, West
Pakistan, and northeastern India, where the tribes are proving difficult to
subdue.

Empire

When one maximal territorial group—tribe or nation—absorbs another,
usually so that the governmental machinery of the one replaces or controls
the political organs of the other, an empire is created. Many nations, including the United States, which administers Indian tribes and other politically dependent peoples, are actually empires, although the word does
not extend to them in popular speech. An alliance or confederation, in
which two or more autonomous maximal groups agree to merge, or to act as
a unit, for certain more or less limited purposes, also represents an empire
in the general sense of the word as used here. Among the Kurds the confederation of tribes is the first clearly nonkin group to make its appearance
(Barth, 1953). A confederation of Kurdish tribes possesses a name, is attached to a particular territory, and recognizes several leaders, who, however, tend to belong to a single tribe. The confederation aids survival by increasing protection from attacks; at the same time it provides an organization effective for carrying out raids on adjacent tribes, perhaps some that
possess desirable pasture land. The Iroquois Indians of the eastern United
States and the southeastern Creek also entered into confederations.

INSTRUMENTAL GROUPS

The groups now to be discussed typically occur within local and maximal
territorial organizations. They represent people organized to work together
for the achievement of some relatively specific goal—like producing automobiles, imparting an education, or waging war. A factory, a school, or an
army is an instrumental group in the sense that it is organized ideally to
carry out some central task regardless of what other individual or cultural
functions it may assume. Kin groups, like the family, or local groups, like a
village, are not so narrowly specialized in purpose. Hence they cannot be
confused with instrumental organizations.

Instrumental organizations generally are found in conjunction with great
technological development such as is afforded by plow or mechanical agriculture. Some such groups, like manufacturing shops, savings associations,

armies, and schools, are somewhat more widely distributed, even being found in company with relatively simple social organizations. They may include mostly kin. In the Nigerian Nupe craftsman's shop the labor force consists of the male members of a family or of several related families (Nadel, 1942:258, 265–269). The sons will inherit the craft of their father. If outsiders join the plant they do so only by virtue of formal adoption into the kin group. The head of the family buys the raw material—iron for blacksmithing, thread for weaving, or wood for carpentry. Proceeds from the sale of the finished product also go to the family head, who is responsible for the needs of the household. At a level removed from such family-based instrumental groups there also exists among the Nupe a nonkin instrumental organization—the craft guild. However, the guilds—for example, that of iron workers—are divided into localized sections, in which all members normally are relatives of one another. The section possesses a titled headman, who is aided by two lower-ranking officials. Highest rank descends hereditarily on the second in command. Craft guilds organize coöperation when the members of one shop cannot meet demands. The order is passed on to other plants belonging to the localized guild section. The head of the blacksmiths' guild also organizes members to secure crude iron, to erect new forges, and for other tasks. He lends guild funds for new equipment and helps to arbitrate disputes. The reader is invited to make his own comparison of Nupe social organization for production with such instrumental groups as factories, trade associations, and labor unions in Europe and America.

Other Instrumental Organizations

The range and types of instrumental bodies will be illustrated by the mutual-aid association, factory and business organization, gangster organization, air base, and school.

1. **Mutual-Aid Association.** African cities are liberally supplied with associations designed to furnish members with mutual benefits. In Leopoldville, Belgian Congo, such mutual-aid associations are organized around people who share the same Christian name or follow a similar occupation or are members of the same tribe (Comhaire-Sylvain, 1950:102–103). Typically in an association of this type a number of people agree to pay small subscriptions regularly to a central treasury. The fund that accumulates may be used to provide gifts for a member's wedding or pay for his funeral, or is distributed periodically to each person in succession, enabling him to make some heavy expenditure, like buying a new suit or bicycle. Mutual-aid associations, designed to meet problems of living in a money economy, are instances of the African "flair" for organization (Herskovits, 1941a:166). Similar savings and insurance bodies can also be found among Negroes in

the United States. They are instrumental by virtue of the narrow goals toward which they are organized although, undoubtedly, other gratifications also are provided for members.

2. **Business Organizations.** The factory or business organizations represent a type of instrumental organization that has been studied much in recent years. The formal nature of such a group is revealed by the organizational chart, which usually shows a series of positions extending in an inverted fan-shape pattern from the president or manager at the top to the workers at the bottom (Gardner, 1946). This formal system of ordering statuses also allocates various duties that are directed toward the goal for which the factory exists. The prestige accorded to an individual is closely related to his position on the chart, each level of which outranks those below it. Deference is extended upward accordingly. A further degree of formality is contributed by the often meticulous job descriptions that a company attaches to positions on an organizational chart. What the organizational chart does not reveal is the existence in the factory of a parallel system of informal organization based on friendships. These relationships often develop out of the kind of grouping imposed by the formal organization. That is, the men engaged on the same tasks or working in the same room become friends. Although not supposed to exist at all, the system of informal organization considerably influences the goal-oriented activities of the factory. The cliques informally set standards of output and fix rates of production. Obviously their norms may not at all match the expectations of management.

The restaurant will serve nicely to illustrate the business organization as a type of instrumental group (W. F. Whyte, 1948). Nearly a quarter of the food eaten by Americans is sold in restaurants and hotels, which serve 50 million meals daily. Eating establishments also constitute social centers where business conferences and friends are able to meet and where ceremonial meals are taken. The instrument goal of the restaurant is to provide food with appropriate service for its customers. To carry out this aim the organization usually has two relatively specialized subsystems, one geared for production (preparing and cooking the food) and the other for service. In a very small establishment a single individual can operate both systems. His clientele is small and only a limited range of food need be offered. In a large restaurant serving many customers and offering a variety of dishes each subgroup involves many persons. A large supervisory staff is required to coördinate both systems. In each subsystem positions are ranked. For example, in the production system persons working on the range outrank those who prepare salads or meat. The fish station is at the bottom of the prestige hierarchy. A waiter or waitress links customer and kitchen force. In this position he or she is in a vulnerable spot to be frustrated. Strains may arise from breakdowns in the production system that interfere with carrying out the waiter's role, or stress may originate from the disagreeable behavior of a customer. When the customer is courteous, however, and the food properly prepared and smoothly provided, considerable satisfaction may accrue to the waiter. He then personally experiences the successful operation of the restaurant in terms of its overall goal. And so it is with any other business. The accomplishment of the instrumental organization's mission is not only rewarding to an abstract organization but satisfying personally to the individual members of the group.

3. **Gangster Organizations.**   Instrumental organizations may be illegal. An example is provided by Murder, Incorporated, a misnamed group despite the fact that it killed at least 63 men in and around New York City between 1931 and 1940 (Berger, 1942). The talented personnel of this organization also worked in other American cities where they were responsible for many more deaths. Six men dominated the organization in New York in addition to its managers in Chicago and Los Angeles. These men did not themselves murder but assigned killings to trigger-men—a specialized homicide staff—who worked for a salary. The managers had extensive interests in other legal and illegal activities, like gambling, from which they received income. Murders were not authorized without a reason acceptable to the heads of the organization. The client who wanted someone put out of the way had to be connected with the organization and the victim had to be in a position to threaten the organization's business interests. In other words, murder was merely a part-goal in the total setup of the group, which existed primarily to control illegal activities.

4. **Air Base.**   The next example of an instrumental organization is furnished by a United States Air Force base, specifically one that has two bombardment wings (Air Force Base Project Staff, 1954; Bates, 1953). In peacetime the goal of such a base is to maintain a state of readiness for air combat in which bombing planes will be used to disintegrate the enemy's warmaking capacity through strategic bombing of industrial and military centers. The peacetime goal is carried out through training with bombers like the B-50 and B-52. From a task-oriented point of view the air base with its 8000 or 9000 people can be divided into four interdependent subsystems. First, there is the executive system. This consists of the men who are engaged in planning work, assigning men to jobs, rewarding and punishing performance, and coördinating the other systems of the total organization. Second, the operations system includes the men who combine the activities and products of the other systems into the final product for which the base is organized—strategic mission flying. In this group are the men who fly the planes and execute the final goal. Third, the maintenance subsystem is engaged in assembling and maintaining the equipment and matériel used by the operations system. Maintenance workers groom and inspect the planes, guns, and electronic equipment employed in bomb-

ing. Finally, the service system of the air base consists of men engaged in moving people and matériel from one place to another, maintaining the biological adequacy of the personnel (by providing meals and medical service, for example), and providing the physical setting in which the acts of the other subsystems can be carried out.

5. **School.** A school is an organization set up for training the young in certain specific tasks or providing them with particular information (Siegel,

A United States Air Force Base Is an Example of an Instrumental Organization (courtesy, U.S. Air Force).

1955). Compared to other so-called professional organizations in America, the school holds relatively low value. Hence, its employees enjoy low prestige which is reflected in low salaries. The school exemplifies a process of communication in which teachers, aided by course materials, transfer information to the children. In this way teachers determine what pupils will learn. Parents and other citizens can also influence the content of learning, but the school, like almost any other instrumental structure, seeks to carry out its tasks with as much autonomy as possible. Such autonomy, of course, can never be perfect.

Additional examples of task-oriented groups could be cited. For example, men and women who administer a city or a nation constitute an instrumental group, one that often is elaborately departmentalized and hierarchically organized. Stores, transportation organizations, newspaper plants, and broadcasting companies represent other task-oriented groups. Social movements, too, require organization to achieve their rather specific programs. A social movement involves a number of people who are organized to achieve some change in culture or the cultural field or who seek to preserve the *status quo*. A case in point are American White Citizens' leagues, which in 1955 and 1956 tried to maintain school segregation in some southern states despite the Supreme Court decision defining such segregation as unconstitutional. The National Foundation for Infantile Paralysis, through the annual March of Dimes campaign, was instrumental in promoting research and therapeutic facilities to bring that illness under control. Social movements may be created to bring pressure on government. In Pakistan the anti-Ahmadiya movement, loosely organized around a core of permanent groups, agitated from 1950 until 1953 to have followers of the Ahmadi sect of Islam declared to be non-Muslims (*Report of the Court of Inquiry, 1954*; Honigmann, 1955 and 1956c).

Bureaucracy

Bureaucratic organization is not found in instrumental groups alone but may appear in so-called associations, to be discussed later. Primarily, however, bureaucracy has been characteristic of large organizations concerned with government, manufacturing, finance, and other goal-oriented activities. Therefore this is an appropriate place to review the concept and to do so primarily with reference to instrumental groups.[2]

Contrary to its popular meaning, bureaucracy is in large part only another name for complex social organization (see pp. 361–364) applied, however, not to a community or society in general, but to an organization. It refers to a highly impersonal group, which, because of its responsibilities, seeks to coördinate systematically the work of many employees. Bureaucracies also serve many people.

The ideal characteristics of a bureaucracy have been noted by Max Weber (1946): (1) The regular activities of the organization are divided systematically among the working members so that a number of specialized part-goals must be executed in order to achieve the final goal. In other words, a bureaucratic organization not only is a specialized group in the community but contains a further number of occupational specialists who each contribute to the final product or mission. (2) The positions in the bureaucracy are organized hierarchically so that each lower office is supervised by a higher one. (3) The activities are carried out according to a formal system of rules and standards that are designed to insure uniformity of tasks, coördination of different tasks, and uniform end products or services. Formal

[2] Much of what follows has been adapted from Blau, 1956.

organization insures predictability. Bureaucracies often are extremely intolerant of informal organization, which introduces unknown and difficult-to-control factors into the system. (4) A bureaucracy is organized rationally. The administrators make decisions without allowing personal considerations to interfere. Jobs are assigned on the basis of qualification, not kinship, tribal membership, or caste. (5) Employment in the organization is protected against arbitrary dismissal and hence constitutes a career. Any particular bureaucratic organization might not show all these characteristics equally, but to the degree that a group shares them it approaches the ideal of a bureaucracy. Specialization, hierarchy, formality, rationalism, and protected employment are designed to promote efficiency and effective operation. Sometimes, however, these means become ends in themselves and actually hamper efficiency.

Bureaucracy is no new development in human culture. It existed in the ancient Middle East 4000 or so years before the Christian era and also in classical Greece and Rome. The rapidly accelerated pace of bureaucratic organization in the modern world can be ascribed largely to the necessity of coördinating increasingly large numbers of people through governmental organizations, to the rise of mass production, and to the large-scale distribution of goods that began with the Industrial Revolution. Also it is related to the increasing specialization of occupations in business. Increased specialization calls for more embracive supervision and coördination to prevent costly breakdowns. Certain special administrative problems facing a community have also encouraged bureaucracy—for example, the need to maintain large irrigation works (see pp. 320–322) and the task of defending extensive national frontiers.

A paramount conflict in bureaucracies resides in trying to preserve initiative and responsibility for the working members and yet preventing spontaneous actions likely to interfere with the group reaching its goal. Careful selection and promotion of qualified personnel are two means of trying to harmonize central control with responsibility. Rules, job descriptions, and explicit operating procedures are other devices suited to the same purpose. The rules in a bureaucracy are often substitutes for face-to-face communication. They are printed in order to reduce diffuseness and misinterpretation (Gouldner, 1954). Where many men must follow the same rules, it is impossible to insure exact compliance by all; but the attempt is made. The rules legitimize punishment but lifting them may be a reward for good performance. Very meticulous application of detailed rules, however, produces inefficiency. The too-conscientious bureaucrat loses sight of the purpose of the standards, which become ends in themselves. It is this malfunctioning in bureaucratic organization that is popularly denoted by the term "bureaucracy."

ASSOCIATIONS

An association (or, as it is often called, a sodality) differs from an instrumental organization in not being oriented so explicitly to particular goals. Ideally speaking, membership is related primarily to the intrinsic satisfaction which the members find in common activities or in being mutually associated. Actually, the distinction between an instrumental group and sodality is relative. By no means is it possible always to determine whether a particular group should be classified in one or the other category. Over a long period members may associate because of common interests. But periodically the group may carry out special programs; for example, the town's Rotarians will sponsor a drive for a new playground, although this is not the primary reason for which Rotary is organized. Many towns in the United States have Parent-Teacher Associations that include parents of school children together with teachers. The PTA mediates between family and school, two groups that are tangent to one another because of overlapping membership (Chapple and Coon, 1942:417–418). In operation the PTA promotes understanding between parents and teachers and reduces the possibility of conflict between the two statuses. In case of conflict the association may seek to restore more harmonious interaction. However, the PTA is not organized toward ends as specific as those of the school. It includes fellowship as a value, which is realized periodically in suppers or other get-togethers.

Classification of associations by type has proved difficult (Lowie, 1948: 294–390). Sometimes such groups are organized mainly on the basis of sex, so that all men in the tribe or local group automatically become members upon reaching a certain age. Sometimes status is ascribed primarily on the basis of age. Men of a certain age constitute a group and pass into a new group as they mature. Possession of a similar achieved status or common experience may be the grounds of organization. Businessmen predominate in Rotary; war veterans make up the American Legion and Veterans of Foreign Wars; Poles and other immigrants in a large city have their clubs. Cutting across sex, age, and common experience as bases of membership is the bifurcation of sodalities into those that are secret and those that are open. Secret groups distinguish themselves by the possession of esoteric knowledge or paraphernalia which may not be communicated to, or witnessed by, outsiders. Open groups also hold meetings limited to members alone, but carefully perpetuated mysteries are lacking.

Sodalities have many social functions ranging from occasional quite instrumental duties to the more general function of knitting the solidarity of the total community or local group. On an individual level they provide adjustive satisfactions which derive from congenial company or from the opportunity to advance one's rank by associating with persons of higher prestige. People in all communities are not equally joiners of associations. The frequency of sodality membership is related to population size, cultural diversity, and extent of occupational specialization. Indians in the northern forest of Canada rarely formed such groups. On the other hand, the Indians who lived along the North Pacific coast of Canada and Alaska or on the Great Plains possessed many associations. In Lost Lake, a modern California town, 2100 people support between 25 and 30 adult and 10 juvenile sodalities. This means, of course, that one person belongs to several of these groups (A. R. Beals and T. McCorkle, 1950:37–39). Americans have been characterized as especially likely to form friendship ties through membership in lodges, fraternities, clubs, and other associations (Mead, 1942a:Chap. 3). Their strong interest in creating social bonds on the basis of common experience may be related to the diversity of backgrounds which Americans possess and to their rapidly shifting life, which prevents them from developing friendships through lifetime residence in some town or neighborhood. Kin groups, too, have little significance in American culture. Vertical mobility, in which each child ideally outdistances the achievement of his parents, further weakens social bonds. The mobile individual is faced constantly with the need of establishing new social relationships. Joining an association is an efficient way of meeting people who belong to one's newly established social level. Hong Kong, a culturally variegated city, also reflects a wide diversity of interests in its club life (Ingrams, 1952:87). Cultural diversity, mobility, and absence of significant kin groups are less satisfactory for explaining the tendency of Africans in tribal territories (i.e., outside of cities) to form associations. A focus on organization is traditional in sub-Saharan African culture.

Associations Based on Sex

Associations based on sex and comprising men more frequently than women occur in many parts of the world. For example, among the Ingalik of the lower Yukon River, Alaska, the men of a village formerly spent much time while not hunting or fishing in the *kashim* or men's clubhouse (Cornelius Osgood, 1940:300). Here they made things, listened to an old man's stories, related experiences, and took their meals. The home-cooked food was brought by women. Habitual occupancy of certain seats in the *kashim* gave men claim to those positions. Unmarried youths slept in the clubhouse and stored their fishing tackle there so that these things would not be endangered by a woman's "breath." Women occupied the *kashim* freely only when the building was used for ceremonies. The *kashim* group in an Ingalik village constituted a noncorporate organization of males the chief function of which probably was to intensify the solidarity of members of that sex. Among the Ona of Tierra del Fuego adult men formed a loose sodality into which adolescent boys were initiated by an elaborate ceremony (Cooper, 1946a:120–121). The charter of the male group included a sense of opposition to women, who, it was believed, had once been dominant over men. Women and uninitiated children had to avoid the initiation hut, from which men disguised as supernaturals emerged to dance publicly. As they danced they threatened with punishment women who failed to obey their husbands. Apparently women accepted the masked dancers as actual spirits. Boys, however, learned the secret of the disguises upon initiation. Remarkably similar initiation ceremonies, also dramatizing the solidarity of men against women, occur in Melanesia. A historic relationship between the two complexes has not been demonstrated successfully.

The tendency for men more than women to be grouped in associations cannot be explained as resulting from a male instinct for "joining" (Schurtz, 1902:47–50, 73). Men are less encumbered with routine activities like preparing food and caring for children. They therefore have larger blocks of time to devote to sodality activities. Their activities are also more diversified and certain associations—interest groups (see pp. 434–435)—build up around the different things that people do.

Associations Based on Age

It is rare for a sodality to be based on age alone, since generally among small-scale exotic people the sexes are separated in their associational life. For example, in Samoa young men belong to the Aumaga but young girls, together with the wives of untitled men and widows, belong to the village Aualuma (Mead, 1928a:55–60). Each sodality combines educational and social functions. Young men in the Aumaga learn to make speeches, to conduct themselves with gravity, and to plan and carry out group enterprises. A girl two or three years past puberty who joins the Aualuma learns the ceremonial roles appropriate to women in Samoan life. Her organization, however, is far less corporate and formally organized than the man's and also less useful as far as the maintenance of Samoan village life is concerned. In this respect the Aualuma is integrated with the general social negligence accorded to women in Samoa.

Dormitories for the use of unmarried men and women are a familiar type of association found in South and Southeast Asia as well as in Melanesia (Majumdar and Madan, 1956:130–137). Membership is not voluntary but is expected when the prospective member reaches an appropriate age. Sometimes such youth houses are bisexual, being occupied both by boys and girls, who pair off for sexual intercourse. The individual usually quits the association with marriage. Life in the group is accompanied by many observances, and members also have particular duties to fulfill for the local group as a whole. During the day they are busy with family tasks, only assembling as an actual group toward evening. Strict secrecy about what happens in the dormitory is enjoined. An administrative hierarchy of peers is capable of imposing punishment for infraction of rules and also coördinates the joint activities of the body. Under the adverse opinions of missionaries and other aliens, youth dormitories are rapidly disappearing.

The best-known associations are those divided into age grades or classes. Age-class systems are common in many parts of Africa, where they consist of a series of sets, grades, or classes through which pass practically all the males in the community.[3] Age-class organization for women is comparatively rare. Although each grade or class in a particular local group is a group, a class, even if scattered, often is conceived of as a single unit for the whole tribe. Youths enter the system by the formation of a new class when they reach a certain age, which, as already pointed out, is determined more by physical appearance than by exact counting of years. Membership in the class is incumbent on every qualified person. Formation of a new age class usually corresponds with puberty ceremonies or some other form of initiation into social manhood. The ceremonies are performed collectively for a number of eligible young males who will henceforth constitute the age set. Members of a set pass as a group from one grade to the next. This transition is automatic. It should be noted that the system stratifies the population according to seniority. It follows that a person's rights and duties, including his role in interpersonal relations, are closely related to his position in the system at a given time. Relations between age mates (i.e., members of the same class) involve obligations of coöperation, solidarity, and mutual help that closely resemble the duties which family members or kin owe to one another.

An important function of age groups is to facilitate the transmission of behavior from one generation to the next. Hence they are most likely to appear in societies where the family or other kin group "cannot ensure, or even impedes, the attainment of full social status by its members" (Eisenstadt, 1956:54). For example, the family cannot prepare the individual for his future roles, or older members block the younger ones' access to prerogatives of social maturity. In hierarchically graded age classes subordination of one age group by another engenders respect for authority and provides a climate favorable for learning. Interaction of an individual with his peers also facilitates learning through mutual identification and imitation. An age class furnishes a communal labor force available for such tasks as clearing the bush for new gardens, maintaining the water supply, waging war, or other useful ends. By assigning responsibilities to various age classes the age-class system assures the performance of tasks important to the community as a whole. Age-grade systems help to integrate a community.

[3] The following material is based on Eisenstadt, 1954; a much more systematic discussion is given in Eisenstadt, 1956. There the age-group concept is defined to include youth organizations and neighborhood gangs in Europe and America.

They bridge kin groups and may span several villages or other territorial segments. A sense of solidarity is engendered in males who do not live together and who have potentially conflicting, segmental loyalties. It is interesting to note that in certain African tribes which lack central government intratribal coördination is achieved by age sets which also possess judicial responsibilities.

Under the system of centralized political control, the age-class system may cease to be autonomous, that is, directed by its own members, and come under the control of the tribal power center. The influence of age classes on the overall behavior of community members is correlated inversely with

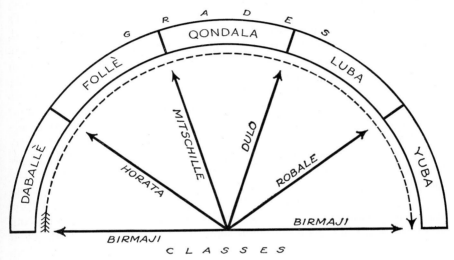

Fig. 26:2.   Classes and Grades in the Galla Age-Class System (after Prins, 1953:33).

the presence of specialized agents of social control. An inverse relationship also exists between the duration of an individual's membership in the system and the degree to which other specialized associations recruit members on some criterion of achievement.

The working of a specific age-class system may be shown by reference to the Galla, an agricultural and herding people of Ethiopia and adjacent East Africa (Prins, 1953:58–80). Here there are 5 classes arranged hierarchically (Fig. 26:2). Every 8 years the members of one class (the Birmaji) move out of the system while a new set of youths re-form it at the lowest grade. Simultaneously, the other 4 groups move each to a higher grade to the accompaniment of a series of status-change ceremonies. Each of the 5 classes is named and the 5 grades each class successively occupies are also named. The fourth grade is divided into 2 periods (not shown on the diagram), the dividing line among some Galla tribes being marked by a circumcision ceremony for all members of the class. Circumcised men in the fourth grade assume political power and responsibility. Men who, as a class, move out of the highest grade (Yuba) and, therefore, out of the system do so at the time when their sons are initiated into the lowest-ranking group (Daballè). Although these initiates are not of the same biological age, in the eyes of the Galla they possess equivalent social status. Figure 26:2 illustrates how members of the Birmaji class are retired from the system 40 years after their entry. Immediately another Birmaji class is formed.

Interest Associations

Sodalities into which members are drawn on the basis of common experience or similar interests are quite common. A diverse variety of groups falls in this category, and some indication of the diversity will now be attempted.

Among the American Plains Indians men who, through a dream or vision, had obtained help from a particular animal or natural phenomenon often formed an association. One of the best known of these is the Bear sodality of the Assiniboin tribe (Ewers, 1955a). Distinguished by special costumes and other paraphernalia the members conducted ceremonies in honor of the bear and coöperated with one another in curing. The same pattern occurred among the Omaha Indians, where curers were grouped in four so-called "doctoring" sodalities, each named after a powerful, postulated patron (Fortune, 1932a). Each group followed its own mode of curing and specialized in different disorders. For example, the Ghost sodality came under the patronage of greatly feared human ghosts. Its members treated delirium, unconsciousness, paralysis, strokes, as well as the dangerous condition automatically acquired when someone dreamed of the dead. Their techniques of curing frequently featured sprinkling with hot water. In addition Ghost doctors possessed the ability to foretell events, especially approaching death. Sometimes they even could avert forthcoming misfortune. The Omaha Indian's search for patrons began at the age of 7 but was conducted more seriously after puberty, when would-be doctors kept wakeful vigils in special places, hoping for a patron to manifest itself and to bestow special abilities on them. Among the Kwakiutl Indians of Vancouver Island in each tribe there likewise existed a number of sodalities comprised of persons who had received power from the same supernatural. The groups formed dual divisions. Traditionally the associations of one division were hostile to those of another (Boas, 1897).

Another type of association is illustrated by the Arioi, chapters of which formerly existed in many Polynesian islands (Williamson, 1939:Chap. 4; Muehlmann, 1955). An Arioi chapter included members of both sexes who were divided into 7 ranks, novices standing at the bottom of the prestige hierarchy. Certain secrets of the organization were revealed only to individuals achieving the highest rank. Appropriate patterns of tattooing and body staining symbolized rank and so did different role behavior. The higher a person's rank, the more heavily tattooed was his body surface. In addition to these grades, the sodality included followers of both sexes who prepared food and otherwise assisted members. Membership imposed the obligation on any but a woman of highest grade to kill any offspring she might produce; female followers were not bound by this rule. The choice of joining the association was voluntary but depended on a relatively involuntary experience, namely, some kind of divine seizure which indicated selection. Considerable honor went with membership and no doubt constituted a motivation unconsciously underlying the selection process. Initiation was celebrated ceremonially and meant bestowing a new name on the candidate. By this name he was henceforth known to members. Each advance in grade received further ceremonial recognition. A novice learned recitations, songs, dances, and other skills. On younger members or lower ranks fell the brunt of the burden of entertaining spectators at an Arioi meeting. This was accomplished through acting, singing, reciting, dancing, and wrestling. Drums and other instruments furnished appropriate music. The dramatic performances and songs celebrated achievements of the supernaturals and also described scenes of love among humans. Some scenes in the dramas involved public copulation, and the songs often celebrated physical love, inciting sexual desire. The Arioi chapter traveled in a group from one island or district to another. Always the sodality was entertained by the local king or chief, sometimes in houses especially prepared for its reception. When evening came the troupe gave its performance, members' bodies stained and ornamented with leaves and flowers. The senior Arioi were among the spectators. After several days the party moved on. Such tours helped to promote social solidarity. Arioi status conferred rights to the property of other people. Within limits, members could seize what they desired. The sodality was considered to be under the protection of certain deities and members were reverenced by other people. The Society Islands' Arioi has become well known for the sexual freedom which its members are supposed to have practiced, the Arioi husbands sharing wives in accordance with what we have called group marriage (see p. 377).[4] It should be recognized that the Polynesians in general were little given to sexual prudery. The Arioi simply may have exaggerated already highly permissive norms governing sexual behavior.

Modern American and Aboriginal Plains Indian Associations

Most modern associations usually do not freely admit all the men or women of a community. They tend to include only certain people and, in one way or another, deliberately to exclude others. By limiting membership in this way, associations function to maintain social distance be-

[4] Muehlmann (1955:99) denies the punaluan family or group marriage.

tween the higher and lower social classes in an American city, at the same time reinforcing solidarity within class boundaries (see pp. 450–451). American interest groups also serve as escalators permitting lower-ranking people to reach more prestigeful social levels. When membership in interest organizations is restricted to persons possessing certain qualifications, like ability to pay membership fees or a background of military service, such membership tends to advertise prestige as well as to constitute an avenue to higher rank (Seeley, Sim, and Loosley, 1956:Chap. 10).

Yankee City, a New England community of 17,000 persons, includes over 800 associations, of which about 357 are more or less permanent. About 6 percent recruited persons from only 2 classes; two-thirds of these contain members from 3 or 4 social classes and only one-tenth from as many as 5 classes. The percentage of members falls as one moves from the upper to the lower social levels of the community (Warner and Lunt, 1941:Chap. 16). What do these persons do as part of their membership role? Much of their behavior in associations is symbolic; that is, the members act symbolically or manipulate and exchange symbols. They take part in dramatic exhibitions, talk, sing, and engage in complex ceremonies. An important function of many of these activities is to tie the members together more closely and so to protect their common interest or perpetuate the group. Some ceremonial activities, like Lincoln's Day programs, bring the members into public interaction with other people. Considerable time during an association's meeting is taken up with making and discussing rules which, in turn, function to define "the status of the members and their office and above all permit the organizational activities of the members to symbolize and state the democratic character of the association" (ibid., p. 200). Occasional meals taken in common represent another means for achieving a sense of unity in the organization.

A study of aboriginal Plains Indian sodalities reveals that the great variety of these groups was, as in modern America, accompanied by relatively few functions (Humphrey, 1941). In some tribes the sodalities were age-graded. Higher ranks recognized bravery and military distinction, ceremonies being replete with symbols of war. Other associations included members linked to the same supernatural, but some groups seem to have been little more than social clubs, held together by a strong bond of companionship. Of course, particular associations also combined several orientations. Many of these organizations admitted women or possessed ladies' auxiliaries. Some Plains sodalities functioned to preserve social order. They policed the communal buffalo hunt, preventing rash individuals from scattering the herd. Some sodality ceremonies promised a plentiful supply of game or military success. Hence they functioned to inspire high morale in these activities. In general, associational membership intensified the bonds of solidarity between adult men and women of the tribe.

Secret Organizations

Mention has been made several times of elements of secrecy in sodality life. Groups restricted to men possess secrets that are kept from or deliberately misrepresented to women. Many associations cultivate an element of the esoteric that, functionally speaking, differentiates members from outsiders, enhances in-group solidarity, and raises the public prestige of the group. This section is limited to associations marked by even more severe secrecy. In West Africa groups of this type play an important role in regulating social life.

Best known of West African secret sodalities is the Poro, a group which can be recognized in numerous tribes, although it has no overall intertribal organization. In Sierra Leone the Poro has a long, though largely unknown, history which the Mende tribe believes ultimately goes back to divine origin (Little, 1948). The strength of the group resides in the spiritual force that its members are felt to possess. Belief in powerful spirits, which are represented periodically by masked members of the association, supports much of the influence that the Poro possesses. Learning about the Poro is not an easy matter for the anthropologist because every member upon entering the sodality takes an oath of secrecy. Breaking this oath will bring illness or death. The Poro meeting ground is closed to nonmembers and always to women and children.

The mighty arm of the Poro reaches directly into political life. The organization is so strong that no individual can hope to occupy public office without also holding sodality membership. Chiefs are expected to protect the group's interests should the latter come into conflict, say, with foreign government policy. In return, rulers are honored regularly by gifts from the group. The Poro also arbitrates in disputes between chiefs and, if necessary, is prepared to enforce its decision by armed officials masked as supernaturals. Administration of the association is vested in senior members, whose offices in a locality are hereditary. Succession to office is preceded by a course of training. Each local chapter is independent of any other, though their rituals and other activities are similar throughout a tribal territory. Occasionally towns and villages send representatives to a larger Poro meeting.

Entry into the Poro demands a fee, as does every advance in grade. Annually the sodality holds a bush school that includes the initiation of new junior members (who are already circumcised). In this way a youth attains social maturity. Prior to participation in the bush school no Mende man may marry or have sexual relations. Failure to be initiated leaves him with little or no social influence. The secrets of the association, including various signs and passwords, are transmitted in the bush school. Knowledge of native law and custom is also inculcated, in part through mock trials.

Even training in road making, bridge building, and trapping is provided. Juniors are examined to be sure that they have learned faithfully. During the period of his absence at the school an initiate is spoken of as having been swallowed by the "devil." Food is furnished by the parents for the "devil" who has swallowed their sons. In dramatic ceremonies the boy finally emerges from the bush, reborn from death and delivered up by the "devil." He has received a new name, in which great pride is taken. Many elements of Poro ritual and the secrecy surrounding them function primarily to intensify the members' feeling of solidarity and to maintain the social power of the organization.

CEREMONIAL KINSHIP

Distinguished from other nonkin organizations are groups formed by people who mutually recognize a nonconsanguineal and nonaffinal kinship relationship. Such kinship may be called ceremonial to distinguish it from true kinship acquired by descent or marriage. Among the best known of these groups is the *Compadrazgo* relationship found in Latin America and Spain. It arises out of the Catholic custom of employing sponsors or godparents on occasions like baptism and confirmation (Foster, 1953).

Among many Anglo-American Catholics godparents and godchildren hardly form a group, although the former may be chosen from an individual's kindred. There is little probability of the ceremonial kin's joining in common activities once the ritual occasion is over. But in Latin America, where the occasions for which sponsors will be sought are quite numerous, a large number of people are drawn into an enduring and regularly exercised *Compadrazgo* relationship. Sponsors are solicited at a child's illness, his first haircutting, the adolescent's first shave, the erection of a new house, and on other occasions. Some people have 25 or more godparents. Most often these are sought on economic levels higher than that which is occupied by the individual's own family. Godparents offer financial and other assistance and are a source of companionship. People related in this way are bound morally to stand together in time of need and danger. In villages where agents of social control are not efficiently developed, *compadres* support one another when disputes arise.

27.

Cleavage in Social Relations

IN NO community does everybody interact indiscriminately with everybody else. Nowhere is it likely, under normal circumstances, that any person will interact equally frequently, or at the same intensity, with every other member of the society. Those who are most respected tend to be segregated from those least respected; the rich are separated from the poor; the most churchly from the most unchurchly; and high government officials from subordinates. Those community members who look to the past may have little in common with, and hence stand aloof from, those who live mainly in the present; aliens (colonial officials, missionaries, language-bound embassy staffs) may interact rarely with the indigenous population. In general terms, social interaction between individuals, groups, or categories is limited by universal factors like age, sex, and kinship as well as by more specialized factors not present in all cultures, like caste, class, physical differences, and national borders.

UNIVERSAL FACTORS LIMITING SOCIAL INTERACTION

All communities contain the relatively young and the relatively old, men and women, and persons who occupy different kinship categories. Some, for example, are mothers-in-law to daughters' husbands whom they must not see or talk to. These are the three universal barriers to social interaction: age, sex, and kinship status.

Age
Nowhere do children and adults, or adults in the prime of life and oldsters, interact with the same likelihood as persons who occupy approximately the same age category. The very young and the very old possess neither the ability nor the inclination to join in the activities of middle-range adults. Adults see little value in including youngsters in their deliberations and may find the interests of the very old uncongenial. This, of course, is not to say that there is no interaction between people in relatively distant age categories. Of course there is. The point is that social interaction tends to be distributed unequally in a society, and age functions as one basis for delimiting areas of social intercourse.

Sex

Communities differ in the degree to which they conceive of men and women in asymmetrical terms—as essentially different from one another, and therefore not able to participate in many of the same situations (Mead, 1949b:Chaps. 2–7). Some cultures, like that of the modern United States, stress the basic equality of the sexes. Under this condition any discrimination based on sex differences becomes highly intolerable. Other cultures, like those of Southwest and South Asia, embody the belief that men and women are essentially different, yet mutually complementary. Sex differences are felt to balance one another: men are strong, bold, and breadwinners; women are weak, modest, and consumers (Honigmann, 1957b: 155–158).

Whether the sexes are regarded in symmetrical or asymmetrical terms, the interaction of men and women is always to some degree limited. The degree of segregation, however, varies. Even in a country like the United States, where the equality of the sexes is affirmed fiercely, nobody questions maintenance of separate dormitories for men and women, or separate barracks and lavatories. More pronounced, if less formally maintained, segregation obtains in many small-scale exotic communities where unrelated men and women rarely associate together. Among Attawapiskat Cree Indians it is extraordinary for even a married couple to take a leisurely walk together in public. In many rural communities in the United States the pattern at social dances is for boys and girls to sit on opposite sides of the room; a girl is fetched from her place by her partner and returned there after she has danced. Even in church men and women may sit apart. Such forms of segregation in public gatherings express a more basic dichotomy between males and females which implicitly is felt to exist.

Kinship

People who stand in certain genealogical and affinal relationships often tend to avoid one another. This basis of limiting social interaction may not be as widely distributed as the previous two but is still common enough to be categorized as universal.

Avoidance between relatives of opposite sex, functionally speaking, reduces the possibility that sexual relations will occur between them. The avoidance between siblings of opposite sex and of a wife's mother may be explained in these terms. Avoidance especially serves this end in social relationships where rules of incest have not become internalized strongly (Murdock, 1949:273). Prevention of incest, in turn, helps to perpetuate marriage outside the nuclear family or larger kinship circle and so contributes to a wider basis of social solidarity and coöperation. A second function of avoidance is to guard against potential conflict between kinsmen. (Other means of escaping such conflict exist: the relatives may treat each other with elaborate respect or be enjoined to joke with, and tease, one another.) Especially in relationships in which a conflict situation is nearly inevitable and is to be avoided at all cost does complete avoidance tend to be the rule (Eggan, 1955). Among the Kaska Indians a man reduces his interaction with his daughter after her marriage and also tends to avoid his son-in-law. Both avoidances suppress potential conflict between these men over which one will initiate action in the new family. It is well to add that residence among the Kaska is matrilocal and the people strongly espouse a value of deference in interpersonal relations (Honigmann, 1949a).

Among the relatives whom a man most often tends to treat with marked restraint or avoidance are his wife's mother (in 78 out of 250 communities), son's wife (in 35), sister (in 30), younger brother's wife (in 18), and parallel cousins (the mother's sister's daughter in 17 communities and the father's brother's in 15) (Murdock, 1949:277).

The Universal Factors and Solidarity

The universal barriers to free social interaction exert a centrifugal force on the social life of the community but seldom introduce any real divisiveness. Overriding age, sex, and kinship as factors limiting social interaction are division of labor based on age and sex, and reciprocity between kinsmen. These latter factors directly insure interdependence and promote social solidarity (see pp. 365–367). However, even avoidance may be socially integrative. Men and women or kinsmen who avoid much or too intimate contact with one another thereby also demonstrate that they share the same standards. When mother-in-law and son-in-law avoid each other they publicly affirm adherence to common ritual values. Like shared values in general, common ritual values help to maintain social solidarity (Radcliffe-Brown, 1939).

Any of the other bases of social segregation to be described in this chapter may serve as common ritual values which enhance the solidarity of those people who express them. A well-nigh essential point is that they be accepted as moral, appropriate, or traditional in the community or group where they occur.

CASTE

Social interaction is limited by membership in different castes. The term "caste" was once readily applied to a rather wide diversity of phenomena. South Asian countries, like India and Ceylon, have traditionally possessed castes. In the United States, Negroes and whites have also been referred to as constituting "color castes" (Dollard, 1937; A. Davis, B. B. Gardner, and M. R. Gardner, 1941:Chap. 2). Certain rather profound differences distinguish the situation in South Asia, where caste bears no relationship to race and, in India at least, is backed by divine sanctions, from that in the United States, where caste ideally stands rejected. These differences have disturbed social analysts faced with the dilemma of applying the same term to both situations (Cox, 1948).

What Is Caste?

As applied to South Asian countries, like India, Ceylon, and, with reservations, Pakistan, five characteristics of caste are significant (Ryan, 1953:19).

1. *Caste is a structural arrangement*. Like any other aspect of social structure, caste refers to the allocation of many people to relatively few status positions that define many of their roles, rights, duties, and social relationships. Caste status also defines the social area in which an individual may look for equals, seek a spouse, and form friendships, and even specifies the part of the village in which he may live or venture. Shares of stock in a corporation or rentals in an apartment house may be restricted by caste. People of different castes have little knowledge about one another.

The caste structure may be accepted or rejected. For centuries castes have been repudiated by some people in India. Today caste goes unrecognized in the legal norms, except for the fact that discrimination on a caste basis is forbidden. On the other hand, some Hindus defend castes as being of divine origin. In Pakistan, caste has no foundation in law or in the ideal tenets of Islam. Yet in many respects the system continues to be adhered to by some people, although far more loosely than in India.

2. *Caste membership is hereditary*. People are allocated by birth to endogamous status categories, castes, membership in which is then ideally fixed for life. Caste membership generally is ascribed patrilineally. The ideal that such membership will remain unchanged is modified in certain cases in which behavior merits punishment by expulsion from a caste. In some parts of South Asia provision is also made for adoption into particular castes, the transition being marked by a public ceremony. Exceptions to the rule of endogamy also occur, notably in the customs of hypergamy and hypogamy permitted by certain castes. In hypergamy a man of a higher-ranking caste takes a wife from a lower category, the children following the father's status. Hypogamy, the marriage of a woman to a man of lower caste, practically is never permitted. Endogamy is also no rule in those few castes of North India and Pakistan which are linked by tradition for marriage purposes. Lohars (Blacksmiths) and Tarkhans (Carpenters) are regarded "just like brother and sister" and may intermarry. Otherwise endogamy is motivated by the fear of spoiling the purity of the descent line. The significance of

this fear in motivating not only caste but local endogamy will become clear in a moment (see point 4 below).

3. *Castes are graded or ranked.* The basis of caste ranking is not always easy to identify; it certainly is not wealth or the value to the community at large of the attached occupational role (if any). On whatever it depends, caste rank is reflected in the social esteem in which an individual occupying that status is held. In India relative caste rank sometimes can be calibrated by the *varna* system. In descending grade there are four *varnas* (sometimes translated as "caste"): Brahman, Kshatriya, Vaisya, and Sudra. Every Brahman caste (*jati*) claims membership in the first, highest-ranking *varna*, though members of one Brahman caste do not claim equality with all other Brahman *jatis*. Theoretically, the rank of any *jati* depends on the *varna* in which it falls. Those which cannot be fitted into any one of these grades are the Scheduled Castes (also called Outcastes, or the individuals are collectively referred to as Untouchables, Harijans, or as constituting a Fifth Caste). Nearly all castes agree on the essential superiority of Brahman castes, though they may resent Brahman privileges. Between closer lying castes relative rank may be more uncertain and often comes into dispute. Furthermore, relative rank within a *varna* is not absolutely fixed. To a large extent the esteem in which a caste is held becomes meaningful only in terms of the caste's relationship to other castes with whose members it is in day-to-day contact.

By adopting more stringent rules of behavior—for example, refusing to allow widows to remarry, rejecting the use of meat, adopting new rituals, or refusing to eat with, or take food from, still lower-ranking castes—a caste in a particular locality can successfully claim higher rank. That is, an advance in position may be acknowledged by its neighbors. Even the Scheduled Castes can "improve their position" if they are willing to "adopt the higher and colder standards of thinking and living that have only been preserved for millennia because those who practiced them would not mix" (Coomaraswamy, 1946:19). To raise rank is not, of course, to attain universal equality.

It should be noted that rank is not necessarily correlated with general social or economic power. Many Brahmans work as household servants, a status in which they take orders from people of inferior caste rank. Brahmans outrank other castes in possession of a putative quality which may be called "purity." From their ranks the priests are chosen. Yet in a village the wealthy landowners may wield far more general power than do the priests (Sarma, 1955:168).

4. *Castes are localized.* A caste may be represented both in a particular locality and over a wider area. Generally it is the localized caste segment that is significant, even though a person feels vaguely that all fellow caste

men, no matter where located, are his kin. Hence it is the local section of a more widely distributed caste that constitutes the real limits to social interaction, the area in which endogamy is practiced. Because caste fellows who live at a distance are unknown it is feared that they may not be of pure endogamous descent. Hence, they are dangerous to select as spouses. When the endogamous local section of a caste receives a distinctive name, and otherwise comes to be distinguished from the larger unit, a new caste (or subcaste) comes into being (Ghurye, 1952:19–23). Through migration this, too, may spread.

5. *Castes and associated rank are identified explicitly.* Unlike the vague categories which Americans recognize by the words "middle class" or "upper class," caste categories are explicit. There is ordinarily no vagueness about the caste to which one belongs or about the role that a particular caste status demands. The identification of a caste is accomplished primarily through its name and by ritual observances which members practice. Such rituals often consist of avoidances that constitute very effective barriers to free social interaction between castes.

Among the most important rituals for expressing caste membership are restrictions placed on eating and associating with people in other castes. As already suggested, these rituals also symbolize relative rank. By altering them, a caste can put forward a claim to superior rank or it can be demoted in grade. Commonest of the eating rules is the refusal to accept water or food from lower-ranking castes. For a Brahman this means any other but a Brahman *jati* of equal or higher rank. There even are castes which assert themselves by refusing to accept from Brahmans any food in the cooking of which water has been used.[1]

Caste rituals sometimes are enforced. The Scheduled Castes, for example, traditionally have been regarded as possessing a putative quality of pollution which can be transmitted by touch and in other ways. Hence not only does an upper-caste man avoid contact with an Untouchable but the latter may be forbidden to draw water from village wells used by higher castes and to enter a Hindu temple lest he pollute it. Quarrels occur when a caste is unwilling to abide by avoidance rites. Because higher-ranking Barbers or priests will not shave members of the Scheduled Castes, the latter have their own endogamous castes of barbers, priests, and other specialists. Almost any imaginable idea or avoidance can become the vehicle for expressing caste rank and membership. Childbirth in South India pollutes some Brahman women for 10 days but women in other

---

[1] That is, *kachcha* food as distinguished from *pukka* food. The latter has been cooked in clarified butter (ghee), without the use of water. Generally people, even Brahmans, are more reluctant to accept *kachcha* than *pukka* food from lower-ranking castes (Ghurye, 1952:7–16).

castes for 11 or 28 days or for as long as 4 months. So, too, with the pollution occasioned by death. Again, in South India for a woman to wear clothes above the waist was formerly an upper-caste privilege. Sudras there are not supposed to study the most sacred Hindu literature. One caste is forbidden to cremate its dead, and Brahmans will not bow to images of supernaturals in a Sudra house. The socially standardized roles which a caste plays in a village or family ceremony—for example, marriage—also express its position.

Other Aspects of Caste in South Asia

Local sections of a caste in South Asia sometimes constitute formal groups. Heading the group is a council (i.e., *panchayat*) of family heads which decides whether caste rules have been infringed and what the punishment shall be for the infraction. Cases of aggression, theft, and adultery between group members will be tried by the council. Penalties take the forms of legal fines, feasts given to caste fellows, expiation, outcasting (ostracism), and even corporal punishment. The growing power of provincial and district government during the British period greatly weakened the power of the caste councils and brought about their practical disappearance.

While castes often are named for occupations (Carpenters, Washermen, Weavers, and others), there is by no means a perfect correlation between such groups and occupation in any given locality. In one South Indian city 83 percent of Brahmans, 56 percent of non-Brahmans, and 45 percent of the Scheduled Caste household heads work in occupations different from their fathers' (Gist, 1954:128). Nevertheless, caste status often limits the occupations which can be chosen without arousing social pressure. In the same South Indian city over half the Brahman household heads were in professional, managerial, business, and clerical positions. Nearly half the non-Brahmans occupied themselves with skilled or semiskilled tasks which carried less prestige, while 46 percent of the Scheduled Caste household heads worked in semiskilled jobs. In a northern Pakistan (Pashto-speaking) village an analysis by the author of 85 Dhobian (Washermen) revealed 16 to be egg dealers, 14 washermen, 10 teachers, and 8 in military service; the rest were distributed in 19 other occupations. Analysis of 46 Najyan (Barbers) revealed 25 to be farmers, 13 barbers, 5 laborers, 2 carriage drivers, and 1 noncultivating landlord.

Caste in South Asia has become a principle of social organization to which many other social divisions in the community readily succumb. It is nearly impossible in parts of India and Pakistan to decide where a caste leaves off and a tribe, religious sect, or even lineage begins. Ethnic and kin groups as well as associations readily become associated with endogamy and symbolic expression of rank and, in nonkin groups, infected with ascribed status. In other words, they become castelike whether or not they can be calibrated with one of the four Hindu *varnas*.[2]

Caste and Solidarity

While caste differences, like primary loyalty to one's kin group, promote strong segmental tendencies in the social organization of the South Asian village or other groups, there are counter-tendencies also at work to maintain in-group solidarity. Not only are the caste differences, to the extent to which they are accepted, an expression of a common faith in certain principles of social organization, but many endogamous categories are linked with one another through division of labor.

The allocation of tasks by caste is known as the *"jajmani* system." A *jajman* is a patron served by an individual known as a *kamin*. Many of the

individuals rendering service belong to so-called menial castes in the village. They have the hereditary right to perform the roles in question. These rights are inherited in the same way as caste membership, and a man who chooses to follow the occupation also inherits his father's clients. The system, in the main, operates without the use of money. A barber shaves his farmer-patron at stated intervals; the carpenter and blacksmith keep the farmer's house, plow, and other implements in repair and are shaved by the barber. Similarly, the priest (a Brahman) offers his services to Hindu farmers in the village. In return, the agriculturalist allocates a traditional portion of each harvest to his *kamins*, including the nonmenial Brahmans.

A Barber Shaving His Patron in West Pakistan.

Other privileges go with a *jajmani* relationship; for example, the *kamin* has rights to sugar cane; treacle, when it is made by a farmer-client; and clothing. Even village beggars form part of this socially integrative system, receiving food daily from each village household in turn. When a specialist,

[2] It may be that the Muslim-Hindu dichotomy failed to become assimilated to the caste principle of social organization. If it had, one could argue, the differences in faith and in associated ritual would have become accepted and friction reduced. In many villages such an adjustment actually had been worked out prior to the partition of the subcontinent. At another level, however, political ambitions gave force to the movement for separate Muslim and Hindu nations, a movement realized in 1947 with the establishment of Pakistan and India (Lumby, 1954; Sharma, 1954).

like the barber, serves a specialist like the Muslim beggar or village bard, he does so free of charge, although the latter may someday play traditional roles at the marriage or death of a barber. Ceremonial duties performed by certain castes constitute an important part of the *jajmani* system (Hocart, 1950:10; cf. Wiser, 1936). For example, in Naggal, a village in Ambala district, Punjab, India, the carpenter supplies a bed and low wooden platform for a bride's wedding; the water carriers carry a groom to the bride's house in a palanquin and also convey the bride to the home of the groom; a barber carries invitations for auspicious ceremonies like weddings; his wife dresses the bride; the sweeper carries news of a death to the bereaved family's relatives (Singh, 1933). For their ceremonial roles *kamins* may receive special monetary remuneration. Today the *jajmani* system shows signs of weakening; cash payment is replacing remuneration in kind and *kamins* are being attracted into agriculture and industry at the expense of traditional occupations (O. Lewis and V. Barnouw, 1956).

Participation in village rituals on the occasion of annual holidays like Diwali and Dasehra also gives members of different castes opportunity to demonstrate certain socially standardized, caste-allocated roles that help to promote local group solidarity (Dube, 1955:Chap. 4).

Distribution of Caste

In the form described here caste is found in South Asia, including India, Pakistan, and Ceylon. Certainly not all of the characteristics mentioned exist in any particular locality. In degree castelike barriers to social interaction also occur in other parts of the world. The camel-herding Bedouin of Arabia, for example, are divided into superior, or Sharif, tribes and inferior tribes. The origin of every individual is known and accepted. Marriage between the divisions is regarded as intolerable; an offender, it is said, would be killed by his own tribe. "The excuse would be that he is spoiling the tribe's blood" (Dickson, 1949:111–112).

SOCIAL CLASS

The word "class" applies to stratified social divisions of various kinds. An observer may perceive objective social strata based on differences of wealth, occupation, education, political power, and many other criteria. Subjectively, people in some communities stratify (i.e., classify) themselves in "psycho-social groupings." They manifest class consciousness by referring to themselves as belonging to a middle class or working class (Centers, 1949). Nearly three-quarters of professional and white-collar workers in the United States identify themselves as "middle" or "upper class" when given four choices: upper, middle, working, or lower class. Seventy-nine percent of all manual workers identify with the "working class." They apparently reject "lower class" because of the unfavorable connotation of the term. Such subjective classes may or may not conform to strata objectively delineated in a community. Whether they correspond or not, class in this sense is a psychological concept.

Classes in a community may be defined or undefined. When people explicitly are aware of the levels into which they fall—nobility, commoners, and slaves, for example—then the community is stratified into well-defined categories based on rank or prestige. The estates of medieval Europe and the castes of India are also defined explicitly (Goldschmidt, 1950:491). When defined or undefined classes act as barriers limiting social interaction they are called "social classes" (Table 35).

TABLE 35.   Relationship of Class and Social Class

Class	A category of people in the community isolated in terms of criteria like occupation, prestige, income, place of residence, birth (e.g., nobility). There are as many classes as there are criteria for distinguishing such strata. Economists use one set of criteria; historians another. A high but not perfect correlation often obtains between criteria. When people in a community are aware of such classes, the classes are defined explicitly. Otherwise they may be undefined.
Social Class	A class in which social interaction, for whatever reason, is more likely to occur with fellow members than with other people in the community.

The work of W. Lloyd Warner and his associates in the United States has made people familiar with six relatively undefined class strata:[3]

Upper-upper class
Lower-upper class
Upper-middle class
Lower-middle class
Upper-lower class
Lower-lower class

What Is Social Class?

Social class may be defined by the following characteristics, which are based mainly on the American scene:

1. *Social class refers to a structural arrangement.* In a social-class system people are allocated to a series of status positions. The system to some degree defines roles, rights, duties, and area of social interaction. The

[3] See, for example, Warner and Lunt, 1941:Chap. 5; Warner, Meeker, and Eells, 1949; and Marquand's novel, *Point of No Return* (1949).

public exhibition of certain behaviors or artifacts (accent, occupation, house, and home furnishings) is the basis upon which neighbors allocate one another to social classes or accept a person's claim to a certain social-class position. Other important matters influencing social-class membership are family background, native or foreign-born origin, friends, and sodality membership. Since many of the behaviors and artifacts which validate a relatively high social-class position are costly, such position is correlated closely with wealth (or income).

2. *Social-class position is validated through behavior.* Children are born into the same social class as parents, but social-class position must be validated by behavior which conforms to social-class values. In India caste membership must also in some measure be validated and can be lost through outcasting, but the explicitness of caste membership and the expectation that it is for life distinguish the caste and social-class systems. Except possibly on upper levels, social-class membership is permeated with the idea of mobility. Ideally, movement is from a lower-ranking social class to a higher one. Americans think of social class as a ladder, i.e., as something along which movement is invited (Mead, 1942a:Chap. 4).

3. *Social classes are ranked.* Any particular social class is a category of people who are believed to be, and accordingly are ranked by other people as, superior or inferior to another category. Different individuals will characterize the rank system in different terms, depending on their own class position. Mr. Substantial Citizen, for example, is aware of a "top level" or "society class" in which some people are "398's but they think they're 400's."[4] The informant then begins to name names: "The Vollners from top to bottom are in . . ." A mill laborer, on the other hand, sees social-class position in terms of wealth and power: "We are poorer, but we are not as poor as a lot of people. . . . The Federated Church has more money in it than any other church in town. . . . Most of these old, landed families around here and some of the wealthy people belong. . . ." But whatever the perception, all informants agree that there is an upper class, whether it is called "Number One," "The Top Class," "The 400," or "The Fancy Crowd." Relative position may be revealed by expressions like "He's one of the Astorbilts," or by relegating somebody to "Nob Hill" or to "the wrong side of the tracks." Interviews may contain still more indirect references that a student of culture can evaluate as ascribing people to superior or inferior positions. Americans place higher value on a college degree than on illiteracy; hence a man called "illiterate" is likely to be ranked below a physician.

4. *Members of a social class tend to marry endogamously but marriage up and down is permitted.* Popular fiction in America, including movies, often refers to the problems of interclass marriage. It is the subject of both humor and tragedy. In India one does not deal lightly with the topic

[4] The paragraph is based on Warner, Meeker, and Eells, 1949:Chaps. 3–5.

of intercaste marriage, although there films describe the difficulties encountered by lovers who come from different castes.

5. *Members of the same social class tend to share a relatively distinct culture.* Socially standardized behavior and artifacts tend to vary with social class. The upper-upper class in America, for example, has a strong feeling for property, particularly for heirlooms and antiques. Such artifacts may link the family with past members. A definite feeling for the importance of family background is another value orientation of that social class. Upper-class values in general tend to be conservative. By the emphasis placed on traditional usages, those people tend to maintain continuity with the community's past (Veblen, 1912:Chap. 8). In the lower and lower-middle classes property is not so strong a value. Money is regarded as something to be spent for relatively transitory satisfactions, not to be saved or invested. Upper- and upper-middle-class people tend to live in large houses which are kept in good or medium condition; lower-middle- and upper-lower-class people live in medium or small houses in medium condition, or small houses in good condition; the upper-lower shares with the lower class houses that are in bad condition (Warner, Meeker, and Eells, 1949:147). Relatively small traits function to distinguish social classes. For example, it has been said that in the lower class when two couples share an automobile each man sits with his wife; in the middle class the two women sit in the back seat, the men in front; in the upper class each man sits beside the other man's wife (Kronenberger, 1954:151). Failure to do the "right thing" in such apparently trifling cases can block social advancement.

Class and Social Segregation

How does the social-class system limit who in a community may have access to whom? Prominent in maintaining social segregation are the mechanisms for maintaining social distance used by upper-class people. These include the use of private schools for children, large private grounds surrounded by fences and hedges, and infrequent use of public conveyances. The topmost class actually has the best chance to express social distance. In other social classes, however, one also refrains from "marrying beneath oneself" or moving into "undesirable neighborhoods." In almost any town or city social classes occupy certain areas in preference to others. A social class may be excluded from renting or building a house in more desirable areas (Warner and Lunt, 1941:10).

As already pointed out, social-class membership often is associated with specific value orientations. Social-class segregation may be motivated by the desire to avoid contact with people whose manners or beliefs are uncongenial. Middle-class people, for example, romantically prefer to believe that class is of no consequence because all men are basically good, or that marriage should be based on compatibility, not income. People who feel differently on these points repel the middle-class person who holds such notions. Certainly people who hold very different values will not be attractive as possible marriage partners (Seeley, Sim, and Loosley, 1956:400). Therefore, marriage tends to be with people who share similar values. And so it is with taste. People who do not share one's class-bound ideas of desirable speech, proper entertainment, or dressing are not congenial company. They even may be embarrassing and so come to be avoided.

Whether based on employment in the same factory or membership in the same school, neighborhood, church, or common fraternity, the clique is an important device for channelizing social interaction between members who belong to the same or closely adjacent social classes (Warner and Lunt, 1941:110–113). A clique is a primary, nonkin group, varying in size from 2 to 30 members. It is completely informal and may be transitory. The members participate in frequent face-to-face relations that lack any specific instrumental end. A person may belong to several cliques simultaneously, with the result that cliques interlock. These groups also are ranked according to the class position of the members. It is through winning acceptance in one or more higher-ranking cliques that an individual who possesses the required wealth and behavior climbs the social-class ladder.

Associations serve much the same function as cliques. Admission to sodalities often is limited through high initiation fees, dues, or a system of "blackballing." The overlap of social classes is usually greater in associations, which are often marked by a good deal of secondary social interaction, than in primary cliques. The country club ranges from middle class through upper class, for example. So broad a range provides excellent opportunities for upward mobility, provided, of course, that the aspirant is accepted by high-ranking cliques in the association. The American Legion and similar interest groups possess even a wider social-class span, including lower- as well as upper-class members.

While the belief that all people do not possess equal social worth happens to be incompatible with one American value, the social-class system, especially when conceived of as a ladder for upward mobility, is quite acceptable. Americans accept social class to the degree that they endorse the belief that achievement is governed less by ability than by ambition and willingness. They do not regard the social-class system as limiting people to the status inherited by birth. Actually, of course, most American workers live in a world of somewhat more limited opportunity; but they do not, therefore, reject the dream of a future that is practically unlimited for themselves or their children (Chinoy, 1955).

Distribution of Social Class

Many communities recognize systems of rank and unequal social worth, but their operation often is too little understood for us to say whether or not they also act as barriers to social interaction. Certainly, rank and social class do not always go together. The presence of slaves in a community does not mean that there necessarily is greatly reduced interaction between them and their owners. Female slaves following their capture possessed low rank among the Kaska Indians. Within a short time, however, marriage absorbed them into the community (Honigmann, 1954c:86, 95, 131). The Kwakiutl and Nootka Indians of Vancouver Island possessed a well-defined rank system, one in which position was marked by many social privileges. Yet there does not seem to have been a social class of nobles who interacted among themselves more than with a lower-ranking category of commoners (Codere, 1957).

A social-class system is a function of population density. Where few people live in a community, segregation on the basis of unequal social worth rarely occurs. Density, of course, depends on dependable subsistence systems like some form of agriculture. Social classes also may appear following the influx of aliens into a community. The system appears readily in association with occupational specialization since, like castes, social classes are based in part on the work which members do.

PHYSICAL DIFFERENCES

Social segregation in the United States is strongly motivated by people's awareness of certain actual or imputed physical differences. It is not quite accurate to refer to this basis of segregation as racial. Race refers to hereditary physical differences characterizing a population. Modern anthropologists do not classify *individuals* racially but work with groups. In discussing segregation based on physical differences, however, one becomes accustomed to hearing individuals freely allocated to one "race" or another. The allocation often is done without much relevance to physical appearance. That is, a person may be isolated by people whom he very much resembles because of evidence that one of his known ancestors was a "Negro." Some Americans frequently impute qualities of superiority or inferiority to individuals on such bases of real or presumed ancestry. The fact that physical characteristics like dark skin and kinky hair cannot be associated reliably with any concrete evidences of inferiority does not deter a number of people from nevertheless adhering to such beliefs.

The Situation in the Deep South[5]

In the southern United States a fundamental social cleavage exists between so-called "Negroes" and "White Folks." People in the latter cate-

[5] Based mainly on A. Davis, B. B. Gardner, and M. R. Gardner, 1941:Chaps. 2–9. All patterns refer to the middle 1930's unless otherwise stated. Popular rather than technically precise use is made of the term "Negro." We are tempted to use the word always with quotation marks. "White" is also not used in any racially precise sense.

gory, by and large, possess higher rank, greater power, and an unequal share of other privileges. These advantages place them in relatively favorable positions compared to the quarter of southern population which is Negro. The social organization of the South is oriented toward maintaining this inequality. At the same time, Negroes are aided to secure an increasing share of the goods and services entering the American market. Four main premises, which often remain unstated, justify the South's social structure and the behaviors to which it gives rise.

1. *Negroes are inherently inferior to whites.* Empirical proof of this proposition is not sought. Neither is behavior ignored which appears to substantiate it. However, contradictory behavior is overlooked more readily or rationalized in order to make it agree with the premise. Biologically and mentally the Negro is believed to be inferior; emotionally he is underdeveloped.

2. *The inherent inferiority of the Negro and his subordinate position in society are "the will of God."* Biblical references are sometimes cited to support the structural subordination of Negroes. Also the argument is heard that the races constitute evidence of God's intention that men should not interbreed freely. (Actually this argument commits the normative fallacy by seeking to derive what ought to be from that which is.)

3. *The Negro is an unsocialized being.* He lacks the same restraints and compulsions by which whites regulate their behavior. He is lazy, without ambition, irresponsible, and works only when his needs are immediate. Anecdotes are drawn upon freely to "prove" these generalizations.

4. *The Negro has an inherently childlike nature.* This is another premise supporting the social subordination of Negroes. Conversely, white folks have the responsibility of looking after the childlike and irresponsible Negro.

The subordination of Negroes is supposed to be acknowledged in relations with whites by "respectful yielding" behavior. Titles like "Sir," "Mister," and "Boss" are signs by which Negroes should show respect. Conversely, a white speaker is careful to avoid such titles when addressing Negroes, except in cases where salesmen serve Negro customers. Subordination is expressed when a Negro uses the back door of a non-Negro dwelling. If he goes to the front door he will not mount the steps but stands below the door and reaches forward to knock. Avoidances imposed on whites in southern so-called race relations also symbolize the relative subordination of the Negro. For example, the white man must not offer to shake hands or make any other gesture symbolic of equality, nor may he eat publicly with Negroes.

Physical differences in the South have traditionally limited social interaction, first, by legal provision in southern states enforcing separate jails, schools, and bus accommodations for Negroes. The Supreme Court decision of 1954 rendered school and bus laws unconstitutional. Segregation also is insisted upon in theaters, churches, swimming pools, restaurants, and even on golf courses and in state parks.

Endogamy is a second important factor limiting social access of the races, and also is maintained legally. Sexual intercourse between white women and Negro men is prohibited. Negro men must be careful lest in approaching white women (even prostitutes) they give an impression of sexual interest. Sexual relations between the two categories, of course, occur. They occasionally even take place between Negro men and white women. The latter, however, tend to be "largely isolated from the white group and little affected by the normal social controls" (A. Davis, B. B. Gardner, and M. R. Gardner, 1941:29). Transitory sexual relations between white men and Negro women are a little more common but the men must conduct such affairs with discretion. Any children born of a mixed union are regarded as Negro.

Third, Negroes and whites are divided on the basis of occupation. Where cotton is the dominant crop, as in the Deep South, division of labor often entails a white landowner's employing white or Negro tenants to cultivate a crop in return for a cash rental or a share of the final harvest. The mutual dependence of one category on another, occupationally speaking, is, of course, an important factor for conditioning social solidarity.

Social Class Among Southern Negroes[6]

Prestige categories restrict the social interaction of Negroes with one another in the Deep South. The social classes, as is true in the United States generally, are largely implicit and undefined. Membership rests on factors like the possession of land, occupation, income, education, skin color, hair form, church and associational membership, talent, manners, dress, housing, and furniture. Three main social levels are distinguishable: upper, middle, and low.

The membership of the Merrymount Bridge Club, consisting of 13 single and 3 married women, is upper class. The members or their husbands mostly are engaged in white-collar professions. The women meet to gossip, hear radio programs, play cards, or, in smaller groups, attend the theater. An example of a middle-class association is the Sunny Sixteen Club composed of 16 mostly unmarried men and women. The men work as taxi drivers and the women have known one another since grade or high school. The members play cards, dance, and drink freely. Most of the women are church members but none belongs to sickness and insurance sodalities such as are popular among lower-ranking Negroes. A group of 7 novitiate preachers, who also hold jobs as laborers, illustrates a lower-class group. The men work together in a planing mill. Until they became interested in

6 Based on A. Davis, B. B. Gardner, and M. R. Gardner, 1941:Chap. 10.

preaching they had been "sinners," spending Saturday nights drinking, gambling, or "chasing" women.

Physical Differences in the North[7]

Physical differences in the northern United States are not without significance in regulating social relations, although the barrier there between Negroes and whites is somewhat weaker than in the Deep South. In Chicago, for example, Negroes generally rank lower than whites. The low social rank closely relates to the presence of Negroes in occupations on which whites place low value. It is also related to the fact that in Chicago, too, whites ascribe to Negroes an inferior mentality, deficient moral sense, and certain childlike qualities. There exists, however, a strong feeling that Negroes deserve privileges of which they currently are deprived. The whites who hold this ideal usually are not ready to change their own behavior toward Negroes in order to allow the latter to secure such rights.[8] Social segregation in Chicago is revealed by the fact that Negroes tend to be housed in a separate section of the city, the so-called "black belt." Although Negroes resent job restrictions, they do not oppose residential segregation with the same vigor, demanding only the right to extend their section of the city as is necessary. Many whites remain opposed to this demand. They fear that if Negroes leave the "black belt" for other sections of the city property values will be lowered. Those neighborhoods will become less desirable for white settlement.

Neither Negroes nor whites in Chicago exert pressure for intermarriage. Endogamy nevertheless operates to restrict social interaction, for marriage between the two categories is rare, though not illegal in Illinois. Sex relations between Negroes and whites are not uncommon, the impersonality of the large city making it relatively easy to carry on such affairs despite the fact that each category frowns on them. Why do these relationships not become permanent, since, as is not the case in the South, they are not legally prohibited? Both Negroes and whites disapprove of mixed marriage. Friends put pressure on persons who propose to establish such a relationship. White employers may invoke economic sanctions against a Negro or white employee who violates the informal rule of endogamy. Finally, it might be difficult to find someone qualified to perform the ceremony. Despite these pressures, in 1938 researchers found 188 families which had been founded through Negro-white intermarriage. In 147 the husband was classified as a Negro. Mostly such men belonged to a relatively low social class. The families founded on mixed marriages encountered some serious prob-

[7] Based on Cayton and Drake, 1946. References are to the early 1940's.
[8] The *New York Times*, for example, has led editorial opinion in favor of desegregation and other Negro rights. In 1957 it saw fit not to approve of a municipal bill making it illegal to discriminate on racial grounds in selling or renting real estate.

lems, including the man's inability to hold onto jobs, difficulty in finding a place to live, and ostracism by friends of both parties. The chief reward seems to have been the"moral satisfaction" realized by individuals who regarded intermarriage as a virtue. Children of mixed unions are generally classified as Negro.

As in the Deep South, Negroes in Chicago are stratified into ranked social classes which function to restrict intracategory interaction. Upper-class people serve as models for imitation, and the degree to which their standards are followed determines the respect in which a person is held. One-third of the Negroes in Chicago belong to the middle social class and hold white-collar jobs or perform manual labor. These are ambitious people, marked by a drive to get ahead. About 65 percent of the population falls in the lower class, a category engaged in supplying manual labor and little-esteemed services to whites and other Negroes. Where the middle class avoids "noisy" or "store-front" churches, the lower class tends to prefer associations of that kind. Lower-class folk interact with a minimum of formality. The family frequently is unstable, partly because of employment hazards. Men, unsure of their economic ability, tend to exalt sexual prowess. Illegitimacy is high. Because the general configuration of behavior in the lower class does not conform to upper- and middle-class standards people in the former stratum receive little respect or social acceptance from higher-ranking Negroes.

LADINOS AND INDIANS[9]

Many Central and South American communities contain two major segments of population between which social intercourse is limited. One is called "Ladino" (in some places "Mestizo") and the other, generally the larger, "Indian." In San Luis Jilotepeque, Guatemala, the former category numbers 1100 persons; the latter 2400. The distinction between the two is essentially cultural. In the community as a whole, Ladinos occupy an advantageous position for rewards like prestige, deference, and other satisfactions. Indians occupy a subordinate status. The two strata have been compared to castes, although the relative ease of crossing from the Indian to the Ladino category suggests that the term has to be redefined sharply to fit this situation.

In San Luis people believe that the Indian-Ladino distinction is based at least partly on inherited physical characteristics. Ladinos are supposed to reveal a large trace of their Hispanic origin. Actually, almost everybody who calls himself Ladino has some Indian ancestry. Yet the stereotype of the Ladino describes him as tall, fair-skinned, blond-headed, and blue-

[9] Based on Tumin, 1952. See also Gillin, 1951, who writes of the same community but calls it "San Carlos," and Billig, Gillin, and Davidson, 1947–48.

eyed while the Indian is held to be shorter, darker, dark-eyed, and the possessor of straight dark hair. The assignment of a person to Ladino status is not based primarily on physical appearance. It depends much on characteristics like literacy, schooling, money; physical possessions like land, clothing, and home; and a style of life corresponding to that of other Ladinos. Hence it is possible for an Indian to change his status by changing his culture, although Ladinos are much more reluctant than Indians to admit this possibility. Prescribed rules of social distance and avoidance, enforced mainly by Ladinos, reduce the possibility of much face-to-face contact between the members of these categories. In many contexts Ladinos exclude Indians from group activity. They forbid the marriage of Ladinos to members of the other category and refuse to let Indians eat from the same table, play in the same fields, or share the same public facilities. Each category maintains separate residential locations, mingles in different street-corner gatherings, and attends its own funerals, school celebrations, and dances. Friendships of great depth are not maintained between the categories. Ladinos rationalize these social barriers as "right." They feel that a rise in the social rank of Indians would lower their own social worth.

Although each category follows separate modes of life, members do interact in certain limited situations. These constitute the mortar that maintains the community as an integrated social system. For example, Ladinos often become godparents of Indian children (see p. 438). They carry out the responsibilities of this role quite faithfully. Both sides participate in the annual Independence Day celebration which rededicates the pueblo to the principles of liberty and affirms loyalty to the nation. Division of labor also knits both categories and makes each responsible in part for the survival of the other. Generally more highly skilled tasks, including clerical work and professional services, are in Ladino hands while Indians more frequently perform manual labor for themselves and for Ladinos.

SEGREGATION IN MODERN SOCIETY

The closely guarded borders of modern nations prevent free interchange of people. Crossing frontiers often involves complicated procedures. Permission must be obtained from the individual's own government, in the form of a passport, and from the host government, which visas the passport after scrutinizing the would-be entrant. Nationalistic sentiments discourage closer identification between nations that would probably weaken national frontiers. There is definite resistance to allowing the emergence of "one world." In 1954 the United States threatened to "do something" about a code of behavior which had been prepared by the United Nations. This reportedly advised employees of that organization to place their loyalty to the international organization before that to their country (*New York Times*, Oct. 11, 1954). The formal organization of nations restricts many kinds of international relations to top administrators. The dealings of these men with one another tend to be highly ritualized and unspontaneous, and in large part are designed to maintain each country's independent influence (Annan, 1952).

FUNCTIONAL ANALYSIS OF SOCIAL SEGREGATION

Social segregation may also be considered as it limits diffusion and assimilation, strengthens unity and solidarity, and stimulates antagonisms. These functions are not as applicable to the three universal barriers—age, sex, and kinship—as they are to segregation on the bases of caste, class, and physical differences. We propose to devote special attention to these latter.

Diffusion and Assimilation

When social arrangements limit the access of people to one another and reduce communication they also limit the diffusion of culture. Women do not share precisely the same values as men, the tastes of social classes diverge, and Negroes retain distinctive attitudes that cut them off from whites (G. Simpson, 1954:68). Such cultural differences, especially when they are made emblematic of category membership, in turn reinforce restrictions on social relations. It is not that reduced social interaction absolutely prevents diffusion and so forestalls cultural assimilation; diffusion does occur, but its rate is slowed down.

Unity and Synergy

As long as the segregation of people by age, sex, kinship, caste, or on any other basis is accepted by all parties, the process of segregation itself offers evidence of a shared social value. When people share a value, it was pointed out, a basis exists for their unity. Not all social segregation meets with social approval. One category may find segregation intolerable. The resentment thus generated constitutes a force which tends to weaken overall social solidarity. On the other hand, even a detested form of social segregation may be associated with occupational division of labor. The categories involved will then be dependent on one another for the satisfaction of wants. This promotes a degree of organic solidarity that counteracts the centrifugal forces at work.

Social segregation, unless equivalent to social separation, always is associated with some degree of synergy. This concept denotes the working together of the separate categories (or, for that matter, of segmental groups) in a society. Each contributes to the adaptation and adjustment of the others.[10] Each segment is rewarded, either economically or in the form of prestige, for the role it plays in the whole interdependent social system. Let culture change devaluate or render useless the service and goods supplied by one of these segments, and the system seriously weakens. Independent nations recognize the value of synergy in time of crisis. They are willing to abandon large measures of sovereignty in order to work together in defense against external aggression. When the danger is passed the unity of the larger group dissipates as segregation tends toward relative social separation (cf. Great Britain, 1951:32). Social synergy is always a matter of degree and may be high or low.

Antagonism

Three conditions favor the rise of antagonism in a situation of social segregation (Lewin, 1948:89): (1) Social segregation is perceived as a threat to the adaptation and adjustment of the members of one or both parties. (2) Attempts to alleviate stress engendered in the situation are frustrated. (3) Flight from a no longer tolerable situation is blocked, either through the cost of social separation or because it is physically impossible.

Barriers to social interaction are especially likely to generate hostility when deprivation and frustration are perceived to follow from them. Rebellion of youth against its adult mentors is a case in point. So are accusations of witchcraft made between two co-wives in a polygynous household. Each of the women is anxious to maximize the advantages of her own children. The existence of one woman's nuclear family is perceived (whether erroneously or not hardly matters) to threaten the well-being of the other group. A boycott instituted by an Indian caste in order to protect its interests, and "racial" boycotts designed to bring about an end to no longer tolerable discrimination are examples of antagonism involving larger numbers.

The absence of overt signs of hostility in a society divided by national boundaries or barriers of caste, class, and physical differences does not mean that people who are disadvantaged by the state of affairs accept the social arrangements. Between people who do not come into regular primary interaction, or who have tenuous relations, conflict tends to remain submerged. As a consequence, opposition itself fails to step up their interaction and bring it to a point where each side could attempt with the aid of the other to rectify difficulties involved (see pp. 465–466). Under such a condition the social cleavage is maintained quite effectively (Coser, 1956:81–85).

---

[10] The concept of synergy is derived from Ruth Benedict's unpublished lectures.

28.

Equilibrium in Social Relations

THE last few chapters have described some forms of social organization. The approach has emphasized form, the morphology of groups rather than the dynamics of their operation. In this and the next three chapters we turn to dynamics. How do groups (and the community as a whole) maintain themselves and continue successfully to carry out the functions for which they are formally or informally organized?[1] Primarily the question applies only to relatively permanent groups like the village, business organization, or nation. The very stability of such organized aggregates suggests that the members are able to maintain more or less intact interaction despite fatigue, illness, death, disputes, strikes, civil wars, and national disasters. Transitory groups are less concerned with the problem of maintaining continuity.

To understand the process by which social stability is maintained some social analysts have found the concept of equilibrium useful. From what sources does social disequilibrium arise? What socially standardized procedures are available for maintaining equilibrium or restoring it after a crisis?

THE EQUILIBRIUM CONCEPT

It is possible to speak of a group as maintaining or losing states of relatively stable equilibrium. Equilibrium exists when, despite internal changes of personnel and activities and in spite of the impingement of external changes on the group, relationships making up the system remain on an even keel. Relative constancy of the group's interaction patterns keynotes equilibrium (Easton, 1956:98). A disturbance in customary interaction, promoted, for example, by the death of a member, indicates disequilibrium. Disturbances of one sort or another are always impinging on group life. Hence it is impossible to speak of any group's ever attaining perfect equilibrium. Although it is useful to assume, and convenient to

[1] When the word "group" is used from now on the reader will keep in mind that an organization, association, village, band, tribe, and empire are all groups. Any one of these may be the community selected for anthropological inquiry (see pp. 16–17). Hence group and community will tend to be used synonymously.

talk about, social equilibrium which exists at a given moment of time, in actuality the state is always being approached or lost.

Relatively stable equilibrium may be recognized from a psychological point of view. A group possesses equilibrium when the members are individually in states of relative adjustment (that is, not disturbed by anxieties, incapacitated, or distracted) and when the members are adjusted to each other harmoniously. Interpersonal relations mesh when a group is in equilibrium. From a more social perspective, a group reveals equilibrium when, following a disturbance or interruption, the members show a tendency to return to what they were doing before. The tendency to return to a previous state of equilibrium often is revealed by a reluctance to leave that state at all. The group tends to avoid change. ". . . Whenever a group of employees in an industrial organization develops a more-or-less successful pattern of adjustment and way of behaving with reference to each other and to things that happen to them in the workplace, they tend to resist changes which will affect these patterns" (Gardner and Moore, 1950:9).

Problems in Equilibrium Theory

A common objection to the use of equilibrium theory cites the fact that social life is so complex, the interrelated variables (people, environment, techniques, artifacts) are so numerous, and change is so omnipresent that it is most transparent nonsense to talk as if a group could ever be in a stable state. An oil burner governed by a thermostat, a steam engine, and even the human body may maintain stable equilibria automatically (the body by homeostasis), but a similar concept is not applicable to groups. This objection has already been anticipated in what was written above. True, social equilibria are never perfect or stable. Rather they constantly are being jeopardized and upset. It need not even be assumed that groups ever reach equilibrium, but only that they try to maximize or approach it (Easton, 1956:100). Man has not yet learned to engineer his social relations in the same expert way that he can design steam engines and much more complicated "thinking" machines.

More serious difficulty arises when social equilibrium, in no matter what degree, is assigned positive value. One then speaks of arrangements that provide equilibrium as good while factors that destroy it are bad. That such a subjective conception of equilibrium won't work is apparent when factors like seasonal change and the cycle of night and day are regarded as disturbances which promote disequilibrium regularly. It makes no sense to call such cycles good or bad. Nor is it easy to prove objectively that a group in relative equilibrium is better off than one in disequilibrium. Subjectively, of course, people may prefer stable social relations. But some readers might also extol the disequilibrium of revolution that promotes intellectual ferment and certain types of social change. Such subjective connotations are not part of the concept as it is treated in these pages. One must avoid "grafting on to the notion of 'equilibrium' certain normative, certain moral layers of meaning. Whatever conduces to the social equilibrium is desirable and right: whatever tends to disturb it is pernicious and wrong" (Wollheim, 1952). This conception makes stability "right" and change, a universal in society, "wrong." Equilibrium theory cannot be used objectively to defend any cultural system or to argue against peaceful or violent revolution.

SOURCES OF DISEQUILIBRIUM

For convenience the sources of disequilibrium may be sorted in three relatively distinct categories: (1) general sources, (2) uncomplementary diversity, and (3) opposition.

General Sources

1. **Social Circulation.** Equilibrium in social relations is being disturbed constantly by social circulation—the loss from, and entry into, groups. Death constitutes such a disturbance, the extent of the disturbance depending on the range of the deceased member's social influence. For example, the death of an infant is not perceptibly upsetting to the equilibrium of a nation and scarcely provides a crisis in a community where high infant mortality is expected. But the death of a president or king, whose direct, indirect, and mediated interaction may have involved millions of subjects, normally is profoundly troubling. The entry of newcomers into a group is disturbing to the extent that their strangeness or inexperience becomes noticeable and interferes with the normal course of activities. The birth of a child, the new employee who joins the shipping room, and the incorporation of several hundred immigrants all interfere with customary activities in the family, factory, local group, and nation. Rituals are important devices for restoring equilibrium in those situations (see pp. 512–513).

2. **Geographical Factors.** Many disturbances arise from geographical environment. Among the most dramatic are storms, earthquakes, and extreme heat and cold. About some such threats little can be done, even in technically highly developed communities. However, the ability to predict a hurricane and other severe forms of weather does allow some preparatory action which helps to reduce the severity or duration of the inevitable disequilibrium. Also originating in the environment are cyclical events like the passage from day to night and from one season to another. Human relations in a modern factory are little disturbed by such alterations. The building is lighted, heated, and insulated from weather. But in communities that live "close to nature" night introduces profound modifica-

tions into social relationships: the family assembles in the house and co-operative work groups break up when it gets too dark to see. Seasonal changes, too, mean technical and social changes. The Eskimo in autumn move to new camps by the sea to hunt through the ice. They establish new rhythms in social interaction. The stormy season in the Pacific keeps fisher-men in the village, where a larger group, therefore, comes to be in active interaction. The poor supply of food in certain seasons among people living close to subsistence levels may intensify anxiety and social hostility.

3. Organismic Factors. Another general source of disequilibrium lies in the rhythms of the human body. Fatigue, for example, disturbs group processes and is followed by an interruption designed for rest. Thereafter, the group may resume. Where menstruation is regarded as dangerous, a woman's menstrual period means that the family must find a new basis of adjustment while she is isolated. Old age may disturb equilibrium in family and village—for example, by reducing the number of food getters. In communities where no compensations are allowed for growing old the oldster may express frustration through aggression, or, what is as real, others may fear that he is hostile and a sorcerer. Illness and accidents underlie absenteeism and incapacity, or otherwise interfere with a person's ability to adjust harmoniously to others, and so contribute to disequilib-rium.

4. Intergroup Relations. Other groups in a society are a potential source of disequilibrium in a particular group. Disturbance may be promoted in at least two ways: (1) Other organizations may be perceived to threaten the group's stability, independence, or tenure. For example, a change in national policy may threaten the operation of certain business establish-ments or labor unions; one nation may threaten another with invasion, punitive action, or underselling in the international market, or a gangster group may extort money from a business. (2) Disequilibrium existing in one group may infect other organizations. Perhaps membership between the two systems is overlapping, so that a man brings his anger from factory to home, a child his anxiety from home to school. The home or school then becomes subject to disequilibrium as the person, unadjusted to himself, disturbs others. Or disequilibrium in a specialized group may interfere with that unit's interdependence with other organizations whose operations are blocked. Labor troubles in a plant, leading to a strike, halt the flow of goods. Other plants dependent on those products must find new sources of supply or continue in serious disequilibrium.

Disequilibrium in a single group may be assumed always to indicate dis-equilibrium in the community as a whole. This, it will be assumed, also radiates into the rest of the society. These assumptions may be held even though the disequilibrium is too slight to perceive outside of the specific group. Generally speaking, the greater the number of groups involved in disequilibrium, the more disturbed will be the stability of the community and society. Hence a perceptible crisis in community life usually means that a number of constituent groups are experiencing persistent and severe disturbances in interpersonal relationships.

General sources of disequilibrium are universal. Those which are not demographic or biological but arise primarily from geographical components of the cultural field are dealt with technically: by building sound houses, developing lighting and heating, or through predicting. Illness, too, in some measure is controlled or eliminated technically by medication and surgery. Little more will be said about technical resources for controlling disequilibrium except that the provision of these is an important administrative responsibility. Socially derived instability (see the next two major sources of disequilibrium) cannot very well be dealt with technologically. Its control involves other measures, to be examined in the next three chapters.

Uncomplementary Diversity

Social interaction, the basis of group organization, is possible as long as the interacting parties are dissimilar enough to find something useful in their relationship (see pp. 355–356). Differences draw people into relationship, but the differences must not be too extreme (Hobhouse, 1924:68–69; G. Wilson and M. Wilson, 1945:48). Complementary diversities induce storekeeper and customer, lawyer and client, administrator and subject, student and teacher, man and woman, or parent and child to interact. On the other hand, a storekeeper who carried goods utterly unrelated to the tastes of his community would hardly draw customers. "Only certain kinds of differences attract each other. . . . They are those which . . . complement each other" (Durkheim, 1933:55). Uncomplementary diversities, in distinction to complementary diversities, are not valued. They are revealed in behavior like failing to coöperate, not coöperating properly, failing to communicate in approved form, or otherwise coming into contradiction with established norms. To the degree that uncomplementary diversities are perceived and noted, they disturb the equilibrium of groups in which they occur. Measures exist in every community to regulate uncomplementary diversity, either by punishing the deviant or by coaxing him back into the area of broad uniformity. We call such measures social pressure (Chapter 30).

Other common examples of uncomplementary diversities include failure to report for an activity or not doing so at the appointed time, inability to execute a task in a skilled fashion, not providing for foreseeable eventualities likely to promote disequilibrium, taking goods belonging to another in an unapproved fashion, and using unauthorized force against others. Sorcery and witchcraft are examples of unauthorized violence, provided the acts are recognized as potentially dangerous. Failure to live up to expected standards; not sharing certain tastes or values; administering authorized punishment in unapproved fashion; engaging in sexual relations with persons excluded from such relationships by virtue of kinship; engaging in sexual acts too early, prior to initiation, or in unapproved fashion; using words outside of approved limits of tolerance; spelling in untraditional fashion; and not abiding by building, driving, and sanitation codes are other examples of uncomplementary behavior. For present purposes the chief significance of such acts is that they pose a threat to the relative stability of human relationships. They upset the harmonious working together of people.

Opposition[2]

Opposition, or conflict, is as fundamental a fact in social interaction as coöperation and collaboration. The culture of any group or community includes measures not only for promoting harmonious social interaction but also for resolving opposition.

Opposition may be the very basis for social organization. For example, many tribes are divided into two rival factions between whom regulated opposition in sports or for office, boasting, and aggression are the order of the day. A village in Latin America is frequently separated into *barrios* between which conflict is expected. Each segment conceives of itself as a tightly knit unit opposed to other units of the same type, yet as belonging to the same village. Without village organization as a framework *barrio* rivalry would have little meaning. Rivalry between the factions probably functions as a safety valve for the safe discharge of aggression generated through group living. It prevents hostility from flaring into uncontrolled violence that might destroy the overall system of organization (Murdock, 1949:90). In other ways, too, opposition takes its place, along with complementary diversity and division of labor (the latter really a form of complementary diversity), as a device which maintains social organization. Opposition between groups functions to help set the boundaries of each group for members. By focusing the attention of members on their organization it contributes to social solidarity.[3] Conflict between groups may signal a state of acute disturbance in the larger community, attention to which is urgently required if social continuity is to be insured. Intergroup conflict gives each group more to do. Hence, functionally speaking, it binds internal relations in such groups more tightly. At the same time it helps to maintain intergroup relations, even if these are in a certain sense

[2] The following section draws much from G. Wilson and M. Wilson, 1945:Chap. 5; and Simmel, 1955.
[3] The balance of this paragraph follows Coser, 1956:Chap. 2. See also Gluckman, 1954a and 1954b.

Opposition May Be the Basis for Social Organization as in the Case of a Group Assembling to Play a Team Game (courtesy, U.S. Air Force).

negative. Other types of relations, in addition to those based on conflict, are likely to follow between those groups. Finally, opposition contributes to tighter social organization because it calls for allies. Alliances bring otherwise loosely related people into tighter social interaction.

Of course, social organization is not encouraged sheerly through opposition. There must also be a measure of basic agreement underlying the conflict. Often this is present. Democrats and Republicans in the United States almost constantly relate to one another in the form of opposition. The intensity of conflict between the parties mounts during election time, especially in a presidential election year. But their opposition rests on some very basic agreements concerning the American form of government, the value of political parties, the style in which a political campaign should be conducted, and a willingness to let a majority or plurality periodically decide the outcome to the conflict. To the extent that agreement over such basic values vanishes and conflict takes place over the basic issues themselves, the community passes from ordinary to radical opposition.

1. **Ordinary Opposition.** Ordinary oppositions occur in particular relationships: between butcher and customer over quality and price; Democrat and Republican over who will hold office; defense and prosecuting

attorneys over which evidence the judge should accept and the jury believe; or between rivals for a girl or in a sports match or chess game. Such opposition hardly threatens equilibrium. It is *expected* to occur and its resolution is achieved quite easily within the framework of rules, laws, and traditions of the community. The course of the conflict is governed by rules and each opponent is willing to see the issue resolved in the framework provided. The normally great capacity of a community to resolve ordinary oppositions should not be surprising. The group expects certain oppositions to arise. It cannot very well carry on its culture without them. The solution of ordinary opposition sometimes requires one of the opponents to quit the group in order to realize his ambition in a new set of social relationships, but this kind of solution is rare.

It is easy to see how certain kinds of ordinary opposition by their regular occurrence strengthen the bonds of social solidarity. Competitions, especially when they are phrased as being for prizes rather than directed toward the elimination of rivals, fall in this category. The ideal (i.e., prize) for which the individuals or groups compete—office, honor, or title—constitutes a value for all the parties and links them despite opposition over which one will attain the goal first (Simmel, 1955:60). In the same way candidates who compete for the position of heading a group or directing in a ceremony testify to the importance of that group or ceremony. They show dramatically that the goal indeed has great social value. This common profession of faith unites the opponents as well as the people who must choose between them.

2. Radical Opposition. The situation is very different with respect to the kind of opposition that is radical (i.e., basic). Radical opposition always is profoundly painful and destructive to equilibrium whatever other general functions it may have. Radical conflict does not occur independently in particular social relationships but is general—permeating nearly all relationships in the group or community. It implies a disagreement over the very values, rules, or premises on which depends the solution of ordinary oppositions. Whereas an ordinary dispute can be resolved by appealing to a jury in prescribed form and accepting that body's unanimous verdict honestly arrived at, radical opposition challenges the rules of evidence, the conventions of courtroom procedure, and even the jury system itself. Ordinary opposition occurs and is ended within a framework of central norms and agreements. Therefore it intensifies the value placed on those norms. The other kind of conflict implies a fundamental disagreement over the central norms (Coser, 1956:73–75). It presses toward a basic change.

It is quite apparent now why basic opposition is difficult to resolve. The very rules or values by which disputes are ordinarily ended are challenged. Neither side wants to give ground or accept the values of the other; so the disequilibrium persists, involving more and more groups. Often, if not always, the same individual supports the conflicting ideas or values. Hence radical opposition may be called "muddled." "Men are divided against themselves as well as against their neighbours" (G. Wilson and M. Wilson, 1945:127). The following example (*ibid.*, p. 126) illustrates radical opposition quite well.

The Nyakyusa . . . lay great emphasis on hospitality. Entertaining his friends is an obligation of a rich man enforced on him not only by conventional pressure—the stingy man loses prestige—but also by fear of witchcraft, "the breath of men," legitimately used by his cheated neighbours. Hospitality is dependent upon polygyny, for only by the labour of more than one wife can a household grow and prepare enough food to entertain well. Christians are thus in a dilemma. They value both monogamy and hospitality. If a Christian take a second wife he is suspended from membership of the Church, probably lives in fear of hell fire, and is ashamed before Christians and pagans alike, for the conflict is not only between Christian and pagan, but within the Christian group itself. If he is inhospitable he is both afraid of witchcraft and again ashamed. Often we saw Christian wives struggling to get through more work than they could manage, in order to entertain as they wished to do. The opposition can only be resolved by social change, economic or religious. Either there must be greater division of labour so that the well-to-do may buy some of their food, more provision of water in the villages, mechanized milling to replace the laborious hand grinding, and the employment of servants; or, on the other hand, the abandonment either of hospitality, or of monogamy.

Yet the Nyakyusa, like most other people who are involved in radical opposition, cannot perceive the internal contradiction of values. They move in largely blind fashion toward trying to resolve a dilemma which they do not understand.

Seventeenth-century England, in which Parliament challenged the authority of kingship, was a period of intense radical opposition (Ashley, 1952:Chap. 4). The opposition over royal power was only one instance of a more basic disagreement between rationalism and traditionalism. In modern Pakistan radical opposition expresses itself in questions like whether a man has the legal right to marry as many as four wives or whether permission to espouse more than one woman has to be secured from a special court. (Actually the overwhelming proportion of married men in that country never take more than a single wife at a time, but that has little bearing on the conflict.) Radical opposition is also expressed in Pakistan in the question whether divorce can occur simply at will or must be secured from a tribunal. Underlying these questions is the opposition over which brand of Islam shall prevail. Traditionalist Muslims deny that customs supported by scripture can be altered through man-made law. Polygyny and the free right to divorce are held to be scripturally sanctioned customs. They are rights which must never be abused or used licentiously and derive directly from God. Reformist Muslims, on the other hand, continue to accept Islam as the true religion but affirm that Parliament may create new, legally enforceable norms and render illegal those that have become obsolete. Some customs may have been appropriate in the past—that is, in a different context of culture—but are not applicable in the modern world. So say the reformists (Honigmann, 1956c). The division of Europe after the Reformation between Catholics and Protestants exemplifies a closely parallel situation of radical opposition. In Pakistan as in Reformation Europe radical opposition promotes a search for ideological innovations through which the basic contradiction will be resolved (Hazard, 1953:217–255).

Radical opposition exists in modern international society, for example, in the issue over nationalism versus internationalism. The great powers— America, England, Russia, France—are quite muddled in their official attitude toward internationalism. First of all, each values being able to control its international relations one-sidedly in order to protect military and economic security. Each seeks to maintain bases, often in colonial territories, and to influence other nations in its orbit. In other words, these countries value a certain type of internationalism; isolation is scarcely conceivable in the modern world. On the other hand, though, the same countries that try to control other nations strenuously resist being brought under any form of international authority that would openly and directly limit sovereignty. This attitude is in contradiction to their attempt to subordinate other sovereign powers in international relations. Let us look at another aspect of the conflict. These countries value self-determination and resist truly international power in their affairs. Yet they contradictorily strive in some measure to control other people whose inclination also is to achieve greater independence or sovereignty. The great powers claim self-determination to be of value at the same time that they delay the goal for colonial possessions. Contradictions are also seen in the way foreign trade and military security press toward some kind of international authority with teeth. At the same time traditional values of self-determination, nationalism, and sovereignty motivate resistance to the adoption of international law.

Communities differ in their capacity to tolerate radical opposition. Totalitarian nations (see pp. 486–487) choke it off sharply (Leites and Bernaut, 1954:60–72; Stahl, 1951:105). Perhaps a community with a long range of historical awareness is able better to resist and limit radical opposition than one with a shorter remembered past. Anyway, heterogeneous modern nations often appeal to the past for a common ground of agreement, and dead heroes of the past, on whom many parties agree, are reverenced publicly (Durkheim, 1933:291). Other things being equal, a larger and more complexly organized group may be in a better position to withstand radical opposition, and to effect compromises, than a small, primary group. For one thing, in a large group everybody cannot interact with everybody else; social segregation limits somewhat the generality of the basic dispute. Small groups cannot tolerate the interpersonal and intrapersonal stress which the radical conflict brings about; hence they tend to dissolve readily under radical opposition.

3. Complex Opposition. Radical opposition is difficult to recognize because rarely does it manifest itself as an open dispute over abstract principles, norms, or the direction of change. Its painful manifestation appears in the form of many ordinary oppositions that beset everyday life. Radical opposition increases the frequency of uncomplementary diversities and breaches of norms. It weakens the mechanisms of social pressure (see Chapter 30) which help to maintain equilibrium by checking uncomplementary differences. Ordinary oppositions which are underlain by radical opposition, and the solution of which then comes to press for changes in rules and basic values, are called complex oppositions. "To the people concerned it seems to be just an ordinary opposition of unusual difficulty, in no way necessarily connected with the other oppositions of the society" (G. Wilson and M. Wilson, 1945:129). The analyst, however, is able to perceive the underlying radical dispute and the way it is linked with other complex oppositions in social life.

Radical Opposition and Scale[4]

Radical opposition and the profound disequilibrium which it promotes reflect uneven culture change: a new idea has not been reinterpreted to accord with traditional concepts; traditional values have not become adjusted to new behavior patterns; or behavior has failed to keep pace with possibilities opened up through new techniques and artifacts. The airplane, cable, radio, and fast water transport have intensified the interdependence of communities in the modern world. However, values of sovereignty, nationalism, and prejudice against new forms of organization hang on. Radical opposition also is rooted in uneven *social* change. Some people in the community have changed faster than others, bringing divergent value systems into conflict. At the same time each party in opposition feels itself attracted to certain advantages perceived to be contained in the other's position. Radical opposition, remember, is muddled.

Uneven social scale is implied in radical opposition. Some people in the group or community are larger in scale than others. The ideas of the large-scale set are in conflict with those of the small-scale one. India under British rule came into active contact with western customs and artifacts. Some of these proved to be acceptable to orthodox and unorthodox Muslims alike and have been incorporated into the contemporary Paki-

[4] From G. Wilson and M. Wilson, 1945:132–136.

stani way of life. Other ideas, the acceptance of which also implies an endorsement of foreign values and, therefore, more intensive societal participation, are at least partly acceptable to nontraditionalist Muslims in modern Pakistan but are rejected by the orthodox. In rejecting the right of Parliament to make laws regulating marriage and divorce the orthodox element comes into conflict with those members of the community who more intensely accept western values and procedures. So, too, the use of modern methods of transportation and communication forces modern nations to intensify their relationships with other countries. This technological pressure is counteracted by nationalistic sentiments that seek to limit the intensity of participation in international society.

The resolution of radical opposition and the disequilibrium to which it gives rise may come, first, through an increase in scale on the part of the narrower-scale elements. Pakistan's orthodox scholars might come to see value in more western-derived customs; modern nations might give up a greater part of their demand for sovereignty in a world tightly linked by machines, trade, and the need for military security. Second, resolution of the disequilibrium promoted by radical opposition can be achieved by a decrease of the wide-scale elements so that they more closely match the narrower. The western-educated elite in Pakistan could give up the doctrine of Parliamentary sovereignty. This second alternative is very difficult because many people (but by no means everyone), however irresolutely, tend to value certain correlates of scale, like development and variety. Finally, resolution may be achieved by a reduction or breaking off of interaction between the parties in opposition. Social fragmentation may occur. This is possible when clear-cut parties or regions are quite firmly committed to different positions. Social fragmentation occurred in the Hopi village of Oraibi when part of that American Indian pueblo moved away to live by itself (L. Thompson, 1950:36). Social fragmentation, which always involves a reduction of scale and hence invites the correlates of smaller scale, may be resisted strenuously. The American Civil War was fought to prevent social fragmentation growing out of the complex opposition over the question of slavery.

In brief, disequilibrium springing from radical opposition can be dissolved through some kind of change. Administrators in a group may try to promote such changes. Primarily, however, the successful end of radical opposition demands innovation—perhaps an ideological origination or borrowing able to bridge the opposing viewpoints. A concrescent position which will override and incorporate conflicting values is called for. Innovations capable of fully satisfying opposed positions in a situation of radical conflict are not come by easily. Having been found, they often are difficult to implement. Hence radical opposition tends to persist while the group or community seeks to protect itself from the full force of disequilibrium by coping with the complex oppositions which are being instigated constantly.

PROCESSES FOR MAINTAINING AND RESTORING EQUILIBRIUM

Every culture includes procedures whose function, at least in part, is to maintain relatively stable equilibrium or to restore a steady state following a crisis. Common processes of this sort, to be examined in the next three chapters, are administration, social pressure (including law and logic), and ritual. Collectively all the processes may be referred to as means of social control (Dahl and Lindblom, 1953:Chap. 4). It cannot be expected that these processes are perfectly efficient in promoting equilibrium. All groups constantly face problems which they cannot manage skillfully, or, perhaps, which people intentionally or unintentionally neglect. Sometimes the very attempt to maintain equilibrium creates fresh, unanticipated problems, as when administrators, seeking to protect a nation from external threat, create stress in the members of other nations.

In any community the maintenance and restoration of equilibrium may be regarded as analogous to negative feedback in certain machines (Sluckin, 1954). Toward the end of the eighteenth century James Watt invented a governor for the steam engine. A momentary increase in the engine's speed produces a reduction of steam flow and so slows down the machine. The same principle is illustrated in the thermostat. An increase in room temperature produces a reduction in heat supply. Temperature tends to remain constant. Analogously one may think of a group as responding in ways that maintain a steady state when members depart from socially standardized norms. But, as already stated, groups are not as efficient as machines, which can maintain a perfectly steady state. On the other hand, an organization is far more original in devising specific means appropriate for dealing with different sources of disequilibrium.

29.

Administration

ADMINISTRATION (i.e., leadership) refers both to a process and to a position, the leader or the policy-making groups, within an organization. From the standpoint of process, administration means making decisions, planning for their execution, disseminating the plans, and, finally, controlling their implementation (Litchfield, 1956; Easton, 1953:131). Occupying administrative positions are kings; chiefs; policy-making bodies, like Congress; top executives of industrial organizations; deans; parents in the family; club presidents and other officers; the commanding officer of an Air Force squadron; his wing commander; the village headman in Africa; the war chief of a Plains Indian military expedition—in short, anyone who makes decisions and follows through on their execution. In some small groups the leader is recognized readily. He is the person who most frequently initiates action to others in group events. That is, he habitually tells groups of people what to do. In a large group, however, the top leaders neither make nor disseminate decisions personally. Rather they are advised by staffs and delegate to lieutenants the power to give orders (Chapple and Coon, 1942:281–283, 330 ff.; Dahl and Lindblom, 1953:230). The top administrators are, however, kept informed concerning the outcome of the administrative process for which they hold primary responsibility.

In what follows the term "administration" will be used both for the process of decision making and to designate those individuals in an organization who work together at all stages to execute that process. Collectively they constitute the administration. The term "administrator" will be used to refer to an individual with clear-cut responsibility for policy matters. Administrators can thus be distinguished from staff members of an administration who assist the top leader.

FUNCTIONS OF ADMINISTRATION

People engaged in administration may be activated by many goals, like job security, high salary, love of power, or the expansion of the organization which they control. These purposes need not be identical with

473

the way an administrative process objectively functions. With respect to equilibrium, the function of administration is to maintain group functioning and to insure realization of the instrumental or other ends for which the organization exists. Groups of whatever sort "embody interests, which demand that leadership take heed of present doubts and future threats" (Selznick, 1949:82). Of course, the sense of responsibility is not evenly distributed among administrators nor are all leaders equally capable of protecting organizational stability. But with these considerations, however serious they may be, this section will not be concerned.

An administration's role in maintaining or restoring equilibrium is manifested in the way it manages to coördinate group activity to further the mutual satisfactions of the members. Various departments of a factory are coördinated in order to maintain a constant (or increasing) rate of production which will allow workers, managers, and investors to obtain their rewards. Among the Nupe of Nigeria the village headman and his council of elders see to it that each family has access to land for cultivation, sites for fishing, and trees (Nadel, 1942:56). The headman also makes sure that certain important ceremonies are performed regularly by the group. Among these same people the head of an extended family organizes the coöperative work of the family members. He stores the grain and supplies tools, housing, and clothing to his sons and their wives (ibid., p. 246). In northern Ghana among the Tallensi, the husband heads the polygynous composite family and organizes the work of his wives, between whom he strives to preserve harmonious relations (Fortes, 1949:126–134). In much the same way the United States Air Force wing commander coördinates the work of the wing's component squadrons and a baseball team manager organizes his players.

The administrator often carries out equilibrium-preserving functions by controlling certain forms of negative pressure through which wrongdoers are brought back into line or punished (see Chapter 30). Toward the end of maintaining suitable behavior the leader likewise uses positive sanctions. Among the Siuai, a people of the Solomon Islands, a man who has won renown becomes a leader or *mumi*. Such a man is a powerful factor in organizing public opinion against wrongdoers. He is also active in expressing anger and censure (Oliver, 1955:443–444).

The leader anticipates future disturbances to equilibrium. Among the Siuai a leader who learns that a man from his neighborhood is planning to marry a girl of loose morals becomes fearful of the trouble she may bring. He tries to dissuade his follower from the marriage. In the same spirit he urges a man to divorce a troublesome wife (Oliver, 1955:443–444). Of course, no leader can predict all crises successfully. Sometimes, despite the most intelligent leadership, breakdowns do occur, disaster strikes, or disequilibrium ensues from circumstances like death or illness. The administrator then proceeds, if possible, to reorganize the group. Should crops have been destroyed in a storm, he directs the members to new resources, encourages replanting, or arranges for an outside loan of food. If death or other loss depletes the group the leader may reallocate duties. Perhaps the disaster is discovered to have been preventable. The administrator will then insure that the new knowledge be applied in the future to prevent occurrences of the same sort.

As the Nupe example cited above indicates, an administrator may oversee the scheduling of certain ceremonies. The Siuai leader organizes feasts. The relationship of ceremonies to equilibrium will be explored below (Chapter 31).

The entrance of new members into a group or community is controlled by administrative decision. The policy may be to admit only qualified workers or immigrants or only congenial members who will not threaten the relationships built up in the group. Members are selected who will not interfere through ineptness with the instrumental goals of the organization or with the pleasure found in mutual association. In the modern world questions regarding "personality" and "ability to get along with others" appear on many application forms. They indicate how formal may be the screening of prospective members before admitting them into the group.

One of the revolutionary developments in western nations has been the trend toward equalizing wealth and providing for the welfare of the relatively poor. These are new administrative responsibilities. Implementing Great Britain's welfare policy means that "about a third of the money raised by taxes is simply taken from one set of citizens in order to be passed on to another . . ." (Lafitte, 1956:545). The transfer is organized by the government with the function of reducing disequilibrium arising from poverty, ill health, or envy and forestalling social movements, like Communism, which promise even more revolutionary change. The widely expanded area of administrative control in the modern world contrasts sharply with the circumscribed duties of chiefs and headmen in the exotic communities often studied by anthropologists. Large numbers of people to be coördinated at home, extensive foreign relations, rapid change, and the displacement of many traditionally sanctioned, automatic modes of behavior—all earmarks of largeness of scale—have helped to swell the chances that disequilibrium will occur in western nations. Even during time of peace, crises of one sort or another occur constantly. Equilibrium, therefore, is far less stable than in a homogeneous community. It is not surprising that modern national governments have tended to embrace ever larger areas of behavior, a move that eventually culminates in totalitarianism (see p. 486; cf. Sorokin, 1947:466, 501).

Administration and Disequilibrium

While an important function of leadership is to maintain or restore equilibrium, experience indicates that relations between administrators and their subordinates may also be accompanied by persistent and severe disequilibrium.

Often disequilibrium in administrative relations is expressed in the form of "boss anxiety." Subordinates worry about the supervisor's opinion. They fear lest he use his power to curtail some of their satisfactions. An arbitrary, inconsistent, cruel, or psychopathological leader especially is likely to inspire fear in the organization he controls. Failure to plan judiciously, in good time, or comprehensively also invites crises that spell disequilibrium. Communication blocks in an organization, such as prevent the upward flow of information on which corrective administrative action might be based, readily lead to trouble. The information that fails to reach the leadership is withheld because it is unpleasant and might bring reproval from those in control. Free flow of communication to an administrator is not as essential as selection of information adequate for the needs of the administrative process. Inadequate selection can be the source of much stress (Jaques, 1951:302).

Where the leader espouses attitudes that are not traditional he may generate divisions where formerly there was consensus. This happened in Afghanistan in 1924 when the king, Amanullah, seeking to make the country more powerful in international affairs, introduced a series of "ultra-modern reforms" (Shah, 1938:138). His own wife traveled abroad unveiled and he sought to abolish *purdah* in general in favor of European dress. He taunted the Muslim scholars and tried to promote schools for girls. These things made him unpopular with a large section of the people and helped to instigate a successful rebellion. Amanullah altered his policies and finally renounced the throne. The case illustrates that even an absolute ruler who fails to live up to group norms "undermines his social rank and hence the presumption that his orders are to be obeyed" (Homans, 1950:426).

AUTHORITY AND POWER

Authority and power (i.e., coercion) are qualities that administrations possess in varying degree. During the twenties, thirties, and forties in India the British government possessed a considerable measure of power but a far smaller degree of legitimate authority in Indian eyes. A Catholic missionary backed by great authority holds little coercive power among Eskimo. Of course, everybody in a social organization possesses some power, the degree depending on his status and experience. A child who successfully appeals for candy has evidenced his power; an expert witness testifying at a trial or hearing may be in a powerful position for helping or convicting the defendant. However, in what follows reference will be not to such forms of power but to coercive power, that is, physical force.

Authority

An administrator possesses authority when the decisions he makes and executes are legitimate in the eyes of the organization in which he acts. He himself is acknowledged to occupy the status of leader and, therefore, expects to be obeyed. People obey him because it is the right thing to do (Simon, 1951). In more complex situations the group may be divided over the authority of an administrator, or over the area in which he can successfully claim authority. A conqueror, for example, may not be recognized by the conquered people for the authority that his own followers claim him to possess.

"Every form of leadership or government claims to be legitimate, but it cannot function unless its legitimacy is accepted" (G. D. Mitchell, 1952: 94). Whence does authority derive? Basically it emanates from the explicit or implicit consent of a group to follow a particular administration and to accept its policies because morally they are justified. The means by which an administration exerts, dramatizes, and reinforces its claim to authority vary considerably from one culture to another. Among the Siuai every prominent man is a leader in his neighborhood. High rank is a necessary condition for effective leadership. To attain prestige the individual must own a clubhouse and be in a position to maintain it by giving frequent feasts. As his prestige grows so does his right to be obeyed (Oliver, 1955: 372–379). In modern nations the authority of an administration derives in large part from recognition that the policy makers were elected or otherwise chosen by constitutional means. Among the Lovedu of South Africa the people do not elect a sovereign. Legitimate authority is established by the Rite of the Door. In this ceremony the door of the royal hut is barred to all but an heir chosen and trained by the previous queen. The choice, however, is secret. Claimants to the throne go to the door and address the deceased, saying who they are. They lightly touch the portal, which, however, is kept shut until the previously chosen claimant comes along. Symbolically speaking, the dead ruler opens the door to her successor, thus publicly validating the latter's right to rule (E. J. Krige and J. D. Krige, 1943:170). In the kingdom of Ankole in Uganda, as in certain other parts of East Africa, succession was limited to the royal descent line and to the strongest of the previous king's sons. Following this ruler's death war broke out, the brothers fighting among themselves until only one remained. By surviving he justified his rightful occupancy of the office (Oberg, 1940:

158). A ceremonial investiture or coronation, in which a deity is invoked to recognize the accession of a sovereign, is frequently arranged. Failure to have been duly crowned may seriously weaken authority.

Charismatic (i.e., nonjural) authority may be distinguished from jural authority. The latter comes from occupying the proper status and having fulfilled prescribed routines or conditions. The successor to the king of Ankole is the eldest son and he has outlived his rivals. Nonjural authority is personal. It is achieved through charisma, "the bath of personality which snares its human environment in trance" (Wolfe, 1951:85). The individual is endowed with distinctive, personal qualities which attract the willing allegiance of followers. Sometimes charisma is revealed through miracle working. The person may claim, or be held, to incarnate a deity. He simply may be a "natural leader" to whose dominance people are eager

The Asantehene, Nana Sir Osei Agyeman Prempeh II, Head of the Kumasi State, Ghana, Wearing Ceremonial Dress (courtesy, British Information Services).

to subordinate themselves. This is how Adolf Hitler initially won his following. In practice charismatic and jural authority can coexist in the same person. Among the Siuai a leader validates jural authority primarily by feast giving, which reinforces his high rank. But only ambitious personalities will use this channel to win renown and acquire leadership (Oliver, 1955:396–441).

Following assumption of office the administrator often is surrounded by wealth and other impressive symbols the function of which is to advertise his status and reinforce the idea of his authority. A large retinue dramatizes exalted status and authority. The same end is achieved by magnificent palaces, spacious grounds, comfortable offices with imposing desks and executive chairs, and dramatic public appearances. Appurtenances like royal robes, wigs, maces, crowns, gold carriages, limousines, or a private railroad car symbolize authority.

The President of the United States appears to make use of relatively few material symbols of his authority; a member of Congress still fewer. This may be related to the diffuse nature of authority in the United States. In Britain the policy makers similarly appear with relatively few symbolic trappings, though the Queen, by whose sole authority Parliament's laws are carried out, is highly visible (Jennings, 1954).

Rituals of avoidance carried out by an administrator as well as rites of deference paid to him are common devices for reinforcing the idea of authority. In the Ashanti states of West Africa (Busia, 1951:26–27):

From the moment that the chief is enstooled his person becomes sacred. This is emphasized by taboos. He may not strike, or be struck by, anyone, lest the ancestors bring misfortune upon the tribe. He may never walk bare-footed, lest when the sole of his foot touches the ground some misfortune befall the community. He should walk with care lest he stumble. If he does stumble, the expected calamity has to be averted with a sacrifice. His buttocks may not touch the ground: that again would bring misfortune. All these taboos remind the chief and everybody else that he occupies a sacred position. He is the occupant of the stool of the ancestors. . . .

Note how vital is the purpose of these observances: failure to observe them threatens misfortune. This threat helps insure that the rituals will be executed faithfully and so contribute to the no less vital function of reinforcing administrative authority.

Inheritance of the paraphernalia of office is a public announcement and validation of the transfer of authority. Possession of the objects symbolizes attainment of the right to be obeyed. The inheritance is less a matter of transmitting things than a transfer, first, of the right to own the paraphernalia and, second, of the authority which that right implies (Gluckman, 1955a:65; Hoebel, 1954:59).

Despite caution taken to preserve it, authority may be lost. For example, authority weakens through failure to exercise it. Hence administrators often contrive to appear in situations where they receive deference and can act out their authority, perhaps by making speeches. Political celebrations, audiences, and durbars to which lesser rulers are invited provide opportunities to exercise authority. Authority may also be usurped, wholly or in part. This happened among the Siuai when a leader, Songhi, asked Tukem from another village to assist him in preparing a feast. Tukem came with a following. In the course of preparations Songhi began to supervise those followers, not through Tukem but directly. After the feast Songhi continued to act in this way with the result that the two political systems were merged and Tukem lost his office (Oliver, 1955:436; 1949:32–33).

Power

Authority should not be confused with power, here meaning the ability to use physical force to compel the behavior of others. Authority is one basis of power but the real test of power comes only when the administrator, challenged in spite of his authority, resorts to force. All modern large-scale government rests on force, although normally this form of coercion exists only in reserve.

Power can by-pass authority. This has happened in many parts of the world where colonial governments came to rule without first acquiring authority. The Canadian government successfully competed with the Iroquois Council of Six Nations and compelled the latter to obey national laws. But the government did not possess authority in Indian eyes (Noon, 1949). Once an administration with power is able to by-pass a weaker leadership backed by authority, there is a high probability that legitimacy will also become attached to the more powerful system.

Although the administrative power-centers of modern nations claim supreme power, this claim is often more ideal than actual. For example, the subordinates on whom top policy makers depend to execute a decision often alter the policy even as they ostensibly carry it out (Blau, 1955: 96–100). Executive power is quite ineffectual wholly to control such reinterpretation. Also the strongest government knows that too callous use of power to enforce unpopular decisions will not only weaken authority but inspire active resistance. Even sovereign nations are careful about creating unfavorable world public opinion; therefore they voluntarily limit the power they possess.

Power not supported by authority is naked power. "Power is naked when its subjects respect it solely because it is power, and not for any other reason" (B. Russell, 1938:97). Naked power is less secure than legitimate power. It tends to attract counterforce, which, as the resistance movements of World War II illustrate, assumes a legitimate character despite attempts to brand it as illegal and to eradicate it by force.

TYPES OF ADMINISTRATION

For a comparative look at administration four types of leadership are distinguished, based on degrees of (1) complexity, (2) traditionality, (3) centralization, and (4) absolutism. These are not independent factors; a particular political system may possess degrees of all of them.

Complexity

An administration in which the leader is kin to his followers, makes decisions in a relatively transitory group, has his role informally defined, and operates by himself without lieutenants or specialized branches is a simple administration (see pp. 361–364). In contrast the government of a modern nation is complex.

The Athapaskan-speaking Indians living in the Northwest Territories, northern Alberta, and British Columbia, Canada, reveal an extremely stripped-down form of administration in their fluid bands (cf. pp. 414–415;

MacNeish, *1956*). Neither bands, tribes, nor kin groups possess clearly defined administration. When several, usually related, nuclear families live together no formal commitments bind them and the band can break up simply at will. The leader of a microcosmic band, perhaps the oldest active male, serves as adviser, coördinator, and expert planner, provided others are willing to listen to his words. No explicit rules govern his role nor do any formal procedures inaugurate him into office. In fact, his authority seems primarily to be charismatic, being based on "prestige gained from his superior abilities and his awe-inspiring powers." His personal influence alone determines the extent to which he will be heeded. Jural authority counts for little. Certainly he controls no reservoir of force with which to compel obedience. Yet without his advice people might go hungry more often, for not only is he experienced in the habits of the game on which people depend but he is "a superior provider and, therefore, in a society where communal distribution of large game is a cardinal rule, a good man to fall in with." A similar, scarcely perceptible pattern of leadership obtained among the northern Algonkians (Honigmann, *1956a*:58) and Caribou Eskimo (Steenhoven, *1956*:35). Simple administration correlates with relatively uncomplex social organization, low population density, relative smallness of scale, and small groups in which interaction is primary.

As scale increases, the administrative structure becomes more complex in the community as a whole. (Groups like the family, with fluid or simple leadership, of course continue to occur.) With complexity goes an increase in the number of people responsible for arriving at administrative decisions and disseminating or executing them. That is, the staffs attached to top policy makers become large, specialized, and hierarchically organized. At its simplest, complexity is indicated when members of an advisory council receive special administrative duties delegated by the top policy maker. In many parts of Negro Africa a ruler is assisted by his "mother" in addition to other advisers. Among the states making up the Ashanti Confederacy the Queen Mother (actually often the ruler's sister) advised the chief and reproved him for misconduct. She controlled marriages in the chiefly lineage, possessed her own council and spokesmen, and superintended certain rituals that safeguarded the army when it went off to battle (Busia, *1951*:19–21). In the United States, where national and state governments carry out more than purely administrative roles (for example, they provide for the mails, inspect food products, and run schools), 1 out of 22 people is on a government payroll. This gives some idea of the size of administrative groups. Complex administration implies full-time specialists. Therefore it can exist only where subsistence techniques produce a dependable surplus.

A quite complex administrative system is illustrated by the government of the Ashanti Confederacy as it existed prior to British rule (Busia, *1951*:

Chaps. 1, 5; and Basehart, 1954). The nine states of the union came under the authority of the head of Kumasi state. He was titled Asantehene. This ruler was legitimized by being installed on a golden stool, symbol of the Confederacy, and by sacrificing to the royal ancestors, who continued to show a close interest in the country's welfare. Each subordinate state of the Confederacy had an equal voice in union councils and manifested strong tendencies toward autonomy that kept the federal organization loose. The power-center supported no army but the states coöperated for mutual defense by providing armed men as need arose (much as did the United Nations in Korea and Egypt). The primary tie of a state to the union was largely voluntary, but the ruler of Kumasi could command a certain amount of force through his own state militia. Kumasi was organized into a number of military companies that cut through clan ties and aggregated unrelated persons under captains. The captains (in some cases sons of the Asantehene) also served as the ruler's councilors and administered territories placed under their control. However, they imposed their rule through traditional village headmen. In the other states rulers worked through a more traditional organization. Each chief was the head of a particular chiefly lineage and his councilors were elders who headed other important lineages. Descent in a lineage was matrilineal; hence a chief could be succeeded only by a duly qualified son of a woman of the lineage. Each lineage head supervised one or more villages in the name of the state chief, but each village also continued to possess its own hereditary headman belonging to the oldest lineage and assisted by the heads of other unilinear descent groups. In addition the young men of a state were organized under a head, the Nkwankwaahene, who, although he had no place in the state council, held influence over his followers. Through him the latter presented their views to the elders and sought to influence the head of the state. The Nkwankwaahene also settled disputes that arose among the younger men.

The size and complexity of an administrative group sometimes lead to the appearance of internal opposition in the organization. Different sections of the group seek to implement conflicting goals. For example, in 1954 the United States State Department favored returning alien German property (including valuable patents) to the former enemy. The Department of Justice objected, claiming that the act would cost American taxpayers millions of dollars and might violate a federal law (New York Times, Aug. 5, 1954).

Traditionality

Positive administration is founded primarily on consent and rests on tradition. Since normally it does not try to execute unpopular decisions to which people are opposed, it need not rely on coercion (Nadel, 1942: 64; Gouldner, 1954:216–217). Positive administration is representative-centered. Policy in the first instance is made by the administrated group and executed by the administrator. In contrast, negative administration is punishment-centered. The decisions arrived at and implemented by the policy makers do not grow from the thinking of the community. They may not be understood or appreciated by the people to whom they are directed. Sometimes they even are resented and resisted. Threat of fine, dismissal, imprisonment, or death compels obedience when resistance appears.

The character of positive administration is revealed in this description of a lineage chief among the Nigerian Tiv: "He was not an executive head. He was more like the chairman of a committee; but with this difference—that power was not delegated to him, but was incorporated in his person; it was organic." The job of the chief was to "implement the will of the group. . . . He gave voice to the decision of the elders, as the spokesman of group authority" (Mead, 1953a:119–120). Like village headmen in Asia, the Tiv chief operated in a social setting in which "law and orderly social behavior [were] based on an accepted pattern of living which only incidentally, not directly, was seen as related to village welfare. A man acted with what amounted to honesty and uprightness because that was the way to act rather than out of social responsibility or out of concern for others" (ibid., p. 52).

Negative replaces positive administration when the interests of group members become diversified, owing for instance, to the rise of opposed special interests. It may be imposed on a community when the people are subordinated by aliens. Because the values of the latter diverge from those of the people being administered, coercion is employed to back policy. This happened among the Nupe of West Africa (Nadel, 1942:65). Formerly the village chief exercised leadership as the executive head of a body of elders who were also family heads. Decisions were born at the bottom and percolated up to the executive. European indirect rule, however, has made the chief an agent of the foreign administration. The policy he now executes is no longer solely that of his village but partly that of the top administration. The chief, for example, is expected to collect taxes, press parents to send children to school, and promote obedience to other, newly imposed, and resented obligations. How has he succeeded in this role? Partly through the additional power put at his disposal in the form of police. Furthermore, should he fail in his work he can be replaced despite the traditionally hereditary nature of his office. In his place would appear a "more willing or more enlightened man, possibly one who had the advantage of education and could thus better see the 'white man's' viewpoint."

The reader should not confuse positive administration with an absence of social pressure. All people seek to maintain equilibrium by pressing one another to retain approved forms of behavior and even applying force toward that end.

Centralization

Centralized administrative organization is indicated when, despite any number of subordinate units, the reins of control eventually lead to a single power-center. In contrast are tribes divided into unilinear kin groups (clans or lineages) each of which claims a territory over which there is no single tribal head. This condition may be called acephalous segmentary social organization (Fortes and Evans-Pritchard, 1940:1–24). Acephalous segmentary tribes, as the name indicates, lack centralized administration. The politically equivalent segments recognize a mutual relationship but have few provisions allowing them to act in concert. Each of the units, therefore, not only regulates its members but exclusively controls its relationships to other units making up the tribe.

Distinction of rank is of far greater significance in centrally than in segmentally organized maximal groups. It has also been noted that when the segments are mainly based on kinship ties they generally are smaller in size than analogous groups united under centralized administration. On the other hand, density of population, in Africa at least, does not seem to vary between the two types of organization nor are there differences in the way subsistence is procured. Historically it is likely that many currently centralized tribes possessed segmental organization. The change in some, but scarcely all, cases may have involved the political ascendancy of one kinship segment. A number of the African centralized tribes also include peoples of several ethnic groups, something not found under segmental organization. The absorption of foreign people could readily have been accomplished through conquest waged by large centralized groups. However, in some parts of Africa voluntary accession to strong kingdoms also has occurred. In centralized maximal territorial groups the ruler and his subordinates command the use of force. In segmented groups, force used by one unit against another is likely to be met by equal force but defeat in such an encounter normally does not result in one segment's establishing political dominance over the other.

In addition to acephalous segmentary and centralized administrative systems, a third type has recently been proposed. It includes tribes with autonomous villages or other units (e.g., bands) which are not based on unilinear kinship. Included are people like the West African Ibo and Mende (Eisenstadt, 1954:100; 1956:120). A system of autonomous villages was common aboriginally in the North Pacific coast culture area. The

Indians of far northern Canada and the Eskimo also fit this third type. The separate bands traveling within a circumscribed territory aboriginally (and even today) were not unilinear kin groups. Neither did they come under a single administrator (see pp. 480–481). Half the communities known to anthropology have no form of administration that transcends the local village or migratory band (Murdock, 1956:133). Perhaps they can be classified as simple acephalous.

Among the Nuba tribes in the Egyptian Sudan both centralized and simple acephalous systems of administration occurred. The Heiban represented a chiefless community consisting of several villages spread along the flank of a hill while the Otoro, also living in a series of hill villages, were coördinated through a chief (Nadel, 1947:146–155, 162–174). Each village contained a number of clans linked by intermarriage, friendship, and vital coöperation. Otoro chieftainship was a recent innovation and it is possible to reconstruct the system of administration existing before introduction of the new trait. At that former period organized attacks on life and property *within* a single hill settlement were more or less controlled. But between contiguous hills belonging to the same tribe armed attacks were normal. Warfare helped men to secure wealth and earn a reputation for courage. Aggression within a village was controlled among the Heiban by fear of leprosy deriving from supernatural sources and by the threat of clan-imposed blood vengeance. But the latter custom, based on balancing death by death, produced considerable disequilibrium. Prior to chieftainship the Otoro also followed blood vengeance but they alternatively allowed the offender's family or clan to balance the scales by surrendering one of its members to the family or clan of the victim. A ceremony of reconciliation followed adoption. It would seem that like chieftainship this alternative to blood vengeance had appeared among the Otoro also only recently, for some kin groups refused to accept a substitute for a victim of murder and insisted on revenge.

The Otoro chief sought to eliminate open tests of strength between kinship segments and aimed to establish unity between the hill settlements. The authority of the British government greatly aided achievement of these objectives. How did chieftainship emerge? Informal administration existed among both the Heiban and the Otoro in the *kweleny,* informal leaders of single settlements with authority based on wealth, supernatural power, personal following, and, no doubt, personality. It was these men who organized raiding parties for swift attacks into enemy country. Their mutual rivalry promoted constant disequilibrium. " 'It is a bad thing,' " said an informant, " 'if you have two big men in the same hill.' " Among the Otoro one of these men, belonging to a hill settlement that he had founded, emerged as paramount over the others. He was himself a foreigner and had introduced an age-grade system (see pp. 431–434) into the tribe, assuming a prominent office connected with that system. Sorcery further helped him to impose control over a number of Otoro hills. After his death a successor effectively extended this rule. At that time British administration appeared and confirmed the chief's right to govern.

Absolutism and Totalitarianism

No administration, whatever its potential power, is perfectly absolute, able to make and execute decisions without any regard to the reaction of the administered population. Polyarchy designates an administrative system containing built-in procedures whereby members of the administered population regularly take part in the decision-making process, registering their approval or disapproval. In the United States and Great Britain, for example, people elect representatives who act as legislators. Americans further elect a President to execute the laws. In Britain the supreme authority, the Queen or Throne, chooses an executive in conformance with the people's choice as it was expressed in the election. The President and Prime Minister are acknowledged to have the right of making certain decisions, some of which must be submitted to the legislature for approval. The executives appoint a number of civil servants for whose actions they retain responsibility. The representative bodies elected by the nation can criticize executive actions and are themselves subject to review when elections come around.

Absolutism refers to an administration that takes a minimum of cognizance of popular reactions to the administrative process. An absolute ruler may have or claim the right to rule without consulting the wishes of his subjects regularly. Absolutism spells dictatorship in the modern world but dictatorship is not the same as totalitarianism. This is the tendency of an administration to control as many areas of living as possible. Strictly speaking, totalitarianism is opposed not to polyarchy but to autonomy over particular areas of living (Friedrich, 1954). The growing pressure to become more totalitarian which exists in practically all nations of the modern world is related to the high degree of interdependence of specialists, groups, and individuals fostered by modern technology. Factories are interdependent and some cannot operate when one of their number goes on strike. Regions are linked so that what happens in one is of concern to others. Schools must be supervised so that they will provide the kind of training needed in industry or government. Even dress and recreation may come under administrative purview—for example, when saving is to be encouraged in the interest of technical development (see pp. 273–278). Totalitarianism represents an attempt to insure equilibrium in a very large-scale community. Modern communications media facilitate totalitarianism. They allow decisions to be broadcast quickly while literacy allows the administration's printed word to be understood by practically any adult. Man has not yet learned to administer himself successfully in totalitarian fashion. In fact, the more totalitarian an administration tries to be, the more it is likely to inspire reactions in favor of autonomy. These reactions seek to protect areas like the family, church, and personal planning from administrative interference (Grodzins, 1956:214).

30.

Social Pressure[1]

IN NO human group does all adherence to custom come automatically. Careful observation does not support the belief that in small-scale exotic communities people never deviate from socially approved rules of behavior and hence never require coercion (Hartland, 1924:138). It is equally untrue that coercion doesn't exist in exotic culture and that anarchy reigns supreme. Everywhere complementary behavior is maintained at least partially through positive inducement and negative sanctions. The latter are what we mean by social pressure.

Complementary differences between people, as already mentioned, are those diversities which are valued and which constitute an essential condition for continued social relations. Diversities are not valued, generally speaking, when they threaten social organization and promote disequilibrium. In order to maintain complementary diversities and reduce undesirable deviance, people who belong to the same group or society exert pressure on one another. The negative sanctions controlling behavior range from those ultimately resting on physical force to some that rely mainly on words. Three main forms of social pressure will be treated in detail: (1) law, which relies on physical force imposed with social approval to achieve a measure of conformity, (2) logic, the basis of which is to expose contradictions between behavior and generally held premises, and (3) convention, which operates through arousing shame and embarrassment. Other possible forms of social pressure will be examined more briefly.

All social pressure ultimately rests on power, but now we no longer use that word only to designate physical force. There are various kinds of power: physical, intellectual, financial, and conventional. When the reader points out to a woman that her hemline is too long for this year's fashion, he is bringing into the open some of his power over another person. Social pressure that works is actualized power. The power of an individual applying social pressure varies with the social worth attached to his status. A king or judge has more power than a prophet who has been abandoned by his followers. But a prophet with a large following may have power to

[1] The general framework of this chapter is based on G. Wilson and M. Wilson, 1945: 49–58.

coerce an administration that controls many armed men. Power is ineffectual when the deviant persists in what he has been doing. Power sometimes is followed by the deviant's separating himself from the group. He does this in preference to giving up his unwelcome action. Although social separation hardly is feasible in all cases of uncomplementary diversity, it may transport the individual beyond the range of social pressure into another group where his behavior is acceptable.

A few words must be said about what social pressure does not mean. Normally speaking, it does not include illegal modes of coercion. Blackmail to compel payment of money and armed robbery scarcely conform to social pressure as the term is used here. Sorcery is not usually in the category of social pressure unless undertaken with the approval of the community (for example, against an enemy). Obviously what is legitimate social pressure in one group may be illicit in another or may become illegitimate under an altered set of conditions. In many African tribes witches were punished for their threat to social equilibrium. But the European administrations in Africa do not recognize the existence of witches. Hence, traditional proceedings against witches have become illegal and subject to social pressure. In an urban gang sexual experience and theft may be approved behaviors. Failure to adhere to the norms will be followed by taunts and other forms of social pressure. These same behaviors, however, in other sectors of the community will be punished if they are found out. Social pressure ". . . is both sectional and general. Every group in a community has its own uniformity which must be maintained by social pressure. . . . Every group must itself conform to a wider uniformity. . . . Confusion arises from the accepted verbal distinction between the organization of larger and smaller groups. The limitations maintained by smaller groups (as schools or trade unions) are called rules. . . . We must use law to include sectional as well as general organization" (G. Wilson and M. Wilson, 1945:51).

Social pressure is not completely identical with rules, norms, or a moral system. Morality or other normative ideas are not within the area of social pressure unless implemented by law, logic, or convention. Social pressure is more than a drawn-up list of norms (like a book of etiquette or a so-called code of laws). Most exotic communities studied by anthropologists lack writing but they hardly lack social pressure. The real test of social pressure lies in what people do when certain norms are transgressed or contradicted.

LAW

Like any other form of social pressure, law operates only when certain norms of conduct are disregarded. Violation of these norms threatens interpersonal adjustment, coöperation, and the maintenance of social organization. It disturbs equilibrium. Through law, economic pressure or physical force is applied to the wrongdoer, presumably as a deterrent against similar behavior in the future.

Law differs from other types of social pressure in terms of the sanctions imposed. In most general terms, legal sanctions to some degree limit the enjoyment of life, limb, or property. Imprisonment, mutilation, death, fines, and destruction of wealth are specific forms of legal pressure. So is the withdrawal of reciprocity. On the atoll of Ulithi in the western Caroline Islands of Micronesia, "law is wholly customary, and in the stricter sense it hardly exists at all, even in rudimentary form, for we do not find that there is any systematic and formal application of force, by some overall authority, to support codified rules of conduct. There are no courts, and no specific sanctions by a central authority. Conformity is due mostly to habituation toward empirically derived ways of life, as well as to fear of social and supernatural sanctions and the need for reciprocity in social behavior" (Lessa and Spiegelman, 1954:251; cf. Malinowski, 1926).

What Is Law?

The word "law" carries two meanings. It designates both the process by which certain kinds of punishment are applied to a deviant whose behavior is unwelcome, and certain kinds of norms, those whose violation brings about the operation of the legal process. Note that not all norms are legal. Those that are fall into two classes: first, those that the community deems so important that it will use force to restrain their violation; second, those which express rights which the community will back by force.[2] In this chapter the word "law" will generally be limited to the social process of applying legal force. Norms backed by such force will be referred to as "legal norms."

To help the reader recognize the main features of law and legal norms a few general propositions will be listed and discussed briefly.

1. *Norms of conduct are legal if one can predict that in the event of violation members of a group will punish the violator by economic sanctions, bodily restraint, or execution.* Posting or otherwise publicly codifying

---

[2] Islamic law, which specifies, for example, that a man may marry not more than four wives, is law in a sense not discussed in this chapter. In religious contexts "law" designates an act that is highly binding because it was enjoined by God or is contained in scriptures. Islamic law was transmitted by God to his prophet, Mohammed, or else it refers to an act practiced, allowed, or condemned by that divinely inspired man (cf. Vesey-Fitzgerald 1955:85). By the present definition a constitution is also probably not law. For who will apply coercion to the nation or province that violates its constitution? North Carolina has gone many years without redistricting the state for elections as its constitution prescribes. The legislators take an oath of office to support the constitution but there is nobody legally to force them, or the people they represent, to implement that charter. Force used against the state (except when used by a higher authority) is, ideally speaking, illegal.

the expected standards of legally sanctioned behavior warns the potential violator that the law will be applied. Hence publicity is a means of inducing conformity without the actual use of social pressure.

The element of predictability is not uniformly present for all legal norms. Culture change constantly results in the creation of new legal norms of which people may be unaware. A conquered people come under legal norms of which they have hitherto been unaware. When people don't rightly know what the legal norms are, violation of such norms will be frequent.

2. *Legislation is a process which declares the norms whose violation will be followed by legal sanctions.* The legislature may also specify the precise punishment to be administered. By its very nature legislation helps to publicize the legally enforceable norms and so helps people to become aware of what will happen if those norms are violated. All legal norms, however, are not made by specialized legislative bodies. The so-called common law consists of traditional (i.e., customary), enforceable norms which sometimes go back to a remote or unknown origin. Common law may be systematized and codified by administrative bodies, as often happens when one community has been conquered by another.

3. *Despite the fact that law rests ultimately on physical force its power is always limited.* For example, the power of a village council or industrial organization to impose laws on members is limited by higher levels of administration. The latter delegate the right to apply coercion. A modern American Indian tribal council cannot impose the death penalty; only a state court may do so. The effectiveness of legal force also depends on the desire of people to avoid suffering. Mostly people do fear the suffering imposed by legal sanctions but sometimes individuals persist in their behavior despite imprisonment. They may even recognize the likelihood of being put to death and accept it. People with this degree of integrity limit the effectiveness of law for controlling uncomplementary diversities. The extremist Doukhobors of British Columbia, Canada, are a case in point. They persist in their resistance to sending children to school, paying taxes, and registering births, deaths, and marriages (Hawthorn, 1955:35). The United States could not enforce the prohibition amendment to the Constitution against altered sentiments of a large number of people.

Certain behaviors cannot be enforced successfully by law—for example, sexual cohabitation, certain relations between parents and children, and maintenance of the state of happiness. These are beyond the power of the most powerful nation. Nor can all rights be guaranteed by law (Cranston, 1956b).

Law in many cultures is limited by the importance attached to the statuses of the parties in a dispute. When the President of the United States speeds through a Maryland township he is less likely to be penalized than an unimportant person. In East Africa if a person does not abide by the decision of the native court (consisting of the tribal chief and council of officers) that body may order confiscation of a specified number of cattle. However, such a measure is not used lightly against a wealthy defendant supported by a strong clan which might threaten to secede from the tribe (Gutmann, cited in Lowie, 1948). In a midwestern American high school the rule against tardiness was enforced by imposing detention after school. If a student could satisfactorily explain his lateness, however, he received a slip excusing him and admitting him to class. An attempt to crack down on lateness by issuing no excuse slips and sending all tardy students to detention was opposed by the superintendent. He said: "You cannot make a rule like that stick in this town. There are students who simply cannot be sent to detention. Their families will not stand for it." The attempt to enforce the new rule failed in the case of the daughter of a prominent family who simply omitted going to the detention room. Instead she kept an appointment at the beauty parlor. No further penalty was imposed (Hollingshead, 1949:185–192). The case shows how a group's ability to enforce law may be limited not only by rank but by social pressure applied from a larger group (the town) in which the first group is a unit. In the same way an African native administration is limited by the superior power of the colonial government.

4. *Legal norms are constantly changing.* Like the rest of culture, to which such norms are closely related, the norms enforced by law are dynamic. New inventions, like the airplane, automobile, and radio, have led to much recent legislation designed to regulate the use of those artifacts. As conditions in culture change, certain norms may cease to be enforced. For example, rules against admitting Negroes to many southern universities in the United States gradually are ceasing to be enforced. The prohibition amendment was repealed from the federal Constitution after a large number of people changed their minds and decided they wanted to drink alcoholic beverages.

The unstable nature of legal norms means that successive judges do not always rule in the same way about similar disputes brought before them. The case of Negro segregation will be discussed in a moment to illustrate this point. The fact that legal norms change means also that the predictability of law is far from perfect. The law possesses a measure of uncertainty, the degree of uncertainty being a function of the rapidity and magnitude of change occurring in other areas of culture.

Legal norms change when they are reinterpreted to make them applicable to current cultural conditions. At one time the Supreme Court of the United States interpreted the Constitution to mean that Negroes could be barred from white schools in the South if at the same time they received "equal" segregated facilities. But in 1954 the Court reversed itself and insisted that segregation itself was contrary to the Constitution and, therefore, illegal and punishable. What had changed in American culture? Obviously many things, and in association with those changes the status of the Negro had become redefined. One change that had an admitted influence on the Court's decision was the new knowledge that had been discovered by sociologists, psychologists, and anthropologists about the correlates of segregation. This indicated that the influence of segregation on Negro personality was probably such that facilities for Negroes could never be the equal of those available for whites. A deep sense of inferiority marked Negroes who grew up with enforced segregation in schools, waiting rooms, buses, and elsewhere. Therefore those facilities could not in any real sense be equal to facilities reserved for whites.

Law often changes as a result of legislation of new legal norms. A superordinate group may legislate for a subordinate one. This occurs in colonial systems. Sometimes such legislation creates acute confusion and stress. In some parts of Africa a Christian who chooses to do so can be married in a church. From then on tribal rights and duties pertaining to the matrimonial relationship are not legally enforceable as far as he is concerned. He comes under English law in the British colonies. Now, under English law adultery is not punishable as it is under tribal law. Hence, a Christian African's wife can commit adultery and remain unpunished while a non-Christian adulteress will be penalized by law. Of course, the Christian African will have grounds for divorce if his wife's unfaithfulness is discovered, but he may not want to take such a relatively drastic action (Parr, 1947; cf. Honigmann, 1956b, and A. Phillips, 1953).

5. *Law does not define what is good.* Law, as the term is used here, designates a way of enforcing certain customs which, normally, people regard as good. Their enforcement is a moral act in the eyes of the group. This is expressed when law is referred to as "justice." But acts are not moral because their omission or commission is punished through law. It sometimes happens that acts of omission or commission which people deem to be immoral are nevertheless legally enforced.

Perhaps this is the appropriate place to point out that the conception of law held in this chapter belongs to the point of view called "legal realism." In essence legal realism insists that law, like the rest of culture, is man-made and not, somehow, discoverable in a realm transcendental to man (G. Hughes, 1956). This conception recognizes no natural "law" which "is binding all over the globe" and alongside which contrary human laws have no validity (Blackstone, cited in Cranston, 1956a). Who would enforce such a transcendental natural law?

Functions of Law

By maintaining an optimal level of coöperation and interpersonal adjustment law facilitates many of those activities which people carry out through social relationships and on which survival depends. A community that restricts a man's right of divorce and requires social approval before divorce is recognized is not simply trying to preserve a family but may be protecting the survival chances of the woman and her dependent children. The following paragraphs are somewhat more specific applications of this general postulate concerning the function of law.

1. *Law limits uncomplementary diversity.* The relatively predictable penalties attached to legally enforceable norms (for example, the rules against theft or killing) function to deter uncomplementary behavior. It is not likely, however, that threats of punishment in themselves are sufficient to restrain unwelcome deviance. The legally enforced norms generally are also regarded as moral, at least as far as they apply to in-group members. Moral sentiments probably are more important than simple threat in restraining uncomplementary behavior.

2. *Law maintains complementary diversities.* Law functions to compel coöperation in certain status relationships. It helps to make the division of labor predictable. The law of contract, for example, specifies what one American businessman can expect when he orders something to be delivered by another. If Jones and Bones, Inc., contract to buy kapok from Rust and Dust, Ltd., they can arrange their affairs, securely expecting that the kapok will be forthcoming. Similarly Rust and Dust can expect that delivery will be accepted and payment made. Each party to the contract proceeds with its affairs, secure in the belief that the contract will be enforced legally if one party defaults. A complexly organized community could not operate in the absence of such security. Theoretically buyer and seller have freedom to decide whether or not to enter a contract. In practice this freedom is becoming somewhat limited in the modern world, where large enterprises or governments control services on which individual consumers depend. A person who wants to light his house with electricity or take a bus to town must accept the contract of the *one* company in his neighborhood enfranchised to supply current or transportation (Anonymous, 1954). His control over the service organization is indirect at best. It depends on his access to the administrators who legislate the terms under which the Public Service Commission may regulate the organizations concerned. When such services are nationalized, as in England, the ordinary citizen's control may be slightly more direct but he hardly is free to set mutually advantageous terms.

The legal enforcement of contracts is also illustrated in Africa. For example, among the Bantu people of East Africa, if custom allows a man to place some of his cattle in the care of another, who will care for them in return for the milk, the owner can expect to receive back all the animals. This right is enforceable through the native court. Similarly, a man who cures illness expects to receive a fee if his efforts are successful. Failure to pay in a reasonable time allows the fee to be recovered in court. A marriage contract exists from the moment the bride's parents agree to the betrothal. Should they later, without a legally recognized reason, refuse to let the marriage take place, they are liable for the return of all the installments of bridewealth and all gifts made to them by the prospective husband and his kin (Piddington, 1950:342).

In Pakistan and other Muslim countries marriage sometimes is concluded through a written contract which, when signed and witnessed, is enforceable in the courts exactly like a commercial contract. In drawing up the contract a woman or her representatives may insist that the husband promise not to marry a second wife (as he is entitled, but not obliged, to do). The woman's right to a marriage settlement is also stated in the contract, together with the amount. However, she may relinquish this right in return for some other right—for example, the privilege to divorce her husband at will (Fyzee, 1949:111–121). The husband having made such stipulations, the community recognizes and supports the wife's right to request legal force, if necessary, to secure obedience to them.

3. *Law limits administration.* In maintaining networks of coöperation law also prevents exploitation of one person by another—for example, the victimization of individuals by administrations. The legally enforceable right of *habeas corpus* issued by a superior court protects the citizen from unlawful arrest. In some situations an administrator may be reluctant to act. The citizen may then apply to a court for a writ of *mandamus*. This orders the person against whom it is directed to carry out his role—for example, to hold an election or to hear a case.

4. *Law controls aggression and sex.* Aggression is an ever present and highly potent threat to group equilibrium. All communities restrain the use of violence, usually through law. Among the Attawapiskat Cree a murderer could expect to be killed legally by a relative of the victim. The act of vengeance could be carried out directly or through sorcery—that is, indirectly (Honigmann, 1956a:64). Among the Azande of the Egyptian Sudan sorcery can legally be directed against an illegal sorcerer but only if the latter is unknown. People believe that the sorcery automatically seeks out the guilty person. Should the culprit be known, however, he must be tried in court. Retaliation by sorcery in the latter case is equivalent to the illegal use of violence (Evans-Pritchard, 1937:389–390).

Sex is another potent disturber of equilibrium but many sex norms are not enforced by the community at large. Often it is left to the family or kin to punish incest, rape, and adultery, the right of private persons to punish with physical means being recognized by the larger community (Lips, 1947:471). In Africa much intertribal variability exists with regard to seduction. In some communities there is no liability unless the girl conceives; in others seduction in any event is punishable (Piddington, 1950: 343). Among the Melanesian Wogeo adultery with the wife of a fellow villager or clansman is not illegal (though it is wrong and punished by other than legal forms of social pressure; see pp. 501–502). If the woman is married to the village headman, however, the adulterer may be executed or the headman will direct sorcery against him. Such extreme punishment is accepted as legal and just by the rest of the community (Piddington, 1950:332; Hogbin, 1938).

5. *Law has independent functions.* Looking at law in its status as a dependent variable related to other aspects of culture, as might be expected, the complexity and formality of law enforcement increase with the scale of the community. Disputes requiring settlement also increase in frequency. Finally, the volume of legal disputes is a function of the amount of interpersonal stress engendered by cultural arrangements. A highly stressful way of life, including one beset by radical opposition, shows many cases of uncomplementary diversity and hence great use of law (as well as other forms of social pressure) to induce conformity (Slotkin, 1950:568–577).

Legal Procedure

Law does not require specialized agents (police, judges, juries) or groups corresponding to the Euroamerican court for its operation. Law may be carried out by the offended individuals or by the general leaders of a group as well as by persons specialized to handle disputes involving legal norms. Certainly groups like the family, school, and many other organizations have no department which specializes in law enforcement. However, the following discussion will refer mainly to maximal territorial groups like tribes and nations.

As already indicated, legal proceedings may be left for the offended individual to carry out with the aid of his kin group, friends, or association fellows. On the opposite extreme stand those communities where legal proceedings are removed from the hands of private individuals and placed in the control of chiefs, kings, or judges. A community may under these circumstances contain a very complex organization of courts specialized for criminal, civil, ecclesiastical, and patent matters. Some courts may be limited to military organizations or may be for appeal. Such a complex legal apparatus is found in large-scale, modern nations. Whereas simple law obtains among food gatherers, specialized law tends to be associated with food production.

Legal procedures not carried out by specialists are sometimes hard to recognize. At a minimum such procedures must involve use of force or economic sanctions applied with the consent of the group or larger community. The element of predictability should also be present, making ignorance no excuse for breaking a legal norm. An Attawapiskat Cree Indian knows that to set a fish trap upstream from a neighbor's trap, with no feeder stream intervening, is liable to bring both a protest and demand for compensation. There are no police to arrest the inconsiderate fisherman and no courts to hear the case. The plaintiff, aware that he is backed by public opinion, confronts the defendant. The defendant, faced by what the public recognizes as a just demand, offers compensation.

If, on the other hand, the community remains unconcerned in a matter of homicide or a dispute, there is no law. From some accounts it appears that among the Caribou and other eastern Arctic Eskimo if one man kills another who has made trouble the local group takes no legal notice. The affair is between individuals alone. If this is true, and vengeance remains purely a private matter among the eastern Arctic Eskimo, then murder among these people is not illegal. Neither is it legal. However, if a man kills too often the group does become concerned and may agree that the habitual murderer should be executed.[3] Among the northeastern Cree Indians murder did carry a legal punishment, one applied much in the same way as among the Eskimo—namely, death by retaliation visited on the murderer himself by a surviving relative. "This retaliation is a self-applied satisfaction, a private punishment, yet tolerated, demanded, sanctioned, and considered as legal by the community" (Lips, 1947:470).

When self-help is the only legal remedy available to members of a community, permanent bad relations, or feuding, are constant dangers. What may happen is that A kills B. This, it will be assumed, is met legally by B's relative who kills A. But now A's relatives may illegally retaliate against the relative of B who avenged the first murder. And so the feud goes on. Hence, self-help as a legal remedy often institutes more disequilibrium than it resolves. It is inefficient. Small wonder that many people without specialized law-enforcement agencies have sought to find substitutes for this kind of law. The substitutes vary. Among the acephalous segmented Tallensi and Nuer there were men who controlled automatic sanctions by which they could end feuding.

If a fight breaks out, the "man of the earth" can restore peace by running between the combatants and hoeing up the earth. The slayer of a man is defiled with blood, and can neither eat nor drink until the "man of the earth" has let the blood of the dead man out of his body. If the slayer resides near the home of the man he has killed, he will live in sanctuary with the "man of the earth" to avoid death at the hands of his victim's kin. The "man of the earth" will then negotiate between the two groups, and try to induce the deceased's kin to accept compensation. This they are bound in honour to refuse; but eventually they will yield when the "man of the earth" threatens to curse them [Gluckman, 1955a:15].[4]

---

[3] For a thorough discussion of Eskimo law see Hoebel, 1954:Chap. 5, and Steenhoven, 1956. Compare with law among the acephalous Plateau Tonga of Northern Rhodesia in Colson, 1953, and Gluckman, 1955a:20–33.

[4] For a first-hand account see Evans-Pritchard, 1940:163–164.

Compare this pattern to that which existed among the Kiowa Indians in the United States:

The Keeper of a Ten Medicine Bundle had a most important legal function because he was the one who presented a peace pipe in a quarrel. The pipe was a basic institution over much of North America for stopping intra-tribal conflict and inter-tribal war. . . . The legal procedure was as follows: it was possible for the relatives of any defendant, fearing for his life, to seek such an owner [of a pipe] and ask him to offer a pipe to the plaintiff. The pipe was offered and almost never refused. Smoking constituted an oath that there would be no further action. Compensation might be stipulated by the plaintiff at that time and could not be refused. The use of the peace pipe involved no judgment as to who was right and who was wrong. Consequently there was no loss of face on either side. The mechanism effectively inhibited a *lex talionis.* . . . Refusing the pipe four times, or violating the injunctions after smoking, called down on the offender's head immediate ill luck, and ultimately, death. . . . There was also a curse of the Ten Medicines that might be invoked by a Keeper against anyone flouting the pipe, but it was usually unnecessary to use it because of the automatic supernatural sanction on a transgressor [J. Richardson, 1940:11].

Where courts appear in small-scale exotic communities they are often presided over by civil administrators rather than by clear-cut judicial specialists. For example, among the Bantu-speaking people of East Africa court is held by chiefs of various levels. They are assisted by men called "remembrancers," chosen for their legal sagacity (Piddington, 1950:346–347). In bringing an action before a court the plaintiff generally reports his complaint to the defendant's chief, who fixes a day to hear the matter. The trial is public and each party shows up with witnesses. Failure to appear is tantamount to contempt of court. Defendant and plaintiff present their sides of the dispute. Anyone in the court may ask questions. Witnesses are interrogated. The case is then discussed, the remembrancers, speaking in ascending order of seniority, pointing out the rights and wrongs and stating the precedents in matters of that kind. The chief sums up the evidence and renders a verdict based on the opinions he has heard. Should the loser wish to appeal from the verdict he may carry the case to the court of a superordinate chief. Here it will be heard all over again.

Quasi-specialized law-enforcement agents are recognizable among the Plains Indians of the United States. In many of these tribes a sodality of warriors executed police functions at the time of the annual tribal bison hunt and at other times. One of the common crimes on the Great Plains was for a hunter to begin running down the bison in advance of the time fixed for the coöperative hunt. This was dangerous because the man who jumped the gun might stampede the herd and make it hard for others to secure food. If the man was caught by the police sodality he might be flogged and his horse destroyed. Later the members might make up the damage they had inflicted. The sodality acting as police also punished people who disturbed the peace during tribal gatherings. A pertinent case may be cited. Among the Kiowa, H got into a fight at the Sun Dance. He was supposed to camp on the south side of the tribal camp circle but felt this area to be too crowded and the ground too rough. So he moved elsewhere. The military sodality policing the circle told him to move back where he belonged but H refused. The police carried his tipi and belongings to where they belonged, whereupon H threatened to shoot a couple of the police. The chief of the sodality warned him but H would not put away his bow. Thereupon the official hit H on the side of the head, knocking him unconscious. When H came to, he glared defiance still. The chief ordered other sodality members to hit H on the head with whatever they held in their hands. Then H moved to where he was supposed to camp (J. Richardson, 1940:22).

Specialist agencies to enforce law do not bring about a complete end of personal retaliation undertaken with community approval. ". . . Even when jurisprudence is far advanced, self-help remains. Ancient Roman law allowed a man to visit direct penalties on a thief taken red-handed" (Lowie, 1948:164). An American is still entitled to defend his house from illegal entry by using force if necessary. A southern town in the United States may countenance lynching of a Negro presumed guilty of raping a white woman, and in many countries a man who shoots and kills his wife's lover may successfully plead the "unwritten law" to escape conviction for murder.

LOGIC

Much has been written about law as a form of social pressure but little consideration has been given to logic as a means for maintaining complementary diversity. "Primarily logic is the avoidance of contradiction between people" (G. Wilson and M. Wilson, 1945:53). And therein lies its equilibrium-maintaining function. Logic facilitates social relations by reminding people of the premises in terms of which, at any given time, behavior is reasonable or unreasonable. Where two disputants hold two utterly different premises there cannot be any logic. Such a situation obtains under radical opposition.

Among the Central African Yao, "a man who tried to charge rent for a garden was severely criticized by the chief who said: 'God made the land (therefore owns it). What right have you to sell it'" (J. C. Mitchell, 1950:8)? If the reader, too, entertained the premise that land belongs to

God, is used by man, but cannot be alienated or transferred from one man to another, he might be in a better position to appreciate the chief's logic. The anthropologist cannot share all the premises or fundamental assumptions of the people he studies but he must be able to recognize when people reason from premises which they generally accept.

A case similar to the Yao matter of charging rent is reported for the New Guinea Arapesh. Here a man attributed to a chief resentment at having to alienate lands to a newcomer. Ascribing such resentment to another person constituted uncomplementary diversity. It contradicted the premise that people were attached to land rather than vice versa. Men sought to bring the deviant back into line by pointing this out. ". . . People belonged to the land, not the land to the people . . ." (Mead, 1935:18).

Examples reporting the use of logic to control behavior are scarce in the ethnographic literature. Such neglect is certainly no evidence for saying that the small-scale, exotic communities frequently studied by anthropologists do not reason or are unable to think logically. Field workers have failed to record instances of such social pressure when they may have observed it. The operation of moral codes, belief in an afterlife, and fear of deities all assume extra significance if one thinks of how they may be applied logically to restrain uncomplementary diversity. When one person warns another that a deity specifically enjoins a certain act, assuming that the community regards the divine injunctions as deserving respect, then that warning can be understood as an appeal to a common premise. The deity's will, it perhaps is added, should not be violated lest some punishment follow. This brings in the assumption that the deity controls the individual's future welfare. Therefore, the argument runs in effect: desist in your behavior for it is in contradiction to what we believe is true.

Whereas law often is applied by an administration, logic tends to be in the hands of everyone. However, it is often wielded by those members of a community who are respected for their knowledge: teachers, scientists, philosophers, priests, or theologians. These specialists may be jealous of their prerogatives. In Pakistan during 1956 a commission made several recommendations for changing the law pertaining to marriage and divorce. The members concluded that the values of Islam had to be reinterpreted to become congruent with other aspects of culture. In modern society, they reasoned, many men could not adequately support more than one wife. Hence, polygyny should not be allowed to occur without express permission given by a special court. The commission tried to justify its recommendations by references to the *Quran*, the Muslim scripture. Theologians objected. They not only contradicted the reasoning of the commission's majority but denied the right of untrained persons to draw conclusions about Islamic matters.

Unequal social change, in which different sections of a community act on different basic assumptions about the world, means that people reason simultaneously from divergent assumptions. One section cannot successfully contradict another under such conditions; for which premises are to prevail? Then logic fails to provide an effective means of social pressure.

Just as the mere threat of law enforcement can insure conformity to legal norms, so the threat of being confronted by contradiction spares the actual imposition of logic. Furthermore, people are able to reason within themselves concerning the logic of some contemplated piece of behavior. Describing how she had to wait on her mother-in-law, kowtow to her, fetch her tea, and wait on her at table, a Chinese wife said: " 'I was never angry or rebellious about it because it was the custom.' " Then came the reflexive application of logic to her uncomplementary tendencies (but the underlying premise remains unspoken): " 'If I rebelled against my mother-in-law, perhaps my mother might have been treated badly by her daughter-in-law' " (Ingrams, 1952:101).

CONVENTION

Convention is a process that seeks to restrain undecorous, rude, and displeasing behavior by invoking shame (G. Wilson and M. Wilson, 1945: 57–58). It is applied to acts which reveal emotional expression: speech, painting, dress, architecture, writing, dancing, style of greeting, and demeanor.[5] Convention seeks to limit uncomplementary forms of expression but it does not always reach deeply enough to limit actual feelings or motives. No more is law able to regulate the impulse life, but only the expression of the impulses. In the absence of radical opposition over standards of beauty and decorum, shame compels the nonconformist either to conform or, through social separation, to enter other social relationships in which his behavior will be accepted as conventional. The importance and frequency of shame used as a form of social pressure are revealed among the Hazara people of Afghanistan. "Time and again our informants explained that a man would be 'ashamed' to do this or not to do that. Men would be ashamed to kill prisoners in war." A girl's father would be ashamed not to give a dowry equal at least to the bridewealth he received and as much more as he could afford. Relatives were ashamed to have an impoverished kinsman marry below his class. Hence they would furnish him with bridewealth. ". . . No man would drink unboiled milk for fear of the ridicule which such an act would excite" (Hudson and Bacon, 1941:251). The Hazara are not atypical in their response to conventional pressure nor is the strength of this sanction to be underestimated. In middle-class America it compels

[5] In brief, art (using the word very broadly) is controlled through convention.

businessmen to wear ties even in hot weather and in India it either kept widows from remarrying or secured their immolation on the husband's cremation pyre.

As with law and logic, the promise of the application of conventional sanctions may be enough to restrain behavior. The student who would like to be careless of grammar and spelling nevertheless follows the rules for fear of what the teacher will say.

It has been suggested that legal sanctions rarely enforce norms of sexual behavior (see pp. 495–496). Sex is an area wherein convention operates strongly. Among the Wogeo, for example, "the adulterer is embarrassed and ashamed, especially if he is insulted in public, when he must listen in silence" (Piddington, 1950:330). Nor are insults slow in reaching a known adulterer. Among these Melanesian people theft, too, is punished by public abuse of the thief. "Only those who are indifferent to their reputation would commit such an offense" (ibid., p. 333). Yet here, as elsewhere, there are some people who cannot be reached by the barbs of public contempt. One Wogeo family partly supports itself by theft.

People rarely can give an explanation for what they brand as indecent or shameful. Among certain Nuba tribes of the Egyptian Sudan "it would be shameful" for women to tend cows; no further reason is necessary (Nadel, 1947:60). But often conventional reasons for adhering to certain norms after a time become rationalized—that is, supported by logic. Thus, among the Korongo Nuba if one drank milk drawn by a woman the teeth would break and fall out (ibid., p. 61). If this explanation comes to be involved in social pressure (for example, in keeping a girl from milking), then logic rather than convention is indicated.

Just as standards of what is decorous, rude, ugly, or improper vary from one community to another, so does the operation of convention. The kissing scenes of American films are hissed off the screen in Latin America. The same audience, however, will complacently sit through a completely nude "art" production (Kinsey, Pomeroy, and Martin, 1948:365). Lower-class people in an American city are likely to be as scornful of petting (which substitutes for premarital coitus in the middle and upper classes) as middle-class folk are about a girl known to have "gone the limit" (ibid., p. 379). While upper-level males frequently read erotic literature and use erotic pictures to augment masturbatory fantasies, lower-level males look on such things as the strangest perversions (ibid., p. 363).

Deeds frowned upon by convention in one community may be enforced by law in another. Or conventional wrongs may, with time, become illegal or illogical (and vice versa) in the same community. Among Jews the avoidance of pork is largely maintained by convention. However, in modern Israel attempts have been made to limit pig raising by parliamentary law (New York Times, Jan. 7, 1954).

OTHER FORMS OF SOCIAL PRESSURE

Law, logic, and convention are major forms of social pressure but they do not exhaust the means which men living in society have devised to restrain uncomplementary diversity in the interest of a stable equilibrium. For example, there is an area of illegitimate pressure by which people more or less surreptitiously try to coerce one another. When workers in a factory slow down production to hurt management financially they may be violating their contract as well as going against direct orders issued by union leaders. A formally organized strike, of course, is legitimate in the United States (as long as it is not undertaken against government) and can be considered an expression of law within the group concerned. Public demonstrations and violent riots directed against an administrative or minority group illustrate another variety of illegitimate coercion. Mass violence appears likely under prolonged frustration which engenders a high level of stress. Other favorable conditions include the presence in the population of persons with a propensity for violence, highly visible rapid change in social organization, and a precipitating incident that triggers conflict (R. M. Williams, 1947:60). "The lack of lawful means for resisting the government is indeed a significant feature of despotism. When such means are not available discontented and desperate men have time and again taken up arms against their government . . ." (Wittfogel, 1957:103). Nations with large-scale irrigation works have developed in their implicit charters a "right of rebellion." In China this right is formulated in the Confucian classics.

Informal and quite legitimate social pressure somewhat resembling law is imposed when consumers, perhaps after an unsatisfactory experience with a product, disregard the wares of a certain manufacturer. This may well lead the plant to alter its standards or could drive the organization out of business. Whenever one person refuses to trust or coöperate with another person he may be trying to exert pressure. Curses are a recognized sanction in many communities. Among the Nyakyusa of Nyasaland a very ill-behaved youth may be cursed by his father (G. Wilson and M. Wilson, 1945:51). Among the Lugbara, living on the Uganda and Belgian Congo boundaries, old men are allowed to invoke ghosts to punish kinsmen who do wrong (Middleton, 1955:259). Fear of automatic retribution for an action is in itself not *social* pressure, though it no doubt operates through the reflexive application of logic by a conscientious individual. Fear of being accused of witchcraft, however, constitutes a rather common form of social pressure (Marwick, 1956; see also pp. 641–642 below).

Regulated Conflict

Combat restricted to champions, like Australian chiefs in western Victoria (J. Dawson, 1881:77), or carefully regulated fighting between small groups of men is difficult to classify under any of the usual forms of social pressure. In western Victoria a dispute is sometimes settled between groups of warriors who fight in pairs. The first wound ends the contest. Among many Eskimo two disputants face each other, alternately delivering straight-armed blows on the side of the head until one is felled and vanquished (Hoebel, 1954:92). These and similar forms of regulated combat allow men to settle disputes without recourse to law and in relatively nonlethal fashion. Aggression is allowed to be expressed against the person who committed an undesirable act but remains bound by rules. The rules may even be enforced legally. Psychologically such contests facilitate the discharge of hostility whose unresolved tension would maintain disequilibrium. Organized rivalry between dual divisions or wards in a village serves the same function (Murdock, 1949:90), and so do games. "A game canalizes potential conflict . . . by bringing about interaction at high frequency but with the rhythmic order imposed by the technique. Games thus prevent conflict . . . [and] provide one of the most important means of preserving equilibrium in a society . . ." (Chapple and Coon, 1942:635).

Eskimo song duels allow conventional sanctions to be imposed on a deviant and at the same time facilitate the discharge of hostility (Hoebel, 1954:93–97). Such contests are highly traditional and governed by explicit rules. The songs follow a traditional style and their aim is to shame the opponent. For example, a too assertive woman is censured in the following song:

> Only now shall I get to hear of such
> That a woman attacks!
> Yes in truth, it is said that you made the first advance,
> You it was, they say, who made the beginning
> In that you acted like a man.[6]

WAR

All war is not social pressure. One group may attack and destroy another for wealth, including land. War may also be carried out in order to secure enemy heads or other trophies with which a ceremony is carried out (Ackerknecht, Nadeau, and Heizer, 1944). Or war may spring from individual motives: men want to raise their rank in the community and are able to do this by winning military honors. This constituted a not uncommon basis of Plains Indian fighting.[7] All such warfare does not directly involve attempts

[6] The source of this song is unknown. The woman in question had violated the rules in the East Greenland sexual game of "putting out the lights." In this game men only are supposed to scramble for partners of the opposite sex (Thalbitzer, 1941:653). For other drum songs see Carpenter, 1955.

[7] It would not appear that Newcomb (1950) effectively refutes the evidence for this statement.

to coerce the behavior of other members in a society. Our interest is in violence undertaken between groups, tribes, or nations with the aim of forcing one party to restrain or alter its behavior. Civil war, directed by a section of a population against an administration, also belongs in this cate gory when it is not solely a struggle for office. Economic sanctions imposed by the United Nations or other international administration is rather closer to law than war, but similar sanctions imposed by one or a few nations on one another may be regarded as a kind of war.

War Versus Law

There are several respects in which war differs from the legal use of force.

1. *Military violence is relatively unregulated.* International agreements limiting the use of certain weapons or techniques (like poison gas) cannot be relied on for the plain reason that as yet there exists no supranational power to enforce such agreements.

2. *War is not undertaken solely against persons guilty of misbehavior.* It involves many people, even children, who do not directly participate in the policy-making process from which a nation's action springs. It threatens belligerents and nonbelligerents alike.

3. *It is difficult to identify uncomplementary diversity in a culturally diversified society.* One nation will accuse another of doing wrong, but the accused party may justify its action in terms of its own standards of conduct. Hence war cannot be conceived of as an attempt to restrain generally agreed-upon unwelcome deviance. A violent action by thugs against the police illustrates the character of war, except that the thugs may themselves perceive the uncomplementary nature of their behavior in relation to the larger community.

4. *Normally law is welcome while war is not.* The imposition of law is generally welcomed by everybody except the deviant to whom it is applied. War, however, is often and at least ideally regretted by all the parties who fight in it. This is true even when one side fights to end an intolerable situation.

Independent Functions of War

War is neither inevitable nor an instinctual component in human behavior. "Warfare . . . may or may not be used in any culture. Where war is made much of, it may be with contrasting objectives, with contrasting organization in relation to the state, and with contrasting sanctions. War may be, as it was among the Aztecs, a way of getting captives for the religious sacrifices. Since the Spaniards fought to kill, according to Aztec standards they broke the rules of the game. The Aztecs fell back in dismay and Cortez walked as victor into the capital" (Benedict, 1934:30–31).

It is also difficult to prove that wars are related to the greater readiness for aggression, learned or otherwise acquired, of one nation compared to another. Wartime propaganda tends to take this line. Some Americans still think of Germany as relatively aggressive in her relations to France and believe that Germans are fond of war. Yet "while the Germans have invaded France three times in less than a century, France, between 1792 and 1813—that is, in less than a quarter of a century—has invaded Germany twelve times" (Leopold Kohr in letter to *New York Times,* Dec. 4, 1950).

There are communities in which organized resort to slaughter never occurs, just as there are people who cannot conceive of a lasting state of peace. The Eskimo belong in the former category. The generations of Americans born since 1914 fall into the second. Clearly, however, there is nothing in human nature that predisposes man to violent conflict. This point is strengthened by the data of archeology which reveal that wars have occurred with different frequency at different points in an area's history. There is no evidence of profound involvement with military conflict in the Middle East before 4000 B.C. Then war becomes progressively more frequent and devastating. The factors behind this increasingly military phase of culture are examined later (Chapter 40). In Europe evidence of warfare is lacking for the long Stone Age. It is also not indicated during the cultural period when agriculture and animal domestication first entered the continent. But with the onset of the Bronze Age, European man finally came to the end of his long period of peaceful existence.

Such evidence suggests that war is dependent functionally on other aspects of culture. Three general independent functions of way may be cited (Sorokin, *1944*).

1. Scale. An important factor in war seems to be the scale of the community. A large population, relatively wide in scale, which depends for food, irrigation water, or ore on other parts of the society rarely allows interference with the sources from which or the routes over which these goods are obtained. A community that exports to foreign markets seeks to protect its trade routes and to keep competitors out of the picture by war if necessary. Loss of autonomy in wide-scale relations is often followed by an administration's seeking to bolster autonomy through overthrowing the conqueror or by renewed empire building.

2. Uneven Change. In a society of closely interdependent communities war may follow a fundamental change in the goals or values of one community when such a change is not simultaneously compensated for in the others. A rapidly rising rate of production without willingness or ability of neighbors to absorb greater surpluses helped to bring on the First and Second World Wars. Technological change, leading to higher energy levels in some parts of the society without corresponding changes in other parts, may instigate war.

3. Radical Opposition. Civil war often is born out of radical opposition and unequal social change inside a national community. Opposing factions become aligned with mutually unacceptable positions. The ordinary mechanisms of social pressure—law, logic, and convention—cannot maintain complementary relations. One side then tries to impose its views forcibly on the other in an effort to end the opposition.

War may also be a function of national power when it reaches a certain critical level. It has been suggested that whenever a nation in relation to some other country, or combination of countries, reaches a certain level of power "it detonates in spontaneous aggression, even as uranium, which is completely harmless below a certain mass, explodes spontaneously . . . the movement it reaches the critical weight" (Leopold Kohr, letter, *New York Times*, Dec. 4, 1950).

LINES OF TENSION IN SOCIAL RELATIONS

War belongs with feuding, sorcery, accusations of witchcraft, and other expressions of hostility that reveal tension in given social relationships. Tension does not occur at random in a society. Often it tends to be related closely to the social structure. Social pressure also tends to cluster around such relationships.

Psychoanalysis has pointed out how the structural relationship of the Euroamerican boy and his father tends to be fraught with tension. Both are rivals for the mother's attention and for other gratifications which she furnishes. Furthermore, the father's status gives him the right to discipline the son, who, in turn, is expected to show respect for the older man. Among the Navaho Indians tension exists between rich and poor, adults and aged, and between younger and elder siblings (C. Kluckhohn, *1944*). The rich do not distribute their wealth freely enough; hence they are disliked. The aged have been neglected and resented because they only consume and do not produce; soon, however, they may die and as ghosts take their vengeance. Hence they are threatening. Elder siblings cared for one in youth. In doing so they promoted frustration and are still conceived of antagonistically. Hostility toward the rich, old, and elder siblings often is projected on actual people occupying those statuses. The Navaho Indian will rationalize his own hostility by seeing it as a reaction to the threat of the other.

Among the Swazi of South Africa hostility is likely to break out between co-wives, who quarrel frequently and accuse one another of sorcery, as well as between people of rank and power who are mutually jealous of one another (Kuper, *1947*:175). A diviner who can "smell out" sorcery will often select as the guilty person someone in a potentially conflictful status relationship to his client.

In the modern world certain international frontiers have long been associated with latent hostility. One of these lines formerly ran through the Middle East, Balkans, and Danzig but recently has moved westward into

Germany. It separates the Soviet and western zones of that country (H. D. Hall, 1948).

Different systems of technology in a community may encourage tensions when the demands of one conflict with the needs of the other. In Lapland the reindeer pastoralists come into conflict with Scandinavian colonists moving north with mixed farming (Collinder, 1949:22–32). Since the seventeenth century a relationship of mutual dependence has grown up between these categories, but instigations to hostility are not absent. In the fall, farmers' haystacks, stored in meadows rather than barns, attract reindeer, whose owners then are charged for the damage caused. The herds also damage standing pasture grass. Agriculturalists, encouraged by the government, have occupied lands which the Lapps regarded as their own. This has provoked conflict. Lapp folk tales tell of Lapps being murdered by farmers. Whether true or not, such stories intensify the conflict and maintain a sense of difference between both groups.

Conflict between American sheep herders and cattle herders is familiar to readers of western fiction. In 1950 Navaho Indian sheepmen who could not find enough grazing land on their reservation moved into grasslands across the border in Utah. The lands were managed by the Department of the Interior but had been leased to white stockmen. Senator Arthur V. Watkins of Utah warned that if further movement off the reserve by Indians continued " 'there may be bloodshed' " (New York Times, Dec. 2, 1950).

31.

Ritual[1]

THE reader probably is prepared to think of ceremonial (i.e., ritual) activity as behavior clearly demarcated from everyday aspects of living. Yet he may have heard that in some communities—for example, Hindu India or the Muslim world—much that the individual does, from the food he eats to his washing and greetings, is ritualized. Ideally it is also expected that a Christian or Jew will live his religion not only on the Sabbath but in nearly everything he does. As a matter of fact, considerably more of the reader's ordinary day than he may realize consists of ceremonial activity. The present chapter will help him to understand the significance of such activity in maintaining and restoring equilibrium in human relationships.

WHAT IS RITUAL?

Confucian philosophers of the second and third pre-Christian centuries spoke of ritual as the orderly expression of feelings appropriate to a social situation (Radcliffe-Brown, 1939). To rephrase this, ritual refers to the symbolic expression of the sentiments which are attached to a given situation. The term "situation" should be taken to include person, place, time, conception, thing, or occasion. Marriage, death, Christmas, and Easter are prominent ceremonial occasions in Europe and America.

A couple of simple instances will show ceremony at work. Upon being received by a host and hostess one murmurs certain appropriate sentiments expressing concern for their health, the weather, or for being late; dinner is received with spoken or unspoken expressions of pleasure (at least displeasure is not revealed); upon leaving one expresses gratitude for having been entertained and this feeling is conveyed with a suitable intonation of

[1] Readers looking for treatment of what is ordinarily called "religion" are advised to read this chapter and then to turn to Chapter 38. The word "religion," however, is not used in any precise, technical sense anywhere in this book. The approach to religious and related phenomena is that of Durkheim (1915), Radcliffe-Brown (1952b:Chaps. 7–8), and Chapple and Coon (1942:Chaps. 20–23). The work of these men has been "away from the attempt to systematize and compare religious *beliefs* [italics ours], away from concern with the genesis and evolution of religions, and towards a study of the" functions of such behavior (F. S. Cohen, 1954:209–210).

sincerity. At a funeral people weep or otherwise express sentiments of commiseration, loss, and seriousness. ". . . It may be that in certain particular cases, the chagrin expressed is really felt. But it is more generally the case that there is no connection between the sentiments felt and the gestures made by the actors in the rite" (Durkheim, 1915:397). The point, of course, is that the appropriate sentiments for particular situations and their expression tend to be standardized. Recurrent events like meeting a friend, entering another's home, marriage, death, departure, Easter, and Christmas possess ideal meanings in most cultures. Thus, Christmas is "a day for the simulation of peace and prosperity" (Levi, 1947:206). It is these ideal meanings that are revealed in ritual behavior, whether such behavior occurs in passing or as a block of activity—for example, a Sunday service in church. Each time such sentiments are expressed they are also reinforced. People who do not feel particularly sorrowful at a certain funeral, or joyous at Easter, or happy to see a guest may nevertheless find such feelings induced in them once they undertake expressions of correct emotion—that is, perform the proper rituals. Ritual expression, of course, occurs in face-to-face interaction and also can be mediated by letter, floral tribute, or other form of gift.

Classification of Ritual

Ceremonial may be classified by whether (1) the expression of sentiments is only incidental to, or dominates, social behavior; (2) it is concerned primarily with expressing deference and respects, or (3) the purpose is to cope with practical problems. Also it can be classified by (4) the nature of the situation in which it occurs. These are not the bases for an exhaustive or systematic classification of varieties of ritual nor are the classes mutually exclusive.

1. Dominance. Ritual may be an attribute of an instrumental activity, like walking, making a purchase, eating with a friend, asking for instructions, or allocating people for a task. Even "for a man to speak one language rather than another is a ritual act" in highland Burma; ". . . it is a statement about one's personal status; to speak the same language as one's neighbours expresses solidarity with those neighbours" (Leach, 1954:49). At the opposite extreme, ritual involves a specific block of activity. A wedding ceremony, victory dance, the Plains Indian Sun Dance, a reception for a distinguished visitor, and the Roman Catholic Mass are in the latter category. These two kinds of ceremony could be called secondary and primary ritual respectively.

2. Rites of Deference. Much ritual behavior, especially when it occurs in the course of ordinary events, is concerned with the expression of pleasure, homage, respect, or similar sentiments in interpersonal relations.

Administrators often are treated with profound respect by their subordinates. Among the Swazi, "no subject stands upright when addressing a chief, or approaches too close. When giving or receiving anything, the subject shuffles forward with bended knee and utters exaggerated praise" (Kuper, 1947:69). In the Indian state of Mandi images of the village deities annually were brought to the palace to offer homage both to the *rajah* (ruler) and to a more powerful deity with which the *rajah* and the kingdom were identified (Punjab Government, 1920:62–63). Consider the following description of a carefully standardized durbar in which the British Viceroy, Dufferin, received the Maharajah of Jodhpore in Calcutta in 1884. Two important persons are showing mutual deference, although one manifestly receives a little more than the other.

A still grander throne than usual was placed for the Viceroy—it was a silver one, with large gold lions for arms; an attendant with a white yak's tail in his hand stood by, lest a fly should trouble His Excellency's composure; a gold embroidered carpet was laid before the dais, and chairs were arranged on either side of it. . . . When the Maharajah reached the door, the Viceroy got up and walked to the middle of the room to meet him, shook hands with him, and motioned him to a chair on his right, while his followers took lower places on the same side. The Maharajah's dress was green and gold; he spoke through an interpreter. . . . "After a short conversation," say the regulations, "the Maharajah's attendants are presented to the Viceroy, and each one holds out to him one gold mohur,"[2] which he touches, thus politely expressing "You may keep it though you are so anxious to give it to me." Then there was another short conversation before the leavetaking. At a signal the Viceroy's attendants brought in two silver vessels; one contained attar of roses, the other some very sticky leaves wrapped up in silver and gold paper. . . . The Viceroy puts a small spoonful of attar of roses on the Maharajah's hand, and gives him a sticky thing to take away with him,[3] and they sit down again, while the Under-Secretary in the Foreign Department does the same for His Highness's attendants, and then they make a final move. The Viceroy again takes a few steps to conduct the Maharajah to the middle of the room, bows to his followers, and they depart with the "same ceremonies as those observed on His Highness's arrival" [Dufferin, 1890:I, 19–21].

The respect which administrators normally are shown and the isolation they maintain help support their authority. Ritual increases the likelihood that their commands will be obeyed. These commands, it may be assumed, function to maintain a degree of social stability. Not only in relations with

---

[2] A gold coin worth about 15 rupees; it is no longer in use.

[3] Probably a serving of betel, i.e., areca nut wrapped in a betel leaf and coated with lime or some spicy substance. Offering "pan" is a recognized gesture of hospitality in India.

superordinates but in any interpersonal situation rites of deference help to preserve a given status relationship and so contribute to stable equilibrium.

3. Instrumental Rituals. The performance of a ritual itself may be intended to achieve some goal, like the happiness or intercession of an ancestor, fertility, or success in an endeavor. A ceremony of this type may be called instrumental in contrast to one which is carried out primarily for the sake of the satisfactions afforded by the event itself. The latter will be called consummatory or expressive. Consummatory rites do not lack functions. A Kaska Indian potlatch, which is a feast given by one exogamous moiety to another, is not intended to achieve any specific result. Functionally speaking, however, it knits the community together by strengthening social solidarity. On the other hand, the Hopi Indian Snake Dance, which constitutes an instrumental appeal for rain, serves an identical function for the village regardless of whether it is a reliable means of bringing about a cloudburst.

4. Rites of Passage and of Intensification. Rituals may be associated primarily with individual status change or mark the simultaneous passage of several individuals from one status to another. Initiation rites, installation and coronation ceremonies, graduation exercises, and death ceremonies mark changes in individuals' customary role behavior. They are rites of passage (*rites de passage*). Rituals of intensification, on the other hand, tend to be performed at regular intervals and in conjunction with cyclical events in culture. Or they may mark the transition from one season to another. Christmas, Easter, Memorial Day, and the fiestas in a Central American village represent rituals of this type.

Functions of Passage Rituals

Passage rituals generally occur at a time in a person's life when he moves from one social position to another. Passage rites build up when the newborn child is presented to the community for the first time, a boy becomes a man, the single person acquires marital status, a woman becomes a mother, a nonleader becomes a leader, and a kinsman is left bereaved. Except for the new leader, these are status changes known in all communities, though they are not always marked ceremonially. The transition from being a warrior to resuming peacetime activities, graduation from school, joining a sodality, and ordination to the priesthood, like promotion to leadership, represent less universal status promotions but they are occasions when ritual often is conspicuous.

The following dependent functions of passage rituals are more or less directly associated with the maintenance of social equilibrium or its restoration after a crisis.

1. *Responsibility is stressed.* Passage rituals serve to facilitate the assumption of new responsibilities by the person whose status has changed. The ceremony functions to insure that actual behavior in the new position will be complementary with expectations held for the role. A passage ritual often ushers the individual dramatically into his new role. The pregnancy avoidances imposed on a pregnant woman, even when they are conceived instrumentally, focus the woman's attention on her forthcoming parental responsibilities. The glowing tributes of a commencement speaker remind the graduating class that a new period of life is at hand. Marriage ceremonies signal the assumption of new roles, both for the wedded couple and for their former associates. The very elaborateness of the ceremony sharpens the break from one style of life, marked by certain habits, to another. Habit is not always easy to unlearn but the "shock" of the public ritual presumably facilitates new learning (Elkin, 1954:166–169).

Passage Rites, Like the Confirmation Ceremony, Mark the Promotion of Individuals from One Status to Another (courtesy, American Swedish News Exchange).

2. *Familiarity is promoted.* Rites of passage help to achieve a smooth working relationship between individuals who have joined in a group. The initiation ceremony of a club, for example, promotes stepped-up social interaction between the new member and others in the association. The rites familiarize both parties with one another. Rites of passage establish equilibrium in new relationships. Birth ceremonies also can be interpreted in this light for they sometimes help a group, the family, to achieve a new equilibrium following the addition of another member. Among the Korwa of Central India, even before the birth takes place an elderly woman narrates anecdotes concerning the achievements of the ancestor who is about to be reborn (Majumdar, 1944:44–46). The rite prepares the family for the new member and for the change which its customary relations will undergo when another joins the group.

3. *Readjustment is aided.* Death ceremonies and other rituals accompanying a disruption in social relations deal with crucial disturbances to equilibrium. Such rites restore stability to the surviving group by helping its members readjust their relationships. Common elements in a death ceremony may be studied for the way they contribute to this function. The survivors often sing, eat, play games, or dance together. Such a stepping up of interaction forces the members to become intensely aware of one another; the

loss is compensated for by extra activity. People may hurt themselves in a funeral ceremony. They thereby are aided to abreact the emotion they feel, to release their tension. Such release, too, facilitates resumption of equilibrium. Where people have certain prescribed roles to play in a ceremony they may be enabled publicly to assume the new status conferred upon them through another's death.

In general, the more important the status of the deceased (measured in terms of the number of people with whom he was in direct, indirect, or mediated interaction), the more elaborate will be the funeral arrangements. The death of an infant is marked by little ritual attention but a king's passing ceremonially disrupts the whole community (Lévy-Bruhl, 1928:209–211). The very disruption of life is a symbolic expression of his importance. The prolonged rituals provide millions of people with a chance to express their loss. At the same time they dramatize the importance of the royal status. In executing the latter function the ceremonies help the successor to maintain authoritative administration.

4. *Solidarity is enhanced.* Status changes disrupt the relatively stable equilibrium which has been established. At the same time, if our theory is correct, accompanying ceremonies act to inaugurate a new period of relative stability. It is likely that joint participation in such rituals strengthens the bonds linking the actors. One way in which this comes about is by confronting the participants with common social values. The ceremonies stress the value of events like birth and marriage, or of important statuses. The community jointly affirms that these things are indeed valuable. Common social values, like common interests in general, symbolize and reinforce the unity of a group, making it better able to withstand threats to stability (Radcliffe-Brown, 1939:151).

Functions of Intensification Rituals

In general terms, cyclical or calendrical ceremonies provide regular opportunities for relatively intense, harmonious, and pleasurable social interaction between people around subjects of social value. To this extent rituals of passage and intensification overlap. In both types social values are put forward prominently and function to promote solidarity. The following specific points amplify and illustrate this more general proposition.

1. *Solidarity is enhanced.* Rites of intensification promote pleasurable interaction. Doing pleasant things together reinforces solidarity in a group. The things people do during the ceremony heighten the pleasure they feel in being together. Christmas parties with their food and drink, factory and church picnics with their games, and annual dinners given by sodalities are examples in point. Such affairs create anew a feeling of belonging (Blau, 1955:132). They increase tolerance for unavoidable future vicissitudes and strains in social living. Thanksgiving and Christmas dinners promote cohe-

sion in the kindred just as unilinear kin group or local group rituals strengthen social bonds in those groups (Radcliffe-Brown, 1952b:Chap. 8). In assessing such functions for a ceremony it is obviously of the greatest importance to know the group or groups which are participating.

2. *Status relationships are activated.* Recurrent ceremonies provide periodic opportunities to activate superordinate and subordinate relationships. Such exercise contributes to the maintenance of the status system and to equilibrium as far as that state hinges on a given system of status relationships. Among the Chukchee of northeastern Siberia the annual Hearth Ceremony occurs in autumn, after the children have returned to the forest from the tundra with the family reindeer. They deliver the animals to the father, their legal owner. The ceremony reaffirms the father's control over the beasts, which for an extended period of time were in the control of the children. The whole family enters a new equilibrium with the start of winter (Chapple and Coon, 1942:509–510).

3. *Values are reiterated.* A ceremony of intensification is often directed to remembering, honoring, or worshiping certain ideas, objects, deceased heroes, or values. The spirit of patriotic sacrifice is commemorated on Memorial Day in the United States (Warner and associates, 1949:Chap. 16); God is honored by the congregation on Saturday or Sunday; the founder of the country is remembered on his birthday; the Tomb of the Unknown Soldier (note the ritualistic use of capital letters) is the scene of ceremonies. What do these targets of ritual have in common? For present purposes it is sufficient to point out that they embody values of great importance. The group that joins in the ritual affirms its unity around these important things. The emotion canalized toward flags, images, or dead heroes also intensifies solidarity. Ideas in radical opposition to the social value (e.g., ideas opposed to military preparedness) will have difficulty in diffusing in the community. The significance of the regularity of such ceremonies should not be overlooked. Regularly people intensify their value system. They are not allowed to forget the sacred elements of their culture. However, there is danger in the very recurrence of ritual. The very habitualness of the experience may deprive it of emotional strength and so weaken its functional importance.

4. *New adjustments are achieved.* Rituals of intensification often occur in conjunction with alterations in the seasonal cycle, with the passage from day to night, or with the change from one technological system to another (land to ice hunting among the Eskimo). Such transitions, although regular, are also associated with upsets in equilibrium. The people change their behavior and customary interaction patterns. For example, the working parent comes home, or, as among the Chukchee, children return from the tundra. Family members now will be associated in different activities. Perhaps they will be together more in the house as the season of field work

comes to an end. All such changes demand that new equilibria be established in human relations. Rituals help to achieve those states.

Other Functions of Rituals

1. *Patriotism is enhanced.* The function of ceremonies in promoting a sense of identification with the community (or group) as a whole is especially important under conditions in which segmental loyalties add a centrifugal pull to the forces making for overall organization. Rituals honoring the nation, its past, those who died in defense of its freedom, or honoring the sovereign, symbol of its unity, function to overcome religious and ethnic group divisiveness. They override struggles between management and labor, rich and poor, and competing philosophies or value systems. In some acephalous segmentary tribes of Africa (for example, the Tallensi) each segment possesses crucial roles in a cycle of rituals that must be completed if *all* the segments are to prosper. Thus the ritual quite directly helps to maintain a mutual sense of awareness and interdependence in an organization without political controls (Gluckman, 1955a:128; Fortes, 1945: Chap. 7).

2. *Conflict is avoided.* Often a ritual consists of one person's avoiding another (see pp. 522–524). While this may be a means of showing respect or recognizing superordinate or subordinate status, a function more directly related to equilibrium is revealed in such expressive action. When a Pakistan youth avoids shaving or smoking in his father's presence he avoids open signs of competition with his father; a man who avoids his mother-in-law among the Kaska or Apache Indians is unable to jeopardize the equilibrium of the matrilocal household through incestuous relations with that woman; a Kaska father who avoids his married daughter and son-in-law again avoids competition, this time with the head of the new nuclear family.

3. *Tension is reduced.* Ritual may involve a letdown in customary avoidances, conventions, or norms. People are allowed, and even encouraged, to do what under normal circumstances would constitute disturbing instances of uncomplementary diversity. Such ritual license reduces tension. "These rites of reversal obviously include a protest against the established order. Yet they are intended to preserve and even to strengthen the established order" (Gluckman, 1955a:109). To start with a simple example, the demurral shown by a bride allows her to abreact the ambivalence felt at the impending status change. She is not fully prepared to assume the new responsibilities. The marriage ritual allows her to act out the negative as well as the positive sides of the transition. Among the Zulu people of South Africa women are legally, if not actually, subordinate to men. This subordination is expressed ritually in the rule that women dress as women and that they shall not herd milk cattle. Yet there formerly occurred a reversal ceremony

at which women dressed like men, carried weapons, drove the cattle to pasture, and milked them. ". . . Performing these normally tabooed actions is a reward and release" (*ibid.*, p. 105). Lifting the rules serves to emphasize them. Therefore ritual license helps to protect the community from deliberate or unthinking uncomplementary diversity during the normal course of events. Swazi ritual abuse of the kingship, when that status is normally highly respected, offers another illustration of license, one that can be interpreted by the same reasoning. ". . . There may be high psychological catharsis and relief in the princes and subjects who are required thus publicly to express hidden resentments. . . . To act the conflicts . . . emphasizes the social cohesion within which the conflicts exist" (*ibid.*, p. 125).

4. *Evil is suppressed symbolically.* Rituals of purposive expiation, purification, or reintegration may be used after a crisis. They function to remove the ripples of a disturbance and to reinstate equilibrium. In an Assamese plains village, "equilibrium . . . is greatly disturbed by an occurrence of illegitimate sex relations. In order to remedy the irregularity the offending parties must invite all fellow members of the *khel* [section] . . . to take part in certain ritual ceremonies" (Goswami, 1954). The ritualization of legal proceedings may be understood as having similar functions. The punishment is somberly declared, its justness is emphasized, and the community is assured that a matter has been dealt with effectively and appropriately.

5. *Anxiety is allayed.* Rituals allay anxiety and therefore maintain personal adjustment, a factor on which interpersonal adjustment depends. The reassurance of prayer, the promise of rain contained in a Pueblo Indian masked dance, and the promise of health suggested in the confident procedure of a Navaho singer curing a patient all contain this anxiety-allaying function. Among the Nyakyusa, when a man dies he goes to join his ancestors. Until the end of the funeral rituals he is on his way. If the ritual is not properly performed he never reaches the ancestors but troubles the dreams and lives of the survivors. " 'If you do not perform the ritual for your father or mother you may go mad or else have a slow and lingering death' " (M. Wilson, 1957:18). Now, does the ritual express people's anxiety and promote confidence or does the very ritual promote anxiety that might not otherwise have appeared?[4] A synthesis between the two theories of ritual in relation to anxiety has been suggested. In the first place, people normally try to cope with anxiety-producing situations. Rituals are used or created to meet this aim. The ritual is not used so much to relieve anxiety as to cope with the problem that aroused the insecurity (see pp. 624–628). Nevertheless, the ritual promotes assurance. Failure to do something in the face of

[4] In connection with this controversy over the relationship between anxiety and ritual see the summary by Homans, 1950:321–330. Also Homans, 1941; Malinowski, 1948:60–70; Radcliffe-Brown, 1939:Chap. 7.

the situation would probably be followed by a perceptible rise in the level of anxiety. Ritual doesn't create the stress, but failure to carry out the rites probably would be stressful.

COMPONENTS OF RITUAL

Once their constituent elements have been examined, ceremonies cease to be the esoteric phenomena that they sometimes appear to be. Basically a ritual consists of one or a combination of the following components: (1) technical manipulations of the physical environment, including the human body, (2) socially standardized interaction between, or isolation from, people, (3) avoidances, (4) material objects which possess symbolic or, at least, strong emotional significance, and (5) collective representations. It is possible to extend this list to include music, dramatization, relatively special forms of speech, and even personality dissociation (trance) as elements of ritual. However, the five components mentioned above and discussed below are the most common and will suffice for introductory purposes (cf. Honigmann, 1953c).

It should be noted in the material which follows how the expressive aspect of ceremony, the key feature of ritual, actually is contained in the component elements of the ritual. The more varied these elements, the more scope to express sentiments bound up with the situation. A handclasp is a simple form of expressing welcome or of graciously terminating an actual interpersonal relationship. But how paltry it is compared to a ceremony that includes decorated streets, flag-waving crowds, a massed band, the presentation of bouquets of flowers, and a banquet. These elements, too, are used to say welcome or farewell.

Ritual Techniques

Ceremonies often prominently feature the manipulation of human bodies or things: a tip of the hat, a genuflection, the consumption of food, washing the hands, building or putting out a fire, imitating fighting, killing an ox, or almost anything else. Some (but not all) such ritual techniques represent relatively commonplace techniques transposed from everyday life into the ceremonial context. Cutting the hair, for example, may mark a child's introduction to the community but the same technique also is used for comfort and adornment. One normally walks to get somewhere but also there is ritual walking, as in processions. Hindus tie cattle to stalls to keep them from straying but they also tie the bride's dress to the groom's garments to symbolize the couple's unity. People slaughter animals for meat but they also do so as an offering to an ancestor or deity. Thereafter they may eat the flesh. Often the commonplace process is performed with heightened care, or in a specially standardized manner, for ritual purposes.

How do techniques come to be selected for inclusion in a ceremony? How do they function in the ritual context? The selection of a technique as a ritual element may be related to one or a combination of the following factors.

1. Symbolic Properties. The technique, often by virtue of its ordinary context or use, serves well to symbolize some analogous idea associated with the ritual. For example, washing is associated with physical cleanliness. In the ritual it often symbolizes another kind of cleanliness—a putative cleanliness of the soul, mind, or heart. Sexual intercourse is known by most people to be associated with conception and reproduction. This makes it a convenient vehicle for symbolizing crop fertility. Where people seriously entertain the premise that like produces like, such ritual techniques may be used instrumentally, that is, to achieve a given end (see p. 627).

2. Pragmatic Utility. Actors in ritual often wish to move from place to place; hence, they adopt an available technique of transportation (walking, riding, driving). Also, people engaged in extended ceremonies become hungry and eat. No matter what additional symbolization may be conveyed by these acts, they are also to be understood from the standpoint of their simple, pragmatic utility in the ritual situation.

3. Attention-Getting Value. The expenditure of energy, care, or wealth in the course of performing a technique calls attention to the ceremony and enhances its importance in public estimation. The slaughter of a valuable animal emphasizes the importance of an occasion or, perhaps, of the target (deity or ancestors) to which the act is directed. "Everyday is not Id," says the Pakistan Muslim. "We don't eat turkey every day," says the American, stressing the special significance attached to a particular holiday on the occasion of which spectacular things happen. Cleaning the house or village prior to a ceremony also serves to express the importance of the forthcoming event. Drawing attention to a ritual in these ways in turn helps to insure other functions attached to the ceremony.

4. Pleasure-Giving Value. A ritual technique may afford pleasure, even while it symbolizes something or draws attention to the occasion. In this sense the technique can make the entire ritual a pleasurable event and this in turn contributes to whatever dependent functions it supports. Singing, eating, drinking to excess, and dancing are techniques whose presence in ritual can be understood in the light of this hypothesis. The pleasure-giving value of ritual techniques also contributes to the persistence of the ceremony over time. People come to look forward to the holiday, perhaps more to its pleasurable aspects than to its ideal meaning.

5. Emotional Abreaction. A technique sometimes provides a means for releasing tension or strong emotion during the course of a ritual. Running, weeping, and mutilating the body are examples. Their presence in certain rituals—for example, those occurring on the occasion of death—should be understood in the light of this property. The abreaction of certain emotions (e.g., grief) may be of fundamental importance for promoting personal adjustment after a crisis. Failure to discharge the emotion effectively may prolong the period over which the disturbance endures.

Sometimes techniques persist in ritual after they have been displaced

Kava Is Being Squeezed into a Traditional Bowl at a Ceremony in Western Samoa (courtesy, New Zealand Embassy).

from everyday life. The burning of candles and the use of horse-drawn transportation are examples from European and American cultures. Everyday techniques may also be abbreviated or tokenized in the ritual context. Communion represents token eating; washing the fingertips in the Mass is a form of abbreviated washing. If the technique is used symbolically it need not be entirely performed in order to achieve its purpose.

A few ritual techniques will now be examined to see how they operate and contribute to equilibrium.

The techniques which loom largest in world ceremony consist simply in manipulating the body. Through these manipulations meanings are expressed symbolically. The nearness of God, an important social value, is brought out in the raised hands of the benediction. Deference to an officer, an act which maintains a given system of status relationships, is shown in the salute. A closed group may be emblemized by a special handshake; using it contributes to the solidarity of the organization. Postures and gestures, of course, become meaningful only if their conventionally assigned meanings have been learned.

Eating is a ritual technique which, because of its association with intimate familial relations, often symbolizes newly established intimacy. It does this when the bride and groom eat together. To offer food also indicates making another person welcome and this in turn strengthens the bonds of interpersonal solidarity. Eating, which manifestly signifies ingestion, may also be used to portray the assimilation of a quality or intangible entity—like God. Often the significance of eating in a ceremony demands knowing the meaning of what is consumed. Cannibalism may express devotion when the body is that of a kinsman but may show degradation when it belongs to an enemy.

Spitting and vomiting less frequently are incorporated in ceremony. Among the Swazi of South Africa a king affirmed his authority by spitting fertility "medicines" over his land (Kuper, 1947:80). The act signified the kingship and its vital importance. Zionist churches in South Africa administer ashes as an emetic, vomiting symbolizing purification (Sundkler, 1948: 233). Purification being a social value, the vomiting links people who belong to the same congregation and also stresses the importance of the collective representation to whose worship the congregation is dedicated.

Social Interaction

Since much ritual occurs in social situations, social interaction is almost invariably a part of that behavior. Here, however, attention is drawn to the fact that the socially standardized expression of sentiments often is accomplished through having people interact with one another in a prescribed, arbitrarily meaningful fashion.

A greeting between two friends is the simplest instance of ceremonious social interaction. Somewhat more elaborate is the announcement that a status change has occurred made by the Aymara headman when he visits each household head in the community and there takes a drink with the host (Tschopik, 1946:540). Congregations meeting at regular intervals to worship under the direction of a specialist minister exemplify another type of ritual interaction. Entertaining one's kindred at a wedding reception, presenting gifts to relatives-in-law, and leaving a calling card at the ambassador's residence are other forms of direct and mediated ritual intercourse. The respect shown between particular kinsmen—for example, by a junior to relatives who are older than he or who have authority over him —is ritual activity (Homans and Schneider, 1955). Sometimes familiarity and teasing are standardized between certain relatives. When such behavior occurs between a man and his wife's sister, for example, it provides "a socially acceptable channel for expressing . . . aggression along with sexual impulses . . ." (Murdock, 1949:282). The aggression derives from the way in which the claims of Ego's wife and her sister's husband frustrate sexual intimacy between Ego and his wife's sister. Joking which is somewhat rough, and at the same time suggestive, carries off the aggression and simultaneously allows discharge of the sexual impulse.

Spectatorship often constitutes an important element in ritual. Such passive interaction allows a ritual cynosure, like a sovereign, bridal couple, or initiated youth, to advertise its importance or a newly assumed status. Spectatorship with applause is a way of showing honor. Furthermore, spectators enhance the importance attached to an occasion and in this way insure the dependent functions of the ritual. Government employees in Washington, D.C., may be given time off from work in order to greet a visiting foreign dignitary. Passive participation in ceremony is directly related to largeness of scale. In small-scale communities it is far less important than it becomes in association with high population density. In much of the modern world millions of people can participate passively in a ceremony through the radio, television, press, or documentary film.

Rituals often include devices which insure that each participant will meet every other or will have a chance to interact with the principal person in the situation. Reception lines and the custom of calling out the names of guests as they arrive accomplish this function. The use of alcohol in ceremonies intensifies the pace at which people interact with each other. The euphoria promoted by liquor presumably intensifies the bonds of solidarity in the group.

A number of rituals, especially those associated with passage from one status to another, involve the temporary isolation of a participant. The Sindhi girl in Pakistan remains in seclusion for some weeks before her marriage. In Africa youths being initiated into an age grade or into the ranks of men spend some months in a bush camp cut off from their families. During this time they are referred to as having died. Their return to the village signifies rebirth. Isolation focuses the attention of the individual on the transition he is undergoing. By being removed from customary social interaction he is better prepared to assume a new role following the ceremony. Finally, the community is given warning to interact with the person in terms of his new social position once the seclusion period is ended. Isolation also stresses the importance attached to a ritual occasion and thereby helps to guarantee whatever other functions the rite possesses. The periodic sequestration of the menstruant in some communities not only expresses the danger postulated to inhere in her condition but effectively prevents her from coming into contact with other people whom she might pollute. The sequestration, therefore, serves directly to guard against uncomplementary behavior.

Avoidance

Enough has been said about avoidance ritual in connection with social organization (see p. 349) to permit only quick recapitulation of how this act, when it is expressive of the significance attached to another person, operates with respect to equilibrium.

The avoidance may isolate certain kinsmen between whom there exists potential conflict or between whom sexual relations are forbidden. Avoidance prevents conflict over who will originate action to whom. The Kaska Indian father tends to avoid his daughter after her marriage; therefore he is not likely to come into conflict with her husband's authority. When certain people are avoided, the action also helps to maintain social distinctions. For example, members of one caste separate themselves from members of another. To keep the castes distinct, in turn, insures the perpetuation of the division of labor that is predicated on the caste system.

Distinguishing, on the one hand, between the primarily ritualistic avoidance of impersonal objects, places, or acts and, on the other hand, matter-of-fact avoidances (like not getting one's feet wet for fear of catching cold) is difficult. Ritually, avoidance is distinguished by its degree of expressiveness. (But remember that ritual expressiveness is a matter of degree; any action can reveal the significance residing in a particular occasion.) In the other kind of avoidance an actor is trying to cope with a problem: not to get sick, to be successful on a hunt, to avoid punishment, to cultivate a rich yam harvest, not to offend a deity. However, in the communities anthropologists often study, many ritual avoidances also are designed purposefully for coping.

The ritual avoidance of some food, certain acts, or objects requires functional explanations different from those which have been assigned to interpersonal avoidances. Some ritual avoidances in the former category may be adaptive in quite direct fashion and thus contribute to equilibrium. For example, the avoidance of pork may help to reduce the incidence of fatal trichinosis in a population; the Eskimo rule against sleeping at the ice edge reduces the danger of a hunter's drifting off on a dislodged floe. But many avoidances remain unaccounted for if only adaptive functions are sought. The Hopi Indian who participates in certain rites must avoid sexual activity during the ceremonial period; Catholics avoid food before going to the Communion table. Such avoidances, closely connected with larger rituals, function to enhance the importance of the ceremonial occasion. They stress that something of great significance is about to happen or is under way. Therefore they reinforce other ends of the ceremony.

Other impersonal avoidances are not bound up with larger ceremonies. Among the Eskimo things from the land and from the sea must not be brought into contact. A Nepalese king never leaves his kingdom to visit another country; if he did so his dynasty would not prosper. Some people avoid the names of the dead; other communities do not use the proper names of parents but refer to these people by the name of an offspring (teknonymy). It is best to look for the explanation of such relatively specific avoidances in the particular cultural context wherein they occur. Generally, however, the following very general function may be suggested: Avoidances create or maintain social values, the recognition of which contributes to social solidarity and consequent resistance to disequilibrium. Anything can become a social value by being treated with respect or avoidance. The very avoidance, if strenuously insisted upon, becomes a paramount, unifying ideal in the culture.

Avoidances pertaining to administrators deserve special comment. They increase the social visibility of the occupant of the status, reinforce the likelihood that his policies will be followed, and so safeguard the equilibrium functions dependent on his role. Avoidances limited to members of a clan, association, or religious sect possess closely analogous functions. They too promote greater visibility at the same time that they set off the group from other groups in the society. The function would seem to be enhanced in-group feeling. This, in turn, also is conducive to social continuity and increases resistance to disruption arising from disequilibrium.

Material Ritual Specifics

The meaning of rituals and their appeal often is made more vivid through certain artifacts, perhaps objects used more or less in their natural state. Such objects, through the meanings they possess, are capable of evoking very strong emotional responses. Think, for example, of a national flag, the Ark in a synagogue, the host in a Roman Catholic Mass, the Sacred Pole of the Omaha Indians (Fletcher and LaFlesche, 1911:229), and the Churingas by which Australian natives remember events of the bygone Dream Time when ancestral heroes walked on earth. The reverence with which such objects are treated (the Sacred Pole was spoken of as though it were a person and was preserved in a shelter) indicates and reinforces the degree of emotion they are capable of arousing. Material ritual specifics also serve as targets of ritual—that is, the ceremony is directed toward them. Often, it would seem, this occurs with the idea of reaching invisible referents for which the artifact stands as a symbol. Among many Plains Indians skin-wrapped objects, called ceremonial bundles, stood for a certain aspect of the universe. The bundles were cherished by Keepers, who acquired their status through a vision, by purchase, or from birth. Rites were addressed to the bundle but are understood better as bringing man into tune with invisible forces of the universe. The bundle acted as a medium in such a relationship. Bundles persist among the Seminole Indians of Florida as well as in other American tribes (W. C. Sturtevant, 1954). Material ritual specifics often consist of modeled human or animal figures symbolizing invisible postulated beings who are believed to control certain aspects of experience.

It is pointless in this general treatment to list exhaustively the kinds of things men associate with ritual. A few examples should give an adequate conception of the range of material ritual specifics. Corn pollen is a widely used specific in the southwestern United States, where a pinch of the stuff touched to the lips and thrown to the sky may promote a blessing (Reichard, 1950:II, 509). Corn meal is no less important in the same cul-

Ritual Specifics, Like the British Crown Jewels, Contribute to the Appeal of a Ceremony and Help to Trigger Off Appropriate Feelings (courtesy, British Information Services).

ture area (*ibid.*, pp. 540–541). Beverages often possess profound expressive value: tea in Japan, India, and Pakistan; beer in Africa (E. J. Krige and J. D. Krige, 1943:287–288), or *kava* in Polynesia.[5] Peyote, used in the ceremonies of the North American Indian church, belongs in the same category.[6] Cattle have a wide use in African ceremonialism (Herskovits, 1926). Among the Tonga of Northern Rhodesia they were killed to celebrate the emergence of the girl from puberty seclusion, during mourning ceremonies (the number proportionate to the importance of the deceased), at rain shrines to ward off drought and pestilence, and to indicate the legal conclusion of marriage (Colson, 1951). Vestments play a

[5] *Kava* is made from the root of *Piper methysticum*. The juice is expressed by squeezing or chewing the root and mixing with water. A mildly intoxicating beverage results. Use of *kava* remains despite the pressure that has been exerted against it by missionaries. The substance depresses the spinal centers controlling movement of the legs. Hence the drinker staggers, although his mind stays quite clear (Deihl, 1932).

[6] Much has been written on peyote. See Brant, 1950; LaBarre, 1938; and Slotkin, 1956.

large part in the church rituals of Euroamerican culture, the color and designs often bearing symbolic meaning. The colors by which holidays like Chanukah, Christmas, and Halloween are marked can be considered ritual specifics just as can the Christmas tree.

A special place among ritual specifics may be reserved for human beings honored in ritual. ". . . In the present day just as much as in the past, we see society constantly creating sacred things out of ordinary ones. If it happens to fall in love with a man and if it thinks it has found in him the principal aspirations that move it, as well as the means of satisfying them, this man will be raised above the others and, as it were, deified" (Durkheim, 1915:212–213). Sovereigns and heroes are examples.

Ritual specifics contribute to the appeal of the ceremony or help to fix its meaning in concrete terms. They are conditioning stimuli that trigger appropriate feelings, the very feelings that are supposed to be experienced in the ritual situation or that the ritual is supposed to express. In this way ritual artifacts do their part in accomplishing the more general functions dependent on the performance of the ceremony. The variety of ritual specifics is a direct index of the elaborateness of the ritual life of a community. Generally speaking (and despite occasional puritan tendencies to reject such objects), the profusion of ritual specifics keeps pace with scale, technical development, and cultural elaboration in general. Great wealth may come to be bound up with ritual specifics and numerous specialized craftsmen be kept busy supplying them.

Collective Representations[7]

Often (but by no means always) rituals are referred to postulated entities—gods, spirits, or bygone heroes. Perhaps the people affirm their dependence on the will of these forces or, like the Navaho Indians, seek to compel the collective representations to act in a manner favorable to man. In many communities of the western world the collective representations are historic personages who are commemorated regularly by the group. They stand for the unity of the organization. Collective representations are among a community's most important beliefs. They are the master symbols which justify given values or a particular system of social organization (Gerth and Mills, 1953:276–277). Their stabilizing influence is clear. Because they are often beyond rational questioning or doubt, and because the values people follow in social relations are backed by the collective representations, the latter concepts do much to preserve group life on an

---

[7] Collective representations are perhaps more in the area of cultural ideology than social organization. At any rate a systematic discussion of the concept is reserved for Chapter 38. We do not, as theorists of religion often do, regard these ideas as the essence of religion. As Sapir (1928) says, "Belief . . . is not a properly religious concept at all, but a scientific one."

even keel. They forestall disequilibrium, especially radical opposition. Rituals periodically remind a group of the collective representations and so maintain the emotional valence of the latter.

AVAILABLE FILMS

Weddings among the Maharashtrians (India), Navaho Indians, Hopi Indians, and in West Africa are pictured in *Hindu Family* (Encyclopædia Britannica Films, 11 min., b. and w.), *Navajo Indians* (Encyclopædia Britannica Films, 10 min., b. and w.), *Hopi Indian* (Coronet Films, 10 min., color), and *Hausa Village* (British Information Services, 22 min., b. and w.). These might be compared fruitfully with *The Royal Wedding*, featuring Elizabeth and the Duke of Edinburgh (British Information Services, 30 min., color).

Several films dealing with initiation ceremonies are not easy to rent in the United States. These include *Making Him Man*, filmed in the Northern Territory of Australia and distributed by Australian Instructional Films (8 min., color or b. and w.); *Foret sacrée* by Waelter and Yatore (35 mm., 70 min., b. and w., in French). Two films dealing with circumcision in Africa are listed on p. 588. Less dramatic is a short section of the Apache girl's puberty dance shown in *Apache Indian* (Coronet Films, 10 min., color). A brief portion of a boy's puberty ceremony is included in Film Images' *Touareg* (15 min., b. and w.), which can be secured from the New York University Film Library.

The following pictures have French commentary or titles and are available in 16 mm. size unless otherwise specified. *Ramdan* describes the month of fasting and the subsequent Id festival as these occur in Tunis. It is produced by the Société des Films, Regent (35 mm., 35 min., b. and w.). *Les Pèlerins de la Mecque*, made under the auspices of the Gouvernement Général de l'Algerie, follows North African pilgrims to the holy places of Mecca (35 mm., 50 min., b. and w.). Harvest sacrifices in the Sahara are shown in *Sacrifices pour la moisson* (B. Champault, 45 min., color, silent); and *Pagodes et fêtes de nouvel an à Luang-Prabang* deals with an Indo-Chinese New Year's festival (J. Gendron, 25 min., b. and w.). *Fiestas* shows Bolivian ceremonies (Cynthia Fain, 30 min., color, silent).

Festival Times (Government of Indian Information Services, 10 min., b. and w.) crowds so much into short footage that it allows little true idea of the significance of Holi, Diwali, and other Hindu and Muslim festivals. Sand painting, a feature of Navaho ritual, is described through *Painting with Sand* (Encyclopædia Britannica Films, 11 min., color). A very fine study of exotic ceremonial is *Trance and Dance in Bali*, narrated by Margaret Mead (20 min., b. and w.). The picture is distributed by the

New York University Film Library. *The Longhouse People*, prepared by
the National Film Board of Canada (24 min., b. and w. or color), shows
an Iroquoian masked curing ceremony and chief's installation.[8] Several
films covering Elizabeth's coronation were produced by British Information
Services. *The Coronation Ceremony* (26 min., b. and w.) relies on draw-
ings, but *Coronation Day* (20 min., color) features the actual ritual.[9] *Her
People Rejoiced* shows the celebration of the coronation in other parts of
the Commonwealth (45 min., b. and w.)

[8] The following papers by Fenton will be found helpful: 1937, 1941b, 1942, 1946.
[9] For possible use with the film are two historical studies of the English coronation
service, by Churchill (1953) and Perkins (1953).

32.

Communication

PRACTICALLY all interpersonal activity depends upon communication. Broadly speaking, communication includes all those procedures by which one person produces a change in another's behavior. This chapter, however, will be concerned exclusively with communication in which one person more or less deliberately seeks to reach a recipient with a message. There is, however, no intention of limiting communication solely to the successful transmission of intended information. Often a message is not received with the meaning it is supposed to convey.

The teacher setting forth facts, the senator on the Senate floor urging his colleagues to see a public issue his way, a package of frozen fish emblemized with a trademark, a propaganda poster caricaturing the enemy as evil, a highway marker warning the motorist of a curve in the road, an orchestra playing Beethoven's *Fifth Symphony*, and a painting in which a painter expresses his conception of reality are all examples of communication. So are the following ramblings of a radio disc jockey on a quiet February night (Anonymous, 1955:27):

And while all the thoughts were being compiled and all the words were being put down on 3 × 5 file cards   a few typewriter ribbons were being changed   and occasionally someone took the time to oil the fielder's mitt   there were things to be written, things to be said and things to be done   and there was a quiet Monday night, February, 1953   a few people were listening   a few people were looking   a few stars were being watched   a few moons were being examined   a few sand dunes were being understood as, in fact, had ever been understood in their brief period of sitting before all the elders. It came to pass that the writing was good   and we've been reading and we've been looking   we've been cleaning windows, washing glasses and smoking cigarettes and from time to time changing typewriter ribbons. We have been clipping fingernails and we've been listening to recordings. We have been eating hamburgers and we've been eating aureomycin.

Communication may be linguistic—involve language—or it may, like writing and printing, be extra-linguistic. In writing, the spoken sounds of language are expressed in graphic signs. Finally, some communication may have no direct relationship to language. Music, traffic signals, railroad semaphores, and dance which tells a story or portrays emotions illustrate nonlinguistic communication (Sapir, 1934a).

SIGNS, SYMBOLS, AND OTHER ELEMENTS

Any form of communication may be studied on two levels. One may note the way in which the technique is executed—for example, how music is made with instruments or how the speech sounds of languages are produced by the vocal organs. Such an approach constitutes an aspect of technology (see pp. 290–291). This chapter will deal only incidentally with the technical aspects of communication. The major interest will be on communication as it involves agreements between people concerning the value, significance, or meaning of the elements used in the communication process. In studying linguistic communication interest will be devoted not to how the sounds of language are produced but to the significant units of verbal communication and how their combination is governed by rules or agreements.

Signs and symbols are two important elements in the process of communicating facts and feelings in social situations. Both point to referents that may be objects, relationships, or states. That is, signs and symbols refer to other events. The deep bow which a subject makes to his ruler refers to the respect he feels (or is supposed to feel); his signature on a contract refers to his promise to act. The distinction between a sign and a symbol can be given succinctly by saying that a sign is designed to prompt an automatic response, whereas people respond to a symbol after no matter how short a period of reflection or thought. A red traffic light is a sign of potential danger if presented in its normal situation, an intersection. People who have learned the meaning will respond by stopping, and proceeding when it turns green. In Pakistan the sound of a *muezzin* calling the faithful to prayer is also a sign if, as is likely, most people respond automatically without understanding the Arabic words he utters. But a poem is different. The words, each a symbol, give information to which the response is not automatic. Understanding increases as a poem is reread. New significance comes to be found in the use of words or in the skillful use of metaphor. A sign, then, is designed to evoke action in relatively direct fashion whereas symbols enable one to conceive of other things. The same words or other stimuli may serve both as signs and as symbols, depending on whether they are intended to evoke overt behavior directly or encourage concept formation (Langer, 1942:Chap. 3).

Animals can learn to respond to many signs but they do not seem to be adept in grasping, say, verbal or written stimuli symbolically. A dog may jump up and look for the family cat on hearing the word "Puff" but he probably does not form a concept of a generalized cat. Unlike a housewife, the dog would not appreciate the picture of a succulent steak on a package of frozen beef. The only way to teach him to respond to a picture is regularly to associate the image with food so that the picture becomes a sign of food to follow. For most shoppers the picture of the steak is symbolic of prime beef, of succulence, and of the consideration that a man will appreciate when he comes to dinner.

Communication, however, involves other elements than discrete signs and symbols. A tone poem, like Sibelius' *Finlandia*, does not, like the word "Finland," point to a referent. Even less does a Mozart concerto suggest specific meanings apart from itself. The communication of music, therefore, appears not to involve either signs or symbols.[1] At a theater the audience reacts not only to words (symbols) of the playwright, or even to the whole drama which constitutes a carefully organized system of symbols, but also to the quality and skill with which the words are spoken and the cast conducts itself. Such elements as quality and skill do not readily fit under the heading of either sign or symbol. Now, an actor's role and a symphony orchestra's rendition of Sibelius or Mozart certainly arise from the signs or symbols in the playwright's script or the composer's score. They also depend on the signs and symbols made by the director or conductor. But the rendition also communicates by virtue of the skill used in rendering the performance. The audience responds to that skill and to the general manner of execution.

Blocked communication occurs when the originator of a communicative act and the person supposed to respond to it in a certain way fail to perceive the same meaning or value in the signs and symbols or in the manner of their execution (A. M. Rose, 1956:44–48). The stranger doesn't understand the legend "Pay here" or misinterprets the word "Private." The person with a certain set of values finds no satisfaction in T. S. Eliot's *The Waste Land* or in the stories in *True Confessions*. Blocked communication also occurs when somebody simply fails to receive messages containing information useful in the performance of his role. An administrator, for example, may not learn of conditions in his organization on which the formulation and execution of policy closely depend. Immigrants may not receive information which facilitates their adjustment to the host community's culture. Members of one social class may fail to learn the values and ideals of another. Blocked communication induces stress, creates misunderstanding, and leads to interpersonal conflict. No community could tolerate the wholly free flow of communication (cf. Chapter 27). What is important is whether the information reaching

---

[1] Naïve musical imitations of animal or city noises are, of course, excepted from this statement. Apparently Langer (1942:Chap. 8) does not agree with the position taken here. She claims that while music is certainly not a sign for feelings, it is a symbol about the musician's feelings. Music is the "language of feeling."

the recipient is adequate for his adaptive and adjustive needs (Jaques, 1951:302).

GENERAL FUNCTIONS

Successful communication of information is basic in maintaining the operation of any group, organism, or machine. Mechanical and biological communication, however, is of no particular interest at this point. The question to be examined in this section is how social communication conditions human adaptation, adjustment, and stress. In the main the discussion will refer specifically to linguistic communication, although what is said also applies in general to other kinds of messages.

Adaptation

Man's relative freedom from instincts (see pp. 817–818) means that he cannot survive unless he learns adaptive behaviors from other individuals who similarly have acquired such knowledge. As a community's degree of technical development increases, the volume of knowledge grows enormous, though, of course, no one American has to learn antisepsis, surgery, safe driving, wheat cultivation, how to shield himself from too great exposure to x-rays, and how to prevent the earth from losing its life-preserving fertility. However, know-how for carrying out all these adaptive skills is transmitted only through communication.

Adaptation depends on social organization—on coöperation, collaboration, and occupational specialization. But it is communication that brings people into partnership and, more important, holds them there even after strains and other evidences of disequilibrium appear. The function of ritual in maintaining social solidarity has already been discussed. Ritual consists overwhelmingly of communication. Social organization periodically is threatened by uncomplementary diversities; life itself is threatened directly by violence or aggression. Social pressure relies on communication to maintain complementary behavior.

Adjustment

The relationship of adjustment to communication is seen whenever a person who is troubled is helped by another individual, like a priest or psychiatrist, who manipulates signs or symbols. Aid may be derived from a cross, words used in prayer, or words which furnish a psychodynamic interpretation of anxiety. To communicate feelings of grief, anger, or joy also contributes to a more stable state for the individual. Rituals often promote such equalization by providing opportunity for the social expression of emotion. Difficulties or misunderstandings between people which complicate living together are overcome through communication.

Social equilibrium, on which intrapersonal adjustment in turn hinges, depends heavily on communication within the group. (1) Communication circulates the information on which the goal-oriented behavior of a viable instrumental group depends. Norms of behavior, how to perform techniques, and when to report what to whom must be communicated for an organization to operate successfully. (2) Communication in a group contributes to equilibrium when the basic values, including faith in the ultimate goal, that keep people in relation are successfully transmitted and periodically renewed. (3) States of disequilibrium when they appear can be dealt with after they are made known to responsible administrators of the group (cf. J. R. Firth, 1950).

Stress

Communication is employed to create or cement existing relationships but it also serves to intimidate or confuse people in social organization and to disrupt group life. This is how the process operates against an enemy in wartime. When certain kinds of information are blocked in whole or part, the blockage may foster disequilibrium and stress. Failure to understand the meaning, or to appreciate the value, of information may weaken coöperation or encourage a sense of frustration.

Man's capacity to use symbols (see pp. 816–817) also imposes on him a special vulnerability to stress which other animals are spared. Such stress occurs when linguistic symbols, words, are treated as the equivalent of the things they represent. People react to the word as though it were the referent. To accuse somebody of being a Communist endows the person thus symbolized with all the vague dread consequences that the word connotes in popular speech. The actual behavior of the person thus designated is of little significance when words are used in this way.

Many words ideally stand for empirical differences in the world being described. But differences may exist in behavior which have no corresponding differences in language. Referents may crop up in language which do not in fact exist in experience or are hard to locate. Language used in these ways leads to muddled thinking (Thouless, 1953:Chap. 7). A patriotic orator in a short space of time may convince his audience that "Russia constitutes a threat to world peace. Russia with its atheistic ideology is a threat to freedom-loving and God-fearing men. The Russian brutality in Hungary indicates the caliber of Soviet international policy." Does the word "Russia" stand for the same referent in each of these sentences? What is the referent? An area of ground? All the inhabitants of European Russia? All the citizens of the Soviet Union? Only some inhabitants of the Soviet Union? Or does "Russia" refer to a rather high order of abstraction, a nation conceived of as an organization of people under government? Clearly the word is not being used very precisely if the reader has trouble in deciding which of these referents is indicated. Yet the United States is preparing to fight a strategic war in which, if it becomes necessary, long-range bombers will be sent across Soviet frontiers to destroy life on a relatively grand scale. Russia, of course, is prepared to do the same. Such vagueness in linguistic communication has been called a "direct threat to our sanity" (Walpole, 1941:67). Many semanticists are devoted to the task of making people more conscious of such "defects" in the way language is used. But it still is true that visitors from another planet might accurately report that

> The race is one of those which use (in this case orally)
>   discrete
> Invariant symbols, recombination of whose elements
> Can in no sort of circumstances be complete
> Or even sound as descriptions of real events.
>
> The 'poem' (at which this, in the biped dialect 'English',
>   is an attempt)
> Is an integration of symbols which may be defined
> As a semantic composition fusing what is thought and dreamt,
> And working in senses and thalamus as well as what is called
>   mind.
>
> .   .   .   .
>
> That 'verse' is better than the race's thought as a whole.
> In general practice they reify abstractions; at
> The price of wars, etc., fail to keep symbols under control.

> [Robert Conquest, "Excerpts from a Report
> to the Galactic Council" (*The Listener*,
> 1954, 52:612)]

LINGUISTIC COMMUNICATION

The greatest proportion of communities studied by anthropology concentrate communication in language. In a large-scale nation, like the United States, face-to-face linguistic communication still remains important but a large volume of information is also put into circulation through extra-linguistic media like printing, telegraphy, or radio. Like any other form, linguistic communication may be described by the kind of conventional agreements that are involved or by the way those agreements are executed in practice. This yields a distinction between language and speech (*la langue* and *la parole*). What linguists call language (*la langue*) consists of an abstraction derived from the flow of the spoken word.

Language (*la langue*) constitutes a vast number of unconsciously made agreements. These include agreements that some sound units (phonemes) will be significant and that certain combinations of sound (morphemes) will be meaningful. The combination *wii* plus *na* in Cree designates the third person singular ("he," "she," "it") but in English "wiener" (often pronounced wii'na) designates a frankfurter. The sound units in this utterance significant to a Cree or English speaker are, approximately, /w ii n/ and /a/. Such agreements between speakers of a language exist despite the fact that only rarely are they codified in written grammars or dictionaries (Laird, 1953:Chap. 1). Tremendous diversity marks the way in which individual members of a community actually use language. Within the implicit agreements on which understanding depends, no two people speak precisely the same way (i.e., use the same idiolect).

The essence of language is, first, to select a basic repertory of sounds from the vast number of sounds that man can potentially produce and, second, to assign, quite arbitrarily, certain combinations of those sounds to certain elements of experience. Learning a language in practice consists in uttering the significant sounds in approved fashion and connecting combinations of them with the experiences to which they are supposed to refer. Thus the name "Professor Richard Smith" refers to a specific individual but "1957 Ford," "house," or "book" refers to a class of events (i.e., objects), the range of the class being quite wide. The words "between," "by," and "into" point not to a class of objects but to relationships between events.

Technically speaking, speech (*la parole*) consists of communicating by means of voluntarily produced, significant sound units. There is nothing instinctive about this process, although the capacity to use language undoubtedly rests on an organic basis (see pp. 815, 845). Speech sounds are largely produced with the lungs, larynx (vocal cords), palates (hard and soft, the latter being the velum), nose, tongue, and lips. However, other organs of the body also come to be involved. Although they may be referred to as "vocal organs" it is obvious that the parts of the body commonly used in speech also possess other functions. The process of speaking consists of expelling a relatively continuous column of air from the lungs and disturbing that column while it is still in the throat or head. (A few languages also include sounds made by inspiring air.) As already illustrated, speech sounds may be classified by the manner in which they are produced (Tables 6 and 7).

Whether language or speech is considered, linguistic communication is certainly, by the definitions adopted in this book, part of culture. The point is raised only because there has been some tendency to speak of "language and culture," as though they were separate systems (Voegelin, 1951; Bittle, 1952).

Families, Dialects, and Argots

Any two or more languages between which genealogical connection can be traced belong to the same language family or linguistic stock.[2] Such languages are derived from a common parent language whose forms can often be reconstructed (see pp. 102–103). Linguists do not agree concerning the number of language families in the world. Some of the world's major families are listed and identified in Table 36. While families tend

TABLE 36.   Some Major Language Families of the World

Family	Distribution and Representative Languages[a]
	A. EURASIATIC[b]
Indo-European	America since contact times, Europe (including Russia), and South Asia (northern India, Pakistan, Afghanistan, and Iran). Languages include German, English, Gaelic, French, Latin, Greek, Russian, Urdu, Hindi, Sanskrit, and Kurdish.
Finno-Ugric	Parts of Europe and Asia. Languages include Hungarian, Esthonian, Finnish, Lappish, and Samoyed.
Ural-Altaic	Southeastern Europe and Asia. Languages include Turkish, Tartar, Uzbeg, Khirghiz, Yakut, Mongolian, Manchu, and Tungus.
Caucasian	In southwestern Asia and southeastern Europe. Includes Georgian.
Sino-Tibetan	Eastern and southeastern Asia. Includes the various Chinese languages, Tibetan, Burmese, and Thai (Siamese).
Paleo-Asiatic	In northeastern Asia. Languages include Chukchee, Kamchadal, and Koryak.
Dravidian	Southern India. Includes Tamil, Malayalam, Telugu, and Brahui (the latter in West Pakistan).
Austro-Asiatic	In northeastern India (where it is spoken by aboriginal tribes) and southeastern Asia. Languages include Munda, Santali, and Mon.
Malayo-Polynesian	In southern Malay Peninsula, Madagascar, Indonesia, Melanesia, Micronesia, and Polynesia.[c]
	B. AFROASIATIC[d]
Hamito-Semitic (also called Afroasiatic)	Southwest Asia, North Africa, and Ethiopia. Languages include Arabic, Hebrew, Berber, Semitic, ancient Egyptian, Amharic, and Somali.
Niger-Congo	Along the Guinea coast, western Sudan, central and East Africa to the Cape of Good Hope. Languages include the Bantu languages (Swahili, Zulu, and many others), Kwa, Mandingo, Yoruba, Nupe, and Ibo.
Macro-Sudanic	Spoken in the eastern (Egyptian) Sudan; includes the Nubian languages.
Central Saharan	In the eastern part of the Sahara desert.
Click (Khoisan)	In South Africa. To this family belong the languages of the Bushmen and Hottentot people.

[2] Larger stocks, or phyla, combining several families sometimes are recognized. Thus Na-déné is a superstock which includes the Athapaskan family, which, in turn, is divided into a number of distinct languages. The distinction between language families and larger stocks will not be emphasized here.

TABLE 36 (*Continued*)

Family	Distribution and Representative Languages[a]
	C. NORTH AND SOUTH AMERINDIAN[e]
Eskimoan	Northern rim of North America, northeastern Asia, and southern Greenland. Includes Eskimo and Aleutian.
Na-déné	Northwestern America and trickling south to the Mexican border. Languages include the Athapaskan group (Kaska, Chipewyan, Sarsi, Apache, Navaho, and others), Tlingit, and Haida.
Penutian	Spoken in Oregon and California. Includes Tsimshian, Sahaptian, Wintu, and Maidu.
Hokan-Siouan	Hokan languages are distributed in Oregon and California; they include Pomo and Shasta. Siouan languages are found in the central United States and include Dakota, Assiniboin, Omaha, Winnebago, Mandan, and Crow. The southern Muskogean languages, including Creek, Choctaw, and Seminole, are also categorized here together with Iroquoian languages like Mohawk and Cherokee.
Algonkian	The Algonkian languages proper are spoken in northeastern and north-central North America. They include Cree, Micmac, Ojibwa, Blackfoot, Cheyenne, Fox, and Delaware. The Salishan and Wakashan language families, spoken in British Columbia and Washington, are also classified here. The former include Bella Coola, Coeur d'Alene, and Kalispel. Nootka and Kwakiutl are representatives of the Wakashan family.
Uto-Aztecan	From the western United States through much of Mexico. Includes Hopi, Zuñi, Comanche, Piman, Ute, Kiowa, and ancient Aztec.
Tupi-Guarani	Eastern South America from the foot of the Andes to eastern Brazil. Includes Siriono, Tupinamba, and Munduruců.
Araucanian	Chile and adjacent Argentina. Includes Mapuche.
Quechumaran	Western South America. Includes Quechua, the language spread by the Inca conquests, and Aymara.
Chibchan	Spoken in northwestern South America and Central America. Languages include Chibcha and Cuna.
Arawak	From Cuba and the Bahamas to Uruguay. Includes Goajiro and Arawak.
Cariban	In the West Indies and eastern South America to eastern Peru. Includes Carib and Choco.

[a] For maps see R. F. Spencer, *1956*.

[b] Unrelated languages include Basque in Europe (spoken in the Pyrenees and perhaps a survival of the pre-Indo-European language family of western Europe) and Japanese, Ainu, and Korean in Asia.

[c] See culture area map of the Pacific, Figure 10:1. The languages spoken by the Australian aborigines are not related to Malayo-Polynesian or any other Asiatic stock. Papuan, spoken in New Guinea, also is an unrelated language.

[d] For a comprehensive review of African language classification see Greenberg, *1954*.

[e] For a comprehensive classification of North American languages see Voegelin and Voegelin, *1941*. The diversity of language in South America is very great.

to be localized continentally there is nothing to prevent any language from being carried to any part of the world.

Within families, then, languages are distinguished. Speakers of the same language constitute a maximal speech community even when they are not contiguously located. The largest speech community of the world is that comprised of Chinese speakers, of whom there are 480 million; then come English (265 million), and Russian (200 million).

A language usually contains several dialects. The speakers of a dialect speak more like each other than like speakers of another dialect. In comparison to a language community, whose members may be noncontiguous, the dialect community is more highly localized. Dialects often form when a section of a larger speech community, speaking a more or less uniform language, is isolated, with the result that innovations enter and become fixed in the language. Should the process continue long enough a new language will come into existence. In other words, dialect differences are relatively small and language differences are greater. Not all dialects of a language are mutually intelligible, however. The Cockney English spoken in London is not too easily understood by a person from Brooklyn, and an American Southerner will have trouble making himself understood in Pakistan. Contiguous dialects, however, are mutually intelligible.

Social class cleavages also correlate with differences in speech. In Washington, D.C., a study indicated that 70 untrained judges listening to short tape recordings of the speech of Washington Negroes could gauge the social level of the speaker accurately. "Persons who grow to adulthood as members of an underprivileged social group may carry a mark of their origin through life and suffer from the various forms of discrimination which society imposes on members of the lower socio-economic classes" (Putnam, 1954; see also O'Hern, 1954). To quote from *My Fair Lady*, such speakers may literally be "condemned by every syllable they utter."

Expressions like "the King's English," "Standard English," and "*Español correcto*" indicate that not all constructions of a language are regarded with equal tolerance. Conformity to one, presumably more correct, form is often valued (Entwistle, 1953:63). Use of the more highly valued form of the language commands greater prestige and tends to be correlated with higher social rank. Teachers use social pressure to induce conformity to the standard form. But sometimes the experts themselves disagree concerning what is correct. Recently some linguists have reacted to the idea of a correct form of language in a startlingly radical manner. They claim that except for the practical difference speech habits make (for example, in getting a job), "there is no such thing as good and bad (or correct and incorrect, grammatical and ungrammatical, right and wrong) in language" (R. A. Hall, 1950:6; cf. Carpenter, 1957).

"A dictionary or grammar is not as good an authority for your speech as the way you yourself speak.

"Words do not have any 'real' meaning as opposed to other 'false' meanings. Any meaning people give to a word is automatically its *real* meaning under those circumstances.

"All languages and dialects are of equal merit, each in its own way.

"When languages change they do not 'decay' or become 'corrupted';

a later stage of a language is worth neither more nor less than an earlier stage" (R. A. Hall, 1950:6).

In areas containing several, mutually unintelligible, speech communities, one of the languages, perhaps in a more simplified form, may constitute the language of intercourse. Swahili in West Africa is such a language, or *lingua franca*. The language of intercourse may be a new language, one blending the vocabularies of several others. Pidgin English ("Business English") in Melanesia is based on Malayo-Polynesian grammar with vocabulary derived from German, English, and other languages, including some native to that region (R. A. Hall, 1955a and 1955b).[3] The movement to make Esperanto a *lingua franca* is analogous to the creation of Pidgin except that it is being deliberately fostered.

Communities with occupational specialization of labor encourage the appearance of specialized forms of language. That is, language comes to contain lexical items or constructions appropriate to the task at hand and emblemizing a group or a category. The East Greenland Eskimo shaman, who acts as the medium for invisible entities, uses special words when he refers to ordinary objects. For example, in his argot wind is called "breathing," earth the "great darkness," and man, "that which resembles a shade" (Thalbitzer, 1930:76). The so-called criminal castes of British India were equipped with quite elaborate argots (Crooke, 1896:I, 215; IV, 187–189). Adolescent slang, the technical terms used in anthropology, and the swearwords of the Yorkshire miners in the pit (Dennis, Henriques, and Slaughter, 1956:214) illustrate argots.

Basic Principles

A few basic facts about language, most of which have at some time or other been contradicted, are worth stating explicitly in order to avoid misunderstandings.

1. *Language is universal.* Except for occasional mutes and similar exceptions, there is no community which does not use language. There are no people so small in scale that they cannot transmit information linguistically. Not only is language universal but it is also very old. Witness the large number of language families in the world that cannot be genealogi-

---

[3] Here is a text and translation from a Roman Catholic hymnbook printed in Pidgin (from Krieger, 1943:49):

Ples bilong mi i namberwan,	Place belong me he number one,
Mi laikim im tasol.	Me like him that's all.
Mi tink long papa, mama tu,	Me think along father, mother too,
Mi krai long haus blong ol.	Me cry along house belong all.
Mi wok long ples i longwe tru,	Me work along place he long way true,
Mi stap no gud tasol.	Me stop no good that's all.

cally related to one another. Divergence between these families has gone
so far since their probable common origin that all resemblances between
them have disappeared (Hoijer, 1956:198).

2. *Language is learned.* It is now generally accepted that a normal child
will, by the age of about 5½, learn to speak the language of those people
who rear it. No person is born with inbuilt patterns of speech. But how
language is taught to a child varies from one culture to another. Baby talk
may be used with children before the regular language is learned. Among
the Papago Indians a special child form of the language is used during
the first five years. In some communities children grow up acquiring simultaneous mastery of several languages. Although certain sounds are easier
for a child to pronounce than others, there is no evidence that any language
is easier for children to learn. For the adult, who comes to learning with
fixed speech habits, the situation of mastering subsequent languages is
usually more difficult. In large-scale communities the individual, as he
changes his job and group or assimilates new words through the press,
radio, and film, continues to learn language throughout his life. In a small-
scale community, however, "once adult status is reached, the range of adult
experience is relatively fixed and unchanging: the language of the adult
likewise remains static" (M. M. Lewis, 1948:45).

3. *Language is relatively autonomous in culture.* Compared with other
areas of culture, like rules of marital residence or social organization, language possesses a large degree of independence from other sectors in the
cultural system. Language is an exception to the generalizations made
earlier about the systematic nature of culture. However, autonomy is not
characteristic of vocabulary. The lexical store of a language manifestly
reflects the activities, interests, and values of the members of the speech
community, and changes in it keep pace with the rest of the culture. But
apart from indisputably distinct dialects and argots, as far as fundamental
grammar is concerned, there really is not much difference between the
English spoken by a Wall Street banker, the American adolescent, and
the underworld criminal (Lévi-Strauss, Jakobson, Voegelin, and Sebeok,
1953:30–31). Some food-gathering Navaho Indians, wandering south from
the New World homeland of the Athapaskan language family, adopted
agriculture, sheep herding, and elaborate ceremonials but did not change
the fundamental structure of their language. Athapaskan in Arizona and
New Mexico is still Athapaskan as it is spoken in Alaska, Yukon Territory,
and the Northwest Territories of Canada. Some writers maintain that
language tends to become simpler as the overall elaboration and degree of
technical development in culture increase (Chapple and Coon, 1942:578–
580). But such a tendency has by no means been demonstrated clearly.

4. *Languages cannot be compared in terms of relative efficiency or*

adequacy. An Oxford University professor advises that ". . . if one wants to get closer to primeval or primordial languages, it is advisable to study savage and barbarous language processes" (Entwistle, 1953:19). Anthropologists have found no reliable way of establishing what a barbarous process of language might be. How can it be proved that the language of the Australian Arunta is closer to early forms of language than, say, English? Spoken languages always are changing. The stock of vocabulary items in the language of a very small-scale, exotic community is just as comprehensive as French, English, or Latin. The sounds of the language may strike the speaker of English as peculiar but let him be assured that English sounds are equally strange and hard to form for foreigners. In short, every language is adequate for the task it has to do. It is adequate for communicating information about elements in culture or significant portions of the cultural field. Change the culture or the field, and people will have to coin or borrow words to deal with the new experience. The Turks had no word for "secular" when they began to westernize their culture; they borrowed one from French. French and English colonists had no ready word for the American Indian's footwear and so borrowed his word, "moccasin." Many other examples of problems similarly met by numerous languages could be cited. Some evidence suggests that communities using the same language differ in the degree to which they will create new words. Australian speakers of English are exuberant improvisers compared to Americans (Pei, 1953:159). But such creativity probably is related to other personality factors and cannot be a function of the language itself.

5. *No language can be translated perfectly into any other.* Yet, and this is equally important, a message expressed in any language can in some form be rendered into any other language. In other words, languages are equivalent, functionally speaking, even though each is specialized for different kinds of experience. There are three kinds of translation (C. Kluckhohn, 1949a:156). First, one word may be substituted literally for another. This is an impossible task when the same words don't occur in different languages. *Gemuetlichkeit* has no precise English equivalent nor does Cree *Niinanaan*—"we," in the sense of I and one or more absent third persons (as distinguished from I and you-who-are-present) (cf. pp. 406–407). Second, the official type of translation allows certain idiomatic equivalents in one language to be accepted for certain words in another. English "God" is rendered *kitchiimanitu* in Cree by Roman Catholic missions (see pp. 657–659). Third, there is translation in which words are sought which will produce the same effect in the second language as in the original. This kind of translation is very difficult. How can the Japanese association of cherry blossoms with spring, or the stork with new hope, be rendered in English without copious and cumbersome footnotes?

6. *Living language is always changing.* Linguistic change occurs in (a) grammar, (b) phonetics, (c) vocabulary, and (d) semantics. (a) Grammatical constructions like "it's me" and "everybody should take off their hat" (replacing "it is I" and "everybody should take off his hat") are becoming increasingly used in American speech. However, the English speech community is less ready to tolerate these usages in written forms of the language. Writing is often more conservative than oral expression. Normative-minded grammarians frequently deplore and resist such modifications and are often successful, at least as far as concerns the standard language. (b) Guardians of language also may seek to control phonetic shifts in language, like the shift from Middle English "acre" (rhymes with "rocker") to modern "acre" or the ongoing change in "forehead" to rhyme with "horrid."

c. Diffusion provides a common source of vocabulary change. From English the Cree Indians borrowed the greeting *watcii* ("what cheer"), and English in turn borrowed "moccasin," "moose," and other words. From Arabic English has derived "admiral," "alcohol," "coffee," "lemon," "magazine," "orange," "sherbet," "sugar," and "zero" plus many others (Walt Taylor, 1933), which accompanied the diffusion into Europe of the objects or experiences to which they refer. These Arabic words diffused long enough ago to have had time to become quite well assimilated to the phonetics of English. Hence they no longer sound foreign. "Courage," from the French, has been more completely assimilated than "rouge" from the same language and both more so than *vis-à-vis*. The Zuñi joking rebuke to an awkward person *suuča ʔintiyan* ("such an Indian") is also fairly well assimilated (S. Newman, 1955:351). World-wide diffusion of science and modern technology is accompanying linguistic diffusion and helping to develop an international vocabulary for those areas of culture. Since the borrowed lexical elements are incorporated into different grammatical systems, however, they are not bringing about a truly international language (Whatmough, 1956:Chap. 4). Vocabulary change through origination apparently is rare, not unlike discovery and invention in general. In English there is resistance to coining new words. Nevertheless, physics has had to coin many names to designate newly discovered fundamental particles. Words like "libido," "defense mechanism," and "Oedipus complex" are also originations. Attempts to purify a language of foreign words may lead to substitutive originations. Thus Germans replaced *die Stenographie* with *die Kurzschrift* (E. H. Sturtevant, 1917). It may be questioned whether "defense mechanism" and *Kurzschrift* are really originations since they merely compound existing lexical forms. However, they do correspond to similar processes of recombination in other areas of culture (see pp. 195–196). Linguistic displacement may occur when a community, sensitive to some area of experience, decides that a word is no longer respectable. It will then be replaced, temporarily, by a more innocuous term. "Toilet" became "water closet" and finally "bathroom," "john," or simply "w. c." (Laird, 1953:63; cf. Nadel, 1954a). The many words for death probably arose in the same way. Origination is encouraged in vocabulary referring to a focus of culture (see pp. 128–129).

d. Over time words lose, or acquire new (added or substitute), meanings. "Jazz" once referred to sexual intercourse and not to a form of music (Laird, 1953:64). Some semantic change occurs through generalization. "Tap" once meant only to draw liquor from a barrel by means of a bung. By generalization it has been extended to cover drawing upon any resource, even on a man's talents (*ibid.*, p. 56).

7. *A word means what it does in a social situation.* The relationship of a word to its referent is purely conventional and not a direct outgrowth of experience. No word is naturally better suited than any other word to designate a particular event. There is no inherent reason why a dog should be referred to by the linguistic form "dog." And, of course, this animal isn't always referred to by that term but by *der Hund, le chien, atim* (Cree), and *kingmiq* (Eskimo). Even in the case of onomatopoeia, words are merely suggested by nature and are not an outgrowth of it. Since the relationship of words to experience is arbitrary, meanings can be altered readily. In fact, word meanings constantly do change. Therefore, it would be foolish to rely on an early-eighteenth-century dictionary for contemporary meanings. It is also not very reliable to depend on a current dictionary for all dimensions of meaning. A word seldom has the same meaning when it is used in different situations. "Be prepared" has one meaning when used as the Boy Scouts' motto, another when issued by a teacher expecting a fire drill, and still another when it appears on a wartime poster. The dictionary gives only the most generalized, or core, meaning. Except for variants, it scarcely suggests the ease with which new associations can be added or old ones displaced. Dictionaries constantly must be revised in accordance with the instability of meanings. Editors collect many illustrations of a word appearing in different contexts. The definition finally published will be based on the different usages (Entwistle, 1953:241).

Functionally speaking, the meaning of a word resides in the work it does. To ascertain the full meaning of any communication it is useful to know the status of the person uttering it, with what motivation as well as in what situation it is spoken, and what response it evokes. The utterance "We forgive those who trespass against us" assumes quite distinct meaning when it is known that these words are used ritually by church congregations on Sunday morning. Few people, knowing this fact, seriously would expect members of the congregation to forgive a business partner or a grocer who swindled or cheated them. How much confusion is promoted by the fact that people refuse to acknowledge the relativity of meaning!

How Languages Are Built

Readers already have been introduced to the two minimal units of significance and meaning, the phoneme and morpheme respectively.

1. Phoneme. The significant sounds of a language, variation of which alters meaning, are called phonemes.[4] For example, varying /p/ to /b/ in English "pin" definitely refocuses the word on a different class of objects. In Cree, however, the voiced labial stop, b, is not a phoneme distinct from the unvoiced labial stop, p. Substituting one for the other changes nothing in a word like *apuu*, "the third-person-singular-sits." Phonemes as such have no meaning but they are significant in the process of conveying meaning. Segmental and prosodic phonemes may be distinguished. In the former category are English /p b u and i/ and many more. Levels of intonation, tone, or stress (for example, the rising voice when one asks a question) are prosodic phonemes. Illustrations in this chapter are primarily confined to the former. Languages can be described as differing in the number and kinds of phonemes used.[5] Chiricahua Apache possesses 31 consonantal phonemes and 16 vowels. These are shown in Table 37. In comparison Greenlandic Eskimo possesses only 3 vowels (high front /i/, high back /u/, and low mid /a/) and the semivowel /y/. In addition there are 14 consonants, as shown in Table 38.

English has a total of 45 phonemes.[6] There are 9 vowels represented in the words "pit," "pet," "pat," "jist," "cut," "hot," "put," /o/ as in New England "coat," and the vowel of British or eastern New England "hot" or midwestern "sorry." In addition there are 3 semivowels: /y w and h/. There are 21 consonantal phonemes: /p t k b d g/; /č/, the initial sound in "chat"; /ǰ/ as in "jet"; /f/; /θ/ as in "thin"; /s/; /š/ as in "shoe"; /v/; /ð/ as in "then"; /z/; /ž/ as in "azure"; /m n/; /ŋ/ as in "sing"; /l r/. Now come the 12 prosodic phonemes. There are 4 stresses in English: primary, secondary, tertiary, and weak (each of which is indicated by a suitable sign). They are respectively illustrated in 4 syllables of the phrase "lighthouse keeper" (one who tends a lighthouse). There are 4 juncture phonemes. Internal juncture normally occurs between words and is illustrated in the compound "night-rate" as contrasted with "nitrate." Terminal sus-

---

[4] Recognition of the phoneme as an element of language is only about 50 years old. The discovery is credited to a Russian, Beaudoin de Courtenay (Lévi-Strauss, 1954a).

[5] Comparing languages in terms of their phonemic structures is not quite as simple as the following examples suggest. If two languages have the voiced labial stop /b/ as a phoneme this does not mean that the allophonic range of each phoneme will be identical (Gleason, 1955:239).

[6] Based on Trager, 1955:1188–1189.

TABLE 37. Phonemes of Chiricahua Apache

	Labial	Alveolar	Blade Alveolar	Lateral	Palatal	Faucal
Stops						
Unaspirated		d			g	
Aspirated		t			k	
Glottalized		t′			k′	ʔ
Nasals						
Continuant	m	n				
Exploded	ⁿb	ⁿd				
Spirants						
Unvoiced		s	š̌	ł	x	h
Voiced		z	ž̌	l	ɣ	
Semivowel					y	
Affricates						
Unaspirated		ds	dš	dł		
Aspirated		ts	tš	tł		
Glottalized		ts′	tš′	tł′		

VOWELS

	Unnasalized	
	Short	Long
Low-central unrounded	a	aa
Mid-front unrounded	e	ee
High-front unrounded	i	ii
Mid-back rounded	o	oo

The same vowels occur in nasalized form.

SOURCE: Hoijer, *1946a:*58–63.

tained juncture is indicated after the word "crowded" in: "The bus was so crowded that we took a cab. Wouldn't you?" Terminal falling juncture is indicated after the word "cab," and terminal rising juncture is marked by the interrogation point at the end of the utterance. Finally, English contains 4 pitches: low, middle, high, and extra high. These are indicated by appropriate numbers as follows:

²I said ³no¹. ³No³? ³That's ²right¹. ⁴No¹.

Some variations of sound in a particular language are irrelevant to mean-

TABLE 38. Consonants of Greenlandic Eskimo

	Bilabial	Mid-palatal	Velar	Interdental Point	Lateral	Alveolar Blade	Point
Stops (voiceless-fortis)	p	k	q	t			
Normal spirants (voiced and voiceless)	β	ɣ	ɣ				
Nasals (voiced)	m	ɲ	ŋ	n			
Lateral spirant (voiced)					l		
Sibilants (voiceless)						s	S

SOURCE: Swadesh, *1946:* 30–31. For vowels see text.

ing and therefore do not represent phonemes. Whether an English speaker utters the vowel in "pin" to rhyme with "bin" or "bean" is nonphonemic. Other variations in the vowel are equally insignificant as long as they don't come too close to the vowels of "pen" or "pan." In Cree substituting b for p in apuu likewise is irrelevant. These nonphonemic variations are the stuff out of which personal variations in speech (idiolects) are derived. They also appear when one speaks hurriedly or under stress. The insignificant variants of phonemes are allophones.

2. Morpheme. A morpheme is the smallest element in language which possesses meaning. "Is," "the-," "small," and "-est" are morphemes of English. Some morphemes may be used alone (when they constitute free forms). Bound forms do not make sense unless used in larger constructions. "The" and "-est" are examples of bound morphemes. In some languages, like French, Algonkian, and Eskimo, most of the morphemes are bound. In English and Chinese many morphemes are free. Languages of the latter type are sometimes called isolating, in contrast to agglutinative and polysynthetic languages that allow a rather large amount of word-building (Bloomfield, 1933:207–208). For example, in Eskimo "I make boots" is kamiliokpuŋa (from kami-, "boot"; -liok-, a bound form indicating the process of manufacture; and -puŋa, the first person singular pronominal suffix). Allomorphs are analogous to allophones. Morphemes that differ in form but have the same meaning, like -s (in "boys"), -z (in "dogs"), and -iz ("roses"), are allomorphs of the same morphene. This morpheme may be designated by any one of the allomorphs. Whichever one is chosen is usually placed in braces; thus: {-s}.[7] Bound morphemes may be used as prefixes, or as suffixes, or may be inserted into a word. A bound form may consist merely of some modification of the constituent phonemes—for example, the change of vowel from "goose" to "geese."

3. Larger Constructions. In linguistic communication morphemes are combined into larger utterances according to patterns called grammar.[8] Grammar may be defined simply as the way morphemes are used in order that they will convey enlarged meaning (Laird, 1953:35). It is a way of putting together ideas in linguistic communication to make those distinctions in experience that a speech community finds significant. Grammar enables speakers of most languages to fix the relative time of an action, specify the actor and the object acted upon, or indicate that the statement is about an incident that occurred or did not occur. Grammar is by no means

---

[7] It can be predicted that in Standard English /-s/ will be used after /p t k f and θ/, -iz after /s z š ž č and j/, and /-z/ after all other consonants and vowels. Other allomorphs include /-en/ used only with the free morpheme "ox."

[8] We pass over the fact that languages also differ in the combinations of phonemes found acceptable. Thus the combination ts occurs in English only at the end of a word but is found more freely in German. Apache phonemes occur in such unfamiliar combinations as sde and nⁿba.

the normative concept which the reader has learned it to be from the way it is taught in many schools. For a linguist grammar does not specify what the speakers of a language should do in order to convey meaning linguistically. It represents the pattern of what they actually do with morphemes when speaking or writing. It is the pattern of the implicit agreements that people follow when they use language. As such, grammar is not fixed but, like the rest of culture, always changing. A person speaks grammatically when he uses the morphemes according to the patterns obtaining generally in his speech community at a given time.

It is in connection with grammar that "parts of speech" enter the picture. Free and bound forms are used in different ways. In English some free forms are nouns and others report the actions of nouns, i.e., verbs. This is an example of categorizing morphemes according to the way they work in larger utterances. All languages contain more than one so-called functional class of forms but not all languages possess the same classes. Early studies in comparative linguistics tried to impose the form categories of Greek, Latin, and English on every language. But these categories do not apply to other languages. Look at Marshallese, the language of the Marshall Islands (Table 39). This has only three form classes (R. A. Hall, 1950:97–100): (1) There are forms to which the personal possessive suffixes (signifying "my," "thy," and "his") may be attached. (2) There are forms which cannot take the personal possessive suffixes, but the owner can

TABLE 39.   Examples of Marshallese Form Categories

Category 1	Category 2	Category 3		
aö, "my property"	*mädak*, "suffering,	FREE	BOUND	
am, "thy property"	pain"	FORMS	FORMS	
bara, "my head"	*nuknuk*, "clothing"	*nga*,	*i-*,	"I"
baram, "thy head"	*ierabal*, "work,	*kwe*,	*ko-*,	"thou"
baran, "his head"	to work"	*e*,	—	"he, she, it"
ituru, "beside me"	*lang*, "sky"	*je*,	—	"we" (1st and
iturum, "beside thee"	*til*, "to burn"			2nd persons)
	bat, "slow, to be	*kim*,	—	"we" (1st and
	slow"			3rd persons)
		kom,	—	"you" (plural)
		ir-	*re-*	"they"

SOURCE: R. A. Hall, Jr., *1950*:97–100.

be indicated by prefixing the phrase *aö*, meaning "my property" or *am*, "thy property." Thus the form "suffering" becomes *aö mädak*, "my suffering" (literally "my-property suffering"). (3) Finally, some forms are substitutes for forms in the previous two categories. They can also be used before a form of types 1 and 2 to identify the actor. These are the most familiar morphemes to a speaker of English, who would call them pronouns. Some Marshallese pronouns occur in two types. One is self-standing (like *kwe*) and the other is a bound form that can be used only with form types 1 and 2. We can now try a sentence in Marshallese: *e-bat am jerabal*, "You work slowly." But what an inadequate translation this is of words that literally say "it-is-slow thy-property work."

Bound morphemes often distinguish number. In some languages, including Eskimo, it is conventional to distinguish three, not two, numbers—namely, singular, plural, and dual. Many languages (but not Eskimo) also indicate the noun's gender with bound morphemes. But this is not, as in French or German, always sex gender. In Cree the suffix of the transitive verb indicates whether an object belongs to the animate or inanimate gender. Thus:

niiwaa′paman teta′puuwin	"I see (inanimate) chair"
niiwaa′pamaw ati′m	"I see (animate) dog"

"Flour," "man," other animals, "snowshoes," and several other nouns are animate. All others are inanimate. Cree speakers no more think of these distinctions when they use language than does a French speaker who refers to the cat with *la* (feminine) and to the dog with *le* (masculine). In Navaho, nouns are categorized by the shape or size of the object to which they refer (C. Kluckhohn and D. Leighton, 1946:Chap. 8). Bound morphemes also may denote tense, but all languages are not equipped to specify the time when an action occurred. This happens to be an aspect of experience about which some people are relatively unconcerned. The Navaho Indians pay little attention to tense but their language is well equipped to designate the relative duration of an act.

Word order may be important in constructing utterances. In English it makes a difference whether one says "The man ate the rabbit" or "The rabbit ate the man." In Eskimo, word order is quite unimportant. In the dialect of Great Whale River, Quebec, one says either:

> *i′nuk naᴠilaw′kuq ukolaca′miq* "Man eats rabbit-*miq*"

or

> *ukolaca′miq naᴠilaw′kuq i′nuk* "Rabbit-*miq* eats man."

In either case the bound form -*miq* suffixed to *ukolacaq* ("rabbit") indicates that this is the referent being acted upon. Move that suffix to *inuk* ("man") and the meaning definitely will be altered.

A simple grammar might consist of only three parts of speech: nouns, used either as subjects or as objects (N_s and N_o respectively); verbs, transitive and intransitive (V_t and V_i respectively), and the truth-value marker (T) to indicate "yes" (Charles E. Osgood and T. A. Sebeok, 1954:105–106). Grammatical analysis might then yield four types of utterances to be used in the imaginary language:

STATEMENTS	QUESTIONS
1. $N_s V_i T$	3. $V_i N_s T$
2. $N_s V_t N_o T$	4. $V_t N_s N_o T$

While such simple syntax is not known for any living language, it serves nicely to illustrate how the linguist synthesizes grammatical patterns from people's speech.

Language and Perception

Analysis of the phonemes and the free and bound forms of a language is sometimes called microlinguistics in distinction to another phase of the subject, metalinguistics. This is the attempt to study the relationship between language and thought or perception (Trager, 1949).

The central assumption of metalinguistics (also called ethnolinguistics and psycholinguistics) holds that each language provides a relatively distinct screen for sifting experience. The real world is largely a world whose form is a function of the way in which a community linguistically refers to elements of experience. No two languages do this in precisely the same way (Sapir, 1929). Different languages emphasize different components of experience. Some stress shape or size of objects; others categorize the world by sex gender. Hopi has three tenses: past, future, and generalized; a verb in the latter is timelessly true. To the ethnolinguist such processes in language imply that different languages govern speakers' thought processes, albeit on an implicit level. Whereas the speaker of English says "when spring comes," making "spring" an abstract nominal analogous to dogs, people, and other things that can arrive or go, the Cree language suggests the seasons to be unfolding or becoming. When the Cree Indian says *eesiikwu'n* he literally says "when it springs." Does this imply a conception of nature different for Cree and English speakers? Metalinguists would say that it does. But a definitive answer to the question requires securing data on perceptual processes which are relatively independent of language. Those data could then be used to verify the role of language in perception (M. B. Smith, 1954:63).

That language reveals a distinctive way of segmentalizing experience has been demonstrated. But perhaps too much should not be claimed for the fact that the Cree Indian, for example, linguistically identifies blue and green with a single linguistic form. After all, he can, if pressed, admit a distinction between those colors. His predicament (if it is a serious predicament) is analogous to the speaker of English who finds himself forced to distinguish different kinds of ice and snow. The reader could, if required, make such distinctions but not as briefly, perhaps, as does the Eskimo. The Eskimo language contains many forms for designating different kinds of ice and snow. For example: *sikuq*, "ice on salt water"; *nilaq*, "ice on fresh water"; *tuvaq*, "heavy ice, safe for walking on"; and *putaq,* "broken drift ice." When it becomes important to make significant new distinctions people usually originate or borrow linguistic means for doing so. Note the terms for elementary particles in physics. On the other hand, without the linguistic forms at hand it is possible that many distinctions in experience simply are ignored. The reader who has read through thirty or so chapters of this book has many more terms (i.e., concepts) in his control for designating characteristics of culture than he possessed when he started reading.

EXTRA-LINGUISTIC COMMUNICATION

An extra-linguistic form of communication depends indirectly on language. The spoken forms of linguistic communication are, for example, represented graphically, or by dots and dashes, or are transmitted and reconstructed into sound electronically.

Writing, the oldest extra-linguistic means of communicating facts and feelings, dates back to about 4000 years before the birth of Christ. Yet

Writing Is the Oldest Extralinguistic Means of Communication. On January 2 Japanese school children compete in writing brush letters (courtesy, Japanese Foreign Ministry).

today, out of a world population of about 2 billion persons, 1 out of 4 cannot read more than a few words or characters (Lewellyn White and R. D. Leigh, 1946:4). In Pakistan and India, where reading the *Quran, Ramayana,* or *Mahabharata* constitutes a meritorious and highly valued act, at least 80 percent of the population is nonliterate.

Writing consists of using graphic signs or symbols to stand for audible ones—either unit sounds or syllables. Reading consists of reconverting the graphic representations into audible, or potentially audible, ones (Kroeber, 1948:235). All writing is not extra-linguistic. Picture writing, which emphasizes the image, does not depend on audible speech sounds, any more than does a Boy Scout's trail blaze (Moorhouse, 1953:Chap. 1).

Such writing has nothing to do with language; it is nonlinguistic. However, pictographic writing comes closer to true writing when independent signs (i.e., ideographs), standing for abstract classes of experience (like fish, man, eating, or royalty), are grouped in various combinations. The meaning is then read from whatever juxtaposition of images happens to have been made. The pictograph for "man" preceded by the sign for "royalty" and followed by the signs for "eating" and "fish" might mean "The king eats fish." Tense markers and other grammatical indicators bring such a system still closer to the spoken language. Chinese writing consists of over 40,000 ideographs, which have become so conventionalized that their meaning can no longer be determined from appearance alone. The Chinese government hopes to replace this system by a phonetic system of writing (Sulzberger, 1956).

The alphabet used in this book originated in Southwest Asia about a thousand years before the present era and has since spread around most of the world. In this system each sign represents one sound, or a combination of more or less closely related sounds. Phonetic writing of this sort has become in turn the basis of new codes—like the Morse code used in telegraphy.[9]

Although the alphabet gave rise to a phonetic system of writing, there are several reasons why the written does not correspond perfectly to the spoken language. (1) Many alphabets lack signs for all the phonemes of the language. This is true of English, in which there are 33 segmental phonemes but the alphabet contains only 26 characters. Representation of the prosodic phonemes is not attempted in ordinary writing. (2) Phonetic change is constant in language but conventions of spelling tend to persist. The speaker says: "He's na gonna go," but the stenographer (unless interested in getting down the actual speech) transcribes the words: "He is not going to go." (3) Some signs used in writing have little to do with the flow of speech. How well do the commas in "He killed moose, deer, beaver, and fox" reflect what happens when these words are normally spoken? Punctuation, which arose in the fifteenth and sixteenth centuries, is largely a matter of convention and does not accurately reflect the pauses (juncture phonemes) of speech (Lloyd and Warfel, 1956:Chap. 4).

The conservatism of writing *vis-à-vis* speech is in part a function of the fear of the linked changes which a modified system of writing might bring about (see p. 188). New ways of representing words graphically would threaten the intelligibility of books written traditionally. These materials will become unreadable except to specialists. It is impossible for twentieth-century Englishmen or Americans to read *Beowulf* or Chaucer without special training. In modern China the written language bridges many mutually unintelligible dialects, much as did the Plains Indian sign lan-

---

[9] Chinese does not use a dot-dash telegraphic code but a code of numbers running from 0001 to 9999. Each number stands for one of 10,000 frequently used ideographs (Moorhouse, 1953:165).

guage (see pp. 555–556). True, in China each speech community reads the ideographs using its own dialect, but a message written ideographically can be interpreted even when writer and reader speak mutually unintelligible dialects. This unity which writing gives to China would disappear with phonetic writing.

Functions of Writing

Writing makes possible mediated social interaction and allows a relatively few people to initiate behavior to a far greater number. Used in this fashion, writing has proved to be of great value for administration and social coördination in large-scale societies. A few more specific dependent functions of writing may be summarily presented.

1. *Writing facilitates the diffusion of new knowledge with relatively few teachers.* Such knowledge sometimes enables people to adapt or adjust more successfully. In 1923 the campaign of the Mass Education Association began in China. The object was to teach 1200 basic characters to illiterate peasants. Between 1933 and 1937 the production of cotton increased 14 times. "This increased production is due to improved agricultural knowledge, and also to the aptitude for handling large stocks which follows the introduction of a proper accounting system" (Moorhouse, 1953:208).

2. *With writing man has become able vastly to supplement his memory and to deal simultaneously with large sectors of experience.* The present author could never talk about the range of subjects covered in this book if written records were not available to help him keep facts straight. History is thin without written records to preserve the past. As a matter of fact, if history is defined as the study of documents, then there can be no history for nonliterate communities. Books are the source of history.[10]

3. *Writing through mediating social interaction has contributed to the impersonality of the modern world.* The writers and processors of the news that is read and heard daily and the authors of books often remain impersonal. Their intentions in writing or publishing cannot be assessed in the light of personal knowledge (Lévi-Strauss, 1954b:113).

4. *Writing facilitates thought and discussion about language itself.* The analytical study of grammar arose after the discovery of writing.

5. *Products of writing sometimes come to be used as means for coping indirectly with problems of living.* To read the Hindu scriptures confers forgiveness from sin; the runic writing of prehistoric northern Europe brought safety to a woman in childbed (see pp. 782–783); and in Pakistan a verse from the *Quran* worn on the body can promote healing.

---

[10] "Book" designates any written literature, whether on clay tablets, rolls of parchment, or bound and folded leaves. The last-mentioned form of a book is called a "codex." The earliest known codex dates from the second century of our era. The greater convenience of codices and their easier concealment may have contributed to their rapid diffusion (cf. Roberts, 1956).

The Mass Media

With the coming of printing, radio, and TV, extensions of writing capable of reaching millions of people in a short time at little cost, the way was open for people in strategic positions to influence the behavior of large populations (Mills, 1956:Chap. 13). It is scarcely surprising that administrations should try to control mass media. For example, in Great Britain radio began as state enterprise. In the United States laws insure each party in an election campaign an equal chance to be heard over a radio or television outlet. Other laws specify what the mass media can report or say about the administration's policies and the occupants of public office. Such controls on communication are, in turn, often resented by those who operate the mass media. Values like "freedom of the press" and the "public's right to know" are cited to defend the press and radio from government controls.

From a functional perspective the mass media offer a large variety of satisfactions. For example, comic strips invite close emotional identification with certain popular characters (*The Sunday Comics, 1956*). (Oral folk tales enjoy the same appeal in small-scale communities.) News accounts encourage the growing intensity of large-scale relationships. The fiction of magazines and radio provides models whose behavior may be imitated. Millions of families become educated to the proper way to react to a dreadful illness, to divorce, or to love and marriage by such communications. The mass media standardize attitudes as well as overt behavior on an international scale.

Any communication which has as its deliberate object influencing behavior for the pecuniary or other special advantages of the communicator or his sponsor, and which pursues that goal by the systematic use of suggestion, persuasion, or allied means, is propaganda (Doob, 1935:75–76). Needless to say, no community devaluates all types of propaganda, and the word, therefore, should be used without normative connotations. In totalitarian nations the mass media are used heavily for propaganda originating from administrators. This also is true of nearly all countries during wartime.[11]

Drum Language[12]

In parts of Africa slit-log or large skin-covered drums are constructed capable of being heard over 3 or 4 miles in daytime and up to 15 miles at night. These instruments are employed in extra-linguistic communication. The basis of the so-called drum language is pitch. Niger-Congo lan-

[11] See the propaganda posters of World War II in *Life*, Dec. 21, 1942.
[12] From Carrington, 1949, and Good, 1942. See also Armstrong, 1955; Carrington, 1953; M. Schneider, 1952; and T. Stern, 1957.

guages—for example, Bantu—make use of pitch phonemes. This means that tone is a significant variable in the speech. The pattern of tone in an utterance of several words transmits information in drum language. For transmission words are chosen with several pitches. These tones are beaten out either on the appropriate ends of a log drum, each end of which is tuned to a different pitch, or on skin drums possessing high and low tones. The tones are interpreted by recipients of the message. Certain expressions, rich in tones, symbolize common ideas. "Only folds, folds hands on his breast" has been chosen by one community to announce that someone is dead. People's drum names are similarly recognizable from their constituent tonal patterns.

NONLINGUISTIC COMMUNICATION

Communication that does not depend on the sound symbols of language ranges from rather involuntary but socially standardized exclamations of pain and joy to certain punctuation marks, the pictorial representation of dreams on a Plains Indian's tipi, or Beethoven's *Fifth Symphony*. Unlike extra-linguistic communications, the transmission of information nonlinguistically occurs in all cultures. But the variety of its types and the number of people it reaches vary with scale.

Gesture

The most common form of nonlinguistic communication relies on body motion or gesture. Kinesics is the term that designates the study of this phenomenon (Birdwhistell, 1952). The units of kinesics are raw kines —movements, like a wink—which can be analyzed into meaningful types of activity called kinemorphs. Each kinemorph not only can be described in its physiological aspect but possesses an agreed-upon meaning, much as does a morpheme. As with language, the meaning of a kinemorph basically depends on the difference it makes in a social situation. Some kinemorphs are defined explicitly; for example, various kinds of winks, the handshake, nod, frown, and many others. Other kinemorphs are part of the implicit culture. Their meaning can be discovered only by studying the gesture in its context. All variations in the way a kinemorph is acted out are not significant but constitute allokines (analogous to the allomorphs of language). Most of the work so far done in kinesics has been confined to developing orthographies for recording.

Since gestural communication is conventional, it follows that no two cultures possess precisely the same system of kinemorphs. The frequency and qualities of gesturing also vary between communities.[13] American

[13] The balance of the paragraph follows Ruesch and Kees, 1956:23–25.

gestures are less ardent than those of some ethnic categories. Italians are more given to expressing themselves in vigorous gesture which reflects the intensity with which they relate interpersonally. Italian body movements are carried out mainly by the face, arms, and shoulders, rarely by the hips or lower extremities. Gestures sometimes even are substituted for words and often they reënact deeds being described linguistically. Jews, on the other hand, use gesture more to support, punctuate, or emphasize words. The lower arm is prominently used while the upper arm is held rigid. Among Germans gesture often expresses covert behavioral states, a reflection of an interest in subtle, internal processes. The gestures are less concerned with communicating details of experience than with revealing clues to an actor's role and social position. The face, region of the spine, eyes, and mouth are used to show "the innermost depths of the soul." In French culture gesture is used quite sparingly but with elegance and precision. Especially are the fingers and face brought into play.

By Gestures the Conductor Engages in Nonlinguistic Communication with Members of His Orchestra (courtesy, RCA Victor).

One of the most explicit forms of gesture is "sign language." If the signs form letters of the alphabet, then we deal with a true extension of language. Often the signs transcend any single speech community and convey discrete ideas. This was the case among the Plains Indians of the United States. Sign language allowed a considerable measure of communication to occur between people who might belong to any of 6 different language families (over two dozen languages). In the sign language of the Plains people, "cold" was indicated by clenching both hands and crossing the arms in front of the chest with a trembling motion. Raising the forefinger and pointing it upward, then reversing the finger and bringing it down meant "chief" (Lowie, 1954:4). The Walbiri people of Central Australia use sign language during initiation. Since the novices are supposed to be dead they do not speak but rely on gesture. Also, in the presence of uninitiated youths older men secretly, through signs, plan the initiation rites which will surprise the novices. Walbiri widows communicate with signs for 12 to 18 months after a husband's death (Meggitt,

1954). Many communities, including the Walbiri, use signs to plan sexual assignations. Among the Kickapoo Indians of Mexico whistling is a prominent feature of the courtship pattern, apparently having replaced the lover's flute (Ritzenthaler and Peterson, 1954).

Object Language[14]

Several other media for nonlinguistic communication illustrate the use of artifacts for conveying information.

Masks constitute a standard communicating device in many cultures. They are used, for example, in ritual and in dramatic performances. Actually masks are but a special instance of communication via clothing and adornment. Dress, tonsure, and adorning the body are widely used to communicate social status, cognizance of the significance of an occasion, and a variety of other messages. To shave or otherwise mutilate the bodies of people guilty of certain kinds of misbehavior has been found effective for advertising their disgrace or their status as prisoners.

Objects suitably arranged and displayed frequently are relied upon to communicate. They may show off a merchant's stock in trade. Often auxiliary printed labels also appear in such displays. The exhibition of museum collections, paintings, or animals at an agricultural exposition con-

The Masks of These French West African Dancers Illustrate One Kind of Object Language (courtesy, French Cultural Services).

[14] Much of what follows is based on Ruesch and Kees, 1956.

stitutes communication. The upper-middle-class house in an American suburb has been called a stage on which visitors play the role of audience while the family displays its possessions. These possessions communicate how well the family has approached the goal of success as measured in material terms (Seeley, Sim, and Loosley, 1956:49–52).

Decoration is in part a statement about the value and significance of the object decorated—for example, a Christmas gift. Decoration also expresses ritually the significance of an occasion. American towns put up the symbols of Christmas when, in late November, they decorate the shopping district with ribbons, lights, and spruce boughs. The Roman Catholic Church conveys the tragedy of the passion and death of Christ by shrouding the church statues during Holy Week.

The invention of photography has augmented communication by allowing use of pictorial messages. Newsreels, picture weeklies, and photographs in the daily newspapers present the news in images that give the audience and readers the impression of having been on the spot where the action happened. Films and posed pictures also convey fictional messages. Whereas the silent movies relied heavily on nonlinguistic pantomime, the advent of talking films reduced dependence on action. The burden of communication came to rest on the dialogue or, in many educational films, narration. Deliberate control of the camera and other aspects of the photographic process can serve to communicate a unique, personal view of the world as seen by a sensitive interpreter. The management of these skills is a task for the producer or director of a motion picture when he coördinates many people and techniques in order to achieve a specific effect.

Telepathic Communication

A message spoken or thought of at a distance and designed to be interpreted by another person without empirically demonstrable means of transmission is probably best regarded as a nonlinguistic form of communication. The investigation of such communication is called parapsychology. Phenomena studied by parapsychology include extrasensory perception (ESP), a term referring to an awareness of events outside oneself without the use of sensory channels of communication. The external event can be an object, an activity occurring at a distance (like an accident), or a covert behavioral state (thought) of another person. Parapsychology also investigates psychokinesics (PK). In this phenomenon the individual "produces an effect upon some object [like a die] in his environment without the use of his own motor system" (Rhine, 1956:193).[15]

Many psychologists remain unconvinced about the actual occurrence of

---

[15] Many of these forms of extrasensory perception and psychokinesics do not represent intentional or social communication. Rather, what is communicated (if anything) illustrates unintentional transmission of a stimulus.

ESP or PK phenomena. But the matter has ceased to be simply one of claims advanced and met by counterarguments. Parapsychology has become an experimental science using carefully controlled techniques and statistical measures (Price, 1955). This research will determine whether at least some kinds of ESP or PK are possible for certain kinds of people. At present, results are neither unduly promising nor wholly negative.

33.

Life Cycle

PRACTICALLY an entire culture may be described from the vantage point of the individual as he moves from conception and birth to death. Such studies have been made. For example, those aspects of Samoan culture that touch the career of a Samoan girl and woman were included in an account of growing up in Samoa (Mead, 1928a). Less systematically, perhaps, large sectors of Hopi and Winnebago Indian culture have been included in autobiographies of members of those tribes (Simmons, 1942; Radin, 1920, 1926). The life-cycle approach refers to a convenient framework for describing situations occurring to the typical individual in a community between birth and death. It is a means of ordering data. The life cycle in any culture refers to how certain socially standardized acts, thoughts and feelings, and artifacts impinge on the maturing individual. The reader scarcely needs to be reminded that individuals in culturally different communities encounter different life experiences as they grow into adulthood and old age.

To avoid undue repetition this chapter will not deal with subjects already comprehensively treated. Some of these appropriately could be included in an examination of life-cycle events—for example, the family and marriage. The life cycle will be subsumed under the following categories: (1) conception, (2) pregnancy, (3) childbirth, (4) child care, (5) adolescence, (6) sexual behavior, (7) adulthood and old age, and (8) death. Since many of these topics involve ideas about the growth and functioning of the body, the chapter marks a transition from social organization to the next major division of culture, ideology.

CONCEPTION

A human life begins the moment that a sperm discharged by the man in the vagina during sexual intercourse makes its way to the uterus and unites with an egg cell or ovum. In rare cases, and only in Euroamerican culture, sperm produced through masturbation is used for artificial insemination. Fertilization of the egg constitutes conception. Contraception refers to any measures that function to prevent conception.

The majority of the world's communities know that pregnancy (and, therefore, conception) is related to sexual intercourse. Such communities recognize the role of the biological father (more precisely, the genitor) in procreation. A few people, notably the Trobriand Islanders and certain Australian aborigines, are reported to be ignorant of the role of coitus in the generative process. Among the Australian aborigines the intangible essence of the human being, the *kuruna*, exists at so-called totem centers where the ancestors in the long-past Dream Time went into the ground. When the *kuruna* enters a suitable woman, in the theory of the Australians, she conceives. In her uterus the formless *kuruna* develops human limbs and other organs, becoming a proper baby. Physiologically no male has anything to do with the process, although natives believe that the *kuruna* normally will not enter a woman who has never had sexual intercourse. Coitus opens up the womb but does not by itself lead to conception (Montagu, *1937, 1938, 1949a*). Recently some doubt has been cast on the generalization that the Australian aborigines actually are nescient concerning the role of physiological paternity. The aborigines' belief concerning the *kuruna*, it is pointed out, accounts merely for the soul of the child. Natives regard the sexual act as also important for it forms the fetus or physical aspect of the new individual (Berndt and Berndt, *1942–44*:244; Berndt, *1951*:231; and Montagu cited above). Future research probably will support the latter viewpoint. Nevertheless, the Australian aborigines seem to place more emphasis on how the spiritual component of human individuality gets its start than on the physical aspect. Their belief, it will be noted, offers a convenient explanation for the manifestly observable fact that not every act of intercourse results in conception. "In his own thought the native is perfectly logical, and in relation to his own system of beliefs, his own framework of reference, his conclusions are perfectly valid" (Montagu, *1949a*:100).

The fact that not every sexual union results in conception also lends support to other exotic beliefs, like the belief that babies are reincarnations of the dead. Among the aboriginal Kaska Indians a child himself might admit to reincarnation by announcing, "I know this country. I been here before" (Honigmann, *1954c*:137). The not uncommon *déjà vu* illusion also may account for such statements. Among some people a birthmark or special aptitude becomes evidence of reincarnation. Some ancestor, it will be recalled, possessed a similar mark on that part of his body or manifested the same aptitude. If not every sex act leads to pregnancy, then this physiological fact is quite congruent with the fairly common belief that repeated copulation is needed to complete conception or to promote fetal growth.

In all N-type communities that continue from one generation to another children obviously are valued enough to be reared to maturity. A woman's failure to conceive not only is a bitter disappointment but may expose her to shame and even constitute grounds for divorce. Sometimes a man will marry a second wife in such circumstances. To prevent or cure barrenness there are many more or less effective remedies. Often these are indirect, involving the manipulation of symbols rather than, say, artificial insemination (see pp. 624–626). Some such remedies actually help to bring about the desired result. They function to prolong the time during which a woman is retained by her husband and, therefore, extend the period during which regular copulation occurs between them and may lead to fertility. Explanations for barrenness vary widely. Rarely is the condition explicitly ascribed to the husband's sterility, unless he manifests obvious impotence. In 6 out of a sample of 64 communities a woman is not considered barren until she has attempted to discover whether her partner is sterile (Ford, 1945:37). Toward this end she copulates with other men, either lovers or, following divorce, a subsequent spouse.

A man has less trouble concealing his sterility than does his wife, especially in a community where adultery is common. There she may conceive with other men and the husband's infirmity will remain undiscovered. The actual genitor in such cases will remain unknown.

In 19 out of 64 communities there is no apparent knowledge that the germ of the fetus—the egg cell—originates with the woman. It is believed that the seed originates with the man somewhat in the same way that plants spring up from seeds planted in the earth. That this may have been the prevailing theory in ancient Egypt is suggested indirectly by a theological text which accounts for creation by a god's masturbation (M. Wilson, 1951a:59). Nine cultures out of 64 believe that both male and female secretions play an important role in conception. Sometimes the woman's contribution is identified with the menstrual blood (which, of course, ceases its periodic appearances once conception occurs). The Kaska Indians see coitus leading to a mixture of bloods which amalgamate in the uterus (Honigmann, 1949a:231). Both matrilineal and patrilineal people recognize a mutual contribution to conception by men and women.

Birth Control and Infanticide

Although all communities value offspring, people sometimes regulate the number of children they produce or avoid reproduction at certain times. Such practices, functionally speaking, are contraceptive. Through abortion women may seek to avoid bearing offspring.

Mainly small-scale, exotic communities seek to avoid pregnancy prior to a girl's marriage, in cases of adultery, and during nursing. The most common as well as most effective means for birth control is abstention from coitus. In many communities people practice avoidances that require temporary periods of sexual chastity but this may not be done deliberately to avoid conception. Nevertheless, any form of continence serves that end. Among the Cheyenne Indians a couple, as a mark of respect to a child, sometimes abstained from sex relations for several years. Naturally they were aware that this would lead to wide spacing of births (Grinnell, 1923). In some communities a woman does not wish to conceive while still nursing a child. Hence, a married couple refrain from coitus during this time. Should lactation last for two or more years, then children will be spaced quite far apart. Sexual frustration for a man is not engendered through such customs when polygyny is part of the culture (Mead, 1953a:226). Missionary influence which eradicates polygyny may indirectly discourage prolonged nursing and encourage frequent pregnancies.

People often try to manage contraception indirectly, through the manipulation of signs and symbols. Among the Kaska Indians one woman pierced the afterbirth of a stillborn fetus with porcupine quills in an attempt to prevent further conception (Honigmann, 1949a:231–232). In a few communities coitus interruptus (i.e., withdrawal) and interfemoral coitus (the latter in parts of East Africa) provide more direct procedures to forestall pregnancy. Among the White Knife Shoshoni Indians, who lived in the sparse desert country of Nevada, a father taught his son to practice withdrawal in order to limit offspring (Harris, 1940:43). Apparently surgery and substances applied locally are rarely used to limit conception.[1] Even when the diaphragm and jelly combination and the condom become available it may be difficult to persuade people who want to limit family size to use these controls. Some persons dislike interfering with the spontaneity of the sex act or feel that mechanical contraceptives reduce the pleasurableness of the experience (Stycos, 1955).

Abortion and infanticide are belated attempts to undo the work of conception. Except in special circumstances, most communities greatly disapprove and punish willful abortion. On the Micronesian island of Yap men object to the practice but women frequently manage to abort. This is done not to avoid the physical difficulties of childbearing (a possible motive for abortion in some communities) but to avoid the change in status that children initiate in a woman's life. She dislikes constantly being tied to the child and the limited opportunities for extramarital sexual affairs, knowing that her husband is not restricted similarly. She recognizes, too, that divorce becomes more difficult with the status of motherhood (D. M. Schneider, 1955:221–222). How do people try to abort an unwanted fetus in small-scale, exotic communities where surgery is never attempted? Medicine taken internally is commonly used for this purpose but some mechanical means is also applied, like kneading the abdomen or jumping

[1] For an excellent study of the reliability of the means used in exotic communities for limiting conception see Lorimer, 1954:100–114.

from heights. A number of abortifacients act as emetics and laxatives, suggesting that people conceive of abortion as analogous to expelling other substances from the body.

Infanticide tends to be practiced by food gatherers, like the precontact Shoshoni or the Eskimo, whose subsistence techniques cannot support large families. It may be used in cases where a child cannot be given to another family in adoption. It is also countenanced in a large number of communities for monstrous births. Communities that dread twins may permit the killing of one or both such children (Ford, 1945:71).

PREGNANCY

Often the first sign of pregnancy that people recognize is cessation of menstruation, although a failure to menstruate does not always indicate pregnancy. Nausea and growth of the breasts and uterus are other signs. Ten of 19 communities in the sample of 64 which recognize pregnancy by cessation of menstruation also calculate the date when birth probably will occur, counting from that time (Ford, 1945:44).

Although a complex series of physiological changes accompanies pregnancy, the amount of cultural fuss made over the event varies from one community to another. Nearly all people impose restrictions on a pregnant woman's diet. Many of the rules in effect reduce her food intake. Sometimes a connection between eating and growth of the fetus is recognized explicitly. At other times certain foods are prohibited because it is feared that they will injure the unborn child. Such an attitude probably is founded on the premise that what a woman eats directly nourishes the fetus. Modern medical practice advises dietary restrictions in order to

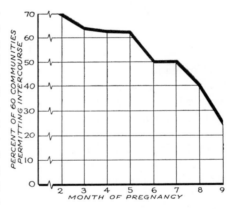

FIG. 33:1. Proportion of 60 Communities Permitting Sexual Intercourse During Various Months of Pregnancy (from Ford and Beach, 1951:216).

facilitate delivery. The reassurance provided by food observances in cases in which a woman is anxious about her condition should not be overlooked. The ritual aspect of these restrictions should also be noted. They express the concern a woman is supposed to feel at this time and call the community's attention to an impending social change.

Sexual restrictions commonly are imposed in pregnancy. Twenty-one out of 64 communities expect a woman to avoid coitus during some period of pregnancy. Such avoidance becomes increasingly frequent as pregnancy approaches the ninth month (Fig. 33:1). Of course, not everybody in a community may abide by this rule or observe the food avoidances. In a sample of 1000 American wives, more than one-quarter said they copulated during the entire period of pregnancy (Ford and Beach, 1951:215). Such intercourse is not dangerous provided that excessive pressure on the woman's abdomen is avoided.

Restrictions on heavy exertion seem to be emphasized less than rules governing eating or sexual intercourse. However, they are not lacking. Prevention of miscarriage is one of their main functions. Exercise frequently is recommended for pregnant women and is advised in western medical practice to promote easy delivery.

Often the husband as well as his pregnant wife follow rules whose intended end is a healthy baby. The man sometimes is forbidden to inflict injury on other people or animals, a prohibition that makes sense if the community believes that like can produce like (see pp. 627–628). It also makes sense in terms of modern psychology. The man's anxiety lest harm befall his pregnant wife or the child is generalized to aggressive (i.e., harmful) acts which he commits.

CHILDBIRTH

Women in small-scale, exotic communities normally do not, as they sometimes are purported to do, give birth without concern, returning to their work within a few hours after delivery (Freedman and Ferguson, 1950). Childbirth seldom takes place without qualified assistance for the parturient. In Europe and America the assistant usually is a male specialist trained in obstetrics. Most other people look to an elderly woman to aid in delivery. She may be a relative, a neighbor, or a specialist midwife. In any event she is someone who herself has given birth, and, therefore, knows what to expect. Her role is adaptive for both mother and child. Only rarely is a priest or shaman called to assist at an especially difficult delivery. His role then usually is to manipulate signs or symbols to overcome difficulties postulated to be hampering birth. Some observances practiced by the pregnant woman and her husband also are directed, in advance as it were, to insure successful delivery.

Anybody not assisting in the actual birth-giving process commonly is excluded from the scene. Men (other than spouses) almost universally keep away (in 45 out of 64 communities, only one reported that they may be present). By decreasing the total number of people present at such a time a community reduces the number of sources through which the woman could become infected. The exclusion of men probably is related to the norms of female modesty. Almost universally the rule is that a woman shall not expose her genitals to men and in delivery such exposure is highly likely. The husband, of course, is in a special category and a few cultures (11 out of 64) recognize his right to be present. Usually he is given a special job to do which effectively prevents him from becoming a nervous spectator. Excluding this man from the birth scene in other communities protects him from a situation in which, because of his identification with the woman in labor, he would experience great stress. Sometimes a husband indirectly assists his wife to give birth, but from a distance. For example, he may be forbidden to smoke, chew, or scratch himself lest he injure the child. He may mimic the birth, taking to bed and going through actions suggestive of labor. The Choroti of central South America believe that the couvade, as the last custom is called, attracts to the man those evil spirits who might interfere with his wife's successful delivery (Ford, 1945:63). Presumably he is able better to cope with them than she is. The father's activities may continue to be restricted during the postnatal period. Apart from its ritual value in calling attention to his new status, the couvade functions to convince a man that he can be of assistance to his wife during this critical time (Ploss, 1871a).

Returning to the delivery, it is interesting to note that in most communities for which relevant information is available women give birth while occupying a sitting position (15 cases). Less commonly the parturient kneels (11 cases) or squats (3 instances). Alternative positions are allowed in 10 communities but rarely does she take the reclining position assumed in modern hospitals. Sometimes the parturient is supported from behind during delivery; she may grasp a stake which has been driven into the ground, or pull on a rope hanging from the ceiling.

Not only the appearance of the baby but also that of the afterbirth is regarded as important by most communities. Such interest is probably related to the fact that should the placenta not be delivered it would form a fatal source of infection. The placenta is disposed of by burial in 30 out of 64 communities, burned in 1, placed in a latrine in 4, and disposed of in alternate ways in 2. Judging from available evidence it is never discarded carelessly, a precaution that definitely is adaptive in view of its infectious nature. The people concerned, however, more probably would point out that careless disposal of the placenta risks its discovery by a sorcerer, into whose hands the child's life would then be committed. No community neglects to sever the umbilical cord from the placenta and most people ligature the stump of the cord in some way, a practice probably preventing occasional hemorrhage and reducing the risk of local infection.

Postnatal Care

Mother and child receive special attention in the period immediately following birth. The majority of communities (48 out of 64) require both persons to remain secluded for some days. They may occupy a special birth shelter or remain isolated in the dwelling. Seclusion is adaptive; it reduces the chances that the mother's still open wounds will become infected through social contact and protects the infant much as does isolation in the modern hospital. The period of isolation further insures that the mother will not resume customary activities until her body has had some chance to heal. Finally, seclusion safeguards other members of the community from contact with the infectious discharge (lochia) that flows for 7 or 10 days after childbirth.

Coitus generally is forbidden to the mother for periods ranging from a week to several months or years following birth. The lacerated genitals thus are protected from infection and the husband is prevented from contact with the infectious lochia. Of course, these are not the rationalizations offered by the people themselves. It is more likely that some communities would cite the woman's uncleanliness from childbirth as a reason for enforcing postnatal sexual continence. Whatever the purpose, these avoidances have adaptive functions for the woman. By preventing a new pregnancy before the baby is strong enough to be weaned from the breast they also safeguard the child's survival. Postnatal dietary restrictions, on the other hand, probably more often are adjustive in their operation. They assure the parents that they are doing everything possible to insure the child's successful development.

Naming

Birth introduces a new member into the family and community. It is useful to designate him in some fashion as early as possible so that he can be referred to conveniently. Names, however, have other purposes than serving merely as appellatives. They may also confer extra power on a person, a power that weakens if the name is used freely. Hence in some cases the first name which a child receives never is used. Instead the person is called by one or a series of nicknames throughout his life. A few people select a name even before a child's birth but allow it to be altered should it be inappropriate sexually. Otherwise, naming usually comes at the end of the postnatal seclusion. Together with other rites occurring at this time it marks the child's ritual introduction to society.

Conventions of naming differ widely. Most people in the world do not follow the Euroamerican custom of assigning both a family surname and a personal name to the child. The surname pattern, however, is diffusing around the world. The Great Whale River Eskimo name children after deceased relatives. A girl may be named after the mother's mother, whose memory the family wishes to perpetuate in the youngster. A woman sometimes lovingly calls her baby *anana*, "mother." Under circumstances like this it sometimes is difficult to say whether a name merely links a child symbolically with an ancestor or is indicative of a belief that the ancestor is reincarnated in the child (Stefaniszyn, 1954). Among the Bessari of French Togoland, West Africa, explicit rules govern naming (Cornevin, 1954). The child's name normally depends both on his order of birth and on the mother's sib. Each sib possesses a fixed series of masculine and feminine names set for first, second, third, fourth, and fifth sons and for five daughters. In the Nataka sib a first son is called Gbati; a first daughter, Numfron. But the Nawale apply the names Kondi and Mutoni respectively. In the Egyptian village of Silwa parents usually choose a child's name (Ammar, 1954:92). For a first child this may be the name of its grandfather or grandmother. As in the rest of the Muslim world favorite names are those similar to the name of the Prophet or those expressing subservience to the will of God.

Teknonymy designates the custom of referring to parents by the name of one of their children ("Father of so-and-so") instead of by their given names. Ritually the custom expresses the altered status of parents.

CHILD CARE

Many variables, including the genetic make-up acquired at the moment of conception and intrauterine experiences, are related to individual personality differences. Anthropologists are less interested in individual differences than in studying elements of overt and covert behavior that are generally characteristic of people in a community. They seek to explain the characteristic personality in terms of experiences that are relatively common to all the community's members. Except possibly for variation associated with class and caste, all parents in a community tend to rear children in similar,

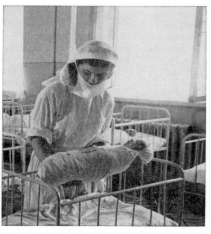

Swaddling Is a Fairly Widespread Form of Early Child Care. A nurse in a Moscow maternity home is holding a stiffly wrapped Russian baby (courtesy, Sovfoto).

socially standardized ways (Mead, 1953b). Each child, therefore, encounters many of the same early experiences and is brought up by models who consistently reinforce one another. Such similarity of early life experiences

is revealed in the common elements of personality that observation shows
to be typical of people living in a community. Of course, each individual
still is a unique organism, different in make-up and idiosyncratic experiences from all other individuals. Aspects of personality regarded as typical

TABLE 40.   Correlation of Five Types of Explanation for Illness with
Handling of Five Systems of Behavior

Type of Explanation[a]	System of Behavior	Comment
Oral explanation. Ingestion of something by the patient is believed responsible for illness. Verbal spells and incantations performed by others also may bring about illness.	For 23 communities where this explanation occurs the average rating for oral socialization anxiety is 12.2. For 16 communities where the explanation is lacking the average rating is 8.94.	The expected difference between the two categories of communities is fairly large and statistically highly significant.
Anal explanation. Defecation is responsible for illness, or the feces or urine brings sickness. Exuviae may also be used for sorcery, including hair clippings and nail parings. Or the ritual charms, curses, and spells and failure of the patient to perform some ritual may bring about illness.	For 10 communities where this explanation occurs the average rating for anal socialization anxiety is 12.1. For 10 communities where this explanation is lacking the average rating is 11.0.	The difference is slight but in the right direction (i.e., the direction predicted by the hypothesis).
Sexual explanation. Sexual behavior is the act, or sexual excretions or menstrual blood the material, responsible for illness.	For 14 communities where this explanation occurs, the average rating for sexual socialization anxiety is 12.2. For 14 communities where this explanation is absent the average rating is 11.2.	The difference is again slight but in the right direction.
Dependence explanation. Soul loss is responsible for illness; or spirit possession brings sickness into the body.	For 13 communities where this explanation occurs the average rating for dependence socialization anxiety is 13.4. For 17 communities where this explanation is absent the average rating is 11.7.	The expected difference is fairly sizable and statistically significant.
Aggression explanation. Aggression or disobedience to spirits is the act responsible for illness. Poison is the material held to produce illness when introjected into the body. Objects used symbolically as weapons may produce illness.	For 17 communities where this explanation occurs the average rating for aggression socialization anxiety is 14.8. For 15 communities where this explanation is absent the average rating is 10.8.	The expected difference is fairly sizable and statistically highly significant.

[a] For the authors' logic followed in grouping certain concepts in each of these categories see J. W. M. Whiting
and I. L. Child, *1953:*150–153.
SOURCE: J. W. M. Whiting and I. L. Child, *1953:*150–164.

of a community's members are referred to collectively as the "typical personality," "modal personality,"[2] or "national character" (Mead, 1942b; Honigmann, 1954b; Haring, 1956). The theory may be summed up in the following postulate: The modal personality in any community is a function of a particular combination of experiences shared by members. These experiences include a relatively similar pattern of child rearing.

Considerably more work remains to be done to test this proposition. Research to date suggests that it is, within broad limits, true. To cite only one important investigation, comparative research suggests that a functional relationship exists between certain aspects of child rearing and the explanations for illness which are current in a given culture (J. W. M. Whiting and I. L. Child, 1953:150–166). The study distinguishes 5 types of explanation for illness: oral, anal, sexual, dependence, and aggression. These are defined in Table 40. Each explanation refers to a system of behavior which may be highly pleasurable or made anxiety provoking in early childhood. For example, in a community where feeding is generous and weaning nontraumatic, the oral system of behavior is gratified rather than surrounded with anxiety. Harsh cleanliness training, severe sanctions on masturbation or sex play, early demands for independence, and strict controls on aggression are anxiety provoking rather than gratifying. The table shows the extent to which each explanation for illness is associated with anxiety induced in the relevant system of behavior during childhood. The researchers conclude that "There is some evidence to support the hypothesis that early socialization anxiety is correlated with explanations for illness. The results for oral, dependent, and aggressive behavior allow the conclusion to be made with considerable confidence."

Early Child Rearing[3]

The newborn individual long remains helpless to maintain his own survival (see pp. 813–814). He requires special, easily digested food (a requirement admirably supplied by the breast milk), must be kept clean, and needs protection. These survival needs are met by child-rearing practices in all cultures.

Care of the child begins practically from birth, when the neonate is washed, a task often performed by someone other than the mother. This

[2] The term "modal personality" is misleading since it suggests that methodologically the field worker counts the number of times various combinations of personality traits recur in a community and then uses the most frequent (i.e., the statistically modal) combination as the type for that group. This is not the procedure usually followed (see, however, Wallace, 1952). Rather, the modal personality picture finally arrived at, after observing a number of different people, synthesizes a number of elements in a composite or ideal type to which no individual corresponds.

[3] For aspects of child rearing not discussed here see Honigmann, 1954b:Chaps. 10–11, and Slotkin, 1954:Chaps. 4–9.

person usually anoints the baby with oil, turmeric, or soft ashes after which he frequently is swaddled or placed in some kind of container (cradle). Food gatherers, who keep on the move, and communities in which babies accompany mothers into the fields usually employ portable carriers that a woman can strap to her back.

During the first few days in some communities the child is not put to the breast. In this period after birth the breasts secrete not milk but a noticeably different substance, colostrum. Apparently colostrum is not injurious if fed to a newborn baby but it may act as a cathartic and so produce bowel movements similar to diarrhea. Perhaps this fact is related to the avoidance of colostrum in the child's diet. In most communities mothers breast-feed their children, although in western countries some children are fed from birth by bottle. The universality of nursing does not mean that this is an instinctive, maternal response. Underlying the custom is the discomfort of the breasts swollen with milk. Nursing relieves the pressure. Erotic gratification

Back-Packing of Children Occurs Among Food Gatherers Like the Great Whale River Cree Indians.

from nursing also may motivate nursing, but more important is the fact that even before motherhood women learn that babies are to be nursed. "So long as the society in which she lives expects her to nurse her offspring as part of her contribution to its wellbeing she will be anxious to do so" (Ford, 1945:78). Specific feeding periods occurring at regular intervals of the day or night (schedule feeding) are rare, taking the world of man as a whole. In general, the baby is fed whenever he signals hunger or other discomfort. Some people are ready to feed young children from the breast whenever they will eat. At night the child normally sleeps with the mother and so readily can receive the breast. Since suckling is one of the child's earliest, emotionally highly toned experiences, and one in which he learns his earliest goal-oriented responses, it is of some interest to note how differently the behavior is executed cross-culturally. Among the Arapesh a baby is fed whenever he will eat; he is treated as a passive thing. The Iatmul, who live in New Guinea, expect the child to claim the breast with some vociferous crying before he is nursed fully and generously. Interestingly, the Arapesh grow up to be relatively passive people but the Iatmul come to be assertive in personality (Mead, 1949b:65–69).

Prolonged breast feeding is common among small-scale peoples. Out of 45 communities for which information is available, in at least 31 children are nursed for 2 years or more. Weaning at 6 or 9 months, something that happens in many white, North American families, definitely is rare (Jelliffe, 1955:123–124).

Other foods usually are given to supplement breast milk while the child still nurses. This pattern prepares the way for weaning, a stage in development that usually presents something of a problem. Children do not outgrow the nursing habit willingly. Techniques for weaning vary but three are common. The first requires removing the child from the mother, perhaps letting him spend some time with grandparents where he will forget the nursing experience (7 cases). Two other ways are to punish the baby for nursing, perhaps by smearing an unpleasant or frightening substance, like pepper or soot, on the nipples (11 cases), or by use of threats (4 cases). There is some suggestion that early weaning is related to standard of living. That is, people who can afford to, wean children earlier than poorer folk (Jelliffe, 1955:130–131). But early weaning steadily is diffusing to other sections of the population where its acceptance is related to four factors: (1) availability of foods that may be substituted for breast milk (like baby foods and certain cereals), (2) prestige associated with use of tinned milk products, (3) government subsidization of the cost of milk powder, and (4) an increase in the number of women who live in cities and who work where they cannot personally tend to their children.

Education

Unless the process is confused ethnocentrically with schooling, it is impossible to find any community lacking education. Not only concerned with presenting facts to a growing individual, education involves the inculcation of values. Actually, the facts taught always are selected in terms of a community's dominant interests and values (cf. Pettitt, 1946).

Taking the world in general, a child's educators rarely are specialist teachers, priests, or governesses. The parents, the parents' siblings, the child's older siblings, and his playmates teach him much that he must know for adaptation and adjustment. From these sources, and usually in informal fashion, he learns how to take solid foods in an approved manner, talk, control elimination, act modestly, relate himself emotionally to others, and distinguish right from wrong (Havighurst, 1953). Gradually he also acquires the ability to form certain socially standardized concepts about his social and physical world. He is made aware that certain people are regarded as better than others; that some animals are menacing but others sustain life, or that the sky is a bowl covering the flat earth. He learns to handle his body with skill in games and in work. From the approval or disapproval of his associates he builds up a conception of himself. If the community is literate he acquires the ability to write and read. Perhaps the earliest literacy is limited to a scripture; the *Quran* serves as a basic text in the mosque schools of the Middle East. With adolescence and adulthood come other learnings which will be referred to in their proper place.

In a small-scale, homogeneous community parents and peers can prepare the individual adequately for the vast majority of his future roles. Schools become important when, as in modern North America, "the goals of education . . . are more and more, the preparation of individuals to fill roles in a highly specialized industrial society and the socialization of children in terms of the middle-class values which are the regulatory ideology of" the culture (Seeley, Sim, and Loosley, 1956:226; cf. Eisenstadt, 1956:163–166). Lower-class children are exposed to this middle-class ideology in an effort to motivate them to leave their lower-class surroundings and values, to become flexible, coöperative, competitive, success-oriented, and able to take their places in a factory or business without friction and with as little disturbance to equilibrium as possible. Schooling in a system of complex social organization also teaches individuals to understand their government and appreciate the responsibilities incurred in contractual relationships (important in a world where organic has replaced mechanical solidarity), and inculcates the ethics that churches no longer can transmit effectively. The greater the degree of occupational specialization, provided that occupations are not strictly hereditary, the more important is formal education or schooling (Loomis and Beegle, 1950:460).

Education is not withdrawn completely from parents in modern society. Even with schoolgoing children parents must still spend time and spare no pains if the youngsters are to meet the demands of the school successfully and so be prepared to secure prestiged social positions and remunerative jobs. Punishment, help with homework, encouragement of diligence, and show of patience are ways in which modern parents prepare children for success in school and in later life. Limiting the number of offspring and sacrificing in order to keep children in school and dressed in appropriate manner are other ways in which parents seek to insure future success. Because middle- and upper-class parents are more inclined, or better able, to perform these services, children on these social levels often earn better grades than lower-class youngsters. More than disadvantaged peers, they are likely to arouse the teacher's interest.[4]

Sometimes in small-scale communities the boy and girl go to separate, so-called "bush schools" where each sex undergoes quite special training

[4] For pertinent reading see the short bibliography in Warner, Meeker, and Eells, 1949: 251–253. Also see Warner, Havighurst, and Loeb, 1944. For an English coal-mining community where children are inadvertently disadvantaged by parents' lack of awareness see Dennis, Henriques, and Slaughter, 1956:234–237.

aided by rigorous discipline. The discipline is applied not by members of the family, who might be lenient and allow an easy pace, but by outsiders. The child is pushed into adulthood by being separated from much that was familiar to him and to which his subadult role had been conditioned. Together in the bush school adolescents learn the details of myths, rituals, and values which it henceforth will be their responsibility to perpetuate. Material ritual specifics and other secrets are revealed in an atmosphere of ritualized solemnity and importance. Sex instruction may also be imparted.

Youth houses, reported for various parts of the world, and especially well known from Melanesia (Malinowski, 1932) and tribal India (Majumdar and Madan, 1956:130–137), are similar in function to the initiation schools. The houses are dormitories in which one sex alone or both in common spend nights until marriage. Much of the group's activity is recreational, but the senior children also instruct their juniors in dances, folk tales, and other traditions. Training is given in living under extrafamilial authority as well as in coöperation and collaboration. The dormitories that accommodate boys and girls afford an opportunity for sex experience and training in sex roles (Elwin, 1947). Among the Nyakyusa of southern Tanganyika, boys after about 11 years no longer sleep in their father's hut but join an age village of their contemporaries, the land being provided by the parents. Here the boys build huts which two or three share until marriage, when each constructs a house for his family in the same village. Their own children will similarly set off to found, or marry into, age villages (M. Wilson, 1951a).

Mutilation

The early part of the life cycle often is associated with deliberate and relatively permanent mutilations of the human body. The manifest purposes of these, as well as their functions, vary considerably so that an adequate functional interpretation would require careful study of the context in which any specific mutilation occurs. For example, scarification or circumcision performed in the bush school probably enhances the dramatic break which a child makes with his past, but enlargement of the ear lobe simply may add to personal attractiveness.

Some mutilations occur very early in life. The earliest of all, probably, is that which flattens the back or other portion of an infant's head. The desired effect is achieved by the way in which the baby is swaddled or bound to a cradleboard. Soon thereafter comes piercing the lobes or helixes of the ears, the nasal septum, lower lip, or cheeks. Ornamental rings and plugs will be worn in the perforations. In parts of Oceania the lobes of the ears are enlarged systematically until sometimes they hang down to the shoulders. In parts of Africa girls systematically enlarge the *labia minora* and may be punished in initiation rites for failing to have done so properly (E. J. Krige and J. D. Krige, 1943:113). Operations on the teeth may come at various times and in varying forms, including extraction of one or more by knocking them free from the gums, filing, and chipping.

Even circumcision may come very early. It does in Euroamerican hospitals, where the operation is performed for reasons of health. More often circumcision occurs some years after infancy and constitutes a badge of proper manhood. In Judaism and Islam relatively early circumcision signifies membership in a body of believers. An analogous genital mutilation for the girl, one with a far more restricted distribution than circumcision, is cliterodectomy, excision of the clitoris (Ploss, 1871b; Laycock, 1950; Young, 1949). People in East Africa have been resistant to giving up cliterodectomy despite pressure from colonial powers. The Kikuyu regard the operation as equivalent to male circumcision (Leakey, 1952:90). In Australia subincision of the penis may substitute for, or follow, circumcision. Two varieties of the operation are known. In one the urethra is slit, sometimes to the very edge of the scrotum; in the other the canal merely is perforated (Basedow, 1927). Women of some Australian tribes dilate the vaginal passage (cf. Ploss, 1871b).

Tattooing and cicatrization are common means of bodily adornment. The latter custom, in which welts are raised in the skin, largely is limited to darkly pigmented people on whose skins tattooing would not show up very well (Gillin, 1948b:310; Coon, Garn, and Birdsell, 1950:54).

Somewhat apart from the mutilations mentioned is the custom of castration. In the Middle East, whence it diffused to Europe, the operation has been performed to produce eunuchs for harem service. In eighteenth- and nineteenth-century Europe it created young males with soprano voices (Heriot, 1956; Penzer, 1936:134–145).

Sex Roles and Temperament

The diversity of sex roles in different cultures indicates quite clearly that a boy is not instinctually equipped to become a proper man, nor a girl a proper woman. Men are not the same, culturally speaking, in different communities; nor are women (Mead, 1935). A boy must learn to behave as males are supposed to act and girls face a similar developmental problem. In some communities the distinction between men and women tends to be blurred. It is almost as if the people expect that a woman could overcome every vestige of her physiological femininity and be able to emulate the man in everything (Mead, 1949b). In other cultures—like those of Pakistan and India—the difference between men and women is accentuated (Honigmann, 1957b).

There always are some individuals who find the role standardized for their sex to be uncongenial in comparison with that of the opposite sex.

In some homogeneous communities no alternative exists to fulfilling indicated status expectations. Men all must fight, compete, or do whatever the cultural ideal specifies. Women must all be passive, gentle, and retiring. The person who is unattracted to the norms specific for his sex has no alternative but to conform. His frustration is often intense. But a number of communities are readier to allow such individuals to assume the dress and habits of the opposite sex and to retain them throughout life (Angelino and Shedd, 1955). These persons become berdaches. Among the Omaha a boy who dreamed of a burden strap or hoe (symbols of female status) could assume certain feminine roles. He used the feminine suffixes of certain words, carried out women's tasks, copied their mannerisms, and let his hair grow like a woman's. He did not necessarily take up homosexual relationships and might marry a normal woman. Confusion between the berdache and the homosexual should be avoided. Among some people of Iraq, in a family whose children have all been girls, one child may assume the role of a man. She follows a masculine profession, earning an income for her parents (Westphal-Hellbusch, 1956:126). Boys in their turn sometimes carry on female singing and dancing roles, even padding the breasts to simulate femininity (Thesiger, 1954:19).

Akin to berdaches were the "manly-hearted women" of the Blackfoot and other Plains Indian tribes (O. Lewis, 1941). Such a woman was assertive, independent, ambitious to accumulate property, and frankly sexual. An ordinary woman did not share these traits. The manly-hearted woman temperamentally may have been unsuited to the relatively retiring role standardized in Plains Indian culture for young women. She also may have been a favorite child and recalled her active, independent childhood when faced with the assumption of more dependent feminine traits.

The Plains Indians generally showed high regard for individuality and personal inclination. They did not expect all individuals to conform to a single ideal norm. In a society that valued chastity, for example, tribes like the Sioux made room for a woman whose career in promiscuity had been validated by a dream. She could even acquire a measure of prestige through forthright sexuality. By accommodating persons with deviant tendencies Plains tribes reduced the likelihood that they would disturb equilibrium through uncomplementary behavior. Their deviance was valued or, at least, accepted within the range of complementary diversity. Of course, no community can provide room for all kinds of deviation.

ADOLESCENCE

More mature relationships, at least with age mates, generally are expected around puberty. At this time the child enters a brief period of adolescence that lasts until the attainment of full sexual maturity. In adolescence the individual begins to assume a considerable share of the adult roles of his culture. In many parts of the world marriage occurs shortly after puberty, especially for girls. In contrast to modern North America, where emotional independence remains incomplete until some years after adolescence, many cultures expect it to be realized within that period. One way of hastening it is through the initiation ceremonies discussed above (p. 432).

Menstruation

Onset of menstruation (menarche) dramatically signals the girl's approaching physiological maturity. It is a time of life recognized ceremonially. Seventy out of 150 communities observe rituals on the occasion of menarche (Ford and Beach, 1951:174). The girl may be honored at this time and confer blessing upon the tribe, as among the Apache Indians (Morris E. Opler, 1941:82–133). In other communities she constitutes a danger to herself and to others and hence is sequestrated in precautionary fashion. This formerly happened among a number of North American Indians (Honigmann, 1954c:123; cf. Benedict, 1934:Chap. 2).

Less than a quarter of a sample of 64 communities entertain any theory to explain menstruation. Most of those that try to account for it either hold the moon somehow to be responsible (6 cases) or else ascribe the onset of the menses to initial sexual intercourse (5 cases). The first theory is explicable by the resemblance between the length of the moon's phases and the duration of the menstrual cycle. But the other belief is more difficult to perceive as in any way logical until one recalls, first, that many people allow premarital sex relations that may begin before puberty and, second, that initial intercourse when accompanied by defloration instigates bleeding. Hymeneal blood is not identical with menstrual blood, but it is doubtful if the distinction would be noted readily. All the people who ascribe menarche to initial copulation also permit considerable premarital sexual freedom to girls (Ford, 1945:9).

Attention paid to menstruation by no means ceases after menarche. Half the sample of 64 communities forbid coitus with a married woman while she is menstruating and an additional 10 prevent close association between husband and wife at that time, thus effectively blocking coitus. Modern hygiene suggests that sexual relations with a menstruating woman may lead to infection. Many people also prevent the menstrual flow from coming into contact with people, food, or other objects. In 19 cases this is done by forbidding a menstruating woman to cook for men; in 6 communities she is urged to keep away from sacred objects; in 9 she must avoid sick persons. In 14 cases the menstruant periodically is isolated in a special shelter, thus effectively preventing her coming into contact with other people and objects. In an additional 6 cases sequestration is less complete.

The woman simply avoids leaving the house, where she remains isolated for the duration of the flow. Another means of preventing contact with the menstrual blood is to provide the woman with a means of collecting the flow. A bark-cloth tampon or menstrual pad which readily can be disposed of performs this function. The more efficient the method for collecting the menstrual fluid, the weaker the restrictions imposed on a menstruating woman. In none of the communities requiring sequestration do women make any use of pads or tampons at this time.

Adolescence a Critical Age?

There was a time not long ago when people thought that adolescence must be a period of conflict and personal distress. This certainly seemed to be true in America, but was it also true in other communities? Did the storm and stress of adolescence bear no relationship to the cultural life in a heterogeneous modern nation? Were they solely dependent on the biological changes of puberty? A study which contributed importantly to answering these questions points out that in Samoa the adolescent girl does not essentially differ from her sisters who have not reached puberty (Mead, 1928a). In other words, adolescence has been proved to be not necessarily a difficult period in a girl's life.

SEXUAL BEHAVIOR

Sexual activity takes a variety of forms. Some of these occur relatively rarely and are disapproved of in many communities—for example, sexual contact with a domesticated animal. Rare and disapproved forms of sexual behavior often are called perversions, a word loaded with normative judgment. Sexual behavior may also appear in relatively disguised form, like target practice with a gun. In this section sexual behavior is defined only in terms of an accompanying physiological disturbance recognized as "erotic arousal" (Kinsey, Pomeroy, and Martin, 1948:157–160; Kinsey, Pomeroy, Martin, and Gebhard, 1953:627–629, 635). Often the goal of sexual activity is a sexual orgasm or climax. There are six chief sources of the human orgasm: self-stimulation (masturbation), nocturnal dreaming to the point of climax, heterosexual petting to climax but without actual intercourse, heterosexual intercourse (i.e., coitus), homosexual intercourse, and contacts with animals of other species. Erotic arousal, like its climax, the orgasm, is normally pleasurable. Arousal (also called tumescence) means a building up of tension in the body that is then abruptly released in the orgasm (i.e., detumescence). In the mature male detumescence may be accompanied by the ejaculation of liquid secretions from the penis. These secretions characteristically contain the sperm on which fertilization depends (see pp. 559–561). Some mature males, like most immature males, can achieve orgasm without ejaculation. Female orgasm is not accompanied by ejaculation though it too is marked by a sudden release of tension that is normally pleasurable.

The phenomena grouped under sexual behavior are extremely sensitive to cultural and other nonbiological stimuli. What is erotic, for example (i.e., leads to erotic arousal), varies considerably from one culture to another. It even varies from one social class in the United States to another. Firm breasts, tattooing on the inside of the leg, or nudity of any kind may be stimulating. Yet not all nudity promotes erotic arousal. In communities where men wear no clothing and women are always practically naked other signs than mere nudity are erotic stimuli. For example, in western South Australia, "the human body . . . is not sexually attractive unless it assumes certain attitudes. As long as the woman's body does not assume a sexually attractive posture, for example with legs apart, or a man's penis does not become erect . . . there is no thought of sex in connection with their bodies" (Berndt and Berndt, 1942–44:320). The degree to which the individual participates in sexual behavior during his life depends very much on the culture of his community. In some communities there is practically a blanket avoidance of all sexual gratification; sex itself is wrong and scarcely to be enjoyed (Kardiner, 1939:23; Murdock, 1949: 263). Other people do not enjoin sexual activity itself but restrict it to special circumstances and forbid it with particular relatives. Out of a sample of 250 communities, 115 are in the latter category and only 3 are in the former (for the rest information simply is unavailable). People who grow up in a community marked by the more accepting attitudes toward sex probably will begin quite young to engage in sexual activity.

A community may vary its attitudes toward the erotic from one point in time to another. The fourteenth century in western Europe was much preoccupied with sex. Women accentuated their breasts and men wore prominent codpieces. Brothels flourished and watering places were centers of assignation. Sexual songs were popular. By the time the nineteenth century came around very different behaviors were held to be acceptable.

It is not surprising that the actual execution of coitus should also vary from one community to another. The amount of sexual foreplay differs. In some places the couple proceeds immediately to copulation with little or no embracing. On the other hand—for instance, among unmarried persons of middle- or upper-class background in the United States—petting techniques like kissing, genital apposition, or stimulation of the female breasts regularly precede coitus or serve as substitutes for intercourse (Kinsey, Pomeroy, Martin, and Gebhard, 1953:Chap. 7). Physiologically one function of sexual foreplay is to induce a high level of sexual tension in each partner, thereby accentuating desire (Ford and Beach, 1951:Chap. 3). Posture during the actual act of coitus is socially standardized (C. Kluckhohn, 1948) though certain patterns recur. It is quite common for the man to squat or kneel before the reclining woman (33 cases out of a sample of 193 communities). He then either moves toward his partner or pulls her toward him so that her spread and raised legs rest on his hips. Other people (35 out of 193) prefer the position customary in Euroamerican culture where the man lies on top of the reclining woman. In a surprising number of cases the woman is allowed to ascend the reclining man (37 out of 193) but how frequently this occurs in a community where it is allowed is not clear. On the whole, the literature contains rather little information about coitus. Not only is such behavior nearly impossible to observe but it normally does not enter conversation, on account of either the ethnographer's or the informant's reticence, or both.

A number of people restrict coitus to certain times (for example, enjoining it during ceremonies, before hunting and warfare, or in connection with some manufacturing process). Such restrictions function to reduce the possibility of conception. A number of communities are concerned lest sexual activity be overdone and lead to permanent debility. The fear of excess may be related to the extreme relaxation that normally follows orgasm. It is unlikely that persons by themselves will normally carry on sexual behavior beyond the point of nervous capacity. Once that point is passed sexual arousal becomes very difficult (Kinsey, Pomeroy, Martin, and Gebhard, 1953:638).

Premarital Sexuality

Sex play often occurs during early years but it is during adolescence that sexual activity becomes prominent. In a sample of 250 communities, 65 fully permit premarital coitus, expecting only that incest rules will be observed. The East African Chewa believe that unless children begin to exercise themselves sexually early in life they will never beget offspring (Ford and Beach, 1951:190). Some 49 more cases conditionally approve such relations (for example, placing restrictions on undue promiscuity or publicity) and 44 explicitly forbid them. This means that premarital sex relations are allowed in 70 percent of the cases for which adequate information is available or 45 percent of the whole sample (Murdock, 1949: 265). Where such behavior is not permitted adults use rather constant supervision, threat, or severe punishment to prevent its occurrence. Unmarried people of mixed sex scarcely may receive opportunities to be together, so closely are girls guarded in some parts of the world. A common device to prevent sexual intimacy consists of placing special value on female virginity, perhaps making it a condition for successful marriage. The Plains Indians allowed special privileges in ritual to a virtuous woman. The American middle class reveals increasing signs of condoning greater freedom of premarital coital relations, at least between couples who are engaged to be married. The same custom is reported for Norway (Rodnick, 1955:56–58).

Where premarital sex relations occur children are not commonly born out of wedlock. Three reasons have been suggested: (1) Coitus is not complete in some communities where sexual intercourse is permitted to occur outside of marriage. The young male does not insert the penis into the vagina but between his partner's thighs (interfemoral coitus) (cf. M. Hunter, 1936:180–183). Or he withdraws a moment before ejaculation. (2) Signs of pregnancy lead to hasty marriage arranged by the girl's parents. (3) Evidence suggests that adolescence is a gradual process and that all the structures in the girl necessary for conception do not become mature until some years after the onset of puberty. This means that the years immediately following the appearance of the secondary sexual characteristics are associated with subfertility. During this time girls are unlikely to conceive or to bear a viable fetus. Considerable data bear out the existence of a period of so-called adolescent subfertility (or adolescent "sterility"). In a southern Appalachian sample of girls those who married at 13 years did not conceive for an average of 7.5 months. At age of 14 the interval was reduced to 6.4 months; 15, to 4.6; 16, to 3.6; 17, to 3.2; 18, to 3.1; 19, to 2.7; and 20–21 years to 2.5 months. Girls who married upon reaching their twenty-second birthday or later tended to conceive in about 2.5 months. Similar data are reported from India (Lorimer, 1954:47). The onset of menstruation, it is interesting to note, apparently is hastened by cultural factors like diet and exercise and seems to be delayed in the tropics.

Extramarital Sexuality

However common premarital sex relations may be, after marriage many communities expect the wife to obtain sexual gratification from her husband alone. A married man's sexual fidelity is controlled less easily than a woman's but it also tends to be expected. Extramarital sexuality is forbidden for both sexes in 28 out of 64 communities but to some degree allowed in 19. It explicitly is forbidden to women in 31 cases. Some evidence indicates that agricultural communities disapprove more severely of extramarital sexual relations than do food gatherers,[5] a finding congruent with the patterns of sexual hospitality and wife lending often found under the latter conditions. Despite its prohibition, adultery commonly occurs. When it does, action often is not taken against the offender other than the spouse, particularly the woman. She may be beaten, mutilated, or divorced. The frequency of adultery, it may be suggested, would make action against the paramour a nearly constant source of disturbance in a community and contribute to weakened in-group solidarity. Wife lending

---

[5] Aubrey Williams, unpublished manuscript, n.d.

(cicisbeism) between friends, or by host to guest, constitutes a device which helps to reduce the incidence of adultery. But a woman sometimes is encouraged to take lovers for the economic help that such men will furnish to the husband (Schwab, 1947:186). In those African communities where women are permitted to marry women, the legal wife can only procreate for her legal "husband" by having sexual relations with men to whom she is not married (cf. E. J. Krige and J. D. Krige, 1943:144).

Disapproved Forms of Sexual Activity

Two means of erotic arousal leading to orgasm are disapproved of in many communities: masturbation and homosexuality.

Self-stimulation is tolerated in some of the sexually more liberal cultures when it occurs in childhood. Stroking a baby's genitals may even be used to pacify the child. Some people, though, do not countenance masturbation even in children and many disapprove strongly of self-stimulation by adults. The reason for disapproval varies. In China masturbation in adults is regarded as a waste of semen which could go for procreation or might be used for the health-giving benefits of coitus (Weakland, 1956:241). In Europe and America masturbation is condemned as immoral and has been held the cause of "every conceivable ill from pimples to insanity" (Kinsey, Pomeroy, and Martin, 1948:513). In the United States, where individuals who go or will go to college more often find sexual gratification in masturbation than in any other sexual activity, millions of young people still live in conflict over this behavior. Yet educators, psychologists, and psychiatrists assure them that "the physical effects of masturbation are not fundamentally different from the physical effects of any other sexual activity . . . any mental harm resulting from masturbation is an outcome of the conflicts introduced by the condemnation" of the activity (*ibid.*, p. 514).

Homosexuality frequently is condemned even when it occurs in childhood. Despite disapproval it tends to be found when either sex finds itself cut off from heterosexual gratification. It occurs in harems, penal institutions, and military groups. Strenuous attempts, however, often are made to discover and eradicate such behavior. One study indicates male homosexuality to be accepted in 54 out of 193 communities and female in 21 (C. Kluckhohn, 1948:340).[6] But the high number of accepting communities undoubtedly includes cases in which berdaches are known, although they may not engage in homosexual relationships (see p. 575). In a few communities male homosexuality is practiced openly before mar-

[6] Out of 190 communities examined by Ford and Beach (1951:130, 133) 49 accept male homosexuality. The berdache is definitely classified as a homosexual in that study. Seventeen communities at least tolerate female homosexuality (again including female berdaches).

riage. The Keraki people of southwestern Papua regard relationships between men and boys as essential for a youth's growth. At initiation a
preadolescent boy spends some months in seclusion attended by an older,
male sponsor. He plays a passive role in sodomy, continuing the relationship for several years (F. E. Williams, 1936:158, 194, 308). In the Egyptian
oasis of Siwah men and boys often form homosexual relationships. Sons are
loaned to friends of a father and may assume the active role in sodomy
(Cline, 1936:43). Although homosexuality is often called by the term
"sodomy," it is by no means certain that sodomy in male sexual relationships is as common as mutual masturbation and oral-genital contacts. In
sexual relationships between women mutual masturbation probably is more
frequent than use of penis substitutes, but information scarcely is adequate
for such generalizations.

Prostitution occurs in many communities where it is not tolerated by
part of the population but is patronized by another, often sizable, section.
It is, therefore, both approved and disapproved. The commercialization of
sex relations is a function of scale and directly correlates with trade and
occupational specialization of labor, of which, indeed, it is a particular
form. Female prostitution is more common than the male variety, although
the latter by no means is unknown. It occurred, for example, in protohistoric Middle America. Female prostitution might well be distinguished
from the custom in which a woman capitalizes not only on her body in sex
relations but more on her personality as a whole. The geisha and Greek
hetaira belong in the latter category (de Beauvoir, 1953:567).

ADULTHOOD AND OLD AGE

Assumption of adult status, it has been pointed out, may be marked by
dramatic initiation ceremonies. It sometimes is symbolized by a distinctive
way of arranging the hair or a special style of clothing. Among the Orokaiva of Papua unmarried girls wear a piece of short bark cloth wrapped
around the hips and supported by a belt. Older women wear somewhat
longer wrap-around skirts and cut their hair short. In some Papuan tribes
no cloth at all is worn until marriage (F. E. Williams, 1930:32–33). In
all communities adulthood marks the assumption of new duties and greater
responsibility.

Learning scarcely ceases with adulthood, although in a homogeneous
community it is likely that the increment of new learning declines with
entrance into this status. Everywhere, though, the adult is faced with developmental tasks like selecting or learning to live with a mate; rearing
children; organizing his or her nuclear family, perhaps within a larger
extended family; executing occupational roles in satisfactory fashion; as-

suming some share of administrative responsibility in the village, nation, tribe, sib, or lineage; helping to enforce social pressure; and, finally, accepting emotionally the physiological changes that come with middle age. Adulthood also brings with it an increased degree of participation in selected cultural activities, but old age means a reduction of the individual's range of cultural and social participation (cf. Barker and Wright, 1955:116).

Old age in most parts of the world is defined by physical condition rather than by elapsed years of life. The individual now learns to restrict his ac-

In Old Age the Individual Learns to Restrict His Activities and Perhaps to Assume a Dependent Relationship with More Active Adults (courtesy, Korean Pacific Press).

tivities to an ever increasing extent. Perhaps he resumes a dependence on more active adults or he may adopt a lower standard of living. He probably already has had experience with the death of parents and children but now may come loss of a spouse and he realistically contemplates his own, not too far off, death.

Reference has already been made to the fact that nearly everywhere adults enjoy higher prestige than subadults. Increasing age, however, does not continue to bring enhanced prestige under all cultural conditions. The social esteem allotted to the aged tends to be greatest in those communities where they control inheritable wealth or where ancestral sanctions exist as a threat. That is to say, when the ancestors are believed to control the fate of the living, the aged continue to be respected until their death. They will soon be very powerful. Respect for the aged may also be withdrawn faster in a heterogeneous community that is changing rapidly than in a homogeneous one where the past continues to be effective as a guide to the future (Mead, 1930:213–214). The treatment of the aged further varies with subsistence technology. A dependable surplus enables oldsters to retire from food production without directly depriving others in the group of food. In a food-gathering community an economic surplus is absent. Hunters rarely can feed more than about three others. In such a setting an unproductive oldster added to a family of several children and a spouse poses a potential threat. The prestige of the aged tends to be low among food gatherers. This low prestige, in turn, makes it relatively easy (but by no means painless) to abandon the infirm oldsters when a band must quickly change its locale to avoid starvation. While a number of hunting and collecting communities on occasion abandoned the aged, this practice was not carried out harshly. The parent or grandparent might be left with a supply of wood and the rest of the group returned as soon as they discovered food. Sometimes, however, they returned too late to prolong the old person's life.

DEATH

Judging from the archeological evidence, the custom of taking deliberate pains to dispose of deceased friends or kin is nearly as old as culture itself. Burial practices go back at least to Mousterian times (Grinsell, 1955; see pp. 740, 858 below). There appears to be a tendency for the elaborateness of funeral customs to increase with level of cultural development and general elaboration, but only to a certain point. Then as wealth increases in the population as a whole, the wealth invested in funerals, tombs, and property deposited with the corpse becomes poorer. "In a stable progressive society the tendency is for the grave-goods to diminish absolutely, or at least relatively; in other words, a diminishing proportion of society's growing wealth is buried with the dead" (Childe, 1944:87).

The corpse often is washed, attired, or wrapped in preparation for its final disposal. Where mortuary specialists are lacking these tasks are performed by persons of the same sex as the deceased, perhaps by particular kinsmen. Communities, therefore, expect that the rules of modesty will continue to be observed even toward a lifeless body. Other signs of respect also are customarily shown to a corpse although this generalization cannot be extended to cover enemy dead. A few communities insist on an autopsy of the corpse, perhaps to diagnose how death occurred. Samoans fear to bury a pregnant woman without cutting the fetus from the mother's body. This operation is performed in the open grave. Were it not done, the fetus would be born as an avenging ghost, according to native belief (Mead, 1928a:133; Quecke, 1952).

Parts of the dead body may be used as powerful specifics through which important ends may be attained. Among the Lovedu of the Transvaal the drums symbolic of the nation, and powerful in bringing rain, formerly were played with a human tibia. Human skulls together with the skin of important men also help to bring rain and fertility among those people (E. J. Krige and J. D. Krige, 1943:127, 273–274). Among the Ute of southern Colorado the tips of fingers, sex organs, lips, and toes were dried and powdered for use by young men to attract girls (Marvin K. Opler, 1940:200). The Andamanese retain the skull of the deceased as an amulet while in Manus it represents the Sir Ghost who protects the household (Fortune, 1935:12–29; Mead, 1930:Chap. 6). In Europe and America the ashes of the dead sometimes are preserved as a remembrance. The relatively rare trait of endocannibalism involves the physical incorporation of the loved one by survivors.

Disposal customs in a community and culture area are notably unstable in time (Kroeber, 1927). In the middle Columbia River area, for example, burial customs in a period of about 200 years shifted from flexed burial to exposure coupled with cremation and then to extended burial. Yet the population basically did not change (Garth, 1952). At any time mortuary customs within a community may vary with the social status of the deceased (Wedgwood, 1927). Conspicuously elaborate burials standing out among many that are less sumptuous often indicate occupational specialization and social class. People who die under abnormal circumstances sometimes receive a distinctive funeral. The major types of disposal are summarized in Table 41.

People often take elaborate symbolic precautions to dissociate the soul (or ghost) of the deceased from living survivors. The funeral party, for example, may follow a circuitous route back from the grave, destroy articles of clothing that belonged to the deceased, and wreck the house in which death occurred. The local group, if normally mobile, moves from the scene of death. Fear of the ghost varies in degree from one culture to another but is especially marked among the Athapaskan Indians of northwestern North America.

Wealth to accompany the deceased or, rather, his spiritual counterpart may be put into the grave or tomb or destroyed on the cremation pyre. Property deposited with a corpse is called *Beigaben* ("that which is given along with"). Prominent in such goods are items like food and tools, the latter usually suited to the sex of the corpse.

TABLE 41. Major Forms of Disposing the Dead

Technique	Description and Alternatives
Ground burial. Includes flexed, seated (or squatting), and extended burial.	The corpse is placed in a simple pit or in a niche dug into the side at the bottom of a grave shaft. The body may be placed in a reclining position but with the knees more or less flexed or it may be laid perfectly straight or placed in a squatting position. Sometimes laying the corpse on one side or the other is favored, perhaps in order to orient it in a certain direction. The orientation of the head and feet may also be significant. Burial in a sitting position requires a grave of narrower dimensions, the corpse being interred with the knees drawn up to the chin. Burial may occur in the floor of the dwelling, in the local settlement, or in cemeteries located on the outskirts of settlements. It may also occur with the corpse in a boat or on a wagon, the entire vehicle being surmounted with earth (see pp. 781–782 as well as p. 784). A cist grave is built up of four vertically placed slabs of stone placed to form a rectangular box.
Cave and tomb interment	Caves may be dug or natural caves utilized in which to deposit the body. When caves are dug into rock for the purposes of containing dead bodies they represent rock-cut tombs. Tombs are also constructed of stone or of artificially made bricks and left on the surface of the ground or, as in Egypt, sunk below ground. Dolmens are tombs made of relatively large blocks of stone (i.e., megalithic tombs) (see pp. 759–761). When covered with a mound of earth such tombs become round or long barrows.
Cremation	The corpse is burned on a funeral pyre after which the ashes or unburnt bones are disposed of further by being thrown into water, interred in a pit, or stored in a pottery or metal cinerary urn. The latter in turn may be stored in tombs, buried in cemeteries (urn fields), or preserved in homes. Cremation spread across the length of Europe during Bronze Age times and then yielded to ground burial in the Iron Age (p. 779).
Surface deposition	The dead body is left on the surface of the ground or on an elevated platform cache. It may be protected from predators by a cairn of stones or left exposed. The Parsis (Zoroastrians) abandon the corpse on mortuary towers where vultures pick the bones.
Secondary interment	This occurs when the body has been buried or allowed to decompose and is then further handled—perhaps exhumed and reburied or the bones put into a tomb. The bones from which the flesh has decomposed may also be gathered and reburied—perhaps with some attempt to reconstruct the skeleton in the grave. The Huron Indians waited from 10 to 20 years before reburial of the corpses and then celebrated a great memorial ceremony.
Mummification and embalming	Deliberate preparation of the body to insure its intact survival as a corpse occurs with cave, tomb, or ground burial. The greatest development has been in ancient Egypt but the process is also known from Australia and the New World. Modern embalming is accomplished by the injection of drugs into the vascular system without removal of the viscera or other organs.

Suicide

While suicide has a world-wide distribution its incidence and techniques vary from one community to another. Many studies have been conducted into the correlates of suicide in Euroamerican culture (Durkheim, 1952 [originally published in 1897]; Halbwachs, 1930; Hurlburt, 1932). Durkheim discovered self-destruction to be correlated inversely with the degree of social solidarity extant in a community and directly with impersonality and anomie. Where people are not closely identified with one another and social norms are not generally accepted, anomie exists and suicide rates tend to be high. Such an explanation, however, is not designed to explain apparent differences in rates of self-destruction between small-scale, homogeneous communities.

In some cultures suicide constitutes an accepted response to certain situations. Among some Eskimo the old people who felt they were a burden on the living sought to rid themselves of life. Doing so assured them of entry into an especially favorable afterworld. Sickness, suffering, and the feeling of uselessness conditioned Eskimo suicide. Kin, however, would try to dissuade a loved relative from choosing this solution to his difficulties. If he persisted in his intention then the kin group would give in. While maladaptive for the deceased, suicide, through the attention it generated, may have contributed to social solidarity in the Eskimo community (A. H. Leighton and C. C. Hughes, 1955). Among the Huron and Iroquois tribes of northeastern North America an aboriginal ambivalence toward suicide crystallized into open condemnation of the practice following receipt of Christian teachings. Here, too, is found a tendency, noted also in other parts of the world, to use suicide as a means of revenge against people who have offended one. This is the principal motive in female suicide among the Iroquois. Men, on the other hand, use self-destruction in an effort to avoid physical suffering and loss of prestige. Children sometimes utilize self-destruction to escape restraint (Fenton, 1941a).

AVAILABLE FILMS

Margaret Mead is the narrator in several short films dealing with child rearing: A Balinese Family (17 min.), Bathing Babies in Three Cultures (9 min.), Childhood Rivalry in Bali and New Guinea (17 min.), First Days of Life of a New Guinea Baby (19 min.). All are black and white and are sold or rented by the New York University Film Library. Family Life of the Navaho Indians is another professional film. It was made under the direction of Margaret Fries and Clyde Kluckhohn and is available from the same source (31 min., b. and w., silent). A portion of a Tuareg boy's life is the subject of Touareg (35 mm., 20 min., b. and w., in French) produced by the Gouvernement Général de L'Algérie. It is available from Film Images,

Inc., 18 East 60th St., New York 22, N.Y. *La circoncision* (30 min., color, in French) and *Rites de la circoncision chez les Mongon* (23 min., b. and w., silent, French titles) deal with the French West African Songhai and Pygmies. They are produced by Jean Rouch and Laboratoires Lavril respectively. Dogon funeral rites are shown in *Sous les masques noirs* (35 mm., 15 min., b. and w., in French), produced by the anthropologist Griaule; and similar ceremonies in Madagascar are shown in *The Bilo*, produced by Nordisk Film Co. under the direction of Paul Fejos (35 mm., 10 min., b. and w.).

34.

Ideology

THIS chapter introduces the third division of culture—ideology. Any socially standardized technique for dealing with the material world and every social relationship is the overt expression of a motive, value, or other idea. Ideology, therefore, is less a hard and fast category of culture than an additional perspective for understanding social life. It is an important perspective, because man's ideas are the bases upon which he acts and judges the activity of others. "The outward facts of any culture are the fruition of its spiritual roots" (Northrop, 1953:311).

Speech, of course, is the channel providing the most direct expression of ideas. But not all concepts are capable of receiving explicit verbal expression. Activity, too, reveals ideology. For example, court cases and other forms of law bring out many of the values about which the members of a community feel most strongly (W. Smith and J. M. Roberts, 1954). A people's heroes and other collective representations reveal some of the most profound aspirations in the culture. Pin-up girl photographs embody the esthetic values of some American males. The attitudes which the Navaho Indians reserve for native music are scarcely esthetic but reveal the value placed on retaining control over hostile forces in the universe (McAllester, 1954:5, 86). The way architecture mirrors attitudes often has been described. When preaching became a value in Methodist chapels in England, the shape of the meeting house changed to emphasize the new trait. The communion table was dwarfed by the pulpit and the shape of the room became square or octagonal so that more of the congregation could face the preacher (Short, 1955). In Roman Catholic churches the prominent altar reveals a primary orientation toward devotion while in many American churches the basements, which are equipped for cooking, eating, and playing, reveal that the church is thought of as a social center as well as a place of devotion.

NATURE OF IDEOLOGY

Ideology, in the sense in which the word is used in this book, includes socially standardized beliefs about the universe and man's place in it; conceptions about the sources of illness and other sorts of danger; attitudes of belonging, allegiance, and identification; sentiments about persons, objects, places, and times; and, finally, values concerning what to do and what not to do. For convenience the ideological sector of culture may also be said to include the material embodiments of ideas, like printed books and pictures.

Operationally speaking, ideology refers to whatever can be learned about the meanings which lie behind a people's response to some significant stimulus. Such meanings are what the psychologist and psychiatrist probe for when they seek to learn how an individual's perceptions are related to his acts. The anthropologist works with communities rather than with discrete individuals but his aim is similar. Behind this definition of ideology lies the assumption that people are constantly organizing, interpreting, and evaluating their world and that they normally respond only to stimuli that possess relevance for their ideology (Masserman, 1946:108).

To illustrate: Suppose that a community balks at the introduction of a new, higher-yielding strain of corn (Spicer, 1952:35–40). The grain is rejected after a brief trial, not because it fails to fulfill the county agent's promise but because the flour paste does not hang together well, the color of the resultant bread is unfamiliar, the flavor unpleasant. This incident contains two divergent perceptions of a single stimulus. Obviously the perceptual framework of the expert differed from the ideology of the community. The inference is clear: ". . . In the system of values of the community, corn quality was more important than corn quantity." The rationalistic county agent "had proceeded on the belief that increased farm production was the only important factor involved."

Most readers will note the difference between the gradual death of an old or sick person and the sudden death of the victim of an accident. Such modes of dying have important significance for us. Many people in the world, though, will not perceive the difference in these modes of dying as really significant. Old age, illness, a wild beast, or a spear—such things have little relevance in their theory of death. In fact, such people may reprove the alien with another way of life who places so much weight on the mere agents of death and ignores the powers who willed the event "and might equally have chosen any other instrument to bring it about" (Lévy-Bruhl, 1923:43).

The fact that socially standardized conceptions of the world vary from one culture to another makes it difficult to speak of "reality" as being much the same for all people. Outside of his hogan a Navaho Indian facing the east sees that

The sage-covered earth is Changing Woman, one of the most benevolent of the gods, who grows old and young again with the cycle of each year's seasons. The rising sun is himself a god who with Changing Woman produced a warrior that rid the earth of most of its evil forces and who is still using his powers to help people. The first brightness is another god, Dawn-Boy. . . . The cone-shaped mountains have lava on their sides, which is the caked blood of a wicked tyrant killed by the Sun's warrior off-spring . . . [A. H. Leighton and D. C. Leighton, 1941:520].

A white man looking at the same landscape sees "the yellow day coming up over miles of sage, a copse of pinyon, three or four yellow pines in the soft light, distant blue swells of mountains, with here and there a volcanic cone. . . ."

Some meaning can be assumed to underlie all human actions except those, like blinking the eye in response to foreign matter, which are re-flexes. Even the discipline of an army and the compliance of a prisoner rest on the meaning which the soldiers and prisoner associate with the com-mands (Hobhouse, 1924:56). Of course, actions often are performed with-out deliberation or conscious intent. Furthermore, the interpretation which people admit for something—the rationalization—need not be taken as the only motivation of their response.

Universality

There are no people without beliefs, values, ideas, and feelings. Although ideology is a universal component of culture, the ideas of different com-munities manifestly vary. Some beliefs are nearly universal, like the notion that events are actuated by other, preceding events. Some values also are widely shared, like the repugnance for in-group killing. But beyond a few such recurrent themes, a bewildering diversity of ideas forces itself on the anthropologist's attention. Americans are most highly motivated when they face a deadline or schedule (D. Lee, 1955:14), whereas in Latin Amer-ica *mañana* expresses a more widespread attitude toward activity. The world is divided into five cardinal points by some people while upriver and downriver, or inland and seaward are the significant directions for others. Therapy may be relegated to the good will of a deity with entire confidence or, as the reader well knows, faith may be restricted to well-tested drugs or surgery. One community may stress allegiance with workers, peasants, or mankind anywhere in the world, while in another only genealogically trace-able kinship ties constitute a bond to be taken seriously.

Obviously, the ideas of small-scale, exotic communities often are incon-sistent or unclear, or fail to recognize what might seem to be obvious dis-tinctions (Jenness, 1935:32). This should not be surprising. What philoso-pher, western or exotic, has escaped having weaknesses in his work brought to light? The Euroamerican scholar heeds his critics and strengthens weak parts of his argument. In subsequent publications he better explains his point of view. Natives, whose views were given informally to a visiting an-thropologist, are unable subsequently to defend their ideas in this fashion even if they had the inclination to do so. In part the contradictions in exotic idea systems stem from the informality of the community's ideology and the absence of ideological specialists who might coördinate and standardize beliefs. Among the Indians of the North Pacific coast of North America individuals in a single tribe "will give completely different accounts of the ancient beliefs as to how the world was supported, and whether the Land of the Dead was across some distant river, somewhere in the sky, or in the underworld" (Drucker, 1955:139). The explanation in this particular case lies not only in the absence of specialists to formalize concepts but in the fact that each lineage or extended family freely employs some mythological episode to explain its own origin. In the process, each social unit tends to construct its own version of how the world was created and how it is organized. Contradictions from still a third source are reported for the Shilluk of the Egyptian Sudan. With them narrating notions about the universe is partly a "creative process" (Lienhardt, 1954b:138–139). Hence, different versions by various narrators are encouraged!

Ideology is derived from experience. Hence it follows that the kind and variety of a community's experiences will influence the ideas which it holds. The larger the community, the greater the variety of experience. Communication with other communities whose members have divergent experiences will also reflect in ideology. In other words, ideology is dependent on scale (see pp. 149–154).

CLASSIFICATION

There are several vantage points for classifying ideology. Certain ideas, like mathematical formulas or rules of conduct, are in the forefront of consciousness (except during lapses of memory). Other ideas are socially standardized on an unconscious level. Their elucidation requires working closely with an individual and, perhaps, using techniques developed by psychoanalysis, like dream analysis. Cautious interpretations of products of fantasy, like motion pictures, also may help to expose some of a community's unconscious ideas. American motion pictures, for example, often show a male hero opposed to a dangerous elderly man associated with a doubtful but attractive woman. The elderly man, whose power the hero must oppose by violence, may correspond to the American's unconscious image of the father (Wolfenstein and Leites, 1950:149–165).

Most anthropologists interested in ideology refer less often to a conscious-unconscious dichotomy than to an explicit-implicit dimension. Following definitions already given (pp. 122–123), the explicit ideology is capable of being verbalized by an informant. Implicit understandings, however, while not unconscious, are inchoate and incompletely verbalizable. They often will be recognized when plausibly put into words by an observer who has inferred them from behavior. Take the conception of social class in the United States as a ladder which one mounts, or sees one's children mount, successfully. Americans are not likely explicitly to conceptualize the class system in those terms. But an anthropologist looking at behavior says that this is how Americans implicitly regard social classes. In return, it is likely that many people of the country would acknowledge the view to be correct.

In Peru, Village Shrines Symbolize the Deity Who Controls the Universe (courtesy, Grace Line).

One might also speak of formal subsystems existing in the largely unformalized mass that is a community's ideology. (Any ideology, we assume, constitutes a system in which changes are likely to ramify beyond the sector in which they occur; but it is a relatively loosely structured system.) The theories of anthropology, beliefs of Catholicism, Marxist doctrine and Hindu idea of God are formalized subsystems of ideas. In a formal idea system selection of new items will be highly conscious, contradictions are avoided or carefully explained, systematization is quite deliberate, and definitions are carefully constructed. Such systems are usually the creation of specialists working in literate communities where their ideas can be set down in writing and passed around for critical study. Note that formal idea systems may express largely implicit conceptions, perhaps through the use of carefully constructed parables and metaphors.

Two Contrasting World Views

Coming to a somewhat different basis of classification, one to which considerable reference will be made in succeeding pages, we find a difference between the personal world view, common to most of the world, and the impersonal orientation that appeared in ancient Greece, post-Renaissance Europe, and America. Table 42 sums up the key points in each of these types of thought. It is usual to refer to these ideological systems as "prescientific" and "scientific" respectively (Albert, 1956:228). Certainly the impersonal world view in Europe and America nurtured itself at the bosom of science at the same time that it encouraged science. But it is not there-

TABLE 42.   The Personal and Impersonal World Views

Personal World View	Impersonal World View
Phenomena in the universe are viewed as the products of personal agents (gods, spirits, ghosts).	Phenomena in the universe are accounted for in impersonal terms.
All or certain parts of nature are treated as though possessing sentience.	Nature is not treated as if sentient.
Concepts about nature do not need to correspond to empirical referents.	Concepts about nature should correspond to observed, empirical referents.
Man is the hub of the universe.	No special place is provided for man in the universe.
Rituals often are used instrumentally as well as expressively.	Rituals primarily are used expressively (to show respect, gratitude, solemnity, and happiness).
Manipulation of signs and symbols (in or out of ritual) often is oriented instrumentally to control natural phenomena.	Nature cannot be controlled indirectly through the manipulation of signs and symbols.
Miracles can occur to alter any recurrent sequences in nature.	Recurrent sequences of nature cannot be interrupted by miracles.

fore identical with science. Nor is the personal world view entirely in the past. Perhaps it never will be wholly displaced from culture.

The personal world view is heavily traditional. It accounts for the phenomena of nature by postulating personal agents or else conceives of the universe as itself possessing sentience—knowing man's needs and deeds. Concepts about the world do not need to be matched against empirical referents in this system of thought. The conception that demons activate a volcano, for example, is not held critically, to be checked against facts and rejected if the facts don't give support. The personal world view is anthropocentric, making man the hub of everything that happens in the world. Since nature is controlled by personal agents, or is itself sentient, and since all that happens occurs with special reference to man, it is possible to influence the world to act in man's favor. Instrumental rituals are employed widely to this end (see p. 512) or else signs and symbols are manipulated quite matter-of-factly to bring about some desired state. Miracles can readily occur, according to the personal world view, and may upset any sequences in nature, no matter how recurrent. This, as was said, is the world view of most of the world. Evidence also indicates that similar beliefs are activated in individuals who ideally espouse the impersonal world view when they are caught up in a situation of great stress (Marvin K. Opler, 1950).

The world view, ideally associated with the tremendously large-scale countries of the west, is impersonal in its conception of nature. It uses no personal gods, spirits, or anthropomorphic entities in its explanations of how the universe is organized and runs. The manipulation of signs and symbols (for example, in prayer, sacrifice, imitation, or ceremonies) is rejected as a means for getting things done unless a connection between the process and the end state (like enhanced social solidarity) can be demonstrated empirically. Symbols and rituals primarily are expressive in this world view, not instrumental. Of course, all this is largely ideal. Even in large-scale communities many people continue to follow a world view in which the determinism of nature is personal and the universe or its rulers are sentient. An impersonal world view was apparent in classical Greece of 500 B.C. (Farrington, 1953:42). Then, as in nineteenth-century Europe, it was forged by men intent on explaining nature solely in empirical terms. Frequently the impersonal world view has run into difficulty. "Every attempt to dislodge man from his pedestal and reinstall him in the kingdom of Nature encountered vigorous protest from philosophical, scientific, and theological authority. For two millennia, natural philosophy was equated with spiritual treason" (Wendt, 1955:139). In the twentieth century this syndrome of thought has come into ideal predominance. Many parts of it are taught in schools as a matter of course. The person who too openly expresses points of the personal world view is today ridiculed or reproved with the same spirit of intolerance that was shown to Copernicus and Spinoza.

Values[1]

Man's ideology possesses two fundamental features, each present in variable degree in any specific instance. A concept primarily may be concerned with what is given rationally or what is probable under certain circumstances. Statements expressing such ideas are: "Two plus 2 equals 4," "This is a phoneme," "A change in any part of the system will be followed by dependent changes in other parts." Such statements express existential concepts. However, ideas may be compounded heavily of affect or feeling. Illustrative statements are: "This is good," "What a beautiful sight," "The scientist should deal as clearly as possible in objective concepts." The concepts expressed are called normative because they imply desirability. Most concepts fall somewhere between the existential and normative extremes. Values are ideas which, although not purely affective like feelings, lean toward the normative end of the continuum. Although containing an existential implication as well as an affective element, a value cannot be altered by attacking the former component alone.

The term "value" refers to an explicit or implicit socially standardized conception of what is desirable or undesirable. Values, in turn, influence selection from available means or ends of action. The values of a community help members decide on the ends of action as well as on permissible

[1] The next two paragraphs are adapted from C. Kluckhohn and others, 1952. See also F. Kluckhohn, 1950.

means to follow in pursuit of those ends. The values themselves are limited by existential ideas regarding what is held to be possible. That is to say, the value system is functionally dependent on the definitions of nature and man which the community holds.

People in any community nevertheless are not seldom attracted by deeds which contradict the positive value system—which, ideally speaking, are held to be undesirable. In-group aggression and illicit sexual relations with another man's wife are widely held to be undesirable. Yet they occur in almost every community. From this it is apparent that, while values constitute one element in motivation, they are not identical with that process. There are other springs to action simultaneously operative in human nature.

Many values contribute to adaptation and adjustment. But some judgments of the desirable hinder these general functions of culture. Some Nuba tribes of the Egyptian Sudan regard generosity as desirable. In conformity with this (and other) values the Nuba use whatever surplus grain remains at harvest time to brew beer, which is liberally distributed. As a result no surplus store of food is accumulated as effective insurance against locusts, drought, or crop failures. Famines hit the Nuba regularly (Nadel, 1947:50). Under the circumstances a value on generosity is not very adaptive. Of course, if any community adopted many values which were profoundly non-adaptive it would not survive long. A value cannot be regarded as eminently suited to survival or adjustment simply because it happens to exist in a community. The general functions of values must be determined analytically and not taken for granted.

To illustrate the concept of values more clearly, a preliminary formulation of what the Navaho Indians regard as desirable may be cited (C. Kluckhohn and D. Leighton, 1946:220–223). Health and strength are good things in life. With the Navaho work becomes possible when one is healthy; industry also is enormously valued. A good appearance is desirable, as are many skills, including speaking, singing, and telling stories; their mastery carries prestige. Thus personal excellence is a positive value but not personal success in the white American sense. The Navaho concept of goodness further stresses "productiveness, ability to get along with people, dependability and helpfulness, generosity in giving and spending." On a more general level a few value orientations of the Navaho Indians are as follows: (1) The universe is a machine which runs according to certain rules. As man acquires knowledge of those rules he can influence events in the universe, even though he cannot escape its threats completely. (2) Nature is more powerful than man and man must adjust himself to nature. (3) Outside of the family one's loyalty is extended in attenuated degrees toward distant biological and clan relatives.

Even academic disciplines are governed by values. For example, the work done by political scientists in the United States is governed by values like liberty, the pursuit of happiness, peace, urban living, and empirical truth (Waldo, 1956:16). Anthropologists specifically value cultural diversity but have little tolerance for ethnocentrism (see pp. 114–117).

The reader will have noted that values may be positive or negative. Negative values are illustrated in the Production Code of the motion-picture industry in the United States. The Code discourages derogatory racial appellations in films and does not see abortion as a fit subject for a motion picture. When abortion, prostitution, illicit narcotics, or kidnapping are dealt with in films they are not to be treated lightly. Detailed and protracted scenes of cruelty are also not to be shown (New York Times, Dec. 12, 1956).

Verification and Maintenance of Ideas

Anthropologists are not concerned with classifying a community's ideas as true or false. Yet people certainly hold existential and normative ideas with some feeling concerning their truth or worth-whileness.

An anthropologist may be able objectively to recognize more or less reliability in the beliefs of the people he studies. He may be able to agree with a native informant who says that oak is harder than pine and hence better for implements receiving hard wear. The temptation to make such comparative assessments of belief is strong. But the examination of particular ideas as true or false is for an anthropologist only incidental to describing exotic ideas faithfully and trying to understand them in the light of a people's own theories of knowledge. Under what circumstances are the ideas of a community retained, displaced, or modified?

Following are some very much overlapping circumstances under which a particular interpretation of the world may be retained or rejected. They represent only a few of the bases by which people verify their existential and normative beliefs.[2] A community may ignore some of these bases or may prefer to use some rather than others for particular classes of ideas.

1. Consensus. Some ideas are held as long as there is social consensus regarding their utility or reasonableness. When new experiences or any of the subsequent bases of verification are called into play, the degree of consensus in the community may decline. For example, since the beginning of the post-Renaissance period of exploration modern man could scarcely defend the notion of a flat world by claiming that "everybody knows it is true." As a matter of fact, western culture has largely come to mistrust the social basis of truth and prefers other bases of verification. Nevertheless, this is still a common ground in Euroamerican culture for accepting some very cherished beliefs, like the practicality of polyarchic administration (see pp.

[2] See also the factors that generally govern cultural persistence (pp. 185–190).

189, 486). Normative ideas are supported primarily on this foundation.

Any increase in scale usually means a greater variety of beliefs or ideas extant in a community. As a result of such increase in variety the whole ideology may become less consistent internally. Contradictions are opened up. This happened in Springtown, Illinois, when isolation declined and the people were confronted with a conception of nature's order different from that which they had held before.

It was believed that successful crops required careful observation of traditional "signs." Lettuce and certain other garden crops must be planted on St. Valentine's day, February 14. Failure to observe this prescription automatically results in a bad crop. Cucumbers must be planted in the "dark moon" and by the Zodiacal "twin" sign. Potatoes and corn must be planted in the dark of the moon. Beans should be planted on Good Friday. In general, the principle seems to have been that plants that grow primarily above the ground should be seeded in "light moon," the others in "dark moon." Things that grow along a vine should be planted when the signs are in the arms [Passin and Bennett, 1943:99–100].

2. Authority. Certain ideas or values will be maintained as long as they are affirmed by a figure of high prestige. It makes little difference whether the authority is directly visible or merely postulated, as in the case of a deity or bygone hero. The content of scriptures is automatically accepted on such a basis. Other beliefs, then, may be verified by their compatibility with scriptural truth.

3. Practicality. Ideas may be held as long as they seem practical in a particular way of life, even though they fail to be implemented or tested empirically. The civil rights which Americans affirm tend to be rights that they can afford to grant in a community at some particular time. A certain number of unrealizable ideals, however, are found in many cultures, despite the recognition that they are incapable of being executed in practice.

4. Logical Consistency. The idea may be held until logical argument shows it to be inconsistent with some generally accepted premises or assumptions. If an idea is demonstrated to be illogical it may be modified or discarded. Perhaps, at the risk of radical opposition, attempts may be made to alter the controlling premise.

5. Reliability. The idea may be held as long as it works in the experience of the community. The activities carried out on its terms reliably lead to expected results in a significant number of cases. This criterion, as noted previously, constitutes the basis of many scientific truths. In science ideas are tested experimentally to assess their reliability. Contrary to what sometimes is believed, not only existential ideas but even values can be verified experimentally, provided that the experimenters can agree on an unambiguous definition of the value. The value must be defined in terms of what perceivable consequences can be expected when the value is implemented (Northrop, 1947). To take an absurdly oversimplified example, the question "Is candy good?" can be answered if "candy" is clearly understood and if "good" in this context objectively means no dental cavities by someone who eats a certain amount of candy over a two-year period. The answer to the question requires discovering empirically whether or not even a single dental cavity appears during the given experimental period. If not even one occurs, then "candy is good."

6. **Analogy.** An idea may be retained when it closely parallels another idea meeting any of the five previous specifications of truth. For example, the idea of using washing to symbolize intangible cleanliness or purity is congruent with the idea that washing can remove physical dirt from the body. The latter idea checks with what happens in an observed experience. Such analogical thinking often supports symbolic techniques for coping with the world (see pp. 624–629).

Ranking Ideologies

It is not uncommon to observe a community's ideology being devaluated by visitors from another group. Aliens reject the gods of another culture as "false." People from large-scale, western communities, who ideally espouse the impersonal world view, disparage the belief that power to get rain or protect crops from marauders resides in signs and symbols. The word "superstitious" often is used to characterize unfavorably reliance on strange deities or on sign-symbol coping. Anthropologists find it wise to avoid this term. They refrain from any subjective evaluation of the beliefs they study.

Attempts to rank exotic ideas as superior or inferior to those of some other community are often in the tradition of evolutionary thinking (see pp. 23–24). That is, contemporary cultures are regarded as living representatives of early ways of life. Early culture, it is assumed gratuitously, was carried by people who reasoned differently from modern man. There is, of course, no sound basis for believing that any contemporary way of life is representative of prehistoric times. Another danger in disparaging people who rely on deities or on sign-symbol means of coping is that it may lead to minimizing the skill with which people who hold such beliefs are able to adapt and adjust. Normally a Melanesian who uses verbal charms to make his garden grow is also a good gardener (within the scope of his available knowledge). Yet the ethnocentric observer puts more stress on the supposedly ineffectual charm than on the labor and skill invested in cultivation. Later it will be seen that the beliefs making up the personal world view frequently have practical significance for adaptation and adjustment (see pp. 629–632).

FUNCTIONS OF IDEOLOGY

How ideology serves the general functions of adaptation, adjustment, and stress probably is already clear to the reader. A few illustrations should suffice to sum up the matter.

By supporting ongoing activities, especially those requiring coöperation, giving them value and meaning, the ideology of a community contributes to survival. Hunting, planting, weeding, trading, and making or repairing tools are tasks not left to chance. Their importance is emphasized by the belief system so that these activities will be executed with fair regularity. The division of labor by sex may be defended by a variety of beliefs about men's strength and women's weakness or danger; so long as the division of labor keeps one sex coöperating with another those ideas promote both adaptation and adjustment. Through ordering, and adding to, knowledge, man increases his level of technical development and so enhances his adaptation. When a community is faced with the threat of enemy force, the attitudes it adopts toward the danger profoundly influence the individual members' chances of survival. Survival may seem to demand resistance, even at the price of many deaths, or surrender may promise to secure the continued existence of the majority.

Adjustment, too, resides in coöperation and social solidarity. To the extent that an ideology enables a community to perceive common meanings in experience it also supports the integrity of social relationships on which adjustment hinges. Certain beliefs function to restore a feeling of security after a crisis. The assurance which a doctor offers to his patients or a priest to his client is adjustive in this sense. The belief that an all-embracive intelligence pervades the universe and controls everything that happens reassures people who recognize their limited ability to control experience. Something has already been said about the role of values and other ideas in discussing the charters by which groups are organized. The concept that physical labor is good, and even the essence of life, is prominent in the charter of Kiryat Yedidim, an Israeli *kibbutz* (Spiro, 1956:Chap. 1). The belief that divine revelation comes directly to every individual without the necessity of priestly intermediaries is a cardinal point in the charter of the more loosely organized Doukhobors of British Columbia, Canada (Hawthorn, 1955). In both of these communities the group itself is a moral value. The Doukhobors (despite the fact that they are fractionated into a number of subsects) see the group as a source of strength. The *kibbutz* sees the group as a means to individual happiness as well as an end in itself. It is interesting that both of these organizations are derived from certain radical ideas formulated in nineteenth-century Russia.

Some concepts enable man to exceed the physiological limits of direct perception. He can imagine what is not empirically visible. Such imaginations, by promoting morale or a feeling of security, may function in the interests of adaptation and adjustment. But it is easy to see that man's creativity also may induce stress. Many of the terrors that beset experience stem from imagination. The view of the world which a person learns may be such as to impose on him a fairly constant load of anxiety. For example, the

Melanesian native of Dobu learns that nearly every person he encounters who does not belong to his mother's lineage is menacing.

Ideology is important in social life. Yet care must be taken not to over-stress the significance of ideas. Often the limiting aspects of normative conceptions are exaggerated. A community's orientation toward the present rather than the future, emphasis on distributing wealth rather than accumulating it, and the trust which people put in kin as opposed to nonkin are cited as making certain kinds of change very difficult if not impossible. Certainly values can and do help to resist diffusion (see p. 227) but incompatible ideas do not necessarily become barriers to change. The ideas may be modified through reinterpretation or overcome by being segregated so as not to conflict with a new practice. Many values in South Asian life, including attitudes to caste, land, and farming, are incompatible with industrialization. Yet the community as a whole does not refuse to industrialize.

35.

Components of the Universe

"UNIVERSE" is used here to designate the very widest perspective which man manages to achieve and all that lies within it. Modern astronomy conceives of a vast macrocosmos in which the universe is a single member. Most communities restrict themselves to a much more limited cosmic perspective. Modern physics focuses down to a microcosmos below the level of the atom—a microcosmos which, of course, remains outside the ken of most communities in the world. Modern science conceptualizes the universe as constituted of space, time, matter, and energy (Shapley, 1954). Fire, water, earth, and air are more familiar components of nature in exotic thought systems.

Man's ideas about nature and himself may be said to deal with the nonhuman and human components of the universe respectively. It should be understood that this distinction between nonhuman and human components is the anthropologist's. Many communities postulate active participation of the human in the nonhuman category. A dividing line between the two, which even modern biology finds difficulty drawing, is scarcely of much concern to those people.

THE NONHUMAN COMPONENT

Either anthropologists have been extraordinarily faithful in collecting data about cosmic and meteorological beliefs or else these areas have attracted a disproportionate amount of attention all over the world. Whatever the reason, in contrast to ideas about the earth, stars, and weather, exotic notions about topography or the physiology and behavior of plants and animals are published much more rarely.

Cosmic Phenomena

Experiments in science have proved that the earth is shaped roughly like a sphere and spins around in space once every 24 hours. As it does so man is exposed to different phenomena of the heavens. However, the sky does not appear quite unchanged from one night to the next. The variations in constellations from season to season and the position of the sun relative to the zenith are partly related to the earth's movement around the sun. The duration of this revolution is called a year. Furthermore, astronomers have shown that the planets possess their own orbits on which they travel around the sun at speeds thousands of miles faster than that of any plane. The sun, earth, and other planets form a highly isolated colony whose nearest neighbor in space, a dim star, is about 25 trillion miles away. Its light takes about 4.27 years to reach the earth. Many of these ideas were discovered quite recently. Until the Middle Ages most Europeans thought that the earth was the center of the universe and that the world was flat. During subsequent centuries astronomers demonstrated that the earth is only one member of the solar system and that this system is only one member of the aggregate of stars constituting the Galactic System. The vast Galactic System is but a single member of an unstable, constantly swelling universe into which the powerful telescope can penetrate only a very short distance.

Many communities regard the earth as the hub of the universe. The earth often is seen as a flat expanse covered by a vault, the sky, in which the stars, planets, sun, and moon are somehow set and move. At the extremities of the flat earth lies water. Such ideas are common and of great antiquity. For example, the Sumerians of the third millennium before the Christian era conceived of the earth as a flat disk with heaven a hollow space enclosed by a solid surface shaped like a vault. Between heaven and earth was air and of this substance the sun and other heavenly bodies were composed. A boundless sea surrounded heaven and earth on all sides (Kramer, 1955:72). Many variations occur in this belief. Some Ojibwa Indians postulate six levels of worlds below the sky, man living on one (Jenness, 1935:28). The Copper Eskimo conceive of four columns of wood holding up the sky, above which is another land, rich in animals (Jenness, 1922:179–180). The space between earth and sky also holds significance for the Eskimo, who endow it with sentience and call it Sila. Sila governs the weather. By withholding storms from these hunting people it makes life possible (Rasmussen, 1932:22–24).

The sun and moon receive more attention than any other heavenly body. People not only recognize the sun as a source of light and heat but often regard it as sentient. The Ojibwa, like other American Indians, appealed to it for help (Lowie, 1954:165; A. Métraux, 1949:564). What astronomers perceive to be shadows of weathered mountains cast on lunar deserts frequently is held to be the outline of a man or animal. In China the moon accommodates both a tree and a frog. Water constitutes the essence of the moon, which, therefore, controls water (Hodus, 1929:187). This idea appears to be related to recognition of the moon's influence on tides. The course of the moon among the stars, according to Chinese popular thought, produces winds. (Of course, today Chinese universities teach astronomy based on verified knowledge obtained through telescopes and careful methods of mathematical calculation.) The conception of the moon as related to menstruation has been discussed under "Life Cycle." When rites are directed to the sun, moon, and other bodies it may be that the ceremonial target less often is the body itself than a conception of the body. Thus for the Nuer the moon is a symbol of God (Evans-Pritchard, 1956:2).

A few constellations are named in many cultures but the configuration of a particular constellation need not correspond to the pattern recognized in modern astronomy. The Navaho Indians expect to find an animal or human figure in star groups and this leads them to extend the area of such a group until they realize their expectation (Haile, 1947:7–11). These same people regard the starry heavens as "a jungled mass of lights," a more orderly arrangement of which was frustrated in a long bygone era by the mythical trickster, Coyote. In Australia, the Aranda regard the stars as divided into tribal groups, much after the fashion of human society (Maegraith, 1932:19–20). The Milky Way, in many cultures regarded as a road or band, sometimes becomes the road followed by the soul en route to the land of the dead (Speck, 1935:50). This conception is especially prevalent in northeastern Canada among the Algonkian tribes. Here too the northern lights are described as dancing souls of the dead (ibid., p. 65). Knowledge of the stars is not useless to small-scale communities. Many people tell the progress of nocturnal time by the position of certain constellations. In the Trust Territory of Micronesia, administered by the United States, stars formerly aided native navigation, and the appearance of certain constellations foretold the onset of different seasons (Kraemer, 1937:134–137). In China, India, and the ancient Middle East, astrology, which attributes certain influences to heavenly bodies and their positions in the mapped heavens, appeared long ago.

Something as unusual as an eclipse of the sun and moon rarely fails to receive a socially standardized explanation. Frequently it is interpreted as an attack on the sun or moon by some evil being. Among the Chukchee of northeastern Siberia the attacker is driven off by people who make noise and threaten with weapons that are flung skyward (Bogoras, 1904–09:314). Popularly, the Chinese associate the attack with a Heavenly Dog (Day, 1940:27).

Meteorological Phenomena

Well-established signs by which to forecast short-term weather changes are known practically everywhere. Modern meteorologists base forecasting on empirical knowledge of how the sun and other natural agencies influence weather. Popular weather portents are familiar to the reader. Many recur in a large number of cultures. There is the belief that a red sky at sunset is an indicator of fair weather on the morrow; a halo around the moon promises rain; winds from certain quarters foretell rain; a rainbow indicates the end of rain. Some of these beliefs no doubt are based on verified observation and may enjoy a greater-than-chance probability of being correct. Or perhaps it is better to say that some signs can be depended on to foretell weather correctly provided that the conditions which make weather do not change. Sudden changes in these numerous and interrelated conditions lower the probability of even scientific meteorology. Not all such beliefs, however, have been tested in experience. Some simply are traditional, nobody taking the trouble to ascertain the proportion of times in which they are correct or incorrect. Weather lore may be expressed in metaphors. The Kaska Indians interpreted dark clouds in the north at sunset as a promise of warm weather. They were a pillow on which the warm weather would recline, it was explained (Honigmann, 1949a:222).

When people try to account for, and not merely predict, weather, they often postulate personal or impersonal sentient agents that control meteorological changes. For the Arctic Eskimo the impersonal but sentient Sila, occupying the space between earth and sky, controls weather. The Greeks saw Poseidon as the author of whirlwinds raised against sailors while Zeus reigned as Lord of Thunder. Among the people of northwestern North America and eastern Siberia a Thunderbird holds the power of Zeus. The Jivaro of the upper Amazon River ascribed thunder to spirits of the dead (Karsten, 1935:381–382). In Africa south of the Sahara rain is recognized as belonging to the often royal ancestors to give or withhold. Rainmaking in that part of the world consists essentially of invocations to the deceased. The Hopi and other Pueblo Indians of the southwestern United States associate rain with nonspecific dead ancestors who, in the form of clouds, bring rain. Elaborate annual ceremonies insure that the needed moisture will be forthcoming (L. Thompson, 1950:123–129). Evidence indicates that the Africans and the Hopi Indians hold these beliefs very seriously.

Another class of beliefs pertains not only to weather but also to other phenomena of nature. The ideas are less explanatory than descriptive and do not lead to trying to control phenomena. Perhaps, also, they are not taken as seriously as the beliefs described in the last paragraph. Examples include the Kaska Indian's notion that winter fog is a sign that a black bear has cubbed in his den (Honigmann, 1949a:223) or the Chukchee conception of two winds, coming from opposite quarters of the compass, being as man and wife (Bogoras, 1904–09:321–322). The fanciful German remark, made when thunder is heard, "They are rolling beer barrels in heaven," also falls in this category of popular fancies.

Hydrographic Phenomena

Communities living near large bodies of water, or those whose members travel on lakes and rivers, possess knowledge about tides, currents, and other hydrographic phenomena. Knowledge, however, often does not include explanations for what is perceived.

The Attawapiskat Cree Indians of northern Ontario live near where the

Attawapiskat River, after it has traveled nearly 300 miles through forest and muskeg, finally enters the salt water of James Bay. The saltiness of the sea puzzles the Indians, who, only half-believingly, account for it in terms of a European ship that was destroyed in a storm. The salt in the cargo distributed itself throughout the waters of the bay making them salty. The regularity of the tides is noted. People make travel plans in such a way as to take advantage of tidal ebb and flow. But the factors controlling tides are not understood. An especially high tide in the lower reaches of the river, where the town of Attawapiskat is located, occurs when the wind blows from the bay. This indicates to the people that wind somehow determines tidal phenomena. But why does the tide ebb again despite the fact that the same wind continues to blow? The rapid flow of the river toward the coast and the rise of the land inland explain why tides do not ascend far upriver.

From their villages on Vancouver Island the Nootka Indians exploited the Pacific Ocean. The beliefs and sentiments reserved for the ocean were quite different from those directed at the forest located inland on the island. An "infinity of dangerous beings lurked in the woods" and various maladies would ensue should a man meet them. "By contrast, the waters contained fewer perils," although certain sources of danger in the sea were also recognized. For the Nootka bathing in ocean, lake, or stream produced various kinds of good fortune, but so did rubbing one's body with plants (Drucker, 1951:153). The marine orientation of the Nootka community is reflected in the prominent place which water occupied in their ideas and in many other aspects of their culture. The tides determined many events of life yet nobody could furnish the anthropologists with an explanation for them. An extremely high midwinter tide was affirmed by informers. As this tide rose and fell "it turned over, then righted again, everything in its path—every stone on the beach." The tide tables do not corroborate this idea, nor do they indicate the extremely low midsummer tide which Nootkans also mentioned.

The Eskimo of Nunivak Island off the coast of Alaska likewise exploited the sea. They "knew well the connection between the tides and the phases of the moon" (Lantis, 1946:171) but we are not told whether they could explain how the moon influenced the rise and fall of the sea water. The Eskimo possessed a rich vocabulary for conceptualizing various kinds of ice, including ice anchored along the shore, broken ice in the open sea, and pond ice.

Plant Beliefs

"Ethnobotany" is a term referring to knowledge which a community possesses about the plant environment. Such knowledge, generally speaking, is eminently practical. The flora usually are appraised in terms of their directly observable properties. Red willow bark among many northern Canadian Indians is perceived to yield a red dye with which moccasins and other objects may be colored. The rapidity with which various woods burn and the amount of heat generated by different woods in combustion are also noted. People act on ideas of the floral environment which are more difficult for a foreign observer to corroborate. The Ingalik Indians believe that birch-bark smoke is disliked by animals, who may smell it on a hunter. Hence, they are careful about getting into the path of such smoke. The same people believe that the bloodlike red sap of alder in contact with a man will destroy his power to catch fish (Cornelius Osgood, 1940:433–434).

Plants often are employed as cures without knowledge of how their properties react on the human organism and certainly without careful observation of the number of cases in which cure follows administration. The so-called "doctrine of signatures" maintains that any object of nature resembling the human form possesses curative properties (Born, 1949a:1099). The mandrake root, which frequently assumes fantastic shapes, enjoyed long popularity in Europe for this reason. In certain cases western medicine has found the drugs of exotic communities to possess empirically demonstrable value. Pharmaceutical companies, therefore, welcome specimens of exotic medicine which can be analyzed chemically to discover if they contain active agents. Some plants are useful for their narcotic or stimulating properties. Native South America is outstanding for the use of intoxicating plants (Cooper, 1949). In order to gather useful plants, native collectors everywhere possess reliable knowledge of the environmental conditions under which certain types of flora grow and the seasons when they are best suited for certain uses.

In Europe, botanical gardens for the observation of cultivated plants may go back to Aristotle's time, but the founding of many famous gardens only came after the sixteenth century (Born, 1949a and 1949b). Landscape gardens, planted for their esthetic value, go back to about 1500 B.C. in Egypt and Assyria and also were laid out by the Aztec Indians of Mexico.

Ethnozoölogy

Ideas concerning animal behavior, it will be understood, have special significance for people who live by hunting and fishing. Their adaptation to a large extent is dependent upon knowledge of where animals may be found and how they may be killed most effectively. Because the structure of useful animals, generally speaking, is more gross than that of plants and is similar to man's, people tend to possess more information about animal biology. Knowledge of animal behavior nearly always is couched in anthropomorphic terms, the species being endowed with feelings and ideas analogous to man's. Some communities believe that in former times the animals were still more human-like and possessed speech. Siberian hunting people especially minimize the distinction between man and other animals. In the possession of tools and weapons man is superior but the animal also has its points of superiority, notably strength and agility. Animals live in closer contact with the supernatural, according to Siberian hunters (Lot-Falck, 1953:Chaps. 2–3). In some places a man's soul may be reincarnated in any animal, or in the distant past men frequently changed into animals. Such metamorphoses involve only an alteration of outward appearance but no change in personality, so close is the resemblance between the human and nonhuman species. The more closely an animal's behavior or structure resembles man's the greater the tendency to align the species with man. The Zoroastrian scriptures classify monkeys as a "species" of man (Zaehner, 1956:75). Such alignment parallels the zoölogist's classification of the anthropoid apes as man's closest relatives. However, in the case of the zoölogist, fossils give direct evidence of a genetic relationship between the two families. Such resemblances, however, cannot explain all cases in which an animal is singled out for special respect or morbid fear. In India the cow comes in this category; among Canadian, Athapaskan-speaking Indians the mink, otter, and wolf belong here, while in western Europe and America snakes arouse special horror. Nor can attitudes reserved for a particular animal always be related to its manifest ferocity or danger. Across Siberia and northern North America respect for food animals commonly is shown by carefully disposing of their bones so that these may be reconstituted into a fresh supply of game (Lot-Falck, 1953:100, 202–210).

As in the case of ethnobotany, beliefs about animals often are based on overt attributes which can be observed readily, rather than on internal organs and processes. But qualities also are imputed to animals which hardly are susceptible of direct observation. The ferocity of a grizzly bear is obvious enough but its readiness to be offended or insulted is an idea of another order. Kaska Indians recognize the species which are commonly designated by Euroamerican naturalists. But in addition they regard some animals as associated with the devil while others are good. Popular European beliefs also account for the disposition of certain animals by linking them as a class with the devil (S. Thompson, 1946:236).

Zoölogical gardens, at first privately built by wealthy men for raising and studying exotic animals, existed in China, Egypt, and Southwest Asia over a thousand years before the birth of Christ. The Greeks and Romans also maintained zoos. Nineteenth-century Europe saw the founding of large public zoölogical gardens like those familiar today.

Ideas About Food

From the standpoint of adaptation, the most important use of plants or animals or animal products is for food. All cultures contain ideas about what people eat. These ideas pertain to taste, nutritional value, and other inherent qualities that foods are supposed to possess. Also there are ideal combinations of food for particular meals or for people at specific points of the life cycle (Mead, 1953a:215–219). It is quite certain that no people eat simply to satisfy hunger. Often food symbolizes social status and rank (J. W. Bennett, 1943). In the Middle East, Pakistan, and Latin America food is classified in terms of whether it is hot or cold. Indians in San Carlos, Guatemala, believe that mother's milk is hot but cow's milk is cold (Gillin, 1951:31). Oranges, cold water, pork, hen meat, rice, and alcoholic beverages are also hot; limes, hot water, beef, fish, and butter are cold. There seems to be some thought that the two categories, being incompatible, should not be taken together, but rules based on this belief are not followed strictly unless the individual is being treated for illness. A pregnant woman is advised to eat hot foods.

Time

Two basic kinds of time have been distinguished: ecological and structural (Evans-Pritchard, 1940:94–107). Ecological time is a reflection of a community's relationship to the geographical environment, whereas structural time is a reflection of people's relationships to one another. Both concepts refer to the succession of events which possess significance for the community. Ecological time is based on regular changes in nature. Without a system for counting years such time measures cannot very well distinguish periods longer than seasons: for example, the season when geese are hunted, when the people travel out of the village to the cattle camps, or when the winds blow from certain points of the compass. Smaller divisions may be based on changes in the moon. Structural time refers to the various status changes that occur in a man's life. A family may plan for a son's career (Seeley, Sim, and Loosley, 1956:66–71) or men in a community with age-grade organization can refer events to the period when they constituted a particular class (see pp. 432–433). Dividing days and years into fixed units might be called definitive ecological time.

Taking the world as a whole, the most common bases for ordering time are the sun's regular rising and setting (the unit called a "day") and the periodic appearance and disappearance of the moon (roughly corresponding to a month). Larger units, corresponding to the year, seem to be almost as common. The reckoning of elapsed "winters" employed by many North American Indians exemplifies an annual division. Counting years by seasons is quite common in the world of man. In Slavonic the word for summer also signifies a year (Nilsson, 1920:97) just as Cree *piipu'n* ("winter") has been reinterpreted to correspond to English "year." Larger divisions of time are much rarer. Hindu thought recognizes a series of eras of human life going back millions of years. Archeologists possess no evidence of human culture beyond some 600,000 years ago; they divide those last 600,000 years into ages based on changes in tools and human behavior (see pp. 736–738). Thus the Old Stone Age was a time when men used only implements of chipped flint; with the New Stone Age came polished stone tools and agriculture. Geologists conceptualize eras of earth history going back some 3 billion years (see pp. 801–802). The difference between the periods of archeology and geology and the Hindu eras is that the former two are based on direct, empirical evidence of change, whereas Hindus postulate events for which no direct evidence is forthcoming.

Many communities observe how the crescent of a new moon grows, wanes, and disappears but do not count or name each such event. They have no lunar calendar. A large number of North and South American Indians, however, name each successive month after some distinctive environmental feature. In northern Canada the new moon appearing about the time when the geese arrive in spring is called "goose moon," and that coinciding with the moose-breeding season in fall is "moon when the moose ruts" (Honigmann, 1954c:32, 34; 1956a:31; Mandelbaum, 1940: 307). Muslims all over the world follow a lunar calendar containing 12 months with Arabic names. This calendar fixes the time when ceremonies commemorating events of Islamic history are to be performed. Thus the month (i.e., moon) of fasting (Ramadan), when no food is taken between sunrise and sunset, commemorates God's gift of the Quran to the ancient Arabs. The Muslim calendar numbers each year, starting from 622 A.D, the year when the prophet Mohammed is said to have left Mecca, the city where he was dishonored, and with his followers journeyed to nearby Medina. For international and business dealings Muslims also follow the western solar calendar based on 365 days arbitrarily divided into 12 months of 28, 30, and 31 days (with an extra day added to February in every fourth year). Now, there are not exactly 12 new moons in a solar year; hence, the traditional Muslim calendar does not coincide perfectly with the solar year but ends some 11 days before the latter. It comes back to the same solar time in about 33 years. Therefore, ceremonies do not occur at the same time (i.e., in the same season) each year. A ceremony celebrated in summer will before long occur in winter. Only after 33 years will it return to summer again. This is a problem that has been noted by all people who follow a lunar calendar exclusively. The solution sometimes attempted is to insert an extra month every few years. The mechanism for intercalation, as the process of adding an extra month is called, rarely is reported in anthropological monographs but it must occur whenever particular ceremonies are supposed to occur in specific seasons. Often intercalation is determined by the appearance of some natural phenomenon that comes only once a year—like the northward-flying Canadian geese or the appearance of the Pleiades (Leach, 1950). Solar calendars, too, are imperfect but the extra day in a leap year keeps them correlated with seasons.

Farming people who seek to correlate their activities as closely as possible with favorable environmental conditions (especially weather) benefit from being able to predict the seasons. They have much to gain from an accurate calendar. Accurate solar calendars have been associated with Southwest Asiatic agricultural communities since about 4000 B.C. The South American Inca do not appear to have possessed a true solar calendar but they built masonry towers carefully spaced in a row along the skyline. From a raised platform in the capital city of Cuzco observers watched the sun as it set behind those towers. When the sun passed the outside tower, about the month of August, it was time to sow early crops. In September, when the two central towers framed the sun, the time for general sowing had come. Perhaps the towers also helped to set the less exact lunar calendar of 12 named months which the Inca followed (W. C. Bennett, 1949:609). The origination of hours of constant length evenly distributed through a day occurred in Babylon (Nilsson, 1920:40). In Europe standard hours remained far less popular than hours which varied in length according to the time of the year, but by the fourteenth century standard units measured by clocks finally were accepted.

Apart from measuring time there also exists a pronounced tendency for man to regard certain periods as more or less desirable for performing particular acts. Unconscious observation over long periods of time may have indicated to the Kuraver and other criminal tribes of India that it is not safe to practice armed robbery in the light of the full moon, which, in turn, is an auspicious time for Hindu ceremonies (Hatch, 1928). The more divisions a community makes in the continuous flow of time, the more elaborate can be their ideas about certain times. Some agricultural communities with calendars, like India and China, also reveal the greatest preoccupation with the significance of various parts of the year, month, and even of the day.

The extent to which people are oriented toward the past and future varies greatly from one community to another. Every group has its own "reference time" (Gouldner, 1956b:37). Relatively present-oriented communities are those which engage in little planning or saving; they probably also tend to be relatively low in technical development. In a Jerusalem neighborhood Jews were studied who had never gotten used to organizing their expenses on a periodical (weekly or monthly) basis (Eisenstadt, 1949). They spent their money readily, with the result that they were often short of money for basic needs. They possessed a very undefined notion of the future. Each moment was ruled by its own particular problem. These people also possessed few continuous relationships. Most had no definite occupation and worked toward no definite goal or social position. In other words, their patterns of social organization and values regarding achievement were integrated with their loose perception of time. People in rural

Greece do not live by the clock, nor do they budget time. Stores open in due course, not on the hour. Church fills gradually and Mass begins when it is full. It is an insult to arrive for dinner on time and dinner is not planned to appear at a predetermined time. Nor is it served with regard for efficient consumption: nuts are not shelled, nor is fruit sliced. Even in cities the prevailing attitude to time persists and people are called "Englishmen" if they arrive on the dot for an appointment (Mead, 1953a:90–92). How different Crestwood Heights, where time is the master! "In Crestwood Heights time seems almost the paramount dimension of existence, not only in the simple sense that all human events occur in sequence . . . but rather because of the pervasiveness of time as a force in life and career patterns. There are constant demands for efficient work (that is to say, for the most economical use of time), for punctuality, for regularity, which call for an acute sense of timing. These are important factors in the estimation of success or failure" (Seeley, Sim, and Loosley, 1956:64).

Few of the communities traditionally studied by anthropologists conceive of time (or, for that matter, space) as wealth. This conception appears in urban culture, particularly in industrial communities. The expression "Time is money" indicates how explicitly Americans accept time as a valuable "commodity," and the fluctuation of rents as one moves farther away from transportation arteries expresses the same value with regard to space.

Space and Distance

The way in which the spatial environment is conceptualized is, like temporal orientation, also related to other elements of culture. For a people who trace descent unilinearly, and who practice unilocal residence, the locality of the unilinearly related relatives will possess a profound significance unknown in communities with bilateral descent and neolocal residence. Transportation developments also help shape the conception of space. Americans conceive of the world as limited and finite. No place is extremely remote. Reference to a "vanished" frontier means that now every place is accessible quickly. Vagueness about the dimensions of the world correlates with isolation and smallness of scale. It is meaningless to tell an Eskimo the number of days required to cross the American continent by a fast transcontinental train. And to express so vast a distance in terms of the time required to cover it by a dog-drawn sled will also be incomprehensible to a man who has never covered even half that distance and cannot conceive of doing so.

Direction often is divided into six cardinal points corresponding to north, south, east, west, nadir (down), and zenith. Perhaps even more than time periods, directions often bear symbolic significance. For example, the west frequently is associated with death. In ancient Egypt the pyramids stood on the west bank of the Nile. In Korea the north is associated with bleakness, cold, and the source of death. Houses are oriented to the south whenever possible. Sometimes a place or object located in a certain direction conditions the meaning of that compass point. Muslims pray while facing the holy city of Mecca. In India or Pakistan, where orientation is of considerable significance, a follower of Islam will not lie with his feet pointing west or north.

Measurement

Most people measure dimensions or distance using the body. Frequent units are the length of the thumb or arm, span of the hand, and pace made with the feet. Among northern Canadian Indians if a manufactured object must correspond to the dimensions of another object (say, a coffin to a body) the length of the latter object is laid off on a stick or cord. Then an equivalent distance can be laid off on the material used in construction. Standardized, conventional units, like the inch, yard, or meter, appear in association with extensive development and specialization. The Inca of Peru, for example, invented the *rikra*, corresponding to about 64 inches, as a unit of land measurement and divided it into *sikya*, or yards (W. C. Bennett, 1949:603). They calculated 6000 paces to a *topo* (equivalent to about 4½ miles) and employed that measure in road building. But units corresponding to the mile scarcely ever are worked out in small-scale, exotic communities, where travel distances tend to be estimated in terms of time required to reach a certain point. Americans using urban transportation continue to use this form of expressing distance when they say that a housing development is only 10 minutes from the center of the city, or an amusement park half an hour from town.

Dry and liquid quantity measures tend to appear in culture in association with heavy trade, markets, and commercial handicraft.

In some parts of the world, notably India and Pakistan, space and volume measures are very highly localized, varying from one place to another. To understand such variation it is useful to recall that the former provinces of undivided India corresponded to ethnic groups which spoke relatively distinct languages and regarded themselves as quite distinct from one another. As the isolation of provinces broke down, provincial units of measurement began slowly to be displaced. British measures are in use for many purposes, including international trade and scientific research. Of course, standards for measurement still vary greatly between modern nations. The reader no doubt is familiar with the problem of trying to convert the units of one nation into those of another. Some examples of such problems are shown in Tables 43 and 44.

TABLE 43.   Some Common Units of Measurement in Selected
Foreign Countries with United States Equivalent

Foreign	United States
Ardeb (Egypt)	5.62 bushels
Batman (Iran)	6.55 pounds
Cantar (Egypt)	99.05 pounds
Cantar (Turkey)	124.45 pounds
Kwan (Japan)	8.27 pounds
Pound (Soviet Union)	0.90 pound
Stater (Greece)	124.16 pounds
Imperial bushel (United Kingdom)	1.03 bushels
Imperial gallon (United Kingdom)	1.20 gallons

SOURCE: Gries, *1944*.

TABLE 44.   Comparison of Some Garment Sizes in Europe and Equivalents
in the United States

Items	Matched Sizes					
Ladies' blouses	U.S.A. and England:	32	34	36	38	40	42
	Continent:	38	40	42	44	46	48
Ladies' sweaters and	U.S.A. and England:	34	36	38	40	42	44
cardigans	Continent:	40	42	44	46	48	50
Junior dresses	U.S.A.:	—	9	11	13	15	17
	England:	9	11	13	15	17	—
	Continent:	34	36	38	40	42	44
Ladies' dresses	U.S.A.:	—	36	38	40	42	44
	England:	34	36	38	40	42	44
	Continent:	42	44	46	48	50	52
Ladies' shoes	U.S.A.:	4½–5	5½–6	6½–7	7½–8[a]
	England:	3½	4½	5½	6½
	Continent:	36–37	37–38	38–39	39–40
Men's hats	U.S.A.:	6⅝	6¾	6⅞	7	7⅛[b]
	England:	6½	6⅝	6¾	6⅞	7
	Continent:	53	54	55	56	57
Men's shirts	U.S.A. and England:	14	14½	15	15½	15¾[c]
	Continent:	36	37	38	39	40

[a] Continuing to sizes 9½–10 in the U.S.A. but to 9 and 43 in England and the Continent respectively.
[b] Continuing to size 7¾ (7⅝ and 62 in England and the Continent respectively).
[c] Continuing to size 18 (45).
SOURCE: "Yards—Meters," a leaflet published jointly by Grieder's stores and Swissair (n.d.).

THE HUMAN COMPONENT

The human component of the universe includes man himself. How do
people in different communities conceive of man in his physical and behavioral aspects?

What Is Man?

Euroamerican culture possesses not one but several definitions of man. For the physical anthropologist man (the Hominidae) is an animal distinguished by a certain physical structure (see pp. 829–831). When only skeletal materials are available it sometimes is very difficult to distinguish the human from certain closely related animals. The Roman Catholic theologian emphasizes that man is a creature possessing an everlasting soul.[1] The chemist may conceive of man as combining in his organism a variety of minerals. Conceptions of man vary according to the perspective from which he is approached. In everyday life, of course, nobody has any difficulty in distinguishing a normal human being from other members of the animal kingdom.

Practically all communities possess some ideas about man's internal as well as external structure and about the way in which his body operates. That is to say, they deal with human anatomy and physiology.[2]

Man's ideas about himself, as they are represented in ethnographic reports, fall into two categories: some derive from directly observable phenomena; others refer to postulated organs, processes, or qualities. Probably the whole world acknowledges that man is composed of components corresponding to muscle, blood, and bone, although the significance attached to them will vary. Agreement would also be high on the uses of certain organs. That the ear serves for hearing, the nose for smelling, and the mouth for eating and speaking will be admitted in practically all idea systems. These conceptions, it will be noted, point to directly observable phenomena. But what about ideas which are concerned with internal organs and processes of the body? Theoretically these are of the same type as beliefs about the limbs or sensory organs of the head. But knowledge about them can be derived only through surgery or autopsy. The internal human organs are hidden from immediate experience. Generally speaking, surgical techniques are not prevalent among small-scale, exotic peoples. The ancient cultures of the Middle East sought anatomical knowledge through dissection, but even European medicine did not find such observation useful until the nineteenth century (Rosen, 1949). At that time the prevailing doctrine inherited from the Greeks, that illness was the result of an imbalance of the humors, was overthrown completely. In its place was installed the conception that particular organs were affected in certain ways to produce disease. Anatomy and physiology were now directed so that more would be learned about those organs, and the symptoms seen by the doc-

---

[1] "Man is a creature composed of body and soul, and made to the image and likeness of God" (O'Brien, 1901).

[2] For ideas pertaining to conception and pregnancy see pp. 560–561 and 563–564. Menstrual beliefs are covered on p. 576.

tor could be related to an anatomical substratum. Appropriate instruments were invented to aid in this sort of observation. Among small-scale, exotic communities, those living by hunting or animal husbandry are best able to gain a considerable understanding of internal anatomy. Observation is based on animal models. The Aleut of the Aleutian Islands go considerably further than this. Here casual observation of animal anatomy is supplemented by human dissection. Even autopsies are carried out to determine the cause of mysterious deaths (Marsh and Laughlin, 1956).

There is another category of ideas about the body. Here belong the ideas which postulate that the heart is the seat of intelligence or emotion, the hair is the source of strength, and the semen essentially is similar to blood. The Burmese and other people do not accept the body as complete at birth. Tattooing, the wearing of charmed jewels and pieces of gold and silver under the skin, or, in the case of girls, piercing the ears, insured adulthood or conferred extra powers of endurance (Mead, 1953a:65, 238).

How far people go in extending their individuality varies. Euroamericans certainly believe that the head and limbs are part of the individual's body, but not leftover foods, cut hair, or excretions of the body. In quite a few communities, especially where sorcerers are feared, people are careful lest their individuality—in forms like nail parings, clipped hair, feces, and sperm—fall into the hands of someone who will use them to invoke injury or death on the owner (Lévy-Bruhl, 1928:115). Still greater generality marks the attitude of the West African Tiv toward their bodies. "A Tiv was continuous with his society and with nature. . . . Elders forced to travel away from 'the land' carefully preserved and brought back some of their excreta, not for fear of evil witchcraft, but so that the potency inherent in the excreta should benefit their own land" (Mead, 1953a:132). The Greeks possess a strong horror toward any loss of body parts; an amputee among them cannot expect the same respect which is accorded to a normal person (ibid., p. 86).

Descriptions of the body as composed of a few basic elements are common, especially among large-scale peoples. For the ancient Chinese these elements were fire, water, wood, metal, and earth (Veith, 1949). In the same country the internal organs were identified and put into classes. The zo are organs of storage: heart, lungs, liver, kidneys, and spleen. The fu are organs of elimination: stomach, large and small intestines, urinary and gall bladders, and a postulated organ called "three burning spaces." Passages are postulated to exist for transmitting blood and pneuma between the organs. Modern biology postulates 14 or so elements in the body which may be observed indirectly by chemical analysis of protoplasm—the ultimate basis of life.

Individual differences in behavior do not go unnoticed by most people, despite occasional assertions to the contrary (Lévy-Bruhl, 1928:11–112, 184).

Of course, all cultures do not stress the significance of personality differences equally. In Samoa, for example, they are quite disregarded, and little interest is taken in questions of motivation (Mead, 1928a). But many people do seek to account for differences in individual behavior. The Navaho Indians regard human nature as a mixture of good and evil. They further account for individual differences by postulating four winds, one of which may enter the body at birth (Albert, 1956:231). If it is the Good Wind, the man will grow up to be honest and do what is right. The Happy Wind makes people good-natured and in other respects good as well. From the Bad Wind only a life of blunders, accidents, and petty misfortune can be expected, while the dreaded Mad Wind produces a mean man—the worst of all possible types. When a community increases in scale and learns about people who live under different climatic conditions, correlations relating human nature to climate may be expected.

Ethnographic literature seems to contain relatively little material on ethnopsychology—ideas about the dynamics of human behavior. Some such ideas will be reviewed in connection with soul and related beliefs immediately below. Comparative studies suggest that the conception of thought as equivalent to action is fairly widespread. It occurs in European Russia, among the West African Tiv, and as a part of Roman Catholic dogma concerning sin (Mead, 1951:Chap. 3; Mead, 1953a:131; O'Brien, 1901:27). Related to this belief is the idea that both good and evil exist in all men, an idea shared by the Great Russians and the Navaho Indians (Mead, 1951: Chap. 3; C. Kluckhohn and D. Leighton, 1946:230).

Soul and Related Beliefs

Probably all people postulate some kind of immaterial fundamental for human life.[3] Most common among these is the soul, which quits the body after death or somehow ceases to exist. More than one soul often is postulated. The Nupe of Nigeria distinguish three intangible parts of the body: (1) Life (rayi) is sent by God and taken back again by him to the sky when the person dies. It is akin to a physical quality, decreasing in old age and during illness. (2) The shadow (fifingi) is that part of man which continues to exist even after the body decays. It becomes manifest in dreams of the dead and haunts the living, especially when the deceased was not given a proper burial. (3) The soul proper (kuci) represents a reincarnated soul

---

[3] To raise a somewhat technical point, it may be that some immaterial entities asserted to exist with the body are not at all concepts by postulation, subject to indirect verification alone, but are of such a nature that they may be verified quite directly by each man through introspection. The Jukun bwi, the name given to the forceful dynamic quality of the individual, may be in this category (Parrinder, 1951:15). That is, the bwi may be the sense of I-ness which is known quite directly. Sometimes one feels more forceful (secure?) than at other times—for example, during depression. It is convenient to say that the bwi is stronger at such moments.

of a dead ancestor in either the father's or mother's line of descent. It enters the body while the latter is yet in the womb. On death it leaves the body and returns to God temporarily. However, contradictorily the Nupe say that the soul remains on earth to watch over survivors. In addition to these parts every person has a double that may be good or evil. Trouble in marriage sometimes arises because a man's double is incompatible with his wife's. The double can give health, property, and safety to its human twin if it is strong but can do little if weak. An evil double brings nightmares and illness (Nadel, 1954b:21–24, 29). Similar *doppelgaenger* beliefs occur elsewhere in the world (Hultkrantz, 1953:353–374). Belief in a duality of souls is general among North American Indians, although with contact and conversion to Christianity these tend to be reduced to one. The dual souls often correspond to two major types: (1) the free, separate soul, which is active while the body remains passive or asleep (for example, it may be held responsible for dreams), and (2) the body soul, which is manifested in breathing, other physical functions, and life itself. Some tribes of the continent distinguish more kinds of souls (Hultkrantz, 1953:Chap. 2).

Much speculation by early anthropologists and psychoanalysts was devoted to the question of how man first hit upon the idea of a soul (Tylor, 1891:I, 428–429; Bastide, 1950:52–53). Their conjectures will not be reviewed here. Not only may souls be ascribed to men but they are bestowed on other parts of the environment—trees, animals, and even inanimate objects. Functionally speaking, soul concepts serve people as explanatory devices. For example, death may be ascribed to the complete loss of the soul, illness to its partial loss, and dreams to the soul's travels and experiences while the individual is asleep. Belief in the continued existence of a soul after death answers the riddle of death for people who find this phenomenon mysterious. Not all people, though, believe in the immortality of some portion of the individual.

Related to, and sometimes hard to distinguish from, the soul are other aspects postulated to form part of man's being. There is the Maori concept of *tupu*—the value or intrinsic quality of one's life (Johansen, 1954:43–47). This notion is hard to translate into English but, briefly, *tupu* refers to repute, honor, or faith. Gray hair in old age constitutes a sign of dwindling *tupu*. Through capturing and enslaving the women of the previous inhabitants of New Zealand, the invading Maori increased their *tupu*. Conversely, a defeat weakens a group's honor, and a slave's life is completely without intrinsic value. The concept connotes the unfolding of a man's life in successful action so that he thrives.

A somewhat different kind of concept is the Burmese *kan*. Health is one of the areas of life maintained through a strong *kan*. At certain points in the life cycle, like pregnancy, the *kan* is weak and the person must take precautions. The *kan* may also be strengthened—for example, by giving wealth to a Buddhist monastery. But nobody can help another person strengthen his *kan* (Mead, 1953a:43–59).

Many anthropologists have sought to explain another Polynesian concept, one more popular than *tupu* and pertaining to man as well as other parts of nature. This is *mana* (Johansen, 1954:84–99). Among the New Zealand Maori *mana* is a postulated, indirectly observable quality that may be participated in (not possessed) by an individual who already possesses *tupu*. It also is revealed in a group and certain objects. Especially does a chief reveal *mana*. Through him, followers and even the land participate in it. The chief's words reveal *mana*; hence they are obeyed. The degree to which any individual reveals *mana* varies. Whatever the degree may be, *mana* endures through the deference received by the person who reveals it. Therefore, *mana* correlates with influence, power, and respect. But *mana* is not the same as personal power nor is *mana* an anthropomorphic force. Perhaps it may be defined operationally as the bond revealed to a Polynesian when a group occupying a given territory holds together and obeys, as well as respects, its head. He understands this bond as pervading all that with which the group comes into contact.

36.

Man and the Universe

TWO different theories of the universe, not closely correlated with the personal and impersonal world views, may be contrasted (Frank, 1951: 38–40). One holds the conception of some single central power, force, or authority regulating everything in the universe like a boss. "Organization . . . [is] conceived as a collection of parts or persons . . . kept together and compelled to operate with greater or less interrelatedness." This is not usually the view of small-scale, exotic communities which anthropologists have studied. Rather in these is found a conception shared by scientists, who conceive of a universe that needs no supreme ruler to keep it running. The cosmos is like a pond or other ecological region in which plants and animals coöperate to maintain a natural balance that allows life to continue. In the second point of view the universe constitutes a self-governing and self-regulated system, one in which man is continuous with the rest of nature (Mead, 1953a:234). Although this general conception exists explicitly or implicitly in most exotic communities, at least four differences mark the self-governing universe found in modern science and in exotic belief systems. (1) In detail the conception of the universe tends to be worked out less systematically among small-scale, exotic peoples. (2) Explanations given for the interrelatedness of things are not verified or tested experimentally but are merely postulated and, sometimes, logically rationalized. It is rare for a member of the Papuan Orokaiva tribes to ask how distant parts of nature may affect each other. He does not even try to rationalize the idea that a field of sugar cane swaying in the wind can upset the stomach of a man who has eaten sugar cane (F. E. Williams, 1934:264). If he is pressed to give an answer to the question starting "how," he refers to the immaterial counterparts—souls—possessed by everything in nature. These immaterial extensions are assumed to be capable of movement. In this way the separate parts of nature can interact. Among the Omaha the concept of an all-pervasive entity, *Wakonda*, linked animate with inanimate parts of the universe and also the part with the whole (Fletcher and LaFlesche, 1911:415; see also pp. 657–659 below). (3) Exotic conceptions often are extremely anthropocentric, making man the hub of the universe (Thurnwald, 1951: 24, 380). For example, among the Navaho Indians ". . . the universe is conceived as a place for man, and all natural phenomena are interpreted as his allies or enemies" (Reichard, 1950:148–149). The anthropocentric point of view and its fate are expressed in the following lines:

The earth was the world and man was its measure, but our minds have looked
Through the little mock-dome of heaven the telescope-slotted observatory eye-
  ball, there space and multitude came in
And the earth is a particle of dust by a sand-grained sun, lost in a nameless
  cove on the shores of a continent.

[Jeffers, 1932:135]

(4) As already pointed out, in most cultures the interrelatedness of the universe is maintained personalistically; that is, parts of nature are conceived after the model of man with his sensory equipment and are capable of volition. Sometimes unseen personal beings are postulated to exist who promote interaction between the parts of nature. A tree-being, for example, allows a tree to crash at the moment when someone is walking within its radius. The western scientific conception, of course, is of a world operating strictly in impersonal terms. Even human beings tend to be analyzed by the aid of impersonal concepts in the science of psychology.

  Although most of the world conceives of a universe in which the parts of nature, including man, are interrelated, this does not mean that people are ready to relate every single phenomenon which they recognize to every other component of their experience. As already noted, all phenomena in nature do not possess equivalent significance for people. Some events are attended to more closely and possess more importance than others. Most people do not work out the conception of an interdependent universe systematically. Their belief in such a system can only be inferred from their behavior. At first glance, such behavior often has struck alien observers as highly irrational or without logical foundation (for such a view see Lévy-Bruhl, 1926:69–70. Also see Lienhardt, 1954a).

THE UNIVERSE AS A BIOSPHERE

  If the universe constitutes an organized system, that is, one in which whatever parts are recognized also influence one another, then from the standpoint of man the universe may be termed a human biosphere: the realm in which human life takes place (Angyal, 1941:101). There is little question that most communities conceive of the universe as such a biosphere. Though few make the conception explicit, it usually can be inferred from other patterns of socially standardized behavior.

  An intelligent responsive universe appears to be a firm part of African speculative thought. Africans explicitly conceptualize some "hidden, mysterious, super-sensible, pervading energy, powers, potencies, forces" that hold the unit together and exist in everything (Parrinder, 1951:10–14). These ideas appear quite clearly among the Lele of the southwest Belgian Congo as they explain the concepts of individual and social ill health (M. Douglas, 1954). In the former a man is feverish or otherwise indisposed; in the latter a village is bad or spoiled. The fertility of women and the success encountered by a communal hunting expedition are somehow linked to social health. At least they are regarded as indicators. When the productivity of hunting declines it is a sign that the village is spoiled. But hunting is controlled by unseen entities. They can be called "spirits," but the Lele never speak of them in anthropomorphic terms. One task of these beings is to uphold the many regulations which people must follow. Especially do they want people to live at peace with one another. Offenses between people are punished by the unseen entities through failure in hunting. Hunting is a male activity which possesses equivalence with childbearing. The communal hunt provides meat for feasts, which are given by the men's associations. These feasts, in turn, induce the unseen entities to facilitate good hunting for the village. The communal hunt "is the supreme religious activity." From a functional point of view it is easy to understand how the value set on hunting helps the people to live in peace with one another, for if they don't do so the hunt will suffer. But the Lele see the matter in more complicated terms. Interpersonal offenses, they say, spoil the village and, through offending postulated entities, interfere with the realization of two goals: children and meat from the hunt.

Many American Indians thought of themselves and the rest of the universe as participating in an abstract power-pool (L. Thompson, 1948). Such a concept goes far to illuminate a number of otherwise puzzling American Indian beliefs. In many North American tribes, for example, the young men sought to enhance their personal abilities by securing a personal helper or guardian spirit (see p. 637). To win such a helper required spending some period of isolation in a lonely place. Here the seeker humbled himself in supplication. Acknowledgment of his request for help came in the form of a dream or vision in which a guardian, a manifestation of the power-pool, promised assistance. Immoral behavior disturbed the power-pool so that automatic retribution brought about illness and other misfortunes. In the thought of some North American tribes, like the Navaho, personalized deities are more prominent than is the abstract power-pool. Such deities seem functionally to be related to the domestication of plants and animals. The Navaho Indian participates in many ceremonies, the purpose of which is to put him in touch or in tune with the Holy People, who, while not all-powerful, insure health, prosperity, and well-being. Some ceremonies are designed to bring rain, help the corn to grow, or provide for a safe journey (C. Kluckhohn and D. Leighton, 1946). The conception of an interrelated universe does not, of course, disappear when anthropomorphic deities are present. ". . . The universe and all the earth people function according to rules. The misfortunes . . . are the results of not following the rules. Navajos hold ceremonials to restore order to the individual by performing exact rituals which will require supernatural forces to withdraw their punishment . . ." (M. Collier and J. Collier, 1948:20).

ROADS TO POWER

In all communities man seeks to retain control over the biosphere he inhabits. Cultures differ in whether they emphasize man's molding the universe to his will or stress the importance of human beings' adjusting to the conditions of the biosphere. Americans often exemplify the former position. In Middle America, "the principal and fundamental goal of Indian cultures is to effect a peaceful adjustment or adaptation of men to the universe" (Gillin, 1952:116; cf. pp. 456–457 *supra*). In contrast the main goal of the more Europeanized Ladino culture in that region "is to effect control of the universe by man. The Indian wishes to come to terms with the universe, the Ladino wishes to dominate it." This does not mean that the Indian is highly passive, fatalistic, or submissive. An attitude similar to the Middle American Indians' has been reported for the Navaho Indians. They conceive of nature as more powerful than man (Vogt, 1951:36; C. Kluckhohn and D. Leighton, 1946:227). The universe is not to be mastered for human ends. Instead, man learns to live with the universe. Again here no passivity is implied. Tools, hard work, living by the traditional way of life, and, sometimes, doing nothing are means of coping and of maintaining harmony with the Holy People, who have great power to help or hinder human beings.

How Man Copes

Whether conceiving of nature as relatively powerful or as the willing servant of man, the means through which people cope with the world fall into two basic categories. These, as other categories that have been described in this book, are not absolutely distinct from each other. Both of the coping mechanisms to be discussed may be found in all communities and may even be simultaneously present in a single situation in which man is trying to deal with some problem. Communities, however, probably differ in the proportion with which one is used in relation to the other.

1. **Direct Coping.** Man copes with the world directly through techniques, social administration, or social pressure applied on people who behave in uncomplementary fashion. Thus, by cutting timber a man acquires material for building a home; through planting crops he provides himself with food; the food is physically harvested and cooked to make it more fit for eating; by threatening punishment human communities reduce uncom-

plementary diversity; through wielding scalpel or forceps man tries to stop or to prolong life or to bring new life into being; from rivers he takes fish, and in factories he coördinates the energy of many people to produce goods. No reader should have any trouble understanding this sort of coping. There is a strong but rather unwarranted temptation to call it "practical" in distinction to coping techniques that belong in the second category. But such a word is ethnocentric, springing from the high evaluation which western man sets on these approaches to nature. It is better to say simply that all people recognize that they can achieve ends by acting on nature or society in this relatively direct fashion. There is no community in which direct coping behavior is not utilized.

2. Indirect Coping with Signs and Symbols. In addition to acting directly on nature or on persons, many communities seek to control the world indirectly through signs and symbols. For example, a man imitates what he would like to see come to pass or crosses his fingers to escape misfortune. During a torrential rain peasants in South Italy stand kettles upside down outside the house in order to bring the downpour to an end (Silone, 1937: 88). Or they pray, with the expectation that God will heed their appeal. Sometimes an individual seeks to develop certain qualities in himself by ingesting or otherwise coming into contact with something which symbolizes the qualities he would like to acquire. He may refrain from eating that which symbolizes an undesirable quality. Bell ringing, drumming, dancing, slaughter, and the integration of all of these techniques into rituals are often regarded as effective means for coping with problems. The instrumental efficacy ascribed to signs, symbols, and rituals used in this way is a firm part of the personal world view.

Unless such behaviors occur merely expressively, that is, without any thought that they will be effective in achieving some desired goal, many readers with an impersonal type of ideology will feel inclined to dismiss them as futile. Here we see the tremendous gap separating the two contemporary world views. In western culture man is not free to act as if a symbol were somehow equivalent to that which it stands for. He does not believe that because an eagle can see long distances it is efficacious to rub under his own eyelids a preparation which includes water from an eagle's eye (C. Kluckhohn and D. Leighton, 1946:231). We can understand talking to another person and promoting a response through symbols (that is, words), but most readers will feel much less confidence in trying to bring about rain, good health, or a swift journey by directing verbal symbols at the physical world, or to personal entities postulated to stand behind it. The distinction between direct and indirect coping is diagramed in Figure 36:1.

In practice it is not always possible to discover when some coping procedure constitutes a direct means of coping and when it is an operation relying indirectly on signs and symbols. This difficulty is acute when nothing is known about the actor's underlying beliefs. Consider a man burning a piece of bark cloth and blowing the smoke into a space inhabited by termites while at the same time he holds a plant possessing certain postulated properties (Evans-Pritchard, 1937:464). Is the Azande man in this situation applying a direct technique of fumigation to get rid of termites or is he op-

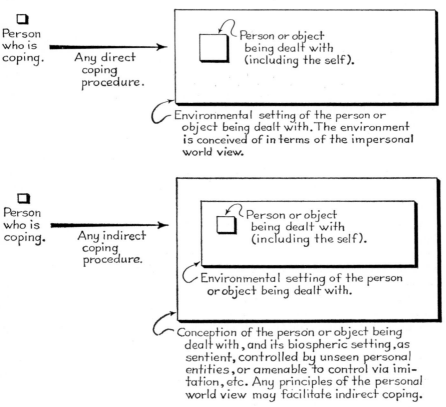

Person who is coping.

Any direct coping procedure.

Person or object being dealt with (including the self).

Environmental setting of the person or object being dealt with. The environment is conceived of in terms of the impersonal world view.

Person who is coping.

Any indirect coping procedure.

Person or object being dealt with (including the self).

Environmental setting of the person or object being dealt with.

Conception of the person or object being dealt with, and its biospheric setting, as sentient, controlled by unseen personal entities, or amenable to control via imitation, etc. Any principles of the personal world view may facilitate indirect coping.

FIG. 36:1. Direct and Indirect Coping.

erating symbolically? It would probably be next to impossible to persuade him to make the distinction or to get him to give a rationalization for the various components of the procedure.

These possibilities do not exhaust the basic ways of behavior by which man seeks to retain objective control, or a subjective sense of power, over his universe. Reference also could be made to prediction, in which the occurrence of one aspect of nature is made the index of another. Further discussion of prediction is reserved for pp. 633–636. Men also seek to control biospheric phenomena, including social relationships, by following rules. Rules actually involve prediction, especially when they more or less guaran-

tee success. In any community some rules will have higher objective reliability than others, regardless of the degree of conviction with which they are
followed. The bulletins issued by American agricultural extension stations
contain tested rules specifying how to raise better grades of tomatoes, chickens, or other products. The rule of planting certain crops when the moon is
visible seems to belong in a category of less reliable knowledge.

COPING INDIRECTLY THROUGH SIGNS AND SYMBOLS

The essence of indirect coping is to treat human and nonhuman phenomena as susceptible to remote individual control. This is done by imita-
tive and other sign-symbol techniques which are designed to act quite
independently of the object's conscious awareness or previously conditioned
response.

Dealing with nature indirectly through signs and symbols is a topic about
which much has been written. Nevertheless, a few additional illustrations
may make the concept more meaningful. From the Orokaiva tribes in
northern Papua, New Guinea, comes this elaborate procedure for promoting rain:

An old woman named Hojavo is reputed to be a rain-maker . . . and con-
sents to show her magical recipe. First she takes a broad striated leaf of the
tree *Gotomo*. (My interpreter points out a resemblance between this leaf and
a certain kind of cloud, which I confess myself unable to see with him.) The
Gotomo leaf is thoroughly crushed and deposited in an earthenware saucepan.
Now the old woman takes a section of banana stalk of the kind called *Andoga*.
This is especially succulent, and as she breaks and squeezes it in her hands
over the pot it sheds a copious rain of drops. Meanwhile she is muttering *Ga
bejo, ga bejo!*—"Rain come, rain come!" Then, when she has squeezed the
Andoga stalk dry, she places it on top of the first leaf and the watery fluid in
the pot, and leaves them in her house. For some reason the rain-maker must
sulk indoors, not venturing out nor even looking at the sky until she relents
and is ready to unmake her magic. To do this she empties the earthenware
pot; she lays out the saturated *Andoga* to dry; she looks into the sky and puffs
her breath at it; she blows into her closed fist and then sweeps her open hand
across the heavens, crying, *Ga tojo, ga tojo!*—"Rain be finished!" [F. E. Williams, 1928:177]

The use of signs and symbols to influence nature may take even more
complex forms and involve the coöperation of a large number of actors. Or
such procedures may be much briefer, consisting of a single whispered
word or momentary gesture. Notice that the word "magic" in the quotation just given does not add anything to the description. It even acts as a
detriment to obtaining insight into the procedure because of the variety
of contexts in which that word has been employed. The quotation brings

out well the imitativeness of the rain-making technique. In trying to stop the rain the woman empties a pot, symbolizing exhaustion. The reader will recall that South Italian peasants also turn a pot upside down to promote the end of the downpour. In the example just given, the words reinforce the symbolism and make it clearer. However, the anthropologist does not help in explaining what, if any, symbolism may be involved in remaining indoors, puffing the breath, or blowing into the closed fist. Perhaps the people could have explained the meaning of this gesture if they had been asked. Or perhaps the meaning could have been deduced by discovering when else people remain indoors, or what meaning puffing one's breath or blowing into a closed space possesses in other contexts of culture. Sometimes rather meaningless words are used for indirect coping. Yet, in the opinion of the community, these may be highly effective when used alone or combined with auxiliary procedures.

Two ideological orientations sometimes are apparent in indirect coping through use of signs and symbols. The procedure may suggest that a part of a person or of nature is being treated as though it actually were the total referent itself. "Contagion-thinking" may then be said to underlie the procedure. Where the desired end merely is imitated, "similarity-thinking" is indicated. The idea of contagion maintains that the part stands for the whole (C. Kluckhohn and D. Leighton, 1946:230–231; Frazer, 1911:52–54); similarity-thinking, on the other hand, holds that like produces like. Not all indirect coping techniques can be classified in one category or the other or even as falling in both simultaneously.

Many of the indirect coping procedures described in ethnographic monographs are designed to influence people and not aspects of the geographical environment. Sometimes the intent is to strengthen a person, perhaps to cure him of illness. The widespread distribution of sign-symbol techniques designed to attract someone of the opposite sex is related to the universality of the problem of finding and retaining a sexual partner. Also familiar are acts designed to cause sickness or death in another person, whether someone within the community or outside. Collectively these latter procedures are called "sorcery." Among the Orokaiva,

If the magician can come by a part of the object or person upon whom he has designs, he will derive an anticipatory satisfaction from putting those designs into effect upon the part in lieu of the whole. If he cannot obtain an actual part of such object or person he will make do with something which has been closely associated. In the case of a human victim, e.g., it will be sufficient to obtain a piece of hair, or one of those red-dyed streamers of areca spathe that the Orokaiva fastens to the tags of his greasy coiffure. It will be sufficient to obtain a tattered fragment of his bark-cloth perineal band, or a scraping of the dirt and sweat which is sometimes present in very available quantity on his skin. A most satisfactory medium is the victim's semen, which,

it is said, can commonly be obtained from a female betrayer. Any such object
. . . which has been in close association with or has belonged to the victim will
serve to personify him, as it were, when the sorcerer wishes to work off his
feelings [F. E. Williams, 1928:190–191].

In some sorcery there is actual contact with the intended victim: ". . .
The magical mixture is prepared first independently of the victim, and is
then brought into contact with him. Sometimes such a mixture may be kept
in a bamboo 'bottle.' When it is called into use the sorcerer creeps on his
victim in his sleep, dips a feather in the mixture, and lightly touches the
sleeper's skin or moistens his lips with it."

The author of the quotation doubts that the sorcerer can be considered
"an out-and-out poisoner" even if genuine poisons are used (*ibid.*, p. 211).
In any community, several types of sorcery (and other indirect coping
procedures used to influence people) may be distinguished: "(1) the cases
where a sorcerer actually practises sorcery but keeps it a secret; (2) the cases
where he makes the fact known that he is practising sorcery or openly pre-
tends or threatens to practise it; and (3) the cases where he is merely supposed by others to practise it." In New Guinea it is suggested that these
categories "stand respectively in a ratio something like 1:10:100" (F. E.
Williams, 1951:20).[1]

Sorcery may be approved or disapproved in a community. Generally it
is approved only when employed against a wrongdoer with the explicit consent of the community or against an external enemy constituting a threat
to the in-group. Inside the community sorcery is illegal. The Azande, who
live in the Egyptian Sudan, permit retaliatory sorcery if a person is presumed to have died from another, unknown individual's sorcery or witchcraft. The sorcery seeks out the unknown slayer.

Some observers seriously have used the words "nonlogical" and "prelogical" to describe indirect coping. It has even been seen as akin to the behavior of the mentally ill. Another point of view, however, sees such activities as
subtly logical, often remarkably clear, and akin to the metaphorical expression of poetry. Consider, for example: Among the Kaska Indians an older
brother ripped open the left sleeve of his coat when his younger brother
first killed a large game animal. This action instigated future abundance.
Instead of remaining hidden, the animals would fall out, metaphorically
speaking, as from a torn garment (Honigmann, 1954c:110).

The Nature of Signs and Symbols in Indirect Coping

People may try to cope indirectly through signs and symbols that consist
primarily of words and gestures, but more commonly they employ a material

---

[1] One of the big problems in studying indirect coping techniques is learning which of
such techniques are put into practice and which are merely ideal. In the latter category
is probably the Mass of St. Secaire, a Mass which is said backwards and involves conditions that rarely could be fulfilled in practice (Rhodes, 1955:60).

specific of one kind or another. The ideas which the community holds about that object or its objective properties often illuminate its use in coping procedures. For example, among the Orokaiva the hibiscus is an ingredient used in symbolic techniques designed to secure successful hunting. The explanation lies in the fact that the natives consider the flower's scarlet color to be like the fresh blood of the pig (F. E. Williams, 1928:189). "The root of a variety of bread fruit was used in sun-magic because it resembled the sun simply in its red-yellow color." The leaf of a towering tree is planted in the same hole with a taro shoot so that the taro will become as big as the tree is big. Pigs also are washed with infusions made from the leaves of that tree. The object is easy to infer. Sometimes the meaning of the specific is more subtle and must be explained by people in the community. For example, a leaf used in making wet weather is selected because of its "damp cold feel." And another one that calms down rough water is efficacious because it wilts a few minutes after it has been plucked (*ibid.*, p. 193). A cold-weather specific is a plant called "dog-tail" "and the virtue . . . was merely in its name. For is not the dog, with its shivering and crouching by the fire, peculiarly sensible of the cold?" Another cold-weather specific among the Orokaiva is a plant that shrinks when the cool of the evening touches it. This is also used as a preparation to make babies sleep because it too appears to sleep. In some instances the symbolism seems apparent to the anthropologist but he cannot verify his belief through native informants. That is to say, the people do not recognize that the specific has the meaning which, it appears logical to the anthropologist, should be present. Why is this so? "It is impossible to be sure of the reason for the use of any particular specific in the first instance; but it is equally impossible to believe that specifics originated in a causeless or haphazard manner. We can only suggest some original association or analogy which may or may not be the true one. . . . The object was in the first instance really a symbol. In the course of time the symbolism was obliterated from memory . . ." (*ibid.*, p. 205).

How Indirect Coping Works

Do people who cope indirectly with the aid of signs, or who deal with the world symbolically, believe in what they do? If the question means whether they use such forms of coping with the expectation that those procedures are efficacious, the answer most anthropologists would give is an unhesitating "yes." Of course, this does not deny that in some communities there may be doubters and that, under conditions of culture change, conflicts ensue over the validity of such behavior. Whether people who use the procedures believe that signs and symbols are not different from more direct forms of coping is a more difficult question. It seems highly likely that where contagious or similarity thinking obtains (where the part is treated as the whole or where like is done to produce like) people would quite readily recognize a distinction between indirect and direct coping techniques. That is, they would recognize a difference between killing a game animal by hitting it with an arrow and imitating the killing in a dance. At the same time they feel strongly convinced of the importance of the symbolization as one step in the successful achievement of the goal. What we suggest is that people are able to perceive that what they do indirectly is not equivalent to directly striking an enemy with a spear or bringing down game with weapons. There is an element of serious pretense in what they do (Marett, 1909:54) just as there is solemn pretense when the carpet is rolled out at the Washington, D.C., airport to honor a distinguished foreign visitor. Of course, the situation is different when no direct mode of dealing with a problem is part of the cultural repertory. For example, if illness is regarded as a visitation by a deity or spirit, then talking to the spirit and urging him to quit the patient is a logically appropriate form of treatment. It cannot be distinguished from a more direct form of therapy unless illness is recognized as having another basis, from which point of view it can be attacked directly—for example, through drugs.

Objectively, indirect coping techniques may not function as the practitioner subjectively believes them to do. Therefore, their maintenance in culture depends on the more or less hidden functions which operate when the techniques are carried out. Following are some possible ways in which indirect coping procedures reward people who use them.

1. Suggestion. At the outset a distinction must be recognized between signs and symbols that are directed against animals or inanimate nature and those used to influence one's own or another's health, welfare, or purpose. The nonhuman components of the universe cannot know what is being done to influence them, but human beings can. Hence the first explanation for the efficacy of indirect forms of coping involves the factor popularly know as "suggestion." Through suggestion, indirect coping comes to possess ascertainable, objective efficacy. In many communities studied by anthropologists curers reiterate the promise of recovery and thus apparently help the body to achieve physiological equilibrium. In the same way knowledge that one has been the victim of sorcery induces depression and, in well-authenticated instances, even has been followed by illness and death (Cannon, 1942).[2]

2. Association with Direct Procedures. Few people omit from gardening such techniques as planting seeds or building a fence to keep out wild animals. At the same time they practice purely symbolic techniques to help their gardens grow. A trapper does not try to get animals without setting or baiting a trap even though he also fortifies the trap symbolically. In other words, there are many situations in which indirect techniques are used only

---

[2] For a review of some literature dealing with thanatomania—illness or death resulting from suggestion or through symbolism—see Honigmann, 1954b:382–384.

in association with more straightforward direct coping operations. The latter, it may be assumed, possess high reliability. That is, they often are successful. If the actor believes that such success will not occur without employment of indirect coping procedures, and if he never experiments or is given other opportunities to see the straightforward techniques used without the sign-symbol auxiliaries, then the latter will give the appearance of working. Naturally, the indirect coping techniques may be working objectively to the degree that they contribute to the assurance with which all the technical operations are carried out. But this is another matter, one which fits better in the discussion of suggestion.

3. Haloing. Another factor apparently contributing to the efficacy of indirect forms of coping may be called "haloing." The African Azande, for example, often discover that a symbolic procedure for coping has failed to achieve the expected results. But they do not generalize from such observations to conclude that all similar procedures are foolish (Evans-Pritchard, 1937:474). Cases in which the measure didn't work tend to be overlooked; those in which the expected sequence occurred may be noted appreciatively and even stressed (perhaps by a specialist practitioner, calling attention to what he has achieved). Such behavior strengthens the community's conviction that the indirect coping procedure is efficacious although, objectively, only low reliability may characterize situations in which it occurs. Haloing is not peculiar to indirect coping but is used to safeguard any fervently held belief in the face of disconfirmation (Festinger, Riecken, and Schachter, 1956:183–184).

4. Consensus. Indirect coping techniques remain subjectively efficacious so long as their underlying assumptions are not questioned or challenged. In other words, indirect procedures normally are logical in the sense of deriving from underlying assumptions. The Orokaiva and Navaho assume to start with that like can produce like in certain contexts. Hence the signs or symbols which they manipulate are logically endowed with validity. Most Americans hold no such assumption and deliberately are discouraged by parents, teachers, and clergy from this kind of thinking. Hence they cannot with conviction execute many indirect procedures. It is a little different with respect to prayer directed to unseen entities. Many Americans assume the existence of powerful deities who are within reach of human supplication. Once this assumption becomes weakened, however, the subjective efficacy of prayer as an indirect form of coping also is destroyed.

5. Social Pressure. The efficacy of indirect coping may rest on the shared nature of the techniques. Other people practicing the same routine give the procedures an aura of certainty or confidence. People actually object if the technique is not executed in a specific situation.

There are other factors that could be added to this list. Among the Azande of the Egyptian Sudan, skepticism is not unknown as far as indirect coping techniques are concerned (Evans-Pritchard, 1937:475). But the skepticism is channeled toward certain acts and certain specialists. By contrast, procedures which are not subject to challenge have their reward value reinforced. Also among the Azande not too much is claimed for such forms of coping; often it is merely implied that they will *help* bring success, not that they guarantee the result absolutely and independently. And, of course, many of the results which they do promise would happen anyway. Only if the people were inclined experimentally would they ever perform the crucial test to discover how often a result would follow without the execution of the appropriate coping procedure. Such an experimental inclination would imply that loss of faith in the coping procedure had already occurred. Some of the factors previously suggested as helping to maintain cultural and ideological persistence also may throw light on the present problem (see pp. 185–190 and 597–599).[3]

Displacement of Indirect Coping

A few things may be said concerning the conditions under which indirect techniques, relying on the manipulation of signs and symbols, tend to be displaced from culture.

1. **Christianization.** Indirect coping techniques which do not postulate sentient powers in the universe have tended to disappear with the rise of doctrines like Christianity, which substitute prayer to superhuman entities. The displacement, of course, has not been complete. Peasants in Catholic Spain or Italy continue to use signs and symbols to protect themselves from postulated sources of danger, like the evil eye, despite the fact that Catholicism frowns on such practices. The use of many indirect coping techniques is prohibited, as a sin against the first commandment, in the *Baltimore Catechism* of the Roman Catholic Church (O'Brien, 1901:163).

2. **Scale.** Forms of coping through signs and symbols, including (but in less degree) prayer and sacrifice, tend to be displaced as the scale of the community increases. Some correlates of scale probably are more closely related to displacement than others. A growing variety of divergent and even conflicting beliefs appears to be most influential in undermining the assumptions on which indirect coping rests.

3. **Felt Inadequacy.** The reader will recall that inadequacy which comes to be perceived in existing cultural elements as substitutes become available is a potent factor promoting successful diffusion of the new with consequent displacement of the old (see pp. 218–219). This factor also holds for the ideas governing indirect coping techniques.

[3] Some 22 factors governing the Azande's faith in indirect coping techniques are listed by Evans-Pritchard (1937:474–478) and should be studied by anyone further interested in this problem. See also D. Lee, 1949:407.

PREDICTION

A familiar means by which man seeks to maintain his own safety, comfort, and success is trying to predict. Prediction is possible once man at least implicitly conceives of his biosphere as constituting an orderly system in which phenomena are interdependent. One thing, therefore, may be an index to another. (1) Prediction may be retrospective (Why did the crop fail or a child sicken?) or it may point to the future (Will it rain? Will the outcome of a venture be successful?). When techniques are used to uncover the unknown or not directly perceivable in the present, we speak of diagnosis. (2) Prediction may involve the performance of highly specialized procedures, like the correlation of large masses of meteorological data which requires a "thinking machine," or the calculation of astrological formulas; or it may be an activity for which little specialized knowledge is required. Anybody may look at the sky to see if rain clouds are present and so foretell rain. (3) Finally, prediction ranges between degrees of objective certainty. It may be reliable in that, more frequently than could be accounted for by chance alone, a technique accurately specifies a past or future event which actually did occur or does come about. Or prediction may be unreliable; the specified events do not occur in a significant number of cases. Probably most popular weather omens possess far less reliability than do the rules for interpreting a mass of meteorological data collected in a modern weather bureau. But it is common knowledge that the weather man is scarcely always right.

Western society has developed highly reliable forms of prediction which require intricate instruments, like barometers, or are based on refined knowledge of the structure of materials. The custom of keeping historical records allows the prediction of automobile accident rates on holiday week ends, of mortality at various ages, and of how many seeds in a packet will germinate. In association with an impersonal world view, prediction rests in the recognition of signs known theoretically and empirically to be related to other phenomena with definite probability. A light signals that the radio or atomic reactor is on because the on-switch regulates the flow of power to the signal lamp. Any point in a series of interrelated phenomena may be a sign of one or more other points in the sequence. An explanation for the connection between the sign or symbol and what follows may be unknown. The problem then is to discover the link. Psychoanalysts regard some dreams as indicators of childhood experiences (retrospective prediction) but many feel that they do not yet possess a satisfactory explanation for the connection between adult dreams and childhood experiences. In association with a personal world view, personalized, sentient, or anthropomorphic forces sometimes are postulated to provide the explanation of why one event is the index of another. Often, though, no explanation is given.

In many communities dreams are regarded as furnishing insight into the future. For example, among the Kaska Indians to dream of fish in the summer promises good fortune in the following winter's trapping; to dream of eating game promises successful hunting; water portends danger of drowning (Honigmann, 1949a:236). The use of an animal's shoulder blade (i.e., scapula) for prediction (called scapulimancy) is distributed in the circumpolar region ranging from Europe through Asia east all the way to Labrador. The bone is heated in fire and the resultant cracks are "read" in order to learn the location of game (O. K. Moore, 1957). The flight of birds or the call of wild animals frequently is regarded as a sign of one thing or another. The Thugi, a former South Asian movement specializing in armed robbery, made a worship out of human sacrifice. They accepted the scream of jungle fowl as a sign that their patron, Kali, wanted them to make an offering (Masters, 1952:Chap. 15). The criminal tribes of that country, like the Kuraver, employed many procedures to find out if all would go well on a criminal expedition which they were planning (Hatch, 1928). If a stone suspended from a string held in the fingers swung like a clock's pendulum success was promised. Or a coin might be buried in one of five piles of earth. Should a man not be able to find it in three guesses the proposed trip was abandoned. One procedure called for two successive handfuls of stones to be seized and flung on the ground. If the first number flung proved to be an odd number and the second even, then success would be certain. To see a kite (a scavenging bird) fly from left to right across a road led the Kuraver to abandon a criminal expedition. Many of these omens may still be observed among the noncriminal, rural population of India and Pakistan. Bodily phenomena, like sneezing, itching, or twitching of surface muscles, often are interpreted as indicators of events to follow. Among the Azande, as well as in other parts of Africa, administering poison to fowls is a means of revealing what is hidden from everyday view (Evans-Pritchard, 1937:258–351). From the behavior of the fowl subjected to the ordeal, especially whether it dies or survives, the Azande receives an answer to his question. Under the orders of a legitimate leader, *benge*, as this ordeal is called, may also reveal the guilt or innocence of a defendant. It is likewise used to discover why a wife has not conceived. Before making long journeys it reveals the outcome and it serves the Azande in a large variety of other situations. The actual administration involves a carefully framed question put to the poison once it is inside the fowl: "If such and such is the case, poison oracle kill the fowl" or "spare the fowl," whatever has been decided (*ibid.*, p. 295). An accused person may be requested to drink oracle poison in order to test his guilt or innocence. Since the poison does not always kill, the outcome is fairly uncertain and hence can be used to decide such questions. No doubt the poison used in *benge* would some-times stun or kill quite without reference to a defendant's guilt. If so, would not that experience undermine the Azande belief in the oracle? Here is a good opportunity to understand how the retention of an oracle in the culture depends on the general ideology of the culture and consensus in the community. The Azande claim not to know whether the poison would work if the question were not put and the other conditions were not ful-filled. More importantly, the anthropologist who asked the Azande this question reports them to be not at all interested in such matters. Nobody "has ever been fool enough to waste good oracle poison in making such pointless experiments," experiments that could be thought of only by a person with doubt, or a person who comes from a different culture with very different assumptions about the organization of the biosphere (*ibid.*, p. 314). The Azande do not regard the action of *benge* to be a natural proc-ess, the way butchering a hen is a natural process to them or consulting a barometer is to a modern meteorologist. But this does not mean that all people who use oracles and consult omens always regard these devices as somehow unnatural or supernatural.

In the northeastern part of Canada the Algonkian Indians foretold the future with the aid of powerful unseen helpers (see pp. 622–623). One de-vice for divination was the shaking-tent, a small lodge in which the diviner is placed while bound. Presently a gust of wind shakes the structure and strange sounds emerge. The unseen helpers of the diviner have come and are speaking through his lips, answering questions asked by the surround-ing audience. When the séance is finished the diviner is found to be free of his bonds. Apparently he was released through the intercession of his powerful attendants (Cooper, 1944; Hallowell, 1942). Unusual events, like a birth occurring feet first, the birth of a human monster, or an eclipse, fre-quently are regarded as portents of danger in many parts of the world (Lévy-Bruhl, 1923:148–158).

The conditions under which any form of prediction is rewarded and thereby retained in culture include those which also govern indirect coping techniques (see pp. 630–631). For example, ordeals may work through sug-gestion when they are administered to guilty people. Through fear the guilty individual may sicken and die. When an oracle promises success in an endeavor, people may work just a little harder to insure the outcome be-cause their morale has been boosted. The hard work, of course, contributes to the success that has been predicted. Haloing also enters here. The misses of a predictive technique are forgotten; the successes, however, are noted carefully. Finally, the maintenance of confidence in routines of prediction depends on having the community's underlying assumptions remain free from contradiction or challenge. It is precisely such challenge which ap-pears under conditions of culture contact, when one way of life is confronted by people who hold different beliefs about the organization of nature.

SPECIALISTS AND THE PERSONAL WORLD VIEW

In certain instances in small-scale communities indirect coping through signs and symbols as well as prediction may be practiced by anybody. On occasion, however, such techniques will be executed by specialists. In Korea "the problems of life are adjusted by having a proper relationship with the world of spirits. Each person can do this to a limited degree himself, but in cases of special difficulties one goes to an individual who has attained through religious experience an unusual intimacy with one or more spirits and is thus in a position to explain and sometimes influence the course of events" (Cornelius Osgood, 1951:245). The degree to which such specialists will be employed to help people, perhaps by warding off or neutralizing threats like those described in the next chapter, depends on the same conditions that support any kind of occupational specialization. In hunting and collecting communities all men and many women are endowed with more than mere physical power and can use it to deal with the unseen aspects of existence. This power may be used for oneself, in behalf of family members and friends, or against a man's enemies. Even when part- and full-time specialists emerge, each individual may continue to engage in private prayer, construct household shrines, and perform symbolic behavior in order to maintain a beneficial relationship between himself and the universe or its personalized controllers.

The terms designating the status of a person who engages in indirect coping vary from one culture area to another. Terms like "sorcerer," "singer," "diviner," "witch doctor," and "herbalist" refer to the activities or goals of such behavior. In sorcery, injury to another person is the goal; the singer prays for something; a diviner works at prediction; a witch doctor seeks out witches; and a herbalist treats illness through plant medicines. In practice these specialties often overlap in the same person. Two relatively distinct types of persons who mediate between man and the universe have been distinguished on the basis of how their status is acquired and validated.

Shaman

The shaman (the feminine form, "shamanin," is rare) is represented by any individual who derives power to control events from direct, personal contact with some sentient portion of the universe. Such an experience normally is not accessible readily but requires specific procedures to be gone through. The shaman's power depends on his ability to win and maintain rapport with this power. "Shaman" itself is a Tungus word, and a classic area for studying shamanism is Central Asia and Siberia whence the phenomenon probably entered the Americas (Eliade, 1951). The principal elements of Siberian shamanism include: (1) a capacity for ecstatic forms of experience, like vivid dreaming, trance, and visions, that mark off the shaman from his fellows; (2) a belief that the shaman can make flights to the sky world and into nether regions; (3) the acquisition of the status through familial inheritance (or else the shaman is selected through a dramatic experience that involuntarily befalls him); (4) the experience that constitutes a call to shamanism—usually a vision, vivid dream, convulsion, or other dramatic illness. Even when the principle of inheritance is followed, the dramatic experience often constitutes validation of a man's qualifications. The induction of a candidate into office sometimes is phrased as involving his death or destruction by spirits. The costume of the Siberian shaman often is ornamented elaborately with many symbols that represent the hidden powers dominating the universe. A drum is a characteristic appendage and, like the costume, enhances the practitioner's abilities.

At a Seance in Mysore, India, an Old Woman Is Asking Advice from the Deity Who Is Possessing the Shaman (Seated). A picture of the shaman's teacher (*guru*) is supported on the chair (courtesy, Edward B. Harper).

Among many North American Indians nearly every young man (less often a woman) sought shamanistic power by going unaccompanied to an isolated place. Here he fasted while wishing (i.e., praying) for a suitable vision or dream. The entities who appeared in the successful fulfillment of the quest differed from one another in strength or power. Hence not all shamans possessed equal capacities. Through public contests involving conjuring and sorcery one shaman could match the strength of his power against that of another. More commonly, validation came through applying such power in curing.

Priest

The concept "priest" covers a far more variable category of individuals than that occupied by the shaman. A priest is a person who has received his power to act as an intermediary between man and the personalized components of the universe by virtue of a strong conviction ("call"), special training, and legitimate consecration. These bases sometimes conflict. A priest convinced of a call to office may be repudiated by his colleagues for his lack of training or for failing to have been consecrated in suitable fashion. John Wesley, founder of Methodism, is an example. Sometimes a priest is also a shaman—he acquires both roles or is legitimized in two different ways for coping indirectly with the world. The two offices should not be thought of as mutually exclusive for either the same individual or the same community. Not only may priests also be shamans, but among the Soara of Orissa, India, shamans inaugurated the hereditary priests into offices (Elwin, 1955:129).

Both a shaman and a priest, whether or not the latter is ordained correctly, may acquire considerable influence and authority. Partly influence may derive through status but more important is possession of an extraordinary personality. Not all shamans in the community will possess an equally strong capacity to command. Individuals who by virtue of their personalities acquire the capacity for leadership have already been mentioned (see p. 478). "Charismatic leaders" include prophets who appear during some time of stress in order to teach new doctrines or to urge a return to true belief. They may claim to have been picked by the personal entities controlling nature. Charismatic leaders also are represented by the *pirs*, or spiritual guides, of Pakistan. In this predominantly Islamic country followers attach themselves to a *pir* in the belief that he can intercede for them with God. Such a notion is rejected as quite fantastic by more orthodox Muslims but does not prevent certain *pirs* from inspiring strong faith.

The relationship between a priest or shaman and his followers varies considerably from one community to another. The prestige of either position by no means is always a high one. Anthropologists do not feel that such specialists knowingly pretend to abilities which they do not themselves believe they possess. In other words, shamans and priests, generally speaking, are not dishonest. When sleight of hand is practiced by them, the aim primarily may be symbolic or is not to hoax so much as it is to help by convincing. However extraordinary these positions may be, the occupants are not therefore mentally ill. No doubt a shaman undergoes experiences which are unusual; to that extent his personality is also unusual or abnormal. Perhaps these statuses often are filled by relatively unusual people. But this does not mean that such specialists regularly are mentally ill in the sense of being gravely disturbed in their interpersonal relationships, ridden by abnormally high anxiety, and unable to solve ordinary problems of living (Devereux, 1956a and 1956b).

Priests and shamans often play a prominent role in helping to readjust an individual or restore equilibrium in a group after a crisis (Chapple and Coon, 1942:Chap. 16). Methods for achieving these ends vary widely but often include rituals and other manipulation of signs and symbols. These procedures reduce emotional disturbance in the people experiencing them. The use of drums to produce rhythms, drugs, and singing are among other techniques which function to promote adjustment. The preacher at a revival meeting relies principally on words when he achieves the same end.

37.

Threat, Danger, and Uncertainty

MAN has been called the lord of creation. In any community and under any way of life he has at his disposal a multitude of means for dealing, in one way or another, with the world in which he lives. Yet nowhere are people invulnerable to threat and danger. Some threats are universal; illness is an example. It is astonishing how widespread is the notion that illness originates externally to the individual (Thurnwald, 1951:61). With this belief is bound up a system of ideas concerning specific sources of illnesses and procedures for healing. Other dangers are more localized. They may arise out of conditions in a particular cultural field (like the threat of drought) or from stresses in the cultural system itself (see pp. 173–175). In this chapter attention is devoted to a few postulated sources of threat, danger, and uncertainty and measures that are taken against them. The chapter continues the topic of the previous chapter: man's relationship to the universe which he structures ideologically.

POSTULATED SOURCES OF DANGER

Six sources of danger are frequently postulated in human culture. Practically all represent conceptions that tend to disappear (or undergo extensive modifications and attenuation) under the influence of Euroamerican culture, although these conceptions are not wholly absent from that way of life. Basically the ideas to be discussed belong to the personal world view (see pp. 593–595). Probably no culture contains all of the threats to be examined. When several are present in the world view of a single community, all may not be of equal importance. In studying these sources of threat the reader will note how appropriate coping techniques follow logically from the nature of the danger and are applied to control or manage it.

Personalized Sentient Entities

Personalized sentient entities frequently are held to control misfortunes like storm, drought, famine, illness, and death. A closer examination of such collective representations will be offered in the next chapter. Specific examples include the last-deceased adult ancestor who among the Manus becomes

the family's Sir Ghost (Fortune, 1935:Chap. 1; Mead, 1930:Chap. 6); Sopono, the Nigerian Yoruba's dreaded god of smallpox (Lucas, 1948:112);
and the ghosts of deceased kin among the Navaho who return to avenge
some offense and portend disaster (C. Kluckhohn and D. Leighton, 1946:
126–127). Possession of an individual by a spirit, which constitutes a frequent
interpretation of illness, belongs in this category of threats. Therapy, then,
requires exorcising or releasing (perhaps through bleeding) the possessing
entity. Sometimes the representation in question is endowed with highly
specialized proclivities, being responsible for only a single affliction or form
of disaster. Quite frequently it is endowed with beneficent as well as malignant powers. The Holy People among the Navaho and the ancestors in parts
of Africa reveal this double nature. The community will then regard it as
essential to keep the entities favorably disposed through some form of attention, perhaps regular sacrifice.

All people who address entities of this type do not do so in order to *request*
aid or favors. The Navaho Indians do not conceive of the Holy People as
possessing any volition; they *must* act when they are addressed properly by
the compulsive force of ritual (Reichard, 1944:41).

One function of stressful representations is that they render the universe
intelligible and, through the derived coping techniques, more manageable.
Ascribing danger to personalized entities also is effective in maintaining general belief in such concepts and thereby insuring whatever other adaptive or
adjustive functions they govern (see pp. 668–669).

Automatic Retribution

A second common conception does not postulate personalized entities
who through vindictiveness or displeasure send calamity. Rather the universe
itself is regarded as sensitive to wrongdoing or to certain events. Under certain conditions the world may become "hot" or "sick." At such times trouble multiplies for man. Among the Lovedu of South Africa, the death of a
ruler, a woman dying in childbirth, and a person struck by lightning all
threaten to make the world hot so that the rain will not fall (E. J. Krige and
J. D. Krige, 1943:120). Symbolic cooling techniques help the community
adjust to this type of disaster. Among certain American Indians an individual's delict can promote automatic retribution upon him and other members
of the community. This follows not from displeasure promoted in a spirit or
anthropomorphic deity but rather from the way in which the universe is
organized. Restoring the upset balance may require simply confession of
wrongdoing. To protect themselves from even inadvertently doing something to disturb balance in the universe people carefully follow rules of behavior.

Belief in automatic retribution also makes the universe more intelligible.
If individual misbehavior is dangerous for an entire community, then, logi-

cally, the public has an interest in how closely people follow rules of good living. Such beliefs, therefore, constitute a basis for checking uncomplementary diversity.[1]

Witches

A human being may be an involuntary vehicle of danger. The term "witch" is applied to a person of either sex who represents a consistent source of danger to other members of his community. He may not deliberately choose to injure others but, owing to some inherited factor, predisposition, or experience (perhaps a sexual relationship with a personalized entity), has become an embodiment of danger. His very presence can cause illness or some other form of trouble. The witch may exert his influence without conscious volition or knowledge yet will confess to witchcraft when confronted with certain circumstantial proofs.

By the very terms in which it is conceived, witchcraft cannot operate on a manifest plane as sorcery can (see pp. 627–628). For example, in medieval Europe a female witch was conceived to have entered a pact with the devil, hence to be in voluntary control of her activities. No doubt some people could visualize the devil and perhaps had entered some kind of relationship with this postulated entity. More persons accused of witchcraft, however, probably had never experienced the particular sequence of events which was supposed to create witches. Yet they confessed. Among the early postcontact Kaska Indians some children were conceived to be witches. It is very unlikely that they had utilized indirect coping techniques to produce evil consequences. However, torture was used successfully to extract confessions from these youthful witches (Honigmann, 1947). Sorcery, then, can be manifest as well as ideal, culturally speaking; witchcraft, however, more nearly always is ideal. The conditions that trigger suspicion of witchcraft, therefore, are of great interest.

Witchcraft accusations often follow existing lines of tension in a community. That is, people with whom the individual has some other reason to be in conflict, or to whom he exists as a rival, may suspect him of bewitching. Periods of culture upheaval and high stress are likely to be associated with outbreaks of witch-fear and witchcraft accusations. In such times people are confronted with many new lines of behavior. Difficult choices frustrate or threaten individuals. The resultant threat and anxiety release themselves through hostility in the form of witchcraft accusations. Furthermore, some people are deviating from traditional customs and values. To accuse them of

[1] In America social regulation of conduct has a different rationale. Disregarding unseen sources of danger, we argue that some limitation on individual behavior is essential in order that all men may enjoy a measure of life, liberty, and property. This conception, however familiar to the reader, may appear very mysterious to someone not familiar with Euroamerican assumptions. In the same way the Soviet Russian theory of social control seems quite incomprehensible to many Americans (Mead, 1951).

being witches is to try to hold their deviant behavior in check (Marwick, 1956; cf. M. Wilson, 1951b, and Nadel, 1954b:Chap. 6)

In many cultures witchcraft accusations function to maintain the existing value system of a culture. That is, the persons most likely to be accused of witchcraft and, perhaps, punished or executed are people who actually do depart from traditional, highly valued forms of behavior. They are not generous, not sociable, or do not coöperate freely. Fear of being accused of witchcraft, therefore, reduces the incidence of uncomplementary diversity.[2] Techniques of discovering who is a witch represent a means of coping with this sort of danger. In Africa such detection is a duty of the witch doctor.

Lightning Rods

Distinct from witchcraft is the belief that an otherwise fairly normal human being at certain times in his life, or in association with some event, enters a condition that makes him dangerous to himself and to others. Hence the person must be secluded or otherwise neutralized—but not, it is important to note, necessarily punished.

Menstruation and birth are common times at which a woman is highly contaminating in many parts of the world. Among a number of American Indian tribes she was secluded carefully at these periods in special camps. The purpose was protection of other people, especially hunters, from the danger which she exuded (see pp. 576–577). To have killed another man, even an enemy, in some places puts one in a dangerous state requiring purification. Such events make the individual a "lightning rod" for danger (Underhill, 1948:5–6).

Among southwestern North American Indians eagle-killing and taking part in a ceremonial pilgrimage (for example, a salt-getting expedition) ushered persons into a dangerous state. The South African Lovedu use the concept of *muridi* to refer to the state of danger originating in certain conditions like death, activities connected with sexual relations (including sexual intercourse, the early period of pregnancy, the birth of twins, and miscarriage), and irregular appearance of the teeth (for example, when a child's upper incisors appear before the lower) (J. D. Krige and E. J. Krige, 1954: 69–70). Healthy people are not visibly affected by *muridi* but can transmit the evil to others whose resistance happens to be weak, like the newborn and the sick. Special precautions are taken to protect the sick from *muridi*. In its more virulent form, called *leridi*, this state of contagious danger infects a warrior who has killed an enemy.

Among the most common functions of lightning-rod beliefs is drawing

---

[2] In the same way the recent United States saw people becoming cautious about joining social movements or espousing certain ideas lest they be accused of supporting left-wing enterprises and Communist ideology. But the people accused of communistic affiliation are not witches in the sense of being inherently disposed to evil.

attention to certain events or to individuals who participate in them. Birth, death, and killing are singled out from ordinary experiences and given special attention. The beliefs also serve to distinguish certain categories of people (for example, women). The practice of purifying the individual as he emerges from this state publicly symbolizes his transition to a new, safe status and, perhaps, to new responsibilities. The conception of a person as being dangerous further possesses explanatory value. Misfortune can be ascribed to inadvertent contact with the sources of contagion or to carelessness by a person occupying that status. Rules enable people to adjust safely to this source of danger.

The next two types of threat primarily account for illness and scarcely enter into the explanation of other forms of calamity unless these happen to be dependent upon illness.

Object Intrusion

In the thinking of some communities an object may intrude itself into the body, provoking illness or death. Sometimes the intruding thing is explained as having been sent by another person, a sorcerer, deliberately to provoke harm. In association with a belief in intrusion, therapy requires removing the object, perhaps by sucking it through the surface of the skin. A carefully palmed sliver of wood or other thing, revealed by the therapist after the sucking has been completed, helps to make the theory of intrusion convincing.

Soul Loss

Loss of a soul may produce illness according to the belief of many people. If the soul is not soon restored to the body its absence may lead to death. The alienation of the soul may be ascribed to the action of a postulated personalized being. Or a sorcerer is held responsible for having stolen this substantial part of man's existence. Cure for the illness lies in successfully restoring the soul. The therapist sometimes announces lengthy trips to far corners of the universe in order to achieve this end. The Central Asiatic Buriat illustrate most of these patterns (Schmidt, 1952:370–375, 422–423). These people think a major source of illness lies in the absence of one or both souls that constitute man's immaterial aspect. In sleep a soul may leave the body to wander in the environment. Should it miss the route back, or be unable to find entry into the body, the sleeper will wake up beset by illness. A postulated entity, Erlik, also may steal the soul.

Other Sources of Threat

The foregoing are major, recurrent sources of danger which people postulate. It is not an exhaustive list.

Illness is often ascribed to a disturbance in the postulated organization of the body. Popular Chinese thought holds that sickness lies in an imbalance of two basic forces pervading the universe, *Yin* and *Yang*. These also form part of the human being. Chinese indigenous medicine also conceives of an imbalance in the five elements of body—fire, water, wood, metal, and earth—producing illness. Or illness could come from an obstruction of the passages carrying blood and pneuma through the body (Veith, 1949). The doctrine of humors in Greek medicine similarly ascribes many human indispositions to internal imbalances. European and American medicine accounts for much illness by postulating internal disturbances which, while sometimes not directly visible, are known from their observable manifestations (Clark-Kennedy, 1957).

Exotic communities do not account for all illness by a single factor nor do they fail to perceive relatively direct conditions as injurious. Fijians recognize three types of disease: "disease of the land," which is sent by *vu* ("spirits"); "disease of the body," resulting from incidental circumstances; and sickness sent deliberately by other persons, i.e., sorcery (D. M. Spencer, 1941). Accidents like drowning, being killed by an enemy spear, or an injury sustained from falling are likely to receive no further explanation in many communities. The association of death with old age similarly is taken for granted. Likewise the periodic increase or decrease in game or fruit does not always involve the direct operation of personalized agents standing behind visible phenomena. Yet many people find it meaningless to ascribe death or drought simply to an accident or old age. The Pondo of South Africa recognize that old age, certain foods, and accidents can produce illness or death (M. Hunter, 1936:272–274). But they also believe illness is due to ancestors or sorcerers. How do they decide when one type of factor—say, the ancestors—is operating, and when the other—old age? The decision "is affective, not rational." Some individuals among the Pondo are inclined, for emotional reasons, to attribute more of such misfortunes to the postulated personalized agents than others. If a diviner is consulted, this specialist always will diagnose illness as due to the willful action of either a sorcerer or an ancestor.

CURING

Techniques of curing could be discussed under the heading of technology. On the other hand, such logical arrangement would disturb the continuity of moving from ideas about threat to procedures for doing something about it. In small-scale, exotic communities curing is often carried out by specialists who mediate between man and the unseen aspects of the universe as the latter are conceived in the personal world view. This is another reason for including the subject at this particular point in the book. No matter how they are conceived, techniques for healing the body and prolonging life are, subjectively speaking, among the most valuable activities engaged in by man. The purpose of the present section is to give a résumé of some of these activities and to show their relationship to underlying ideology.

Classification of Curing Procedures

No satisfactory way of classifying curing practices has yet been found. Nor do all such practices constitute techniques in the sense in which that word has been used (see pp. 290–291). The therapist, priest, or psychiatrist who listens sympathetically is performing no technical manipulation of his environment. So, too, with confession among the Eskimo. Perhaps a distinction between technical and nontechnical routines of curing helps as an initial classificatory device. The usefulness of the distinction, though, is limited.

Diagnosis

There are communities which value diagnosis as much as curing. In parts of India a man is esteemed highly if he can identify the affliction troubling a patient and if he gives a favorable prognosis. The identification and promise of cure give reassurance to the suffering individual and his kin. Because they have come to expect such services from a therapist, the aloof, western-trained physician is not highly respected. He arouses little confidence if he addresses the patient with words like: "What is troubling you?" Those people are accustomed to diagnosticians who will tell them what is wrong (Carstairs, 1956:131).

Often diagnosis involves retrospective prediction. What did the patient do to become ill? In other cases the object is to discover what living person, sorcerer or witch, is responsible for the affliction. The diagnostician also may seek to learn if the illness springs from soul loss or object intrusion. What specific personalized entity sent the trouble?

Forms of diagnosis vary. Without attempting classification but merely as examples, we note that the Navaho Indians prefer hand trembling as a means of learning what is troubling a person (C. Kluckhohn and D. Leighton, 1946:148). Calling on a postulated entity to tell him what is wrong with the patient, the diagnostician waits for his arm to shake violently. The way it trembles provides the information sought. The Manus consult a female medium, always a woman with a dead male child (Mead, 1930:77–78). The child has become the medium's control and links her with other collective representations. Messages from the unseen realm of the universe are communicated through odd whistling sounds which issue from the woman's lips. When interpreted they reveal what is displeasing some personalized entity and motivating him to trouble his living descendants.

In any community diagnosticians are likely to be shrewd judges of their neighbors, with whose behavior they are closely familiar. It is relatively simple for a Manus medium to ascribe the illness of a woman to her dead husband's jealous ghost. For it is common knowledge in the village that the widow is planning to remarry. Sometimes, however, the diagnostician's power rests on little more than a suspicion of wrongdoing. If, as is common in Africa, the diagnostician is a relative stranger from another village he must play his role by ear. Among the Lovedu the diviner ostensibly reads the answer to what is troubling the patient in the bones (or dice) that he throws (E. J. Krige and J. D. Krige, 1943:228). At the same time he keeps up a stream of conversation and questioning lasting several hours. "You have been greatly troubled," he says. Does the face of the client show agreement? If so, the diagnostician expands on the kind of trouble. He always is ready to backtrack if the patient's manner suggests that he has gotten on the wrong track. "The procedure . . . is a subtle process combining suggestion, free association of ideas, and techniques of leading the client and inspiring confidence."

Preventive Medicine

Preventive medicine is not unknown in small-scale, exotic communities. It occurs whenever the ideas concerning the cause of illness suggest behavior to be performed or avoided in order to remain healthy. Rules for good living, even though they contain no hint of germ theory, are a kind of preventive medicine. At least they work to the extent of giving people a feeling of confidence, which, perhaps, fortifies morale and so indirectly helps to maintain a healthy organism. A Burmese man learns to be careful on days which his horoscope says are unlucky (Mead, 1953a:66). Also in the category of preventive medicine is the Aleut custom of bathing in the sea in order to promote strength and vigor (Veniaminov, 1840) and the Apache girl's puberty rite in which she runs around a course for health and strength (Morris E. Opler, 1941:82–133). Most of the Pondo in South Africa cut off the top joint of the little finger of the eldest child and of every alternate child thereafter in order to prevent illness. For alternate children, however, merely a bit of flesh may be removed from the finger in order to attain the insurance (M. Hunter, 1936:264–265).

Surgery

Surgery outside of the orbit of Euroamerican medicine usually is limited to wound treatment, setting of broken and dislocated bones, and blood letting.[3] Wounds are treated through the application of herbs and other preparations; suturing, with animal sinew or thorns; and trying to stop the loss of blood. Tourniquets and cauterization both are applied to stop bleeding. These techniques are known in aboriginal North America, Oceania, and Africa. The treatment of broken bones is not always accomplished success-

---

[3] The discussion of surgery follows Ackerknecht, 1947.

fully in small-scale, exotic communities. Nevertheless, frequent attempts are made to deal with the problem, including even use of splints. Bloodletting is nearly universal in its distribution but is often carried out to release postulated agents of illness from the body. The most common techniques for opening the arteries or veins are scarification, cupping (in Africa with thorns placed over the incision), venesection (mainly in North and South America), and, more rarely, use of leeches. Boils and abscesses frequently are opened by lancing them. The Japanese sometimes seek to relieve obstructions in the vessels carrying blood and pneuma by puncturing the body surface at any of 365 points. For this purpose special needles are employed. Or else an opening is provided in the skin by blistering the surface. This is done by burning a small cone of dried, powdered leaves on the skin (Veith, 1949: 1199–1200).

Amputation of frozen body parts was attempted aboriginally by North American Indians (as well as Eskimo). In a few other places limb amputation occurs, and the excision of the neck glands to cure sleeping sickness has also been reported from parts of Africa. Amputation in such forms as circumcision or cutting off the finger joints in mourning should also be mentioned, although their aim is not therapeutic. Trepanation, surgical opening of the skull, has received considerable attention from anthropologists.[4] The reasons for trepanation are not always clear, especially when the only evidence consists of trepanned skulls recovered from burials. Cutting the newborn child free from the placenta by severing the umbilical cord is, of course, a universal instance of surgery. True Caesarian section, performed during the life of the mother, is rare. Under somewhat unclear circumstances it is reported to have occurred among the Baganda of East Africa (R. F. Spencer, 1949). Removing the fetus from the womb of a dead woman is not at all uncommon. The Samoans, for example, out of fear that a partly developed fetus will be born as an avenging ghost, always cut it from a deceased mother's body. The operation is performed in the open grave before an audience of villagers (Mead, 1928a:133). In 715 B.C. Rome prescribed a similar operation by law.[5]

Drugs

The ingestion of animal, plant, and mineral substances in an effort to promote cure is common everywhere in the world. Generally speaking, most people use such materials with little empirical knowledge of their action on the body. Exceptions occur in the case of emetics, cathartics, and similar agents. Nor are personalized entities always imagined to reside in the drugs.

[4] Five papers comprising an entire issue of *Ciba Symposia* (Vol. 1, No. 6, 1939) are devoted to the subject.
[5] The entire issue of *Ciba-Zeitschrift* (1952), 11:4706–4736) is devoted to Caesarian section.

The leaves, roots, animal parts, or earths may simply be components of the biosphere which possess the capacity to heal.

Use of drugs about which little is known concerning their composition or action in the body is called polypharmacy. In distinction, specific pharmacy is based on beliefs about how the ingested substances are constituted in relation to the organization of the body.

Other Forms of Treatment

Another remedy is the sweat bath, widespread in North and South America but also known among the Finns and Slavs (Krickeberg, 1939). Among American Indians it was prepared by bringing very hot stones into a small, airtight hut and then pouring water on them. One or several men (rarely women) might take the bath together. The treatment frequently availed for removing a postulated impurity (like the danger incurred in enemy killing), for strengthening the body, and obtaining relief from certain ailments. A plunge in cold water followed the steaming. The enema, usually made of gourds or leather and provided with a reed tube, also enjoyed widespread currency in North and South America (Heizer, 1944). In the Amazon region the Indians made a rubber-bulb syringe which diffused to Europe via the Portuguese (Ackerknecht, 1949).

Drumming, praying, and singing are common adjuncts to therapy, sometimes being incorporated into more or less elaborate ceremonies lasting several days. Navaho Indian culture includes a repertory of several curing chants. Choice depends on the diagnosed source of trouble and the family's ability to pay (C. Kluckhohn and D. Leighton, 1946:153–154). The chants occur in 2-, 3-, or 5-night forms. Also short excerpts may be tried out on the patient. If improvement is noted after the experiment, the whole chant may be sung. Most chants consist of songs; prayers; herbal medicines; sweat bathing; use of an emetic; the making, and depositing, of prayer sticks; a bath in yucca suds; and consecration of the house. Dry painting on buckskin or sand using pollen, corn meal, or crushed flowers occurs in Holy Way and Evil Way chants (*ibid.*, p. 150). The designs painted in this way represent stories about the Holy People or else symbolize sacred forces (lightning; animals of the mountains; or the bluebird, symbol of happiness).

In many communities (as with ourselves) a tentative approach to different remedies or therapies is common. The Navaho experimental approach to chants has been described. The Chiricahua Apache first attacked illness with herbs, massage, or bloodletting. If these means did not succeed in effecting cure, and if indications showed the illness to derive from a personalized entity or to have been sent by a sorcerer, then a specialist was called in to perform a four-day ceremony. Direct reassurance is a prominent note in many of these healing practices. It is communicated to the patient through prayer or other use of language; the attitude of the curer; the cost of the therapy, which magnifies the importance of the occasion; and the expectant attitude of the patient's relatives and friends.

Euroamerican medicine is distinguished by two basic features: (1) Little deliberate use is made of signs or symbols to effect healing except in psychiatry. However, the "bedside manner" of a skilled physician and the advertisements for patent medicines represent such techniques. (2) Ideally no remedy—including surgery—is employed until its action has been ascertained reliably through experimentation or it is justified theoretically. Knowing how and why something works makes possible quite accurate prediction of results in western therapy.

Therapeutic Practices and Child Rearing[6]

Do certain curing procedures bear a functional relationship to patterns of child rearing? To answer this question an experiment has been conducted; Five types of therapy were distinguished: (1) oral, (2) anal, (3) sexual, (4) dependence, and (5) aggression-performance therapy.[7] These terms are defined in Table 45, column 1. Communities for which sufficient information was available were identified to see whether they used one or more of these forms of therapy. Each such community was rated by three raters for the degree to which child-rearing practices (1) indulge the child orally (for example, through generous, long nursing and mild weaning), (2) do not enforce urinary and anal controls harshly or very early in life, (3) are easygoing about sex (including masturbation and heterosexual play in children), (4) indulge the child's tendencies to be dependent and do not insist on early independence, and (5) are permissive with reference to aggression. These five areas of behavior (listed in column two of Table 45), we should note, correspond to the five types of therapy. It was hypothesized that if a community regularly indulged any of these areas of behavior in children it would practice a form of therapy making specific use of behavior falling in that area. The greater the initial satisfaction (estimated by each rater on a scale of from 1 to 7 but then summed up for each community on a scale of from 3 to 21), the greater will be the use of therapeutic practices which require the performance of responses belonging to that system. Table 45 indicates weak but fairly consistent support for the hypothesis that thera-

---

[6] This section is based on J. W. M. Whiting and I. L. Child, 1953:114–210. See also p. 568 *supra*.

[7] These types were formulated strategically to meet certain expectations deductively derived from the fixation theory of psychoanalysis. According to this theory the derivation of gratification through oral, anal, or genital body zones in early childhood will make those bodily zones primary in the value system of the individual. That is, positive fixation develops on the zone or on the system of behavior associated with it. Gratification of dependence or aggressive responses in childhood similarly leads to a fixation on those modes of behavior in later life. Fixation is defined as referring to a strong potential for oral, anal, genital, dependence, or aggressive responses to evoke reward.

peutic practices are dependent functionally on the initial satisfaction of oral, anal, sexual, dependence, and aggressive systems of behavior.

An alternative hypothesis, namely, that if early anxiety is regularly ex-

TABLE 45.   Therapeutic Practices and Patterns of Child Rearing

Form of Therapy	Initial Satisfaction	Comment
Oral performance therapy. The practice involves swallowing something —for example, food, herbs, or medicines.	The 40 communities practicing oral therapy possess an average rating of 14.2 for oral satisfaction in childhood. But 21 communities without evidence of such therapy show an average rating of only 13.6.	The difference in ratings between the 2 groups of communities is small but in the right direction (i.e., the direction predicted by the hypothesis).
Anal performance therapy. Defecation and urination (regarded as theoretically equivalent) possess therapeutic value.	The 14 communities where such therapy is present possess an average rating of 12.1 for anal satisfaction in childhood. But 30 communities without evidence of such therapy show an average rating of 12.0.	The difference is even smaller than for oral performance therapy but again is in the expected direction.
Sexual performance therapy. Only 4 communities were found which regard sexual intercourse as possessing therapeutic value. Only for 2 of these are data about child rearing sufficient to permit rating.	The only 2 communities where sexual intercourse is used therapeutically yield an average rating for sexual satisfaction of 18.5. The 51 communities without evidence of such therapy show an average rating of only 12.3.	This is a large and statistically significant difference in the expected direction.
Dependence performance therapy. Prayer, assumed to reveal dependence on supernatural beings analogous to the child's dependent behavior, possesses therapeutic value.[a]	For 30 communities using prayer as a therapeutic procedure the average rating for early dependence satisfaction is 14.1. For 27 communities without evidence of such therapy the average rating is 14.9.	The difference is not only small but contrary to what is predicted by the hypothesis. Hence the hypothesis is contradicted at this point.
Aggression-performance therapy. The material believed to be responsible for the illness is destroyed; or else destruction of the supernatural agent is symbolized; he is tricked or told to desist.	For 31 communities using such therapeutic practices the average rating for early aggression satisfaction is 11.2. The 25 communities without evidence of such therapy reveal an average rating of 10.5.	The difference is small but in the direction predicted by the hypothesis.

[a] We have pointed out that such an assumption may not be justified. All people do not petition collective representations to act. Some, like the Navaho Indians, command them (see also p. 674).

SOURCE: J. W. M. Whiting and I. L. Child, *1953*:144–199.

perienced in any of these areas of behavior then the community will use a therapeutic practice involving the undoing or avoidance of such behavior, is slightly better sustained. In particular, statistically significant indication exists that: (1) Communities which induce severe anal anxiety in children (through toilet training or demands for modesty) also standardize washing, cleansing, adherence to rules of cleanliness, and retention of feces as practices for getting over sickness. (2) Communities which demand early independence in children and fail to indulge dependence also tend to isolate a sick person or to remove him from his home for the duration of the illness.

Therapists

A therapist is any person—shaman, priest, layman, or physician—who attempts to cure illness. In communities without even part-time occupational specialization therapists scarcely can be distinguished from laymen except in the situation where they practice. Aboriginally among the Indians of the northern forest of Canada (for instance, the Kaska or Cree) every man was a shaman. That is, he could utilize his acquired power for therapeutic ends. In any locality one or a few men might become especially renowned for successful cures. They would be consulted more frequently, and with greater confidence, than others and were rewarded for their services. These men corresponded to incipient part-time therapists. In addition the circumpolar people knew herbal cures whose use and efficacy did not depend directly on the therapist's being a shaman.

In many communities the roles of shaman (or priest) and therapist are indistinguishable. However, a division of roles and ideology may occur, through reduction segregation (see pp. 235–236). The qualifications for each type of position then differ, and mastery of specific technique replaces contact with spirits or consecration as the basis of status validation. As therapy becomes a full-time specialism, knowledge and procedures in this area increase. In place of informal instruction acquired by watching or assisting a therapist more formal systems of learning appear. With increasing complexity of social organization, formally organized groups of therapists arise. These make explicit provision for passing on their knowledge to qualified students. In the history of medicine full-time therapists who made provision for the formal training of successors emerged in South Asia, China, the Middle East, and Europe.

In the relatively large-scale countries of North or East Africa, Latin America, Pakistan, and India people today have opportunity to consult a variety of curers. Some therapists represent the persistence of traditional forms of therapy; others have been trained in Euroamerican medicine. In Ethiopia a priest is consulted first for illness (Barkhuus, 1947). If he proves ineffectual a traditional therapist is called in. He is a man who inherited his knowledge from his father and is licensed to practice under a recent national law. In addition, an illegal practitioner is available for consultation, a therapist who attempts to cure primarily by the manipulation of signs and symbols. Finally, if all of these fail, there is the physician trained in the European tradition of medicine. In Pakistan traditional *hakims* practicing a version of ancient Greek medicine, chiropractors, homeopaths, naturopaths, and so-called allopathic physicians all have been influenced by the diffusion of therapeutic ideas from European culture.

Amulets

A familiar means of escaping from threats is to wear an amulet or display one in a suitable place. The form and material of the amulet depend upon how people structure universal order. In Siberia iron is regarded as very effective for warding off hostile spirits and the dangers they represent. The teeth, claws, or other parts of animals also serve as amulets. They guarantee success in hunting and are valuable for certain sorts of protection. Weapons, like a bow and arrow, hung above a cradle protect a child from hostile forces (Lot-Falck, 1953:93–98). In the Muslim world of the Middle East and South Asia verses from the Quran are worn on the body to insure personal safety. Contrary to official Catholic doctrine, members of the Catholic Church frequently use medals and other ritual specifics instrumentally rather than expressively.

38.

Collective Representations

IN THE course of referring to the threats that people recognize and attempt to cope with, reference has already been made to postulated agents that control nature. Such causative agents usually are immaterial ("spiritual") but at times are believed to assume human form and may even beget children with human beings (Lowie, 1924:99–100, 122–123). The purpose of this chapter is to continue in a more systematic way the examination of these and closely related beliefs.

At the outset two kinds of collective representations will be distinguished. First are those sentient aspects of the universe which constitute sources of help, fear, or ambivalence. At times we have referred to these as "supernaturals" but that word is unsuitable because not all people recognize a distinction between natural and supernatural realms in the universe. Briefly they may be designated as sentient or S-type collective representations. In the second category are more or less authenticated historic personages whose memory is commemorated regularly. Perhaps they are honored because from them the present way of life has been derived. Both types of conceptions inspire ceremonies, often instrumental in the case of the first and purely expressive in the second. The difference between the types largely is one of degree. Only a few years may separate a tomb whose occupant merely is honored from one that is visited in order to communicate with the sentient aspect of its occupant. Both these conceptions are conveniently called collective representations.[1]

Communities differ in the amount of attention they pay to such conceptions. In a sacred community many ceremonies and much of everyday life are referred to collective representations. What one eats, wears, and avoids doing or saying is rationalized with reference to those central and important beliefs which constitute a cultural focus in the sacred community (see pp. 128–129).[2] The secular community makes few references of this sort. Behavior there is justified in quite different terms.

[1] The term is adapted from Durkheim (1915). See also Lévy-Bruhl, 1926:Chap. 1, and the discussion on pp. 526–527 supra.

[2] The reader is reminded that A. Huxley's imaginative, large-scale Brave New World (1932) represents a sacred community in which much of life is referred to Fordsie. Speaking generally, however, industrial communities are predominantly secular rather than sacred.

CHARACTERISTICS

Collective representations occur in all societies and are associated with both personal and impersonal world views. Only a very general definition can cover a word with such broad range. Hence the collective representations may be defined simply as referring to certain concepts, presumed to be at least partly independent of the individual (therefore excluding the soul), which are important in the thinking of a community. As already suggested, importance may vary in degree from a sacred community on the one hand to a secular community on the other. A few additional general characteristics may be noted.

The importance with which collective representations are held may be traced to several factors. In the first place, the regular occurrence of these concepts in ritual reinforces the extreme significance attached to them. But it is their original significance which recommends them for ritual attention. The fact that these concepts frequently symbolize central values of the community (they may even symbolize the community itself) certainly conditions their importance. In many cases S-type collective representations are valued profoundly because of the important things in life—fertility, illness, success—which they control.

Unlike certain concepts (like "red," "table," or "shoe") collective representations usually cannot be sensed directly.[3] As long as the belief system remains unchallenged, people show little interest in verifying these conceptions empirically or even in proving their existence logically. George Bernard Shaw (1916) points out that many Christians prefer Luke's account of the Annunciation and early life of Christ, although that Gospel is the most literary and, presumably, the most difficult to verify of all. Theoretically, collective representations constitute concepts by postulation. Such concepts, it will be recalled, may be verified only through the observable phenomena deduced to follow from their existence. A concept by postulation is defined in a way that predicts what empirical manifestations are to be sought if the existence of the concept is to be ascertained (Northrop, 1947:1–101). For historic figures such consequences reside in documentary and other tangible evidence surviving into present-day times. A believer may postulate that a deity manifests his existence through regular cycles of growth, illness, reproduction, and death. These processes of nature, the believer will maintain, are controlled by the deity and through them the deity is known. Atheists and agnostics challenge such reasoning as well as reasoning which seeks to prove God's existence logically. Many believers, on the other hand, see no

---

[3] An exception will be noted below (pp. 681–684) in connection with concepts like Brahman, the central conception of Hindu theology, which can be sensed directly through mystical experience.

The Roman Catholic Mass Dramatically Reënacts the Death of Jesus Christ on a Cross. It is offered to honor and thank God, to help remit sin, and to obtain blessings (courtesy, Japanese Foreign Ministry).

need of arguments. They accept the collective representations on faith alone. Among the logical proofs of God's existence is one in which St. Thomas Aquinas pointed out that motion or change manifestly exists in the world. Being and events come to exist. Therefore nature contains things which *are* while at the same time these phenomena are capable of not being. Things are graded in degrees of perfection mixed with imperfection. Finally everything that exists has an end which is proved by the aptitude of everything to produce its own specific consequences. From these observations Aquinas concluded that one is obliged to admit an unmoved mover and uncaused cause, one which can never lack existence, is purely perfect, as is the first principle and ultimate end of all goals. Such a cause he called God.[4]

Collective representations often are modeled or described in characteristic poses or situations. For example, Christ is shown as a shepherd, God is represented as light, and the Hindu deity Ganesha is sculptured with an elephant's head. Krishna (who is merely an *avatar*, or form, of Vishnu) sometimes is pictured as an amorous cowherd. Washington in reproductions of the famous painting is familiar in the act of crossing the Delaware River. Such images often depict outstanding qualities which the collective representation symbolizes. The socially standardized ways of representing these figures pictorially or otherwise constitute the iconography of a culture. Collective representations must be distinguished from emblems, like the eagle; from ritual specifics, like the cross or a flag; and from decorative design. The American eagle and the nation's flag are not collective representations.

Origins of the Beliefs

Early students of culture were greatly interested in how the idea of collective representations first appeared in human ways of life. Edward Tylor (1891) saw the origin of the belief in "spiritual beings" to lie in simple animism, or beliefs about "souls of individual creatures" capable of existence after death (*ibid.*, p. 426). This belief he in turn accounted for as arising in response to early man's puzzlement about the difference between a living and a dead body and between the sleeping and waking states. "Ancient savage philosophers" postulated an element in the body which was responsible for life but which could leave the body temporarily or permanently, "a thin unsubstantial image . . . a sort of vapor, film, or shadow . . ." (*ibid.*, p. 429). Such simple animism expanded to include the idea that animals, plants, and objects also possessed souls. Man began to conceive of places where the soul went after death. Then came belief in spirits like elves, fairies, or deities modeled on man's primary conception of his own soul; belief in specialized deities, responsible for agriculture, childbirth, or other activities; and, finally, the reduction of multiple deities to a single "Almighty Creator" (*ibid.*, p. 332). Belief in spiritual beings on all of these levels was "suggested and maintained by the direct evidence of the senses of sight, touch, and hearing." The spirits appeared in dreams or visions and such experiences clinched the argument for their existence (*ibid.*, p. 189).

---

[4] For a critical examination of this argument see Randall and Buchler, 1942:Chap. 13. A simpler logical proof of God's existence goes like this: Everything in nature, including nature itself, must have a cause. It is manifestly futile and inadmissible to look for this cause in nature itself. If these premises are granted, then it follows that the cause of nature must be sought outside of nature. But this is the supernatural, or God.

Marett (1909:Chap. 1), while claiming to avoid any dogmatic statements about origins, saw the belief in "spiritual beings" emerge from man's reaction to phenomena like thunderstorms, death, or disease. These experiences arouse "the emotions of Awe, Wonder, and the like. . . ." Overcome by such feelings men are led "to objectify and even personify the mysterious or 'supernatural' something. . . ." Natural phenomena are personified and from this animatism animistic beliefs in spirits may arise.

In another famous theory Émile Durkheim (1915) accounted for beliefs in collective representations by ascribing such conceptions to projections of states induced in man through social living. Durkheim also sought to avoid conjecturing about the origin of religious beliefs. Instead he sought for the "ever present causes" which are functionally related to such beliefs. People who live in small-scale, exotic communities, he reasoned, do not possess the insights of sociologists or anthropologists. They cannot conceive naturalistically of coöperative activities' producing enthusiasm and arousing morale in men. Nor can they understand the dynamics of social pressure. Instead they project the source of social joy and social constraint on external forces. Collective representations in some measure enable man to objectify his own social relationships. Religion is not a hallucination or collection of falsehoods but is grounded in the ever present reality of social life.

Many of these men were concerned with explaining how the idea of personalized sentient entities first appeared in culture. Theories concerning the origin of religion make interesting reading but none is better supported by facts than any other. Anthropology has largely abandoned the question of how belief in deities originally arose.

MAJOR TYPES

The most often recurrent collective representations may be grouped under six heads. These, numbered by the order in which they are treated below, are:

SENTIENT (S-TYPE)	NONSENTIENT
1. Impersonal sentient entities	4. Postulated realms
2. Personalized sentient entities	5. Historic events and places
3. Zoömorphic sentient entities	6. Historic heroes and public figures

Impersonal Sentient Entities

It is with some hesitation that concepts like *Manitu* and *Wakonda* are referred to as entities. It is by no means certain that the word "sentience," designating an anthropomorphic-like awareness, quite fits these conceptions. No better word suggests itself, however, to designate the idea of a living force pervading everything in which people participate and on occasion manifesting itself. Through this force the systematic order of the universe is maintained. *Manitu* is an Algonkian Indian word for this concept held by the Cree, Ojibwa, Blackfoot, and Menomini. *Wakonda* belongs to the Siouan-speaking Indian tribes, like the Sioux, Assiniboin, and Omaha. Since the ethnographic coverage is rich for the aboriginal Omaha, impersonal sentient entities will be illustrated mainly by reference to *Wakonda*.[5]

For the Omaha Indians, living in what is now Nebraska, *Wakonda* represents a "mysterious life power permeating all natural forms and forces and all phases of man's conscious life" (Fletcher and LaFlesche, 1911:597). It is the source of all life and the invisible force which maintains the integrated operation of the universe. *Wakonda* is also an ethical process in the sense that to it may be traced punishment for dishonesty and undutifulness. As a sanction, however, the force manifests itself through natural phenomena— for example, lightning bolts. The word cannot logically be translated as "spirit" because there is another Omaha word, *wanonxe*, which carries this meaning.

Like many sentient collective representations, *Wakonda* served the aboriginal Omaha as an explanatory device. A person who complained against misfortunes with which he did not know how to cope could be reassured by the advice that "this is ordered by *Wakonda*." In the same way God among Christians is a powerful symbol through which personal adjustment may be restored. The Omaha explained tears as a device originated by *Wakonda* to provide relief for human nature. The term *Wakonda* frequently occurred in personal prayers and ceremonies, especially in those rituals which had the welfare of the entire tribe as their goal. In these ceremonies songs were sung supplicating *Wakonda* and other collective representations. The songs assured man that his prayers for food or assistance had been heard. Very freely, one such song runs as follows:

It is done, I say
A majestic one, a female one,
A little calf, you shall have, I say.
That which is difficult to accomplish, you shall have, I say [*ibid.*, p. 295].

A pipe sometimes was smoked during the prayer. Afterwards the pipe might be left lying in the place where the appeal to *Wakonda* had been offered. However, in all smoking rituals the pipe itself remained relatively unimportant. The real symbol or offering was the tobacco. Words were unnecessary in prayers. Repetition of the name *Wakonda* sufficed to call the mysterious process into operation and also, one suspects, to reassure a troubled person. At meals a small portion of food dropped into the fire constituted a gift to *Wakonda*. Appeals for help could also be made to animals and natural forces which symbolized *Wakonda*. For the Omaha they represented "certain facul-

[5] The following material is drawn from Fletcher and LaFlesche, 1911. See also W. Jones, 1905.

ties and powers individualized, so to speak. . . . The life which informs them, like that which informs man, is continuous and unbroken, emanating from the great mystery, Wakon'da" (*ibid.*, p. 589). At puberty a youth went through a ceremony in which he appealed to the "great power" for help throughout his future life. Meanwhile he kept his thoughts fixed on a good life, one that would include success in hunting and war. In the same way, it was believed, long ago when the people had been weak and poor they had sent their children to a lonely place and made them cry to *Wakonda* for strength. From that original event, in the minds of the Omaha, the puberty rite has come.

Proofs of the existence of the power lay, first, in motion. ". . . All actions of mind or body are because of this invisible life" (*ibid.*, p. 134). The orderly succession of the seasons and of day and night also revealed *Wakonda* and were "one method by which Wakon'da taught man to be truthful, so that his words and acts could be depended on" (*ibid.*, p. 608). Proof also resided in being; in the "permanency of structure and form, as in the rock, the physical features of the landscape, mountains, plains, streams, rivers, lakes, animals, and man." *Wakonda* dwelt in healing herbs and became active through an invocation uttered to those herbs by a curer. Through this force the dead continued to live in close relationship to the living. Also by virtue of it a part could be treated as equivalent to a whole. Signs and symbols could be used to induce the help of *Wakonda*. By scattering partly masticated corn over the fields a certain clan was able to appeal to *Wakonda* to prevent small birds from attacking the fields. Smoking the pipe itself constituted a symbolic form of address. Words spoken and unanimous decisions taken in the tribal Council of Seven Chiefs originated with *Wakonda*. Through the chiefs the power maintained in-group peace and order, engineered out-group relations, and generally promoted tribal welfare. In other words, administration was a sacred process to the Omaha. No direct material symbols of *Wakonda* existed. The Seven Chiefs, of course, symbolized the force and so did the Sacred Pole. The latter, however, had many more complex associations. It stood, in fact, for all the tribe, the Seven Chiefs, and the abstract unity of the tribe. *Wakonda* created all these things which at first were only in the mind of the great power moving as spirits "in space between the earth and the stars" (*ibid.*, p. 570). Through the power of *Wakonda*, however, they descended to earth and became material objects or persons. Some confusion has arisen from the application of the word to anything mysterious or inexplicable. Thunder, a gun shell, and a fictive monster are all spoken of as *wakondas* but are not to be regarded as representative of *Wakonda* itself.

Some Christians conceive of God as formless, impersonal, and sentient, although the more familiar personalistic conception seems to be more significant to most Americans. Al-Ghazzālī, a twelfth-century Persian philosopher and mystic, writing for Muslims said: ". . . There are many who ignorantly cling to an anthropomorphic view of Him, there are few who cherish a transcendental pure conception of Him, and believe that He is not only above all material limitations but even above the limitation of metaphor"

Girls Offer Food at a Hindu Shrine in Bali (courtesy, Indonesian Embassy).

(quoted in Alī, 1946:53). The Hindu Brahman—the Immutable Absolute—which is continuous with each individual's soul also falls in this category, although more anthropomorphic collective representations enjoy greater popularity among India's people. Hindu theologians have interpreted the latter concepts as referring to forms of Brahman. Such concepts appeal to people because of their greater specificity.

Personalized Sentient Entities

Examples of personalized (i.e., anthropomorphic) collective representations are not difficult to secure. Sentient entities are personalized when people conceive of them as resembling and behaving like human beings even though possessing extraordinary abilities not shared by ordinary mortals.

Illustrations include the *orisas* of the Nigerian Yoruba (Lucas, 1948): Esu, who is conceived of as evil but whose anger can be avoided by money offerings and whose help can be secured to inflict injury on an enemy; Ifa, who controls the unknown future and of whom myths recount that he was once a person and an extraordinarily skillful diviner; Sopono, the god of smallpox; and Ogun, associated with war and iron, who is also controller of hunting. Soldiers and blacksmiths look to Ogun for protection while hunters sacrifice to him. Any piece of iron, the forge, anvil, sword, spear, or a dart, is a material symbol of this collective representation. There are many more *orisas* including Olorun, who is omnipresent, omniscient, omnipotent, the judge of people in this and the next world, and the creator. He is located in the sky. To the people Olorun is of relatively little importance despite his superordinate position over the many subordinate deities.

The Fijian *vu*, male and female entities never seen by human beings, also fit in the present category (D. M. Spencer, *1941*). They have personal names and are thought of as falling into several types. Some are fair-skinned girls and others belong to the class of cannibalistic old women. Certain *vu* are associated with particular localities like waterfalls. Some always are dangerous but others can help as well as hurt. Still others are thought to enter into voluntary or involuntary relationships with people who thereby acquire their powers. People serve a *vu* and by their daily offerings keep the latter at their disposal. The *vu* regulate social conduct. For example, a *vu* attached to a particular clan punishes failure to carry out birth, marriage, or death rituals. In this way belief in the *vu* serves to maintain the ceremonies plus whatever adjustive functions the ceremonies possess in the life of the community. V*u* also avenge the injury of one person by another and thus help to control aggression. The power of the *vu* is manifested in illness. Following is an incident illustrating how the *vu* through their control of illness indirectly help to control uncomplementary diversity.

Semi, a man of Wauosi, and Senitoutou met and fell in love at sight. Although Senitoutou had promised to marry another youth, she and Semi eloped to Nasauthoko and were married there. The girl's clan relatives were furiously angry but the young people disregarded them and went to live in Wauosi. Although it was their duty, Semi's people neglected to make either the betrothal or the marriage ceremonies to Senitoutou's clan. It was not long before Semi and Senitoutou became afflicted with disease, and their trouble was diagnosed as . . . resulting from the fact that the *vu* of Senitoutou's clan was angry because Semi's people had not made the ceremony of betrothal [*ibid.*, pp. 23–24].

Ancestors represent a fairly distinct type of anthropomorphic sentient entity. Among the Papuan Orokaiva of New Guinea the ghosts of ancestors may send success to a gardener, reveal new cures to a therapist, or help a hunter locate wild pigs. Ancestral displeasure most often is manifested through illness. Frequent offerings of tobacco and betel are intended to keep the good will of these powerful forces, who are also addressed through prayers and invited to attend dances given by their living descendants. In African kingdoms a man's own ancestors are important enough but far exceeding them in significance are the royal ancestors. Among the Lozi of northwestern Rhodesia the villages at which kings and certain princesses, princes, and queens are buried become capitals for their neighborhood (Gluckman, *1951*:29–31). Each king or noble selects such a village where he or she will be buried. In it he places a number of counselors and priests. The dead chief still rules and does so by striking the neighborhood with misfortune or granting good crops, big catches of fish, or many children. Any royal grave can afflict any member of the royal line wherever he may be and bring misfortune to the whole kingdom. People make offerings at the royal graves through resident priests. In extreme conditions the king may go personally to make offerings at the grave of a recalcitrant ancestor.

Among the Lovedu of the Transvaal nobody thinks much of the creator god but each family attends carefully to its ancestors, "who guard one in death as they did in life" and are responsible for the fertility of the field (E. J. Krige and J. D. Krige, 1943:Chap. 13). The ancestors frequently "complain" by sending illness or other misfortune. Chiefly such behavior is explained as part of the nature of people when they "sleep." Grounds for complaints are improper burial and neglect, or they may arise for no reason at all. Prayer, and beer poured on the ground are directed to ancestors. Sometimes shrines are built to the dead and animals are dedicated to them. Objects which were once in the ancestors' possession contain special power for healing. A dead queen is the most powerful ancestor in the country of the Lovedu and it is she who legitimizes the new occupant of the royal office by opening a door kept closed to all but the rightful candidate (see p. 477). The living queen is the chief rain maker, but this power is linked to the ancestors and is not solely her own. The skin of a deceased counselor constitutes an important specific through whose agency the queen derives a measure of her power to bring rain (*ibid.*, p. 274).

The heroes of aboriginal Australian culture fit in this category of collective representations although they overlap with plant, animal, and other sorts of group totems (see pp. 366–367). The Australian hunters are divided into local groups or bands.[6] Within each local group the men who have been initiated form an association. The major functions of this group are to perpetuate myths connected with landmarks in the geographical environment and to perform ceremonies to increase resources like animals, rain, and yams, on which life depends. The association's activities often are directed not to totems but to ancestral heroes that are somehow linked to totems. The myths, narrated and dramatized by the members, recall the travels and adventures of these heroes, who lived in a mythological period— the Dream Time. The territory of a local group also includes sites located on the "paths" taken by the Dream Time heroes. At these sites the hero is supposed to have performed certain acts; at one he rested; at another he disappeared or turned into a stone. At one site he may have deposited the human and other souls which await incarnation in human or animal births. Along the paths are secret storehouses containing ritual paraphernalia, to be described later. Since the paths are continuous from one local group to another, and even from one tribe to another, they bind several groups who have no overall political organization. Increase rites for rain or yams at a territorial site benefit not only the group living in the territory but all people depending on those things for livelihood. Thus common values—rain, yams, or kangaroos—plus the knowledge that adjacent groups are carrying out ceremonies for their increase contribute to social solidarity.

[6] Discussion based on Elkin, 1954:Chaps. 6–8.

Who were the Dream Time ancestral heroes? They are not true ancestors as much as they are creators. Things are as they are because they were so instituted by the heroes who lived long ago. They made life possible for mankind. Yet they did not do so once and for all. The activities of the associations are necessary to continue to make the world suitable for human survival. Sometimes the Dream Time heroes are referred to as human beings bearing totemic names and sometimes as the totemic species itself. Some were humans who took the forms of totems. At any rate, ". . . the totem symbolizes the ancestor or hero whom the members commemorate" (Elkin, 1954:195). The association's ceremonies fall into three types. First are lengthy initiation ceremonies in which boys learn the lore of the association and become responsible adults. A second kind is predominantly expressive, reënacting the doings of the heroes who crossed the band territory. The members wear painted symbols of the heroes or of animals associated with the ancestors. The costumes and songs which are chanted function to perpetuate tradition. A third class of ceremony is the increase ceremony, aiming to increase natural species or to insure rainfall. Usually performed at sites which are themselves symbols of the heroes, these rituals give men the assurance of controlling nature in some measure. Increase ceremonies do not operate automatically but through the agency of the hero. How the ceremonies work is not made explicit by the natives. The association seeks to perpetuate not only the totemic species of the local group but also other animals, plants, and natural phenomena which are associated with the particular heroes whose sites are in the territory.

Ritual specifics figure in all these rites, including the *churingas* and bull-roarers. A *churinga* is a flat stone or slab of wood, reputedly part of a hero's body, engraved with abstract designs which possess meaning. Generally speaking, the older a *churinga*, the more valuable it is deemed to be. Bull-roarers are wooden devices usually swung around the head to make a distinctive noise. Some are too large to be used in this way. Also incised with symbolic designs, the bullroarer, like the *churinga*, symbolizes a hero or totemic ancestor. These objects are concealed from uninitiated youths and women. In the belief of the Australian natives, *churingas* and bullroarers possess tremendous value. To touch them is an inspiring act for they mediate the life and power of the Dream Time heroes to the living. To rub them on the sick gives strength. Human blood is sometimes allowed to fall on the sacred emblems during increase rituals.

Zoömorphic and Phytomorphic Sentient Entities

If people postulate invisible animal-like entities which produce, understand, or respond to human difficulties, are such conceptions not anthropomorphic rather than zoömorphic in nature? If we admit this problem of classification, the present category may nevertheless be useful to indicate that people also focus fear and dependence on entities pictured as possessing animal and plant forms.

In many communities an imaginary animal is postulated as heading the whole species. "Thus we find everywhere the legend of a king of the serpents," whose crown may be stolen, as well as rulers of the wolves, deer, boars, hawks, owls, and other animals (W. I. Thomas and F. Znaniecki, 1927:I, 208). Whether the importance which these ideas enjoy is sufficient to make them collective representations may be questioned. The nature "bosses" of the Kaska Indians and Siberian peoples are a better case (Honigmann, 1949a:217; Lot-Falck, 1953:54–55). These people conceive of some "chief bear" or "mother caribou" who stands behind, and controls, the respective species, allowing members to be killed for food. However, not all nature (or even animal) rulers possess zoömorphic characteristics.

Destiny animals in Chichicastenango, a town in Guatemala (Bunzel, 1952:274), illustrate zoömorphic collective representations very well. The people believe every individual's life is linked to an animal or other natural object. If the destiny animal is killed, then the man to whom it is linked will also die. Sudden death is explained in terms of this assumption. Complications lie in the fact that nobody in Chichicastenango knows to which animal his fate is linked. People hope and pray that they may meet a destiny animal, for such encounters are lucky events. Sometimes the animal speaks when he is encountered and calls his ward by name. The belief in personal guardian spirits who are animals is called nagualism and is distributed generally in Central America (Brinton, 1894).

Belief in a powerful snake from which men and animals have descended is popular in the tropical forest of South America (Gillin, 1948a:855). The Nupe *Bukpe* lives in the shape of a crocodile and brings disease and drought. But his evil propensities can be controlled through performance of the annual *Bukpe* ritual. Inhuman monsters which inspire fear also belong in this category. It is often difficult to tell from published accounts whether individual animals or an abstract species is regarded as the collective representation.[7]

Sentient plant entities do not appear to be very popular in the world of man. Concepts like Mother Potato or Spirit of the Cassava, encountered in Andean and tropical South America, probably are regarded better as personalized entities. The same point can be made for many "nature spirits." Among the Nupe of Nigeria "vaguely anthropomorphous" entities are said

---

[7] Lévy-Bruhl (1926:96; 1928:Chap. 1) ascribed the lack of discrimination between individual and species to a special talent of "primitive thought." Such thought adheres to the "law of participation" (*a* can be both *a* and not-*a* at the same time) rather than the "law of contradiction." A simpler explanation suggests itself, namely, that people simply do not feel the need to make a distinction. In the same way the reader, when he says "I wish I had a dog," is not consciously distinguishing between possession of an individual dog and "dog" generically considered.

to inhabit the inanimate parts of nature, like hills, trees, watercourses, the bush, and so forth. These entities are sexed and may be friendly or hostile. Small amounts of food, including honey, are left for them to find or are dropped in a river (Nadel, 1954b:26–27). The behavior ascribed to them would seem to warrant their classification as personalized and sentient. However, there is no hard and fast line between such categories.

Postulated Realms

Many people postulate other worlds or realms than the one in which they live. Usually these realms are the places to which the dead go. Not all people are equally concerned with a future existence. The Aymara of Peru follow an apparently Christian-derived conception of heaven and hell but with "no deep conviction regarding ultimate retribution (either reward or punishment) nor, for that matter, any very clear notions of the mode of life in the hereafter" (Tschopik, 1951:217). According to one informant life in heaven is much like that on earth. Outside of the Euroamerican cultural tradition, an afterworld based on the idea of retribution or compensation for earthly conduct or suffering is quite rare. Instead, life beyond death constitutes simply a continuation of mortal existence.

A number of communities regard the future state as depending on a person's status or mode of life while alive. Warriors or those slain in battle may have a separate destination from other men, as also might women who died in childbirth and individuals who perished through drowning. This means, of course, that these communities conceptualize several planes of continued existence.

Sometimes the postulated realm of life after death can be neither imagined nor directly sensed. In official Roman Catholic ideology heaven is a concept of this very abstract type. ". . . Our ideas, however abstruse, however poetic, are inadequate, must be inadequate, to the supernatural reality; not by their intensity, but in their very quality, the joys of Heaven elude us" (Knox, 1955).

Historic Events

Literacy enables the past to be preserved for future generations, which, depending on the meaning they assign to that previous time, are able to commemorate certain events in the continuous flow of history. Historic events that also are collective representations are ideas about past events regarded as having been important in the career of the community. The earliest evidence of such attitudes toward the past applies to Egypt and Chaldea during the first millennium before Christ, a period when both countries lived under foreign domination. Rome in the second and third centuries of the present era also did much looking back to the building of the Roman Empire. Similar conceptions are quite apparent in practically every large-scale, modern nation. Mussolini's Italy harked back to the glory of imperial Rome. Americans have long commemorated a number of historic events: Christmas, the birth of Christ; the signing of the Declaration of Independence, celebrated July 4; and a day to memorialize soldiers who died in national service, Memorial Day. More recent is the celebration of Pearl Harbor Day, when, in the words of a celebrant speaking at the scene of the event, "The U.S.S. Arizona was lost. Hundreds of her gallant crew died here in keeping with the finest traditions of the United States Navy. Free men, they stayed with their ship, fighting to the last breath. Today we are here to honor the memory of those men, our shipmates. . . . I am sure the Arizona's crew will know and appreciate what we are doing" (*New York Times*, Dec. 8, 1951).

Nonsentient Heroes and Public Figures

Nonsentient heroes and public figures who become collective representations through their perpetuation in culture help to keep alive values and aspirations. Such men may have helped to make a community what it is or given it a heritage whose preservation still is valued. In celebrating notable events of the past it usually is impossible to avoid commemorating the men who manifested heroism or some other idealized quality in those events. Sometimes the heroes remain anonymous, as in the Pearl Harbor tribute quoted above. (Note the suggestion of their sentience.) At other times specific names may be mentioned, as when Stalin in 1941 urged Communist troops to "be inspired in this war by the valiant images of our great ancestors—Alexander Nevsky, Dimitry Donskoi, Kuzma Minin, Dimitry Pozharsky . . ." (Bilibin, 1952). This speech was significant because prior to that time the Soviets had invested Czarist times with little positive significance.

The hero as a collective representation in modern large-scale communities differs from sentient and nonsentient culture heroes patterned in terms of the personal world view in that his existence is often clearly, if indirectly, verifiable. Exceptions appear, of course, like St. Philumena, who may never have existed although miracles are claimed to have resulted through her intercession, and St. Josephat of India, who is apparently a European reinterpretation of Gautama, the Buddha (letter, *The Listener*, June 7, 1956). The achievements of the modern hero, if not his personal qualities, potentially are replicable by living men. Both types of heroes shade into each other. The Christ of history occupies one category; the Christ of miracles falls into another. Modern nations become quite objective about bygone heroes without giving them up as collective representations. An editorial states: "It may even be true, as some scoffers say, that Lincoln has become 'the great American myth.' It could be true that the cult of 'Lincolnolatry' has obscured the man and most of the facts about him." Nevertheless, he remains a hero who receives (or should receive) reverence. "The man symbolizes . . . personal goodness and social righteousness. . . . The true dignity of a great simplicity" (*New York Times,* Feb. 12, 1951).

Note on Supreme Beings

Beliefs in high gods and supreme beings are world-wide but this does not mean that they are universal in the sense of occurring in every culture. Not infrequently a community holds a conception of a supreme sentient being but attaches little importance to the idea.

The Inca Viracocha was high god, creator of the world, and culture hero. He instructed man in many arts and was worshiped in special temples through prayer and sacrifice. However, his popularity always remained somewhat less than that of the Sun and other lesser deities, perhaps because of his relatively late emergence as a collective representation (A. Métraux, 1949:560). At the southern tip of South America, in Tierra del Fuego, the Ona and Yahgan recognized supreme beings (Cooper, 1946a, 1946b). Among both peoples the names of these high gods were rarely mentioned. Instead people spoke of "the highest one" or "that one there above," referring to the deity's abode in the sky. In neither case was the high god a creator, but he did punish men by death. In the Yahgan initiation ceremonies the moral instructions given to boys and girls were described as representing the will of the supreme being. Since the high god is described as without body, wife, or children he may correspond to an impersonal sentient entity. A bit of food thrown into the fire among the Ona constituted a gift for "the one above." Prayers, consisting largely of complaints, sought the supreme being's intercession in event of illness. Shamans, who cured, influenced weather or hunting, and aided warriors, derived their power from the ghosts of dead shamans, not from the high god. Much of Negro Africa entertains the idea of a supreme being but rarely is he a target of worship. Exceptionally, among South African tribes like the Zulu and Swazi, who have banded together to form national states, the supreme being appears as a "national God to whom national and official sacrifices and prayers are directed" (Pettersson, 1953:171). The reigning king leads those ceremonies. A few anthropologists have suggested a tendency for a supreme being to become important as social organization becomes more complex. The supreme god then symbolizes the total network of social relationships in the community, which are themselves tightly coördinated through administration and overlapping associations (Chapple and Coon, 1942: Chap. 23).

Monotheism has emerged historically a few times in connection with high gods. It has taken the form of a movement, often claiming to be inspired by the supreme deity, seeking to eradicate all other sentient collective representations. Despite the ideal monotheism of Judaism, Christianity, and Islam, it is likely that many followers of these ideological systems continue to attribute to other collective representations powers which, ideally, belong to God alone.

COLLECTIVE REPRESENTATIONS IN CULTURE

This section will look at some functions of collective representations. It will be convenient to consider these beliefs, first, as the independent and, second, as the dependent variable. Phrased in other words: What does man derive from his belief in collective representations? How do those beliefs take shape in a particular cultural system?

The Independent Variable

In most general terms, the collective representations of a community contribute to the adjustment of individual members and in doing so help to preserve equilibrium in social relations. The adjustive functions of S-type representations reside in their definition as symbols of security, love, compassion, retribution, and justice. Ancestors and deities, for example, act as pillars of dependence and sources of comfort. They can be invoked to remedy distress. The very idea of a watchful symbol may assist people to retain confidence and morale in the face of the recurrent crises which they encounter.

The adjustive functions of sentient collective representations also derive from the definition of these as explanatory symbols. Through them the believer is provided with a means for accounting for many events which affect him and the community and for which any other available explanation is unsatisfactory.

Whether symbolic of compassion or explanation, collective representations that are sentient usually lend themselves to control—for example, through prayer and sacrifice. Therefore they offer people a means for coping with threat, danger, sorrow, and uncertainty.

For man to surrender himself to a powerful symbol who is entitled to obedience and reverence in a large-scale, highly impersonal society provides a means of escape from unpleasant feelings of aloneness and limited effectiveness (Fromm, 1950:Chap. 3). Adjustment, then, may lie in identifying with the overwhelming power of the postulated sentient or even nonsentient entity.

Both sentient and nonsentient collective representations function to maintain consensus over the values obtaining in a community and thereby help to reduce uncomplementary diversity. They limit the probability of radical opposition. A god, saint, or hero embodies the ideals around which people are organized. In recognizing the importance of the conception, the ideals on which social solidarity hinges also are affirmed. When a sentient representation is conceived of as sanctioning behavior through his control of reward or punishment, further protection is furnished to the maintenance of complementary diversities. The hope of heaven or fear of hell serves the same end.

Where collective representations include moral sanctions, their function with respect to enforcing complementary behavior may be indirect or direct (Cooper, 1931). Indirect enforcement of standards is illustrated by the belief that happiness or misery in a future life depends upon following certain rules of behavior in this world. Also the ideas that personalized sentient entities protect their devotees from immoral people and from acts like theft or murder indirectly enforce approved conduct. As for directly sanctioning behavior, sentient entities may be conceived of as quite immediately punishing immoral acts and rewarding good deeds. While the belief that collective representations enforce morality is not found in all cultures, its distribution shows no obvious relationship with particular forms of subsistence technology or with complexity of social organization.

Sentient collective representations also may promote stress. Their definition as the source of punishment or cause of illness, drought, or other unpleasant circumstances heightens anxiety. The unknown will of sentient beings as well as the fear of offending them induces a sense of uncertainty.

There may be times when a series of catastrophes undermines faith in the traditional principles of order. The believer may see unbelievers, often from another society, carrying out forbidden acts without fear of retribution. When such conditions appear, it is not uncommon for a special type of leader to arise. He announces a new conception of the deities or a fresh message inspired or directly revealed by them, perhaps in a vision or some other ecstatic experience (Boisen, 1951; Wallace, 1956a and 1956b). The insight which the prophet has received in time becomes organized into a system with new rituals. The leader wins followers through his earnestness and enthusiasm, and by virtue of the adjustive satisfactions provided by what he preaches. Final success of his doctrine also depends on its internal consistency, on the degree to which it possesses anchorage points in cultural tradition, as well as on factors governing diffusion in general (Chapter 15). The distinction between a successful "revitalization movement" and an unsuccessful attempt at such a movement is often small. Successful prophets usually do not believe themselves to be the deity, although their following may deify them. Patients in a mental hospital on the other hand, who may also be convinced of the validity of their message, more often tend to believe that they are God, Jesus, or a similar entity. Society neither believes nor follows the unsuccessful prophet. He becomes socially inconvenient even to his close associates and is certified as insane and hospitalized (Wallace, 1956b:272–273).

The Dependent Variable

How do conceptions of invisible sentient entities and man's relationship to them arise? What determines the attitude with which nonsentient heroes are regarded?

In a large-scale community with an impersonal world view men ideally do not credit their deities with explanatory functions. Here is one example of how the character of collective representations depends on other elements in the ideological system, particularly the degree to which that system accounts for the way the universe is organized. As knowledge of nature increases, the conception of sentient entities is modified or the beliefs may even be displaced (R. Firth, 1948). A belief of this sort will be abandoned when it no longer fulfills significant functions, like providing hope, explanation, or even fear. With new and, presumably, more reliable conceptions of how the universe is organized and operates, much has happened to man's faith in S-type collective representations. In the western world collective representations have come to be held by many people as expressive symbols of truth, goodness, and other socially standardized values. In paying homage to such concepts those people, sometimes quite self-consciously, reiterate their faith in those virtues. They do not petition a sentient collective representation to do anything for them. Fixing attention on the concepts is perceived by them to have an adjustive function.

Not only is the definition of sentient collective representations dependent upon the kind of knowledge available for explaining the organization of nature, but it is related functionally to the kinds of problems that people living by a particular way of life encounter. The collective representations are dependent on man's fears, uncertainties, and other values. As these change, the belief system also undergoes modification. The explanatory functions assigned to the S-type representations likewise are conditioned by what people do. Obviously, a hunting and collecting community does not possess deities who control the growth of crops.

Man's relationship to the collective representations tends to be congruent with the way in which the individual regards himself and others in a particular community. The representations are a projection of his general role in, and conception of, social relations (Kardiner, 1945:426–429). Among the Comanche Indians of the southern American Plains procedures for soliciting aid from personalized sentient entities are devoid of any sense of sin, retribution, expiation, or forgiveness (ibid., Chap. 3). This is quite consistent with the character of Comanche life. During his growth the Comanche individual encounters few anxieties and does not learn to distrust himself. Punishment is not used for children; parents do not become objects of mixed hatred and attraction, and the individual finds it unnecessary to repress many strong forbidden drives. "The result is emphasis on the achievement aspect of activity and not on the anxieties with which it may be associated" (*ibid.*, p. 87). People are secure in their ability to deal with the outside world. These qualities are reflected in the individual's relationship to the controlling forces of the universe. "In view of the fact that in early relations to the father obedience plays such a small role and punishment is not used as a means of implementing discipline, we would not expect suffering or conformity to discipline to be a means of soliciting this power. The technique of solicitation is merely to express the wish to have it and to render oneself worthy of possessing it by a demonstration of strength, endurance, or determination. Not helplessness but resourcefulness is a claim for power" (*ibid.*, p. 92).

On the Indonesian island of Alor different conditions operate (*ibid.*, Chap. 6). Here there is little opportunity for an individual to form strong attachments to his parents. Even young children often experience hunger while the missing mother remains away from the village working in the gardens. Teasing and deception of children prevent the child from developing a favorable image of himself. No strong expectations are held out toward the father, who is absent a good part of the time. Neither parent is highly dependable and at no point in his life "does the individual have the opportunity to think highly of himself" (*ibid.*, p. 163). He does not trust his ability to achieve results through action. The situation is almost directly reversed from the Comanche Indians. Ancestors are the important sentient entities to which these people attend. The dead, however, are not placated nor are their powers exaggerated. Good things are never sought from this source. This is entirely consistent with the attitudes toward the parents, whose images also never become inflated and on whom strong expectations do not develop. The ancestors are fed and feared though they are not idealized. The individual obeys their presumed wishes reluctantly and grudgingly.

The congruence of collective representations with the social organization was noted in another way by Aristotle, who in *Politics* wrote that "the opinion which universally prevails, that the gods themselves are subject to kingly government, arises from hence, that all men were, and many are so now; and as they imagined themselves to be made in the likeness of the gods, so they supposed their manner of life must needs be the same" (Aristoteles, 1913:3). The reference, of course, is to the tendency to set up pantheons modeled on human administrative systems. One can go even further and point out how often the deities are organized into families and have children, as mankind does.

Weak administrative organization among the Fox Indians, who flourished in the Great Lakes region of the United States, was reflected in their conception of the pantheon (W. B. Miller, 1955). The Fox possessed a profound aversion to any system of superordinate-subordinate power relations. Their culture contrasts with Euroamerican life, in which the "vertical authority relationship is a fundamental building block" serving to coördinate social relationships. The European pantheon—for example, as illustrated in Greek culture—contains an elevated supreme being who coördinates a series of subordinate personalized entities arranged in a hierarchy of descending power deriving from the supreme power source. The priesthood is arranged in a similar hierarchy. The Fox Indians present a contrasting picture. Here an impersonal sentient entity, *Manitu*, is at the center. This power circulates to, and is withdrawn from, other beings, including natural phenomena like Rain, Lightning, Corn, Fire, and Man. Possession of *Manitu* power is never assured; an entity with superior power can destroy it in another. Man, too, can gain power and lose it—for example, by neglecting his obligations. There is no supreme coördinating deity in the rather disorderly Fox pantheon. And the Indian's social life also lacks any central administrative source of power. The Fox repertory of collective representations contains no heroes of the stature of Ulysses, Moses, or Washington. Living heroes who receive popular tribute similarly remain unrecorded. "The relations between gods, and between gods and men, as they are depicted in Fox religious mythology, are based on Fox ideals of right and proper interpersonal relations" (*ibid.*, p. 283). Even parents did not act the part of chief disciplinarians, nor did they stringently enforce dependence. Rank and prestige are unelaborated phenomena in Fox social life. Certain leadership offices, like that of a village chief or war leader, certainly existed, but the authority behind their decisions was not binding. "Just as each individual related himself directly to the source of supernatural power, each individual participating in organized activity related himself directly to the body of procedural rules governing that activity. He was free to select and execute appropriate modes of action . . ." (*ibid.*, p. 285).

The elaborateness of any system of collective representations, including the detail with which the functions and personalities of the concepts are defined or expressed in myths, is related functionally to the elaboration present in other areas of culture, including the complexity of social organization. Directly, of course, elaboration of the belief system depends on the activities of specialists who are able to devote themselves to this topic.

Malevolent features in conceptual representations may reflect specific ambiguities and uncertainties in human relationships which induce stress in their participants. The Heiban and Otoro, two Nuba tribes living in the Egyptian Sudan, share many cultural elements but differ sharply in how they conceive of the universal order (Nadel, 1955). Both communities accept the importance of ghosts. But only the Heiban elaborate ghost beliefs into a theory of ancestors who possess power over the living. For them the dead may be helpful as well as threatening to their living progeny. Constant readiness exists to detect signs of anger in the ancestors, when, for example, illness and disaster strike. In addition, both groups believe in a supreme being but differ in how to approach him. The typical Otoro ritual is quiet and reserved. The Heiban as a rule approach the high god in an excited and angry mood. They abuse the deity for his lack of concern and his weakness. The Heiban in general appear to be more tense and pessimistic in their outlook on the universe including its postulated forces. These qualities apparently reflect anxieties encountered in the course of growth and in social relationships. Adolescence, for example, is not a clear-cut transition to new roles and responsibilities. The step-by-step system of age grading found among the Otoro is lacking. Among the Heiban, wives join the unilinear kin group of their husbands but their adoption remains incomplete. Their loyalty continues to be bound up in part with their own families. Anxieties over the success of the marriage are encouraged through this arrangement. Finally, although male homosexuality occurs in both communities, the Otoro allow the homosexual to lead a respectable life as a woman. The Heiban regard him simply as abnormal. These aspects of Heiban life are seen as conditioning the pessimism of the people, which is reflected in the malevolent patterning of the collective representations.

To derive the collective representations from the character of social relationships and personal tensions existing in a community is not to claim that each generation invents anew these important beliefs. The learning of the belief system proceeds like any other learning. It starts in childhood when the social heritage first is passed on from one generation to another. What these hypotheses do suggest is that changes elsewhere in the cultural configuration will be accompanied by reinterpretations of the collective representations. However, difficulties in reinterpreting such beliefs often arise, especially in large-scale communities where the particular belief system is in the hands of specialists—historians and theologians—and has been set down in writing. The formal ideas, especially, will change very slowly compared to the popular, informal, and, perhaps, partly implicit conceptions held by most of the community. Should these radically new conceptions be expressed in speech or writing they are called heretical. Often interdependent belief systems come into being under such conditions to which the names "great" and "little" traditions have been assigned (Marriott, 1955; Redfield, 1956b:Chap. 3). The former is cultivated in schools, temples, and monasteries by priests and philosophers; the latter works itself out in the daily life of the people.

Collective Representations in Ritual

The sentiments attached both to sentient and to nonsentient collective representations derive primarily from, and are reinforced by, the regular occurrence of those concepts in ritual. The dramatic, emotionally stirring context in which the ritual presents the concepts gives them a different character from other ideas which man acquires. They become set apart from ordinary ideas, in other words acquiring a special ("sacred") character (Chapple and Coon, 1942:551).

There are three main ways in which collective representations occur in ritual situations.

1. *The ritual may commemorate or honor a collective representation.* Indirectly, as already pointed out, people in honoring a sentient or nonsentient entity may also be affirming the importance of the values and ideals attached to the figure who is being praised in the ceremony. Sunday church services, devoted to the honoring of God, and patriotic rallies on the birthdays of heroes illustrate ceremonies carrying this function.

2. *The ritual may be designed to effect some kind of response from a sentient collective representation.* For example, participants may use the ceremony to command, or to press themselves on, the entity's attention. People may petition for specific benefits, like rain or health. It is worth repeating that all ritual is not petition. Navaho Indians pray with the words:

> Safely may my young men move about
> Safely may we live.
> Safely may we move as a group
> May my people follow the pollen trail in the future.
> Being safe on all sides may we dwell.
> May earth people be safe [Reichard, 1944:44].

But the Navaho through these words are not asking the Holy People to protect them. Through the prayer they compel the sentient entities to act.

In another sense, too, what sounds like petition may upon deeper insight be revealed in quite another light. The Roman Catholic Mass for Pilgrims and Travelers asks God to "direct my steps according to Thy word, and let no iniquity have dominion over me" (Lasance, 1952:1481). From this prayer it is apparent that the Mass is not said in order to guarantee a safe journey. Rather it expresses the congregation's self-committal to the will of God. Of course, this is the formal meaning of the ritual. How it is interpreted in popular thought may be quite different.

3. *The ritual may seek to prevent some kind of response from the collective representation.* Some ceremonies seek to isolate or exorcise a malevolent entity in the same way that people are avoided or shunned in order to escape unpleasant consequences felt to proceed from them. An example is seen in the Navaho rite of exorcism, in which the ritualist works symbolically, either moving evil out into a limited area or preserving a limited space as a protective circle. In "evil-chasing chants" the object "is to restrict the territory over which evil can operate" (Reichard, 1944:15).

There seems to be little question that in the past several hundred years in Europe and America the amount of respect and awe reserved for sentient collective representations has declined. "Human affairs around the world seem more and more commonly to be decided without reference to supernatural powers" (Wallace, 1956b:277). The question of whether man can safely dispense with such beliefs without accumulating additional stress remains unanswered. An increase in behavioral disorders of a neurotic character and the "paranoid deification of political leaders and ideologies" are what one writer expects to see emerge from this state of affairs (ibid., p. 278). Over a somewhat longer period of time the importance accorded to nonsentient collective representations has constantly increased. It is probably fair to say that some of the most dramatic ceremonies in Euroamerican culture are directed toward the latter types of beliefs.

MYTHS

In addition to their frequent occurrence in rituals, collective representations are also maintained through myths. Myths occur in many forms. In communities without writing, the oral narrative suffices for the transmission of tales about the origin of the world and the role the collective representations may have played in that achievement. In communities with writing, myths take their place with history and in some cases may be difficult to distinguish from objective historical accounts. In communities with mass media of communication, the film, radio, and television drama become the vehicles for relating the mythological achievements of a hero or a deity. So-called "mythologicals" constitute an important output of the Indian film industry, the second largest such industry in the world. In the plot of one of these pictures a king finds himself in a dilemma over whether or not to be a party to human sacrifice, and thus to reclaim himself in the eyes of his parents. He decides to sacrifice an 8-year-old child of poor parents but the child is rescued from the sacrificial fire by the popular Lord Krishna (Screen, May 7, 1954).

In a large-scale community with an impersonal world view, people may doubt many of their historically unauthenticated myths. The myths, however, are not displaced immediately even with such doubt. They may be enjoyed as fantasy or be reinterpreted to fit the new situation. Thus the creation tale of Genesis continues to be taught in school and church, sometimes being reinterpreted as an analogy of the creator's actual powers. Little point exists in classifying myths as true or untrue. People may know their myths are not accurate historically and yet retain them for the powerful emotional satisfaction they provide.

The dependent functions of myth are varied. In helping to maintain collective representations myths also help promote consensus in the community, consensus around those important values on which solidarity in turn depends. All myths are not concerned with collective representations. Some explain, emphasize, or make dramatic certain portions of the community's way of life in terms of past struggles, hopes, and aspirations (Redfield, 1956a:367). Perhaps the *status quo* is interpreted dramatically as having been won through some notable struggle. The myths of American history, like the account of the Revolutionary War, belong in this category. Other myths are more cosmic and explain the origin and organization of the universe. They may contain the justification for using certain signs and symbols in indirect coping.

Myths shade off into fictions—true or fabricated tales that people tell, read, act, or view for pleasure. Fictions embody none of the importance reserved for myths.

AVAILABLE FILMS

Art, Life and Religion (9 min., b. and w.) was made in the Northern Territory of Australia. It describes an old man painting a piece of bark with ocher and then drawing a lizard with white clay. Rock paintings are also illustrated. These paintings, constituting "a link with nature," aid the Dream Time heroes to increase the food supply. The picture is available from Australian Instructional Films, Ltd., Sydney, Australia. *Les hommes qui font la pluie* (35 min., b. and w., in French) depicts Yenendi rites for rain among the African Songhai. The producer is Jean Rouch of the Musée de l'Homme. The ceremonies and prayers are addressed to the wind, earth, rainbow, lightning, and other collective representations. *L'invention du monde* (35 mm., 45 min., b. and w., in French) in a poetic manner reviews creation myths through architecture, cave paintings, masks, and ritual objects from various parts of the world. It is produced by Zimbacca and Béouin. For a similar sort of picture, which, however, illustrates only one tale, see *The Loon's Necklace,* distributed by Encyclopædia Britannica Films (10 min., color).

39

The Pursuit of Knowledge

THE preceding chapters furnished in brief compass a review of what the world of man believes. Attention also was given to how man acquires his knowledge of the seen and unseen world and how that knowledge persists from one generation to another. The purpose of this chapter is to sum up some points already made and to inquire more intensively and from a comparative point of view into the sources of knowledge and the bases on which beliefs are held. These are subjects about which philosophers have written much and on which they are by no means always in agreement.

EXPERIENCE AND REASON

Basically, as was said, all knowledge derives from experience. Yet, paradoxically, man does not "see," or experience, all that he comes to know. He does not, for example, see atoms, collective representations, or, in paddling a canoe, the relationship between fast water and the increase in the boat's speed when going downstream. At least he does not come to know these things with the same immediacy with which he perceives the blue of the sky, the house in which he lives, or the crops growing in his garden. This introduces again the distinction between directly and indirectly perceived knowledge. All man's concepts gravitate toward one or another of these opposite poles: concepts by inspection, which are demonstrated by pointing to the referent, which, in turn, can be sensed directly, and concepts by postulation, which, if they exist, can be demonstrated only indirectly. That is, the person who holds a concept by postulation says, in effect: "If the concept exists then under conditions so and so, such and such observable phenomena may be sensed directly. These will be proof of the concept by postulation." Not all people subject all concepts by postulation to empirical test. It may be enough to prove such postulates by logic—that is, through reasoning alone. Of course, in testing for the existence of a concept by postulation by looking for certain empirical consequences of its existence, use also is made of reason.

In many cases knowledge consists of inferring predictable relationships —for example, between fast water and the speed of a canoe. Such relationships cannot directly be seen. Obviously, people do not "see" much that they know! Knowledge depends to a great extent on reasoning from what is seen or otherwise sensed. One way in which cultures become different is by virtue of the fact that people draw different relationships between the entities they see and postulate. Also they apply their reasoning to different phenomena. They do not reason differently, it is important to emphasize, but only apply their biologically given capacity for reason to different concepts. Putting this in other words: Each culture includes a relatively distinct conception of reality. The conception of one community tends to make its members blind to reality as perceived in another. No one view exhausts reality. It does not follow that a true and final picture of how the world is really constituted would be obtained by summing up all conceptions of reality. Such an additive summary would constitute a bizarre collection of incompatibilities. Anthropology surveys but does not sum up ideologies. From such surveys it seeks to discover the common bases upon which people come to acquire their ideas.

Is Logical Reasoning Universal?

Not a little has been written about the supposed illogicality of small-scale, exotic peoples. One prominent study of the African Azande begins by distinguishing between the mystical and common-sense notions of those people (Evans-Pritchard, 1937:12). The former "attribute to phenomena suprasensible qualities which . . . are not derived from observation or cannot be logically inferred from it. . . ." Common-sense ideas, however, "attribute to phenomena only what men observe in them or what can logically be inferred from observation." In a sense the distinction between mystical and common-sense ideas approaches the difference between concepts by postulation and by inspection. Note, though, that we have insisted that both sorts of concepts derive in some degree from experience. Suprasensible qualities, like the soul, are not observable directly. But should people try to prove the existence of a soul, this could be done only through some application of logical reasoning from given premises that are accepted in a particular community. What the author of the quotation just given implies in his distinction between mystical and common-sense notions is only that Europeans or Americans cannot logically infer an Azande's mystical notions because alien observers employ their own peculiar premises. Culture-bound premises blind the person to another system of reality. That the Azande do not or could not sustain their beliefs logically is dubious. As a matter of fact the excellent documentation of Azande ideology in the book which has been cited indicates quite clearly that the Azande do logically rationalize their "suprasensible postulates." For example, the belief that a witch can produce death or other unfortunate events is logical in terms of the Azande premise that no event can be explained fully unless witchcraft is taken into consideration (*ibid.*, p. 71). Furthermore, there exist premises by which to deduce logically the existence of witches through a séance or some other form of diagnosis (*ibid.*, pp. 148–182). Azande witch doctors act on these premises plus their knowledge of local scandals when they identify somebody as a witch. Furthermore, there is a premise in Azande thought which says that "one witch can see another witch." Therefore, the suspicions of a witch doctor who is himself a witch are particularly well founded (*ibid.*, p. 187). Now, such premises are utterly untenable to most Euroamericans and entirely incongruent with the impersonal world view. For a Euroamerican student of culture to employ these premises for purposes other than trying to understand the Azande, while at the same time maintaining the impersonal world view, would really be to act illogically. But that doesn't mean that the Azande are illogical.

Lévy-Bruhl (1926) has argued that small-scale, exotic people are "prelogical" because they ignore the "law of contradiction" by which one is bound to assert that *a* cannot be both *a* and not-*a* at the same time.[1] A witch cannot be both asleep in a hut and flying on a broomstick during the same night. A man cannot be in a distant country and also under the direct control of a sorcerer by virtue of the latter's owning a portion of the victim. In place of the "law of contradiction" such people (or, as he called them, "primitives") adhere to the "law of participation," which allows *a* to be both *a* and not-*a* simultaneously. In other words, they reason differently. Most anthropologists believe that statements which posit different procedures of reasoning for mankind are based on an inadequate understanding of cultures. If a community *for certain purposes* assumes a symbol to be equivalent to that which it represents, this does not mean that in response to a direct question of whether both things are really equal a difference would not be admitted. Because the impersonal world view ideally rejects the notion that a symbol can be equal to its referent, the adherent of that world view classifies such an idea as illogical or prelogical. No attempt is made to discover whether the other community's members can distinguish between symbol and referent. Of course, whether they make such a distinction also depends on their values and on whether the distinction possesses any significance for them. "What the comparative study of culture, based on first-hand contact with many peoples, has taught is that all peoples think in terms of certain premises that are taken largely for granted. Whatever the chain of reasoning employed, the logic is dictated by these assumptions. Granting the premises, the logic is inescapable" (Herskovits, 1948:73).

Of course, nobody would claim that everybody always thinks logically and never errs in reasoning (see pp. 499–500). But such illogicality occurs everywhere, in all cultures, and has nothing to do with alleged cultural differ-

---

[1] Later he abandoned this point of view. See Lévy-Bruhl, 1949.

ences. Furthermore, all people (with the exception perhaps of highly skeptical philosophers) take much of their knowledge for granted and feel no
compulsion to prove it. The premises required for proof may be so highly
implicit as to be unavailable to the community's average member. This is
clearly the case with ourselves. How many readers can defend logically their
belief in science as a reliable source of truth? As already pointed out, the
impersonal world view prefers concepts which are demonstrable empirically.
If somebody suggests that a man can be in two places at one time, we demand to know how this is possible. Many exotic communities, however,
know from dreams that they can be both asleep in their homes and away
from home simultaneously. They do not concern themselves with the "how"
of the matter. The personal world view is far less likely to raise questions of
this sort.

Reason and Truth

Truth reached through reason or logic alone differs from statements
which can be tested through experience. Logically, John can be shown to
be both mortal and immortal, depending on the premise accepted. The
premise chosen can be defended in terms of further reasoning. But empirical
verification of John's mortality or immortality can come only after one
has carefully defined "John" and conducted a crucial experiment. The story
is told of the Chancellor of a European university who had hung a goose
outdoors in the fall. It was cut down and stolen. Rumor said that the bird
had been taken by the son of a young professor. The professor called on the
Chancellor and explained why it could not have been his son who stole the
goose. After listening the Chancellor said: "Your irrefutable logic has convinced me that it could not have been your son—but I saw him cutting
down the goose."

"Cabalism" is the term applied to a purely rational and esoteric form of
attaining truth which is scarcely subject to experimental testing. Some
Muslims believe that the *Quran* was first revealed by God to Mohammed
on the twenty-seventh day of the month of Ramadan. The only proof offered
is that the verse referring to the revelation of the *Quran* contains 27 words,
and the expression "Lailat-ul-Qadr," referring to the night of the revelation,
contains 9 letters and occurs 3 times in the verse, thus also adding up to 27.
In a different category from cabalists are humanists, who also use reason to
defend some conception about the world (see pp. 26–29).

Many people in western society have become impatient with a purely
rational basis of truth. They tend to devalue pure reason in favor of scientific
prediction as the test of truth. In many circumstances they reject as meaningless questions which cannot be reduced to terms admitting of experimental verification. This is the modern temper, one that science has introduced into Euroamerican culture. Perhaps because normative questions

of right or wrong, good or bad are notoriously difficult to answer empirically, and yet are important in social life, a reaction to such a one-sided conception of truth may be at hand. Certainly all communities do not insist that the only significant truth is that which can be demonstrated through the senses.

Freedom of Inquiry

Where incompatible views of reality exist in radical opposition to each other, experience shows a tendency for the proponents of one view to force others to acknowledge the truth as they see it. Or else limits may be placed around the pursuit and dissemination of knowledge, especially if those activities follow unorthodox or dangerous directions. The western world ideally espouses freedom of inquiry and the right to communicate the results of study. Yet, despite ideal protestations to the contrary, it is doubtful that freedom of inquiry, any more than freedom of religion or any kind of other freedom, can ever be full, absolute, and complete in any society. Examples of suppression of the right to disseminate truth are not hard to find. Communists are not welcome to pursue the Marxist version of truth in American universities, and in Egypt a professor of theology was threatened with trial in El Azhar University Court for questioning the obligatoriness of the annual fast of Ramadan, pillar of Islamic beliefs (*Dawn*, June 14, 15, 1955). "Men of power, whether monarchs or millionaires or Marxists, only allow criticism when it does not go so far as to threaten policies" (Arnold Nash, quoted by Kneller, 1955:123). Many modern countries reveal a tendency to be "exclusive and intolerant" and consciously to ridicule and reject intellectual effort. Proponents of such attitudes press toward narrowness of scale. They refuse "to acknowledge the greatness of other times and other lands" (Kennan, 1953).

BEYOND THE SENSES

With the exception of a few mystics, American and European thinkers in general show little inclination to know things more immediately than through concepts which can be communicated verbally, logically defended, and tested. But there is a way of knowing which abandons concepts. The world can be known with great immediacy, no concepts coming between knower and known.

In South Asia certain thinkers are convinced that all definite, determinate things like flowers, people, human passions, and even scientific laws are fleeting or transitory (Northrop, 1946:Chap. 10).[2] Why should man attach himself with conviction and passion to transitory things when experience

[2] The following summary is based on Northrop, 1953:74–82, but the scriptural quotations have been selected by the present author.

reveals something which is not transitory? "I don't know what to call it. Arbitrarily I name it Tao," the Way (Wang, 1946:62). Buddhist scholars name it Nirvana; Hindu thinkers, Brahman. One must understand clearly that Tao or Brahman cannot be seen, heard, or felt. Unlike sense objects,

Membership in a Buddhist Convent May Help These Girls to Surrender Attachment to the Definite, Transitory, and Determinate Things of the World (courtesy, Japanese Foreign Ministry).

it is indeterminate and indefinite. It is not discovered through the senses, for the senses reveal only transitory phenomena. Despite the fact that the Brahman cannot be seen, heard, or felt, and that it is timeless and spaceless, it can be known. It *is* known when a person rids himself of all sensed objects and becomes conscious only of the background out of which the sensed objects, including himself, arise as determinate parts. Because such experiences are not to be conceptualized directly in words, eastern philosophers usually express them metaphorically. The *Upanishads*, written several hundred years before Christ, are full of directions for knowing Brahman. Here are some: "By the Self one knows form and taste and smell, by the Self one knows sound and touch and the joy of man with woman: what is there left in this world of which the Self not knows? *This is That thou seekest*" (Ghose, 1953:71). " 'Where one sees nothing else, hears nothing else, understands nothing else, that is the Infinite. Where one sees something else, hears something else, understands something else, that is the finite. The infinite is immortal, the finite is mortal' " (Macnicol, 1938:183).

The *Tao Te Ching* of Lao Tzu, a book probably dating from the fourth century before Christ, follows the same method:

If the Tao could be comprised in words, it would not be the unchangeable Tao:
[For] if a name may be named, it is not an unchangeable name [E. R. Hughes, 1942:144].

> The world may be known
> Without leaving the house;
> The Way may be seen
> Apart from the windows.

> The further you go,
> The less you will know [*Tao Te Ching*, 1955:100].

The Brahman or Tao is that out of which the sensory perceptions of the knower arise. Out of it also appear the objects which are conceptualized. Into it the self and the sensed objects may at will dissolve or disappear. Knowing Brahman or Tao, then, consists in identifying completely the knower and the known. It is a way of fusing oneself through feeling with the entire universe. The goal of such knowledge may be called the undifferentiated esthetic continuum as well as the Way, Tao, or Brahman.

As the reader may have gathered, Asian scholars do not merely seek to know the undifferentiated esthetic continuum. They elevate such an experience to a high value. It becomes desirable to dedicate oneself to the "indeterminate, all-embracing immediacy which is Brahman and to give up determinate desires and actions, treating them as the worldly and transitory things which they are" (Northrop, 1953:78). To surrender attachment to the transitory may mean that man lives in the world and deals with sense objects while yet escaping the world through nonattachment. This is the reiterated advice of the popular Hindu scripture, the *Bhagavadgita* (1951). The three following quotations from that book represent the advice of Lord Krishna to a troubled man:

> Thinking about sense-objects
> Will attach you to sense-objects;
> Grow attached, and you become addicted;
> Thwart your addiction, it turns to anger;
> Be angry, and you confuse your mind;
> Confuse your mind, you forget the lesson of experience;
> Forget experience, you lose discrimination;
> Lose discrimination, and you miss life's only purpose [*ibid.*, pp. 48–49].

The world is imprisoned in its own activity, except when actions are performed in the worship of God. Therefore you must perform every action sacramentally and be free from all attachments to results [*ibid.*, p. 52].

> The illumined soul
> Whose heart is Brahman's heart
> Thinks always: "I am doing nothing."
> No matter what he sees,
> Hears, touches, smells, eats;
> No matter whether he is moving,
> Sleeping, breathing, speaking,
> Excreting, or grasping something with his hand,
> Or opening his eyes,
> Or closing his eyes:
> This he knows always:

"I am not seeing, I am not hearing:
It is the senses that see and hear
And touch the things of the senses."

He puts aside desire,
Offering the act to Brahman.
The lotus leaf rests unwetted on water:
He rests on action, untouched by action [*ibid.*, p. 71].

"In other words, one accepts the determinate, earthly deeds and facts of life for whatever they may be, ugly or beautiful, with indifference or nonattachment. One is in the dirt of the world, but not of it" (Northrop, 1953: 79). The *Tao Te Ching* expresses the same thought:

The business of learning is one of day by day acquiring more,
The business of the Tao one of day by day dealing with less.
Yes dealing with less and less
Until you arrive at inaction [E. R. Hughes, 1942:158].

The reader should not believe that all Asians live by nonattachment. They do so no more than all Westerners regulate their lives by scientific method. Both goals remain ideals to most men. But such ideals possess relevance for appraising means and ends, and even people who do not live by those values are affected by them. In Asia, for example, rules, expressing as they do determinate meanings attached to some experience, assume a relatively unimportant place in life. They readily are violated, with the result that a certain easygoingness about rules results (Ryan and Straus, 1954). In India western-educated leaders are countering this tendency by extolling determinate virtues like honesty, promptness, or "discipline." The consequences of evaluating highly the undifferentiated esthetic continuum are under fire from imported western attitudes which attach high importance to determinate things.

MAGICAL THOUGHT

"Magic" is a word that entered anthropology from everyday speech and lacks clearly denotative, technical meaning. Even by students of culture it has been employed loosely. The word continues to enjoy wide currency in ordinary usage, where it designates behavior ranging from wonder-working on the stage or at a social party (more precisely designated as "conjuring") to the easy, fluid performance of a substance ("Works like magic!" claim the ads). The usual definitions apply the word to actions which an observer deems objectively to rest on false premises. Treating a symbol as though it were equivalent to its referent is, therefore, magical. A belief that planting in the light of the moon will be successful also is labeled "magic." Trying to cure illness by sucking it from the body is either magical or "quasi-magical." The phrase "from magic to science" reveals how magic is identified with error, or at least with a kind of belief no longer accepted by the observer. The policy in this book has been not to stress the truth or falsity of exotic beliefs. Therefore, any use of "magic" which tends to identify some behavior with error manifestly is inappropriate.

As used in this book, magic designates primarily an attitude toward any aspect of experience. It is, therefore, strictly a way of knowing or believing. Magic designates the tendency to attach unfailing significance to some configuration of events (G. Wilson and M. Wilson, 1945:72–89). When defined in these terms, magical thinking stands at the opposite pole from another kind of thought in which events do not have necessary significance but merely are more or less probable, true by agreement, appropriate under stated conditions, or relative to some time and place. These are ideas that some readers may find difficult. Are not some conclusions always or inevitably true and some events necessary and, therefore, magical? The conclusion that "2 and 2 equal 4," the spelling of some word, and the dictionary meaning of a term appear to be necessary only when their conventional character is overlooked. These things are true only by agreement. The relative or conventional character of rules and definitions often is overlooked in favor of more magical attitudes.[3]

The following fictional incident (Silone, 1937:116–119) illustrates the magical attitude, which fails to recognize the relative nature of conventional agreement:

Four youths playing settemezzo had started a quarrel about the king of diamonds. In settemezzo the king of diamonds is the most important card. Matalena only had two packs of cards, and in both the king of diamonds was so worn and easily recognizable that it was impossible for the game to be fair. Daniele Maglietta made a proposal to avoid disputes.

"Since the king of diamonds is recognizable, let us substitute, say, the three of spades for it. The king of diamonds, which is recognizable, will count as the three of spades, and the three of spades, which is indistinguishable from the rest, will count as the king of diamonds."

"That's impossible," Michele Mascolo objected. "It would be impossible, even if we all agreed to it."

[3] As Bridgman (1938:64–66) says, ". . . This feeling of necessity is one of the things that I have lost; I used to have the unquestioning conviction that the conclusion of the syllogism had to follow from the premises, but now I have lost it and cannot even recapture the conviction that there is meaning here. . . . Even the statement of the syllogism itself in its most guarded form: 'If a is b and if c is a then c is b' does no more, at least as far as my own analysis can find, than sum up in compact form my past experience: namely, whenever I have encountered an a which was b, and a c which was an a then always I have noticed that c was also b. . . . The certainty of a description of past experience always has to be safeguarded against illusion or error. . . ." (Inner quotation marks around the terms of the syllogisms have been omitted in transcribing this quotation.)

"Why?"

"It's obvious," said Mascolo. "The king of diamonds is always the king of diamonds. He may be filthy, or marked, or have holes in him, but he's still the king of diamonds. This, for example, is a pipe. You ask me why. It's obvious. It is a pipe because it is a pipe. In the same way the Pope is the Pope. Why? Because he is the Pope. The king of diamonds is the king of diamonds in the same way. That's what he is and that's what he remains."

Magic, by an extension of the primarily ideological definition given above, also covers activity or other behavior that follows from a conviction of an inevitable significance residing in some person, place, thing, or action. Magic, then, can be identified in practice only by knowing the attitudinal state from which it springs. Illustrative examples may make this clearer.

It must be understood that anything can be surrounded by magic. The magic of birth ascribes an inevitable quality to the circumstance of birth. Twins, for example, may be regarded with such absolute horror (true in some places in Africa) that they are killed immediately. The birth of a child with a caul may carry a conviction about that child's future success. The magic of race seizes upon some combination of hereditary features, like skin color and hair form, and regards them as linked with some necessary quality inherent in all members of the race. How deeply felt the magical sentiments may be, is realized when even some white Americans eager to manifest good will find it impossible to eat with Negroes. Of course, many whites and Negroes in the South adhere to segregation because it is appropriate rather than absolutely necessary. A magical morality is a morality which is inflexible and intolerant. The exact way in which an act is executed becomes the sole criterion of its value. With a nonmagical morality the spirit in which the act is done also assumes significance and no act is taken to be the unfailing residence of moral value. The African Nyakyusa place magical value on the symbols of generosity. The stingy man feels the threat of his neighbors. If he fails to feast them on stated occasions, "their righteous anger will, he believes, cause illness to himself or his family. But so long as meat or beer is provided on the appropriate occasions the intention of the host is irrelevant. Certain details of material execution are taken as intrinsically right" (G. Wilson and M. Wilson, 1945:92). Magicality may appear in history when unfailing "value, significance, and sanctity" are attached to a particular period—the past, present, or future. The traditional in a way of life may be treated magically as well as, sometimes nowadays, that which is new.

In some countries magicality declines with age. Questioned about rules of games, Swiss children aged 6 to 10 years thought that rules could not be changed. As the age of 12 was approached, practically all the children thought that rules could be altered, provided the players all agreed. The children's actions corresponded to these beliefs (Piaget, 1923:Chap. 1).

Somewhat different results were obtained in questioning American Indian children (Havighurst and Neugarten, 1955:Chap. 5). Judging from Swiss norms it would be expected that by about age 12 practically all subjects would have said that it was all right to change the rules and that people of their own age could do so. Instead, among Indian children only the Navaho of Shiprock approached "this level of freedom" in the case of 11- to 13-year-olds. ". . . The other Indian tribes all showed a slower development toward moral autonomy than did Piaget's children" (*ibid.*, p. 135). The order of "moral constraint" for the tribes varies. Zuñi children are consistently marked by strong magical attitudes; Papago and Sioux come next, and then Zia and Hopi. "The order of constraint for the various Indian groups is *not* the same as their order of assimilation of white culture" (*ibid.*, p. 136). The Sioux are probably the most assimilated but the children stand high in degree of moral constraint. Magical attitudes are suggested in the attitudes of some rural Liberian traders who refuse to accept Queen Victoria shillings because "dem ole Mammy go die; him money go die too" (Schwab, 1947:180).

All procedures for coping with the universe indirectly through signs or symbols are *not* magical by the definition adopted here. The African Azande, for example, ". . . always admit that the issue of a rite is uncertain. No one can be sure that his medicines will achieve the results aimed at." Such tentativeness is the opposite of magicality. The Azande do not feel the same confidence in sign-symbol procedures that they do in direct forms of coping. They acknowledge that a person who has lost all sense of shame will also not be deterred by symbolic measures undertaken against a thief. Only " 'good men heed magic.' " The Azande prefer to supplement direct forms of coping with indirect techniques but not to substitute the latter for the former (Evans-Pritchard, 1937:466–467).

Magic is no stranger to many people who ideally espouse the impersonal world view. Americans often accept the conclusions of experts with unquestioned confidence, feel utterly convinced of the universal practicality and ultimate triumph of democracy, or capitalism, and deem Christianity to be necessary for everybody's salvation (cf. Marwick, 1956:491). Many people, however, having become familiar with other beliefs and other ways of doing things, weaken in their final, exclusive commitment to any doctrine. "No student at all familiar with studies of the past fifty years in the field of comparative cultural anthropology can well remain a dogmatic follower of any culture or any religious faith, so much has been shown about how different human beings, under different circumstances, have coped with their problems" (Stokes and Mace, 1953:237). But with increased relativity also may come uncertainty, a lack of sureness, a want of poise.

Magical thinking in a community tends to decline with expanding scale and also in response to the greater variety of behaviors which living in a large-scale society brings to a community. Where there are many ways of doing things and of interpreting the world, can any one way be final, inevitable, or necessary? Beliefs loosen, admitting an element of tolerance. Considering magic as the independent variable suggests that magical attitudes promote a sense of assurance, confidence, and security. Magically held values insure social consensus and therefore help to maintain the equilibrium and integrity of the group as well as the adaptive and adjustive functions dependent on social solidarity. Perhaps man cannot do without some magical attitudes. His very faith in tolerance and relativity may acquire magical strength. Magical beliefs also limit uncomplementary diversities. That which is held to be absolutely true or final can be contradicted only by a very bold heretic indeed.

For the same reason that magic declines with scale, magical thinking limits scale. It holds people back from contact with the new and prevents intense relations with people who follow a different way of life or possess different physical features. Rationality, the cold dispassionate estimate of the value of an act, is also inhibited by magical thought. The significance of an act cannot be separated analytically from the act itself. "If the particular execution of an act is taken as the unfailing residence of that action's value then the particular execution cannot be altered without impairing the action's value" (G. Wilson and M. Wilson, 1945:92). How magical thought patterns limit origination, and thereby elaboration, is illustrated by a few examples taken from the first national elections held in independent India (Trumbull, 1952). Because of the high rate of illiteracy each political party relied on a recognizable symbol. Emotionally powerful symbols, like the cow, could under no circumstances appear in this context, quite apart from the fact that they might lend themselves to exploitation. Two or 3 million women could not qualify as voters because they refused to reveal their own or their husband's name to a stranger.

SCIENCE

Science consists largely of systematically relating ideas, the relationships then being tested through some experimental technique. In some fields, like astronomy, geology, and sociology, experiment in the narrow sense of isolating and manipulating specific variables remains restricted. Stars, mountains, and people cannot be manipulated freely. But experimentation is not the essence of science. The basic goal of science lies in prediction, and the important object is to discover predictable relationships between events. Experiments simply offer a useful means of verifying hypotheses assumed to be predictive. Prediction can also be carried out through the systematic observation of the heavens, the earth, or the interaction of people. Through purposeful and controlled observation one may discover whether hypotheses are true or false.

As already indicated, science can be distinguished from the natural-history method of simple observation and careful description. Also it is different from technology. When a man seeks to repair a broken tool, his action bears little relationship to the work of the scientist who, having conceptualized certain phenomena, proceeds to test those propositions. "We must not . . . confuse the satisfactory solution of specific technological problems with the creation of a theoretical system of nature, even if the former may set the stage for the latter. The invention of new machines and the resolution of specific problems of practical life often occur without recognition of the general principles involved in either" (Nagel, 1948:250).

In the sense of the term as used here, science first appeared in Egypt some 2000 years before the Christian era. It started approaching its climax in fifteenth- or sixteenth-century Europe. Possibly the climax came in the twentieth century. From Europe scientific thought diffused very slowly to other parts of the world (Farrington, 1953; Butterfield, 1950:Chap. 5).

Using other definitions than the one used here, several observers have sought to identify science in small-scale, exotic cultures. Sometimes the process of reasoning about nature is made the indicator of "science." As already shown, science demands empirical observation; it should not be confused with reason. Reason, it is agreed, constitutes a universal form of behavior and also an indispensable foundation of science. Some writers maintain that successful techniques of agriculture, ceramics, and metallurgy appearing in the Middle East several thousand years ago constitute the beginning of science. Such crafts show that man had discovered sound relationships between the facts of nature (Farrington, 1953:72). Even evidence of a dugout canoe dating from the Stone Age is regarded as representing the application of then existing knowledge or science (Childe, 1936:6). That man applies his discoveries and in doing so alters his life must be granted. But it is no more sound to identify science with discovery and invention than to describe the selection of stones for stone tools as geology, or pottery making as chemistry (*ibid.*, pp. 49–50).

Science is defined as the systematic attempt to derive predictable relationships about events with the expectation that these relationships will be tested. Everybody constantly makes tentative suppositions which are proved sound when the expected results follow (Ruesch and Bateson, 1951:26). But there is nothing systematic in this. Many people even experiment in a casual fashion. Nuba farmers in the Egyptian Sudan, for example, deliberately try out new types of grain or new plots of land (Nadel, 1947:18). This casual approach to the search for knowledge is not full-fledged science. It is doubtful whether science, considered as the specialized and systematic pursuit of new knowledge, even developed out of such casual experimentation. Science has its roots in attempts to reason systematically about the world, an activity that itself is not universal but has appeared several times in human history. Systematic reasoning was known in the ancient Middle East, including Egypt; occurred among the protohistoric Greeks; and was carried on in the European Middle Ages (Whitehead, 1925:Chap. 1; Barber, 1952:49 ff.). Dissatisfaction with truth obtained solely by reason moved men to test systematically, and via prediction, their rationally derived propositions. Then science appeared.

Functions of Science

The major independent and dependent functions of science may be summed up briefly.

1. *Science thrives in a climate of rationalism.* At the same time, science encourages a detached attitude of inquiry that recognizes no limits other than those imposed by available means and knowledge. A critical approach not only to the material world but also to the events of social life is fostered.

2. *Science depends on an economic surplus.* A high rate of research cannot be maintained without a substantial economic surplus that will allow researchers to be spared from the duties of getting a living. Scientific research has been most productive in the relatively rich countries of the world and today lags most in the relatively underdeveloped areas.

3. *Science fosters technical development.* But development increases only to the extent that the newly discovered knowledge is capable of being applied to the control of the physical world and man is willing to apply it.

4. *Science encourages impersonality and nonmagicality.* The factors which condition events are conceptualized by the scientist in abstract and general terms. They are assigned a stated probability of bringing about certain phenomena. Faith in personalistic explanations tends to be weakened in association with such thinking. No necessary connections between events can be entertained when occurrences become a matter of higher or lower probability rather than of certainty.

As these functions suggest, science is directly associated with largeness of scale. The cultures in which science flourishes all belong to large-scale communities.

Part Six

GROWTH

OF WESTERN CULTURE

Of all that was done in the past you eat the fruit, either rotten or ripe.
T. S. Eliot (*1934:20*)

. . . *Posterity judges by facts and not by pretensions.*
Alexander Dumas (*1952:169*)

40.

The Middle East

THE area including what today is called Egypt, Israel, and the other countries of Southwest Asia as far east as the borders of Afghanistan and Pakistan records the earliest farming villages and large-scale civilizations found anywhere in the world (Fig. 40:1). The evidence is remarkably free from question. This is also a region to which modern western culture owes many of its constituent traits and complexes, including agriculture; sheep, goat, and cattle domestication; metallurgy; the alphabet; and religions like Judaism, Christianity, and Islam.

Five successive periods, shown in Figure 40:2, sum up the prehistory and protohistory of this region (Steward, 1949a; 1955:Chap. 11). They are: (1) the Preagricultural era, a long-enduring period of prehistory, when people lived by food gathering without agriculture or domesticated animals other than the dog; (2) the era of Incipient Agriculture, which saw the first more or less tentative efforts at food production (direct archeological evidence of this period is very rare in the Middle East and, for that matter, elsewhere in the world); (3) the Formative period, marked by the introduction of new techniques and the further mastery of old ones, including basketry, pottery, weaving, metallurgy, and construction in wood and stone; (4) the era of Regional Florescent Nations, which saw the diffusion of culture over a wide area together with the growth of maximal units of administration, including empires; and (5) the era of Cyclical Conquests, during which no new basic techniques entered culture but militarism grew, together with the size of political units. As the name suggests, this was a time of recurrent warfare.

No claim is made that a similar unfolding of these stages took place independently in Egypt and in Mesopotamia. It is not assumed that farming, animal husbandry, political kingship, metallurgy, irrigation, and writing were invented several times. No doubt marked diffusion linked the subregions of the Middle East, where no serious natural barriers limit intercourse. But diffusion by itself accounts only for how parts of culture came to be distributed according to a certain spatial pattern. It does not explain any recurrent functional relationship that might exist between certain traits (Steward, 1955:182).

FIG. 40:1. Some Countries of the Modern Middle East and Other Place Names.

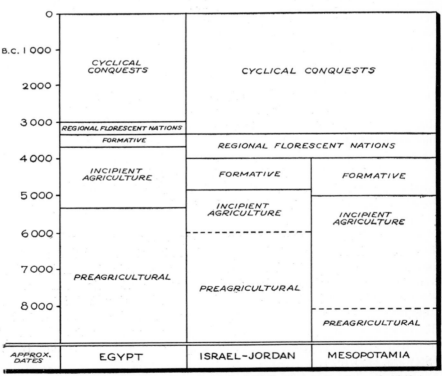

FIG. 40:2. Periods of Culture Growth in the Middle East (After Steward, 1949a).

The object of this chapter will be to see in functional terms how the culture of Southwest Asia altered from one of these periods to the next. The survey inevitably extends from the range of prehistory into the era of written history (see pp. 34–35). Thanks to the increasing volume of documents for the four millennia prior to the Christian era, greater specificity becomes possible in reconstructing cultural content in the later periods. The aim is not to furnish exhaustive accounts of archeological discoveries or political events. Nor will all the known local phases of early culture be described. The aim is to omit many details and to attempt meaningful synthesis. The readings specified in the chapter will refer the reader to more detailed sources. Most of the dates before 3000 B.C. are likely to be revised through future research. They must be regarded as very approximate.

THE MILIEU

The five cultural eras will be treated as manifested in the archeology of three broad subareas (Fig. 40:1): (1) Egypt (actually, mainly the Nile Valley), (2) Israel-Jordan (including sometimes Lebanon and eastern Anatolia, as Asiatic Turkey is called), and (3) Mesopotamia. The latter, strictly speaking, refers to the land of the Tigris and Euphrates rivers but here includes part of Syria, Iraq, and Iran. With Arabia there is no need to be concerned. Farther east lies the Indus River Valley of Pakistan, where civilization also grew up but to which only incidental reference will be made. This general region, extending in an arc from the Nile to the Indus, is often called the Fertile Crescent.

Geographically the Middle East today occupies one of the hottest and driest zones in the world, a desert belt stretching from North Africa to northwestern India (Childe, 1952:Chap. 2). A few river valleys traverse the desert: the Nile, Euphrates, Tigris, and Indus of Pakistan. Another feature of the area is the relative absence of internal physiographic barriers. The Mediterranean Sea with the Caucasus, Elburz, and Hindu Kush mountains form the northern border of the zone.

Long ago the Middle East received more rainfall than it does today. While northern Europe was glacier covered, regular winter rainstorms from the Atlantic passed over North Africa and Southwest Asia. Rivers and lakes, the beds of which have become dry, carried off the rainfall. Parkland and savannah made green at least parts of what (outside of the irrigated oases) today is largely a bare landscape. Many animals found life possible in this environment and human hunters preyed on the available store of food. Even after the main ice sheets receded from Europe at the end of the Pleistocene, the storms continued to cover the Middle East as they blew in from the Atlantic. But around 5000 B.C. the storms began to settle down on their present northern track. Desert conditions set in and have left only the river valleys and a few other oases fertile.

Differences within the area are recognizable. Thus Egypt is divided between the open, marshy, and readily accessible plain of the delta, and Upper Egypt, which consists of a narrow rift, the Nile Valley, bordered by rocky walls (Childe, 1952:Chap. 3). The rocky walls are occasionally broken by the dry, eroded gorges of old streams. Desiccation in the surrounding countryside probably made the fertile valley a favorite dwelling place for man and animals in the fifth millennium. Later the valley naturally proved quite defensible, especially since the surrounding country was unfavorable to the growth of potentially hostile powers. Egypt had more to fear from her neighbors in Southwest Asia. Rival empires found it easy to spread in and beyond Mesopotamia and in spreading they fell on one another and encroached on Egyptian sovereignty. Mountain people in the east and north also made forays on the rich, fertile plain of Mesopotamia. The dearth of stone and wood in the lower Tigris-Euphrates Valley meant that the people who settled in this fertile land had to depend considerably on trade. In Iraq and Syria the land is higher and some valleys still today receive enough water through rainfall for crops and pasture. The relatively isolated, protohistoric people of these valleys were not readily managed by the nations of the plain, which, however, saw real value in the stone and wood resources of the elevated country.

This brief picture of the environment indicates a situation especially favorable for irrigation farming. It is a little rash but nevertheless plausible to say that the Middle East might not have become the cradle of civilization had it not assumed desert conditions almost simultaneously with the invention and adoption of food production.

PREAGRICULTURAL PERIOD

The Preagricultural era is largely known from its stone implements. These change from highly generalized (i.e., all-purpose) hand axes to more specialized projectile points, scrapers (presumably for working animal skins), and stone blades. Control over the chipping of stone became ever greater during the hundreds of thousands of years occupied by the Preagricultural period. Toward the end of the era, namely, in the Middle Stone Age, very small implements, called microliths, started to be made. Their use is not known.

Still speaking only in terms of tools, the Preagricultural period ended at about the time when, in addition to chipping flint into useful forms, men began to grind closer-grained rocks, after preliminary pecking, into shape. The New Stone (Neolithic) Age, as this succeeding period is often called, is better remembered for the fact that it saw the introduction of the earliest food production. Hence, here it is called the period of Incipient Agriculture. Pottery, too, was introduced in this period.

It is difficult to go far beyond artifacts in reconstructing the Preagricultural way of life. The people were hunters. Judging from hunting-collecting communities that have been studied ethnographically, we may state that undoubtedly they moved around a great deal, following game and collecting vegetable food. As already mentioned, this region, now largely desert except where irrigation permits cultivation, once was forested and rich in game. Stone Age Egyptian sites often lie near the Nile but on high terraces which escaped annual flooding. Later, with the coming of farming, people moved down to the valley floor to take advantage of the rich alluvial soil and water. In Mesopotamia, Preagricultural sites are not found on the plain either (much of which was covered by the Persian Gulf throughout the period) but in the northern highlands—for example, in the Elburz Mountains —where, too, some very early, though not the earliest, agricultural sites have been uncovered. Shortly before the end of the Preagricultural period a new weapon, the bow, appeared in Egypt. It probably had diffused from farther west in North Africa. Also relatively late in time stone mortars appeared. They doubtlessly served for grinding flour from wild grains. Communities must have been small, culturally quite homogeneous, and self-sufficient. Specialists did not ply diverse activities nor could there have been any significant degree of trade. Fighting no doubt broke out on occasion but organized war was not possible as long as population density remained low.

PERIOD OF INCIPIENT AGRICULTURE

The best available evidence, including radiocarbon dating, indicates that the food-producing revolution, which was to usher in many profound cultural changes, began in the hilly flanks of the region east of the Mediterranean Sea before 6000 B.C. (Braidwood, 1952:10–13). These flanks still possess sufficient rainfall today to support a spring crop. Conditions may have been favorable to cultivation even say 9000 or 10,000 years ago. Sites like Fayum, located at what is now a dried-up lake bed in northern Egypt, and Tasa on the upper Nile are considerably later in time.

One of the earliest sites of Incipient Agriculture is Karim Shahir in northern Iraq (Fig. 40:3). The date is about 6000 B.C. Mortars indicate the use of cereals but their cultivation is not evidenced directly. Polished celts (Fig. 42:3) may have served as hoes but the accompanying sickles might have been used as well for harvesting wild grain. Hotu and Belt caves in the Elburz Mountains of northern Iran contain a sequential record of cultural growth from the Middle Stone Age (which radiocarbon dating suggests extended from about 8500 to 6135 B.C.) to nonceramic, pottery, and food-producing horizons (Coon, 1951b, 1952; cf. pp. 46–48). In the upper Middle Stone Age levels of Belt cave (levels 17 to 11) the gazelle and ox are abundantly represented by bones. Sheep and goats are much rarer. In the subsequent, early farming levels (10 to 8) the ox practically disappears, to reappear together with the pig, in probably domesticated form, in the pottery levels (7 to 1). The consumption of seal declines as other food became available. The relatively large number of immature sheep and goats killed from level 7 upward (immature specimens outnumber mature ones) suggests that the people slaughtered mainly domesticated kids and goats, perhaps leaving the adults to supply milk and wool. The appearance of pottery about 5000 B.C. (level 7) marks the end of the era of Incipient Agricul-

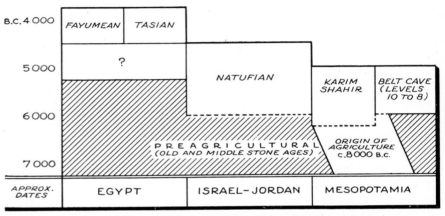

Fig. 40:3. Some Phases of Culture in the Period of Incipient Agriculture.

ture. Early ceramics are wide, open, flat-bottomed bowls of simple profile without handles or spouts. In level 3 other wares begin—including red, brown, and gray types of pottery, some decorated with painted lines and cross-hatching. The stimulation for some of this ware probably came from other places. In Hotu cave a sterile gap follows the pottery layers. Only centuries later did copper, bronze, and iron-using people reoccupy that site.

A probable reconstruction of the Belt cave culture, based on a detailed analysis of evidence, contains three points which research in the Elburz Mountains may be able to test: (1) During Late Stone Age times the inhabitants were hunters of the gazelle, wild ox, sheep, and goat. They began to domesticate the goat in this phase. (2) Sheep came next to be domesticated but still without plant cultivation. (3) With the adoption of cereal cultivation (suggested by sickle blades and celts in the last 8 levels), weaving, pottery, and cattle domestication also appeared. Plants as a new source of food allowed many sheep and goats to be spared for their milk and wool. It is now that the bones of immature animals come to exceed those of adults (Coon, 1951b:50).

A dated summary of the phases of culture leading from the Middle Stone

Age to the Neolithic Age, or the period of Incipient Agriculture, in northern Iran is given in Table 46.

TABLE 46. Appearance of Agriculture and Animal Husbandry, Northern Iran

Cultural Data	Approximate Radiocarbon Date (B.C.)
Late Neolithic: pottery, grain, pigs, cows	5330 ± 260
Early Neolithic: sheep, goats, no pottery	5840 ± 330
Dry Mesolithic culture	6620 ± 380
Wet Mesolithic culture	9530 ± 550

SOURCE: Coon, *1954*:143.

The Natufian phase, named from the site Wadi Natuf, near present-day Jerusalem, has also been found in several caves in different parts of Israel and Jordan, including upper levels of the long-inhabited cave of Mount Carmel. Natufian culture is characterized by microlithic blades and points, blades to serve as sickles, and stone objects that may have been provided as hoes or picks. There is no direct evidence of food cultivation, but stone mortars and pestles may have been used to grind grain as well as red ocher. With stone engraving tools the people carved animal heads on the handles of long bone sickles in which flint teeth were set end to end. A dog skull testifies to the domestication of at least that animal but ox and pig bones may also belong to domesticated varieties. Bone harpoons and other hunting weapons indicate that food gathering certainly provided some measure of subsistence. Bone pins and awls, pendants, bone carved to resemble deer's teeth, beads, a flint-chiseled phallus, and a stone-carved human head are other elements comprising the Natufian phase. These people practiced removal of the incisor teeth, a custom also found in Africa. The dead were buried in tightly contracted, or, somewhat later, flexed position.

In Egypt the earliest known farming phases were relatively late but still included considerable hunting and fishing (as indicated by an abundance of arrowpoints, harpoons, and barbless hooks for angling) along with wheat, barley, and animal domestication. The Fayumean phase has received a radiocarbon date of 4145 B.C. ± 250; it is better taken as belonging to the Formative era. Bones of cattle, sheep, goats, pigs, and cats presumably belong to domesticated species that provided people with skins, meat, and other products, as well as companionship. Harvested grains were stored in clay storage jars or mat-lined pits sunk into the ground. To break the earth for planting, farmers used chipped flint hoes, but whether crops were watered artificially cannot be said. Wooden sickles used by harvesters contain the usual small flint teeth. Mortars and pestles used in late Stone Age times were replaced by saddle-shaped querns, about 20 inches long and 10

inches wide. These were used with rubbing stones (i.e., manos). Natufian
pottery was decorated with incised lines filled with white paint. Vessels also
received an interior blackening by being inverted over fire. Ivory ornaments,
baskets, leather, and linen garments (the latter made from cultivated flax)
represent new crafts. The absence of house remains suggests that shelter
may have been of reeds or some other impermanent material. Stone palettes
for grinding and mixing pigments indicate a form of bodily adornment.
Beads of ostrich shell and stone were also used. Tasa has about 40 graves
that contain evidence of careful burial, the corpse being flexed and wrapped
in skin mats or straw before interment in oval-shaped pits. In death the
hands covered the face. Few *Beigaben* accompanied the deceased.

The earliest farmers are shown by the archeological record to have used
stone tools. Favored by a relatively sedentary way of life they were developing new skills, like ceramics, woodworking, weaving, and work in hard stone,
which would constitute the bases of future specialization. Burnished and
painted pottery and carved sickle handles show that time and effort were
also devoted to the nonutilitarian expression of feeling. The overall picture
is one of communities possessing little internal specialization and living in
great isolation from one another, yet exposed to diffusion. For all practical
purposes these communities remained self-sufficient, only a few luxury goods
being secured in trade. Thus at Fayum clamshells have been found that apparently originated along the Red Sea. The male generative organ carved in
flint by the Natufians (later, similar phallic sculpture came to be modeled
in clay) was probably designed to symbolize reproduction—perhaps of food
plants as well as offspring. A focus on death or burial appeared in Egypt
that was to persist for centuries.

FORMATIVE PERIOD

The Formative era is marked by the substantial accumulation of new capital. In addition to tools and a varied assemblage of ornaments, social capital is recognized in houses, graves, basketry, pottery, woodwork, spun thread,
woven fabrics, animals, and, of course, agricultural land. But some of the
techniques represented in this wealth began with the very inception of agriculture. However, in the period now entered, mastery of them increases.
Among the most important new techniques is metallurgy. Metal along with
the smith's equipment is added to capital goods. Wealth begins to be employed in a small way to symbolize the status and prestige of individuals in
society.

Each of the phases of the Formative period in the Middle East was spread
over a relatively broad territory, indicating that diffusion had been stepped
up from the previous era. New forms of political organization also made
their appearance and bestowed on man the ability to coördinate relatively

large human aggregates. The use to which this new power would be put remains to be seen.

Representative Sites

In Mesopotamia the Formative is known from Jarmo, Hassuna, and Samarra sites, as Figure 40:4 indicates, located near the headwaters of the

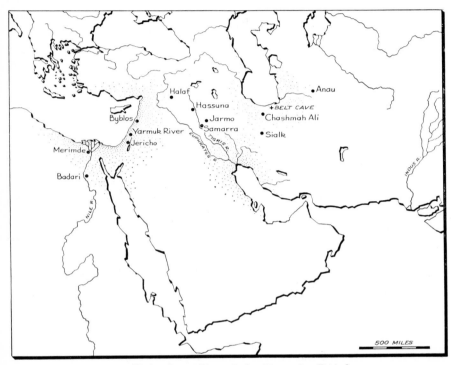

FIG. 40:4.   Some Sites of the Formative Period.

Tigris River at the edge of the highlands in northern Mesopotamia. Levels 7 to 1 of Belt cave really belong to this era (see pp. 697–698) and so do Tepe Sialk and Chashmah Ali, located near modern Teheran, and Tell Halaf in eastern Syria on a tributary of the upper Euphrates.[1] The center column of Figure 40:5 shows levels 18 to 9 of the Jericho site to be Formative. Pottery appears only late in level 9. In Egypt, Formative culture is known from Merimde, located at the southern apex of the Nile delta, and Badari, in Upper Egypt near Tasa. Sand in the refuse heaps at Merimde testifies to the encroaching desert that possibly contributed to the eventual

[1] The words "tepe" and "tell" refer to mounds that represent the debris of vanished settlements.

abandonment of the site. Badarian culture, representing a continuation and elaboration of the Tasian phase, may be partially a creation of Negroid people who moved into the Nile Valley from the south and mixed with earlier inhabitants. The Formative era has also been called the Early Chalcolithic ("copper-stone") or Copper Age as well as an era of Peasant Efficiency.

In the hills of northern Iraq, Jarmo offers an early village assemblage that has been dated by radiocarbon technique as having flourished between 5270 and 4630 B.C. Houses were made of firmly packed mud, occasionally on a stone foundation. Pottery was introduced by diffusion rather than local invention. Villagers also installed baked-in-place clay basins scooped from the house floors; these probably were storage pits, such as also turn up in Jericho. Portable clay vessels appear in the last third of the Jarmoan phase,

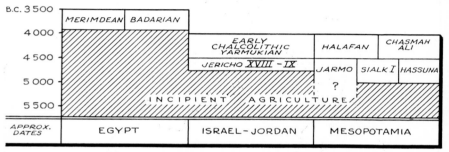

FIG. 40:5. Some Phases of Culture in the Formative Period.

when containers were also carved from stone. Female and animal figurines were modeled in clay. A single carved stone phallus has been discovered. Saddle querns and carbonized grains of wheat and barley point to plant cultivation. However, it is possible that the cereals may have been collected in the wild state. People did gather wild peas and a kind of pistachio nut. About 95 percent of the animal bones belong to the sheep, goat, cattle, pig, and dog, and 5 percent to other species. An extremely large proportion of the slaughtered animals were yearlings. This is indirect proof that such animals were domesticated and not hunted and also suggests, as at Belt cave, that the adults were too valuable to eat. Here as in nearby Hassuna the ax and adze provided relatively specialized cutting tools, suggesting the importance of woodworking (Braidwood and Braidwood, 1950). Circular as well as rectangular houses characterize the earliest Hassunan mode of life.

Jericho, in Jordan, furnishes a stratified site where successive changes in Formative culture can be observed. The lower levels of the mound reveal a way of life (sometimes called Tahunian) also found at other places in Israel and Jordan. Arrowpoints and microliths are abundant. Traces exist of a building with stone foundations and a floor of limestone chips smoothed over with lime. Similar floors were made farther north at Byblos in Lebanon. The structure was rebuilt no less than six times and probably served for worship. Evidence of agriculture is absent on these levels. But food gatherers cannot be expected to have erected a substantial building like this one. Only on level 9 do pottery and saddle-shaped querns, on which flour was ground with a rubbing stone, show up. Mortars and pestles continue. Undoubtedly farming had been practiced for some centuries by the time this phase was reached. Before pottery, people at Jericho set clay-lined storage bins into the house floors. When portable vessels made their appearance they at first remained sun-dried and unfired. Then pots came to be baked and painted. Out of clay people also fashioned unbaked figurines of human beings and animals. Species are difficult to ascertain, so little interest or skill did the makers devote to realistic modeling.

Artifacts from the Yarmukian phase in Israel include a large number of chipped flint objects and some large cutting tools possessing a cutting edge given by polishing. Stone sinkers for nets are evidence that the people fished. The nets and spindle whorls in turn testify to spinning. Pottery, of course, was also made. The bones of calves, sheep, and goats suggest pastoralism, and the dog was likewise domesticated. Although sickles bearing flint teeth, mortars, and querns have been recovered, direct traces of agriculture are still lacking. In addition to phallic stones a number of schematic female figurines prominently displaying the sexual characteristics may be evidence of some kind of collective representation who was conceived of as a female charged with maintaining fertility. But this is largely conjecture.

Cultural Reconstruction

Although hunting and fishing with nets and traps continued to supply a measure of food during the Formative period, the importance of food gathering shrank into relative insignificance alongside agriculture. The boomerang was used in Badari, perhaps as a hunting device. The farmers succeeded in cultivating harvests larger than had ever before been taken from the land. This is demonstrated by the large storage pits used to preserve crops. The Formative was a time for marshaling available technical resources rather than introducing basic innovations. Sickles and stone implements for breaking the earth remained practically unchanged from earlier times. Carefully prepared, mud-walled, shallow threshing pits equipped with drains may represent a new development.

Growing control over material is also evidenced in ceramics. Very fine pottery came to be made in time, being symmetrically modeled in a great variety of shapes and decorated with burnishing as well as quite elaborate painting. Samarran pottery is interesting for the way in which the decoration follows the limits that would be imposed in trying to weave designs in a basket. In other words, instead of taking advantage of the freedom allowed by painting on a flat surface, the draftsman arranged his design in zones and deliberately made his animal figures angular, no doubt thereby satisfying traditional tastes. This makes an interesting instance of reinterpretation (see pp. 237–241). Pottery ovens, containing a means for controlling the draft and capable of reaching a temperature of 1200° F., appear at the end of the period.

If a Halafan vessel design belonging to this period really represents a man in a chariot, then it constitutes the earliest evidence of the wheel. Stone tools were still used almost universally, but Egypt, Israel, and Mesopotamia witnessed the first hammering of naturally found pieces of pure copper into desired shapes. Casting the metal in open molds to form pins, beads, and drills for boring stone marks a transition from the Formative to the era of Regional Florescent Nations and will be discussed below.

Habitations were diverse but usually substantial. The Merimdeans lived in oval houses erected in pits and walled with reed mats. Later mud walls came to be constructed. A ladder served the occupants for entry and exit. The dwellings were aligned in lanes and contained raised fireplaces. In Mesopotamia multiroomed mud houses were used before the close of the period. Streets in Tell Halaf were paved with cobblestones. Of nonresidential structures only temples may be recognized, like the shrine at Tell Halaf, located in the center of the village.

Burials contain evidence that people took pains with their bodily appearance. Nose plugs, beads of hard, precious stone, combs, and various styles of fixing the hair and beard are indicated over the entire area. Men wore bracelets and women painted their eyes with malachite ground on rectangular slate palettes. Linen and leather provided material for clothing.

Trade increased during the Formative period but mainly enabled people to secure luxury goods not available locally. In Egypt, basalt for vases together with ivory, shells, turquoise, and copper was imported by the Badarians. Perhaps they sent out expeditions for these products, supporting the travelers with food. Clay models show that these Nile people possessed boats. From the Persian Gulf shells were brought across the mountains to Sialk while the Tell Halaf folk quarried volcanic glass for export. There may have been three kinds of specialists living in the larger villages: traders or sailors, metallurgists working with copper, and administrators or priests. Some of the luxury goods traded probably functioned to reinforce the authority and power of administrators. One suggestion that social inequalities were known by this time lies in the way some Badarian dead are buried apart from others. Their graves are also somewhat larger. Seals for stamping ownership marks on goods may reflect a rising consciousness of individual property and its unequal distribution.

Burial patterns diverge between Egypt and Mesopotamia. In the former, preoccupation with death continues. The Merimde phase includes burials within the house, the flexed corpse facing east; Badarians interred their dead in single graves grouped into cemeteries and without much regard for directional orientation. The corpse was wrapped in linen and skins and, pacing the communities' growing wealth, was accompanied by rich *Beigaben*, including figurines and live cattle, goats, and dogs. Weapons are scarce in all burials of this period, suggesting (in combination with evidence like the absence of specialized military traits) that fighting did not greatly occupy the self-sufficient peasant villagers. However, the first wall went up around Jericho at this time. Mesopotamia practiced flexed burial. *Beigaben* remained scarce, as in Preagricultural times.

It is hard to infer much of the ideological life of the people. Female figurines carved in ivory or modeled in clay were distributed from Egypt to Mesopotamia. They again suggest a female collective representation (a so-called "mother goddess"). Perhaps she was postulated to control the growing crops on which people depended so heavily for life.

Several problems faced by the early farmers are plausibly inferred (Childe, 1946). First, animals, land, and crops provided a temptation for hungry robbers, some of whom may have had little interest in cultivation or lacked fertile lands of their own. Second, drought, flood, frost, and hail periodically threatened the crops and herds. When these threats materialized they spelled famine for the self-sufficient village, whose resources were too small to tide it over a bad year. The threat of bad harvests would remain for many centuries. In India not until the coming of railroads and increased crops from newly irrigated lands did famines finally come under control (Griffiths, 1952:180–189). A third problem stemmed from the luxury imports of some villagers. To continue or to increase the enjoyment of these satisfactions payment had to be forthcoming. The buyers had to be ready to give up a greater measure of self-sufficiency and to contrive to increase the exportable surplus. If all the village did not share in the luxuries, then those who did had to accumulate the necessary wealth for payment. Evidence from the period of Regional Florescent Nations will indicate how well they succeeded.

PERIOD OF REGIONAL FLORESCENT NATIONS

Had agriculture remained confined to the highlands and along rivers, being carried out by hand alone, perhaps the world would not so soon have seen elaborate temples and tombs, well-defined class structure, or powerful administrators controlling great riches and many people. That the Middle East around 4000 B.C. began to manifest these features seems closely related to two basic farming innovations that appeared simultaneously: irrigation and the plow. Before examining the dynamic significance of these elements some representative sites of the period will be mentioned.

Representative Sites

About 4000 years before the Christian era, at about the time that agriculture, pottery, and village life finally reached the British Isles, Mesopotamian culture spread from the highlands into the lower Euphrates and Tigris valleys (Fig. 40:6). Here is situated the type site of Ubaidan culture—Al Ubaid (Fig. 40:7). The Proto-Sumerian settlers of Ubaid and other cities of the plain had probably migrated from the north. They moved into an

FIG. 40:6. Northern and Southern Mesopotamia. Map shows river mouths in protohistoric era.

extremely fertile alluvial plain near the estuaries of the rivers. In the fifth millennium Sumer was a swampy country, subject to regular flooding. The settlers found a climate considerably warmer than in the north. Although they drained some of the marshes for fields, the country continued to shelter much wild life so that fishing (from boats) and hunting were highly productive undertakings. Date palms grew wild. The Ubaid people and their neighbors exploited these and other resources, including the fine alluvial mud, which they made into bricks or, later, baked into writing tablets (Chiera, 1938:17–18). Some customary resources were lacking, like flint, stone suitable for building, timber, and copper. These materials had to be imported from the northern highlands. From the start, therefore, the people of the plain became dependent on trade. From the Ubaid phase grew Su-

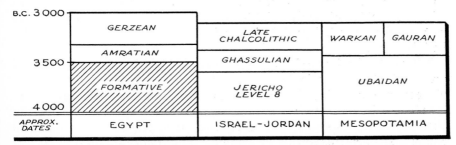

Fig. 40:7. Some Phases of Culture in the Period of Regional Florescent Nations.

merian culture. It is not certain, however, that the Sumerians were descended physically from the people of Al Ubaid and adjacent cities; perhaps fresh invasions brought a new population into the estuary country. Certainly Sumerian culture shows continuity with the Ubaid phase and links it to that of Early Dynastic times. Ubaidan culture was widespread in the river valley and extended as far as Tepe Gawra, located a short distance north of Nineveh. Here in the highlands Gauran, a later phase of northern Mesopotamian culture, grew up. Ubaidan material is also found on the lowest levels of Ur. Later material from that site belongs to the Uruk phase, which for present purposes is subsumed under the term "Warkan." Jemdet Nasr on the Tigris is, with Warka, an important site of the southern, or Warkan, phase of Regional Florescent Nations. Warka in turn gave rise to Erech, the Biblical city. Susa, located east of Sumer, received influences from these cities but manifests distinct traditions of its own. Sialk continued to be occupied during Regional Florescent Nations. Meanwhile, far away on the plateau of Turkestan in Central Asia, Anau, a site occupied since Halafan times, borrowed elements from the culture of Sialk.

In Egypt the period is known from Amrah, a hundred miles upriver from Badari, as well as Gerzeh, farther down the Nile. Elements from the latter phase traversed the length of the river in northern Egypt. Gerzean culture shows strong affinities with Asia even though it also continues the Amratian tradition. These facts show how the Formative tendency for distinct ways of life to spread and bring about subregional uniformities became intensified during the period of emerging nations.

Technology

Agriculture expanded in both the Egyptian and Mesopotamian river valleys as canals were dug to drain or irrigate new land. Before the end of this period was reached use of the wooden plow fitted with a wooden mattock helped further to increase the area of land that could be cultivated by an individual family. The ox, or some other tractable animal, harnessed to the plow furnished a new source of energy for supplementing human brawn. In the Mesopotamian delta harvests were now taken with clay sickles set with the familiar microlithic flint teeth. New crops included the date in the east and the grape in Egypt. Wine probably joined beer as a popular alcoholic beverage.

Why did a family need the larger harvest which the plow enabled it to produce?[2] The answer lies in growing interdependence. The food-producing villages were becoming closely linked to other groups in the larger society. The matter is understandable if one keeps in mind that the era of Regional Florescent Nations also saw the growth of urban centers and in them the rise of craftsmen specializing in manufacturing, trade, administration, and ritual. These specialists no longer produced the food they and their families needed to survive. A thousand years earlier many such specialists could not have been supported. Farmers could not have produced enough surplus through manual agriculture alone. Now, though, the animal-drawn plow enabled human productivity to be increased. A surplus easily could be produced above what a family needed or desired to consume. Markets for that surplus existed in the towns and cities. Farmers became specialists. They spent their working time producing crops in return for the services of manufacturers, traders, and other specialists. Exactly how some of the latter, especially administrators and ritual leaders (both offices may have been combined in the same person) managed to persuade the food producers to part with wealth is not entirely clear. Written records in the succeeding period of Cyclical Conquests attest to feudalism and tenancy. That is, the farmers owed dues or rent to the landowners (in Mesopotamia, ideally speaking, to the god and temple), who, in turn, supported many craftsmen. Shepherds represent another specialism of the time. The shepherd's crook, which the Catholic Church uses as a ritual symbol carried by a bishop, is known from the Gerzean phase.

---

[2] The reader is invited to check the following analysis against the functional interpretation of agriculture on pp. 315–317. Also see the significance of industrial manufacturing for urbanization, discussed on pp. 335–340.

Most dwellings contained only a single room and were made of mud bricks that had been dried in the sun. The houses were roofed with wood. Doors in Mesopotamia pivoted in stone sockets. Furniture increased a little, starting with stools and ending with beds. Temples grew in elaboration. In southern Mesopotamia, at Eridu, the first temple was only about 9 feet square. The people's successful adaptation in their new environment was followed by successive reconstructions of the building until it became over 40 feet long and was mounted on a platform (ziggurat) that kept it above flood levels of the river. Later the size reached 77 by 40 feet and the platform 87 by 52 feet before going on to reach cathedral proportions in the Warkan phase. Pillars, limestone-faced platforms, and whitewashed walls painted with polychrome frescoes helped to make temples even more imposing. Egyptian rock-cut tombs foreshadow the monumental structures to come.

In Al Ubaid and elsewhere, instead of working only with rare pieces of natural copper which could be hammered into shape, coppersmiths learned to reduce copper ore to metal and, later, at Jemdet Nasr, to separate silver from lead. Reduction meant heating with charcoal certain stones that did not look in the least like metallic copper. But "they are fortunately brightly colored and so the sort of stones early man looked for as pigments or charms" (Childe, 1946:69). The discovery that these stones could be transformed into metal greatly enlarged the supply of that substance. Both reduction and the subsequent casting of molten metal required high temperatures. Yet bellows for this purpose are not ascertainable directly in the Middle East before 1500 B.C. The development of metallurgy probably was favored by the advantages of the new substance over stone (e.g., metal is more durable and can be cast into various shapes) as well as by the scarcity of stone in deltaic Mesopotamia. The coppersmiths produced pins, drills, adzes, axes, razors, harpoons, knives or daggers, saws, chisels, and figurines. In Israel copper arrowpoints quite displaced the stone variety. In most places, though, ax and adze blades also continued to be made of stone. In Israel, for example, stone tools were not displaced wholly until about 2500. Gold and silver were cast as well as copper but the rarity of these metals scarcely permitted their use for tools. The discovery of bronze, an alloy of tin and copper, was a momentous event in prehistory. Not only did it bring into existence a stronger metal—one promptly adopted for a variety of tools —but it also stimulated trade. Deposits of tin ore are relatively rare and the bronzesmiths of the Middle East had to look far afield for a dependable supply of this metal.

The incomplete archeological records furnish only a partial idea of the variety of dress during the fourth millennium. Amratian and Gerzean patterns of women's dress included white skirts worn, perhaps, with the breasts exposed. Men wore the penis sheath. Such sheaths today are primarily found in the southwest Pacific but also occur in Africa and South America (Birket-Smith, 1946:209). In southern Mesopotamia women also wore little clothing. Shaving, leaving only a beard, and wigs for women (worn after they had shaved the head) occurred in Egypt and Mesopotamia. Ornaments were of gold, silver, copper, ivory, precious stone, and tortoise shell. Stone palettes on which to mix body paints persist from earlier times. The margins were decorated with elaborately carved animal and hunting scenes. The use of hunting as an element in representational art is characteristic of the culture of Regional Florescent Nations. Another contemporary object from Egypt is a board game. The clay playing board is divided into 18 squares; the accompanying dozen game pieces are of clay coated with wax.

Land and sea transport reached new peaks of efficiency. On land the wheel could hardly have been practical for transportation until, close to the end of the period, the ox and ass replaced human energy as the motive power for the cart. Some idea of early wheeled vehicles may be obtained by moving ahead to the Early Dynastic phase (Cyclical Conquests). Wheels then were from 20 to 30 inches in diameter and consisted of 3 pieces of wood clamped together with wooden struts. Leather tires may have been held in place by copper nails—the nails are definitely shown in models and paintings. They project from the rims like cogs. Copper bolts or leather thongs secured the axle to the body of the wagon. Collars for the draft animals were accompanied by metal rings which passed through the harness beast's lips and attached to reins.

Ships are known from a model in a late Ubaid grave and from wall and vase paintings belonging to Gerzean culture. Egyptian vessels were large, fitted with cabins. Some even possessed the amenity of a canopy. A single painting exhibits a sail but most of the boats are shown propelled with oars, a helmsman sitting in the stern. One vessel in a Gerzean painting is unusual; it may have been of foreign origin, perhaps from the Israeli coast or lower Mesopotamia. Other evidence of heavy foreign commerce is at hand. Egypt, for example, secured wood from Syria, cedar and marble from the Aegean region. Southern Mesopotamia brought down stone, wood, and metal from the northern highlands.

Social Organization and Ideology

Irrigation, drainage canals, and temples furnish indirect proof that during the period of Regional Florescent Nations efficient means existed for securing large-scale social coöperation through administrative devices. The administrators, whose beginnings were seen in the Formative era, now possessed considerably more power over larger aggregates of people. Toward the end of the period they became eager to impose that power on political systems held together by other administrators. In Egypt, originally the home of small, independent nomes (from the Greek *nomos*, meaning "law"), each with its ruler and divine symbols, kingdoms emerged, one in the north and the other in the south. City-states, actually towns with their surrounding countryside, coalesced in Mesopotamia. Simultaneously these nations of the plain armed to defend themselves against one another and from the onslaughts of raiders from the hills, who partially subsisted on the plunder taken from the rich cities. Devastation of cities came frequently toward 3000 but nearly always they sprang up again. The satisfactions afforded in one way or another by urban life must have been great.

Administration no doubt benefited from an origination that appeared at both ends of the Fertile Crescent late in Regional Florescent Nations—writing. The technique apparently originated in the temples of Mesopotamia, where it helped in keeping track of who had donated tribute, paid rent, or offered his tax to the house of the god. The earliest writing may have been purely pictographic, that is, dependent solely upon pictorial representations for the signification of objects and the symbolization of ideas. However, the earliest *known* writing from Sumer includes, in addition to pictographic signs, other signs more highly conventionalized. In Mesopotamia writing began with the use of a pointed instrument to draw lines in soft clay. Soon a stylus possessing an end that was shaped like the blade of a wedge came to be employed. Hence the term "cuneiform" ("wedgelike") to describe the writing. With a stylus the scribe impressed, rather than drew, the signs on which communication depended. It was a labor-saving innovation which also hastened the increasing conventionalization of the pictographs. In addition to saving time and energy the stylus possessed other developmental features. With a pointed instrument signs were often likely to be torn out when lines crossed. Drawing the point across the wet material heaped up clay in the direction of the line and so blurred the outline of the completed sign. These difficulties were overcome by impressing rather than drawing the lines (G. R. Driver, 1954:33).

Surviving early writing from Mesopotamia often reveals several meanings for single signs. Thus the sign for "male organ" also communicated the idea "to stand up." Sometimes plural meanings became segregated and attached to separate signs, thereby increasing the number of characters to be learned. Another early process consisted in modifying a sign by additional strokes, or combining two distinct signs, in order to express further concepts. Thus the sign for "great" and "man" were fused to read *lugal* or "king." This latter process naturally facilitated the communication of abstract ideas without increasing the number of characters. But it also contributed to confusion. Some signs that already possessed several meanings now came to acquire still further meanings in combination with one another. Determinative signs, serving to indicate the class of an object or idea, were invented to overcome such confusion. However, Mesopotamia scribes soon had to memorize 2000 or more signs standing for more than that number of concepts. A system for writing numbers dates from close to the end of the period.

Toward the end of Regional Florescent Nations at Jemdet Nasr some signs, in addition to the other duties they carried, came to represent syllables. The sign for *ti*, "arrow," which in some contexts also signified *til*, "life," now came to be read simply as it sounded, "ti" or "til," without reference to meaning. With the agreement that signs could stand for syllables, any words containing those syllables as component elements could be written. The pictograph or ideograph had become a phonogram. Man was on the road to a phonetic alphabet in which each sign would stand for a distinct sound unit.

Seals were made in the shape of cylinders so that their pictographic designs could readily be impressed on a clay tablet or the clay seal of a vessel. In Mesopotamia where they originated, such seals are both narrative and purely decorative. The former show a man feeding a temple herd, a ceremony, or a huntsman defending a calving cow against a lion. The latter contain figures, like a lion-headed eagle, that the cylinder rhythmically repeats as it makes its mark.

Graves and tombs offer insight into the ideological life and social stratification of the predynastic Middle East. In Egypt the early focus on death and burial continued, but component customs became more elaborate. The Amratians painted and tattooed the corpse, which was then doubled up and wrapped in skins and mats for interment. Direction possessed special significance, the corpse being laid on the left side, head facing south, hands shielding the eyes. *Beigaben* were numerous, including weapons; but clay and ivory models of animals soon came to substitute for flesh and blood creatures in what may represent a partial retreat from magical thinking about the future life. Dogs, however, still were buried with their masters. Differences in the size of a grave and quantity of *Beigaben* testify to rather strong class differences. In Gerzean times graves increased in size, the pits sometimes being walls with bricks on which a fresco might be painted. Other graves were provided with a ledge, or side recess, such as still receives the body in parts of Pakistan and the Middle East. Corpses faced west. Just before dynastic times Egyptian tombs came to be cut in rock and gradually moved above ground. Northern Mesopotamia appears to have lacked cemeteries. The dead lie scattered in the village. But in southern Ubaid the corpse was buried in extended position and adult graves were grouped in regular cemeteries. However, children remained close to home, being interred among the houses. At Eridu brick cists were constructed. With time, the Lower Mesopotamians came to prefer very contracted attitudes in their burials. Secondary deposition was also practiced, the flesh being allowed to decompose before the skeleton was interred in clay boxes or house models.

Throughout the period Mesopotamia maintained a lead on Egypt in a number of basic inventions: the wheel, animal traction, copper, bronze, mud brick, and, probably, writing. Yet Egypt was never long in learning about these innovations. Both regions remained closely matched for development and elaboration. The importance of diffusion in culture growth is once more indicated.

CYCLICAL CONQUESTS

The final period of culture growth in the Middle East encompasses 3000 relatively well-studied years that are within the range of history. The period often is divided into a Bronze and subsequent Iron Age. The Bronze Age opened on a world in which man had won a considerable measure of emancipation from immediate dependence on nature. Through farming, irrigation, animal power, the wheel, plow, and metals he had increased his power of control. By administration, trade, and military organizations he could coördinate large numbers of people. Production was heavy enough to relieve some men from subsistence techniques and manufacturing. These specialists devoted their time to ritual, painting, sculpture, administration, writing, and thought, thus contributing to further cultural elaboration. Finally, man had managed to short-circuit time and space with writing. It is, after all, to that very invention that modern man owes his knowledge of the Middle East during the three pre-Christian millennia.

The Slowing Down in Development

The millennia between 8000 and 3000 furnish an impressive record of human inventiveness leading to increasing development. Many of the basic inventions on which western civilization still depends appeared during this epoch. Considered as a whole, since about 10,000 years ago the growth curve of human culture has never declined (see pp. 280–282). Development, however, has not always proceeded at the same rate. A period of gradual leveling off occurred during the 3000 years of Cyclical Conquests. The full explanation for this arrest is not available but it has been postulated that events in the period of Regional Florescent Nations evoked certain internal contradictions in Middle East society (Childe, 1936:Chap. 9). Relatively great wealth was being produced but, at the dawn of Cyclical Conquests, much of it was concentrated in the hands of kings, priests, and the persons associated with those leaders. The mass of the population possessed little direct share in prosperity. ". . . Socially they were sinking toward the status of tenants or even serfs" (ibid., p. 229). How did the concentration of wealth in the hands of a few arrest development? The craftsmen and farmers who, presumably, had made many of the important capital originations of an earlier day had then lived in a relatively egalitarian social system. Now they lived under rulers who were scarcely human, claiming, as they did, divinity or the special protection of gods. Rulers with these affiliations did not much patronize the search for new means of development. Perhaps they felt confidence in the extraordinary patrons who oversaw them. Perhaps their very prosperity lulled them. Also, with their recently acquired ability to recruit the labor of many subjects and slaves, the wealthy rulers had little need of labor-saving devices. The specialist craftsmen, who might be expected to make discoveries and inventions, worked primarily to satisfy this ruling class. Their position in society was not competitive. They felt little need to develop labor-saving devices with which to hold or win markets. Finally, an anti-intellectual climate was maintained through reliance on dogma. This led men to ignore the advantages of experimentation and observation. In sum, technical developments promised few rewards in the social and ideological climate that existed after the rise of the early dynasties.

External contradictions also beset the communities. Nations were not self-sufficient. At first they had seen no alternative to giving up wealth in exchange for imports. Presently, infatuated with power, they tried to regularize delivery of goods by force or by conquering the sources of supply. Revolts of dissatisfied subjects in turn undermined stability. The resultant warfare stimulated many military inventions but, as is not unknown from other eras, relatively few that were suited to peaceful ends (see pp. 202–203). In large measure warfare destroyed rather than produced wealth. Directly or indirectly it destroyed people, the producers of wealth and the ultimate sources of innovation.

Verification of this complex interpretation of the facts is difficult. The reader will find abundant evidence of militarism, class differences, and divine kingship in the period of Cyclical Conquests. That these variables acted to limit developmental originations is not entirely sure. Certain alternative hypotheses are not more satisfactory. To say that people's inventive ability ran out, or that people lost the ability to apply discoveries to practical problems, is scarcely an explanation. Perhaps development had proceeded as far as it could, given the available sources of energy. Anyhow, the next spurt in the curve did not come until man learned to harness inanimate sources of power to do his work—namely, the stored power in coal, oil, and water.

Subperiods

Five subperiods will be followed in describing the culture history of Cyclical Conquests. These divisions are not based on changes in cultural regularities as much as they follow political events. They are based on a distinction between centuries of social stability and so-called "dark ages" marked by great instability. The subperiods are (cf. Fig. 40:8):

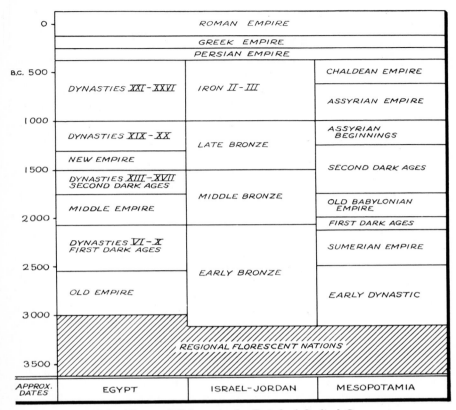

Fig. 40:8. Phases of Culture in the Period of Cyclical Conquests.

1. *Initial Conquests:* Old Empire and Early Dynasties of Egypt and Mesopotamia respectively; corresponds to the Early Bronze Age; from about 3000 to 2500 in Egypt and to 2000 in the rest of the area.
2. *First Intermediate period* (First Dark Ages): from 2500 to 2000 in Egypt but lasting only a few centuries, around 2000, in the rest of the area.
3. *Second Conquests:* Middle Empire of Egypt and Old Babylonian Empire of Mesopotamia; roughly the first half of the Middle Bronze Age; from 2000 to about 1800.
4. *Second Intermediate period* (Second Dark Ages): starts around 1700 and ends shortly before 1500 in Egypt; lasts until about 1400 elsewhere.
5. *Successive Conquests:* the centuries marked by the Egyptian New Empire and by the far-flung empires of Assyria, Persia, Greece, and Rome that quickly succeeded each other; corresponds to the Late Bronze and Early Iron Age; lasts through the Roman Empire.

Initial Conquests: 3000 B.C.

1. Administration and Kingship. The transition from Regional Florescent Nations to Initial Conquests in Mesopotamia was marked by the growing power which each of the petty nations (i.e., city-states)—Kish, Erech, Ur, and others—exerted on its neighbors. In Egypt the new period saw the unification of the two kingdoms into a united Egypt.[3] The union of Upper and Lower Egypt gave rise to what is usually called the Old Kingdom. In keeping with definitions adopted earlier, it may also be called the Old Empire.

The economic interdependence of the florescent nations probably contributed an incentive for empire building. The nations probably saw their viability to lie in reducing hostile sources of power. Empires grew out of the realization of this goal. Out of political combinations and recombinations emerged the Sumerian Empire, headed by Sargon I. Based in Akkad, by 2550 it stretched to the Mediterranean coast. Expansion on this scale means that war came to play a focal role in the culture of Initial Conquests. Such an inference is sustained by the evidence of weapons, armor, and various defensive devices that have been recovered from contemporary sites. In Egypt, Initial Conquests began with copper weapons but before the Old Empire came to an end bronze had diffused from Mesopotamia and was in use by armies. The bodies of fighting men who carved out empires on the Nile and in Southwest Asia were departmentalized by function. In dynastic Ur there was a heavy and light infantry while other specialists drove ass-drawn chariots. For defense, cities became surrounded by monumental walls. Beth Yerah stood inside a mud-brick bastion 28 feet thick and sloping on both sides. Ur lay enclosed in walls 26 feet high and 77 feet thick at the bottom. Such defenses did not render the city dwellers invulnerable and many fortified settlements met destruction.

In international affairs the expanding nations learned both the use of power and the threat of power; cold wars alternated with hot ones. How little has changed in this respect is apparent in the message which Enmerker, king of Erech, sent to Aratta, a city controlling a region rich in metal and stone. The ambassador of Enmerker spoke thus to the king of Aratta: "Your father . . . has sent me to you . . . and thus says my king: . . . Do not flee like a bird into the nest, Aratta cursed by the pure. . . . Like a place destroyed I shall destroy [you]. . . ." Successive threats of this type

---

[3] Nobody knows how many independent nations existed during the era of Regional Florescent Nations. By Aristotle's time 160 such organizations are said to have maintained themselves in Greece alone. In 1955 the total number of independent nations in the world was 87, according to the United Nations. Even if a few areas in which foreign sovereignty is not acknowledged, and not successfully enforced, were added to this figure, the total would not be much greater. Such a tabulation offers some idea of how political power has become unified in the world.

made the people of Aratta ready to hail Enmerker as their new ruler (*New York Times*, Mar. 2, 1947; Kramer, 1955:Chap. 3). The wealth contained in the imperial capitals leaves no doubt that from one standpoint at least such international organizations were successful. There, of course, lies an important explanation for their persistence. Yet the unequal distribution of the wealth constituted a factor that never allowed power to be consolidated or become stable.

Naked power obviously did not suffice to rule. The early dynasties rationalized their desire to govern through various dogmas of legitimization, of which our own—popular election—was not one. In Mesopotamia early kings ruled in the name of gods. The king dwelt in the residence of the god as the latter's servant. In Egypt the king was a divinity, not the mere servant of one. Later Mesopotamia also borrowed this belief. Imposing houses, elaborate burial rites, and monumental tombs expressed symbolically the exalted status of these paramount administrators. In Ur the bejeweled bodies of kings and queens rested in wood, clay, or wicker coffins along with golden ornaments and the seal of office. Multiroomed underground tombs housed the dead and their retinue. Limestone for one Third Dynasty tomb, brought from at least 30 miles away, faced the chamber, in which rose 3 corbeled domes. *Beigaben* included ornate harps, chariots, asses, wagons, oxen, retainers (some wearing golden headdresses), soldiers with gold-, silver-, and copper-pointed spears and copper helmets. One king went into death accompanied by 62 retainers; his widow with 25. In Egypt kings were interred in pyramids, structures that succeeded brick-lined shafts 10 feet deep and chambered at the bottom. At first only a single superstructure was built over the tomb. Later the Egyptians mounted a series of buildings one on top of the other in pyramid form. These structures were sited along the west bank of the river, on a rock substratum that was not likely to crack (Edwards, 1947:Chap. 7). The bedrock was leveled and smoothed with great skill and the pyramid laid out so that the base formed a nearly perfect square, each side of which faced one cardinal point. Local stone formed the causeway, on which fine limestone blocks and granite columns could be moved. The gangs that cut this stone painted their names ("Vigorous Gang," "Enduring Gang") on the blocks, where some may still be read. Copper saws and chisels aided by moistened quartz, sand, and other abrasives probably helped to cut the material. Sometimes the quarrymen dug through undesirable stone to reach a substance of higher quality. Some limestone blocks weighed 200 tons; the lighter ones only from 2 to 50 tons. Without the use of the pulley only inclined ramps aided the movement of these megaliths to the desired positions. To build the Great Pyramid (Fourth Dynasty) may have taken 20 years and over 100,000 men annually. Symbolically speaking, the tombs allowed a dead ruler to ascend to the sun. Into them, after funeral ceremonies that lasted for weeks, went the mummified body as well as the viscera and many *Beigaben* which, when not stolen by grave robbers, afford an intimate glimpse of early dynastic Egyptian life. The people believed that life continued after death but that it required material sustenance. The preservation of the corpse was also essential for survival. In time, however, statues representing the dead man came to substitute for the body.

Finally, great magicality surrounded the status of the ruler and no doubt added to his capacity to rule. In Egypt, as in parts of Africa today, the fertility of the land depended on the Pharaoh (cf. Seligman, 1934).[4] The king stood for *maat*—order, truth, and prosperity—qualities that existed as long as he was there to guarantee the regular course of nature (Frankfort, 1948:54-64). The special importance or sacredness of the royal person was expressed symbolically in many rituals that functioned to keep alive the idea of the king's potent qualities and special status. In more material fashion, tribute and taxes swelled the king's wealth. Some rulers were more rapacious than others (Kramer, 1955:Chap. 6) but ultimately this income supported many people: the king's family, staff, retainers, perhaps military officers, and craft specialists who worked for the palace and created beautiful things for the ruling class. Possession of these objects further enhanced the prestige of that class in public eyes. In the end none of the elaboration and magicality surrounding kingship worked with much success. No regime remained free from the threat of internal and external revolt.

2. Patterns of Living. Cities were large in area as well as in influence. During the thousand years of Initial Conquests the area of Ur expanded from one-third of a square mile to 3¾ square miles. The population may have reached 24,000 in the Third Dynasty, a record for this period. Trade was extensive and routes linked practically all parts of the Middle East. The camel came into use for transport as early as the Egyptian Fourth Dynasty (2500) and may have originated in Mesopotamia. General use was not made of this animal, however, until about 900 B.C. Volume of trade and regularization of tribute or taxes greatly depended on writing. Business instruments like bills, receipts, notes, and letters of credit were committed to writing at this time and the use of checks long predates coinage. Weighted bars of gold or silver also served as media of exchange.

In Egypt a pictographic-ideographic script, known as hieroglyphic writing, finally appeared to replace earlier pictographs. In it the signs for concrete objects were stretched to cover related ideas (the sign of the sun, for example, also representing the idea of "day"). As in Mesopotamia, combinations of signs expressed more complicated ideas. Presently the pictographs and ideographs came to serve as phonograms, expressing words and syllables in rebus fashion. The phonograms, however, do not take over. For

---

[4] "Pharaoh" originally meant "palace" and only in the XVIII Dynasty did the word come to be used as a term of respect for the ruler.

thousands of years they merely accompany the pictograph-ideographs. What happened in Mesopotamia, when pictographs were conventionalized through the agency of the stylus, giving rise to cuneiform writing, did not occur in Egypt. Something else took place. Egyptians wrote with pen and ink on papyrus (made from the pith of sedge pressed toegther after being laid down in crosswise layers). For practical purposes a simplified and very cursive script, known as hieratic writing, came into use for papyrus. The more realistic pictographs and ideographs persisted for tombs and ritual. Thus two styles of writing arose, specialized for different circumstances.[5] Nor did writing mean the displacement of pictographic seals by which a witness signed documents or men agreed to contracts. Cylinder seals, known since Regional Florescent Nations, now came to be pressed on flat, thin pieces of clay that sheathed business documents like an envelope, making the latter tamper-proof.

By this time the Egyptians used a 365-day calendar. It was divided into 12 months of 30 days each, 5 extra days being added to fill out the remarkably regular interval between floodings of the Nile. While not precisely accurate, losing at least six hours annually, the calendar survived until 238 B.C. Then, over great opposition, a leap year of 366 days was added every 4 years so that, as a contemporary observed, ". . . the case may not arise that some of the festivals which are celebrated in Egypt in the winter should come to be observed in the summer" (Watkins, 1954:23).

The city folk enjoyed a varied diet, including in Mesopotamia the meat of oxen, sheep, doves, ducks, chickens, and fish; dates; figs; cucumbers; butter; oil; and cakes of grain flour. Around 2500 the horned buffalo was introduced in this country, apparently deriving from Asia Minor. A great variety of amusements, including dancing and music, were available. The harp and lyre were popular instruments. Rural areas of the country saw clay sickles disappear, being replaced mainly by wooden implements still armed with flint teeth. Bronze and copper sickles were very rare. The wealthy folk, on the other hand, made much use of metal. Almost every form of vessel formerly made in clay now appears in silver, gold, or copper. For royalty there were even saws, chisels, and weapons of gold or silver.

3. Ideology. Written records show considerable preoccupation with theological thought. Despite lack of direct evidence, it is reasonable to deduce that in some degree such thinking extends into previous periods as well. Various collective representations were symbolized: in Egypt, a solar deity by a winged disk; Nekhbet by a vulture's head, and Neith by a shield across which two arrows ran diagonally. No doubt each of these deities had devotees. Various craftsmen worshiped their particular patron gods. Mesopota-

---

[5] An amusing illustrated account of two modern Egyptologists corresponding in hieroglyphics and being forced to create new signs to express concepts like "television" was printed in the *New York Times*, May 26, 1956.

mian worshipers approached the gods naked, as a ritual gesture of respect.

Powers of carefully trained priests extended in many directions. In Mesopotamia they taught subjects like arithmetic and geometry in the temples and collected taxes. At least some found bribery irresistible. A conscientious king has left his reproach of their conduct. The temples included women who ritually prostituted themselves; presumably they acted the role of a servant to the god.

Medicine in Sumer used a diversified number of ingredients: mineral, animal, and plant. However, most medicine, according to a medical text dating from the end of the third millennium, was botanical. Preparation of remedies sometimes involved many steps and on occasion internal remedies were administered in beer (Kramer, 1955:Chap. 9).

A more famous text of the third millennium deals with a man who, blessed with wealth and friends, is overrun by sickness and suffering. This Sumerian "Job" suffers through no apparent fault of his own. In the end God, moved by his prayers and torments, relieves him of misfortune (ibid., Chap. 14). Destined to survive for an equally long time was the deluge tale of Sumer:

> . . . for seven days and seven nights,
> The flood had swept over the island
> And the huge boat had been tossed about by the windstorms on the
> great waters. . . .

This tale presumably diffused to Babylonia and eventually to the Israelites for inclusion into the Bible (ibid., Chap. 21). A well-known Egyptian book of the period consists of a father's exhortations to his son. Obedience, faithfulness to tradition, and ambition are extolled, especially for men who would follow careers in public service.

First Intermediate Period: 2500 B.C.

Apart from specific political calamities like the revolt of the Egyptian nobles in 2300 and the rebellion of Sargon's subject nations, two cultural factors appear related to the onset of the First Dark Ages: the centralization of administration and the diffusion of culture.

1. **Centralization of Administration.** With all lines of administration centered in a small but powerful social group, any interference with the exercise of government had to be disturbing. When this happened the mutual interdependence of communities, which had been guaranteed by the powerful empires, dissolved. Irrigation canals became clogged and food supplies in towns dwindled. The weakened nations in the fertile plain attracted the attention of raiders from the hills who had never been included successfully with the imperial frontiers. Their arrival increased confusion and anarchy. Specialists were thrown out of work and lawless elements in the relatively

dense population met little opposition. Disorganization lasted until an administration proved strong enough to restore order and productivity.

The political revolts against sovereigns that instituted the First Intermediate period may also be regarded as rising out of the unpopular policies of central administrations which had not learned to rule successfully. Magical thinking and ritualism centering around the king failed to hold together the empire in Egypt. Rebellion against the king—source of *maat*—was profoundly disconcerting. As somebody wrote: "The country turns around like a potter's wheel" and "Great and small say: 'I wish I were dead' " (Frankfort, 1948:86–87). The petty nobles, who successfully reinstated the autonomy of the small-scale nomes (provinces), prevented imperial reorganization for nearly 400 years. Reactions came in the form of popular agnosticism and hedonism. "Make holiday and weary not therein: Behold it is not given to a man to take his property with him" (J. A. Wilson, 1951:114).

2. Trade, Expansion, Diffusion. Not only had the commercial and political expansion of the Regional Florescent Nations spread new cultures but they had introduced knowledge of new forms of social organization and of the use of power in social relations to people who may not have realized clearly the advantages of such devices. The tribute-paying regions supplying raw material to cities like Ur now sought to wrest advantages from their overlords through organizing after the fashion of the latter. The social energy thus canalized came to be used for revolt and conquest. Thus in 2400 the Guti (of Gutium, lying east of Nineveh) descended on the Sumerian Empire. For a hundred years the weakened Sumerians resisted. Then they fell back under the Amorites led by Hammurabi, who reinstated centralized administration in Southwest Asia.

The royal pyramids of Egypt were raided for their wealth. Funerary customs that previously had been limited to royalty began to be diffused to the common people. Of course, many people did not have the wealth to permit emulation of royal funerals but specialists were willing to supply miniature models of boats, granaries, and the images of servants and artisans for interment. Such *ersatz* grave goods appear to reflect further weakening in the strength of belief in an afterlife. They suggest that some people no longer believed quite so firmly that elaborate funerary treatment guaranteed a happy afterlife. The extension of royal prerogatives to nobles and commoners also reflects a diminution of faith in the divinity of kings, who, anyway, had failed to hold their realms intact. Yet this was also a time when popular opinion felt that everyone must expect to answer to the gods for his conduct. If a man's faults exceeded his virtues he could never hope to join the deities (J. A. Wilson, 1951:120). In the monuments memorializing the wealthy there is a sloughing off of care or skill. Artistic expression seems to have been less highly valued. Meanwhile the disturbed times kindled interest in the past,

Sumerian historians sought to reconstruct the past, mixing conjecture with fact. At the same time they recorded the present for the benefit of their successors.

During the First Intermediate period civilization grew up in the Indus Valley, or what is now West Pakistan. The cities there enjoyed only rare contact with Mesopotamia but the initial currents of diffusion undoubtedly originated in the Tigris and Euphrates valleys. Like those streams the Indus also flowed through desert, and the region provided the same combination of circumstances that had encouraged culture growth in Mesopotamia. Urbanization was a dominant feature of Indus Valley civilization. The walls of Harappa possessed a circumference of 2½ miles and enclosed many elaborate houses built of baked brick. The largest building measured 150 by 56 feet and appears to have been a granary rather than a temple or tomb.

Second Period of Conquests: 2000 B.C.

From the standpoint of political history this is the period when Hammurabi of Babylon established a strong central government whose power he carried to the Mediterranean coast. In Egypt the Pharaohs of the Sixth Dynasty were restored through a popular revolt against the local nobles. However, the Middle Empire scarcely expanded beyond the frontiers of the Nile and the Sinai peninsula, which connects Africa with Asia. In part Egypt's failure ever to spread her power was probably related to geographical factors. Cataracts on the Nile limited southward boat travel while uninhabited deserts on the west and east offered no worth-while target for conquest. Also there were no nearby centers of power threatening Egypt whereas any city of the Tigris and Euphrates plain was highly vulnerable to its nearby rivals. When Egypt finally expanded she did so by moving across the Sinai desert into Asia. Perhaps the long absence of the wheel from Egypt also kept the country from carrying conquest far afield.

The early centuries following the start of the second millennium are notable for the rise in the Middle East of people speaking languages not belonging (like Egyptian or Babylonian) to the Hamito-Semitic family. These people—for example, the Medes in the west and the Hittites in Anatolia—spoke Indo-European languages. They appear on the scene at about the same time that the Greeks, belonging to the same stock, descended to the Mediterranean and the Aryans entered India (Hencken, 1955:39–44). The original home of the Indo-European people has not been fixed but originally they may have been localized in southeastern Europe or the plain north of the Black Sea (see pp. 102–103). Eventually they would dominate the political scene in both Southwest Asia and Europe.

Taxation had hitherto scarcely been lacking but in Second Conquests a systematization of the process appears to have taken place. The expenses of administration also increased. Mesopotamia added compulsory military service, increased the size of the army, and elaborated the system of legal administration. Under Hammurabi the Babylonians fostered the dogma of divine monarchy, regarding the king as an incarnated divinity. Legal norms specified new offenses (always a function of a rapidly changing way of life). Treason and sedition were listed as punishable offenses. In Egypt crimes against the monarchy deprived a man of a suitable funeral and, ideally, of life after death. Yet neither threat of punishment nor curses for the enemies of government (something Egypt had already tried in the Old Empire) could eradicate rival claims to power. No more do modern secret police, the F.B.I., and laws against subversion guarantee internal security. Administrations took more part in apprehending criminals, including presumed sorcerers, and bringing them before the courts. Pardons could not be granted without the consent of a victim or his family. The Middle Bronze period, then, is a period in which personal autonomy came to decline rapidly in the wider circle of social relationships as government regulation increased (see pp. 153–154). This may also be seen in the organization for production and distribution. The Babylonian Empire regulated by law conduct of partnership and agency, the making of wills, and collection of interest. Even price fixing occurred and sellers of goods or specialists remained legally responsible for their product or service. At the same time constitutional limitations on rule were accepted, at least nominally, by the power centers. Actually the autocratic power of kings was not to disappear before nearly 4000 more years.

For convenience in exchanging goods, merchants in Egypt reckoned value in terms of rings fashioned from copper and other metals. These continued in use until displaced by coinage in the sixth century. Much of a nation's wealth came from agricultural products raised by serfs who were attached permanently to a piece of land. The labor of a distinct class of slaves, however, was also available for production.

Second Conquests saw the horse hitched to a chariot made with light, spoked wheels. In Egypt secondary originations were made in the sail. Bronze and copper provided a large and varied supply of metal implements, including even hair curlers to serve the esthetic need of Egyptian women.

The times saw the first codified law (Kramer, 1955:Chap. 7). This Mesopotamian innovation may be understood as a function of the growing complexity of social life, close contact between people of different cultural traditions promoted through conquest, and writing by which to codify injunctions. One function of codification, it may be deduced, was to make explicit the customary and statutory legal norms of an administration in areas where they were not traditional and where the people, perhaps, did not respect the new ruler. A strong tendency became apparent to remove the process of law from private hands. An aggrieved person still had to bring the accused into court, but that body, consisting of temple priests, administered punishment. Legal norms recognized social inequalities so that punishments varied according to the rank of the offender and the plaintiff. Injury to an aristocrat constituted a far more serious offense than the same act committed against a commoner. However, an aristocratic offender was also dealt with more seriously. Apparently a member of the ruling class was expected to feel a greater sense of social responsibility and to manifest greater self-control.

In the area of ideology physiological research contributed empirical knowledge about the functions of the heart, liver, and other human organs. New drugs came into use for treating illness. The medium of cuneiform writing allowed discoveries in medicine and other fields to be recorded and also encouraged the setting down of more speculative ideas. Cuneiform diffused widely throughout Southwest Asia, enabling many languages to be written. With the spread of the script went texts, like myths, omens, and prescriptions. From such records modern scholars learn that Egypt now developed a highly abstract theory of an impersonal, nonanthropomorphic cosmic intelligence, "the Word that was God." In this intelligence the idea of a universe was originally conceived as a step in creation (J. A. Wilson, 1951:59). Babylonians recorded the already old Gilgamesh Epic, a poem centering on a youthful ruler (Heidel, 1946). It recounts the deeds of this hero, Gilgamesh, and his unsuccessful search for immortality. A portion of the epic tells of a flood sent by the gods from which some people saved themselves by building a vessel which they shared with representatives of all the animal species. Much thought revolved around the nature of sin, destiny, and the human will. A Pharaoh expressed his skepticism about the afterworld in the Dialogue of a Misanthrope with His Soul. Here, as in the Job story, a good man of gentle spirit falls victim to gross injustice. His world is pictured as corrupt and dishonest.

Egypt invented a "pseudo-alphabet" at about this time, using a relatively few phonograms to represent consonants. Thus the sign for *ri*, "mouth," came to be used for the spoken words *ra, re, ri, ru*. Finally it came to stand for initial *r* in any word. However, various ways existed of representing the same consonants. Therefore this cannot be regarded as a true alphabet. The Egyptians mainly used this new type of writing to spell out foreign words and proper nouns.

The Babylonians made wide use of mathematics and worked with the sexagesimal numerical system. That is, they counted not decimally but in sixties. The utility of such a unit lies in its ready divisibility not only by 2, 5, and 10 but also by 3, 4, 6, 12, and 15. Modern science and technology still find this system of numeration convenient for dividing the circle into 360 parts or 60 minutes. While the Babylonians cannot be credited with invention of the zero concept (an innovation independently made later in India and again by the Maya Indians of Guatemala), their scribes did have a sign to represent "naught" (Kroeber, 1948:468–472; Chiera, 1938:156; Childe, 1936:155–156).

Second Intermediate Period: 1700 B.C.

Once more the Egyptian nobles revolted and fought each other to capture the throne. In the middle of their struggle the Hyksos (including Indo-European-speaking Hurri) drove south in horse-drawn chariots and seized control of the intervening country as well as Egypt (1788). They restored order. Revolution and war with Elam had weakened the Old Babylonian Empire and into that power vacuum now stepped the Indo-European Kassites (1749). From the Hyksos the Egyptians adopted the horse and chariot. Within 200 years they used these developments to establish their own brief empire. The Dark Ages renewed the attention which Mesopotamians paid to wall building. Double and even triple walls surrounded some cities. Inclined ramps, wide enough for only a single chariot, gave access to the gateways. These defenses, of course, were far from perfect but they probably succeeded in slowing down the onslaught of the bronze-armored warriors who drove on wheels.

This anarchic period may have witnessed the earliest alphabetic writing. Specimens have been found in the extreme southwestern corner of Asia. Unfortunately, the signs cannot be understood so it is largely conjecture to call them alphabetic at all. At Byblos in Phoenicia inscriptions on stone and metal that may go back to 2000 contain signs not numerous enough to be a part of a pictographic or ideographic script. Yet they are also too numerous for an alphabet. Similarly with inscriptions from the mines of Sinai, dated between 1850 and 1500. From 1500 we have clay tablets from Ugarit, on the Syrian coast, written with 20 or 30 signs resembling both earlier Phoenician characters and Babylonian cuneiform. Apparently they represent an attempt to assimilate cuneiform to an already existent alphabet. These and other forms of contemporary writing indicate that phonetic writing did not burst into existence full-blown nor did it derive directly from cuneiform. Perhaps the hieroglyphic consonantal alphabet of Egypt stimulated numerous parallel attempts to achieve alphabetic scripts in Southwest Asia at this time. By 1000 B.C. the achievement certainly had been completed and was ready for diffusion to Greece, Rome, and, eventually, western Europe and America. How this alphabet became modified in diffusion has often been told (Diringer, 1948; Moorhouse, 1953).

Successive Conquests: 1500 B.C.

The restoration of government in Egypt came considerably earlier than the consolidation of power in Mesopotamia, where nearly the whole second millennium was marked by a bitter struggle for supremacy between Assyria and Babylonia, nations speaking nearly the same Semitic language. Around 1000 B.C. the Assyrians won out and in 700 there began a period of imperial splendor, the Sargonid period, marked by some of the most lavish architecture that had yet appeared. Sargon II, ruler of the Assyrian Empire, lived in a palace 975 feet wide and 1100 feet long. It lay within the mile-square walls of Khorsabad. The arrangement of the palace halls and council chambers was calculated to show off as dramatically as possible the royal power and the visitor's comparative impotence. Eating and dining halls were connected with bathrooms (Frankfort, 1954:74–78).

The highly unstable equilibrium in the land was finally upset by the rise of the Persians, who partitioned the empire, giving half to Nebuchadnezzar (605–563), head of the New Babylonian (Chaldean) Empire. Eventually the Indo-European Persians themselves took control of the whole Middle East and were followed by the European-based empires of the Greeks and Romans. Then occurred a heavy diffusion of Greek culture into the area—the Middle East became Hellenized (Gomme, 1935:756–774).

Accompanying the struggle between mighty power centers were restless movements of people that contributed to instability. In the Israel-Jordan sector the indigenous Canaanites unsuccessfully sought to block the Israelite migrations. The latter people, in turn, later sought to confine the newly arrived Sea People (Philistines) to the Mediterranean coast and quite succeeded. The Israelites (or Jews) were originally a tent-dwelling pastoral people organized only in clans and lacking overall administration. They apparently wished to settle down as farmers and perceived Canaan to offer a favorable land. In 1025 B.C. the Israelites organized a consolidated kingdom. The efforts of various powers since that date to exterminate the kingdom or the professors of Judaism is a familiar story.[6]

Successive Conquests is notable for its military aspects: standing armies larger than any so far established, new techniques of fighting, heavy bows, long lances, battering rams, and metal breastplates, shields, and helmets. In Egypt the army included mercenaries, among them a large Negro contingent. The horse was indispensable for imperial administration. Even a small kingdom like Israel required cavalry, and at Megiddo King Solomon constructed stables large enough to accommodate 450 animals. Artillery featured a wheeled platform upon which the attackers could be raised to wall level. The forerunner of modern steel tanks appeared, leather-covered vehicles shielding soldiers who manned the battering ram with which the city walls were assaulted. Warships rode the rivers, their sides strengthened by lines of metal shields and fitted with a sharply pointed ram, presumably useful in attacking and sinking enemy vessels. City walls now came to be of stone set in

[6] Incidentally, the Bible contains much information about the culture of the land of Canaan. However, that book was not begun until the ninth century B.C. and the Israelites had moved in from the southeast, via Egypt, as long before as the fifteenth century.

mud mortar. The cleverly designed indirect-access gateway required a sharp right turn to enter. An Assyrian device consisted of leaving the passage through the massive walls open to the sky at intervals. Archers posted in these skylights constituted a second line of defense in cases where the outer gates had been forced.

The remaining high points of these crowded centuries will be summed up under the major categories of technology, social organization, and ideology (including religion).

1. **Technology.** The most important event in Successive Conquests was the slow adoption of iron following 1400. By 1000 the people of Israel and Jordan employed iron daggers, axheads, and swords. By 600 they had abandoned flint-toothed sickles for iron ones. The new harvesting implements allowed about twice as much grain to be harvested in a given period of time. Following 600 a wide variety of iron tools—including adzes, saws, and chisels—came into use. The ability to control metalworking grew throughout the last millennium. Among objects testifying to rising skill are bronze statues weighing nearly two tons. These must have required considerable ingenuity to construct in view of the limited capacity of available crucibles.

Housing varied considerably, not only between localities but between the elaborate, stone-built palaces of kings and the mud-brick shelters of the common folk. For lighting wide use was made of saucer-shaped oil lamps provided with a pinched spout containing the wick. People often burned crude oil, or petroleum, which, of course, was not refined. Houses were commonly furnished with beds, stools, and tables. A type of oven used for baking unleavened bread resembled ovens that are still used in twentieth-century Lebanon and West Pakistan. It consisted of a clay cylinder two feet high. Thin round cakes of dough were plastered against the inner surface after the oven had been preheated (Benzinger, 1927:65). Cities grew very large and administrators had their abilities taxed more than ever before to provide for the needs of urban populations. One problem was water, and the first aqueducts date from this period. The one that fed spring water into Nineveh spanned valleys on arches and must have constituted a contemporary engineering triumph.

Irrigation was a mainstay for supporting the swollen population. On occasion heavily silted canals had to be abandoned but fresh ones were at once opened up. The *shaduf* enabled water to be lifted in cases where the fields were too high to receive flowing canal water. This device, which is probably older than the first millennium, consisted of a moving pole supported on a fulcrum. The shorter end was weighted and could be depressed with slight effort to hoist a filled receptacle on the longer, forward end. In the Greek and Roman centuries animal-operated water wheels and grinding stones facilitated irrigation as well as milling. Oxen drew the plows, which were often fitted with seed drills for sowing. The same animals trampled the grain in threshing unless the newly originated ox-drawn threshing sled was employed. The garlic, onion, pepper, lettuce, fig, lentil, and olive were among the common foods. Olives and sesame seeds provided valuable oil. In Assyria grains were stored in elevated, high, cylinder-shaped silos (very much resembling those still in use) that were mounted by ladders. The assortment of cultivated plants, animals—cow, sheep, goat, and horned buffalo —together with fish taken from rivers and canals assured quite a varied cuisine, at least for those people who could afford to choose their foods. Confections, cake, beer, and wine were also used in addition to unleavened and raised bread. The latter consisted of fermented dough.

2. Social Organization. The large empires which were involved in the Successive Conquests were forced by size to decentralize many tasks. In Egypt the large, feudal landholders retained responsibilities like tax collecting, while the Persian Empire, which included Egypt and Aryan-speaking India, was organized into provinces by difficult-to-manage satraps. Special agencies for the administration of justice, price fixing, and collection of taxes took their place along with large military departments. Corruption posed an ever present problem. In Egypt the ideal impartiality of law frequently had to be stimulated by royal exhortations. Legal punishments tended to be severe and death was the penalty for many crimes. Means of execution included poisoning, impaling, hanging, crucifixion, and other techniques.

Mesopotamian kings, although they lived in well-furnished houses and controlled stupendous wealth, ceased to claim divinity or divine descent. They were content to be acknowledged as men of great wisdom, power, and excellence—"kings of kings." Nevertheless the link between collective representations and kingships did not completely dissolve. Oracles helped to validate succession to the throne by revealing divine assent. At the coronation priests anointed the new ruler in the name of the leading deity. Political control over large areas and many people facilitated the importing of scarce resources. Solomon sent thousands of his subjects to foreign lands to cut wood and hew stone. Naturally trade flourished and the rise of specialized "trading people" can be traced to this time. The Phoenicians devoted themselves mainly to shipping. Their galleys, propelled by sails and banks of oars, reached Sardinia, Spain, and other Mediterranean ports. Growing use was made of the camel for desert travel. Related to the volume of trade is the inauguration of inns for travelers and the search for new media to facilitate the exchange of different commodities. Stamped bars of lead served this function in Assyria as early as the fourteenth century and may have replaced partially the use of precious metals. In 700 Lydia, a nation in Anatolia, inaugurated the use of coins made of electrum, an alloy of gold and silver. Cylinder seals continued to identify an individual's property until late Assyrian times, when a return to the earlier stamp seal occurred.

Slavery represented an important social relationship. War brought slaves and sometimes the poor sold themselves or their children as means of paying off a debt. In Assyria four years was the statutory maximum term of debt slavery. As is not unusual in a slave system, some bondsmen, despite their status, achieved a considerable measure of wealth and power, operating their own enterprises and even owning slaves in their own name.

3. Ideology. In Egypt a change in cultural focus becomes noticeable as temples become more prominent than tombs (pyramids tend to disappear during Second Conquests). The interest in tombs continued, however, pyramids being replaced by underground burial chambers, sometimes cut out of solid bedrock. The murals in these tombs reveal the horrors associated with the afterworld. Grief is a prominent expression on the human features represented in grave art. In Israel-Jordan the corpse was interred in rock-cut family tombs each of which accommodated several generations. Some people first allowed the flesh to decompose before the bones were interred in a limestone casket and entombed. In Mesopotamia interment took place in basketry, wooden, or clay coffins. Late in the period they came to be provided with a glazed window at the head. The Assyrian Empire accompanied pronounced change in thinking about the afterworld. No longer were the dead individually provided with food. Instead collective offerings were brought to temples periodically and offered in memory of the departed. *Beigaben* practically disappeared. The custom of placing the name of the deceased and a sketch of his life on tomb or casket dates from around 300 B.C. in Israel and Jordan.

In Canaan and Persia much ritual was carried out under the open sky, in sanctuaries containing small shrines or altars. The Hebrew synagogue appeared around 400 as a place where people could assemble to hear readings of the scriptures. By this time, 3000 years after the first use of writing, certain written versions of tradition had come to be held as the word of God. The official editing of the Old Testament began about 650; the first five books (Pentateuch) were pronounced divinely inspired around 400. Other books of the Bible succeeded to this status during the following centuries. Temple and palace were separate but the king still constituted an important link between the world and the gods. Hence, temple and palace were located near one another. In both Egypt and Mesopotamia a special tone of voice for ritual purposes probably long ago had made its appearance. By no means is a special manner of speaking universally found as an element in religious performances. Very likely, then, this Hebrew-Christian tradition also originated in the Middle East.

Thought continued to emphasize morality. Confession of sins to gods, established in Egypt by 1300, may indicate a particularly strong sense of socially engendered guilt. The device of using collective representations to relieve this feeling passed directly into Christianity, as did the Babylonian penitential hymns and prayers.

Collective representations were numerous. Every nation had its own protective symbols, which sometimes became imperial symbols. In addition, family gods were worshiped in clay models. Perhaps in the latter category is the image of an obviously pregnant female which became prominent in Canaan about the time of the Israelite invasion. But similar "mother goddess" figures are of great antiquity in the Middle East. Identification of a particular collective representation with a national government meant that allegiance to rival figures automatically introduced a potential cleavage or weakness in political organization.

Movements to synthesize polytheistic conceptions into a relatively monotheistic belief system, which began to appear during Successive Conquests, may have been related to this threat. In Egypt the priests successfully resisted such an innovation introduced by the Pharaoh, Ikhnaton. The Neo-Babylonian Empire took Marduk, a rather minor god, and made him the principal deity of the nation. Similarly incomplete monotheism in Assyria resulted in the elevation of Ashur, together with Ishtar, his consort, to supremacy over other gods. Attempts in both areas were under way to reduce the number of gods by merging various ones. Among the Israelites prophets boldly declared only Jehovah to be god; the deities of other people were false and nonexistent. Such a point of view has remained a firm part of Christianity. Instead of regarding royal personages as incarnations of divinity, people believed that all men are children of God. The personal relationship between man and deity which emerged again anticipated Christianity. It is tempting to see centralization of the pantheon as related predictably to centralization of imperial power (Chapple and Coon, 1942:555–556). However, the Greeks and Romans, who established the largest empires in the area, did not find monotheism attractive and regarded other people's gods quite tolerantly. In Persia the half-legendary Zarathustra (Zoroaster) sometime around the year 600 paralleled Moses and the other Hebrew prophets in revealing a scripture, the *Avesta*, to his people. He too preached of one powerful god and urged that faith in others be abandoned. The divine source of the *Avesta*, the god Ahura-Mazda, is known to Americans for his name which has been appropriated for a light bulb.

Thought in the final pre-Christian millennium contained profound historical nostalgia. The Egyptians revived old styles of sculpture, former personal names, and even nearly forgotten gods. Nebuchadnezzar restored the city of Babylon and deliberately sought to emulate the glories he perceived in Hammurabi's reign. In part such resuscitation and celebration of the past hinged on the practice of writing. Literacy enabled the past to survive in greater detail than ever before. Ritualization of the past may have functioned to promote social solidarity around an administration. The past became an abstract symbol rallying community identification. Both Nazi Germany and

Fascist Italy sought to intensify nationalistic feeling by using the past as a collective representation.

Writing helped to preserve the memory of what happened but it also invited men to try to erase or alter the past by manipulating records. When Ikhnaton sought to establish monotheism in Egypt his goal was to raise Aton to the status of an only god. Therefore he ordered the name of Amon, a rival collective representation, to be erased on inscriptions wherever found (J. A. Wilson, 1951:Chap. 9). The diffusion of the alphabet during these and subsequent times is shown in Table 47.

TABLE 47.   Diffusion of the Alphabet

Country or People	Century When Alphabet Arrived
Southwest Asia	10th–11th B.C.
Israelites	9th
Greece	9th
Italy	8th
Carthage	8th
North India	3rd
Britain	1st
South India (Dravidians)	4th A.D.
Ethiopia	4th
Scandinavia and Russia	10th
Mongolia	14th
Korea	15th
Manchuria	16th

SOURCE: Kroeber, 1948:531.

Medical technology in Egypt possessed a highly specialized vocabulary (i.e., argot) that reflected the large amount of more or less reliable knowledge which had been acquired by its highly specialized practitioners. Doctors long ago had begun to distinguish between natural illnesses and those brought on by postulated entities. Specialists included gynecologists, oculists, and others. General practitioners were truly general, even providing cosmetics for their clients. The medical texts include carefully prepared case studies in which diagnosis and prognosis are discussed for specific diseases. In addition to medicines, the enema and circumcision served as curative or preventive techniques, and the Egyptians may have used chemical suppositories for contraception.

41.

European Periods of Food Gathering

THIS chapter will describe European culture as it was during nearly 600,-
000 years of the Pleistocene period. Long and intensive archeological research has made the continent of Europe one of the best known as far as prehistory is concerned. The next chapter will cover the arrival in Europe of
civilization, as manifested in traits like plant and animal domestication, village and town life, metallurgy, large-scale warfare, and writing.

Five successive periods of early European culture can be distinguished:
(1) the Paleolithic era of food gathering, distinguished by the use of chipped
stone, ivory, antler, and bone implements;[1] (2) the Mesolithic era of food
gathering, distinguished by essentially the same raw materials but more
specialized types of tools; (3) the era marked by the arrival of agriculture and
animal husbandry, the Neolithic; (4) the era that saw the growth of Mediterranean civilization in the Aegean region, the Bronze Age; and (5) the
Bronze and Iron ages in central, western, and northern Europe, here called
the Era of Awakening Frontiers (Fig. 41:1). Periods 1 and 2 correspond to
the Preagricultural era in the Middle East and the Paleoindian period of
North America (see pp. 789–791). The correlation of these periods with
one another in different parts of the continent, and with the culture-historical
periods in Southwest Asia/Egypt, is given in Fig. 41:1. The present chapter
is concerned only with the periods of Paleolithic and Mesolithic food gathering.

PLEISTOCENE GLACIATIONS

The term "Pleistocene" designates the "recent" period of earth history.
(The succeeding Holocene period refers to the "wholly recent.") The recent
geological period is notable for its glaciations, a phenomenon immediately
called to mind when the word "Pleistocene" is heard. Although the factors
which produced these glaciations are not well understood, traces on the
earth's surface leave no room for doubt that successive ice movements really
took place.

[1] The terms "Paleolithic," "Mesolithic," and "Neolithic" mean "old," "middle,"
and "new stone" respectively.

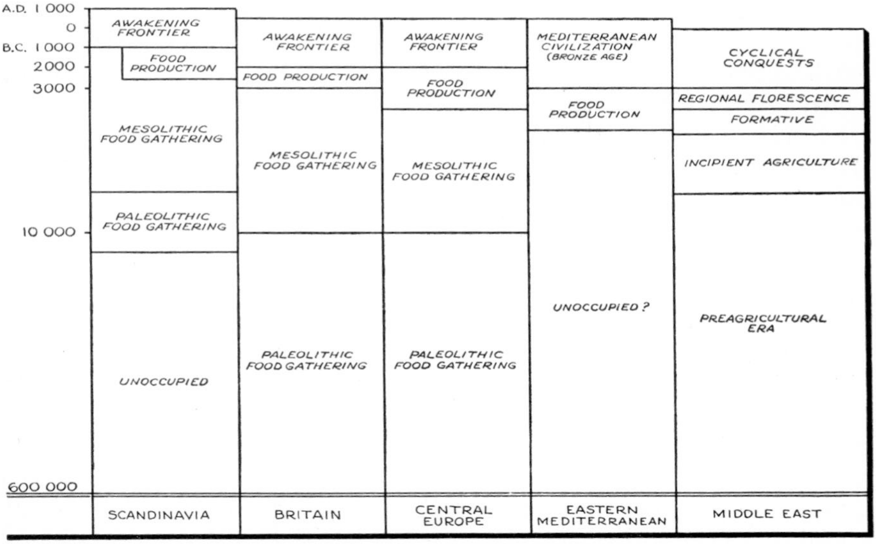

	SCANDINAVIA	BRITAIN	CENTRAL EUROPE	EASTERN MEDITERRANEAN	MIDDLE EAST
A.D. 1000 / 0	AWAKENING FRONTIER	AWAKENING FRONTIER	AWAKENING FRONTIER	MEDITERRANEAN CIVILIZATION (BRONZE AGE)	CYCLICAL CONQUESTS
B.C. 1000 / 2000 / 3000	FOOD PRODUCTION	FOOD PRODUCTION	FOOD PRODUCTION	FOOD PRODUCTION	REGIONAL FLORESCENCE / FORMATIVE
	MESOLITHIC FOOD GATHERING	MESOLITHIC FOOD GATHERING	MESOLITHIC FOOD GATHERING		INCIPIENT AGRICULTURE
10 000	PALEOLITHIC FOOD GATHERING			UNOCCUPIED ?	PREAGRICULTURAL ERA
	UNOCCUPIED	PALEOLITHIC FOOD GATHERING	PALEOLITHIC FOOD GATHERING		
600 000					

Fig. 41:1. Main Eras of European Prehistory and Protohistory, Showing Correlation with Cultural Eras of the Middle East.

Glaciers did not come or recede all at once. Four major European stages of ice advance are commonly recognized, interspersed with three relatively warm, interglacial stages (Table 48).[2] Each such stage lasted thousands of years. An interglacial stage, during which the ice sheet retreated and disappeared, actually lasted long enough for semitropical animals, like the ele-

TABLE 48. Divisions of the Pleistocene[a]

Division	Glacial and Interglacial Stages
Upper Pleistocene	Fourth (Wuerm) Glaciation Third Interglacial
Middle Pleistocene	Third (Riss) Glaciation Second Interglacial
Lower Pleistocene	Second (Mindel) Glaciation First Interglacial First (Guenz) Glaciation

[a] Read from bottom up.

phant, rhinoceros, tiger, and hippopotamus, to displace cold-weather fauna, like the mammoth and bison. The climate of Europe at the height of an interglacial stage was warmer than it is today, 10,000 or so years after the last retreat of the ice front. Gradually, as an interglacial stage ended, giving

[2] Also see Figures 41:3, 41:4, and, for dates, p. 852.

rise to a fresh advance of ice, forests yielded to grass-covered steppe. The steppe was visited by summer and winter storms. These storms blew snow in winter and in summer deposited a fine dust, or loess, in the open country. Today loess deposits constitute an important topographical feature in southern England, France, Central Europe, Russia, and China ("country of the yellow earth" refers to the loess cover). Gradually the steppe still beyond the reach of the glacier became moss-covered tundra, marshy and frozen in winter like the modern Arctic north of the tree line. All the glacial ice did not descend from the polar regions. Each mountain belt in Europe was a center of glaciation, ice moving into the surrounding territory. The names of the glacial stages, Guenz, Mindel, Riss, and Wuerm, although commonly applied to the whole of Europe, actually refer to stages discovered in the Alpine region. Here, too, evidence of two so-called final oscillations, or retreats, have been observed, the Laufen and Achen (Fig. 41:4). In northern Europe the mass of ice was far more extensive than in the south. It even invaded the sea, at the height of a glacial stage covering the water with an unbroken ice sheet several thousand feet thick. Table 48 shows the glacial and interglacial stages categorized according to three major Pleistocene subdivisions.

With the end of the fourth, Wuerm, stage (starting 15,000 years ago), Europe's climate gradually warmed up. Shortly after 8000 B.C. the process of warming intensified, inaugurating the Hypsithermal (also called Altithermal) period, the end of which came to be felt around 1000 B.C. (Fig. 41:2). The end of the warm Hypsithermal severely influenced the move-

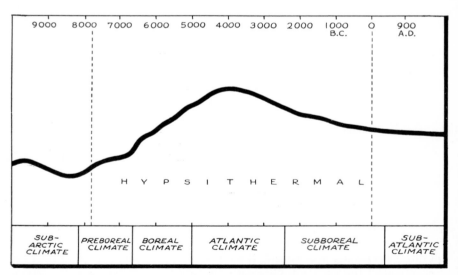

Fig. 41:2. Temperature Graph for the Past 12,000 Years (After Antevs, 1955; Deevey and Flint, 1957).

ment of people in northern latitudes. Following the Hypsithermal came a cool-moist period, cold enough in the north to have promoted glacial advances in the Scandinavian and Alaskan mountains. It is then that modern geographical conditions came to be established in the northern hemispheres.

North America also saw four glacial advances during the Pleistocene but they are identified by different terms from those used for their European counterparts (see the chart on p. 852). In Africa, pluvial (rainy) periods corresponded approximately to glacial periods. Their significance for dating will be apparent in dealing with primate evolution on that continent (Chapter 45).

Paleolithic Geography

The culture history in Europe begins with the first Pleistocene glaciation or, possibly, somewhat earlier. So-called eoliths ("dawn stones"), supposed to have been used in their natural state without further shaping, sometimes are found in pre-Pleistocene geological deposits. Finders of such objects, however, have had difficulty in getting their discoveries accepted as bonafide tools. Evidence of deliberate human shaping or use must be clear before such an object will be accepted as an artifact.

During the Old Stone (Paleolithic) Age, lasting from the first through the fourth glacial stage (the ice retreated relatively late in Scandinavia), man inhabited several areas on the European continent. His range, of course, was governed by the extent of glaciation. No Paleolithic implements have been recovered from the Balkans, Greece, Crete, and the Aegean islands. Perhaps interest in the latter three areas has been concentrated too exclusively on classical remains, to the neglect of earlier periods of culture. The Old Stone Age is known from adjacent Anatolia, an area that, archeologically speaking, is better classified with the Middle East. The Paleolithic is represented abundantly in western Europe, especially in France, Spain, and southern Britain. It is well to keep in mind that Britain did not become an island till after Pleistocene times.

Paleolithic Subperiods

Three overlapping Paleolithic subperiods are recognized: Early, Middle, and Late (Table 49 and Movius, 1956:50). The Lower and Middle Paleolithic periods are limited largely to western Europe but the Upper Paleolithic is distributed more widely, extending into southern Russia. For obvious reasons, Scandinavia and northern Britain (Scotland) remained uninhabited until the final retreat of the last glaciation.

Each of these major periods can be divided into a number of component industries or cultures (see pp. 39–41). The main Paleolithic industries and cultures are shown in Figures 41:3 and 41:4. All of the traits making up a particular industry or culture did not occur together at the same time or place. The reader must keep the fact of local variation in mind as he reads the following highly generalized description of European prehistory.

Instead of being able to study total ways of life, like the ethnologist or archeologist working with later phases of culture, the Lower Paleolithic prehistorian is restricted to dealing with different types of stone tools. Each such type represents a different way of fabricating stone. Hence it is customary to speak of Paleolithic industries—or stone-tool traditions—rather than cultures. The tools are almost the sole evidence of culture during the greater part of the Pleistocene. Figure 41:3 includes the major industries of the first three glacial and interglacial stages. Some of these last into the fourth (Wuerm) glacial stage (Fig. 41:4), thereby enduring for hundreds of thousands of years. While changes from one industry to another or in their spatio-temporal distributions are important for reconstructing prehistory, in itself an industry reveals little about the total round of life. Upon reaching the fourth glacial stage, however, the assemblages become richer. Terms like "Aurignacian" and "Magdalenian" refer to full-blown phases of culture rather than only to traditions of stoneworking.

Industries of the Lower and Middle Paleolithic

No doubt varied resources were employed by men living in Lower and Middle Stone Age times but only stone implements survive. These are found largely in the open rather than in caves or under rock shelters, suggesting that man had not yet begun to inhabit natural shelters to the extent that he would toward the close of the fourth (Wuerm) glaciation. Tools of the early Ice Age are unspecialized and consist primarily of hand axes and flakes that served many purposes. Evidence of painting, sculpture, or engraving does not exist but this does not mean that men who lived then lacked the

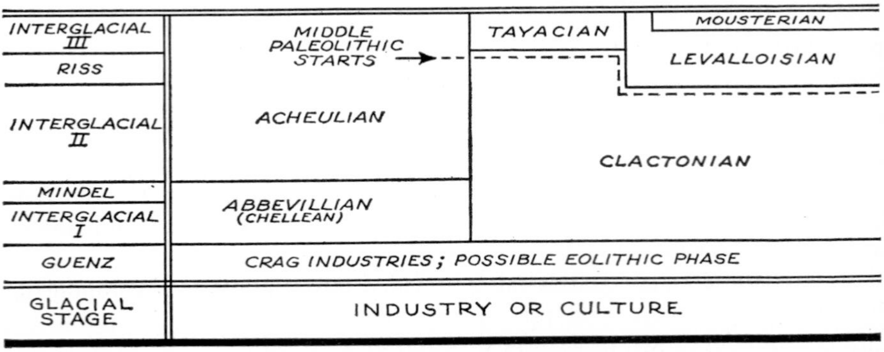

GLACIAL STAGE	INDUSTRY OR CULTURE		
INTERGLACIAL III	MIDDLE PALEOLITHIC STARTS →	TAYACIAN	MOUSTERIAN
RISS			LEVALLOISIAN
INTERGLACIAL II	ACHEULIAN		
		CLACTONIAN	
MINDEL INTERGLACIAL I	ABBEVILLIAN (CHELLEAN)		
GUENZ	CRAG INDUSTRIES; POSSIBLE EOLITHIC PHASE		

Fig. 41:3. Paleolithic Industries in the First Three Glacial and Interglacial Stages.

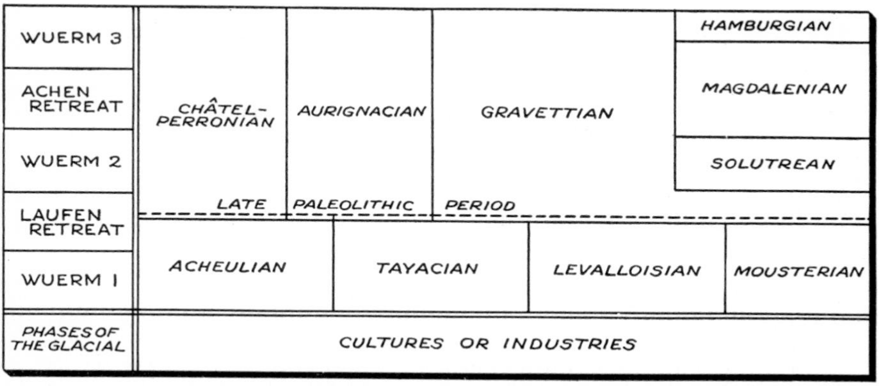

PHASES OF THE GLACIAL	CULTURES OR INDUSTRIES				
WUERM 3					HAMBURGIAN
ACHEN RETREAT	CHÂTEL-PERRONIAN	AURIGNACIAN	GRAVETTIAN		MAGDALENIAN
WUERM 2					SOLUTREAN
LAUFEN RETREAT	LATE PALEOLITHIC PERIOD				
WUERM 1	ACHEULIAN	TAYACIAN		LEVALLOISIAN	MOUSTERIAN

FIG. 41:4. Paleolithic Cultures in the Fourth (Wuerm) Glacial Stage (Substages of the Wuerm Glaciation Not According to Scale).

capacity to appreciate skillful workmanship or beauty. The symmetry and careful manufacture of later hand axes have impressed modern observers, who suggest that the makers found the deliberate control of technique intrinsically satisfying. The finished objects may have been used not only mundanely but also in ritual (Coon, 1954:56). Finally, the Lower and Middle Paleolithic periods are noteworthy for the long periods over which certain techniques or artifacts persisted. Change came slowly, at least in those areas of culture available for study by archeology.

Five main industries, together with Mousterian culture, will be described for the Lower and Middle Paleolithic. The reader is urged to refer frequently to Figures 41:3 and 41:4 in order to keep the relative chronology of these industries clearly in mind (see also the sequence summary in Table 49).

1. Crag Industries. Apart from even more dubious eoliths, possibly the earliest traces of culture in Europe consist of stone flakes, rough biface stone axes, and cores of flint trimmed only along the cutting edge (called choppers or chopping tools) recovered from the very earliest glacial marine deposits in southeastern England. The several Crag industries suggest that man lived in western Europe before the height of the first glaciation. But not all archeologists accept this interpretation. The Crag industries sometimes are held to represent later Paleolithic implements washed into first glacial marine deposits.

2. Abbevillian. Dating mainly from subtropical first interglacial times, and distributed in western Europe (England, Belgium, France, Spain, and Italy), Africa, and southern Asia are biface hand axes of the Abbevillian (formerly called Chellean) tradition.[3] The hunters who executed the Abbe-

[3] The change in nomenclature is related to finding the industry in its original geological stratum at Abbeville in the Somme Valley of northern France. At Chelles the stratum postdated the geological stage in which the axes first had been used. Calling these tools bifaces signifies that flaking occurred on both surfaces.

TABLE 49.   Correlation of Paleolithic Periods, Industries, and Cultures

Period and Duration	Industry or Culture
Lower Paleolithic The period extends from the first (Guenz) glacial into the early part of the fourth glacial. For present purposes it may be said to terminate with the third interglacial.	Crag, Abbevillian, Clactonian, and Acheulian industries. The common feature of these industries is the use, for many purposes, of biface hand axes or, in some cases, cruder chopping tools. In addition flake implements were used, including Clactonian flakes struck from a previously prepared core.
Middle Paleolithic The period extends from the second interglacial into the first part of the fourth (Wuerm) glacial stage. *a*	Levalloisian and Tayacian industries; Mousterian culture. A feature in this period is the ability to obtain specialized flakes from cores of flint containing a previously prepared striking platform. Hand axes continue.
Late Paleolithic The period is entirely within the fourth (Wuerm) glacial stage of the Upper Pleistocene.	Châtelperronian, Aurignacian, Gravettian, Solutrean, Magdalenian, and Hamburgian cultures. These cultures share the making of blades and an interest in representational or decorative art.

a Probably in parts of Europe the Middle Paleolithic survived into the latter part of the fourth glacial stage.

villian technique secured large cores of flint from which they detached flakes on both surfaces in order to make an irregular cutting tool ranging in length from 4 to 6 inches. How the flakes were detached remains in doubt. Either the core was struck with a hammer of some sort or it was struck against a stone anvil. At any rate the process was controlled sufficiently to produce tools of fairly standardized form. Some Abbevillian hand axes (also called *coups de poing* and fist axes) are oval; others lozenge-shaped or triangular. Regardless of form, the tools probably all served the same general purpose. What precisely they were used for is difficult to say. The flakes detached in the process of manufacture also found employment without being further trimmed or shaped. Some culture historians believe that the distribution of these core tools in Africa indicates that the followers of the Abbevillian tradition moved into that continent, along with other warm-weather fauna, when the glacial ice invaded Europe for the second time.

3. **Clactonian.** All communities in the first interglacial stage did not make Abbevillian hand axes. Some, in addition to using chopping tools (flaked on one surface or on both sides but only along a single cutting edge), employed flake tools secured by deliberately striking a flint core against a fixed stone anvil. To insure getting a usable flake the flint worker first prepared the core in a rather unsystematic way. It is the technique of striking flakes off from an unsystematically prepared core, and then shaping the

resultant flakes by further (secondary) chipping (or retouching), that is denoted by the term "Clactonian."[4] The industry, marked by increasing control over stone material, survived until the third (Riss) glacial stage, after which it appears to have merged with another technique for preparing cores, the Levalloisian, and to have given rise to the Tayacian industry. Both the latter continued in France into the fourth (Wuerm) glacial stage. Tools made according to the Clactonian tradition show up in Central Europe and Asia north of the spine formed by the Alps, Balkans, and Caucasus. The Clactonian industry, then, is noteworthy for the radical change introduced in flake preparation

4. Acheulian. The Abbevillian hand-ax tradition was succeeded in second interglacial times by a new approach to the fabrication of biface core tools. Hand axes were now made smaller. Available specimens from Europe, Asia, and Africa indicate greater skill in preparing the core. The cutting edges of the implement were made regular by the application of secondary chipping. To these innovations the term "Acheulian" is applied.[5] Tools of this type are often found in association with flakes prepared in the Clactonian tradition and these tend to increase as the Acheulian tradition persists. The European distribution of the industry is the same as the Abbevillian except that Germany is better represented. This industry also testifies to man's growing command of working flint.

5. Levalloisian. Beginning around the end of the second long interglacial stage is another innovation in flake manufacturing. This, the Levalloisian,[6] involved the careful blocking-out of a desired shape on a core from which was then detached an oval-shaped flake or, if the length was more than twice the width, a blade (Movius, 1953:166). The flake was struck off by a final blow delivered on the striking platform of the prepared core. This technique may have arisen from the Clactonian tradition. In the Levalloisian industry the core underwent more careful preparation, being more painstakingly trimmed. With time the Levalloisian technique assumed still greater mastery over material. Tools prepared in this tradition occur in France, Britain, Germany, and Asia and extend far into Africa. People who executed the technique also often made Acheulian hand axes. In southern France a blending of Levalloisian and Clactonian influences during the third interglacial stage gave rise to a new industry, the Tayacian, that continued into the next glacial period.[7]

---

[4] The type site is Clacton-on-Sea, in Essex, England. A Clactonian industry has also been discovered at Swanscombe, Kent, in the Thames Valley (see p. 856).

[5] From Saint-Acheul, located in the Somme Valley of France. The final stage of the Acheulian tradition is sometimes called Micoquian from La Micoque in south-central France, Department of La Dordogne.

[6] From Levallois, the type site, on the outskirts of Paris.

[7] Tayacian is named after Tayac, a commune in the French Department of La Dordogne.

6. **Mousterian.** In a narrow sense, Mousterian also refers to an industry of flake chipping.[8] It is easy to mistake a Mousterian flake for a Levalloisian. Both were struck from a systematically prepared core. The Mousterian core is generally described as "discoidal" and the Levalloisian as a "tortoise" core but more technical considerations lie behind these names than need be gone into here.[9] For present purposes such technical considerations may be ignored. Mousterian also constitutes a phase of culture possessing these elements: heart-shaped hand axes of relatively small size; triangular flakes with a sharp apex suggesting their use as spear or lance points; flakes with one chipped edge—side scrapers—and others with a semicircular notch (notched scraper) that may have been used to smooth down spear or lance shafts; flakes with a beak, useful for engraving and called "beaked gravers"; chisel-like flakes with a transverse cutting edge, called "burins" and probably used to make slots in wood or bone; balls of limestone and quartz, the function of which is unknown although they may indicate hunting with a bola; perforated animal teeth, no doubt worn for adornment; deliberate burial of the dead with joints of meat and tools; the use of fire to cook meat; and cannibalism. The latter trait is revealed by the condition of some of the human bones found in Mousterian contexts. Levalloisian, Mousterian, and Acheulian industries are all apparent in Mousterian culture.

Portions of the Mousterian assemblage appear in both cave and open-air sites distributed in Spain, Portugal, France, and Germany. Such sites thin out toward Britain in the west and Austria and Hungary in the east. The phase began in the warm period of the third interglacial but persisted into the fourth (Wuerm) glacial stage. Human skeletons associated with Mousterian tools do not resemble modern forms of man but are usually Neanderthaloid (see pp. 857–858). The chief significance of the Mousterian phase of Paleolithic culture is the appearance in it of clearly specialized flint implements: projectile points, two kinds of scrapers (one, perhaps, used for skins with which man protected himself from the cold as the final ice stage drew near), and engraving tools. Burials, personal adornment, fire, and cannibalism all may have occurred earlier in Pleistocene Europe but this is the first time that so many elements of Paleolithic culture have been found together.

Cultures of the Late Paleolithic

A fresh glance at Figures 41:3 and 41:4 shows that culture did not change abruptly as the third interglacial gave way to the fourth, and last, major ice advance. The Acheulian, Tayacian, and Levalloisian industries persisted into the first phase of the new cold period. The final stage of the fourth, Wuerm,

---

[8] The type site is a rock shelter at Le Moustier in south-central France, Department of La Dordogne.

[9] It has also been argued that the Mousterian industry is a degeneration of the Levalloisian (Lévi-Strauss, 1952:42).

glaciation, however, is marked by dramatic cultural innovations. The full expression of these heralds the Late Paleolithic era, in some respects one of the most spectacular cultural periods of human history.

The distinctive features of Late Paleolithic culture (some of which are foreshadowed in the transitional Mousterian phase) include: increasing use of cave shelters as well as evidence of man-made dwellings; use of projectile points and blades; hitherto unused resources for culture building, like bone, antler, and ivory; in France and Spain, mural paintings on cave walls; sculpture; engraving; and carving (Leakey, 1954). Considerable blending of traditions occurred in this period indicating extensive contact between communities. To use the special concepts of economics: the Late Paleolithic was marked by a substantial increase of capital. Some of this was productive capital—new tools and weapons. Some was social capital, representing not so much an increase in wealth as means to augment the capacity of the people to produce more wealth (Spengler, 1956). Examples include sculptured figurines, the meaning of which is lost; caves, painted and engraved, serving as habitations or, conceivably, as ritual shelters; and additional forms of ornament. Obviously the break between the Middle and Late Paleolithic was not sharp. Continuity therefore existed between both phases of culture in techniques, artifacts, and general mode of life.

The principle phases of Late Paleolithic culture now will be described.

1. Châtelperronian. Distributed in France and Germany and ranging eastward into Crimea and Israel, the distinctive blades that mark this culture may have originated in western Asia.[10] Hand axes continue in a typical Châtelperronian assemblage. Large end scrapers (the scraping edge being along the short axis of the implement) largely replace Mousterian side scrapers. Pointed blades, corresponding to the steel portion of modern knives, but made of flint, were made in several forms. Sometimes they were blunted on one edge but at other times left plain. Burins continued to be manufactured, and perforated canine teeth of the stag and fox maintained an earlier Paleolithic pattern of animal teeth for adornment. Points for a spear or lance were made of bone, at times with the butt end divided by a slit, the function of which remains unclear.

2. Aurignacian. The Aurignacian contemporaries of Châtelperronian communities lived in the mountainous parts of France and Central Europe where caves were abundant. The culture ranged into western Germany, Italy, Czechoslovakia, Austria, Hungary, Rumania, Bulgaria, Crimea, Turkey, and Israel.[11] The people hunted the cave bear and engraved, or painted in

---

[10] The name is derived from Châtelperron, Department of Allier, in central France. Formerly known as Lower Aurignacian, the culture is sometimes classed with Gravettian (see below) and called Périgordian after a region in southwestern France.

[11] Formerly called Middle Aurignacian, the type site is Aurignac, Department of Haute-Garonne, southern France.

red and black, the profiles of this and other animals on cave walls. Bear skulls possessed special significance and were arranged in a systematic pattern on the cave floor. Certain tools common to the Châtelperronian assemblage, like split-base bone points and blades, both edges of which possess a shallow notch, were also made by Aurignacians. Notched blades, however, are more typical of the latter. Several varieties of engravers reflect the interest of the people in representational art. A new form of end scraper—thick, with a flat base but a back that rises like the keel of a boat, the so-called keel-shaped scraper—appeared for the first time, together with bone needles containing an eye for threading. That such needles also meant tailored clothing in place of draped skins is not easy to verify. In addition to engraved and painted animal profiles the Aurignacians sculptured human torsos which suggest that some special significance may have been attached to the vulva. Their hands painted on cave walls sometimes show missing finger joints. Whether the joints were severed deliberately or not is again hard to say.

3. Gravettian. Mammoth, bison, reindeer, and wild horse provided the basis of life in the Gravettian phase and also supplied ivory and antler for manufacturing. The Gravettians were distributed in Wales, England, Spain, France, Italy, the Rhine Valley, upper Danube, Kurdistan, and the south Russian plain.[12] In western Europe they lived in caves but on the eastern loess plains of the continent they built quite substantial shelters. At Gagarino on the Don River, in the Ukraine, Soviet archeologists have discovered a saucer-shaped excavation that was originally over a foot deep and about 19 by 15 feet across. Large mammoth tusks in the depression suggest the diet of hunters who may have erected a large skin shelter in this locality. In Siberia similar excavations contain a center hearth consisting of a shallow basin with a stone slab at the bottom and slabs of stone on edge at either side. At Kostienko on the Don a hollow oval measuring 106 feet in length and 49 feet wide contains remains of 9 or more hearths spaced 6 or 7 feet apart. This may represent a communal winter house accommodating several nuclear families.

A distinctive implement of Gravettian culture was the Gravette blade. This was drawn out to a sharp point and given the suggestion of a tang by means of which it may have been hafted. Needles were still made. Curious perforated sections of antler horn, known as *bâtons de commandement*, have aroused much speculation. The name given them suggests that these implements symbolized authority but this is as much pure fancy as the idea that they constituted rods for guiding harnessed reindeer, horse bits, dress fasteners, basketmaking devices, shaft polishers, or clubs. In Germany the Gravettians excavated Mousterian stone artifacts and reworked them for further use. Ornaments included bracelets, nose plugs, and beads carved from bone

---

[12] The type site is La Gravette in the Department of La Dordogne.

and ivory or made by perforating shells and animal teeth. Such objects, along with food and tools, also went into graves, the corpses being covered liberally with red ocher. The representational art features small figures, carved from ivory or soft stone, of women with pendant breasts and heavy buttocks. Such "Venus figurines" are best known from Willendorf, a site on the Danube. In France similar images were carved on cave walls. From one site comes a carved block of limestone, about 11 by 17 inches, illustrating what appears to be a scene of coitus. Another larger tablet bears the relief figure of a woman 17 inches high. In southern Russia sculptured figures of the mammoth and cave lion have been discovered, and in France and Spain animals were painted or engraved on cave walls.

4. Solutrean. Sites yielding Solutrean remains occur in central and western Europe but are rare in England and absent in Italy, the Balkans, and southern Russia.[13] Solutrean culture itself may have originated in Hungary or, according to another opinion, in southeastern Spain under North African influence. Many of the implements are already familiar: Gravette blade, end scraper, and engraving tools indistinguishable from Châtelperronian, Aurignacian, and Gravettian. Distinctive is a "laurel-leaf" flake (point), from 2½ to 7 inches long, carefully worked. Slimmer blades occur that also may represent spear points. The processing of bone shows considerably less skill (or, what is more likely, care) than does work in stone. Hearths in one site are set so close together that a communal dwelling is suggested but in France the Solutreans usually lived in caves. For subsistence these people hunted the wild horse, cave lion, hyena, bear, hare, marmot, mammoth, wild cattle, and reindeer. Fossil shells were sometimes perforated for suspension. Apart from figures of animals engraved on stone blocks and carved in the round, the Solutrean phase contained relatively little interest in representational art.

5. Magdalenian. In France, Spain, and parts of Belgium, Switzerland, southern Germany, western Czechoslovakia, Poland, and the Ukraine the Paleolithic draws to a close with Magdalenian culture.[14] Hunting of the reindeer, bison, mammoth, and other animals occurred in conjunction with fishing so that the implement assemblage included a large number of bone and ivory points and harpoon heads. The latter were at first barbed on only one side but later on both. The spear thrower (i.e., atlatl) came into use then and can be counted as man's first machine. The keel-shaped scraper, Gravette blade, polished bone needle, and engraving tools link Magdalenian with Gravettian and Aurignacian ways of life. The *bâtons de commandements* also persist and are finished quite elaborately with a high polish and

[13] The name derives from the village of Solutré in the Department of Saône-et-Loire, east-central France.

[14] Named from the type site La Madeleine, a rock shelter in the Department of La Dordogne. The culture is a continuation of Gravettian and Aurignacian traditions. In England, Gravettian continues in Creswellian culture.

engraved surface. Blades of reindeer horn were decorated with sculptured
animal figures. Could such blades have served the function of daggers?
Many of the flint tools were made by detaching ribbons of flint 7 to 9
inches in length. These probably served as knives but show none of the
careful secondary chipping of the Solutrean phase. In some places the
terminal Magdalenians made relatively small flint implements which herald
the microlithic artifacts of the Mesolithic period (see pp. 747–748). Human
crania provided rather morbid drinking vessels. Flat, oval-shaped pendants
of stone and bone may have symbolized bullroarers. Ornament in Germany
included mollusc shells somehow transported overland from the Mediterranean. One French Magdalenian burial is of great interest for the fact that
the bones were arranged in the grave to represent a human skeleton. The
original dismemberment probably took place elsewhere and, perhaps, was
done deliberately. Other kinds of burials also are known and often contain
a skeleton sprinkled with red ocher and covered with slabs of stone. The
bâtons de commandement constitute a favorite type of *Beigaben*. Representational art is rich, particularly in France and northern Spain (Fig.
41:5). The art includes profiles of animals, done on cave walls in mono-

Fig. 41:5. Centers of Late Paleolithic Representational
Art.

chrome; polychrome animal scenes, spectacular in their naturalistic poses; life-size carvings; and figures of bisons and other beasts modeled in clay. The rock shelter of Le Roc aux Sorciers, near Angles (Department of Vienne) contained a life-size relief sculpture of a horse, group of ibexes, and three life-size women depicted from the waist down. The carvings "suggest a degree of sensitivity and even sophistication which are hard to visualise even in much later ages" (Garrod and St. Mathuring, 1952). At the nearby Cave of Louis Taillebourg was found a sculptured head of a Magdalenian man. It shows him with a black beard, muffled to his chin with a fur garment below which he seems to be wearing a fur undergarment (Garrod, 1949). Older cave paintings, often located in relatively inaccessible parts of the cave, sometimes are covered over with later work. Portable art includes carvings on stone, bone, ivory, and antler; engraved implements—like harpoons or batons—and a few sculptured human torsos. Generally animals are the favorite subject matter and their execution is highly naturalistic. The purposes behind the cave paintings and sculptures frequently have been discussed. One common explanation associates them with rituals designed to secure an increase in the food supply. However, there is no evidence that Magdalenian man painted or carved with this intention in mind.

6. **Hamburgian.** From northern Holland and Germany come remains of a culture associated with people who wintered in southern forests and then moved north in the summer to hunt wild fowl, reindeer, and fish on the Arctic tundra.[15] Keeled and end scrapers, burins, tanged points, pointed flakes or blades, and, perhaps, bone hooks constituted the Hamburgian tool assemblage. Heavy implements, like the ax, are absent. On occasion the people weighted a reindeer with stones and threw it into a glacial bog, probably as an offering to some collective representation.

MESOLITHIC ERA OF FOOD GATHERING[16]

As the glaciers withdrew from Scandinavia and rose from valley bottoms farther south, substantial alterations took place on the earth's surface. Water returned to the ocean and sea levels rose. At the same time removal of the weight of the ice mass enabled the surface of the land to lift. Most importantly, the climate ameliorated (Fig. 41:6). This brought about a change in flora and fauna. Forests crept north over the tundra. Animals like the reindeer, horse, or bison, easy to hunt because they roamed in herds, were replaced by solitary species like the elk, bear, and deer. Profound alterations in European culture followed. Caves and rock shelters ceased to be used much as habitations. A large part of the subsistence needs came to be met by collecting nuts and shellfish as well as through fishing. The cultures which

[15] The type site is near the city of Hamburg.
[16] This section is based largely on J. G. D. Clark, 1932, 1936, 1952.

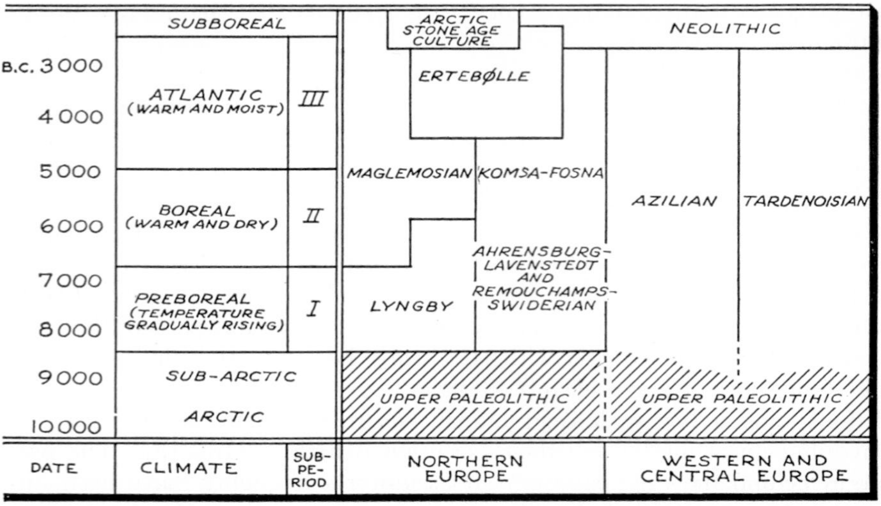
SUBBOREAL
ARCTIC STONE AGE CULTURE
NEOLITHIC
B.C. 3000
4000
5000
6000
7000
8000
9000
10000
ATLANTIC (WARM AND MOIST)
III
ERTEBØLLE
MAGLEMOSIAN
KOMSA-FOSNA
AZILIAN
TARDENOISIAN
BOREAL (WARM AND DRY)
II
AHRENSBURG-LAVENSTEDT AND REMOUCHAMPS-SWIDERIAN
PREBOREAL (TEMPERATURE GRADUALLY RISING)
I
LYNGBY
SUB-ARCTIC
ARCTIC
UPPER PALEOLITHIC
UPPER PALEOLITIHIC
DATE
CLIMATE
SUB-PE-RIOD
NORTHERN EUROPE
WESTERN AND CENTRAL EUROPE

FIG. 41:6. Mesolithic Phases of European Culture.

existed between the Old Stone Age, in its Pleistocene setting, and the first signs of food production belong to the Mesolithic, or Middle Stone Age. Figure 41:6 includes the main phases of Mesolithic culture.

Instead of describing in detail each of the Mesolithic ways of life this section will sketch some of the general features of the era. The reader must once more bear in mind that local variation was more important than will be indicated.

Culture of the Middle Stone Age

Reflecting the growth of forests on the warming postglacial tundra was a prominent item in the Mesolithic tool assemblage, the ax. Absent during subperiod I in the plain stretching from Holland to Poland, the place of this tool could hardly have been taken by the variously sized flakes or tanged flint points that belong to this period. In the second subperiod, during which alder, elm, oak, and lime trees began to enter the still predominantly birch and pine forests, the new tool made its appearance along with a large assortment of other implements for woodworking: wedges, bow drills, chisels, and gouges. The Maglemosean hunters, who ranged from eastern England to the Baltic, used both axes and adzes (cf. Cole, *1954a*). Often these artifacts consisted of cores of flint shaped by chipping but also of close-grained stone shaped by pecking and grinding.[17] Added with time was a long and slender pickax. Some of the adzes consisted of a single piece of bone or antler mounted on a staff through a shaft-hole. In other cases the stone

[17] The word "Maglemosean" refers to "big bog." The type site is Maglemose, located on the island of Seeland in the North Sea.

blades were hafted in an antler sleeve mounted on a wooden shaft. If Paleolithic hand axes are not counted, then this period is marked by the origination and rapid diffusion of the true ax.

For food many Mesolithic communities turned to shellfish and other sea products, especially pike. They also hunted land animals, like the urox, elk, hart, boar, bear, otter, beaver, fox, marten, porcupine, and many varieties of birds. Collected vegetable products included berries, nuts, and wild seeds. The importance of shellfish in the diet of communities located along the indented coasts of Scandinavia may be judged from the mounds of refuse that give the Ertebølle phase its name. These kitchen middens often reached 100 yards in length, up to 55 feet in width, and 3 to 5 feet in depth. Examination of the shells mixed with animal bones reveals that the people who occupied the seashore sites ate oysters, cockles, mussels, and periwinkles. The Ertebølle culture lasted until domesticated animals arrived in the region.

Mesolithic folk used dugout canoes and sledges (probably hand-drawn). Food-getting equipment included fish nets made from bast fibers and suspended from bark floats; barbed and plain bone hooks; fire-charred pikes or lances; spears; throwing sticks, or the boomerang; bone leisters; funnel-shaped fish traps; and, of course, bone and horn harpoon heads. In southern Europe when the reindeer disappeared harpoon heads came to be made of stag horn. The material posed a problem because the inner core of this substance is soft, leaving only the outer section fit for use. Man's inventive response was the flat harpoon. The bow, a North African Paleolithic invention, became common in Europe at this time. Arrows were tipped with bone and stone points that were sometimes barbed. Perhaps dogs assisted Mesolithic man's hunting. In the Ertebølle phase a larger type of dog was introduced. He may indicate the beginning of animal traction.

Microlithic (i.e., pygmy) flints first began to be manufactured in Late Paleolithic times (see p. 744) but they may be regarded properly as a sign of the Mesolithic era. Tardenoisian culture, distributed in Britain, Belgium, southwestern Germany, and Poland particularly, is rich in small flakes of flint trimmed in a variety of geometric shapes: triangles, crescents, lozenges, rhomboids, trapezes, and points marked with a concave base.[18] Making these implements required no little skill. They were removed from carefully prepared cores and then trimmed, often with considerable wastage of material. The microliths (usually less than three-eighths of an inch long) are too small to have been used in their natural state. Some of the less retouched pygmy flints have been found set in slots provided in bone points, but this by no means makes clear the purposes for which the more carefully processed ones

---

[18] The type site is at Fère-en-Tardenois, Aisne, France. The culture is not rich in wood-cutting implements and the people preferred to cope with the problem of forests by avoiding them. They located camps on sandy or rocky places and along the margins of lakes.

were made or the meaning of their geometric shapes. It is well to note that microliths have recurred several times in culture history. Whether all other pygmy-flint traditions can be traced to the European Mesolithic one is not at all certain (Burkitt, 1929:16).

Also not clearly understood is the meaning of the painted pebbles bearing red-painted designs which were richly represented in Azilian culture.[19] The designs predominantly were geometric but in some cases may have been intended to represent stylized human figures (Fig. 41:7). These, in turn, have

FIG. 41:7.   Some Designs from Azilian Painted Pebbles (from Macalister, 1921:529–530).

been related to stylized figures found in certain Spanish cave paintings (Macalister, 1921:529). Conjecture has held that the pebbles were protective amulets, served as a kind of coinage, and constituted playthings. In one site some have been found carefully broken in two, suggesting that they were objects of great importance.

From the eastern Baltic area comes a blunt cylindrical head of wood whose use likewise is not clear; it may have been used to club moulting fowl or trapped animals. It seems to lack any connection with the cross- or star-shaped mace, often made of soft soapstone and decorated with incised lines, found in the Arctic Stone Age culture. The precise use of the latter similarly remains unknown.

The listing of Mesolithic implements can go on, indicating the varied stock of capital equipment which man in this period possessed. People used awls of bone and horn; netting needles; burins of Late Paleolithic forms; various kinds of scrapers; knives and daggers of stone, bone, and horn; and, in the Arctic Stone Age phase, slate knives (sometimes slightly curved or "banana-shaped" and also strongly semilunar, like the modern Eskimo woman's tool). Other objects of slate finished by grinding also belong to this late Mesolithic period. In the Ertebølle culture appears the first pottery of northern Europe: large, rough storage jars with a pointed base and flaring rim, together with oval, saucer-shaped lamps in which oil may have been burned. The pots were made by building up successive coils of clay and then,

[19] Le Mas d'Azil, in the Pyrenean Department of Ariège, is the type site. The painted pebbles are limited to northern Spain and France, but other parts of the Azilian assemblage extend through Central Europe to the Danube and perhaps even farther east.

sometimes, burnishing the surface with a smooth pebble. Potters were not too adept at controlling the heat in firing. Pottery continues into the Arctic Stone Age, a food-gathering way of life that tarried in northern Scandinavia and Russia after food production already had been established in northern Europe (see below). Here the clay vessels came to be decorated with lines of dots impressed with a comb (comb marking). Mesolithic jewelry included perforated shells and animal teeth; pins and bracelets of bone; and beads or pendants of amber. The use of combs, made of bone, already has been mentioned.

Forms of shelter are difficult to detect. Tardenoisian culture, with its absence of heavy equipment, has been found in caves and rock shelters but these people also built habitations in shallow excavations. Judging from sparse evidence, the houses had an oval ground plan. They were about 15 feet long and 8 feet wide, possessing a central hearth. From Yorkshire, England, a settlement 220 by 240 square yards is known and assigned by radiocarbon dating to between 7100 and 7900 B.C. The shelters themselves cannot be reconstructed but it is clear that the village was built on a corduroy platform laid down on the marshy surface of a lakeshore. Platform dwellings and round huts (10 to 13 feet in diameter) formed part of the Arctic Stone Age. In the latter phase the ski and sled probably appeared for the first time in northern Europe.

It is somewhat easier to reconstruct the ceremonial treatment of the dead. West European Tardenoisians doubled up the corpse and interred it in rubbish heaps accompanied by ornament and implements. One Azilian site in Bavaria yielded 20 neatly severed human skulls arranged in a circle facing west and covered with red ocher and perforated animal teeth. Ertebølle folk were buried fully extended in shallow graves and without *Beigaben*. Some of these burials have been found in the kitchen midden sites but others, so far unfound, must have been prepared away from the settlements. The Arctic Stone Age people continued to inter corpses among the dwellings, sometimes adding a circle of stones around the grave. Cannibalism is suspected to have been practiced in the Maglemosean and Ertebølle cultures.

Mesolithic people did not remain content to make only utilitarian objects. Animal figurines carved from amber were decorated with incised lines as were certain tools; similar images were engraved on stone; finely drilled holes arranged in patterns constituted a favorite form of decoration in Maglemosean culture. The Tardenoisians sometimes decorated cave shelters with rather impressionistic hunting scenes but the period of Late Paleolithic mural painting definitely is over. Naturalistic animal carvings on cliff walls, dating from the Arctic Stone Age or later, recall the former period. These carvings represented reindeer, elk, bear, halibut, and sea birds. The same people also sculptured animal images out of bone and horn.

Tarriance in North Europe

Many features of the Mesolithic period persisted in Scandinavia until 2000 or 1500 B.C., more than a thousand years after agriculture had spread into the central and western parts of the continent. In parts of Sweden and Norway hunting and fishing continued as important subsistence activities even after the use of domesticated plants and animals. The Vikings and later Lapps placed considerable reliance on bone and stone for tools at the same time that they employed iron and bronze. The situation parallels that found in the circumpolar region of the New World, where stone tools and food gathering persisted long after greater cultural development had appeared southward. Tarriance, therefore, is a characteristic phenomenon in Arctic and sub-Arctic cultures, one related to the marginality of the circumpolar region (see pp. 185–186).

AVAILABLE FILMS

The excavation of a Paleolithic hand ax and exploration of Lascaux and Gargas caves in France are featured in *La trace de l'homme*, produced by the Compagnie Artistique de Production et Adaptation Cinématographique (20 min., b. and w., French narration). The paintings of Lascaux receive a leisurely examination in *Lascaux: Cradle of Man's Art*, produced by Gotham Films (17 min., color). *Story of Prehistoric Man*, by Coronet Films, is short and rather elementary (11 min., color).

42.

Civilization in Europe

CIVILIZATION emerges in Europe with the diffusion of agriculture, animal husbandry, pottery, metallurgy, and many other traits from the world of the Middle East and their incorporation into a distinctive, new cultural configuration. As Fig. 41:1 indicated, the arrival of food production in the eastern Mediterranean occurred when in Southwest Asia and Egypt culture entered the era of Regional Florescence. In Scandinavia, agriculture arrived much later.

Three periods conveniently sum up the emergence of European civilization. They cover: (1) the arrival of food production with associated elements (often called the Neolithic Age), (2) the growth of Mediterranean (Aegean) civilization, and (3) the overlapping period which saw civilization move to the frontiers of central, eastern, and northern Europe. The plan of this chapter is to treat each of these periods in succession, although, as Figure 41:1 revealed, in some regions a new one began before the previous one had ended in some more marginal region of the continent. For each period prehistory will be examined in four geographical regions: (1) Aegean or eastern Mediterranean (including, sometimes, a look northward into the Balkans and southern Russia), (2) Central and South-Central Europe (including Italy), (3) the Atlantic countries, especially Great Britain, and (4) Scandinavia.

Geographically each of these regions differs from the others (Fig. 42:1). In Greece and Crete agricultural plains are as scarce as the summer rains. Streams that run with torrents during the summer show only dry beds in winter. Overland communication between the inhabited valleys is cut off by steep mountain slopes, numerous inlets, and treacherous streams. From early times commerce used the sea, encouraging the rise of pirates. North of the Greek peninsula, highland continues to the Transylvanian Alps (cut through, however, by the easterly flowing Danube) and Carpathians. East of the Carpathians lies the southern Russian plain—a country of rich earth.

Central Europe includes the European plain stretching from eastern England into Russia. Precipitation occurs in summer and winter but the long and cold winter hardly allows agriculture. The western part of the plain is favored by considerably warmer winters, a factor perhaps related to its

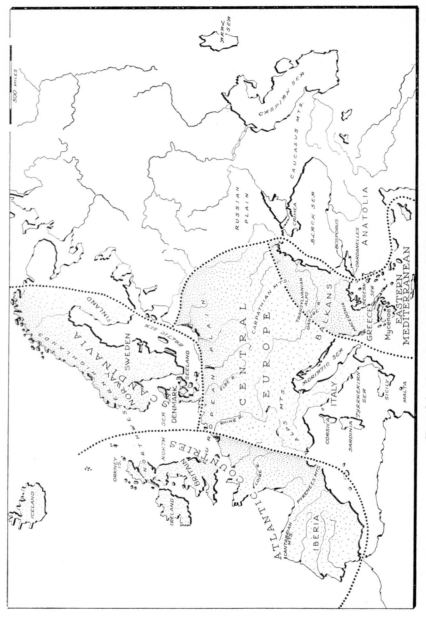

Fig. 42:1. Some European Regions and Place Names.

heavy infiltration in late prehistoric times when the climate of Europe grew colder. The Alps separate this plain from the Italian peninsula.

The Atlantic countries—Portugal, Spain (together both countries make up Iberia), France, Belgium, Britain, and Ireland—experience relatively mild winters. They are also well watered, but the climate mostly is too cold for winter farming.

North of the European plain (but in the south occupying a small part of it) lies Scandinavia, a name embracing Denmark, Norway, Sweden, and Finland. The coastal climate, particularly in Norway, is relatively mild, especially so when its northern location is taken into account. Inland the weather is colder. The explanation for the generally milder climate as one moves westward in Europe lies in the moderating influence of the ocean, whence blow the prevailing winds. Precipitation in Scandinavia is more abundant toward the west, the rain-bearing winds being largely excluded from Sweden by the northwestern highlands.

ARRIVAL OF FOOD PRODUCTION

In no sense does the diffusion of culture from Southwest Asia and Egypt to Europe represent a simple transfer of ready-made elements which came to be executed in the new setting exactly as they were in the old. "The Oriental impulse was blended and transformed into a diversity of essentially European cultures" (Hawkes, 1940:284). The Neolithic Age, as the period when food production arrived in Europe is also called, meant the introduction of innovations like cereal agriculture; domestication of cattle, pigs, sheep, and goats; and new crafts like ceramics, textile weaving, and the making of bricks. Although wild cattle and pigs lived in Mesolithic Europe, the earliest domesticated varieties do not represent local types, indicating that domestication did not originate on the continent. Similarly, cultivated cereals like wheat and barley are not related to the wild European grasses but appear to be more at home in Egypt or northern Mesopotamia.

The earliest diffusion of mixed farming into the eastern Mediterranean probably involved several actual migrations of people who carried the new way of life. This is indicated by the slight importance which the earliest villagers attached to hunting. Refuse heaps contain relatively few wild animal bones. Perhaps population pressure lay behind the migrations, or increasing desiccation may have led to a search for better-watered terrain. Europe in the fourth millennium, when mixed farming was first implemented, existed in the relatively warm and moist Atlantic climate phase (Fig. 41:2). By the time the new way of life reached western Europe drier conditions had already set in. Yet irrigation never became necessary there and even the deterioration of climate, about 500 years before the Christian era (the end of the Hypsithermal), did not force the displacement of plant cultivation except in northern Scandinavia. Neolithic colonists probably entered Europe through several gateways. From Southwest Asia some could have crossed the Bosporus or Dardanelles, entering European Turkey and the Balkans. Others may have moved along the island bridges from Anatolia to Greece and then on to the Balkans and Central Europe. From North Africa another gateway led to Spain and then to France and Britain, the latter by this time being separated from the mainland. From the eastern Mediterranean islands, where civilization first flourished, subsequent waves of colonists appear to have moved westward as far as the Straits of Gibraltar and then north (Fig. 42:2). Others entered Jugoslavia and followed the Danube

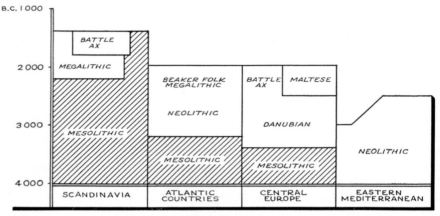

Fig. 42:2.   Some Neolithic Cultures of Europe.

into the European plain. The reader should not think of these migrations as deliberate expeditions each of which occurred only once. Many separate shifts and thrusts influenced, and became blended with, one another to a complicated degree.

The period here called Arrival of Food Production corresponds to the Formative era in the Middle East. The alternative name Neolithic (i.e., New Stone) refers specifically to the growing importance of grinding or polishing stone in manufacturing implements. But it is also used with a much wider connotation to denote a whole complex of elements that tend to recur together: agriculture, animal husbandry, relatively sedentary village life, pottery, and ground stone tools.

Among the most common Neolithic implements of polished stone is the celt (although celts were also occasionally chipped from flint or some other, easily fracturable, stone). Measuring about 4 or 5 inches long and 2 inches wide the implement is more or less pointed on one end and round in cross section. It carries a sharp, convex cutting edge at the other end (Fig. 42:3). Whether or not such tools were hafted and used as axes is not quite clear.

They could also have served as wedges for splitting wood. In eastern Europe the celt (or so-called shoe-last celt) was longer. It reveals a flat under surface, while the upper surface is fairly convex. One end is blunt but the other possesses a sharp cutting edge. It is supposed that this celt may have been hafted and served as a hoe. Another common element of European Neolithic culture is the socketed stone ax containing a hole for hafting. One famous type is the battle ax, used as a weapon. Some forms of battle axes are shown in Figure 42:4.

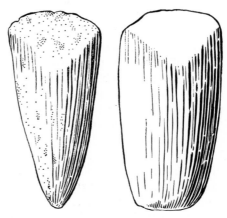

FIG. 42:3.   Neolithic Celts from Western Europe (After Burkitt, 1929:105).

Eastern Mediterranean

Permanent villages, around which farmers artificially maintained the fertility of their fields, accompanied the arrival of food production in Cyprus, Crete, Greece, Macedonia, and the Balkans. Eastern Mediterranean crops included barley, wheat, and, somewhat later, figs, pears, almonds, peas, and beans (J. G. D. Clark, 1952:114). The ground may have been broken for cultivation by means of polished stone, shoe-last celts. Cereals were harvested with flint sickles. Cattle were domesticated while weapons like the sling,

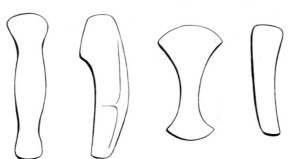

FIG. 42:4.   Battle Axes in Outline (After Burkitt, 1929:121).

bow, spear, and fishhooks helped in exploiting another source of meat and fish. Other early implements included polished stone adzes and axes, flint and bone scrapers, stone querns for grinding grain, blades of chipped stone, and needles of bone and horn. Clay spindle whorls attest to spinning and, perhaps, also indicate weaving. Stone beads and pendants—sometimes in the form of miniature axes—bone pins, and shell ornaments provided adornment. To this early assemblage new forms of wealth were gradually added. Pottery and kilns for firing it came first. The surface of the early vessels was often burnished to a high finish. In Crete stratigraphy reveals the introduction of a black, incised ware that in time replaced plain burnished vessels. The incised lines were filled in with white paint. After a while Cretan pottery began to be painted, spiral and meander designs especially being popular. The period of newly arrived food production closes with the introduction of copper, probably native copper, that was cast into desired forms. Objects made of copper remained small, probably because of a limited supply of metal. Stamp seals, obviously derived from Mesopotamia, point to a growing consciousness of wealth and property.

Aegean houses had rectangular and circular ground plans. In Cyprus the latter type (called a *tholos*, "a circular room"—*tholoi*, plural) reached diameters of from 13 to 20 feet. Larger structures of the same plan, perhaps temples, later came to be constructed. In Crete some early farmers lived and buried the dead in caves. From a later Neolithic horizon Cretan houses are known which rested on stone block foundations and probably were built of sun-dried brick. In Greece and the Balkans early dwellings were rectangular and gabled, of mud brick or wattle and daub, and included clay ovens. Beaten clay gave the floors of Aegean houses a hard surface. In time dwellings increased in size and some settlements came to be surrounded by quite massive fortifications heralding a militaristic phase of culture.

The Neolithic farming folk contracted the bodies of the deceased before subjecting them to burial. Almost everywhere people made small female figurines of clay or stone; they show women standing, sitting, and squatting. Some became so conventionalized that they scarcely can be recognized. The use of these figurines may be conjectured. Perhaps they indicate a collective representation, one conceived of as having power over plant growth and human fertility. Signs of trade and specialization are not revealed in the local settlements of early Aegean food producers. Nor are indications of war apparent here or in the Balkans until just before the end of the era.

Central Europe

The formative influences from the eastern Mediterranean took hold only slowly in the deciduous forests of the central European plain. The earliest farmers sought sandy, pervious soils which, despite their forest cover, would be easier to cultivate than heavy loams. The trees, of course, had to be cleared for agriculture and cleared often, for the early Danubian cultivators did not occupy permanent settlements as the Aegeans did. The central Europeans practiced shifting cultivation, moving on to clear new sites when the soil in one place became exhausted. They must have found the ax and adze extremely valuable tools. A settlement included about 12 or 15 households that supported themselves by domesticating wheat, barley, cattle, pigs, and sheep as well as by intensive hunting. In time some communities became pastoral specialists, especially rearing sheep. In this region it is likely that some cultivators were not colonists from the Mediterranean coast but food gatherers who learned techniques of food production as these diffused via the Danube Valley. The shoe-last celt again seems to have provided a hoe. Dwellings, rectangular in ground plan and with a gabled roof, were partly sunk into the excavated loess and seem to have been large enough to accommodate several nuclear families. In the houses stood domed ovens coated with clay. Household pottery remained plain but was furnished with lugs, often in the form of animal heads, and decorated with incised spiral and meander designs. Early pottery copied the shapes of gourds, but the later kind recalls leather vessels used to hold liquids. Incision gradually gave way to decoration with stabs of a sharp tool (stab-and-drag technique). Temples were not constructed, but elevated granaries constituted prominent village features. People dressed in skin and textile garments.

Here, as in the Aegean region, settlements remained self-sufficient. However, stone for adzes and querns as well as shells for ornament were imported. Trade increased somewhat later in Danubian culture and, at about the same time, weapons and fortifications assumed a more prominent place in the total configuration. The dead were flexed before interment. They were showered with red ocher and *Beigaben*. Clay figurines of women were made, as well as skillfully modeled figures of bulls, doves, and houses.

Around 2300 early Danubian culture began to spread across Central Europe, borrowing local cultural traditions. Where the Danubian folk went they set themselves up as a ruling class. Through these migrations of a people, also known as the Battle-Ax Folk, the Indo-European language probably made its way across much of Europe. "Theirs was a masculine hero-worshipping, warrior-pastoralist mentality" (Davison, 1951:116). Drinking vessels in the timber-lined graves of warriors suggest a pattern of heavy drinking in masculine company that was to last for millennia. Mounds of earth were raised over warrior tombs, the bodies being covered with red ocher. The stone battle ax, by which these migrants have become known to anthropologists, was undoubtedly influenced by the type of metal ax contemporaneously used in Mesopotamia. Female figurines disappeared from the Danubian assemblage with the appearance of the Battle-Ax Folk.

Switzerland of the Neolithic period is well known for its settlements of pile dwellings built on lake shores. The lake dwellers hunted deer and other animals, caught fish with nets, set fish traps, and raised wheat, barley, peas, and lentils. Wild fruit provided auxiliary items of diet, and cattle, sheep, goats, and pigs furnished meat and perhaps dairy products. Flax and wool thread was used in weaving but skin clothing continued to be worn. Bone, ivory, and wooden beads as well as combs belonged to this culture.

Some early farmers in northern Italy also built houses on piles while others found it more convenient to build round houses sunk into the earth for a depth of several feet. They were walled with pliant splints of wood covered with clay (wattle and daub construction). The earliest Italian pottery was fired in an open blaze after having been decorated with incision or finger marking. Terra-cotta spindle whorls indicate spinning. Female figurines perhaps symbolized a deity with characteristics similar to her counterpart in the Aegean and the Danube Valley.

Malta reveals an interesting Neolithic culture that provides a transition to western Europe. The most striking feature is the use of enormous slabs of stone for extensive temple building. The structures themselves possessed an elliptical ground plan and several rooms. In one of these a 7-foot, obese female figure has been discovered. Many smaller figurines were also made, as well as statues of ordinary mortals, carved altars, ax-shaped amulets, and pottery decorated with incised spiral designs filled with white or red paint. Obviously the Maltese of the third millennium possessed great skill in social organization. Otherwise how could the large temples have been built or soil carried up the slopes of barren hills to provide gardens? Military weapons, however, are rare in the archeological record. Priests may have wielded political power, possibly aided by concealed human beings who acted as oracles. A slit cut in the stone wall of a hidden temple room suggests a device for transmitting instructions on which priestly authority perhaps rested.

Atlantic Countries

In Britain the cultivation of wheat and barley entered simultaneously with the domestication of sheep, goats, and cattle. The new techniques came in with immigrants who at first avoided much contact with the sparse Mesolithic population. Later, when fusion between the two ways of life did occur, a distinctive Neolithic culture appeared, one quite different from that of the continent. Cereal grains originally were ground on a flat-topped stone slab with a stone mano. Frequent use soon wore a depression in the quern. Saddle-shaped querns did not reach England until the close of Neolithic times. Hunting continued to be practiced by early food producers and the preparation of both wild and domesticated animal skins constituted work of some importance. Pottery quickly diffused from the farmers to people who still practiced food gathering and who executed the new technique with relatively little skill or care. Dependence on flint tools continued, the material being extracted from deep mines sunk into the soft chalk downs of southern England where the formative farming cultures remained concentrated. Antler picks helped in prying loose the stone.

Causeway camps were one of the striking constructions of the early British farmers. Each consisted of a series of concentric rings of ditches, the excavated earth being banked up on the inner side. Numerous solid causeways of undisturbed soil divide the ditches. At one place four concentric ditches enclose a total area of 11½ acres. Semisubterranean huts, possessing an oval ground plan varying from 6 to 8 to 10 by 25 feet, were erected in the center of such a location. The functions of the causeway camp are not entirely clear. Perhaps the places were used in autumn when a large proportion of young livestock had to be slaughtered owing to the lack of winter feed. Certainly building the camps involved some ability to coördinate many hands. The stone slab houses at Skara Brae in the Orkney Islands, with their stone benches and shelves, are probably somewhat later in time than the causeway camps.

Coming to ceremonial patterns: female figurines and phalli carved out of chalk no doubt possessed ritual significance. The causeway builders followed a custom of erecting long earthen barrows (100 to 400 feet long) over turf or pole enclosures. Skeletons of the deceased were moved into these tombs some time after death had occurred. In certain cases partial cremation preceded inhumation but *Beigaben* were rare. In western England, northern Ireland, and nearby Scotland interment of cremated and uncremated bodies took place in tombs constructed of huge slabs of undressed stone. These megalithic structures fell into several types: some enclosed only a single chamber while others contained several chambers entered through a passage. Such burial chambers housed several generations of dead; presumably they served some kind of large kin group. An earthen barrow was heaped over the stone structure and a curb of stones placed around the flanks of the mound. *Beigaben* in the megalithic tombs generally remained slight but included food, pots, and ornaments.

Although local groups enjoyed a high measure of self-sufficiency and autonomy, signs of trade are not wholly lacking. In certain localities of southern England and Wales flint axes were manufactured in large quantities and exported to other parts of the country. Scotland even secured flint from Ireland for use in toolmaking. Some villages specialized in ceramics.

Not only in Britain but all along the Atlantic coast the late Neolithic period saw the construction of megalithic tombs. Structures very much alike in size and form are distributed from Sardinia and Corsica across France, Spain, and Portugal to Ireland, and north into Scandinavia. They have created much interest and speculation. One theory holds that while sparse Mesolithic people could bury their dead in caves, the expanding Neolithic population ran out of cave space and built the megalithic tombs as substitutes (Wheeler, 1935:185). Few archeologists accept this as a sound interpretation of the facts. Precisely where the megalith tradition originated is hard to determine. In Iberia people migrating from southwestern France introduced such tombs when they set themselves up as rulers of a prosperous local population. They removed gold, silver, copper, and lead from the country, constructed bridges and aqueducts, and imported luxury goods from

Stonehenge Was One of the Megalithic Sanctuaries of Bronze Age Britain (see p. 778) (courtesy, British Information Services).

Africa, Sicily, and Troy. This phase of culture, marking a transition to the Bronze Age, clearly derived certain of its elements from the eastern Mediterranean.

The Beaker Folk probably had their origin in the culturally diverse, late Neolithic, ethnic groups of Spain. Their name derives from so-called bell beakers in which they took their drink, a squat, cuplike clay vessel with a rounded base and S-shaped profile, decorated with horizontal bands applied by a pointed instrument. The people who made this container occupied round huts 10 or 16 feet in diameter and specialized in trade. Their migrations can be traced through France, Germany, and Britain. With them they carried amber, copper, gold, callais (a green stone used for ornament), and more precious stones. Where they could trade they settled and farmed. Like modern Gypsies they knew no homeland. The Beaker Folk are responsible for the diffusion of many new forms of wealth throughout the Atlantic and central European countries.

Scandinavia

Megaliths and food production based on animal and plant domestication came in together in northern Europe. The oldest chambered tomb was the dolmen, a 4-sided polygon room reaching a height of 6½ feet, the entry being on the eastern or southern side. Sometimes a mound of earth, a barrow, surmounted the dolmen, the outer edges being ringed with stones. Passage graves, consisting of a chamber entered by a covered passage, came next in time. The walls and room were constructed of large blocks of stone, the spaces filled with smaller ones. The chambers ranged from 13 to 23 feet in length and reached heights of 4 or 5 feet. These structures always were buried under a mound of earth. Finally, the stone surface cist came into use for housing the dead. Consisting of a long, rectangular chamber made of raised stone slabs, it usually reached lengths of 8 to 13 feet, rarely as much as 33 feet. Frequently these too were covered by earthen barrows. In such chambers the dead lay surrounded by implements, pottery, and ornaments. Occasionally fires were built in the tombs, a practice also known from other parts of western Europe. Examination of the skeletons of Scandinavian Neolithic graves reveals that most people died between 20 and 30 years of age and that some 13 percent of the burials show sign of dental caries.

Much of the pottery of the region was decorated by punctuation and cord-marking. Bone and amber provided material for ornaments that included amber beads shaped like double axes. Buttons of amber were provided with an opening bored through in the form of an inverted V. Battle axes came with the Battle-Ax Folk. Maces made of volcanic rock possibly possessed ritual significance. The use of stone tools hung on in this northern region long after copper and bronze came into use in Central Europe. Flint daggers found in the stone tombs sometimes possess a handle that clearly was inspired by the shape of metal models. Stimulus diffusion must have been operative.

The Battle-Ax Folk when they came into northern Europe buried their dead in single graves covered with low mounds. Each body lay on its side, the knees bent. A layer of stones at the bottom and sides enclosed the early shaft grave. Later this form gave way to a burial pit walled with timber. *Beigaben* included a battle ax, earthenware beaker, disk of amber, and string of amber beads. Perhaps the Battle-Ax people were the first Germanic-speaking (i.e., Indo-European) settlers to reach Scandinavia.

GROWTH OF AEGEAN CIVILIZATION

Rising on Neolithic foundations European civilization first appeared in Crete and Greece. From here it radiated into the other regions of Europe. The story of that diffusion belongs to the next section (pp. 769–784).

The wealthy nations of the Middle East eagerly offered their surplus production in exchange for copper, tin, silver, timber, dyestuffs, and marble supplied by the people of southern Europe. Knowledge of smelting, bronze casting, and less technical matters reached the Aegean region, where population had begun to expand during the 1500 years of the Neolithic. This population came to be organized under efficient administration. Specialists appeared—administrators, sailors, traders, pirates, and ritualists—supported by the farmers' surplus. The culmination of these beginnings came with Late Minoan civilization in Crete and Late Helladic (or Mycenaean) culture in Greece (Fig. 42:5). In the sections which follow, Crete and Greece (the

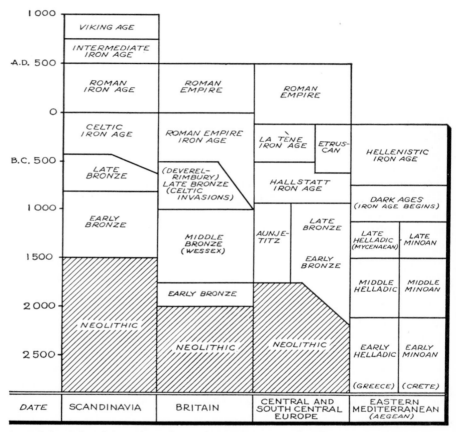

FIG. 42:5. Cultural Growth on the Awakening Frontier and in the Aegean (the European Bronze and Iron Age Periods).

Minoan and Helladic traditions) will be treated as a single unit. This, of course, does not mean that all the elements to be described could be found in all parts of the Aegean region.

Early Minoan and Early Helladic

The early centuries of the Bronze Age belong to Crete, a small island heavily influenced by Egyptian and Southwest Asiatic cultural currents.

Mainland Greece received its impetus to cultural growth from Crete and Anatolia, the latter a part of the Southwest Asiatic culture area.

Aegean Neolithic communities slowly became transformed into a way of life symbolized by imports like carved stone vases; amulets in the form of monkeys, human limbs, or mummies; tweezers for depilation; palettes of stone for paints and unguents; penis sheaths; and stamp seals of Egyptian type. From Southwest Asia, Crete received cast copper axes with a hole through the head for hafting; pottery; button seals, and the technique of glazed painting for ceramics. Another trade arm reached toward the northern frontiers and brought to Crete raw copper, tin, and amber of Baltic origin. Seagoing vessels propelled by oars sailed from the Aegean to Anatolia, Egypt, the Israeli coast, westward to Sicily and, perhaps, Spain, loaded with wine, olive oil, and other goods. Near Cretan and Greek harbors, villages grew into prosperous trading and manufacturing towns. The earliest phase of Aegean civilization still had a peaceful, commercial character. However, before reaching the middle Aegean culture we find that towns had become fortified.

Specialization stands revealed in the products of jewelers, goldsmiths, coppersmiths, and lapidaries. Great skill was shown in the designing of gold ornaments. But the volume of specialized production remained quite low and towns stayed small. However, the plow came into use for cereal cultivation and with it the farmers' output would increase to supply a growing urban population. Figs, grapes, and olives were added to the stock of cultivated plants, their products, as already pointed out, reaching foreign markets.

Little is known about dwellings. The mainland Greeks lived in long rectangular or oval houses. Villages occupied the same sites long enough for the accumulated debris to raise mounds. Early Cretan houses do not depend on windows for light and probably received sunlight from one or more light wells such as remained a standard architectural feature throughout Cretan prehistory. Dwellings show a complexity of rectangular rooms, as in the late Neolithic building shown in Figure 42:6 (A). In some cases the mud walls of dwellings were decorated with hard, rough stucco.

Burial took place in family or communal tombs, either natural caves or stone chambers. The body was placed on the floor in a contracted position. Circular (*tholos*) tombs in Crete measured from 13 to 40 feet in diameter but do not appear to have been vaulted in early times. Religious ritual apparently took place in the open air, for elaborate temples are not yet indicated. Ritual specifics included female figurines (they remained in use through the middle and late phases of the Aegean Bronze Age—i.e., through the Late Minoan and Late Helladic periods), phalli, and double axes of copper or lead (a type not yet used for woodworking). Later the female statuettes came to be accompanied by a youthful male companion—perhaps a son of the goddess.

(A)   (B)

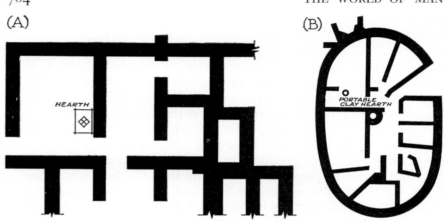

Fig. 42:6. Cretan Houses. A, late Neolithic house from Knossos showing portions of adjacent dwellings (1 inch = 177 inches); B, oval house of Middle Minoan Age (1 inch = 200 inches) (both after Pendlebury, 1939).

Middle Minoan and Middle Helladic

Three important events keynote the middle period of early Aegean culture: (1) the rise of an administrative and commercial class on the mainland and in Crete, (2) the wheel, used to make pottery and for transportation, and (3) invention of an ideographic script in Crete. Palaces served as administrative headquarters during the middle period and contained rooms for worship, manufacturing, and warehousing. On Crete, where these buildings were not fortified as strongly as on the mainland, the palace of Knossos occupied a site that had been used for habitations since Neolithic times. It measured some 40 feet square in this period. Around such palaces towns grew into comfortable cities served by aqueducts. Single-story grew into double story houses with both rectangular and oval ground plans. Clay pipes at Knossos carried water and served as drains. Even a bathtub has been recovered from the ruins of this phase. Clay lamps of various forms burned oil and provided light. Polychrome wall paintings and reliefs in the palace at Knossos depict both animals and human beings.

The four-wheeled cart implies the existence of roads, construction and maintenance of which helped administrators to exercise and strengthen their power. The potter's wheel furthered specialization in the field of ceramics and left the housewife with time for other activities. The Minoan script apparently constitutes an example of stimulus diffusion, deriving ultimately from the scripts of Egypt and Sumeria. The system of writing underwent a number of rapid transformations in the centuries which followed its origination (Diringer, 1948:Chap. 3). Sea traffic, shipped in vessels reaching 70 feet in length, carried Cretan pottery to many parts of the eastern Mediterranean and brought ores of copper and tin from as far away as Britain. A system of standardized weights and measures facilitated commerce. Bronze came into widespread use for weapons like the dagger and rapier, as well as for caldrons and a variety of tools, including the sledge hammer. The single-bladed ax was displaced by a double-headed variety already known in Sumeria. Here is the prototype of the distinctive weapon of the Battle-Ax people (see pp. 755, 761). A gaming table found in Crete points to some kind of board game resembling chess and played with ivory draughtsmen. On the mainland individual cists or jars came into use for burial. Interment sometimes took place in the house floor. Hill sanctuaries provided an appropriate setting for rituals.

The Middle Minoan period ended in some kind of widespread disaster, probably an earthquake, followed by the eruption of disastrous warfare in which the palace at Knossos was thoroughly razed. The invading armies may have come from Greece.

Late Minoan and Late Helladic

With the Late Minoan-Helladic period, the culture climax and center of influence and military power shifted from Crete to Greece (where the period is known as Mycenaean, from the city of Mycenae). This culture largely had been derived from Crete but now it underwent a period of florescence in the course of which much of the Aegean world acquired a relatively uniform way of life. This, of course, indicates a large amount of far-flung interaction, particularly trade. Political unity, however, was lacking, as is made quite clear in Homer's epics. The Late Helladic phase belongs to a people whom that poet called Achaeans. While Homer's work cannot be construed as documentary history (he lived during the ninth century B.C. and Mycenae collapsed in about 1300), it illuminates the period, as do the plays of Aeschylus.

The independent cities, like Mycenae, which exerted administrative power over the surrounding countryside, became highly prosperous. Large shares of wealth were invested in arms with which to defend their prosperity. Chariots, organized armies, cavalry, fortified citadels, shields, leather and bronze helmets are symptomatic of one component of the ethos. Weapons included the sword, dagger, spear, sling, and arrows tipped with barbed points. Toward the end of the Late Helladic phase iron was welcomed for reducing the cost of the huge quantities of weapons that fighting consumed. Cities made strenuous preparations to resist destruction. In nearby Asia, Troy (which feared much from mainland armies) stood within walls 16 feet thick yet could not withstand the Greek onslaughts. In Greece and Crete government was in the hands of wealthy warrior-princes who lived in citadels surrounded by large towns. A Late Minoan palace at Knossos had a basement 360 by 240 feet and a first story of 160 by 360 feet. Bathtubs with carbonized wood nearby suggest that hot water could be provided on demand for the royal bath. Palace frescoes show male and female acrobats (toreadors) performing somersaults over charging bulls. The representational art, however, reveals little historical consciousness such as will appear in Greece during a later cultural era. Cultivated flower gardens around the palaces made a striking contrast to this militaristic element in the culture. Upon death Mycenaean kings were buried in deep shaft graves accompanied by rich *Beigaben*. Commoners were interred in rock-cut or brick tombs. Worship was directed to several, largely female, deities. A woman may even have headed the Greek pantheon.

The towns not only exported goods to a world which reached from Egypt and Israel to Bulgaria and Sicily but also planted colonists abroad. Those in Asia Minor and Syria carried with them many Mycenaean elements. Decked sailing vessels over 100 feet long served this commerce, and guarded roads and bridges supported overland traffic. Road building took full advantage of the natural contours of the land. Urban specialists included masons, potters, tanners, cobblers, metalworkers, sculptors, painters, carpenters, wainwrights, jewelers, lapidaries, merchants, soldiers, administrators, and architects. The farmers, too, had become specialists who supplied themselves and other consumers with wheat and other food. For their dress men wore knee-length kilts, and women wore flounced or straight skirts with embroidered hems.

For a closer look at Mycenaean culture one can examine the archeological reports of specific sites—for example, the excavations at Mycenae itself.[1] While the identity has not been proved conclusively, the city of Mycenae near the close of the Aegean Bronze Age "corresponds admirably with our idea of the stronghold which was the capital of Agamemnon" (Wace, 1949: 23). With this idea in mind, the pillaged tomb 42 feet in diameter located outside the walls of the city, and containing the body of a woman, has been called Clytemnestra's burial chamber (Fig. 42:7). It dates from about 1300 B.C. Dominating the city is the citadel placed on the crest of a precipice and surrounded by walls 20 feet thick. Within this fortress three building styles may be recognized: (1) cyclopean, the walls of huge limestone blocks, dating prior to 1500 B.C., (2) structures of large blocks of limestone hammer-dressed, dating from about 1300 B.C., and (3) buildings of carefully fitted blocks of stone dating about 200 B.C.—which is long after Mycenaean times. The citadel guards a slab-enclosed circle over 80 feet wide containing 6 shaft graves with 19 bodies buried in contracted positions. Quite clearly these belonged to a royal dynasty. The faces of the men had been covered in death with golden masks. On their chests lay golden breastplates, perhaps of Irish gold. Children's bodies were wrapped in sheet gold. Weapons, drinking cups, and other *Beigaben* accompanied the bodies. The palace is situated on the summit of the citadel, a road zigzagging to the entrance where a cobblestone courtyard gave access to the grand staircase leading to the throne room. "This would have been the Palace of Agamemnon and his bride Clytemnes-

---

[1] The following description is based on Wace, 1949; see also the illustrations of Late Minoan artifacts in *Illustrated London News* (1952), 220:58–60.

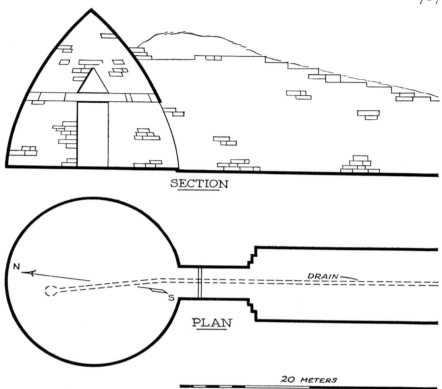

SECTION

PLAN

N

S

DRAIN

20 METERS

Fig. 42:7. Sketch of Clytemnestra's Tomb, Mycenae (After Wace, 1949:Fig. 6).

tra. . . . It was here that the grim tragedy so brilliantly dramatized by Aeschylus would have been enacted" (*ibid.*, p. 90). The ordinary houses were made of brick laid on stone foundations. Doors and thresholds consisted of wood and the doors swung on bronze pivots. They could be barred with stout timbers. Windows were small and not yet glazed. Stone or clay lamps burning olive oil gave light. Charcoal braziers as well as central hearths provided heat. The rich used vessels of precious metals; the poor remained content with containers of lead and earthenware. Food included mutton, goat, pork, more rarely beef or fowl; also wild deer, boar, hare, wild fowl, fish, oysters, mussels. The vegetable portion of the diet consisted of wheat, barley, pears, beans, lentils, and vetches; also the pear, apple, fig, pomegranate, plum, and various nuts. Much wine was drunk. As elsewhere in the Mediterranean during the Late Bronze Age, Mycenaeans adopted the fibula, or safety pin, an object originally derived from Central Europe (Fig. 42:8). Mycenaeans also wore ornaments of precious metals, glass, amber, and terra cotta.

Around 1300 B.C. Mycenaean civilization collapsed. Foreign trade dropped

off (perhaps partly owing to unrest in the Middle East) as military invasions descended from the northern Macedonian frontier, destroying and
plundering. The invasions brought the Dorian Greeks to the shores of the
Mediterranean. These people
were hardly (as was once believed) the first Indo-European-
speaking people in that region.
Recently an important discovery
was made with the decipherment
of the Minoan Linear B script,
records in which were found at
Knossos and Mycenae. It dates from about 1400 B.C. This script, which had
replaced the earlier ideographic script of Middle Minoan times, very clearly
was used to write Greek (i.e., Indo-European).

FIG. 42:8. Simple Bronze Fibula, Bronze Age,
Italy (Scale ½) (After Peet, 1909:352).

Hellenistic Period

Following the Dorian invasions a period of reduced scale and cultural
decline settled over the Aegean cities. Foreign trade and the standard of living diminished as local groups relapsed into relatively greater self-sufficiency.
Crete suffered a tremendous loss of population as people abandoned coastal
cities and fled into the hills. The island was ruled from robber castles, other
forms of social order breaking down. From these dark ages the reader passes
into the full light of history, or into the era of classical (i.e., Hellenistic)
Greece. During the last millennium before the Christian era Hellenistic culture spread far beyond the Aegean area (de Burgh, 1947:Chaps. 4–6).

Two kinds of vessels, ships specialized for cargo carrying and war, symbolize the prosperous Hellenistic Greeks. Piracy, which had long flourished
in the Aegean, naturally also benefited from the all-time high which foreign
trade now hit. The alphabet reached the mainland about 750 B.C. and coinage sometime after 700. Temples eclipsed palaces in importance while former
royal tombs became shrines where worship was offered to bygone heroes and,
indirectly, to a commemorated past. Poets and dramatists also looked back
to Late Helladic heroes who had fought in the Trojan War. Astronomy,
geography, mechanics, mathematics, physics, and philosophy were actively
pursued. Grammarians discovered the principles governing use of the Greek
language. In medicine and other disciplines as well, empiricism became a
special virtue and unverified speculation was condemned. Between 600 and
400 B.C. several scholars adopted a thoroughly impersonal world view (see
pp. 593–595). But a naturalistic approach to experience was not allowed to
go unchallenged. Powerful men like Plato interfered and a full-fledged
science failed to develop in classical Greece (Farrington, 1953).

The Greeks were still organized in small independent kingdoms (city-
states). In many cases hereditary monarchs agreed to limit their power and

granted constitutions. Strong loyalties linked people with these small political units. Among the cities stood Athens, populated by 250,000 free persons plus slaves. The cities fought one another, conquest leading to renewed fighting for independence. Trade and athletic festivals, like the one held every four years at Olympus to honor Zeus, together with common collective representations, gave the cities some basis of unity and helped to enlarge their scale. Commerce and colonization went hand in hand. Rich merchants patronized literature and representational art, particularly sculpture. They also struggled for a share in political power and thereby contributed to a nearly perpetual state of disequilibrium. Those who were defeated in these struggles were sent abroad as colonists. Great imperial wars were fought as the Aegean entered its own era of Cyclical Conquests (see pp. 713–714). Athens defeated Persia and tried to organize an empire of her own which the other city-states resisted. The Greek cities plunged into the Peloponnesian War, a struggle that accomplished little beyond weakening them all. Thereupon all Greece was easily absorbed into the rapidly expanding empire of Philip, a Macedonian. His son, Alexander, carried that empire, together with a good share of Hellenistic culture, as far east as India.

THE AWAKENING FRONTIER

The food-producing revolution, which brought a high degree of specialization, as well as urbanization, commerce, war, and piracy, to the Aegean, developed much more timidly elsewhere in Europe. The central Mediterranean, however, being far less marginal to the Aegean than Britain or Scandinavia, received Minoan and Helladic cultural influences with little delay. Etruscan and Roman power grew out of that basis. The reader who recalls the cosmopolitan culture of Spain at the close of the Neolithic (see pp. 759–760) will understand how greatly the Mediterranean Sea facilitated cultural transmission. Elsewhere in Europe the full flush of cultural elaboration scarcely appeared before the Renaissance.

Despite the slowness of the European frontier's cultural growth, the continent during Bronze Age times was not in a wholly quiet slough. Populations constantly kept on the march in the fashion of the Battle-Ax Folk. Some of this movement no doubt sprang from local population pressure; in part it stemmed from covetous intent; partly, too, it was connected with trade. The Bronze Age in the Aegean stimulated a vast demand for ore and the continent supplied a large part of that need. In return, finished metal products of Mediterranean manufacture reached into the heart of Europe. The people who accepted these goods at first possessed as little knowledge of the underlying metallurgical process as contemporary steel-tool-using Eskimo or Brazilian Indians have of steel manufacturing. Soon, however, Europe began to make its own bronze. But bronzesmiths did not set up shop everywhere. Hence trade continued to be important both for ore and in finished wares.

The European Bronze Age coincided with the subboreal climate, a relatively dry phase favorable for the opening of new farms in hitherto unexploited forests. The forests were beginning to thin out. The climate especially favored pastoralism by encouraging growth of more grassland for pasture. These factors, no doubt, also influenced the amount of population shifting that went on during Europe's Bronze Age. From the archeological point of view, one result of this movement was to distribute a considerable number of common elements from Britain to the Black Sea.

Central Europe

First the Bronze Age will be described and then the Iron Age, which culminated in the period of Roman rule.

1. **Bronze Age.** The demand for ores and the need for markets that would absorb the surplus production of Aegean craftsmen helped to beam Minoan and Helladic Bronze Age culture northward. In the first phase of this diffusion, the Danubian and Battle-Ax ways of life disappeared or were absorbed into a relatively new culture. Centers of this early Bronze Age culture grew up along the trade routes leading to amber deposits in the north, tin and copper mines, mountain passes, and ports through which the amber and ores filtered to the Aegean shores. The routes followed by the traders are still traceable, partly through buried hoards of finished or half-finished articles (Fig. 42:9). Despite the importance of trade, wheeled vehicles remained absent during most of the central European Bronze Age.

When European bronzesmiths began to manufacture their own metalware, some of the objects they produced revealed definite affinities with Middle Eastern and Aegean prototypes—for example: pins with a head of twisted metal shaped like a knot, and lunar pendants similar to Anatolian forms. Axes and other tools show a more independent style while the violin-bow fibula (i.e., safety pin) was a local invention that in time would circle the globe. Bone and stone implements continued in use for some time, along with metal tools. The forms of the latter were also sometimes imitated in bone. Pottery continued to be made by hand, in some cases also exactly copying Middle East types. The potter's wheel did not arrive in Europe until the Iron Age. Long before that, however, wheel-made vessels containing wine and other products had been imported from Mediterranean countries. Weapons are conspicuous in the Bronze Age assemblage: daggers, leaf-shaped swords, and short rapiers useful as both dagger and thrusting sword. Swords came to be weighted toward the point, making them into an effective slashing weapon replacing the battle ax. They continued as the standard European fighting tool for centuries. Cities remained absent throughout the Bronze Age. One explanation lies in the fact that specializa-

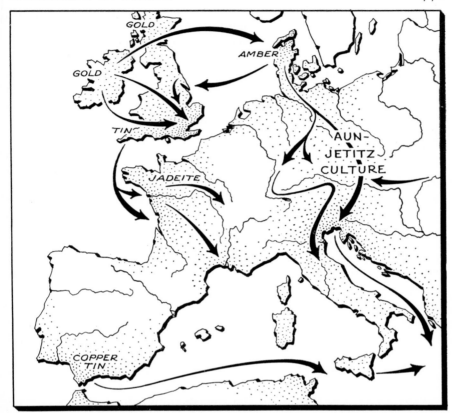

Fig. 42:9. European Trade Routes in the Second Millennium B.C. (After Wheeler, 1935:Fig. 6).

tion, too, remained very limited compared to that in the Aegean region. Also, the Mediterranean-type plow, with which surplus agricultural products could be cultivated, did not arrive north of the Alps until Late Bronze times along with bronze sickles and new crops like spelt, oats, and beans. In Middle and Late Bronze times the pattern of shifting cultivation, which had been introduced into Europe by the Danubians, changed to one in which settled fields were tilled—two sets, one being cropped while the other lay fallow.[2]

The pig became a staple article of diet but hunting and fishing remained important as additional sources of meat. With the advent of the Late Bronze Age, sheep and goats assumed quite an important place in the economy, somewhat displacing cattle and pigs. Two other innovations of the Bronze

[2] Later a three-field system appeared where climate allowed, one crop of wheat sown in the spring, another in the fall, and a summer crop of other products.

Age are razors (replacing tweezers) and cremation. After the corpse had been burned, the ashes, carefully purified of charcoal and cinders, were collected in urns. These then were buried along with additional vessels containing food and unguents. The Middle Bronze urn fields constitute true cemeteries. In them it is difficult to perceive traces of class distinction. In some places certain graves were covered with a round barrow of earth, about 5 feet high and 30 feet in diameter. These may belong to chiefs. The urns themselves measured about 9 inches high and were covered by a shallow dish.

Aunjetitz may be taken as a representative Bronze Age phase of culture. Known from a cemetery near Prague, the same way of life was spread over a broad area in which several trade routes converged from the north. The working of bronze was introduced into the Aunjetitz phase by the Bell Beaker Folk and other immigrants. Settlements tended to be located in valleys favorable for farming. Houses were round, and partly sunk below the surface of the ground, or rectangular. Cemeteries reveal much about the culture. The dead were generally buried in a contracted position, lying on the right side facing south. *Beigaben* included pottery vessels and dishes, tools, and a wealth of pins. The Aunjetitz people cast bronze in elaborate molds, trading the resultant implements for amber, gold, shell, and ivory, materials which they themselves worked into ornaments. No doubt trade was in the hands of traveling merchants or peddlers who left family behind as each covered a sales territory. Rich profit came to both the smiths and other craftsmen.

Italy may justifiably be included in Central Europe, and during the Early Bronze Age many innovations reached the southern peninsula from the Danube Valley. Later, Etruscan and Roman culture drew more heavily on Greece. Then Italy assumed a definitely Mediterranean cultural character. Extensive cemeteries in the north, with contracted burial, reveal the presence of large, permanent Bronze Age settlements. The plow came into early use and metal became cheap enough to be employed for agricultural tools like sickles. Crossing the Alps, traditions of cremation and urn burial found their way south where they continued to be practiced until the second Christian century.

2. Iron Age. For the sake of continuity the Italian peninsula will be described before the central European region. In Italy knowledge of iron-working was first introduced from the eastern Mediterranean and from here it spread northward through the Alpine passes. The Italian Iron Age opened shortly after 900 B.C. Two hundred years later it gave rise to Etruscan culture.[3] This culture spread as far south as the Tiber, settlers reclaiming land by constructing efficient drainage canals. The Etruscans were a wealthy peo-

[3] The following summary of the Etruscan phase follows Pallottino, 1955.

ple whose living patterns clearly reveal Hellenistic influence that probably derived from Greek trading colonies located in Etrurian ports. The Etruscans themselves sailed widely and established trading outposts in the western Mediterranean between the eighth and sixth centuries. Here they exported iron, bronze, and leather goods, in return importing gold, silver, and ivory. Not surprisingly they soon dislodged the Greeks from this trade. After they dominated it themselves they became responsible for much cultural diffusion on the Italian peninsula and elsewhere. The names of Roman deities, like Minerva, Neptune, and Mars, were used by the Etruscans; the custom of a personal name coupled with a hereditary family name may have originated here, and the Romans secured the Greek alphabet from these people.

Archeological excavations in Etruria reveal streets laid out in an orderly grid pattern and cities that had an efficient water supply. Socially the people never formed a compact political unit but remained content with a loose confederation dominated by one of the city (or regional) states. As in Greece, sports contests helped to create a sense of solidarity between the autonomous units, while conquest also led to the creation of several small empires. The government started as a monarchy but, as elsewhere in the Mediterranean between the sixth and fifth centuries, eventually became republican. The symbol of authority, a bundle of rods bound around a battle ax, was revived in Mussolini's short-lived Italian empire. Some collective representations of the Etruscans clearly originated in Greece: Jupiter, Juno, Mercury, Venus, and others. Prediction through consulting animal entrails (i.e., haruspicy) found much favor. It formed an important activity of the priests and lasted into the Roman phase of Iron Age culture. Death involved a sorrowful journey to a fearful subterranean abode of the souls. Profound pessimism came to be associated with this concept; but a belief in salvation, to be attained through ritual, also existed, although it does not appear to have been very popular. In temples worshipers offered live animals, food, drink, and statuettes before images. Tombs were cut from solid rock, walled structures sometimes being added. Habitations gradually grew from rectangular one-room structures covered by gabled roofs to multiroomed dwellings with porticoes. Cushions, chairs, footrests, bronze candelabra for candles, and oil lamps furnished the home. Men wore a short kirtle or skirt, loincloth, sandals, and cap. The upper part of the body remained uncovered except for a loose mantle. Such relative nakedness declined after the advent of the toga. Women at all times wore a skirt and mantle.

Many elements of Etruscan culture, including names of deities, alphabet, and a fondness for athletics and gladiator sports, became incorporated into the culture of Rome. No effort will be made to deal here with this historic culture, whose roots grew in a small republic that overthrew Etruscan domination in the sixth century before the present era. Attention must be given, however, to the influence which the Roman community came to exert over Iron Age Europe.

North of the Alps the Hallstatt Iron Age (named from Austrian urn fields) ushered in a growing predominance of cheaper iron over bronze. Bronze pretty well became a luxury metal. The typical Hallstatt assemblage, which included ox-drawn carts, a variety of weapons, chariots, horseback riding, fireplaces, andirons, and spits, pocketknives, and iron tripods from which to suspend bronze caldrons, spread across Europe. During the succeeding La Tène period (the type site is in Switzerland) the custom of burying certain dead in chariots or wagons drifted across Central Europe. Such burials, apparently of wealthy, Celtic chieftains, were accompanied by weapons and much food, including quarters of beef, joints of pork and mutton, hares, fowl, and in one case even a plate of frogs. The sword remained the main weapon and its construction shows considerable command of ironwork. For example, the body was made of hard iron while the edge was left soft, allowing repairs to be made readily by hammering. The shield belongs to the Iron Age and may have been devised as a defense against bow-thrown javelins. In the La Tène period such familiar objects as the anvil, hammer, saw, pick, awl, sickle, and pitchfork assumed their modern shapes. Iron locks and keys appeared but wooden locks may be earlier still. Whereas the Bronze Age plow with its narrow share had been suited to conserve moisture in dry soil, the wetter climate and heavier soils that now began to be exploited in Central Europe called for a heavier instrument, one that would turn a furrow and help the soil to drain. A new type of plow was invented, one bearing a broad share that sliced the earth and could be provided with a moldboard to turn the sod. Wheels helped oxen to draw these heavy farm implements. The stalling of cattle is first attested from the early part of the Iron Age and is probably related to the increasingly cold climate that followed the end of the postglacial warm spell (i.e., Hypsithermal period). Houses varied in type. A rectangular Hallstatt building in Germany measured 62 feet long and 23 feet across. It was built on a foundation of vertical posts and contained two hearths. Lengths were usually shorter than this (between 45 and 52 feet, perhaps). The presence of double hearths suggests two-family occupancy. Oval huts were also built, one measuring about 28 by 23 feet. Roofs were gabled, timber or wattle and daub providing the walls. The first upright looms date from Hallstatt times. Rotary mills for grinding grain as well as the potter's wheel entered Europe during the Iron Age and a new cereal, rye, was also introduced. Amulets were shaped like axes, human feet, animals, or human beings. An especially popular ornament consisted of a glass pendant shaped like a human mask. Inhumation and cremation constituted parallel forms of disposing of the dead. Cremation did not disappear until the advent of Christianity.

True urban centers are still rare in Iron Age Europe. War, however, was endemic. Social organization rested on local tribes, each of which spoke a distinctive dialect and retained political independence. A few fortified places were strategically located across trade routes where customs duties could be levied. These centers are hardly comparable to the Aegean cities of the Iron or preceding Bronze Age. Two ethnic groups inhabited Central Europe: the Germans, east and north of the Rhine, and the Celts, farther west and along the Danube. The Celts first menaced the Mediterranean cities; after them came the Germans. Around 449 A.D. two Germanic tribes, the Angles and Saxons, left northwestern Germany and settled in England. This event has since been credited with much significance.

3. Roman Empire. The Romans threw their imperial net around the Celts and Germans, who at the same time provided a welcome market for mass-produced Roman manufactures. The volume of trade flowing north effectively swamped markets which previously had been reserved for local craftsmen. Latin became the language of commerce. Roads were built in order to enable the Roman power better to knit the fragmented country. Roman towns grew up as seats of administration. From Roman literary sources emerges a fairly comprehensive picture of the culture of the central Europeans, particularly of their quarrelsomeness and heavy drinking. They used two-horse chariots for fighting; carried shields; wore ornate helmets surmounted with figures of birds, animals, or horns; and in victory beheaded their enemies. The head trophies were then slung around horses' necks. Villages remained without walls; in time of trouble people quit the wattle and daub habitations for fortified places. Furniture and other amenities hardly figured in these houses compared to the richly furnished, contemporary dwellings of the Mediterranean world. Meat was eaten with the fingers, although metal and clay dishes were used. From the garden came onions, fennel, parsnips, turnips (important in winter; after the Renaissance their place was taken by the New World potato). Milk and cheese held important positions in the diet and Mediterranean wines provided a welcome addition to native beers. Flax and wool furnished material for spinning. The clothing of the Celts and Germans instead of being cut like Roman wear was tailored and included wide trousers for men. Shoes were of leather. In the north some German tribes still dressed in skins, including sealskins. A priesthood (including the little-known Druids among the Celts) instructed young men and acted as judges.

The Romans recruited these frontier people into the imperial army, which thus became an important avenue of cultural assimilation. Italian soldiers not infrequently married native women, and Roman schools were opened in garrison towns. In time Christian missionaries came north, introducing another Middle Eastern ritual system, following others that had previously made their entry. Romanization gained for Europe "a lasting sense of unity, peace and ordered government, a common language and an education . . . in urban life" (S. N. Miller, 1935:491).

Britain

Archeologically the British Isles have been well studied and they will be used to show the growth of culture along the Atlantic frontier during the Bronze, Iron, and Roman periods. To be kept in mind is the relatively marginal position of Britain in relation to the rest of Europe. Its location delayed the diffusion of many continental elements, including bronze, new techniques of farming, the moldboard plow, and the rotary quern.

1. **Bronze Age.** The British Bronze Age was initiated by the invasion of the Beaker Folk carrying the S-shaped vessels that accompanied them even in death. From the region of the North Sea came another invasion, this one by a people with a Battle-Ax culture. The way of life that followed the contact of these two ways of life resembled a blend of Neolithic and other novel elements. The key activity was pastoralism, which assumed dominance over farming. Hunting also reëmerged into greater prominence. "The development is really a proper response to environmental conditions in the temperate zone. . . . Here, with the rudimentary agricultural science and equipment at first available, an economy based on hunting and on farming with emphasis on pastoralism yields an easier return than a predominantly agricultural one—within, of course, very narrow limits" (Childe, 1940:35). These subsistence patterns demanded considerable mobility; nevertheless shallow excavated dwellings continued in use. Some were 10 feet long and 4 feet wide; others were round and about 5 feet in diameter. Weapons assumed greater prominence, starting with the introduction of bronze battle axes and stone wrist guards which offered protection from the recoiling bowstring. Daggers, axes, halberds, and rapiers were manufactured in bronze and copper. Metallurgy seems to have had its climax in Ireland and from here the Beaker Folk imported many metal weapons. Flint mining at last practically disappeared in England. Early Bronze Age Ireland was also the home of the lunula, a thin disk of gold cut in the form of a crescent and worn over the breast, suspended from a chain or cord. Geometric designs decorated the surface. The lathe was introduced and carpenters produced quite elaborate scepter staffs, boxes covered with sheet gold, and other luxury goods. Weaving of wool and flax (a newly introduced plant) may have been introduced at this time. The plow itself did not reach Britain till the arrival of land-hungry Celtic invaders, who introduced a renewed agricultural focus with Deverel-Rimbury culture in Late Bronze times. The "Celtic field" pattern, which can still be detected in British soil, consisted of planting in irregular squares, the length of which was determined by the distance a pair of oxen could plow without a breather. After a short rest the animals were

turned around. The square shape may also be related to the custom of double plowing, the plow crossing its own tracks during the second go-over. The Celtic invaders, who were pushed across the Channel by continental unrest, introduced the horse, a new type of sword weighted in the blade, armor for horses, shields, and eventually iron. Bronze, however, had been growing steadily cheaper and a wide variety of objects were made in that metal including chisels, gouges, hammers, tongs, small anvils, sickles, caldrons (symbols of wealth), razors, and everyday knives. The clay mold, replacing one made of carved stone, helped to cheapen the production of bronze artifacts.

The Bronze Age promoted a considerable volume of trade, although in the main commerce remained confined to luxury goods. Not only were objects of bronze and gold exported from Ireland, and tin from Cornwall, to other parts of England, but Irish gold and bronze were transshipped to northern Europe in exchange for amber. The British focus on commerce, therefore, goes back to an early start. Burial hoards of bronze objects suggest traveling merchants who spread metal products widely. With trade went an expanded base of occupational specialization: metalworkers, traders, sailors, rulers, weavers. And, of course, farmers or pastoralists became increasingly specialized as they, too, no longer provided for all of their needs unaided. An emerging wealthy class is indicated by certain elaborate burials. In these, cremation was followed by placing the bones in a wooden coffin and interring it under a barrow. In Middle Bronze times the custom of urn burial began, the cinerary vessels being cord-marked. Sometimes they were buried under a wooden post or in a stone circle. In one case 11 oaken posts enclosed an area 36 feet in diameter wherein a pit was dug to contain two urns. Outside the palisade stood a ditch lined with birch poles, interrupted by a causeway flanked by two gateposts. Another palisade surrounded the ditch. Most burials, however, contain practically no *Beigaben*.[4] Urn burial diffused swiftly through Britain, just as it did through Central Europe. Common people's urns went into cemeteries while barrows accommodated the remains of administrators and, perhaps, wealthy merchants. Judging from the size of the cemeteries, an expanding population and enlarging villages can be inferred.

Some effective system of social administration must have helped to build

---

[4] An early Soviet explanation (cited in Childe, 1940:75) is interesting but does not hold up well cross culturally. "In a communistic society a person's possessions being what he used, and wore, and very often made himself . . . were naturally buried or cremated with his body. But now they have become commodities, wealth, sources of prestige, and symbols of status. The accumulation of commodities may then become an end in itself, and that not only for the individual, but for that more enduring unit, the family. . . . It was in the family's interest to accumulate gold ornaments, bronze swords, and cauldrons, not to bury them in a grave or consume them on a pyre. To put it bluntly, the greed of the heirs discouraged extravagant funerary furniture."

the megalithic sanctuaries prominent in British Bronze Age culture. The best known are Avebury and Stonehenge. Originally Avebury consisted of a series of stone circles with an avenue, also lined by megaliths, leading to the sanctuary. When rebuilt, a 30-foot ditch, interrupted by causeways, was added. (Note the persistence of the ditch-causeway complex in British pre-history.) The ditch enclosed 28½ acres. Stonehenge also underwent several rebuildings. The central ring consisted of megalithic blocks standing about 30 feet high. Eight feet of the upright slabs were embedded in the ground. Carved tenons on top fitted into mortised holes on the underside of stone lintels. Such techniques belong to carpentry, whence they may have been adopted. Some of the stone in Stonehenge originally came from southern Wales and probably was transported by sea before being dragged overland. (For an illustration of Stonehenge see p. 760.)

2. Iron Age. The Celts who introduced iron were peasants and not skilled craftsmen. Early ironwork was executed on a relatively local basis. Yet the volume of Bronze Age trade did not diminish. Bronze still had many uses. The bronzesmiths withdrew to peripheral regions, where iron reached only slowly, and here continued their craft, even turning out new objects like horse bits and mirrors. The Celtic invasions contributed much to the intensification of agriculture, the average family cultivating about 5 acres a year. The farmer used 3 fields, 2 of which lay fallow at any one time. In place of the simple scratch plow a moldboard device enabled the soil to be turned over thoroughly. Dried grain kept well in bell-shaped pits. These were dug 8 to 10 feet deep, 6 feet wide on top, and 10 feet wide in diameter at the bottom. It is estimated that a family stored 55 bushels (about 2750 lbs.) of grain annually.[5] Round houses were widespread during Early Iron times, circular constructions being another of the persistent elements of British prehistoric culture (though by no means unknown elsewhere). The rotary quern facilitated grinding grain into flour, but beans and other vegetables were cultivated in addition to grain. Pork became an extremely popular food. Four-wheeled carts, drawn by oxen and horses, allowed transportation; the two-wheeled chariot, with wheels 3 feet in diameter and cased in iron rims, facilitated warfare. Another application of the wheel occurred in pottery making. The popular safety pin also became a standard item of dress or adornment.

The prevalence of military traits shows the Iron Age to have been a period of great unrest. Isolated family farms came to be surrounded by a palisade, sometimes with a ditch outside. Hill forts appeared and steadily became more elaborate. They were encircled by ditches and ramparts enclosing from 14 to 24 acres. The number of such forts and castles suggests a very fragmen-

[5] This would roughly equal about 2000 lbs. of wheat flour consumed yearly. If the average family included 2 adults and 3 children the average per capita consumption of flour may have been 333 lbs. a year, compared to the American figure of 140 lbs. in 1951.

tary pattern of political administration, each political unit strenuously resisting incorporation into a larger body. There were also castles with walls 14 to 15 feet thick enclosing 170 acres and also surrounded by a ditch or moat (Toy, 1955:Chap. 3). In Scotland at a somewhat later time castles were built with double walls, each 12 to 15 feet thick at the base. The sling with clay pellets represented a new military weapon. The first towns date from the period just before the Roman invasion. Although little more than expanded villages, they housed a variety of specialists (quern makers, metallurgists, potters, smiths, leatherworkers, and merchants). They also provided markets for the surrounding agricultural district. Currency bars of lead and iron were used in some commercial transactions. Ornate chariot burials attest to the distinction existing between common folk and the wealthy chiefs under whose orders the forts and castles were raised. The aristocrats supported a number of specialists, like wainwrights and armorers, and probably rewarded their fighting arm primarily with loot taken in battle. The lavish graves of aristocrats contained variegated *Beigaben*, including joints of pork, weapons, and, sometimes, horses and wives or retainers. Over them rose a barrow. In Iron Age times the Bronze Age pattern of cremation began to be reversed by a taste for inhumation.

3. Roman Empire. Caesar's invasion occurred in 55 B.C. It was facilitated by the constant strife that divided the petty rulers of Britain and prevented organized resistance. A process of Romanization ensued in which temples, houses, baths, and market towns were built; Mediterranean costume was introduced to the aristocracy, and Latin learning was encouraged. Coinage facilitated trade. So did newly introduced weights and measures and roads which the Roman army built in order to protect its administration. For nearly 400 years Britain remained a Roman province. Even after the withdrawal of the imperial garrisons the invasion of Germanic tribes, like the Angles and Saxons, failed to displace Roman culture entirely.

Some people lived comfortably during the early Christian centuries, particularly in the towns. The whole range of cultural variety in the Roman Empire became available to Britons, provided they possessed the means to avail themselves of this richness. Italian craftsmen laid out mosaic floors and painted frescoes on interior walls. From Italy came ceramics, sculpture, wine, oil, glass, and bronze. Some of these objects were no doubt intended for Romans who wished to live in familiar surroundings but, of course, wider diffusion inevitably occurred. Peasants mostly lived in round mud-plastered huts or timbered houses which were still enclosed by ramparts and ditches. Gradually they began to plaster and paint the walls, used tile for roofing, and adopted portable furnishings of Roman origin. To support the foreign administration everybody paid a tax. Peasants paid according to acreage of plowland and pasture, merchants on horses and vehicles, and artisans on earnings. The Romans believed that "there can be no peace among nations without arms, no arms without pay, and no pay without tribute" (quoted in Winbolt, 1945:103). Not only material goods from the Mediterranean reached Britain but also new religions. For the worship of living and deceased members of the imperial house special temples were built. Deities like Jupiter, Juno, Minerva, and others had their priests (Romans, to be sure). Syncretism took place between Roman and Celtic deities and also found expression in new ritual systems. Finally, eastern religions which had reached Rome from the far end of the Mediterranean, including Christianity, crossed the Channel and were accepted.

Scandinavia

Northern Europe, especially proceeding northward in Norway and Sweden, properly can be called a frontier, a marginal area, in relation to the progressive elaboration and development occurring in the Mediterranean oikumene. In Central Europe, even, copper had assumed a prominent place in manufactures before the end of the Neolithic Age. But in the far north the metal remained rare and stone was retained as the major material for weapons and other implements even after the start of the Bronze Age.

1. **Bronze Age.** The archeological record of Scandinavia reveals a very gradual penetration of bronze daggers, axes, and swords from central European manufacturers. At first these never were placed in graves. Once the casting of axes, celts, spearheads, knives, buttons, combs, razors, tweezers, chisels, and safety pins started (before the end of the Early Bronze Age), a supply of these objects came to be employed as *Beigaben*. In the same period gold ornaments, including arm and finger rings and diadems, were imported from Europe and Britain. Amber probably was the most important item shipped from Scandinavia in return for these imports. Dry codfish, however, may also have been exported from a relatively early time. Silver remained absent throughout the Bronze Age. The sheep, goat, and ox provided animal flesh while millet and oats joined wheat and barley as cereal crops. Cultivation of millet, however, soon ceased. The ox-drawn plow made possible more extensive cultivation. Cranberry wine is known to have been used in Early Bronze times; fermented drinks made from grain were in use by the Iron Age.

Burials afford detailed information about dress patterns. Men wore a kirtle reaching to the knee. It fastened over the shoulder with straps, in addition to being girdled at the waist. A longer cloak draped over the shoulders was held with a pin. In addition men protected the feet with cloth or leather shoes and covered the head with a cap. No trousers are indicated. Faces were clean-shaven. A woman dressed in a close-fitting jacket with sleeves, light short skirt reaching to the knees or a little beyond, supported with a belt containing a bronze plate, and a hair net that covered her short hair.

Weaving employed thread spun of wool mixed with the hair of the red deer.

Many dead were housed under barrows 9 to 13 feet high that capped megalithic stone structures. In Norway and Sweden plain stone cairns were also erected over burials, often on promontories. Gradually cremation appeared in the Early Bronze period as a popular alternative mode of disposing of the dead. The bones of the burnt burials initially were deposited in full-length graves or oak coffins—an interesting example of token persistence (see pp. 184–185). Later plain earthenware cinerary urns came to be used. They were buried with practically no *Beigaben*. Mounds, too, ceased to be built over graves although sometimes burials intruded into older barrows. The custom of enclosing some graves in a rim of stones shaped like a boat suggests a belief that the afterlife involved a journey. The pattern anticipates the Iron Age boat burials. Ritual is indicated by the so-called votive offerings buried or sunk in lakes and streams. The custom recalls a trait in Hamburgian culture, but now the offerings included axes, swords, daggers, small boats of gold, gold-coated axes, and sun images in bronze. These objects were often deposited in pairs. A taste for striking and flamboyant decoration dominates the Late Bronze Age. Even the safety pins became monstrous in size. Gold was fairly abundant but it was all imported. Great skill had been attained in bronze casting. Objects produced from this metal included decorated tools, and statues of human beings, ships, and fish.

2. Iron Age. Iron objects secured in trade showed up during the Late Bronze period. The early ironware was also imitated in bronze just as bronze objects had earlier copied stone forms. Very slowly bronze began to diminish in importance.

The Iron Age coincided with a period of relative cultural decline in Scandinavia (see p. 282). Partly this seems to have been closely related to the unrest in Central Europe, where Celtic migrations probably disturbed channels of trade on which the north depended. This factor may also explain the extreme slowness with which iron penetrated the circumpolar region. Furthermore, the weather of Scandinavia was growing colder as the postglacial Hypsithermal came to an end and the Little Ice Age began (Deevey and Flint, 1957; see also Fig. 41:2). In some cases destitution reached quite an extreme degree and population migrated southward. In Norway farming retreated from 68° latitude to 60° at this time.

An interesting example of persistence appears in the working of stone. Iron Age soapstone vessels made to serve as cooking pots were exported widely from Scandinavia. They recall the Eskimo use of soapstone, though these Arctic industries probably are not related genetically. In places domestication of the chicken and goose now appeared. Cremation burials commonly involved bent or ruined weapons. Votive offerings included coats of mail,

wooden shields, and live animals. Sometimes these were laid in a boat that
was then sunk in a bog, perhaps as a thanksgiving offering following a battle.
Even a wagon might be disassembled and the parts scattered in a bog. From
such finds archeologists learn that Iron Age wagons were made of very
hard ash wood, the wheels consisting of a single piece rimmed with an iron
tire. For ritual purposes, at least, wagons were elaborately decorated with
bronze.

Scandinavia entered history when Pytheas, a Greek explorer, reached the
region in 300 B.C. His reports do not seem completely reliable but speak of
the threshing of corn (i.e., grain) indoors because of the wet climate rather
than, as in his country, outdoors.

3. Roman Iron Age. Roman political control did not encompass Scandinavia but cultural influences from the Italian nation and its central European provinces certainly reached the region. Coins, weights, bronze vessels,
glass, scissors, distaff for spinning, and spurs are some innovations. Gradually
products originating in the Mediterranean were replaced by goods manufactured in the European provinces of the Empire. New weapons included
double-edged swords, throwing spears with barbs, and armor. A brooch in
the form of the swastika was popular and rye entered as a new farm crop.
Some Danish graves were equipped with luxurious furnishings as cremation
disappeared. In the more ornate graves, undoubtedly those of chiefs, complete banquet services have been found, including beakers, jars, and wine
ladles. Some of the beakers bear scenes from the *Iliad*. Such vessels constituted a traditional diplomatic gift made by the Romans to German frontier rulers. Meat, fermented drinks of malt and berry juice, and ornaments
for women also constituted *Beigaben*. Graves, however, were not equipped
with weapons. While such burial complexes thin out in Norway and Sweden,
the basic pattern, somewhat attenuated, persists. In those countries even
interred cinerary urns were surrounded by weapons and drinking paraphernalia. A small piece of gold in the mouth of the corpse (or in the urn of
ashes) suggests that people thought the deceased had to pay a fee for his
journey to the afterworld. Votive offerings, including coats of mail, broken
weapons, helmets, horses, and boats, still went into bogs.

Writing reached the Germanic tribes during the Roman Iron Age. Stimulus diffusion no doubt underlies the origination of the runic alphabet
containing 24 letters. The origin, however, quickly became mythologized,
being attributed to gods. The more northerly Scandinavians received the
system of writing in diffusion along with the myth. Runic writing appears
to have been used hardly at all for communication. Primarily it served as a
technique for indirect coping. "It was primarily the magical power of writing which caught the imagination . . . and it was this conception that
determined the character of the alphabet formed according to their own
views and purposes" (Shetelig and Falk, 1937:217). Many of the surviving

"runes" are verses written to insure victory in war, safety at sea, or safe delivery in childbirth.

4. Intermediate Iron Age. During the fifth and sixth centuries of the present era gold in relative abundance from the plundered cities of the Mediterranean reached Scandinavia and largely replaced other *Beigaben* in Danish graves. North of that country burials became especially elaborate, accompanied by much wealth. Barrows, persisting from megalithic times, at length began to disappear. Some burials occurred in boats, a pattern that continued into the Viking age. Memorial stones bearing runic writing were erected on graves. Generally only the names of the writer and the deceased were given. People lived in rectangular houses that provided less security than nearby fortifications, which were built in great number. Located on high places, forts often consisted of bare stone ramparts without mortar. A reservoir inside made provision for a siege. Kings coördinated the social energy needed to construct forts and were likewise responsible for much of the unrest prevalent in the area. Rulers struggled against one another for commercial advantages. After death they were buried in splendor along with weapons, horses, bridles, hounds on leash, hunting falcon, rich stocks of food, and ornate iron helmets resembling those of the Roman cavalry. All these goods were assembled in ships over 30 feet long. Ship burials became more elaborate in the seventh and eighth centuries as the power of rulers extended over larger maximal units of administration. *Beigaben* for common people declined very noticeably.

5. Viking Age. Pirate raids from the ninth to the eleventh centuries forcefully introduced the Germanic tribes of Scandinavia to other parts of Europe and carried pioneer settlers to Iceland, Greenland, and, perhaps, America. In larger numbers colonists settled in Scotland and other parts of western Europe. On British coasts large Viking fleets established winter bases and fortified camps. From these the Danes conquered England. Behind these raids and colonizations lay a rising population, power given by effective forms of administration under kings (several kingdoms coöperated in a raid), a worsened climate that made northern farming perilous, and a heroic tradition. Many foreign goods found their way home, including Irish bronze vessels, saddlery, and ornaments; British bronze caldrons, buckets, silver vessels, weapons, and wheat; western European glassware and pottery. From Europe the Vikings learned to cultivate cabbages, turnips, and other garden vegetables. For some of these goods the Vikings paid, exporting soapstone cooking vessels, dried cod, and silver twisted into interlocking rings, useful as ornament and coinage. Foreign coins in great variety also helped to support commerce. In the ninth century the first Scandinavian coins came from the mint.

A Viking village has been excavated in the Shetland Islands off the Scottish coast. It covered two acres in its earliest phase (Hamilton, 1949). A stone-paved path traversed the settlement. The long rectangular houses stood on a slope, stone-walled cattle enclosures being located farther downhill where they would not drain into the dwellings. The houses had two or three rooms. Walls were of stone and turf 3 or 4 feet thick, the roofing of thatch. Apertures in the gable allowed light to enter, and higher up was located the smoke hole. One building houses a bronze smithy. The excavation has yielded evidence of spinning, weaving, bone combs, animal- and ax-headed pins, hanging lamps, soapstone and clay cooking vessels, dice, and accompanying slate gaming boards with their playing pieces.

Viking men still wore a knee-length kirtle and long cloak fastened with a brooch. The woman's skirt reached to the feet. She added a short cloak for greater warmth. Her hair was bound in a knot at the nape of the neck and then hung loose down the back. In death Danes, whether cremated or interred, were accompanied by few *Beigaben,* but in Norway and Sweden up to one-third of a man's wealth found its way into the grave, regardless of which form of disposal occurred. Boat burials are especially spectacular and the custom diffused from royalty to other people who could afford it. Some royal burials required vessels over 60 feet long, a burial chamber being erected midships. The freight of these liners included mast, oars, gangplank, tents, wheeled wagon, beds, domesticated animals, and, in some cases, human beings. Over all went an immense barrow.

Viking culture represents both the persistence and florescence of pre-Roman central European and Scandinavian cultures. In Central Europe the growth assumed a different direction under especially strong Mediterranean influence. The influence of Rome thinned out to the north and here the German tradition continued and flourished. Twentieth-century western European values regard the Viking boat burials with their ostentatious show of wealth, the Wagnerian heroic tradition, and the pirate raids as uncivilized and vulgar. Such a point of view itself is largely derived from Mediterranean civilization that has cut off western man from his earlier, Iron Age traditions.

AVAILABLE FILMS

Most of *The Beginning of History,* released by British Information Services, is concerned with the Neolithic, Bronze, and Iron ages of Britain (48 min., b. and w.). Bronze casting, forts, and the monuments of Avebury and Stonehenge are well treated. Other films include *Ancient World Inheritance* (11 min., color) and *Ancient Rome* (11 min., color), both by Coronet Films.

43.

Man in the New World

THE aboriginal inhabitants of North and South America have at various times been identified with the Lost Tribes of Israel and as descendants of Carthaginians and Phoenician survivors. A few people have even argued for an independent evolution of man in the New World, one unconnected with hominid evolution in the Old. Such speculations have been replaced by recognition of evidence pointing to the Indian's Old World origin and subsequent migration to America in a number of movements covering a prolonged period.

ARRIVAL OF THE FIRST AMERICANS[1]

The oldest cultural remains in North America go back about 25,000 years.[2] This date, corresponding with the latter part of the Pleistocene, assumes special significance when it is learned that toward the end of the Ice Age the central plain of Alaska and lowlands bordering on Bering Strait and the Arctic coast remained unglaciated. Somewhat later an ice-free corridor opened along the eastern slope of the Rockies leading from Alaska into the plains of Canada and the United States. On and off during this same period ice or land bridges connected Alaska with Asia. An unglaciated passage from Central Asia probably also offered access to the Pacific coast. Entry from Asia, therefore, was quite feasible around 25,000 years ago and passage southward in the new continent posed no insuperable difficulties. The cultural finds of early date distributed between Alaska and Mexico furnish clues to the route followed by the earliest Americans. Around 6000 B.C. man reached the southernmost tip of South America (Sellards, 1952:95).

The Asiatic origin of the American Indian naturally implies a similar origin for early cultural elements found in the New World. Such elements derived from pre-Neolithic and Neolithic modes of life. Stone tools of very early age resembling Mesolithic microliths have been recovered from the north Bering coast of Alaska. Successive waves of culture, each somewhat different from the last, entered the Bering gateway over a relatively long

[1] Based on F. H. H. Roberts, 1953.
[2] Perhaps even to the third interglacial stage if certain recent claims are verified.

period, carried by fresh hunting and fishing migrants. The culture traits they
brought spread by diffusion to still earlier arrivals. The number and character
of these early migrations, while they cannot be reconstructed in detail, presumably bear some relationship to the linguistic stocks in North and South
America (see pp. 100–101) and to the three periods of indigenous Ameri-

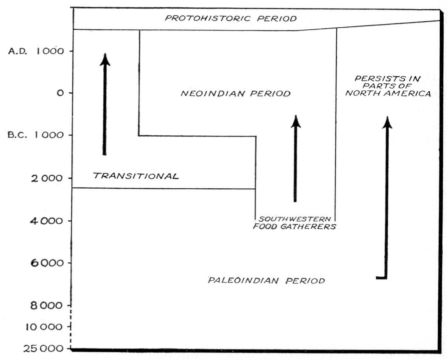

Fig. 43:1.   Major Periods of North American Indian Culture.

can culture history that will be the subject of this chapter: (1) an early
Paleoindian followed by (2) a Transitional, and finally (3) a Neoindian
period, marked by definite signs of cultural florescence in some parts of the
United States, Central America, and South America (Fig. 43:1). Central
and South American culture history is not covered in the following pages.

Recently a comprehensive sequence of New World culture growth in both
continents has been suggested. While not to be followed in this book, the
periods are given in Table 50 so that the reader can better appraise the significance of the Mayan, Aztec, and Andean civilizations in New World culture history. Note the great discrepancy between the growth levels achieved
in Central and South America as compared to North America.

TABLE 50. Periods in North, Central, and South American Culture History

Period	Characteristics
1. Early Lithic Stage	Use of rough and chipped stone tools; no polishing or grinding of stone; work in bone and horn unimportant; no permanent dwellings. The sites of this stage have been found in association with extinct elephants and bison in the western plains of the United States (Sellards, *1952*).
2. Archaic Stage	Grinding and polishing enter as new techniques of stoneworking together with more variegated cultural assemblages. Also new are heavy woodworking tools, like the ax and adze, as well as milling stones, mortars, and pestles. Other significant archaic elements include slate points and knives, atlatl weights, bola stones, and stone tubes.
3. Preformative Stage	Agriculture is introduced but it is merely another, and not necessarily the most important, food resource. Hunting and collecting are still followed. Basketmaker culture in the Southwest belongs here.
4. Formative Stage	Maize and/or manioc agriculture are associated with "the successful socioeconomic integration of such agriculture into well-established sedentary village life; pottery, weaving, stone carving, and ceremonial buildings are diagnostic of the American formative. Such cultures extend from the Southwestern U.S. through Middle America to the Andes Mountains starting in the second millennium."
5. Classic Stage	The criteria are subjective, including "aesthetic excellence, religious climax, and general florescence." Diagnostic are "fine specialized craft products for burial furniture, ceremonial uses, or as luxury items." Intellectual interests and the arts flourish. Only Central America and Peru reveal cultural phases belonging to this stage. In the Guatemalan (Maya) and Mexican (Aztec) regions this stage opens about 300 B.C. and in Peru around the start of the present era.
6. Postclassic Stage	The dominant tendencies are urbanism, secularism (i.e., nonreligious leadership), and militarism, the trends of which can be seen earlier, and widespread movements of people and idea systems. The Maya and Aztec postclassic phases started between 800 and 900 A.D. In the Andean Highlands the period opens around 1000 and ends in 1532 A.D.

SOURCE: Willey and Phillips, *1955*.

American and Middle East Culture Growth

If agriculture began in the Middle East before 6000 and in North America about 4000 B.C., then in the ensuing 3000 years culture grew far more rapidly in the Old World than it did north of the Rio Grande River (Fig. 43:2). By the end of 5500 years of agriculture, when the Europeans arrived, North American Indian culture still had not attained the levels of elaboration and development found in Egypt or Mesopotamia by the end of the era of Regional Florescence. South of the Rio Grande, however, the situation was considerably different. Florescence among the Maya of Guatemala and in

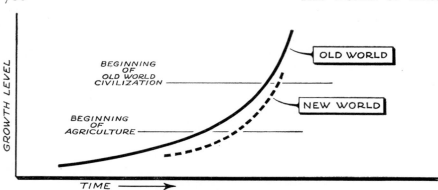

FIG. 43:2.   Comparison of Growth Curves in Old and New World Cultures (after Dittmer, 1954:97).

the central Andes of Peru and Bolivia came before or with the beginning of the Christian era (Classic Stage in Table 50).

How can the cultural retardation of North America be explained?

1. Marginality. Just as all parts of the Old World did not become centers of elaboration, so North America remained a tract where the more spectacular levels of culture growth failed to penetrate. Centers whence cultural elements could flow into the continent existed to the south: the Aztec, Maya, and Andean civilizations. Unlike the country of Southwest Asia, however, environmental conditions, including tropical forest and mountainous terrain, did not favor rapid, widespread diffusion. Distances, too, were much greater. Some diffusion between Central America and the United States certainly occurred. Agriculture, at least some pottery styles, and other elements of Neoindian culture presumably originated there. But environmental barriers and geographical marginality kept the level of cultural transmission low.

2. Low Energy. Energy for culture building remained seriously limited even after the food-producing revolution occurred in North America. Sources of energy other than human muscle power remained unavailable. In highland South America the llama served as a pack animal and boats may have been propelled with wind power. The sparsity of population north of the Rio Grande limited trade and specialization so that more efficient transportation machines could have played no major role. No doubt, in time this poverty of demographic resources would have disappeared as agriculture became more productive and capable of supporting large communities. Except in a few regions, like the Mississippi Valley, this did not occur before the invasions of Europeans began.

3. Slight Specialization. The absence of true metallurgy north of the Rio Grande meant the absence of an important stimulus for specialization. Men specializing in metals or other elaborate techniques, like administrators with large groups to manage, encourage additional specialists who will provide them with food and other goods. Such specialization, in turn, encourages discovery and invention leading to cumulative enrichment of culture. But these stimuli to specialization appeared only incipiently in North America.

4. Invasion. Time was insufficient to allow civilization to emerge in, or diffuse to, North America. Obviously time did not stop in 1600 or 1700 A.D. when the archeological record ceases. Rather, what happened was the arrival of a culture embodying a very high level of technological development. In terms of the energy it allowed to be harnessed, the new way of life diverged utterly from the indigenous. This, plus the ethnocentric attitudes of the Europeans, allowed few complementary relationships to be established between them and the Indians. The newcomers showed little cultural tolerance toward the people whom they conquered (it does not follow that the native Americans manifested equal unreadiness to synchronize their culture with that of the Europeans). Immigrant priest, captain, and ordinary household head were intent either on destroying the Indian culture or quickly transforming it on European terms. When the aliens seized power and deprived the Indian of land and other resources, the colonists quite directly cut off access to those indigenous resources on which native life had been founded. The situation so abruptly created hardly favored selective borrowing of European elements and synchronized change in the aboriginal culture such as has occurred in parts of Africa (like the Guinea coast) or Melanesia (for example, among the Manus). Some Neoindian communities, like the Pueblo Indians, resisted the invaders and cultural transformation. To do so they shrank within themselves. Their deliberately constricted societal role likewise did not encourage culture growth.

PALEOINDIAN PERIOD

As with the Lower Paleolithic horizon in Europe, knowledge of the very earliest period of American culture history is primarily restricted to traditions followed in stone tool manufacture.[3] The most widely distributed technique of early flint work in North America, which, however, was not the earliest, resulted in the production of carefully finished fluted points (Fig. 43:3). Mainly such implements, named from a flute or channel running from the base and left by skillfully removing a long flake, have been discovered along a north-south line from Alberta and Saskatchewan to New Mexico and Arizona. The frequency diminishes northward, ruling out an Asiatic origin. These artifacts are also rare on the Pacific coast. What looks like a spur turns northeast from the southwestern states, crosses the Mississippi, and follows the Ohio into western Pennsylvania, New York, and Ontario.

[3] The following several paragraphs follow F. H. H. Roberts, 1953; Sellards, 1952; and Willey and Phillips, 1955.

Fluted points vary in form and in the degree to which they are channeled. Some reach 4 inches or more in length and an inch in width; others are 2 inches or less long and below a half-inch wide. The dating of sites containing fluted points formerly depended entirely on the relative age of the earth strata wherein they were found or on associated bones of extinct animals.

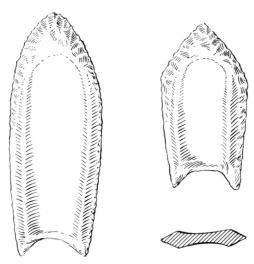

FIG. 43:3.   Fluted Implements (after Sellards, 1952).

More recently radiocarbon dating applied to associated organic remains has allowed somewhat greater precision. In northern Colorado a site (Linden-meier) containing fluted points, bones of extinct animal species (including a camel), as well as bones of animals still found in the region has been dated geologically from the Mankato (post-Pleistocene) glacial stage (see chart on p. 852). Several radiocarbon dates of Mankato organic material yield an average date of about 9500 B.C. A similar site near Lubbock, Texas, according to carbon-14 analysis, dates from between 8200 and 7500 B.C. A Wyoming site containing a somewhat later type of fluted projectile head dates from between 5200 and 4700 B.C.

Closer examination of certain of these early (but not earliest) sites offers dramatic clues to postglacial hunting methods. In Roberts County, Texas, fluted bone points and a scraper have been found in association with the remains of several elephants. Reconstructing what may have happened suggests that the animals met their death at a water hole. What agency snuffed out their lives is hard to determine but the artifacts suggest that, whatever happened, a band of hunters was not too far off and promptly sought to make use of the hides and, perhaps, flesh. From the valley of Mexico; Roosevelt

County, New Mexico; Weld County, Colorado; and elsewhere in the Southwest the evidence shows that Paleoindians killed elephants with fluted points mounted on lances or spears (Sellards, 1952:17–46). Extinct forms of bison were hunted in Kansas, New Mexico, and Colorado. In Union County, New Mexico, a site containing remains of 32 bison, 19 projectile points, and other artifacts indicates a mass kill by Paleoindians armed with fluted-point weapons. Probably the early hunters preferred to stalk large animals which were weakened from drought or which had become bogged down in mud and deep snow. In some cases men may have prompted bison stampedes in which some beasts became crushed nearly to death and could then be killed. Such an interpretation agrees with the number of skeletons often found associated with fluted points.

Some of these early communities specialized less in hunting than in gathering. Wild seeds were milled on large flat querns with rough manos. Other stone tools are most unspecialized, consisting of all-purpose flint cores and casually dislodged flakes. Such was the Cochise way of life. Crafts included skin work and stone and bone fabrication. From one cave 75 pairs of sandals have been recovered, dating from between 7400 and 6700 B.C. (Sellards, 1952:85). Such so-called gathering cultures persisted for a long time in the Southwest, gradually giving rise to a new way of life based on agriculture. The early Paleoindian period yields none of the elaborate portable and mural art characteristic of the Upper Paleolithic in Europe. Geometric ornamentation on bone tools and a few carved human heads found near Henderson City, Texas, reveal no strong decorative or representational traditions.

Later Paleoindian Period[4]

Material surviving from a somewhat later period of Paleoindian culture in North America is considerably more varied. It is marked by the addition of ground-stone implements in addition to those of chipped stone, bone, antler, and shell. The use of natural copper becomes frequent in some regions of the United States. Points, scrapers, and blades of chipped stone are abundant, some of the knives revealing great skill in secondary chipping. Heavy woodworking tools include axes and adzes, sometimes grooved. Polished-stone celts really may be ungrooved axheads or all-purpose implements. Drills were an important element, one related to the profusion of perforated ground stone artifacts. Bone supplied awls, true needles, hooks and short, needle-like gorges for fishing, and spear points.

It did not take long for hunters who arrived in the belt stretching from Minnesota and Wisconsin east to New England to discover possibilities in nuggets of natural metallic copper. The substance was abundant and promptly came to be shaped by hammering into the ax, adze, chisel, harpoon

[4] Also known as the Archaic period. It should be clear that elements to be mentioned do not occur in all sites dating from this period.

point, gorge for fishing, and other objects. The forms followed those of the respective stone or bone implements. Use of natural copper persisted for a long time but mainly for ornaments, its use for utilitarian objects quickly declining.

Grooved stone balls probably indicate hunting with the bola but the spear thrower was a more common weapon. For additional leverage on the atlatl, stone weights (so-called banner stones) were mounted at the forward end of the device. The harpoon also occurs in certain sites of this period. Shaft straighteners of several types were made of antler and stone. Dogs were kept, or raised themselves, in the vicinity of the hunters' camps and may have assisted in hunting. The net, weighted with notched stone sinkers, helped augment the food supply with fish. The persistence of gathering as another auxiliary subsistence technique is indicated in flat grinding stones and manos as well as by stone mortars used with pestles of the same material. Such objects were pecked from close-grained rock, like lava. Some communities settled near shell-fishing grounds. Their refuse heaps, although smaller, recall the kitchen middens of Scandinavia (see pp. 747–748). Basketry appears to have been a late Paleoindian innovation but pottery remained lacking. Its arrival marks a new phase in culture.

The presence of nonutilitarian objects, like sandstone palettes for mixing red and yellow ocher or the variety of beads (shell, animal teeth, stone, and bone worked into tubular shapes), spells interest in personal appearance. Some kind of board game was played with bone counters bearing incised designs. Stone pipes remain rare but began to be used toward the end of the period. Tubular in shape, they resemble cigar holders more than the familiar elbow pipe. Presumably smokers, or their wives, gathered and dried a wild form of tobacco. Smoking and maize would become two of the most widely diffused elements of New World culture.

The American hunters of the pre-Christian millennia possessed only modest capital equipment, which fact undoubtedly is reflected in their simple social organization. Trade and occupational specialization were insignificant. Use of natural copper for artifacts never led to true metallurgy and promoted little or no specialization, every man continuing to shape tools mainly for himself. Casting of metallic copper or reduction of ores never appeared north of the Rio Grande. Each region of the country to some extent possessed a culture reflective of geographical conditions. Linguistic differentiation must also have been present and together with variation in ideas and values probably accounted for greater regional variation in culture than appears in the archeological record. Survival for small bands need not have been difficult in a favorable climatic period and with such elements as we have mentioned. Population density remained extremely limited, and other conditions for cultural elaboration, too, were absent.

TRANSITIONAL PERIOD

A transition from Paleoindian to Neoindian culture occurs in certain parts of North America with the introduction of pottery. Whether pottery originated in the New World or in Asia and by what routes it diffused are questions impossible to answer categorically. A Middle American origin has been suggested, with diffusion carrying ceramics to the eastern United States via the Gulf coastal plain. Another stream of diffusion from Asia has also been argued and is not beyond possibility (Tolstoy, 1953). In the Southwest, where agriculture is nearly 6000 years old, pottery has not been found for a date earlier than about 500 A.D. In eastern areas, where pottery had appeared by 2500 B.C., ahead of farming, it accompanied few other innovations. The major new elements in the transitional period include greater use of polished stone implements, hunting with the bow and arrow; the semilunar, or Eskimo woman's, knife (distributed from the Central States to New England), weaving without the loom, and increased ceremonialism accompanying disposal of the dead. Matting probably had coexisted with basketry from the start but indirect evidence now shows fiber textiles to have been manufactured by use of a simple plaiting technique. None of these innovations remade the way of life of food gatherers in the way that agriculture soon would do.

Early American ceramics varied rather little from one region to another. Hence a suggestion of the general pattern involves little difficulty. Vessels were thick, coarse, and unpainted. Firing or baking was far from skillfully executed. Conoidal or rounded bottoms give the ware a resemblance to the pottery of the Beaker Folk while cord-marking recalls another widespread early European (and Asian) ceramic trait (see pp. 760–761). Other forms of decoration included punctuation, sometimes linear or arranged in bands, incision with a sharp instrument, dentate stamping, and basketry impression. With the adoption of pottery, clay also came to be employed for making tobacco pipes of both tubular and elbow varieties.

The first experiments with food cultivation very probably occurred during the transitional period, so that period gradually merges into the subsequent, Neoindian, era of food production.

NEOINDIAN PERIOD

Neoindian culture means agriculture and therefore marks the development of many American Indian cultures from a food-gathering to a food-production technology. Neoindian as here defined extends from the earliest beginnings of farming to the relatively elaborate, late prehistoric Pueblo and

Mississippi cultures. Another procedure would be to divide this period into Preformative (Incipient Agricultural) and Formative stages (Willey and Phillips, 1955; see Table 50). If New World culture growth in general can be compared to that of the Middle East, then the Neoindian period probably corresponds to the era of Incipient Agriculture there, plus a large part, or the whole, of the Formative era (see Chapter 40).

New World farming is not derived from Asiatic centers of agriculture in the way European agriculture stems from the latter region (Sauer, 1936; Carter, 1945). Farming in the Americas developed in several centers of South and Central America. There followed an interchange of crops between those centers resulting, at least outside of the geographically specialized tropical forest of South America, in a small, integrated assemblage of domesticated plants diffusing as a complex. The corn-bean-squash complex, which is important in North America, presumably originated in Central America, spreading north and south. The earliest radiocarbon date for presumably domesticated corn in the United States is 3651 ± 290 b.c., or nearly 6000 years ago. Other cultivated plants may be older still but this date can be taken provisionally as marking the start of food production north of the Rio Grande.

The domesticated plants of the New World (except the potato, but including maize, beans, cassava, and squashes) are best adapted to a tropical or semitropical environment, although some do quite well in a continental climate, like that of the north-central United States, where hot summers are the rule. Cassava, a starchy root, has not been cultivated successfully outside of the tropical forest region. Other than the turkey, no animals were domesticated for food. Dogs made an occasional appearance in the cuisine of some regions. In highland South America the llama and alpaca were raised for transportation and wool respectively.

Part Seven

MAN AND CULTURE

But the most important experiment for settling the value of racial distinctions—one for which the resources of science are too small, and only the history of the world suffices—is now for the first time in progress. The introduction of the so-called lower races into the circle of the higher civilization, and the overthrow of the barriers which once were raised high against such introduction, is not only a brilliant feat of humanity, but at the same time an event of the deepest scientific interest. For the first time millions of what was considered the lowest race—the blacks—have had all the advantages, all the rights and duties of the highest civilization thrown open to them; nothing prevents them from employing all the means of self-formation which—and herein lies the anthropological interest of the process—will necessarily be transformation. If we could say today with approximate certainty, what will become in the course of generations of the 1,200,000 of negro slaves who have within the last thirty years been freed in America, and who will, in the enjoyment of freedom and the most modern acquisitions of culture, have multiplied to 100,000,000, we could with certainty answer the question as to the effect of culture upon race distinctions.

FRIEDRICH RATZEL (1896:I, 17–18)

Part Seven

MAN AND CULTURE

44.

Organism and Culture

A BASIC distinction between living man and the other animals is the human being's possession of culture.[1] No doubt other animals also exhibit instances of socially standardized behavior and even transmit some such behavior to offspring through learning. But the volume of socially standardized behavior in modern man is tremendously greater than in any other species of the animal kingdom. It would be strange indeed if this distinction were unrelated to other features which set modern man apart from his companions in the animal kingdom.

Symbolization, language, and capacity to learn are probably the basic features of the human organism that condition culture. But other elements of man's structure and functioning also underlie the traits of culture. The argument to be elaborated in this chapter might be summed up as follows: If man were constituted differently with respect to any single organic feature, like erect posture, milk glands for the female, prehensile forelimbs, or small number of young at one birth, other things remaining equal, culture would also not be as we know it. By itself no feature of man's organism is sufficient to produce culture. It is only together, in a configuration that must include capacities for abstract thought (i.e., symbolization), language, and learning, that the elements of the human organism can be said to provide the biological bases of culture. Perhaps some day, when other worlds have been explored, it will be possible to test experimentally the proposition that terrestrial culture derives from the nature of man as we know him. Until a culture-bearing organism is found that is constructed or functions differently from man, any proof of the relationship which we argue exists between culture and the human organism remains logical and subject only to the test of common sense. Perhaps it is worth while to say definitely that relating culture to a biological base is not claiming that culture is purely biological (McGill, 1954:Chap. 1).

---

[1] It might as well be admitted at the outset that "man" is an ambiguous word (see pp. 827–831). The distinction between the Hominidae (i.e., man in general) and certain other animals is not clear cut, especially when only skeletal remains are available for study. The anthropologist does not define man as an animal in possession of culture. There have been forms of the Hominidae (for example, the South African Man-Apes described on pp. 850–853) for which no clear-cut evidence of culture has been discovered.

MAN'S POSITION IN THE ANIMAL KINGDOM

The major purpose of this chapter, then, is to outline the relationship between the structure and functioning of man's organism and culture. In addition, a brief attempt will be made to sketch the evolutionary appearance of certain features of that organism. This task is continued in Chapter 45. It is easier to reconstruct the appearance of structural characters of animals than to trace the evolution of their functioning. The reason, of course, lies in the largely skeletal nature of the evidence of evolution. The behavior of early animals has left few traces and only tentatively can one suggest from living animals how similar ancestral forms might have behaved. The genetic fallacy maintains that because modern and extinct forms of life resemble each other structurally they must also have behaved in similar fashion (Dowling, 1946:423). Consider the resemblance between the red and the spotted deer. Morphologically both animals are quite similar but the spotted deer breeds all year round while the red variety has only a short mating season (Zuckerman, 1932:25). With this caution in mind, the reader may regard the present chapter as continuing the work of the last four chapters which inquired into the growth of culture. In a sense the search now turns to the origins of culture with the assumption that these lie in the record of man's evolution (Kroeber, 1948:69).

Taxonomy

The manner in which biologists classify forms of life is ascribed to the eighteenth-century Swedish naturalist, Linnaeus, or Karl von Linné. Modern taxonomy, using Latin and Greek morphemes, conceptualizes the relationship between different forms of life by arranging them according to evolutionary relationship and similarity in fundamental build. Animals fundamentally alike (except for slight racial or individual differences) comprise a species. As Table 51 indicates, man today constitutes a single species, *Homo sapiens*. A number of species having several physical features in common are grouped into a genus. The single species of living man fits into the single living genus *Homo*. Note how the species name is coupled with the generic name to designate a particular animal: *Homo sapiens*, modern man; *Felis leo*, lion; *Felis domestica*, the house cat; and so on. Taxonomists classify a number of genera which share certain fundamental features into a family. Modern and earlier genera of man, regardless of whether or not they possessed culture, fall into the family Hominidae, a word rather inadequately translated "humans" and better defined as designating animals with relatively large brains, a retracted face that lacks a snout, reduced canine teeth, and erect posture. Families possessing related physical characteristics constitute a suborder. The Hominidae have been classified with apes and mon-

TABLE 51. Man's Position in the Animal Kingdom

Selected Characters for Classification	Taxonomic Classification	Evolutionary Antecedents
Man is an animal.	Kingdom: Animal	The first animal-like plants probably arose from an undifferentiated form of life about 1½ billion years ago.
He is constituted of many cells.	Subkingdom: Metazoa	The Metazoa derived from some form of Protozoa (one-celled organisms) in the Proterozoic era, about 825 million years ago.[a]
As an embryo man reveals a notochord, the evolutionary antecedent of the bony spinal column.	Phylum: Chordata	The earliest chordates probably evolved from an extinct coelenterate, like the polyp or jellyfish, in the Ordovician period of the Paleozoic era, about 420 million years ago.
Man possesses an internal skeleton, his brain is contained in a bony case (cranium), and his central nervous system is housed in a jointed backbone or vertebral column.	Subphylum: Vertebrata	The ancestor of the first vertebrate may have been a small fishlike animal lacking a spinal column which lived in the Silurian period, about 350 million years ago.
In his hairy, warm-blooded body man possesses lungs and a 4-chambered heart; his body is separated by a diaphragm into a pleural (lung) and an abdominal cavity; the female suckles her young, which are born alive. There are usually 2 sets of teeth, the "milk" teeth and the permanent ones. On each jaw there are 2 long canine teeth.	Class: Mammalia	The mammals evolved from an early reptile in the Permian period, about 220 million years ago, at the close of the Paleozoic era.
The human female is a mammal who carries her unborn young in a placenta, a membrane through which nutritive, respiratory, and excretory materials are exchanged.	Subclass: Eutheria	Probably the Eutheria derived from a tree-dwelling marsupial animal which bore immature young and kept them in a pouch. The evolution of Eutheria may have occurred in the Cretaceous period of the Mesozoic era, about 140 million years ago.
Man like other eutherian mammals is characterized by a flexible skeleton, nails instead of claws, a grasping hand, a thumb or big toe opposable to the other digits, omnivorous diet, and a strong sense of sight along with a reduced sense of smell. The brain is	Order: Primates	The Primates evolved from an early insect-eating mammal resembling tree shrews in the Paleocene period of the Cainozoic era about 70 million years ago.

TABLE 51 (*Continued*)

Selected Characters for Classification	Taxonomic Classification	Evolutionary Antecedents
large and the snout (muzzle) shortened.		
The eyes of this Primate are relatively large and face downward. The foramen magnum tends to be under rather than in back of the skull; the hands are partly freed from locomotion (a characteristic found in all Primates), and the brain is larger.	Suborder: Anthropoidea (Comprises monkeys, apes and man. Man resembles the apes more than he does the monkeys. Hence man and the apes are grouped as a single superfamily, the Hominoidea.)	The first anthropoids evolved from tarsier-like insect eaters in the Oligocene period, some 45 million years ago.
Among the Primates man belongs to the family that walks on two limbs (except in infancy) and possesses a very large brain. Relative to the apes his arms are short and his legs long. The canines are very much reduced.	Family: Hominidae	The earliest hominids probably appeared in late Pliocene times.
Modern man through culture reveals capacities for symbolic thought, language, and learning. Also he lacks any vestige of snout or brow ridges. His large skull cavity contains about 1500 cubic centimeters.	Genus: *Homo* Species: *sapiens*	The morphological features of modern man first appear around Middle Pleistocene times (see p. 850).

^a For a chart of geological eras and their subdivisions see Table 52.

keys in the suborder Anthropoidea because all three families share certain characteristics. Beyond the suborder is the order. The order of Primates includes animals which possess a relatively large brain compared to non-Primates, dependence on sight rather than smell, nails instead of claws, an opposable thumb on fore or hindlimbs or both, and eye orbits in front rather than on the side of the head. Monkeys, apes, and humans share these traits. Lemurs are also Primates, although not completely clawless. Orders fall into larger categories. Thus the subclass Eutheria includes all the animals that prior to birth nourish the young in a placenta. Man, of course, is a Primate belonging to the subclass Eutheria and to the class of hairy, warm-blooded animals that suckle their young—the Mammalia. The mammals are divided into subphyla. Animals, like mammals, with a solid brain case and jointed backbone fall into the subphylum Vertebrata and into the phylum Chordata. Chordates are animals which at some point in their life history, between the embryo and the adult stage, have a flexible cellular rod—the notochord—on the dorsal (back) surface of the body. Some fish retain the notochord throughout their existence. In man's embryological development it is replaced by the bony spinal column. The 12 phyla into which all the multi-celled animals are divided constitute the subkingdom Metazoa. Together with unicellular animals, the Protozoa, the Metazoa make up the animal kingdom. The following classification sums up man's position in the animal kingdom:

Kingdom: Animal
   Subkingdom: Metazoa (multicelled)
      Phylum: Chordata (chordates)
         Subphylum: Vertebrata (animals with backbones)
            Class: Mammalia (mammals)
               Subclass: Eutheria (placental animals)
                  Order: Primates ("the first")
                     Suborder: Anthropoidea (manlike)
                        Family: Hominidae (human)
                           Genus: *Homo* (from Greek word "same")
                             Species: *sapiens* ("wise")

Some very explicit rules guide taxonomic classification and extend into writing. For example, names of genera and higher categories are always capitalized but not so the second words in names of species. Names of genera and species are distinguished in print by a different type face, usually italics. Generic names are considered Latin singulars but higher names are plurals (George Gaylord Simpson, 1945:24–25).

Dating

Table 51, column 3, refers to the geological periods used in dating events in biological evolution and earth history. A fuller geological time scale is presented in Table 52. Remember, such charts are to be read from the bottom up.

According to Table 52, life originated over one billion years ago and multicellular animal life a little less than one billion years before the present. The Paleozoic, or era of ancient life, saw animals and plants emerge from the sea. In the Mesozoic mammals originated from reptiles and in the Cainozoic gave rise to the earliest Primates, from whom monkeys, apes, and man evolved during the last 45 million years.

LIFE, ANIMALS, AND CULTURE[2]

Man shares certain biological characteristics with all other forms of life. As an animal he possesses both generalized animal features—traits widely distributed among living animals—and more specialized features. The specialized characters of the human organism are limited to man or at the most are shared with the other Primates.

[2] Based on Guyer, 1937:15–149.

TABLE 52.   Geological Time Scale and Major Evolutionary Events

Major Eras (or Ages)[a]	Suberas	Periods	Evolutionary Significance	Million Years Ago[b]
	Quaternary	Holocene (modern period) Pleistocene	Genus *Homo*	1
Cainozoic (age of modern forms of life)		Pliocene	Man probably originated in this period	15
	Tertiary	Miocene	Larger apes	35
		Oligocene	Monkeys, apes	45
		Eocene	Lemuriformes, tarsiiformes, and lorisiformes	55
		Paleocene	First Primates	70
Mesozoic (middle age of life)		Cretaceous	Placental mammals	140
		Jurassic	Birds	170
		Triassic	Mammals	200
Paleozoic (age of ancient life)		Permian	Reptiles	220
		Carboniferous	Insects	275
		Devonian	Land animals (Amphibia)	320
		Silurian	Land plants	350
		Ordovician	Chordates (fishes)	420
		Cambrian	Starfish and snails	520
Proterozoic (age of very early life)			Metazoa	825
Archeozoic (age of primeval life)			Protozoa	1550
Azoic (lifeless age)			Origin of the earth	3000

[a] The Proterozoic and Archeozoic together are sometimes called the Precambrian era.
[b] All dates are highly approximate and likely to be revised with new evidence.

The General Nature of Living Things

1. **Protoplasm.** All living (i.e., organic) forms, whether plant or animal, resemble each other in that beneath their more or less solid, but not impermeable, exteriors they are constituted of protoplasm, the semiliquid basis of life and hence of culture. For without life there could be no culture. Protoplasm is organized into microscopic units or cells whose business includes absorbing nutritive elements from the environment and ejecting waste prod-

ucts. Culture, it will be recalled, is very much concerned with provisioning the human cells with life-sustaining materials.

2. Growth and Reproduction. Orderly growth and reproduction are other characteristics evidenced by living things. Communities possess socially standardized procedures which encourage and direct the growth process, particularly in children, provide for reproduction of the species, and dispose of organisms that have ceased to live and grow.

3. Irritability. Plants and animals are alike in their capacity to respond to stimuli outside themselves—light, heat, and more complex excitants. The biologist calls this characteristic of life "irritability." The stimuli capable of acting on modern man are tremendously more varied than those to which plants and other animals respond and include words as well as other signs and symbols which men make in order to influence other men. Fundamentally the organization of society is dependent on the irritability of the human organism.

4. Adaptation and Adjustment. Finally, life requires adjusting to the organism's biosphere, the realm which comprises the organism and its environment (Angyal, 1941:100). Survival is a function of the organism's changing as certain external conditions alter. For man adaptation and adjustment are more complex processes than they are for other animals or plants. This is chiefly because his biosphere includes many more features relevant for life and comfort. When an anthropologist studies culture he observes the complicated way in which man sustains life and adjustment in the biosphere.

Generalized Animal Nature

Although sharing some of the characteristics of plants, animals possess distinctive features of their own. As much as possible the following section is arranged so that man's most generalized animal features are discussed first. Those follow which appeared relatively late in evolution and so are not shared as widely with other animals.

1. Plants and Animals the Basis of Subsistence. Most plants (apart from some parasites and fungi) secure nourishment in the form of simple chemical elements extracted from soil or water. These are then converted into organic compounds in the plant's body. An animal, however, subsists on plants or other animals. It takes nourishment in the form of ready-made organic compounds. Every community shares certain socially standardized means of securing energy-providing food—whether through hunting, collecting, fishing, or agriculture—and preparing it for consumption. Earlier chapters have shown how subsistence techniques vary with other aspects of culture. Many of man's social relationships have as their end the provision, distribution, or preparation of foodstuffs, and the regulation of those activities has become one of the major roles of modern government.

2. Mobility. Starting with the one-celled Protozoa, animals generally (excepting sponges, corals, oysters, and the like) are more mobile than plants. They possess specialized organs of locomotion like fins, legs, or wings. Mobility is related closely to culture, entering into many socially standardized activities, from food getting to recreation and religion. Culture extends the organs of locomotion and so enables man to exploit a larger portion of his environment than any other animal manages to cover. Boats, submarines, snowshoes, toboggans, planes, automobiles, and animals trained for riding fulfill this function. Exploration, flight, courtship, piracy, drama, trade, war, suicide, and exile (at least, in a certain sense) are some culture patterns based on the generalized animal feature of mobility.

3. Sensory Equipment. An animal's organs of mobility would be of little use without some means for exercising control over them. The more complexly organized species possess specialized sense organs with which to learn about the world: eyes, nose, and ears. Protozoa, too, are capable of responding to stimuli but it is in the multicelled Metazoa that highly specialized cells for sensory perception and muscular coördination appear. The human central nervous system reveals receptor-effector organs of great complexity and efficiency. With such organs animals may efficiently direct their mobility for rewards like food and sex and in the interest of flight, attack, and play. Much of culture rests on the ability to coördinate stimuli and to furnish appropriate responses. Food getting, activities leading to the solidarity and equilibrium of groups, and theories about how the world is organized all depend on man's ability to receive and discriminate between stimuli and to produce voluntary and involuntary responses with various parts of the body. The capacity for symbolization allows modern man to interpret his sensory impressions in many diverse fashions and to respond to them in highly subtle ways.

4. Sexual Reproduction. Sexual reproduction, in the widest sense of the term, extends even further in the animal kingdom than specialized receptor-effector systems. Certain Protozoa, like *Paramecium*, exchange cellular materials when they come together to conjugate; another unicellular creature, *Volvox*, produces specialized cells, spermatozoa and ova, that unite. With the appearance of the reptiles animals came to be divided into separate sexes, each distinguished by special organs that produce and facilitate the union of spermatozoa and ova. In the mammals, and especially the Primates, there appears a distinct state of tension of hormonal origin, the sex drive, that motivates sexual behavior. Sexual reproduction, therefore, constitutes a very generalized feature of animal nature. Nearly all contemporary communities that perpetuate themselves through sexual reproduction standardize the manner in which the sexes come into relationship for copulation. Around the sex drive are erected some of the most careful precautions found in social life. For example, people in certain statuses are forbidden to become reproductive partners; sexual union is prohibited at certain times and places, and some modes of union are disallowed. In some communities even thinking about copulation may be interdicted for certain statuses. The double standard governing sex relations in many communities rests on the biological fact that only the female conceives through sexual intercourse. Furthermore, no community fails to seize on the biological differences which exist between men and women and to make these the grounds for different behavior. Sexual division of labor is universal. Some people go further than others in elaborating these biological differences; a few cultures almost deny that there are any significant differences between men and women (Mead, 1949b).

Obviously, a good deal of culture is related to the generalized animal capacity for sexual reproduction. But sexual reproduction and the underlying sex drive cannot by themselves account for those aspects of culture. Customs of courtship, marriage, romantic poetry, pornography, and rules governing expression of the sex impluse can be understood only as they are conditioned by man's capacity for symbolic thought and extremely reduced repertory of automatic reproductive responses. Man lacks the sexual instincts of some of the other animals and so may learn diverse ways of satisfying the sex drive, some of which may be forbidden.

5. Mammary Glands. In common with practically all mammals, the human female possesses specialized organs which in certain circumstances produce milk. This is used to rear offspring to an age where they can survive on other foods alone. The relationship between the occurrence of female mammary glands and culture is quite extensive. In the first place, most communities which perpetuate themselves through sexual reproduction standardize certain procedures for nursing the young. The standardized mode of nursing, in turn, constitutes one of the earliest channels through which an infant learns habits for responding to the external world. Nursing implies weaning, which has come to pose an additional adaptive problem for mammals (F. L. Clark, 1953). It is the female who bears children and possesses milk glands for feeding them. Such biological specialization is related to the fact that all over the world women rather than men remain in close association with children after they are born. The woman's role as food giver gives her great influence in educating and forming the personality of offspring (Menninger, 1942:41; Mead, 1949b:Chaps. 3–4). The family also can be understood in this context. In association with sexual division of labor this group is adaptive for women, whose specialized biological functions limit their ability to engage in subsistence pursuits as diversified as those followed by men. The early dependence of infant on mother together with the protracted period of early helplessness may condition man's social nature. Human beings normally avoid extended periods of aloneness and welcome sociability. Culture, of course, is founded on human gregariousness. It depends on learning, coöperation, and collaboration for its existence.

The breasts, man's mammalian heritage, have become associated with ideas and values quite independent of their nutritional function. Consider the "erotic fetishist value given to women's breasts in contemporary America. . . . The cleft which separates the breasts is almost the greatest object of erotic curosity; and a number of English films in which actresses wore Restoration costumes have been considered too indecent to be shown to the American public without fichus" (Gorer, 1948:77–78).

A Biological Basis of Coöperation?

Is there a biological basis for coöperation, one more specific than infantile dependence, which man shares with the rest of the animal kingdom? Evidence of coöperative behavior among animals has been marshalled by a number of writers. These men do not deny that such behavior is matched by egotistic manifestations but, generally speaking, the coöperative tendencies are seen as somehow having the edge (Allee, 1943). The struggle for existence, it is concluded, cannot be the primary factor in evolution (see pp. 825–827). The continued existence of different species depends not only on each one's successfully overcoming competitors but also on the fact that in each species animals live in groups (for example, offspring live with parents) the members of which help one another (Montagu, 1951a:24–26).

The evidence of coöperation among animals is undeniable but any general "biological basis" for such behavior remains difficult to specify. Yet coöperativeness is described as a "biologically determined . . . drive" (ibid., p. 101). A related difficulty lies in the nature of some evidence cited in favor of widely shared coöperative tendencies. This is sometimes so general that it covers practically all forms of nonconflictful interaction between animals, including sexual intercourse to reproduce the species. It has been discovered, for example, that in a toxic solution goldfish survive longer in company than individually. In that way each comes to share the dose that would be fatal to any one fish alone. Also their secretions combine to help neutralize the poison (Allee, 1938:56–57). It may be questioned if in this example the basis of survival is really *social*. That term usually implies that two or more organisms are consciously aware of each other. Deliberate social coöperation between farmer and city dweller or mother and offspring enables the urbanite or child to survive. Does the holding together of cells to form a multicelled animal exhibit the same elements found in the organization of a human community? The two kinds of phenomena would seem to be quite different (Montagu, 1951a:36). A third difficulty with the theory that coöperation is "the most important factor in the survival of animal groups" and individuals (*ibid.*, p. 26) lies in the attempt to establish coöperation as somehow more natural, or more important, than conflict. Little or no attention is paid to antagonism as a widespread element in animal life. Coöperation is endowed with moral value. Being "indispensable" it also becomes good. Such a moral argument is legitimate if it does not mislead one into believing that moral value somehow can be proved by what is given in nature. *Even if it could indubitably be demonstrated empirically and experimentally that survival depends on coöperation, in itself that would not make coöperation either good or bad.*

Such close examination of the social coöperation theory is worth while because it illustrates a common fallacy. A similar error in reasoning has been committed by a number of well-intentioned persons who seek to base some ethical idea on the facts of biology. The mistake lies in equating what should be with what is. It may very well be true that not enough attention has been given to the fact that animals do not survive through struggle as much as by mutual protection, succor, and general coöperation. It is not necessary to identify any specific organic basis for such behavior to demonstrate that it is true. Yet proving it true does not lead directly to the conclusions that "when behavior is not coöperative it is diseased behavior" and "to love thy neighbor as thyself is . . . perfectly sound biology" (Montagu, 1949b:21). Such statements are normative, not existential. It is as value judgments that they must be defended—in the tradition of the humanities—not as biological facts.

Structure and Behavior

The survey of how generalized animal features of the human organism enter into man's way of life has scarcely touched on all possible features relevant for understanding the relationship of culture and organism. For example, fatigue is a widely shared animal reaction and also conditions culture. So, too, does the mammalian trait (shared by birds) of warm-bloodedness which necessitates protection from extremely low temperatures in order for the animal to survive. In the absence of fur or feathers man secures this protection by stripping other animals of theirs, and by building shelter and fire. The animal organism is vulnerable to illness and injury. Cultures include procedures for curing and repairing diseased, torn, or broken parts of the body. Specific organs appearing in the course of evolution, like movable jaws and teeth, could also be linked with features of culture.

Man shares several elements of behavior with other animals that cannot easily be related to common organic features. These include playing, living in groups, using shelter, conflict, aggression, and the establishment of a hierarchy of dominance (peck order) when associated in groups (Leuba, 1954). But perhaps the case has been demonstrated sufficiently. The structure and functioning of the organism which man shares with a considerable sector of the animal kingdom does enter into culture. In themselves, however, these traits are not sufficient to produce culture.

MAN'S MORE SPECIALIZED ANIMAL NATURE

We now will examine aspects of the human organism not widely shared in the animal kingdom but rather closely limited to man or other Primates. The following relatively specialized features have been selected as those most significant for understanding the organismic foundations of culture: (1) biped posture, flexible shoulder girdle, and inflexible foot; (2) flexible hand; (3) visual acuity; (4) a reduced hairy skin covering; (5) year-round sexual responsiveness; (6) infantile helplessness and adult longevity; (7) large size; (8) a large, complex brain with which is bound up an extensive capacity for symbolic thought; (9) enormous plasticity, meaning the relative absence of fixed, goal-oriented responses; and (10) reliance on a heavy protein diet.

Upright Posture and Flexible Arm

Mobility characterizes the animal kingdom, but most animal species provided with four limbs utilize all for locomotion. Some 70 million years ago, when certain insect-eating mammals became arboreal, limbs became specialized. The rear ones began to support the body while the forelimbs served early Primates to pick up and fasten onto objects. Specialized hind and forelimbs persisted in anthropoid apes too large to live in trees all the time. But for a long time specialization remained only partial because the front limbs continued to assist in locomotion. They could be used for manipulation only when the animal was not swinging from trees or walking but sat or stood erect on its hindlimbs. Modern apes still use the forelimbs to support movement. However, not many millions of years ago an anthropoid gradually made its appearance in whom the arms remained wholly emancipated from locomotion, at least after infancy.

Man inherited from his Primate ancestors a shoulder in which the arms can pivot and swing in nearly any direction. Such freedom for the forelimbs might have possessed special value for tree-swinging apes but its use is different in living Hominidae, who, outside of playgrounds or gymnasiums, do not brachiate. The flexible shoulder, nevertheless, remains an asset on the assembly line or baseball field, and for the house painter.

The design of many items of material culture is related to upright posture —including doors, chairs, library shelves, diving boards, and the height of rooms. Many patterns of behavior—like offering obeisance by bowing, practically all athletic sports, courting, and dancing—make use of this hominoid characteristic.

The Hand

At the extremities of Primate forelimbs are pendactylous hands with widely separated fingers equipped for grasping. These extremities serve Primates for feeding, handling, feeling, fighting, and holding onto the rungs of branches or ladders. Many activities which four-footed terrestrial mammals carry out with the teeth, in the arboreal Primates are allocated to the hands. Making possible this shift, it is important to bear in mind, is the fact that the forelimbs no longer support the animal's body constantly. Pendactyly, which originally made its appearance with the reptiles, counted for little as

How Many Generalized and Specialized Animal Features Can You Discern in This Picture of an Eskimo Hunter? (courtesy, Hudson's Bay Company).

long as freedom to use the digits was inhibited by the necessity of quadruped living. Its potentialities were enlarged still more when the Primates developed a lengthened thumb that could be opposed to the other digits. In the Primates claws gave way to flattened nails below which lay highly sensitized fingertips. For arboreal creatures, which frequently balance on relatively narrow tree limbs, the grasping hand and opposable thumb are highly adaptive. Opposability and sensitive fingertips also allow apes to pick up and handle fine objects and to use simple tools. Sewing, weaving, ceramics, and many other intricate processes of manufacture, as well as music, writing, painting, and money changing are some elements of culture that depend on man's specialized hand. With his flexible fingers man has been able to provide additional "limbs" outside of himself by making tools and weapons (Crawford, cited in Hooton, 1947:135). Tools, in turn, provide vehicles for more efficient movement, machines for utilizing nonhuman energy sources, and much other apparatus.

Visual Acuity

Terrestrial vertebrates possess a receptor-effector apparatus relying heavily on the sense of smell. The long snout of animals like the bear and dog gives prominence to the nose, which is kept close to the ground where food is likely to be found. The eyes lie on the side of the head. When the Primates took to trees the olfactory sense became of less immediate use for survival. In the branches food must often be grasped with the forelimbs while at the same time the animal balances to keep from falling off or grips with its hind-limbs. The same conditions which favored the emergence of prehensility rewarded reliance on vision rather than smell. The evolution of Primates was accompanied by the eyes, moving to the front of the head from their lateral position. At the same time the snout reduced and the face flattened out.

Indicative of the importance of visual information in human behavior is the fact that two-thirds of all nerve fibers entering man's central nervous system come from the eye (Gerard, 1957:429). Olfactory sensation holds attenuated importance in modern culture. Vision, together with hearing, far more significantly governs adaptation, adjustment, and stress. Primary social interaction is based on visual recognition of fellow members. Secondary interaction depends heavily on visually based writing and reading. Modern man in large part estimates with the aid of sight or appearance the degree of trust and value he can put in a sexual or business partner. Subsistence techniques often involve sighting animals or fruit, recognizing by visual signs the readiness of crops, or distinguishing by appearance edible from inedible resources. Culture could be described as largely a system of conventional visual and auditory cues which govern behavior with reference to persons, places, and things.

Like the eyes of other anthropoids and certain mammals, man's eyes combine their action to produce only a single fused image on the brain. This gives his vision a sense of depth which, judging from anatomical evidence, is probably lacking among the majority of living vertebrates. Stereoscopic vision, interacting with a flexible hand, permits the quick performance of many tasks which require judgment of distance, from threading a needle to lighting a cigarette. Let the curious reader try to perform these operations while keeping one eye shut!

Reduced Hairiness

The so-called "hairy apes" are far less hirsute than many warm-blooded vertebrates in whom feathers or thick hair acts as a protective layer in addition to the skin and helps retain body heat. The hairs insulate the animal by enclosing a layer of "dead air." In the course of Primate evolution leading to anthropoid apes and man, the hairy covering seems to have grown thinner and eventually all but disappeared. The human body is literally naked except for the head and a few other places. Lacking natural means of protecting his internal body temperature, man turned to clothing, shelter, and heating for adaptation. Where climate calls for these modes of adaptation every culture includes patterns for maintaining a warm atmosphere around the vulnerable organism. In the tropics clothing, including a turban or solar topee, helps decidedly to avoid sunstroke. For hair alone, on an unpigmented skull at least, does not offer efficient protection against ultraviolet radiation.

Year-Round Sexual Readiness[3]

Among most mammals, females are fertile only during one or two short periods of the year, when they are receptive to copulation. At such times, when they are said to be in heat or estrus, glands secrete hormones into the blood stream producing sexual restlessness. It is then that the female may seek out a partner for mating. The estrus cycle, however, does not mean a complete absence of sexual behavior at other times. Among certain mammals, like the rabbit, llama, and camel, females are ready to copulate at any time, whether they are in heat or not. Among primates, particularly monkeys, apes, and man, female sex readiness is not governed so closely by estrus as in other mammals. Female monkeys or apes are inclined to allow sexual intercourse even when not in heat, although readiness to engage in sex behavior is more pronounced during estrus. Even some human females report cycles of intense erotic arousal around the time of ovulation, the period when estrus occurs in many mammals. But, of course, they remain responsive during the rest of the menstrual cycle as well.

The evidence suggests that physiological factors became of diminished importance for regulating female sexual behavior during the course of mammalian evolution. Year-round sexual readiness characterizes the human female. What about males? Among some mammals the male of the species also reveals cyclical periods of sexual activity. In the larger number of mammals, however, male sexual arousal may come at any time. This is true of man. Therefore the human animal of both sexes manifests year-round sexual readiness.

What cultural concomitants can be traced to the permanence of the human sexual impulse? In every community which practices sexual reproduction some provision exists for a sexually ready male and female to satisfy sexual tension. Perhaps no culture manages to extend this provision equally for all individuals but a tendency in that direction is apparent. Such arrangements, whether accomplished through marriage, sexual hospitality, concubinage, or prostitution, not only provide year-round sexual opportunities but

---

[3] Much that follows is based on Ford and Beach, 1951:Chaps. 11–12, and Zuckerman, 1932:Chap. 5.

at the same time help to reduce conflict between erotically aroused males or females over access to sexual objects.

From a biological point of view the substained relationship between the sexes in the human family is conditioned by sexual omnireadiness. A female who nearly always is willing to accept coitus gives a male a biological incentive for marriage (LaBarre, 1954:44). Proof of this statement is seen in the other anthropoids, the monkeys and apes. Among these, it will be recalled, the female also is willing to copulate at other than periods of estrus. It is significant, then, to find a tendency for those males also to form relatively permanent alliances with females. The situation is different among the mammals generally. With some exceptions, associations there are constantly being broken and remade as estrus goes and comes (Zuckerman, 1932:147).

If a human female will accept coitus in any season then it follows that her baby can be conceived and born at any time. All year some females are rendered unfit to survive by themselves during the period when they are advanced in pregnancy, engaged in parturition, or busy caring for the young (see pp. 353–354). But the family is an ever present group in which one or more adult males are normally on hand to collect food and provide protection for the dependent female. A neat instance of synergy in social arrangements is revealed. To start with, a man is partly induced to remain with a woman by the constant availability of sexual satisfaction. Sexual relations lead to reproduction. Although the husband's sexual access to his wife is now temporarily interdicted, he still remains her companion, providing subsistence and protection. "The child possesses the breast, the father the sexuality of the mother: on this biological bargain the family is founded" (LaBarre, 1954:124).[4] Obviously the word "bargain" does not mean an explicitly formulated transaction such as one strikes with a second-hand clothing dealer. Communities very strongly resent a male who refuses to fulfill his obligations to a sexual partner whom he has impregnated. The revolutionary significance of contraception lies partly in the fact that it allows sexuality to be indulged in freely without the consequences of offspring and the responsibilities that they impose.

Man's capacity for symbolic thinking makes him unique in the way he seeks to elaborate his ever present sexual interest. Various qualifications must be present in a partner before he or she adequately can satisfy the erotic drive. Man constructs fantasies that become partial substitutes for physical satisfaction and seeks variety in the forms of sexual behavior.

---

[4] In carnivorous species of mammals, among which males and females do not form permanent alliances, the female restricts her hunting in an area close to her litter, or allows the young to gorge on milk in order to survive her prolonged absences, or some other pattern of adaptation comes into play (Etkin, 1954:136).

Human Helplessness

From the lemurs, monkeys, and apes to man, offspring are born smaller, more helpless, and immature. The period required to learn to walk, to be weaned, and to achieve social independence constantly increases (LaBarre, 1954:54; Hooton, 1947:231–254; Schultz, 1936:267). Table 53 compares a

TABLE 53. Rates of Development for the Rhesus Monkey, Chimpanzee, and Man

| | Age in Weeks | | |
	Rhesus Monkey	Chimpanzee	Man
Raises head and upper chest	birth	2	13
Head steadily erect while sitting	½	2	16
Stands on all fours	1	20	42
Walks on fours (creeps)	1	20	45
Sits unsupported	9	24	23
Biped standing	10	39	54
Biped walking	—	43	58

SOURCE: Riesen and Kinder, 1952:168.

monkey and an ape with man in several items of development. The human infant's retardation is apparent in all but its capacity to sit unsupported. A few other available facts may be cited: Growth is completed in 3 years among lemurs, 7 years among monkeys, 11 years among apes, but takes 20 years for man. Suckling is similarly protracted from a few weeks in monkeys to a year or more in humans. In consequence of the slow pace of growth, early human survival for a long time depends upon adults who provide the child with subsistence and with protection from predators, cold, or heat, and generally maintain its comfort. It is interesting that along with their increased term of early helplessness, the Hominoidea rarely give birth to more than one offspring at a time (Schultz, 1948). A single offspring seems to be optimally adaptive. With only a small number of young to care for at any one time human parents can devote sufficient care to help them all survive.

Transmission of any community's large store of culture from one generation to another is facilitated by the long period of human helplessness (Fiske, 1909). Children too young to survive unaided are required to learn to behave according to the parental generation's standards and values. Parents themselves acquired many of those standards during their own period of subadult dependence. In this way culture acquires its superorganic aspect. The extended dependence of child on adult creates the problem of insuring that every normal individual eventually will reach a point where he can assume the degree of independence (i.e., "emotional maturity") appropriate to his social status. One doubts if members of any other species fail to grow up in the way that humans sometimes do. Becoming-a-man and other status-promoting rituals, as well as a variety of rewards and threats, are employed universally to insure the successful transition of the young to adult status. Long-term early dependence may also be related to the dependent relationships that individuals in some communities are expected to form with collective representations and with authoritative figures in society. Human desire for company and the anxiety promoted by aloneness also may be conditioned in part by the biological dependence of children on adults (Muensterberger, 1955). And once more the family is implicated. The group meets survival problems arising from protracted juvenile dependence as well as from the increased term of pregnancy. Human helplessness is prolonged by an extended period of gestation lasting 266 days in man compared to 150–160 days in monkeys, 110–150 days in lemurs, and less in tree shrews.

Size

Man in his fullness of growth is the second largest Primate. He is exceeded in height and weight only by the gorilla. The difference is stupendous. Gorillas weigh up to 547 pounds (248,000 grams). This does not mean that man holds second place for the size or weight of each body part. In length of ear, for example, *Homo sapiens* is below the macaque, gibbon, and chimpanzee; in foot length he comes after the orang-utan, gorilla, and chimpanzee, while in brain weight he exceeds all the Primates (Schultz, 1936:437, 446).

It is hard to imagine what culture would be like if man approached the smaller mammals in size—say, if he had the 8-inch-long body of the tarsier. Culture is geared to an animal large enough to manipulate tillers, sails, kayaks, and toboggans; to use tools like the ax and sickle, or weapons like the sword; to climb trees or cliffs for honeycombs; to haul in fish nets and cultivate fields with the hoe and plow. The relatively giant size of man has certainly bestowed on him a large measure of command over his smaller contemporaries in the animal kingdom.

Expanded Brain, Symbolization, and Language

What would quadrupeds, lacking prehensile hands or a developed sense of sight, do with modern man's brain? If their behavior came under the dominance of instincts they would have little or no use for such an organ for they would have no need to learn from one another. Such speculation is intended to show the close evolutionary tie between the human brain and man's other, relatively unique features. This organ must have been especially adaptive in a large animal, born without instincts, long dependent on adults for survival, with hands free to handle the environment on which it could focus its stereoscopic eyes.

The size of the brain may be measured directly by weighing the organ or indirectly by measuring the capacity of the cranial vault in which it lodges. Some comparative measurements of animal brains are given in Tables 54 and

TABLE 54. Some Comparisons of Brain Weight

Species	Weight in Kilograms
Blue whale	6.8
Chimpanzee	0.33–0.44
Dog	0.08
Elephant	4.0–5.7
Gibbon	0.09
Grizzly bear	0.39
Horse	0.53–0.71
Orang-utan	0.30–0.37
Man	1.32

SOURCE: Kroeber, *1948:75.*

55. We emphasize that in actual brain weight and skull capacity man always comes out ahead of any other Primate. In proportion to body size man's brain is also heavier than that of most Primates. The human brain weighs in at 2 percent of the body weight, the gibbon's at 1.67, orang-utan at 0.52, rhesus monkey at 1.43, and marmoset monkey at 3.82. Structurally modern

TABLE 55. Comparisons of Some Brain Sizes

Species	Cranial Capacity (cubic centimeters)
Chimpanzee	400
Gibbon	98
Gorilla	549
Orang-utan	416
Man (modern)	1300–1450

man's brain differs from that of any other living Primate brain in the extent of gray matter or cortex, the stuff on which thought depends.

Structurally the *sapiens'* brain (the only one of the Hominidae whose brain is known from direct observation) is quite intricate. It has five major regions. (1) Above the spinal cord lies the medulla oblongata, a vital center that regulates internal processes like breathing and kidney action. Damage here is followed by rapid death. All fibers carrying impulses between the brain and the body muscles pass through the medulla. (2) Just above this point is the cerebellum or "little brain," a center that controls posture and balance. (3) The hypothalamus and thalamus are situated near the center of the head where they control temperature, appetite, activity, and inactivity. Together the hypothalamus, thalamus, and medulla make up the evolutionarily oldest parts of the brain. (4) Across the top of the head lie the cerebral hemispheres, both of which make up the cerebrum. This part of the brain became tremendously expanded in the mammals. A layer of gray matter consisting of millions of cells (it is about 100 cells deep) sheathes the hemispheres and is called the cerebral cortex (cortex means "bark"; the cortex is sometimes called the neopallium, from "pallium," meaning "cloak"). Receptor-effector coördination through which the organism responds to stimuli takes place in the cortex. Here, as well as in the frontal lobes (see below), sensory perceptions are screened and acted upon in terms of the accumulated resources of the organism. Interdependent areas of the cortex are concerned with auditory, optic, and tactile stimuli as well as with speech and motor activity in various parts of the body. The extent of cortical area specialized for each of these functions is proportional to the intricacy of the actions performed. Thus, the area of the human cortex concerned with speech is very large. The cortex also works interdependently with the "old brain." (5) In front of the brain lie the frontal lobes. They operate to maintain discrimination and control over the organism's responses.

Animal evolution has involved not merely increase in brain size but expansion of the cortex and frontal lobes. Man's cortex exceeds the ape's fourfold. It seems quite safe to conclude that man's outstanding capacity for symbolic thought is connected intimately with growth of the gray matter. Increase in the cortical area has been brought about primarily through the convolutions, or folds, in the cerebrum. These grow more numerous as one moves from the non-Primates to man. Sixty-five percent of the human cortex is on the internal surfaces of the fissures of the brain.

What does culture owe to the capacity for symbolization, whose primary locus is no doubt the cerebral cortex? Human behavior in general is much influenced by sign-symbol processes (Chapter 32). In man the almost automatic link between perception and reaction marking other animals has been broken and these processes have become relatively independent. Man's acts are not immediate reactions to his last impressions; they may be delayed, following the stimuli by many days, weeks, or even years. Responses may constitute very elaborate products of imagination like novels, plays, ballets, and operas.

Culture and symbolization are practically equivalent. Some definitions of culture even make the term refer only to the agreements by which people regulate behavior. Communication, as was pointed out, is basically a process of symbolic manipulation. Through language, in turn, much standardization of behavior occurs. Man's symbol-using proclivity allows him to endow experience with many diverse meanings and values. And so the human being creates poetry, prejudices, and ideological systems ranging from religion to science.

With his brain man became a "time-binding" animal, able to conserve and utilize the past in the present (Montagu, 1953). Far more than any other animal man remains aware of his past. Sometimes accumulated experience recalled from bygone times helps him to solve problems. Occasionally such solutions are applied inappropriately. Where once they were useful, in the new situation they won't work. Man also possesses the ability, founded on symbolization, to anticipate the future. From such anticipations he derives both a feeling of security and, sometimes, a sense of dread.

The capacity for symbolic thought, contributing to processes of origination and cultural borrowing, has been responsible for the great multiplication of man and his spread over the globe. No other Primate and few other animals have managed to adapt in such a diversity of environments.

Eulogies are common when even the most sober natural historians describe how the brain works. We have tried not to lose sight of the fact that much of human stress also depends on symbolization. No other animal displays quite the unreason, folly, and impracticality of man, allowing himself to be haunted by imaginary fears or frightened by words, those mere images of things (Langer, 1944).

Language consists of agreements concerning meaningful and significant sounds. Speech, in turn, depends closely on oral techniques. Man's mouth is characterized by a lower jaw which, in contrast to that of the other living Hominoidea, is not joined in front by a horizontal plate of bone, the simian shelf (Hooton, 1947:166–169).[5] Both halves of the hominid jaw are braced by chin bones. The space thus opened up and broadened in the floor of the mouth allows relatively free movement to the tongue, facilitating speech. It is hardly likely that language could have arisen without the human juvenile's extended dependence on adults. Phonemes, morphemes, and the rules of combining them have a chance to become established and transmitted in stable groups like the family.

Plasticity

Man learns most of his behavior through social interaction or through personal experience. An instinct-bound animal, on the other hand, cannot add much to its heritage. Man's plasticity, his freedom from instincts, marks the end of a major trend in evolution. Keeping pace with the expanding brain, the number of unlearned responses has steadily declined, giving animals opportunity for enlarging the capacity for symbolization and learning. Apes

[5] Evidence indicates that the simian shelf is a specialization not present in the common ancestor of the living apes and man.

clearly show themselves capable of learning although they continue to manifest responses, like nest building, which they need not be taught.[6] Few such innate goal-oriented responses are left in humans. A few automatic reflexes remain, like tearing in response to a foreign body in the eye, coughing when an obstruction lodges in the esophagus, and blinking if an object approaches the eye, but they are not usually classified as instincts.

Human plasticity makes possible the wide range of cultural diversity which is the subject of many of the preceding chapters. Man everywhere shares certain likenesses, but communities have grown in different directions. No inbuilt mechanisms determine how man shall travel from place to place or how he will mate, use speech organs, eat, use his hands, or perform practically any other voluntary act.

Protein Diet

Man is the only intensive protein-eating Primate. He usually prefers milk, eggs, beans, and meat to a steady routine of vegetables and fruit. Such specialization of diet, at least with respect to meat, is partly dependent on man's size and erect posture, which enable him to kill large and even dangerous animals for food. Apes are principally frugivorous, using their long canines to rip through the tough rinds of fruit. Man is omnivorous—eating "everything" (vegetable foods as well as meat)—but has a specialized kidney structure for carrying off the protein wastes he regularly accumulates. The food quest of hunters, the prized place of the pig in Melanesian feasts, large-scale pastoralism, commercial cattle farming, dairying, and the place of cheese in many cultures are some traits related to man's taste for proteins. The cracked bones left by fossil men indicate that this taste enjoys considerable antiquity.

PHYLOGENY AND CULTURE

Little evidence supports the assumption made by Sigmund Freud and Carl Jung that each individual at birth possesses a phylogenetic heritage of thought tendencies derived from previous generations or even from mammalian evolution. The theory has been carried furthest by Jung, who postulates a collective unconscious deriving part of its content from prehuman ancestry. This heritage, he holds, is capable of motivating behavior and especially manifests itself in dreams or folklore. "There are present in every individual, besides his personal memories, the great 'primordial' images . . . the inherited powers of human imagination as it was from time immemorial.

---

[6] Just as a child does not learn to walk or talk without appropriate experience, so the instincts do not appear independently of experience. For example, female rats with no experience in moving things like bits of paper and string do not build nests when they become pregnant (Beach, 1954:96).

The fact of this inheritance explains the truly amazing phenomenon that certain motifs from myths and legends repeat themselves the world over in identical forms. It also explains why it is that our mental patients can reproduce exactly the same images and associations that are known to us from the old texts" (Jung, 1953:64).

Thus he explains the similarity of dreams and folk tales from one part of the world to another. The collective unconscious also accumulates wisdom or experience, which, therefore, does not need to be acquired anew in each generation. Jung's theory resembles the rejected theory in biology which held that traits acquired by an individual could be transmitted through heredity to future generations. Experiments have failed to demonstrate the soundness of that proposition. To avoid the implication that experience as such is inherited, Jungian psychologists hold that ". . . rather . . . the brain itself has been shaped and influenced by the remote experiences of mankind." From those experiences arose "physiological paths" that still manifest themselves in our behavior (Fordham, 1953:24). Proving or disproving the inheritance of brain pathways is difficult and biologists are mostly too skeptical to test the theory rigorously.

Avoiding Some Fallacies

Two related fallacies entrap people's thinking about the relationship of man and culture: the culturalistic and biological fallacies.

1. Culturalistic Fallacy. Some sociologists have identified human nature with socialization. They deny that the baby at birth is yet a human being. Such a viewpoint, of course, is basically a matter of definition. It also appears in the thinking of some anthropologists who define man only by evidence of culture. Unless signs of fire or tools are found in association with fossil anthropoids the latter are not classified as human. Such positions fail to recognize that culture is not implanted in man but rather is grounded in animal nature. Once this relationship is admitted then a specifically human nature no longer can be demarcated neatly from a more generalized animal nature. The organic and superorganic are not only continuous but interdependent. Animal nature also limits culture. No human being is wholly plastic, that is, capable of being molded in any direction. For that reason all cultures reveal certain recurrent elements. All over most men eat, move around, mate, live in groups, sleep, use tools, talk, use signs and symbols, and make decisions. But, of course, what people eat, say, symbolize, or decide exhibits great variability. Yet even this variability is grounded in biology, stemming as it does from an organism emancipated from instincts. To ignore the biological basis of culture is to commit the culturalistic fallacy (Bidney, 1953:150–151).

2. Biological Fallacy. Whereas the disciplines which concentrate on social behavior often over-evaluate culture, students of biology are more likely to over-biologize their data. They sometimes see culture as wholly a matter of the organism's structure and functioning without dynamic properties of its own. Animal nature offers man the ability to feel, react, and create symbols. The symbols he creates, whether in the form of a cross, swastika, or stars and stripes, are not determined wholly organically; neither are the responses which man gives to those symbols. For if the response to symbols were entirely biological, then no generation would ever neglect to pay respect to the cross, for example; regardless of culture, every people would salute the stars and stripes. The same symbols would recur from one community to another. Hence, there are aspects of human behavior which cannot be understood fruitfully by considering the structure and functioning of the organism alone.

The biological fallacy crops up in the work of criminologists who look for recurrent physical characteristics distinguishing criminals. Apparently demonstration of biological stigmata in criminals is sufficient to support the assumption of these scholars that criminal behavior is also hereditary. One study sees the American criminal (i.e., a person born in the United States, convicted and serving a sentence for crime) as shorter than his noncriminal contemporaries, lighter in weight, "poorer" in body build, with a smaller head, straighter hair, shorter and broader face, prominent but short nose, narrow jaws, and small yet broad ears (Hooton, 1939:127–128). Except for the "poorer" body build, all these characteristics are objectively measurable. Yet repeated attempts to test the correlation of these traits with criminality have not been successful (Lessa, 1943:15–26). Nor do the so-called "criminal tribes" of India, which specialize in what society considers crime, constitute a biologically homogeneous lot (Majumdar, 1944:186). What constitutes a crime or a criminal varies so much from one period of time to another and between communities that it is hard to see how crime can be biologically inherited. The words just written may be declared criminal overnight—say, as a result of a foreign conquest or a revolution—yet the author's heredity has not changed!

Similar thinking is indicated in those more subjective aspects of somatotyping which seek to demonstrate scientifically an organic basis for certain traits of personality. Every individual, it is held, can be classified by his somatotype, that is, by the amounts of each of three components shown in various regions of his body. These components are (1) endomorphy, soft roundness; (2) mesomorphy, square muscularity and heavy bones; and (3) ectomorphy, linearity and fragility of build. Every individual in different degree bears some of each in his externally visible constitution, but the proportion of any component varies from one person to another (Sheldon, 1940). Not only is a correlation held to exist between a person's somatotype and his temperament, but it is held that constitution in some as yet unknown way produces temperament. Individuals in whom soft round tissue predominates (endomorphs) tend to be relaxed and sociable; they enjoy physical comfort and social approval. Mesomorphs, as one might expect, are aggressive, noisy, and fond of dominating other people. Ectomorphs, with their fragile, linear build, are inhibited and fond of privacy (Sheldon, 1942). More recently a study has demonstrated that boys with a specific type of constitution are more likely to become juvenile delinquents (Sheldon, 1949). A positive association links juvenile delinquency and predominant mesomorphy or moderate endomorphy. It should be borne in mind that the research in question has been conducted in the United States, where heavy muscular build and aggressive "masculinity" popularly are assumed to go together. More serious is the fact that other workers seeking to test some of these studies have been unable even to repeat the initial measurements. Apparently a large element of subjectivity resides even in estimating a somatotype (Snodgrasse, 1951:38). Not being able to determine the somatotypes objectively makes it difficult empirically to prove or disprove a link between personality and biological factors.

45.

Evolution of the Organism

HOMO SAPIENS had established himself in the Old World—Africa, Europe, and Asia—before the end of the fourth glacial stage, or before 15,000 B.C. Even before that time his representatives had crossed Bering Strait and entered the New World. Between 7130 and 6230 B.C. (radiocarbon dates) *Homo sapiens* reached the Straits of Magellan, the southernmost area of South America. The purpose of this chapter is to look much further back into *sapiens'* evolution.

In biology evolution refers to the process by which new species or organisms come into being. Generally speaking, the evolutionary record shows life forms becoming increasingly complex, although occasionally the reverse trend is also manifested. Grass, for example, evolved from a more complex lily-like ancestor (Dodson, 1952:183–187). Animal evolution has been in the direction of increasing size, but again not inevitably. Biological evolution, whether or not it is manifested in increased complexity and size, in itself implies nothing about progress or greater fitness for survival. The dinosaurs in Mesozoic times reached tremendous size but seem to have been poorly equipped for adaptation. They became extinct, while generally smaller reptiles, birds, and mammals propagated their kind.

The immediately preceding chapter described the organismic roots of the human culture. Here the aim will be to show how that organism appeared. Emphasis will go to those features of man—prehensile hands and expanded brain, for example—which are, logically speaking, most intimately related to culture.

LOOKING FOR ADAM[1]

In 1859 Charles Darwin published his *Origin of Species* and advanced the theory of natural selection. This states three main points. (1) All plants and animals reproduce in excess of the number that can survive. Hence, there exists competition for survival. (2) The members of any species differ from one another; some intraspecies differences are insignificant but others may

---

[1] This section is based on Dodson, 1952:Chaps, 1–5; also see Wendt, 1955:Chaps. 1–6.

help or hinder the individual organism's chances in the struggle for survival. (3) Those members of a species tend to survive and to reproduce their kind which biologically are best fitted for adaptation; i.e., they are able to compete successfully for survival.

Darwin could not explain adequately how intraspecies differences arise. He remained unaware of Mendel's theory of genes, a theory that provided a vitally important key to how evolution occurs. It is interesting that in 1858 another Englishman, A. L. Wallace, completed an essay containing practically the same theory of evolution which Darwin had discovered independently. Darwin's views nearly instantly achieved world-wide acceptance. Then, not so much because of the controversy aroused (for that still has not yet fully abated), the early enthusiasm declined. Interest in natural selection as a basic process in evolution did not revive until the 1920's, when gene theory came to account for the origin of those individual differences that successfully underwent selection (see pp. 864–865).

EVIDENCE OF EVOLUTION[2]

Two types of evidence that evolution occurred may be distinguished: indirect and direct. As the reader will see, the direct evidence makes it difficult to accept any position which radically denies that animals without backbones gave rise to fishlike vertebrates who emerged from the sea and in turn developed into mammals from which the Primates, including man, derived.

Indirect Evidence

Indirect evidence of evolution consists primarily of certain data in ecology, comparative anatomy, embryology, and race formation. By themselves these data do not conclusively prove evolution to have occurred. Far more direct proof is provided by paleontological data.

1. Ecology. The distribution of plants and animals on the earth's surface is such that those geographical areas which have been isolated for the longest time possess the most differentiated forms of life. Inhabitants within the same geographical area, however, tend to resemble one another. An explanation for such differentiation lies in the process of natural selection, through which plants and animals become specialized and better suited to their physical surroundings. Resemblances within an area indicate that relatively similar specialized modifications are suited for survival and that possibilities for adaptive modification are limited.

2. Anatomy. Evidence indirectly pointing to evolution comes from the data of comparative anatomy. Man shows a number of vestigial bodily struc-

[2] Based on Dodson, 1952:22–86.

tures, including pointed canine teeth, tail bones (the so-called caudal vertebrae), vermiform appendix, and body hair. When man is compared to other mammals these characters are shown to be very much reduced from the latter's homologous structures. In man these structures also tend to have attenuated functions. Apparently the living mammals, so far as homologous characters are concerned, remain somewhat closer to their original evolutionary forms with respect to those traits, whereas in man more radical change has taken place.

3. Embryology. Data from embryology tell a similar story. The human embryo shows successively fishlike, mammalian, and finally Primate characteristics (not to mention signs of still more simple forms of life that appeared on earth earlier). The stages through which the embryo passes also resemble the embryological development of other animal species and appear to be the product of a long inheritance. Similar phases are revealed in fossils dating from successive geological epochs.

4. Raciation. When some members of an animal species are geographically isolated they will in time become a relatively distinct subspecies or race. Some of the racial characters may be adaptive for particular environmental conditions. A race is a potential new species; that is, the race is a stage available for further evolutionary diversification. "If it is once admitted that local races can be produced in this way, then it seems natural to infer that the differentiation of species has occurred in the same manner" (W. E. L. Clark, 1956:5).

Direct Evidence

The fossil-bearing rocks which make up the crust of the earth offer direct proof that plants and animals passed in step-wise fashion from ancestral to later forms. Study of fossils is called paleontology.

"Fossil" usually designates a quickly buried, dead organism whose organic matter has been replaced by some petrifying or mineralizing substance taken from the earth (Lull, 1935:5–11). In that way the organism becomes incorporated into the crust of the earth and highly resistant to destruction. Despite this customary usage, the word is also applied to organic remains preserved in ice, oil, amber, and frozen soil as well as to a cast of some no longer surviving organism impressed in hardened earth. Other things being equal, the more deeply buried the fossil, the older its age. Buckling of the planet's surface and other geological processes limit the usefulness of this age-depth rule. In practice, dating a fossil depends on identifying the geological period when the particular rocks in which it is contained were laid down. Other associated fossil evidence may give much help in dating. Flora and fauna vary from warm to cold periods of earth history, and the general character of the fossils, by giving evidence of climate, therefore provides clues to the age of the rocks. The great incompleteness of the fossil record becomes apparent from the fact that most plants and animals do not fossilize upon death. Rather they decay through weathering or are eaten by predators so that the skeletal structures are broken up beyond all hope of recognition. Where anything escapes destruction it is usually the hard parts of the animal—bones and especially teeth. These then may undergo fossilization. Fossils provide direct evidence about earlier forms of life and the stages through which evolution proceeded. Often many evolutionary stages are lacking in the fossil record. Paleontological reconstruction of what happened in evolution then remains tentative and subject to revision as additional information is discovered.

How Paleontologists Work[3]

Digging for fossils is a specialized undertaking. A paleontologist does not sink a spade at random. Knowing that fossils occur in sedimentary rocks, like sandstone, shale, slate, or limestone, the seeker after fossils selects such rocks when they also happen to be contemporaneous with the species in whose early history he is interested. He would not, for example, examine rocks of the Mesozoic geological era in the hope of finding fossil apes because he already knows that apes did not appear until the succeeding era. Having found a rock formation of approximately correct age, the explorer, walking down a ravine, along a stream, or by a bluff, may be rewarded with clues to what lies buried below the surface. His eye catches sight of a fragment of bone. In further exposing the fossil he may uncover a quarry containing several skeletons. Small steel implements, whisk brooms, and even camel's-hair brushes help in careful excavation of the fragile relics.

Although the paleontologist remains primarily dependent on the fossil evidence, back in the laboratory he often tries to put flesh on the hard parts or skeleton. Reconstruction of the organism's soft parts is easy when the tissues have left their imprint on bone. Thus, heavy jaw muscles are reflected in the bony ridges of prehistoric human skulls. Recourse to far more speculative methods is necessary to reconstruct how an extinct animal behaved. The paleontologist sometimes fills in the picture of body structure and behavior by examining living creatures who closely resemble the ancient form. The procedure is fraught with danger. Even though the living species has descended from the fossil ancestor, drastic divergences may have taken place.

HOW EVOLUTION OCCURS

That evolution did occur is fairly well demonstrated. How it took place is by no means fully understood. The basis of the process is certainly genetic. Evolution rests on mutation, that is, on random chemical changes

[3] Based on Andrews, 1945:37–41.

occurring in the genes. The gene concept will be explained below.[4] What an individual becomes is dependent partly on his environment and partly on the genes which he has inherited from both parents. The genes control the expression of those physical characters from whose fossil imprint evolution can be reconstructed. If a mutant gene (i.e., a mutation) is inherited by an offspring and is manifested through a change in physiological appearance or functioning; if the change is adaptive, equipping the individual for survival; and if the mutation, plus other, subsequent mutations, spreads or multiplies in an isolated population through inbreeding—then in time a new race and, still later, a new species will come into being. Evolution is taking place.

Darwin emphasized that as differences appear in a species some are more likely to be adapted for survival than others. Those members of a species tend to multiply or spread which are best able to compete for survival. But early evolutionists could not explain how intraspecies differences arose in the first place. The theory of the genes and, particularly, discovery of the process of mutation helped considerably in solving that problem.

Natural selection arises from the fact that at the same time that mutations are occurring all plants and animals reproduce in excess of the number that actually survive.[5] Whether a mutant gene will enter the gene pool of a local population, and so be perpetuated, depends heavily on whether the mutation makes the animal who inherits it better suited for competition or hinders its chances in a given environment. If the alteration is lethal then the organism may die soon after birth. Death, of course, means the end of reproduction as far as that particular mutation is concerned. It disappears from the breeding population until it once more shows up through chance. Alterations that favor animals for survival increase according to the frequency with which they occur in a population. They become perpetuated and fixed. Some modifications neither favor nor hinder survival in a given environment. These neutral characters also stand a better chance of being maintained through succeeding generations than do lethal alterations. Unlike the mutation itself, the survival of a mutation in many cases is not a matter of chance. Take the case of the colon bacteria. Most of these are killed if a small amount of streptomycin is added to their environment, namely, the large intestine. In any large collection of colon bacteria, however, a few cells survive the poison and reproduce. They inherit a mutation which confers resistance to streptomycin and are likely to die in an environment free from this antibiotic! Mutant bacteria which are resistant to streptomycin are produced once in a billion cells and arise by chance regardless of whether the antibiotic is

---

[4] As the following section makes clear, evolution depends on the same process that produces those smaller variations in a species called racial. Hence, the discussion of evolution overlaps with the section on race formation in Chapter 46. More detailed attention to mutation and associated processes whereby the mutation becomes distributed in a population will be found in the following chapter.

[5] The rest of this paragraph is based on Dobzhansky, 1953:294–300.

present in the environment or not. (Hence, the environment does not produce the mutation.) The mutant bacteria multiply best in an environment that favors them by removing competition for survival in the form of normal bacteria. This the streptomycin does.

Since most animals by the very fact of their existence are already adapted to their environment it is not difficult to understand why mutations often prove disadvantageous in a particular milieu. (This assumes that the milieu itself remains more or less unchanged while mutation occurs.) For this reason, too, mutations which are responsible for relatively small variations, that is, which do not upset the adaptation of the organism in its stable environment, are most likely to be perpetuated.

Rates of evolution do not remain constant from one time to another. For example, fairly rapid evolution tends to occur during periods marked by great geological changes. The theory of natural selection provides an explanation for this relationship. Periods of drastic environmental change pose serious survival problems for a relatively immutable species. Those successive biological changes that suit the altered conditions confer survival advantages. In stable times, of course, almost any change might be disadvantageous and altered species do not appear so readily. Therefore, evolution (but not mutation!) slows down when geological conditions remain constant. Care must be taken not to infer that the geographical modifications produce the mutant genes.

WHAT IS MAN?

As we have already indicated, a difficult problem of distinguishing between man and certain of the other Primates faces the paleontologist, who works only with fragmentary skeletons. Considering the close resemblance between apes and men, both of whom possess a bony skeleton built according to the same general plan, how does an investigator know whether a given piece of fossil evidence represents an early form of man or a very manlike ape?[6]

Classification of Man

The anthropoid apes—African chimpanzee and gorilla, East Asiatic orangutan and gibbon—possess sufficient anatomical similarities to warrant grouping them in a single zoölogical family, the Pongidae. Man belongs in another family, Hominidae. Many morphological resemblances occur between pongids and hominids and constitute grounds for grouping both of these families in a larger category, or superfamily, Hominoidea. The hominoids, as the accompanying chart indicates, fit into a still larger order, the Primates, which include also monkeys, lemurs, tarsiers, and lorises.

[6] The rest of the section follows W. E. L. Clark, 1955:Chap. 1.

THE LIVING PRIMATES

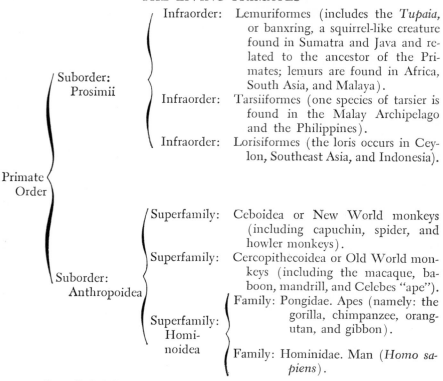

Primate Order

Suborder: Prosimii

Infraorder: Lemuriformes (includes the *Tupaia,* or banxring, a squirrel-like creature found in Sumatra and Java and related to the ancestor of the Primates; lemurs are found in Africa, South Asia, and Malaya).

Infraorder: Tarsiiformes (one species of tarsier is found in the Malay Archipelago and the Philippines).

Infraorder: Lorisiformes (the loris occurs in Ceylon, Southeast Asia, and Indonesia).

Suborder: Anthropoidea

Superfamily: Ceboidea or New World monkeys (including capuchin, spider, and howler monkeys).

Superfamily: Cercopithecoidea or Old World monkeys (including the macaque, baboon, mandrill, and Celebes "ape").

Superfamily: Hominoidea

Family: Pongidae. Apes (namely: the gorilla, chimpanzee, orangutan, and gibbon).

Family: Hominidae. Man (*Homo sapiens*).

SOURCE: George Gaylord Simpson, *1945*:61–68.

Returning to man or, to use a more precise designation, the Hominidae: several subclasses within this family are commonly recognized. The world today is peopled by a single species—*Homo sapiens*—which, however, is not to be recognized in fossil evidence dating from before the middle of the Pleistocene period. Yet fossils have come to light dating from the start of the Ice Age which are also classified with the Hominidae because, in a general way, they resemble the living representatives of *Homo sapiens.* Hence, the Hominidae include both *sapiens* and an unfixed number of non-*sapiens* species which became extinct. Evidence of culture's having been associated with a fossil form of man is *not* the basis for classifying that fossil with *sapiens* or with the Hominidae. Culture, as indicated by deliberately fabricated tools or other artifacts, is older than *Homo sapiens* and not all Hominidae finds reveal such evidence. The Pongidae, too, include not only the living apes but also currently extinct types known only from fossil remains. No evidence of deliberately fabricated tools has ever been found associated with a fossil pongid.

Pongid and hominid fossils differ in degree. This very fact makes classification difficult. Furthermore, the classifier often has few anatomical features to use in making the assignment. His data of necessity are limited to the hard parts of the body: skull, teeth, and other portions of the skeleton. With such evidence before him the paleontologist will, ideally, avoid having his decision determined solely by the age of the geological level in which the skeletal materials were found. To close one's mind to the possibility that hominids existed before the Quaternary era would, of course, lead to relegating all fossils found in Tertiary deposits to the Pongidae regardless of their appearance. Nor does the paleontologist base his judgment solely on a comparison of discrete, individual characters (like size of teeth, length of arm, or size of cranium). For this reason when the evidence for a fossil form is limited to a single character (for example, a fragment of jawbone) taxonomic status is very difficult to assess confidently. The judgment of pongid or hominid status is made on the basis of the *total morphological configuration* of the available material, that is, all the known physical characters taken in combination. The mere size of a canine tooth in an otherwise hominoid jaw is not by itself sufficient to indicate whether the owner was ape or man, even though large canines rarely occur in the Hominidae. A large, tusklike lower canine in combination with other features, like a measurable gap (diastema) between upper incisors and canine teeth and a lower jaw in which the teeth are set in the shape of a parabola (rather than forming an inverted U-shaped arc), offers far more satisfactory grounds for assigning the particular fossil to the pongid rather than the hominid family.

Naturally, the actual process of studying anatomical remains requires more technical knowledge than these simple illustrations indicate. Knowledge of major trends in evolution substantially assists the specialist for he will then base his judgment on characters most relevant for classification. For example, the evolutionary emergence of the Hominidae from the Pongidae involved development of fully erect, biped posture. Hence the form of the hindlimbs rather than the forelimbs is especially pertinent evidence for putting a form in one family or the other.

The same general methodology outlined for classifying a fossil as pongid or hominid in structure applies to making further classification within the Hominidae, that is, to determining whether a given form of man is *sapiens* or non-*sapiens*. When such judgment is necessary, features of the skull and jaw become more relevant than parts of the lower skeleton because, according to the paleontological record, skull and jaw underwent rapid evolution once the Hominidae appeared.

Configurations of Men and Apes

In relatively nontechnical terms, the evolutionary trend by which the Hominidae departed from the Pongidae included the gradual appearance of hominid characters like an upright skeleton, a foot specialized for locomotion, loss of opposability in the great toe, exploded brain, and others listed in the first column of Table 56. In contrast, the evolutionary process which led to the living anthropoid apes produced such diagnostic features as the simian shelf (or plate of bone bracing the lower jaw [see p. 817]), rela-

TABLE 56.   Some Evolutionary Trends Leading to Appearance of Men, *Homo sapiens*, and Living Apes

Hominidae	Pongidae (living)
1. Progressive modification of the skeleton in the direction of upright posture and biped locomotion, including specialization of the foot for support.	Modification of the skeleton in the direction of becoming specialized for brachiation; relatively long fore-limbs.
2. Thumb opposable; this facility is lost in the great toe.	Thumb and great toe both retain the opposability gained in earlier evolution.
3. Reduction of facial prognathism, the face becoming increasingly flat and retracted under the brain case. At the same time the chin emerges.	Some prognathism retained; there is no chin.
4. Reduction in the size of the jaw and those areas of the skull where masticatory muscles attach.	Development of massive jaws and associated strong, muscular ridges and crests on the skull where masticatory muscles attach.
5. Reduction in size of canine teeth and disappearance of the diastema (gap) between upper canine and incisor; early wearing down of the teeth to a flat surface; reduction of molars.	Enlargement of the canine teeth, which interlock when they meet; measurable diastema; molar teeth large.
6. Development of an evenly rounded, U-shaped dental arc (Fig. 45:1).	Teeth continue to be arranged in parabolic form (Fig. 45:1).
7. Marked and rapid expansion of cranial capacity (implying larger brain).	Ultimately there occurs only a limited expansion of the brain.
8. High and rounded skull vault.	Relatively flat skull vault retained.
9. Mastoid processes (bony extensions of the skull projecting down behind the position of the ears) develop early and regularly.	Mastoid processes develop rarely if at all.

Homo sapiens

1. Skeleton adapted to fully upright posture; limb bones relatively slender and straight.
2. Muscular ridges on the cranium not strongly marked; ridge above eyes (i.e., the supraorbital torus) moderate and not forming an uninterrupted shelf of bone.
3. Rounded occipital (back of the head) region.
4. Foramen magnum facing directly downward.
5. Prominent mastoid processes.
6. Jaws and teeth of relatively small size.
7. Definite chin.
8. Spherical skull vault with a mean capacity of about 1350 or 1400 c.c.
9. Rounded and approximately vertical forehead.

SOURCE: Adapted from W. E. L. Clark, *1954*:387–388; *1955*:48, 110, 111; Schultz, *1955*.

tively long arms specialized for brachiation (tree-swinging), massive jaws, and others shown in the second column of the table. Evolution of hominids and pongids did not, of course, manifest itself only in skeletal features. Among other hominid characters that must have appeared were prolonga-

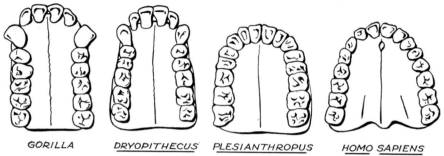

GORILLA   DRYOPITHECUS   PLESIANTHROPUS   HOMO SAPIENS

FIG. 45:1. Pongid and Hominid Dental Arcs (from Howells, 1945:100).

tion of helplessness in the offspring following birth, slowing down of growth, and reduction of body hair.

Around the middle of the Ice Age, or Pleistocene period, the single living species of the Hominidae, *Homo sapiens*, emerged. The total morphological configuration includes a high forehead, foramen magnum (through which the central nervous system connects with the brain) facing downward in the base of the skull, rounded back of the head, small jaws and teeth, definite chin, spherical skull vault, and other characters listed at the end of Table 56.

BACKGROUND OF PRIMATE EVOLUTION

It will be recalled that life on a hitherto lifeless earth first started somewhat less than 2 billion years ago in the Archeozoic era.[7] How the chemical revolution producing protoplasm came about is not known. In time, however, thousands of species of protozoa, one-celled animals, were occupying the ancient seas. Their imprint remains in what was once soft mud and they have also left traces of their carbon in the earth's surface. Each protozoön had a nucleus that stored genetic material. In this genetic material mutations occurred. These probably led to the transition from one-celled to multicelled animals—the Metazoa. The earliest marine metazoa, appearing in the Proterozoic era, were, of course, still without backbones. The paleon-

[7] See the geological time scale in Table 52. The major geological eras given there are (in order of greatest remoteness from the present): the Azoic (lifeless), Archeozoic (primeval life), Proterozoic (very early life), Paleozoic (ancient life), Mesozoic (middle life), and Cainozoic (modern life). Further subdivisions in some of these eras will be referred to when necessary.

tological record indicates that over the next several million years the early
invertebrates multiplied into a great diversity of forms: worms, sponges,
jellyfish, snails, starfish, and many others.

From Backbone to Lungs

Following the Proterozoic came the Paleozoic, or era of ancient life, from
which fossil evidence is quite abundant. Considerable is known, too, about
the history of the earth during the ensuing 300 million years of the Paleozoic
(Read, 1949). This was an epoch of repeated floods that brought submer-
gence and again emergence to great land masses. Each such climatic sequence occupied millions of years. Early in the Paleozoic half of North
America lay under water. Great volcanic outbursts buried large portions of
the Old and New Worlds with ash and lava. After that, the earth's crust
crushed together (like a crumbling piece of paper). In the New World this
movement pushed up the Appalachian Mountains. The Paleozoic closed
with a widespread glaciation in which parts of South America, South Africa,
India, and Australia lay under huge masses of ice. From the standpoint of
evolution equally dramatic events occurred. In the realm of plants, the first
trees and mosses appeared. Vertebrate forms of animal life quit the sea for
the land.

Animals with backbones evolved from earlier chordates, in whom the
place of the backbone is taken by the notochord, an elongated, rodlike
sheath filled with a gelatinous substance. The notochord gives firmness with
extreme flexibility to the organism. In existing species of this type the central
nervous tract lies above the notochord. True vertebrates, the earliest of
which may have possessed only a round mouth for sucking, nostrils, ears,
but no jaws, evolved from chordates. Median and tail fins aided their locomotion. Lacking were paired fins on the under surface of the body such as
later developed into limbs.[8] Direct fossil evidence of the earliest vertebrates
has still to be discovered. Perhaps some day the rocks will yield a lamprey-
like fossil. Living lampreys exist in fresh and salt water. In form they resemble an eel. Paired fins are absent and the round mouth is essentially a cuplike sucking disk. Attaching themselves to other fish, lampreys prey on the
hosts' flesh, a rasping tonguelike structure substituting for jaws.

Next came the appearance of jaws and paired limbs (actually fins, as we
are still dealing with fishes). The new organs must have been adaptive in
enabling their bearers to become more active predators. Paired fins facilitated movement and speed while jaws allowed food to be taken in large
pieces and ground down for consumption. Finally lungs were added to the
assemblage of paired fins and jaws. Lungs may have been especially suitable

[8] The following account of vertebrate evolution follows Romer, 1941:Chaps. 1, 3, 5,
9, and 14.

for fish living in the unsettled conditions of the Paleozoic.[9] Drought and flood based on heavy rainfall alternated. "If the streams and ponds . . . tended to dry up, the water would become stagnant and foul" but with "some sort of membranous lung sac . . . developed in the throat, a fish in such a pool could come to the surface, gulp down air, and breathe atmospheric oxygen . . ." (Romer, 1941:27).

On the Land

Perhaps 80 million years separate the earliest chordate, with its notochord, and the primitive lunged fish, ancestor to all modern terrestrial and air-breathing animal forms, including man. By the time the first quarter of the Paleozoic era had ended, several basic features which were to be incorporated in the Primate organism had evolved: the backbone, two sets of paired ventral fins (corresponding to four limbs), jaw, and lungs. For what happened next, imagine some aggressive, active, backboned, lunged animals leaving the sea for a more extensive career on land. Such an event occurred in the Devonian period of the Paleozoic era.[10] The earliest land vertebrates were amphibious—at home in both air and water. When an animal spent time in both water and land, mutations in the direction of limbs would favor terrestrial survival. Perhaps such enhanced adaptability contributed to the diversification of limbed creatures. Some, like the labyrinthodonts of the succeeding Carboniferous period, grew as large as crocodiles. New methods of absorbing air into the lungs evolved. Supplanting use of gills, breathing probably came to be accomplished (as in modern amphibians) by throat muscles used to swallow air. The ear came to include a diaphragm, the eardrum, that amplified sound. Hearing, it may be inferred, possessed greater survival value on land than in the water.

Paleozoic amphibians gave rise to reptiles. When early reptiles began to lay eggs on land, emancipation of life from the water was complete. The break may have occurred as early as Permian times, that is, in the final era of the Paleozoic. Reptiles did not become prevalent until the succeeding, Mesozoic, era, which is also known as the Age of Reptiles.

Geologically the Mesozoic remained relatively quiet after the tumult of the earlier period. Floodings and subsidences continued, however. In the middle of the Mesozoic (Jurassic period) the American cordillera (Sierra

[9] In 1939 considerable excitement followed the catching of a coelacanth off the coast of South Africa. Here is a modified descendant of one of man's early ancestors, a lunged fish with fins containing a fleshy lobe within which is a skeleton, the whole comparable to a land animal's leg. Other coelacanths have since been taken. To zoölogists their discovery has been like the shock of discovering an existing dinosaur.

[10] The periods of the Paleozoic in the order of their occurrence are: the Cambrian, Ordovician, Silurian, Devonian, Carboniferous, and Permian. There is no need to be concerned with the further division of each of these.

Nevada) was formed and then (in the final Cretaceous period) the Rockies themselves heaved up.[11] Meanwhile reptiles continued to evolve in their limbs, backbones, muscles, hearts, lungs, and other organs as they adapted themselves to a terrestrial existence. Breathing probably came to involve chest rather than throat muscles. The first trace of small cerebral hemispheres marked evolution in the brain. These appendages to the so-called old brain continued to evolve accompanying increased ability to "record" past experience in memory. But the reptile brain still does little more than receive sensations, the animal acting directly upon the incoming stimuli. Reptilian teeth are peglike and undifferentiated from one another, a condition that will also alter with the mammals.

The Mesozoic saw some reptiles grow as large as dinosaurs while others evolved into birds. Another line gradually assumed mammal-like forms from which true mammals finally arose, animals that no longer laid eggs. Reptilian mammals in the Triassic period already possessed mechanisms for maintaining constant body temperature. Following Mesozoic times, mammals spread rapidly over the earth while reptiles tended to disappear. Hence the Cainozoic era is often called the Age of Mammals.[12]

Mammals

Mammals, it will be recalled, are animals which nurse their young, which are born alive after a period of existence within the mother's body. Other mammalian features include constant, high body temperature, an external surface covered with hair, sweat glands, a much enlarged brain, and more efficient appendages for locomotion. The mammalian brain reveals enlargement of the cerebral hemispheres. Mammals are further distinguished by the separation of the nostrils from the oral passage. They possess an external ear flap and grow two successive sets of teeth (the so-called milk and permanent sets). Teeth of mammals are differentiated into four types: incisors that function for shearing, canines, and premolars (sometimes called bicuspids in man) which, together with molars, are adapted for grinding. A Jurassic mammal is known with 64 teeth (4 incisors, 1 canine, 5 premolars, and 6 molars in each of the 4 quarters of the mouth). In the Tertiary era mammals evolved with only 44 teeth arranged in each half of the mouth according to the following dental formula: $I\frac{3}{3}$ $C\frac{1}{1}$ $P\frac{4}{4}$ $M\frac{3}{3}$ (Fig. 45:2). This means that each of 4 quarters of the mouth contained 3

[11] Three periods make up the Mesozoic: the Triassic, Jurassic, and Cretaceous. There is no need to be concerned with the subdivision of these into smaller units.

[12] The Cainozoic is sometimes divided into two suberas: Tertiary and Quaternary. The Tertiary contains five periods. In order of occurrence these are the Paleocene, Eocene, Oligocene, Miocene, and Pliocene. The Quaternary includes the Pleistocene (i.e., "recent") period or Ice Age, and the "wholly recent," or Holocene.

incisors, 1 large canine, 4 premolars, and 3 molars.[13] Free replacement of teeth ceases with the mammals. That is, lost members of the second set are never regained (except through modern dentistry). Typical Mesozoic mammals remained small (about the size of a mouse or rat) and arboreal. Although they were carnivorous, their diminutive build hardly equipped them to secure game larger than insects or worms. Eggs of reptiles and birds probably also figured prominently in their diet. Cainozoic mammals showed definite increase in size, which,

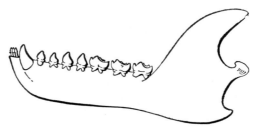

FIG. 45:2.   Early Mammalian Dental Pattern (after W. E. L. Clark, 1956:25).

together with the growing brain, would finally enable mammalian species to take over the world.

Earth-shaking changes mark the geological history of the Cainozoic, the geological era in which we live. "Volcanic outbursts proceeded on a gigantic scale, the grandest mountain-belts of all times [Alps and Himalayas] were erected, violent earthquakes rocked great segments of the crust, the continents were enlarged and came to stand higher," and, finally, shortly before the present, a vast glaciation spread over much of the northern hemisphere (Read, 1949:228). Mammals survived through this upheaval. At the start of it there appeared the present self-styled rulers of the world, the Primates.

EVOLUTION OF PRIMATES TO MAN

Fossil remains of Primates are disappointingly scarce. Most of these animals, being arboreal, lived mainly in forested regions, which are unfavorable for fossilization. Hence, considerably more is known about the evolution of certain mammals, like the horse or elephant, than about Primates.[14] Living members of the order fall into two main suborders (see p. 828): (1) the Prosimii, consisting of squirrel-like lemurs, the loris (or banxring), and tarsiers, all living in tropical environments, and (2) the Anthropoidea, comprising monkeys, apes, and man.

The earliest Primates, probably originating from insect-eating tree shrews in the Paleocene period, may have resembled the modern *Tupaia*. If we proceed on this analogy, very early Primates were small, were diurnal in habits

[13] Hominidae's dental formula, given for ready reference, is I$\frac{2}{2}$ C$\frac{1}{1}$ P$\frac{2}{2}$ M$\frac{3}{3}$ or a total of 32 teeth.

[14] See the map showing occurrence of nonhominid Primate fossils in the Old World in Patterson, 1955:15.

(that is, active by day and sleeping by night), and possessed 5 clawed digits on each limb. The forelimbs, to some degree freed from functions of locomotion, could be used to manipulate environmental objects or convey food to the mouth.

The fossil of a pre-Primate, *Indrodon*, possessing some of these characters has been found dating from the middle of the Paleocene period. *Indrodon's* dental formula, $I\frac{2}{2}$ $C\frac{1}{1}$ $P\frac{4}{4}$ $M\frac{3}{3}$, reveals a typical Primate feature: 2 rather than 3 incisors. The total number of teeth has taken a further reduction. It is now 40 rather than 44, approaching closer to the Hominidae's 32.

The Modern Ring-Tailed Lemur Is a Descendant of Eocene Lemuroids Like Notharctus (courtesy, New York Zoological Society).

Evolution of Lemuriformes

North America in the lower and middle Eocene epoch marks the setting in which *Notharctus*, a lemuroid[15] creature measuring 11 to 14 inches in length, flourished. His dental formula remains unchanged from the pre-Primate *Indrodon's*. Other European Eocene lemuroids, however, evolved a jaw with only 36 teeth distributed as follows: $I\frac{2}{2}$ $C\frac{1}{1}$ $P\frac{3}{3}$ $M\frac{3}{3}$.

Modern lemurs cannot provide a reliable key to the structure and behavior of early lemuroids but a look at them familiarizes one with the remote Primate ancestors.[16] In body size living lemurs vary from a few inches to about two feet. Locomotion involves all four limbs, but the digits on these limbs (except the second on the hind extremities) possess flat nails in place of claws. The dental formula generally corresponds to that of their Eocene predecessors. Thumb and great toe both are capable of being opposed to the tips of the other four digits. Whereas the forelimbs can be rotated, the hindlimbs cannot and tend to be more rigidly specialized for support. Possessing hairy coats and elongated snouts with nostrils placed in a naked, moist muzzle, like a cat's, lemurs are also equipped with large round eyes lying, Primate fashion, in front of the head. Compared to non-Primate mammals of the same size, lemurs are large-

---

[15] The suffix *-oid* means "like."
[16] From Hooton, 1942:Chap. 11; Montagu, 1951b:37–39.

brained, though the unconvoluted cerebral hemispheres are still quite small. Tails vary in size or may be absent. In habit lemurs are mostly nocturnal. They inhabit a relatively closely defined territory. Some lemur species have been described in which the female rejects the male for copulation outside of the estrus period. An annual breeding season is thus indicated. They give birth to litters containing several young. With Old World monkeys, lemurs share a penis bone. In most lemurs the upper incisors are greatly reduced while the lower incisors and canines project forward like a comb. This is a late evolutionary specialization not found in Eocene fossils.

Evolution of Tarsiiformes

Early tarsioids may have been a North American innovation but by the middle of the Eocene period tarsioids are known from Europe. Judging from skeletal evidence they were small animals despite a considerably expanded brain case. Presumably they descended from a generalized lemuroid ancestor and possessed the same dental formula. Judging from *Amphipithecus*, an upper Eocene fossil from Burma, the third premolar shows marked reduction in size, which seems to herald its eventual extinction.

Looking at the modern tarsiers may be helpful.[17] Indonesian adult tarsiers approximate the size of a two-weeks-old kitten, but they possess a very much longer tail. Digited extremities, opposable thumb and big toe, claws retained on two toes, and an insectivorous diet are distinguishing features. The face or snout shows marked reduction that may have accompanied attenuation in the importance of the olfactory sense compared to the visual. The tarsier's eyes also are set in front of the head. Like the hindlimbs with their extreme specialization for hopping, the large eyes are late evolutionary features in which modern tarsiers do not resemble their more generalized Eocene ancestors. Note that increasing differentiation of hindlimbs from forelimbs is characteristic of lemurs, tarsiers, and man. As in lemurs, the relatively large tarsier brain is not convoluted but the cerebral hemispheres are larger in proportion to the rest of the brain. Tarsiers tend to live in bisexual pairs and have only one well-defined annual breeding season. They give birth to a single young at a time and do not construct nests. Unlike lemurs, but like the Hominoidea, female tarsiers menstruate. There is no penis bone as in lemurs and Old World monkeys.

What happened to the Eocene tarsioids? It has been suggested that one line may have developed into a generalized monkey and another into an ape. But considerably more evidence is required to confirm such detailed reconstruction. Clearly Eocene tarsioids gave rise to modern tarsiers. There is also evidence that one tarsioid line evolved to develop the same features that were appearing in the line of monkey evolution (just as happened also

[17] From Hooton, 1942:Chap. 10; Montagu, 1951b:39–43.

with a line of lemurs in Madagascar). Cases of parallelism, while not exactly common in evolution, are also not entirely unexpected.

Lorisiformes

The several species of existing lorisiformes have been somewhat neglected for study by naturalists. Also little is known of their evolution prior to the Pliocene period, when they appear in India. Today they are small, arboreal, furry animals with short, pointed snouts, quite big eyes, and no tail. Hind-limbs and forelimbs are differentiated, and as in lemurs and tarsiers, the second toe generally possesses a claw instead of the customary nail. The loris is nocturnal and omnivorous, eating birds, insects, eggs, and fruit. Some authors classify it as a lemur (Hooton, 1942:315–319).

Monkeys and Their Missing Ancestors

With monkeys the evolutionary record draws closer to man. This is indicated in the chart on p. 828 where the Lemuriformes, Tarsiiformes, and Lorisiformes are segregated into the Prosimii, a suborder of Primates, while the monkeys, apes, and man share the second suborder, Anthropoidea.

Living monkeys fall into two divisions: Old World (Cercopithecoidea) and New World (Ceboidea). Both share an essentially manlike eye, a capacity to sit upright and to manipulate objects with prehensile forelimbs when not engaged in locomotion, and a relatively larger brain. New World monkeys are also called platyrrhine monkeys because of widely separated nostrils turned sideways, a feature they share with lemurs and tarsiers. They continue to have three premolars and, at times, prehensile tails. Old World monkeys are catarrhines, possessing nostrils set close together and facing downward like those of apes and man. In size they exceed the New World family and possess a shorter tail or none at all, more flattened nails, and particularly long canines. Only two premolars are in each quarter of the mouth, giving them the same dental formula that is shared by apes and man: I$\frac{2}{2}$ C$\frac{1}{1}$ P$\frac{2}{2}$ M$\frac{3}{3}$ (Fig. 45:3). Within Old and New World monkeys some pronounced variations in structure and behavior characterize the different species. Most monkeys are arboreal, though the baboon, mandrill, and Barbary ape prefer a terrestrial environment. A summary of some of the features of living monkeys is given in Table 57.

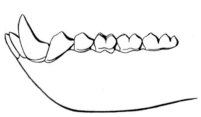

Fig. 45:3. Old World Monkey Dental Pattern Shared by Apes and Man (after W. E. L. Clark, 1956:27).

At this point the reader may expect the description of a generalized fossil monkey, one from whom the New and Old World superfamilies branched off. No monkey fossils earlier than the Miocene epoch have so far been dis-

TABLE 57. Some Structures and Behaviors of Living Monkeys

New World Monkeys (including howler, spider, and cebus monkeys)	Old World Monkeys (including baboon, mandrill, macaque, mangabey, Barbary ape [all with elongated snouts], and the shorter-faced langur, guerezas and proboscis monkeys)
1. Dental formula: $I\frac{2}{2} C\frac{1}{1} P\frac{3}{3} M\frac{3}{3}$.	Dental formula: $I\frac{2}{2} C \frac{1}{1} P\frac{2}{2} M\frac{3}{3}$.
2. Generally possess a less-projecting muzzle than Old World contemporaries.	Fall into two groups, one with projecting muzzle and the other with a generally retracted snout.
3. Wide partition between nostrils, which are directed sideways (platyrrhine).	Nostrils are set close together and are downward-facing (catarrhine), separated by a narrow septum.
4. Long, prehensile tail is common.	Tail is short or absent but thumb and great toe possess great capacity for movement.
5. Lack cheek pouches.	Cheek pouches enable food to be stuffed into the mouth and masticated at leisure.
6. Lack ischial callosities.	Possess ischial callosities—naked patches of thickened skin over the haunch bones such as also occur in apes. This area becomes inflamed and enlarged when the female is in estrus.
7. Only the cebus monkey possesses a penis bone.	Penis possesses well-marked bone.
8. The extent to which sexual intercourse is limited to the time of estrus is not clear.	Sexual intercourse is engaged in by many Old World monkeys regardless of estrus.
9. The ruthless dominance behavior found among Old World monkeys is absent, generally speaking, and sexual jealousy is less apparent.	In some species (e.g., baboon and macaque) dominance behavior is ruthless, the animal capable of dominating a group acting with such extreme selfishness that subordinate members are scarcely permitted to eat. The less ascendant animals live in a constant state of intimidation and often use sexual presentation in attempts to placate the more aggressive ones.

SOURCES: New World Monkeys: Hooton, *1942*:233–274; Zuckerman, *1932*:51. Old World Monkeys: Hooton, *1942*:178–231; Zuckerman, *1932*:50.

covered. By Miocene times apes had already begun to flourish. Cercopithecoid monkeys probably diverged from the Primate line leading to the Hominoidea as early as the late Eocene or (at the very latest) in the Oligocene epoch. The Ceboidea probably separated even earlier. Many more fossils are required before details of monkey evolution can reasonably be suggested.

Fossil Anthropoid Apes

One speculative reconstruction of what next happened in Primate evolution derives the anthropoid (i.e., manlike) apes from a generalized monkey, presumably of the catarrhine type. As just pointed out, however, a suitable fossil parent to make this sequence plausible remains to be discovered. Possibly the apes, which made their first appearance in the Oligocene period,

TABLE 58. Structures and Behaviors of Living Apes

	Chimpanzee	Gibbon	Orang-utan	Gorilla
1. *Distribution:*	Congo and Niger River drainages and southern Egyptian Sudan to Lake Victoria.	Assam, Burma, Indo-China, Malay Peninsula, and Indonesia.	Sumatra and Borneo; fossil remains are known from Java and southern China.	Lowland country east of southern Nigeria to the Belgian Congo; also mountainous region of eastern Congo to southern tip of Lake Tanganyika.
2. *Size and skin color:*	Average weight is 110 lbs. for males and 88 lbs. for females; maximum height, 5 and 4 feet respectively; skin color under hair-cover varies from almost black to coffee, pigmentation deepening with exposure.	Averages from 11 to 15 lbs., there being little difference between the sexes; stature rarely exceeds 3 feet; skin color usually black under a woolly coat.	Male averages 165 lbs. (with maximum of 200 lbs. being recorded) and female 81 lbs. Height is about 50 inches in males and 44 inches in females. Hairs are longer than in any other anthropoid. Skin color brownish but ordinarily not as dark as in gorilla and some chimpanzees; face hairless.	Average weight is about 420 lbs. but some individuals reach 500 lbs. or more; males measure about 5 or 6 feet. Skin color increases with age and ordinarily is black.
3. *Skull, brain, and jaw:*	Brain case is low-vaulted; forehead low; continuous supraorbital torus, the size of which grows with age. Cranial capacity averages about 400 c.c. for males and 366 for females. Projecting jaws with very thin lips but no chin. To support the heavy jaws thick musculature almost conceals the animal's neck. Foramen magnum located far back on skull base. Incisors and canines are large, relative to man, and canines interlock, giving rise to diastema. The third molars are reduced and degenerate.	Skull is low, the cranial capacity averaging 97 c.c. The brain, however, is large compared to body weight. Forehead low and brow ridges not very prominent; poise of the skull on the vertebral column is not typical of a pronograde animal. Third molars are reduced and often lacking; incisors small; canines tusklike and interlocking.	Bony crests cross the back of the low skull vault but are not continuous in front. The male carries another crest from fore to aft on top of his skull. Heavy musculature hides the neck. Cranial capacity is about 416 c.c. for males and 336 for females. In comparison to body size, the orang's cranial capacity is one-fourth that of man's. Forehead is relatively high; foramen magnum situated back on the base of the skull. Unlike gorilla, chimpanzee, and man, eye orbits are almost circular. Massive jaws bulge forward; cheek pouches in the male; teeth, especially canines, are large.	Brain case is low; heavy brow ridges above the eyes, and another crest runs the length of the head to meet a transverse-running ridge of bone at the back of the head where the head is flat and heavy nuchal muscles slope to the animal's back. Cranial capacity averages 549 c.c. for males and 459 for females. Brain is only $\frac{1}{150}$th of body weight compared to $\frac{1}{50}$th in man. Jaw chinless, lips thin, and upper incisors massive; tusklike canines; heavy molars.

840

4. *Torso and limbs:* Chest is deep but the female breasts are relatively inconspicuous; pelvis narrow and buttocks little developed. Upper limbs are long, reaching to the knee or below when the animal is upright; legs are short. Locomotion is with the weight borne on forelimbs or, more precisely, on the knuckles, the hindlimbs swinging between them as the animal moves in a somewhat sideways fashion. Arm-swinging through trees is practiced, though not for any great distance. Erect posture in walking is used occasionally, e.g., while carrying something, but the knees always remain bent. The thumb is diminutive; great toe massive, projecting like a thumb, and capable of grasping.

5. *Range and diet:* Individual nests are built in leafy trees or branches, the task taking 3 to 25 minutes depending on whether distraction occurs. Diet is vegetarian. Chimpanzees do not remain restricted to a definite territory.

6. *Sex:* Estrus occurs with swelling of sexual skin at intervals of about 36 days, animal remaining responsive to coitus for about 4 days at this time. Some

Torso and limbs: Shoulders and hips are broad but the breasts are rather flat, nipples lying high. Forelimbs are very long but the legs are sometimes longer than in man; forelimbs can touch ground when animal stands erect. Posture is normally upright when standing and, of course, while brachiating, for which gibbons are very well equipped. Can cover 20 feet in 2 or 2½ swings; 90 percent of locomotion is by brachiation. The thumb on the narrow hand is longer than in chimpanzee and orang-utan but shorter than man's. Thumb not "clearly" opposable to other fingertips; teeth often used to hold objects.

Range and diet: Gibbons remain in a fairly well-defined territory ranging from 30 to 100 acres; intruders in territory are dislodged. Diet primarily vegetarian but eggs, insects, and young birds are also eaten.

Sex: Males and females remain together even when estrus is completed. Estrus recurs at 29-day intervals but copulation occurs at other times as well,

Torso and limbs: Breasts as large as in man; nipples situated below the armpits. Chest circumference is greater than man's and shoulder breadth is also great. Arm measures 924 mm. compared to chimpanzee's 789 and man's 773 mm.; hindlimb is 545 mm. compared to chimpanzee's 577 and man's 882 mm. Orang has longest foot of any Primate. Progression is by brachiation or on all fours, the elbows slightly extended, support being at least partly on the inner edge of the hand. Forelimbs are so long that even in quadrupedal position the animal seems to be walking erect. Erect posture is possible but quickly fatiguing. Thumb is very small and starts so far back toward the wrist that it can reach only to the middle of the palm. Great toe small but larger than thumb, opposable, and often devoid of nail. Heel scarcely developed.

Range and diet: Migration over long distance; nests built in trees, probably nightly. Diet is vegetarian, mainly fruit.

Sex: No data.

Torso and limbs: Forelimbs extend very far, especially the forearm, but length is not as exaggerated as in orang and gibbon. Trunk and legs are relatively short. Animal habitually moves on all fours, bearing weight on knuckles. (One reason being that, as in the chimpanzee and orang-utan, the hand cannot be bent back to bring the palm at right angles to the extended arm. Monkeys can do this as can young humans.) When gorilla occasionally stands erect the knees are bent. Unlike other apes, does not sidle in walking. Is an accomplished brachiator. Thumb too short for man's range of opposability; other fingers are webbed to first joint. Great toe massive but shorter than chimpanzee's; heel better developed.

Range and diet: Nests built daily in trees or, for mountain-dwelling species, on the ground, avoiding thorny plants. Diet largely vegetarian though they can learn to eat meat in captivity.

Sex: No data. Presumably sex drive is most intense during estrus. Emotional expression from many sources is commonly shown by beating on the chest with both

TABLE 58. (*Continued*)

Chimpanzee	Gibbon	Orang-utan	Gorilla
females will accept coitus in any period of the sexual cycle but others are more independent. Rape occurs and homosexual mounting is not infrequent, especially when invited by a sexually aroused female. Masturbation is common.	young being born in any season.		fists. One purpose in this is probably to startle an observer.
7. *Social life:* Animals generally associate in groups of from 4 to 14 individuals but whether polygamous or monogamous is not clear. Group members differ in dominance, the most subordinate also being most inclined to share food upon demand or even spontaneously.	*Social life:* Groups range from 2 to 6 animals, the minimal group being a bisexual pair but more frequently consisting of 2 parents and 2 young; thus monogamy is indicated. Gibbons are not markedly competitive or aggressive, animals rarely taking food from less dominant fellows. Dominance behavior does occur, however, and is dependent on personality, not sex.	*Social life:* Little known but males are said to live alone except when mating; gregariousness seems absent.	*Social life:* Little studied; dominance behavior has been noted. Groups are under the control of a single polygynous male who, when he is overcome by more powerful competitors, may take to solitary life.
8. *Learning:* Considerable learning is possible, including use of food and other tokens as rewards for work; animal can learn to use these in a vending machine. Stereoscopic vision seems indicated and colors can be distinguished.	*Learning:* Ability to learn is attested though seems to be not very high.	*Learning:* Ability seems indicated but manual skill is relatively limited.	*Learning:* Gorillas can learn to perform simple tasks, like drawing food closer by means of a stick, but learning ability appears inferior to chimpanzees'.

842

sources: Chimpanzee: Hooton, *1942*:Chap. 1; see also Yerkes, *1943*. Gibbon: Hooton, *1942*:Chap. 4. Orang-utan: Hooton, *1942*:Chap. 3. Gorilla: Hooton, *1942*:Chap. 2.

evolved from some tarsioid ancestor without an intervening monkey-like phase (W. E. L. Clark, 1956:57–58). Available facts fall far short of these conjectures. For one of the earliest apelike fossils of Oligocene age, *Parapithecus*, the evidence consists of most of a lower jaw (mandible) found in the Fayum depression of northern Egypt. *Parapithecus* was no giant Primate. The jaw measures only 36.5 mm. in length (about an inch and a half), less than half the size of the jaw of a modern gibbon, smallest of the living apes (Table 58). Thirty-two teeth are arranged according to the dental formula I$\frac{2}{2}$ C$\frac{1}{1}$ P$\frac{2}{2}$ M$\frac{3}{3}$, shared by the living Old World monkeys, apes, and men. Certain features in the way the cusps are arranged on the molars, while seemingly a most esoteric and technical matter to the nonspecialist, are an additional reason for classifying *Parapithecus* with the Hominoidea. The width of the mandible suggests a relatively expanded brain. The other Oligocene pongid, *Propliopithecus*, also comes from Egypt. Judging from the evidence, in this case also a partial lower jaw, he was larger than *Parapithecus* and about the size of a gibbon.

A wide morphological gap separates *Propliopithecus* from the fossil Hominoidea of the Miocene. The earliest of these, with which alone we need be concerned, were discovered in western Kenya beginning in 1909.[18]

The wealth of data recovered in that region makes it safe to say that by Miocene times a profusion of types of apes must have been flourishing there. In fact, East Africa may well have been the center of hominoid evolution. The principal East African fossil Hominoidea are described in Table 59. All knowledge about these creatures, it should be kept in mind, is derived largely from skull fragments and isolated teeth. Few other portions of the skeleton have been recovered. To sum up the characters of the East African Miocene apes: Although large, they were built more lightly than the living Pongidae and in several other ways were not so specialized. Such familiar apelike features as heavy supraorbital ridges, large incisor teeth, and a fully developed simian shelf are specialized developments which appeared later in evolution, when pongids also became heavier and the arms specialized for brachiation. A hominoid creature like *Proconsul* (assuming that the limb bones mentioned in the note in Table 59 belong to that genus) *could* have been ancestral to both the tree-dwelling Pongidae and ground-walking Hominidae. Perhaps both families diverged in the Miocene epoch or earlier from a generalized hominoid like *Proconsul* (W. E. L. Clark and L. S. B. Leakey, 1951:114).

Anthropologists have suggested that apes of the lower Miocene, in the

---

[18] Occasional reference will be made to post-Miocene European and South Asian representatives of the early pongids; but detailed description of *Pliopithecus*, from the upper Miocene of Europe, or of *Bramapithecus*, *Ramapithecus*, and *Sugrivapithecus* from South Asia would have little bearing on the evolutionary links leading to the emergence of the Hominidae. By the time they lived, hominid evolution must have begun.

TABLE 59.   East African Hominoidea from the Miocene Period

Genus and Species	Description
Genus *Limnopithecus* (including *Limnopithecus legetet* and *Limnopithecus macinnesi*).	A relatively small creature about the size of living gibbons and perhaps ancestral to these. May himself be derived from *Propliopithecus*.
Genus *Proconsul* (including *Proconsul africanus*, represented by a nearly complete skull, *Proconsul nyanzae*, and *Proconsul major*).	Species varied in size from animals smaller than the chimpanzee to about the stature of the gorilla. Canines and jaws powerfully constructed; prognathism pronounced, but there is no supraorbital torus in *P. africanus*, which is surprising, even if the fossil is that of a female. Brain capacity must have been very limited. The dental formula is $I\frac{2}{2}\ C\frac{1}{1}\ P\frac{2}{2}\ M\frac{3}{3}$. Perhaps *Proconsul* was ancestral to the gorilla.

NOTE: Certain isolated limb bones cannot directly be connected with any of the species mentioned in this table but are usually linked with *Proconsul*. These bones indicate a foot built to bear the stresses and strains associated with rapid movement and suggest quadrupedal locomotion rather than brachiation. Deducing from overall body size, locomotion was probably terrestrial. The long bone of the leg implies lightness of build, a character also suggested by the skull of *P. africanus*.

Genus and Species	Description
Genus *Sivapithecus* (including *Sivapithecus africanus* and also species from the Pliocene in South Asia).	The jaws are medium large, the premolars and molars broad. *Sivapithecus* is more generalized and primitive than *Dryopithecus*.
Genus *Dryopithecus* (including *Dryopithecus fontani* and Pliocene species from Europe and South Asia).	About the size of a modern chimpanzee, the Dryopithecinae also show relationship to the orang-utan and gorilla. In general more specialized than *Sivapithecus* and therefore relatively closer to the living apes. (Limb bones of European species imply a lightly built, agile animal whose arms were not specialized for tree-swinging.) The cusp pattern of the molars closely resembles that of the Hominidae. Unlike other Miocene apes, *D. fontani* shows an incipient simian shelf, a feature common to living apes but absent in man.

SOURCES: W. E. L. Clark and L. S. B. Leakey, *1951*; W. E. L. Clark, *1956:55–63*.

fashion of living pongids, occasionally supported themselves on hindlimbs, leaving forelimbs free to manipulate their environment. This situation would have been favorable for perpetuating gene mutations controlling certain neural (or brain) modifications like rapid growth of the cerebral hemispheres. Each such mutation that increased learning capacity or led to improved use of forelimbs for making and handling tools would have extended the survival chances (Greenman, 1945). The lower jaw without a simian shelf would have favored perpetuation of similar mutations leading to linguistic communication. In thus arguing that a hypothetical terrestrial hominoid lacking a simian shelf was in a favorable position to transmit mutations favorable for human culture, nobody claims *Proconsul* or *Sivapithecus* possessed language or used tools.

What happened to the East African Miocene apes? (1) By late Miocene and early Pliocene times their large-bodied descendants had radiated from Africa into Europe and Asia (see the accompanying chart). Land bridges facilitated this movement, as Figure 45:4 indicates. The small canines, graceful U-shaped dental arc, and reduced prognathism of Pliocene apes like *Ramapithecus* and

The Chimpanzee and Other Anthropoids Occasionally Support Themselves on Hind Limbs Only, Leaving the Fore Limbs Free to Manipulate the Environment (courtesy, Yerkes Laboratories of Primate Biology, Orange Park, Fla.).

Summary of Early Pongidae

Period	Years Ago (million)	Generalized Forms ⟶ Specialized Forms
Pliocene	15	*Oreopithecus* (Europe) / *Ramapithecus* (Asia) / *Sugrivapithecus* (Asia) / *Bramapithecus* (Asia)
Miocene	35	*Pliopithecus* (Europe) / *Dryopithecus* (Africa, Europe, Asia) / *Sivapithecus* (Africa, Asia) / *Proconsul* (Africa) ⎫ (*Did the crucial mutations leading to* / *Limnopithecus* (Africa) ⎬ *human culture occur here?*)
Oligocene	45	*Propliopithecus* (Africa) / *Parapithecus* (Africa)

Note that the evolution of the fossil apes moved from relatively generalized to increasingly specialized forms.

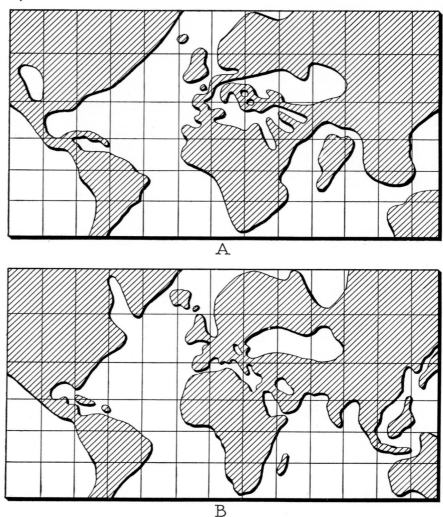

Fig. 45:4. Land Masses of the Tertiary. The upper figure (A) shows the world of the Miocene and the land bridges of the Old World across which the Miocene apes may have migrated. The lower figure (B) shows the continent during the Pliocene period and the land bridges that may have served any Hominidae extant at that time (from Coates, 1952:28).

Bramapithecus may have paralleled similar characters already possessed by an as yet unknown, contemporary hominid. These lines presumably became extinct, for living apes do not resemble those Pliocene pongids. (2) Speculatively, it may be suggested that another lines of descendants evolved into the South African Man-Apes (Australopithecinae), of whom more will be heard (see pp. 850–853).

HOMINIDAE AT LAST

The preceding summary of Primate evolution through the fossil Pongidae may have seemed to be long in coming to the focal topic, man. Man's known tenure on earth—a mere million years—indeed *is* brief compared to the perhaps 70 million years of Primate history.

Sound evidence remains to be discovered for any hominids earlier than the Pleistocene. None are known from the Pliocene or late Miocene. Until such data come forward let the reader imagine a gap in evolutionary knowledge extending from the divergence of pongids and hominids (presumably in Miocene times) to the emergence of Lower Pleistocene forms of man. No doubt the Hominidae before long will be traced back another 3, 5, or more million years but even that will constitute a relatively short span of life. This section deals with the appearance of man. A deliberate effort has been made to avoid going beyond the sparse facts in trying to connect different fossil forms in terms of genealogical relationship. Limited agreement exists between the people who have drawn up speculative human family trees. Nor has any point been seen in reporting various conflicting theories of this sort (for some see Kroeber, 1948:55). What follows purports to be a cautious record of the facts arranged according to a theory which recognizes three forms of man—Protoanthropinae, Paleoanthropinae, and Neanthropinae; the second is more *sapiens*-like than the first, and the last is indistinguishable from living races. These morphological classes refer solely to anatomical characters and never to intellectual or culture-building capacity.

Table 60 provides the reader with a handy listing of the main fossil Ho-

TABLE 60. Summary of Some Early Hominidae

Nomenclature	Provenience	Brief Identification of Evidence
A. PROTOANTHROPINAE		
Australopithecinae	South Africa; dating from the Lower to the Middle Pleistocene.	The South African Man-Apes, a subfamily of Hominidae, are known from many skull, jaw, and limb bones. The cranial capacity ranges from 450 to 600 c.c.
Meganthropus paleojavanicus (or *Pithecanthropus paleojavanicus*)	Java; Lower Pleistocene is suggested but stratigraphic evidence is poor.	A jaw fragment with 3 teeth in position indicating giantism but fundamentally not different from *Pithecanthropus*.
Atlanthropus (including Ternifine Man)	Algeria and Morocco; 2nd glacial stage (Lower Pleistocene).	Ternifine Man is known from 3 jaws, which resemble *Pithecanthropus* material from Java and China, and Acheulian-like hand axes.

TABLE 60. (*Continued*)

Nomenclature	Provenience	Brief Identification of Evidence
Pithecanthropus (including *P. erectus*, *P. robustus*, and the Modjokerto child)	Java; finds have come from horizons believed to correspond to the 1st and 2nd interglacial stages (Lower and Middle Pleistocene).	Best known from parts of several skulls, a left thigh bone, and part of a jaw bone. Cranial capacity averages 860 c.c.
Sinanthropus pekinensis (or *Pithecanthropus pekinensis*)	China, near Peiping; 2nd interglacial.	Remains of some 40 individuals found, although no complete skeletons. Crania capacity averages 1075 c.c.

B. PALEOANTHROPINAE

Nomenclature	Provenience	Brief Identification of Evidence
Homo rhodesiensis (including Saldanha Man)	Northern Rhodesia; date uncertain. The Saldanha skull cap has been dated from the 4th glacial stage (Upper Pleistocene).	Rhodesian Man manifests a strange combination of ape-like and human features in his skull. Cranial capacity is around 1300 c.c.
Homo heidelbergensis	Germany; 1st or 2nd interglacial (Lower or Middle Pleistocene).	A single large, heavy lower jaw with teeth.
Florisbad Man	Orange Free State, South Africa; early Upper Pleistocene.	Portions of a flat-vaulted skull with prominent torus.
Homo neanderthalensis (including the La Chapelle-aux-Saints, Monte Circeo and Krapina finds)	Various parts of Europe and Southwest Asia; extends from the 3rd interglacial to the start of the 4th glacial (Upper Pleistocene).	Nearly a hundred individuals have been recovered, some in association with artifacts of Mousterian type. Cranial capacity averages around 1460 c.c.
Solo Man	Java; perhaps 3rd interglacial (Upper Pleistocene).	Eleven skulls and skull fragments with 2 shin bones. Cranial capacity averages 1200 c.c.

C. NEANTHROPINAE
(*Homo sapiens*)

Nomenclature	Provenience	Brief Identification of Evidence
Kanam Man	Western Kenya; date in some question but may have lived any time between start of the Kageran and end of the Kamasian pluvial (i.e., 1st glacial to 2nd interglacial stages). Probably Middle Pleistocene.	Fragment of a lower jaw bearing suggestion of a chin.
Kanjeran Man	Kenya; Kamasian pluvial or somewhat later (Middle Pleistocene).	Mainly fragments of several skulls with modern features.
Swanscombe Man	England; upper 2nd interglacial (Middle Pleistocene).	Skull fragments of a single individual; cranial capacity about 1300 c.c.
Fontéchevade Man	France; 3rd interglacial (Upper Pleistocene).	Skull bones lacking a supra-orbital torus.

TABLE 60. (*Continued*)

Nomenclature	Provenience	Brief Identification of Evidence
Steinheim Man	Germany; 3rd interglacial (Upper Pleistocene).	A nearly complete skull; cranial capacity about 1100 c.c.
Ehringsdorf Man	Germany; second half of the 3rd interglacial (Upper Pleistocene).	Portion of a skull with high vault but prominent brow ridges; cranial capacity perhaps 1450 c.c.
Mount Carmel Man	Israel; 3rd interglacial (Upper Pleistocene).	Several skeletons showing great variability between individuals but *sapiens* features are quite pronounced.
Saccopastore Man	Italy; 3rd interglacial (Upper Pleistocene).	Several skulls showing strong brow ridges, low vault, but cranial capacity between 1200 and 1300 c.c.
Boskop Man	Transvaal; 3rd interglacial (Upper Pleistocene).	Skull cap, mandible, and limb bones; vault quite flat but cranial capacity large.
Cro-Magnon Man	Various parts of Europe; 4th glacial (Upper Pleistocene).	Several complete skeletons of tall stature and high skull vault that reaches 1600 c.c.
Chancelade Man	France; 4th glacial (Upper Pleistocene).	Another Upper Pleistocene race, distinguished by "keeled" skull and wide cheeks.
Grimaldi Man	Near Monaco, Europe; 4th glacial (Upper Pleistocene).	Two skeletons revealing some prognathism and relatively long legs and forearms; supposedly Negroid in type.
Capsian.[a]	Kenya; 4th glacial (Upper Pleistocene).	Several complete skeletons, supposedly Caucasoid in type.
Afalou Man	Algeria; Upper Pleistocene.	Several skeletons with heavy torus, high vault, and prominent chin.
Wadjak Man (*Homo wadjakensis*)	Java; Upper Pleistocene.	Two incomplete skulls suggesting the Australian aborigine type and containing about 1600 c.c.
Upper Chou Kou Tien Man	China, near Peiping; 4th glacial or postglacial (Upper Pleistocene or Holocene).	Several adult and immature skeletons showing great variability between individuals but all quite *sapiens*.

[a] This term is chosen to include the finds from Gamble's Cave, Naivasha Rock Shelter, and Olduvai described in Cole, *1954b*:96–101.

minidae. Like the accompanying chart it is divided into morphological categories. While such classification has been deplored as needlessly multiplying terms (W. E. L. Clark, 1955:9), it may help the nonspecialist to order facts. A glance at the chart reveals no close correlation between morphological type and geological date. Some neanthropic hominids derive from

Chronological Classification of Morphological Human Types

Pleistocene Division	Protoanthropic Man	TYPES Paleoanthropic Man	Neanthropic Man (*Homo sapiens*)
UPPER PLEISTOCENE — IV Glacial		Eyasi Man	Cro-Magnon, Chancelade, Grimaldi, Capsian, Afalou, Wadjak, and Upper Chou Kou Tien Men
UPPER PLEISTOCENE — III Interglacial		Solo Man, Neanderthal Man, Florisbad Man	Fontéchevade, Steinheim, Ehringsdorf, Saccopastore, Boskop, and Mount Carmel Men
III Glacial			
MIDDLE PLEISTOCENE — II Interglacial	*Sinanthropus*	Heidelberg Man	Swanscombe Man Kanjeran Man Kanam Man
II Glacial	*Australopithecinae* *Meganthropus* *Atlanthropus*		
LOWER PLEISTOCENE — I Interglacial	*Pithecanthropus*		
I Glacial			

Only relatively datable forms mentioned in Table 60 are shown. Rhodesian Man has been omitted because of great uncertainty about age. In doubtful cases (e.g., Heidelberg Man) the most conservative estimate was chosen when grounds for choice existed.

Middle Pleistocene strata and others are Upper Pleistocene in time. Paleoanthropic fossils persist into late glacial times. Only the Protoanthropinae are restricted in time and they even overlap with modern forms of man.

Protoanthropic South Africans

The so far earliest attested Hominidae lived in South Africa. Originally labeled Australopithecinae (i.e., southern apes), a fairer approximation of their now increasingly recognized hominid position warrants the title "South African Man-Apes." East Africa, it will be recalled, seems to have been the early center of pongid evolution (see pp. 843–845). From there also come more dubious bits of evidence suggestive of the possibly very early existence of *sapiens* in that part of the world (see pp. 855–856). However, Africa cannot therefore be accepted as the cradle of man. The Australopithecine fossils do not date from early enough geological horizons to warrant their acceptance as ancestral to other early forms of man (like *Pithecanthropus*, for example). The latter are contemporaries of the Australopithecinae rather than descendants. If future evidence should be found allowing the South African Hominidae to be pushed a million years or so further back in time, then, on morphological and geological grounds, they might be accorded parental status.

The eponymous fossil skull of the Australopithecine subfamily of Hominidae—*Australopithecus africanus* (the so-called Taungs skull)—was found by Raymond Dart at Taungs, Bechuanaland, in 1925. Then, in 1936, Robert Broom, another South African anthropologist, discovered *Australopithecus transvaalensis* (whose name later became *Plesianthropus*) in the Transvaal. That find consisted of several skulls and jaws belonging to adults and young people, together with a number of limb bones. Still more recent finds of Australopithecine fossils include *Australopithecus prometheus*, *Paranthropus robustus*, and *Telanthropus capensis*. (Some of these no doubt could be combined into a single genus.) The South African Man-Apes occupied a rather long span of time. Fossil evidence of *Australopithecus prometheus*, for example, dates from the Kageran pluvial period while *Paranthropus* and *Telanthropus* are from the Kamasian. According to the way these periods have tentatively been correlated with glacial stages the Australopithecinae so far discovered lived in Lower and Middle Pleistocene times (Oakley, 1954:16), *Zinjanthropus* maybe as long ago as 1,750,000 years ago.

Considered in their overall morphological configuration, the Australopithecinae belong with the Hominidae rather than the Pongidae. Supporting such a decision is the combination of small incisor and canine teeth (smaller than in living apes), evenly rounded dental arc, and the absence of heavy brow ridges together with indications of an emerging forehead. A pyramidal mastoid process is characteristic of both children's and adults' skeletons, and the location of the foramen magnum indicates that the head did not hang forward like an ape's but sat poised on top of the spinal column. The evidence of the foramen magnum in conjunction with the shape of hip and limb bones indicates that the Australopithecinae probably walked erectly. It has been said that the limb bones, taken alone, might easily be mistaken for those of *Homo sapiens*. Different significance attaches to the large molars, large jaw, overall pygmoid stature, and remarkably small skulls. Cranial capacity ranges from 450 to 650 c.c. Nevertheless the total picture is that of well-defined hominid rather than pongid creatures.

It is still unknown whether these protoanthropic Hominidae fabricated tools according to agreed-upon traditional designs. South African anthropologists point to fractured baboon skulls found in association with Australopithecine fossils. The fractures, it is asserted, "could only have been

Divisions of the Pleistocene

Conventional Dates	Stage	Climate and Fauna in Europe	Conventional Division of European and East African Climates		North American Glacial Stages	Proposed Revised Dates[b]
15,000	Recent[a]	Modern			Mankato	
	Fourth (or Wuerm) Glaciation (97,000 yrs.)	Cold and occasionally temperate; reindeer, elk, bison, mammoth, woolly rhinoceros, cave bear.	Upper Pleistocene	Gamblian Pluvial Period	Wisconsin Glaciation	− 14,000
100,000						− 75,000
	Third (Riss-Wuerm) Interglacial (65,000 yrs.)	Warm; cave lion, elephant, rhinoceros.		Interpluvial	Sangamon Interglacial	
200,000	Third (or Riss) Glaciation (53,000 yrs.)	Cold; mammoth, woolly rhinoceros, cave bear.	Middle Pleistocene	Kanjeran Pluvial Period	Illinoian Glaciation	−103,000
300,000	Second (or Mindel-Riss) Interglacial (193,000 yrs.)	Mild to warm; elephant, extinct rhinoceros, hippopotamus, sabre-toothed giant.		Interpluvial	Yarmouth Interglacial	−125,000
400,000				Kamasian Pluvial Period		−175,000
	Second (or Mindel) Glaciation (47,000 yrs.)	Cold; mammoth, woolly rhinoceros.			Kansan Glaciation	−200,000
500,000	First (or Guenz-Mindel) Interglacial (65,000 yrs.)	Warm; southern elephant, Etruscan rhinoceros, wild horse.	Lower Pleistocene	Interpluvial	Aftonian Interglacial	−265,000
600,000	First (or Guenz) Glaciation (49,000 yrs.)	Cold		Kageran Pluvial Period	Nebraskan Glaciation	−290,000
	Preglacial[c]	Warm-temperate climate becoming colder; land fauna at start of Pleistocene include elephant, rhinoceros, and hippopotamus.				

[a] Definition is local. Does not occur until 8000 or later in Scandinavia.

[b] If these dates and the revised duration of the stages represented were to be accepted, the chart would, of course, have to be redrawn.

[c] Not to scale.

Also shown are correlations of glacial stages with African climatic periods. Pluvial periods are very tentative; the whole matter of these climatic stages is by no means clearly known. Chart is adapted from Broderick, *1948:*59; Wendt, *1955:*238; Zeuner, *1952;* and Emiliani, *1955.*

inflicted by implements held in the hands or by the crushing hands themselves" (Dart, 1949:5). Overlooking the margin of doubt indirectly admitted in this quotation, it may be pointed out that apes also occasionally use tools but do not fabricate objects according to socially standardized patterns. Direct evidence of artifacts made by the South African Man-Apes is still missing.[19] In 1947 Australopithecus prometheus (cranial capacity is 650 c.c.) was found under circumstances that suggested use of fire. Whether the blaze was indeed man-made and controlled is by no means indicated.

Evolutionarily speaking, the Australopithecinae perhaps represent an independent hominid offshoot from the Miocene fossil apes, which then underwent evolution parallel with that of other Hominidae. Already in Lower Pleistocene times larger-brained forms of Hominidae were in existence. It is reasonable to infer for them a relatively long period of previous evolution.

Early Giants?

Available data are too few to reconstruct the overall morphological configurations of Gigantopithecus and Meganthropus, sometimes regarded as early giants who lived in Southeast Asia. The former became known from three very large molars purchased from Hong Kong druggists by a persistent searcher for fossil man, G. H. R. von Koenigswald. Where they were found originally and from when they date are unanswerable questions. The teeth are about twice the size of those of a full-grown modern gorilla and no less than six times the dimensions of Homo sapiens'. The arrangement of the cusps has been called "less complicated than in anthropoids" but the teeth themselves have been regarded as evidence of an early giant hominid. A number of anthropologists regard the teeth as belonging to a pongid whom they call Gigantopithecus blacki. The diagnosis of ape is strengthened by discovery in China of a mandible asserted to belong to this genus and dating from Middle Pleistocene times (New York Times, Mar. 17, 1957; Straus, 1957).

Meganthropus paleojavanicus exists in the remains of a lower jaw discovered at Sangiran, in Java, by the same von Koenigswald. Geologically the find dates from the Lower Pleistocene. In size the teeth (2 premolars and the first molar) and jaw are again remarkably large, although the molar is about a third smaller than those of Gigantantopithecus. In height and thickness the jaw exceeds that of any known hominid though presumably the mandible of Gigantantopithecus would be larger. Any hint of a chin is lacking. In reconstruction, the dental arc is intermediate between that of the Pongidae and Hominidae. Claims that here are remains of an early race of giants are not very well founded. It has been maintained that Meganthropus, to the de-

[19] For some ingenious arguments based on indirect evidence see Bartholomew and Birdsell, 1953:490–491.

gree that he is known from the jaw fragment, cannot be separated from the genus *Pithecanthropus*. Even the size falls within the range of variation that may be expected if judgment is based on the range of variation shown by living *Homo sapiens* (W. E. L. Clark, 1955:86–87).

Pithecanthropus and Sinanthropus

Eugene Dubois, a Dutch physician, found the remains of *Pithecanthropus erectus* in 1891 and 1892 near Trinil in north-central Java. His discoveries consisted of some teeth, a portion of a skull cap, and a thigh bone. All came from a geological formation of Middle Pleistocene date or, more precisely, from a period contemporaneous with the second interglacial stage in Europe. Dubois first argued for the hominid status of the fossil but later, when public opinion swung around to this point of view, he changed his mind and described *Pithecanthropus* as an ape. Between 1936 and 1941 G. H. R. von Koenigswald excavated portions of additional crania and also a jaw as well as the immature *Modjokertensis* skull. All but the latter belong to the same geological horizon as *Pithecanthropus erectus*. The 2-year-old Modjokerto child, however, pushes the antiquity of *Pithecanthropus* back to the Lower Pleistocene, perhaps to first interglacial times. *Pithecanthropus*, as this group of fossils will be called, therefore lived in Java long enough to be a contemporary of China Man (i.e., *Sinanthropus*), a fossil discovered through the efforts of Davidson Black and Franz Weidenreich. The remains of about 40 individuals were taken from a series of natural caves located near the town of Chou Kou Tien, 42 miles from Peiping (Peking). Hence the name bestowed on them collectively: *Sinanthropus pekinensis*. The remains date from Middle Pleistocene (second interglacial) times. Morphologically, little distinguishes *Pithecanthropus* from *Sinanthropus*.

Pithecanthropus shared a tropical jungle valley with a number of now extinct species of rhinoceros, lion, hippopotamus, and elephant. In appearance he possessed a heavy skull, no chin, quite prominent and continuous brow ridges, low and receding forehead, and a cranial capacity ranging from 775 to 900 c.c. (The *Modjokertensis* skull has been estimated to contain 700 c.c. compared to 1000 c.c. for a modern European child of that age.) Separating upper canines from incisors was the diastema, or gap, that accommodates the large lower canine. The large jaws were also markedly prognathous. Teeth were set in the graceful arc characteristic of the Hominidae. Judging from limb bones (which are hardly distinguishable from modern man's), *Pithecanthropus* probably stood erect, reaching perhaps 5 feet, 7 inches. Going now to Chou Kou Tien, *Sinanthropus* also possessed a heavy skull but no chin, beetling brow ridges with scarcely sign of a forehead, and a cranial capacity averaging about 1075 c.c. The canines were not prominent. The upper level of the range of variation puts the skull well within the range of *Homo sapiens* (W. E. L. Clark, 1955:98). Upright posture is indicated but in stature the Peiping hominid may have averaged only 5 feet, 1 inch. As already mentioned, no striking differences distinguish these fossils from Java and China. Hence they have been classified in a single genus, *Pithecanthropus*, in which the so-called *Meganthropus* mandible may also belong.[20] The major characters distinguishing the Pithecanthropinae are low cranial capacity, flattened skull vault, heavy jaw, evenly rounded dental arc, slight overlap of the canines with occurrence of the diastema, and erect posture (W. E. L. Clark, 1955:103).

Sinanthropus controlled fire and probably used it to cook meat. He had also replaced large canines with cutting tools made of a type of stone not available around Chou Kou Tien.[21] Little energy went into shaping those implements. Yet definite specialization is indicated in the choppers, scrapers, points, and hammerstones. Some bones found in the caves may also have served as tools. That these second interglacial people were omnivorous is suggested by the combination of hackberry seed shells and animal bones. Some of the hominid skulls are themselves fractured, suggesting that an attempt had been made to reach the brain. Cannibalism, therefore, also seems to have been a cultural trait of *Sinanthropus* as it was of several other Pleistocene hominids (Oakley, cited in Grinsell, 1955:809).

Early Moderns

Sinanthropus from Middle Pleistocene times possessed culture but was not *Homo sapiens*. From East Africa come reports of men living in Middle Pleistocene times who corresponded to modern men morphologically and also used socially standardized implements. The reader will discover, however, that the evidence for *sapiens* at this early date is quite fragmentary and many anthropologists accept it only with considerable reserve.

Kanam Man, from the Kavirondo Gulf in western Kenya, was found in 1932 by L. S. B. Leakey. The slim evidence consists of a lower jaw, containing definite indications of a *sapiens* chin, found in a geological stratum containing remains of extinct fauna. Dating is much influenced by the associated animal fossils. Some of these flourished in the Kageran pluvial period without, however, disappearing until Kamasian pluvial times (see p. 852). Correlating these periods with European glacial stages or even with the grosser Pleistocene divisions must be very tentative, but indications are that Kanam

[20] Hence China Man should be retitled *Pithecanthropus pekinensis*, and *Meganthropus* would become *P. paleojavanicus*.

[21] The origin of tools may be related functionally to the adoption by early hominids of a partially carnivorous diet at the same time that the canines were becoming reduced. With the hands freed from locomotion sharp pieces of stone provided an alternative cutting instrument. The shift from a strictly herbivorous diet (which apes follow, at least in the wild state) to a predominantly carnivorous one also allowed the Hominidae sufficient time to fashion tools. In contrast to herbivores, who eat nearly all the time, carnivores are better able to store energy (Oakley, 1954:19–21).

Man could have existed at any time between the start of the first glacial and the end of the second interglacial periods. A conservative age, dating to the first half of the Middle Pleistocene, is used in this book. Roughly shaped chopping tools found in the deposit containing the Kanam jaw have a typological affinity with the early choppers used in South and East Asia during second interglacial times. They *may* have been used by Kanam Man.

Kanjeran Man is known from fragments of four skulls and part of a leg bone found in western Kenya by Leakey in the late thirties. Some of these fossils (skull 1 and parts of skull 3) were discovered on the ground surface, others (skulls 2, 4, and parts of 3) in a geological deposit containing Chellean hand axes and the bones of extinct fauna. These animals flourished at the time of the Kamasian pluvial and during the subsequent interpluvial or even later (roughly the Middle Pleistocene). Surface and buried finds bear about equal degrees of mineralization. Hence they may be contemporaneous. Reconstruction of skull 1 results in a heavy, thick-walled cranium lacking brow ridges but manifesting signs of a vertical forehead. The limb bone suggests upright posture.

These East African fossils are fascinating because they suggest the existence of neanthropic man during Middle or earlier Pleistocene times. They make *sapiens* a contemporary of the Australopithecinae and Pithecanthropinae. If sound, the evidence suggests that several genera of man simultaneously occupied the world in early glacial times and each made tools according to socially standardized designs. But the perplexing matter is knowing how much faith to put in the Kanam and Kanjeran data. One can only wait for future finds that may throw further light on those forms.

Very much better authenticated are the neanthropic remains of Swanscombe Man, originally found in southern England in 1935 and 1936 by A. T. Marston. The sparse finds include two hominid skull bones associated with bones of an elephant, rhinoceros, and red deer, as well as artifacts of Acheulian type. An additional fragment was discovered in 1955 with additional stone artifacts. The geological evidence suggests an upper second interglacial date. Chemical (fluorine) analysis of the bones confirms that age. Thus nearly indubitable evidence of Middle Pleistocene *Homo sapiens* is on hand. Reconstructing the thick bones of the cranium suggests a globular skull vault with a capacity of about 1300 or 1350 c.c. and no brow ridges. If any trust can be put in a cast of the inner surface of the skull, then Swanscombe Man possessed cerebral hemispheres quite as complicated in their convolutions as those of living men.

Up until a few years ago two additional fossils furnished proof of the existence of *Homo sapiens* during the second and third interglacial stages. The Galley Hill skeleton and Piltdown skull and jaw belong to England, the former having been found as far back as 1888. In 1949 fluorine analysis of the Galley Hill bones showed that they could not be as old as the third interglacial (as had been claimed). The fluorine content averaged 0.34 percent.

But the range of authenticated Pleistocene material bearing this age and from the same geographical region is from 1.7 to 2.8 percent. Fossils from the fourth glacial range from 0.9 to 1.4 percent. Geologically recent bones contain from 0.05 to 0.3 percent fluorine; the skeleton from Galley Hill falls into the latter group. The association of the bones with stone tools normally found in third interglacial deposits must therefore have been accidental, though how the skeleton came to intrude into the particular stratum has not been explained. The Piltdown skull and mandible, originally found in 1911–12 by Charles Dawson, a lawyer, long puzzled some anthropologists, who found it inconceivable that the apelike jaw could belong to the very neanthropic cranium. Fluorine analysis justified their skepticism by demonstrating that jaw and skull indeed were not contemporaneous. Closer study then showed that the jaw, belonging to a living species of orang-utan, had deliberately been stained to make it look old. The skull, in turn, dated from Upper Pleistocene times, when, of course, the existence of *Homo sapiens* is certified. There can be no doubt that the two pieces had been planted together in second interglacial gravels in order to perpetrate a deliberate hoax (Washburn, 1953; Weiner, 1955). At this writing the perpetrator of the fake remains unidentified.[22]

Neanderthal and Other Paleoanthropinae

The facts suggest that at least two basically different types of stone-tool-using Hominidae inhabited the Middle Pleistocene Old World. While the Pithecanthropinae roamed in eastern and southeastern Asia *Homo sapiens* lived in Europe and perhaps in Africa. That the also contemporaneous Australopithecinae used tools is not proved. The archaic strain represented by the Pithecanthropinae does not disappear but continues into Upper Pleistocene times, albeit in somewhat attenuated form.

Neanderthal Man (*Homo neanderthalensis*) is the best known of the late archaic, or Paleoanthropic, forms of man. He is known from over a hundred skeletons that have been coming to light in Europe and western Asia since the middle of the nineteenth century (Keith, 1929:Chaps. 8–10). The range of his existence lasts from the warm third interglacial stage to the cold, wet fourth glacial. Extinct mammals were associated with a number of Neanderthal finds, and the broken skulls of some specimens suggest that Neanderthal Man preyed on his own kind. This, along with associated evidence of fire, carefully prepared burials, and stone tools (Mousterian type), constitute direct evidence of culture.

The average Neanderthal male stood about 5 feet, 4 inches tall; the woman 4 feet, 3 inches. Long arms and short legs, large extremities, large head with

---

[22] Piltdown is not the only forgery of fossil evidence. In the eighteenth century German students near Wuerzburg modeled various fantastic objects in clay and then baked the images. They left the "fossils" where their credulous professor found them (Wendt, 1955:18–19).

prominent ridges in back (the point of muscular attachment), together with low forehead and cranial vault are characteristics suggesting his relatively archaic morphological status. The heavy brow ridges, massive jaws, and receding chin found in protoanthropic Hominidae are also present. Neanderthal's cranial capacity, however, stands high, averaging 1460 c.c. and ranging from 1300 to 1625. Casts of the interior of the brain have been attempted in order to learn something about the structure of the Neanderthal brain. If such reconstruction possesses validity (which is far from certain) then Neanderthal possessed relatively small frontal lobes (see pp. 816–817), a deficiency, it is suggested, which might have led to his gradual extinction. However—and this undermines the somewhat ethnocentric argument buttressed by brain casts made by *sapiens* anthropologists—Neanderthal culture reveals increased ability to control the working of stone; possible hafting of stone tools in handles; ability to kill large creatures, like the rhinoceros, bear, and during the colder centuries mammoth; and quite obvious signs of funerary ritual (see p. 740). The demonstrable morphological gap separating the Neanderthals from *Homo sapiens* is not reflected in the cultural stream that is continuous from Middle to Upper Paleolithic times.

Neanderthaloid remains have been divided into two groups, one "classical" (or extreme) and the other "generalized." The skeletons found at La Chapelle-aux-Saints, a rock shelter in southern France; Monte Circeo, a cave overlooking the Mediterranean south of Rome, and at least some skulls from Krapina in Croatia are "classical" Neanderthals. The bones are heavy and thick, brow ridges continuous and large. No sign of vertical forehead exists and the molar teeth show a peculiar enlargement of the pulp cavity which extends downward to the roots (taurodontism, a condition occasionally found in modern Caucasoids and reported in some Eskimo skulls). The "generalized" Neanderthals are of neanthropic proportions and probably preceded the "classical" type. They lived in the third interglacial period. Skeletons from the caves on the slope of Mount Carmel in Israel, as well as the Steinheim and other neanthropic fossils, used to be put in this category. There is no sound reason for distinguishing generalized Neanderthals from *Homo sapiens* (W. E. L. Clark, 1955:Chap. 2). That position is adopted in Table 60 and the chart on p. 850. It is possible that further study may show *Homo neanderthalensis* to constitute an aberrant evolutionary strain of early *sapiens*, one which became extinct during the cold of the fourth glacial. The dead-end status of the fossil is expressed in the sonnet "Neanderthal" by Marijane Allen (*New York Times*, Nov. 15, 1956):

> "Intriguing specimen, behold the jaw . . ."
> Beholding him, I wonder what befell
> when prophets found no future to foretell?
> Those furrowed brows, I wonder what he saw
> standing where oblivion whipped him raw
> with chilly winds? What encroaching hell

drove him to the caverns of Dussel[23]
to die, with what raw hunger in his craw?
What hunger for tomorrow had that race
evolving deathward down an aberrant track?—
limping to extinction without grace
because the Breeder overlooked some lack
unknowable to us. "Behold the jaw . . ."
Unfutured race, I wonder what *it* saw.

Rhodesian Man, named after a robust skull found by miners at Broken Hill, Northern Rhodesia, in 1921, may be another late archaic, but the fossil evidence cannot be dated. The robust construction of the skull, if it could be correlated with an Upper Pleistocene horizon, would suggest an African Neanderthaloid.[24] The brow ridges are the widest ever seen on any hominid. Cranial capacity has been estimated by different authorities as 1280 and 1400 c.c. Upright posture is indicated from the position of the foramen magnum. The portions of an associated limb bone, which are more *sapiens* in type, have been shown to be of the same age as the cranium (W. E. L. Clark, 1955:76). Eyasi Man, from northern Tanganyika, seems to be a related form. The pieces of three crania were recovered between 1934 and 1936 by Kohl Larson from a lake bed from the Gamblian pluvial period (latter half of Upper Pleistocene). Such a date is confirmed by associated species of extinct animals. Judging from the position of the foramen magnum, the heavy Eyasi skull, with its pronounced brow ridges, hung forward on the body of the hominid carrier. Like the possessor of the 1932 Florisbad skull from South Africa, whose construction is similar, Eyasi may be a variety of Rhodesian Man and hence also an African Neanderthaloid.

The discovery of *Homo soloensis* in central Java between 1931 and 1936 suggests that descendants of *Pithecanthropus* survived at least until the third interglacial stage and perhaps longer. Solo Man's relatively robust skulls, with low foreheads and heavy brow ridges, again show evidence that they might have been hacked open, perhaps by cannibals. The crania range in size from 1160 to 1316 c.c. and possess a skull vault higher than that of *Pithecanthropus*. Judging from the position of one foramen magnum, the head may not have been too well poised but rather hung forward. Stone and antler implements, including a barbed spearhead, associated with the skulls demonstrate quite skillful workmanship.

Another paleoanthropic fossil is the Heidelberg lower jaw taken from a sand pit near the village Mauer, not far from Heidelberg, Germany, in 1907. The teeth are relatively small for so massive a mandible and the canines definitely are not enlarged. There is no chin. Associated animal fossils suggest an

[23] The reference is to the Duessel River in whose valley (i.e., *thal*) near the gorge of Neander the first recognized discovery of Neanderthal Man occurred. Cf. Kroeber, 1948:94.
[24] However, Keith (1929:Chaps. 20–21), who gives a good summary of the circumstances of the discovery, believes that the skull is from the Lower Pleistocene.

early Pleistocene date but estimates have vacillated between the first and second interglacial stages. The significance of the earliest date should not be overlooked. If sound, it represents the earliest European hominid.

Late Moderns

With the close of the fourth glacial stage the Paleoanthropinae disappear and modern man, *Homo sapiens*, takes over on all the continents of the Old World. If the robust Neanderthals left descendants in the population of Europe, such traces are not readily apparent.

The reader will recall that *sapiens* made no sudden emergence. Neanthropic man may have existed in early second interglacial times. Very probably he lived in southern England during this warm period. In the equally favorable third interglacial times evidence becomes more abundant, as Table 60 and the chart on p. 850 indicate. Note that Fontéchevade, Steinheim, Ehringsdorf, Saccopastore, and the Southwest Asiatic Mount Carmel people were contemporaries of more archaic Paleoanthropinae. With the latter some Neanthropinae (like Saccopastore) overlap morphologically.

These finds, since they are essentially *sapiens* in quality and add little to the history of human evolution, need only slight attention. The Steinheim skull, found in 1933, possesses strong supraorbital ridges and a low cranial vault but the forehead is amply formed and the total morphological configuration conforms closely to modern man. The Ehringsdorf cranium (1925) consists of a fragmentary brain case. The brow ridges are heavy but signs of a vertical forehead and pyramidal mastoid processes are apparent. It cannot really be distinguished from *Homo sapiens*. The cranial capacity may be about 1450 c.c. The Mount Carmel skeletons are a mixture of *Homo sapiens* and *Homo neanderthalensis* or a transition from one to the other. Because the Neanderthaloid morphological configuration does not dominate, the skeletons may be regarded as essentially neanthropic or *sapiens*.

Portions of two skulls ascribed to Fontéchevade Man were found in southern France in 1947. As with Swanscombe Man, the bones are thick but do not reveal brow ridges and are not demonstrably different from those of *Homo sapiens*. The antiquity of the finds is well attested and kinship with Swanscombe seems probable (Vallois, 1949). Third interglacial neanthropic material also has been found in South Africa, notably the Boskop skeleton.

Coming now to the final glacial stage, the best-known fossils undoubtedly are those belonging to Cro-Magnon Man, whose skeleton has been found in western Europe and Southwest Asia. He represents, however, only one of the neanthropic races of the period.[25] Outstanding features of Cro-Magnon include a high forehead, a high vaulted skull with cranial capacity of as much as 1600 c.c., a broad face, strong chin, and stature reaching 6 feet. An-

[25] Upper Pleistocene discoveries are comprehensively summarized in Keith, 1929:Chaps. 4–7; Chancelade and Grimaldi men are described in Chap. 5.

other *sapiens* race is represented in the Chancelade skeletons distributed in France and Germany. They belong to a shorter hominid who possessed slightly developed brow ridges and wide cheeks. A crest running the length of the cranium recalls some Mongoloid skulls bearing a similar feature. Hence the thought has occurred that, perhaps, a Mongoloid race inhabited Europe toward the end of the Pleistocene. Whether so or not is a question demanding evidence better than any now available. Grimaldi Man, represented by skeletons of a woman and boy found on the Italian Riviera, has been held to constitute proof of a Negroid European race but that conjecture may also be pigeonholed for the present. Meanwhile Capsian Man in East Africa supposedly appeared quite Caucasoid in type while his contemporary, Afalou, in Algeria, was just becoming high vaulted and strong chinned, though retaining rather prominent brow ridges. The Upper Pleistocene fossil hominids clearly show marked racial differences but that the variants correspond to living races is less easy to support.

In Southeast Asia modern man is represented by the Wadjak and related races known from Australian discoveries, Talgai and Keilor men. From the upper levels of the famous caves at Chou Kou Tien come highly mixed skeletons that fully authenticate the existence of *sapiens* in East Asia by the end of the Pleistocene epoch.

Cro-Magnon and the other Upper Pleistocene races of *sapiens* remained hunters. In Europe Cro-Magnon subsisted on the horse, reindeer, and then the new animals which entered the continent as the climate grew warmer. All Cro-Magnon Man's life was not passed in caves. In South Russia (Gagarino) he sank oval dwellings into the ground and roofed them with logs and soil. Skin clothes were tailored and sewn with needles. Carved female figurines with exaggerated buttocks were kept out of some sentimental regard. At Předmost, in Moravia, a tomb 13 feet long and over 7 feet wide has been uncovered, the burials interesting for their intermediate position between *Homo sapiens* and *Homo neanderthalensis*. The Cro-Magnons continued cannibalistic practices and in Hungary some skulls were shaped into drinking cups.

Neoteny in *Sapiens* Evolution[26]

The failure of neanthropic forms of man to be limited to late geological times poses something of a puzzle. Ideally one would expect a direct correlation between time and development: the longer the elapsed time, the more *sapiens*-like the morphological development. But such a close correlation between geology and morphology is not apparent in the paleontological record. Hence the question: From what ancestors and by what means did early moderns evolve? The explanation proposed requires additional sup-

---

[26] The following discussion is based on Montagu, 1955.

port before it is fully acceptable. It is the theory of neoteny (or paedomorphism), the theory that youthful (including fetal) characters of an ancestor are sometimes retained in the adult stage of the descendant.

Modern man, it will be recalled, is diagnosed, among other characters, by the presence of a high, rounded cranial vault. Such a cranium, it is now fairly clear, did not first appear at the close of the Ice Age but in the middle of the Pleistocene epoch or even earlier (see pp. 855–856). The high, rounded vault is closer to the crania of fetal apes than to those revealed by adult Pongidae. May it be that the neanthropic cranium is not evolutionarily specialized but rather generalized and, therefore, more primitive than the rugged Neanderthal cranium? The theory of neoteny accepts this classification and proceeds to explain it by assuming a mutation in early Pleistocene times which produced relative retardation of somatic development. As a result of this mutation, offspring of the animal in which it occurred failed to achieve the developmental status of the ancestor but instead retained relatively juvenile characters. A mutation of this sort could have spread rapidly throughout a small, isolated breeding population so that the rugged features of a Protoanthropic ancestor would quickly have been lost or, better, replaced by the almost fetal characters of that ancestor.

A glance at the foetal skulls of most Primates shows how essentially similar they all are, with smooth round crania and small jaws. Such Primates as the gorilla, which subsequently develop large jaws and teeth and heavy supraorbital and occipital ridges, have differentiated furthest away from the foetal standard. . . . Those, such as man, which show a progressively stronger tendency to retain the smooth skull and small jaws have differentiated least. . . . Evolution up to [modern] man has not been marked by a progressive reduction of simian features as is usually assumed; it is distinguished by failure to attain the simian degree of differentiation in a number of physical characteristics.

Not all modern human physical characters are foetalized, of course. A highly-arched nose, large mastoid process, prominent chin and the human foot are quite the reverse [Abbie, 1952:84].

Neoteny, the retention of fetal or juvenile characters in an adult, particularly in the head region, explains the rather sudden evolution of *Homo sapiens* in Hominidae history. It is not assumed that a neotenous mutation occurred only once in hominid evolution. It probably happened several times in early hominid populations. That such a mutation had any selective advantage is by no means indicated.

AVAILABLE FILM

Monkey into Man describes some social and other habits of the baboon and anthropoid apes. A comparison is drawn with human traits (20 min., b. and w., Library Films).

46.

Race

THE last two chapters dealt, first, with the relationship between culture and the biological organism and, second, with the evolution of some of the biological features that help to shape ways of life or distinguish modern man. This final chapter turns to those small, hereditary variations that distinguish different populations within the species *Homo sapiens*. The distinction between races, it will become clear, is hardly as sharp as popular belief would have it. Nor is the subject directly relevant for understanding the world which man has created through culture.

Where one race has been responsible for some origination—for example, East Asiatic Mongoloids invented gunpowder, paper, and printing—nothing has prevented another race from borrowing and using it. Mongoloids easily mastered military techniques, industrial processes, and, more recently, the ideology of Communism, all of which originated with presumably non-Mongoloid races. If races are not characterized by unequal abilities to build culture, neither have they reliably been associated with differences in moral quality, intellectual ability, or overall superiority and inferiority.

Evidently the race concept means quite different things to the anthropologist and to the public-spirited citizen who urges segregation or integration. For some Americans any person who is socially designated as a "Negro" is a full-fledged member of the Negro race. The anthropologist's conception of race has been influenced much by the work of geneticists. For him the concept applies not to discrete individuals but to a socially or geographically isolated population which, by virtue of frequent inbreeding, has come to differ from another such population in (1) certain physical characters or (2) the frequency of the genes that help to produce those characters. Thus the frequency of blue eyes and blood type A, or of the genes that produce those characters, tends to be greater in northern Europe than in East Africa. The pattern of gene frequencies, which sometimes can be inferred from overt characters in a population, is called the genotype of the race. The observable characters themselves make up the phenotype. A race may be defined genotypically or phenotypically. "In both cases the procedure must be primarily quantitative. . . . Certain characters or genes may be totally absent, and when this is so we can make a qualitative distinction. More generally the distinction will be quantitative. The characters or genes which are present will be present in different proportions in different groups . . ." (J. Huxley, 1941:125).

GENES AND RACE

A race arises out of the same processes that lead to species evolution. Among nonhuman animals, distinct races evolve into different species when isolation is great enough to insure that the population breeds primarily within itself. There is little chance that the races of modern man will become differentiated into species. It is safer to guess that as the scale of human society continues to increase, racial differences will increasingly become blurred.

Racial differences are hereditary, being transmitted from parent to offspring in the process of reproduction. Although men for a long time have been interested in heredity they scarcely understood the process until recently. Then it was discovered that the offspring of parents are not simply a blend of parental characters. Rather, discrete parental characters, like the mother's brown eyes or the father's blood type, are passed on as units of inheritance. Unit characters include colors, dimensions, organs, chemical peculiarities, physiological functions, sex (maleness or femaleness), sensory acuity, and other phenotypical traits. Sometimes more than one gene is involved in producing a physical trait.

Every individual starts life as a single, fertilized egg cell, called a zygote, which then undergoes a complicated course of biological growth. The zygote is a product of the union of two germ cells, a single-cell ovum and a single-cell spermatozoön. Normally myriads of spermatozoa are introduced into the woman's body during an act of sexual intercourse but only one of these is needed to fertilize an ovum. With the union of ovum and spermatozoön a fusion of the nuclear material of each germ cell takes place. The nuclei of the germ cells contain thousands of genes arranged in threadlike fashion on chromosomes. The genes, which remain invisible with the most powerful microscope, are units of inheritance. The human zygote contains 46 or 48 chromosomes, half that number being derived from each parent.[1]

Individuals therefore inherit not specific features of the biological organism but genetic capacities to grow, to develop certain organs, and to

[1] Not only the germ cells contain chromosomes and genes but every cell in the body does. These cells have the full complement of 48 (or sometimes, according to recent discoveries, 46) chromosomes arranged in pairs. In the formation of the ovum and sperm cells (a process called meiosis), a special type of nuclear division takes place so that the nucleus of those cells contains only 23 or 24 chromosomes—one of each pair. Then at fertilization the full complement is restored, the individual receiving one of each pair of chromosomes from each parent.

perform certain kinds of behavior. The genes do not control inheritance un-aided. Any biological character is a product of both heredity and environ-ment. Genes can cause nothing independently of an environment, which enables them to carry out their work. There is little point in saying that certain characters are the product of nature (genes) and others the product of nurture (i.e., environment or experience). Everything that an animal does, every movement made, every pound it gains is jointly the product of genes working out their potentialities in an environment. Some physical characters of the organism are more autonomous or stable than others. They do not change readily when the outside environment changes. Examples include the type of blood which the individual carries, his hair form and eye color. Other characters are highly unstable: the skin darkens with exposure to sun, and fat is added or subtracted from the body according to diet. Stat-ure is unstable. A sample group of European Jews and Bohemians born in the United States were taller than their parents born overseas but the chil-dren of Sicilians born here were shorter (Kaplan, 1954:784–885). For pur-poses of race classification anthropologists have favored working with features that are least affected by environmental variation.

Genetics of Blood Types

The way genes work, the nature of heredity, and the use of genotypical factors in distinguishing races may be illustrated with reference to the dif-ferences in blood found in the human species (W. C. Boyd, 1953; W. C. Boyd and I. Asimov, 1955:Chap. 8). The liquid portion of the blood, called plasma, contains various kinds of cells as well as a large complement of water. Most numerous are the red blood cells, which contain certain chemicals known as blood-group substances. Two of these substances are simply called A and B. A person whose red blood cells contain substance A possesses type A blood (of which there are two varieties, A_1 and A_2); someone with B sub-stance possesses type B blood. Some people's plasma contains red blood cells with both substances A and B; they belong to type AB. Other people lack both these substances and are referred to as type zero (or, more usually, O).

Whether a person is of blood type A, B, AB, or O depends on the genes he has received through inheritance. With one exception,[2] all chromosomes and their constituent genes are paired. For every gene, then, there is a second gene governing the same character. Paired genes may or may not be identi-cal. They may affect the same character—say, blood type—in the same way or in different ways. Whenever two genes for a particular trait are identical, the person carrying them is homozygous for that character; if they are not identical he is heterozygous for the trait. If a child receives two A genes, one

[2] The so-called X-Y chromosomes which determine the sex of the embryo.

from each parent, he is, genotypically speaking, AA (or homozygous for blood type of the A—B—O series).

Supposing a person who is homozygous for blood type A marries a person who is homozygous for type B. The offspring will inherit an A gene from one parent and a B gene from the other. The offspring will be heterozygous for this particular trait. Should an AA individual marry an OO individual, the children will again be heterozygous. Phenotypically, however, the children will belong to the A blood type because the A gene is dominant over O.[3]

The gene for blood substance B is also dominant over O. Supposing now that an AO man marries an OO woman. In that case there is a theoretically equal chance that the man will pass on in his sperm cell an A or an O gene. The woman's ovum will contain only O genes. Hence the child can be either AO or OO, genotypically speaking. He will manifest blood type A or O.

Apart from the A—B—O series there are other blood-group substances which are inherited completely independently of the A and B substances. For example, an individual may have blood substances M or N in his red blood cells and belong to blood types M, N, or MN. There are a dozen so-called Rh blood types. Some people have Rh-negative blood (having inherited two Rh genes, one from each parent, for this gene is recessive). Rh-positive type blood is produced when a person inherits at least one Rh gene. An Rh-positive baby conceived in an Rh-negative mother is in danger of having its red blood cells destroyed and may die before birth or shortly after unless transfusions are arranged in time.

Races or breeding populations may be determined on the basis of differences in the frequency with which blood types are represented (see pp. 874–875). Generally speaking, type O is most common in the world, with A, B, and AB following in that order. But the proportion of each varies from one population to another. For example, Asia is ahead of any other continent in the frequency with which blood group B occurs. From blood-group frequencies gene frequencies may be calculated for the population.

Genetics and Racial Variation

When a child resembles one parent or the other in physical features like hair color, nose form, type of blood, or the ability to taste phenyl-thio-carbamide (PTC) it is not because the offspring has inherited his hair, nose, blood, or taste buds in any direct, material way but because he has inherited genes capable of bringing about those characters. In the same way, a breeding population tends to perpetuate genes which produce physical characters diagnostic of race.

---

[3] In other words, the O gene is recessive. This does not mean that the O type will be extinguished in the population, for individuals with at least one O gene are always being born from matings with persons homozygous for O or from persons with genotypes AO and BO who mate with one another or with OO persons.

No two human beings except identical twins have exactly the same genes for the same traits. A man and woman who mate never possess precisely similar genotypes, and neither parent transmits his total genotype to an offspring. Hence phenotypically no offspring completely resembles his parents. If children born of the same parents inherit parental genes but possess different genetic make-ups, therefore differing in their biological structure and functioning, then it follows that in a breeding population no two individuals will be identical. This could happen only in the case of identical twins who started life as a single egg cell fertilized by a spermatozoön. It is utterly fallacious to talk as if all Negroids, Caucasoids, or the members of any other racial division were precisely alike.

A basic process in the formation of new races and in evolution is mutation. As already explained in Chapter 45, a mutation involves a change in the chemical composition of a chromosome or even a single gene. It marks the appearance in the individual's genetic make-up of a character which he did not inherit from an ancestor but which (assuming the mutation occurred in the germ cells and not in other cells of the body) can be inherited by one of his descendants. It is through such relatively random (i.e., unpredictable) changes in genetic structure that new characters appear in the store of genes possessed by a given population. A mutation, then, transmitted through heredity, receives a chance to develop under suitable environmental conditions.

Most mutations transmitted to an offspring produce only slight changes in observable characteristics. For example, a mutation may bring about a slight reduction in the size of the bristles of the fruit fly. Many mutations are more or less lethal. That is, they express themselves in characters that hinder the survival chances of the offspring who inherits them. Such genes obviously tend to disappear because the bearers who inherited them tend to die without reproducing. They may, of course, recur through future mutations. The perpetuation or extinction of mutant genes, depending on how they affect survival chances, is the process of natural selection emphasized by Darwin. Some mutations do not prove lethal, but individuals manifesting the new physical trait are shunned as breeding partners or have less opportunity than other persons to engage in sexual reproduction. Such genes will also tend to be reduced in frequency or may be extinguished completely from the population. This process is called social selection (Montagu, 1951b:287–295). The accumulation of new characters in a population through mutations that confer survival advantages, whether the process be natural or social selection, leads to the emergence of a new race. If differentiation is carried far, then a new species will have evolved.

Race formation is partly a matter of chance. This is the case when a character confers no natural or other selective advantage on a population. Under such circumstances the significant factors are (1) territory sufficient to allow increase in population size without loss of isolation and (2) relatively small size of the group in which mates are sought. If a breeding population is small (as it was during the greater part of human history when the basis of subsistence was food gathering), a particular mutant gene possessing neither positive nor negative survival value may spread rapidly in the group. The smaller the population and the greater its isolation, the more chance that the gene will become fixed in nearly all members. On the other hand, there is equal possibility that a particular gene will be lost through failure of the individual possessing it to reproduce. In large populations such fluctuation scarcely would be noticeable. Accidental increase or decrease in the frequency of particular genes is called genetic drift. Through this process it is possible for populations which started with similar genotypes but became isolated from one another to develop along different lines, diverging in nonadaptive characters as some genes are lost and as others become more frequent (Montagu, 1950:329).

Genetic drift may be illustrated by an analogy. Two brothers named Jones each join an immigrant band moving into a new territory. One brother has seven sons who all have sons of their own and so on. Family names are inherited patrilineally. The band remains isolated so that no new names are added and none of the children leaves the territory. In a few generations the proportion of people named Jones may have grown from, say, 1 to 5 percent. The other brother has no sons. Hence, in the same period of time the name Jones disappears from the other community. If instead of family names the trait happened to be a hereditary blood type, then extinction or spread of the gene differentiating one population from the other would illustrate genetic drift (Dunn, 1951:23).

Territoriality

From the standpoint of territoriality, or isolation, three types of animal variation may be distinguished (J. Huxley, 1941:117).

1. Low Intragroup Variability. In most wild species of animals the population in any one locality presents relatively little variability. Of the variability shown, some reflects differences in individual genetic make-up. Genetic variability is slight in an isolated population compared to that existing between populations in different localities.

2. Racial Variation. Between populations isolated in different territories (or, in the case of man, populations that are socially segregated despite their presence in a common territory), marked racial variation is often perceivable. Variability tends to increase, the longer and more firmly the populations are isolated. Such variability is especially marked if geographical differences between the territories are extreme, as between northern Europe and Central Africa. Clearly drift and natural selection have been at work. The geographical environment, perhaps, has operated to select certain adaptive physical characters (see pp. 825–827). The Jewish ghetto of Rome has been relatively segregated for more than 2000 years (Dunn and Dunn, 1957). Marriages are usually endogamous and, in the past three or four generations at least, in- and out-migration have not been great. A comparison of blood-group frequencies between the ghetto and the surrounding population shows interesting variations, although by and large the genotype resembles that of Mediterranean people in general. Nearly 27 percent of a sample of Jews belonged to blood type B, whereas in a sample of Catholic Italians not more than 12 percent possess this substance in their red blood cells. Five percent of the Jewish population was marked by an Rh gene rare among Italians or Europeans in general. This 5 percent represented a tenfold greater incidence of the gene than was found among non-Jewish Italians.

3. **Race Mixture.** Often, particularly in man, populations are incompletely isolated geographically. They possess overlapping ranges or else social segregation is incomplete. The region of overlap reveals every possible combination of traits characteristic of each population. Variability is very high. The overlap area could as easily be assigned to one race as to the other. If sufficient distinctive characteristics are present, the population might be regarded as a race distinct from the Forest Negroes to the south or the Mediterranean race to the north. This third type of variation introduces race mixture. Man's propensity for migration, together with his nearly unique ability to learn modes of adaptation suitable for new environments, encourages race mixture (see pp. 875–881). An area of human racial overlap need not be on the boundary of two localized breeding populations. Representatives from quite distant breeding groups may migrate into a tract of territory where another population is already established. This happened when several Negroid and Caucasoid races came to the New World.

Man's isolation generally is much less than that of the other animals. Hence, in man, after incipient divergence of populations, new branches of those populations come together again. Isolation ceases to be associated with the formation of new species. Should isolation, both geographical and social, become much less frequent, racial variation will be reduced in the world. There are, however, strong forces at work to prevent this from happening.

Adaptive Functions

The opinion once widely held that racial characters were without adaptive significance has now been abandoned. It now is assumed that many genetically controlled racial differences "serve, in the long run, to suit races to different environments, or to different phases of a single environment" (Coon, Garn, and Birdsell, 1950:4). It even is assumed to be "quite likely that all of the traits in which peoples differ have adaptive value" (Garn, 1957:221).

The thesis that some racial differences are adaptive in certain environments or under particular ways of life may be illustrated with reference to

body build. Two extreme terrestrial environments are those marked by dry
heat and extreme cold. The first is characteristic of the deserts of North Africa, East Africa, and Australia. The people living here appear to be specialized for climatic conditions. They are "lean, skinny men, with long arms and
legs, short, shallow bodies, and narrow hands and feet" (Coon, Garn, and
Birdsell, 1950:36–37). Other animals living in deserts also tend to have long,
slender bodies. With this body build the skin surface which people like the
Saharan Tuareg expose to the air is great in proportion to total volume and
weight. They present a maximum of body surface to the air for evaporation
and cooling. The body constitutes a radiation device which, functionally
speaking, is designed for cooling (Fig. 46:1).

People who live around the Arctic Circle tend to be short, around 5 feet

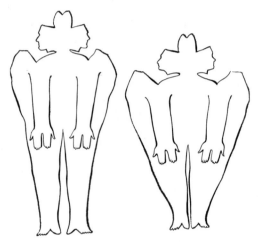

Fig. 46:1. Two Types of Body Structure. These
figures are drawn with the skin flattened out. A,
Lean, shallow, 150-lb. body adapted for ready
cooling in dry heat: B, thick-set 150-lb. body
adapted for heat preservation in extreme cold
temperature (from Coon, Carleton Stevens,
Garn, Stanley M., and Birdsell, Joseph B.,
*Races: A Study of the Problems of Race Forma-
tion in Man,* 1950, courtesy of Charles C.
Thomas, Publisher, Springfield, Illinois).

tall. They are thick-set, with chunky bodies, thick wide chests, short legs,
short toes and fingers, and small fat-covered wrists and ankles. Such a body
type presents relatively little skin surface to the air for cooling. It radiates
little heat in proportion to volume and weight and, therefore, is adapted to
an environment of extreme cold.

The correlation of body size and environment has been expressed in
Bergmann's Law. This holds that within a single warm-blooded species, the

races in colder climates are larger than those in warmer climates. The Pygmies are no exception to this rule. Those who live in the hot Congo are smaller than those living on the cool slopes of the mountains of Ruanda-Urundi (Coon, 1955:263). The explanation of Bergmann's Law is simple (M. T. Newman, 1953). The larger body has the smaller skin surface in proportion to mass ("volume and mass increase as the cube of linear measurements and surface only as the square"). Chunkier builds, as already noted, achieve the same end (Fig. 46:1). In cold climates the size of the appendages and extremities of the body tends to decrease, thus further reducing the amount of body area exposed to air. The ears of several North American rabbits, for example, grow shorter as distance north increases. The distribution of male stature in the New World shows a conspicuous concentration of shorter people in warmer latitudes despite the great deal of intracontinental migration that has occurred (M. T. Newman, 1953:315). The short Eskimo are only partially an exception to this correlation of stature and latitude. Their short stature is explained by their relatively short legs, the reduction of which, as explained before, is adaptively suited to heat retention. In the past, the presence of different statures among the American Indians would have been explained as a function of a series of migrations of racially distinct populations to the New World. It is doubtful, though, if body size could have survived unaltered over from 2000 to 20,000 years and under various environmental circumstances. Instead it seems more likely that adaptive changes in New World peoples have been taking place since these continents were first populated and they still continue to occur (R. W. Newman and E. H. Munro, 1955). Races are not stable.

Adaptation also is illustrated in the correlation of skin color and the amount of light which falls on a given part of the earth's surface. Dark skin is related to a heavy deposit of melanin in the epidermis. Albinos lack this substance but Caucasoids possess varying quantities. Negroids possess much melanin. Dark skins absorb more visible solar radiation than do lighter ones but prevent the invisible ultraviolet rays from penetrating deeply. Ultraviolet light is potentially harmful. Hence it follows that the pigmented skin of Negroids, which acts as a filter of ultraviolet light, is adaptive under tropical conditions marked by abundant, direct sunlight (Coon, Garn, and Birdsell, 1950:53). In the reduced light of northern climates, however, and in association with a diet deficient in vitamin D, Negro children show greater susceptibility to rickets than do white children. What is adaptive in one environment may be quite unsuited to another. A dark outer surface of the iris of the eye also serves to screen ultraviolet light. Under cloudy conditions a light (i.e., blue) eye is not a disadvantage but what adaptive functions it may possess is unknown (ibid., p. 79).

Several other racial characters exhibit adaptive advantages. For example, the beardless Mongoloid face is suited to a cold environment where a hirsute (e.g., Caucasoid) face would collect frost. The hairless Negroid body is adapted to the tropics where hair would interfere with the radiation of heat (Coon, 1955:268). People who plod through forests, cold, and snow have heavy bones while desert people are built with light skeletons. The breadth of the face is probably related to the amount of chewing that is done, which, in turn, is related to the subsistence techniques of a population.

The reader should not think of the geographical environment or culture as directly producing hereditary physical traits. These characters are controlled by genes. Certain genes (perhaps appearing suddenly through mutation or else carried by migration) are advantageous in a given environment or in association with a given way of life. External conditions then favor capacities inherent in the genes; other conditions fail to bring them out so strongly or may even eradicate the bearers of such genes.

Culture and Race

Indications have been given that racial characters may be examined profitably as a dependent function of culture. That is to say, while racial differences do not help to explain cultural differences, culture is significant for understanding some aspects of race formation.

The maintenance of racial varieties within the human species is related to the fact that men and women do not mate promiscuously or at random but within a social or geographic population isolate. The size of the breeding group is partly a function of scale, variables dependent on scale, and level of technical development. If transportation facilities are increased and values governing contact with aliens broaden accordingly, then the diffusion of genes across former barriers is bound to occur. Racial differences, then, are bound to grow weaker (C. Stern, 1950). Where a subsistence system, like food gathering, or value placed on exclusiveness keeps breeding populations small and isolated, conditions are favorable for the fixation of certain characters in the population perhaps in accordance with natural selection or drift.

While culture and culture change do not directly influence heredity, indirectly they exert an influence on the gene pool of a population by affecting birth rate, migration, or breeding habits. College students in America tend to produce fewer children than persons without higher education. Their genes are partially withdrawn from the gene pool. Imprisonment, military service, and removal of one sex from a community for work in distant labor camps, plantations, and mines all affect the transmission of heredity. Variables like reproductive longevity of individuals, and the ability of offspring to reach age of reproduction, or of groups to protect their integrity through social pressure, administration, ritual, or war and so remain intact for breeding, also influence genetic change in the population (Coon, 1950:247).

Even fertile men do not produce spermatozoa constantly. Rest from sexual intercourse contributes to the production of sperm sufficient for fertilization. Jobs that force a man to absent himself from his wife, customs of enforced continence during ceremonial and other occasions, and avoidance of intercourse with a menstruating or lactating wife provide opportunities for sperm replenishment. They therefore increase the chances that a mated couple will produce offspring carrying their genes (*ibid.*, p. 252).

Mutation in the germ cells can be induced through cultural arrangements. Men in the twentieth century have succeeded in producing several kinds of radiation, including x-rays and the radiation of nuclear fission. Strong doses of such radiation penetrating the ordinary cells of the body can be fatal. Sometimes damage is confined to the germ cells. The consequent mutant genes may express themselves in new forms of pigmentation, organ shapes, physiological function, or skeletal abnormalities. Because they are recessive, not all mutations are detectable in offspring during the first generation. The mutant germ cells may not be revealed for several generations or until two people carrying the recessive mutant gene mate (Auerbach, 1956:Chaps. 2–5).

CLASSIFICATION OF RACES

Herodotus spoke of human beings as belonging to a number of *ethnea*.[4] However common it may be to translate the singular form of the word *ethnos* as "race," Herodotus did not base his divisions on physical traits. His term is perhaps better rendered as "ethnic group," an aggregate of people who feel a sense of unity on the basis of common traditions, a common language, or other aspect of culture. Attention to ethnic groups rather than races also characterized the Romans and persisted through the Middle Ages. In Renaissance artists like Da Vinci and Duerer is found the origin of the practice of measuring human features. Albrecht Duerer, who lived from 1471 to 1528, measured body parts with great care and so came to recognize several physical types in the German population. The anatomist Andreas Vesalius (1518–64) carried on the work. Like Duerer, he paid special attention to the shape of the head. In 1775 J. F. Blumenbach wrote *On the Natural Variety of Mankind* and laid the foundation of physical anthropology. From him comes the term "Caucasian." He insisted on the basic unity of mankind and emphasized that racial differences were differences in degree rather than kind. The nineteenth century saw many attempts at racial classification based on measurement as well as rather constant confusion between races and ethnic groups. In the middle of the century Joseph de Gobineau

[4] The paragraph is based on J. Huxley, A. C. Haddon, and A. M. Carr-Saunders, 1936:Chap. 2.

advanced the idea that the "Aryan races" possessed superiorities over others. The term Aryan (i.e., Indo-European) eventually came to be narrowed down to an ethnic group that spoke Germanic languages. However, Christ and Dante among others have been awarded honorary membership in that collectivity despite their anomalous linguistic position. Gobineau's point of view became highly popular in Germany. In fact it was given state support by the totalitarian National Socialist government of Adolf Hitler.

Anthropometry and anthroposcopy, respectively meaning measurement and inspection of the human body, including its skeleton, constitute the standard bases of race classification. These techniques are applied to yield measurements and ratios of the head, nose, and other body parts, as well as stature seated and standing. Anthroposcopically the color and quality of the skin, hair, and other anatomical features are assessed. Testing for blood type recently has been added to the standard techniques of race classification (Montagu, 1951b:440–511). The organismic features dealt with by these techniques are relatively trifling. "Absence of great and outstanding biological differences among the various subgroups of Homo sapiens has forced the classifiers of living man to deal with anatomical minutiae" (Titiev, 1954: 116). Among the most common characters used in classifying races are the texture, form, and color of the hair; amount of body hair; skin pigmentation; form of the nose, face, lips, and ear; and presence of an eyefold. Head shape, body build, stature, the proportions of the limbs, shape of the pelvis, and female breast shape are other traits of which use is made. Naturally, many of these features cannot be used when only skeletons are available for classification. The various blood-type series have already been mentioned and are becoming of increasing importance for classification.

Although a much larger number of races will be found listed in nearly any guide to physical anthropology, four main divisions of Homo sapiens are readily distinguished: Mongoloid, Negroid, Australoid, and Caucasoid. Except for the third, each of these is relatively isolated on the earth's surface. But each has also fanned out from its characteristic habitat. Some distinguishing physical characteristics of the racial divisions are given in Table 61.

Within each of these major segments of the world's population it is possible to distinguish additional races. Anthropologists do not agree on precisely how many nor are they much concerned with the question. The racial divisions do not each contain an equal number of constituent races. In the first place they are not all of the same size, the world containing relatively few Australoids compared to Mongoloids. Then, too, all the subdivisions have not been studied equally. Far more is known about the Caucasoid racial divisions than about the Negroid races and more about the Negroids than the Mongoloids.

Using primarily blood-group gene frequencies on the basis of localization, six somewhat different races have been distinguished. These, briefly described, are:[5]

> *Australian:* Low or no B, low M, and no A_2.
> *American Indian:* Low or no B, low N, and no A_2.
> *Asian:* High B, high Rh_z, no A_2.
> *African:* High B, high Rh_o, some rh, high A_2.
> *European:* Moderate B, moderately high rh, moderate A_2.
> *Early European* (found in Pyrenees region): No B and
>   very high rh_1.

National, religious, and similar aggregates, like speech communities, rarely coincide with racial populations. That is, all the members of such a category rarely constitute a single breeding population isolated from other aggregates. Jews are not a race but, to venture one of a series of possible definitions, a religious category distributed all over the world. In any particular region (for example, Rome; see p. 869) strong isolation of Jews from the neighboring population may lead to race formation, but Jews as a whole possess no hereditary traits in common. The Anglo-Saxons are not a race but presumed descendants of two tribes, the Angles and Saxons, who have interbred with the descendants of many other tribes and nations. The Chinese are a nation, although some people of Chinese birth or parentage also hold citizenship in other nations. There is no Chinese race; the nation contains several relatively distinct breeding populations. Aryans (perhaps better called Indo-European speakers) represent a linguistic stock and obviously do not constitute a single breeding population.

Sometimes races are designated by terms that also apply to language or tribal communities. For example, the word "Dravidian" signifies both a language stock found mainly in South India and a subdivision in the Australoid racial division. Vedda, the name of a food-gathering people in Ceylon, signifies another Australoid race. The precise meaning of such labels will come from the contexts in which they are used.

RACE MIXTURE[6]

People have never been wholly stable. Migration, invasion, and resettlement have always operated to encourage the mixture of races. Transportation developments over the past 500 years have accentuated such contacts. A new kind of race mixture has emerged. In place of invasion or migration promoting interbreeding between different Negroid races or between genet-

---

[5] From the following list it is apparent that there is more than one type of A blood; A_2 designates a second main variety of A. There are at least six types of blood in the Rh series (W. C. Boyd, 1953:236–237, 240–241).

[6] This section follows Shapiro, 1953.

TABLE 61. Some Distinguishing Physical Characters of Four Major Racial Divisions

	Mongoloid	Negroid	Australoid	Caucasoid
Hair:	Dark brown to brown-black; straight in form and coarse in texture. Body hair very scant.	Dark brown to brown-black; wavy to curly in E. Africa and frizzly in S. and W. Africa and Melanesia. Body hair very scant.	Dark brown to brown-black; wavy to curly. Body hair is abundant among the Australians but scanty among the Vedda of Ceylon and the Dravidians of S. India.	Light blond and straight in N. Europe, light brown in central Europe, and dark brown and curly in S. Europe, N. India, and Pakistan. Texture is fine in N. Europe to medium in S. Europe, N. India, and Pakistan. Body hair usually profuse.
Skin:	Light brown with a saffron undertone to yellow-brown.	Light brown to brown in E. Africa; dark brown to brown-black in W. Africa and Melanesia. The Bushman in S.W. Africa has yellow-brown skin.	Light brown among the Ainu to dark brown in S. Asia and Australia.	Pale, ruddy white in N. Europe to light brown in the south. Dark brown in S. India.
Face:	Height is medium in N. China but low in the south; broad cheekbones arched and projecting (i.e., "high"). The root of the nose is moderately low and broad; the bridge straight, broad, and low, with broad wings and a forward-directed tip that tends to incline down.	High and narrow in E. Africa to medium in height and breadth in W. Africa and Melanesia. Only the Bushman face is broad and high. The root of the nose is moderately high and narrow in E. Africa to low and broad in the west. The bridge tends to be weakly convex and low with the wings narrow in E. Africa and very wide in W. Africa and Melanesia. The tip is directed forward.	Narrow among Australians and Vedda, medium among the Ainu and Dravidians. The nasal root is depressed, the bridge low, broad, and mostly straight among Dravidians and Vedda to concave among Australians and Ainu.	High and narrow in N. Europe to medium in height and breadth in S. Europe, N. India, and Pakistan. Cheekbones are not projecting. The nose is high with the bridge straight (W. Europe, S. Europe, parts of India-Pakistan), concave (N.E. Europe), or convex (S.E. Europe and S.W. Asia). The wings are narrow to moderate with tip directed forward in much of Europe and India-Pakistan but upward in N.E. Europe and down in S.E. Europe and S.W. Asia.

Eyes: The eye is medium to dark brown; fatty; the eyelid, when the eye is open, often disappears behind an overhanging "Mongolian eyefold." Color, medium to dark brown.	The eyefold often covers the eyelid in the center of the eye in W. Africa and among the Bushmen. Color is mainly dark brown to brownblack.	The eye is light brown among the Ainu to dark brown elsewhere.	The eyefold does not usually overhang the eyelid, although in N. Europe the fold may cover a portion of the eyelid. Color is blue, gray, or hazel in N. Europe to medium or dark brown elsewhere.
Lips: Moderately thick.	Moderately to very thick, with eversion of some mucous membrane apparent in W. Africa.	Medium except for the thickness occurring among Dravidians.	Thin in N. Europe to moderately thick in the rest of Europe and India-Pakistan.
Ears: Moderate in size with deeply rolled outer edge or helix.	Small and not deeply rolled.		Moderate in size and heavily rolled.
Head: Broad and moderately high except for longheadedness in N. China and among American Indians.	Long and moderately high, though Pygmies of Africa and Melanesia are broadheaded.	Very long heads occur among Vedda; the Australians and Dravidians are longheaded and the Ainu are intermediate.	High and long in N. Europe but broader in S. Europe, S.W. Asia, and India-Pakistan.
Body: The body is muscular, tall in N. China and among some American Indians ranging to short and moderately tall elsewhere. Buttocks of female are moderately prominent. Pelvis is moderately broad and deep. Legs tend to be short relative to trunk length. Breast is disk-shaped.	The body is muscular with marked linearity in E. Africa. Tall in E. Africa to moderately tall in W. Africa and Melanesia. The Pygmies of Africa and Melanesia are very short. Female buttocks are generally moderately prominent to very prominent among Bushmen. Pelvis narrow and very deep. Arms and legs long relative to trunk length; forearm and lower leg relatively long. Breast conical.	Stature generally short but Australians are tall.	The body is muscular and tends to be heavy. Tall in N. Europe and N.W. India, moderately tall in central and S.E. Europe, short in S. Europe and the rest of India. The female buttocks are generally prominent. Pelvis broad and shallow. Arms and legs not disproportionately long. Breast is hemispherical.

SOURCES: R. L. Beals and H. Hoijer, *1953*:163; Krogman, *1946*; Montagu, *1951b*:299–346.

ically akin Mongoloid races, intermixture has come to take place between racial divisions themselves. Under the former type of race mixture offspring differed only slightly from parents. But when mixture occurs between parental populations markedly different in physical characters and genetic make-up, then the offspring are also highly distinct. Race mixture of this sort has been increasing in the world since about 1500 A.D.

Population movements leading to race mixture occurred on an unprecedented scale in the post-Columbian period. Many hitherto isolated parts of the world found themselves hosts to colonial and commercial envoys from Europe. Spain gained control of the Philippines, the Dutch acquired Indonesia, England and France moved into India. Millions of immigrants quickly succeeded the first explorers, adventurers, and dissenters who set foot in the New World and they brought with them 15 million African Negroes. Then Russians penetrated east of the Ural Mountains into Asia, and the Chinese flowed into Southeast Asia, the East Indies, and other parts of the continent.

Nobody knows how many racial hybrids resulted from this reshuffling of population. Such people are not always easy to recognize and may be brought up in ignorance of their family history. In the United States census, individuals of mixed ancestry are not returned as racially mixed but as Negroes and this makes any estimation of the number of hybrids highly speculative.

Hybrids

Hybrids are often accorded special treatment in a community but this is not inevitably the case. In Latin America the fact of mixed parentage is less important than in the United States. Regardless of ancestry it is the way of life which the individual follows that tends to determine whether he will be classified as Indian or Mestizo. Hybrids who adopt Spanish dress and costume are regarded as non-Indians while those who continue to speak the native language and wear traditional garb are Indians. In Brazil a similar situation prevails with reference to Negroid people. "There is not growing up a relatively permanent mixed racial stock, like the 'Cape Coloured' of South Africa. . . . The Brazilian mixed-bloods are absorbing the blacks and are themselves in turn being absorbed by the predominantly European population" (Pierson, 1942:345). Hybridization constitutes no problem in such countries.

Probably most of the world's racial hybrids are to be found in North and South America and the West Indies. The population may contain as many as 28 million Indian-white crosses (mostly in Latin America) and about 8 million mulattoes, or Negro-white crosses. These figures suggest that racially mixed people comprise at least one-sixth of the population of the western hemisphere. An estimated 6 million hybrids reside in other parts of the world, most of them in Southeast Asia. Are the 40 or 50 million hybrids in the world biologically inferior to other people, born of parents belonging to the same racial stock? Information regarding three well-documented cases of race mixture—Pitcairn Island, Jamaica, and Hawaii—may be examined for an answer to this question.

Pitcairn Island

This tiny South Pacific island was settled in 1789 by 9 British sailors, 12 Tahitian (Polynesian) women, and 6 Tahitian men. None of the native men left offspring, but the colony increased by leaps and bounds until in 1856 the 200 Pitcairn Islanders moved to larger Norfolk Island. A few returned to Pitcairn and in 1953 about 1000 descendants of the original colony lived on both islands (not counting immigrants). Nearly completely separated from other communities, the Pitcairn Islanders did not have to cope with any disabilities imposed on them because of their hybrid status.

. . . It is evident to anyone visiting the island that here is a well-organized settlement, conducting its own affairs successfully under a system devised by the islanders themselves. Like people anywhere, of course, they vary, but the visitor is invariably impressed by the pleasant, friendly manners of the islanders, their charm, their hospitality and self-confidence. There is no trace here of a people conscious of inferiority. They are all literate and have from the earliest days maintained a school system of their own efforts. Equally notable is the vigour of their church. Previously adherents of the Church of England, they were converted to Seventh Day Adventism at the end of the last century. The way in which they made this shift in adherence is typical of their wisdom in managing their own affairs. In making the change, the community was faced with a situation that might have been serious in its consequences. The population was divided on the issue of conversion, and, recognizing the danger of a tiny community being split between two rival Churches, decided to put the matter to a vote, with the minority pledged to go along with the expressed wish of the majority. Thus the whole community unanimously adopted Seventh Day Adventism and preserved the religious unity of the colony [Shapiro, 1953:39].

Culturally the island reveals both Tahitian and English elements. Before European contact brought new material goods, clothing was made of bark cloth and cooking followed the Tahitian tradition. Houses resembled English houses except for a thatched roof.

Did the 200 people who lived on Pitcairn Island in 1936 reveal the worst behavioral traits of both parental groups? "As far as the Pitcairn islanders are concerned, I can offer no objective data on their psychological or moral qualities. None, to my knowledge, is available. Certainly there have been many published impressions of these traits of the islanders and most of them are enthusiastic" (Shapiro, 1953:41). Visitors have found them "moral, upright, and virtuous" despite the fact that they sprang from mutineers. The anthropologist who studied them found an intelligent and attractive people. Their physical condition was "excellent." Inbreeding has produced no physical deformities. There are no signs of mental deficiency. These things are true despite the fact that there has been no resident physician or nurse on the island. Shapiro, the anthropologist who undertook the study, sees evidence of "hybrid vigor" in Pitcairn. The offspring are probably bigger than their parents just as a cross-bred grain or animal often exceeds the parents in size. An initially high birth rate, which has since declined, lends no support to the thesis that race mixture leads to biological degeneracy.

Jamaica

Following the Spanish conquest of this West Indian island, the Arawak Indian population became extinct. Negroes had been introduced shortly after contact and East India coolies came later. In the 1920's 18 percent of the population consisted of mulattoes. These products of Negro-white crossings were studied by Davenport and Steggerda. They examined Negro descendants of West African slaves, whites living on the island, and hybrids, or so-called Browns, resulting from crossing between the two populations. The authors find the Browns inferior to both parental groups biologically and intellectually. In height and weight the hybrids fell below both parent races.

Doubt has been expressed over whether the authors chose their samples fairly. Many Browns in the sample are between 16 and 20 years old. Hence they may not have reached mature physical development. Stature and weight may not be important characters when it comes to estimating biological adequacy. Critics also point out that Davenport and Steggerda took the resident whites to represent one of the parent groups that contributed genes to the Browns. These whites, coming from various parts of the world, are highly varied. Some arrived too recently to have contributed anything to the Brown mixture. The study includes no descendants of early Spanish settlers of the type that did mix intensively with the Negroes.

Psychologically, as determined by 26 tests, the Negroes of Jamaica surpass the whites in musical ability but are inferior in planning and judgment. The Browns are generally inferior to both parent races. Reëxamination of the scores suggests that the Browns actually are similar to Negroes in test performance. There is, of course, the very real possibility that the tests, by relying highly on education, language, and culture, favored the whites at the expense of the Negroes and Browns. This is a common problem with intelligence tests applied to exotic cultural groups.

Hawaii

In the Hawaiian Islands, Polynesians, Caucasoids, and Mongoloids have produced an array of hybrids. At the same time the territory evidences little racially based friction or prejudice. These results may stem from the fact that when Americans and Europeans first settled in the islands they found natives in positions of authority and accorded respect to the indigenous rulers. Intermarriage with native royal families was sought because of the wealth and prestige which it brought. Racial tolerance was encouraged under those early conditions. The pattern of tolerance continued and even was extended to include Japanese and Chinese who arrived in the islands. At present mixed Hawaiians are especially favored as marriage partners by all racial groups. Mixed Hawaiians are expanding at a more rapid rate than all other categories of the population. They are probably destined to become the major element in Hawaii's population.

An examination of these cases of race mixture conclusively indicates that there exists in man no instinctual antipathy to cross-breeding. Such an instinct, it sometimes has been argued, protects the human stock from deterioration. The evidence scarcely supports the belief that biological deterioration predictably follows race mixture.

AVAILABLE FILMS

Most of the films dealing with genetics and race are elementary and have been prepared primarily for high school and lower grades. *Brotherhood of Race* (10 min., color) is an animated cartoon produced by the Anti-Defamation League. *Man, One Family* presents J. B. S. Haldane and Julian Huxley speaking on the race theories of the Nazis (British Information Services, 17 min., b. and w.). Coronet Films offers *Heredity and Environment*, which contains a brief discussion of genetics (10 min., b. and w.). *Heredity*, by Encyclopædia Britannica Films, covers the same ground (10 min., b. and w.). *The Color of Man*, produced by University of California Educational Film Sales, is a more mature account of the agencies that influence skin color (10 min., b. and w.).

BIBLIOGRAPHY

Abbas, Ahmad, Khwaja. 1955. *Inqilab.* Jaico Book Edition. Bombay, Jaico Publishing House.

Abbie, A. A. 1952. A New Approach to the Problem of Human Evolution. *Transactions of the Royal Society of South Australia,* 75:70–88.

Ackerknecht, Erwin H. 1947. Primitive Surgery. *American Anthropologist,* 49:25–45.

Ackerknecht, Erwin H. 1949. Medical Practices. In: Steward, Julian H. (ed.), *Handbook of South American Indians.* Vol. 5, *The Comparative Ethnology of South American Indians.* Bureau of American Ethnology, Bulletin 143.

Ackerknecht, Erwin H., Nadeau, Gabriel, and Heizer, R. F. 1944. Scalp and Head Trophies. *Ciba Symposia,* 5:1654–1684.

Ackoff, Russell L. 1953. *The Design of Social Research.* Chicago, University of Chicago Press.

Adair, John, and Vogt, Evon Z. 1949. Navaho and Zuñi Veterans: A Study of Contrasting Modes of Culture Change. *American Anthropologist,* 51:547–561.

Adam, Leonhard. 1948. "Virilocal" and "Uxorilocal." *Man,* 48:12.

Agreement Between Canada and the United States on the Establishment of a Distant Early Warning System in Canadian Territory. 1956. *The Arctic Circular,* 9:23–31.

Ailleret, Pierre. 1950. Energy in Its International Aspects. In: UNESCO *Discussion Theme 1951,* "Energy in the Service of Man." Paper No. 4. Paris, UNESCO, offset printed.

Air Force Base Project Staff. 1954. *The Organization and Performance of Bomb Wings: Studies in Complex Social Systems in Action, Summary Report.* Chapel Hill, Air Force Base Project, Institute for Research in Social Science, University of North Carolina, Technical Report No. 25, mimeographed.

Albert, Ethel M. 1956. The Classification of Values: A Method and Illustration. *American Anthropologist,* 58:221–248.

Albrecht, Milton C. 1954. The Relationship of Literature and Society. *American Journal of Sociology,* 59:425–436.

Ali, Mrs. Meer Hassan. *See* Mīr Hasan 'Alī, Mrs. B.

Alī, Syed Nawāb. 1946. *Some Moral and Religious Teachings of al-Ghazzālī.* Lahore, Sheikh Muhammad Ashraf.

Allan, W., Gluckman, Max, Peters, D. U., and Trapnell, C. G. 1948. *Land Holding and Land Usage Among the Plateau Tonga of Mazabuka District: A Reconnaissance Survey, 1945.* The Rhodes-Livingstone Papers, No. 14.

Allee, Warder C. 1938. *The Social Life of Animals.* New York, W. W. Norton and Co., Inc.

Allee, Warder C. 1943. Where Angels Fear to Tread: A Contribution from General Sociology to Human Ethics. *Science*, 97:517–525.

Allen, Rosemary A. 1955. Changing Social Organization and Kinship Among the Alaskan Haidas. *Anthropological Papers of the University of Alaska*, 4:5–13.

Allport, Gordon W. 1954. The Historical Background of Modern Social Psychology. In: Lindzey, Gardner (ed.), *Handbook of Social Psychology*. Vol. 1, *Theory and Method*. Cambridge, Mass., Addison-Wesley Publishing Co., Inc.

Ammar, Hamed. 1954. *Growing Up in an Egyptian Village (Silwa, Province of Aswan)*. London, Routledge and Kegan Paul, Ltd.

Anderson, Frank G. 1955. The Pueblo Kachina Cult: A Historical Reconstruction. *Southwestern Journal of Anthropology*, 11:404–419.

Anderson, Oscar Edward. 1953. *Refrigeration in America*. Princeton, Princeton University Press.

Andrews, Roy Chapman. 1945. *Meet Your Ancestors: A Biography of Primitive Man*. New York, Viking Press.

Angelino, Henry, and Shedd, Charles L. 1955. A Note on Berdache. *American Anthropologist*, 57:121–126.

Angyal, Andras. 1941. *Foundations for a Science of Personality*. New York, The Commonwealth Fund.

Annan, Noel. 1952. British Foreign Policy: The Situation Today. *The Listener*, 47:43–44, 58.

Anonymous. 1954. Freedom of Contract—Reality or Delusion? By a Barrister. *The Listener*, 52:854–856.

Anonymous. 1955. Channel Cat in the Middle Distance. *Explorations*, 5:26–29.

Antevs, Ernst. 1955. Geologic-Climatic Dating in the West. *American Antiquity*, 20:317–335.

Aristoteles. [1913.] A *Treatise on Government or The Politics of Aristotle*. Translated by William Ellis. London, J. M. Dent and Sons, Ltd.

Armattoe, R. E. G. 1949. Civilization and Molar Decay in Western Europe and Africa. Abstract. *American Journal of Physical Anthropology*, 7:281–282.

Armstrong, Robert G. 1955. Talking Instruments in Africa. *Explorations*, 4:140–153.

Ashley, Maurice. 1952. *England in the Seventeenth Century (1603–1714)*. Harmondsworth, Penguin Books.

Auerbach, Charlotte. 1956. *Genetics in the Atomic Age*. Fair Lawn, N.J., Essential Books, Inc.

Bacon, Elizabeth. 1946. A Preliminary Attempt to Determine the Culture Areas of Asia. *Southwestern Journal of Anthropology*, 2:117–132.

Baechlin, Peter, and Muller-Strauss, Maurice. 1952. *Newsreels Across the World*. Paris, UNESCO.

Banfield, Edward C. 1951. *Government Project*. Glencoe, Ill., The Free Press.

Barber, Bernard. [1952.] *Science and the Social Order.* Glencoe, Ill., The Free Press.

Barker, Roger G., and Wright, Herbert F. 1955. *Midwest and Its Children.* Evanston, Ill., Row, Peterson and Co.

Barkhuus, Arne. 1947. Native Medicine in Ethiopia. *Ciba Symposia,* 9:724–728.

Barnes, Harry Elmer, and Becker, Howard. 1938. *Social Thought from Lore to Science.* Two vols. Boston, D. C. Heath and Co.

Barnes, J. A. 1947. The Collection of Genealogies. *Journal of the Rhodes-Livingstone Institute,* 5:48–55.

Barnett, Homer G. 1953. *Innovation: The Basis of Cultural Change.* New York, McGraw-Hill Book Company, Inc.

Barth, Fredrik. 1953. *Principles of Social Organization in Southern Kurdistan.* Universitets Etnografiske Museum, Bulletin 7.

Barth, Fredrik. 1954. Father's Brother's Daughter Marriage in Kurdistan. *Southwestern Journal of Anthropology,* 10:164–171.

Bartholomew, George A., Jr., and Birdsell, Joseph B. 1953. Ecology and the Protohominids. *American Anthropologist,* 55:481–498.

Bartlett, Frederic C. 1946. Psychological Methods for the Study of "Hard" and "Soft" Features of Culture. *Africa,* 16:145–155.

Basedow, Herbert. 1927. Subincision and Kindred Rites of the Australian Aboriginal. *Journal of the Royal Anthropological Institute,* 57:123–156.

Basehart, Harry W. 1954. Ashanti Society and Kinship Structure. Paper Prepared for the Social Science Research Council, Summer Seminar on Kinship, mimeographed.

Bastide, Roger. 1950. *Sociologie et psychanalyse.* Paris, Presses Universitaires de France.

Bates, Frederick L. 1953. *The Coordination of Maintenance Activities in Bomb Wings: Synchronization and Performance.* Chapel Hill, Air Force Base Project, Institute for Research in Social Science, University of North Carolina, Technical Report No. 16, mimeographed.

Bateson, Gregory. 1944. Cultural Determinants of Personality. In: Hunt, J. McV. (ed.), *Personality and the Behavior Disorders.* Two vols. New York, The Ronald Press Company.

Bateson, Gregory, and Mead, M. 1942. *Balinese Character.* New York, New York Academy of Sciences.

Batten, T. R. 1954. *Problems of African Development.* Two vols. Second ed. London, Oxford University Press.

Beach, Frank A. 1954. The Individual from Conception to Conceptualization. In: *Current Trends in Psychology and the Behavioral Sciences.* Pittsburgh, University of Pittsburgh Press.

Beals, Alan R. 1955. Interplay Among Factors of Change in a Mysore Village. In: Marriott, McKim (ed.), *Village India.* Memoirs of the American Anthropological Association, No. 83.

Beals, Alan R., and McCorkle, Thomas. 1950. *Lost Lake.* Kroeber Anthropological Society Papers, No. 3.

Beals, Ralph L., and Hoijer, Harry. 1953. *An Introduction to Anthropology*. New York, The Macmillan Company.

Beardsley, Richard K. 1953. *Hypotheses on Inner Asian Pastoral Nomadism and Its Culture Area*. Memoirs of the Society for American Archaeology, No. 9.

Beattie, J. H. M. 1955. Contemporary Trends in British Social Anthropology. *Sociologus*, 5:1–14.

Bell, Quentin. 1949. *On Human Finery*. New York, A. A. Wyn, Inc.

Belo, Jane. 1949. *Bali: Rangda and Barong*. Monographs of the American Ethnological Society, No. 16.

Belshaw, Cyril S. 1954. *Changing Melanesia*. Melbourne, Oxford University Press.

Benedict, Ruth F. 1934. *Patterns of Culture*. Boston, Houghton Mifflin Co.

Benedict, Ruth F. 1946. *The Chrysanthemum and the Sword*. Boston, Houghton Mifflin Co.

Benedict, Ruth F. 1948. Anthropology and the Humanities. *American Anthropologist*, 50:585–593.

Bennett, John W. 1943. Food and Social Status in a Rural Society. *American Sociological Review*, 7:561–569.

Bennett, John W. 1946. The Interpretation of Pueblo Culture: A Question of Values. *Southwestern Journal of Anthropology*, 2:361–374.

Bennett, John W., and Tumin, Melvin M. 1948. *Social Life: Structure and Function*. New York, Alfred A. Knopf.

Bennett, John W., and Wolff, Kurt H. 1955. Toward Communication Between Sociology and Anthropology. In: *Yearbook of Anthropology 1955*. New York, Wenner-Gren Foundation for Anthropological Research, Inc.

Bennett, Wendell C. 1949. Numbers, Measures, Weights, and Calendars. In: Steward, Julian H. (ed.), *Handbook of South American Indians*. Vol. 5, *The Comparative Ethnology of South American Indians*. Bureau of American Ethnology, Bulletin 143.

Benzinger, I. 1927. *Hebraeische Archaeologie*. Third ed. Leipzig, Verlag von Eduard Pfeiffer.

Berger, Meyer. 1942. *The Eight Million*. New York, Simon and Schuster, Inc.

Bernays, Edward L. 1956. American Public Relations. *Gazette*, 2:169–177.

Berndt, Ronald M. 1951. Influence of European Culture on Australian Aborigines. *Oceania*, 21:229–235.

Berndt, Ronald M. 1952–53. A Cargo Movement in the Eastern Central Highlands of New Guinea. *Oceania*, 23:40–65, 137–158, 202–234.

Berndt, Ronald M. 1954. Reaction to Contact in the Eastern Highlands of New Guinea. *Oceania*, 24:191–228, 255–274.

Berndt, Ronald M., and Berndt, Catherine. 1942–44. A Preliminary Report of Field Work in the Ooldea Region, Western South Australia. *Oceania*, 12: 305–330; 13:51–70, 143–169, 243–280, 362–375; 14:30–66, 124–158, 220–249, 338–358; 15:49–80, 154–165, 239–275.

Berndt, Ronald M., and Berndt, Catherine. 1954. *Arnhem Land*. Melbourne, F. W. Cheshire.

Berreman, Gerald D. 1955. Inquiry into Community Integration in an Aleutian Village. *American Anthropologist*, 57:49–59.

Bhagavadgita. 1951. Translated by Swami Prabhavananda and Christopher Isherwood. New York, Harper & Brothers.

Bidney, David. 1953. *Theoretical Anthropology*. New York, Columbia University Press.

Bilibin, Ivan. 1952. The Soviet Attitude to the Past. *The Listener*, 47:178–179.

Billig, Otto, Gillin, John, and Davidson, William. 1947–48. Aspects of Personality and Culture in a Guatemalan Community: Ethnological and Rorschach Approaches. *Journal of Personality*, 16:153–187, 326–368.

Birdwhistell, Ray L. [1952.] *Introduction to Kinesics: An Annotation System for Analysis of Body Motion and Gesture*. Louisville, University of Louisville.

Birket-Smith, Kaj. 1930. Folk Wanderings and Culture Drifts in Northern North America. *Journal de la Société des Américanistes*, 22:1–29.

Birket-Smith, Kaj. 1946. *Geschichte der Kultur*. Second ed. Zurich, Orell Fuessli Verlag.

Bittle, William E. 1952. Language and Culture: A Comment on Voegelin's View. *Southwestern Journal of Anthropology*, 8:466–471.

Blanguernon, Claude. 1954. The Schools for Nomads in the Hoggar. *Fundamental and Adult Education*, 6:8–14.

Blau, Peter M. 1955. *The Dynamics of Bureaucracy*. Chicago, Chicago University Press.

Blau, Peter M. 1956. *Bureaucracy in Modern Society*. New York, Random House, Inc.

Bloch, Bernard, and Trager, George L. 1942. *Outline of Linguistic Analysis*. Baltimore, Linguistic Society of America.

Bloomfield, Leonard. 1933. *Language*. New York, Henry Holt and Co.

Bloomfield, Leonard. 1946. Algonquian. In: Hoijer, Harry, *et al.*, *Linguistic Structures of Native America*. Viking Fund Publications in Anthropology, No. 6.

Blue, John T., Jr. 1955. Conceptual Errors Common in the Teaching of Sociology. *Social Forces*, 33:286–289.

Boas, Franz. 1897. The Social Organization and the Secret Societies of the Kwakiutl. *Report of the United States National Museum for 1895*, pp. 311–737.

Boas, Franz. 1932. *Anthropology and Modern Life*. New and revised ed. New York, W. W. Norton and Co., Inc.

Bogoras, Waldemar G. 1904–09. *The Chukchee*. Three vols. Memoirs of the American Museum of Natural History, No. 11.

Bogoras, Waldemar G. 1929. Elements of the Culture of the Circumpolar Zone. *American Anthropologist*, 31:579–601.

Boisen, Anton T. 1951. The Development and Validation of Religious Faith. *Psychiatry*, 14:455–462.

Borges, Jorge Luis. 1955. Mutations. *Explorations*, 4:21.

Born, Wolfgang. 1949a. Early Botanical Gardens. *Ciba Symposia*, 11:1099–1116.

Born, Wolfgang. 1949b. The Garden in History. *Ciba Symposia*, 11:1094–1098.

Bose, Nirmal Kumar. 1956. Some Observations on Nomadic Castes in India. *Man in India*, 36:1–6.

Bossard, James H. S., and Sanger, W. P. 1952. The Large Family System—A Research Report. *American Sociological Review*, 17:3–9.

Bouquet, A. C. 1951. *Comparative Religion*. Harmondsworth, Penguin Books.

Bowers, Alfred W. 1950. *Mandan Social and Ceremonial Organization*. Chicago, University of Chicago Press.

Boyd, Mary. 1956. Political Development in Western Samoa and Universal Suffrage. *Political Science*, 8:44–67.

Boyd, William C. 1953. *Genetics and the Races of Man: An Introduction to Modern Physical Anthropology*. Boston, Little, Brown and Co.

Boyd, William C., and Asimov, Isaac. 1955. *Races and People*. New York, Abelard-Schuman.

Brade-Birks, S. Graham. [1955.] *Teach Yourself Archaeology*. New York, Roy Publishers.

Braidwood, Robert J. 1946. Artifacts. In: *Human Origins: An Introductory General Course in Anthropology. Selected Readings, Series II*. Second ed. Chicago, University of Chicago Bookstore, mimeographed.

Braidwood, Robert J. 1952. *The Near East and the Foundations for Civilization*. Eugene, Oregon State System of Higher Education.

Braidwood, Robert J., and Braidwood, Linda. 1950. Jarmo: A Village of Early Farmers in Iraq. *Antiquity*, 48:189–195.

Brant, Charles S. 1950. Peyotism Among the Kiowa-Apache and Neighboring Tribes. *Southwestern Journal of Anthropology*, 6:212–222.

Brelsford, William Vernon. 1946. *Fishermen of the Bangweulu Swamps*. The Rhodes-Livingstone Papers, No. 12.

Bridgman, P. W. 1938. *The Intelligent Individual and Society*. New York, The Macmillan Company.

Brinton, Daniel G. 1894. Nagualism: A Study in Native American Folk-lore and History. *Proceedings of the American Philosophical Society*, 33:11–71.

Brock, J. F., and Autret, M. 1952. *Kwashiorkor in Africa*. FAO Nutritional Studies, No. 8.

Broderick, Alan H. 1948. *Early Man*. London, Hutchinson's Scientific and Technical Publications.

Brown, G. Gordon. 1944. Missions and Cultural Diffusion. *American Journal of Sociology*, 50:214–219.

Brown, G. Gordon, and Hutt, A. McD. B. 1935. *Anthropology in Action*. London, Oxford University Press.

Bruner, Edward M. 1955. Two Processes of Change in Mandan-Hidatsa Kinship Terminology. *American Anthropologist*, 57:840–850.

Bruner, Edward M. 1956. Cultural Transmission and Cultural Change. *Southwestern Journal of Anthropology*, 12:191–199.

Buck, Peter H. *See* Hiroa, Te Rangi.

Buecher, Karl. 1901. *Industrial Evolution*. New York, Henry Holt and Co.

Bunzel, Ruth. 1952. *Chichicastenango: A Guatemalan Village*. Publications of the American Ethnological Society, No. 22.

Burkitt, Miles Crawford. 1929. Archaeology: 1. Stone Age. In: *The Encyclopædia Britannica*. Vol. 2, fourteenth ed. Chicago, Encyclopædia Britannica, Inc.

Busia, K. A. 1951. *The Position of the Chief in the Modern Political System of Ashanti*. London, Oxford University Press.

Butler, Nicholas Murray. 1912. *Why Should We Change Our Form of Government?* New York, Charles Scribner's Sons.

Butterfield, Herbert. 1950. *The Origins of Modern Science 1300–1800*. London, G. Bell and Sons, Ltd.

Canada. Department of Mines and Resources. Northwest Territories and Yukon Services. Lands and Development Services Branch. 1949. *The Book of Wisdom for Eskimo*. Translated into syllabic by Samuel G. Ford. Translation into Eskimo (Roman characters) by Cyril Wingnek. Ottawa.

Cannon, W. B. 1942. "Voodoo" Death. *American Anthropologist*, 44:169–181.

Carpenter, Edmund. 1955. Eskimo Poetry: Word Magic. *Explorations*, 4:101–111.

Carpenter, Edmund. 1957. Grammar Is Snobbish Nonsense. *Maclean's Magazine*, 70:2, 43–45.

Carr, E. H. 1955. The Bolshevik Revolution in Perspective. *The Listener*, 53:697–699, 742–744.

Carreira, António. 1953. La polygamie parmi les groupes ethniques de la Guinée Portugaise—contributions à l'étude de l'institution de la polygamie dans les territoires africains. Abstract. *African Abstracts*, 4:66.

Carrington, John F. 1949. *Talking Drums of Africa*. London, The Carey Kingsgate Press Ltd.

Carrington, John F. 1953. Communication by Means of Gongs. *Explorations*, 1:24–33.

Carstairs, G. Morris. 1956. Medicine and Faith in Rural Rajasthan. In: Paul, Benjamin D. (ed.), *Health, Culture, and Community*. New York, Russell Sage Foundation.

Carter, George F. 1945. *Plant Geography and Culture History in the American Southwest*. Viking Fund Publications in Anthropology, No. 5.

Casagrande, Joseph B. 1952. Ojibwa Bear Ceremonialism: The Persistence of a Ritual Attitude. In: Tax, Sol (ed.), *Acculturation in the Americas*. Proceedings and Selected Papers of the XXIXth International Congress of Americanists.

Caudill, William. 1952. *Japanese-American Personality and Acculturation.* Genetic Psychology Monographs, No. 45.

Caudill, William. 1953. Applied Anthropology in Medicine. In: Kroeber, A. L. (ed.), *Anthropology Today.* Chicago, University of Chicago Press.

Caudill, William, Redlich, F. C., Gilmore, H. R., and Brody, E. G. 1952. Social Structure and Interaction Processes on a Psychiatric Ward. *American Journal of Orthopsychiatry,* 22:314–334.

Cayton, H. R., and Drake, St. Clair. 1946. *Black Metropolis.* New York, Harcourt, Brace and Co.

Centers, Richard. 1949. *The Psychology of Social Classes.* Princeton, Princeton University Press.

Chadwick, E. R. 1949. Fundamental Education in Udi Division. *Fundamental Education,* 1:9–21.

Chapple, Eliot D. 1952. The Training of the Professional Anthropologist: Social Anthropology and Applied Anthropology. *American Anthropologist,* 54:340–342.

Chapple, Eliot D. 1953. Applied Anthropology in Industry. In: Kroeber, A. L. (ed.), *Anthropology Today.* Chicago, University of Chicago Press.

Chapple, Eliot D., and Coon, Carleton S. 1942. *Principles of Anthropology.* New York, Henry Holt and Co.

Chiera, Edward. 1938. *They Wrote on Clay.* Chicago, University of Chicago Press.

Childe, V. Gordon. 1930. *The Bronze Age.* Cambridge, Cambridge University Press.

Childe, V. Gordon. 1936. *Man Makes Himself.* London, Watts and Co.

Childe, V. Gordon. [1940.] *Prehistoric Communities of the British Isles.* London, W. R. Chambers Ltd.

Childe, V. Gordon. 1944. *Progress and Archaeology.* London, Watts and Co.

Childe, V. Gordon. 1946. *What Happened in History.* Harmondsworth, Penguin Books.

Childe, V. Gordon. 1949. *Social Worlds of Knowledge.* London, Oxford University Press.

Childe, V. Gordon. 1951. *Social Evolution.* London, Watts and Co.

Childe, V. Gordon. 1952. *New Light on the Most Ancient East.* Fourth ed. London, Kegan, Paul, Trench, Trubner and Co.

Childe, V. Gordon. 1953. *What Is History?* New York, Henry Schuman.

Childe, V. Gordon. 1956. *Piecing Together the Past.* New York, Frederick A. Praeger.

Childs, M. W., and Cater, D. 1954. *Ethics in a Business Society.* New York, Harper & Brothers.

Chinoy, Ely. 1954. *Sociological Perspective.* Doubleday Short Studies in Sociology, No. 2.

Chinoy, Ely. 1955. *Automobile Workers and the American Dream.* Garden City, Doubleday and Co., Inc.

Chitale, Venu. 1950. *In Transit.* Bombay, Hind Kitabs, Ltd.

Churchill, Randolph S. 1953. *The Story of the Coronation*. London, Derek Verschoyle.

Clark, F. Le Gros. 1953. The Weaning of the Human Child. *Nutrition*, 7:82–89.

Clark, John Grahame Douglas. 1932. *The Mesolithic Age in Britain*. Cambridge, Cambridge University Press.

Clark, John Grahame Douglas. 1936. *The Mesolithic Settlement of Northern Europe*. Cambridge, Cambridge University Press.

Clark, John Grahame Douglas. 1952. *Prehistoric Europe: The Economic Basis*. London, Methuen and Co., Ltd.

Clark, Wilfrid E. Le Gros. 1954. The Antiquity of *Homo sapiens* in Particular and of the Hominidae in General. *Science Progress*, 42:377–395.

Clark, Wilfrid E. Le Gros. 1955. *The Fossil Evidence for Human Evolution: An Introduction to the Study of Paleoanthropology*. Chicago, University of Chicago Press.

Clark, Wilfrid E. Le Gros. 1956. *History of the Primates*. Fifth ed. London, British Museum (Natural History).

Clark, Wilfrid E. Le Gros, and Leakey, L. S. B. 1951. *The Miocene Hominoidea of East Africa*. British Museum (Natural History), Fossil Mammals of Africa, No. 1.

Clark-Kennedy, A. E. 1957. *Human Disease*. Harmondsworth, Penguin Books.

Cline, Walter. 1936. *Notes on the People of Siwah and El Garah in the Libyan Desert*. General Series in Anthropology, No. 4.

Clough, Shepard B. 1951. *The Rise and Fall of Civilization: An Inquiry into the Relationship Between Economic Development and Civilization*. New York, McGraw-Hill Book Company, Inc.

Coates, Adrian. 1952. *Prelude to History*. New York, Philosophical Library.

Codere, Helen. 1955. A Genealogical Study of Kinship in the United States. *Psychiatry*, 18:65–79.

Codere, Helen. 1957. Kwakiutl Society: Rank Without Class. *American Anthropologist*, 59:473–486.

Cohen, Felix S. 1954. Transcendental Nonsense and the Functional Approach. In: Hayakawa, S. I. (ed.), *Language, Meaning and Maturity*. New York, Harper & Brothers.

Cohen, Lillian. 1954. *Statistical Methods for Social Scientists*. New York, Prentice-Hall.

Cole, Sonia M. 1954a. Differentiation of Non-Metallic Tools. In: Singer, Charles, Holmyard, E. J., and Hall, A. R. (eds.), *A History of Technology*. Vol. 1, *From Early Times to Fall of Ancient Empires*. Oxford, Clarendon Press.

Cole, Sonia M. 1954b. *The Prehistory of East Africa*. Harmondsworth, Penguin Books.

Collier, John. 1947. *The Indians of the Americas*. New York, W. W. Norton and Co., Inc.

Collier, Mary, and Collier, John, Jr. 1948. Navajo Farmer. *The Farm Quarterly*, 3:20–22.

Collinder, Björn. 1949. *The Lapps*. Princeton, Princeton University Press.

Collins, Henry B. 1954. *Arctic Area*. Program of the History of America: I, Indigenous Period, No. 2. Comisión de Historia, No. 68. Instituto Panamericano de Geofrafía e Historia, Mexico D.F.

Colson, Elizabeth. 1951. The Role of Cattle Among the Plateau Tonga. *Human Problems in British Central Africa*, 11:10–47.

Colson, Elizabeth. 1953. Social Control and Vengeance in Plateau Tonga Society. *Africa*, 23:199–211.

Comhaire-Sylvain, Suzanne. 1950. *Food and Leisure Among the African Youth of Leopoldville (Belgian Congo)*. Communications from the School of African Studies, n.s., No. 25.

Commager, Henry Steele. 1949. Portrait of the American. In: Chase, J. W. (ed.), *Years of the Modern*. New York, Longmans, Green and Co.

Conant, James B. 1952. *Modern Science and Modern Man*. New York, Columbia University Press.

Conklin, Harold C. 1954. An Ethnoecological Approach to Shifting Agriculture. *Transactions of the New York Academy of Sciences*, 17:133–142.

Coomaraswamy, Ananda K. 1946. *The Religious Basis of the Forms of Indian Society; Indian Culture and English Influence; East and West*. New York, Orientalia, offset printed.

Coon, Carleton Stevens (ed.). 1948. *A Reader in General Anthropology*. New York, Henry Holt and Co.

Coon, Carleton Stevens. 1950. Human Races in Relation to Environment and Culture with Special Reference to the Influence of Culture upon Genetic Changes in Human Population. In: *Origin and Evolution of Man*. Cold Spring Harbor Symposia on Quantitative Biology, No. 15.

Coon, Carleton Stevens. 1951a. *Caravan: The Story of the Middle East*. New York, Henry Holt and Co.

Coon, Carleton Stevens. 1951b. *Cave Explorations in Iran 1949*. Philadelphia, The University Museum, University of Pennsylvania.

Coon, Carleton Stevens. 1952. Excavations in Hotu Cave, Iran, 1951; A Preliminary Report. *Proceedings of the American Philosophical Society*, 96:231–249.

Coon, Carleton Stevens. 1954. *The Story of Man*. New York, Alfred A. Knopf.

Coon, Carleton Stevens. 1955. Some Problems of Human Variability and Natural Selection in Climate and Culture. *The American Naturalist*, 89:257–279.

Coon, Carleton Stevens. 1957. *The Seven Caves*. New York, Alfred A. Knopf.

Coon, Carleton Stevens, Garn, Stanley M., and Birdsell, Joseph B. 1950. *Races: A Study of the Problems of Race Formation in Man*. Springfield, Ill., Charles C. Thomas.

Cooper, John M. 1931. The Relations Between Religion and Morality in Primitive Culture. *Primitive Man*, 4:33–48.

Cooper, John M. 1932. Incest Prohibitions in Primitive Culture. *Primitive Man*, 5:1–20.

Cooper, John M. 1941. *Temporal Sequence and the Marginal Cultures*. The Catholic University of America, Anthropological Series, No. 10.

Cooper, John M. 1944. The Shaking Tent Rite Among Plains and Forest Algonquians. *Primitive Man*, 17:60–84.

Cooper, John M. 1946a. The Ona. In: Steward, Julian H. (ed.), *Handbook of South American Indians*. Vol. 1, *The Marginal Tribes*. Bureau of American Ethnology, Bulletin 143.

Cooper, John M. 1946b. The Yahgan. In: Steward, Julian H. (ed.), *Handbook of South American Indians*. Vol. 1, *The Marginal Tribes*. Bureau of American Ethnology, Bulletin 143.

Cooper, John M. 1949. Stimulants and Narcotics. In: Steward, Julian H. (ed.), *Handbook of South American Indians*. Vol. 5, *The Comparative Ethnology of South American Indians*. Bureau of American Ethnology, Bulletin 143.

Cormack, Margaret. 1953. *The Hindu Woman*. New York, Bureau of Publications, Teachers College, Columbia University.

Cornevin, R. 1954. Names Among the Bessari. *Southwestern Journal of Anthropology*, 10:160–163.

Cort, David. 1954. *The Big Picture*. Indianapolis, Bobbs-Merrill Co., Inc.

Coser, Lewis A. 1956. *The Functions of Social Conflict*. Glencoe, Ill., The Free Press.

Cottrell, Fred. 1955. *Energy and Society*. New York, McGraw-Hill Book Co., Inc.

Cox, Oliver Cromwell. 1948. *Caste, Class, and Race*. Garden City, Doubleday and Co., Inc.

Cranston, Maurice. 1956a. Rights and Conscience. *The Listener*, 55:552–553.

Cranston, Maurice. 1956b. Rights and Law. *The Listener*, 55:49.

Creedy, Frederick. 1939. *Human Nature Writ Large*. Chapel Hill, University of North Carolina Press.

Crooke, William. 1896. *The Tribes and Castes of the North-western Provinces and Oudh*. Four vols. Calcutta, Office of the Superintendent of Government Printing.

Cumming, John, and Cumming, Elaine. 1955. Mental Health Education in a Canadian Community. In: Paul, Benjamin D. (ed.), *Health, Culture, and Community*. New York, Russell Sage Foundation.

Cunnison, Ian. 1957. History and Genealogies in a Conquest State. *American Anthropologist*, 59:20–31.

Curwen, E. Cecil, and Hatt, Gudmund. 1953. *Plough and Pasture: The Early History of Farming*. New York, Henry Schuman.

Dahl, Robert A., and Lindblom, Charles E. 1953. *Politics, Economics, and Welfare*. New York, Harper & Brothers.

Daniel, Glyn E. 1950. Archaeology Links Geology to History. In: *Ideas and Beliefs of the Victorians*. London, Sylvan Press.

Darling, Malcolm. 1947. *The Punjab Peasant in Prosperity and Debt*. Fourth ed. London, Geoffrey Cumberlege, Oxford University Press.

Dart, Raymond A. 1949. The Predatory Implemental Technique of Australopithecus. *American Journal of Physical Anthropology*, 7:1–38.

Das, Rasvihary. 1953. The Concept of Man and the Philosophy of Education in the East and West. In: *Humanism and Education East and West*. Paris, UNESCO.

David, F. N. 1953. *A Statistical Primer*. London, Charles Griffin and Co., Ltd.

Davis, Allison, Gardner, Burleigh B., and Gardner, Mary R. 1941. *Deep South*. Chicago, University of Chicago Press.

Davis, Kingsley, and Blake, Judith. 1956. Social Structure and Fertility: An Analytic Framework. *Economic Development and Cultural Change*, 4:211–235.

Davis, Kingsley, and Golden, Hilda Hertz. 1954. Urbanization and the Development of Pre-Industrial Areas. *Economic Development and Cultural Change*, 3:6–24.

Davison, Dorothy. 1951. *The Story of Prehistoric Civilizations*. London, Watts and Co.

Dawson, James. 1881. *Australian Aborigines*. Melbourne, G. Robertson.

Day, Clarence B. 1940. *Chinese Peasant Cults*. Shanghai, Kelly and Walsh, Ltd.

de Beauvoir, Simone. 1953. *The Second Sex*. New York, Alfred A. Knopf.

de Bie, Pierre. 1954. The Teaching of Sociology, Social Psychology and Social Anthropology. In: *The University Teaching of Social Sciences: Sociology, Social Psychology and Anthropology*. Paris, UNESCO.

de Burgh, W. G. 1947. *The Legacy of the Ancient World*. New and revised ed. Two vols. New York, The Macmillan Company.

Deevey, Edward S., and Flint, Richard Foster. 1957. Postglacial Hypsithermal Interval. *Science*, 125:182–184.

de Grange, McQuilkin. 1953. *The Nature and Elements of Sociology*. New Haven, Yale University Press.

Deihl, Joseph R. 1932. Kava and Kava Drinking. *Primitive Man*, 5:61–67.

de Jong, J. P. B. de Josselin. 1952. *Lévi-Strauss's Theory of Kinship and Marriage*. Mededelingen van het Rijksmuseum voor Volkenkunde, Leiden, No. 10.

Dennis, Norman, Henriques, Fernando, and Slaughter, Clifford. 1956. *Coal Is Our Life*. London, Eyre and Spottiswoode.

Desai, Akshaya R. 1954. *Social Background of Indian Nationalism*. Bombay, Popular Book Depot.

Deutsch, Karl W. 1953. *Nationalism and Social Communication: An Inquiry into the Foundations of Nationality*. New York, Technology Press of the Massachusetts Institute of Technology and John Wiley and Sons, Inc.

Deutsch, Karl W. 1954. *Political Community at the International Level*. Doubleday Short Studies in Political Science, No. 1.

Devereux, George. 1956a. Normal and Abnormal: The Key Problem of Psychiatric Anthropology. In: *Some Uses of Anthropology: Theoretical and Applied*. Washington, D.C., The Anthropological Society of Washington.

Devereux, George. 1956b. The Origin of Shamanistic Powers as Reflected in a Neurosis. *Revue Internationale d'Ethnopsychologie Normale et Pathologique*, 1:3–13.

Dice, Lee Raymond. 1955. *Man's Nature and Nature's Man*. Ann Arbor, University of Michigan Press.

Dickson, H. R. P. 1949. *The Arab of the Desert*. London, George Allen and Unwin.

Diringer, David. 1948. *The Alphabet*. New York, Philosophical Library.

Dittmer, Kunz. 1954. *Allgemeine Voelkerkunde: Formen und Entwicklung der Kultur*. Braunschweig, Friedr. Vieweg und Sohn.

Dixon, Roland B. 1928. *The Building of Cultures*. New York, Charles Scribner's Sons.

Dobzhansky, Theodosius. 1953. The Genetic Basis of Evolution. In: *Scientific American Reader*. New York, Simon and Schuster.

Dodd, Stuart Carter. 1947. *Systematic Social Science*. American University of Beirut, Publications of the Faculty of Arts and Science, Social Science Series, No. 16.

Dodson, Edward O. 1952. *A Textbook of Evolution*. Philadelphia, W. B. Saunders Co.

Dollard, John. 1937. *Caste and Class in a Southern Town*. New Haven, Yale University Press.

Doob, Leonard W. 1935. *Propaganda, Its Psychology and Technique*. New York, Henry Holt and Co.

Douglas, Mary. 1954. The Lele of Kasai. In: Forde, Daryll (ed.), *African Worlds: Studies in the Cosmological Ideas and Social Values of African Peoples*. London, Oxford University Press.

Dowling, J. W. 1946. Relative Archaism: A New Fallacy and Mr. Toynbee. *Journal of Philosophy*, 43:421–435.

Driver, G. R. 1954. *Semitic Writing from Pictograph to Alphabet*. Revised ed. London, Oxford University Press.

Driver, Harold E., Cooper, John M., Kirchhoff, Paul, Libby, Dorothy Rainier, Massey, William C., and Spier, Leslie. 1953. *Indian Tribes of North America*. International Journal of American Linguistics, Memoir 9.

Drucker, Philip. 1951. *The Northern and Central Nootkan Tribes*. Bureau of American Ethnology, Bulletin 144.

Drucker, Philip. 1955. *Indians of the Northwest Coast*. New York, McGraw-Hill Book Co., Inc.

Dubalen, Marie T. 1955. *The Worker Priests*. Student League for Industrial Democracy Research Tracts, No. 3, mimeographed.

Dube, S. C. 1951. *The Kamar*. Lucknow, The Universal Publishers, Ltd.

Dube, S. C. 1955. *Indian Village*. London, Routledge and Kegan Paul, Ltd.

Dube, S. C. 1956. *Some Problems of Communication in Rural Community Development*. Ithaca, Cornell University India Program, mimeographed.

Dubin, Robert. 1951. *Human Problems in Administration*. New York, Prentice-Hall.

Dubois, J. A. 1924. *Hindu Manners, Customs and Ceremonies*. Translated by Henry K. Beauchamp. Third ed. Oxford, Clarendon Press.

Dufferin, Harriet (Marchioness of Dufferin and Ava). 1890. *Our Viceregal Life in India, Selections from My Journal, 1884–1888*. Two vols. London, John Murray.

Dumas, Alexander. 1952. *The Three Musketeers*. Translated by Lord Sudley. Harmondsworth, Penguin Books.

Dunn, Leslie C. 1951. *Race and Biology*. Paris, UNESCO.

Dunn, Leslie C., and Dunn, Stephen P. 1957. The Jewish Community of Rome. *Scientific American*, 196:118–128.

Durkheim, Émile. 1915. *The Elementary Forms of the Religious Life*. Translated by Joseph Ward Swain. London, George Allen and Unwin, Ltd.

Durkheim, Émile. 1933. *On the Division of Labor in Society*. Translated and edited by George Simpson. New York, The Macmillan Company.

Durkheim, Émile. 1952. *Suicide: A Study in Sociology*. Translated by John A. Spaulding and George Simpson. London, Routledge and Kegan Paul.

Durrad, W. J. 1922. The Depopulation of Melanesia. In: Rivers, W. H. R. (ed.), *Essays on the Depopulation of Melanesia*. Cambridge, Cambridge University Press.

Easton, David. 1953. *The Political System: An Inquiry into the State of Political Science*. New York, Alfred A. Knopf.

Easton, David. 1956. Limits of the Equilibrium Model in Social Research. *Behavioral Science*, 1:96–104.

Eaton, Joseph W. 1952. Controlled Acculturation: A Survival Technique of the Hutterites. *American Sociological Review*, 17:331–340.

Edwards, I. E. S. 1947. *The Pyramids of Egypt*. Harmondsworth, Penguin Books.

Egerton, A. C. 1951. Civilization and the Use of Energy. In: *UNESCO Discussion Theme 1951: "Energy in the Service of Man."* Paper No. 1. Paris, UNESCO, offset printed.

Eggan, Fred R. 1955. The Cheyenne and Arapaho Kinship System. In: Eggan, Fred (ed.), *Social Anthropology of North American Tribes*. Enlarged ed. Chicago, University of Chicago Press.

Eichelberg, Gustav. 1950. Utilization of Energy. In: *UNESCO Discussion Theme 1951: "Energy in the Service of Man."* Paper No. 3. Paris, UNESCO, offset printed.

Eisenstadt, S. N. 1949. The Perception of Time and Space in a Situation of Culture-Contact. *Journal of the Royal Anthropological Institute*, 79:63–68.

Eisenstadt, S. N. 1954. African Age Groups, A Comparative Study. *Africa*, 24:100–113.

Eisenstadt, S. N. 1956. *From Generation to Generation: Age Groups and Social Structure*. London, Routledge and Kegan Paul.

Eliade, Mircea. 1951. *Le chamanisme et les techniques archaïques de l'extase*. Paris, Payot.

Eliot, T. S. 1934. *The Rock*. London, Faber and Faber, Ltd.

Elkin, A. P. 1951. Reaction and Interaction: A Food Gathering People and European Settlement in Australia. *American Anthropologist*, 53:164–186.

Elkin, A. P. 1954. The Australian Aborigines. Third ed. Sydney, Angus and Robertson.

Elwin, Verrier. 1947. *The Muria and Their Ghotul*. London, Oxford University Press.

Elwin, Verrier. 1955. *The Religion of an Indian Tribe*. Bombay, Oxford University Press.

Embree, John F. 1950. Thailand—A Loosely Structured Social System. *American Anthropologist*, 52:181–193.

Embree, John F., and Dotson, Lillian Ota. 1950. *Bibliography of the Peoples and Cultures of Mainland Southeast Asia*. New Haven, Yale University, Southeast Asia Studies.

Emiliani, Cesare. 1955. Pleistocene Temperatures. *Journal of Geology*, 63:538–578.

Emmanuel, Pierre. 1954. The End of France's Worker Priests. *The Listener*, 51:598–600.

Entwistle, William J. 1953. *Aspects of Language*. London, Faber and Faber.

Erasmus, Charles John. 1952. Changing Folk Beliefs and the Relativity of Empirical Knowledge. *Southwestern Journal of Anthropology*, 8:411–428.

Etkin, William. 1954. Social Behavior and the Evolution of Man's Mental Faculties. *The American Naturalist*, 88:129–142.

Evans-Pritchard, Edward Evan. 1937. *Witchcraft, Oracles and Magic Among the Azande*. Oxford, Clarendon Press.

Evans-Pritchard, Edward Evan. 1940. *The Nuer: A Description of the Modes of Livelihood and Political Institutions of a Nilotic People*. Oxford, Clarendon Press.

Evans-Pritchard, Edward Evan. 1951a. *Kinship and Marriage Among the Nuer*. Oxford, Clarendon Press.

Evans-Pritchard, Edward Evan. 1951b. *Social Anthropology*. London, Cohen and West, Ltd.

Evans-Pritchard, Edward Evan. 1956. *Nuer Religion*. Oxford, Clarendon Press.

Ewers, John C. 1955a. The Bear Cult Among the Assiniboin and Their Neighbors of the Northern Plains. *Southwestern Journal of Anthropology*, 11:1–14.

Ewers, John C. 1955b. *The Horse in Blackfoot Indian Culture, with Comparative Material from Other Western Tribes*. Bureau of American Ethnology, Bulletin 159.

Farquhar, John Nicol. 1929. *Modern Religious Movements in India*. London, Macmillan & Co., Ltd.

Farrington, Benjamin. 1953. *Greek Science*. One-vol. ed. Harmondsworth, Penguin Books.

Feldmesser, Robert A. 1953. The Persistence of Status Advantages in Soviet Russia. *American Journal of Sociology*, 59:19–27.

Fenton, William N. 1937. The Seneca Society of Faces. *The Scientific Monthly*, 44:215–238.

Fenton, William N. 1941a. *Iroquois Suicide: A Study in the Stability of Culture*. Bureau of American Ethnology, Bulletin 128, Paper No. 14.

Fenton, William N. 1941b. Masked Medicine Societies of the Iroquois. *Smithsonian Report for 1940*, pp. 397–430.

Fenton, William N. 1942. *Songs from the Iroquois Longhouse: Program Notes for an Album of American Indian Music for the Eastern Woodlands.* Smithsonian Institution, Publication No. 3691.

Fenton, William N. 1946. An Iroquois Condolence Council for Installing Cayuga Chiefs in 1945. *Journal of the Washington Academy of Sciences*, 36:110–127.

Festinger, Leon, Riecken, Henry W., and Schachter, Stanley. 1956. *When Prophecy Fails*. Minneapolis, University of Minnesota Press.

Firth, J. R. 1950. Personality and Language in Society. *Sociological Review*, 42:37–52.

Firth, Raymond. 1946. *Malay Fishermen*. London, Kegan Paul, Trench, Trubner and Co., Ltd.

Firth, Raymond. 1948. Religious Belief and Personal Adjustment. *Journal of the Royal Anthropological Institute*, 78:25–44.

Firth, Raymond. 1951. *Elements of Social Organization*. London, Watts and Co.

Firth, Raymond. 1952. Notes on the Social Structure of Some South-Eastern New Guinea Communities. Part II, Koita. *Man*, 52:86–88.

Fischer, J. L. 1955. Avunculocal Residence on Losap. *American Anthropologist*, 57:1025–1032.

Fiske, John. 1909. *The Meaning of Infancy*. Boston, Houghton Mifflin Co.

Fitzgerald, Charles Patrick. 1952. *Revolution in China*. London, Cresset Press.

Flannery, Regina. 1953. *The Gros Ventres of Montana*. Part 1, *Social Life*. The Catholic University of America, Anthropological Series, No. 15.

Fletcher, Alice C., and LaFlesche, Francis. 1911. *The Omaha Tribe*. Annual Reports of the Bureau of American Ethnology, No. 27.

Flexner, Abraham. 1930. *Universities, American, English, German*. New York, Oxford University Press.

Ford, Clellan S. 1945. *A Comparative Study of Human Reproduction*. Yale University Publications in Anthropology, No. 32.

Ford, Clellan S., and Beach, Frank A. 1951. *Patterns of Sexual Behavior*. New York, Harper & Brothers.

Forde, C. Daryll. 1949. *Habitat, Economy and Society*. Seventh ed. New York, E. P. Dutton and Co., Inc.

Forde, C. Daryll. 1950. Anthropology—The Victorian Synthesis and Modern Relativism. In: *Ideas and Beliefs of the Victorians*. London, Sylvan Press.

Fordham, Frieda. 1953. *An Introduction to Jung's Psychology*. Harmondsworth, Penguin Books.

Forster, Edward Morgan. 1927. *Aspects of the Novel*. New York, Harcourt, Brace and Co.

Fortes, Meyer. 1945. *The Dynamics of Clanship Among the Tallensi*. London, Oxford University Press.

Fortes, Meyer. 1949. *The Web of Kinship Among the Tallensi*. London, Oxford University Press.

Fortes, Meyer. 1954. A Demographic Field Study in Ashanti. In: Lorimer, Frank (ed.), *Culture and Human Fertility*. Paris, UNESCO.

Fortes, Meyer, and Evans-Pritchard, Edward Evan. 1940. *African Political Systems*. London, Oxford University Press.

Fortune, Reo F. 1932a. *Omaha Secret Societies*. Columbia University Contributions to Anthropology, No. 14.

Fortune, Reo F. 1932b. *Sorcerers of Dobu*. New York, E. P. Dutton and Co., Inc.

Fortune, Reo F. 1935. *Manus Religion*. Memoirs of the American Philosophical Society, No. 3.

Foster, George M. 1953. Confradía and Compadrazgo in Spain and South America. *Southwestern Journal of Anthropology*, 9:1–28.

Frank, Lawrence K. 1951. *Nature and Human Nature*. New Brunswick, Rutgers University Press.

Frankel, Sally Herbert. 1953. *The Economic Impact on Under-Developed Societies*. Oxford, Basil Blackwell.

Frankfort, Henri. 1948. *Ancient Egyptian Religion*. New York, Columbia University Press.

Frankfort, Henri. 1954. *The Art and Architecture of the Ancient Orient*. Harmondsworth, Penguin Books.

Frazer, James George. 1911. *The Golden Bough*. Vol. 1, *The Magic Art and the Evolution of Kings*. Third ed., two parts. London, Macmillan & Co., Ltd.

Frazer, James George. 1922. *The Golden Bough*. One-vol. abridged ed. New York, The Macmillan Company.

Frederiksen, Svend. 1952. Henrik Lund, A National Poet of Greenland. *Proceedings of the American Philosophical Society*, 96:653–659.

Freedman, L. Z., and Ferguson, V. M. 1950. The Question of "Painless Childbirth" in Primitive Cultures. *American Journal of Orthopsychiatry*, 20:363–372.

French, David H. 1948. *Factionalism in Isleta Pueblo*. Monographs of the American Ethnological Society, No. 14.

Freud, Sigmund. 1913. *The Interpretation of Dreams*. Translated by A. A. Brill. New York, The Macmillan Company.

Fried, Jacob. 1955. Forty Years of Change in a Hawaiian Homestead Community: Anahole. *Rural Sociology*, 20:51–57.

Friedrich, Carl J. 1954. *Totalitarianism*. Cambridge, Mass., Harvard University Press.

Fromm, Ehrich. 1950. *Psychoanalysis and Religion*. New Haven, Yale University Press.

Fuchs, Stephen. 1950. *The Children of Hari*. Vienna, Verlag Herold.

Fyzee, Asaf A. A. 1949. *Outlines of Muhammadan Law*. Calcutta, Oxford University Press.

Gamble, J. I. 1952. Changing Patterns in Kiowa Indian Dances. In: Tax, Sol (ed.), *Acculturation in the Americas*. Proceedings and Selected Papers of the XXIXth International Congress of Americanists.

Gandhi, Mohandas Karamchand, Mahatma. 1940. *An Autobiography or the Story of My Experiments with Truth*. Second ed. Translated by Mahadev Desai. Ahmedabad, Navajivan Publishing House.

Gardner, Burleigh B. 1946. The Factory as a Social System. In: Whyte, W. F. (ed.), *Industry and Society*. New York, McGraw-Hill Book Co., Inc.

Gardner, Burleigh B., and Moore, David G. 1950. *Human Relations in Industry*. Chicago, Richard D. Irwin, Inc.

Garn, Stanley M. 1957. Race and Evolution. *American Anthropologist*, 59:218–224.

Garrod, Dorothy. 1949. Finding the Earliest Realistic Portrait in the History of Man. *Illustrated London News*, 215:i–iv, 91–92.

Garrod, Dorothy, and St. Mathuring, S. 1952. The Master Sculptors of 12,000 Years Ago Revealed. *Illustrated London News*, 220:454–457.

Garth, Thomas R. 1952. The Middle Columbia Cremation Complex. *American Antiquity*, 13:40–56.

Gast, Marceau. 1954. A Class in the Hoggar Mountains. *Fundamental and Adult Education*, 6:71–75.

Gaster, Theodor H. 1955. *The Holy and the Profane*. New York, William Sloane Associates.

Geddes, W. R. 1954. *The Land Dayaks of Sarawak*. Colonial Research Studies, No. 14.

Gerard, R. W. 1957. Units and Concepts of Biology. *Science*, 125:429–433.

Gerschenkron, Alexander. 1952. Economic Backwardness in Historical Perspective. In: Hoselitz, B. F. (ed.), *The Progress of Underdeveloped Areas*. Chicago, University of Chicago Press.

Gerth, Hans, and Mills, C. Wright. 1953. *Character and Social Structure*. New York, Harcourt, Brace and Co.

Ghose, Aurobindo, Sri (translator). 1953. *Eight Upanishads*. Pondicherry, Sri Aurobindo Ashram.

Ghurye, G. S. 1952. *Caste and Class in India*. New York, Philosophical Library.

Giedion, Siegfried. 1948. *Mechanization Takes Command*. New York, Oxford University Press.

Gilfillan, Colum S. 1935. *The Sociology of Invention*. Chicago, Follett Publishing Co.

Gillin, John. 1948a. Tribes of the Guianas. In: Steward, Julian H. (ed.), *Handbook of South American Indians*. Vol. 3, *The Tropical Forest Tribes*. Bureau of American Ethnology, Bulletin 143.

Gillin, John. 1948b. *The Ways of Men: An Introduction to Anthropology*. New York, Appleton-Century-Crofts, Inc.

Gillin, John. 1951. *The Culture of Security in San Carlos*. Middle American Research Institute, The Tulane University of Louisiana, Publication No. 16.

Gillin, John. 1952. Ethos and Cultural Aspects of Personality. In: Tax, Sol (ed.), *Heritage of Conquest*. Glencoe, Ill., The Free Press.

Gillin, John, and Murphy, E. J. 1950–51. Notes on Southern Culture Patterns. *Social Forces*, 29:422–432.

Gist, Noel P. 1954. Caste Differentials in South India. *American Sociological Review*, 19:126–137.

Gladwin, Thomas, and Sarason, Seymour B. 1953. *Truk: Man in Paradise*. Viking Fund Publications in Anthropology, No. 20.

Gleason, H. A., Jr. 1955. *An Introduction to Descriptive Linguistics*. New York, Henry Holt and Co.

Gluckman, Max. 1949. *Malinowski's Sociological Theories*. The Rhodes-Livingstone Papers, No. 16.

Gluckman, Max. 1951. The Lozi of Barotseland in North-Western Rhodesia. In: Colson, Elizabeth, and Gluckman, Max (eds.), *Seven Tribes of British Central Africa*. London, Oxford University Press.

Gluckman, Max. 1954a. Political Institutions. In: *The Institutions of Primitive Society*. Oxford, Basil Blackwell.

Gluckman, Max. 1954b. Succession and Civil War Among the Bemba: An Exercise in Anthropological Theory. *Human Problems in British Central Africa*, 16:6–25.

Gluckman, Max. 1955a. *Custom and Conflict in Africa*. Oxford, Basil Blackwell.

Gluckman, Max. 1955b. Review of E. A. Hoebel, "The Law of Primitive Man." *Man*, 55:93–95.

Goffman, Erving. 1956. *The Presentation of Self in Everyday Life*. University of Edinburgh, Social Sciences Research Council, Monograph No. 2.

Gokhale, B. G. 1952. *Ancient India, History and Culture*. Bombay, Asia Publishing House.

Goldenweiser, Alexander. 1937. *Anthropology*. New York, Appleton-Century-Crofts.

Goldman, Irving. 1955. Status Rivalry and Cultural Evolution in Polynesia. *American Anthropologist*, 57:680–697.

Goldschmidt, Walter. 1950. Social Class in America—A Critical Review. *American Anthropologist*, 52:483–498.

Goldstein, Marcus S. 1954. Longevity and Health Status of Whites and Nonwhites in the United States. *Journal of the National Medical Association*, 46:83–104.

Gomme, A. W. 1935. The Greeks. In: Eyre, Edward (ed.), *European Civilization, Its Origin and Development*. Vol. 1, *Prehistoric Man and Earliest Known Societies*. London, Oxford University Press.

Good, A. I. 1942. Drum Talk Is the African's Wireless. *Natural History*, 50:69–74.

Goodenough, Ward H. 1951. *Property, Kin, and Community on Truk*. Yale University Publications in Anthropology, No. 46.

Goodenough, Ward H. 1956. Residence Rules. *Southwestern Journal of Anthropology*, 12:22–37.

Goodwin, A. J. H. 1953. *Method in Prehistory*. Second ed. Cape Town, South African Archaeological Society.

Gorer, Geoffrey. 1948. *The American People*. New York, W. W. Norton and Co., Inc.

Gorer, Geoffrey. 1953. National Character: Theory and Practice. In: Mead, Margaret, and Métraux, Rhoda (eds.), *The Study of Culture at a Distance*. Chicago, University of Chicago Press.

Gorer, Geoffrey. 1955. *Exploring English Character*. Complete ed. London, The Cresset Press.

Goswami, M. C. 1954. The Social Structure of an Assamese Village. *Man*, 54:27–28.

Gouldner, A. W. 1954. *Patterns of Industrial Bureaucracy*. Glencoe, Ill., The Free Press.

Gouldner, A. W. 1956a. Explorations in Applied Social Science. *Social Problems*, 3:169–181.

Gouldner, A. W. 1956b. Some Observations on Systematic Theory, 1945–1955. In: Zetterberg, Hans L. (ed.), *Sociology in the United States of America*. Paris, UNESCO.

Great Britain. Secretary of State for Commonwealth Relations. 1951. *Basutoland Medicine Murder*. London, H.M. Stationery Office.

Greenberg, Joseph H. 1953. Historical Linguistics and Unwritten Languages. In: Kroeber, A. L. (ed.), *Anthropology Today*. Chicago, University of Chicago Press.

Greenberg, Joseph H. 1954. Studies in African Linguistic Classification: VIII. Further Remarks on Method: Revisions and Corrections. *Southwestern Journal of Anthropology*, 10:405–415.

Greenberg, Joseph H. n.d. "Violence Texts." Unpublished paper, mimeographed.

Greenman, Emerson F. 1945. Material Culture and the Organism. *American Anthropologist*, 47:211–229.

Gries, Caroline G. 1944. *Foreign Weights and Measures with Factors for Conversion to United States Units*. Washington, U.S. Department of Agriculture, Office of Foreign Agricultural Relations, mimeographed.

Griffiths, Percival. 1952. *The British Impact on India*. London, Macdonald.

Grinnell, George Bird. 1923. *The Cheyenne Indians*. Two vols. New Haven, Yale University Press.

Grinsell, Leslie V. 1955. Death and the After-Life. *Nature*, 176:809–812.

Grodzins, Morton. 1956. *The Loyal and the Disloyal: Social Boundaries of Patriotism and Treason*. Chicago, University of Chicago Press.

Grosse, Ernst. 1896. *Formen der Familie und die Formen der Wirtschaft*. Freiburg i/B, J. C. B. Mohr.

Gruber, Jacob W. 1948. Irrigation and Land Use in Ancient Mesopotamia. *Agricultural History*, 22:69–77.

Guyer, Michael F. 1937. *Animal Biology*. Rev. ed. New York, Harper & Brothers.

Hagood, Margaret J. 1939. *Mothers of the South: Portraiture of the White Tenant Farm Woman*. Chapel Hill, University of North Carolina Press.

Hagood, Margaret J., and Price, Daniel O. 1952. *Statistics for Sociologists*. Rev. ed. New York, Henry Holt and Co.

Haile, Berard. 1947. *Starlore Among the Navajo*. Sante Fe, Museum of Navajo Ceremonial Art.

Halbwachs, M. 1930. *Les causes du suicide*. Paris, F. Alcan.

Hall, Edward T., Jr., and Trager, George L. 1953a. *The Analysis of Culture*. Prepublication edition for criticism and discussion; reproduced for the authors with the assistance of the American Council of Learned Societies. Washington, offset printed.

Hall, Edward T., Jr., and Trager, George L. 1953b. *Human Nature at Home and Abroad*. Washington, Foreign Service Institute, Department of State.

Hall, H. Duncan. 1948. *Mandates, Dependencies and Trusteeship*. Washington, Carnegie Endowment for International Peace.

Hall, Robert A., Jr. 1950. *Leave Your Language Alone!* Ithaca, Linguistica.

Hall, Robert A., Jr. 1955a. *Hands Off Pidgin English*. Sydney, Publications Pty., Ltd.

Hall, Robert A., Jr. 1955b. Innovations in Melanesian Pidgin (Neo-Melanesian). *Oceania*, 26:91–109.

Hallowell, A. Irving. 1926. Bear Ceremonialism in the Northern Hemisphere. *American Anthropologist*, 28:1–175.

Hallowell, A. Irving. 1938. The Incidence, Character, and Decline of Polygyny Among the Lake Winnipeg Cree and Saulteaux. *American Anthropologist*, 40:235–256.

Hallowell, A. Irving. 1942. *The Role of Conjuring in Saulteaux Society*. Publications of the Philadelphia Anthropological Society, 2:1–96.

Hallowell, A. Irving. 1945. The Rorschach Technique in the Study of Personality and Culture. *American Anthropologist*, 47:195–210.

Hallowell, A. Irving. 1949. The Size of Algonkian Hunting Territories: A Function of Adjustment. *American Anthropologist*, 51:34–45.

Hamamsy, Laila Shukry. 1957. The Role of Women in a Changing Navaho Society. *American Anthropologist*, 59:101–111.

Hamilton, J. R. C. 1949. The Vikings in the Shetlands. *Illustrated London News*, 215:859–863.

Handlin, Oscar. 1955. *The Positive Contribution by Immigrants*. Paris, UNESCO.

Hanks, Lucien M., Jr., and Hanks, Jane Richardson. 1950. *Tribe Under Trust*. Toronto, University of Toronto Press.

Haring, Douglas G. (ed.). 1956. *Personal Character and Cultural Milieu*. Third rev. ed. Syracuse, Syracuse University Press.

Harris, Jack S. 1940. The White Knife Shoshoni of Nevada. In: Linton, Ralph (ed.), *Acculturation in Seven American Indian Tribes*. New York, Appleton-Century-Crofts.

Harrison, H. S. 1954. Discovery, Invention, and Duffusion. In: Singer, Charles, Holmyard, E. J., and Hall, A. R. (eds.), *A History of Technology.* Vol. 1, *From Early Times to Fall of Ancient Empires.* Oxford, Clarendon Press.

Hart, Hornell. 1948. The Logistic Growth of Political Areas. *Social Forces,* 26:396–408.

Hartland, E. S. 1924. *Primitive Law.* London, Methuen and Co.

Hatch, William J. 1928. *The Land Pirates of India.* Philadelphia, J. B. Lippincott.

Havighurst, Robert J. 1953. *Human Development and Education.* New York, Longmans, Green and Co.

Havighurst, Robert J., and Neugarten, Bernice L. 1955. *American Indian and White Children.* Chicago, University of Chicago Press.

Hawkes, Charles Francis Christopher. 1940. *The Prehistoric Foundations of Europe to the Mycenean Age.* London, Methuen and Co.

Hawkes, Charles Francis Christopher. 1954. Archeological Theory and Method: Some Suggestions from the Old World. *American Anthropologist,* 56:155–168.

Hawthorn, Harry B. (ed.). 1955. *The Doukhobors of British Columbia.* Vancouver, The University of British Columbia Press.

Hazard, Paul. 1953. *The European Mind, The Critical Years 1680–1715.* New Haven, Yale University Press.

Heath, Dwight B. 1955. Sexual Division of Labor and Cross-Cultural Research. Unpublished paper read at annual meeting of the American Anthropological Association, Boston, Nov. 18.

Heidel, Alexander. 1946. *The Gilgamesh Epic and Old Testament Parallels.* Chicago, University of Chicago Press.

Heizer, Robert F. 1944. The Use of the Enema Among the Aboriginal American Indians. *Ciba Symposia,* 5:1686–1693.

Heizer, Robert F. 1953. Long-Range Dating in Archeology. In: Kroeber, A. L. (ed.), *Anthropology Today.* Chicago, University of Chicago Press.

Hencken, Hugh. 1955. *Indo-European Languages and Archeology.* Memoirs of the American Anthropological Association, No. 84.

Henry, Jules. 1941. *Jungle People.* New York, J. J. Augustin.

Henry, Jules. 1951. The Economics of Pilagá Food Distribution. *American Anthropologist,* 53:187–219.

Henry, Jules, and Spiro, Melford E. 1953. Psychological Techniques: Projective Tests in Field Work. In: Kroeber, A. L. (ed.), *Anthropology Today.* Chicago, University of Chicago Press.

Heriot, Angus. 1956. *The Castrati in Opera.* London, Secker and Warburg.

Herman, Mary W. 1956. The Social Aspect of Huron Property. *American Anthropologist,* 58:1044–1058.

Hermanns, P. M. 1953. Polyandrie in Tibet. *Anthropos,* 48:637–641.

Herskovits, Melville J. 1924. A Preliminary Consideration of the Culture Areas of Africa. *American Anthropologist,* 26:50–63.

Herskovits, Melville J. 1926. The Cattle Complex in East Africa. *American Anthropologist*, 28:230–272, 361–388, 494–528, 633–664.

Herskovits, Melville J. 1941a. *The Myth of the Negro Past*. New York, Harper & Brothers.

Herskovits, Melville J. 1941b. Some Comments on the Study of Culture Contact. *American Anthropologist*, 43:1–10.

Herskovits, Melville J. 1948. *Man and His Works*. New York, Alfred A. Knopf.

Herskovits, Melville J. 1953. *Franz Boas: The Science of Man in the Making*. New York, Charles Scribner's Sons.

Hesse, Hermann. 1929. *Steppenwolf*. Translated by Basil Creighton. New York, Henry Holt and Co.

Hewes, Gordon W. 1948. The Rubric "Fishing and Fisheries." *American Anthropologist*, 50:238–246.

Hiroa, Te Rangi (Buck, Peter H.). 1934. *Mangaian Society*. B. P. Bishop Museum, Bulletin 122.

Hiroa, Te Rangi (Buck, Peter H.). 1945. *An Introduction to Polynesian Anthropology*. Bernice P. Bishop Museum, Bulletin 187.

Hobhouse, Leonard T. 1924. *Social Development*. London, George Allen and Unwin, Ltd.

Hobhouse, Leonard T. 1956. The Simplest Peoples. Part I, A Comparative Study. Part II, Peace and Order Among the Simplest Peoples. *British Journal of Sociology*, 7:77–119.

Hobhouse, Leonard T., Wheeler, G. C., and Ginsberg, M. 1915. *The Material Culture and Social Institutions of the Simpler Peoples*. London, Chapman and Hall, Ltd.

Hocart, Arthur Maurice. 1950. *Caste: A Comparative Study*. London, Methuen and Co., Ltd.

Hodus, Lewis. 1929. *Folkways in China*. London, Arthur Probsthain.

Hoebel, E. Adamson. 1949. *Man in the Primitive World*. New York, McGraw-Hill Book Co., Inc.

Hoebel, E. Adamson. 1954. *The Law of Primitive Man: A Study in Comparative Legal Dynamics*. Cambridge, Mass., Harvard University Press.

Hogbin, Herbert Ian. 1938. Social Reaction to Crime: Law and Morals in the Schouten Islands, New Guinea. *Journal of the Royal Anthropological Institute*, 68:223–262.

Hohenthal, W. D., and McCorkle, Thomas. 1955. The Problem of Aboriginal Persistence. *Southwestern Journal of Anthropology*, 11:288–300.

Hoijer, Harry. 1946a. Chiricahua Apache. In: Hoijer, H., *et al.*, *Linguistic Structures of Native America*. Viking Fund Publications in Anthropology, No. 6.

Hoijer, Harry. 1946b. Linguistic History. In: *Human Origins: An Introductory General Course in Anthropology. Selected Readings, Series II*. Second ed. Chicago, University of Chicago Bookstore.

Hoijer, Harry. 1956. Language and Writing. In: Shapiro, Harry L. (ed.), *Man, Culture, and Society*. New York, Oxford University Press.

Hollingshead, August B. 1949. *Elmtown's Youth*. New York, John Wiley and Sons, Inc.

Holmberg, Allan R. 1950. *Nomads of the Long Bow*. Washington, Smithsonian Institution, Institute of Social Anthropology, Publication No. 10.

Homans, G. C. 1941. Anxiety and Ritual. *American Anthropologist*, 43: 164–172.

Homans, G. C. 1950. *The Human Group*. New York, Harcourt, Brace and Co.

Homans, G. C., and Schneider, David M. 1955. *Marriage, Authority, and Final Causes*. Glencoe, Ill., The Free Press.

Honigmann, John J. 1947. Witch-Fear in Post-Contact Kaska Society. *American Anthropologist*, 49:222–243.

Honigmann, John J. 1949a. *Culture and Ethos of Kaska Society*. Yale University Publications in Anthropology, No. 40.

Honigmann, John J. 1949b. Incentives to Work in a Canadian Indian Community. *Human Organization*, 8:23–28.

Honigmann, John J. 1952. Intercultural Relations at Great Whale River. *American Anthropologist*, 54:510–522.

Honigmann, John J. 1953a. European and Other Tales from the Western Woods Cree. *Journal of American Folklore*, 66:309–331.

Honigmann, John J. 1953b. *Information for Pakistan: Report of Research on Intercultural Communication Through Films*. Chapel Hill, Institute for Research in Social Science, University of North Carolina, mimeographed.

Honigmann, John J. (ed.). 1953c. *Theory of Ritual, A Book of Readings and Cases*. Chapel Hill, University of North Carolina Bookstore, mimeographed.

Honigmann, John J. 1954a. An Anthropological Approach to Sex. *Social Problems*, 2:7–16.

Honigmann, John J. 1954b. *Culture and Personality*. New York, Harper & Brothers.

Honigmann, John J. 1954c. *The Kaska Indians, An Ethnographic Reconstruction*. Yale University Publications in Anthropology, No. 51.

Honigmann, John J. [1954d.] *Some Patterns of Bomb Squadron Culture with Special Reference to Airmen*. Chapel Hill, Air Force Base Project, Institute for Research in Social Science, University of North Carolina, Technical Report No. 16, mimeographed.

Honigmann, John J. 1955. Radical Opposition in National Culture: A Case Study. *Davidson Journal of Anthropology*, 1:169–180.

Honigmann, John J. 1956a. The Attawapiskat Swampy Cree: An Ethnographic Reconstruction. *Anthropological Papers of the University of Alaska*, 5:23–82.

Honigmann, John J. 1956b. Culture and the Courts: A New Field for Applied Anthropology. *Social Problems*, 3:154–160.

Honigmann, John J. 1956c. Intensional Orientation and National Unity: A Case Study from Pakistan. *ETC: A Review of General Semantics*, 13:108–115.

Honigmann, John J. 1956d. Notes on Sarsi Kin Behavior. *Anthropologica*, 2:17–38.

Honigmann, John J. 1957a. Interpersonal Relations and Ideology in a Northern Canadian Community. *Social Forces*, 35:365–370.

Honigmann, John J. 1957b. Woman in West Pakistan. In: Maron, Stanley (ed.), *Pakistan: Society and Culture*. New Haven, Human Relations Area Files.

Honigmann, John J., and Carrera, Richard. 1957. *Some Themes in Pakistan National Culture*. Studies in Pakistan National Culture, No. 4. Chapel Hill, Institute for Research in Social Science, University of North Carolina, mimeographed.

Hooke, Samuel Henry. 1953. Babylonian and Assyrian Religion. London, Hutchinson's University Library.

Hooton, Earnest A. 1939. *Crime and the Man*. Cambridge, Mass., Harvard University Press.

Hooton, Earnest A. 1942. *Man's Poor Relations*. Garden City, Doubleday and Co., Inc.

Hooton, Earnest A. 1947. *Up from the Ape*. Revised ed. New York, The Macmillan Company.

Hornell, James. 1950. *Fishing in Many Waters*. Cambridge, Cambridge University Press.

Howells, William W. 1945. *Mankind So Far*. Garden City, Doubleday and Co., Inc.

Hsu, Francis L. K. 1953. *Americans and Chinese*. New York, Henry Schuman.

Hudson, Alfred E., and Bacon, Elizabeth. 1941. Social Control and the Individual in Eastern Hazara Culture. In: Spier, L., Hallowell, A. I., and Newman, S. S. (eds.), *Language, Culture, and Personality, Essays in Memory of Edward Sapir*. Menasha, George Banta Publishing Co.

Hueper, W. C. 1948. *Environmental and Occupational Cancer*. Public Health Reports, Supplement 209.

Hughes, Edward. 1952. *North Country Life in the Eighteenth Century*. London, Oxford University Press.

Hughes, Ernest Richard (ed. and trans.). 1942. *Chinese Philosophy in Classical Times*. London, J. M. Dent and Sons, Ltd.

Hughes, Graham. 1956. What Makes Law? *The Listener*, 56:659, 663, 665, 706–707, 711.

Hultkrantz, Ake. 1953. *Conceptions of the Soul Among North American Indians*. The Ethnographical Museum of Sweden, Monograph Series, Publication No. 1.

Hume, David. 1911. *A Treatise of Human Nature*. Two vols. London, J. M. Dent and Sons, Ltd.

Humphrey, Norman D. 1941. A Characterization of Certain Plains Associations. *American Anthropologist*, 43:428–436.

Hunter, C. Bruce. 1956. *Tribal Map of Negro Africa*. New York, The American Museum of Natural History.

Hunter, Monica. 1936. *Reaction to Conquest: Effects of Contact with Europeans on the Pondo of South Africa*. London, Oxford University Press.

Huntingford, George Wynn Brereton. 1950. *Nandi Work and Culture.* Colonial Research Studies, No. 4.

Hurlburt, W. C. 1932. Prosperity, Depression, and the Suicide Rate. *American Journal of Sociology,* 37:715–719.

Hutton, Graham. 1954. Britain's Bloodless Revolution. *The Listener, 51:* 559, 579.

Huxley, Aldous. 1932. *Brave New World.* New York, Doubleday and Co., Inc.

Huxley, Julian. 1941. *Man Stands Alone.* New York, Harper & Brothers.

Huxley, Julian, Haddon, A. C., and Carr-Saunders, A. M. 1936. *We Europeans.* New York, Harper & Brothers.

Hyman, Herbert. 1955. *Survey Design and Analysis.* Glencoe, Ill., The Free Press.

Ikbāl 'Alī Shāh, Sirdar. [1938.] *Modern Afghanistan.* London, Sampson Low, Marston and Co., Ltd.

Ingrams, William Harold. 1952. *Hong Kong.* London, H. M. Stationery Office.

International Institute of Differing Civilizations. Record and Proceedings, 28th Meeting. 1953. *Programmes and Plans for Rural Development in Tropical and Subtropical Countries.* Brussels, International Institute of Differing Civilizations.

International Labour Office. 1953. *Indigenous Peoples.* Geneva, International Labour Office.

Iyer, L. K. Anantha Krishna. 1909. *The Cochin Tribes and Castes.* Madras, Higginbotham and Co.

Jacobs, Melville, and Stern, B. J. 1947. *Outline of Anthropology.* New York, Barnes and Noble, Inc.

Jaques, Elliott. 1951. *The Changing Culture of a Factory.* London, Tavistock Publications.

Jaspan, M. A. 1953. A Sociological Case Study: Communal Hostility to Imposed Social Change in South Africa. In: Ruopp, Phillips (ed.), *Approaches to Community Development.* The Hague, W. Van Hoeve, Ltd.

Jeffers, Robinson. 1932. *Thurso's Landing and Other Poems.* New York, Liveright, Inc.

Jelliffe, D. B. 1955. *Infant Nutrition in the Subtropics and Tropics.* Geneva, World Health Organization.

Jenness, Diamond. 1922. *The Life of the Copper Eskimos.* Report of the Canadian Arctic Expedition, 1913–18, Vol. 12, Part a.

Jenness, Diamond. 1935. *The Ojibwa Indians of Parry Island. Their Social and Religious Life.* Bulletin of the Canadian Department of Mines, National Museum of Canada, No. 78.

Jennings, Ivor. 1954. *The Queen's Government.* Harmondsworth, Penguin Books.

Johansen, J. Prytz. 1954. *The Maori and His Religion in Its Non-Ritualistic Aspects.* Kobenhavn, I Kommission Hos Ejnar Munksgaard.

Johnson, Frederick. 1951. *Radiocarbon Dating.* Memoirs of the Society for American Archaeology, No. 8.

Jones, J. A. 1955. *The Sun Dance of the Northern Ute*. Bureau of American Ethnology, Bulletin 157, Paper No. 47.

Jones, V. R., and Jones, L. Bevan. 1941. *Woman in Islām*. Lucknow, The Lucknow Publishing House.

Jones, William. 1905. The Algonkin Manitu. *Journal of American Folklore*, 18:183–190.

Jung, Carl G. 1953. The Psychology of the Unconscious. In: Jung, Carl G., *Two Essays on Analytical Psychology*. Translated by R. F. C. Hull. New York, Pantheon Books.

Kaberry, Phyllis M. 1939. *Aboriginal Woman, Sacred and Profane*. Philadelphia, Blakiston Co.

Kahn, Fritz. 1954. *Design of the Universe*. New York, Crown Publishers, Inc.

Kaplan, Bernice A. 1954. Environment and Human Plasticity. *American Anthropologist*, 56:780–800.

Kardiner, Abram. 1939. *The Individual and His Society: The Psychodynamics of Primitive Social Organization*. New York, Columbia University Press.

Kardiner, Abram. 1945. *The Psychological Frontiers of Society*. New York, Columbia University Press.

Karrer, P. 1955. Curare Alkaloids. *Nature*, 176:277–280.

Karsten, Rafael. 1935. *The Head-Hunters of Western Amazonas: The Life and Culture of the Jibaro Indians of Eastern Ecuador and Peru*. Societas Scientiarum Fennica: Commentationes Humanarum Litterarum, Vol. 7, No. 1.

Katz, Daniel. 1953. Field Studies. In: Festinger, Leon, and Katz, Daniel (eds.), *Research Methods in the Behavioral Sciences*. New York, The Dryden Press.

Keith, Arthur. 1929. *The Antiquity of Man*. Second ed., two vols. London, Williams and Norgate, Ltd.

Kennan, George F. 1953. The Right to Differ. *The Listener*, 50:93–94.

Kennedy, Raymond. 1943. *Islands and Peoples of the Indies*. Smithsonian Institution, War Background Studies, No. 14.

Kennedy, Raymond. 1945. *Bibliography of Indonesian Peoples and Cultures*. Yale Anthropological Studies, No. 4.

Kenyon, Kathleen M. 1952. *Beginnings in Archaeology*. New York, Frederick A. Praeger.

Keur, John Y., and Keur, Dorothy L. 1955. *The Deeply Rooted: A Study of a Drents Community in the Netherlands*. Monographs of the American Ethnological Society, No. 25.

Kimball, Solon T. 1955. Problems of Studying American Culture. *American Anthropologist*, 57:1131–1142.

Kinsey, A. C., Pomeroy, W. B., and Martin, C. E. 1948. *Sexual Behavior in the Human Male*. Philadelphia, W. B. Saunders Co.

Kinsey, A. C., Pomeroy, W. B., Martin, C. E., and Gebhard, P. H. 1953. *Sexual Behavior in the Human Female*. Philadelphia, W. B. Saunders Co.

Klimek, Stanislaw. 1935. *Culture Element Distributions*: I. *The Structure of California Indian Culture*. University of California Publications in American Archaeology and Ethnology, Vol. 37, No. 1.

Klimm, Lester E. 1956. Man's Ports and Channels. In: Thomas, William L., Jr. (ed.), *Man's Role in Changing the Face of the Earth*. Chicago, University of Chicago Press.

Klineberg, Otto. 1935. *Race Differences*. New York, Harper & Brothers.

Kluckhohn, Clyde. 1944. *Navaho Witchcraft*. Papers of the Peabody Museum of American Archaeology and Ethnology, Harvard University, Vol. 22, No. 2.

Kluckhohn, Clyde. 1948. Sex as an Anthropologist Views It. In: Deutsch, Albert (ed.), *Sex Habits of American Men*. New York, Prentice-Hall.

Kluckhohn, Clyde. 1949a. *Mirror for Man*. New York, Whittlesey House.

Kluckhohn, Clyde. 1949b. The Philosophy of the Navaho Indians. In: Northrop, F. S. C. (ed.), *Ideological Differences and World Order*. New Haven, Yale University Press.

Kluckhohn, Clyde. 1953. Universal Categories of Culture. In: Kroeber, A. L. (ed.), *Anthropology Today*. Chicago, University of Chicago Press.

Kluckhohn, Clyde, and Leighton, Dorothea. 1946. *The Navaho*. Cambridge, Mass., Harvard University Press.

Kluckhohn, Clyde, and others. 1952. Values and Value-Orientation in the Theory of Action. In: Parsons, Talcott, and Shills, Edward A. (eds.), *Toward a General Theory of Action*. Cambridge, Mass., Harvard University Press.

Kluckhohn, Florence R. 1950. Dominant and Substitute Profiles of Cultural Orientations: Their Significance for the Analysis of Social Stratification. *Social Forces*, 28:376–393.

Kneller, George F. 1955. *Higher Learning in Britain*. Berkeley, University of California Press.

Knox, R. A. 1955. Survival After Death. *The Listener*, 54:1043–1044.

Koebben, André J. 1954. L'héritage chez les Agni: L'influence de l'économie de profit. *Africa*, 24:359–363.

Kollmorgen, Walter. 1942. *Culture of a Contemporary Rural Community, The Old Order Amish of Lancaster County, Pennsylvania*. U.S. Department of Agriculture, Bureau of Agricultural Economics, Rural Life Studies, No. 4.

Kossoris, Max D. 1953. Workmen's Compensation Laws. I. An Appraisal. *Monthly Labor Review of the U.S. Bureau of Labor Statistics*, 76:359–366.

Krader, Lawrence. 1955. Ecology of Central Asian Pastoralism. *Southwestern Journal of Anthropology*, 11:301–326.

Kraemer, Augustin Friedrich. 1937. *Zentral Karolinen*, Part I. *Lamotrek Gruppe, Olei, Feis*. Ergebnisse der Suedsee-Expedition 1908–1910, Vol. 10, Pt. 1.

Kramer, Samuel Noah. 1955. *From the Tablets of Sumer*. Indian Hills, Colo., The Falcon's Wing Press.

Krause, F. 1924. *Wirtschaftsleben der Voelker*. Breslau, F. Hirt.

Krickeberg, Walter. 1939. The Indian Sweat Bath. *Ciba Symposia*, 1:19–25.

Krieger, Herbert W. 1943. *Island Peoples of the Western Pacific: Micronesia and Melanesia.* Smithsonian Institution, War Background Studies, No. 16.

Krige, E. J., and Krige, J. D. 1943. *The Realm of a Rain-Queen.* London, Oxford University Press.

Krige, J. D., and Krige, E. J. 1954. The Lovedu of the Transvaal. In: Forde, Daryll (ed.), *African Worlds: Studies in the Cosmological Ideas and Social Values of African Peoples.* London, Oxford University Press.

Kroeber, Alfred Louis. 1927. Disposal of the Dead. *American Anthropologist,* 29:308–315.

Kroeber, Alfred Louis. 1931. The Culture-Area and Age-Area Concepts of Clark Wissler. In: Rice, S. A. (ed.), *Methods in Social Science—A Case Book.* Chicago, University of Chicago Press.

Kroeber, Alfred Louis. 1936a. *Culture Element Distributions: III. Area and Climax.* University of California Publications in American Archaeology and Ethnology, 37:101–116.

Kroeber, Alfred Louis. 1936b. So-called Social Science. *Journal of Social Philosophy,* 1:317–340.

Kroeber, Alfred Louis. 1939. *Cultural and Natural Areas of Native North America.* University of California Publications in American Archaeology and Ethnology, Vol. 38.

Kroeber, Alfred Louis. 1940. Stimulus Diffusion. *American Anthropologist,* 42:1–20.

Kroeber, Alfred Louis. 1944. Configurations of Culture Growth. Berkeley, University of California Press.

Kroeber, Alfred Louis. 1945. The Ancient *Oikumenê* as an Historic Culture Aggregate. *Journal of the Royal Anthropological Institute,* 75:9–20.

Kroeber, Alfred Louis. 1948. *Anthropology.* New ed., revised. New York, Harcourt, Brace and Co.

Kroeber, Alfred Louis. 1955a. History of Anthropological Thought. In: *Yearbook of Anthropology 1955.* New York, Wenner-Gren Foundation for Anthropological Research.

Kroeber, Alfred Louis. 1955b. Linguistic Time Depth Results so Far and Their Meaning. *International Journal of American Linguistics,* 21:91–104.

Kroeber, Alfred Louis, and Kluckhohn, Clyde. 1952. *Culture: A Critical Review of Concepts and Definitions.* Papers of the Peabody Museum of American Archaeology and Ethnology, Harvard University, Vol. 47, No. 1.

Krogman, Wilton M. 1946. The Races of Mankind. In: *Human Origins: An Introductory General Course in Anthropology. Selected Readings, Series II.* Second ed. Chicago, University of Chicago Bookstore.

Kronenberger, Louis. 1954. *Company Manners.* Indianapolis, Bobbs-Merrill Co., Inc.

Kuper, Hilda. 1947. *An African Aristocracy.* London, Oxford University Press.

LaBarre, Weston. 1938. *The Peyote Cult.* Yale University Publications in Anthropology, No. 19.

LaBarre, Weston. 1954. *The Human Animal*. Chicago, University of Chicago Press.

Lafitte, François. 1956. Social Aims of the Contemporary State. In: Pryce-Jones, Alan (ed.), *The New Outline of Modern Knowledge*. London, Victor Gollancz, Ltd.

Laird, Charlton. 1953. *Miracle of Language*. Cleveland, The World Book Co.

Lal, B. B. 1952. New Light on the "Dark Ages" of Indian History: Recent Excavations at the Hastināpura Site near Delhi. *Illustrated London News*, 221:551–553.

Lambton, Ann Katharine S. 1953. *Landlord and Peasant in Persia*. London, Oxford University Press.

Landon, Kenneth P. 1949. *Southeast Asia, Crossroad of Religions*. Chicago, University of Chicago Press.

Langer, Susanne K. 1942. *Philosophy in a New Key*. Cambridge, Mass., Harvard University Press.

Langer, Susanne K. 1944. The Lord of Creation. *Fortune*, 29:127–128, 139–154.

Lantis, Margaret. 1946. *The Social Culture of the Nunivak Eskimo*. Transactions of the American Philosophical Society, Vol. 35, Pt. 3.

Lasance, F. X. 1952. *The New Roman Missal*. New York, Benziger Brothers, Inc.

Layard, John W. 1928. Degree-Taking Rites in South West Bay, Malekula. *Journal of the Royal Anthropological Institute*, 58:139–223.

Layard, John W. 1942. *Stone Men of Malekula*. London, Chatto and Windus.

Laycock, H. T. 1950. Surgical Aspects of Female Circumcision in Somaliland. *East African Medical Journal*, 27:445–450.

Leach, E. R. 1949. Some Aspects of Dry Rice Cultivation in North Burma and British Borneo. In: Digby, A. (ed.), *Technique and Economic Organisation Among Primitive Peoples*. Advancement of Science, Vol. 6, No. 21.

Leach, E. R. 1950. Primitive Calendars. *Oceania*, 20:245–262.

Leach, E. R. 1954. *Political Systems of Highland Burma*. Cambridge, Mass., Harvard University Press.

Leakey, L. S. B. 1952. *Mau Mau and the Kikuyu*. London, Methuen and Co., Ltd.

Leakey, L. S. B. 1954. Graphic and Plastic Arts. In: Singer, Charles, Holmyard, E. J., and Hall, A. R. (eds.), *A History of Technology*. Vol. 1, *From Early Times to the Fall of Ancient Empires*. Oxford, Clarendon Press.

Lebon, J. H. G. 1952. *An Introduction to Human Geography*. London, Hutchinson's University Library.

Lee, Arthur. 1954. Climate and Our Fish Supply. *The Listener*, 51:779–781.

Lee, Dorothy. 1949. Being and Value in a Primitive Culture. *Journal of Philosophy*, 46:401–415.

Lee, Dorothy. 1955. Freedom, Spontaneity and Limit in American Linguistic Usage. *Explorations*, 4:6–14.

Lee, Norman E. 1955. *Travel and Transport Through the Ages.* Cambridge, Cambridge University Press.

Lee, Shu-Ching. 1953. China's Traditional Family, Its Characteristics and Disintegration. *American Sociological Review,* 18:272–280.

Lee, Thomas E. 1954. The First Sheguiandah Expedition, Manitoulin Island, Ontario. *American Antiquity,* 20:101–111.

Lees, R. B. 1953. The Basis of Glottochronology. *Language,* 29:113–127.

Leighton, Alexander H., and Hughes, Charles C. 1955. Notes on Eskimo Patterns of Suicide. *Southwestern Journal of Anthropology,* 11:327–338.

Leighton, Alexander H., and Leighton, Dorothea C. 1941. Elements of Psychotherapy in Navaho Religion. *Psychiatry,* 4:515–523.

Leighton, Dorothea, and Kluckhohn, Clyde. 1947. *Children of the People.* Cambridge, Mass., Harvard University Press.

Leiris, Michel. 1951. *Race and Culture.* Paris, UNESCO.

Leites, Nathan, and Bernaut, Elsa. 1954. *Ritual of Liquidation: The Case of the Moscow Trials.* Glencoe, Ill., The Free Press.

Leroi-Gourhan, André. 1943. *Évolution et techniques: L'homme et la matière.* Paris, Éditions Albin Michel.

Leroi-Gourhan, André. 1945. *Évolution et techniques: Milieu et techniques.* Paris, Éditions Albin Michel.

Lessa, William Armand. 1943. *An Appraisal of Constitutional Typologies.* Memoirs of the American Anthropological Association, No. 62.

Lessa, William Armand, and Spiegelman, Marvin. 1954. *Ulithian Personality as Seen Through Ethnological Materials and Thematic Test Analysis.* University of California Publications in Culture and Society, Vol. 2, No. 5.

Lesser, Alexander. 1933. Cultural Significance of the Ghost Dance. *American Anthropologist,* 35:108–115.

Leuba, Clarence. 1954. *The Natural Man.* Doubleday Papers in Psychology, No. 1.

Levi, Carlo. 1947. *Christ Stopped at Eboli.* Translated by Frances Frenaye. New York, Farrar, Straus and Co., Inc.

Lévi-Strauss, Claude. 1949. *Les structures élémentaires de la parenté.* Paris, Presses Universitaires de France.

Lévi-Strauss, Claude. 1952. *Race and History.* Paris, UNESCO.

Lévi-Strauss, Claude. 1954a. The Mathematics of Man. *International Social Science Bulletin,* 6:581–590.

Lévi-Strauss, Claude. 1954b. The Place of Anthropology in the Social Sciences and Problems Raised in Teaching It. In: *The University Teaching of Social Sciences: Sociology, Social Psychology and Anthropology.* Paris, UNESCO.

Lévi-Strauss, Claude, Jakobson, R., Voegelin, Carl F., and Sebeok, T. 1953. *Results of the Conference of Anthropologists and Linguists.* International Journal of American Linguistics, Memoir 8.

Lévy-Bruhl, Lucien. 1923. *Primitive Mentality.* Translated by Lilian A. Clare. New York, The Macmillan Company.

Lévy-Bruhl, Lucien. 1926. *How Natives Think*. Translated by Lilian A. Clare. London, George Allen and Unwin, Ltd.

Lévy-Bruhl, Lucien. 1928. *The "Soul" of the Primitive*. Translated by Lilian A. Clare. New York, The Macmillan Company.

Lévy-Bruhl, Lucien. 1949. *Les carnets du Lucien Lévy-Bruhl*. Paris, Presses Universitaires de France.

Lewin, Kurt. 1948. *Resolving Social Conflicts*. New York, Harper & Brothers.

Lewin, Kurt. 1951. *Field Theory in Social Science*. New York, Harper & Brothers.

Lewin, Kurt. 1952. Group Decision and Social Change. In: Swanson, G. E., Newcomb, T. M., and Hartley, E. L. (eds.), *Readings in Social Psychology*. New York, Henry Holt and Co.

Lewis, M. M. 1948. *Language in Society*. New York, Social Science Publishers, Inc.

Lewis, Oscar. 1941. Manly-Hearted Woman Among the North Piegan. *American Anthropologist*, 43:173–187.

Lewis, Oscar. 1949. Plow Culture and Hoe Culture—A Study in Contrasts. *Rural Sociology*, 14:116–127.

Lewis, Oscar, and Barnouw, Victor. 1956. Caste and the Jajmani System in a North Indian Village. *The Scientific Monthly*, 83:66–81.

Lewis, W. Arthur. 1955. *The Theory of Economic Growth*. London, Allen and Unwin, Ltd.

Li An-Che. 1949. Tibetan Family and Its Relation to Religion. *Asian Horizon*, 2:25–36.

Lienhardt, R. Godfrey. 1954a. Modes of Thought. In: *The Institutions of Primitive Society*. Oxford, Basil Blackwell.

Lienhardt, R. Godfrey. 1954b. The Shilluk of the Upper Nile. In: Forde, Daryll (ed.), *African Worlds: Studies in the Cosmological Ideas and Social Values of African Peoples*. London, Oxford University Press.

Lindgren, Ethel John. 1938. An Example of Culture Contact Without Conflict: Reindeer Tungus and Cossacks of Northwestern Manchuria. *American Anthropologist*, 40:605–621.

Linton, Ralph. 1936. *The Study of Man*. New York, Appleton-Century-Crofts.

Linton, Ralph (ed.). 1940a. *Acculturation in Seven American Indian Tribes*. New York, Appleton-Century-Crofts.

Linton, Ralph. 1940b. Crops, Soils, and Culture in America. In: *The Maya and Their Neighbors*. New York, Appleton-Century-Crofts.

Linton, Ralph. 1943. Nativistic Movements. *American Anthropologist*, 45: 230–240.

Linton, Ralph. 1952. Cultural and Personality Factors Affecting Economic Growth. In: Hoselitz, Bert F., *The Progress of Underdeveloped Areas*. Chicago, University of Chicago Press.

Lips, Julius E. 1947. *Naskapi Law*. (*Lake St. John and Lake Mistassini Bands*.) *Law and Order in a Hunting Society*. Transactions of the American Philosophical Society, 37:379–492.

Litchfield, Edward H. 1956. Notes on a General Theory of Administration. *Administrative Science Quarterly*, 1:3–29.

Little, Kenneth L. 1948. The Poro Society as an Arbiter of Culture. *African Studies*, 7:1–16.

Little, Kenneth L. 1951. *The Mende of Sierra Leone*. London, Routledge and Kegan Paul, Ltd.

Little, Kenneth L. 1953. Social Change in a Non-Literate Community. In: Ruopp, Phillips (ed.), *Approaches to Community Development*. The Hague, W. Van Hoeve, Ltd.

Liu, Gaines K. C. 1952. The Silkworm and Chinese Culture. *Osiris*, 10:129–194.

Lloyd, Donald J., and Warfel, Harry R. 1956. *American English in Its Cultural Setting*. New York, Alfred A. Knopf.

Logan, Frank A., Olmsted, David L., Rosner, Burton S., Schwartz, Richard D., and Stevens, Carl M. 1955. *Behavior Theory and Social Science*. New Haven, Yale University Press.

Logan, W. P. D. 1954. Social Class Variation in Mortality. *Public Health Reports*, 69:1217–1224.

Loomis, Charles P., and Beegle, J. Allan. 1950. *Rural Social Systems*. New York, Prentice-Hall.

Lorimer, Frank (ed.). 1954. *Culture and Human Fertility*. Paris, UNESCO.

Lot-Falck, Eveline. 1953. *Les rites de chasse chez les peuples sibériens*. Paris, Gallimard.

Lounsbury, Floyd G. 1953. Field Methods and Techniques in Linguistics. In: Kroeber, A. L. (ed.), *Anthropology Today*. Chicago, University of Chicago Press.

Lowie, Robert H. 1912. On the Principle of Convergence in Ethnology. *Journal of American Folklore*, 25:24–42.

Lowie, Robert H. 1924. *Primitive Religion*. New York, Boni-Liveright.

Lowie, Robert H. 1937. *The History of Ethnological Theory*. New York, Farrar and Rinehart.

Lowie, Robert H. 1948. *Social Organization*. New York, Rinehart and Co., Inc.

Lowie, Robert H. 1952. The Heterogeneity of Marginal Cultures. In: Tax, Sol (ed.), *The Civilization of Ancient America*. Selected Papers of the XXIXth International Congress of Americanists.

Lowie, Robert H. 1953. Alleged Kiowa-Crow Affinities. *Southwestern Journal of Anthropology*, 9:357–368.

Lowie, Robert H. 1954. *Indians of the Plains*. New York, McGraw-Hill Book Co., Inc.

Lowie, Robert H. 1956. Boas Once More. *American Anthropologist*, 58:159–164.

Lucas, J. Olumide. 1948. *The Religion of the Yorubas*. Lagos, C. M. S. Bookshop.

Lull, Richard Swann. 1935. *Fossils: What They Tell Us of Plants and Animals of the Past*. New York, The University Society Inc.

Lumby, E. W. R. 1954. *The Transfer of Power in India.* London, George Allen and Unwin, Ltd.

Lynd, Robert Staughton, and Lynd, Helen Merrell. 1929. *Middletown.* New York, Harcourt, Brace and Co.

Macalister, R. A. S. 1921. *A Text-book of European Archaeology.* Vol. 1, *The Palaeolithic Period.* Cambridge, Cambridge University Press.

McAllester, David P. 1954. *Enemy Way Music: A Study of Social and Esthetic Values as Seen in Navaho Music.* Papers of the Peabody Museum of American Archaeology and Ethnology, Harvard University, Vol. 41, No. 3.

Macbeath, Alexander. 1954. The Author of "The Golden Bough"—III. *The Listener,* 51:217–218.

McCabe, Louis C. 1951. World Sources and Consumption of Energy. In: *UNESCO Discussion Theme 1951, "Energy in the Service of Man."* Paper No. 2. Paris, UNESCO, offset printed.

McGill, Vivian J. 1954. *Emotions and Reason.* Springfield, Ill., Charles C. Thomas.

McGranahan, D. V., and Wayne, I. 1948. German and American Traits Reflected in Popular Drama. *Human Relations,* 1:429–455.

MacNeice, Louis. 1940. *Poems: 1925–1940.* New York, Random House.

MacNeish, June Helm. 1956. Leadership Among the Northeastern Athabascans. *Anthropologica,* 2:131–163.

Macnicol, Nicol (ed.). 1938. *Hindu Scriptures.* London, J. M. Dent and Sons, Ltd.

Maegraith, Brian G. 1932. The Astronomy of the Aranda and Luritja Tribes. *Transactions and Proceedings of the Royal Society of South Australia,* 56: 19–26.

Majumdar, Dhirendra Nath. 1944. *The Fortunes of Primitive Tribes.* Lucknow, The Universal Publishers, Ltd.

Majumdar, Dhirendra Nath, and Madan, T. N. 1956. *An Introduction to Social Anthropology.* Bombay, Asia Publishing House.

Malinowski, Bronislaw. 1926. *Crime and Custom in Savage Society.* New York, Harcourt, Brace and Co.

Malinowski, Bronislaw. 1927. The Life of Culture. In: Smith, G. Elliott, Malinowski, Bronislaw, Spinden, Herbert J., and Goldenweiser, Alexander, *Culture: The Diffusion Controversy.* New York, W. W. Norton and Co., Inc.

Malinowski, Bronislaw. 1932. *The Sexual Life of Savages.* London, Routledge and Kegan Paul, Ltd.

Malinowski, Bronislaw. 1944. *A Scientific Theory of Culture and Other Essays.* Chapel Hill, University of North Carolina Press.

Malinowski, Bronislaw. 1945. *The Dynamics of Culture Change: An Inquiry into Race Relations in Africa.* Edited by Phyllis Kaberry. New Haven, Yale University Press.

Malinowski, Bronislaw. 1948. *Magic, Science and Religion.* Glencoe, Ill., The Free Press.

Mandelbaum, David G. 1940. *The Plains Cree*. Anthropological Papers of the American Museum of Natural History, Vol. 37, Part II.

Mandelbaum, David G. 1941. Culture Change Among the Nilgiri Tribes. *American Anthropologist*, 43:19–26.

Mann, Michael. 1953. Village Industries and Community Development. *Overseas Education*, 25:89–91.

Mann, Stuart E. 1946. Basks and Mediterraneans. *Man*, 46:101–102.

Marett, Robert Ranulph. 1909. *The Threshold of Religion*. London, Methuen and Co., Ltd.

Marett, Robert Ranulph. 1920. *Psychology and Folklore*. London, Methuen and Co., Ltd.

Marquand, John. 1949. *Point of No Return*. Boston, Little, Brown and Co.

Marriott, McKim. 1955. Little Communities in an Indigenous Civilization. In: Marriott, McKim (ed.), *Village India: Studies in the Little Community*. Memoirs of the American Anthropological Association, No. 83.

Marsh, Gordon H., and Laughlin, William S. 1956. Human Anatomical Knowledge Among the Aleutian Islanders. *Southwestern Journal of Anthropology*, 12:38–78.

Martin, Paul S., Quimby, George I., and Collier, Donald. 1947. *Indians Before Columbus*. Chicago, University of Chicago Press.

Marwick, Max G. 1952. The Social Context of Cewa Witch Beliefs. *Africa*, 22:120–135, 215–233.

Marwick, Max G. 1956. The Continuance of Witchcraft Belief. *The Listener*, 55:490–492.

Mason, J. Alden. 1950. The Languages of South Amercian Indians. In: Steward, Julian H. (ed.), *Handbook of South American Indians*. Vol. 6, *Physical Anthropology, Linguistics and Cultural Geography of South American Indians*. Bureau of American Ethnology, Bulletin 143.

Mass Observation. 1943. *The Pub and the People: A Worktown Study*. London, Victor Gollancz, Ltd.

Masserman, Jules H. 1946. *Principles of Dynamic Psychiatry*. Philadelphia, W. B. Saunders Co.

Masters, John. 1952. *The Deceivers*. New York, The Viking Press.

Maude, Roy L., and Maude, Angus. 1950. *The English Middle Classes*. New York, Alfred A. Knopf.

Maurer, Herrymon. 1955. *Great Enterprise: Growth and Behavior of the Big Corporation*. New York, The Macmillan Company.

Mauss, Marcel. 1950. *Sociologie et anthropologie*. Paris, Presses Universitaires de France.

Mayers, Lewis. 1955. *The American Legal System*. New York, Harper & Brothers.

Mead, Margaret. 1928a. *Coming of Age in Samoa*. New York, William Morrow and Co.

Mead, Margaret. 1928b. *An Inquiry into the Question of Cultural Stability in Polynesia*. Columbia University Contributions in Anthropology, No. 9.

Mead, Margaret. 1928c. The Rôle of the Individual in Samoan Culture. *Journal of the Royal Anthropological Institute*, 58:481–495.

Mead, Margaret. 1930. *Growing Up in New Guinea*. New York, William Morrow and Co.

Mead, Margaret. 1934. *Kinship in the Admiralty Islands*. Anthropological Papers of the American Museum of Natural History, 34:181–358.

Mead, Margaret. 1935. *Sex and Temperament in Three Primitive Societies*. New York, William Morrow and Co.

Mead, Margaret. 1942a. *And Keep Your Powder Dry*. New York, William Morrow and Co.

Mead, Margaret. 1942b. Educative Effects of Social Environment as Disclosed by Studies of Primitive Societies. In: Burgess, E. W., Warner, W. L., Alexander, Franz, and Mead, Margaret, *Symposium on Environment and Education*. Supplementary Educational Monographs, No. 54.

Mead, Margaret. 1947a. The Application of Anthropological Techniques to Cross-National Communication. *Transactions of the New York Academy of Sciences*, Vol. 9, series II, pp. 133–152.

Mead, Margaret. 1947b. The Implications of Culture Change for Personality Development. *American Journal of Orthopsychiatry*, 17:633–646.

Mead, Margaret. 1947c. *The Mountain Arapesh*: III. *Socio-Economic Life*. Anthropological Papers of the American Museum of Natural History, Vol. 40, No. 3.

Mead, Margaret. 1949a. Character Formation and Diachronic Theory. In: Fortes, Meyer (ed.), *Social Structure, Studies Presented to A. R. Radcliffe-Brown*. Oxford, Clarendon Press.

Mead, Margaret. 1949b. *Male and Female*. New York, William Morrow and Co.

Mead, Margaret. 1951. *Soviet Attitudes Toward Authority*. New York, McGraw-Hill Book Co., Inc.

Mead, Margaret. 1953a. *Cultural Patterns and Technical Change*. Paris, UNESCO.

Mead, Margaret. 1953b. National Character. In: Kroeber, A. L. (ed.), *Anthropology Today*. Chicago, University of Chicago Press.

Mead, Margaret. 1953c. The Study of Culture at a Distance. In: Mead, Margaret, and Métraux, Rhoda (eds.), *The Study of Culture at a Distance*. Chicago, University of Chicago Press.

Mead, Margaret. 1955. Children and Ritual in Bali. In: Mead, Margaret, and Wolfenstein, Martha (eds.), *Childhood in Contemporary Cultures*. Chicago, University of Chicago Press.

Mead, Margaret. 1956a. *New Lives for Old*. New York, William Morrow and Co.

Mead, Margaret. 1956b. Some Uses of Still Photography in Culture and Personality Studies. In: Haring, D. G. (ed.), *Personal Character and Cultural Milieu*. Third rev. ed. Syracuse, Syracuse University Press.

Mead, Margaret, and Calas, Nicolas. 1953. *Primitive Heritage*. New York, Random House.

Mead, Margaret, and Macgregor, Frances Cooke. 1951. *Growth and Culture*. New York, G. P. Putnam's Sons.

Mead, Margaret, and Métraux, Rhoda (eds.). 1953. *The Study of Culture at a Distance*. Chicago, University of Chicago Press.

Meadows, Paul. 1950. *The Culture of Industrial Man*. Lincoln, University of Nebraska Press.

Meggitt, Mervyn. 1954. Sign Language Among the Walbiri of Central Australia. *Oceania*, 25:1–16.

Menninger, Karl. 1942. *Love Against Hate*. New York, Harcourt, Brace and Co.

Merriam, Alan P. 1955. The Use of Music in the Study of a Problem of Acculturation. *American Anthropologist*, 57:28–34.

Métraux, Alfred. 1949. Religion and Shamanism. In: Steward, Julian H. (ed.), *Handbook of South American Indians*. Vol. 5, *The Comparative Ethnology of South American Indians*. Bureau of American Ethnology, Bulletin 143.

Métraux, Alfred. 1953. Réactions psychologiques à la christianisation de la vallée de Marbial (Haïti). *Revue de Psychologie des Peuples*, 8:250–267.

Métraux, Rhoda, and Mead, Margaret. 1954. *Themes in French Culture*. Stanford, Stanford University Press.

Middleton, John. 1955. The Concept of "Bewitching" in Lugbara. *Africa*, 25:252–260.

Miller, Delbert C., and Form, W. H. 1951. *Industrial Sociology*. New York, Harper & Brothers.

Miller, S. N. 1935. The Roman Empire in the First Three Centuries. In: Eyre, Edward (ed.), *European Civilization, Its Origin and Development*. Vol. 2, *Rome and Christendom*. London, Oxford University Press.

Miller, Walter B. 1955. Two Concepts of Authority. *American Anthropologist*, 57:271–289.

Mills, C. Wright. 1951. *White Collar: The American Middle Classes*. New York, Oxford University Press.

Mills, C. Wright. 1956. *The Power Elite*. New York, Oxford University Press.

Mintz, Alexander. 1953. The Failure of a Propaganda Campaign Attempting to Influence the Behavior of Consumers in the National Interest by Predominantly Selfish Appeals. *Journal of Social Psychology*, 38:49–62.

Mīr Hasan 'Alī, Mrs. B. 1917. *Observations on the Mussulmauns of India*. Second ed. Edited with notes and an introduction by W. Crooke. London, Humphrey Milford, Oxford University Press.

Mitchell, G. Duncan. 1952. The Parish Council and the Rural Community. *Journal of African Administration*, 4:93–100.

Mitchell, J. Clyde. 1950. Preliminary Notes on Land Tenure and Agriculture Among the Machinga Yao. *Human Problems in British Central Africa*, 10:1–13.

Mitchell, J. Clyde. 1956. Labour Migration and the Tribe. *The Listener*, 56:646–647.

Mitchell, J. Clyde, and Barnes, J. A. 1950. *The Lamba Village: Report of a Social Survey*. Communications from the School of African Studies, University of Cape Town, n.s., No. 24.

Montagu, M. F. Ashley. 1937. Physiological Paternity in Australia. *American Anthropologist*, 39:175–183.

Montagu, M. F. Ashley. 1938. *Coming into Being Among the Australian Aborigines*. New York, E. P. Dutton and Co.

Montagu, M. F. Ashley. 1949a. Embryological Beliefs of Primitive Peoples. *Ciba Symposia*, 10:994–1008.

Montagu, M. F. Ashley. 1949b. The Origin and Nature of Social Life and the Biological Basis of Cooperation. *Main Currents*, 7:14–22.

Montagu, M. F. Ashley. 1950. A Consideration of the Concept of Race. In: *Origin and Evolution of Man*. Cold Spring Harbor Symposia on Quantitative Biology, Vol. 15.

Montagu, M. F. Ashley. 1951a. *On Being Human*. New York, Henry Schuman.

Montagu, M. F. Ashley. 1951b. *An Introduction to Physical Anthropology*. Second ed. Springfield, Charles C. Thomas.

Montagu, M. F. Ashley. 1953. Time-Binding and the Concept of Culture. *Scientific Monthly*, 77:148–155.

Montagu, M. F. Ashley. 1955. Time, Morphology, and Neoteny in the Evolution of Man. *American Anthropologist*, 57:13–27.

Montandon, G. 1937. *La civilisation Ainou et les cultures arctiques*. Paris, Payot.

Montgomery, Arthur. 1939. *The Rise of Modern Industry in Sweden*. London, P. S. King and Son, Ltd.

Mooney, James. 1896. *The Ghost-Dance Religion and the Sioux Outbreak of 1890*. Annual Reports of the Bureau of American Ethnology, No. 14.

Moore, Harvey C. 1954. Cumulation and Cultural Processes. *American Anthropologist*, 56:347–357.

Moore, Omar Khayyam. 1957. Divination—A New Perspective. *American Anthropologist*, 59:69–74.

Moorhouse, Alfred C. 1953. *The Triumph of the Alphabet*. New York, Henry Schuman.

Morgan, Lewis H. 1877. *Ancient Society, or Researches in the Lines of Human Progress from Savagery, Through Barbarism to Civilization*. New York, Henry Holt and Co.

Morice, A. G. 1928. The Fur Trader in Anthropology; and a Few Related Questions. *American Anthropologist*, 30:60–84.

Morris, H. S. 1953. *Report on a Melanau Sago Producing Community in Sarawak*. Colonial Research Studies, No. 9.

Morris, J. N. 1955. Coronary Thrombosis: A Modern Epidemic. *The Listener*, 54:995–997.

Movius, Hallam L., Jr. 1953. Old World Prehistory: Paleolithic. In: Kroeber, A. L. (ed.), *Anthropology Today*. Chicago, University of Chicago Press.

Movius, Hallam L., Jr. 1956. The Old Stone Age. In: Shapiro, Harry L. (ed.), *Man, Culture, and Society*. New York, Oxford University Press.

Muehlmann, Wilhelm E. 1938. *Methodik der Voelkerkunde*. Stuttgart, Ferdinand Enke Verlag, 1938.

Muehlmann, Wilhelm E. 1955. *Arioi und Mamaia*. Wiesbaden, Franz Steiner Verlag GMBH.

Muensterberger, Warner. 1955. *On the Biopsychological Determinants of Social Life*: In memoriam *Géza Rhoeim*. Psychoanalysis and the Social Sciences, No. 4.

Mukerji, Dhan Gopal. 1924. *My Brother's Face*. New York, E. P. Dutton and Co.

Murdock, George Peter. 1934. *Our Primitive Contemporaries*. New York, The Macmillan Company.

Murdock, George Peter. 1949. *Social Structure*. New York, The Macmillan Company.

Murdock, George Peter. 1950. Family Stability in Non-European Cultures. *The Annals of the American Academy of Political and Social Science*, 272: 195–201.

Murdock, George Peter (ed.). 1951a. *Outline of South American Cultures*. Behavior Science Outlines, 2. New Haven, Human Relations Area Files.

Murdock, George Peter. 1951b. South American Culture Areas. *Southwestern Journal of Anthropology*, 7:415–436.

Murdock, George Peter. 1953. *Ethnographic Bibliography of North America*. Second ed. Behavior Science Bibliographies. New Haven, Human Relations Area Files.

Murdock, George Peter. 1954. Sociology and Anthropology. In: Gillin, John (ed.), *For a Science of Social Man*. New York, The Macmillan Company.

Murdock, George Peter. 1955a. Changing Emphases in Social Structure. *Southwestern Journal of Anthropology*, 11:361–370.

Murdock, George Peter. 1955b. North American Social Organization. *Davidson Journal of Anthropology*, 1:85–95.

Murdock, George Peter. 1956. Political Moieties. In: White, Leonard D. (ed.), *The State of the Social Sciences: A Reappraisal of the Problems, Methods and Goals of the Social Sciences at Mid-Century*. Chicago, University of Chicago Press.

Murdock, George Peter, and Goodenough, Ward H. 1947. Social Organization of Truk. *Southwestern Journal of Anthropology*, 3:331–343.

Murdock, George Peter, Ford, Clellan S., Hudson, Alfred E., Kennedy, Raymond, Simmons, Leo W., and Whiting, John W. M. 1950. *Outline of Cultural Materials*. Third rev. ed. Behavior Science Outlines, No. 1. New Haven, Human Relations Area Files.

Murphy, Gardner. 1953. *In the Minds of Men*. New York, Basic Books, Inc.

Murphy, Robert F., and Quain, Buell. 1955. *The Trumai Indians of Central Brazil*. Monographs of the American Ethnological Society, No. 24.

Nadel, Siegfried Frederick. 1942. *A Black Byzantium: The Kingdom of Nupe in Nigeria.* London, Oxford University Press.

Nadel, Siegfried Frederick. 1947. *The Nuba: An Anthropological Study of the Hill Tribes in Kordofan.* London, Oxford University Press.

Nadel, Siegfried Frederick. 1951. *The Foundations of Social Anthropology.* London, Cohen and West, Ltd.

Nadel, Siegfried Frederick. 1952. Witchcraft in Four African Societies: An Essay in Comparison. *American Anthropologist,* 54:18–29.

Nadel, Siegfried Frederick. 1954a. Morality and Language Among the Nupe. *Man,* 54:55–57.

Nadel, Siegfried Frederick. 1954b. *Nupe Religion.* London, Routledge and Kegan Paul, Ltd.

Nadel, Siegfried Frederick. 1955. Two Nuba Religions: An Essay in Comparison. *American Anthropologist,* 57:661–679.

Nagel, Ernest. 1948. The Development of Modern Science. In: *Chapters in Western Civilization.* Two vols. New York, Columbia University Press.

Naroll, Raoul S. 1950. A Draft Map of the Culture Areas of Asia. *Southwestern Journal of Anthropology,* 6:183–187.

Newcomb, W. W., Jr. 1950. A Re-examination of the Causes of Plains Warfare. *American Anthropologist,* 52:317–330.

Newman, Marshall T. 1953. The Application of Ecological Rules to the Racial Anthropology of the Aboriginal New World. *American Anthropologist,* 55:311–327.

Newman, Russell W., and Munro, Ella H. 1955. The Relation of Climate and Body Size in U.S. Males. *American Journal of Physical Anthropology,* 13:1–17.

Newman, Stanley. 1955. Vocabulary Levels: Zuñi Sacred and Slang Usage. *Southwestern Journal of Anthropology,* 11:345–354.

Nilsson, Martin P. 1920. *Primitive Time-Reckoning.* Lund, C. W. K. Gleerup.

Noon, John A. 1949. *Law and Government of the Grand River Iroquois.* Viking Fund Publications in Anthropology, No. 12.

Norbeck, Edward. 1954. *Takashima: A Japanese Fishing Community.* Salt Lake City, University of Utah Press.

Northrop, F. S. C. 1946. *The Meeting of East and West, an Inquiry Concerning World Understanding.* New York, The Macmillan Company.

Northrop, F. S. C. 1947. *Logic of the Sciences and the Humanities.* New York, The Macmillan Company.

Northrop, F. S. C. 1953. *The Taming of the Nations.* New York, The Macmillan Company.

Oakley, Kenneth P. 1954. Dating of the Australopithecinae of Africa. *American Journal of Physical Anthropology,* 12:9–27.

Oberg, Kalervo. 1940. The Kingdom of Ankole in Uganda. In: Fortes, Meyer, and Evans-Pritchard, Edward Evan (eds.), *African Political Systems.* London, Oxford University Press.

O'Brien, Thomas J. [1901.] *An Advanced Catechism of Catholic Faith and Practice.* Chicago, John B. Oink.

Odum, Howard M. 1953. Folk Sociology as a Subject Field for the Historical Study of Total Human Society and the Empirical Study of Group Behavior. *Social Forces*, 31:193–223.

Oestreich, Nancy. 1948. Trends of Change in Patterns of Child Care and Training Among the Wisconsin Winnebago. *The Wisconsin Archeologist*, 29:39–140.

O'Faolain, Sean. 1947. *The Irish*. Harmondsworth, Penguin Books.

Ogburn, William F. 1950. *Social Change*. New ed. New York, The Viking Press.

Ogburn, William F., and Nimkoff, Meyer F. 1946. *Sociology*. Boston, Houghton Mifflin Co.

O'Hern, Edna Mae. 1954. The Status Significance of an Isolated Urban Dialect. Abstract of dissertation presented to the School of Social Science of the Catholic University of America.

Oliver, Douglas L. 1949. *Studies in the Anthropology of Bougainville, Solomon Islands*. Papers of the Peabody Museum of American Archaeology and Ethnology, Harvard University, No. 39.

Oliver, Douglas L. 1955. *A Solomon Island Society*. Cambridge, Mass., Harvard University Press.

Olmsted, David L. 1953. Comparative Notes on Yoruba and Lucumí. *Language*, 29:157–164.

Opler, Marvin K. 1940. The Southern Ute of Colorado. In: Linton, Ralph (ed.), *Acculturation in Seven American Indian Tribes*. New York, Appleton-Century-Crofts.

Opler, Marvin K. 1950. Japanese Folk Beliefs and Practices, Tule Lake, California. *Journal of American Folklore*, 63:385–397.

Opler, Marvin K. 1956. Cultural Anthropology and Social Psychiatry. *American Journal of Psychiatry*, 113:302–311.

Opler, Morris Edward. 1941. *An Apache Life-Way*. Chicago, University of Chicago Press.

Opler, Morris Edward. 1945. Themes as Dynamic Forces in Culture. *American Journal of Sociology*, 51:198–206.

Opler, Morris Edward. 1946. An Application of the Theory of Themes in Culture. *Journal of the Washington Academy of Sciences*, 36:137–165.

Oppenheimer, J. Robert. 1953. The Sciences and Man's Community. *The Listener*, 50:1075–1077.

Osgood, Charles E., and Sebeok, Thomas A. 1954. *Psycholinguistics: A Survey of Theory and Research Problems*. Supplement to the *Journal of Abnormal and Social Psychology*, Vol. 49, No. 4.

Osgood, Cornelius. 1936. *The Distribution of the Northern Athapaskan Indians*. Yale University Publications in Anthropology, No. 7.

Osgood, Cornelius. 1940. *Ingalik Material Culture*. Yale University Publications in Anthropology, No. 22.

Osgood, Cornelius. 1951. *The Koreans and Their Culture*. New York, The Ronald Press Co.

Pakistan, Government of, Ministry of Law. 1956. *The Constitution of the Islamic Republic of Pakistan.* Karachi, Manager, Government of Pakistan Press.

Pallottino, M. 1955. *The Etruscans.* Translated by J. Cremona. Harmondsworth, Penguin Books.

Parr, Martin. 1947. Marriage Ordinances for Africans. *Africa, 17:1–7.*

Parrinder, G. 1951. *West African Psychology.* London, Lutterworth Press.

Parsons, Elsie Clews. 1906. *The Family: An Ethnographical and Historical Outline.* New York, G. P. Putnam's Sons.

Passin, Herbert, and Bennett, John W. 1943. Changing Agricultural Magic in Southern Illinois: A Systematic Analysis of Folk-Urban Transition. *Social Forces, 22:98–106.*

Patai, Raphael. 1951. Nomadism: Middle Eastern and Central Asian. *Southwestern Journal of Anthropology, 7:401–414.*

Patai, Raphael. 1953. *Israel Between East and West.* Philadelphia, Jewish Publication Society of America.

Pater, Walter. 1925. *The Renaissance: Studies in Art and Poetry.* Library ed. London, Macmillan & Co., Ltd.

Patterson, Bryan. 1955. The Geological History of Non-Hominid Primates in the Old World. In: Gavan, James A. (ed.), *The Non-Human Primates and Human Evolution.* Detroit, Wayne University Press.

Paul, Benjamin D. 1953a. Interview Techniques and Field Relationships. In: Kroeber, A. L. (ed.), *Anthropology Today.* Chicago, University of Chicago Press.

Paul, Benjamin D. 1953b. Respect for Cultural Differences. *Community Development Bulletin, 4:42–47.*

Peet, Thomas Eric. 1909. *The Stone and Bronze Ages of Italy and Sicily.* Oxford, The Clarendon Press.

Pei, Mario. 1953. *The Story of English.* Philadelphia, J. B. Lippincott Co.

Pendlebury, J. D. S. 1939. *The Archaeology of Crete: An Introduction.* London, Methuen and Co., Ltd.

Penzer, N. M. [1936.] *The Harēm.* Philadelphia, J. B. Lippincott Co.

Peristiany, J. G. 1954. Pokot Sanctions and Structure. *Africa, 24:17–25.*

Perkins, Jocelyn. 1953. *The Crowning of the Sovereign of Great Britain and the Dominions Overseas: A Handbook to the Coronation.* Second ed. London, Methuen and Co., Ltd.

Pettersson, Olaf. 1953. *Chiefs and Gods: Religious and Social Elements in the Southeastern Bantu Kingship.* Lund, C. W. K. Gleerup.

Pettitt, George A. 1946. *Primitive Education in North America.* University of California Publications in American Archaeology and Ethnology, No. 43.

Pettitt, George A. 1950. *The Quileute of La Push: 1775–1945.* University of California, Anthropological Records, Vol. 14, No. 1.

Phillips, Arthur. 1953. Marriage Laws of Africa. In: Phillips, A. (ed.), *Survey of African Marriage and Family Life.* London, Oxford University Press.

Phillips, Philip, Ford, J. A., and Griffin, James B. 1951. *Archaeological Survey in the Lower Mississippi Alluvial Valley, 1940–1947.* Papers of the

Peabody Museum of American Archaeology and Ethnology, Harvard University, No. 25.

Phillips, Philip, and Willey, Gordon R. 1953. Method and Theory in American Archeology: An Operational Basis for Culture-Historical Integration. *American Anthropologist*, 55:615–633.

Piaget, Jean. 1923. *The Moral Judgment of the Child*. Translated by Marjorie Gabain. New York, Harcourt, Brace and Co.

Pickthall, Mohammed Marmaduke. 1930. *The Meaning of the Glorious Koran*. London, George Allen and Unwin, Ltd.

Piddington, Ralph. 1950. *An Introduction to Social Anthropology*. Edinburgh, Oliver and Boyd.

Pierson, Donald. 1942. *Negroes in Brazil*. Chicago, University of Chicago Press.

Pike, Kenneth L. 1947. *Phonemics, A Technique for Reducing Language to Writing*. University of Michigan Publications in Linguistics, 3.

Pittman, Dean. 1948. *Practical Linguistics*. Cleveland, Mid-Missions.

Ploss, H. H. 1871a. *Die Maennerkindbett (Couvade), seine geographische Verbreitung und ethnographische Bedeutung*. Leipzig, Hinrichs' Verlag.

Ploss, H. H. 1871b. Die operative Behandlung der weiblichen Geschlechtstheile bei verschniedenen Voelkern. *Zeitschrift fuer Ethnologie*, 3:381–397.

Price, George R. 1955. Science and the Supernatural. *Science*, 122:359–367.

Prins, A. H. J. 1953. *East African Age-Class Systems*. Groningen, J. B. Wolters.

Progress in Asia: The Colombo Plan in Action. 1953. London, H. M. Stationery Office.

Punjab Government. 1920. *Punjab Gazetteers*. Vol. 12-A, *Mandi State*. Lahore, Superintendent, Government Printing, Punjab.

Putnam, George Nelson. 1954. The Status Significance of an Isolated Urban Dialect. Abstract of dissertation presented to the School of Social Science of the Catholic University of America.

Putney, Gladys J., and Putney, Snell W. 1954. A Field Evaluation of Acculturation Theory. Ph.D. Dissertation, Department of Sociology, University of Oregon.

Quecke, K. 1952. Der Kaiserschnitt an der Toten. *Ciba-Zeitschrift*, 11:4711–4716.

Radcliffe-Brown, A. R. 1939. *Taboo: The Frazer Lecture, 1939*. Cambridge, Cambridge University Press.

Radcliffe-Brown, A. R. 1946a. Meaning and Scope of Social Anthropology. In: *Human Origins: An Introductory General Course in Anthropology. Selected Readings, Series II*. Second ed. Chicago, University of Chicago Bookstore, mimeographed.

Radcliffe-Brown, A. R. 1946b. A Note on Functional Anthropology. *Man*, 46:38–41.

Radcliffe-Brown, A. R. 1952a. The Comparative Method in Social Anthropology. *Journal of the Royal Anthropological Institute*, 81:15–22.

Radcliffe-Brown, A. R. 1952b. *Structure and Function in Primitive Society.* London, Cohen and West, Ltd.

Radin, Paul. 1920. *The Autobiography of a Winnebago Indian.* University of California Publications in American Archaeology and Ethnology, 16:381–473.

Radin, Paul (ed.). 1926. *Crashing Thunder, The Autobiography of an American Indian.* New York, Appleton-Century-Crofts.

Rand, Christopher. 1949. Our Far-Flung Correspondents: The Egg Family. *The New Yorker,* 25:52–60.

Randall, John H., Jr., and Buchler, Justus. 1942. *Philosophy: An Introduction.* New York, Barnes and Noble, Inc.

Rasmussen, Knud. 1932. *Intellectual Culture of the Copper Eskimo.* Report of the Fifth Thule Expedition 1921–24, Vol. 9.

Ratzel, Friedrich. 1896. *The History of Mankind.* Translated from 2nd German ed. by A. J. Butler. Three vols. London, Macmillan & Co., Ltd.

Ray, Verne F. 1942. *Culture Elements Distributions: XXII, Plateau.* University of California, Anthropological Records, Vol. 8, No. 2.

Read, H. H. 1949. *Geology: An Introduction to Earth-History.* London, Oxford University Press.

Redfield, Robert. 1939. Culture Contact Without Conflict. *American Anthropologist,* 41:514–517.

Redfield, Robert. 1946. Anthropology: Unity and Diversity. In: *Human Origins, An Introductory General Course in Anthropology. Selected Readings, Series II,* Second ed. Chicago, University of Chicago Bookstore, mimeographed.

Redfield, Robert. 1947. The Folk Society. *American Journal of Sociology,* 52:293–308.

Redfield, Robert. 1953a. *The Primitive World and Its Transformations.* Ithaca, Cornell University Press.

Redfield, Robert. 1953b. Relations of Anthropology to the Social Sciences and to the Humanities. In: Kroeber, A. L. (ed.), *Anthropology Today.* Chicago, University of Chicago Press.

Redfield, Robert. 1955. *The Little Community.* Chicago, University of Chicago Press.

Redfield, Robert. 1956a. How Human Society Operates. In: Shapiro, Harry L. (ed.), *Man, Culture, and Society.* New York, Oxford University Press.

Redfield, Robert. 1956b. *Peasant Society and Culture.* Chicago, University of Chicago Press.

Reece, B. Carroll. 1954. *Tax-Exempt Foundations. Report of the Special Committee to Investigate Tax-Exempt Foundations and Comparable Organizations.* House of Representatives, 83rd Congress, 2nd Session, on House Resolution 217. House Report No. 2681, 83rd Congress, 2nd Session. Washington, Government Printing Office.

Rees, Alwyn D. 1950. *Life in a Welsh Countryside.* Cardiff, University of Wales.

Reichard, Gladys A. 1944. *Prayer: The Compulsive Word.* Monographs of the American Ethnological Society, No. 7.

Reichard, Gladys A. 1950. *Navaho Religion: A Study of Symbolism.* Two vols. New York, Pantheon Books.

Report of the Court of Inquiry Constituted Under Punjab Act II of 1954 to Enquire into the Punjab Disturbances of 1953. 1954. Lahore, Superintendent, Government Printing.

Rhine, J. B. 1956. Parapsychology. In: Pryce-Jones, Alan (ed.), *The New Outline of Modern Knowledge.* London, Victor Gollancz, Ltd.

Rhodes, Henry T. F. 1955. *The Satanic Mass.* New York, Citadel Press.

Richardson, F. L. W., Jr. 1949. Introduction: The Near East. In: Linton, Ralph (ed.), *Most of the World.* New York, Columbia University Press.

Richardson, F. L. W., Jr. 1955. Anthropology and Human Relations in Business and Industry. In: *Yearbook of Anthropology 1955.* New York, Wenner-Gren Foundation for Anthropological Research.

Richardson, Jane. 1940. *Law and Status Among the Kiowa Indians.* Monographs of the American Ethnological Society, No. 1.

Riesen, Austin H., and Kinder, Elaine F. 1952. *Postural Development of Infant Chimpanzees.* New Haven, Yale University Press.

Riesman, D. 1950. *The Lonely Crowd.* New Haven, Yale University Press.

Riley, Carroll L. 1952. The Blowgun in the New World. *Southwestern Journal of Anthropology,* 8:297–319.

Rioux, Marcel. 1956. Remarques sur les concepts de schème and de modèle culturels. *Anthropologica,* 2:93–106.

Ritzenthaler, Robert F., and Peterson, Frederick A. 1954. Courtship Whistling of the Mexican Kickapoo Indians. *American Anthropologist,* 56:1088–1089.

Rivers, William Halse Rivers. 1900. A Genealogical Method of Collecting Social and Vital Statistics. *Journal of the Royal Anthropological Institute,* 30:74–82.

Rivers, William Halse Rivers. 1906. *The Todas.* London, Macmillan & Co., Ltd.

Rivers, William Halse Rivers. 1910. The Genealogical Method of Anthropological Inquiry. *Sociological Review,* 3:1–12.

Roberts, Colin. 1956. The Book as the Creation of Christianity. *The Listener,* 56:92–94.

Roberts, Frank H. H. 1953. Earliest Men in America. *Cahiers d'Histoire Mondiale,* 1:255–277.

Robertson, Archibald. 1952. *How to Read History.* London, Watts and Co.

Robertson, George Scott. 1896. *The Kafirs of the Hindu-Kush.* London, Lawrence and Bullen, Ltd.

Rodnick, David. 1955. *The Norwegians; A Study in National Culture.* Washington, Public Affairs Press.

Roe, Frank Gilbert. 1955. *The Indian and the Horse.* Norman, University of Oklahoma Press.

Róheim, Géza. 1925. *Australian Totemism: A Psycho-Analytic Study in Anthropology.* London, George Allen and Unwin, Ltd.

Romer, Alfred Sherwood. 1941. *Man and the Vertebrates*. Third ed. Chicago, University of Chicago Press.

Rose, Arnold M. 1954. *Theory and Method in Social Science*. Minneapolis, University of Minnesota Press.

Rose, Arnold M. 1956. *Sociology, The Study of Human Relations*. New York, Alfred A. Knopf.

Rose, Edward. 1947–48. Innovations in American Culture. *Social Forces*, 26:255–276.

Rosen, George. 1949. Medical Thought and the Rise of Specialism. *Ciba Symposia, 11*:1126–1134.

Rossman, Joseph. 1931. War and Invention. *American Journal of Sociology*, 36:625–633.

Rouse, Irving. 1951. *A Survey of Indian River Archeology, Florida*. Yale University Publications in Anthropology, No. 44.

Rousseau, Jean Jacques. 1913. *The Social Contract and Discourses*. Translated with introduction by G. D. H. Cole. London, J. M. Dent and Sons, Ltd.

Rubin, Morton. 1951. *Plantation County*. Chapel Hill, University of North Carolina Press.

Ruesch, Jurgen, and Bateson, Gregory. 1951. *Communication: The Social Matrix of Psychiatry*. New York, W. W. Norton and Co., Inc.

Ruesch, Jurgen, and Kees, Weldon. 1956. *Nonverbal Communication*. Berkeley, University of California Press.

Russell, Bertrand. [1938.] *Power: A New Social Analysis*. New York, W. W. Norton and Co., Inc.

Russell, J. C. 1948. *British Medieval Population*. Albuquerque, University of New Mexico Press.

Ryan, Bryce F. 1953. *Caste in Modern Ceylon*. New Brunswick, Rutgers University Press.

Ryan, Bryce F., and Straus, Murray A. 1954. The Integration of Sinhalese Society. *Research Studies of the State College of Washington*, 22:179–227.

Sansom, G. B. 1951. *The Western World and Japan*. New York, Alfred A. Knopf.

Sapir, Edward. 1924. Culture, Genuine and Spurious. *American Journal of Sociology*, 29:401–429.

Sapir, Edward. 1927. The Unconscious Patterning of Behavior in Society. In: Dummer, E. S. (ed.), *The Unconscious: A Symposium*. New York, Alfred A. Knopf.

Sapir, Edward. 1928. The Meaning of Religion. *The American Mercury, 15*: 72–79.

Sapir, Edward. 1929. The Status of Linguistics as a Science. *Language*, 5:207–214.

Sapir, Edward. 1934a. Communication. In: *Encyclopedia of the Social Sciences*. Vol. 4. New York, The Macmillan Company.

Sarma, Jyotirmoyee. [1955.] A Village in West Bengal. In: *India's Villages*. Calcutta, West Bengal Government Press.

Sauer, C. O. 1936. American Agricultural Origins: A Consideration of Nature and Culture. In: *Essays in Anthropology in Honor of Alfred Louis Kroeber.* Berkeley, University of California Press.

Sawyer, William A. 1951. Medical Care in Industry. *The Annals of the American Academy of Political and Social Science,* 273:151–159.

Schaff, A., and Ehrlich, S. 1950. Dialectical Materialism in Political Science. In: *Contemporary Political Science.* Liège, UNESCO.

Schapera, Isaac. 1943. *Native Land Tenure in the Bechuanaland Protectorate.* Lovedale, South Africa, The Lovedale Press.

Schapera, Isaac. 1950. Kinship and Marriage Among the Tswana. In: Radcliffe-Brown, A. R., and Forde, Daryll (eds.), *African Systems of Kinship and Marriage.* London, Oxford University Press.

Schmidt, Wilhelm. 1939. *The Culture Historical Method of Ethnology.* New York, Fortuny.

Schmidt, Wilhelm. 1952. *Der Ursprung der Gottesidee.* Band 10. 3 Abteilung: *Die Religionen der Hirtenvoelker. 4. Die Asiatischen Hirtenvoelker.* Muenster i. W., Aschendorffsche Verlagsbuchhandlung.

Schneider, David M. 1947. The Social Dynamics of Physical Disability in Army Basic Training. *Psychiatry,* 10:323–333.

Schneider, David M. 1953a. A Note on Bridewealth and the Stability of Marriage. *Man,* 53:55–57.

Schneider, David M. 1953b. Yap Kinship Terminology and Kin Groups. *American Anthropologist,* 55:215–236.

Schneider, David M. 1955. Abortion and Depopulation on a Pacific Island. In: Paul, Benjamin D. (ed.), *Health, Culture, and Community.* New York, Russell Sage Foundation.

Schneider, David M., and Homans, George C. 1955. Kinship Terminology and the American Kinship System. *American Anthropologist,* 57:1194–1208.

Schneider, M. 1952. Zu Trommelsprache der Duala. *Anthropos,* 47:235–243.

Schultz, Adolph H. 1936. Characters Common to Higher Primates and Characters Specific for Man. *Quarterly Review of Biology,* 11:259–283, 425–455.

Schultz, Adolph H. 1948. The Number of Young at Birth and the Number of Nipples in Primates. *American Journal of Physical Anthropology,* n.s., 6:1–23.

Schultz, Adolph H. 1955. Primatology in Its Relation to Anthropology. In: *Yearbook of Anthropology 1955.* New York, Wenner-Gren Foundation for Anthropological Research.

Schurtz, Heinrich. 1902. *Altersklassen und Maennerbuende.* Berlin, Georg Reimer.

Schwab, George. 1947. *Tribes of the Liberian Hinterland.* Papers of the Peabody Museum of American Archaeology and Ethnology, Harvard University, 31.

Scott, Jerome F., and Lynton, R. P. 1952. *The Community Factor in Modern Technology.* Paris, UNESCO.

Seeley, John R., Sim, R. Alexander, and Loosley, E. W. 1956. *Crestwood Heights.* New York, Basic Books.

Seligman, Charles Gabriel. 1934. *Egypt and Negro Africa: A Study in Divine Kingship.* London, George Routledge and Sons, Ltd.

Sellards, E. H. 1952. *Early Man in America.* Austin, University of Texas Press.

Selznick, Philip. 1949. *TVA and the Grass Roots.* University of California Publications in Culture and Society, No. 3.

Shah, Sirdar Ikbal Ali. *See* Ikbāl 'Alī Shāh, Sirdar.

Shapiro, Harry L. 1953. *Race Mixture.* Paris, UNESCO.

Shapley, Harlow. 1954. Cosmography. *American Scientist, 42:*471–486.

Sharma, M. S. Mantreshwar. 1954. *Peeps into Pakistan.* Patna, Pustak Bhandar.

Shaw, George Bernard. 1916. *Androcles and the Lion.* New York, Brentano's.

Shaw, George Bernard. 1945. *Major Barbara, a Screen Version.* Harmondsworth, Penguin Books.

Sheldon, William H. 1940. *The Varieties of Human Physique.* New York, Harper & Brothers.

Sheldon, William H. 1942. *The Varieties of Temperament.* New York, Harper & Brothers.

Sheldon, William H. 1949. *Varieties of Delinquent Youth.* New York, Harper & Brothers.

Shetelig, Haakon, and Falk, Hjalmar. 1937. *Scandinavian Archeology.* Translated by E. V. Gordon. Oxford, Clarendon Press.

Shimkin, D. B. 1953. *The Wind River Shoshone Sun Dance.* Bureau of American Ethnology, Bulletin 151, Paper No. 41.

Short, H. L. 1955. Changing Styles in Nonconformist Architecture. *The Listener, 53:*471–474.

Sieber, S. A., and Mueller, F. H. 1950. *The Social Life of Primitive Man.* Third ed. St. Louis, B. Herder.

Siegel, Bernard J. 1955. Models for the Analysis of the Educative Process in American Communities. In: Spindler, George D. (ed.), *Education and Anthropology.* Stanford, Stanford University Press.

Silone, Ignazio. 1937. *Bread and Wine.* Translated by Gwenda David and Erich Mosbacher. New York, Harper & Brothers.

Simmel, Georg. 1955. *Conflict.* Translated by Kurt H. Wolff. Glencoe, Ill., The Free Press.

Simmel, Georg. 1957. Fashion. *American Journal of Sociology, 62:*541–558.

Simmons, Leo (ed.). 1942. *Sun Chief, the Autobiography of a Hopi Indian.* New Haven, Yale University Press.

Simon, H. A. 1951. Authority. In: Dubin, Robert (ed.), *Human Relations in Administration.* New York, Prentice-Hall.

Simpson, George. 1954. *Man in Society.* Garden City, Doubleday and Co., Inc.

Simpson, George Gaylord. 1945. *The Principles of Classification and a Classification of Mammals.* Bulletin of the American Museum of Natural History, 85.

Singh, Sher. 1933. *An Economic Survey of Naggal, a Village in the Ambala District of the Punjab.* The Board of Economic Inquiry, Punjab, Punjab Village Surveys, No. 5.

Slotkin, James S. 1950. *Social Anthropology.* New York, The Macmillan Company.

Slotkin, James S. 1954. *Personality Development.* New York, Harper & Brothers.

Slotkin, James S. 1956. *The Peyote Religion: A Study in Indian-White Relations.* Glencoe, Ill., The Free Press.

Sluckin, W. 1954. *Minds and Machines.* Harmondsworth, Penguin Books.

Smith, Edwin W. 1927. *The Golden Stool: Some Aspects of the Conflict of Cultures in Modern Africa.* London, The Society for the Propagation of the Gospel in Foreign Parts.

Smith, M. Brewster. 1954. Anthropology and Psychology. In: Gillin, John (ed.), *For a Science of Social Man.* New York, The Macmillan Company.

Smith, Michael G. 1952. A Study of Hausa Domestic Economy in Northern Zaria. *Africa,* 22:333–347.

Smith, Michael G. 1953. Secondary Marriage in Northern Nigeria. *Africa,* 23:298–323.

Smith, Watson, and Roberts, John M. 1954. *Zuñi Law. A Field of Values.* Papers of the Peabody Museum of American Archaeology and Ethnology, Harvard University, Vol. 43, No. 1.

Smith, Wilfred C. 1946. *Modern Islām in India.* Second Indian ed. revised. London, Victor Gollancz, Ltd.

Snodgrasse, Richard M. 1951. Crime and the Constitution Human: A Survey. *The Journal of Criminal Law, Criminology and Political Science,* 42:18–52.

The Social Science Research Council Summer Seminar on Acculturation, 1953. 1954. Acculturation: An Exploratory Formulation. *American Anthropologist,* 56:973–1002.

Sorokin, Pitirim A. 1944. The Causes of War and Conditions of a Lasting Peace. In: *Approaches to World Peace. Conference on Science, Philosophy and Religion in Their Relation to the Democratic Way of Life.* Fourth Symposium. New York, Harper & Brothers.

Sorokin, Pitirim A. 1947. *Society, Culture, and Personality: Their Structure and Dynamics.* New York, Harper & Brothers.

Sorre, Maximilien. 1948. *Les fondements de la géographie humaine.* Tome II, *Les fondements techniques.* Two parts. Paris, Librairie Armand Colin.

Sorre, Maximilien. 1951. *Les fondements de la géographie humaine.* Tome I, *Les fondements biologiques.* Paris, Librairie Armand Colin.

Spear, Percival. 1951. *Twilight of the Mughuls.* Cambridge, Cambridge University Press.

Speck, Frank G. 1935. *Naskapi: The Savage Hunters of the Labrador Peninsula.* Norman, University of Oklahoma Press.

Speiser, Felix. 1922. Decadence and Preservation in The New Hebrides. In: Rivers, W. H. R. (ed.), *Essays on the Depopulation of Melanesia.* Cambridge, Cambridge University Press.

Spencer, Dorothy M. 1941. *Disease, Religion and Society in the Fiji Islands.* Monographs of the American Ethnological Society, No. 2.

Spencer, Robert F. 1949. Primitive Obstetrics. *Ciba Symposia,* 11:1158–1188.

Spencer, Robert F. 1954. The Humanities in Cultural Anthropology. In: Spencer, R. F. (ed.), *Method and Perspective in Anthropology.* Minneapolis, University of Minnesota Press.

Spencer, Robert F. 1956. *An Ethno-Atlas.* Dubuque, Iowa, Wm. C. Brown Co.

Spengler, Joseph J. 1956. Capital Requirements and Population Growth in Underdeveloped Countries: Their Interrelations. *Economic Development and Cultural Change,* 4:305–334.

Spicer, Edward H. 1952. *Human Problems in Technological Change.* New York, Russell Sage Foundation.

Spindler, George D. 1955. *Sociocultural and Psychological Processes in Menomini Acculturation.* University of California Publications in Culture and Society, Vol. 5.

Spiro, Melford E. 1954. Is the Family Universal? *American Anthropologist,* 56:839–846.

Spiro, Melford E. 1956. *Kibbutz: Venture in Utopia.* Cambridge, Mass., Harvard University Press.

Srinivas, M. N. 1952. *Religion and Society Among the Coorgs.* Oxford, Clarendon Press.

Stahl, Kathleen M. 1951. *British and Soviet Colonial Systems.* London, Faber and Faber, Ltd.

Stanton, Alfred H., and Schwartz, Morris S. 1954. *The Mental Hospital.* New York, Basic Books, Inc.

Steenhoven, G. van den. [1956.] *Report to the Department of Northern Affairs and National Resources on a Field-Research Journey for the Study of Legal Concepts Among the Eskimos in Some Parts of the Keewatin District, N.W.T., in the Summer of 1955.* Ottawa, Department of Northern Affairs, mimeographed.

Stefaniszyn, B. 1954. African Reincarnation Reexamined. *African Studies,* 13:131–146.

Steiner, Franz. 1954. Notes on Comparative Economics. *British Journal of Sociology,* 5:118–129.

Stern, Bernhard J. 1949. Some Aspects of Historical Materialism. In: Sellars, R. W., McGill, V. J., and Farber, M. (eds.), *Philosophy for the Future.* New York, The Macmillan Company.

Stern, Curt. 1950. Man's Genetic Future. *Scientific American,* 186:68–74.

Stern, Theodore. 1957. Drum and Whistle "Languages": An Analysis of Speech Surrogates. *American Anthropologist,* 59:487–506.

Steward, Julian H. (ed.). 1946–50. *Handbook of South American Indians.* Six vols. Bureau of American Ethnology, Bulletin 143.

Steward, Julian H. 1949a. Cultural Causality and Law: A Trial Formulation of the Development of Early Civilizations. *American Anthropologist,* 51:1–27.

Steward, Julian H. 1949b. South American Cultures: An Interpretative Summary. In: Steward, Julian H. (ed.), *Handbook of South American Indians*. Vol. 5, *The Comparative Ethnology of South American Indians*. Bureau of American Ethnology, Bulletin 143.

Steward, Julian H. 1955. *Theory of Culture Change*. Urbana, University of Illinois Press.

Stewart, Omer C. 1954. The Forgotten Side of Ethnogeography. In: Spencer, Robert F. (ed.), *Method and Perspective in Anthropology*, Minneapolis, University of Minnesota Press.

Stoetzel, Jean. 1955. *Without the Chrysanthemum and the Sword*. New York, Columbia University Press.

Stokes, Walter R., and Mace, D. R. 1953. Premarital Sexual Behavior. *Marriage and Family Living*, 18:234–249.

Straus, William L., Jr. 1957. Jaw of Gigantopithecus. *Science, 125*:685.

Sturtevant, E. H. 1917. *Linguistic Change*. Chicago, University of Chicago Press.

Sturtevant, William C. 1954. The Medicine Bundle and Busks of the Florida Seminole. *The Florida Anthropologist*, 7:31–70.

Stycos, J. Mayone. 1955. Birth Control Clinics in Crowded Puerto Rico. In: Paul, Benjamin D. (ed.), *Health, Culture, and Community*. New York, Russell Sage Foundation.

Sultan Muhammad Shah, Sir Agha Khan. 1954. *The Memoirs of Aga Khan*. New York, Simon and Schuster.

Sulzberger, C. L. 1956. 6,000 Characters in Search of an Alphabet. *New York Times*, July 18, 1956.

The Sunday Comics: A Socio-Psychological Study with Attendant Advertising Implications. 1956. Chicago, Science Research Associates.

Sundkler, Bengt G. M. 1948. *Bantu Prophets in South Africa*. London, Lutterworth Press.

Suttles, Wayne. 1951. The Early Diffusion of the Potato Among the Coast Salish. *Southwestern Journal of Anthropology*, 7:272–288.

Swadesh, Morris. 1946. South Greenlandic (Eskimo). In: Hoijer, Harry, and Others, *Linguistic Structures of Native America*. Viking Fund Publications in Anthropology, No. 6.

Swadesh, Morris. 1951. Diffusional Cumulation and Archaic Residue as Historical Explanations. *Southwestern Journal of Anthropology*, 7:1–21.

Swadesh, Morris. 1952. Lexico-Statistic Dating of Prehistoric Ethnic Contacts. *Proceedings of the American Philosophical Society*, 96:452–463.

Swadesh, Morris. 1955. Towards Greater Accuracy in Lexicostatistic Dating. *International Journal of American Linguistics*, 21:121–137.

Swanton, John R. 1946. *The Indians of the Southeastern United States*. Bureau of American Ethnology, Bulletin 137.

Swanton, John R. 1952. *The Indian Tribes of North America*. Bureau of American Ethnology, Bulletin 145.

Tao Te Ching. 1955. Translated by R. B. Blakney. New York, New American Library.

The Task Ahead, Progress of the Colombo Plan for Co-Operative Economic Development in South and South-East Asia. 1956. Colombo, Colombo Plan Information Unit.

Tawney, Richard Henry. 1920. *The Acquisitive Society.* New York, Harcourt, Brace and Co.

Tax, Sol. 1955. The Integration of Anthropology. In: *Yearbook of Anthropology 1955.* New York, Wenner-Gren Foundation for Anthropological Research, Inc.

Tax, Sol, Eiseley, Loren C., Rouse, Irving, and Voegelin, Carl F. (eds.). 1953. *An Appraisal of Anthropology Today.* Chicago, University of Chicago Press.

Taylor, Clyde Romer Hughes. 1951. *A Pacific Bibliography.* Wellington, N.Z., The Polynesian Society.

Taylor, Griffith. [1951.] *Urban Geography.* New York, E. P. Dutton and Co., Inc.

Taylor, Walt. 1933. *Arabic Words in English.* Oxford, Clarendon Press.

Thalbitzer, William. 1930. Les magiciens esquimaux, leurs conceptions du monde, de l'âme et de la vie. *Journal de la Société des Américanistes,* 22:73–106.

Thalbitzer, William. 1941. *The Ammassalik Eskimo.* Second part. Meddelelser om Grønland, 40:569–739.

Theodorson, George A. 1953. Acceptance of Industrialization and Its Attendant Consequences for the Social Patterns of Non-Western Societies. *American Sociological Review,* 18:477–484.

Thesiger, Wilfred. 1954. The Ma'dan or Marsh Dwellers of Southern Iraq. *Royal Central Asian Journal,* 41:4–25.

Thomas, William I., and Znaniecki, Florian. 1927. *The Polish Peasant in Europe and America.* Second ed. Two vols. New York, Alfred A. Knopf.

Thomas, William L., Jr. (ed.). 1956. *Man's Role in Changing the Face of the Earth.* Chicago, University of Chicago Press.

Thompson, Laura. 1948. Attitudes and Acculturation. *American Anthropologist,* 50:200–215.

Thompson, Laura. 1950. *Culture in Crisis: A Study of the Hopi Indians.* New York, Harper & Brothers.

Thompson, Stith. 1946. *The Folktale.* New York, The Dryden Press.

Thouless, Robert H. 1953. *Straight and Crooked Thinking.* Revised and enlarged ed. London, Pan Books, Ltd.

Thurnwald, Richard. 1950. *Der Mensch geringer Naturbeherrschung: Sein Aufstieg zwischen Vernunft und Wahn.* Berlin, Walter de Gruyter and Co.

Thurnwald, Richard. 1951. *Des Menschengeistes Erwachen, Wachsen und Irren: Versuch einer Palaeopsychologie von Naturvoelkern.* Berlin, Duncker und Humblot.

Titiev, Mischa. 1954. *The Science of Man.* New York, Henry Holt and Co.

Titiev, Mischa. 1956. The Importance of Space in Primitive Kinship. *American Anthropologist,* 58:854–865.

Tjomsland, Anne. 1950. The White Potato. *Ciba Symposia,* 11:1255–1284.

Todd, Arthur James. 1933. *Industry and Society.* New York, Henry Holt and Co.

Toennies, Ferdinand. 1940. *Fundamental Concepts of Sociology.* Translated by C. P. Loomis. New York, American Book Co.

Tolstoy, Paul. 1953. Some Amerasian Pottery Traits in North Asian Prehistory. *American Antiquity,* 19:25–39.

Toy, Sidney. 1955. *A History of Fortification, from 3000 B.C. to A.D. 1700.* London, William Heinemann, Ltd.

Trager, George L. 1949. *The Field of Linguistics.* Studies in Linguistics, Occasional Papers, No. 1.

Trager, George L. 1955. The Language of America. *American Anthropologist,* 57:1182–1193.

Trumbull, Robert. 1952. Unprecedented Experiment in Democracy. *New York Times Magazine,* Jan. 20, 1952, pp. 9, 41–42.

Tschopik, Harry, Jr. 1946. The Aymara. In: Steward, Julian H. (ed.), *Handbook of South American Indians.* Vol. 2, *The Andean Civilizations.* Bureau of American Ethnology, Bulletin 143.

Tschopik, Harry, Jr. 1951. *The Aymara of Chucuito, Peru. I, Magic.* Anthropological Papers of the American Museum of Natural History, Vol. 44, Part 2.

Tumin, Melvin M. 1952. *Caste in a Peasant Society.* Princeton, Princeton University Press.

Tylor, Edward B. 1891. *Primitive Culture: Researches into the Development of Mythology, Philosophy, Religion, Language, Art, and Custom.* Third ed. revised. Two vols. London, John Murray.

Underhill, Ruth M. 1948. *Ceremonial Patterns in the Greater Southwest.* Monographs of the American Ethnological Society, No. 13.

United Nations, Statistical Office, Department of Economic and Social Affairs. 1951. *Demographic Yearbook.* Third issue. 1954, Sixth issue. New York, United Nations.

United States, Department of Commerce, Bureau of Foreign Commerce. 1954. *Investment in Pakistan.* Washington, Government Printing Office.

United States, Department of Labor, Bureau of Labor Statistics. 1940. *Problems of Workmen's Compensation Administration in the United States and Canada.* Bulletin 672.

Ure, Andrew. 1835. *Philosophy of Manufactures.* London, C. Knight.

Useem, Andrew, and Useem, Ruth Hill. 1955. *The Western-Educated Man in India.* New York, The Dryden Press.

Vallois, Henri V. 1949. The Fontéchevade Fossil Men. *American Journal of Physical Anthropology,* 7:339–362.

Vance, Rupert B. 1929. *Human Factors in Cotton Culture.* Chapel Hill, University of North Carolina Press.

Van den Bergh, G. 1956. *Unity in Diversity.* London, Batsford.

Vaughan, Elizabeth Head. 1949. *Community Under Stress: An Internment Camp Culture.* Princeton, Princeton University Press.

Veblen, Thorstein. 1912. *The Theory of the Leisure Class*. New York, The Macmillan Company.

Veith, Ilza. 1949. Introduction of Chinese Medicine in Japan. *Ciba Symposia*, 11:1193–1201.

Veniaminov, I. 1840. Notes on the Islands of the Unalaska District. Translated by Benjamin Keen for the Human Relations Area Files. Unpublished.

Vesey-Fitzgerald, S. G. 1955. Nature and Sources of the Sharī'a. In: Khadduri, Majid, and Liebesny, Herbert J. (eds.), *Law in the Middle East*. Vol. 1, *Origin and Development of Islamic Law*. Washington, The Middle East Institute.

Vickers, Geoffrey. 1956. The Pound of Flesh. *The Listener*, 54:1113, 1127.

Viereck, Peter. 1956. *The Unadjusted Man: A New Hero for Americans*. Boston, The Beacon Press.

Voegelin, C. F. 1945. Relative Chronology of North American Linguistic Types. *American Anthropologist*, 47:232–234.

Voegelin, C. F. 1951. Culture, Language, and the Human Organism. *Southwestern Journal of Anthropology*, 7:357–373.

Voegelin, C. F., and Voegelin, E. W. 1941. *Map of North American Indian Languages*. Publications of the American Ethnological Society, No. 20.

Voget, Fred W. 1956. The American Indian in Transition: Reformation and Accommodation. *American Anthropologist*, 58:249–263.

Voget, Fred W. 1957. The American Indian in Transition: Reformation and Status Innovations. *American Journal of Sociology*, 62:369–378.

Vogt, Evon Z. 1951. *Navaho Veterans: A Study of Changing Values*. Papers of the Peabody Museum of American Archaeology and Ethnology, Harvard University, Vol. 41, No. 1.

Vogt, Evon Z., and O'Dea, Thomas F. 1953. A Comparative Study of the Role of Values in Two Southwestern Communities. *American Sociological Review*, 18:645–654.

Wace, Alan John Bayard. 1949. *Mycenae: An Archaeological History and Guide*. Princeton, Princeton University Press.

Wagley, C. 1940. The Effects of Depopulation upon Social Organization as Illustrated by the Tapirapé Indians. *Transactions of the New York Academy of Sciences*, Series 2, 3:12–16.

Waldo, Dwight. 1956. *Political Science in the United States of America*. Paris, UNESCO.

Waley, Arthur. 1949. *The Way and Its Power*. London, George Allen and Unwin.

Wallace, Anthony F. C. 1952. *The Modal Personality Structure of the Tuscarora Indians as Revealed by the Rorschach Test*. Bureau of American Ethnology, Bulletin 150.

Wallace, Anthony F. C. 1956a. New Religions Among the Delaware Indians, 1600–1900. *Southwestern Journal of Anthropology*, 12:1–21.

Wallace, Anthony F. C. 1956b. Revitalization Movements: Some Theoretical Considerations for Their Comparative Study. *American Anthropologist*, 58:264–281.

Walpole, Hugh R. 1941. *Semantics: The Nature of Words and Their Meaning.* New York, W. W. Norton and Co., Inc.

Wang, Kung-hsing. 1946. *The Chinese Mind.* New York, John Day Co., Inc.

Warner, W. Lloyd. 1947. *The Social System of a Modern Factory.* New Haven, Yale University Press.

Warner, W. Lloyd, and associates. 1949. *Democracy in Jonesville.* New York, Harper & Brothers.

Warner, W. Lloyd, Havighurst, R. J., and Loeb, Martin B. 1944. *Who Shall Be Educated?* New York, Harper & Brothers.

Warner, W. Lloyd, and Lunt, Paul S. 1941. *The Social Life of a Modern Community.* New Haven, Yale University Press.

Warner, W. Lloyd, Meeker, Marchia, and Eells, Kenneth. 1949. *Social Class in America.* Chicago, Science Research Associates.

Washburn, S. L. 1953. The Piltdown Hoax. *American Anthropologist,* 55:759–762.

Waters, Frank. [1942.] *The Man Who Killed the Deer.* New York, Farrar and Rinehart, Inc.

Watkins, Harold. 1954. *Time Counts: The Story of the Calendar.* New York, Philosophical Library.

Watson, Francis. 1956. Holier than Thou. *The Listener,* 55:49–50.

Watson, James B. 1952. *Cayuá Culture Change: A Study in Acculturation and Methodology.* Memoirs of the American Anthropological Association, No. 73.

Weakland, John H. 1956. Orality in Chinese Conceptions of Male Genital Sexuality. *Psychiatry,* 19:237–247.

Weber, Max. 1922. Methodische Grundlagen der Soziologie. In: Weber, Max, *Gesammelte Aufsaetze zur Wissenschaftslehre.* Tuebingen, Mohr.

Weber, Max. 1946. *From Max Weber: Essays in Sociology.* Translated by H. H. Gerth and C. Wright Mills. New York, Oxford University Press.

Weckler, J. E., Jr. 1943. *Polynesians, Explorers of the Pacific.* Smithsonian Institution, War Background Studies, No. 6.

Wedgwood, Camilla H. 1927. Death and Social Status in Melanesia. *Journal of the Royal Anthropological Institute,* 57:377–397.

Weiner, J. S. 1955. *The Piltdown Forgery.* London, Oxford University Press.

Welch, James. 1953. Christian Thinking in Nigeria. *The Listener,* 50:542–543.

Wendt, Herbert. 1955. *I Looked for Adam.* Translated by James Cleugh. London, Weidenfeld and Nicolson.

Wermlund, Sven. 1951. Culture, Behavior, and Patterns of Behavior. *Theoria,* 17:276–290.

Westermarck, Edward A. 1921. *The History of Human Marriage.* Fifth ed. Three vols. London, Macmillan & Co., Ltd.

Westphal-Hellbusch, Sigrid. 1956. Transvestiten bei arabischen Staemmen. *Sociologus,* 6:126–137.

Whatmough, Joshua. 1956. *Language: A Modern Synthesis.* New York, St. Martin's Press.

Wheat, Joe Ben. 1954. Southwestern Cultural Interrelationships and the Question of Area Co-tradition. *American Anthropologist*, 56:576–591.

Wheeler, R. E. Mortimer. 1935. The Prehistoric Era in the West. In: Eyre, Edward (ed.), *European Civilization, Its Origin and Development*. Vol. 1, *Prehistoric Man and Earliest Known Societies*. London, Oxford University Press.

Wheeler, R. E. Mortimer. 1954. *Archaeology from the Earth*. Oxford, Clarendon Press.

White, Leslie A. 1948. The Definition and Prohibition of Incest. *American Anthropologist*, 50:416–435.

White, Leslie A. 1949. *The Science of Culture*. New York, Farrar, Straus and Co.

White, Leslie A. 1950. The Individual and the Culture Process. In: *Centennial, Collected Papers Presented at the Centennial Celebration, Washington, D.C., September 13–17, 1948*. Washington, American Association for the Advancement of Science.

White, Leslie A. 1954a. The Energy Theory of Cultural Development. In: Kapadia, K. M. (ed.), *Ghurye Felicitation Volume*. Bombay, Popular Book Depot.

White, Leslie A. 1954b. Review of "The Nature of Culture" by A. L. Kroeber, and "Culture: A Critical Review of Concepts and Definitions" by A. L. Kroeber and Clyde Kluckhohn. *American Anthropologist*, 56:461–468.

White, Llewellyn, and Leigh, Robert D. 1946. *Peoples Speaking to Peoples*. Chicago, University of Chicago Press.

Whitehead, Alfred North. 1925. *Science and the Modern World*. New York, The Macmillan Company.

Whiting, Beatrice Blyth. 1950. *Paiute Sorcery*. Viking Fund Publications in Anthropology, No. 15.

Whiting, J. W. M., and Child, Irvin L. 1953. *Child Training and Personality*. New Haven, Yale University Press.

Whittlesey, Derwent. 1949. *Environmental Factors of European History*. New York, Appleton-Century-Crofts, Inc.

Whyte, William Foote. 1943. *Street Corner Society*. Chicago, University of Chicago Press.

Whyte, William Foote. 1948. *Human Relations in the Restaurant Industry*. New York, McGraw-Hill Book Co., Inc.

Whyte, William H., Jr. 1956. *The Organization Man*. New York, Simon and Schuster.

Willems, Emílio. 1944. Acculturation and the Horse Complex Among the German-Brazilians. *American Anthropologist*, 46:153–161.

Willems, Emílio. 1955. Protestantism as a Factor of Culture Change in Brazil. *Economic Development and Cultural Change*, 3:321–333.

Willey, Gordon R., and Phillips, Philip. 1955. Method and Theory in American Archeology. II: Historical-Developmental Interpretation. *American Anthropologist*, 57:723–819.

Williams, Aubrey. n.d. Sentiment Regarding Adultery in Tillage and Non-Tillage Communities. Unpublished paper.

Williams, Elgin. 1947. Anthropology for the Common Man. *American Anthropologist, 49*:84–90.

Williams, F. E. 1928. *Orokaiva Magic.* London, Oxford University Press.

Williams, F. E. 1930. *Orokaiva Society.* London, Oxford University Press.

Williams, F. E. 1934. The Vailala Madness in Retrospect. In: Evans-Pritchard, Edward Evan, Firth, Raymond, Malinowski, Bronislaw, and Schapera, Isaac (eds.), *Essays Presented to C. G. Seligman.* London, Kegan, Paul, Trench, Trubner and Co., Ltd.

Williams, F. E. 1936. *Papuans of the Trans-Fly.* Oxford, Clarendon Press.

Williams, F. E. 1940. *Drama of Orokolo: The Social and Ceremonial Life of the Elema.* Oxford, Clarendon Press.

Williams, F. E. 1951. *The Blending of Cultures: An Essay on the Aims of Native Education.* Papua and New Guinea, Official Research Publication, No. 1. (A republication of Territory of Papua Anthropology Report No. 16.)

Williams, Phyllis H., and Straus, Robert. 1950. Drinking Patterns of Italians in New Haven. *Quarterly Journal of Studies on Alcohol, 11*:51–91, 250–308, 452–483, 586–629.

Williams, Robin M., Jr. 1947. *The Reduction of Intergroup Tensions.* Social Science Research Council Bulletin 57.

Williamson, Robert W. 1939. *Essays in Polynesian Ethnology.* Edited by Ralph Piddington. Cambridge, Cambridge University Press.

Willis, Elizabeth Bayley. 1955. *Survey of Uttar Pradesh (India) Handicrafts: Production and Export Market Possibilities.* New York, United Nations Technical Assistance Program.

Wilmer, Harry A. 1953. A Hitherto Undescribed Island: An Approach to the Problem of Acculturation. *American Scientist, 41*:456–463.

Wilson, Godfrey, and Wilson, Monica. 1945. *The Analysis of Social Change.* Cambridge, Cambridge University Press.

Wilson, John A. 1951. *The Burden of Egypt.* Chicago, University of Chicago Press.

Wilson, Monica. 1951a. *Good Company: A Study of Nyakyusa Age-Villages.* London, Oxford University Press.

Wilson, Monica. 1951b. Witch Beliefs and Social Structure. *American Journal of Sociology, 56*:307–313.

Wilson, Monica. 1957. *Rituals of Kinship Among the Nyakyusa.* London, Oxford University Press.

Wilson, Robert N. 1954. The Undergraduate Social Scientist. *Social Science Research Council Items, 8*:25–29.

Winbolt, S. E. 1945. *Britain Under the Romans.* Harmondsworth, Penguin Books.

Wiser, William Henricks. 1936. *The Hindu Jajmani System.* Lucknow, Lucknow Publishing House.

Wissler, Clark. 1923. *Man and Culture.* New York, Thomas Y. Crowell Co.

Wissler, Clark. 1938. *The American Indian*. Third ed. New York, Oxford University Press.

Wissler, Clark. 1943. The Archaeologist at Work. *Natural History*, 51:120–134.

Wittfogel, Karl A. 1957. *Oriental Despotism: A Comparative Study of Total Power*. New Haven, Yale University Press.

Wolf, Eric R., and Palerm, Ángel. 1955. Irrigation in the Old Acolhua Domain, Mexico. *Southwestern Journal of Anthropology*, 11:265–281.

Wolfe, Bernard. 1951. *The Late Risers*. New York, Random House.

Wolfenstein, Martha. 1953. Movie Analysis in the Study of Culture. In: Mead, Margaret, and Métraux, Rhoda (eds.), *The Study of Culture at a Distance*. Chicago, University of Chicago Press.

Wolfenstein, Martha, and Leites, Nathan. 1950. *Movies: A Psychological Study*. Glencoe, Ill., The Free Press.

Wollheim, Richard. 1952. The Significance of Vilfredo Pareto. *The Listener*, 47:64–65.

Wooton, Barbara. 1950. *Testament for Social Science*. London, George Allen and Unwin, Ltd.

The Worker-Priests: A Collective Documentation. 1956. Translated by John Petrie. London, Routledge and Kegan Paul.

Worsley, Peter. 1955. The Trumpet Shall Sound. *The Listener*, 54:597–598.

Wortis, Joseph. 1950. *Soviet Psychiatry*. Baltimore, Williams and Wilkins Co.

Woytinsky, Wladimir S., and Woytinsky, E. S. 1953. *World Population and Production*. New York, Twentieth Century Fund.

Yaroslavsky, E. 1956. Religion in the U.S.S.R. In: *The Communist Conspiracy: Strategy and Tactics of World Communism*. Part I, *Communism Outside the United States*. Washington, Government Printing Office.

Yerkes, R. M. 1943. *Chimpanzees*. New Haven, Yale University Press.

Young, E. Hills. 1949. Female Circumcision in the Sudan. *Anti-Slavery Reporter*, 5:13–15.

Zaehner, R. C. 1956. *The Teachings of the Magi*. London, George Allen and Unwin.

Zeuner, Frederick E. 1952. *Dating the Past*. Third ed., revised and enlarged. London, Methuen and Co., Ltd.

Znaniecki, Florian. 1952. *Modern Nationalities*. Urbana, University of Illinois Press.

Zuckerman, S. 1932. *The Social Life of Monkeys and Apes*. London, Kegan, Paul, Trench, Trubner and Co., Ltd.

INDEX OF NAMES

INDEX OF SUBJECTS